# FALLS CHURCH:
# By Fence and Fireside

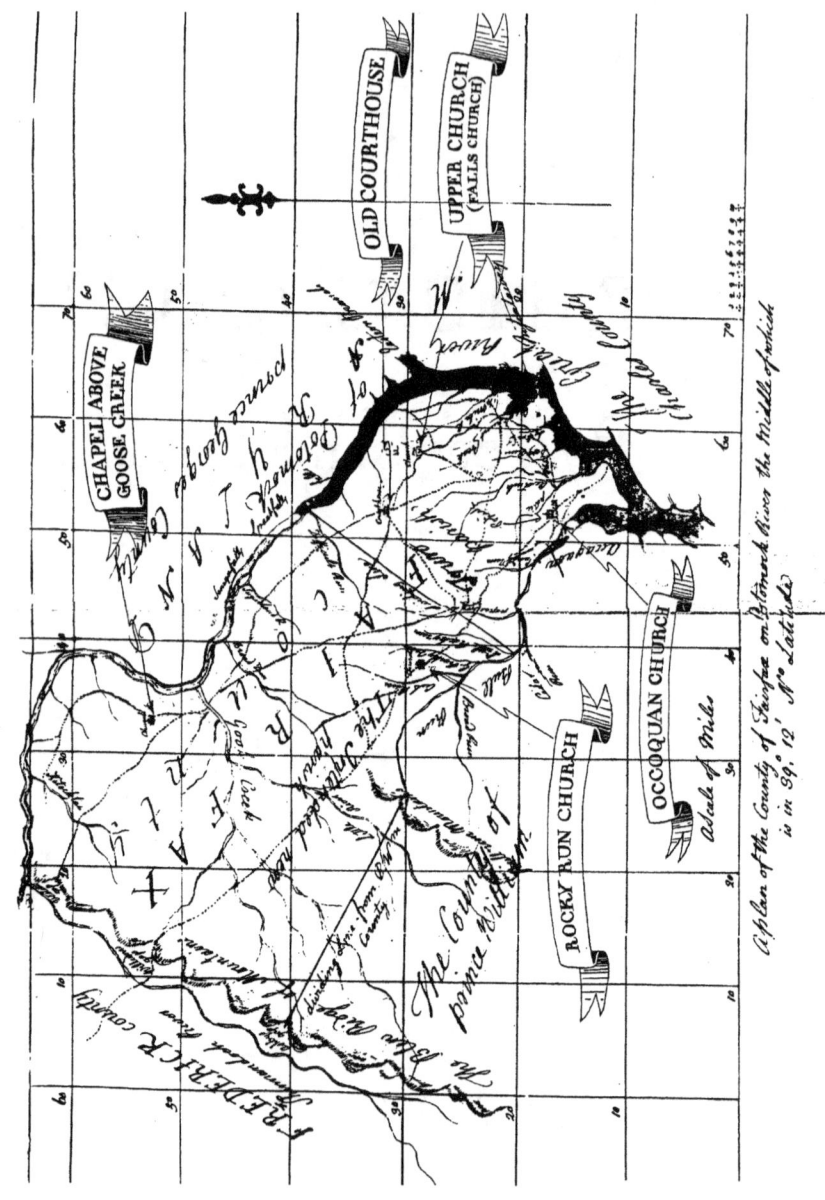

### THE FALLS CHURCH

The Church as it appeared in 1956, showing the original front on Fairfax Street. Begun in 1765 and completed in 1769, this building was erected by Colonel James Wren from his own design. The wing shown to the right was a later addition.

(Photo courtesy Porter Studio)

**A note on the map used for the end papers of this book.** *The original of this map, in the Library of Congress, was discovered there in 1928 by the Hon. R. Walton Moore (an announcement was made in the Washington Post of February 26). This copy was apparently purchased in Baltimore. The map was presumably drawn after 1745 (when Rocky Run Church, near Centreville, was erected), and before 1748 when Cameron Parish was founded (map shows "The Intended New Parish"). Churches noted on this map are:*

1) *Occoquan (now Pohick) on its old site between Occoquan and Pohick Run.*
2) *Upper Church (Falls Church) built 1733, on the present site.*
3) *Chapel Above Goose Creek (Big Spring on Rt. 15 near Leesburg) built 1735.*
4) *Rocky Run Church at Newgate (now Centreville) built 1745. The map shows the old Court House at Freedom Hill, now Tysons' Corners. The roads are shown in more complete detail on this map than on the Fry-Jefferson map published in 1755.*

# Falls Church
— Virginia —

# By Fence and Fireside

Melvin Lee Steadman, Jr.

HERITAGE BOOKS
2007

# HERITAGE BOOKS
*AN IMPRINT OF HERITAGE BOOKS, INC.*

**Books, CDs, and more—Worldwide**

For our listing of thousands of titles see our website
at
www.HeritageBooks.com

A Facsimile Reprint
Published 2007 by
HERITAGE BOOKS, INC.
Publishing Division
100 Railroad Ave. #104
Westminster, Maryland 21157

Copyright © 1964 Melvin Lee Steadman, Jr.

Copyright © 1995 Beverley T. Thomas

Library of Congress Catalog Number: 64-8065

— Publisher's Notice —
In reprints such as this, it is often not possible to remove blemishes from the original. We feel the contents of this book warrant its reissue despite these blemishes and hope you will agree and read it with pleasure.

International Standard Book Number: 978-0-7884-0203-6

# DEDICATION

To my wife and my parents

*for every reason*

## SUBSCRIBERS

*The publication of this book was greatly aided by those who subscribed to the limited Presentation Edition.*

Mr. & Mrs. William A. Albaugh, III
Mr. & Mrs. William S. Bailey, Jr.
Col. Perry L. Baldwin
Carrie Alberta Ball
Mr. & Mrs. Samuel Baritz
Ardis V. Basham
Mr. & Mrs. William M. Baskin
Cecil P. Bell
John W. Bell
Mrs. Landon C. Bell
William Landon Bell
Miss Essie F. Birch
Milton T. Birch
Mr. & Mrs. Morgan Birge
Mr. & Mrs. Warren Riley Birge
Katherine Garner Bishop
Mr. & Mrs. Kenneth Bolen
Mr. & Mrs. Mel H. Bolster
Alice L. & Lee Briggs
Charles and Martha Ann Brown
Mr. & Mrs. Horace E. Brown, Jr.
Mrs. Horace E. Brown, Sr.
Hugh R. Brown
Mrs. Meres G. Brown
James R. & Estelle Bryant
Mr. & Mrs. Clarence L. Buck
Mr. & Mrs. Richard K. Burns
Mr. & Mrs. Raymond L. Burt
Col. & Mrs. Harry Lee Campbell
Anna Cooper Cerio
Mr. & Mrs. Thomas P. Chapman, Jr.
Mrs. Guy N. Church
Mr. & Mrs. Charles C. Clark, Jr.
Mr. & Mrs. R. B. Clark
George Fulton Collins, Jr.
Mr. William H. Condon, Sr.
Mrs. John Pryor Cowan
Mr. & Mrs. Walter F. Cronin
Samuel J. Dennis
Mr. & Mrs. Wayne V. Dexter
Mrs. Ira J. Dietrich
Hon. John A. K. Donovan
Mr. & Mrs. W. J. Driver
Mrs. I. Greenwood Duncan
Mr. & Mrs. Thomas G. Eastham
William Fitzhugh Edmonds
Aveline Flagg Edwards
Charles T. Edwards
Nancy & Marshall Edwards
Mrs. John C. Elliott
Minnie D. Ellison
William H. Ellison
Hon. & Mrs. Guy O. Farley, Jr.
Mr. & Mrs. Harry A. Fellows, Jr.
Hon. & Mrs. Herman L. Fink

Hon. Robert C. Fitzgerald
Mrs. Edmund Howard Flagg
Dorothy B. Fox
Mr. & Mrs. Donald S. Frady
Charles E. Gage
Mrs. Kathleen Riley Gage
Harry James Garcia
Mr. & Mrs. Julian N. Garcia
Mrs. Alan Freeman Garner
Lynn P. Gentry
Mr. & Mrs. Burns N. Gibson, Jr.
Mr. & Mrs. W. Franklin Gooding
Miss Ruth L. Gordon
John Kenneth Gott
Douglas M. Graves
J. Robert Grille
Hon. Charles M. & Nancy H. Hailey
Courtnay C. Hamilton, Jr.
Mr. & Mrs. William H. Hansbarger
Charles J. Hedetniemi
Dr. Edwin B. Henderson
Dr. Edwin M. Henderson
Dr. James H. M. Henderson
Mr. & Mrs. U. H. Henry
Mr. & Mrs. A. Burke Hertz
Mr. & Mrs. Grant G. Hilliker
Hon. Omer L. Hirst
Josephine Theo Howard
Nancy Joan Huff
Miss Eloise Dexter Hunter
Dr. & Mrs. Harold M. Johnson
Mr. & Mrs. Thomas R. Jones
Mr. & Mrs. Albert Kay
Mr. & Mrs. Roy Robert Keith
Miss Mabel Louise Kennedy
Ruth K. Kerley
George Harrison Sanford King
Agnes & Marvin Kirby
Karl H. Knickmeyer
Mr. & Mrs. Robert F. Kohlhaas
Munson H. & Ruth Reeves Lane
Mr. & Mrs. James S. Lay, Jr.
Mr. & Mrs. Albert H. Lester
J. Leo Lynch
Julia & Colin McCollin
N. A. McDaniel
Mr. & Mrs. Robert B. McDowell
Mr. & Mrs. Harry A. McGinnis, Sr.
Flossie C. McNicol
Mr. & Mrs. Atherton H. Mears
Mr. & Mrs. Ewell G. Moore, Jr.
Mr. & Mrs. Louis T. Olom
Mr. & Mrs. Robert J. Parcelles
Mr. & Mrs. John G. Payne
Mrs. Martha T. Peach

Mr. & Mrs. O. C. Pearson
Jewell H. Pedersen
Charles A. Pendleton
David & Mary M. Persinger
E. Lakin & Gloria L. Phillips
Mr. & Mrs. Vail W. Pischke
Mrs. Esther Kincheloe Podolnick
Dr. Nelson Podolnick
Mrs. Howard C. Porter
Mr. & Mrs. Quentin R. Porter
Mr. & Mrs. Keith Price
Hon. & Mrs. Edgar A. Prichard
Thomas F. Probey
Mr. & Mrs. Nick Rajacich
Annabel R. Rathman
Mr. & Mrs. Lee M. Rhoads
Mr. & Mrs. Sam Houston Riley
Virginia Edwards Russell
Mr. & Mrs. E. Edward Schefer
David H. Scull
William W. Semenuk
Mr. & Mrs. William C. Shreve
Mr. & Mrs. Donald Hilary Sides
Harold Silverstein
Dr. & Mrs. J. Arol Simpson
B. M. Smith
Calvin W. Smith, Jr.
Mr. & Mrs. Victor B. Spector
Miss Josephine Stambaugh
Mr. & Mrs. Mayo S. Stuntz
Mr. & Mrs. David Thoburn Styles
Miss Elizabeth Morgan Styles
Mr. & Mrs. Francis Holmes Styles
Mr. Michael Hogan Styles
Neal Chapline Swaim
Philip Melville Talbott
Mr. & Mrs. John E. Taylor
Franklin Thackrey
Tunis Donaldson Thorne
La Rue Van Meter
Cdr. USN(Ret.) & Mrs. Harvey O. Vogel
Miss Ada Walker
Mr. & Mrs. Herschel C. Walling
Mildred Thorne Weaver
Mr. & Mrs. Harry E. Wells
John R. Williams
Laura Payne Wolford
Mr. & Mrs. J. Roger Wollenberg
Mr. & Mrs. Walter W. Woodside
Raymond Fitzhugh Wrenn
Richard Fitzhugh Wrenn
Mr. & Mrs. Robert B. Wright
Marie Hirst Yochim

*IN MEMORIAM*

Horace E. Brown, Sr.
Sheldon Scott & Mary Brigham Cline
John Graham, Jr.
Mason Hirst
Mrs. Fannie M. Shreve
David Whitman

# ACKNOWLEDGEMENTS

It is impossible to list the names of all who have helped with this project. But I cannot overlook some of my dear friends and neighbors who have been so patient and loyal. The sustained interest and generosity of Mr. and Mrs. Charles E. Gage has guided me along the way. Their good counsel and courtesy has been as sterling as that of parents to child. The good pen of J. O. Martin corrected many of my errors. My late dear friend, Jacob S. Payton, discussed many of the chapters with me. A special debt of gratitude must be tendered Richard K. Burns, Librarian of the Falls Church Library, for his helpful advice and many kindnesses. Mr. Burns has served as project manager and is really responsible for the publication of this book.

The Historical Development Commission of the City of Falls Church has, through its first chairman, Colonel Guy N. Church, and past and present members, encouraged me in preparing the manuscript.

My cousins, Captain and Mrs. Walter Towner Jewell, have done much to assist me in my work. They have spent long hours in cemeteries and in uncovering records of other days. Amid other duties, they have never failed to be a shelter in the storm.

My dear ones . . . Mother and Dad, my sisters, Ruthie and Mildred, were my first companions in my historical ventures. Life at home was always warm and loving, and thus it was that a youngster was able to wend his way into the long ago.

My life has been enriched by a lovely family. Beth, my companion of almost eleven years, has been at my side through College and Seminary, a behind-the-scenes spark to my various historical undertakings. My son, John Payton, has added his special glow to my days. My two-year-old daughter, Betsy, has surrounded my work of more recent days with her merry smile. My parents-in-law,

Ada and Emerson Powell, have answered distress calls as babysitters, always cheerfully responding to our every need. Mrs. E. Frank Taylor, Regent of the Falls Church Chapter, Daughters of the American Revolution, and many other members of that organization gave hours to the tedious but all-important task of indexing the volume.

Many friends and relatives, "whose name is legion," have assisted me. Some of them have joined the Church Triumphant, but a listing of their names, too, is placed here with gratitude: Miss Ella Virginia Ball, Captain and Mrs. John F. Bethune, Miss Essie F. Birch, Miss Mary N. Birch, Mrs. Flora Crossman Birch, Mr. and Mrs. Horace E. Brown, Mr. John E. Coe, Miss Sallie A. B. Coe, Miss Minnie D. Ellison, Mrs. George B. Fadeley, Mr. and Mrs. E. H. Flagg, Mr. Willis L. Gordon, Miss Ruth L. Gordon, Mr. Mason Hirst, Honorable Omer Lee Hirst, Mr. and Mrs. Herbert Nelson Hirst, Mrs. Clarence M. Hirst, Mrs. E. Allen Hildebrand, Captain and Mrs. Walter Towner Jewell, Mr. and Mrs. Marvin Hirst Kirby, Mr. David Leonard, Jr., Mr. Daniel McCauley Mills, Mr. Charles G. Mankin, Mrs. Blanche Mills Scheid, Mr. and Mrs. Carroll V. Shreve, Mrs. Prentiss A. Shreve, Mr. Frank M. Steadman, Sr., Mr. and Mrs. Melvin Lee Steadman, Sr., Mr. and Mrs. Howard R. Steadman, Mr. Charles A. Stewart, Miss Elizabeth Tabb Stewart, Mr. Samuel H. Styles, Miss Elizabeth Morgan Styles, Mrs. J. Spencer Thorne, Miss Ada Walker, Dr. Macon Ware, Mrs. Russell D. Weaver, the Reverend Raymond Fitzhugh Wrenn, and Mrs. Eldred Martin Yochim.

It is fitting to acknowledge those in official position at this time through whom the indispensable support of the City of Falls Church was given to this project:

*City Council:* Charles M. Hailey, Mayor; Samuel J. Dennis, Thomas G. Eastham, Charles J. Hedetniemi, Thomas R. Jones, Lee M. Rhoads, and Harold Silverstein.

*Board of Trustees of the Public Library:* Mrs. Robert B. McDowell, Chairman; Mrs. Frank Acosta, Mel H. Bolster, Mrs. Kermit Overby, Miss Elizabeth M. Styles, J. Hugh Rose, and Robert B. Wright.

*City Manager:* Harry E. Wells.

And finally a brief note as to some of the special circumstances surrounding the final stages of publication. Portions of these chapters were written over the past 18 years, some of them as notes without real thought of publication. After publication was finally assured, the time for updating, for verifying and for polishing was sharply limited. While every effort was made to make the book as complete and as accurate as possible, sources were not available for checking every possibility of error, and for any which may have remained I ask the reader's indulgence. I appreciate the permission, freely given, to reproduce certain copyrighted material; if through oversight or through inability to trace copyright ownership I have included any items without proper arrangement I will appreciate being notified and will make the necessary corrections in future editions.

In selecting families for the second portion of the book, in general those coming to Falls Church after World War I, and those of Fairfax County not intimately connected with the life of Falls Church itself, were eliminated, but even among the others the accessibility of information has determined in large part the treatment which could be accorded them. Preference has also been given to family material not already published in book form.

## *Illustrations*

The sources of many of the illustrations in this book are noted in the captions. The cover illustration, showing "Big Chimneys" as it appeared in the late eighteenth century, is by F. Erle Prior, an artist of note and long-time resident of Falls Church. Mr. Prior used an old photograph of "Big Chimneys," and sketches made by the author, with the help of his grandmother, in 1947/48.

Copy-work on many of the photographs was done by Porter Studios and by Charles E. Gage. Many other photographs were given or loaned to the author by the families involved.

# Contents

|  | Page |
|---|---|
| Acknowledgements | i |
| List of Illustrations | vi |
| Introduction—Hon. Omer L. Hirst | viii |
| Foreword—"A Moment at My Fireside" | x |
| "Home Town" by Harry Kinzie, Jr. | xiii |

## Chapter

| | | |
|---|---|---|
| 1 | Some Common-Place Boundaries | 1 |
| 2 | The Church on The Road to The Falls | 11 |
| 3 | The Old Brick Church | 21 |
| 4 | Roads and Wayside Taverns | 32 |
| 5 | Drum, Fife, and Cannon | 45 |
| 6 | By a Broken Fence | 49 |
| 7 | To Mend a Broken Fence | 71 |
| 8 | The Methodists | 92 |
| 9 | The Baptists | 110 |
| 10 | The Presbyterians | 116 |
| 11 | The Roman Catholics | 122 |
| 12 | Schools, Pencils and Books | 128 |
| 13 | Public Service and Organizations | 145 |
| 14 | Rails and Ties By Fence and Field | 186 |
| 15 | Location and Natural Resources | 194 |
| 16 | Neighbors Over The Fence | 197 |
| 17 | Friends and Neighbors At the Fireside | 206 |

# BIOGRAPHICAL AND GENEALOGICAL SKETCHES
## Families

| | | |
|---|---|---|
| Abbott ............................. 219 | Elliott ............................. 305 | Nourse ........................... 395 |
| Adams ............................ 221 | Ellison ........................... 307 | Osborn ........................... 395 |
| Adams-Wren-Watters | Erwin ............................. 311 | Payne ............................. 396 |
| Cemetery ..................... 238 | Fadeley .......................... 313 | Jacob Payne ................. 400 |
| Albertson ........................ 239 | Febrey ............................ 314 | Porter ............................ 402 |
| Archibald Lamon | Fellows .......................... 317 | Quick ............................. 403 |
| Anderson ..................... 239 | Flagg .............................. 318 | Read .............................. 403 |
| Joseph Anderson ............. 240 | Ford ............................... 322 | Rice ................................ 404 |
| Auchmoody ..................... 240 | Daniel S. Gordon ............ 322 | Riley ............................... 406 |
| Bailey (of Bailey's | Willis Leonard Gordon .... 324 | Row ................................ 411 |
| Cross Roads) ................ 241 | Gott ................................ 326 | Sebastian ....................... 412 |
| Lyman M. Ballard ............ 245 | Gunnell .......................... 328 | Sewell-Sewall ................ 414 |
| Barbor ............................ 245 | Hawxhurst ..................... 332 | Sherwood ....................... 415 |
| Barrett ............................ 246 | Henderson ..................... 333 | Shotwell ......................... 417 |
| Bartlett (of "Home Hill") .247 | Hirst ............................... 333 | Shreve ............................ 418 |
| Beach .............................. 250 | Hiett ............................... 336 | Soule .............................. 424 |
| Bethune .......................... 250 | Hull ................................ 337 | Sprankle ......................... 424 |
| Birch ............................... 251 | Ives ................................. 339 | Steadman ....................... 425 |
| Almond Birch ................. 269 | Kirby ............................... 341 | Stewart ........................... 429 |
| Bowen ............................ 271 | Klock .............................. 345 | Talbott ............................ 432 |
| Bramhall, and | Lee ................................. 346 | Taylor ............................. 432 |
| "Hollywood Farm" ...... 272 | Leonard .......................... 347 | Terrett ............................ 433 |
| Broadwater ..................... 272 | Lindsay ........................... 348 | Thompson (of |
| Brown ............................. 278 | Lloyd .............................. 353 | "Big Chimneys") ......... 434 |
| Brunner .......................... 280 | Lynch ............................. 354 | Thorne ........................... 437 |
| Burke (of "Royal Lodge") 281 | Maben ............................ 359 | Torreyson ...................... 440 |
| Chappel .......................... 282 | Mankin ........................... 360 | Trammell ....................... 441 |
| Church ........................... 284 | Marr ............................... 366 | Tripp .............................. 444 |
| Clover ............................. 287 | McCauley ....................... 366 | Turner ............................ 445 |
| Coe (of "Mt. Hope") ........ 287 | Merry .............................. 368 | Wakefield ...................... 445 |
| Crossman ........................ 288 | Mills ............................... 370 | Walker (of "Chestnut |
| Crump ............................ 291 | Minor ............................. 372 | Grove") ........................ 449 |
| Darne .............................. 292 | Moran ............................. 378 | Watkins .......................... 451 |
| Donaldson ...................... 301 | Munson .......................... 380 | West ............................... 453 |
| Duncan ........................... 302 | Murray ............................ 382 | Wheeler ......................... 461 |
| Eastman .......................... 303 | Mutersbaugh .................. 391 | Wren (Wrenn) ............... 463 |
| Edmonds ........................ 304 | Nelson ............................ 393 | |

At the End of the Fence Row ............................................................. 521

## APPENDIX

Bibliography ............................................................................................. 522
Roll of Elected Mayors ............................................................................ 524
Population and Tax Data ........................................................................ 525
List of Tithables, 1748/9 ......................................................................... 526
Facsimiles of Vestry Book pages 1733-1757-1760 ............................... 538
Broadside—"Hollywood Farm" sale .................................................... 541
Index ......................................................................................................... 542

# LIST OF ILLUSTRATIONS

FIRST SECTION, Following Page 72
Fig.
1. Falls Church, 1861 (Leslie's)
2. So. Washington and W. Broad Streets, 1904
3. Falls Church Market, ca. 1920
4. Falls Church Garage, ca. 1920
5. Falls Church Bank, ca. 1920
6. Brown's Corner, ca. 1890
7. Mankin's Pharmacy, 1904
8. Spofford & Church, 1880's
9. First P. O. Building, ca. 1895
10. Broad Street, 1907
11. Broad Street with Silver Maples
12. E. Broad Street, ca. 1900
13. Original Falls Church Bank Building
14. Toll Gate, 1874
15. West End Station
16. Elliott's Store, ca. 1904
17. The Falls Church, 1862
18. Interior, The Falls Church
19. Baptismal Font, The Falls Church
20. First Congregational Church, 1904
21. Dulin Methodist Church
22. Original Crossman Methodist Church, 1904
23. First Sanctuary, Presbyterian Church
24. Columbia Baptist Church, 1861
25. Original Second Baptist Church (colored) ca. 1872
26. Original St. James Catholic Church, ca. 1889
27. Civil war panoramic views (Leslie's)
28. Confederate treed (Leslie's)
29. Pickets skirmishing (Leslie's)
30. The Misses Scott being taken prisoner
31. Hangman's Tree
32. Jefferson School, 1891
33. Virginia Training School, 1904
34. "Maury," the Bailey home
35. Old Lynch house
36. "Arringdon Hall"
37. "Tallwood"
38. "Home Hill"
39. Birch House
40. "Highland View"
41. "Mount Pleasant," 1890's
42. "Mount Pleasant," 1960's
43. "Walnut Hill"
44. "Gum Aysle"
45. "The Mount"
46. "Hollywood Farm"
47. "Cherry Hill"
48. The Spite House
49. Ellison House, ca. 1890
50. Ellison House, 1950

SECOND SECTION, Following Page 200
Fig.
51. East End, Spanish-American War
52. Tents at East End
53. Scenes at Camp Alger
54. Digging cut for trolley line
55. Railroad depots, East Falls Church, 1921
56. Fourth of July celebration, Eagle House Hotel
57. "Uncle Pete" Gillam
58. Original D. C. corner boundary stone
59. Brick walk, Broad Street, 1917
60. Judge Joseph S. Riley
61. Wm. H. G. Lynch
62. Albert Wren
63. Dr. Louis E. Gott
64. Elery C. Walker
65. Minor F. Chamblin
66. Frederick F. Foote
67. Edmund Flagg
68. America Virginia (Scott) Darne
69. Miss Mattie Gundry
70. Eastman Family
71. M. E. Church
72. Harry A. Fellows
73. Ellen Lightfoot Lynch
74. Ella Febrey Talbott
75. Joseph E. Birch and wife
76. Barbara (Ball) Prigg
77. Isaac Crossman
78. The Mankin brothers
79. William Gwynn Coe and wife
80. James I. Brown
81. Mrs. Louisa (Marrs) Henderson and children
82. Ellison Family
83. Thorne Family
84. Presbyterian picnic
85. Map of Falls Church, 1879
86. Falls Church central district, 1879
87. 1801 map of Northern Virginia
88. Map of Falls Church, 1890
89. Sherwood home
90. Mankin Home House
91. Crossman home
92. Eastman house
93. "Longview"
94. Original Columbia Baptist Church (Brady)
95. The Falls Church, 1862 (Brady)
96. The Falls Church, with fence (Brady)
97. "Church Hill" in 1890's
98. "Church Hill" in recent years
99. Southgate house
100. Pond House
101. Mankin's store, 1904
102. "Cloverdale"
103. Foote painting of Broad Street in 1860
104. Frank Lloyd Wright house
105. "Montpelier"
106. Cutting of maple trees, N. Washington Street
107. "Mount Hope"
108. "Fair Mount"
109. Annual Report, Finances of Falls Church, 1888

# INTRODUCTION

We in our time live at the beginning of the Metropolitan Age. Population increases and technological progress alike push us toward vast urban-suburban agglomerations. While this new pattern has much to offer, including a new and rising standard of living, the yearning for neighborhood and for the human values involved in neighborly living remains to be satisfied. We find ourselves thinking nostalgically about the towns we knew or read about and wondering if something precious is by way of being lost as our old towns lose their identity in the encroachment of urbanization.

The American town deserves its place in American history. It has left its mark upon us, and it is well to reflect upon and preserve for posterity some recollection of the Falls Church that used to be, for out of that Falls Church and in its mold has come the modern city, the Falls Church of today, in which progress and stability are so happily blended.

There has always been something special about Falls Church, not only as a town in the conventional sense, but also as a cross-section of Northern Virginia. Not long ago it was a farmers' town, because the dairy farms and truck patches lay just outside to the north, the south, the east, and the west. It was a commuters' town, blessed with two electric railways linking it with Georgetown and Washington. It was a meeting point of north and south, not only geographically but in its mixture of Union and Confederate veterans, all of whom could marvel at the Army doings at Camp Alger or later in France.

It has always been a cultivated town in its interest in books and schools, and, in fact, owes its independent city status today to the dissatisfaction of its citizens in 1948 and 1949 with the school system of the neighboring county of which it was then a part. Most of all, it has always been a home folks town where people of diverse backgrounds of religion, race, and of economic circumstance met in genuine neighborliness, each contributing toward making Falls Church a delightful and interesting community. Such current achievements as a public school system of exceptional quality and city hall and city library buildings that are outstanding for architectural excellence are at once characteristic of that community and indicative of the tastes and standards of its people.

As one who has seen a tall, sleek office building replace his grandfather's house in the inevitable and not always bad change that is the rule of life, I am grateful to Melvin Steadman for showing us the beginnings and the being of Falls Church, at once so typical and so special.

Omer L. Hirst
*27th Senatorial District*
*The General Assembly of Virginia*

AUTHOR'S FOREWORD

# A MOMENT AT MY FIRESIDE...

... during the time when a young boy learns from his grandmother of the long ago. The maternal grandmother speaks of the Falls Church of her girlhood, when a small town fireside burned in a small town way. The Grandmother, Mrs. Herbert Nelson Hirst (nee Ellen Elizabeth Mankin), had spent many pleasant hours during the late 1880's by the old worm wood fence surrounding "Big Chimneys," the home of her maternal ancestors. This ancient fireside had warmed old and young since the late 1690's. The old spring house was a young girl's play house, and the warm sun shone with many a merry ray over her pleasure. At the "Big Chimneys" fireside her own Grandmother Lynch, as little Elizabeth Ellen Lightfoot, had learned what all young girls have learned before and since.

The grandchild listened with rapt attention as once more lambs played over the meadows at "Big Chimneys"; and somehow Aunt Mary Lynch's salt-rising bread came anew from the big chimney oven. Old friends took on new life: the many Negro families that had blended their own life with the "Big Chimneys" soil; Mrs. Mary Williams at her Toll Gate; Mother Mary Birch on an errand of mercy; hymn-singing local crusaders marching on John Brush's Saloon—all this, and peppermint sticks from the local store, too!

Thus the grandchild was wrought in the fabric of Falls Church, and as he wandered by fence row and chimney peak, the saints and sinners of yesterday seemed to call to him for some special word. The road he walked was narrow and winding, edged with maple and wild shrubs, laced with a tangle of honeysuckle and laurel. Here and there amid Virginia's dogwood, local songsters sang their song of Falls Church. All winter muddy and full of ruts, all summer deep in dust, old Shreve Road had its drawbacks. But, like its native place, it had an undeniable, unalterable charm.

As the child grew into manhood, the honeysuckle tangle and fence row gave way steadily to strangers with their new ways. The echoes calling with their ancient lyre seemed to demand attention. Thus it is that you have come to pause a moment at my fireside. The old-fashioned nose-gay given by a grandmother to her grandchild has been surrounded by names and dates from neighboring firesides and a modern Court House. No doubt the nosegay could be better—but such as this is, a grateful grandson passes these things to all who love and value old Falls Church.

—Melvin Lee Steadman, Jr.

The Parsonage, Pender.
Fairfax, Virginia
February 19, 1961.

The Parsonage
Gainesville, Virginia

(This glance at Falls Church by fence and fireside was begun at the family residence, Antrim, Falls Church, Virginia, January 28, 1946.)

## HOME TOWN

You can't build a home town.

The cleverest architects and the most determined builders in the world never designed or erected a home town.

And yet the world is full of them, revolves around them, would fall apart without them.

They are hard to find. They hide behind streets and buildings and trees and houses, until they look just like ordinary towns.

You could be looking right at a home town, and unless you belonged there or came from there, you'd never know it. That is, until you had learned some of the many magical things that make up a home town.

Home towns are made up of bowling teams, borrowed cups of sugar, first names and easy hello's. They are noted for father-and-son banquets, tricycles in driveways, football heroes, village belles, neighborhood belles, belles of the block and many assorted sweethearts... all of the latter being the most beautiful in the world.

Home towns have plenty of nearby fields for Saturday Indian massacres, quantities of evening breeze to help the sounds of choir practice get around, and one of the world's best back-yard wireless systems.

They're long on lodge meetings, school meetings, business meetings, town meetings, meetings in the drug-store, in the barbershop, or in somebody's kitchen after the show. All are characterized by a wealth of opinion, freely given, freely disputed, but never forbidden.

Home towns are heated in winter by steaming coffee pots, cooled in summer by small boys whizzing down the sidewalk after dark on bicycles. They are lit up by the sparkle of tinsel on Christmas baskets down at the firehouse. They are shaded by a wealth and profusion of family trees whose minutest branches are known to all.

Home towns are warm, wonderful places.

They're happiness, family-style. They're the star-spangled excitement of a Fourth of July afternoon with its unashamed patriotism. They're George the butcher, Scout Troop Three, the price of potatoes, and the Galworthy girl getting married.

People living a life and dreaming a dream together.

And home towns **are** hard to find . . . unless you know just where to look!

In your heart.

—Harry Kinzie, Jr., in The Fairless Hills News
reprinted in the Reader's Digest, August, 1952

# CHAPTER 1

# Some Common-Place Boundaries

Old land surveys are full of remarkably common-place boundaries: so many feet to a red oak, an old stump, or a heap of stones. The ancient Indian fields used for grain and meadow were called "poison-fields" by the early settlers. The Chantilly section of Fairfax County retained this distinctive name for more than a century. After all, if trees and brush were not found growing on land, it must be poisoned. The Indians had consistently burned over these fields, always carefully leaving a "fence" of old trees. Occasionally a friendly and tumbling brook acted as a natural barrier. But fences that are friendly are not binding, and the early settlers were determined to keep their vaguely defined boundaries in bonds. Sapling fences, some dubbed with stone, served as the earliest fences in Virginia, and these were sought after, fought for, and sued about.

Fairfax County was settled by a cross section of wayward and aimless persons, as well as the straight-laced and narrow. Of course, in between, were the more cheerful and less radical elements, even as we find the native of today. An endless procession, both motley and dignified, yeoman and cavalier, indentured and free, made its way painfully over trails that knew not the upper crust any more than the lower. Religious dissenters (Protestants from Maryland, French Huguenots, Anabaptists, and many Quakers) found shelter in Fairfax County. The countryside was marked by contrast, a virgin land which was the scene of great achievements, personal triumphs, and significant contributions to human progress. The early settlers set a pattern for gracious living. Skilled artisans at Alexandria, Leesburg, and Fredericksburg practiced their craftsmanship and rivalled the best of Europe. Observant farmers in Loudoun and Fairfax discovered and practiced methods of tillage which restored fertility to the soil. Statesmen imbued with the spirit of this new world formulated principles of individual liberty, and etched them deep on the surface of American life. From Fairfax County George Washington and George Mason went forth to write with quill pen and speak with eloquent tongue a deathless plea for a free nation.

Fairfax County, scene of this restless and revolutionary activity, was formed in 1742 from Prince William County. Prince William was formed in 1730 from Stafford, and the latter was formed in 1663 from Westmoreland. Westmoreland County was partitioned in 1653 from Northumberland, which was a frontier county formed in 1648. Thus, what is now the City of Falls Church, was once part of all of these political subdivisions. Loudoun County was taken from Fairfax in 1757. This was followed later by the County of Alexandria, D.C., which is now Arlington.

All of the area mentioned was part of the Northern Neck, which was without defined boundaries other than the land which lay between the Potomac and Rappahannock Rivers. This domain was by inheritance the sole proprietary of Thomas, Sixth Lord Fairfax and Baron of Cameron, a descendant of Lord Culpeper, to whom, with others, the royal grant was made by Charles II. Lord Fairfax's holdings consisted of five million two hundred and eighty-two thousand acres of land.

Leading the procession of settlers who claimed the land were the explorers. Among the earliest and best known of these was that most interesting early Virginian, John Smith, "Captayne and Admirall of New England." On June 16, 1608, Captain Smith, with a party of explorers, entered the Potomac (as he writes it, "Patawomeck") River in an "open Barge neare three tuns burthern," as he relates in his *Generall Historie*. But even Smith couldn't overcome the Great Falls of the Potomac, or even the Little Falls. Progress was halted at Little Falls, and the party moved inland along an old Indian path into what is now Fairfax County. This Indian path is now Little Falls Street. On his voyage up the Potomac Smith encountered "three or foure thousand Savages" who were so "strongly paynted, grimed, disguised," that he was certain so many "spirits from Hell could not have shewed more terrible." Smith speaks of being entertained by the local Indians at Tauxenent (or Toags) which was on the site of the future Washington holdings at Mount Vernon.

This section of Virginia was originally part of the confederacy of the Indian Chief ("Emperor") Powhatan. This well-known Virginian was absolute ruler of a highly developed society of Indians. By his many wives he was the ancestor of many present-day Americans. He was the father of "Princess" Pocahontas, who was later baptized Rebecca. Born about 1595, Pocahontas died in England in 1617, the wife of John Rolfe.

Little evidence remains of this Indian society. One reminder, however, is on Wilson Boulevard below 7 Corners, where a sign, "Powhatan Spring," stands in front of a lovely home. "Powhatan Springs," according to local tradition, was where Powhatan held his fall councils and harvest festivals. Tribesmen from all over the confederacy would gather here at an appointed time and hold council. Water from Powhatan Spring was considered to have health-giving qualities, and, previous to the automobile era, representatives of Harper's Livery Stables in Washington, D.C., regularly came to fill five-gallon jugs which were delivered to purchasers in the city.

At the dawn of the seventeenth century, three distinct groups of Indians, representing three different linguistic stocks, occupied Virginia. In Falls Church there is record of only one permanent camp, and that was located on a farm formerly owned by Isaac Crossman on Lee Highway near Columbia Street.[1] Professor Proudfit in an article in the *American Anthropologist* refers in detail to the principal Indian village, Nacotchtanke, and locates the other village sites within the old lines of the District of Columbia. One, denoted as number five, "near the mouth of Four Mile Run," was in the vicinity of Falls Church, and that already mentioned, on the Crossman farm, was denoted as number six.

Other nearby camps included Nameroughquena, across the old Long Bridge from Washington, and Assomeck, below Alexandria. Also near Alexandria was a camp called Namasingakeut. The powerful Doegs and Susquehannocks who roamed in this area, probably vied for these sites as a base for their hunting and trading expeditions. One tribe operated an extensive soapstone quarry at Falls Church.[2]

The Indians and the settlers were seldom on friendly terms—and it is no wonder! In recent years bones have been found indicating that some of the terrible Susquehannocks may have been eight feet in height. Smith commented that the local Indians had broad noses flat and full at the ends, and had "great bigg lippes, and wyde mouthes..." He says the Patawomeck Indians camped along the Potomac.

In 1675, the Indian problem came to a climax in the "Susquehannock War." Following this, the procession of local settlers increased. Previously, the Virginia and Maryland sides of the Potomac suffered greatly from Indian aggression. The local Indians crossed the Potomac to attack the settlers in 1675, beginning a war of typical guerilla tactics, including theft and depredation.[3]

For about a year or more the war was fought in a desultory manner in Virginia and Maryland, with the result that the Indians were permanently driven from the area. A first-hand account of the war is to be found in a letter, dated July 13, 1705, from Thomas Matthews (Burgess from Stafford County) to the Honorable Robert Harley, Esquire, English Secretary of State.

In his letter Matthews wrote that "About the year 1675, appear'd three prodigies in that country, which from th' attending disasters, were looked upon as ominous presages." He then speaks of a comet "streaming like a horse taile westwards" every evening for a week, and "fflights of pigeons in breadth nigh a quarter of the midmemisphere, and of their length was no visible end..." This sight put the "planters under the more portentious apprehensions, because the like was seen (as they said) in the year 1640 when the Indians committed the last massacre, but not after, untill that present year 1675." The third of the "prodigies" was swarms of "fflyes about an inch long, and big as the top of a man's little finger, rising out of spigot holes in the earth, which eat the new sprouted leaves from the top of the trees without other harm, and in a month left us."

3

Matthews relates that his overseer, Mr. Pimmitt, had agreed to hire Robert Hen as herdsman. Hen lived about ten miles above the Matthews plantation. On the way to church on one Sunday morning in the summer of 1675, the people saw "Hen lying thwart his threshold, and an Indian without the door, both chopped on their heads, arms and other parts, as if done with Indian hatchetts, th' Indian dead, but Hen when ask'd who did that? answered Doegs, Doegs, and soon died, then a boy came out from under a bed, where he had hid himself, and told them, Indians had come a break of day and done those murders."

Matthews goes on to say that from "this Englishman's bloud |blood| did (by degrees) arise Bacons rebellion with the following mischiefs which overspread all Virginia and twice endangered Maryland..."

Matthews also gives an account of the excursion by Captain Giles Brent and Colonel George Mason against the Indians.[4] At the same time that Brent and Mason attacked, Colonel John Washington, a great-grandfather of George Washington, with a Virginia force, joined Major John Truman's Maryland troops in a campaign against the Indians on Piscataway Creek, Maryland. This John Washington, with Nicholas Spencer, was the original proprietor of what later became Mount Vernon, having been granted a patent on March 1, 1675.

One of the small streams emptying into the Potomac near the Chain Bridge bears the name of John Pimmitt, who was overseer for Thomas Matthews. It has borne his name since 1675. Doeg Run, which flows into the Potomac at the northern boundary of Mount Vernon, takes its name from the Doeg tribe of Indians.

By 1660, land patents were secured by the early settlers from the Proprietors of the Northern Neck. Earlier, the colonial land patents were issued by the Governor (who was appointed by the Crown) or by his deputies. The Northern Neck Charter, dated September 18, 1649, to Lord Culpeper, Lord Hopton, and others, was granted by Charles II in recognition of their sacrifices made on behalf of his father, during the time of Cromwell.

The major settlements in this section of Fairfax County took place about 1675/90. At first glance it would seem that the procession of pioneering population was slow in reaching this immediate section. The earliest of these people were almost entirely English. Among the later comers were the German, Dutch, Swiss, and French. The Scotch-Irish and Quakers came down from Pennsylvania in a steady tide. These later people settled in that section now in Loudoun County and also in Jefferson County (now in West Virginia).

Many early settlers came because of eloquent accounts sent back to England and also because enterprising adventurers were willing to pay the passage over. For those who came as indentured servants, these often had a very hard time of it. Many were well-educated but poor men, like William Buckland, Architect of Gunston Hall, who became foremost in his field in America.

Land grants were given those who rendered public services, such as clergymen and physicians. If a man paid the passage of one immigrant, the Proprietor gave him one hundred acres of land (one hundred acres more for the immigrant's wife, and fifty acres for each child). If a person could recruit five or more additional immigrants, he was given two thousand acres. Any one who acquired one thousand acres in Maryland was entitled to become "Lord of a Manor" with feudal rights. In Virginia, "King" Robert Carter owned three hundred thousand acres, William Fitzhugh owned fifty thousand acres of land. The large majority settled on smaller tracts, and these included artisans and small farmers.

Land was the measure of wealth, and the basis of a highly cultured aristocracy. Great houses such as Mount Vernon, Gunston Hall, and The Mount rang with the merry sounds of frequent parties and dances. Fox hunting, dining, music, and dancing were cultivated.

Towns did not grow up, although some small trading posts did. Each plantation was a self-contained unit. Life centered about the plantation, where the planter in his mansion, surrounded by his family and retainers, was a patriarch mildly ruling and entertaining every one. It was the life of the family and not of the great world, and produced that intense attachment to the soil which is a characteristic of Virginians to this day. The public or political character of Virginians corresponded to their private one, haughty and jealous of their liberties, impatient of restraint, symbolized in men such as Mason, Jefferson, Washington, and a host of others.

The land was originally covered with virgin timber except for meadows and corn fields used by the Indians. The forests were sacrificed for tobacco culture. By 1635, tobacco cultivation had become one of the most profitable enterprises in Virginia. The expanding European market assured the planters of a steady demand for all that they could produce. Negro slaves did most of the work over many hundreds of acres of tobacco. By rapid consumption of nitrogen and potash, the tobacco plant exhausted the soil. Former tobacco fields were soon heir to brush and scrub pine. This continued until John Alexander Binns, of neighboring Loudoun County, found a method to revive fertility. His method consisted of liming, deep plowing and five-year crop rotation. Publicized in 1803, these methods became known as the "Loudoun System," and drew praise and support from Thomas Jefferson.[5]

Alexandria was the only town of any importance near the Falls Church during colonial days. Between the time of its first importance, until the establishment of Georgetown, then in Maryland, and now part of the District of Columbia, Alexandria received all of the so-called "up-county" trade. "Up-county" included that vast area west to the Blue Ridge. The population of Alexandria increased during the boom following the Revolutionary War, and commerce in the same bounding way. Between 1791 and 1796, exports from Alexandria tripled to an annual value of more than one million dollars, and it was the most important shipping center for produce from the Valley. By 1820, more than half the wheat in North America was raised in Virginia and Maryland, with Baltimore at that time the flour milling center of the world, and a city of seventy-five thousand people.

Dumfries was also an important town with a good harbor, and many ships lay at anchor bound for the greater world. The present day community at Dumfries gives little evidence of the colonial town, and, later, as the seat of the District Court, the busy home of lawyers and merchants.

Following the Revolution, Baltimore was the most important foreign shipping point. General Henry Mankin established the first regular line of packet ships adapted to passenger as well as freight traffic between Baltimore and Liverpool. The first ship put on the line was the Franconia, Captain Smith (familiarly known as "Long John Smith") was in command. Colonel Benjamin Musgrove Mankin, a merchant and planter at Dumfries, (and grandfather of George and Charles Mankin, early merchants at Falls Church), was among the first from Virginia to make use of the Baltimore traffic to Europe. As Quantico Creek (through which the trade from Europe passed) filled with silt, it was apparent to Mankin and other Dumfries area merchants, that the community was on its way out.[6]

The west shore of the Potomac was the last of the Tidewater fringe to be settled, as indicated earlier, and conditions were frontier-like, primitive and hard. In 1669 Governor William Berkeley granted to Captain Robert Howsing some "six thousand acres of land situate. . .upon the freshes of Potomac River on the west side." This tract was purchased by Colonel John Alexander, and settlement soon followed. Nicholas Spencer and John Washington patented the original Mount Vernon estate. Spencer came to Virginia in 1657 from Cople, Bedfordshire. He later returned to England, where he died in 1699. During his stay in Virginia, he served the Colony as Burgess, Secretary of State, President of the Council, and was acting Governor from 1683 until 1689. His son, John Spencer, possessed the joint tenancy of the five-thousand acre Mount Vernon tract with John Washington. Young Spencer also inherited Albany, a large estate in Cople Parish, Westmoreland, from his father. The family continued active in affairs of that section, (then in Stafford, now Fairfax), and a daughter of John Spencer, Frances, married John Ariss. Their son, John Ariss, Jr., lived in Fairfax County, and was the Architect of Payne's Church near Fairfax Court House.

Another large holder was William Fitzhugh. Portions of his land were within the present-day boundaries of Falls Church. William Fitzhugh and George Brent were agents for the Proprietors of the Northern Neck from 1693 until 1700, and maintained a land office at Woodstock, Stafford County. A patent (Brent to Fitzhugh) dated October 1, 1694, conveyed twenty-one thousand, nine hundred and ninety-six acres of land, including the Ravensworth tract at Annandale.[7]

In 1726 Simon Pearson and John Fitzhugh patented one thousand two hundred and nine acres of land on Middle Run (called the "Horsepen" of Great Hunting Creek). This land lay between Falls Church and the tract patented by William Fitzhugh in 1694. On March 4, 1730, Simon Pearson and Gabriel Adams patented seven hundred and eight acres north of Falls Church, running back to Brandymore Castle, which was probably an early name for Minor's Hill.

The late Charles Stetson, in his *Four Mile Run Landgrants*, says that Carlyle Fairfax Whiting added to the extensive estate he had acquired by the will of his grandfather, John Carlyle of Alexandria, by purchasing sixty-seven acres near Falls Church from Simon Pearson.[8]

Other large planters were the Gunnell, West, Trammell, Darne and Wren families. In 1784 Sampson Trammell was living two miles west of Falls Church, and this is where General Washington and Dr. Craik stopped for dinner on their journey to Washington's western land.[9]

By deeds made in 1786 and 1796, Simon Pearson conveyed land on the Leesburg Road west of Falls Church, in trust for Peletiah Graffort for life, and in remainder to her son, John Pearson. Major Charles Little was another land holder near the Falls Church. His residence, Cleesh, was formerly the seat of Colonel John Colville, south of Great Hunting Creek, but he also owned a plantation on the Falls Church Road. This seems to have been in the area included in National Memorial Park Cemetery. Captain John Harper of Alexandria had a summer place, Walnut Hill, near Falls Church.

Colonel Robert Lindsay settled on four hundred acres which is now bounded by what is now Idylwood Road and west of Falls Church. He added to his estate, and his home, erected in 1745, and still standing, was called The Mount.

The location of Falls Church has always been its great advantage, and the source of its settlement and continued progress. Part of the Metropolitan area of Washington, D.C., it has thus become tied to government expansion. From 1791 until 1846, the western boundary of the original District of Columbia terminated at Falls Church. The boundary markers are still in existence to remind us of this fact.

The original plan of Washington City, as approved by Act of Congress on July 16, 1790, included a tract of ten miles square, carved from Virginia and Maryland.[10] This rectangular tract was marked at intervals by stones four feet high. The surveyor hired to mark out the site was Andrew Ellicott of Philadelphia. He was instructed by President Washington, through Secretary of State Jefferson, to "proceed by the first stage to the Federal territory on the Potomac for the purpose of making a survey of it," and Charles Pierre L'Enfant was instructed to "prepare a plan of the city."

Ellicott arrived in Georgetown before the middle of February, and had completed his first line of survey, and was four days advanced on the second line when on March 9, 1791, Major L'Enfant reached Georgetown to begin work.[11] With Ellicott was an assistant, Benjamin Banneker, who was, according to the *Georgetown Weekly Ledger* of March 12, 1791, ". .an Ethiopian whose abilities as a surveyor and astronomer clearly prove that Mr. Jefferson's concluding that race of men were void of mental endowments was without foundation." This self-taught quadroon was a remarkable mathematician. Part of his training came from his grandmother, a white woman named Mary Welch.

Before the end of the next year, Major Ellicott had completed his survey. On January 1, 1793, he reported to the District Commissioners with "singular satisfaction," that he had completed the "four lines comprehending the Territory of Columbia." These lines were opened and cleared forty feet wide, "that is, twenty feet on each side of the lines limiting the Territory..." He reported that he had set up square milestones, "marked progressively with the number of miles from the beginning of Jones' Point, except as to a few cases were the miles terminated on a declivity or in water; in such cases, the stones were placed on the nearest firm ground, and their true distances and miles and poles marked on them." On the sides facing the District was inscribed: "Jurisdiction of the United States," and on the opposite sides "Virginia," or "Maryland," as the case existed. On a fourth side was inscribed the year and the position of the magnetic needle on the compass.

On March 29, 1791, Washington, accompanied by three District Commissioners, Mayor Daniel Carroll, Dr. David Stuart, and Thomas Johnson, together with Major L'Enfant and Major Ellicott, rode over as much of the line as could be easily reached, and on the evening of the next day signed and sealed the definite agreement with the owners of the land for the District.

The first stone laid for the boundary was at Jones Point, Alexandria, and this was the focal point of Masonic rites conducted by General Washington on Friday, April 15, 1791. The mayor and people, together with members of the various local Masonic Lodges, assembled, and at three o'clock waited on the Commissioners at "Mr. Wises's," and there a glass of wine was drunk by all to the following toast:

> May the stone we are about to place in the ground remain an immovable monument of the wisdom and unanimity of North America.

The following was the order of parade to Jones Point: first, the Town Sergeant, followed by the Mayor, Honorable Daniel Carroll; the Surveyor, Major Ellicott; his Recorder, the Aldermen, members of the Common Council (who were not included in the Masonic Order); and those listed as "strangers" (guests). Following these came the Worshipful Master of Masonic Lodge Number 22, with Dr. David Stuart at his right and the Reverend James Muir at his left, the Lodge marching in "usual form," followed by the citizenry.

The Reverend Mr. Muir, in his address at Jones Point, said in part:

> From this |corner| stone may a superstructure arise whose glory, whose magnificence, whose stability, unequalled hitherto, shall astonish the world and invite even the savage of the wilderness to a shelter under its roof.

The Virginia portion of the District of Columbia was returned to the Commonwealth by the United States, and the "Document of Recession" was signed on September 7, 1846, by President James K. Polk. The area was not returned to Fairfax County, and a new political subdivision, Alexandria County, was created. Because of the confusion created in postal operations (due to the adjacent City of Alexandria) the name was changed to Arlington in 1922 in honor of the old Custis-Lee home.

The present day boundary of Arlington County follows the old District line adjacent to Falls Church. In Falls Church only two stones are extant, one on Van Buren Street, and the important western marker on Meridian Street. Each is protected by an iron fence erected by the Falls Church Chapter, D.A.R. A third stone was located on Upton Hill (now Willston) at Seven Corners, but this was disturbed by recent construction.

The stones marking the boundary were of sandstone from Aquia Creek in Stafford County. Each stone was to be twelve inches square and twenty-four inches out of the ground. The cornerposts were to be thirty-six inches, but the one at Falls Church is the same size as the intermediate stones. Evidently a mistake was made, as there is a thirty-six inch stone at a point called number three on the southest line. The western stone at Falls Church bearing the words, "West Corner" is the only stone bearing a notation of the corner, probably because of the mistake in height. This stone bears the date 1791, and the compass reading, probably 2° 0' East. The number of minutes is uncertain, but may be 10, 20, 30 or perhaps 00. This stone should be exactly ten miles from the south corner, but, according to a survey by the Coast and Geodetic Survey in 1879, actually is ten statute miles and 230.5 feet therefrom. This is remarkable accuracy to come out of the wilderness of 1791.

## FOOTNOTES

[1] Proudfit, Samuel Victor, "Aboriginal Occupancy of the District of Columbia," in Columbia Historical Society *Records*, volume 25, 1923, p. 182, et. seq. See also, *American Anthropologist*, (published by the Anthropological Society of Washington), volume 2, p. 225, et. seq., July, 1889. "Ancient Village Sites and Aboriginal Workshops in the District of Columbia," beginning on page 243, is of special value.

[2] *Ibid.*

[3] An account of the war can be found in *Economic and Social Survey of Fairfax County* (University of Virginia Record Extension Series, Vol. VIII, No. 12), August, 1924, by Lehman Nickell and Cary J. Randolph, Charlottesville, University of Virginia Press, page 8, article by Thomas R. Keith.

[4] *Historical Magazine*, Vol. I, page 65 (article "The Fall of the Susquehannocks"); Rowland, Kate Mason, *The Life Of George Mason, 1725-1792*, G. P. Putnam's Sons, 1892, Vol. I, page 9 *et. seq.*; and Force, Peter, *Tracts*, Vol. I, tract VIII.

[5] An article on the life of John Alexander Binns can be found in *William & Mary Quarterly*, 2nd series, volume 2, page 20, *et. seq.* This was written by Rodney H. True.

[6] Steadman, Melvin Lee, Jr., *The Mankin Family of America, 1677-1964*, 3 volumes, MS., 1964. A biographical sketch of General Henry Mankin is in the files of the Maryland Historical Society.

[7] Embrey, Alvin T., *Waters of the State*, Richmond: Old Dominion Press, 1931, pp. 109-10.

[8] Stetson, Charles W., *Four Mile Run Land Grants*, Washington, D.C.: Mimeoform Press, 1935, p. 74.

[9] Washington, George, *Diaries*, Volume 2, page 279.

[10] Proctor, John Clagett, *Proctor's Washington and Environs*, Washington, D.C., 1949, p. 102, *et. seq.*

[11] For a biographical sketch of L'Enfant, see Saemmerer, H. Paul, *The Life of Pierre Charles L'Enfant Planner of the City Beautiful*, etc., Washington, D.C.: National Republic Publications, 1950.

CHAPTER 2

# The Church on The Road to The Falls[1]

Falls Church is unique in at least one way. It is the only Falls Church in the United States. It was the name of a church before it was the name of a village; therefore the present city owes its existence to a church rather than to a store, court house, or landmark. It is fitting to give a history of the church to which the city is indebted. At the time the church, later called "Falls Church" was founded, there was nothing in this area except plantations and small farms, and here and there an occasional Ordinary (tavern). The road to the Little Falls of the Potomac was intersected by the road from Alexandria to Leesburg, once known as Middle Turnpike, and now known as Leesburg Pike (Broad Street). It was at this crossroads "on the road to Little Falls" and about three miles distant, that the Falls Church was built.

In 1730 Prince William County was taken from Stafford County, above Chappawamsick Creek and Deep Run, and along the Potomac River, to the "Great Mountains." This became known as the Hamilton Parish boundary when that parish was created. By an Act of the General Assembly, May, 1732, Hamilton Parish was divided, effective the following November, into two parishes. One of them was marked or bounded "By the river Ockoquan, and the Bull Run, (a branch thereof,) and a course from thence to the Indian Thoroughfare of the Blue Ridge Mountains." (Indian Thoroughfare was later Ashby's Gap.) That portion which remained in Prince William retained the name of Hamilton Parish, "and all that other part of the said county, which lies above those bounds, shall hereafter be called and known by the name of Truro." Truro Parish was later divided into smaller parishes, which include the Parishes of Cameron, Fairfax, Shelburne (all instituted in colonial days) and the later Parishes of Johns, Upper Truro, McGill, and a portion of Meade. Truro Parish was named for the ancient parish of that name in Cornwall, England.

Truro Parish was instituted by Act of the Assembly which provided that the sheriff of the County should summon the freeholders and housekeepers to meet and to elect so many of "most able and discreet persons in the said

Parish as shall make up the number of Vestrymen in the said Parish twelve and no more." This order was complied with, and the following "most able and discreet persons" were elected: Charles Broadwater, John Lewis, Richard Osborn, Gabriel Adams, and Edward Emms. The vestry book states that these men "together with Dennis McCarty, John Heryford, and Edward Barry, having taken the oaths appointed by Law, and Subscribed to be conformable to the doctrine and discipline of the Church of England, took their places in the Vestry accordingly."

The first vestry meeting was held on November 7, 1732, at which time Edward Barry was nominated and elected clerk. John Heryford and Edward Emms were chosen churchwardens for the next year, and were "sworn accordingly." The vestry book here begins for the first time, with recitation of the Act of the Assembly instituting the parish. The second meeting was held March 26, 1733, and at that time John Sturman and Giles Tillett were added to the vestry, and also listed are the names of Francis Awbrey (of Awbrey's Ferry) and William Godfrey, not previously mentioned. At this meeting it was decided to build the first Falls Church: "Ordered: that the Churchwardens give publick notice to workmen to appear at the next Vestry to be held for this parish to agree for the building of a church at the cross roads near Michael Reagans in this parish."

At the meeting held April 16, 1733, Michael Ashford was declared on oath a vestryman of the parish and "subscribed to the test." At this time an agreement was made with the Reverend Lawrence DeButts to preach three times a month for one year, "at Occoquan Church, the new Church, or William Gunnell's, (Falls Church) and at the Chappell above Goose Creek for the sum of eight thousand pounds of tobacco clear of the Warehouse charge and abatements,—And the said DeButts doth further agree to and with the Vestry aforesaid, that in case he fails, or is by the weather prevented to preach at any of the places aforesaid, any of the times aforesaid, tobacco shall only be levied for him in proportion to his service." Mr. DeButts preached eight sermons for the parish during the year assigned him, and received 1,970 lbs. of tobacco. He moved to Maryland at the end of the year.

The first Falls Church congregation to which DeButts ministered, seems to have been established through the efforts of William Gunnell. Gunnell was a native of Westmoreland County, and settled in what is now Falls Church in 1729. In that year he was issued two patents of land, one for four hundred and the other for two-hundred fifty acres, to border on Four Mile Run. A portion of this land was just north of where the church was erected, and the second on the south side of the Run, adjoining Thomas Pearson's patent on the west. In the spring of 1730, Gunnell applied to James Keith a minister of Hamilton Parish, to serve the congregation he had established in his home, consisting of Thomas Pearson, Michael Reagan, and others. Services were held occasionally by Mr. Keith, and the congregation became known as "William Gunnell's Church." Mr. Keith served until the coming of Mr. DeButts in 1733, and received 10,544 pounds of tobacco for his services. Keith was a colorful figure and was the maternal grandfather of Chief Justice John Marshall.

From 1733 (building of the first church) until 1765-69 (building of the present brick church) the history is often confusing owing to a difference of name for the church. First appearing as "William Gunnell's Church," it was known after 1733 and until about 1757 as Upper Church," to distinguish it from the "Lower Church" of the parish (or "Occoquan Church," the original Pohick Church). At the time that Truro Parish was created from Hamilton Parish, the small beginnings of these two congregations were already in existence, as was the congregation of the "Chappell above Goose Creek," (near the Big Spring on the road to Point of Rocks outside of Leesburg in Loudoun County.)

The records concerning the first Falls Church, a wooden building, are given in the vestry book. On June 9, 1733, Colonel Richard Blackburn agreed with the Vestry of Truro Parish (consisting of John Sturman, Dennis McCarty, Michael Ashford, William Godfrey, Giles Tillett, Gabriel Adams, Edward Barry, John Hereford and Edward Emms) to build this first Falls Church:

> Whereas Mr. Richard Blackburn has this day agreed with this Vestry to build a Church at the Cross roads near Michael Reagans in this Parish of the following dimentions; Vizt: Forty feet in length, two and twenty foot wide, and thirteen foot pitch, to be weather boarded, Covered, and all the inside work perform'd and done after the same manner the work upon O̶c̶c̶o̶q̶u̶a̶n̶ Pohick Church is done, for the sum of thirty three thousand five hundred pounds of tobacco.

William Godfrey and Michael Ashford were "to take care that the work upon the church be well and sufficiently done and performed." Dr. Douglas Southall Freeman in his *George Washington* (Vol. 1, page 54) gives the above quotation from the Vestry Book and states: "It is quite probable, though it cannot be stated positively, that this was the first church ever attended by George Washington."

Michael Reagan gave the land for the Falls Church, but failed to give a deed to the Vestry. He later sold his property to John Trammell. On March 20, 1746, by deed recorded in the Fairfax Court House, John Trammell transferred "by deed of bargain and sale to the Vestry of Truro Parish in Fairfax County" a certain parcel of land containing two acres "where the Upper Church now is, to be laid off in such manner as the Vestry shall think proper, to include the said Church church-yard, and spring, and all appurtenances to the said premises." Trammell received fifty shillings sterling for the land.

The name Falls Church first appears in the old Vestry Book on November 28, 1757, when John Lumley, Clerk at "Falls Church" and Alexandria was ordered paid 2,000 lbs. of tobacco for his services. Prior to this entry the church was called "Upper Church." It is interesting to note that at one time the church may have been referred to as "Little Falls Church." Bishop Meade refers to the church by this name.[2]

The contract awarded on June 9, 1733 is the earliest record concerning the building at Falls Church. By order of the vestry dated October 13, 1734,

John Trammell was paid 320 pounds of tobacco for "grubbing a place for a church." Under the same date, the Vestry ordered that Richard Blackburn be paid 16,750 pounds of tobacco "for his plans for building a church;" and Joseph Johnson was ordered to "read at the chapels," for which he was to receive 1,300 pounds of tobacco. By this date the new building was at least partly in use. Another building was being constructed for the church at Goose Creek, and became known as "Goose Creek Chapel." On June 10, 1733, Capt. Francis Aubrey was paid 2,500 lbs. of tobacco for building the chapel.

Richard Blackburn, the architect of Falls Church, was a prominent Prince William resident, and a son of Col. Thomas Blackburn, an early settler. His daughter, Julia Anne Blackburn, married Justice Bushrod Washington, who inherited Mount Vernon from General Washington. Jane Charlotte Blackburn, niece of Julia Anne (Blackburn) Washington, married John Augustine Washington, last private owner of Mount Vernon.

Colonel Richard Blackburn is noted in the records as a "builder of skill." He designed the original house at Mount Vernon, now part of the present mansion. The Blackburn home, Rippon Lodge, built in 1725, and named for his ancestral home in Rippon, England, still stands today in what is now Prince William County, and is owned by a descendant, Richard Blackburn Black. Rippon Lodge is a story-and-half frame building with a gabled roof and three dormer windows. The dormer windows project over the balustraded roof of a recessed porch which has six small Doric columns. In the interior, the hall and dining room have richly carved paneling. In the upper hall is an aperture in the north wall which formerly led to a secret stairway. This stairway connected with a tunnel extending from the basement to a ravine.

In the yard is a brick office which Blackburn used, and a building called the guardhouse with iron-grilled windows. In this structure Thomas Blackburn quartered soldiers during the Revolutionary War.

The Reverend Charles Green was the first resident clergyman appointed to the Falls Church and the other churches of the parish. He was settled in 1737 and served until 1764. Green is of special interest because of numerous marginal notes which he made in the Vestry Book. Dr. Green was recommended to the Vestry by Captain Augustine Washington. The following is the Vestry Record of August 19, 1736:

> At a Vestry held for Truro Parish this 19th. day of August, 1736, present: Jeremiah Bronaugh, Church Warden; Dennis McCarty, Augustine Washington, Richard Osborn, John Sturman, Wm. Godfrey, James Baxter, Edward Barry, and Thomas Lewis, Vestrymen. Mr. Charles Green, being recommended to this Vestry by Capt. Augustine Washington as a person qualified to officiate as a Minister of this Parish, as soon as he shall receive orders from his Grace the Bishop of London to qualify himself for the same. It is therefore ordered by this Vestry, that as soon as the said Green has qualified himself as aforesaid, he be received and entertained as Minister of the said Parish. And the said Vestry do humbly

recommend the said Charles Green to the Right Honorable Thomas Lord Fairfax for his letters of recommendation and Presentation to his Grace the said Lord Bishop of London to qualify him as aforesaid.

In 1748 Colonel George Mason of Gunston Hall was elected to the Vestry, and continued to serve in this capacity for the next thirty-five years. He was loyal to his church in every way, and served on the building committee of Pohick Church,[3] and the Falls Church.

The material in the old Vestry Book concerning the Falls Church at this time is scant. Some references are of interest, however:[4]

> October 12, 1747: Mary Bennett, sexton, Upper Church, 400 pounds of tobacco.
>
> October 10, 1748: Mary Bennitt, sexton, Upper Church, 400 pounds of tobacco.
>
> October 8, 1749: Mary Bennitt, sexton, Upper Church, 460 pounds of tobacco.

In 1749 the parish was divided, and the "Upper Parish called Cameron." This was done between October 10, 1748, and February 19, 1749. On this last date John Wilber Danty was ordered paid 1,000 pounds of tobacco for services as Clerk at Upper Church. At the meeting held February 19, 1749, the following were present: the Reverend Charles Green, Minister, Hugh West, Colonel George Mason, James Hamilton, Colonel Charles Broadwater, Daniel McCarty, Colonel William Payne, Colonel Abraham Barnes, Thomas Wren, Robert Boggess, and John Turley, Gentlemen. At this meeting it was ordered that an addition be built to the Upper Church according to a plan presented to the Vestry by Charles Broadwater, who "undertakes to do the same and finish and complete it by the laying of the next Parish levy for the sum of 12,000 pounds of tobacco which is then to be levied for him."

On October 9, 1749, John Wilber Danty, Clerk at Upper Church, was ordered paid the usual 1,000 pounds of tobacco for his services. Mary Bennitt was serving as sexton at the usual price of 460 pounds of tobacco. Jacob Remey was ordered paid "out of proportionable part 1,950 pounds of tobacco" for "paling in the New Church, making horse blocks and tarring church, etc." It was also ordered that the Vestry was to meet on the third Monday "in February next" at the Glebe House "to see what repairs are wanted to it and the New Church and the Church Wardens are ordered to give notice to workmen to appear there to undertake the work and also to repair the Pohick Church and the Vestry House."

On August 8, 1749, a meeting was held to appoint Processioners for the parish to "procession" (establish all land boundaries within the parish for the purpose of tithe collection).[5] It was ordered that John Trammell and John Harle procession "all the patented lands between Difficult Run and Broad Run and that they perform the same sometime in the month of October or November next and report their proceedings according to law." Anthony Hampton and William Moore were to procession all the patented lands between Broad Run and the south side of Goose Creek, as far as the fork of Little River, and that they were to "perform the same sometime in the month of October or November next and report their proceedings according to law."

A "new church" (later called Rocky Run) was ordered built during the 1745-6 period, on Blackburn's plan of the Falls Church, and the description is very complete. To what extent it follows Blackburn's plan is not known, but some adaptation was made. The plan for the "New Church" (voted upon at the Vestry meeting of May 21, 1745) follows: "That a Church be built at or near the spring nigh Mr. Hutchinson's and the Mountain road," of the following dimensions: 40 feet long, 22 feet wide and 13 feet pitch. The building was to be weather-boarded with 3/4 inch feather-edge plank, quartered and beaded; shingled with 18 inch pine shingles; sawed frame, and frame worked ceiled with quartered plank; beaded, "and floored with 1 1/4 inch plank with proper cornice under the eaves with pulpit, desk, [and] communion table." The new church was to have "Communion table, pews, doors, windows & seats *after the manner of the upper Church* and all proper facings and mouldings; and window shutters to be shingled with single tiers weather boarded with eights and filled with tens and brads; locks and hinges that are necessary for the same."[6]

The salary of John Wilber Danty as Clerk of the Upper Church was raised 200 pounds, when on October 2, 1752, it was ordered that the clerk of Upper Church "read prayers every intervening Sunday." At this same time Colonel Charles Broadwater and Colonel Abraham Barnes were appointed Church Wardens for the ensuing year. By the time of the Vestry meeting of November 22, 1754 William Donaldson had been appointed the Clerk of Upper Church, and Mary Bennitt continued as sexton.

On September 17, 1755, it was ordered: "That the several tracts of land that have their beginnings between Hunting Creek and the Potomac the road that leads from Awbrey's Ferry to the UPPER CHURCH be processioned sometime in the month of December next." John Dalton, Thomas Harrison, John Hunter, and Nathaniel Smith were to "attend to see the same performed and that they take an account of their proceedings therein and return the same to the next Vestry after the same shall be performed."

At the time of the meeting of November 29, 1756, Mr. Lumley was serving as Clerk of Upper Church and receiving 1,000 pounds of tobacco as salary. At the time of the Vestry held Nov. 12, 1759, Thomas Lewis was Clerk and Gerard Trammell was sexton.

October 25, 1762, has been called the most important date in the history of the Parish. Under this date the following is entered into the Vestry Book: "*Ordered, that Geo. Washington, Esqr. be chosen and appointed one of the Vestrymen of this Parish in the room of William Peake, Gent., deceased.*" At the Court House in Fairfax is the following record under date of February 15, 1763: "George Washington, Esqr., took the oaths according to

Law, repeated and subscribed to the Test, and subscribed to the Doctrine and Discipline of the Church of England in order to qualify him to act as a Vestryman of Truro Parish."

Three generations of the Washington family were Vestrymen of the Parish. George Washington's father, Captain Augustine Washington, who was sworn "one of the members of this Vestry, took his place accordingly" on November 18, 1735, served for many years. The Reverend Charles Green (under initial of "C.G.") wrote on the margin of the Vestry Book: "A.W. a fourteenth Vestryman, father of L.W. [Lawrence Washington] the other Burgess when Truro Vestry was dissolved." Lund Washington, a kinsman and manager of Mount Vernon, also served on the Vestry.

Under date October 25, 1762, it was also ordered that the sexton at the Falls Church be allowed 560 pounds of tobacco.

The present Falls Church was voted upon by Truro Vestry, but actually built by Fairfax Vestry, after the division of the older Parish. The following is the record calling for the erection of the building which now stands at 145 South Washington Street:

At a Vestry of Truro Parish held at the Falls Church March 28th, 1763, Present: Henry Gunnell, Wm. Payne, Jun., Ch. Wardens; John West, William Payne, Chas. Broadwater, Thos. Wren, Abra. Barnes, Dan'l. McCarty, Robt. Boggess and Geo. Washington, Vestry Men who being there met to examine into the State of the said Church greatly in decay & want of repair & likewise whether the same should be repaired, or a new one built, and whether at the same Place, or removed to a more convenient one, and likewise to view the Addition built by Mr. Charles Broadwater, and what he hath been deficient in the work.

Resolved it is the Opinion of this Vestry that the old Church is rotten and unfit for repair, but that a new Church be built at the same place. Resolved that James Wren and Owen Williams do value the work to be done by Mr. Broadwater on the new Addition, that is, the price of Glazing three Windows & Plastering the said House, together with materials necessary for the same, and make report to the next Vestry.

Ordered that the Clerk of the Vestry Advertise in the Virginia and Maryland Gazettes for Workmen to meet at the said Church on the 29th Day of August next, if fair, if not the next fair Day to undertake the Building a Brick Church to contain 1,600 Feet on the Floor, with a suitable Gallery & bring a Plan of the Church and price according to the same.

"Ordered that the Church Wardens employ Workmen to repair the Windows on the North side & the East End of the old Church and repair the Shutters of the new Addition."

Copy                  Henry Gunnell
                         Wm. Payne

N.B. This Vestry was held when I was sick, and could not attend —the above Orders were sent as above, signed by Messrs. Gunnell

& Payne, and I thought fit to record the same—tho' in point of Time it should have been before the Last one. John West Junr.

At the vestry meeting held October 3, 1763, the following were present: Charles Green, Minister; Wm. Payne, Jr., and Henry Gunnell, Church Wardens; George William Fairfax, Thomas Wren, William Payne, Abraham Barnes, Charles Broadwater, John West, and George Mason. Mr. Green was voted 17,280 pounds of tobacco as salary. Gerard Trammell (sexton at the Falls Church) was voted 560 pounds of tobacco. Trammell also served as the constable. Some 30,000 Pounds of tobacco was levied towards building the Falls Church, to be sold by the Church Wardens for cash at the best price. It was ordered that George William Fairfax and George Washington, be appointed Church Wardens for the ensuing year. The Vestry was instructed to meet at Alexandria the third Tuesday "of March next" in order to agree with workmen to undertake the "building of a church at or near the old Falls Church;" and that the Church Wardens advertise in the Virginia and Maryland Gazettes six weeks, and for workmen to produce the plan and estimated expense. (Signed by Charles Green and George William Fairfax, Church Wardens). The advertisement published in the Maryland Gazette follows:

> Virginia, Fairfax county, March 20, 1764
> Notice is hereby given to any Person or Persons, who are willing to undertake the Building of a Brick Church at the Falls in Truro Parish in the County aforesaid, (to contain 1600 feet superficial Measure, with convenient Galleries), That on the Third Monday in June next, there will be a meeting of the Vestry, at what is commonly called the Upper Church; At which Time and Place, any Person or Persons, who will undertake the same, are desired to attend, with their Plans, and Estimate of the Expense, and to give Bond, with good Security, to the Church wardens of the said Parish, for his or their true performance.
> George W. Fairfax
> George Washington  Church Wardens.

There is no record of a meeting held on the third Monday in June, 1764. However, Colonel James Wren produced a plan which was accepted by the Vestry and constructed the present building. This plan was the basis for the one used for the present Pohick Church, and for Christ Church at Alexandria.

The meeting held April 26, 1765, dealt with the division of the Parish. February 1, 1765, Truro Parish was divided, and a new parish formed called Fairfax Parish. Truro Parish was divided "from Colonel Washington's Mill to John Monroe's, and thence to Difficult Run, the upper Parish called Fairfax." The division was favorable to the new parish, and unfavorable to the older parish. Hence, the House of Burgesses, meeting in 1765, revised the parish boundaries, making them more equal. The bone of contention was that Washington and his immense Mount Vernon estate had been placed in Fairfax Parish. At the first meeting of Fairfax Parish (March 28, 1765)

Washington was elected a Vestryman. The following names are of the first Vestry of Fairfax Parish: John West, Charles Alexander, William Payne, John Dalton, George Washington, Charles Broadwater, George Johnston, Townsend Dade, Richard Sanford, William Adams, John Posey, and Daniel French. The life of the new parish after the first division was but four months. There is no evidence that the Vestry ever met for organization. The revision of the parish boundaries having taken place in May, Washington was elected a Vestryman of Truro Parish again in July. The Falls Church and the church at Alexandria (Christ Church) fell within the bounds of the new parish, where they remain to this day. It was left to the Vestry of Fairfax Parish to complete the new edifice at Falls Church, which was done by 1769.

Details concerning the completion of the church are found in both Vestry Books. On February 3rd and 4th, 1766, at the home of William Gardner (at which time Washington was present) the following was recorded: "It appearing from an order of the Vestry bearing date the 25th day of March 1763 that there was a deficiency in the work which ought to have been done to the Falls Church by Mr. Chas. Broadwater and that persons were appointed to view the same and report and no report appearing upon the records of this parish it is ordered that the Church Wardens do inquire into the same and report accordingly."

Again, on July 10, 1766:

"At a Vestry held for Truro Parish, July 10, 1766, Mr. Edward Payne one of the Church Wardens having reported to this vestry that he had applied to the persons formally appointed to view the work which ought to have been done on the Falls Church by Mr. Chas. Broadwater and that they denied having any order to view the same and refused to concern themselves: Ordered: That Thos. Price do view the work done to the Falls Church and report what deficiency appears in the same and that Mr. Edward Payne do apply to the vestry of Fairfax Parish to appoint a workman to view the same and that the said do report as aforesaid and that Mr. Edward Payne attend the viewing on behalf of this parish and to apply to the said vestry to appoint one of their members to attend the same on behalf of their parish."

A meeting was held at the Glebe on February 23, 1767, (at which time George Washington was present). The following was reported: "A report being made to this vestry by Jas. Wren and Thos. Price two workmen empowered by a formal order of this vestry to view the work done to the Falls Church and to report what deficiency appeared in the same etc., by which report there appears to be a deficiency of 9 £ 14 s. 6 p. Ordered: That the Church Wardens of this parish apply to Maj. Chas. Broadwater the undertaker of said work for the sum and account with the vestry of Fairfax Parish for their proportion of the same when it is received. Ordered: That a vestry house be built at the new church. . ."

## FOOTNOTES

[1] *The Vestry Book of Truro Parish* (November 7, 1732-May 18, 1832) is the basis for the history of Falls Church (the Church). It is now in the manuscript collections of the Library of Congress, Washington, D. C., having been placed there by the Vestry on April 20, 1924. The Vestry Book was lost to sight for many years, and in 1824 Bishop Meade could not find it. After the War Between the States it was found by the Rev. Philip Slaughter. It was purchased by him and presented to the Vestry of Pohick Church. A photostat copy is retained at Pohick Church. The book of Vestry Minutes was kept separate from the Parish Register, which recorded events such as birth, death and marriage. However, a few records of baptism are to be found in the first few pages of the book.(It is of interest to note that the practice of keeping systematic records of births was first adopted by the Clergy in England about 1538 to prevent disputes regarding inheritance. From this beginning evolved all other interest in maintaining a Parish record.) The Vestry Book of Truro Parish is particularly valuable since it contains numerous autographs of George Washington, George Mason, and others.

For further study there is an excellent manuscript volume (of which only several copies were made) having the following title page: "The Falls Church/The Old Colonial Church/Near the Falls of the Potomac/1733-1940/Charles A. Stewart, S.W. |Senior Warden|/ February, 1941." A copy was placed in the Falls Church Library (the church library), one in Richmond, and an additional copy is owned by the Stewart family. This latter copy was made available to the author.

[2] Bishop William Meade, *Old Churches, and Families of Virginia* published by Lippincott, 1857, volume I, page 256.

[3] Pohick Church, originally called Occoquan Church, was first located on land now owned by the Cranford Memorial Methodist Church near Lorton. Cranford Memorial, first called "Lewis Chapel," met on alternate Sundays at Pohick Church. The first Lewis Chapel was built on the old Pohick Church site. A marker on the grounds has this inscription: "Site of the First Pohick Church, 1730-1774." "Pohick" comes from "Pohickory" the Indian name for the hickory nut tree. This is found in some records as "Pokecory." Pohick Run was probably the source of the name for the Church—since it was built nearby. For other information on Cranford Memorial Church, and later history of the old site, see *Cranford Memorial Methodist Church* (One-hundredth Anniversary), August 4, 1957, *Historical Presentation* by Miss Susan Annie Plaskett.

[4] The name Bennett is spelled several ways in the record.

[5] The Parish had charge of "Such matters as related to the relief of the poor, the medical care of the sick, charges for burial of the dead, the maintenance of the blind, the lame, and the maimed, also of foundlings and vagrants. . . ." Stewart, *A Virginia Village,"* p.p. 34-35.

[6] Andrew Hutchison deeded two acres of land to the Vestry for the "New" Church—which was later called "Rocky Run Chapel." Hugh Thomas contracted to build the building for 24,500 pounds of tobacco. "Rocky Run Chapel" was located near the modern community of Centreville (Old New Gate) on the Fairfax-Loudoun border.

CHAPTER 3

# The Old Brick Church[1]

The Vestry Book of Fairfax Parish begins on August 26, 1765. Under the first date (August 26, 1765) the following is recorded in reference to Falls Church:

> Ordered that Samuel Hamon be appointed Reader at the Falls Church.

The following are other references to the church:

> (November 30, 1765) To Thomas Wren, Reader at the Falls Church, 750 lbs. tobacco.

> (December 30, 1765) Gerrard Trammell agreed to do the usual at the Falls Church for 400 lbs. tobacco as Sexton. Thomas Wren is appointed Clerk for the Falls Church.

> (October 16, 1766) To Thomas Wren at the Falls Church, 1,000 pounds of tobacco. To Gerrard Trammel[1], Sexton at the Falls Church, 560 lbs. tobacco. Ordered, That the Church Wardens advertise the want of a Glebe to be bought, and those inclined to sell Land let them meet at the Falls Church the first Monday in March ensuing, or send in their proposal.

> (October 16, 1766) An Order of the Vestry of Truro Parish was produced to this Parrish desiring a view of the work done to the Falls Church by Charles Broadwater—they having appointed Thomas Price to view the work desires us to appoint another workman to join in Conjunction with him. (James Wren and William Payne were appointed).

> James Wren was elected a Vestryman on November 15, 1766 in place of Edward Blackburn who resigned.

At a regular meeting of the vestry held November 27, 1766, the Church Wardens were directed to advertise the construction of two churches to be 2,400 square feet, each built of brick, "from outside to outside," and "the walls to be raised to admit of galleries." One of these was to be "where the old Falls Church now stands," and the other "at Alexandria."

The "undertakers" (contractors) met on January 1, 1767, and "James Wren produced a plan sixty feet by forty, which was made choice of, and agrees to Build the same for Five Hundred and Ninety-nine pounds and Fifteen Shillings." This plan was to be used for both buildings. It was "Ordered that the Church Wardens apply to the Clerk of Prince William for an abstract of the deed Relative to lands at and adjoining the Falls Church."

James Wren's plan as entered in the Vestry Book reads as follows:

> The church at the Falls and Alexandria to be 28 ft. from the foundation, that is 3 bricks and a half to the sleepers, 3 bricks to the water table and 2 1/2 from thence. The Quoins and arches to be rubbed brick; the Pediments to the doors rubbed work in the Tuscan order; the outside of the wall to be done with place bricks. The mortar to be two thirds lime and one sand; the inside half lime and half sand; the isles [aisles] to be laid with tile or flags;[2] the lower windows to contain eighteen lights, each of 9 x 11, and the upper windows 12 lights each, besides the compass head; the sashes of the lower windows to hang with weights and pulleys and to be clean of sap; to have medallion cornice under the eaves; the roof to have three pair of principal rafters, or as the workmen call it a principal roof to be framed in the best manner and to be covered with inch pine or poplar plank, laid close to shingle on; the shingles to be made of the best juniper-cypress, three quarters of an inch thick, eighteen inches long and to show six inches.
> —The floors to be laid with inch and a quarter pine plank and to be raised four inches above the isles [aisles] the pews to be three feet six inches high besides the coping, with doors to all to be neatly wainscoted, with quarter round on both sides, and raised panel on one, and to be neatly capped with some handsome moulding — the seats to be 12 x 13 inches broad, the outdoors to be folding and in width — Feet, hung with proper hinges locks and bars, to be raised pannelled on both sides, locust sills to the frame and the architrave. The altar piece, pulpit and canopy to be completed in Ionic order. The walls and ceiling to be well plastered with three coats and with a cove cornice. The whole to be neatly painted and finished in the best manner. The isles [aisles] to be six feet.

The cost of building the Falls Church was £600. It was begun in 1767 and being complete, turned over to the Vestry in December, 1769. As to the materials used, Bishop Meade[3] writing during the 1850's states that the proportions of lime and sand in the mortar was the "very reverse of the proportion of this day, and which accounts for the greater durability of ancient walls. The shingles were to be of the best Cypress or Juniper, and 3 quarters of an inch thick, instead of our present half inch." Bishop Meade wrote: "A gallery never was erected in the Little Falls Church." However, the first building may have had a gallery. In 1740 three of the notables of the parish asked permission to construct a gallery, at their expense, at the west end of the church. This was to be for the exclusive use of their families. The rector was one of the petitioners, though he signed "Charles Green, Doctor of Physick."

There is a tradition that the bricks in the church walls were brought from England, and brick was often used as ballast. However, it is well known locally that the bricks in the Falls Church were made by Colonel James Wren and William Wren, at their kiln. Although "bricks from England" is a pleasing tradition, it is pointed out by numerous authorities that it is not altogether probable. Only a very few were imported by the colonies. Nearly everywhere in Virginia can be found excellent deposits of brick clay, Thus the material was cheap and near at hand. The ships out of England were small, and every available inch of space was packed with manufactured and much-needed items. The "bricks from England" theory in all probability came to popular thought by the fact that the trade phrases of the makers were "Dutch" and "English" style brick. The Wren kiln was about three-fourths of a mile east of what is now Dunn Loring, one block south of the W. & O.D. Railroad on Shreve Road.[4]

The Vestry ordered that George Washington pay to Alexander Henderson the sum of £8 being the balance of £9 — 14 s. 6 p. received from Maj. Chas. Broadwater "for a deficiency on the Falls Church." This was the conclusion of a drawn-out discussion. Washington's name appears less and less in the Vestry Book. On February 24, 1784 (in the same year that the civil functions of the Vestry ceased) it was reported: "At a vestry held for Truro Parish at Colchester the 22nd day of February 1784, John Gibson, gent., is elected for a member of this Parish in the room of his Excellency, General Washington who has signified his resignation in a letter to Dan'l. McCarty, Esq."

The meeting of Fairfax Parish, held December 20, 1769, was attended by: Townsend Dade, Church Warden; James Wren, Church Warden; William Payne, John Dalton, Charles Broadwater, Richard Sanford, William Adams, Daniel French, Edward Dulin, Thomas Shaw, and Henry Gunnell. "It is agreed by the Vestry that Mr. James Wren has *completed* the work on the *Falls Church*, agreeable to his contract and that his bond be delivered to him, and that they have received the same for the use of the parish. Ordered: That Mr. James Wren and Townshend Dade do Allott the seats for the parishioners according to dignity. It is ordered that the old church be sold immediately and be removed by the last of February, a distance sufficient from the new building and the purchaser to give bond and security payable next June, come twelve months, and if it is not removed by that time that the property be vested in the Parish again."

The old building which seems to have been in use right up to 1769, was sold to John Brawner for 7 pounds, 10 shillings. It stood somewhat southwest of the present building.[5]

The Vestry of Fairfax Parish met twenty-seven times between December 20, 1769 and March 24, 1777, and the business at hand was more or less routine. In 1772 it is noted that Bryan Fairfax had resigned as vestryman and John West, Jr., was appointed in his place. Upon the death of Townsend Dade in 1777, John Muir was elected to the Vestry.

Benjamin West who was appointed in 1769, continued as Clerk of Falls Church until 1773 when John Ball was appointed to that office. Ball served until after 1776 at an annual salary of 1,000 pounds of tobacco. In 1779 Elisha Powell served as Clerk of Falls Church at a reduced salary of 750 pounds of tobacco.

Gerard Trammell served as Sexton of Falls Church from 1767 until 1776. His salary between 1767 and 1770 was at a rate of 560 pounds of tobacco yearly. Between 1770 and 1776 the salary was 500 pounds yearly.

With the appointment of the Clerk for Falls Church in November, 1779, references to the Church in the Vestry Book of Fairfax Parish ceased, and no furthur action is noted. On October 1, 1792 Thomas Davis was appointed Rector of Fairfax Parish and his assistant was the Reverend Bernard Page. Since the Vestry gave Page liberty to preach at two churches in Fairfax Parish, it is assumed one was Christ Church, Alexandria, and the other Falls Church.

The Vestry of Fairfax Parish on April 7, 1793 consisted of the following persons: Richard Arrell, Charles Broadwater, Richard Conway, Baldwin Dade, William Darrell, Nicholas Fitzhugh, William Herbert, John C. Hunter, Robert T. Hooe, Philip R. Fendall, William Payne (Church Warden), and Roger West (Church Warden). Of these, Broadwater and Payne had served 'since before 1769. The other names are relatively new and most of them were residents of Alexandria.

Among the clergymen who have served Falls Church have been a number of well-qualified and exceptionally fine men. The first was the Reverend Lawrence DeButts. DeButts served Truro Parish from April 16, 1733, until October 11, 1734. At the meeting of Truro Vestry held April 16, 1733, an agreement was made with Mr. DeButts to preach three times a month for one year, at Occoquan, [Pohick] New Church [Falls Church] and the Chapel at Goose Creek. He preached eight sermons during this time, and received 1,970 pounds of tobacco in payment. DeButts later moved to Maryland.

The Reverend John Holmes and the Reverend Joseph Blumfield are mentioned in the Vestry Book under date of October 11, 1736. They seem to have ministered in the Parish. Mr. DeButts is mentioned in the parish records of August 19, 1736.

An incomplete list of clergymen who have served the Falls Church follows:

### TRURO PARISH

| | |
|---|---|
| James Keith (Hamilton Parish) | 1730-1733 |
| Lawrence DeButts | 1733-1734 |
| John Holmes and Joseph Blumfield | 1734-1736 |
| Lawrence DeButts | 1736-1737 |

## TRURO PARISH

| | |
|---|---|
| Charles Green | 1737-1764 |
| Lee Massey | 1767 |

## FAIRFAX PARISH

| | |
|---|---|
| Townsend Dade | 1767-1777 |
| William West | 1778-1779 |
| David Griffith | 1779-1789 |
| Bryan Fairfax | 1790-1792 |
| Thomas Davis | 1792-1806 |

### From the Seminary

| | |
|---|---|
| Launcelot Minor | 1833-1837 |
| Edward Lippit | 1837-1840 |
| R. T. Brown | 1842-1843 |
| William F. Lockwood | 1847-1852 |
| R. T. Brown | 1855-1861 |

(Dr. Joshua Peterkin, student at the Seminary in 1834, should be included at some undetermined point in the above list. Dr. Joseph Packard refers to his first sermon at Falls Church, apparently when Peterkin was a student.)

### War Between the States

During the War Between the States the church was used by both Confederate and Union Chaplains until the building was converted into a stable. The only person known by name to have used the building was the Reverend Dr. Mines, Chaplain of the Second Maine Regiment, as reported in *Harper's Weekly* of August 3, 1861.

### Clergymen since the War

| | |
|---|---|
| Right Reverend Bishop Horatio Southgate | 1874 |
| John McGill | 1877 |
| Frank Page | 1878-1889 |
| J. Cleveland Hall | 1891-1892 |
| R. A. Castleman | 1892-1895 |
| John McGill | 1895-1899 |
| George S. Somerville ("Restoration Rector") | 1899-1908 |
| W. E. Callender | 1908-1912 |
| John McGill | 1913 |
| Andrew G. Grinnan | 1913-1917 |
| R. A. Castleman | 1917-1931 |
| Clarence S. McClellan | 1932-1934 |
| W. Leigh Ribble | 1935-1945 |
| Francis W. Hayes, Jr. | 1945-1958 |
| J. Hodge Alves | 1958- |

\* \* \* \* \* \* \* \* \* \*

The Reverend David Griffith, who served from 1779 until 1789, was the last to serve a full congregation at Falls Church, as the building was finally abandoned.[6] The Reverend Bryan Fairfax was an ardent Royalist before the Revolution. Son of William Fairfax of Belvoir, he was ordained

25

in 1786 by Bishop Seabury. Fairfax was confirmed as the eighth Lord Fairfax by the English House of Lords in 1800. His tombstone in Ivy Hill Cemetery, Alexandria, reads as follows: "In memoriam — Right Hon. and Reverend Bryan, Lord Fairfax, Baron of Cameron. Rector of Fairfax Parish. Died at Mount Eagle August 7th, 1802 aged 65 years."

Of the other men mentioned, a few facts have been obtained about some of them. Townsend Dade was a native of Virginia, and was ordained by the Bishop of London in 1765.

Mr. Dade preached to his scattered parishioners from 1767 to 1777. They included those at Falls Church and at Alexandria (Christ Church) where he preached on alternate Sundays. In 1778, after strong pressure was brought to bear on him, he was forced to resign because of "conduct unbecoming." Two years later he was succeeded by the Rev. Bryan Fairfax. A year after his arrival (1791) the Glebe was valued at 1,000 pounds, current money.

Mr. Dade received twenty shillings for a wedding or funeral, and it took only fifteen of these to buy a choice acre of land. The prospective rector was allowed a commission of fifty per-cent for procuring books and ornaments for the church. His congregation did not bear a heavy burden on him, if we can judge from other accounts. The Reverend Charles Green on a list of tithables of Fairfax County compiled during the 1740's, commented that his loss of congregation was due to Papists, Presbyterians, and Anabaptists in the Parish. Mr. Green writes (when he had Goose Creek Chapel under his care): "I never had one communicant, though several times prepared to administer the sacrament."

Edward R. Lippit (1837-1840) was appointed Professor of Systematic Divinity at the Seminary near Alexandria in 1826. Launcelot B. Minor served from 1833 until 1837. He went as a missionary to Africa upon leaving Falls Church. While in Africa he walked over burning sand forty miles during one day, and it was from this and other exertions that his life was shortened. Minor walked to the Falls Church, a distance of six miles, taught Sunday School and held services. It was his custom to walk the six miles back to the Seminary and engage in services there.

Dr. Joseph Packard (1812-1902) in his interesting work, *"Recollections of a Long Life,"* mentions many of the men who served at Falls Church. He also tells of visiting an old lady near Falls Church, a Mrs. Hopkins. She was more than ninety when she died, and remembered the kiln where the bricks for Falls Church were made, and had played in it as a child. Dr. Packard also states that Francis Scott Key, author of the "Star Spangled Banner," preached at the Falls Church. As early as 1816 Key was appointed Lay Reader at St. John's, Georgetown, being recommended as one "whose talents and piety" rendered him capable to exercise this office.

The Reverend William Meade, distinguished Bishop of the Church, preached at the Falls Church on one occasion for one hour and a half, the last third to the Negroes present. This was reported by Dr. Packard, who was present, and who also preached there. Packard also accompanied Bishop

John Johns to Falls Church on his visitation, and heard him preach. According to Dr. Packard the Bishop had not decided "what sermon to preach until he should see the congregation." After looking upon the congregation the worthy Bishop selected the text: "Many shall seek to enter in and shall not be able."

A great debt is owed to the students of the Theological Seminary who kept the church from falling into complete decay. Others who preached here from the Seminary were: Richard Wilmer (later Bishop); W.H. Kinckle, Churchill J. Gibson, and George W. Shinn.

Bishop James Madison, first Protestant Episcopal Bishop of Virginia visited Falls Church and preached here. Bishop Kinsolving, Bishop of Brazil, received Confirmation in Falls Church.

After the war the church was almost a complete ruin until it was revived by Bishop Southgate, formerly missionary Bishop in Constantinople.

The home of the Parish minister was known as the Glebe. While this term is not familiar to us today, it represented an ancient Anglican practice which had its beginning prior to 1302. The rector was supplied with a farm and house as part of his salary. The original Glebe of Truro Parish was called a "Mansion House" and was 24 x 24 x 10. A description of this building is to be found in the *Virginia Gazette* for August 14, 1752.[7] It called for a building of 1,200 square feet of brick, one story high, with cellars below, and with "convenient rooms and closets as the land will allow."

The first Glebe for Fairfax Parish is now 4527 17th St., Arlington, and is the home of Senator and Mrs. Frank L. Ball. The present house, however, has one wing erected 1820, and the foundation of the dwelling erected in 1775.

On December 30, 1765 the Reverend Townshend Dade presented his credentials at Alexandria as the first rector of Fairfax Parish. He was given an additional 2,500 pounds, on account of the lack of a Glebe. On this same day the Church Wardens were ordered by the Vestry to take steps to procure a Glebe. It appears that nothing suitable was found until 1769, when the church agreed conditionally to pay £800 for four hundred acres, the property of Townshend Dade, Sr., father of the rector. The son agreed to erect and repair buildings and make a "glebe compleat," within five years. However, he did not comply with the conditions, and the vestry turned elsewhere.

At this time there was a tract of five hundred acres which was rentable for 2,500 pounds of raw tobacco. On May 12, 1770, the following was written in the Fairfax Vestry Book: "An offer being made by Daniel Jennings of his tract of land for a Glebe, it is agreed to hold a vestry at the plantation of the said Jennings on Thursday next, being the 17th instant, in order to view the said land."

The meeting was held on the appointed date, with eight Vestrymen present, two of whom were Church Wardens (Mr. Dade, the Rector, and James Wren); and the result was an agreement to purchase the land for 15 shillings an acre. Today this same land is valued at more than $20,000,000. It has been remembered in names such as Glebe Road, (road to the Glebe), Glebe

Hill, Glebe House, and Glebewood. The modern boundary of the old Glebe would be approximately Glebe Road, Wilson Boulevard (as far as Clarendon Circle), Washington Boulevard to Jackson Street, and from that point to Spout Run and Old Dominion Drive.

The following is from the Vestry Book:

> It is agreed with Daniel Jennings to take the land whereon he lives, containing, as is supposed to be, about four hundred and more acres. The said Daniel Jennings agrees that Mr. George West, the surveyor, is to lay off the different pattents, at his expense, adjoining, to find the real quantity now in his possession, for which the Church Wardens and Vestry agree to pay him at the rate of fifteen shillings per acre. The said Daniel Jennings is to make sufficient deeds for the same, with a general warrantee, on or before the fifteenth day of September next ensuing, and to deliver up all the premises on the land on the fifteenth of December next, except the dwellinghouse and kitchen, which he reserves for his use until the first day of May next ensuing. The Church Wardens and Vestry agree in consideration of the said premises to pay him, the said Daniel Jennings, one half of the amount of said land the first day of November, the other half or remainder on the first day of November which shall happen to be in the year 1771.

This land was first patented in 1713 by the Reverend James Brechin of Westmoreland County, and contained, at the time, seven hundred-ninety-five acres. The land was drained by the upper waters of Spout Run (tributary of the Potomac) and Lubber Run (tributary of Four Mile Run). Daniel Jennings was the son of Daniel Jennings, Sr., who was the first official surveyor of Fairfax County. The Glebe touched the lands of George Mason of Gunston Hall. The survey of Mr. West showed the land to contain five hundred-sixteen acres.

Since the Jennings buildings did not meet the needs of the rector, in 1773 the Vestry (meeting at the home of Dade) engaged Benjamin Ray to build a Glebe house and necessary buildings, for which he was to receive 653 pounds of tobacco, the payment "to be made in common currency, that is, dollars at six shillings, and half Joes" (a "Joe" was a Portuguese coin worth at that time about $8.81) "in proportion."

The following is the description of the house to be constructed, as found in the Vestry Book:

> A Dwelling house to be built on the Glebe land, 42 feet in the clear. The walls from the foundation to be two bricks thick to the water table, and one and a half from that to the Top. The cellar to be four feet under ground and to include the dining room and passage in it, and from the bottom of the cellar to the upper part of the second floor to be eleven feet. Two partition walls in the cellar under the gurders, of brick, nine inches each, with proper doors into the cellar and through the partition, with good and sufficient locks and hinges to them, with the cellar cleared out.

The chimneys to be seven feet above the ridge. The frame of the lower floor to be sawed out of white oak or poplar, clear of sap. The upper framing to be sawed out of white oak or poplar, to be got very substantial and well framed. The bricks to be laid in mortar, two thirds lime and one sand, for the outside, and inside half and half. The floors to be laid with inch and a quarter pine plank. The upper floor to be gruved and tounged, the stairs to run up in the passage with hand rail and banisters, and a door underneath to go down into the cellar, with a broad step ladder. All the doors on the lower floor to have six panels each, and frames to have double architraves. The doors of the upper floor to have four panels each, and the frames to be cased with a bare ege and beed, the room doors below to have brass locks, and them above to have Japaned locks with swivels and hung with good and sufficient hinges. Nine large windows below, with eighteen lights in each, ten by eight, with inside shutters to them, four end windows, eight lights each ten by eight. Six Dormer windows, twelve lights, ten by eight, with good and sufficient frames, with locust sills to all six cellar windows, with locust frame and bars, and the frames of all the windows to be cased agreeable to the doors. Two portals, the one is the half the other, in the dining room, to have the upper door glass, the passage door the front side to have four lights of glass fixed in the frame above the door, the closets in the plan omitted. The roof to be latted and shingled with the best Juniper Cyprus shingles, got eighteen inches, and shew six Good and sufficient steps made of locust to all the out doors, a plain Cornish under the eaves and a large board up the ends. Chear and wash boards to all the rooms and them in the hall and dining-room to be neat, the other plain, The whole building to be lathed, plastered, white washed, and painted with plain colors as the Minister shall direct, and everything to be done to make said Building compleat in a plain, neat and workman like manner and agreeable to plan annexed.

A Kitchen to be built on the Glebe land, twenty feet by sixteen feet, in the clear, and eight feet pitch, with an inside chimney of brick, six feet in the clear, a pair of stairs to run up on the one side, and a closet on the other. The frame to be sawed out of white oak, and sides and ends to be weather boarded with clap boards clear of sap, the roof to be covered with feather edge shingles to be got out of red oak, and well saped. The inside fitted in with brick and the floor laid with brick or soil, and under pinned, and the loft laid with plank, one plank door and one window, eight lights, and a window in the loft with a shutter, proper shelves and dressers put up, the eaves boxed and barged, with corner boards to be painted, the sides and roofs to be tared, the whole to be well framed, and everything done to make the said Kitchen compleat in a plain workman like manner.

In addition to the mansion and kitchen, the specifications called for a "darey, |dairy| 12 feet square, a "meet |meat| house," 12 feet square with "pigeon roof;" a barn to be 32 by 20 feet, with a frame sawed out of white oak; a stable, 24 by 16 feet of sawed logs; a corn house, 16 by 10 feet; a "house of office," |toilet| to be 8 by 6 feet; and a garden 100 feet square, enclosed by pales five feet high, "neatly headed." The whole lay-out was to be completed by November 1, 1775. In 1774 provision was made to construct a hen house, 16 by 10 feet, with two ballard doors.

Thomas Jefferson led the dissenting churches in a campaign against the established church during the Revolutionary period. Although the church was separated from the state after 1776, by an act of the Virginia Legislature, it was allowed to keep its Glebes through the efforts of George Mason of Gunston Hall. In 1802, however, a law was passed confiscating the Glebes and turning them over to the county Overseers of the Poor. When the Fairfax Glebe became part of the District of Columbia in 1801, its fate was delayed. In 1811 a suit was brought against the overseers of the poor to prevent them taking the Glebe lands. The United States Supreme Court stepped in during the year 1815, and ruled that the title of the Glebe actually belonged to the Alexandria Church (called Christ Church in 1811). An objection was made to the effect that the Falls Church had claim to one half of the lands, and it was not legally the property of Christ Church, but of the Vestry of Fairfax Parish. However, since the Falls Church had been abandoned as a place of worship, this was not effective.

The old Glebe burned in 1808, and was not rebuilt until 1820. Having gained a clear title, the Vestry sold the land to General John Mason and Walter Jones, who married a daughter of Charles Lee. The price was twenty four dollars an acre (or in all, $13,367.34). On the original foundations of the old Glebe Mr. Jones built a house, now the oldest wing of the present mansion. Mr. Jones maintained his residence in Washington, where he conducted his law practice using the Glebe for other purposes. The main (octagon) portion of the present house was erected during the 1870's by The Honorable Caleb Cushing.

The last owner of the whole tract of land was New York Congressman John Peter Van Ness. He purchased Mr. Jones' half in 1826 at a public sale, Mr. Jones having defaulted on a note for $1,700. He purchased Mrs. Mason's half in 1836 for $2,500. In 1847 subdivision was begun. In 1870 Caleb Cushing (President Pierce's Attorney General) gained title to the last one hundred acres and the present house for $6,000. It was sold for $1,800 and divided thirteen years later. The present house has many notable features. One is a stairway in the octagon added by Cushing about 1883. The octagon was added to the house as an art gallery, being one room with balconies. On top of the octagon is a flying eagle, said to have been presented to Cushing by the people of Spain. Two acres remain with the house.

The Rectory of the Falls Church (about 1900-1912) was the Oak Street house until recently occupied by Mr. and Mrs. G. Torreyson Reeves. The Reverend George S. Somerville lived there in 1904. Bishop Southgate lived in what was later the Burns N. Gibson home opposite the church.[8] The next Rectory was the old A.D. Lounsbury home, a Falls Church landmark for more than a century, which is at the corner of Fairfax and East Broad Streets. This has been sold and a Rectory purchased in Broadmont.

## FOOTNOTES

[1] *The Vestry Book of Fairfax Parish* is the basis of the history of Falls Church after 1765. The original is in a bank vault in Alexandria. It is not available to scholars. However, the late Mary G. Powell made a handwritten copy which she gave to the D.A.R. Library, Washington, D. C. This copy is kept in a locked cabinet there, and is available to those interested. (The Present Vestry Book of the Falls Church begins November 27, 1873.) The author is in debt to the late Charles A. Stewart who made extracts of various records concerning the old Church, including those after 1873. These were kindly loaned by his daughter, Miss Elizabeth Tabb Stewart.

[2] During the War Between the States Union troops converted the old church into a stable, and at the time removed the floors and brick aisle. Mr. H. C. Ryer obtained one of the aisle bricks at the time (1864) and presented it to the church on November 7, 1918.

[3] *Old Churches and Families of Virginia*, p. 251.

[4] According to the late William Nathan Lynch some of the bricks, probably the rough bricks, were burned in a kiln about 300 yards west of the Church on the old Fairfax Road. Traces of the kiln could be seen as late as 1945 near the C. C. Walters home.

[5] An order of the Fairfax Vestry dated February 8, 1768, was "that James Wrenn fix the church as near the north side of the old church so that it fronts directly south."

[6] Mr. Griffith was a close personal friend of George Washington, and served as chaplain of the Third Virginia Regiment during the Revolutionary War. He died in 1789.

[7] Thomas Waite agreed to build the Glebe in October 1752. By 1759, "tho' often admonished" Waite had not completed his work. His contract was annulled and William Buckland, distinguished architect of George Mason's Gunston Hall, completed the work and was paid the balance due Waite.

[8] Built for a Rectory prior to the War Between the States, and often called the "Wilson House."

## CHAPTER 4

# Roads and Wayside Taverns

At the time of the First World War it was a common sight to see herds of cattle moving along the Leesburg Pike through Falls Church toward Washington. The largest slaughter house in this vicinity was at Rosslyn, and was conducted on a profitable basis for many years. Local farmers would arise about four o'clock in the morning, and, with four or five neighbors to help, would drive the cattle to be slaughtered. They arrived in Rosslyn about nine o'clock.

Times have changed rapidly and all we see today to remind us of our once rural area is an occasional plow horse and wagon.

In early colonial times, the life of the colony centered around the parish church. Here the social and religious affairs of life were attended to. The location of a church was determined by a main road, and the location selected was usually accessible to water. There were sometimes two or three churches in each parish, and an occasional "chapel of ease." The latter was located in a remote neighborhood and served from one of the churches. Church location was controlled by a desire to make the meeting place central to principal plantations, and the main road offered a carriage-way for the faithful. Once a neighborhood was selected, the exact location was determined by a good spring of water, as the parishioners came over hot and dusty roads in summer, and often man and beast refreshed themselves after travelling half the length of the county. The spring near "Big Chimneys" was convenient to the Falls Church.

In colonial days two main arteries of travel intersected at what became Falls Church. One was the road from Fairfax to the ferry near Little Falls and the other, known in early times as the Great Road and later as Middle Turnpike, extended from Hunting Creek (Alexandria) through Leesburg to the Shenandoah Valley. The name Middle Turnpike was applied because it lay between the Little River Turnpike, from Alexandria westward, and the Georgetown Turnpike, from Georgetown to Dranesville, where it joined the Georgetown Pike. It is interesting to note that the minutes of the Town Council of Falls Church, mentioned this as Middle Turnpike until that part of it within the town limits was named Broad Street. Broad Street has long been known locally as the Leesburg Pike.

Leesburg Pike (Route 7) is said to be one of the oldest roads in America in continuous use. It was originally an Indian trail about two hundred and thirty miles long, extending from Tidewater (in the vicinity of Williamsburg) to what were known as "the valleys beyond the mountains," or beyond the Blue Ridge. It passed through the counties of New Kent, King William, Caroline, Spotsylvania, Stafford, and Prince William, crossing the Occoquan at Colchester into Fairfax. From Colchester it passed by way of Accotink, Washington's Old Mill, over the fords at Little Hunting Creek and at Great Hunting Creek, into Alexandria.

From Alexandria the Indian trail followed two routes, varying from one to twelve miles apart as the branches passed on their way to the mountains. One of these passed through Fairfax County by Falls Church and Dranesville, through Loudoun County by Leesburg and Clark's Gap in the Catoctin Mountains and by Hillsboro to Key's Gap in the Blue Ridge Mountains. It was over this branch that General Sir Peter Halket's historic Forty-fourth Regiment of British Regulars, a part of General Braddock's army, marched, in April, 1755, on the disastrous expedition against the French and Indians.

The other part of this Indian trail passed from Alexandria through Fairfax one mile southwest of the present court house, through Loudoun County by Aldie near the Bull Run Mountains, to Snicker's Gap in the Blue Ridge. A considerable extent of this branch is also known as Braddock's Road,[1] from the fact that a part of Braddock's wagon train passed over it.

It was over this road that George Washington and George William Fairfax journeyed to the Shenandoah Valley to survey the lands of Thomas, Lord Fairfax. In 1753, at the age of twenty-one, as a messenger from Governor Dinwiddie to the French Commander (with a commission of Colonel), Washington passed over it again on his route to Great Meadows.

Mr. J.O. Martin wrote of this road:

". . . Dolley Madison, wife of the President, fled along this same road to Leesburg, when the British burned the White House at Washington, and over this same road was borne the body of Nellie Custis, George Washington's adopted daughter, who died in the Valley of Virginia, near Berryville, at an advanced age, and who was laid to rest at Mount Vernon."

Miss Ada Walker wrote the author concerning Mrs. Madison's route:

"I was told that Dolley Madison fled over Chain Bridge, spent the night at Smoot's and went on from there to Leesburg Pike."

Leaving Langley Mrs. Madison went to Falls Church by Little Falls Road, according to a local tradition. It would seem out of the way for Mrs. Madison to have used the Little Falls Road, but it may be that this was the only road leading to the Pike that was not being searched. It is known that the old "Big Chimneys" at Falls Church was searched by the British, since the President was thought to be there.

Mr. Martin points out, in a recent communication, that when he wrote of Dolley Madison, he probably had in mind that portion of the Leesburg Pike which lies between the place where the Georgetown Pike joins it at Dranesville and the home to which she fled, near Leesburg, and that he was probably not thinking of Mrs. Madison in connection with Falls Church.

In the Virginia Historical Society at Richmond is a photostat of an undated and unsigned map of Fairfax County made about 1748, used as the end papers of this book. It was drawn to illustrate a proposal to divide Truro Parish and establish a new parish at the upper end of the county. A line was drawn straight across the county from the Potomac at the mouth of Difficult Run to Bull Run at the mouth of Little Rocky Run. Written above the line is "The Intended new Parish." Among the landmarks on the map are Pohick Church shown between the Occoquan and Pohick Run, the Falls Church, then known as Upper Church, the Rocky Run Church, established 1745, and the Fairfax Court House at Freedom Hill, near Tyson's Corner, which was used until 1752. Also shown is the glebe of Truro Parish. These buildings were the principal public buildings in Northern Virginia at the time. Since Rocky Run Church was established in 1745, and the Court House continued at Freedom Hill until 1752, it is thus determined that the map was made between those dates.

Some interesting comments on early roads were made in an article by Mrs. Sally Ortolani from an interview with Mr. Mason Hirst of Annandale, who is currently compiling a history of Northern Virginia.[2] Mrs. Ortolani wrote:

> According to Mr. Mason Hirst, local real estate agent and compiler of historical data, Annandale was an Indian trading post as early as 1685—long before George Washington was born. It is believed that buffalo once roamed this far East and that Rolling Road was first a buffalo trace and then became an Indian portage path. The early name of Springfield Road was Backlick Road, which probably had its origin in the time of the buffalo.
>
> Rolling Road was built in 1692 by Lord Culpeper as a means of rolling the large hogsheads of tobacco from Ravensworth to the warehouses at Colchester on the Potomack, as it was then called. Ships regularly called at the port to load the tobacco for England and other foreign countries, where it was in great demand. It is said to be the oldest road this side of Williamsburg, and has been in constant use through the years. This year the old Rolling Road bowed to progress and was hard surfaced to better take care of the increased traffic.

The designation of various "rolling roads," arose from the practice of transporting the tobacco to the various shipping points in hogsheads in which were adjusted a pair of rude shafts, and thus in the way of a garden roller drawn to its destination.

Guinea Road was known as the "Rolling Road to Colchester Warehouses." The first warehouse in this vicinity was authorized in 1730 on the south side of Hunting Creek "upon Broadwater's land." The site was found unsuitable, and the establishment of a warehouse "upon Simon Pearson's land upon the upper side of Great Hunting Creek," was confirmed in 1732 by the General Assembly.

Hunting Creek has changed little since that time in some respects. It is a marshy resting place for ducks in autumn and winter. In the vicinity in 1676 a "fort or place of defence on Potomac River" was built as a protection from the Susquehannock Indians. In 1740 a public ferry was established "from Hunting Creek warehouse, on land of Hugh West. . .to Fraziers Point in Maryland." This was the ferry which the old records refer to so often as "the ferry."

An old building which stood until recent years on Fairfax Street adjacent to the Gibson apartments near the Falls Church was originally a tobacco storage warehouse connected with the Falls Warehouse. It was a long one-story building made of logs. Mr. W.B. Bryan wrote concerning this Warehouse:[3]

> The Parish Church of Fairfax was known as Falls Church, and was located some 6 miles to the west of the site of Washington and so named from the proximity of the Little Falls of the Potomac. Here was located a tobacco Inspection House, as well as one at Alexandria, but it may be concluded from the placing of the principal Church of the Parish at the Falls, as it was called, although several miles from the banks of the river, that it was then regarded as more central to the members of the Parish than Alexandria, where what was known as a minor Church, or Chapel of Ease, was located.

A number of references to the Falls Warehouse date back to the Colonial period. On September 19, 1755, Townshend Dade, Henry Gunnell, James Donaldson and Owen Williams were recommended to the Governor "as proper persons for Inspectors at the Falls Warehouse."[4] On January 12, 1764, it was ordered by the Fairfax Court that "Sampson Trammell, William Noding, Hugh Conn, and William Trammell, or any three being sworn, view the most convt. [convenient] way for a Road to be Opened from the Great Falls to Difficult Run to meet a Road to be cleared from thence thro' part of Fxx. [Fairfax] County to the Fall's Warehouse and Report."[5]

The Warehouse was in need of repairs when on November 23, 1768, it was ordered that John Dalton and Henry Riddell "view the Falls Warehouse and agree with workmen to make the necessary repairs."[6] Apparently Daniel French of Rose Hill (contractor of Pohick Church) agreed to repair the building. On August 21, 1769, it was ordered that Charles Broadwater, Bryan Fairfax, and William Adams, Gentlemen, or any two of them "view the work performed by Daniel French at the Falls warehouse and report to the next Court."[7] The gentlemen appointed did not carry out the order, and it was entered again on September 19, 1769, and the names of Henry Gunnell and John Dalton were added, this time with the stipulation that any three were to view the work done by French.[8] On October 16, 1769, the following order was recorded:[9]

35

Ordered to be certified to the Treasurer that Daniel French, Gent., has performed work and buildings at the Falls warehouse to the amount of Sixty-five pounds ten shillings and it is ordered that the Inspector account with the Treasurer out of the Rents of the said Warehouse to the amount of the above sum.

On March 21, 1769, it was "Ordered that the Inspectors at the Falls warehouse provide weights."[10]

The old Court Order Books provide complete information as to appointments and other matters related to the Falls Warehouse. Local residents can be traced along the route to the Warehouse, and mention is frequently noted concerning the maintenance of the road to "the Falls Warehouse."

Tobacco played an important part in local life, and its connection with the development of this area is yet to be written. The early Virginians spent many hours at regulating the tobacco trade. The first permanently effective legislation providing for inspection of tobacco was passed by the Virginia Legislature in 1730. Numerous attempts were made in prior years to provide assurance of quality to foreign purchasers. As early as 1619 sworn viewers were employed to inspect tobacco. The first warehouse act was passed in 1712, providing for the establishment of public warehouses at points not more than one mile from navigable water. It was followed by an act passed in 1713 providing for official inspection. So much objection was encountered, however, that the act was vetoed by the King, in 1717. A protracted depression which began in 1725 brought renewal of interest which culminated in the Act of 1730. It has been said that this was probably the most constructive type of marketing legislation passed in the colonial period, and its influence was profound.[11]

The following is taken from a book entitled *Bookkeeping Methodiz'd: or a Methodical Treatise of Merchant-Accompts according to the Italian Form*, (Dublin: MDCCLXIII), Chapter VII, Section I:

> The purchasing of tobacco in the colonies, is now, by an inspection-law, made easy and safe both to the planter and merchant. This law took place in Virginia in the year 1730, but in Maryland not until the year 1748. The planter, by virtue of this, may go to any place, and sell his tobacco, without carrying a sample of it along with him; and the merchant may buy it, though lying 100 miles, or at any distance from his store, and yet be morally sure both with respect to quality and quantity.
>
> For this purpose, upon all the rivers and bays of Virginia and Maryland, at the distance of about twelve or fourteen miles from one another, are erected warehouses, which generally take their name from the bays or creeks on which they are situated. Those on the south side of Potomack River are, Wicomico, Coan, Yeocomico, Nomony, Mattox, Boyd's-hole, Caves, Acquia, Quantico, Occoquan, Huntin-creek, and Falls. Those on the north side of Rappahannock are Indian Creek, Deep Creek, Glascocks, Totuskey, Nailors, Bray's Church, Gibson's, Falmouth. On the south

side of that river are, Urbanna, Hob's-hole, Port Royal, Fredericksburgh, etc. To these warehouses all the tobacco in the country must be brought, and there lodged, before the planters can offer it to sale. And men of good character, generally planters, two for each warehouse, chosen yearly by the county-court in Virginia, and by the vestry of each parish in Maryland, are commissioned by the governor, and appointed inspectors of all tobacco brought to their respective warehouses. Before their admission to that office, they are obliged to give oath and bond, with security in 1000 £ sterling to the faithful discharge of the same. Their salaries vary from 25 to 60 £ in that currency, according to the importance of the place where they serve. Their business is, to examine all the tobacco brought in, receive such as is good and merchantable, condemn and burn what appears damnified or insufficient.

The above is followed by several pages of discussion and details concerning the further handling of the tobacco trade, methods and forms used in connection with the export handling, accounting, and other matters.

What is now known as Little Falls Street was once a tobacco or "Rolling Road." Little Falls Street in Falls Church was once part of the road to the Little Falls of the Potomac, and crossed the Leesburg Pike (Broad Street) about in front of the present day Odd Fellows Hall. The road meandered through the vacant field near the Bowling Alley: This road passed Big Chimneys Tavern, and connected with the road (Fairfax Street) beside the old Falls Church. Fairfax Street, often called "old back road," or by the more dignified "Courthouse Road," by older residents, passed, near Hillwood Avenue behind the old Birch home, connecting with Wilson Boulevard.

Great Falls Street, which intersects Little Falls Road in Falls Church, is another old road. A well-known local tradition, coming from several independent sources, maintains that George Washington surveyed this road as a route to the Potomac Canal.

Shreve Road at West Falls Church follows a colonial access road which was used by the Wren, Darne, and Lindsay families. It was not until 1869, however, that it was laid off and under public control, although it was extended for public use as far as Backlick Road (now Lee Highway) below Mills Crossroads (Merrifield). Shreve Road was named for William Henry Shreve of "Mount Pleasant" (the old Lindsay home) who presented a petition to the Fairfax County Court in October, 1869:[12]

> ... [for] a county road from a point on the Middle Turnpike road about one fourth of a mile north of the crossing of the Alexandria Loudoun and Hampshire Railroad to a point on the road leading from Falls Church to Fairfax Court House and passing through the lands of Daniel H. Barrett, Lewis Sewall, Albert Wren, Elizabeth Wren, Robert Darne, and J.W. Gaylord, being about two and a half miles in length.

This petition was signed by William H. Shreve, J.C. DePutron, Archibald Sherwood, Seth Osborn, William H. Ellison, Charles H. Bramhall, Charles

Kirby, Francis A. Kirby, Benjamin F. Johnson, John R. Darne, James Payne, John B. Burke, J.C. Haycock, John L. Koon, Levi Parker, G.C. Powell, William McCauley, James Donaldson, Benjamin Klock, George W. West, Arthur B. West, Andrew Bedle, (Beedle)—"by Concent,"—Mary E. Mills, Lemuel Mills, John C. Mills, Robert Sherwood, Alfred Moore, John Moore, E.O. Powell, Tobias Roby, N. Humphrey, Robert S. Porter, and N.C. Hunter.

William H. Shreve presented this petition with a motion for the proposed road to the October, 1869 Court, and by January, 1870, the road was declared opened and damages assessed. Three large land owners, Daniel H. Barrett, Elizabeth Wren, and Robert Darne, gave right of way on October 13, 1869.

One of the first ramblers erected in the Falls Church area was a house on this road called "Wallhaven," built by Mr. and Mrs. Ralph McMillan Turner.[13]

In the W.P.A. Guidebook[14] is an account of the "New Church Road," put through in 1742:

> From an Indian trail along the Potomac emerged the Potomac Path, along which developed Dumfries, Colchester, and Alexandria. Branching from this road at Cameron Run on Hunting Creek was a road, known as 'The New Church Road,' in 1742, that extended by Falls Church to Vestal's (now William's) Gap and then to Winchester.

Leesburg Pike has been in use for many years, and was long the most important road in this vicinity. When the pioneers set out to new lands "beyond the mountains," it was over it that they travelled. The pike, for many years but a mud-hole, was made of logs in later years (a "corduroy road") for the convenience of the mail carriers. Along this route, to finance the pike, toll gates were erected.

John and Mary Williams maintained a toll gate at the north corner of Cherry Street and East Broad Street, from 1853 until the 1880's. It was the earliest toll gate in this area. The Williams home was a little house which was built about 1770. It was directly back of the toll gate house. The house was of clapboards over log, as so many of the older homes were, and had shutters and a wood shingle roof. Mrs. Charles E. Mankin (Ann Valinda Lynch) and her mother, Mrs. W.H.G. Lynch, often visited the Williams family. Mrs. Mankin recalled eating dinner there at one time, and remarked that Mrs. Williams' biscuits and Virginia ham were delicious. The water used by the household was drawn from an old shallow well beside the house, with an oaken bucket. The bucket hoops were of brass, and were shined, as Mrs. Mankin termed it, "so you could see your face in it." She also remarked that the water was as "clear as a bell," an old expression often associated with the tone of a bell, but which later denoted sight.

In later years a toll gate (before 1912) was established on the N.W. corner of Leesburg Pike and Shreve Road, opposite the site of Green's Blacksmith Shop. The toll house was opposite "Tops." The building was later used as a garage by Mr. Julius Willet, who purchased it from the State when no longer in use. It was a white clapboard structure, like an average single car garage, with a gabled roof. Mr. Walter Follin (called "Billy Goat" because of his beard) was a long-time toll keeper. According to the author's father, it cost 10¢ to go through the gate with a pony and wagon. To avoid the toll he and his child-hood playmates crossed through Gordon's Field, and this became Chestnut Street at Antrim. The toll building was torn down in 1952.

On the outskirts of Falls Church, near Munson's Hill Towers, is a portion of an old road used before the Revolution. J.O. Martin wrote concerning this road:[15]

> You ascend and descend a few small hills, pass an old home called Munson Hill, which was there before the war, and come to the place where the winding road from Washington, now called Wilson Boulevard, joins the highway. This road, incidentally, was in use before the Revolution. You'll recognize the place if you will watch for the telephone cables, for here the cable lines from Washington to the South cross the highway and branch off, one line going along an old road toward Richmond and the other cutting off through the woods to Lynchburg. The old square-pole line from Norfolk meets the Washington cable at this point, too. Probably the telephone men who built it in 1897 did not realize that the section of it they built between Falls Church and Dumfries followed an emergency road built in a hurry by the Fairfax militia for the wagon trains and the beef cattle of the American and French armies on the way to Yorktown.[16] The soldiers went by the Chesapeake but the wagon trains proceeded more slowly by land, crossing the Occoquan at Wolf Trap Shoals in order to avoid the ferry. In Prince William County this road, usable only in spots, is now called the Telephone Road.

Mr. Charles Stetson writes of an early road leading from the ferry to Falls Church, which became Wilson Boulevard, called Awbreys Road named for nearby land-owners, John & Mary Awbrey. In late colonial days the Awbreys owned the ferry. The name "Awbrey's Road" was used until the early part of the present century. A Vestry record of Truro Parish dated September 17, 1755, making mention of this road, recites: "Ordered That the several tracts of land that have their beginnings between Hunting Creek and the Potomac the road that leads from Awbrey's Ferry to the Upper Church [Falls Church] and the road that leads from Cameron [Parish] to the Upper Church. . ."

Leesburg Pike (Route 7) was once an Indian trail, and was well worn long before white men discovered it. The late Mr. Prentiss A. Shreve recorded some of its history in an article entitled "Know Your State and County," in *The Providence Journal*, September 30, 1944:

> Prior to about 1888 there was no public road leading from the Leesburg Pike to what is now Dunn Loring, and travel over this route was entirely over a private road by the old Lindsay cemetery and through the Klock and Shreve estates. The trough-like bed of this old road is clearly discernible near Mr. Klock's home and elsewhere and finally merges into an old colonial roadbed to be

easily seen at the turn of the present road entering Dunn Loring and opposite Mr. Sparshott's home. The present road was cleared of trees after the survey by a man who received $60 for the job.

I have been asked to outline the old Leesburg Road that preceeded the present improved highway. This I can only partially describe, and would be grateful for any assistance from someone having the story of the old route. I will attempt to carry it along for several miles, and leave off at some undetermined point, and of which point I am not familiar. Beginning near West Falls Church the old roadbed seems to speak for itself as it passes through the Flagg and Leonard Farms and about 300 feet north, back of the old Caton home at Lemon Road and Leesburg Pike, on through the Carlin (now Redd) farm, just back of the Whitney home, passing on up the hill in front of Mr. Dave Patterson's, through Falls Church orchards, then becoming lost until around the bend it is again found passing up through the Mills properties, continuing through the Buell and Rozier Kidwell farms to the Gallows Road, where it crosses and becomes the road now used at the old George Merry home, passing the old Watts farm (now Madrillon Farms) and on by the Sherman home to the sawmill at Flint Hill (the old Court House) and from there I am puzzled as to its directions and its point of contact with the present pike.

Early laws of the State made provision for the roads. One such order in 1657 stated that the settlers were to "Keep roads cleered yeerly." It has been said that Virginia's turnpikes in ante-bellum days were America's most complete adventure in the realm of good roads. In colonial days the roads were under the care of the county surveyor. If he failed to keep up his section of the road, the grand jury was prompt in dealing with him, as evidenced by this record: "We present the surveyor of the road from the Falls Church to Rock Creek for not having a sign post erected at the forks of the road." After the War Between the States, part of the tax on each head of a family was to work on the road a certain amount of time each year. The roads were plowed, scraped, and cleaned. In Falls Church during the 1880's and '90's, the Road Machine was run by Robert Nourse.

In 1789, the Fairfax and Loudoun Turnpike Road Company located a new road to the valley, later known as the Little River Turnpike, already mentioned. Now route 236, which junctions at Fairfax Court House with Ox Road (now route 123), it has been in continuous use since that time.

The Aqueduct Bridge, which was near the present Key Bridge over the Potomac, was established about 1790, and replaced a ferry which was in operation during colonial days. This bridge enabled the local farmers to ship produce to the Washington market at less expense. The stone pier at the Virginia end of the old bridge, to the west of the Key Bridge, can still be seen. The present Key Bridge, named in honor of Francis Scott Key, author of our National Anthem, was opened to traffic January 17, 1923. The Key mansion stood near the Georgetown end of the bridge until recent years. The old Long Bridge, downstream, was constructed in 1809, and was replaced by the 14th Street Bridge. The Union troops fled back to Washington over Long Bridge after the Bull Run Battle.

On the evening of June 17, 1940, Mrs. George R. Reeves, Mrs. Charles E. Gage, Mr. H.C. Walling, and others met at the home of Mrs. Frank Birch (312 East Broad Street) to interview Mr. William Nathan Lynch. Mr. Lynch said:

> Years ago, there were two ways for people from Virginia to get to the City of Washington: First, over the Chain Bridge, which received its name because it was hung by a chain. There was no charge to go over it; second, by the ferry and the Aqueduct Bridge. It cost 25 cents per person to cross on the ferry and 2 cents per person to walk across the bridge. These ferry boats were called 'Whistle Steam-boats;' and had an up-and-down engine and carried about 125 tons of coal.

Along the route to Falls Church were numerous taverns of a varied sort. Mrs. Wakefield, an early English visitor to Virginia, wrote: "We can scarcely pass ten or twenty miles without seeing an ordinary," by which she meant an inn or tavern. "They all resemble each other, having a porch in front, the length of the house almost covered with hand-bills. They have no sign. These Virginia taverns take their name from the person who keeps the house, who is often a man of consequence."

The first tavern near the Falls Church was at the old cross roads, where Little Falls Road intersected Leesburg Pike. For many years Colonel James Wren owned a tavern near the Church. It was recommended by Thomas Jefferson and was still in existence in 1808. It was at Colonel Wren's Tavern, according to tradition, that Colonel George Washington, Colonel George Mason and others of the Truro Vestry met, upon at least one occasion. "Big Chimneys" was also an Ordinary, and was located directly opposite the Falls Church. It was at one of these that a young English visitor stopped in 1776. This young aristocrat, Nicholas Cresswell, noted in his *Journal* of Wednesday, September 18, 1776:[18]

> Left Alexandria in company with Harry McCabe. Dined at the Falls Church. Got to Leesburg in the evening.

Lindsay's old Tavern (after 1865 the Mills home) was established, according to local tradition, in 1720. If in business this early, the founder was not a Lindsay, although the Lindsays did own it for many years following 1745. The tavern was located on Leesburg Pike between Falls Church and Tyson's Corners, or Peach Grove. A 1920 era house now occupies the site adjacent to George Marshall School and the old well is still in use. Tradition long entrenched, says General Washington refreshed himself at this well. It is a likely tradition since his diary records several trips "up the pike."

The late Mr. David Leonard of Five Oaks, was the source of all the data we have on Lindsay's Old Tavern. During an interview with him on October 17, 1947, he told the author how the old tavern appeared during his childhood, following the War Between the States. Mr. Leonard said that it seemed not to have changed since the time it was built; he could not discern an addition to the building. Lindsay's was a log story-and-a-half building similar to Big Chimneys, with a stone foundation, and large brick end-chimneys. Four dormer windows were in the front roof, facing the pike. A porch, perhaps a later addition, was on the southeast side of the building. The windows were typical of the 1720 era, and had Dutch shutters. A door was in the center.

The Tavern was torn down about 1912. At that time the floors, of heart white pine, were worn thin. Originally 2" thick, the knots in the pine did not wear down, and were about half an inch above the floor. The floors were random and pegged together.

A duel of honor was fought in the yard during colonial days, in which both men were killed. They were buried behind the Inn.[19] Another story told by Mr. Leonard, and which he obtained from a member of the Mills family, was that of a guest "drunk as a Lord," who killed another guest in the main room. The bloodstain was on the floor until the building was torn down.

Liquor was supplied to the inn from a local source. A still was located on what is now a portion of the Benjamin Klock property—perhaps this was the Trammell still, at any rate, Mr. Leonard seemed to think so. Among items bequeathed by Gerrard Trammell (in a will dated Nov. 16, 1775, at Fairfax Court House) was a "still and warm pone mash" left to a grandson and namesake, Gerrard Trammell.

The local laws were maintained with much diligence by the county sheriff, who lived half the length of the county away from the inn. One such law was enacted on March 20, 1755, when the Fairfax Court ordered a positive set of rates to be posted on the door of each tavern in the county. It states that all "soldiers or expresses of his Majesty's Service paying ready money" were to have one-fifth deducted. The rates from the old 1755 Order Book at Fairfax follow:

|  | s. | d. |
|---|---|---|
| For a gill of rum and so in proportion | 8 |  |
| Nank Brandy | 20 |  |
| Virginia Peach or Apple Brandy | 6 |  |
| New England Rum | 2 | 6 |
| Virginia Brandy from grain | 4 |  |
| Arrack the quart made into punch | 8 |  |
| For a quart of red or white wine | 2 | 6 |
| For a quart of Maderia wine | 2 | 6 |
| For all the other low wines per quart | 1 | 6 |
| English Strong beer pr. do.[20] | 1 | 3 |
| London beer, called Porter pr. do. | 1 |  |
| Virginia strong beer pr. do. |  | 7½ |

| | | |
|---|---|---|
| Cyder, the quart bottle | | 4 |
| English Cyder       pr. do. | 1 | 3 |
| For a gill of rum made into punch with loaf sugar, 6 d., but with fruit | | 7½ |
| For do. with brown sugar | | 4½ |
| For a hot diet with small beer or Cyder | 1 | |
| For a cold diet | | 6 |
| For a gallon of Corn or oates | | 4 |
| Stableage and fodder for a horse 24 hours or one night | | 6 |
| Pasturage for a horse for small amt. of time | | 4 |
| For a night lodging with clean sheets, 6 d., otherwise nothing. | | |

There were many other small inns-of-a-sort in and around the Fairfax-Falls Church area, probably mere "tippling houses." By 1668 "small tippling houses," or drinking bars, became so numerous in Virginia that a law was passed limiting each county to one at the court house and one at a public landing and ferry. Concerning the quality of the Virginia tavern, the Duc de la Rochefoucauld, a visitor from France, said that the inns in the back country of Virginia were preferable to the inns in many of the most inhabited parts of New England.

The food consumed was usually plain but always in plenty. The Indians of Virginia boiled beans, peas, corn and pumpkins together and the early colonists grew to like this stable dish. The pumpkins grew in abundance in this area. During the great flood of 1750, hundreds of them growing near the banks of the Potomac were swept into the water. Hence the flood was called the Pumpkin Flood.

## FOOTNOTES

[1] A good account of "Braddock's Road," is to be found in *Historic Highways*, by Archer B. Hulbert, Vol. IV.

[2] *The Falls Church Echo*, October 19, 1951, "Progressive Annandale is Rich in Local Tradition."

[3] Bryan, W. B., *A History of The National Capital*, New York: The MacMillan Company, 1914, Volume 1, page 82.

[4] Fairfax County records, *Order Book 17 (part 2) 1754-56*, page 417.

[5] Fairfax County records, *Minute Book (beginning March, 1764)*, page 12.

[6] Fairfax County records, *County Court Book 1768-1770*, page 65.

[7] *Ibid*, page 218.

[8] *Ibid*, page 231.

[9] *Ibid*, page 240.

[10] *Ibid*, page 105.

[11] From a letter from Charles E. Gage, noted authority on tobacco, February 11, 1963. Mr. Gage sent the author a condensed version of a lengthy paper read by L. C. Gray before the American Agricultural History Society in December, 1926, under the title *The Market Surplus Problems of Colonial Tobacco*. A footnote by Dr. Gray, formerly of

the U. S. Department of Agriculture, states that the contents of the paper were mainly abstracted from a larger study of southern agriculture before 1860.

[12] This Petition was found among unclassified material on file at Fairfax Court House, and a photostatic copy and a Shreve family copy are in the author's file.

[13] The Davis family has done much to develop the Shreve Road section of West Falls Church. Jackson Drive, intersecting Shreve Road, was named for Thomas Jackson Davis, born in Prentiss County, Mississippi, on November 14, 1875, and who died in Virginia, October 8, 1949. He was the son of William Jackson Davis and Mary Elizabeth Blassingame, grandson of William Addison Davis and Martha Kilburn, great-grandson of John Davis who married Nancy Wakefield of Virginia.

Thomas Jackson Davis married Docia Barnes, daughter of Marion Barnes and Margaret Rosanna Waters, a descendant of Lieutenant Edward Waters who came to Virginia in 1608 with Sir Thomas Gates and Sir George Somers as a member of the London Company to settle Jamestown. He married Grace O'Neal, called "Lady Grace," who was first cousin to Admiral James O'Neal, famous in the naval service of Charles I and whose wife was a maid of honor to the queen.

Thomas Jackson Davis and Docia Barnes Davis had three children: James Frederick, born September 10, 1908, Marion Elizabeth, born December 3, 1909, and Martha Louise born October 24, 1913.

Mr. Davis and family came to Virginia from Mississippi in the early thirties. The land on Shreve Road which he developed was a small tract that was a re-development of "Oldewood." This was in the mid-forties after he retired from the Treasury Department. A road running at right angles to Jackson Drive was named Martha's Lane for his younger daughter who once owned property adjoining it. Martha Davis married Vernon Plummer Leitch of Anne Arundel County, Maryland. Mrs. Leitch is a well-known local historian and civic leader. The Leitches now live at "Deerlick Cottage" in Buckland, Virginia.

James Frederick Davis, the son, married Mildred Carter Martin, a descendant of "King" Carter. They have one son, James Frederick Davis, Jr., called Fred, who owns and operates the Davis Gun Shop in Falls Church. Mrs. James Frederick Davis is Postmaster and Mr. Davis is Assistant Postmaster at Merrifield.

Marion Elizabeth Davis married Ralph McMillan Turner of Spartanburg, South Carolina. They lived on Shreve Road for a number of years. Mr. and Mrs. Turner built "Wallhaven." Mrs. Turner, now a widow, owns and operates the "Bird in Hand" Antique Shop in Buckland, Virginia, a favorite stopping place for many Falls Church residents who cherish the old and beautiful.

Thomas Jackson Davis, his wife and Ralph Turner are buried in the National Memorial Park Cemetery.

——Interview, May 22, 1964, with Martha Davis Leitch

[14] *Virginia, A Guide To the Old Dominion*, W. P. A., 1941, page 89.

[15] Sleepy Hollow Road.

[16] J. O. Martin, *Over the Concrete*, page 18.

[17] Charles W. Stetson, *Four Mile Run Land Grants*, Washington, D.C.: Mimeoform Press, 1935, page 9.

[18] *The Journal of Nicholas Cresswell (1774-1777)*, New York, Lincoln Macveagh, The Dial Press, 1924, page 162.

[19] D. M. Mills, age 91 years, recalls six graves behind the old Tavern. Mr. Mills was born in the old Tavern and grew up there.

[20] "pr. do." or "per ditto" referring to per quart.

## CHAPTER 5

# Drum, Fife, and Cannon

On June 7, 1755, George Washington noted in his diary that Sir Peter Halket, with the First Brigade of Braddock's army, was to begin his march to the Ohio. On the following day, they camped in the Falls Church yard, having marched from Shooter's Hill, (now Masonic Hill), in Alexandria, along what is now the Leesburg Pike.

Most of these men did not return from their ill-fated expedition to expel the French and Indians from English Ohio.

Earlier, February 20, 1755, General Edward Braddock landed at Hampton, and met in Williamsburg, to consult Governor Dinwiddie. Shortly thereafter he was joined by Commodore Keppel, whose squadron of two ships-of-war and several transport ships were anchored in the Chesapeake Bay. On board were two prime regiments of about five hundred men each, one commanded by Halket, the other by Col. Dunbar. The troops landed at Alexandria from the ships named "Norwich," "Seahorse," "Garland," and "Nightingale"; 1,300 men in all.

Sir Peter Halket was an interesting figure, and deserves comment here. He was a man of great ability, and utterly fearless. When ordered by the Duke of Cumberland to fight against the Pretender, Halket would not, since he wished James to be his king. With great courage he refused to do so, saying, "His Royal Highness is master of my commission, but not of my honor." He was captured by Charles Edward in 1745, and released by special parole to the Duke of Cumberland.

In his First Brigade, Halket commanded 984 men, including 700 Grenadier Guards of the 44th Regiment and two independent companies from New York, commanded by Capt. Rutherford and Capt. Gates. Capt. Gates was the same person to whom Burgoyne would surrender in the Revolution, and who came close to replacing as Commander-in-Chief the same George Washington who was then Braddock's aide. Also under Halket were Capt. Polson's Carpenters, two companies of Virginia Rangers, and forty nine Maryland Rangers under Capt. Dagworthy.

45

Sir Peter Halket was shot during the ensuing battle. This was reported to an English paper, which announced that "Sir Peter Halket of Pitfirrane, Bart," was killed in the action near Monongahela River "july ye 9th 1755." His son, Major James Halket, was also killed, while bending over the corpse of his father. After the war, another son came back to find the bodies of his father and brother. The bones were found interlocked.

Other than the brief visit to the yard of the Falls Church by Halket, nothing of any interest is on record concerning activity during the remainder of the war.

Less than twenty years later, the Revolutionary era opened with great excitement in Fairfax County. The famous *Fairfax Resolves* drafted by Colonel George Mason were adopted, and Colonel Charles Broadwater recruited soldiers for a local militia company in the Falls Church. There is an old tradition that the Declaration of Independence was read from the steps of old Falls Church in mid-July, 1776. Among Revolutionists active from Falls Church area were Colonel James Wren, Colonel Charles Broadwater, Colonel Charles Little, and others. Col. Charles Little, of "Cleesh," was not appointed a full Colonel of the Fairfax Militia until May 22, 1787. Charles Simms was commissioned by the governor as Colonel-Commanding, of the reorganized Fairfax Militia, June 22, 1785 *(Fairfax Order Book.* 1783-1788*)*.

Thomas Jefferson led the campaign for the separation of Church and State, so much a symbol of old England. Many of the old church buildings in Virginia were thereafter abandoned. Nor was the Falls Church exempt from the scars of this strife, during which twenty-three Virginia Parishes succumbed. The Vestry ceased its civil functions in 1784. After 1790, the building of the Falls Church ceased being used as a place of worship. Later, it was repaired by Captain Henry Fairfax, grandson of the former Rector, Bryan Fairfax. The records from 1827, about the time the building was repaired, until 1861, are lost, having been destroyed (it is thought) by Union troops during the War Between the States.

One Revolutionary hero who lived near Falls Church should not be overlooked. This was John Follin. According to records at Arlington Cemetery, Mr. Follin died April 17, 1841, and was buried in the family cemetery at Falls Church. He was reinterred in Lot 294-A of Arlington National Cemetery, where a proper monument was erected to his memory. Mr. Follin was a native of the Falls Church area. He enlisted in the navy from Alexandria, was captured, and taken a prisoner of war to Plymouth, England, and from there was transported to Gibraltar. Follin was flogged several times because he refused to serve in the British Navy. The British claimed the right to his services as a British subject. John Follin married twice, and was father of thirty children, twenty-one from his first marriage, nine from the second. One of these children died within recent years.

The Revolutionary War closed on a note of hope for the new "American Citizens" of Fairfax County. Many left their native county for "the West." This migration from Fairfax County extended to Kentucky and later, during the 1820-1840 period, to Missouri and elsewhere. A large number of settlers from the Falls Church area, including old families named Darne, Wren, Blackburn, Davis, and Broadwater, settled Callaway County, Missouri.

The War of 1812 was one of great excitement, but little action. Captain Nicholas Darne was a hero of this war, as was his kinsman, Robert Darne. The latter served under his father-in-law, John Wren, in the Fairfax Militia. An old tradition has it that during the war a search for the President was made in the Falls Church vicinity. It is well known among descendants of the Thompson-Lightfoot family that their home, Big Chimneys, was searched, but no written evidence has been found to support this.

During this same time the old Falls Church was open on the public highway and falling into ruin. The first reference to the Church after 1790 is in the annual report of the Convocation of The Protestant Episcopal Church under date May 14, 1823. At that time the petition of one John Moore was read in which he represented that "he was, on the 10th instant, duly elected a lay deputy to represent the interests of the Congregation of the Falls Church, in Fairfax Parish..." Moore was not seated, however, no congregation being in existence to elect him. He possibly took his authority from some former members or officials. These included, no doubt, members of the Darne and Wren families, although most of them were by this time members of The Methodist Church.

In 1824 the Marquis de Lafayette revisited America, and toured each of the twenty-four states. At every stop he was acclaimed with dinners, dances, and speeches. A tradition has it that he took off his hat to the old Falls Church when he passed it, enroute to Leesburg from Alexandria. He was for a short time a guest at Big Chimneys, opposite the Falls Church. At Alexandria the Masonic Lodge gave a great banquet in his honor. The toast given at that time by Edward Arthur May, maternal grandfather of Charles E. and George W. Mankin of Falls Church, is preserved in the family bible.

In 1827, Henry Fairfax contributed to the restoration of the abandoned church. About this time Bishop Meade visited the building and wrote of it:

> The exercises of the Seminary being over, I next directed my steps to the Falls Church, so called from its vicinity to one of the falls of the Potomac River. It is about eight miles from Alexandria, and the same from Georgetown. It is a large oblong building, and like that near Mount Vernon, has two rows of windows, being doubtless designed for galleries all around, though none were ever put there. It was deserted as a house of worship by Episcopalians about forty years ago. About that period, for the first, and it is believed last time, it was visited by Bishop Madison. Since then it has been used by any who were disposed to occupy it as a place of worship, and the doors and windows being open, itself standing on the common highway, it has been entered at pleasure by travelers on the road and animals of every kind. Some years since, the attention of the professors of our Seminary, and of some of the students were drawn towards it, and occasional services performed there. This led to its partial repair.

The church is mentioned in the annual report of the Convocation of the Protestant Episcopal Church in 1833. It is mentioned also on May 16, 1838, and it is stated in this report that communicants numbered 13, and of this number, 6 were added in the year concluded. Also it was noted that one funeral was held in the church and 3 white and 1 colored person baptized. It was reported that a Sunday School and Bible Class was in "flourishing condition." and that funds have been "raised for the repair of the church which will be put in complete order, it is expected, by the middle of July."

In the report of May 15, 1839, the Lay Delegate seated from Falls Church was Cleveland K. Nelson. Mr. Nelson reported the building "thoroughly repaired" and an enclosure of the burial plot was soon to be completed. At this same time the Rector, the Rev. Edward R. Lippett, stated:

> At the time of the last report |our| Sunday School was the only one in that neighborhood. Since that period one has been opened in the Methodist Chapel, |Fairfax Chapel| about a mile distant, which has diminished very much the attendance of our School.

However, 38 scholars and 10 teachers were reported at the Falls Church. On May 30, 1840, Henry Fairfax was seated as Lay Delegate, and also in 1841. In 1843 Henry Dennison was seated as Lay Delegate, and 16 members reported. In 1850 Arthur Lee Brent was seated in this same capacity. The report of 1861 listed 22 communicants. This is the last reference prior to the War Between the States.

Captain Henry Fairfax who financed the restoration of the 1830's and 1840's, deserves extended mention.[1] He was a hero of the Mexican War, and at the outbreak of the war organized a company called the *Fairfax Volunteers*. A graduate of West Point, Fairfax had a good military background. The Fairfax Volunteers sailed to Mexico with the regiment of Virginia volunteers under command of Colonel John F. Hamtramck. Upon arriving in Mexico, Fairfax devoted his energy and zeal in defense of his country. He died at Saltillo, a victim of the climate, August 16, 1847. As he wished, his body was brought home and buried in the Falls Church yard. A tablet in his memory was placed on the front wall of the church. Though later destroyed, its inscription was quoted in an 1861 issue of *Harper's Weekly*. In 1917 a tombstone bearing the same inscription was erected over his grave.

HENRY FAIRFAX
In memory of Henry Fairfax
An accomplished gentleman,
A sincere Christian, An up-right magistrate,
Died in command of the Fairfax Volunteers
At Saltillo, Mexico, 1847. But for his munificence
this church might still have been in ruin.
Erected by the Virginia Chapter of the
National Society of the Daughters of Founders
and Patriots of America, 1917.

[1] The Fairfax Home, "Ash Grove" is located on Leesburg Pike near Tyson's Corners. The widow of Henry Fairfax sold it to Alvord Sherman in 1850, and it is still a Sherman home.

## CHAPTER 6

# By a Broken Fence

An old worm fence, silver brown and gray with the luster of many years, marked the boundary of Williston Clover's farm. Enclosing a corn field of several acres, the fence followed Leesburg Pike in its meandering from Hangman's Tree to a spot near where the Presbyterian Church was built, but at that time, on the brink of the North-South struggle, was a spot occupied by Dr. Simon Groot's Academy.

Young Nat Lynch tilled corn in this same field during the late 1860's, but was at more dangerous labor during the war. Dusty and hot blue coats began to swarm the Pike in 1861. Tempers ran higher than the corn and were longer than the fence rows. Nat's father, enterprising blacksmith with an extensive establishment including a wheel wright, tempered with the South. Although a Marylander by birth, William H.G. Lynch was more Virginian than his eight years residence in Falls Church would indicate. His shop became the center of Falls Church "Rebel" activity. Arrested under suspicion several times, imprisoned at Alexandria, and questioned at length, Lynch did not give an inch, nor did the authorities find the source of information. They never suspected young Nat, who had his father's order to perch on the fence rail and count the Blue Coats as they rode into the Village.

Northern visitors of the paying kind left Star Tavern with the advance of McDowell's army in early spring. Their Republican twang and close-mouth manners made it expedient for their return to the rock from whence they were hewn. Even General McDowell could not guarantee their safety. The Village life took on grim aspect. Short, quick, and dignified William Gwynn Coe, Baltimore and Catholic bred, left the red-brick and double-door Methodist Chapel, and Falls Church went behind closed doors. The old Falls Church, like its Baptist and Methodist counterparts, was a pawn for both Blue and Gray. All was not quiet on the other side of the Potomac, and Honest Abe Lincoln, who drank from the wrong political cup, was an outcast on the Falls Church side.

Falls Church eyes cast longing glances toward Richmond, and news spread

49

over fence and fireside: the Virginia Assembly had passed the Ordinance of Secession on April 17, 1861. On the following May 23rd, local residents voted on secession. On the evening of the same day orders were given for the Federal troops in Washington to enter Virginia. They entered by four lanes: by steamer down the Potomac from Washington to Alexandria; by the old Long Bridge; by the Aqueduct Bridge at Georgetown; and by the Chain Bridge. Participating in this action were Ohio, Michigan, Massachusetts, Rhode Island, New York, New Jersey, and District of Columbia troops, about 10,000 men in all.

Falls Church went underground, and part of a system of defense for Washington City was extended to within its confines. A later historian, Charles A. Stewart, comments in his *Virginia Village:*[1]

> After the first battle of Bull Run a systematic plan for the defense of the National Capital began to take shape. At that time the commanding heights four miles west of Alexandria and six miles from Washington was occupied by the Confederates, Falls Church being the head-quarters of General Longstreet.

Longstreet's headquarters was in the house later known as the Lawton House, on the crest of Lawton Road.

The *Richmond Examiner* of September 19, 1861,[2] states that Longstreet's headquarters "had been established at Fairfax C.H. and about Sept. 9, had been advanced to Fall's Church." Later blue-clad General George B. McClellan occupied the Star Tavern.

In August and September 1861, while McClellan was reorganizing the Army of the Potomac, the Confederate army lay in the vicinity of the Fairfax Court House, with its outposts and picket lines extending in a curve from a point below Alexandria on the Little River Turnpike, over to Mason's, Munson's, and Upton's hills, to a point on the side of Falls Church near Arlington (then Alexandria) County. In front of this line lay the Union pickets and outposts.

Falls Church was the most advanced post of General McDowell's Corps when on August 3, 1861, a correspondent of Harper's Weekly writing "from the scene of action" describes the old Falls Church as it appeared at the beginning of the war:

> On this page we illustrate Fall's Church Fairfax County Virginia from a sketch by our special artist with General McDowells "corps d' armee.' This is the most advanced post of our army in Fairfax County and has been the scene of several picket skirmishes. Falls Church was built in 1709 and rebuilt as an inscription on the wall informs us by the late "Lord" Fairfax, whose son the present "Lord" Fairfax is supposed to be serving in the rebel army. The title "Lord" we may observe is still given to the representative of the family. The inscription on the old church reads as follows: "Henry Fairfax an accomplished gentleman , an upright magistrate, a sincere Christian, died in command of the Fairfax Volunteers at Saltillo, Mexico, 1847. But for his munificence this church might

still have been a ruin." Service was held in the old church two Sundays since, Rev. Dr. Mines Chaplain of the Second Maine Regiment officiating and most of the troops in the neighborhood present.

The Confederate outpost nearest Washington was on Munson's Hill, about a mile from the center of the village, and five miles from Georgetown. It was occupied by a force of Virginia cavalry under the command of Colonel J.E.B. Stuart, later a major-general who fell in battle. One writer stated: "The Confederate flag on Munson's Hill could be seen from the dome of the Capitol, a continual eyesore." General O.O. Howard wrote: "Reference to this audacious flag pointed the speech of many a brave orator that fall while criticising the slowness of McClellan. Munson's Hill armed the On-to-Richmond press with pithy paragraphs."

*Frank Leslie's Illustrated,* published in New York, was a popular newspaper of its day. In the issue of September 21, 1861, is a sketch of "The rebel fortifications of Munson's Hill—The rebel position nearest the Union lines, three mile Southwest of Arlington Heights." At the bottom of the same page is a sketch "by the special artist" with General McClellan, depicting the "Skirmishing between the pickets of the two armies, near Munson Hill."

In the issue dated June 29, 1861, is a very clear sketch of Falls Church Village, showing the arrival of the Second U.S. Cavalry, Company B, on Wednesday morning, June 19th. This gives a view of Lieutenant Charles Tompkins arriving at the Star Tavern to take command of the village. The old Columbia Baptist Church can be seen in the background. The write-up accompanying the sketch follows:

### FALLS CHURCH

This is a village in Virginia, about eleven miles from Alexandria and four miles from Vienna, and is situated on the Alexandria, Loudoun and Hampshire Railroad. Our artist has sent us an interesting sketch of the arrival of Lieutenant Tompkins and his gallant Company B. at that Village. It will be remembered that Lieutenant Tompkins has already distinguished himself by the dashing charge at Fairfax Court House and also by his subsequent rescue of two of his men, who were taken prisoners by the rebels. It was in this brilliant skirmish that he met in combat and wounded Colonel Ewell, a former associate, but one of the rebel leaders, who has thus been placed hor de combat for the present.

Tompkins, a Virginian, was born at Fort Monroe, November 13, 1843. He entered the Union Army at Brooklyn, N.Y., and on June 1, 1861, was awarded the Medal of Honor at Fairfax Court House. The citation stated that he had twice charged through the enemies lines and taking a carbine from an enlisted man, "shot the enemy's Captain."

In the early part of the war, a raid was made by a "masked battery" of Confederate soldiers on a train near Vienna, in which several Falls Church men were involved. *Leslie's* reports the incident as follows:[3]

RAILWAY TRAIN CONVEYING THE FIRST OHIO VOLUNTEERS, FIRED INTO BY A SECESSION MASKED BATTERY, NEAR VIENNA.

Official Report of Brigadier-General R.C. Schenck.

To Lieutenant General Scott:

I left camp with six hundred and sixty-eight rank and file, and twenty-nine field and company officers, in pursuance of General McDowell's orders to go upon this expedition with the available force of one of my regiments. The regiment selected was the First Ohio Volunteers. I left two companies, Company H and Company I, in the aggregate one hundred and thirty-five men, at the crossing of the road. I sent Lieutenant-Colonel Parrott, with two companies of one hundred and seventeen men, to Falls Church and to patrol the woods in that direction. I stationed two companies, Company E, Captain Paddock; Company C, Lieutenant Woodward (afterwards joined by Captain Pease); Company G, Captain Bailey; and Company H, Captain Hazlett—total, two hundred and seventy-five men.

On turning the curve slowly, within one-quarter of a mile from Vienna, were fired upon by raking masked batteries, of I think three guns, with shells, round-shot and grape, killing and wounding the men on the platform and in the cars, before the train could be stopped. When the train stopped the engine could not, on account of damage to some part of the running machinery, draw the train out of the fire. The engine being in the rear, we left the cars and retired to the right and left of the train through the woods. Finding that the enemy's batteries were sustained by what appeared about a regiment of infantry and cavalry, which force we have since understood to have been some fifteen hundred South Carolinians, we fell back along the railroad, throwing out skirmishers on both flanks, and this was about seven p.m. Thus we retired slowly, bearing off our wounded five miles to this point, which we reached at ten o'clock.

The following is a list of the casualities:

Captain Hazlett's Company H—Two known to be killed, three wounded, five missing.

Captain Bailey's Company G—Three killed, two wounded, two missing.

Captain Paddock's Company E—One officer slightly wounded.

Company C—Captain Pease, and two missing.

The engineer, when the men left the cars, instead of retiring slowly, as I ordered, detached his engine, with one passenger car, from the rest of the disabled train and abandoned us, running to Alexandria, and we have heard nothing from him since. Thus we were deprived of a rallying point, and of means of conveying the wounded, who had to be carried on litters in blankets. We wait here holding the road for reinforcements. The enemy did not pursue.

I have ascertained that the enemy's force at Fairfax Courthouse, four miles from Vienna, is now about four thousand.

When all the enemy's batteries opened upon us Major Hughey was at his station on the foremost platform car. Colonel McCook was with me in one of the passenger cars. Both these officers with others of the commissioned officers, and many of the men, behaved most cooly under this galling fire, which we could not return, and from batteries which we could not flank or turn, from the nature of the ground. The approach to Vienna is through a deep cut in the railway. In leaving the cars and before they could rally, many of my men lost their haversacks or blankets, but brought off all their muskets, except it may be a few that were destroyed by the enemy's first fire, or lost with the killed.

Robert C. Schenck,<br>Brigadier-General.

It cannot be doubted that the affair was a miserable blunder, running into the country of an active enemy, cooped up in railroad cars, without first making a thorough examination of the locality by scouts, is an act of combined madness and stupidity. It is true they have found out the masked battery, but it was in the same way that the Irish pilot found out the rock—by running the ship on it. Such gross carelessness in our superior officers must discourage and dishearten our brave soldiers. Profound confidence in their leaders is one of the chief elements of military success, confidence once destroyed and the army is demoralized.

To remedy this blunder General McDowell has advanced a large force towards Vienna. The Secessionists have, of course, retreated, removing their guns and fallen back upon Fairfax Court House, upon which point it is supposed a strong movement will be made, having first found that no masked batteries are in the way.

On Tuesday, June 18, 1861, General Tyler and the Connecticut troops arrived at Vienna at 3:30 in an effort to strengthen the Union forces there. A sketch of this action can be found at page 100 of the June 29, 1861 issue of *Leslie's*.

In the issue of *Leslie's* of October 26, 1861, pages 360-361, are two full length pictures of Falls Church. The first, "A View in Falls Village, Virginia, occupied by the National Forces, General Smith's division showing Taylor's Tavern and the Northern Extremity of the Town." This sketch gives a full front view of William Taylor's Tavern, and on the next page under heading of "Illustrations," appears the following account:

VIEW IN FALLS VILLAGE, VA.

By the recent withdrawal of the Rebel Army, Falls Church has again come into our possession, and is now the headquarters of General Smith, who commands one division of our army. On the advance of the National troops on the 29th of September, an unfortunate collision took place between Baker's California regiment and Baxter's Pennsylvanians, each regiment mistaking the other as enemies. The error was not discovered until several volleys had been fired, and many killed and wounded.

Another sketch on the same page is entitled "Panoramic View of the Village of Falls Church, Mason's Hill, and the Surrounding Country, taken from the works now building by the National Troops on Munson's Hill." Given in this sketch is a view of the Union Troops erecting a new fort, Mason's Hill, Union pickets, Rebel pickets attempting to shell General Wadsworth's Headquarters, Falls Church, and the Rebel pickets on the ridge. All of this is listed under the picture. The following account (under "Illustrations")[4] tells of the Panoramic View:

PANORAMIC VIEW OF FALLS CHURCH AND THE SURROUNDING SCENERY

Munson's Hill, which was occupied by the rebels in their recent advance, and imperfectly fortified by them, is now held by the National troops, who are engaged in entrenching it in a formidable manner. It commands a wide view to the southwest in the direction of Manassas, including Mason's Hill, the Village of Falls Church, and many other points which the events of the war have made famous.

The evacuation of Munson's Hill was an event of considerable importance to the U.S. Government. This can be seen in a letter written by a correspondent to the *Washington Star*, dated from Munson's Hill, September 29, 1861 and appearing in that newspaper on the following day:

Your correspondent came up to this famous locality this afternoon, and found things much changed since his last visit, when the pickets on either side were industriously popping rifle-ball courtesies at each other, under cover in the corn-fields, between this place and Bailey's Cross Roads, three quarters of a mile distant. Now, the road (Leesburg Turnpike) leading to the hill was lined with visitors in carriages, on horse-back, and on foot, pushing boldly along to get a close look at the much talked of eminence. Among the visitors just leaving as I arrived was Secretary Seward.

The New York Thirty-seventh regiment was in occupancy of the hill—at least such portion of the regiment as was not straggling around the neighborhood committing depredations. The deeds of this regiment (formerly McCunn's) done on yesterday will doubtless receive an investigation at the hands of Gen. McClellan. They were certainly of the most disgraceful character. Several dwellings, with barns and outhouses, were set on fire and wholly consumed. Amongst these was the house and barn of Rev. Mr. Lipscomb. Valuable furniture, pianos, large mirrors, feather beds, etc., were destroyed wantonly, and in one instance the officer of a cavalry regiment was so much incensed by these outrageous acts of vandalism that he compelled the miscreants to suspend their villanous (sic) work at the point of the pistol.

This (Thirty-seventh) Regiment will need some active discipline to make it any credit to the service. On yesterday Lieut.-Col. Burke found it necessary to shoot private William Moran through the head for insubordination. The men of the regiment were murmuring their discontent at this prompt punishment, into the ear of every visitor, and were not at all loth to use such phrases as that 'poor Moran was murdered for doing nothing at all.'

Later in the day I saw an officer (a captain) of this regiment endeavor to raise a squad, first by entreaty, next by imperative orders, to go with him to put a stop to the depredations of their comrades. Three or four of them finally obeyed with a very bad grace, and the inquiry, having previously passed among them, "Shall we go?"

The "fort" on Munson's Hill I find to be perhaps 300 yards long in the circuit of its parapet, the whole being nothing more than infantry breast-works, having however a rather formidable "Quaker Gun," in the shape of an ash log with a dab of black paint at the butt to represent the muzzle. Such other and more valuable guns as they may have had here had been carefully removed by the Confeds when they withdrew their pickets previously. At the earth-work to the rear of Munson's Hill the retreating Confederates had left six sections of stove-pipe mounted in the six embrasures, and some rather formidable looking (at a distance) earthworks upon Mason's Hill proved, on the occupation of that point by our troops, to be just about of the same bogus nature.

The stars and stripes which have displaced the "stars and bars" here, now float from a small pine tree nearly upon the apex of the hill. There is a quantity of straw on the westerly slope of the hill, but nothing to indicate that the enemy has ever been here in any force.

The bivouac fires of our troops can now be seen two or three miles in advance of this point towards the enemy's House. The Garibaldi Regiment is bivouacked at Bailey's Cross Roads, and the New York 8th (German Regiment) by the Arlington Mills.

Before the end of 1861 many new fortifications on the south side of the Potomac were erected. On September 24th, General W.F. Smith's division crossed the Chain Bridge and Fort Ethan Allen and Fort Marcy were commenced on the heights commanding the bridge. General Smith occupied Falls Church as shown in the *Leslie's* sketch already quoted.

Scouting parties of both armies ranged through the woods and meadows of Falls Church. One such expedition by the local Union forces was written up in *Leslie's* of December 14, 1861:

### SCOUTING PARTY NEAR FALLS CHURCH

> These everyday incidents in war are generally so similar in detail as to be monotonous in the description, although in reality few things send the blood with a livelier gallop through the heart then to accompany one of them, either as artist or Special Correspondent. The value of life is never so palpable as when the next step may bring us upon the muzzle of a rifle, or a hand to hand encounter with a desperate son of the south. The annexed sketch represents a small party of cavalry scouting in the vicinity of Falls Church, the scene of the late unhappy skirmish, where nearly 30 of our gallant men were either captured or slain. We are glad to learn that General McClellan contemplates issuing an order forbidding these private ventures into the Fox's den. If a correct list were drawn up of all who have been murdered in these imbecile rushes into danger, the community would be horrified at the extent of the losses.

Of the many tales which have been handed down to this day, the most interesting is that of a humorous capture in an old chestnut tree, first told the author by the late Willis L. Gordon. Mr. Gordon said that the story was told him by Frank Williams, one of Mosby's men. He stated that the old tree was located on the road to Falls Church near the old Merry home just beyond the Dunn Loring Road, near the present day Providence Baptist Church. The author did not think he would find documentation for this story, but *Leslie's* gave the following account in their issue of October 26, 1861 at page 353, under a drawing by the artist in the field in the paragraph:

### A REBEL TREED

> Capture of Lieutenant H.J. Segal of the Insurgent army near Falls Church, by Lieutenant-Colonel Winslow and Captain Shattuck, of the New York 37th from a sketch by our artist attached to General M'Clellan's command.

The following appears separately:

### TREEING A REBEL NEAR FAIRFAX

> Our artist has sent us so amusing an account of the capture of Lieutenant H.J. Segal of the Confederate army, that we regret we can only epitomise the particulars. On Friday the 4th of October, a scouting party of 18 men under Lieutenant Colonel B. Winslow and Captain L.B. Shattuck, of the 37th Regiment N.Y.V. were out in the vicinity of the enemy's lines about five miles from

Falls Church, in the direction of Fairfax. As they were proceeding in silence and caution through a dense wood, they heard the tramp of horses and the jingle of sabre scabbards. The Lieutenant-Colonel and the Captain ordering their men to halt went to reconnoitre. In a short time one of them came upon an open space where they saw four rebels seated under a large chestnut tree, by the side of the road, and engaged in eating chestnuts. The Confederates saw him and sprang upon their horses. The officer crying in a loud voice "Charge!" by the time the scouting party had got up the four "Gallant" horsemen were beyond pursuit. The men were about gathering up the spoils of the Victory, which consisted of four sabres, two revolvers, four coats and blankets, when they saw a horse tied to a tree by the roadside. A further search revealed its master perched upon the lower limb of a large chestnut—whither he had climbed with his sabre to lop off the fruit. A dozen rifles pointed at his breast soon brought him to reason, and he surrendered himself a prisoner. When he got down and felt safe, he began to 'blow' with true Southern chivalry; and, when brought before General McDowell, cooly boasted that at the battle of Bull Run he had aimed repeatedly at the General, but had always missed. General McDowell smiled, and said that he would send him somewhere where he would not have another chance for some time.

Mr. Gordon said that in the early part of this present century he and his wife were riding in their carriage up the pike during a hard storm which had come up after they had left their home. They passed the Dunn Loring Road, and decided to pause under the tree until the worst seemed over. The great branches of the old tree crossed the road, and offered ample protection. As they pulled away, (having gone about fifty feet), a bolt of lightning split the ancient landmark into pieces.

The following article concerning Munson's Hill is taken from page 292 of *Leslie's* for September 21, 1861:

## MUNSON'S HILL, NEAR WASHINGTON

During the last few weeks, Munson's Hill, 'a prominence' about five miles from Chain Bridge, has become a spot to which all eyes have been directed. It is on the northern side of the Leesburg turnpike, about one mile from Bailey's Cross-roads, where our pickets are stationed, and about three miles this side of Falls Church, which is in full possession of the enemy. It commands no road excepting the Leesburg turnpike, the Columbia turnpike being sheltered by thick woods up to the crossing. Its defenses are unimportant, being simple breastworks of considerable extent, but not ditched, and not embrasured for artillery. Those who saw the deserted works at Fairfax Court House and Centerville will understand just how little these are worth, for they are of exactly the same order. The elevation of the hill is not great, and its summit can be approached to within a few hundred yards from the north, under cover of heavy woods. At present its only distinction lies in its proximity to our lines. It is the nearest of a series of defenses which have been planted along the Leesburg road, which extend to some distance above Chain Bridge. The rebels, however, hold positions nearer to the Potomac than Munson's Hill. Four miles beyond the Chain Bridge, opposite our right, they have a small force, and their pickets approach a little nearer. Thence they run down, through by-lanes and fields, irregularly, toward the Orange and Alexandria Railroad, which they hold, up to the spot where it is crossed by the Four Mile Run. In this neighborhood they have strong pickets, which frequently come into collision with those sent out upon our side from Balls X-Roads. Hall's House, a little to the west of Ball's Road was a point of perpetual contention. From the four mile Run the rebel outposts cross directly to Munson's Hill, on the slope of which they descend to within a half mile of Bailey's Roads. From this point down to Benton's Tavern they hold the Columbia turnpike, and thence stretch across in almost a straight line to near the mouth of Occotink Run, the last place at which our pickets meet them.

The following is a copy of the report of Colonel J.E.B. Stuart to General Longstreet:

Headquarters, Munson's Hill, August 28, 1861.

General:

I inclose a list of killed and wounded (1 killed and 6 wounded). I have no time for a detailed report on the affair of yesterday, but I acquainted Rev. D. Ball, chaplain of my regiment, as well as Major Skinner, with all the particulars, and requested them to inform you last night, which I hope will answer for present. As soon as it was fair light this morning I had a piece of rifled cannon, Washington Battery (Artillery), brought clandestinely in position to bear on Bailey's Cross-Roads and fired four shots, distance being by the shots 1,350 yards. The shots took effect admirably, dispersing the entire force at that point, and developed what it was my object to ascertain—that they had no artillery there. Munson's Hill is a fine place for a battery, and is more capable of defense than Mason's Hill. The fire of artillery dispersed also a long line of skirmishers, who ran precipitately without being in the slightest danger from its shots. The 1st Regiment is at Falls Church, and I have directed its commander to hold himself in readiness to move up to my support, or act to the left as circumstances indicate. Two companies of that regiment are ordered to occupy the ridge along Upton's. I sent back Beckman's section of artillery, as the men were pretty well used up from fatigue and hunger, and I am now going to send back to Mason's Hill Major Johnson's command, and relieve those companies of your command here, who have been out so long, and send them back to Falls Church.

I believe this a fine line of defense; I mean the line passing through this and Mason's Hill. Every inch of the road is visible from here to Bailey's Cross Roads. The force now here and at Falls Church I consider sufficient for the present, and the best school of practice possible for our troops. I consider the enemy's design not to meet us outside their trenches in force pretty well developed. Please send this to General Johnston for me.

Most respectfully, your obedient servant,
J.E.B. Stuart,
Colonel, Commanding.

J. Longstreet, Brigadier-General.

P.S. The scattered fragments of the force at Bailey's Cross-roads reassembled, and I have the place in position to stir them up again whenever the group is in sufficient force to warrant the expenditure of our ammunition.

J.E.B.S.

In the September 28, 1861 issue of *Leslie's* at page 310, is an item concerning the defenses at Bailey's Crossroads and at Munson's Hill. The picture, at page 311, is entitled: "Bailey's Cross Roads, Virginia—the advanced posts of the Federal Pickets, Munson's Hill one mile in the distance—from a sketch by our special artist with General McClellan's command." The article follows:

### BAILEY'S CROSS ROADS AND MUNSON'S HILL

The advance position held by the Union Pickets in Virginia is Bailey's Cross Roads, at the crossing of the direct road to Fairfax Court House and the Leesburg turnpike, about five miles to the South-West of Long Bridge. It is evidently regarded by General McClellan as important strategically, and has been held by him with great tenacity. Never of high architectual pretensions, the few buildings that remain show the dilapidation and ruin incident of war, and make the place less attractive than before. It is but about a mile from the rebel position on Munson's Hill, which is in full view.

During the summer of 1862, incidental to the recapture of Munson's Hill, there was an engagement and bombardment. The affair began at the Union position at Fort Head (Tyson's Cross Roads). The residents of Falls Church were forced to flee for safety. As Wadsworth's shells fell around the old colonial church, the citizens, in carts and on foot, fled to the Dulany farm, later the home of Silas Tripp, now Greenway Downs. Here they were forced to remain several weeks. Troops in the abandoned Village turned pigs out, forced their way into dwellings, and ruined gardens. Several citizens took their cows with them to Dulany's, and the milk spoiled because of the lack of means to keep it cool. They cooked on an old cookstove with the help of an ancient colored servant of Mr. Dulany. The men put the stove out in the pasture, and it was in use all day.

On November 20, 1861, President Lincoln reviewed the Union troops "en masse" on the old Bailey farm near the crossroads, which was the greatest assembly of troops in one place ever assembled on the American continent at that time. In October previous, Falls Church became the headquarters of the Union army, and General McDowell's corps billeted in the village. These troops were stationed there at the time of the "Grand Review." The following write-up of this event, which covered front pages of leading American newspapers of the time, is taken from the December 14, 1861, issue of *Leslie's*:

GRAND REVIEW OF THE NATIONAL ARMY AT WASHINGTON. SEVENTY THOUSAND MEN ON THE FIELD.

The review held by General McClellan on Wednesday, the 20th of November, presented a spectacle never witnessed on this side of the Atlantic, for on that day nearly 70,00 patriot soldiers stood in arms ready to meet the enemies of their country, who combine the two-fold characters of rebels and brothers.

The spot chosen for the review was the open plain adjoining Bailey's Cross Roads, and the adjacent hills, Mason's and Munson's. We have described and illustrated these localities so often that we shall content ourselves by adding that Bailey's Cross Roads are situated eight miles from Washington, in the direction of Fairfax Court House, at the junction of the Columbia turnpike and the Alexandria and Leesburg turnpike. Between the Cross Roads and Munson's Hill, a mile and a half distant towards Falls Church, is a plain two miles in length, which was prepared by clearing off the fences, filling up the ditches, etc., for this grand display.

At half-past nine o'clock the General commanding, attended by all his staff officers, left his headquarters, escorted by a column of 18,000 regular cavalry. The array was most imposing as this splendid cortege moved through the streets, the cavalry marching by platoons until it reached the bridge, where it was compelled to march by columns of four, and afterwards defiled along the road leading by Arlington Heights to the review ground. Gen. McClellan was plainly attired. As he rode in advance of his numerous retinue he was loudly cheered.

In the upper and lower divisions, Gen. McCall's and Gen. Heintzelman's from which a march of some eight or ten miles had to be made, the troops were astir at from two to three o'clock in the morning, and were on the march long before daylight. All of the seven divisions on the Virginia side of the Potomac were represented in the review, but enough were left in each to supply double the usual picket force to guard the camps, and a reserve in addition strong enough to repel any attack in force the enemy could make.

As early as nine o'clock the head of the column of Gen. Blenker's division the headquarters of which are nearest to Bailey's began to arrive at the grounds from the Washington road. Soon after Gen. McDowell's advance guard appeared on a road entering the grounds from the same direction, but farther to the west. Next came the head of Gen. Franklin's column, approaching from the Alexandria road; and soon after the division of Gen. Smith began to enter the grounds from the direction of Falls Church. Gen. Fitz John Porter was next on the ground, bringing his forces by still another road. The troops now poured in from all directions, those under Gen. Heintzelman following Gen. Franklin's division, and the column of Gen. McCall succeeding that of Gen. Smith, and continued without cessation until half-past eleven o'clock.

The scene now was most exhilarating—more than 20 Generals, with their staffs, numbering above 150 horsemen, were dashing hither and thither arranging their divisions—which presented a total of above 70,000 men, including seven regiments of cavalry, numbering nearly 8,000 men.

At a quarter past 11 o'clock the President of the United States entered the grounds in his carriage, followed by the Secretary of State, also in his carriage, and by the Secretary of War and Post-Master General, accompanied by Mrs. General McDowell and by two daughters of General Taylor on Horseback. The party were escorted to a slight elevation near the centre of the area, marked by a white flag, where they were soon joined by General McClellan and his staff. The cavalry escort was formed in line on the left. The seven regiments of volunteer cavalry, and the entire artillery present, were placed on the outer margin of the grounds. The infantry were formed into columns by divisions in mass. Everything being now in readiness, a salvo to the President and General-in-Chief were fired by four batteries of artillery designated for that purpose.

In the meantime the President and Secretary of State, Secretary of War and Assistant Secretary of War, alighted from their carriages, mounted horses and prepared to accompany General McClellan in his review of the lines. This occupied about an hour and a half. Then commenced the march of the troops past in review. The honor of leading the column was assigned the First Rifle Regiment of Pennsylvania Reserve, or the Bucktails, which was with General McClellan in Western Virginia. The divisions then passed in the following order:

First—General McCall's division, composed of the brigades of Generals Mead, Reynolds, and Ord.

Second—General Heintzelman's division, composed of the brigades of Generals Sedgwick, Jamison and Richardson.

Third—General Smith's division, composed of the brigades of Generals Hancock, Brooks, and Benham.

Fourth—General Franklin's division, composed of the brigades of Generals Slocum, Newton and Kearney.

Fifth—The division of General Blenker, composed of the brigade of General Stahl and of two brigades commanded by senior Colonels.

Sixth—The division of General Fitz John Porter, composed of the brigades of Generals Merell, Martindale, and Butterfield.

Seventh—The division of General McDowell, composed of the brigades of Generals King and Wadsworth, and a brigade now commanded by Colonel Frisbie.

Upon the right of the General commanding during the review were the President, the Secretary of State, the Secretary and Assistant Secretary of War, Quartermaster-General Meigs, and the Prince de Joinville. Mingled with his staff were General Sumner, and from time to time a number of the division and of the brigade Generals whose forces were in the review. Upon the ground were also all the rest of the Cabinet officers, and a number of Foreign Ministers and their families, grouped in carriages and on horseback around the carriage of the President, which containing Mrs. Lincoln and some friends, was immediately opposite to the position of the Commanding General. Among these were Governor Andrew and lady, of Massachusetts; the Misses Stewart, nieces to Colonel Scott, Assistant Secretary of State, and lady; Hon. Montgomery Blair, Postmaster-General, and lady, and two daughters of General Taylor; Mrs. General McDowell, Mrs. General Smith; Francis P. Blair, senior, Esq., W. Russell, of the Times, Frank Leslie's Artist, etc.

One of the most interesting features of the day to many was the martial music, played by more than 50 bands, most of which were of the first order. The consolidated band in General Butterfield's brigade numbered 120 pieces, and played with excellent effect, while the brigade was passing in review, a quickstep entitled "The Standard Bearer Quickstep," composed for and dedicated to General Butterfield.

The whole review was most admirably conducted. Infinite credit is due to General McDowell, who was the commander of the review, for the promptness with which his vast column was moved.

Present at this review was Mrs. Julia Ward Howe.[5] During the review a reported movement of the enemy resulted in the dismissal of some of the troops, and General McDowell's division marched back along the Columbia Turnpike to its camp on the Arlington Heights. At this same time some spectators returned along this same route to Washington. In one of these carriages rode Governor and Mrs. John A. Andrew, of Massachusetts, Julia Ward Howe, and the Reverend James Freeman Clarke, Mrs. Howe's pastor. It is told how on either side marched soldiers, filling the roadway, and at this time the occupants of the carriage and the soldiers began to sing "John Brown's body lies a-mouldering in the grave." This song led the Reverend Mr. Clarke to say to Mrs. Howe: "Mrs. Howe, you ought to write some new words to that tune." Mrs. Howe replied, "I wish I might."

The next morning in the gray of early dawn at old Willard's Hotel in Washington, the words of the "Battle Hymn of the Republic" took form in Mrs. Howe's mind, and she wrote them out. One old tradition in Falls Church has it that Mrs. Howe, Governor and Mrs. Andrew and party stopped at the Munson home for refreshment, and it was there that she made notes for the hymn.

One of the unfortunate incidents of the war was the "Reed Affair." Two brothers, according to tradition, settled in Falls Church, and both were active in the Baptist Church. It is known that the Reverend H.W. Reed was pastor of Columbia Baptist Church when it affiliated with the Potomac Association of the Baptist Church in 1857. It is also established fact that John B., said to be a brother of H.W. Reed, was also a resident of the Village at the time of the war. H.W. Reed is said to have been a native of New York, and John B. Reed was a native of Connecticut. H.W. Reed probably moved from Falls Church after 1861, as the records of the Union and Confederate Army (Series II, Vol. 2) shows that H.W. Reed testified in the treason trial of one Asa Hodges who was released on July 2, 1862. He is remembered in Falls Church as a Union man and there was quite a bit of bitterness toward him in the Village.

John B. Reed, native of Connecticut, was a farmer and also preached at Columbia Baptist Church during the period 1862-1864. Mr. Reed was captured and shot as a spy by Mosby's men. The following is quoted from *Mosby's Rangers* by James J. Williamson, of Company A (published in 1909 by Sturgis & Walton, New York):

> (October 1864) Montjoy, with Company D, and with Bush Underwood as guide, moved off towards Falls Church and at night prepared to attack the camp. The pickets were captured, and some of our men were leading horses out of the stables, when the camp was aroused. The blowing of a horn, which at first was thought by our men to denote the assembling of a party of coon hunters, was discovered to be a signal given by a citizen named Reed to alarm the camp. Reed was shot by one of our men. The enemy, now thoroughly aroused, opened fire, which in the darkness did no damage. Three or four negro infantry were killed; 6 prisoners and 7 horses were brought out.

The Misses Emma and Lottie Reed (who later changed their surname to "Read") told the story of the death of their father to many in the Village, among whom were Mack Crossman, Willis L. Gordon, E.H. Flagg, and William N. Lynch. All of those mentioned with the exception of Mr. Crossman, gave the information to this writer. Mr. Gordon stated that Miss Emma Reed informed him that the pickets (mentioned by Mr. Williamson) were captured at their station between Little Falls Street and Hangman's Tree (across from the Reed home). The Misses Reed stated that Mosby had previously caught John B. Reed sending a message concerning the movement of Confederate troops to the Union officials. The message was in the hands of an old Negro whom Mr. Reed hired to go between the lines to the outskirts of the Village (near what is now Oak Street).

The official report of the Union Colonel Birdsall follows:

> BIRDSALL to TAYLOR, Oct. 19th, 1864: About 2 a.m. on the morning of Oct. 18, a force of Mosby's men estimated at 75, entered Falls Church village, halted at the church (brigade hospital), and after breaking open the barn of Mr. Sines, a citizen who lives opposite, and taking therefrom 5 valuable horses, passed up the Alexandria and Lewinsville pike toward Vienna. The post at the junction of the Lewinsville road with the pike, consisting of one Corporal and three men of the Sixteenth New York Cavalry, was captured, with one horse. A negro named Frank Brooks, belonging to the citizens home guard of the village, was shot dead while attempting to assist the picket in making defense. Mr. J.B. Reed, a citizen and a member of the same guard, with one of his negro employes, were taken prisoners at the same time. Mr. Reed was afterwards brutally murdered by the party who captured him, in a dense pine wood near Hunter's Mill,[6] and his body has been found and brought into his house. An attempt to kill the negro taken with Mr. Reed was also made, and the rebels, supposing him dead, left him in the woods. He escaped afterwards, however, and has but a slight wound in the head, with the loss of an ear, blown off by a pistol shot. There is no doubt concerning the murder of Mr. Reed, as the surgeon, who has made an examination of the body, states that the skull at the base of the brain is blown to atoms, and the flesh about the wound is filled with powder, as if the pistol had been placed close to the head. The negro who escaped brings information that at or near Vienna, the force which visited Falls Church was joined by a reserve party of 100 or more men.

It is said that Mosby had a good deal against J.B. Reed, including obtaining information from wounded Confederate soldiers who were staying in the Church which was the hospital. This information was given to the Union army. Mrs. Reed received a note from Mosby that she would not be molested if she wished to obtain her husband's body. With an aged Negro driving the wagon, Mrs. Reed and her fourteen year old daughter, Lottie, went to Fort Head at Tyson's Corners for the body. Mr. Reed was buried in the Village Cemetery (the Episcopal Church yard). A stone in the yard also gives data on Mrs. Reed and the daughter Charlotte.

The Reed home was later sold and the large house built by Mr. Duryee (later Miss Gundry's School) was erected on the site. Misses Emma and

Lottie (Charlotte) Reed lived until their death in a small house directly across from the Dulin Chapel on East Broad Street.

There is an interesting sequel to the "Reed Affair." A number of years ago, before the First World War, Mack Crossman was visiting in Knoxville, Tennessee, and while there met a gentleman who told an interesting story. Learning that Mr. Crossman was from Falls Church, the gentleman told how he had been among the group of Mosby's men who shot J.B. Reed. He overlooked this as an incident of war, but said it was a constant source of regret to him that they had "killed the Negro" with Reed, since the Negro was innocent. The gentleman was delighted to learn that the Negro had survived, (with the loss of an ear) and was content as a servant of the Crossman family in Falls Church!

The following report concerns the arrest of Mr. Augustus Klock of The Mount:

> Headquarters Cavalry Brigade,
> near Fort Buffalo, Va.
> August 25, 1864
>
> To Lieut. Colonel J.H. Taylor from H.M. Lazelle, 16th New York Cavalry, Comdg. Cavalry Brigade:
>
> A picket-post, consisting of a corporal and 3 men (near this camp) of the Sixteenth New York Cavalry, was attacked at 2 a.m. to-day by a party of mounted rebels; 4 horses and 2 men were taken; 1 man badly wounded and the corporal escaped. August Klock, a citizen living near Falls Church, was arrested by Mosby yesterday near Vienna, and was released this morning. He states that Mosby on releasing him told him to inform me that he (Mosby) had sent Major W.H. Forbes and Captain Manning, Second Massachusetts Cavalry, to the penitentiary, in retaliation for the confinement of Jack Barnes and Phil Trammell, two of Mosby's men.

Fort Buffalo was established by the Twenty-first New York Infantry at what is now called Seven Corners late in 1861. Their officers were: Colonel Wm. F. Rogers, Lieutenant Colonel Adrian R. Root, Wm. H. Drew, Horace G. Thomas, Chester W. Sternberg, Majors Wm. H. Drew and Edward L. Lee. This regiment was recruited in Buffalo, N.Y.,[7] and was an outgrowth of the 74th New York Militia, mustered into U.S. service May 20, 1861, at Elmira, for three months. They left for Washington, D.C., on June 18th, and on August 31st, the regiment was attached to Wadsworth's brigade—McDowell's division at Fort Cass, thence to Upton's Hill at Falls Church. Earthworks in Oakwood Cemetery dating from this period are still visible. This was winter quarters for the regiment in 1862, and they "broke camp for the general advance movement" March 10, 1862.

The local "Battle of the Peach Orchard" is well-known to old-time residents, but the author has not found an official account of the event. Mrs. John F. Bethune makes reference to the battle as follows:[8]

...and the local battle of the Peach Orchard derived its name from fruit trees growing on what is now the Riley place. That house, too, was confiscated by the soldiers and its old mahogany furniture was used for horse troughs.

The Falls Church was damaged by Union soldiers during the war. The extent of the damage was great, including the removal of all of the furniture and the floor. The soldiers removed the windows and doors on the lower floor. The marks where the new brick was inserted (below the windows) are still visible. These bricks were torn out so that the horses might be taken out with ease when the church was used as a stable. Mr. Charles A. Stewart wrote in his *Virginia Village* concerning this matter:

> The damage done to the Church according to Mr. George B. Ives was done by a company of Union Cavalry on picket duty under the command of a captain of the regular army. He permitted his men to tear out the floor of the church and use it as a stable...The building might have been damaged beyond repair had it not been for Mr. George Ives and the late Mr. John Bartlett who reported the matter to General Augur the military governor of this district by whose orders the Captain was arrested and further desecration prevented.

During this time the tablets containing the Lord's Prayer and the Ten Commandments were taken to Alexandria or Georgetown, and shipped to a church in Hartford, Connecticut. The late Mr. Benjamin R. Shreve (who was 100 years old on December 1, 1948) told how he accompanied his sister, Barbara, a nurse, to the old church with food for Confederate prisoners. This was at the time the church was being used as a hospital, prior to being used as a stable. He saw the soldiers removing the furniture from the building, including the tablets. He said that the old high pulpit (similar to that in Pohick Church) was opposite the double doors facing Fairfax Street.

Other than some bricks from the original aisle, only two articles of furnishings remain. One is a chalice which was returned to the church in 1952. It was part of the Communion Silver used at the church and was taken by a Union soldier (said to have been named Simpson). Part was taken to Ames, Iowa, and the rest to New York. This was on exhibit at a silver collector's convention, and when recognized by the "Falls Church, Truro Parish" on it (by one who was a member of the old Church) was withdrawn from the exhibit. This was within the past ten years. The other original piece of furnishing is the old stone baptismal font.

"And thereby hangs a tale."

During the war a soldier stopped at the Star Tavern and handed Mrs. W.H. Erwin (later Mrs. Auchmoody) a box marked to be sent home. The soldier was on his way to battle. He remarked that it contained a "relic of the old church Washington attended." Mrs. Erwin decided that this relic would never get to its destination. She hid the font in her attic, and later in the cornfield. After the war was over she returned the font to Bishop Southgate.

The following extracts are taken from *A Virginia Village* by Charles A. Stewart:

The attack at Munson's Hill was on August 31, 1861. (Report of Colonel George W. Taylor of the 3rd New Jersey Infantry dated Sept. 2, 1861):

General: The pickets of the enemy having for some time been extremely annoying to outposts on Little River Turnpike and on the road leading from thence to Chestnut Hill, I decided on making a reconnaissance in person with a small force with the view of cutting them off. Accordingly I marched with 40 men volunteers from two companies of my regiment on the morning of August 31, at 3 a.m. and keeping to the woods arrived soon after daylight at or near the point a little beyond at which I desired to strike the road and cut them off. Here we were obliged to cross a fence and a narrow corn field where the enemy who had doubtless dodged our approach through the woods lay in considerable force. .

While in the corn we were suddenly opened upon by a rapid and sharp fire which our men whenever they got sight of the enemy returned with much spirit. Scarce two minutes elapsed when I found three men close to me had been shot down. The enemy being mostly hid I deemed it prudent to order my men to fall back to the woods distant about thirty yards which I did.

At the same time I ordered enough to remain with me to carry off the wounded but they did not hear or heed my order except two. With these we got all off as I supposed the corn being thick but Corporal Hand; Co. 1 who when I turned him over appeared to be dying. I took his musket also the musket of one of the wounded and returned to the woods to rally the men. I regret to say that none of them could be found nor did I meet them until I reached the blacksmith shop three-quarters of a mile distant.

Here I found Capt. Regur Company 1, with his command re-enforcing him with twenty-five men of the picket then in charge of Capt. Vickers 3rd regiment N.J. volunteers, with the latter he immediately marched back to bring in Corporal Hand and any others still missing. He reports that on reaching the ground he found the enemy in increased force and did not re-enter the corn field in which I think he was justified. I should have stated that quite a number of the enemy were in full view in the road when we jumped the fence and charged them and that each man in the charge, Capt. Regur leading by my side, seemed eager to be foremost; nor did one to my knowledge flinch from the contest until my order to fall back to the woods, which fortunately they misconstrued into a continuous retreat to our pickets. The enemy seemed to have retreated very soon after as the firing had ceased before I left.

The 3 wounded men are doing well except one. As near as I can ascertain, there were 3 of the enemy shot down.

The whole affair did not last 10 minutes.

The officers with me were Capt. Regur, Co. 1, 1st Lieut. Taylor, and 3rd Lieut. Spencer; both of the same company. . .

(Signed by George W. Taylor, Col. 3rd N.J. Volunteers, and addressed to Gen. Philip Kearney.)

Sept. 4, 1862, Brig. Gen'l. A. Pleasanton from his camp near Fort Albany, in his report to Brig. Gen. R.B. March, Chief of Staff, written at 5 a.m. states that he is about to be off with the sixth cavalry and two other companies for Falls Church where he expects to make his headquarters and from whence he will scout as directed. He suggests that the telegraph be extended to Falls Church, and asks that supplies for his command be forwarded by railroad to a point opposite Falls Church. At 8:30 a.m. his message states that from reports received by him the impression is that the enemy is going to cross the Potomac at Walker's Landing. At 12:45 p.m. he reports from Falls Church that the enemy's advanced pickets on the Leesburg and Georgetown turnpike are three-fourths of a mile this side of Difficult Creek and that a regiment of Mississippi cavalry, the Jeff Davis Legion is at the bridge over the creek. At 1:30 p.m. from Falls Church his dispatch to the Chief of Staff states that the squadron on the Vienna road reports the enemy to be approaching from that direction in some force; that one of his men has been badly wounded in a skirmish. Gives it as his opinion that the enemy is only making a show of force to conceal his movements on the upper Potomac.

On Sept. 4, 1862 at 6:45 p.m. from Upton's Hill Brig. Gen. J.D. Cox commanding division, makes the following report to A.V. Colburn ass't. Adjutant General: 'The firing upon General Pleasanton's command was from possibly three pieces of light artillery. The small-arm fighting was confined to the head of the enemy's column deployed as skirmishers with some dismounted men or infantry, it is not certain which. The pickets of Pleasanton's command Eighth Illinois and Eighth Pennsylvania did not come beyond the edge of the woods one and a half or two miles above Falls Church and no large numbers were actually seen. The reports sent by Gen. Pleasanton were necessarily those brought in by his men. A regiment of cavalry with two light pieces rapidly handled would account for all the demonstration I could see with my glass but there may have been more. General Pleasanton's cavalry being ordered away we shall not have cavalry to scout the country till General Buford arrives. Scouts report all quiet toward Fairfax and Little River Turnpike.

August 16, 1863, skirmish at Falls Church, no circumstantial reports on file. (This may have been the "Battle of the Peach Orchard.")

July 18—21, 1864, Scout from Falls Church, Va., Col. Henry M. Lazelle, 16th N.Y. Cavalry commanding Brigade writing under the date of July 21, 1864, from headquarters cavalry brigade near Falls Church, Va., to Lieut. Colonel J.H. Taylor Assistant adjutant General and Chief of Staff reports the return to camp of a portion of a party of ten men sent under charge of second Lieut. Gray 13th N.Y. Cavalry on Monday evening last. About 4 o'clock a.m. today while between Sangsters and Fairfax Station was ambushed by a party from fifty to sixty; loss of five men, taken prisoners and seven horses. . .

## FOOTNOTES

[1] Page 62.
[2] Page 3.
[3] Issue of June 19, 1861, page 109.
[4] From page 362. On page 379 of *Leslie's* for November 2, 1861, is a sketch entitled "A War Incident" showing the burning of haystacks on Munson's Hill "by the Rebels in their evacuation of that position, on September 29th."
[5] See *Service with the Sixth Wisconsin Volunteers* by Rufus R. Dawes, pp. 28-29; and Florence H. Howe, *The Story of the Battle Hymn of the Republic,* pp. 50-53.
[6] Hunter's Mill was between Tyson's Corners and Herndon.
[7] Vol. 2, page 65, *The Union Army.*
[8] *A Brief History of Falls Church Virginia,* by Lucina M. Bethune, 1923, page 6.

## THE OLD FALLS CHURCH
Fairfax Co., Va.

'Twas eve when I stray'd to the old church-yard
   And mused mid the shade of its oaks;
Not a sound the deep stillness marr'd
   Save the wood-pecker's hammering strokes.

As if driving the nails in the old coffin-lids
   Of folks that were buried a century ago;
And the song of the shrill Katydids
   Seemed chanting their requiem too.

With reverence I gazed on the moss covered graves
   Of those who had long been at rest;
I knew they had passed life's troubl'd waves
   And I felt that to lie so were blest.

I turned mine eye where the old church stands
   So simple majestic and strong;
And marvell'd at the work of our forefathers hands,
   That had mouldered in death for so long.

When first it was built by our fore-father's then,
   With labor, with care, and with cost,
All around was a wilderness drear,
   Or a few lone dwellings at most.

But now the wilderness blooms
   And 'blossoms like as the rose;'
Footsteps are heard 'round their grey toombs
   Which cannot disturb their repose.

Stout sons of the north, mid their smiling homes,
   Surround the Old Falls Church,
And the sounds of thrift may stir the bones
   Of the old folks that lie under cedar and birch.

Now I've sung my lay of the Old Falls Church
   And my spirit has flown to the olden time;
I've thought of those who loved it much
   And in fancy have heard the old bells chime.

    ...January 18, 1860, *The Democratic Mirror*
    Leesburg, Loudoun County, Va., page one.

## CHAPTER 7

# To Mend a Broken Fence

A broken fence is a sign of broken spirits. The fields of Falls Church were dismal in 1866. Even the wild laurel and honeysuckle could not hide the seared soil and blood stained rocks. The Virginia worm fence rows were part of the past, as were many of the old cedars which lined the way. Cold and homesick soldiers both Blue and Gray had warmed themselves by bonfires made of their substance, for cold knows no better.

Union men suffered as much as the Rebs. They were foreigners still, for the most part, and the climate-seekers of the 1850's, many of them old men, longed for the rolling hills of New England. In such a depressed spirit, one of them, Quaker garbed and spare old Talmadge Thorne, wrote his long-time friend, Governor William Enos of Dutchess County, New York. Conflicting emotions engulfed him as he wrote:

> Since peace has been proclaimed the Union men of Fairfax do not like President Johnsons Experiment of Reconstruction, in Pardoning the Rebels, by the gross or whole sale, and in stopping the Confiscation of their property. . .a Union man has no Say now,. . .we are trampled down by the Rebs, was before the war, through the war, and after the war, and if Congress does not do something for us, we are in a bad fix.

If more men like Sumner and Stephens were in the Halls of Congress, he continued, with a Butler for Governor of Virginia, the Union men would be safe. He complained that suffering had been great, "our property Confiscated or taken, families stripped and men Imprisoned for nothing only adhearing to the Government of the United States."

It seemed clear to Thorne that in putting down the Rebellion, (as he called it) the property of the Rebs ought to "make the Union men whole." He also complained that Union men and Freedmen were on a par, which was not to his liking. Ah! to be young again, he would soon "bid adieu" (*a duw* as he spells it) to Virginia. In his quaint spelling, he was certain the Rebs had "been Thouraley wipt.," but had not received their deserts.

Thorne and some others were circulating a Petition "to have Gov. Pierpont Removed and a Provisional Governor appointed." He says he had not returned to his farm, as it might not be safe (this was on February 8, 1866). This Union sympathizer speaks of a "young man by the name of Gould" (probably Dr. James Burr Gould) who was halted on his own farm and fired at. The cap of the pistol exploded, and before the second shot he had spurred his horse, and "laying Close to his Saddle the Second Shot past over him." As he made good his escape, Gould noticed the gruesome hole prepared for his grave.

In Loudoun County, by Thorne's account, two soldiers, one a Rebel, the other a Yankee, took two horses, but were caught in the act. The Yankee was sent to prison, "and the Johnny...cleared." He moaned for the "managin" of "Some of your Simpathisers with them," which was intended for a good cure. They had suffered every thing but death for four years. But it was worth it, beyond description, too. Thorne wrote that he would "rather Leave that [suffering for the sake of his country] as a Legacy to my Children than gold (than to have it Said their Father was a Traitor)."

He goes on to inquire about a law suit, "Myers vs. Thorn," and instructs his Lawyer, Stuart, by his friend Enos, to "Bluff Myers if he possibly can." "I don't See how I Can ever pay that Claim or at present...it worries me I have Lost So much..."

The scars of war were soon erased from the surface of village life, but Falls Church could never forget the horror and suffering. People were poor—with the exception of more recent residents from the North. But dignity and breeding overcame the lack of material comfort, and the pioneer fortitude inherited from their ancestors stood them in good stead. Falls Church, always a friendly community, soon accepted new neighbors and the aftermath of war led to a more compact community life. A number of new residents hailed from Maine. Among the earliest to come was Benjamin W. Pond of Bangor, who settled in 1873. He was followed the next year by Milton S. Roberts of Waterbury, G.A.L. Merrifield of Kennebec, and T.T. Fowler. A few former Union soldiers returned to Falls Church as private citizens, attracted by the beauty and peace of the small hamlet. Bringing with them sturdy New England character, these men and women created a wholesome atmosphere in the village, and Falls Church soon became the largest town in Fairfax County. Men like Major M.S. Hopkins (who returned and built his beautiful home with the white columns which stands today across from the State Theater), added the best from their way of life to Falls Church.

After a long hard struggle, the Falls Church was repaired, and on November 27, 1873, the congregation was reorganized and Vestry chosen: George E. Porter, Senior Warden; Sackett Duryee, Junior Warden; N.F. Graham, Treasurer; Jacob C. DePutron, Secretary; George G. Ely, H.J. England, and Levi Parker. The Communicants listed in the Vestry Book for 1878 were: Mattie Frances Archer, Maggie Archer (sister to Mattie), Miss Mary Ball, L.M. Blackford, Mrs. E.F. Crocker, Mrs. George G.

Fig. 1.—"The village of Falls Church, Va. — Arrival of the Second U.S. Cavalry, Company B, Lieutenant Tompkins, on Wednesday morning, June 19th (1861) — From a sketch by our Special Artist accompanying General M'Dowell's Command": Frank Leslie's New York Illustrated for June 29, 1861. The building with the star is the "Star Tavern," now the site of the Falls Church Bank. Note that Washington Street (Lee Highway) did not exist. The Columbia Baptist Church shows in the distance, beyond the tobacco and candy store owned by Mariah Watkins.

Intersection of South Washington & West Broad Streets, 1904. Fig. 2, above, shows present site of the Falls Church Bank. The first small building is the shoe shop owned by George Thomas, a highly respected Negro leader; the building with the porch is the Star Tavern.

Fig. 3, below, shows the Falls Church Market and, on right, Gardner's Apothecary. This was later the site of the stone building housing the Falls Church Garage and subsequently Kent's Cleaners, but now demolished for street widening.

Views along East Broad Street about 1920. Fig. 4, above, shows Falls Church Garage during construction. At far left, Mariah Watkins' candy shop. (See Chapter 6) Fig. 5, below, shows the Bank on the right.

Fig. 6—"Brown's Corner," about 1890, across from Star Tavern.

Fig. 7—Mankin's Pharmacy, 1904. The first building constructed as a pharmacy, built 1897 by Charles Edward Mankin, until 1963 located on No. Washington St. just below the State Theater.

Fig. 8.—Spofford and Church (picture made in the 1880s.) This building, still standing in 1964, was next to the Falls Church Bank. Shown (l to r): Dr. George B. Fadeley, Dr. George T. Mankin, Edward Kimball, and Dr. Merton E. Church.

Fig. 9—First building erected for a Post Office, about 1895. (From oil painting made about 1940). Building at right was replaced by Robertson's 5 & 10¢ Store.

Fig. 10—Broad Street at Washington, looking Westward, 1907.

Fig. 11—Broad Street under the arch of silver maples from the Munson Hill Nursery, given in the '90s by Dr. Nodine.

Fig. 12—E. Broad St., corner of Washington. Building at left was John Brush's saloon (see Chapter 7); later a bakery; at time of picture, about 1900, was Mankin's Notions and Dry-Goods Store; after World War I replaced by Ware's Pharmacy.

Fig. 13—Original Falls Church Bank Building.

Fig. 14—Falls Church Toll Gate. This sketch made by Henry J. Morgan on September 12, 1874 shows the Toll House which stood on what is now the corner of Cherry and East Broad Streets, in front of Jefferson School. Nancy Williams was collecting toll. Mr. Morgan placed himself and his wife in the carriage. Original owned by Miss Elizabeth M. Styles.

Fig. 15—West End Station on Washington & Old Dominion R.R., where tracks crossed West Broad Street. Stood from about 1870 to 1945.

Fig. 16—J.C. Elliott's Store at East Falls Church, later Snyder's Hardware. (Picture about 1904).

Fig. 17—The Falls Church, 1862, showing heavy shutters; Union cavalrymen in churchyard. (Picture taken before wartime damage).

Fig. 18—Interior, The Falls Church, prior to remodeling in the 1960s when wall and windows shown in picture were removed.

Fig. 19—Baptismal Font in The Falls Church, the only fixture surviving from the earliest colonial period; hidden during the War Between the States under the porch of the Star Tavern, and later returned.

Fig. 20—First Congregational Church, in 1904. This building, much remodeled, became the Police Station and is now the Washington House of the Falls Church Womens Club, next to the State Theater.

Fig. 21—Dulin Methodist Church, in 1947.

Fig. 22—Original Crossman Methodist Church, in 1904 (Erected 1875, Demolished 1963).

Fig. 23—The first Sanctuary of the Presbyterian Church, shortly after it was built in 1884; still a part of the building in 1964.

Fig. 24—Columbia Baptist Church, on East Broad Street, from Harper's Weekly, August 3, 1861, showing roof of the old Falls Church in the right background. This building was used for the first meetings of the Crossman Methodist Church, and it later became the Lyceum and housed the Jefferson Institute in 1875. The present church is on a different site.

Fig. 25—Original building of the Second Baptist Church (colored) about 1872, shown in its last days.

Fig. 26—Original building, St. James Roman Catholic Church, pictured about 1889; it stood on South West St. where St. James Cemetery is now located.

Fig. 27—Illustrations from Frank Leslie's New York Illustrated for October 26, 1861, "from a sketch by our special artist attached to General McClellan's Command." The upper picture was captioned "View in Falls Village, Virginia, occupied by the National Forces, General Smith's Division, showing Taylor's Tavern, and the northern extremity of the town." The tavern was at what is now Seven Corners. The lower one was captioned "Panoramic view of the village

Rebel Pickets along this Ridge.

of Falls Church, Mason's Hill, and the surrounding country, taken from the works now building by the National Troops on Munson's Hill." Identified, from left to right, were "Fairfax Seminary, Union Troops erecting a new Fort," "Union Pickets," "Mason's Hill," "Rebel Pickets attempting to shell Gen. Wadsworth's Headquarters," "Falls Church Village," "Rebel Pickets along this Ridge."

Fig. 28. A Confederate Treed, from Leslie's. (See Text.)

Fig. 29—"Skirmishing between the pickets of the two armies, near Munson's Hill — the Hill in the distance" Leslie's, September 21 1861.

Fig. 30. The Misses Scott being escorted to prison, from Harpers (See text.)

Fig. 31—Hangman's Tree, used during the War between the States after the Battle of the Peach Orchard.

Fig. 32—Jefferson School, as it appeared in 1891.

Fig. 33—Virginia Training School, 1904. This house, erected by the Duryee Family, was later a school for feeble-minded, owned by Miss Mattie Gundry. It stood on the "Tyler Gardens" tract about opposite Little Falls Street where it intersects West Broad.

Fig. 34—"Maury," the Bailey home near Bailey's Crossroads, about 1870. Here Lincoln stayed during the Grand Review in 1861. It was later used as a summer hotel accomodating guests from the Willard in Washington. The part on the right is the original colonial house; a wing not shown extended still further to the right giving the whole structure 101 rooms.

Fig. 35—The old Lynch house, 100 block of E. Broad, built before 1790. First house in Falls Church to have Venetian blinds.

Fig. 36—"Arringdon Hall," built by Major Marcus S. Hopkins and still standing across from the State Theater.

Fig. 37—"Tallwood," 708 E. Broad St., built during the 1870s by Yale Rice: formerly home of Dr. Milton Eisenhower and for 6 months the residence of Dwight D. Eisenhower. (As it appeared in the 1880's.)

Fig. 38—"Home Hill," still standing on Lawton Road, erected in the 1840s by John Bartlett, used as headquarters by Gen. Longstreet (CSA) and by Gen. McDowell (USA); later the home of Gen. Henry W. Lawton.

Fig. 39—Birch House, 312 East Broad, home of members of the Birch family since 1835, now the residence of Miss Essie F. Birch.

Fig. 40—"Highland View." Home of Edmund Flagg (1815-1890) and still owned by his descendants.

Fig. 41—"Mount Pleasant," erected by Robert Lindsay in 1770, became the home of the Shreve family for whom Shreve Road was named. Shown during the 1890s. The woman standing 3rd from right was Barbara Shreve Melville, the Confederate nurse and spy.

Fig. 42—Picture of "Mount Pleasant" taken prior to its destruction in 1963 to make way for a new highway.

Fig. 43— Walnut Hill," 1509 South West St., once called "Granite Hill," the Colonial home of the Minors and Sewalls. The first Roman Catholic mass in Falls Church was celebrated in this house.

Fig. 44—"Gum Aysle," 311 South West St., built by the Parker family in the 1840s. Extensively remodeled.

Fig. 45—"The Mount," in Falls Hill, erected in 1745 by Col. Robert Lindsay.

Fig. 46—"Hollywood Farm," West Broad St. near George Mason School, built 1750. Broadside pictured elsewhere offered house for sale in 1876.

Fig. 47—"Cherry Hill," Colonial House, home of Judge Joseph S. Riley and of his children Mrs. Margaret Parker and J. Harvey Riley the noted ornithologist

Fig. 48—"The Spite House," erected after 1800. See text.

Fig. 49—The Ellison House at the corner of Broad and West Streets, erected prior to 1860, birthplace of Judge Francis Ellison of Red Bluff, Calif., shown about 1890 prior to remodeling; home of Andrew Ellison and of his son the Hon. Wm. H. Ellison.

Fig. 50—The same house in 1950. Standing until the late 1950s, the Falls Church Public Library was housed here for several years.

Ely, Mrs. E. Galpin, Jabez Koon, Cassius F. Lee, James M. Mason, Miss Ella Moore, Miss Elizabeth Moore, Miss Gertrude Moore, Miss Carrie Parker, Miss Mary F. Parker, Mrs. Levi Parker, J.C. DePutron, Miss Minnie Payne, Miss Artemisia Scott, Silas D. Tripp, and Mrs. Uber.

Mr. and Mrs. William Fitzhugh Edmonds wrote a delightful paper containing their recollections of the old Falls Church in the 1890's. It follows:

## "RECOLLECTIONS"

At the request of our Rector, the Rev. J. Hodge Alves, we will endeavor to bring to you a picture of the life and activities of the Falls Church as we knew it many years ago. We hope you will be able to visualize, as you look back over the years with us, the charm and serenity of this ancient building and the beauty of nature surrounding it.

In the 1890's we were children in the Sunday School, and later, teen-agers in the choir, members of the Girls' Friendly Society and the Brotherhood of St. Andrew. At that time the interior of the Church was quite crude, the flooring being of lumber furnished by the U.S. Government after the departure of the Union Army. The boards were of different widths and contained many knots, also knotholes. Our pitiful attempt to cover them resulted in one strip of sombre carpet up the center aisle from door to chancel.

A chimney was built on the north side of the church, when the Parker family discontinued the use of their summer kitchen and donated the bricks. If one looks carefully, the scars may be distinguished on the outside wall. Two huge stoves were set in boxes of sand, one on each side and directly in line with the side door, the pipes being held by wires suspended from the ceiling. Mr. John Lynch, the sexton, built the fires on Saturdays and tended them carefully to be sure that the church would be comfortably heated for the three o'clock service on Sunday. The Vestryroom, made of flooring planks, occupied the south corner of the church and was reached by the side aisle. The pews were of white pine, made by a local carpenter, and as we remember, they were most uncomfortable.

The church yard was protected on the front and sides by a thick evergreen hedge, with three strands of barbed wire running through it. There was a heavy iron double gate at the entrance, made by Mr. W.N. Lynch, the village blacksmith. This was locked during the week. The walk leading to the church was gravel and became very muddy at times. The maple trees on either side were given by Mrs. Huber who, with her family, attended the church for many years. Honeysuckle grew in profusion back of the church, furnishing a barrier that discouraged intruders. Mr. Philip Edmonds, who was Junior Warden at the time, was designated "Captain" by the Rector; his duty being to summon the vestrymen to fight the honeysuckle in the church yard twice a year. They descended upon it with scythes, sickles and rakes. After several days, they emerged the victors. The Rev. Dr. John McGill was our Rector at that time, and Mr. Silas D. Tripp our Sunday School Superintendent.

Our three Sunday School teachers were Miss Maude Hodgkin, Miss Jessie England, and Mr. George Nicolson. We thought them perfect, in spite of the fact we were often mildly rebuked for playing tag over the graves.

There were less than 300 residents in Falls Church at that time, so with five churches in town you can well imagine that the attendance in each was small. The first wedding ceremony to be performed in the church after the Civil War was that of Selina M. Slade and Philip M. Edmonds when the Rev. John McGill joined them in holy matrimony on October 25, 1877. In their old portfolio we found one of the first bulletins. Unfortunately it has been mislaid so we can't recall who the Rector was at that time. However, we do remember that he was asking each member of the congregation to increase his pledge to more than ten dollars a year, as it was becoming increasingly difficult to meet expenses.

On June 8, 1892, Mary Edwards Riley and Samuel Holmes Styles were united in marriage by the Rev. J. Cleveland Hall. Evidently flowers played no part in church weddings at that time for the couple had to obtain special permission from the Bishop to decorate the altar.

The outstanding event of our church year was Christmas. A huge tree was placed near the chancel and trimmed with glass icicles, strands of tinsel, strings of popcorn and the traditional painted candy fruit. This was not supposed to be eaten, but how we longed to take just one bite. Our gifts were usually books, and for each child there was a small box of highly colored candy.

The day that Miss Mattie Gundry moved to Falls Church was a fortunate one for our church. She bought the Schuyler Duryea house, (situated on the present site of Tyler Gardens), and opened a school for mentally retarded children. She became quite active in the church and was a generous contributor, her first pledge being $50.00 a year. With her in our midst, we felt that our future was assured. It was due to her generosity that the unsightly boards that enclosed the vesting room were removed, and red velvet curtains on brass rods were substituted. With our finances in better shape, it was decided that our next greatest need was a carpet, so many yards were bought and for many weeks the women, sitting on the floor, sewed strips together. At last the auspicious day dawned, and we proudly walked into the church on red, wall to wall carpeting.

Miss Carrie Parker for many years gave of her strength and time to pump the old organ and direct the choir. Our lawn parties were big events. All members attended with their entire families. All day the men turned ice cream freezers while the women baked cakes and set up tables. The children put candles in the Japanese lanterns and the boys strung wires from which to hang them. These parties were usually held on Dr. Hodgkin's lawn. Perhaps many of you will remember his spacious old home on the hill, now the site of Tower Square Shopping Center.

Our next project was a cross for the altar. Mrs. James Oden, sponsor of the Girls' Friendly Society, offered the use of her side yard for the erection of a summer house in which to serve refreshments. The Vestry accepted, and for several summers the girls sold ice cream and cake. At the same time, the Altar Guild and small groups of the church women, worked on their individual projects, so before too long, our goal was reached and, with pride, we presented the cross that still adorns our altar.

We sincerely hope that these recollections will prove to be of interest, not only to the present congregation, but to future generations that attend this old colonial church.

Maude Morse and William Fitzhugh Edmonds<br>December 1960

A movement led by Joseph S. Riley and others during 1873 and 1874 led to incorporation. On March 30, 1875, the Town of Falls Church was incorporated by Act of the Legislature,[1] and on April 13, 1875, the new town began its career with the following officials duly installed: Dr. John J. Moran, Mayor; H.J. England, Clerk; E.F. Crocker, Town Sergeant; and the following Councilmen (called Aldermen): Dr. J.J. Moran, George B. Ives, J.E. Birch, T.T. Fowler, Isaac Crossman, J.J. Carter, and Dr. L.E. Gott. The Act of March 30, 1875, was successively amended in 1879, 1890, and 1894. The town boundaries were defined (as amended March 2, 1894):

> So much of the territories in the counties of Fairfax and Alexandria, together with all the improvements and appurtenances thereunto belonging, as is contained in the following boundaries, to-wit: Beginning at the corner of Alexandria and Fairfax Counties, on J.C. DePutron's farm; thence to the corner of J.C. Nicholson and W.S. Patton, in Mistress Ellen Gordon's line; thence to the corner of Sewell and L.S. Abbott on the new cut road; thence to the corner of A.A. Freeman and Mrs. Henry J. England on the Falls Church and Fairfax Court House road; thence along centre of said road to centre of bridge over Holmes Run; thence easterly in a straight line to the northwest corner of the colored Methodist Church on the road leading to Annandale; thence easterly to the crossing of the Alexandria and Georgetown roads at Taylor's corner; thence along the north line of said Taylor's estate; thence to a pin oak tree near Dr. L.E. Gott's spring; thence to a stone on the property of J.A. and Mrs. J.H.C. Brown formerly the northeast corner of John Brown's barn; thence to the crossing of Isaac Crossman's and Bowen's line on the chain bridge road; thence to the place of beginning is and shall continue forever to be a body politic and corporate under the name and style of the town

of Falls Church, and shall possess and exercise the rights and powers conferred on towns by the general laws of this State and shall be subject to the restrictions and limitations imposed by said law in so far as the provisions thereof are not in conflict with the provisions of this act. [2]

Mr. Charles E. Gage made this comment on the Act of Incorporation: "... Judge Riley, who went to Richmond and lobbied through the Act of Incorporation, gave me to understand that one of the impelling reasons behind it was the deplorable conditions in the village due to unregulated sale of drink. Apparently there was so much loafing and drinking that ladies could not walk about without embarrassment."

The old Minute Books of the Town Council are on file in the City Hall. Book One, beginning April 13, 1875, and closing June 30, 1884, gives a complete picture of the formal organization of the Town. Some of the first pages give us a taste of the earliest official acts:

> The Board of Councilmen of Falls Church met at Jefferson Hall Falls Church, Va., April 13, 1875.
> PRESENT
> J.J. Moran, Geo. B. Ives, J.E. Birch, T.T. Fowler, Isaac Crossman, J.J. Carter, Dr. L.E. Gott.
>
> The oath of office was duly administered by Justice E.F. Crocker. The board was called to order, the vote called, present and absentees marked by the clerk.
>
> On motion of Ald. J.E. Birch, Dr. J.J. Moran was elected by acclamation, chairman 'pro tem.'
>
> An amendment was offered by Ald. Fowler, that Ald. Moran be elected permanent chairman, which was carried.
>
> E.F. Crocker was sworn to perform the duties of Town Sergeant by the Clerk.
>
> Ald. Dr. J.J. Moran on taking the Chair offered a few well timed, earnest remarks, upon the urgent necessity of the organization, and the unlimited good that must inevitably result to the prosperity and peace of the place, and the good of the people.
>
> Moved by Ald. Fowler that when the board adjourns, they shall adjourn to meet two weeks from this date—passed.—
>
> Moved by Ald. Fowler that the Clerk notify the Hon. James Love, Atty., for the Commonwealth of Fairfax Co., Va., that the Council of Falls Church has been duly organized, agreeable to an act passed by the Legislature of Va., 'passed and approved March 30th, 1875,' incorporating the Town of Falls Church, Fairfax Co., Va.—passed—
>
> The notice was written and duly signed, and by order of the Chair was handed to Mr. J.S. Riley to deliver to the Hon. James Love in person.

Moved by Ald. Ives to adjourn to meet at this place two weeks from this night.—passed—

        H.J. ENGLAND, Clerk.

Tuesday—Jefferson Hall, April 27th, 1875. A heavy storm of wind and rain prevailing, no meeting of the board of Councilmen occurred.

        H.J. ENGLAND, Clerk.

May 4, 1875, Council met pursuant to a call by the Chair at Jefferson Hall.

### PRESENT

Ald. Moran, Birch, Ives, Crossman, Fowler, Gott.

After enjoying a social chat, and failing to complete any business, the Council on motion of Dr. Ald. Gott adjourned for one week at this place to meet at 8 o'clock p.m.

        H.J. ENGLAND, Clerk.

May 11, 1875, Council met pursuant to adjournment.
Present: Ald. Ives, Birch, Fowler, Crossman, Chair. Moran.

Ald. Fowler was chosen Clerk pro. tem.

It was moved and voted that the clerk be instructed to call a meeting of the voters of Falls Church to put in nomination candidates for the several offices of the Town. Said meeting to be held Saturday night next at 7½ p.m., at Lewis Crump's shop.

It was voted that two councilmen be appointed by the Chair to act in concert with the Clerk as Judge of Election. The Chair appointed J.E. Birch and Dr. L.E. Gott as such associates.

Council adjourned for one week.

        H.J. ENGLAND, Clerk."

  The minutes do not show how the first officers were appointed before the election. The councilmen are called Aldermen, which is a term common in New England. On page four of the first *Minute Book*, the result of the first election is given. This election was held at Dr. Lloyd's house, which was on the site of Peoples Drug Store near the Falls Church Bank, and once known as Wiltshire's Undertaking Parlor.

  The Council met in various places until the Town Hall was built. The first Town Hall was until recently the Police Station. The building was larger in its early day, and had a bell tower on top. The first meeting (April 13, 1875) was held at Jefferson Hall, or the old Columbia Baptist Church on East Broad Street. The Council rented the "rear room, first floor," for $50.00 per year.

At the election of May 27, 1875, held at Dr. Lloyd's, the following were elected: Councilmen — J.J. Moran, J.E. Birch, George B. Ives, T.T. Fowler, J.J. Carter, Dr. L.E. Gott, Wells Forbes; H.J. England, Clerk; and E.F. Crocker, Town Sergeant.

The following extracts from the old Minute Books are of interest:

### Streets and Roads in Falls Church

December 21, 1875. Petition presented for a road from Green's Blacksmith Shop to B.F. Shreve's.

February 25, 1876. Councilman Fowler moved that prayers of petitioners for a road from Green's Blacksmith shop to the corner of the county road on lands of B.F. Shreve's the same to be thirty feet wide be granted.

May 5, 1876. Moved by Councilman Ives that the petition for a road from the Middle Turnpike to Dr. Gardner's be accepted and prayers of petitioners be granted. (Little Falls Street from Broad to Columbia).

July 24, 1876. Committee approved rebuilding the bridge on Middle Turnpike near Mr. Archibald Sherwood's gate.

July 31, 1876. To determine the best method of disposing of the water near the crossing of the "new" turnpike and Middle Turnpike roads. (Lee Highway).

August 7, 1876. Committee reported it best to "take down the hill near Dr. Lloyd's barn or old mill and fill up the turnpike near the post office and put in a trunk and sluice main across Middle Turnpike." (Dr. Lloyd's barn, or old mill, refers to old Kerr Mill behind the Star Tavern. At that time the Post Office was in a room in the old tavern.)

October 9, 1876. Petition presented by Councilman Forbes for condemning that portion of Fairfax and Georgetown Pike from Middle Turnpike Road to corporate limits and make same one of the streets of the town. Appropriate action ordered.

October 30, 1876. Motion of Councilman Osborn ordered to condemn that portion of Fairfax and Georgetown Pike between the Post Office and corporation limits recommended.

January 8, 1877. On motion of Councilman Riley the mayor was requested to draft a petition for the purpose of condemning that portion of the Fairfax and Georgetown Turnpike that is within the corporate limits.

February 5, 1877. On motion of Councilman Riley, ordered that councilmen sign a petition to the Legislature for condemning that portion of Fairfax and Georgetown Turnpike within the corporation.

### On Bonds

January 22, 1877. On motion of Councilman Riley a petition of freeholders for the purpose of bonding the corporation was read—action deferred until the next meeting. February 13, 1877, committee appointed to draft ordinance for this action. February 19, 1877, report of committee is accepted. Purpose of bonds not stated, but it is thought they were for roads.

February 13, 1877. J.C. DePutron was requested to address the council, representing President Barst of the proposed narrow-gauge railroad.

February 13, 1877. Committee consisting of Riley, Osborn and Ives appointed to draft an ordinance to be submitted to the people for purpose of bonding the town. By separate motion, ordered that the gentlemen not residing in the corporation be added to the committee.

February 19, 1877. Ordinance read and accepted.

February 21, 1877. Bonding election judges appointed to assist the sergeant: Weeks and Birch.

February 26, 1877. On motion of Councilman Riley, bonding ordinance amended by striking out the name of Councilman Seth Osborne and substituting William Corcoran.

February 26, 1877. Date changed from April 2 to April 9.

March 6, 1877. Committee appointed to draft bonding ordinance.

March 19, 1877. Ordinance for bonding the town for $10,000 reconsidered. New ordinance reported by committee adopted. April 24 set for election. Question: "Whether the said Town of Falls Church shall subscribe to the capital stock of the Washington, Cincinnati, and St. Louis Railroad Company, not exceeding $10,000. (Note: There are in the thirty-two pages of the ordinance provisions for stations, crossings, maximums of passengers for adult, children (½), commutation $5.00 per mo.)

April 9, 1877. Bonding election postponed to the fourth Thursday.

May 14, 1877. Public meeting set for May 22 to answer bonding question.

\* \* \* \* \* \* \* \* \* \* \*

The following are extracts of interest from the town records:

On August 20, 1875, George M. Thompson was elected sergeant in the room of Alderman Crocker who refused to qualify.

December 27, 1875. Made unlawful to ride or drive a horse on any sidewalk in Falls Church.

February 18, 1876. Committee appointed to define limits of sidewalks on "Middle Turnpike" (and at this meeting provided for the setting out of shade trees).

Dr. L.E. Gott resigned on May 11, 1876, at which time his resignation was accepted. On that same date the resignation of H.J. England as Clerk was accepted. This action was revised May 23rd, and Mr. England allowed to withdraw his resignation. The council records do not give a reason for this action.

July 1, 1876, the new council sworn (by Dr. J.J. Moran) as follows: Wells Forbes, Joseph E. Birch, George B. Ives, T.T. Fowler, Seth Osborn, E.F. Crocker, H.D. Weeks, Councilmen. George M. Thompson was sworn in as Town Clerk and F.F. Foote, Jr., Town Sergeant. On the fourth ballot, the council elected T.T. Fowler to serve as Mayor.

August 14, 1876. Councilman Crocker elected clerk, resigned as councilman and qualified as clerk. Election of a councilman to fill Mr. Crocker's place came up October 9, 1876, at which time J.S. Riley was elected.

On January 22, 1877, the town charter was amended. On motion of Councilman Joseph E. Birch, the committee of Councilman Ives, Osborn, and Fowler (with the mayor) were approved to draft and circulate a petition for amendment to the charter relieving taxpayers of the county tax.

\* \* \* \* \* \* \* \* \* \* \*

An influx of new people into the community was constant during the 1870 period. Among them were the families of Charles H. Buxton, Professor W.W. Kingsley, George W. Mankin, and Charles E. Mankin. G.W. Mankin purchased the old Brush Saloon and opened a general store in the building, which he conducted for a short time. He later sold the building to his brother, Charles E. Mankin, who opened there the first bakery in Falls Church in 1880.

Falls Church fires were no longer open and bright. Victorian plush-tasseled lambrequins and the many other evidences of the ginger-bread fancy had arrived. The old open firesides, black with soot, but cheerful and certain, were part of yesterday.

Typically Victorian houses began to encroach on the cornfields and pastures. Charles Mankin, caught up in Victorianism, built his "Home House": hip-roof, with iron ornamentation from Curtin & Butts Foundry at Alexandria—including adamant plaster, some stain glass, and heavy wood mantles with green marble trim. George Simms, Mankin's Architect, did better by his client and friend than did some others. Schuyler Duryee and his sprawling mansion on the old John Reed property next to the Mankin Home House, installed cedar paneling and blue stain glass in his main hall.

Some were content with the older, less ornate (and more enduring) fashions. The Widow Ellen Lightfoot Lynch lovingly cared for her 1790 era cottage; Judge and Mrs. Riley's beautiful "Cherry Hill" was a show-place reflecting the best of other days; Joseph Birch's old home, with a face-lifting (fortunately in keeping with its past) was still of the old school. Other places, including Miss Lottie Reed's, George Mankin's (Clover House), "Spite" House, and a host of others yet unsung, were little changed.

During the 1870's[3] a "Crusade" was waged by the ladies of Falls Church. The object of their wrath was John D. Brush's Saloon. Brush, a Confederate veteran, opened his Saloon on the present site of the drug store (opposite Brown's) at the traffic light. The building he erected amid the pines which clustered at the edge of Clover's corn field, was two stories with a two-deck front porch. The porch, steps and all, was the gathering place of the local male population. "Sandy" James a local Negro, (called Sandy because he had red hair) enjoyed playing his harmonica while he sat long hours on the steps.

The Saloon was a source of embarrassment to the community, and the ladies decided to do something about it. The leaders of the movement were Mrs. Joseph E. Birch and Mrs. William H.G. Lynch, both persons of high moral and spiritual character. They soon enlisted Mrs. A.D. Lounsbury, Mrs. John E. Febrey, Mrs. Henry W. Febrey, Mrs. James Brunner, Mrs. A.D. Torreyson and Mrs. George Ives to their cause. Many others joined them, but their names are not now known.

The ladies met each afternoon and evening until they were successful. Meetings were held in their homes and a chain of prayers was offered for divine assistance. The children went with them to the meetings. To avoid the chance of their young ears hearing of "Demon Rum," games were devised to distract them. One game sent them out to the wood lot (and everybody had one)—to "pick up chips." This meant picking up wood chips and putting them in baskets for use in kindling fires. Afterwards they were permitted to play other games and eat cookies.[4]

A vigil was maintained on the front steps of the Saloon, and hymns of praise and supplication offered (to the kind accompaniment of Sandy James on his harmonica). Appropriate Scriptures were read and an uncomfortable feeling spread amid the tables and along the bar. Business fell off, the Saloon closed, much to the satisfaction of the community. Even the owner was glad to be rid of his troubles!

Falls Church was Crusade-minded during the 1870's and '80's. The community was Church conscious. A local clergyman, J.H. Waugh, of Dulin Chapel, made a revealing comment in a report dated December 4, 1880:[5]

... I can but believe, that if the churches in the town of Falls

Church, were less in number by one half at least our own church in that community, to say nothing of other churches—would be much more largely aggressive. — Seven congregations of white persons in a town with a population of whites and blacks, not over eight hundred, and with six of the seven congregations having public worship at the same hour, is in my judgment a planting of churches so thickly and a multiplying of pastors so largely, as to preclude even the expectation of a large annual accession of members, in the case of any one of the churches. We have it is true the largest congregation in the town; and in it some as intelligent, liberal, and devoted Methodists as I have ever had the happiness of knowing.

On April 21, 1898, Congress declared war on Spain.

The next important event in the life of the new town was the establishment of Camp Alger near Falls Church. This completely changed the life of the community, and once more war brought the name of Falls Church to the pages of every major newspaper in the country.

The summer of 1898 was a most eventful one in Falls Church. No such stirring scenes had been witnessed here since the days of the Civil War. Troop trains arriving or departing, drills at camp and practice marches through the town, martial music from many bands, reveille and taps, all contributed to impress the town folk with the fact that the country was at war.

President McKinley and General Graham personally selected a tract of land, "The Wilderness," farm of Mr. C.L. Campbell, for the site of Camp Russell A. Alger, first camp of the war. This farm in colonial days was known as "Cleesh" and was owned by Colonel Charles Little. It was named Camp Alger in honor of the Secretary of War. On a hill, in what is now National Memorial Park, was the headquarters of the Signal Corps.

On May 16, 1898, Maj. Gen. William M. Graham, U.S.V., assigned orders to the troops assembled at Falls Church. General Graham assumed command on May 23, 1898.

The tents of the provost guard pitched at the electric railway terminus at East End with pickets posted at various street corners made Falls Church appear like a town under martial law. Under all the circumstances the conduct of the troops was admirable. The homes of the citizens were thrown open to the soldiers doing picket duty in the village, and the ladies of the place vied with each other in contributing to the comfort of sick soldiers at the camp.

Captain Joseph E. Willard, owner of Willard's Hotel, in Washington City, personally outfitted a company and was captain and the company was designed as Company I. Captain Willard was a son of Captain Joseph C. and Antonia (Ford) Willard. Mrs. Willard, better known as "Ann Ford," was a full Lieutenant in the Confederate Army. The title was conferred on her for meritorious service to Stuart and Mosby during the War Between the States.

At the time of the war, Miss Antonia Ford was a gay and charming belle of Fairfax Court House. At the outbreak of the war, she volunteered her services as a spy, and was responsible for the capture of General Edwin H. Stoughton on March 8, 1863. Her home, built in 1800, is a large brick building, and was later the home of Thomas R. Keith. It is related how Ann entertained Federal officers to spy upon them. Major Willard (provost marshal) arrested her, and she was taken to Old Capitol Prison in Washington. As one historian wrote of Major Willard, "he delivered the lady to a Federal Prison, but later worked for her release and eventually married her." The Willards were a prominent family, and Joseph E. Willard owned a beautiful mansion near the Court House. Captain Willard served as U.S. Ambassador to Spain. A daughter of Captain Willard married Archie Roosevelt, son of President Theodore Roosevelt.

The following is a Roll of Company I, in the author's file:

SOLDIER'S MEMORIAL, Spanish-American War of 1898. 3d Virginia, Volunteer Infantry, Fairfax Light Infantry, U.S.A. Company I.

### OFFICERS

Captain, Joseph E. Willard; 1st Lieut. Arthur I. Flagg; 2nd Lieut. Stephen R. Donohoe.

*SERGEANTS:* First, Richard C.L. Moncure; Q.M., Guy Huntington; Thomas B. Love, John C. Chichester, Elton Renney, Lamar Munroe.

*CORPORALS:* Charles H. Ford, James W. Ballard, Charles Y. Oliver, Robert T. Lester, Boyd Watson, Samuel E. Davis.

Hospital Corps—Maurice G. Buchwald, Roy Wakefield.
Musicians: Sigismond Boernstein, George Maben.
Artificer: Harry T. Selecman.
Wagoner; Carl G. Moffett.

WILLIAM NALLE, COLONEL COMMANDING.

### PRIVATES

Adams, Harry D.
Adams, Robert I.
Allen, Jacob I.
Armstrong, Charles A.
Arnold, Christian F.
Arnold, Charles P.
Baggott, James W.
Ballard, Hiram C.
Besley, James L.
Brooke, Ernest A.
Carrico, John A.
Carmichael, Richard H.
Cleveland, William E.
Carroll, John L.

Collins, Edward L.
Collins, Harry
Crowell, Harvey M.
Cullum, Pickins C.
Curtiss, Harvey E.
Davis, George W.
Davis, John P.
Davis, Lasrence E.
Davis, Olin
Donovan, William
Evans, Edward G.
Everett, Lloyd T.
Farquhar, Charles B.
Farroll, Patrick

83

Fisher, Samuel T.
Follin, Vernon
Ford, Ernest R.
Frye, Edward M.
Ford, John
Goodwin, Harry I.
Graham, Alfred M.
Groves, William
Gunnell, Moss
Hall, Quincy
Hoffman, Morris W. H.
Hutchinson, Robert Lee
Jonas, Joseph
Kendall, John F.
Kenyon, Howland
Kidwell, William W.
Kinsloe, James L.
King, Wallace
Laing, Walter
Lynn, Andrew M.
Manley, Eddie R.
Marks, August S.
Martin, Eugene L.
Martin, Ernest S.
Melville, Charles B.
Milstead, Ernest
Moore, Beverly J.
Moore, Robert L.

O'Connor, Thomas L.
Payne, John B.
Pettitt, John M.
Patton, George J.
Powell, Robert L.
Powell, William F.
Reid, Silas L.
Renney, John E.
Ritchie, Joshua A.
Robertson, John H.
Rust, Willie H.
Sanborn, Merton C.
Sangston, Lawrence
Selecman, John R.
Selecman, Odie L.
Sloper, Thomas E.
Smith, George H.
Spalding, George C.
Speer, George B.
Spindle, Gilbert B.
Sprigg, Clarence B.
Stone, George E.
Spindle, Zeno H.
Tilghman, Henry S.
Trammell, Albert W.
Trumble, Edwin
Williams, Ernest
Wilson, Daniel B.

Organized at Fairfax Court House, Va., May 14, 1898, Mustered into the United States Service at Camp Lee, Richmond, Va., May 22, 1898.

The first troops to arrive at Camp Alger were the District of Columbia Volunteers.[6] They were followed by the Pennsylvania Volunteers, and later came troops from Massachusetts, Rhode Island, Connecticut, New York, New Jersey, Ohio, Illinois, Indiana, Michigan, Missouri, Kansas, Tennessee, and Virginia, all forming the second army corps of the Spanish-American War. During May, 1898, there were 922 officers and 17,467 men. In June there were 1,103 officers and 26,002 men. In July there were 1,183 officers and 29,747 men. In August, there were 1,347 officers and 33,755 men. On May 24th, troops then on duty were organized into the First Division, three brigades of three regiments each, and by orders given on the 9th of June 1898, the Ninth Massachusetts Volunteer Infantry and the 33rd and 34th Michigan were constituted as a separate brigade. On June 9th, the separate brigade mentioned was assigned as the First Brigade, third division. On August 2, 1898, a second brigade was organized, composed of the First Connecticut Volunteer Infantry, and the Third Virginia Volunteer Infantry. The First Brigade consisting of the Massachusetts and Michigan troops left Camp Alger for Santiago de Cuba on the 22nd and 24th of June, 1898. Troops of the Second Brigade were returned to their states to be mustered out on September 7 and 8, 1898.

After the Aguinaldo capture by General Funston it was a Falls Church man who commanded the gun-boat which conveyed the captive around the island of Luzon to Manila. When the Maine was sunk two jackies from Falls Church escaped with their lives. One of these was Charles Galpin, who lost his hearing as a consequence. Mr. Galpin was a marine.

Mr. Willis L. Gordon, a meat merchant of the town, was given a pass signed by President McKinley and others, stating that he could pass any picket line while delivering meat to the army. This pass is still in his family.

General Henry Ware Lawton had made his home in Falls Church prior to the war, in what is known today as "Lawton House," or "Lawton Manor," a house which was built some time prior to the War Between the States and which served as Longstreet's headquarters. General Lawton was killed in a battle in the Philippines, and his death was felt to be a personal loss to his Falls Church neighbors. He is still remembered by many older residents as the man who walked in the village streets with a gold-topped cane! A glass case in the Smithsonian Institution in Washington, D.C., contains relics, including his sword and uniform, given by Mrs. Lawton.

During the war, President McKinley often visited the Camp, and was present at a Grand Review in 1898. Miss Ada Walker was an eye-witness. The review was scheduled to show the strength of the U.S. forces stationed here, and the prominent and elect of Washington were on hand. The review stand was erected near what is now Tremont Inn, on Lee Highway, near the branch which runs through National Memorial Park. The major portion of this was parade grounds, and the central camp was located across the road nearer Fairfax.

President and Mrs. McKinley and the Cabinet were present. In honor of the President, the 8th Ohio Volunteers (his native bodyguard) were the first on the grounds in full splendor. They came onto the grounds from the direction of Horseshoe Hill. Miss Walker tells the story of one New Jersey lad who had lost his white pants, and his long white Canton flannel underwear served the purpose. According to Miss Walker he had given away some of the buttons on his blouse, and needed a pin or two. He appealed to Harry Walker (who clerked in the drug store) and Mr. Walker turned to his sister for aid. Miss Walker stated that his "leggins were his salvation, with them, and standing very straight he looked o.k."

One of the soldiers stationed at Camp Alger was a future poet and author—Carl Sandburg. In his book, *Abraham Lincoln, The War Years*,[7] Sandburg writes:

> Though it was not my fate to see battle action as a soldier, I did in 1898 wear the same light-blue trousers and dark-blue jacket with brass buttons as the troops of the Army of the Potomac, and near Falls Church, Virginia, only a few miles from the Capitol

dome, I lived in a tent, answered roll call six and seven times a day, cut saplings and built myself a bunk, more than once made a practice march in hot weather carrying the first weeks a Springfield rifle, later a Krag-Jorgensen rifle, cartridge belt, canteen, and blanket roll.

Another soldier who later became famous was Barrett O'Hara. Mr. O'Hara, a member of Congress from Illinois, visited the spot of his soldier-life on February 15, 1950. He told of his visit in a speech published in the *Congressional Record* for February 20, 1950:

> ... after the House had adjourned, and before joining up at the commander in chief's dinner, I had driven out past Falls Church down the Lee Highway to the place where now there is a national cemetery on one side of the road and on the other side a tavern and a few other buildings. This was the site of Camp Alger 52 years ago, forgotten by this generation, although the service it rendered 33 years after the end of hostilities in 1865 in healing the still sore wounds of sectional warfare, deserves a better fate than oblivion. It was the camp of the Spanish-American War near the National Capital, and on the soil of Virginia, where regiments from the North and the regiments from the South, again wearing the same uniform, pitched tents together and trained as reunited brothers to fight the battles of the Republic.
>
> Only one person did I find who ever had heard of Camp Alger, so forgotten by the present generation is the war of 1898 that healed the wounds of the war of 1861-65 and started the United States of America on the road to world leadership. I pass his name to the surviving soldiers and sailors of the Spanish-American War with the hope that to him they will send messages of their appreciation. Melvin Steadman is 17 years old and in Falls Church he is known as its historian because every inch of rich historical interest in that locality he has charted with a fidelity to accuracy that could come only from love of country and from willingness to subject himself to the hard, grinding labor of research. He had not fallen into a modern trend of forgetting the Spanish-American War, or of minimizing its far-reaching repercussions. He not alone knew the general site of Camp Alger, but he was able to direct me to the spots where every regiment was camped.
>
> I selected the place by the roadside as best I could where I had stood 52 years ago with my distinguished colleague from Michigan |Mr. Woodruff| of the same regiment, with other boy soldiers from Michigan and from Massachusetts, infantrymen of the Ninth Massachusetts largely from the district now represented by our distinguished majority leader, waving our hats and screaming a welcome to the regiment just in from Tennessee at the head of which marched Col. Cordell Hull, later to become our great Secretary of State.
>
> That night, 52 years ago at Camp Alger, on the soil of Virginia,

the tents of the boys from Tennessee were spread beside the tents of the boys from Michigan and Massachusetts. Again the country was at war and it was a united country. God grant that it ever shall remain such and that under the influence of its leadership the world in which we live shall itself be a world united in peace and brotherhood.

\*\*\*\*\*\*\*\*\*\*\*

Water was scarce during 1898 because of the large numbers of troops stationed here. The Army hauled water from Washington in large white-painted barrels,.and one of them was placed in front of Mankin's Notions & Dry Goods Store.

Soldiers stood guard around the clock to prevent anyone from poisoning the water. Many wells were sunk at Dunn Loring, where the troops came by train, if they did not get off at East Falls Church. They also had a post at Dunn Loring.

The little red brick Post Office building (now a cleaning establishment) was built several years prior to the war by Mr. Charles E. Mankin. During the war it was found necessary to enlarge the building because of the volume of mail coming to Camp Alger, and the back wing was added.

When the troops were recalled at the close of the war, Falls Church quieted down to a more normal pace, but was for the first time what one writer called "cosmopolitan Falls Church." Many local girls married soldiers, and ties were made with other states. The village of Falls Church lingers today in the memories of former Camp Alger soldiers. Typical of these is Congressman Barrett O'Hara (R) of Illinois, who called on this author for information concerning the location of the camp, as it was the first time he had made a trip here in many years.

At Camp Alger was the home of a fine Negro, fondly called "Ike." Isaac Norment was a graduate of Oberlin College, as was his wife. During the war they opened their home to General Butler, and it served as his headquarters.

### The Village of Falls Church in 1892

(The following account of Falls Church as it appeared in 1892 is taken from the unpublished autobiography of the late Charles A. Stewart.)

... My wife and I first went to Falls Church in Sept. 1892 and lived there about a year, making some very pleasant acquaintances and a few friends that ever after remained faithful. It was in the summer of 1894 that I built a six-room cottage at East End, as it was then called, and became from the fall of that year a permanent resident of the town. The town of Falls Church at that time had about 1,100 inhabitants and the only means of transportation to Washington except by horse back or horse drawn vehicle, was by the steam cars on a branch of the Southern Railway extending from the junction with the main of the R.F. & P.R.R. near Alexandria to Round Hill at the foot of the Blue Ridge Mountains.

Most of the heads of families in the town were government employees and commuted by way of the railroad to Washington, entering that city at the Sixth Street Depot, now the site of the Mellon Art Gallery, just one short block from Pennsylvania Avenue. The train took about an hour to reach Washington from Falls Church, and the commuters generally became well acquainted in their travels back and forth.

Falls Church then as now had but few characteristics of a Virginia town. It was really a "New England Village" as many of its leading citizens were New Englanders. Raised as I had been in a section of Virginia made up mostly of Scotch-Irish ancestry who were noted for their cordiality and hospitality, it was hard for me to become acquainted with the business-like, matter-of-fact New England Yankees. But when you learned to understand them, you were impressed by their sterling qualities and could but admire their quiet undemonstrative home life. I learned to affiliate with my Yankee neighbors and we got along nicely in our daily associations. The characteristics of the town were entirely different from any other town in the State. The residents were more or less cultivated people from every section of the country. Their work was at the National Capital; most of them were on the government pay roll. Many did not concern themselves about local affairs. Some were experts in their profession, with perhaps a reputation extending to other countries; yet in Falls Church they might be but little known and without influence in local politics. Their interests centered at the capital of the nation and often these intelligent and well-read experts knew but little of State affairs and perhaps could not tell you the name of the Governor of the State. Such people lived in Falls Church for a home only. They cultivated their pet hobbies around their own firesides and concerned themselves but little about their neighbor even if he lived next door.

The Southern habit of wives gossiping over back yard fences was never practiced. Each family kept strictly in its own grounds and visited in formal way when they did exchange calls. Many of the Department clerks of Northern birth were industrious Sunday workers; each Sunday the head of the house dressed in overalls put in the day cultivating the vegetable garden, mowing the lawn, trimming the hedge, doing repairs around the house or kept busily engaged in his work-shop all day long. To the man from the South this method of spending the Sabbath shocked his religious principles as taught and practised in what is called the "Bible Belt." Besides it appeared to him vulgar and common-place and not the proper way for those raised in genteel society to act. It appeared thoroughly plebeian; but the Sunday worker here was not self-conscious and he lost no standing in Village social circles. [8]

The year 1900 dawned, without excitement, but the population was fast growing. In 1890, there were 792 people living in Falls Church; and by 1900 there was a twenty-seven per cent increase. Many government employees discovered Falls Church. Among these were G.A.L. Merrifield, Milton S. Roberts (both of the Pension Bureau); Albert P. Eastman of the War Department; and George F. Rollins of the Treasury Department.

On April 6, 1917, Congress declared war on Germany. The people of Falls Church responded to the war effort with their characteristic patriotism and carried on a vigorous program of war work. Falls Church contributed her quota of men, not without sorrow, for some lost their lives for their country. Liberty Loan drives were held, and the people did all that they could to help. A company of State Troopers was organized by Captain John F. Bethune, with R.R. Farr and A.B. Piggott as lieutenants.

Of the many who were honored during the war were Edward G. Fenwick (Distinguished Service Cross and French Croix-de-Guerre); Stephen McGroarty (cited for gallantry in action); Colonel George M. Newell (Legion of Honor and made a Chevalier); and Sgt. Milton Roberts Westcott (cited by the Commander-in-Chief, Meritorious Citation Certificate). In 1918, Stephen McGroarty and Ralph Stambaugh were killed on the front in Europe.

Upon the outbreak of World War Two, the community responded once more with the same vigor and patriotism. Among the men who lost their lives were Corbin Braxton Bryan III, Daniel C. Budd, William Ulysses Chinn, Thomas J. Cunningham, William S. Fought, Roy L. Gilbert, Warren L. Hawley, John M. Koutsos, Norman E. Leppert, Lindon R. Marshall, Paul F. Martin, Raymond Jacques Martin, Reuben C. Moffat, Joseph W. Patterson, Jr., Philip E. Pergande, William P. Sheers, Ralph E. Smith, Linwood F. Spencer, Benjamin S. Stalcup, Victor T. Turrou, Edwin M. Ward, Jr., and James V. Whitmer. Of the 98 reported dead from Fairfax County, 22 were from Falls Church.

During the early part of the war Dwight D. Eisenhower stayed at the home of his brother Milton Eisenhower (the old Rice house "Tall Wood," at 708 East Broad Street). In his book, *Crusade in Europe,* on page 24, President Eisenhower mentions the house as the house he had not seen in the daylight. Ann C. Whitman, Personal Secretary to the President on April 4, 1955, stated in a letter to the author:

> The President spent some time in Dr. Milton Eisenhower's home in Falls Church during 1941. It was a particularly hectic period in the President's life, and he does not recall many of the details of his existence, outside of the strenuous and long working hours.

After 1917 Falls Church lost most of its small town character and reached City status at the close of World War Two. It is difficult to give an adequate description of Falls Church prior to 1917, and after 1898. Here is an account written in 1907:

> Falls Church, one of the most beautiful suburban communities in Virginia, is situated on the boundary line between Alexandria

and Fairfax Counties, six miles from Washington, and contains a population of 1,100. It was incorporated in 1875, and on account of the large area included within its corporate limits, it is frequently styled "the town of magnificent distances." The Bluemont branch of the Southern Railroad and the Washington, Arlington and Falls Church Electric Railway pass through the town, furnishing excellent transportation facilities between Falls Church and the cities of Washington and Alexandria. The Southern Railway operates five trains daily each way during the year, with one or more extras during the summer period. The electric cars run every half hour during the day, and as late as 12 o'clock at night. Commutation rates of travel on both roads are low, making it more economical to reside here than in Washington. The Great Falls and Old Dominion Electric Railway, constructed last year, is only two miles distant and it is confidently expected that it will be extended to Falls Church in the near future. The residents of the town are mostly business men of Washington city and Government employees, who, being people of culture, have not spared expenses in beautifying and making comfortable and attractive their homes.

The beautiful shaded and well-paved streets, the tastefully and conveniently constructed cottages, together with the ample gardens and large and beautiful grounds surrounding them, make Falls Church one of the most attractive towns in Northern Virginia. The moral and religious tone of the town is of the highest order. The licensed sale of liquor within one mile of the corporate limits of the town is prohibited by the charter, and thus is secured almost absolute freedom from the vices and annoyances that surround communities where intoxicating liquors are sold. There are ten churches, one excellent graded school, one private kindergarten school, one training school and sanitarium, a banking and trust corporation, a fire department, a public library, a public hall with comfortable lodge rooms, where the Masons, Odd-Fellows and Good Templars hold their meetings; two steam railway stations, two electric car stations, three postoffices, a printing office, three medical doctors, one dentist, three attorneys-at-law, twelve contractors and builders, drug store, feed store, bakery, two notion stores, seven grocery stores, paint and hardware store, three meat and provision stores, two wood and coal yards, feedmill, broom factory, two lunch rooms, two blacksmith and wheelwright shops, two funeral directors, livery stable, plumber and gas fitter, lumber yard, shoe shop, three barber shops, and six real estates agents. On account of the excellent moral environment, the high altitude and general healthfulness of Falls Church, it is considered one of the most desirable suburbs of Washington City. The land is gently rolling, well drained, very productive, and especially adapted to poultry-raising and fruit culture, and on account of present low prices (compared with the prices of similarly situated property with respect to Washington City and the Maryland side of the Potomac River), it is being rapidly taken up by prosperous and progressive people. ⁹

FOOTNOTES

¹ *Acts of The General Assembly, 1874-75*, pages 403-405.
² Although the Act of Incorporation provided for the name of the new town as "Falls Church," some were not satisfied. Several attempts were made to change the name. According to a letter to the editor of the *Virginia Register* of December 5, 1885, the name "Churchall" had been suggested as a name for the town.
³ The date is uncertain, but was most likely 1874. John Brush was admitted into membership at Dulin Chapel on January 19, 1873, but was suddenly expelled without comment in 1874. Since the Methodist Episcopal Church, South, expelled persons connected with the liquor traffic, it is likely that this was the reason, and thus the time of the "Crusade."
⁴ Details of the Crusade were given the author by Mrs. Herbert Nelson Hirst (who talked with her Grandmother Lynch) and Mrs. Frank L. Birch.
⁵ *Steward's Book, East Fairfax Circuit, 1869-81*, pages 114-115. This book is on file in the Jacob Simpson Payton Library of the Methodist Historical Society of Northern Virginia.
⁶ For other details see *Washington, Past and Present*, 1930, John C. Proctor, Editor, Chapter XXXVII, under title "Spanish-American War" by Colonel Leroy Herron.
⁷ Volume I (Foreword, page ix).
⁸ Stewart, *My Story*, Volume I, Pages 222-224.
⁹ Pages 8-10, *Industrial and Historical Sketch of Fairfax County, Virginia* published by the County Board of Supervisors and a Committee (M. D. Hall, S. R. Donohoe, Franklin Williams, Jr., M. E. Church, and J. S. Pearson), 1907.

CHAPTER 8

# The Methodists

Among the early Methodist preachers in this area were Robert Strawbridge, Philip Gatch, William Watters, Richard Owings, William Duke, Martin Rhodda, and Francis Asbury. These men were products of one of the greatest religious movements ever to sweep this continent. Philip Gatch was converted on April 26, 1772, under the influence of Richard Owings,[1] first native Methodist local preacher in America.

Philip Gatch wrote of his Circuit in 1774:

> We found the circuit to be very laborious; some of the rides quite long, and only one hundred and seventy-five members in the circuit.

Gatch was the second native-born itinerant, entering the ministry when but twenty-three years of age. During the Revolution, assisted by William Watters, he began the work in Georgetown. While preaching on a street corner in Georgetown, a mob gathered and threatened him. Gatch stood firm and unwavering, and continued to preach the Gospel. The mob incensed, attacked him, covered his body with tar and feathers, and tossed him into the Potomac River. The tar inflamed an eye, which caused loss of sight which he never recovered. This early preacher later became a distinguished Judge in Ohio.

When the Methodist Conference met at Baltimore on May 21, 1776, Gatch attended, although still suffering from his experience at Georgetown. His report to the Conference indicated that one hundred-sixty new members had been added to his circuit, then called Frederick Circuit.[2] The bounds of his work included Frederick County, Maryland, which at that time embraced what later became Montgomery, Washington, Allegheny, and Carroll Counties. The circuit, which also included Northern Virginia, had been under the pastoral care of Robert Strawbridge and William Watters and other early heroes of Methodism.

Frederick Circuit was divided by the Conference of 1776 and the new

Circuit was called Fairfax. The bounds of Fairfax Circuit extended from Dumfries to Leesburg, and from the Potomac to the Blue Ridge. During the Revolutionary conflict the Circuit lost twenty-one members, but prospered after the war. In 1791 the Circuit reported a membership of seven hundred ninety-eight.

Robert Strawbridge prepared the way for Gatch and the others. He was an Irish Methodist, and a native of Drumsnaugh on the River Shannon. Coming to Frederick County, Maryland, in the 1750's,[3] Strawbridge formed societies on both sides of the Potomac and in Pennsylvania. The Society at Leesburg was no doubt a product of his work.

It is well established that a Society was formed in Falls Church, at "Church Hill," the home of Colonel William Adams, soon after the conversion of Mrs. Adams in 1773. The early meetings were held in the Adams home, and later, sometime prior to November 21, 1779,[4] a building was dedicated which may have originally served the Minor family as a barn. This was soon named Fairfax Chapel.

Bishop Francis Asbury makes a number of references to Fairfax Chapel in his *Journal*. The first is dated May 4, 1780:[5]

> . . . preached at the chapel in Fairfax—and met Mr. Griffith, an Episcopal minister, who was friendly; and we spent the afternoon together.

The Reverend Mr. Griffith was minister of Fairfax Parish and served the Falls Church.

Harry Hoosier, sometimes called "Black Harry" in the old records, was the first Negro Methodist Preacher. His first recorded sermon was preached in Fairfax Chapel. Bishop Asbury tells of the event on Sunday, May 13, 1781:[6]

> Preached at the chapel; afterward Harry, a black man, spoke on the barren fig-tree. This circumstance was new, and the white people looked on with attention.

At the time Asbury was a house guest of Colonel William Adams. By the 17th of May he was in Leesburg.

On April 22, 1783,[7] Asbury rode north from Petersburg, and reached Colonel Adams in time to preach. He refers to Fairfax Chapel as "Adams' Church."

Bishop Thomas Coke followed the "Asbury trail" to Falls Church. He was a guest at Perry Hall, the mansion home of Harry Dorsey Gough, near Baltimore, on May 28, 1785, when he left there and "traveled about fifty miles" to Falls Church. On Sunday, May 29th, he wrote in his *Journal*:[8]

> I preached and administered the sacrament at the Falls-church, as it is called. It was the quarterly-meeting.

It is interesting to note that the Quarterly Conference was held in the Falls Church and that Methodists were using it for some of their work. It was a much larger building than Fairfax Chapel. Coke was a priest of the Anglican Church, and was entitled to administer the Holy Communion.

George Washington knew that the Methodists were using the Falls Church. In a letter dated from Mount Vernon, August 23, 1786, he wrote in regard to the Falls Church: . . ." of what religion the people thereabout now are, I am unable to say. Most probably a medley as they have had Methodist, and Baptist Preachers of all kinds among them."[9] William Watters used the Falls Church as late as 1798.[10]

Bishop Asbury preached at the Chapel on Saturday, October 13, 1798:[11]

> We had a long ride to Fairfax chapel, where we came in about twelve o'clock. In consequence of my affliction of body and mind I was but poorly prepared to preach; however, I attempted a gloss on I Peter II, 1,2,3. Here I saw and conversed with my old friend William Watters.

On Monday, the 15th, Asbury went to Alexandria, where he preached. Between 1783 and 1810, he made twenty-two recorded visits to Alexandria. Asbury was again at Fairfax Chapel on Thursday, April 25, 1799:[12]

> The general fast day—I attended at Fairfax chapel; Philip Bruce gave a discourse upon those words of our Lord, "And then shall they fast in those days." As I was unable to preach, I gave an exhortation from the subject. . .I rest on Friday at William Watters.' Saturday, rode to Alexandria.

Asbury frequently mentions his "old friend Billy Watters." Watters was the first native born itinerant Methodist Preacher in America. His home and farm was located about three miles from Falls Church, near present day Chesterbrook. He built his house there in 1783, and it stood until the past few years. This early pioneer is buried on his farm. A tombstone, erected in 1892 by the Virginia Conference of the Methodist Episcopal Church, has the following inscription:[13]

> (*Front*) In memory of Rev. William Watters, the first Itinerant Methodist Preacher in America, born Oct. 16, 1751, died March 29, 1827.
> (*Right side*) He was a pioneer, leading the way for the vast army of American Methodist Itinerants having the Everlasting Gospel to preach.
> (*Left side*) Fervent in spirit, prudent in counsel, abundant in labors, skillful in winning souls, he was a workman that needed not to be ashamed.
> (*Reverse*) Also his wife Sarah Adams. Erected by the Virginia Conference of the Methodist Episcopal Church.

Fairfax Chapel was located in the present day bounds of the Crump and Crossman lots in the northeast corner of Oakwood Cemetery. During the summer of 1798 the older log and clapboard structure was replaced with a larger building. In 1819 this was in turn replaced by a larger brick building.

Colonel George Minor of "Minor's Hill," an early convert, gave the Methodists permission to use this land. Colonel Minor was a brother-in-law to William Watters and son-in-law to Colonel William Adams. However, Minor failed to deed the land to the Society. Following the death of the Colonel, his heirs, in consideration of one penny, deeded the property to the Methodists on November 14, 1818.[14] This deed, from George Minor, Daniel Minor, William Minor, John Minor, Hugh W. Minor, Ann Minor, Philip H. Minor, Smith Minor, and Thomas J. Minor, children of George Minor, deceased, was to William Watters, William Carlin, Wesley Adams, Samuel Marcey, Edward Bates, John Childs and John Adams, "now trustees of the METHODIST MEETING HOUSE near the Falls Church. . ." The deed recited that their father, "the aforesaid George Minor Decd., did in his lifetime give his bond to the then trustees of the old meeting house to convey one acre of land to said trustees & their successors forever for the use and benefit of the METHODIST SOCIETY."

The trustees mentioned in the deed were appointed by the Fairfax County Court on June 21, 1818. Witnesses to the deed included: John A. Summers, Benjamin Shreve, and Richard Thompson.

The deed, like that of the Falls Church, was recorded many years after the Church actually came into possession of the land. The first Falls Church, erected 1733, was not deeded until 1746.

The late Prentiss A. Shreve made a memorandum concerning his understanding of the early history of Fairfax Chapel:[15]

> . . . a committee was asked to secure a site on which to build the Fairfax Meeting House. It so happened, as recorded at Fairfax Court House that my paternal and maternal great-grandfathers, Benjamin Shreve and Horatio Ball served on that committee. . . This site was the north-east corner of what is now Oakwood Cemetery, in Falls Church, and the following year a frame building was erected to be followed some years later by a brick church with a gallery, made accessible by a flight of exterior stairs to be used by the colored people who attended the same services.

Mr. Shreve wrote from family tradition, and it may be that the earlier wooden chapel is the one he had in mind.

Little is known about the original appearance of Fairfax Chapel. Mr. H.C. Walling in the 75th Anniversary History of Dulin Chapel in 1944, gives some record of the 1819 building:

> Fairfax Chapel was of the usual type but exceptionally large and pretentious for its time and place. It was built of red brick instead of the usual frame construction, and the fittings were very well constructed. It was about 40 by 60 feet and 20 feet high to the ceiling. It had a high pitched, shingle roof, with no steeple. There were two doors at the front opening directly into the church sanctuary—one door for the men and one for the ladies. It had a gallery above the entrance where the colored people sat. The

inside walls were smooth-finished. There were eight large windows, four on each side, set in deep recesses in the thick walls. It was furnished with a single section of pews in the center, with aisles on each side. The pews and pulpit were plain and substantial and were hand-made from native wood. The building was hidden from the Leesburg Pike and the surrounding high points in a grove of trees.

Fairfax Chapel was in the old Baltimore Conference of the Methodist Episcopal Church until the War Between the States, when the building was destroyed and the bricks used by the 22nd New York Regiment, U.S.A., to build chimneys for their winter quarters. This occurred during the winter of 1862. Services were suspended early in the spring of 1861 with the advance of McDowell's army. The pastor, William Gwynn Coe had moved to Accomac County, Virginia, where he formed an independent Church consisting of the former Methodist Churches in Northampton and Accomac. Near the church was Taylor's Tavern, where on September 29, 1861, with the advance of the National Army, General Smith and his division encamped. Later the U.S. Government paid for the destruction of the building.

Among the names listed as members of classes in Fairfax Chapel in 1859 (written in the neat hand of Dr. W.G. Coe) are:

*Class No.* 1, Richard Southron, Leader. William Ball, Sarah Ball, Frances Southron, Mary Allison, Barbara Shreve, William Shreve, Mary Shreve, Samuel Birch, William Birch, Julia Birch, Mary J. Ball, Amanda Ball, Henry W. Febrey, Margaret Febrey, John E. Febrey, Mary F. Febrey, Moses A. Febrey, Caroline Febrey, Sarah Shreve, Barbara Shreve, Susan Shreve, Elizabeth Ball, Louisa Ball, Salmon Childs, Catharine Childs, Albert Wrenn, James Wrenn, George W. Shreve, Nicholas Febrey. *Class* 2, Benjamin F. Shreve, Leader. Andrew Ellison, William Ellison, Elizabeth Ellison, Lewis A. Crump, Abby Crump, Joseph E. Birch, Mary E. Birch, William Lynch, Virginia Mortimore, Margaret Eskridge, Isabella Eskridge, Elizabeth Lynch, John W. Lynch, William Dulin, John W. Sinclair, James Robey, Nelson Wrenn, Daniel S. Gordon, Amanda S. Gordon, Benjamin F. Ball, and William Clarke.

The Dulin Methodist Church and the Crossman Methodist Church of today were the two churches founded after the War Between the States from the original Fairfax Chapel congregation.

The Methodist Church in Falls Church has been under several jurisdictions. From 1819 until 1870 it was part of the Fairfax Circuit, and of the Baltimore Conference from 1770 until 1939. The East Fairfax Circuit was established from the southern section of the Baltimore Conference. The Annual Conference of 1870 changed the name of East Fairfax Circuit to Falls Church Charge. The constituency of this circuit was reduced to Dulin Chapel and Langley by the Annual Conference of 1873. Chesterbrook was added to the Falls Church Charge in 1906, when services were begun in the school house there. In 1922 the Langley-Chesterbrook Charge was formed and the Merrifield and Dunn Loring Churches were added to the Falls Church

Charge. Dulin Chapel (after January, 1945, "Dulin Methodist Church") became a station appointment in 1941.

The close of the War Between the States found the Methodists of Falls Church in a position which was not promising. They owned an acre of land and a cemetery, and the foundation of their former building; no pastor, and the reduced congregation (with no money) was divided into two groups: those "southern" in sympathy and those "northern" in sympathy. Services for the "southern" group (later part of Dulin Chapel) were held in various homes of the congregation, principally the homes of Benjamin Shreve, William Shreve, and Joseph E. Birch. The eighteen members of the "northern" party (later Crossman Church) met elsewhere, principally in the home of Isaac Crossman.

Early in 1866 arrangements were made with the Episcopalians to hold services in old Falls Church.[16] The "southern" group appointed a committee consisting of Benjamin F. Shreve, Henry W. Febrey, and Daniel S. Gordon to call on Bishop John Johns of the Episcopal Seminary to arrange for the use of the church. The desired permission was obtained, but Bishop Johns made the remark that the Methodists should erect a building as soon as possible, as "two old ladies cannot agree for very long in the same house!" Dr. Joseph Packard of the Seminary preached to the Methodist group from time to time. Later a Methodist Minister, the Reverend A.B. Dolly, did active work among them.

Dulin Methodist Church is the oldest Methodist Church in Falls Church today. It was named for Mr. William Dulin, a former member of Fairfax Chapel, who gave the ground. On May 20, 1867, Dulin deeded two acres to the trustees of the Methodist "Meeting House" to build a "new Methodist Episcopal Church, South." The trustees were: Daniel S. Gordon, Henry W. Febrey, Joseph E. Birch, John E. Febrey, Charles Kirby, Ambrose Cook, and Benjamin F. Shreve. The deed, in the name of these men, was recorded at Fairfax Court House on June 12, 1868. Under provisions of the document, the property is to revert to the Dulin Heirs if ever used for other than church purposes.

Mr. William Dulin had no heirs, as he was a bachelor. Heirs of his brother live in Washington, D.C.

Mr. Dulin was a large land owner and before the war owned the Campbell Tract near present-day National Memorial Park. He was a slave owner, a great fox hunter, and a lover of dogs and horses. He gave all of his personal possessions to General J.E.B. Stuart at the time of the War Between the States and went to Baltimore to live, where he remained until the war was over. After the war he returned to Falls Church and lived with Trueman Brush until his death before 1879. He was buried from Dulin Chapel and Mr. William H.G. Lynch was one of the Pallbearers.

The building of Dulin Chapel[17] was done by the members of the congregation, assisted by two colored boys from Alexandria who made the brick from clay taken from a pit which became the basement of the old parsonage. William P. Speer was the architect and supervised construction. His son,

Horton Speer, walked eight miles every day from his home near Fairfax to assist in laying the brick, according to Miss Essie Birch. The original entrance was in the south wall. The building was brick with a low gable, clear windows and green painted shutters. The church had a large balcony across the back which served as a choir loft. The pews were arranged in a single section in the center with side benches against the wall of each side. The building was heated by two large wood-burning stoves, one on each side of the sanctuary.

Dulin Chapel was dedicated (according to a stone in the gable of the side tower) on May 30, 1869, and the service was conducted by Dr. Munsey of Tennessee. The first parsonage was built in 1873 by James Brunner and his son George. This building served as the parsonage until 1956. The church was extensively repaired and remodeled in 1892, when the tower and present entrance was added, the roof raised two feet in the center, the alcove built and the balcony removed. This work was done under the leadership of the pastor, Dr. James E. Armstrong, brother-in-law of Dr. William Gwynn Coe (who was pastor before the War Between the States). The stained glass windows were added at this time. The contractor was Augustus Davis, Jr., a member of the church. The Sunday School addition was made in 1926 and was constructed as a duplicate of the original (remodeled) church. Stanley Higgins drew the plans, and the entire building was pebble-dashed and stuccoed.

The addition was dedicated February 23, 1927, by the Reverend Homer Welch, who was the pastor. In 1940, Mr. P.H. Lichau, in memory of Emma and Annie Lichau, donated the old house and lot on the southwest corner of the church grounds to extend and improve the appearance of the surroundings. This had been the home of the first mayor of Falls Church, Dr. J.J. Moran.

During the forenoon of March 20, 1943, a fire damaged the building to the extent of $8,400.15, which was fully covered by insurance. Services were held in Madison School, and the building was reopened after extensive repairs and remodeling. Under the leadership of George G. Oliver, the present enlarged sanctuary and Sunday School addition were completed.

The following memorial windows, erected by members of the families represented, are in Dulin Church: Daniel Smith Gordon, 1811-1884; Henry W. Febrey, 1828-1881; Margaret A. Febrey, 1830-1915; William H. Shreve, 1812-1890; John Ball; James G.W. Brunner, 1830-1911; Catherine Jane Brunner, 1831-1918; Ernest F., (1893-1893) and Margaret A., (1899-1913), children of Ernest J. and Grace W. Febrey; William M. Ellison, 1859-1924; Lillian B. Ellison, 1861-1921; William H. Shreve, 1852-1922; William H. Torreyson, 1835-1910; Mary E. Torreyson, 1835-1921; Joseph E. Birch, 1818-1892; Mary E. Birch, 1836-1901; Mildred Birch, 1902.

## CROSSMAN METHODIST CHURCH

Crossman Methodist Church was an outgrowth of the "northern" branch of the Fairfax Chapel congregation. The seventeen members who were of northern sympathy met in the basement of the old Columbia Baptist Church on East Broad Street for a number of years. The Reverend L.M. Nickerson, Presiding Elder of the Richmond District of the Methodist Episcopal Church lived at Falls Church prior to 1872 and held occasional services. The seventeen members of his congregation included the following:[18] Mr. and Mrs. Talmadge Thorne, Mr. and Mrs. Jacob M. Thorne, Mr. and Mrs. Lewis Crump, Mrs. M.S. Roberts, Mr. and Mrs. William Ellison, Henry Parker, Isaac Crossman, Mrs. Almond Birch, Mr. and Mrs. E.D. Darling, Mrs. Elizabeth Hubbell, Mrs. Charles Perrigo and Mrs. Sarah Sprangle. Of this group, only Mr. and Mrs. Crump and Mr. and Mrs. Ellison had been members of Fairfax Chapel at the outbreak of the war.

In 1872 the Reverend R.A. Scott was sent as the first permanent pastor of this small group, and his charge included five churches: Falls Church (later called Crossman Chapel); Accotink, Flint Hill (now Oakton); Arlington and Lincolnia.[19] Preaching services were held at Falls Church every Sunday morning, and in the afternoon and evening the pastor would preach at two of the other appointments alternately. There were no denominational Sunday Schools in the village at that time, but a union school was held in the Baptist Church building with Mr. C.H. Buxton serving as superintendent.

At the time of the reorganization of the Methodist Episcopal Church in 1873, Crossman Church fell under the jurisdiction of the Alexandria District of the Virginia Conference. Two Annual Conferences of the Virginia Conference of the Methodist Episcopal Church were subsequently held in Falls Church. The first was on March 2, 1892, with Bishop John M. Walton presiding, and the second, March 10, 1899, with Bishop Daniel Goodsell presiding. In 1904 the Virginia Conference was dissolved and Crossman Church, with a large part of the Alexandria District, was placed in the Washington District of the Baltimore Conference, the Reverend Dr. Nailor, Presiding Elder.

To further define the circuit connections, it appears that about 1901 the so-called "New Charge" was formed, comprised of Arlington, Accotink, and Lincolnia. Fairfax and Vienna were then added to Falls Church, which, together with Oakton, made four appointments in the circuit. Fairfax was dropped the following year, and no further change was made until the spring of 1911 when Vienna was transferred to Arlington, leaving Falls Church and Oakton as the only appointments on this charge. Crossman Congregation (at that time known as The Methodist Episcopal Church of Falls Church) then became self-supporting and a station appointment.

Sometime during the year 1874[20] a subscription list was circulated and sufficient funds received to justify immediate construction of a Church building. Mr. Isaac Crossman donated the lot upon which the Church was built. Two plans were submitted—one by Mr. George W. Hubbell and the other by Mr. E.D. Darling. The latter plan was accepted and the building begun. The large base timbers in the new building were hewn in the forest near Chesterbrook by the Reverend David Mutersbaugh, local preacher and farmer. Although work was begun in 1875, the building was not completed until 1876, and was dedicated in August of that year. As soon as the building was enclosed the basement was fitted up for use and a Sunday School was organized with Mr. J.M. Thorne as superintendent. Mr. Thorne held this office until his death in March, 1907, with the exception of one year. Dr. S.S. Luttrell served in the position during the vacation of Mr. Thorne. In 1907 Mr. M.E. Church was elected Superintendent and continued in this office until after 1914.

At the Dedication Service in August, 1876, the local residents joined with the Crossman congregation in their celebration. The Reverend A.J. Porter, Presiding Elder, officiated. The Reverend Richard Norris, of Wesley Chapel, Washington, D.C. assisted. Dinner was provided for all those who came from a distance.

The first wedding celebrated in the new building was that of Rudolph F. Kittlets of Fortress Monroe and Ida M. Porter, daughter of the Reverend A.J. Porter, of Falls Church. This wedding took place on May 8, 1889, the Reverend J.S. Wickline, officiating. In 1914 it was noted that only four weddings had taken place in the Church in the previous thirty-eight years.

During the pastorate of Mr. Wickline, a movement was organized for the building of a parsonage which was completed in 1889. This building served until it was torn down in 1957 to enable the congregation to build the new sanctuary which was opened on September 22, 1957. Among the large contributors to the parsonage fund was Mr. Stephen Cowling of Accotink, who pledged $500.00. Mr. Henry Turner advanced $1000.00 without interest and this was paid back in installments of one hundred dollars per year as rental for the parsonage. At that time the minister paid rent for his home and under the new arrangement was to credit the church with $100 each year on his salary. Mr. E.D. Darling, who built the Church, was engaged to build the parsonage. According to his plan and contract, Mr. Darling erected the building for about $2,000.00. The remaining indebtedness was paid off under the pastorate of the Reverend U.S.A. Heavener in 1900.

During the construction of the parsonage, some of the ladies of the church, led by Mrs. Darling and Mrs. Wickline, held a meeting and organized a Ladies' Mite Society with the following officers: Mrs. S.C. Wickline, President; Mrs. E.D. Darling, Vice-President; Miss Corrie Cooksey, Secretary; and Miss Jennie Thorne, Treasurer. The following were members: Mrs. E.D. Darling, Mrs. Ball, Mrs. Thorne, Mrs. Abbott, Mrs. Center, Mrs. Kimball, Mrs. Roberts, Mrs. Birch, Mrs. Hubbell, Mrs. Sprangle, Mrs. Turner, Mrs. Church, and some others. This Society secured furnishings for the new parsonage and continued to raise funds for various purposes.

In 1903, Miss Ethel M. Payne, Miss Carrie A. Ball, and others, suggested and contributed toward the purchase of a pipe organ for the Church, and succeeded in raising $250. In April, 1913, through the influence of the Reverend G. Ellis Williams, Mr. Andrew Carnegie made an offer to donate one-half of the cost of the organ. The organ was purchased and installed in December, 1913. To provide suitable housing for the organ, an organ loft, and a new roof were added. A subscription list was circulated and $2,000.00, or more, was pledged. Mr. Darling was awarded the contract, and work was commenced in September and the educational building completed early in 1914.

In January, 1910, it was suggested that the Sunday School be organized in accordance with the plan submitted by the International Sunday School Association. Mr. M.E. Church was a leader in this movement, and an organization effected with the following officers: F.E. Parker, President; W.L. Fox, Secretary; O.B. Livingston, Treasurer; and H.C. Houston, Teacher. A. Charter was applied for, and the following were charter members: Rev. L.M. Ferguson, F.E. Parker, A.J. Potter, W.L. Fox, O.B. Livingston, M.E. Church, E.H. Follin, G.C. Round, J.C. Follin, W.H. Rogers, Allen Stevens, Harvey Follin, and H.C. Houston. On the first Sunday of March, 1910, this class commenced regular work.

Not long after the organization of the Men's Class, the women of the Church organized and the following were officers: Mrs. Sallie B. Viands, President; Mrs. Bertha Livingston, Secretary; Mrs. Marcia Parker, Treasurer; and the Reverend L.M. Ferguson, Teacher. On March 12, 1912, this class obtained a charter from the International Sunday School Association, which bears the following names as members: Sallie B. Viands, Emilie Church, Fannie Stevens, Frances Darling, Edith Haskell, Edith Bean, Lillian Birch, Marcia Parker, Nellie Crossman, Teco Cogswell, Bertha Livingston, Jane Cobb, Edith Jewell, Ethel M. Payne, Mabel Kennedy, Margaret Birch, Hattie Dickinson, Kate Carrell, Carrie Ball, and Miss Wandling.

The Intermediate Girls Class was organized on November 29, 1912, under the name of "Buds of Promise," with the following officers: Maybelle Church, President; Dorothy Haskell, Secretary; Dorothy Swift, Treasurer; and Mrs. Katie Carrell, Teacher. The following were charter members: Maybelle Church, Laura Lowe, Dorothy Haskell, Marguerite Dickinson, Louise Haskell, Dorothy Swift, Hattie Follin, and Blanche Mabin.

In 1913 a Cradle Roll Department was organized with Mrs. C.C. Ball as Superintendent. The following were members in 1914: Gladstone Ellis Williams, Boynton Parker Livingston, Louise Catherine Chanel, Helen May Chanel, Annie Twitchell, Margaret L. Swift, Merton E. Church, Jr., Arthur J. Potter, Jr., Kathleen Virginia Birch, and John Wesley Mabin.

Crossman Methodist Church has a new building, erected in 1957, and the old building has been torn down. The building erected in 1876 originally had a tall steeple with dormer windows, which was torn off prior to 1930 when the timbers began to rot. The new building is of brick colonial design.

The Educational Building detached from the old Church was erected about 1932. A new Parsonage was purchased in Broadmont in 1955.

Crossman Church united with Dulin Chapel to obtain restitution for the loss of Fairfax Chapel.

On December 22, 1904, representatives of the Quarterly Conferences of the Crossman Methodist Episcopal Church and the Dulin Chapel Methodist Episcopal Church, South, consisting of J.M. Thorne and the Reverend D.C. Hedrick of the Crossman Church and William M. Ellison and the Reverend W.H. Woolf of the Dulin Chapel, met and organized to take action for the prosecution of their claim against the United States for the unwarranted destruction of Fairfax Chapel.[21] On January 11, 1905, William M. Ellison was given power of attorney to take all legal steps before the Court of Claims to secure an adjustment of this claim and the payment of the award. Mr. Ellison was to receive twenty percent of the amount awarded for his professional services. On February 7, 1906 Mr. Martin introduced in the First Session of the 59th Congress a Bill for the relief of the trustees of the Methodist Episcopal Church of Falls Church, reading as follows:

> Be it enacted by the Senate and House of Representatives of the United States of America in Congress assembled, That the Secretary of the Treasury be, and he is hereby authorized and directed to pay, out of any money in the Treasury not otherwise appropriated, the sum of four thousand dollars to the trustees of the Methodist Episcopal Church of Falls Church, Virginia, for damage done to the property of said Church by the armies of the United States during the late War between the States.

This bill was referred to the Court of Claims, on June 13, 1906, by resolution of the United States Senate under the Tucker Act of March 3, 1887. The case was brought to a hearing on loyalty and the merits on March 16, 1908. Mr. William M. Ellison appeared for the claimants, and the Attorney General, by Mr. P.M. Cox, his assistant, and under his direction, appeared for the defense and protection of the interests of the United States.

The Court of Claims of the United States found the following facts:

> I. The Methodist Episcopal Church of Falls Church, Va., as a church, was loyal to the Government of the United States throughout the late Civil War.
>
> II. During the said war the church building described in the petition, situated in Fairfax County, Va., was torn down by soldiers belonging to the Twenty-second New York Regiment without authority therefor, who used the material thereof in the construction of chimneys and other structures in their camp.[22] The reasonable value of the building at the time and place was the sum of sixteen hundred dollars ($1,600), for which no payment appears to have been made. The value of the material so taken and used is not shown.
>
> III. The foregoing claim was never presented to any department of the Government prior to its presentation to Congress and reference to this court by resolution of the United States Senate, as herein before set forth in the statement of this case, and no satisfactory evidence is adduced showing why the claim was not earlier presented.

These findings were certified to the President of the Senate on December 21, 1908, and were referred to the Committee on Claims on January 4, 1909. An appropriation of $1,600 was included in the Omnibus Claims Act, approved March 4, 1915 (*Public Law* 289). After deducting attorney's fees of $320.00, the remainder of $1,280 was divided equally between Dulin Chapel and the Crossman Church as successors to Fairfax Chapel.

## ROSTER OF MINISTERS

(According to records of the Conference of Methodist Preachers held in June, 1773, at Philadelphia, there were 1,160 members of Methodist "Societies" in America, and 10 preachers. Of this number, 500 were in Maryland, 200 in New Jersey, 180 each in Philadelphia and New York, and 100 in Virginia. The ten preachers were Thomas Rankin, George Shadford, John King, William Watters, Francis Asbury, Robert Strawbridge, Abraham Whitworth, Joseph Yearbry, Richard Wright, and Robert Williams. By the Conference of May 25, 1774, held at Philadelphia, Frederick Circuit was created, which included Fairfax County. It had 175 members, and Philip Gatch and William Duke were appointed to it.)

| Date | Name of Clergyman | Number of Members | |
|---|---|---|---|
| | *(Frederick Circuit)* | White | Colored |
| 1774 | Philip Gatch, William Duke............... | 175 | |
| 1775 | William Watters, Robt. Strawbridge, Francis Asbury[23] ............................. | 30 | |
| | *(Fairfax Circuit)* | | |
| 1776 | William Watters, Thomas McClure, Adam Fornerdon[24] .......................... | 350 | |
| 1777 | Daniel Ruff, John Cooper, Thos. S. Chew, Isaac Rollins .............. | 330 | |
| 1778 | William Watters, Daniel Duvall .........(numbers not given) | | |
| 1779 | William Gill, Edward Bailey .............. | 309 | |
| 1780 | Philip Cox, ..................................... | 361 | |
| 1781 | Francis Poythress, Michael Ellis ........ | 301 | |
| 1782 | Ignatius Pigman, Samuel Watson........ | 262 | |
| 1783 | Jonathan Forrest, David Abbott.......... | 310 | ([25]) |
| 1784 | Joseph Everett ................................. | 317 | |
| 1785 | Simon Pile ..............................(numbers not given) | | |
| 1786 | Richard Owings, John Fidler .............. | 260 | 0 |
| 1787 | Michael Ellis, Adam Cloud ............... | 270 | 0 |
| 1788 | Amos G. Thompson, James Thomas .. | 350 | 18 |
| 1789 | Thos. Bowen, John Chalmers, Benjamin Snelling................................ | 474 | 76 |
| 1790 | Samuel Breeze, Lewis Dawson .......... | 775 | 175 |
| 1791 | Thornton Fleming, Stuart Redman .... | 657 | 141 |
| 1792 | George Cannon, Stuart Redman ........ | 675 | 114 |
| 1793 | George Cannon ................................. | 520 | 50 |
| 1794 | Andrew Nichols, Elijah Sparks............ | 540 | 50 |
| 1795 | John Bloodgood, Lewis Browning ...... | 363 | 61 |

| | | | |
|---|---|---|---|
| 1796 | Morris Howe, John Chalmers | 347 | 62 |
| 1797 | Daniel Hitt, Thomas Lyell, Curtis Williams[2 6] | 335 | 52 |
| 1798 | Curtis Williams, Benj. Essex | 337 | 52 |
| 1799 | John Pitts, Joseph Stone | 328 | 47 |
| 1800 | Seely Bunn, John Philips | 300 | 47 |
| 1801 | Seely Bunn | 282 | 48 |
| 1802 | Hamilton Jefferson, Frederick Stier | 261 | 52 |
| 1803 | Hamilton Jefferson, Joseph Hayes | 441 | 95 |
| 1804 | Hamilton Jefferson, John Bell | 647 | 172 |
| 1805 | Joseph Rowen, James Smith | 619 | 143 |
| 1806 | Frederick Stier, John Richards | 600 | 150 |
| 1807 | Christopher Frye, Joseph Stone | 618 | 188 |
| 1808 | Andrew Hemphill, Joseph Stone | 648 | 172 |
| 1809 | E. Matthews, J. Rowen, Joseph Frye | 746 | 228 |
| 1810 | Benedict Reynolds, Joseph Frye | 803 | 269 |
| 1811 | John Watson, John W. Bond | 330 | 184 |
| 1812 | Richard Tidings, Oliver Woodworth | 337 | 229 |
| 1813 | John White, John Macklefresh | 324 | 119 |
| 1814 | John Davis, James Sewall | 382 | 124 |
| 1815 | John G. Watt | 375 | 120 |
| 1816 | Nicholas Willis | 303 | 164 |
| 1817 | Daniel Hall | 360 | 200 |
| 1818 | Alfred Griffith | 385 | 204 |
| 1819 | Alfred Griffith | 400 | 204 |
| 1820 | Richard M'Allister | 377 | 188 |
| 1821 | Richard M'Allister | 352 | 180 |
| 1822 | Gideon Lanning | 336 | 119 |
| 1823 | Robert Burch | 369 | 157 |
| 1824 | Robert Burch, John G. Watt | 350 | 150 |
| 1825 | James M'Cann, J. G. Watt | 340 | 130 |
| 1826 | Samuel Kennerly | 330 | 132 |
| 1827 | Charles B. Young, Richard Bone | 422 | 99 |
| 1828 | S. L. Booker, J. G. Watt | 405 | 82 |
| 1829 | J. Paynter, W. O. Lumsden | 281 | 78 |
| 1830 | Chas. Kalbfus | 270 | 100 |
| 1831 | John A. Henning | 292 | 120 |
| 1832 | John Houseweart, Wm. Evans | 261 | 114 |
| 1833 | R. Bond, A.A. Reese, J. Chalmers | 441 | 149 |
| 1834 | C. Parkinson, A. Compton | 435 | 150 |
| 1835 | W. Evans, L. F. Morgan | 369 | 147 |
| 1836 | E. R. Veitch, David Thomas | 380 | 120 |
| 1837 | Eldridge R. Veitch, Elisha P. Phelps | 358 | 88 |
| 1838 | Wesley Howe, Wm. O. Lumsden | 350 | 80 |
| 1839 | Wm.O.Lumsden,LaytonJ.Hansberger | 313 | 19 |
| 1840 | Thomas Wheeler, G.W. Israel | 300 | 109 |
| 1841 | C. A. Davis, Wm. H. Laney | 315 | 77 |
| 1842 | John W. Osborne, Wesley Rohr | 312 | 102 |
| 1843 | James Watts, Benj. F. Brooke | 435 | 161 |
| 1844 | James Watts, Chas. E. Browne | 422 | 137 |

| | | | |
|---|---|---|---|
| 1845 | R. T. Nixon, Wm. L. Murphy | 389 | 111 |
| 1846 | R. T. Nixon, Thomas Cornelius | 366 | 121 |
| 1847 | M. G. Hamilton, J. W. Kelly | 344 | 90 |
| 1848 | M. G. Hamilton, J. W. Kelly | 339 | 95 |
| 1849 | Wm. Prettyman, John Landstreet | 320 | 105 |
| 1850 | Wm. Prettyman, J. E. Ryland[27] | 275 | 80 |
| 1851 | Joshua M. Grandin, John H. Ryland | 376 | 90 |
| 1852 | Joshua M. Grandin, Wm. O. Lumsden | 400 | 96 |
| 1853 | John W. Hoover, Washington W. Welsh, Wm. O. Lumsden | 346 | 97 |
| 1854 | John W. Hoover, James H. Knotts, John W. Bull | 372 | 45 |
| 1855 | David Thomas, Thaddeus B. M'Falls | 350 | 25 |
| 1856 | David Thomas, R. R. Murphy | 376 | 60 |
| 1857 | John W. Tongue, Samuel Dickson[28] | 392 | 71 |
| 1858 | John W. Tongue, Samuel Dickson[29] | 288 | 50 |
| 1859 | William G. Coe, Harrison M'Nemar[30] | 301 | 61 |
| 1860 | William G. Coe, G. H. Zimmerman (East Fairfax—W.C. M'Gruder) | 300 | 57 |
| 1861 | R. M. Lipscomb, J. H. Beckwith (During 1861 J. S. Gardner also preached in the Circuit.) | 306 | 55 |
| 1865 | Wesley Hammond | | |
| 1868-69 | Andrew B. Dolly, Wesley Hammond | | |

*Note*—In 1850, the Methodist Episcopal Church, South, assigned their first clergyman to the Fairfax Circuit area. Apparently preachers from both organizations worked in the same community. It is not clear just what arrangements were made. The figures given as to membership are unusual. In 1853, the above list gives 346 white members, 97 colored. In this same year, the Fairfax Circuit, M. E. Church, South, lists 205 white and 5 Negroes in membership.

## MINISTERS APPOINTED BY THE METHODIST EPISCOPAL CHURCH, SOUTH TO FAIRFAX CIRCUIT

| Date | Name of Ministers | Number of Members | |
|---|---|---|---|
| | | (White) | (Colored) |
| 1850 | K. Adams | 89 | — |
| 1851 | John D. Blackwell | 156 | 4 |
| 1852 | Wm. G. Foote | 214 | 4 |
| 1853 | Wm. E. Judkins | 205 | 5 |
| 1854 | Wm. E. Judkins (Fairfax Mission to be supplied) | 100 | 2 |
| 1855 | Alexander G. Brown | 90 | 31 |
| 1856 | Peter F. August | 106 | 10 |

| | | | |
|---|---|---|---|
| 1857 | Thomas J. Bayton | 91 | 1 |
| 1858 | Thomas J. Bayton | 91 | 1 |
| 1859 | Henry C. Cheatham | 147 | 2 |
| 1860 | Wm. G. Hammond | 107 | 1 |

## MINISTERS OF DULIN CHURCH

| Name of Clergyman | Date |
|---|---|
| Presley B. Smith | 1869-1871 |
| L. H. Crenshaw | 1871-1875 |
| W. G. Hammond | 1875-1877 |
| Rumsey Smithson | 1877-1878 |
| J. H. Waugh | 1878-1881 |
| Presley B. Smith | 1881-1884 |
| J. S. Haddaway | 1884-1886 |
| J. W. Duffey | 1886-1890 |
| W. A. Wade | 1890-1891 |
| James E. Armstrong | 1891-1893 |
| J. T. Williams | 1893-1895 |
| A. M. Cackley | 1895-1899 |
| George T. Tyler | 1899-1901 |
| J. H. Boyd | 1901-1902 |
| W. H. Woolf | 1902-1906 |
| J. L. Kibler | 1906-1909 |
| B. W. Bond | 1909-1910 |
| J. R. Andrew | 1910-1912 |
| W. D. Keene | 1912-1914 |
| J. B. Henry | 1914-1918 |
| O. W. Lusby | 1918-1921 |
| S. V. Hildebrand | 1921-1924 |
| G. D. White | 1924-1925 |
| J. R. Wood | 1925- |
| Paul Warner (supply) | 1925-1926 |
| Homer Welch | 1926-1929 |
| C. H. Cannon | 1929-1933 |
| W. D. King | 1933-1937 |
| P. C. Helmintoller | 1937-1941 |
| H. P. Baker | 1941-1942 |
| W. S. Courtney | 1942-1944 |
| H. S. Southgate | 1944-1948 |
| George G. Oliver | 1948-1953 |
| Richard M. Robertson | 1953-1962 |
| James W. Smith | 1962-present |

## MINISTERS OF CROSSMAN CHURCH

| Name of Clergyman | Date |
|---|---|
| R. A. Scott | 1872-1875 |
| E. P. Phelps | 1875-1876 |
| J. S. Byers | 1876-1879 |
| (David M. Mutersbaugh, Assistant) | 1877-1880 |
| A. J. Porter | 1879-1880 |
| William H. Forsythe | 1880-1881 |
| C. W. Ball | 1881-1882 |
| J. E. Evans | 1882-1883 |
| Samuel A. Ball | 1883-1884 |
| William T. Schooley | 1884-1885 |
| J. M. Pascoe | 1885-1886 |
| J. S. Wickline | 1886-1890 |
| Stephen P. Shipman | 1890-1893 |
| Samuel A. Ball | 1893-1898 |
| U. S. A. Heavener | 1898-1901 |
| W. F. Miller | 1901-1903 |
| Samuel A. Ball | 1903 |
| D. C. Hedrick | 1903-1904 |
| G. S. Painter | 1904 |
| J. E. Amos | 1905-1908 |
| L. M. Ferguson | 1909-1912 |
| G. Ellis Williams | 1912-1915 |
| Merritt Earl | 1915-1921 |
| Charles F. Boss, Jr., Junior Preacher | 1915-1917 |
| M.F. Lowe, Junior Preacher | 1917-1918 |
| J.M. McCauley, supply, Junior Preacher | 1918-1919 |
| D.H. Martin, Junior Preacher | 1919-1920 |
| S.R. Murray | 1921-1926 |
| E.F. Fielding | 1926-1929 |
| G.L. Conner | 1929-1931 |
| E.B. Wilcox | 1931-1939 |
| J. C. Sinclair | 1939 |
| Herman McKay | 1940-1941 |
| J. R. Hendricks | 1941-1945 |
| A. R. Mays | 1945-1947 |
| W. J. Groah | 1947-1951 |
| A. P. Roach | 1952-1955 |
| H. A. Harrell | 1955-1960 |
| J. C. Fink | 1960-1961 |
| E. L. Hylton | 1961-1963 |
| C. Roy Everett, Jr. | 1963-present |

## FOOTNOTES

[1] Richard Owings is buried in the Old Stone Church Methodist Cemetery, in Leesburg.

[2] The first work in Virginia, later within the bounds of the Frederick Circuit, was at Leesburg. Here, on May 11, 1766, a lot was deeded on which the now famous Old Stone Church was erected. This was the first deeded land to Methodists in America, ante-dating the John Street, New York site, long thought to be the first, by two years. See Melvin Lee Steadman, Jr., *Leesburg's Old Stone Church*, Virginia-Craft Printing Company, Manassas, Virginia, 1964; and an article by the same, "The First Methodist Deed in America," published in WORLD PARISH (official publication of the World Methodist Council), Volume VII, No. 11, pages 19-32.

[3] See "The Case of the Stolen Pig" by Melvin Lee Steadman, Jr., in *The New Christian Advocate*, Volume III, No. 9, pp. 32-34. Also, *How Methodism Came* by Mrs. Arthur Bibbins (edited by Richard Larkin Shipley and Gordon Pratt Baker), The American Methodist Historical Society of the Baltimore Annual Conference, 1945.

[4] On Wednesday, November 17, 1779, a prayer meeting was held in the Falls Church neighborhood. On the following Sunday, the 21st, William Adams, a young Methodist preacher, was ill in his bedroom, but was taken downstairs with the family "intending in the evening to preach at the preaching-house," but was not able to do so. Thus there was a "preaching-house" by that date. See *The Arminian Magazine*. Volume 1, Philadelphia: Prichard & Hall, 1789, pages 132/33.

[5] *The Journal of the Rev. Francis Asbury*, New York: Bangs & Mason, 1821, volume I, page 282. Hereafter *Journal*.

[6] *Journal*, volume I, page 328.

[7] *Ibid.*, volume I, page 356.

[8] *The Arminian Magazine*, Philadelphia: Prichard & Hall, 1789, volume 1, page 397.

[9] *Writings of George Washington.*, edited by Fitzpatrick, 1932, volume 28, page 527.

[10] Bishop Asbury recorded in his *Journal* (volume 1, page 315) on Saturday, April 22, 1798: "I heard of brother Watter's preaching at the Fall church, a faithful funeral sermon." This was reported to him, no doubt, by William Adams, with whom Asbury had dinner that day in Colchester.

[11] *Journal*, volume II, page 330.

[12] *Ibid*, volume II, page 343.

[13] Copied by the author when he first visited the spot, with Charles E. Gage, on August 6, 1949. William Watters did effective work in this area as well as in numerous other localities. Plans are now being made to clear the cemetery where he is buried and to maintain it in a suitable fashion.

[14] Fairfax County, *Deed Book R # 2, page 13*.

[15] Loaned by his widow and copied by the author in 1949.

[16] On May 26, 1867, William Gwynn Coe, former pastor of Fairfax Chapel, noted in his Sermon Book: "Falls' Ch: (Prot. Episc.) for Ffx.Ch.: Congregation—Luke XVIII, 22." In this abbreviated form Dr. Coe noted that he preached a sermon to the Fairfax Chapel Congregation at the Falls Church.

[17] Records of Dulin Methodist Church and the East Fairfax Circuit (in custody of the Secretary of the Records Committee)—complete typescript by Mrs. Walter Towner Jewell, 1954, in the author's file.

The *75th Anniversary History* of Dulin Chapel Methodist Church, published in 1944, written by H. C. Walling and others, has been used in this chapter. *A History of the Old Baltimore Conference* by Dr. James E. Armstrong, King Bros., 1907, should be carefully studied. Thanks are also due to a lady in Falls Church for loan of papers passed down from her grandfather, name withheld by request.

[18] This was the congregation in 1875.

[19] This information and other data in this article were taken from the "Brief History of the Methodist Episcopal Church, Falls Church, Virginia" compiled in 1914 by the Reverend G. Ellis Williams and H. C. Houston, and published in *Souvenir Program and History, 1872-1914, Re-opening Services January Eleven to Eighteen Inclusive*, etc.

[20] The congregation used the old Baptist Church on East Broad Street for a number of years. An *Agreement,* dated October 1, 1874, between Joseph E. Birch, President of the Jefferson Institute, and Isaac Crossman, was loaned to Crossman Church by the author on April 27, 1961. By this agreement, in consideration of $25.00 "expended in repairing the Hall or upper room," Birch agreed that the "Methodist Society shall have the use of the upper room of said Jefferson Institute building, for one service, or meeting, each Sunday . . . " for one year.

[21] A paper, torn and faded, states that the undersigned, "Trustees of 'Fairfax Chapel' before its destruction," claimed that ". . . this Chapel was used as a Military Hospital by the U. S. Army under the Command of General Wadsworth, during the winter of 1861-'62; and finally utterly destroyed during the winter of 1862, by the soldiers. . ." They also stated that some of the "present Trustees were appointed, as such, in the year 1827—more than a quarter of a century ago." Signers included W. R. Birch, Horatio Ball, James Payne, Henry W. Febrey, and B. F. Shreve. The paper was addressed to "Mr. Secretary—." While not dated, and the address torn, it was apparently part of the file included in an earlier attempt to obtain funds from the Government. The paper is in private hands.

[22] The other structures referred to are said to be two small buildings on the "Munson Hill" farm. They were built as winter quarters.

[23] Under numbers, Fairfax is listed as a station in Frederick Circuit with 30 members, the Circuit with 336 members.

[24] Fairfax a separate Circuit with 350 members; Frederick, at the same time with 359 members.

[25] The difference in numbers each year was due, no doubt, to the high rate of those dismissed for not conforming to the rigid Methodist standard of conduct.

[26] Fairfax and Alexandria.

[27] Membership statistics from this date include the number of Local Preachers and probationers (those in a waiting period prior to membership). In 1850 white probationers numbered 101, colored 11.

[28] Seven churches listed in the Fairfax Circuit, valued at $20,000. Also, one parsonage worth $2,000, a library of 350 books, and a Sunday School membership of 280.

[29] Only 5 churches were listed in 1858. What happened to the two additional listed the preceding year? It may be the circuit was divided.

[30] The parsonage in 1859 was located at Fairfax Court House, but Fairfax Chapel at Falls Church was the leading church on the Circuit. This is ascertained from the fact that the author's wife's grandfather, Walker Peyton Conway Coe, son of the Reverend William Gwynn Coe (then pastor of Fairfax Circuit), was born at the parsonage at Fairfax Court House October 2, 1859.

CHAPTER 9

# The Baptists

The earliest record of the Columbia Baptist Church is dated 1856, but there were Baptist preachers in Fairfax County more than one hundred years earlier. The beginning of the Baptist movement in Northern Virginia has been traced to the evangelistic efforts of Edmund Hayes and Thomas Yates, who were members of Sater's Baptist Church of Maryland as early as 1743. The first Baptist Church in Virginia was established at Burleigh, Isle of Wight County, in 1714. In 1770 there were six Baptist Churches in the state and in 1774 there were fifty-four. The established church fell into disfavor with the rolling tides of the Revolution, and many were added to the rolls of dissenting churches. The Baptist movement obtained a strong hold in aristocratic King & Queen County and in Fauquier County.

Jeremiah Moore was among the early itinerant Baptist preachers of Fairfax County. Born in Prince William County on June 7, 1746, son of William and Angelia (French) Moore, he grew up in the Church of England. Early in life this future Baptist was a Lay Reader for Dettigen Parish in Prince William County. During the Revolutionary War he served as a corporal in the Virginia Line. At the age of twenty-six Moore professed the Baptist covenant, and was baptized by the Reverend David Thomas of the Broad Run Baptist Church at New Baltimore in Fauquier County. Shortly afterwards Moore began to preach and was especially successful in Fairfax County.

Moore felt that a man had the God-given right to preach the Gospel. For those who were not members of the Church of England, preaching was difficult and against the law. Moore refused to submit to the laws of Virginia requiring a license to preach, probably because he could not comply with the rules of the Established Church. The civil authorities of Fairfax County (on order of the Church of England by authority of an Act of 1643) arrested Moore while he was preaching near Colvin's Mill on Difficult Run in Fairfax County, and he was imprisoned in Alexandria. From the window of the prison Moore continued to preach.

The imprisonment of Jeremiah Moore was echoed throughout Virginia. Patrick Henry came to his defense in 1773, and in his argument exclaimed: "Great God, Gentlemen, a man in prison for preaching the Gospel of the Son of God."

Upon his release Moore went back to work. Through his efforts Back Lick Baptist Church was established in upper Fairfax County, and from this church came the charter members of the First Baptist Church of Alexandria. Moore also established Frying Pan Baptist Church at what is now Floris (formerly "Frying Pan") near Herndon. The original Frying Pan building is still standing and the old pulpit from which Moore preached is still in use.

Jeremiah Moore died in February, 1815, at his home "Moorefield," near present day Vienna, and was buried there in the family cemetery. In recent years the D.A.R. has erected a monument to his memory. Moore left numerous children, and a prominent descendant was the Honorable R. Walton Moore of the State Department.

Although it appears that Baptists have lived here since the early Colonial period, it was not until sometime prior to August 7, 1856, that seven Falls Church Baptists (under the leadership of Deacon and Mrs. Dexter Kingman) formed a congregation.[1] Their names follow: Deacon and Mrs. Dexter Kingman, Mr. and Mrs. William Kingman, Mr. and Mrs. Caleb Reed, and Mrs. Josiah Galpin. They were later joined in their efforts by Mr. and Mrs. Weston.[2] They first met in Groot Hall, and the Reverend Stephen Prescott Hill of the First Baptist Church, Washington, D.C., was engaged to preach every other Sunday as a supply pastor. The records of First Baptist Church disclose that Mr. Hill informed his church that he was serving as supply pastor of Columbia Baptist Church on April 10, 1857.

Columbia Church has been a member of three Baptist Associations: the Columbia Association of Baptist Churches, composed of churches in the District of Columbia and Virginia, sometime prior to August 7, 1856; the Potomac Association, from 1857 until 1952; the Mount Vernon Association which was organized August 28, 1952 in the stone edifice of Columbia Baptist Church. This church was one of the charter members of the new Association. The old Columbia Association was formed in 1819.

The following is taken from the minutes of the Potomac Association of 1857:

> Columbia — This is a new church recently constituted and just received into our body. Its prospects are very flattering having recently had a glorious revival during which some fifty or sixty were baptized and added to the church. Its Pastor is Rev. H.W. Reed. They contributed to our Treasury $18.75.

The first building of Columbia Baptist Church was on East Broad Street, the site of the old Parish Hall of the Falls Church. It was erected by Dexter Kingman, who donated the lumber and part of the labor. While the building was erected in 1857, the deed was not recorded until April 5, 1859 (Fairfax Deed Book B-4, page 165). The deed was from Lester and Sarah F. (Darne)

Lloyd to Dexter Kingman, James Bennett, and Thatcher Perkins, trustees of the Columbia Baptist Church. The property contained one-half, acre, and the purchase price was $100.

This first building was constructed of hewn timber and clapboard. It was painted white with brown trim, and had a tall steeple. A picture of the building appeared in the August 3, 1861 issue of *Harper's Weekly*.

The Reverend Hiram W. Reed mentioned in the 1857 Association Report continued as pastor of the church until the outbreak of the War Between the States. His name does not appear in the 1860 U.S. Census of Fairfax County, and he apparently moved before the taking of the Census. The records of the Union and Confederate Army (Series II, Vol. 2) shows that H.W. Reed testified in the treason trial of one Asa Hodges who was released on July 2, 1862. Reed was a native of New York.

The next pastor was John B. Reed (Read) born in Connecticut in 1814. His wife was Charlotte E. Reed, and both were active in the work of the church. His daughter, Miss Emma Reed, served for many years as President of the Woman's Missionary Society. Reed was a well known Union Sympathizer during the War. A communication of August 10, 1863 from G.A. DeRussy, Brigadier General, to Lt. Col. J.H. Taylor of the Union Army, disclosed that Mr. Reed, a resident of Falls Church, knew the location of Mosby's headquarters only five miles from Falls Church and that Mosby's men had infiltrated the Union ranks influencing Union men to desert. Reed was executed as a spy, and this story is given in the chapter on the War Between the States.

Columbia Church was used as a hospital by the Union Army during 1862/63. It was also used by the Confederate Army. There are no records of the Potomac Association for 1861/64 since the Association found it impossible to meet because of the war.

For the fourteen years between 1865/79 the church maintained a skeleton organization, as reported to the Association by the Church Clerk, Dr. Peter Hogan. There was no pastor during this time and services were held intermittently. In 1869 a revival was held by the Reverend William Early, and the late Judge John Francis Ellison of California (a native of Falls Church) was converted.

The Church was reorganized in 1880 by the Reverend W.S.O. Thomas, and the membership consisted of twenty-four persons including: Mr. & Mrs. S.S. Everett, Mrs. John B. Reed, Charlotte Reed (wife and daughter of the Rev. John B. Reed); Mr. & Mrs. Thomas Hillier, Mrs. Steven Thomas Smoot, Dr. and Mrs. Peter Hogan, Mr. Greenbury Gaither, Mr. Wright, Mrs. Rawlings, Sally Rawlings, Mrs. Berry, Mrs. Silas D. Tripp and Mrs. John P. Bartlett. The Reverend Mr. Thomas remained for three years, and resigned to become Assistant to Dr. H.M. Wharton of the Brantley Baptist Church of Baltimore.

During the period 1883-1906, the church had a net increase of sixty-three members and contributions rose from $272.00 in 1883 to $708 in 1906. The period 1907-1917 saw the membership of the church increase from 100 in 1907 to 189 in 1917 and during the same period the contributions increased from $708 to $2,937. It was during the later period, that the lot at the corner of Washington and Columbia Streets was purchased, with the idea of constructing a new church. The transaction was handled by the Reverend W. S.O. Thomas, and funds for the down payment were given by the Ladies Aid Society of the Church. This was the beginning of the stone Columbia Baptist Church.

The Building Committee, appointed by Mr. Thomas, consisted of W.S. Hoge, Jr., Chairman; M.E. Church, T.J. Northrup, George W. Hawxhurst, J.L. Shotwell, Charles B. Quick, Van Quick, T.B. Snoddy, and Charles A. Berger. All Protestant churches of Falls Church were represented on the Committee.

The first spade of earth was turned by Russell Thomas and W.S. Hoge, III, sons of the Pastor and Chairman of the Building Committee. The stone work was done by Mr. Seoane. The carpenter work was contracted by Thomas Hillier and later by Jechonias L. Shotwell. The stained glass windows over the pulpit of this stone building are the original windows from the original St. James Catholic Church of Falls Church, which was located on South West Street, on the site of the present St. James Cemetery. They were procured by Mr. Hillier, with the assistance of Mr. Seoane, when the old Catholic Church was torn down.

Columbia moved from the old building to the stone church on the fourth Sunday of June, 1909. The Pulpit chairs in the stone church are the original furniture from the first edifice of Columbia Baptist Church. They were refinished and reupholstered about 1928 and have been in continuous use since that time. The old building was torn down and replaced by the Episcopal Parish Hall. The church bell was removed to the Merrifield School.

The church has memorials to many of its members and families. Tablets were erected in memory of the Reverend Ulysses Simpson Knox, Pastor 1918-1943, and to Edward Taylor Fenwick, who served as Superintendent of the Sunday School for many years. Mr. Fenwick was later elected Superintendent Emeritus. Jechonias Lewis Shotwell and Charles Harmon Lane, were elected Deacons Emeritus in recognition of their long service to the Church.

In 1919, the mortgage on the stone building was burned and the structure dedicated with appropriate ceremony. The Educational Building wing was added in 1925, at a cost of $25,000.00. On June 26, 1941, the debt on the Educational Building and Parsonage was liquidated in an Anniversary Service. Dr. Ernest F. Campbell, of the First Baptist Church, Alexandria, preached a sermon entitled: "Will the Church Deliver?"

During 1918/43 the membership increased from 167 to 527 persons and the contributions increased during the same period from $3050.00 to $8,713.34.

The church membership increased during the six years between 1944 and 1950 from 556 to 853 persons. Contributions increased from $14,675.00

to $33,749.00. In addition there were substantial contributions to the building fund.

Columbia Baptist Church has sponsored Bon Air Baptist Church, Boulevard Baptist Church and Providence Baptist Church. In each instance a number of Columbia's members have become part of the new organizations and assisted in their formation. Columbia rendered financial assistance and furnished equipment.

The enlargement program at Columbia began in August, 1944, when the abutting property was purchased from Mrs. Charles A. Berger. This was followed by the purchase of the Martin property for $18,000.00, the Finnigan property for $18,000.00 and the Head property for $24,000.00. The Finnigan and Head properties were used for Sunday School facilities.

The building committee, consisted of Ray S. Via, John Donohue, M.R. Walters, James Perrin, James L. Shotwell, J.B. Moore, W.S. Hoge, Jr., S.S. Landess, James Anderson, W.C. Massie, Jr., R.B. Clark, Leonard Rubright, Lila Mae Via, Edith Colby, Fannie Roberts, Callie Beard, Pauline Winn, Frank M. Steadman, Dale C. Dillon, Palmer Fletcher, Edward G. Fenwick, W.C. Eubank, Clarence L. Shotwell, and Nellie Rogers.

The Architect selected for the new brick structure, was Eimer Cappelmann and the builder was E.L. Daniels. The cornerstone of the new building was laid on December 10, 1950. The speaker of the occasion was Dr. Edward H. Pruden, Minister of the First Baptist Church, Washington, D.C. The Committee on the laying of the cornerstone consisted of George T. Reeves, Edward G. Fenwick, and Dale C. Dillon. The Church was dedicated on October 21, 1951.

On January 2, 1952, J. Lewis Shotwell, Chairman of the Executive Committee, reported the cost of the building: building $179,245.63, furniture and fixtures $22,836.30, architectural fee, $10,907.00, sodding, landscaping and parking area, $5,457.57, and a miscellaneous item of $5,567.99, making a total cost for the new building of $224,014.40. (This does not include the purchase price of the Berger and Martin properties at a cost of $30,000.00.) The membership of the church increased from 853 to 1276 during 1950/53, and contributions increased from $33,000.00 to $55,900,00. Since 1953 the building has been substantially enlarged and the membership greatly increased.

The Church has maintained a Sunday School since 1880. A complete report is set forth in the Minutes of the Potomac Association and Mt. Vernon Association. For the year 1953, the Superintendent reported an enrollment of 1,420 persons with an average attendance of 804 persons each Sunday. A graded Sunday School has been maintained for many years. It has Departments for all ages, Nursery through Adults.

The following have served as Superintendents of the Sunday School since 1880: S.S. Everett, A.M. Wheeler, J.S. Garrison, Eli J. Northrup, S.M. Proudfit, W.P. Graham, E.J. Galpin, Franklin Williams, Jr., Thomas Hillier, J.E. Hild, Reuben Ilsley, J.S. Parrott, E.M. Updike, J.L. Shotwell, J.G. Herndon, W.T. Parrott, Edward T. Fenwick, U.P. Gibson and M.R. Walters.

## ROSTER OF MINISTERS 1856-1964

| | |
|---|---|
| Stephen P. Hill | 1856-1857 |
| Hiram W. Reed | 1857-1860 |
| John B. Reed | 1860-1864 |
| W.S.O. Thomas | 1880-1883 |
| Hugh P. McCormick | 1883-1884 |
| George E. Truett | 1885-1887 |
| Frank Berkley | 1888 |
| Timothy W. T. Noland | 1889 |
| J. B. Clayton | 1891 |
| S. J. Barbor | 1892-1895 |
| J. W. Kincheloe | 1897-1898 |
| A. W. Graves | 1899-1906 |
| W. S. O. Thomas | 1907-1917 |
| Ulysses S. Knox | 1918-1943 |
| Cecil H. Franks | 1944-1950 |
| Richard M. Stephenson | 1950-present |

### FOOTNOTES

[1] The basis of this chapter is notes compiled by the Honorable Frank M. Steadman, who has long been interested in the history of Columbia Baptist Church. His *History of Columbia Baptist Church* was published in 1954 by the Church, and this was enlarged for the booklet *1856 To 1956, A Story Of The First Hundred Years Of Columbia Baptist Church.*

[2] William S. Kearns was another early member. Dr. William Gwynn Coe noted in the Fairfax Chapel (Methodist) Class List that Kearns withdrew August 2, 1860, "to join Baptists." [Original record on file at Dulin Methodist Church.]

CHAPTER 10

# The Presbyterians

A committee of the Baltimore Presbytery in 1812 reported to that body that "three places southwest of the Potomac invited attention." and Professor William Maffitt, then a member of the Presbytery, was directed to devote as much time as possible to developing work in these areas. They were: Falls Church, Centreville, and Difficult. Mrs. John F. Bethune wrote in 1934:[1]

> ... Rev. William Maffitt, one of the four ministers who participated in the funeral services of George Washington, Dec. 18, 1799, held occasional services. No further work was done until 1843, when an influx of Presbyterian and Congregational families made it possible to organize a church. Under the leadership of Commodore Thomas A.C. Jones, U.S.N., a church was established at Lewinsville, Virginia; and the services of Rev. L.H. Christian were engaged.

The Lewinsville Presbyterian Church, "mother" of the Falls Church Presbyterian Church, was established October 17, 1846. The Church was established by the Presbytery of Winchester, and the building (torn down in 1955) was dedicated January 3, 1847. The first elders at Lewinsville were: Amzi Coe (whose home was in Falls Church) and B. Gilbert.

In 1848 Amzi Coe held meetings in his home and in other residences at Falls Church, and formed a congregation. The meetings were later principally in the home of A.E. Lounsbury. The Lounsbury home (until 1954 the Rectory of the Falls Church) is located across the street from the present Presbyterian Church. These meetings resulted in regular Sabbath worship, held twice a month at Falls Church. The congregation was a branch of the Lewinsville Church. In 1850 services were being held in Groot Hall, which stood adjacent to the present church.

This building, Groot Hall, erected by Dr. Simon J. Groot, was used as a community building. The work at Groot Hall was under the direction

116

of Dr. B.F. Bittinger. The church prospered until services were suspended due to the War Between the States.

By 1861 it was thought that the Virginia Presbyterian churches might decide to join the newly-organized southern branch of the Presbyterian Church, but, on October 4, 1865, the congregation of Lewinsville notified the Presbytery of the Potomac, (which had been formed for Washington and nearby Virginia and Maryland in 1858) that it wished to continue under its jurisdiction.

Many of the congregation at Falls Church were anxious to become a regular church. These included, Dr. B.F. Bittinger, A.E. Lounsbury, Amzi Coe, Seth Osborn, and Col. Daniel O. Munson. This group decided that Falls Church was to be the site for the new church. Shortly thereafter Groot Hall was purchased for a permanent church home, and was occupied free from debt due largely to the valiant efforts of the ladies of the congregation.

The deed is dated June 26, 1866, and the building was dedicated the following November 30th. The Reverend Dr. John Chester preached the dedicatory sermon. The Reverend H.P. Dechert served as supply for Lewinsville and Falls Church from 1866 until 1870 and was active in forwarding the purchase of Groot Hall. Mr. Dechert also served as principal of Groot Hall Academy. The first elders of the church were: A.E. Lounsbury, Spencer A. Coe, Miles C. Munson, and A.P. Douglass.

The first full-time minister of the Falls Church Presbyterian Church and Lewinsville Church was the Reverend David Hoge Riddle, who succeeded Mr. Dechert in 1870. Mr. Riddle was installed as minister of the church (and of the Church at Lewinsville) on April 25, 1873, at which time the new organization was officially established and recognized as the "Presbyterian Church of Falls Church, Va." The first trustees (serving three-year terms) were George B. Ives, Charles H. Buxton, Albert H. Ives, Daniel O. Munson, Schuyler Duryee, Ira F. Munson, and Nicholas Van Voast.

A new congregation was formed at Ballston |now Parkington| in Alexandria |now Arlington| County which was also served by Dr. Riddle. On October 22, 1876, a house of worship was dedicated at Ballston, but it was not an independent congregation until 1895.

Under the leadership of Dr. Riddle, the present church edifice was built in 1884, and was formally dedicated in October of that year. It was subsequently enlarged and remodeled in 1954. The stone used in construction of the building was taken from the Falls Church Quarry and the red stone used for the trim was brought from Seneca, Maryland, by way of the old Chesapeake and Ohio Canal. The builders were William Palmer & Son. Mr. Palmer contributed his labor "as an offering to the Lord in commemoration of the event of his conversion into the church." Mr. William Nathan Lynch assisted in hauling the stone and contributed the iron work supporting the roof of the church.

The building was dedicated October 30, 1884, while yet unfinished. The Reverend W.A. Bartlett of the New York Avenue Presbyterian Church,

Washington, D.C., assisted in the dedicatory service, while Dr. Riddle, the pastor, outlined a history of the founding of the church.

Dr. Riddle served as minister until 1890, when he resigned to accept a call in Kent, Ohio, and later held charges at Havre de Grace, and Emmitsburg, Maryland. He retired because of failing health in 1907, and returned to Falls Church, where he made his home with his sister, Miss Sue Riddle, until his death on December 11, 1911. Frequently during the period he served as supply in his old pulpit and in other local churches. Dr. Riddle and his sister organized the first Sunday School class for the local Negro population. He received his Doctor of Divinity Degree from Jefferson College (now Washington & Jefferson College) in 1902.

The Bible used in the dedication and organization services of the Falls Church Presbyterian Church was a large pulpit Bible, given Dr. Riddle by his mother, Mrs. Elizabeth Brown Riddle. The mother purchased it at the time of his birth, January 27, 1846. Dr. Riddle used this Bible during his lifetime. It was printed by J.B. Lippincott & Company of Philadelphia, 1846.[2]

The family record, which is torn, has this inscription written by Dr. Riddle: "Birth—Kate Riddle Vroom, Daughter of G.D. and K.R. Vroom, 9th November 1863."

In 1950 the Lewinsville Presbyterian Church acquired an old quilt which was presented to the minister of the church in 1852, and which contained one hundred and eight names of members of the church. The quilt was presented to the Reverend B.F. Bittinger, who was installed as minister on May 30, 1852. It was inherited by his brother, Henry E. Bittinger of "Sharon," Fairfax County, and was contributed by the latter's widow to the Chevy Chase Presbyterian Church. It was to go to a church in Darmstadt, Germany, with other gifts.[3] Mrs. George Davis, Secretary of the Chevy Chase Church, noticed that written in ink on one of the squares were the words "Rev. B.F. Bittinger, Installed Pastor of the Lewinsville Presbyterian Church, May 30, 1852."

The names on the quilt squares follow: Harriet N. Woodworth of "Summer Hill"; Mr. and Mrs. Calvin Woodworth, of "Fairview"; Mrs. Sarah C. Gilbert, of "Greenwood"; William C. Crocker, of "Glenair"; Jane E. Crocker, of "Glenair"; Mr. and Mrs. Phelps; Mr. James Crombie, of "Sunyside"; Mr. and Mrs. Tenant; Mary Child-Lucy Klock; Robert Judson—Miles C. Munson; Mr. G.B. Phillips, of "Linvale"; Mr. and Mrs. Seaymaker; Mr. and Mrs. Ball, of "Glenwood"; Mr. and Mrs. Child; Milton Woodworth, of "Summer Hill"; Mr. and Mrs. Wright; Mr. and Mrs. Perkins, of "Lake Borgne"; Mr. and Mrs. Coe, of "Mt. Hope"; Mr. B.T. Carpenter, of "Red Hill"; Amanda Ellison; Sarah D. Crocker, of "Glenair"; Mr. and Mrs. Barrett; Mrs. Julia Palmer; Mr. and Mrs. Ives; Mrs. Sharley G. Woodworth, of "Summer Hill"; Caroline Sherman, of "Ash Grove"; Mrs. M.E. Beall, of "Sharon"; Mr. and Mrs. Klock; Mr. and Mrs. Parker, of "Gum Asyle"; Mr. and Mrs. Hatch; Mrs. M.N. Dulany, of "Benvenue"; Dr. and Mrs. Grant; Aurelia R. Crocker, of "Glenair"; Mrs. Abigail Williams, of "Sunnyside"; Mr. and Mrs. Steele;

Mr. and Mrs. Seth Osborne; Mrs. Mary C. Crombie, of "Sunnyside"; Cyrus Osborne; Thomas ap. Catesby Jones, U.S.N., of "Sharon"; Mrs. Sarah C. Phillips, of "Linvale"; Charley Crocker; Martha S. Swink; Mr. John Gilbert, of "Greenwood"; Mrs. Norval Wilson, of "Ingleside"; Mrs. Anna Crocker, of "Glenair"; Harriet Woodworth, of "Fairview"; Mr. and Mrs. Sage; Mr. and Mrs. Ransom, of "Woodburn"; Anna M. Carpenter, of "Red Hill"; Mrs. Sarah Crocker; Mr. and Mrs. Younglove; Mrs. Martha C. Ball, of "Woodbury"; Mrs. Henry Bittinger, of "Sharon"; Mark C. Jones, of "Sharon"; Mr. and Mrs. Sherwood; Mrs. Gorham, of "Hebron"; Mr. Dorr Crocker; Mr. Arthur Lee Brent; Mrs. I.K. Gorham, of "Hebron"; James H. Crocker, of "Glenair"; Timothy Munson—Ann Munson; Mr. William Woodworth, of "Summer Hill"; Mrs. Ellen H. Crocker; Mr. and Mrs. Gacen, of "Prospect Hill"; Mary A. Woodworth, of "Summer Hill"; Mr. Francis Crocker, of "Glenair"; B.D. Carpenter, of "Red Hill"; Malcolm W. Woodworth, of "Summer Hill"; Mr. Scott Crocker; Henry Coe—Marietta Coe, of "Mt. Hope"; M.T. Jones, U.S.N., of "Sharon"; D.P. Palmer; Nancy Fish—Eliza Coe; Mrs. Sarah Carpenter, of "Red Hill"; Mr. and Mrs. Mase, of "Anchorage"; Mrs. Storer, of "Grandview"; Mrs. Mary W. Jones, of "Sharon"; Martha C. Jones, of "Sharon"; and Mr. and Mrs. Squier of "Lake Borgne."

Among the names on the old quilt which are of local interest, were the following: Lucy Klock, who resided at "The Mount"; Miles C. Munson of "Pendennis"; Mr. and Mrs. Parker of "Gum Asyle" (now the home of Dr. Lanier on South West Street); the Coe family of "Mt. Hope"; and the families of Barrett, Ives, Osborn, Fish and Swink.

The following memorial windows are in the Falls Church Presbyterian Church: Elizabeth Brown Riddle; Ives and Vanderwerken families; Stephen McGroarty; Capt. and Mrs. M.S. Roberts; Miss Carrie Parker; Mr. and Mrs. Yale Rice; and John Rice.

### ROSTER OF MINISTERS 1812-1964

| | |
|---|---|
| William Maffitt, Baltimore Presbytery | 1812 |
| L.H. Christian | 1843 |
| B.F. Bittinger | 1852 |
| H.P. Dechert | 1866-1870 |
| David H. Riddle | 1871-1890 |
| Davis L. Rathbun | 1890-1900 |
| Robert A. Davison | 1900-1918 |
| William R. McElroy | 1919-1923 |
| Alton B. Altfather | 1924-1961 |
| Floyd W. Ewalt, Present Minister | 1961- |

### LIST OF ELDERS
(With the year of their election)

| | |
|---|---|
| Albert E. Lounsbury | 1873 |
| Miles C. Munson | 1873 |
| Spencer A. Coe | 1873 |
| Albert H. Ives | 1873 |

Charles H. Mix ................................................................... 1876
Albert P. Douglass............................................................. 1877
William J. Allen ................................................................. 1882
George B. Fadeley.............................................................. 1897
Charles H. Buxton ............................................................. 1908
George W. Hawxhurst ....................................................... 1908
Andrew M. Smith .............................................................. 1908
E.C. Hough ........................................................................ 1920
Isaac A. Rullman ............................................................... 1920
J.V. McNary ...................................................................... 1920
Charles N. McGroarty ....................................................... 1922
Henry P. Noble .................................................................. 1922
Everett E. Tillett ................................................................ 1927
H.A. Hollins ....................................................................... 1929
J.P. Thompson ................................................................... 1930
H.E. Brown ........................................................................ 1933
Frank H. Eastman .............................................................. 1933

## LIST OF SUNDAY SCHOOL SUPERINTENDENTS

H.P. Dechert ................................................................ 1866-1869
Spencer A. Coe............................................................. 1869-1870
James W. Sargent ......................................................... 1871-1873
Albert E. Lounsbury ..................................................... 1874
Spencer A. Coe............................................................. 1875-1884
William J. Allen ........................................................... 1885-1889
A.E. Lounsbury ............................................................ 1890-1891
M.M. Erwin .................................................................. 1892
E.C. Hough ................................................................... 1893-1913
Andrew M. Smith ........................................................ 1914-1915
Isaac A. Rullman .......................................................... 1916-1917
Frank H. Eastman ......................................................... 1917

## FIRST CONGREGATIONAL CHURCH

The First Congregational Church of Falls Church was abandoned due to a loss in membership, in 1910, at which time the remaining members became communicants of the Falls Church Presbyterian Church. It is for this reason that some notice of the First Congregational Church is given here.

The First Congregational Church of Falls Church was organized in October, 1875, and was recognized by the Congregational Council on May 20, 1876. Services were held in the old Columbia Baptist Church on East Broad Street until 1879, when the church edifice was built. This building was later a Police Station, having served for many years until 1953 as Town Hall. The building originally had stained glass windows, a steeple, and a fine-toned bell. The sanctuary seated three hundred, and the Sunday School was in the rear of the building. The bell purchased in 1881 was rung on all public occasions.

The first minister was the Reverend J.W. Chickering, Jr., who was followed by L.B. Platt. After the building was abandoned, it was used as a gymnasium, later as a grade school, and Town Hall. It housed the Falls Church Library during the 1940's.

The following article appeared in the *Falls Church News* of January 21, 1898:

> Rev. H.P. Higley, of Washington, D.C., will preach in the Congregational Church Sunday morning.
>
> The Ladies Aid Society of the Congregational Church met Thursday at the home of Mrs. A.C. Rorebeck. They made arrangements to give a dinner on Washington's birthday.

The late Mr. Charles A. Stewart wrote concerning the organization of the church:

> At its organization 25 members united in forming the church. At that time it was thought by some that another church in such a small town would result in dissension among the Christian people. Such was not the intention of this church. At its first annual meeting a resolution was unanimously adopted expressing 'good wishes toward every church of Christ in this place, and its readiness and desire to co-operate with them in every good work.' The other churches responded in a Christian spirit, and the pastors and churches of this town have always cordially worked together in the cause of the Master.

In 1904 the officers of the church were: George F. Rollins, M.H. Brinkerhoff, George W. Poole, Trustees; Dr. J.B. Gould, Treasurer; Frank H. Eastman, Clerk; Miss Gertrude Nourse, Superintendent of Sunday School; George F. Rollins, G.A.L. Merrifield, Albert P. Eastman, Deacons; and Mrs. Albert P. Eastman, Mrs. Helen C. Raymond, Deaconesses.

The following are some of the clergymen who served the church: J.W. Chickering, Jr., L.B. Platt, Nov. 1877-June, 1880; A.L. Park, Nov. 1881-Dec. 1882; Wm. W. Jordan, May 1883-Oct. 1885; F.W. Tuckerman, Sept. 1886-May, 1890; R.E. Eels, Feb. 1891-Dec. 1891; J.H. Jenkins, Jan. 1893-July 1897; Arsene Schmavonian, May 1899-May 1901; Franklin Noble, Dec. 1901-1904.

In September, 1961, after years of service as police station, town hall, recreation center, library, and general meeting place, the old Congregational Church was sold to the Woman's Club of Falls Church for $18,514. It was extensively remodeled and is now their headquarters.[4]

## FOOTNOTES

[1] *Our Church—Its History*, in the *Golden Jubilee Booklet*, Falls Church Presbyterian Church, October 19, 1934, page 7. The author was Mrs. John F. Bethune.

[2] This Bible was presented to the Church during the Anniversary celebration held February 10, 1963. It was placed in the Church files by the author in memory of his maternal grandmother, Ellen Mankin Hirst.

[3] From the February 16, 1950 issue of *The Providence Journal*. This quilt was later placed in the Lewinsville Church.

[4] *Northern Virginia Sun*, September 12, 1961.

CHAPTER 11

# The Roman Catholics

St. James Church was established in 1873 as a mission of St. Mary's Church, Alexandria. It was not separated from that congregation until 1892. It is said that St. Mary's is the oldest Roman Catholic parish in the state. Established on March 17, 1778, St. Mary's was made a parish in 1795, and the first building was erected in 1796. Concerning the origin of St. James Church, Mr. J.O. Martin wrote:[1]

> Sixty years ago the few Catholics in the vicinity of Falls Church were served on a mission basis from the church at Alexandria. Reverend John Kane, Jesuit, came once a month to say Mass in the home of Mrs. Sabilla (or Sabina) Sewall, who lived in the old house that still stands at the top of the hill beyond the graveyard, on the road that leads from Mr. Shreve's store to the Lee Highway. [2]

Twenty-five years ago Roman Catholics made up less than two per cent of the population of Virginia. There were few adherents in earlier years and most of these immigrants from Maryland and Ireland. Until after the Revolutionary War the Roman Catholic Church, like certain other churches, had no official existence in the state. The Church of England was the established Church with government support.

In 1871 there was no Catholic Church between Alexandria and the Blue Ridge Mountains, with the exception of the little church at Fairfax Station, built at the time of the construction of the Southern Railroad to serve the spiritual needs of the Irish laborers who helped to build the road. The establishment of a congregation at Falls Church was the first attempt in a general way to extend the service of the church into the vast area to the west.

Mrs. Gibson Terrett was one of the first to work toward this goal. Among the records of St. James Church is a leaf torn from a notebook, on which is written, in the hand of the bishop who later became Cardinal Gibbons:

Mrs. Gibson Terrett is authorized to solicit contributions which will be devoted to the erection of a Catholic Church at Falls Church, Fairfax County, Virginia.
James Gibbons,
Bishop of Richmond.
May 19, 1873.

Mr. Martin says: "Mrs. Terrett did solicit contributions, proof of which may be seen on two other notebook pages—the names of the contributors. These names—except in a few cases—are not familiar names in Falls Church, and it is likely that several of them were not Catholics. It ought to be mentioned that Mrs. Terrett, the solicitor, was one of the chief contributors." The contributions were in small sums, one and two dollars.

On June 30, 1873, Mrs. Terrett gave Father Kane the sum of $76.00 for which he duly receipted on the paper containing the list of names. On September 1, 1873, Mrs. Terrett sent Father Kane an additional $50.00. Erection of a small wooden building was begun in that same year, much of the labor being contributed. The work was under the supervision of the late Mr. Thomas Hartwell Walker and his son Ewell Walker.[3] This first chapel was located on the corner of Fowler Street and South West Street in West Falls Church, on the lot now occupied by the St. James Cemetery. The house adjoining the property (on Fowler Street), once a home of the Lightfoot family, was the Rectory. It was built in 1892. The church building was clapboard and the windows were clear glass, with the exception of two stained windows above the altar, which are now in the rear wall of the stone sanctuary of the Columbia Baptist Church (erected in 1909). The chapel had a steeple and bell. The ground was donated by Miss Sabilla Sewall.

Among the early communicants of the first church were the following families: Carlin, Peyton, McCauley, Murnane, McCarty, Beattie, Burke, Stewart, Nelson, Sewall, Terrett, Crowell, and Crimmins. Some of these names are still to be found on the rolls of the church.

The present St. James Church was extensively remodeled and enlarged in recent years. The portion of the building facing Spring Street (the old front) was erected in 1902 by contributions, due largely to a large gift of money donated by Mrs. Thomas Fortune Ryan, wife of the millionaire financier.[4] At the time it was built, the church was called the "best example of Gothic architecture in the state." This lovely building was designed by Mr. A.O. Von Herbulis, an architect of some note who lived near the church, and who was a communicant. He also designed the rectory. Members of the family still live in the parish.

The Sisters of Perpetual Adoration from Louisiana established a school in 1905 in the old Sherwood home which stood where St. James School now stands. The Sherwood home also served as a temporary convent. A good portion of the money to build a new brick school and convent was given by Mrs. Ryan. The convent was used until 1964[5] and the school was torn down during World War Two to make way for the present building.

In 1904 the enrollment at St. James Church was three hundred-twenty-five members. The church is now one of the largest in this vicinity, serving not only Falls Church but a large area in Fairfax County. The membership runs into the thousands. Four priests serve the congregation and six Masses are said every Sunday.

When the mission at Falls Church came into existence as a parish in 1892, Bishop Augustus Van de Vyver appointed Father Edward Tierney (later Monsignor Tierney) as minister. He was formerly pastor at the church in Lynchburg. Father Tierney remained at St. James Church until 1897. He served St. James, Fairfax, Manassas, and Leesburg as missions during 1892-97.

In July, 1897, Father Tierney was appointed minister of the Cathedral Church of St. Peter in Richmond, and his successor was Father John Bowler. In November, 1899, Father Bowler succeeded Father Tierney at St. Peter's and Father Tierney returned to St. James. In October, 1904, due to a large increase in members Father Tierney was given an assistant, Father Lackey. Father Lackey was later minister at St. Charles Church in Clarendon. Two Masses were said each Sunday at Falls Church and one Mass each at Fairfax and Leesburg during this period.

In January, 1910, Father A.J. Van Ingelgem came to St. James. In 1925 he celebrated his Golden Jubilee—fifty years in the priesthood, fifty years of service to his fellow man. On that occasion a celebration was held at West Falls Church, which was attended by priests and others from every part of the Richmond Diocese. Many honors were heaped on "Father Van," as he was affectionately known. He was decorated by the King of his native country, Belgium. Mr. J.O. Martin made the historical address at the Anniversary party. Mr. Martin told of the early history of the church and particularly Father Van's work in connection with it.

Father Van's career is given in detail because he was beloved by the entire community. Father Van gave freely of his energies and personal funds to the work in Falls Church. He did not accept a salary and lived frugally. When presented a purse of more than $1,000 at his jubilee, he turned it over to the church to pay off a debt on the heating system.

Father Van Ingelgem came to the United States from Belgium, where he had become a priest twenty-five years previously, and where for a time he taught philosophy in the University of Loùvain. He came to this country specifically to do missionary work with the Negro people of the South.

A short time after his arrival (and before taking up his duties in the missionary field) he was asked to go to Newfoundland and conduct a mission there for the French-speaking people of that community. He did so with great success. While still in Newfoundland, Bishop Van de Vyver, of the Diocese of Richmond (who had known Father Van while both were students in Belgium)—wrote to him and asked him to come to Virginia. Thus, Father Van came to begin his work in this state.

Father Van was forty-eight years old when he arrived in the United States. Reared in an atmosphere of refinement, culture and learning, he represented a family of material wealth and social standing. Mr. Martin wrote:

> And yet this good man chose to leave all that behind him and to come to Virginia to do missionary work among the colored people. He came to Virginia, knowing little of the language or the habits or customs of the people. He came from a community where he was a highly-respected person to a community where he was just an unknown foreign priest, in a land where priests were scarce and perhaps sometimes under unjust suspicion.

But priests were badly needed in Virginia to conduct parish work, and after a few weeks Bishop Van de Vyver appointed him pastor at Staunton, where he remained for six years, doing missionary work on the side among the people of the Valley and the nearby foothills.

In 1906, Father Van and Father Thomas Waters, later Monsignor Waters, pastor at the Sacred Heart Church at Norfolk, were appointed members of a mission band, with the whole diocese as their field. They were the only members of the band and they went all over Virginia, conducting missions for Catholics and others, traveling by horseback, train, wagon, or whatever other means of transportation might be available.

They published a little magazine, editing it while they traveled. It was called the Catholic Virginian. It is interesting to note that the weekly newspaper now serving the Diocese of Richmond bears the same name.

The headquarters of the mission fathers was Danville, Va.

Three years later Father Van was appointed minister at "Oak Ridge," the Virginia estate of a wealthy layman. From a poor missionary traveling around on horseback among the poor and lowly and preaching constantly, he became pastor of a rich man's private chapel with practically nothing to do. This was not his mission. Once when the owner of the estate sent word to Father Van that he should not preach to the people in the surrounding country, as he, the rich man, feared that Father Van would use his name in making converts, Father Van sent him back a message that the Church has other recommendations than the names of millionaires who happen to be members of it.

After a few months at "Oak Ridge," the Bishop appointed Father Van as his secretary. But Father Van felt that he had not come from Belgium to Virginia for a comfortable post, having given up a similar position in the old country. Prevailing upon the bishop, he was at length appointed minister at St. James. Father Van immediately set out to establish missions. When the parish was founded, it had two missions, Fairfax Station and Leesburg. In 1913, Father Van built St. John's Church at El Nido; in 1917 he built a church at Purcellville; and in 1923 he built the church at Herndon. There was also a church built at Pleasant Valley, a mission of Fairfax Station. All of these missions were attended by the assistant pastor of St. James, assisted by two priests of the religious houses at Washington. In 1922 the Fairfax Station mission was made a parish, and Father Valentine Cuervas, then assistant at St. James, became first pastor. In 1926 Leesburg was made a parish and Father Joseph Govaert, then assistant at St. James, became first pastor.

Where formerly there was only one little mission—West Falls Church—there were in 1931 four parishes, each with missions. The first of those parishes to be separated from the mother parish was Clarendon, in 1899. Father Lackey, then assistant at St. James, was made the first pastor. Later, a mission was established at Cherrydale. The parish of Fairfax Station had missions at Pleasant Valley, Bailey's Cross Roads, and Centreville. The parish at Leesburg had missions in Herndon and Purcellville.[6]

The original territory covered by Father Van and his assistant extended from below Clarendon to the Blue Ridge Mountains—an area of about 2,400 square miles, much of which was rugged country. The mode of travel was by horseback and wagons. The electric line to Bluemont was also used in their work. There were occasions, when two days were required to make a sick call.

Mr. Martin wrote of an incident in Father Van's career which gives an idea of the task he faced and conditions of the time:

> Let me digress here a minute to give you a detail or two regarding the building of the church at El Nido. How much money do you suppose Father Van had in hand to start that church? Just $42—plus a tremendous faith that God would provide the way of getting the rest. And the people had faith, too. One man had no money, having a large family to support, but he had a good cow, the milk of which was used for the family table. He said they would do without milk for a while and sold the cow for $50, and turned the money in to the building fund. And it was not long before God so prospered him that he had money enough to buy his cow back. And he did—the same cow.

In 1905 the first building for the St. James School was erected, constructed of brick. This was torn down in 1948 to make way for the present Colonial-style structure which was opened September 27, 1948. The new building cost $250,000. It was dedicated on October 10, 1948, by the Reverend Peter L. Ireton, Bishop of Richmond.[7] The Dedication address was by the Right Reverend Msgr. Edward B. Jordan, Vice Rector of Catholic University. The school opened with an enrollment of five hundred, and was enlarged, in the winter of 1950, and again in 1956. The school, like the church, serves not only the city, but part of Fairfax County. Enrollment now exceeds two-thousand pupils.

In 1907 the first Villa Maria Academy and the Sisters' Chapel were built. About 1924 the Sisters of the Immaculate Heart of Mary, from Pennsylvania, were established in residence in place of the original group.

St. James Church was extensively enlarged and remodeled in 1951-52. The Mass of Dedication was held on Sunday, October 12, 1952. Present at the time was the Pastor, the Reverend E.V. Mullarkey, and the Most Reverend Peter L. Ireton, Bishop of Richmond. The Church is now cruciform in shape and has about thirty stained glass windows, including a rose window above the main altar. This particular window has sentimental significance for the older families of the parish as it is dedicated to the memory of Sister Mary Callesta, a nun who taught the first-grade children of St. James School.

In the territory originally served by the Church at Alexandria, with missions at Fairfax Station and Falls Church, there are now numerous parishes, including St. Anthony's at Culmore, St. Ann's at Westover, and St. Michael's at Annandale, where new churches have been built in recent years. There are new parishes at Vienna and Fairfax.

*Ministers* 1874-1964

| | |
|---|---|
| Dennis John O'Kane (Kane), S.J. | 1872-1891 |
| Edward M. Tierney | 1892-1897 |
| John J. Bowler | 1897-1899 |
| Edward M. Tierney | 1899-1910 |
| A.J. Van Ingelgem | 1910-1931 |
| Edward V. Mullarkey | 1931-1953 |
| Paul Keller | 1953-present |

### FOOTNOTES

[1] From a ms. article, *In Sixty Years,* compiled in 1931 by J. O. Martin, p. 1. We now know this street as South West Street. The home, "Walnut Hill," is now occupied by Major Coggins. The name of Miss (not Mrs.) Sewall is correctly Sabilla.

[2] The basis of this chapter is from the writings of Mr. J. O. Martin who kindly loaned his manuscripts to the author. The first is a speech by Mr. Martin which he gave at the Golden Jubilee of Father Van Ingelgem, 1925; and the second is a manuscript article, *In Sixty Years* written June 5, 1931 by him in which he pointed out the progress of the congregation since 1872. I have also talked extensively with the late Messrs. David Leonard, Jr., and Willis L. Gordon; as well as with the author's aunt, Velva Lee (Wakefield) Steadman. Several clippings from local newspaper files have been consulted.

[3] Statement of the late Willis L. Gordon and Mrs. Howard R. Steadman. Mrs. Steadman is a granddaughter of the late Sarah Jane (Thompson) Caton, first wife of John Wesley Caton and second wife of Thomas Hartwell Walker.

[4] Contractor and builder was Thomas Hillier, who also built the rectory.

[5] A new building was completed in the spring of this year.

[6] The Church at El Nido, called the Church of St. John the Evangelist, was built in 1913 by Father Van. The Purcellville Church (St. Francis de Sales) was built in 1921 after having held services for some time in the home of Mr. Notley Ball. In 1928 the Mass was offered in the Herndon Hotel and in 1931 St. Joseph's, Herndon, was built.

[7] From an article in the Washington, D.C., *Washington Post,* October 11, 1948.

CHAPTER 12

# Schools, Pencils and Books

Writing during the seventeenth century, the Bishop of London said that the lack of schools in Virginia was a consequence of "their scattered planting." Because of the feudal set-up of Virginia life, the planter provided tutors for his children. A travelling school master would occasionally settle and open a "field school," but these were rare.

About 1702, according to a tradition handed down to Mrs. W.H.G. Lynch (born 1826) a school was established at the crossroads, now Falls Church. This date seems very early for this area. However, it is known that a substantial log building was erected for a school in 1780, and stood until the outbreak of the War Between the States. This school was attended by Ellen Lightfoot (later Mrs. W.H.G. Lynch), and her sisters, Mary Ann Lightfoot (later Mrs. John W. Lynch), and Jane Lightfoot. They attended the school from 1836 until 1850. The Misses Lightfoot lived at "Big Chimneys," home of their maternal uncle, Nathan Thompson.

Mrs. W.H.G. Lynch told her granddaughter (the author's grandmother) that she was selected to "set the copy" for the students of the school. Her handwriting was considered outstanding, and the selection was a distinction. The lesson was copied on her slate and the other pupils would attempt to imitate her Spencerian style.

The old 1780 building was of log construction, and was put together with large wooden pegs. It had "double-crossed" shutters on the windows. The floor boards were wide and rough. The teacher sat on a platform which was in the middle of the room. According to Mrs. Lynch, the roof was made of hand-hewn shingles, which in her day were covered with moss. A gable front faced the road, with a large hand-made wooden door and a single window. The windows had sixteen panes. At the back of the large room was a fieldstone fireplace. The foundation was also of stone. The logs were kept whitewashed.

No greater contrast in conditions could exist than between the school life of the "good old days," and that of the far better times of today. The school house of yesterday was poor, small, and uncomfortable, with scant furnishings (benches and tables), few and uninteresting books, tiresome, indifferent, and unreasonable methods of teaching, and heavy severity of discipline which left its mark. Yet, even with all of these disadvantages (certainly they did little to inspire), such schools produced some of the greatest scholars, statesmen, and gentlemen this world has ever known.

The type of school represented by the old log school was what was sometimes called "an old field" school, because such a school was usually located in an abandoned field. A few neighbors would unite to hire a teacher, too often a poor one, who taught short terms. A bell was rung at eight o'clock in the morning, to call the pupils together. The school closed for a recess at eleven, opened again at one, closed at four. All sessions began and closed with prayer. On Wednesday and Saturday the children were taught the questions and answers in the Catechism and the Book of Common Prayer of the Church of England.

The average salary for a "qualified teacher" was sixty-seven cents a week with room and board. Teaching was not easy. Few lead pencils were used, as they were expensive. In 1761 Faber's pencils were put on the market, and one Peter Goelet advertised lead pencils in New York in 1786.

The clothing worn to school by the pupils would make a modern child self-conscious. The author's great-great-grandmother (Ellen Lightfoot) wore a dress skirt with a draped over-skirt, called a polonaise. She also wore a Basque, which was a tight-fitting waist, and a "body button up." The "body button up" was worn over the corset and according to Miss Ada Walker, "the whole outfit weighed about three pounds but was not half as eye-catching as the present day bare-skin get-up."

Text books were few. John Locke in his "Thoughts Concerning Education" (1690) says the method of teaching children to read in England at that time was always "the ordinary road of Horn-book, Primer, Psalter, Testament, and Bible." These, according to Locke, "engage the liking of children...."! When the scholar was beyond the Horn-book, and the Primer, he was ready for "Lilly's Grammer." This was a wretched thing. It named twenty-five different kinds of nouns and devoted twenty-two pages of solid print to declensions of nouns; contained seven genders, with fifteen pages of rules for genders and exceptions!

The old log school in Falls Church having served its purpose, it was torn down about 1858. Mrs. John F. Bethune wrote concerning this school:[2]

> In 1873 the first public school was established. Prior to this a private school had been maintained near the Episcopal Church.

The old log school was on the site of the Henderson home between what is now 121 South Washington Street and the Alma Shop.

Groot Hall Academy was established at an early date, and apparently was the second school in Falls Church. Groot Hall was erected about 1845 by

Dr. Simon J. Groot "for religious and other services" for the community. The building was torn down about the time of World War I. It was made of clapboard painted white and had two stories with front gable. About 1850 the Presbyterians in Falls Church (offspring of the Lewinsville Presbyterian Church) held services in this building, which they later purchased for their Church. The Presbyterian congregation used the first floor for church and Sunday School and their pastor, the Reverend H. P. Dechert (1866-1870) was principal of the school held upstairs. During the period 1880-1900, a private school was conducted in this building. In 1892 Miss Mamie Castleman, sister of the beloved Rector of the Falls Church, became principal. She opened it as a private school. The tuition was $5.00 per month, and this fee was later raised to $8.00, according to Ellen Mankin Hirst, who attended the school. Among students of the school before 1900 were Will Edmonds, Hattie Graham, Clara Graham, Percy Tripp, Robert Hoskinson, and Bessie Rice. A student was permitted to select any subject he wished.

According to the late Prentiss A. Shreve, Groot Hall served as the first Town Hall for Falls Church. Mr. Shreve also said that a Mr. Brown maintained a school there at one time.

A Mr. and Mrs. Owens maintained a private school in the Old Baptist Church. Mr. Owens taught the boys and Mrs. Owens taught the girls. This school was closed in 1861 and reopened after the war. A private school was in a building where the stone arch building is at the corner of Broad and South Washington Street (at the traffic light). A Miss Smith was the teacher in 1857 when the late Benjamin R. Shreve was a student.

Prior to 1874 a private school was opened in the old Columbia Baptist Church, with Miss Lou Ball as the teacher. After 1874 the "Thomas Jefferson Institute," first public school in Falls Church[3] was established in this same building. When the brick Jefferson Institute was erected, the builder, Richard Ratcliffe Farr, remarked to Mrs. Charles E. Mankin that he put a double foundation under the building because it took a hundred years of need to appropriate money for the school, and he knew it would be another hundred years before more funds would be raised! He was almost right. The bricks in the Jefferson building were fired in the yard. The building was one of the finest in the state, and was the most outstanding feature of the community for many years. It originally had green shutters. Jefferson Institute was built for a school, and was never used for anything else prior to 1956. Due to an incident that occurred there during the childhood of the author's grandmother, when some boy put the pigtails of several young misses in their glue pots (part of the desk equipment), it has been called the "glue factory."

The following are recollections of old Jefferson written by two former students, Ada Walker and Professor William H. Ellison. They were published, in an extended form, in a volume entitled "Memories of Old Jefferson Institute, Falls Church, Va.," by Ada Walker, June 10, 1964. Fourteen copies were made of this publication.[4]

By Ada Walker

I first saw the Jefferson Institute in 1886 when I was eleven years old. My seatmate and I spent the noon hour cleaning the plaster off the window glass in our room, using chips from the wood pile and plain water.

The building was completed in 1882 after a period of some 6 or 7 years of organization and fund raising, during most of which time classes were conducted in the old Columbia Baptist Church on East Broad Street. The money was raised by the people of the Falls Church community, by subscription. Fairfax County furnished the seats, blackboards, water buckets, and paid the teachers.

The basement had two rooms—a school room in front and a furnace room in the back. The first floor had two class rooms, and the top floor had a large stage across one end, and seats in the rest of the room. At one time it was used as a class room. Mostly it was used for commencement exercises, and later we outfitted it as a gymnasium.

Three teachers took care of all who came, and taught from the first to the eighth grade. Each teacher had from 40 to 60 pupils.

The school was built by people who knew how. It would have stood for many years, and would have made a wonderful museum.

With our fathers, we children gave the school a lovely flag, a dictionary, a bible, and a clock for the Principal's room.

Among the children about my age in Jefferson Institute was a small boy who was so eager to learn that he attracted the special attention of the principal. He was William H. Ellison, otherwise known as Bill. Just as this booklet was in the final stages of preparation, I received a note from Bill enclosing a clipping from the Santa Barbara California News-Press of April 3, 1964, concerning plans adopted for conferring the honorary degree of Doctor of Laws on Prof. Ellison the following Wednesday, April 8, 1964. The occasion was the Carter Anniversary Ceremonies of UCSB. Following are excerpts from the newspaper clipping.

> Prof. Ellison is the first retired UCSB (U. Cal. Santa Barbara) faculty member to be presented with an honorary degree from his own University. . . .
>
> Born in Virginia, Prof. Ellison received his B.A. degree from Randolph-Macon College in 1904. . . . He later studied at Pacific Theological Seminary and served several years in the ministry. He then turned to graduate work in history and earned his M.A. and Ph.D. degrees at UC Berkeley campus.
>
> For nearly a quarter of a century he taught at Santa Barbara where he gained a reputation as a stimulating teacher. . . .
>
> Recognized as an authority on California history and on the Indians of the American Southwest, Prof. Ellison has a long record of research and publications. His writings include seven books and

numerous articles in prominent historical journals. He was selected by his faculty colleagues as the 1958 Faculty Research Lecturer in recognition of his scholarly achievements.

He served as President of the Pacific Coast Branch of the American Historical Assn., and assisted in the founding of the association's journal, *Pacific Historical Review.*' He has been president and director of the Santa Barbara Historical Society, president of the Southern California Branch of the National Association on Indian Affairs, and active in several other scholarly societies.

Since its founding, he has been a sponsor of the California Historical Foundation, and in recognition of his work in Franciscan history, in 1932 he was elected corresponding member of the Academy of Franciscan History. In 1955 he was named the first Wyles Board Fellow at Santa Barbara.

His wife, the former Ruth Doolittle, is an associate professor of art, emeritus, at UCSB.

## *A TEACHER WHO LIVES IN MEMORY*
By Prof. William H. Ellison
University of California

Think for thyself.
One good idea but known to be thine own
Is better than a thousand
Gleaned from fields by others sown.

Across a continent and down the corridors of time—three score years and ten plus, in fact—I still remember a man. Everyone of the school and community addressed him as "Mr. Brown" during the years 1890 to 1893 when he was Principal of the Jefferson Grammar School of Falls Church, Virginia. The lines quoted above were written in the autograph album of Ada Walker, one of the school's bright pupils. Whether original with Mr. Brown or written by another, these lines speak from the mind and heart of the Quaker school principal and teacher we knew in the last three years of his life.

It would be easy to digress at this point as one thinks of the impact of some teachers on those taught, the why of it, and if in our differences today in methods and facilities we have moved so far as we think. My considered observation as to why Mr. Brown effected the impact on me and others that he did is that he possessed the spiritual and intellectual equipment of a great teacher which in any day would have made him "a teacher who lives in memory."

James Isaac Brown was born in Loudoun County, Virginia. Life ended for him at Falls Church in 1893 at the age of 44. When he was a child his father died leaving a wife and four small children. He was partly of Quaker descent, lived some of his boyhood days among Quakers, and was brought up in the Quaker religion. How he acquired his education we never learned, but what he was and did marked him as a broadly and deeply educated person. A daughter thinks he had some training in a Quaker college and graduated from William and Mary.

This Quaker educator had taught a number of years in the schools of Loudoun County before coming to the Jefferson school in Falls Church. At Philomont, Loudoun County, Mr. Brown married one of his pupils, Miss Sarah Tavenner, who bore him three daughters, Ivy, Mary Byrd and Myrtle.

Mr. Brown was about five feet and ten inches in height. His face tended toward roundness. He had dark hair which was beginning to take leave of him, and he wore sideburns and a cropped goatee. He moved with steadiness and a confident air, carried himself erect, and from the first at Falls Church had the respect of the community, the churches, and the youth of all ages in the school.

Like the good Quaker that he was, Mr. Brown did not make his religion obtrusive. Soon after coming to the Falls Church school he became a regular attendant at the morning service of a church in the community. Why he selected the one he did in the proud little town of Falls Church, with its population of 975 and its seven churches, but with no Quaker society, can be deduced with relative certainty. In retrospect, considering the man and the churches, it seems quite clear to the writer that Mr. Brown chose the inconspicuous and small Baptist church of the town as his place of corporate worship because of its democracy, the simplicity of its service, and its absence of pretensions about status.

In his youth, James Brown had been blinded in one eye when a bit of red hot iron struck an eyeball. In spite of this handicap, the young persons he taught came to feel that he knew much about them, and that with his one eye he could see about everything that went on. Some would say good naturedly that he must have eyes in the back of his head.

Great respect for Mr. Brown developed quickly among the boys and girls of the Falls Church school. This was evidenced when on occasion he would leave his room briefly to look after administrative details as principal, or for other purposes, and would say to a pupil, "Take your work to my desk and look after things until I return." There would rarely be any disorder or inattention to study while he was absent from the room.

A case of Mr. Brown's authority being respected in his absence occurred one day when at recess he sent two girls, Ada Walker and "Maggie" Riley, to fetch a pail of water. The old school pump gave no help. The well was nearly dry. They went across the turnpike to Mr. Joe Birch's well about 100 yards away to fill their bucket. When they were nearly back the school bell rang. The pupils rushed up the broad board steps except one Charley ——— who stealthily went under the open steps. "Maggie" refused to go up the steps but daring Ada went ahead with the pail of water. When she got above Charley who was looking up, she let him have the bucketful, then went into the school room and banged the empty bucket down in its place on the platform. The principal-teacher asked her to explain. She told him what had taken place. Saying to Ada, "Take my chair," he went out after Charley, took him to the gym for a warming up, and sent him home for dry clothes. Mr. Brown returned to his class room to find it in as perfect order as if he had been present all of the time.

That Mr. Brown's power of moral suasion was not confined to its exercise in dealing with the very young was shown one day in the way he cooled off an angry man. The teacher of the middle grades was at times an impulsive and cruel disciplinarian. One day he made bruises on a boy with the heavy plank he used in punishing him. It was rumored at the school that the punished boy's angered father would visit the school to beat up the boy's teacher. Some pupils in Mr. Brown's room saw through windows the angered father coming up a path to the school. The excitement of the young people caused Mr. Brown to look out. He too saw the angry man approaching. Saying calmly to a pupil, "Take my chair," he went outside and met the man at the front steps. What was said in the man-to-man talk, as the two men sat on the schoolhouse steps, was not heard by others. This we know: in a little while, some pupils glancing out the windows saw the father unexcitedly walking back down the path away from the school just as unperturbed Mr. Brown returned to his orderly room.

An incident in which the exercise of authority in an unusual way had results for the persons directly involved, and for all in the upper classes of school, was Mr. Brown's dealings with two thirteen year old boys who entered into a fight with loud words and blows as the room was assembling at the end of a recess. At once the principal called the boys to the platform. They came apprehensively as he walked around them with two strong switches in his hand. He did not ask them what their trouble was. "Face one another," he said to them. "Double up your fists," he directed. "Now fight," he commanded. They hesitated. "Fight, I say," he said firmly. The boys went at it. Mr. Brown then went to switching their backsides with vigor, saying at the same time, "Fight, fight, I say." Soon both boys were bawling. "Stop everything," the kindly principal said after a few embarrassing moments for the boys. They looked at one another smiling sheepishly as they spontaneously shook hands. "Now we are all friends," Mr. Brown said, as the boys went to their seats.

The natural dignity and spiritual insight of Principal Brown, which were always present with him as a teacher, had the effect of awakening something in the persons taught. This was manifest one day in the reading and study of the poem, "Forty Years Ago," in *Mc-Guffey's Fifth Reader*. When about half through the poem, following the reading of the fourth stanza's closing verses,

> And kneeling down to take a drink
> Dear Tim, I started so,
> To think how very much I've changed
> Since forty years ago,

there occurred a little light laughter by some of the thoughtless. Not in the manner of a rebuke, Mr. Brown said meaningfully, "You can be sure that none of this will seem amusing to you forty years from now." The way and the spirit in which the words were spoken awakened the minds and hearts of the youth in the class. As if by magic the poem seemed to take on new meaning for them. They became at once alive to the beauty and meaning of what was being studied, as the writer knows because he was there.

There was little of the authoritarian in principal-teacher Brown either in the management of the school as a whole or in his classroom. Rarely did it become necessary for him to arbitrarily exercise the power vested in him by the state in dealing with the thoughtless or slightly vicious. His willingness to listen with openness of mind to serious proposals presented by groups of earnest pupils gave him greatly respected moral authority. At the same time, it made him an approachable person.

Because of the kind of man their principal-teacher was, there was no hesitancy on the part of some older girls and boys in presenting to him a request that had to do with a change in the daily opening exercises for his room. He had followed a practice of reading briefly from the Bible and the singing of some stanzas of a familiar religious song. One day a group of the pupils in good spirit put to him the question, "Mr. Brown, why can't we sing 'college songs' at the opening of school?"

In his usual kindly manner, their teacher replied, "Maybe we can, but you will have to let me think it over until tomorrow. There might be reasons why I could not grant your request."

On the next day when he told the interested group that their request was approved, he asked them who would pick out the songs and lead the singing. They told him to leave it to them.

A few days later the young people of the room sang with enthusiasm their first "College Song." Where or how so many of them learned this particular song, "There Is a Tavern in This Town." I do not know. Principal Brown sat quietly with his arms folded until the song was concluded. With no apparent feeling, he broke the strange silence as the song came to its close by saying, "If that is a good example of college songs, I think we'll sing no more of them."

This was not the end. The older girls went to their approachable teacher acknowledging that they had made a mistake. They asked if they might not try again. Their plea was granted. The next day when the singing of "The Spanish Cavalier" was concluded, Mr.

Brown said pleasantly, "That is more like it, and you will do even better than that," and they did.

Another concession granted had to do with baseball. Boys out of school working in the village would talk to the older boys of Jefferson School about trying to arrange a midday game on the school grounds. The school boys would then approach the school principal with respect to such a game. He did not find their request unreasonable. The result was that on occasion he would cancel the morning and afternoon recesses for the upper and middle grades, add the time to the noon hour, and thus provide an hour and a half for the game. A few townspeople came to these occasional games, and the upper and middle grades of the school turned out *en masse*. Not only did the pupils have a happy time but good feeling was increased in school and community.

When James Isaac Brown was the principal of and a teacher with the upper grades of the Jefferson school, this was the only grammar school in Falls Church. There was no high school nearer than the small Central High School in Washington. Some youths who had finished with the grammar school grades would ask permission to continue another year for additional work in English or in mathematical subjects. Surveying was looked into by a few, one of whom in a few years became county surveyor. Acceding to requests as Mr. Brown was wont to do, he organized a class in Physics, which he taught himself, using as a text-book, Steele's *Fourteen Weeks in Physics*.

One of the boys, with only the background in advanced work under the versatile and highly educated Principal James Brown went to an academy some seven years later to make preparation for college entrance. With no academic training other than that received in the Jefferson school, he was able in a semester there to do a year's work in English, a year's work in Latin, in which he led the class, and two years of work in secondary school Mathematics with a perfect record.

The Jefferson School in Falls Church was housed in an architecturally unattractive three storied brick building. It was so solidly built that being in the path of a tornado about 1891 did not disturb the building, except to take away its entire tin roof while Principal Brown with utmost calmness, assisted by other teachers, kept the terrified pupils within its strong walls during the few minutes of the twister's passing.

Last summer a visitor from the west coast, where he had lived for many years, accompanied by his wife, with difficulty made his way up the almost obliterated path leading from the turnpike to the site of the old school he had attended in his youth. He was shocked when he came to the end of the path to find only a disorderly pile of broken bricks where he had hoped to find an old school building. As he looked about, he found himself stirred by nostalgic memories "that linger like perfume of dried roses about the heart of the day that is gone." In answer to his inquiry as to what had lately happened there, a lady nearby informed him that a year earlier in spite of much protest bull-dozers and heavy machinery had with difficulty, because of the solidity of the structure, razed the old landmark that belonged to the spot where it had been so long.

It is not strange that among the few persons still living, who were taught by Principal Brown within the strong walls of the Jefferson school building, there are persons well past four score years of age who remember vividly much that he taught them. They can recall bits from poems that he read and studied with them, lines from an oration like Charles Sprague's "The American Indian," points made by Webster and Hayne in their great debate, clarification of puzzling items in English grammar, and the way he led to solution of a difficult mathematical problem.

As several of us past four score years of age looked back and remembered, it was clear to us that the qualities which made James Isaac Brown an unforgettable character and person were kindliness with firmness, approachableness, understanding of young people at different stages of their growth, humility, intellectual clarity, an undefinable something that inspired confidence in him, and a quiet forcefulness. His remarkable ability to teach persons at different ages with such skill that they forgot neither the subject taught nor the teacher, led us to agree as we talked together after many years of separation, that this teacher of the long ago was not only a remarkable man but the best teacher we ever had, whose death at the early age of 44 was a great educational loss.

The following is a copy of a clipping from the Washington, D.C., *Evening Star* of April 18, 1956 issue:

### JEFFERSON SCHOOL, BELFRY AND ALL, RETIRED AT 81

Battered but unbowed, the old Jefferson School in Falls Church has been retired for school purposes.

The two-story brick building which has pigeons in its belfry is 81 years old (sic).

The belfry is old Jefferson's proudest possession. Modern schools have their fancy tiled walls, intricate mazes of corridors, cafeterias, libraries and assorted other doodads.

### BELFRY DISTINGUISHED IT

Old Jefferson had none of these. Just six classrooms, only five of which were school-worthy.

But that belfry, long since denuded of the big resonant bell, was something an old building could be proud of. Now the pigeons roost in its vents. But the indignities an old building suffers from the feathery folk can be taken in stride. At least the birds are company.

Built in 1875 by public subscription the building has been used continuously as a school until last Friday. At one time in its long career it was a high school.

Last week the 180 fourth, fifth and sixth graders who used Old Jefferson moved into a $300,000 addition to the city's Mount Daniel School.

School officials said they couldn't possibly estimate how many children were educated in the building during the past 81 years. But they know of at least one child who graduated and returned years later as a teacher.

A few old-time residents of the city recall how the big bell used to echo through the country streets. It could be heard two miles away, according to their stories. When the big bell became too much of a weight for the sagging belfry to bear it was taken down and put in storage.

Old Jefferson may not be permitted the luxury of a graceful retirement. City officials are making plans to restore the building, possibly for use as a museum.

Standing looking up at Old Jefferson's belfry, listening to the wind hum through the vents and thinking about the restoration plans, it's easy to imagine the old building chuckling complacently to itself:

'There's life in Old Jeff yet.'[5]

An article in the *Fairfax Herald* of December 8, 1899 stated that the "reports of the teachers of the public graded schools of the town [Falls Church], made to the clerk of the School Board for the third month of the term show an enrollment of 154 scholars. . . ." In 1904-05 the enrollment reported was 147. The principal at the time was Professor E. C. Sine, and his staff included Miss Fanny Weedon, Miss Lottie Dyer, and Miss Ida N. Ball. The Board of School Trustees included J. W. Brown, Chairman; R. J. Yates, Clerk; and Judge Joseph S. Riley. Judge Sangster was principal about 1888. Mr. Yates also held this office at one time. Some of the names of former teachers are: Miss Mamie Castleman, Mrs. Miller (who taught the primer, first and second grades), Miss Minnie Birch, Mrs. Fanny Buggs (of Farmville, Va.), Miss Florence Leeds, Professor Heaton, Miss Maud Riley, M. D. Hall (later Fairfax County Superintendent of Schools), Mr. Brown, Mrs. Lillian Divine Birch, Miss Rockwell, Miss Arnold, Miss Annie Coe, and Miss Mary Parker.

Many stories cling to the old building. One such tale concerns a student named Walter Kerr. It seems that Professor Heaton usually chose the best boy in the class to ring the bell. One week Walter was chosen, and was "always on the job." About the middle of one afternoon, during the course of an extra dull session, Walter, alas, fell asleep. The discussion centered around Alexander Graham Bell. Walter was conscious enough to hear the word "Bell." Immediately he jumped up and rang the closing bell. Children raced outside. Finally the astounded teachers gathered some of the students together, explained what had happened, and the day was declared a holiday for all—except poor Walter!

Old Jefferson served as a high school until 1945. Apparently it was used as combination high school and grade school from an early day. Later the grade school (during the early 1900's) met in the old Columbia Baptist Church and the Congregational Church.

Another school known as "Jefferson School" was opened in 1880 near West Falls Church. This was soon known as "Ford School," having been built on land donated by Clark Ford. The building stood near the Leesburg Pike between "Highland View" (the Flagg home) and "Ford Hill," now on the corner of Idylwood Road. The school house was originally in the valley to the left of the Ford house, but the late S. W. Flagg had it moved nearer the house and it was used as a barn.[6] The building was torn down in 1952. At the Idylwood Road corner Mr. Ford maintained an underpass for use of his cattle, and this was used until after 1890.

Mr. Ellery C. Walker was one of the principal contributors to the Ford School, and also hauled stone for the foundation. The building was of clapboard, and well built. Mr. Webster Klock contributed the carpenter work. The school was abandoned in 1910. Sunday School for the neighborhood was once held there. In order to raise funds for support of the school, Mr. Robert Nourse lectured there on Dr. Jekyll and Mr. Hyde. Edmund Flagg (1815-1890) gave special lectures at the school.

At one time Ford School had fifty pupils. Miss Ada Walker has an autograph book presented her by her teacher at Ford School for good behavior, the only such award given in Fairfax County. The inscription on the fly-leaf reads:

*"Presented to Ada Walker by her teacher. J. Thomas Kidwell. Nov. 9, 1885.*

*Go forth thou little volume:*
*I leave thee to thy fate.*
*To love, and friendship truly.*
*Thy leaves I dedicate."*

The following served as teachers at Ford School: Miss Mary Parker (1881-1882); Henry Barrett (1882-1884); Miss Bessie Diggs (1884-1885); J. Thomas Kidwell (1885-1886); Walter Kirby (1886-1887); Rose Kidwell, Sarah Marr, Carrie Marr, Bessie Shreve, Kate Moore, Charles Richards, Blanche Mills, and Lula Stewart.

Among the students of the school were the children of the following families: Klock, Leonard, Flagg, Patterson, Sherwood, Walker, Caton, Money, Darne, McCauley, Ford, Wren, Shreve, Melville, Mills, Kirby, and Gorham.

A Kindergarten was attended in 1886-87 by Ellen Mankin in the present-day Raymond Lee home on North Washington Street. Miss Clistie Hefner, a private teacher, taught there. The Brown children also attended the school. Another school attended by Ellen Mankin was one built and owned by H.W. Lloyd. According to Mrs. Charles E. Gage, a girl's school was conducted by three Misses Moore in the old Lawton house before it was occupied by the Lawton family. Mrs. Gage also said that Mrs. Forbes (whose daughter married Mack Crossman) built a private frame school building on Columbia Street opposite the present Crossman home. The school was later the residence of Mr. Channel and the site is now part of the land on which the addition to Columbia Baptist Church was built.

The Falls Church School Board purchased the Old Congregational Church and it was used for school purposes for a number of years. Prior to 1920 the school board decided to buy the "Eagle House" Hotel which stood on the present site of the State Theatre. The following is an undated printed statement in the author's file:

> Tentative Plan for the Purchase (by the Townspeople) of the Inn property on Washington Street, Falls Church, Virginia, for emergency use by the School Board.
>
> The property, which contains about three acres and has a very good frontage on Washington Street, can be purchased for the sum of $11,000, and as it adjoins the Congregational Church property (now owned by the school) it might prove a very desirable site for the erection of a new school building in the future.
>
> (Here follows a long description of terms, subscription, and other matters).

This property was not purchased. The School Board finally purchased the property where Madison School was built. A full account of the purchase of this property is contained in an article in the Washington, D.C., *Evening Star* of August 26, 1923, under title: *Buy School Site at Falls Church*. The article reveals that the Board paid $4,850 for two parcels of land, and the proposed building (now Madison School) was to cost $50,000. The two parcels made up a site of about two and a half acres. One lot of an acre and a quarter faced Washington Street, and is the one upon which the building is located. The rear tract was part of the old Lawton property. The lot facing Washington Street was purchased from M. E. Church. Mr. Church purchased it (with the brick house now owned by Mrs. Rowan) for $9,000, and sold the vacant land to the School Board for $3,000. The Lawton property sold at the rate of $1,500 an acre. The sale was handled by John M. Garner, who acted as attorney for the Board. The School Board already owned four acres at East Falls Church, and they applied to the Court for permission to sell it, to raise enough money for the current purchase.

The purchase contract called for the opening of a street through the Lawton tract from Columbia to Broad (now Lawton Road); and for the extension of Great Falls Street to the new street, between the Merrifield home and cottage. Both are in use today. The following in the article makes reference to old Jefferson: "As soon as the building is ready for occupancy the present Jefferson building will be turned over to the county school board under an agreement, as yet informal, to establish in it a four-year accredited county high school for the southern part of Fairfax County."

Another source states that "No definite action has been taken looking to disposal of the present primary building on Washington Street, but it is the intention of board members that it shall be turned over to the town without cost, to be used as a town hall and council room and place of public assembly."

In a printed circular published by the Board on September 23, 1924, it is noted that Russel Edward Mitchell of Washington, D.C. was the architect. On September 23rd it was estimated that the cost of this building would not be "over $75,000." The building was to be of "modern design and attractive appearance to be constructed of brick and tile or of native stone if found more economical. There will be 10 class-rooms besides principal's room and library and an assembly room seating 400 or more."

The following article is from the *Evening Star* of September 21, 1926:

### SCHOOL DEDICATED AT FALLS CHURCH
*County Officers Take Part in Exercises
At New Building on Lee Highway.*

The new elementary school building, which has just been completed here, was dedicated last night with an impressive program in the auditorium. Charles A. Stewart, chairman of the school board, who presided at the occasion, announced that the building has been named the Madison School and gave a brief account of the efforts by citizens, school board and town officers for a new school building, which began four years ago.

He commended the work of the special committee which resulted in an amendment to the town charter making a school board issue possible, and also that of former Mayor H. A. Fellows and his special committee who sold the bonds.

The building, which is located on the Lee Highway in the center of the town, is a handsome structure of native stone, with brick facings, and contains 14 rooms, with modern heating, lighting and plumbing fixtures. Five of the rooms have new furniture throughout, including pupils' desks and teacher's tables and chairs. The pupils will enter the building from side streets and playgrounds are all in the rear.

Grading and planting of shrubbery remains to be done. Russel E. Mitchell of Washington was the architect.

S. A. Rohwer, clerk of the School Board, showed slides displaying the receipts and expenditures on the building. The total cost to date is $86,501.70 and receipts from various sources amounted to $86,202.61, leaving a deficit of $299.09 to be met out of this year's appropriation.

The sum of $329, which was raised by the children of the school, was used to furnish a new piano.

Former Mayor Fellows, in speaking of the value of the building to the town, said that it, with the new roads, was but a forerunner of other improvements.

Prof. Fletcher Kemp, division superintendent, Arlington County, and at one time principal of the Falls Church schools, spoke of the rapid growth of both counties, which will necessitate more such buildings. He also urged loyal support of the teachers.

Prof. M. D. Hall, division superintendent of Fairfax County, who has served for 40 years, gave much of the credit to the vote and influence of the women of the county. He compared the value of Fairfax County property 40 years ago, at $24,000, with the present valuation of $500,000.

Harris Hart, State superintendent of public instruction, placed Virginia and Texas at the head of the educational list in Southern States, and said the present public school acts as a public service station to the children of the land. He urged continued cooperation in improving the service.

Representative R. Walton Moore of Fairfax, in stressing the need of public education, also urged better home discipline and ascribed the prevalence of crime in this age to a definite lack of the influence of home and church, such as existed in former years.

Representative Moore said his father was the first superintendent of Fairfax County and he was one of the first teachers.

The Music Study Club, under direction of C. N. McGroarty, gave the following selections: "Come Where the Lilies Bloom"; "The Old Road"; "The Bells of Aberdovey" and "Greeting to Spring."

Rev. R. A. Castelman gave the invocation and Rev. U. S. Knox the benediction. Following the exercises the building was thrown open for inspection and patrons were introduced to the new principal, Miss Hobbs, and her staff of teachers.

A three-year high school will be maintained in the former Jefferson building this year, and by another year the board expects to have a complete four-year course.

The following figures are taken from a printed statement, "New Public School Building" published September 23, 1924 by the School Board (consisting of C. A. Stewart, S. A. Rohwer, and Mrs. W. A. Fravel):

### "SCHOOL ENROLLMENT"

| | |
|---|---|
| 1900 | none taken |
| 1903 | 119 |
| 1905-06 | 172 |
| 1910-11 | 234 |
| 1915-16 | 238 |
| 1920-21 | 404 |
| 1922-23 | 403 |

School building in Falls Church since World War II has been at a rapid pace. The Oak Street Elementary School was opened September 7, 1948. The December 9, 1949 issue of the *Falls Church Echo* announced the purchase of the twenty-five acre "Wayside" tract at West Falls Church from S. W. Flagg for $40,000. This land, with a frontage of 1,600 feet on Leesburg Pike and 600 feet on Haycock Road, is now the site of George Mason School. The contract to build the school was awarded to B. & J. Construction Company of Washington, D.C., which submitted a bid of $680,952. Ground was broken for an addition to the building on January 13, 1951. In accordance with the suggestion of Mr. William C. Warner (a local school teacher) the building was named George Mason, in honor of the statesman of Gunston Hall. Edmund Flagg was also suggested as a fitting name for the new school. George Mason School was dedicated on October 11, 1952.

## VIRGINIA TRAINING SCHOOL (MISS GUNDRY'S)

The Virginia Training School, an Institution for mentally retarded children, was located at what was formerly 309 West Broad Street, on a twenty-acre trace now the site of Tyler Gardens Apartments.

The idea for such a school originated in the mind of Miss Mattie A. Gundry, who came to Falls Church with the purpose of establishing and devoting her entire life to the school. In 1893[7] Miss Gundry, and a partner, Miss Weller, rented the old Bartlett-Buxton house (later Lawton Manor) and named it Gun-Well School. Gun-Well School was the genesis of Virginia Training School. The following notice appeared in *The Fairfax Herald* of December 8, 1899:

> Mr. Schuyler Duryee has sold to Miss Mattie Gundry the balance of the property at Falls Church, containing about eleven acres for $2,500.

In the year 1899, now the sole owner, Miss Gundry moved into the Duryee mansion. The Duryee house was erected about 1870 by Schuyler Duryee. His eldest son, with several other ambitious young men in Falls Church, established a printing press in a small building to the rear of the main house, and published *The Falls Church News*.

The buildings, including the enlarged mansion, a dormitory, and others, were taken down between December, 1946, and February, 1947, to make way for the Tyler Gardens Project.

Miss Mattie Gundry was a colorful resident of Falls Church for over fifty years. Born December 25, 1863 in Dayton, Ohio, she was the daughter of Dr. Richard and Martha (Fitzharris) Gundry. Her father was a native of London, and her mother a native of Dublin, Ireland. Miss Gundry attended public schools in Dayton and Athens. She was a graduate of the Ohio University.

The family of four brothers and three sisters came to Maryland in 1886. Miss Gundry attended the Maryland Art School, and graduating in 1891, taught art in the Baltimore Normal School. The same year she was given charge of the Maryland State School for the Feeble Minded. This was a natural course for her to follow, as her father, her three brothers, a niece and a nephew were all noted psychiatrists.

Miss Gundry realized the great need for such an institution in the South. Coming to Falls Church and attracted by the beauty and peace of the country, Miss Gundry decided to locate here.

Miss Gundry started with three pupils. These she patiently taught useful living, infusing into them the traits of her own splendid character, some finally attaining the goal of self support. The industrial occupations taught in the school included art and the handicraft of rug making. The only one of its kind in the South, Virginia Training School soon took its place as the second largest such institution in the United States.

Miss Gundry was deeply interested in Falls Church, and was the first woman to serve on the Town Council—serving three terms under Mayor H. A. Fellows. Appointed by the Governor as Secretary of the Commission to inspect County institutions including the jail and the County House, Miss Gundry promptly recommended that the inadequate and disgraceful poor house should be burned down! It was not long before a modern and sanitary structure was built.

In 1910 Miss Gundry was appointed Director of the Falls Church Bank, a position she held until her death. This outstanding humanitarian held membership in numerous organizations, including The American Association on Mental Deficiency of which she was a member for fifty years. Miss Gundry contributed various pieces of literature on mental deficiency, including articles in *The Journal of Mental Deficiency*, and two booklets: "Education of Defections of the Child" and "Management of Defective Girls."

Miss Gundry was a life-long member of the Republican Party, and was originally an Episcopalian, later a member of the First Church of Christ, Scientist, of whose building she was the architect.

An artist of note, Miss Gundry won first prize for her entry at the Chicago World's Fair. Architecture was her favorite avocation. She died on November 19, 1947 and was buried in the Loudoun Park Cemetery, Baltimore, Maryland.

### FOOTNOTES

[1] Statements made by Ellen (Lightfoot) Lynch to her granddaughter, Ellen (Mankin) Hirst (the author's grandmother), have been extensively used. Original papers of the School Board (courtesy of Mrs. Charles E. Gage) have been used, and miscellaneous clippings quoted.

[2] Bethune, Lucina M., *Brief History of Falls Church*, published by the Falls Church Chapter, D.A.R., 1923, page 5.

[3] Records are in the author's files connected with the establishment and first year of the Jefferson Institute in 1875-76.

[4] Suburban Business Service, Arlington, Va., 1964.

[5] Jefferson School was torn down in November, 1958.

[6] Statement of the late E. H. Flagg to the author, June 14, 1948.

[7] In a "Falls Church Letter" dated April 25, 1893, and published in *The Telephone* of Hamilton, Va. (issue of April 28th) it is stated that Miss M. A. Gundry and Miss Weller of Maryland had rented the Lawton Place "for a year and have opened a school for training children."

CHAPTER 13

# Public Service and Organizations

*The Post Office*

In 1661 the Virginia Assembly voted into law what was a custom as early as 1658, that planters must forward "all letters superscribed for the service of his Majesty or publique," and the penalty for failure to do so was 350 pounds of tobacco. The Colonial Court of Virginia enacted legislation for sending official letters from one plantation to another in 1657. The real beginning of the colonial postal system goes back to a grant from William and Mary of England to Thomas Neale, February 17, 1692, for a full twenty-one year period. Neale was required to pay six shillings and eight pence per year for this favor, and was also granted the postal concession for the West Indies.

A court favourite, Neale was Master of the Mint, and received permission to conduct private lotteries. His Deputy Agent was Andrew Hamilton, former Edinburgh merchant and later a Governor of New Jersey. Neale himself never came to the colonies. The Virginians supported the Neale Patent, and a postal service was established through the efforts of Governor Andros, formerly Governor of New York, and worked with difficulties. It cost no more to direct a letter from New England to the West Indies or to Europe than to Maryland or Virginia. The rate was nine pence to Maryland, and in the direction of Virginia, twelve pence.

On May 1, 1693, Andrew Hamilton's inter-colonial post service began a weekly run between Portsmouth, N.H., and Virginia. These operations were maintained at a loss for several years, and Neale dropped the concession to Hamilton and a Mr. West in 1698. The Crown repurchased the Neale grant in 1710 and Parliament designated New York as the center of its postal operations, with John Hamilton (son of Andrew Hamilton) as Post Master.

In 1710 a postal service was in operation between New York and Virginia with a six-week period required for a return trip between these two points. John Dickenson, writing of this early route, said:[1]

145

There was [in 1717] a settled post along the main line of communication through the Northern Colonies and Virginia and Maryland. The distance between Boston and Williamsburgh [Virginia] was completed in four weeks, except in Winter, when double that time was required.

In 1695 a Postal Route along the Potomac on the Virginia and Maryland side was organized, and the first post rider hired. This trip extended as far as Philadelphia at one time. John Perry was the first rider, and made regular trips eight times a year.

Envelopes came into general use in 1840, and prior to that time letters were folded and sealed with wax.

The earliest known stopping place on the mail route in Falls Church was "Mt. Hope" the old Coe-Duncan house on Oak Street near West Broad Street. At this same time the Big Chimneys Tavern was a stopping place for mail riders. The Post Office at Falls Church after 1850 was in the Star Tavern. The first Post Master at Falls Church, Charles Upton, of "Upton Hill," was appointed by the President on June 11, 1849.

Charles Horace Upton was a native of Salem, Mass., and a graduate of Bowdoin College. He came to Falls Church in 1837 and engaged in "agricultural and literary pursuits." He was Post Master for eleven days! The second Post Master, Dr. Simon J. Groot, was an early physician in Falls Church. Upton continued to live near Falls Church, and in 1861 was elected as the first Republican representative to Congress from Virginia. He later was Consul General to Switzerland, and died in 1877.

The Falls Church Post Office served about one hundred twenty-five families in its infancy. This service was later expanded to meet the need of a growing community. At about the same time as the Johnstown Flood the Potomac River rose, and mail delivery was interrupted. A group of Falls Church men, including M.E. Church, J.W. Brown, Eli Northrup and Post Master, Charles E. Mankin, took turns in rowing the flooded Potomac for the mail bag.

The Post Office was moved during the 1880's from the Star Tavern to George Thomas' Shoe Shop. This Shop was located in a small building attached to the Star Tavern. It was later housed in Mankin's Notions & Dry Goods Store, where Miss Ellen (Ella) Lynch was assistant Post Mistress.

The first building erected for the use of the Post Office was a red brick building owned by Charles E. Mankin. The building, erected in 1895 by Padgett Brothers of Alexandria, is still standing. It cannot be recognized today, having a new front, and is adjacent to the former Robertson's 5 & 10¢ Store. During the Spanish-American War, with Camp Alger located near Falls Church, the mail became so heavy that double doors were cut in the rear of the building and a room added to care for this increase. After Mr. Mankin went out of office, he leased the building to Frank Crocker who was the new Post Master. Mr. Mankin held his commission as Post Master during both administrations of Cleveland, and his daughter Ruth C. Mankin (now Mrs. E.A. Hildebrand) held her commission under Wilson.

About the time of World War II, the United States Post Office Department purchased from the Crossman heirs the corner lot at Columbia and Washington Streets, with the view of locating a permanent Post Office Building for Falls Church. However, in 1949, it was decided that the site was no longer desirable. Accordingly, the government purchased from Miss Elizabeth M. Styles and others, a lot of ground on the corner of Little Falls Street and West Broad Street, a portion of the Riley farm. The price paid was $12,000, plus the Crossman lot.

The Post Office is currently housed in a rented building opposite the proposed site of the new building.

The following list of Post Masters of Falls Church, with dates of their appointment, is taken from a letter dated August 22, 1951 from Mr. Victor Gondos, Jr., of the Industrial Records Branch, National Archives, Washington, D.C. to the author:[2]

|  |  |
|---|---|
| Charles H. Upton | June 11, 1849 |
| Simon J. Groot | June 22, 1849 |
| Charles A. Orton | October 10, 1859 |
| William A. Moore | April 5, 1860 |
| George B. Ives | April 18, 1862 |
| Edward J. Birch | April 22, 1872 |
| Albert E. Lounsbury | June 27, 1881 |
| Charles E. Mankin | August 27, 1885 |
| Edwin F. Crocker | June 20, 1889 |
| Samuel R. Newlon | May 31, 1893 |
| Edwin F. Crocker | May 7, 1897 |
| George W. Hawxhurst | September 7, 1906 |
| Vanderbeet Quick | July 13, 1907 |
| Ozias B. Livingston | February 25, 1909 |
| Emmett W. Skinner | February 26, 1915 |
| Ruth C. Mankin | May 9, 1919 |
| Virginia T. Quick | June 5, 1924 |
| Virginia Austin (acting) | June 23, 1928 |
| Byron Austin | December 20, 1928 |
| Clarence M. Sale | July 1, 1933 |
| B. Frank May | March 31, 1945 |
| Walter Sealock | March, 1954 |
| W. Edwin Scheid | July, 1963 |

Falls Church has been called unique since it was perhaps the only town of less than eight hundred residents to have three independent Post Office units, the one at East End, the one in "the Village," established 1849, and the one at West End (West Falls Church). The West End Post Office was established primarily to accommodate Edmund Flagg, who lived at nearby "Highland View." Due to his activities as author, real estate man, politician, and lawyer, his mail was especially heavy. Among the names he suggested for the new Post Office at West End (established 1888) were: Westfall, Westchurch, Ellison, Sherwood, West Grove, West End, and KaOka. Westchurch was favored by Mr. Flagg, but West End was designated by the Post Office Department.

The original directions issued to William M. Ellison, dated August 7, 1888, include the following statements: "Sir: The POSTMASTER GENERAL has established a Post Office by the name of West End in the County of Fairfax and State of Va., and appointed you POSTMASTER thereof. . ."

Edmund Flagg wrote the following letter to the Post Office Department which is of interest in this connection:

           West End,
           Fairfax County, Va.
           Oct. 20/88.

Hon. A.E. Stevenson,
 First Assistant Post Master General.

Sir: The Post Office recently established by your order at this place proves to be of very great benefit to a large number of citizens, and they are exceedingly gratified; but I am requested to submit to you very respectfully that if they could be favored as are the offices below and above them on the Railroad with an evening as well as a morning mail from Washington, they would be still more benefited. Indeed, if they could be supplied with but one mail daily they would greatly prefer that it should come in the evening, since they have been accustomed to receive nearly all their letters and papers at the Falls Church office heretofore at that time. They would suggest that a pouch from Washington would bring the evening papers of that city and the New York papers of the morning otherwise delayed until next day.

 I have the honor to be &c &c,
          Very respectfully,

          Edmund Flagg.

The Post Office at East End was established during the Spanish-American War. The original building is standing.

## NEWSPAPERS

*The Advertiser,* a weekly newspaper, was published in Falls Church in 1878. Little is known of this paper excepting that D.W. Whiting was publisher. *The Morning Sun* was published in 1884/85 as a weekly, and this was issued by the Morning Star Company of Falls Church and Washington, D.C. No issues of either paper are known to have survived.

A paper, the *Virginia Register,* was established early in 1885. The only known copy, volume 1, number 26, dated December 5, 1885, is in the author's file. A Saturday publication, of which William Taylor was editor and publisher, the *Register* survived for several years and suspended publication about 1890. Taylor's office of publication and print shop was located in a building at the rear of the Star Tavern.

The following is an advertisement in the December 5th issue:

"THE REGISTER. Published every Saturday, (If paid strictly

in advance, only $1.50). Advertising Rates Low, considering circulation. Wm. Taylor, Editor & Publisher. With good workmen, the best presses and new type, we are prepared at the Register Job Printing Establishment to get up WEDDING INVITATIONS, FINE CIRCULARS, CARDS, BILL-HEADS, TAGS, STATEMENTS, &c. &c., Posters a specialty—Printing done in any color.

The *Register* was succeeded by the *Falls Church News* about 1890. In 1895 Edward F. Rorebeck, a real estate agent, was the editor. A copy in the author's file is dated January 21, 1898. About 1900 the name was changed to *The Falls Church Monitor*. It continued under the same management until about 1920, when it was discontinued. At one time M.E. Church was editor and R.C.L. Moncure was manager.

The following is a copy of a bill in the author's file:

O.H. DAVIS                                          B.E. WILLIAMS
Falls Church, Va. Mar. 1, 1902
TO MONITOR PRINTING CO.
DAVIS & WILLIAMS, Props.

Mr. "Bon-Tons"

To Balance a/c          5—
Recd. Payment Mar. 27/02 Davis & Williams Pr. [per] A.D. Swift.
JOB PRINTING OF ALL KINDS.     Falls Church Monitor
                                                Alexandria County Monitor

The "Bon-Tons" was a local social club.

The Monitor shop was in the old Star Tavern building, using the *Register* equipment. Burress Williams and Olin Davis also did the reporting for the paper.

The two copies of the first Falls Church newspapers contain much of interest. The advertisements are especially interesting. In 1885 porterhouse steaks were selling for eighteen cents a pound, round steak ten to eleven cents, "choice breakfast bacon" fourteen cents and corned beef, four to five cents. The *Register* is filled with other items. One is the "Travelers' Guide," listing the schedules of the Washington, Ohio and Western R.R. (predecessor of the W. & O.D), whose ambition of reaching Ohio and points west had reached Round Hill in neighboring Loudoun. The passenger trains leaving the Baltimore & Potomac Station in Washington at 9 a.m. were to arrive in Round Hill at 11:47 a.m. The announcement continued: "the mail trains make close connection at Round Hill with Daily Line of Stages to and from Winchester, Berryville and Snickersville. Also at Leesburg with Daily Stages to Aldie and Middleburg. All passenger trains make close connection at Vienna with Sissons Line of Stages for Fairfax Court House."

The *Register* also reported in 1885 that a "Falls Church lady, Miss Emma Read, received three premiums at our State fair, held recently at Richmond, for exquisitely fine crochet and fancy work. Although deprived entirely of sight, Miss Read does much work in finer taste than most young ladies who are blest with vision. Miss Read is a graduate of the Institute of Staunton, where Miss Lula Mankin of this place still continues her studies."

Another paper published at Falls Church was *The Press*, a weekly published on Friday by S.B. Shaw, editor and publisher. The issue of November 26, 1909, in the author's file, is Volume II, No. 21. *The Press* paper was established about 1907.

In 1940 *The Falls Church Echo* (now the Sun-Echo) was established by Richard Eaton, who had been an announcer and newscaster with Washington Radio Station WOL. On May 15, 1946, Mr. Eaton sold the paper to Charles G. Manly, who in turn sold it to Roosevelt Der Tatevasion in January, 1950. *The Falls Church Echo* was combined with *The Herndon Sun* after 1950.

*The Fairfax Standard*, locally owned and published, was established during the period of World War II.

## CEMETERY SITES

The first public cemetery in Falls Church was in the Falls Church yard. Burials have been made there since the earliest times, but most of the old stones have long since disappeared.

Oakwood Cemetery near what is now Seven Corners, was originally a Methodist Cemetery. Fairfax Chapel, the first Methodist Church in Falls Church, was located where the graves of the Crump and Crossman family are now located. During the War Between the States many of the stones were used in line defenses by the 121st New York Regiment. The only one which has survived in its original location has the following inscription:[3]

> Samuel Hyson, Died Feby 5th 1853 aged 45 yrs. 11 mo. Yea though I walk through the valley of the shadow of death I shall fear no evil...

A copy of all of the tombstone inscriptions in the cemetery, made in June, 1949, gives a total of 1,165 burials. However, many are buried there without markers.

The following records have been loaned by Miss Essie Birch, and deal with the transfer of the old Methodist property to the public:

>Falls Church, Va.
>May 24th 1884.

To his Honor Judge Keith of the Circuit Court

Dear Sir,

> The undersigned Trustees would respectfully ask leave of Your Honor to sell and transfer unto the Falls Church Cemetery Company, a certain lot of land known as "Fairfax Chapel Lot" lying in the Corporation of Falls Church and being the property of the Methodist Episcopal Church.

The property is not needed for church purposes and it is the desire of all interested that it be disposed of in the manner indicated.

We would therefore petition Your Honor to make such an order as may be necessary under the Act of Jan. 31-1884 (a copy of which is hereunto attached).

It would simplify matters greatly if J.M. Thorne of the M.E. Church and Jno. E. Febrey of the M.E. Church, South, (both churches being interested) could be appointed Special Trustees to make the sale.

Trusting that Your Honor will consider our petition at the June term of your Court in Fairfax. We are very Respectfully,

                        Your Obdt. Servants

    Talmadge Thorne
    Isaac Crossman
    Almond Birch
    L.A. Crump           Trustees
    D.S. Gordon
    Joseph E. Birch

---

Talmadge Thorne, Isaac Crossman, Almond Birch, L.A. Crump, D.S. Gordon, and Joseph E. Birch, trustees, holding the legal title to a certain parcel of land lying within the corporate limits of the town of Falls Church and County of Fairfax, and known as "Fairfax Chapel Lot" this day filed their petition asking leave to sell said lot or parcel of land and the court being satisfied by evidence taken in open court that a sale of said lot under the provisions of and out of the General Assembly of Virginia approved January 31st 1884 would be proper and in accordance with the wishes of the congregation interested therein doth adjudge order and decree in accordance with the prayer of the said petition that T.M. Thorne and John E. Febrey who are hereby appointed commissioners for the purpose and proceed to sell and convey the lot hereinbefore mentioned to such person or persons or corporation and upon such terms and conditions as the trustees above named may desire and said commissioners shall report their proceedings under this decree to the next term of this court, and it is further ordered that the petitioners pay any costs which have been or may be hereafter be incurred in this behalf.

The deed to the property is filed in Liber E.N. 5, folio 114, of the land records of Fairfax County. Attached to the deed is a map "Field notes of a Cemetery Lot at Falls Church Fairfax Co. Va. made this 27th day of Nov., 1884 under direction of Messrs. Febrey, Gordon and Birch. Attest — Wm. N. Reed Surveyor."

The deed was dated May 13, 1885, "between Jacob M. Thorne and John E. Febrey, Special Commissioners appointed by the Circuit Court. . . of the first part. . . and Frank L. Birch, William N. Febrey, Jacob M. Thorne,

Wm. P. Graham, George A.L. Merrifield, Spencer A. Coe, and Isaac Crossman, as Trustees of the Falls Church Cemetery Company. . ." In consideration of one dollar the tract containing "about four acres two roods, and twenty perches of land more or less" was conveyed and the cemetery was opened in the following months.

The Oakwood Cemetery originally had iron gates which closed at 6 p.m. and was surrounded by a hedge.

Inside the cemetery are earthworks thrown up during the War Between the States.

The following article is from *The Falls Church News* of January 21, 1898:

### OAKWOOD CEMETERY ASSOCIATION

The annual meeting of the Trustees of the Oakwood Cemetery was held in the office of M.E. Church on Monday evening at 7 p.m.

The Trustees present were, Messrs. W.N. Febrey, President; E.J. Northrup, Secretary; G.A.L. Merrifield, Treasurer; Frank Birch and Wm. Allen.

The officers made their reports of the past year. All of the old officers were re-elected.

About 1930 the trustees decided to develop the portion of the cemetery containing the old earthworks. However, only one lot had been sold in this new section when the project was abandoned. This was the Steadman lot which is consequently the only one in the new part. The trustees wished to buy the lot back, but the family refused to sell it. In 1954 the broomsedge in this "new" part was removed, and the streets paved. It is said the old earthworks will be left as they are, and additional lots will be sold.[4]

Among persons buried in the cemetery are many of the old residents of Falls Church and two national figures, Edmund Flagg, diplomat and author; and George D. Mitchell, founder of *Pathfinder Magazine*.

### NATIONAL MEMORIAL PARK CEMETERY

This cemetery, outside of the corporate limits, was a portion of the old Campbell farm, "The Wilderness," and of the Albert Wren farm. This cemetery has attracted national attention because of the Fountain of Life by Carl Milles. It received a write-up in *Life Magazine* (August 30, 1948), and many subsequent articles in magazines and newspapers. The fountain has incorporated in it a group of thirty-six life-size nude figures.

### THE FALLS CHURCH BANK

The Falls Church Bank was granted a charter on June 26, 1906, and opened its doors on July 30 at 113 W. Broad Street, in an old building still standing just west of the present bank building. The first building was formerly a drug store owned by M.E. Church. Dr. George B. Fadeley was the first President. The first depositor on July 30, 1906, was S.H. Anderson, who at that time was manager-caretaker of the A.M. Lothrop estate at what is now Wilson Boulevard and McKinley Road. By December 31, 1906 the Bank had two hundred fifty depositors. The Bank had an initial capital of $25,000.

Early directors included M.E. Church, William M. Ellison, J.L. Davenport, George W. Hawxhurst, A.H. Barbor, Miss Mattie Gundry, G.A.L. Merrifield, and Dr. J.B. Gould. Dr. Gould was first Vice-President, and Mr. Hawxhurst first Secretary-Treasurer. Dr. Fadeley served as President until his death in 1941, and was succeeded by Carroll V. Shreve. Mr. Horace E. Brown, second depositor when the Bank opened, served for a number of years as Vice-President.

In 1922 the East Falls Church Branch was opened with A.H. Barbor as manager. The institution now has fifty-four employees, fifty of them at the main office, and two each at the West End Shopping Center Branch and the East Falls Church Branch. George Hawxhurst was the first employee of the bank and its only one for a long time. When he needed help, Miss Ethel Payne (later Mrs. J.H. Marr) was employed as Bookkeeper.

The following is taken from a bulletin issued by the Bank in 1917:

George B. Fadeley, M.D., President; James B. Gould, D.D.S., First Vice-President; M.E. Church, Real Estate, Second Vice-President; George W. Hawxhurst, Clerk Council, Cashier; Miss Mattie Gundry, Proprietor of Gundry Home and Training School; A.H. Barbor, Real Estate; H. Scott Ryer, Clerk P.O. Dept.; W.M. Ellison, Attorney-At-Law; Horace E. Brown, Merchant; George T. Mankin, Real Estate; G.A.L. Merrifield; Miss Carrie A. Ball, Book-keeper and Note Teller.

## *FALLS CHURCH FIRE DEPARTMENT*

The Falls Church Volunteer Fire Department was organized in 1898. The old-fashioned method of fire fighting ("the bucket brigade") was found useless when the old Kerr Mill burned in Falls Church prior to 1898. By 1899 two Chemical Carts were purchased for local use. They were first used when the summer kitchen at the "Home House" of Charles E. Mankin burned in that year. The following is from an order of the Town Council of July, 1899:

> The town council of Falls Church will levy a special tax of 15 cents on the $100 in the rate of taxation for the purchase of chemical engines for the fire department of that town. It is proposed by the council to purchase three chemical engines, one large one for the center of the town and two smaller ones to be located at East and West Falls Church respectively.
>
> —(*Fairfax Herald*, July 28, 1899)

The large engine was placed beside Brown's Store, and held fifty-five gallons of chemicals. It was drawn by hand. Later the carts were taken to the local blacksmith and rigged for a horse. The first fire house was at East Falls Church adjacent to the present building.[5]

Robert E. Kendrick was the first president of the Fire Department, and the carts were hand drawn at various times by early firemen—Robert L. Harmon, Joe Royston, and Edward Kimball. The Department was organized on a purely voluntary basis and was incorporated in 1925. The first powered apparatus acquired was "Tom"—a cherished Model T engine which now occupies a position of honor in the fire house. It is used for exhibition in local parades.

The present brick fire house was erected in 1934 when the limits of the town extended well beyond the site. Later, when East Falls Church "seceded" to Arlington County, the county line was established through the building. One difficulty encountered since the secession was in 1943 when a "blessed event" occurred in the middle of the line, and it still remains undecided whether the child was born in Fairfax or Arlington!

Officers in 1904 were: Chief Engineer: Dr. J.B. Gould; Fire Wardens: (1st Ward) George T. Mankin; (2nd Ward) Edgar A. Kimball; and (3rd Ward) D.B. Patterson.

Ground for a new building has been purchased at Antrim on the corner of Shreve Road and Chestnut Street in West Falls Church. The site was cleared on October 13, 1962, but no other work has been done.

## THE FALLS CHURCH LIBRARY

The Falls Church Library was established in 1899, and the first books were stored on shelves in a small building near the corner of East Columbia Street and Lee Highway. This building, later a garage, was torn down about 1951. Although this was the first community library, there was a library in the Dulin Chapel M.E. Church, South, of which Ross Wright was librarian about 1880.

The Woman's Club sponsored the library of 1899, the present library being largely due to their untiring efforts and support. According to *A Catalogue of Books* published in 1903, the library was then governed by a "Board of Control of Thirteen." The Library was open for three hours on Tuesday, Thursday, and Saturday. The following is taken from the 1903 catalog:

> To provide the necessary funds for expenses in conducting the Library the nominal amount of $1.00 per annum is charged for the use of the books. Permanent membership, $5.00. A total of 650 books now in the Library. New and popular Books are constantly being added.

The officers in 1903 were: Pickering Dodge, President; Dr. George B. Fadeley, Vice President; William A. Ball, Secretary; and George W. Hawxhurst, Librarian. The Board of Control of Thirteen in 1903 consisted of Professor W.W. Kinsley, Dr. Tunis Cline Quick, Dr. George T. Mankin, Dr. Merton E. Church, Mr. E.C. Hough, Mrs. G.A.L. Merrifield, Dr. J.B. Gould and Miss Belle C. Merrifield.

The Village Improvement Society aided in collecting books for the Library by requesting each member to bring a book for the Library at its monthly meetings. When the Library Association was disbanded in 1909 it had a collection of about seven hundred and fifty books.

The Library was in the little building owned by Mr. George W. Hawxhurst (on East Columbia Street) from 1899 until 1906. Miss Nellie Hawxhurst was custodian and issued books upon request. In 1906 the books were moved to a room in the rear of the Post Office. Mr. Hawxhurst, then Post Master, and Miss Nellie Hawxhurst (assistant to her father) continued to issue books. The Association disintegrated, and for several years the books were stored in this back room, many disappearing in the course of time.

When the Civic League (a woman's organization) was formed in 1913, one of their first projects was to rescue the library from oblivion. They started with about five hundred volumes, including the old stock. Since 1913 the library has been in continuous operation. The Library was moved to an alcove in the front of the old Congregational Church building and was later moved to East Falls Church. Through the generosity of Dr. M.E. Church, the Library was housed in the building next to Brown's Meat Market at East End. Here the Library was open two afternoons a week, using first the subscription method of one dollar per year, but changing later to a fee system of five cents a week for each book and two cents a day for overtime. About 1916 the League joined the Federation of Woman's Clubs and changed its name to the Falls Church Woman's Club.

Mrs. John F. Bethune tells the following story in a manuscript history which she sent the author:

> There was no heat in that building [referring to the one in East Falls Church] but there was a fireplace in the room used for the Library. The frugal ladies, preferring to spend their funds for books rather than for firewood, decided that each member should bring one or two sticks of wood to each meeting.

A Library Committee was named each year, composed of women who were willing to devote one or two afternoons a month to library service. Mrs. George B. Fadeley and Mrs. Peveril H. Smyth were among the early chairmen. In 1919 the library returned to the old Congregational Church building, which was owned by the School Board. Mrs. Samuel H. Styles was Chairman of the Library Committee at the time of removal. She retained the position until ill health forced her resignation in August, 1945. Mrs. Styles devoted her time and talents in building the library into an efficient system. It will always be a monument to her memory. Her assistants were: Mrs. George B. Fadeley, Mrs. P.H. Smyth, Mrs. Charles Marshall, Mrs. Frederick W. Jones, and Mrs. John F. Bethune.

The Falls Church Library, after much wandering, has now been settled in a lovely colonial-type building on the corner of Park and Virginia Avenues. From the Murphy Building, opposite the site of the old Episcopal Parish Hall, the book collection was moved in 1950 to the Ellison House at the corner of West and West Broad Streets. In 1955 a new move took the library to a brick residence near the corner of Lawton Road, at 201 East Broad Street. Henry H. Douglas was appointed Librarian during this period.

Impetus for the present handsome quarters came with a gift of land from the "Cherry Hill" estate of the Riley family. This lot was a gift from Miss Elizabeth Morgan (Betty) Styles and her brother, the Honorable Francis H. Styles. Miss Styles, like her mother, Mrs. Mary Edwards (Riley) Styles, in whose honor the ground was given, has a deep interest in the development of facilities for a better community.

Ground breaking ceremonies for the new building were held on August 19, 1957. The $210,000 structure was ready for occupancy in May 1958.[6] Authorized by bond referendum in 1956, the new library was built with an eye toward future expansion.

On the ground floor is the "Virginia Room" which houses a collection of Virginiana. This collection, greatly enriched by gifts from Riley estate, by courtesy of Mrs. Charles E. Gage, will prove to be of lasting value to the community.

The library is governed under the direction of a seven-member board appointed by the City Council for three-year terms. Members of the board when the new building was opened were: Mrs. John W. Bonnell, Chairman; Mrs. Mary Persinger, Carl W. Clewlow, Miss Elizabeth M. Styles, Edgar Vandivere, Mrs. Harry Myers and Dr. Robert Moore.

The present Librarian is Richard K. Burns who has brought the library into its best focus. Mr. Burns, an authority on early American folk songs, has, through his interest and effort, brought about the publication of this book.

## FALLS CHURCH TELEPHONE COMPANY

The Falls Church Telephone Company was incorporated by an Act of the General Assembly dated February 29, 1888. It was incorporated in the name of Robert Morrison, W.H. Doolittle, Schuyler Duryee, E.J. Northrup, Dr. T.M. Talbott, D.O. Munson, and M.E. Church. They were granted the right to erect lines of wire, to acquire and hold real estate, to purchase other lines, and to connect with other lines. The regular annual meeting was to be held in Falls Church, "at some convenient place."

The following article is from *The Press* of November 26, 1909:

### RECEPTION

One of the most enjoyable occasions of the season was a reception given by Dr. Church, president and general manager of the Falls Church Telephone & Telegraph Co., at his residence Saturday evening, to the employes of the company.

About thirty-five were present, and President Church gave an informal talk on the duties of the employer and employes to each other, especially dwelling upon the necessity of fidelity and integrity in the employes for the success of the company and of the operators, after which a program was rendered consisting of vocal and instrumental music, by the Misses Seay, Adams, Ball, and Mrs. Potter.

Miss Alice Davis read a selection on the "Troubles of the Telephone Operator," after which refreshments were served.

We are unable this week to give the names of all those present.

## BOY SCOUTS OF AMERICA

There are a number of groups of the Boy Scouts in Falls Church but for the purpose of this history the early and original organization will be mentioned.

In 1914 the Broken Arrow Patrol, Troop # 101, was under the direction of Scout Master Dr. Julius H. Parmelee. Among the members about that time were: Frank M. Steadman, Donald Lee, and Billy Billingsley. The Broken Arrow Patrol participated in the inauguration of President Wilson.[7]

## CHILDREN OF THE AMERICAN REVOLUTION

The Falls Church Chapter, C.A.R., was organized November 11, 1957, in the home of Mrs. N. Currell Pattie in North Arlington. The organization was effected by the organizing president, Mrs. Vernon H. Gaston. The first officers were installed by Mrs. C. Marbury Seaman, senior state president of the C.A.R. Mrs. Seaman was the guest speaker and addressed the young people, all descendants of Revolutionary heroes and under eighteen years of age, on the "Future of Our Young Citizens."

Officers installed by Mrs. Seaman were: Ann Morgan, president; Rebecca Jones, vice president; Ruth Ellen Steadman, secretary; and Deborah Davis, chaplain.

A tea for the new Society, atwhich members of the Falls Church Chapter, D.A.R., were present, was held after the formal meeting. The Falls Church Chapter, D.A.R., sponsored the new group.

The first regular meeting was held at the home of Rebecca Jones, 902 Highland Street, in January, 1958. Mrs. Thomas A. Annan was present, as Senior President. Other guests at this meeting were mothers of the members of the C.A.R.[8]

The fifth anniversary was celebrated on November 11, 1962.[9]

## CHILDREN OF THE CONFEDERACY

The J.E.B. Stuart Chapter, Children of the Confederacy, was organized prior to 1900. A program of an "Entertainment" in the author's file is dated Monday, April 23, 1900. The front cover, of white paper, has a red and blue design. At the top are crossed flags—the Confederate Battle Flag and the Flag of Virginia. The "Entertainment," held at Odd Fellows Hall, included dancing at 8 p.m. Dances included the Waltz, Quadrille, Two-Step, Lancers, Virginia Reel, and Home Sweet Home,

## THE CLUB

"The Club" was an exclusive social organization established in Falls Church prior to 1882. The only record known is in the form of an invitation and program issued to Mr. and Mrs. Edmund Flagg of "Highland View." On the envelope is printed: "The Club, Falls Church, Va." and on the front is written: "Mr. and Mrs. E. Flagg." Inside of the envelope is a printed card with a nosegay of red roses in the upper right hand corner. This reads: "Mr. [Flagg] and Lady. The pleasure of your company is respectfully desired to attend a Private Social SOIREE, at the Residence of Mr. Flagg, on Thursday, Eve., March 29th, 1883. Compliments of Nellie R. Patterson, Ella Q. Lynch, S.T. Howard, D.B. Patterson, Committee. Dancing to commence at 7 o'clock."

The second card is pink in color, and reads: "Office of the Secretary of THE CLUB. Falls Church, Va., Dec. 26, 1882. Mr. & Mrs. E. Flagg—You are informed that the Holiday Meeting of THE CLUB will be held at the residence of Mr. J.J. Shipman on Friday Evening, December 29, 1882, at 7:30 o'clock. You are requested to be present. Very Respectfully &c., Andrew J. Shipman, Secretary." The enclosed card reads: "The ladies are requested to provide Refreshments."

The following is the printed program of the Thanksgiving Celebration held in 1882:

THANKSGIVING CELEBRATION—THE CLUB—At the residence of Mr. Edmund Flagg. Thursday, November 30, 1882.

ORDER OF EXERCISES.

Music — Chorus.
Essay — Mr. Edmund Flagg.
Music — Miss Shipman & Mr. Martinez.
Recitation — Mr. C.H. Buxton.
Music — Quartette.
Recitation — Miss Mary Parker.
Music — Mrs. W.W. Kinsley.
Oration — Mr. D.H. Riddle, Jr.
Thanksgiving Festivities.

## THE CHRISTIAN ENDEAVOR SOCIETY

The Christian Endeavor Society was organized at Falls Church on July 20, 1888, composed of young people from all of the Protestant churches in the community. The following were early members: Lynn S. Abbott, Professor and Mrs. H.F. Lowe, Miss Sue Riddle, the Reverend W.S.O. Thomas, the Reverend D.H. Riddle, Andrew Smith, Harry Coe Febrey, John Seay, Frank Hinkins, Wirt Kinsley, and Will Eastman.

Christian Endeavor met every Sunday evening at 6:15 p.m. in the old Groot Hall (of the Falls Church Presbyterian Church). The following were officers in 1904: Andrew M. Smith, President; Miss Raydelle B. Shaw, Vice

President; Jesse Varcoe, Secretary; Miss Emma Seaman, Corresponding Secretary; and Milton Thorne, Treasurer.

## DAUGHTERS OF THE AMERICAN REVOLUTION

The Falls Church Chapter, Daughters of the American Revolution, was organized on June 7, 1910, at the home of Mrs. Swan Sinclair, with Mrs. Charles Gibson of Vienna as Organizing Regent. The Chapter was organized through the efforts of Mrs. W.E. Callender, and was named for the old Falls Church. The following were charter members: Mrs. J.A. Albrecht, Mrs. John S. Barbour, Mrs. H.C. Birge, Mrs. W.E. Callender, Mrs. F.R. Dudley, Mrs. Augustus Duffey, Mrs. Charles E. Gage, Miss Caroline E. Hudgins, Mrs. David Irwin, Mrs. George N. Lester, Mrs. H.T. Miller, Mrs. Henry E. Mott, Mrs. Leo G. Parker, Mrs. Swan Sinclair, Mrs. Samuel H. Styles, Mrs. S.A. Sutton, Mrs. Jonas T. Unverzagt, Mrs. Robert E. Thornton, and Mrs. H.A. Fellows. Mrs. Callender was the first Regent.

The Chapter has been very active in the field of local and national history. Some of the accomplishments include: October 6, 1911, a marble marker, imbedded in the walls of the old Falls Church was unveiled. A vesper service in this church, sponsored by the Chapter, was held in June and became an annual custom. In 1912-14, the will of Martha Washington was returned to the Fairfax Court House through the efforts of Mrs. John S. Barbour, Regent. It was stolen during the War Between the States, and was found in the collection of Pierpont Morgan. Mrs. Barbour was also responsible for a state-wide interest in a memorial to Colonel George Mason of "Gunston Hall," which took the form of a fence about his grave. In 1914-16 a fence was placed by the Chapter around the Western Boundary Stone of the District of Columbia on Meridan Street. In 1923 a community celebration was held, sponsored jointly by the American Legion, the Woman's Club, and the D.A.R., to celebrate the Fourth of July. At this time Mrs. John F. Bethune read her history which was later printed. In 1926 Mrs. John F. Bethune and others started a movement to save the old Washington Tulip Tree in the Falls Church yard.

### ROSTER OF REGENTS

| | |
|---|---|
| Mrs. W.E. Callender | 1912-1912 |
| Mrs. John S. Barbour | 1912-1914 |
| Mrs. Robert Formad | 1914-1916 |
| Mrs. Eugene MacNair | 1916-1918 |
| Mrs. Harry A. Fellows | 1918-1920 |
| Mrs. Elida C. Hough | 1920-1922 |
| Mrs. Samuel H. Styles | 1922-1924 |
| Mrs. Harry E. Moran | 1924-1926 |
| Mrs. John F. Bethune | 1926-1928 |
| Mrs. Pearce Horne | 1928-1930 |
| Mrs. C.N. McGroarty | 1930-1932 |
| Miss Gertrude Orr | 1932-1934 |

Mrs. William S. Brown ................................................1934-1936
Miss Gertrude Orr ......................................................1936-1937
Mrs. John F. Bethune ................................................1937-1939
Mrs. Harry E. Demarest ............................................1939-1941
Mrs. E.A. Capen.........................................................1941-1943
Mrs. E.A. Capen.........................................................1941-1943
Mrs. W. Leigh Ribble ................................................1943-1945
Mrs. D.G. Farragut....................................................1945-1947
Mrs. N.C. Pattie ........................................................1947-1949
Mrs. Ray Thomas .......................................................1949-1951
Mrs. E.J. Lintner .......................................................1951-1953
Mrs. H.E. Moran .......................................................1953-1954
Mrs. Edward G. Fenwick ..........................................1954-1956
Mrs. Eldred Martin Yochim ......................................1956-1962
Mrs. E. Frank Taylor ...........................................1962-present

## THE FALLS CHURCH HISTORICAL SOCIETY

There was an organization called "The Falls Church Historical Society" during the 1920-1940 period, but this group was not active, nor was it formally organized. The first meeting of the organization now known as The Falls Church Historical Society was on April 13, 1955, at the City Council room. A name for the society was discussed, and the name The Falls Church Historical Society was suggested by Mrs. Geneva Shepherd.

The second meeting was held on May 23, 1955, at the City Recreation Center, behind the old Falls Church Parish House on East Broad Street. Discussion about the organization of the society continued. The third meeting was held on October 6, 1955, in the City Council room. At that meeting the Reverend Melvin Lee Steadman, Jr., spoke on the history of Falls Church from the manuscript of this book. At the fourth meeting, November 3, 1955, also in the City Council room, the Reverend Francis W. Hayes, Jr., spoke on the history of the old Falls Church and the return of the Communion Cup. The fifth meeting was held on December 1, 1955, and Mr. La Rue Van Meter spoke on the organization and function of the Falls Church Historical Commission.

Charter members of The Falls Church Historical Society are: Mr. & Mrs. Wm. M. Baskin; Miss Essie Birch; Miss Nell V. Boyd; Mrs. Blanche Browder; Mr. & Mrs. Horace E. Brown; Colonel and Mrs. Harry L. Campbell; Mr. & Mrs. John P. Cowan; Mr. & Mrs. Guy N. Church; Senator & Mrs. Charles R. Fenwick; Mrs. E.H. Ferrell; Mr. William T. Finley; Mr. William W. Follin; Mrs. Maya Freeman; Mr. & Mrs. Charles E. Gage; Mr. & Mrs. Norman E. German; Mr. Edward German; Mrs. E.P. Harrison; Mr. & Mrs. A.L. Haycock; the Reverend Francis W. Hayes, Jr.; Mr. Robert H. Hough; Mrs. Philippe G. Jacques; Mr. Virgil Carrington Jones; Mrs. Margaret King; Mrs. E.J. Lintner; Mr. & Mrs. F.W. Maher; Mrs. Charles G. Manley; Mrs. John J. McNeely; Mrs. John D. Neely; Mr. John F. O'Gara; Mr. & Mrs. Thos. A. O'Halloran; Dr. & Mrs. Nelson Podolnick; Mrs. Lawrence M. Proctor; Mrs. Nicholas J. Proferes; Mr. & Mrs. George T. Reeves; Mr. &

Mrs. Robt. Rochester; Mr. & Mrs. Robt. L. Saintsing; Mrs. G.M. Shepherd; Mr. Victor B. Spector; Mr. Harold J. Spelman; Mrs. David R. Strobel; Miss Elizabeth M. Styles; the Reverend & Mrs. Melvin Lee Steadman, Jr.; Mr. & Mrs. E. Frank Taylor; Mr. Cuyler Taylor; Mr. La Rue Van Meter; and Mr. and Mrs. Floyd G. Wellman.

## THE FALLS CHURCH POULTRY ASSOCIATION

The Falls Church Poultry Association was organized sometime prior to 1911. On December 12, 13, 14, 1911, the first annual Show was held at Falls Church. At this time A.H. Barbor was President; S.E. Hutton, Vice President; H.E. Demarest, Secretary; and T.C. Rich, Treasurer. Directors included A.H. Barbor, S.E. Hutton, V.A. Zahn, P.H. Smyth, D.P. Swope, E. McNair, J.J. Haskell, T.C. Rich, Frank Poston and H.E. Demarest.

## FALLS CHURCH WOMAN'S CLUB

The Falls Church Woman's Club was originally the Civic League. The present structure of the club took form in 1947. It was the first member of the Fairfax County Federation to have its own clubhouse, "The Washington House," once the First Congregational Church. The newly remodeled building was dedicated on May 3, 1959.[10]

## INDEPENDENT ORDER OF GOOD TEMPLARS

Falls Church Lodge, Independent Order of Good Templars, was the "Pioneer Lodge" of the State. The Falls Church Lodge was organized April 16, 1867, as Lodge No. 1. The meetings were held every Tuesday night in the Star Tavern, and later in the Old Baptist Church and Odd Fellows Hall. In 1904 there were eighty-five members in good standing. The object of the order was the prohibition of liquor traffic by the will of the people. William Henry Greenbury Lynch was the founder of the Good Templars. George W. Hawxhurst was also an early and outstanding leader in the movement. In 1904 Falls Church was headquarters of the Grand Lodge of the State.[11] Mr. Hawxhurst was Grand Secretary of the State, and he filled the position for thirty-two years. The following were officers in 1904: Henry Hawxhurst, Chief Templar; Jesse Varcoe, Past Chief Templar; Miss Laura Summers, Secretary; George W. Hawxhurst, Financial Secretary; Mrs. J.H. Garretson, Treasurer; J.H. Marr, Marshal; Miss Raydelle S. Shaw, Chaplain; Miss Catharine Foley, Vice Templar; G.C. Kesterson, Guard; Walter Kerr, Sentinel; Mrs. M.M. Erwin, Organist; J.H. Garretson, Lodge Deputy; Mrs. George W. Hawxhurst, Superintendent of Juveniles.

## INDEPENDENT ORDER OF ODD FELLOWS

### Falls Church Lodge Number 11.

Falls Church Lodge No. 11, Independent Order of Odd Fellows, was organized October 24, 1890. Their large brick Hall on West Broad Street was erected shortly afterwards, largely through the generosity of Charles

E. Mankin, an early member and official of the Order. Padgett Brothers of Alexandria, (childhood school mates of Mr. Mankin in Bishop Whittle's School) erected the building in 1891. The Washington, D.C., *Evening Star* called it a "monument" to the memory of Mr. Mankin. In 1904 there were seventy-four members.

## THE LANTERN CLUB

The Lantern Club is a unique organization and a product of Falls Church's intellectual life.[1,2] Perhaps the most convenient way to start the life story of the Lantern Club would be to find out the date and place of the first meeting, and perhaps the names of those present, and then proceed to set down the simple facts in logical order.

That orderly procedure would probably be all right if the Lantern Club were a conventional organization. But it isn't. It is one of the most unconventional groups in the country. The writing of its history, therefore, should not be done in conventional style.

The history of any organization, even one which is dull and formal and in large part useless (which the Lantern Club isn't), need not begin with the first meeting.

Before there can be an organization or a meeting somebody must have an idea. The period between the birth of the idea and the translation of it into action could be an interesting interval. It certainly should be a period of preparation.

Perhaps the careful preparation which preceded the organization of the Lantern Club is what has insured the long life it has enjoyed—long, at least, when one considers the high mortality among organizations in general.

The Lantern Club did not come into being as a result of a vague idea lightly tossed off between drinks, and the work of bringing together the people who might become members was not done in haphazard fashion. The club was put together with painstaking care.

In view of the preceding statements it may seem odd to the reader that the idea for the Lantern Club was born in a bus. Among the people who rode the bus between Washington and Falls Church in the summer of 1933 were Ralph Staebner and J.O. Martin. Mr. Staebner was an employee of the Internal Revenue Department and Mr. Martin worked for The Chesapeake and Potomac Telephone Company. Both liked to talk. But there was nothing unusual about that. Most people like to talk. They differed from most men in that they talked about ideas rather than about things. Those sessions on the bus were pleasant but really not long enough for a first-rate discussion, and there were not enough people involved.

These two bus-mates finally arrived at the idea of organizing a group in Falls Church for academic discussion. Mr. Staebner knew a man who he felt would be interested and the idea was discussed with him. He was definitely interested. The man was Barkley Wilcox, Pastor of the Crossman Methodist Church. Wilcox was young, educated, enthusiastic, friendly, and a practical thinker. He joined Mr. Martin and Staebner as one of the founders.

The three men knew what they wanted in an organization and they knew the type of member needed to make it a success. They were determined to get that type even if they had to hand-pick the original membership. And that's exactly what they did.

Falls Church was then a small community. The names of the telephone subscribers were all together in one place in the local telephone directory.

Meeting one evening to draw up a list of prospective members, the three founders used the telephone list as a guide. They went from A to Z, checking each name carefully, if recognized, and freely discussing the merits of the owners of the respective names.

The idea was that at least one of the conspirators would know something about nearly everybody in town who had a telephone, and if one of the three turned thumbs down on a particular individual that was enough to keep the name of that individual from going on the list.

The three men went about their task in a serious but lighthearted way, and some of the well-known individuals in the community might have been shocked and grieved could they have heard the comments made about them.

Founder J.O. Martin, distinguished citizen, author, and gentleman, now deceased, tells us the rest of the story:

> When the list was completed there were only 40 names on it. A letter of invitation was drafted and sent to those who had made the grade.
>
> As far as I can recall, nothing was said to anybody by word of mouth. Nobody was called up and asked to attend. Nobody was asked what did he think of the idea. The usual ballyhoo methods were entirely discarded. Those invited to the meeting could come or stay away. If enough came to organize a little club, a little club would be organized. If only two or three came, that would be evidence that the idea was "not so hot," as the youngsters say.
>
> The organization meeting was held at the residence of Mr. Wilcox on the evening of October 16, 1933. Seventeen men came, including the original three. During the meeting each man gave some facts concerning his own personal background, a procedure which is still followed with new members. Several states were represented—more than a dozen. About 90% of those present had attended college. About 25% of those present had the degree of doctor. Only two of those present had been born in Falls Church.
>
> The temporary chairman explained the form of organization which the three organizers had thought out. First, there wasn't to be any name until one had attached itself to the organization by force of common usage. Until that time the members could refer to it simply as "the club." The club had been in existence six months before a name finally evolved. It came into being as a result of the thoughtfulness of one of the members who lived

on a dark street. He hung out a lantern to guide the members up a few steps to his front yard.

The next idea offered was that there would be no officers. Having no business to transact, and no dues, and no letters to write, and no notices to send out, there would be no need for a president, a secretary or a treasurer.

It was decided at the first meeting that meetings would not be held on any definite day of the week, as that would automatically shut out some of the members who had certain evenings tied up—such as those who attend lodge meetings on the third Tuesday or Chess Club on the second and fourth Thursdays. Instead, it was agreed to meet on or about the sixteenth day of the month. The date and place of the following meeting was—before notices were introduced—set by those at the current meeting, and a member who was absent from that meeting had no rights (with regard to the time or place of the next meeting) which those present were bound to respect.

In the beginning, it was customary for somebody present at a meeting to volunteer his home for the following meeting, and he thereby became the committee on arrangements for that meeting. His job was to furnish the refreshments—free—and to think up a subject for discussion. That arrangement still prevails, except that volunteers are few.

As in the beginning, members are seldom urged to attend a meeting. They can attend or stay away, as suits their pleasure, and they will be neither praised nor chided. No minutes are written, no records are kept, no motions are made.

The members are not voted in. It has been the custom from the beginning that a member can bring a friend, and if the friend seems to be socially acceptable he is accepted. In the beginning, nobody brought to a meeting any man who was not apparently acceptable then and later to all the rest.

The attendance has varied from about eight to about twenty, and the subjects have varied from college football to national politics.

The preceding paragraphs contain the story of the idea back of the organization and the steps taken to translate that idea into action. But a complete history of the Lantern Club for the quarter of a century it has been in existence is more difficult, for in the original plan no records were to be kept. However, one member did keep a few notes, unofficially, of some of the early meetings, and later, when we started to send out notices, one of the other members started a notebook containing the names of those who were considered members at the time, and it was followed by other notebooks.

Information from the various miscellaneous sources mentioned, as well as from copies of speeches, has been made into the supplements which follow, and the reader is asked to accept these supplements as part of the history of the club.

Copy of letter sent to those who were
selected as prospective members of the
Lantern Club

Dear Mr.—

Believing that there is need in Falls Church for a group or organization in which educated and socially-minded men may find mental stimulation or informal contact with their fellows, the men whose names appear at the bottom of this letter are endeavoring to organize such a group and they solicit your cooperation.

Here's the idea. Falls Church probably has a greater percentage of college-trained men or men of like character than any other town in Virginia except perhaps one or two of the college towns. But because Falls Church is spread all over the map, and also because apparently no effort has been made to get them together, these men do not know one another. All of them are missing many hours of congenial contact simply because there is no one group now in existence which appeals to all of them. It is true that there are in our town many worthy organizations, but each of them was organized for a purpose different from that which we have in mind.

If we can interest from a dozen to twenty-five men in the idea we can meet about every two weeks, with perhaps something to eat, and discuss matters of interest. We have no object in mind except the mental pleasure of those taking part. We are not seeking to build streets or install sewers or promote business or to advance the interests of any political candidate, or to improve the morals of the town, or to bring about any reform in anything or anybody. We simply feel that there is room in our town for an organization in which men who like fellowship may meet and talk with like-minded men.

If you feel likewise, come to the organization meeting on Monday evening, October 16, at 8 p.m., at the residence of Mr. Wilcox, on Washington Street, next to the M.E. Church.

Yours sincerely,

Organization Committee

*Supplement A*

List of those to whom was extended
the original invitation to join.

Rev. A.B. Altfather—Pastor of Presbyterian Church. Was present at first meeting. Not a member in 1958.

A.L. Anderson—Government employee. Became a member after January 1, 1934. Now dead.

H.O. Bishop—Engaged in public relations work. Did not become a member. Afterwards left Falls Church.

J.T. Bowen—Probably Government employee. Did not become a member. Now dead.

Dr. Charles Brooks—Government employee. Present at first and later meetings. Left Falls Church after retirement.

Rev. R.A. Castleman—Pastor of The Falls Church. Present at first meeting and perhaps some of the subsequent meetings. Now dead.

E.A. Chapman—Government employee. Did not become a member. Afterwards left Falls Church.

Guy N. Church—Real estate. Present at first meeting and probably some of the subsequent meetings. Not a member in '58.

Jack Cline—Washington Evening Star. Present at first meeting and probably some of subsequent meetings. Not a member in 1958.

W.A. Cushman—Government employee. Became a member previous to Jan. 1 1934, and remained a member until he moved to California. Now dead.

Alvah Daughton—Physician. Did not become a member.

Dr. W.W. Diehl—Government employee. Present at first meeting. Still an active member.

Guy Ervin—Attended at least one meeting before Jan. 1, 1934. Not a member in 1958.

Dr. R.J. Formad—Government employee. Did not become a member.

Charles E. Gage—Government employee. Present at first meeting. Still an active member.

Martin Haertle—Became a member after Jan. 1, 1934. Moved away from Falls Church.

C.P. Scott—Did not become a member.

R.S. Holmes—Did not become a member.

Harold Kennedy—Government. Attended first meeting and later meetings. Moved from Falls Church area after retirement.

Col. R.S. Keyser—Marines. Attended first meeting and later meetings. Afterwards moved from Falls Church.

E.W. Marcellus—Did not become a member.

C.M. Matheney—Government. Attended first meeting and later meetings. Moved from Falls Church.

W. Middleton—Became a member after Jan. 1, 1934. Not a member in 1958.

George M. Newell—Colonel in World War One. Became a member after January 1, 1934. Moved from Falls Church.

W.A. Pierce—Government.—Became member after Jan. 1, '34. Now dead.

Dr. Merritt Pope—Government. Became member after Jan. 1, '34. Moved from Falls Church.

Loren Pope—Son of Merritt. Newspaper man. Attended first meeting and later meetings. Moved from Falls Church.

Dr. E.V. Miller—Government. Attended first meeting and later meetings. Moved from Falls Church.

Erle Prior—Artist. Attended first meeting. Still an active member.

G.A. Ransom—Physician. Member before Jan. 1, 1934. Now dead.

F.G. Reddington—Government. Did not become member.

Neil Stevens—Government. Member before Jan. 1, 1934. Moved from Falls Church.

Phil Talbot—Did not become a member.

Thurlow White—Did not become a member.

Sargent White—Government. Member after Jan. 1, 1934. Still an active member.

Fred Wright—Did not become a member.

P.C. Yates—Did not become a member.

Louis W. Weld—Attended first meeting and later meetings. Moved away from Falls Church.

Thomas Martin—Lived at Dunn Loring. Attended first meeting and probably later meetings.

### Supplement B

List of those in attendance at first meeting, which was held at the residence of Barkley Wilcox on October 16, 1933:

A.B. Altfather; Charles Brooks; R.A. Castleman; Guy Church; Jack Cline; W.W. Diehl; Charles Gage; Harold Kennedy; C.M. Matheny; Loren Pope; F.E. Prior; Louis Weld; E.B. Wilcox; H.C. Staebner; J.O. Martin; E.V. Miller; Thomas Martin (Dunn Loring).

### Supplement C

The following were on the original list of those invited, but they did not attend the first meeting. They did attend at least one meeting prior to January 1, 1934.

W.S. Brown; R.A. Cushman; Guy Ervin; Col. R.S. Keyser; Merritt Pope; C.A. Ransom; Neil Stevens.

The following were on the original list of those invited, but did not attend a meeting until after January 1, 1934.

A.L. Anderson; Martin Haertle; W. Middleton; W.A. Pierce; Col. George Newell; Sargent White (Mr. White is still a member in 1958).

The following were not on the original list but became members at one of the meetings in the latter part of 1933.

Tom Dixcey; Mr. Gray; Oscar Kiessling (Dr. Kiessling is still a member in 1958).

New members who came in between January 1 and March 15, 1934, but who were not on the original list of those invited to join.

Mr. Ashby; Edwin Kennedy; Dr. Hanks; Dr. Barr; Dr. Hill; Dr. Hamilton.

The following were among the members in 1937, and have not been previously mentioned, and may have come in at any time between 1934 and 1937.

J.W. Blailock; Roger Blake; Ray Soderberg; A.B. Grow; E.G. Bienhart W.A. Ribble; Louis Coyner; M.A. Murray; O.G. Snyder; Paul Ferris; W.E. Wandel; Wilbert Woodson; J.B. Holland.

The following were among the members in 1940 and have not been previously mentioned and may have become members at any time between 1934, or during that year, and 1940.

Dr. Henry Knowles; R.W. Bennett; Dale Dillon; Geo. Holliday; A.D. Neale; Malcolm Smith; John Donovan; John Turnbull; Roy Blough; Larry Laing; Paul Brown; Willard Smith; F.R. Fosberg; Benton Westfall; Tom Probey; Clarence Shotwell; Rev. J.B. Hendricks; Earle Hamm; J.H. Branson; E.W. Berkley; Perry Crittenden; James E. Martin; Carl Kinsley; Norman McKay; Elmer Pauly; Francis P. Miller; Titus Snoddy; P.G. Storm. (Malcolm Smith and Larry Laing are still active members in 1958. Carl Kennedy continued a member until he became incapacitated.)

## *Supplement E*

When one of the bureaus of the Department of Agriculture was set up at Beltsville, Md., some of those who were members of the Lantern Club and residents of Falls Church were transferred to Maryland, and wished to establish a Lantern Club there. It was decided that the new club would be a chapter of the old one and accordingly a group from Falls Church journeyed out to Beltsville to get it going with due ceremony.

A lantern was presented and credentials given in a speech which described the original club as having been started by Diogenes.

* * * * * * * * * * *

When Bob Cushman was moving to California some of the

members thought he might be able to get a Lantern Club—or chapter—started there. At a meeting in which he was bade farewell a lantern was presented and credentials given.

\* \* \* \* \* \* \* \* \* \*

When Col. Tom Sands was moving to Minneapolis after World War Two he was given a lantern, plus credentials, with the idea that he would start a chapter in Minneapolis. A copy of the speech made on that occasion and a copy of the certificate have been preserved and they are included—that is, copies of the copies—in these notes.

\* \* \* \* \* \* \* \* \* \*

When Harry Doyle was preparing to leave Falls Church for California in the latter part of 1957 he was presented a lantern and given authority to start a chapter in California.

*Supplement E*
Part 2

Speech at the time of the presentation of
lantern and certificate to Colonel Sands

Once more we are called upon to bid a fond farewell to one of our members who is leaving our fair village to take up residence in a distant state. He goes forth with our good wishes and with a more tangible token of our esteem—our lantern.

To some of our newer members that lantern, the beams of which have long lighted the feet of outstanding gentlemen and scholars to our meetings, may be just a lantern. But a few of the old-timers know that this lantern has a history which is inextricably (but not inexplicably) tied up with the history of this ancient and honorable organization.

For the benefit of the neophytes among us, may I give you a brief résumé of how our original lantern was acquired.

You have heard of Diogenes, of course. You have heard of how he searched the world for an honest man, carrying a lantern to help him in his purpose. But history would have you believe that the search was begun and concluded in ancient times, and that the results were pretty poor. That's where history was wrong. The truth of the matter is that the search extended right on down to recent years and that it ended in Falls Church. In this town Diogenes found not only one honest man but three.

To those three men he entrusted his lantern and besought them to seek out and organize other honest men and encourage them to meet frequently and indulge in honest talk, in which hypocrisy would have no part. They accepted the trust and did bring together a group of such men, and the light of Diogenes' lantern continues to shine—no longer in search of honest men, but in gilding with its beams both knowledge and wisdom.

Diogenes guessed that such a group would grow and that other honest men in distant places would want to establish similar groups and so he gave to the original group the authority to establish chapters or branches.

Because it is essential that each group have a lantern, he decreed that the original lantern be passed on to such new chapter as may be established and that a new lantern be acquired by the parent organization.

Twice in our history have we passed on the lantern to a departing member who wished to establish a chapter elsewhere, and it is with pleasure that we pass on our present lantern to such a worthy person as Colonel Sands, knowing that he will cause it to shine in worthy places.

So that no man may question his authority, we have prepared a certificate, signed by all of the members here present, giving him the right to start a chapter in Minneapolis. It is expressly stipulated, however, that this authority does not confer on the chapter about to be established the right to establish new chapters or to pass on the lantern. That right is specifically reserved by the parent chapter.

Colonel Sands, it gives me great pleasure to present to you the Lantern of Diogenes and the accompanying certificate of authority.

### Certificate

Know all men to whose attention this document shall come that Thomas Sands, Colonel in the United States Army and a resident of Falls Church, Virginia, having signified his intention to return to the wilds of Minnesota and resume his practice of law which was interrupted when he responded to the call of his country, and having expressed his desire to establish in the general neighborhood of the Great Lakes and the headwaters of the Mississippi, and particularly in the settlement known as Minneapolis, a chapter of our beloved organization, The Lantern Club, and having signified his willingness to abide by our traditions and our high standards.

Be it known that we, the members assembled at a meeting of the Lantern Club, held at the residence of the said Thomas Sands on the evening of January 10, 1946, acting under the authority of our beloved founder, George W. Diogenes, do give and grant to the said Thomas Sands the right to establish a chapter at Minneapolis, in the State of Minnesota, and as a token of such authority do present him our official lantern, which, in turn, will become the official lantern of the Minneapolis Chapter.

Possession of this lantern does not give any right to start new chapters. All such new chapters must stem from the parent organization.

### *Supplement F*

(At a meeting held at the home of J.O. Martin in December, 1957, Harry Doyle, who was getting ready to move to California, was presented a lantern. J.O. couldn't find his copy of the presentation speech on a similar occasion and was obliged to draw upon his memory for the words of the speech, which he did, adding something new here and there, mostly foolishness, and having little or no foundation in fact.)

Another little piece of business here tonight is the presentation of a lantern to a member, Mr. Harry Doyle, who is leaving for California. Our lantern will light his way, figuratively speaking, and will assist him in organizing a branch of the Lantern Club on the Pacific Coast. This makes the second of our lanterns to go to—or at least to start for—California. As far as I know the first one produced no results.

We took another lantern out to Beltsville, Md., several years ago and started a branch there, and that one, I understand, did all right for a while but is now in a state of suspended animation. A third lantern went with a departing member, one Colonel Sands, to Minneapolis. I understand from Larry Laing that Colonel Sands did succeed in starting a branch there, but whether it survived I do not know.

Before turning our present lantern over to our present departing member it may be in order to relate, especially for the benefit of our newer members, the story of the lantern.

I realize, of course, that a lot of legends are to be taken with a grain of salt, and I hasten to assure you that you are at liberty to accept or reject this one, just as you choose.

I suppose you have all heard of Diogenes, that peripatetic old Greek who went around with a lantern, seeking an honest man. The story goes that in his travels Diogenes finally reached Falls Church, where he found not only one honest man, but three. Of course, that was back in the days before the great influx of newcomers completely changed the character of our fair city.

Diogenes was so delighted with finding what he had been looking for that he gave the lantern to the three honest men. It was no great sacrifice on his part. He didn't need it any more. Besides, it was pretty badly beaten up. The metal was dented in several places, the chimney was cracked, and it smoked and smelled as no good lantern should.

Diogenes suggested that the three form a little club and use the lantern as a symbol and a source of inspiration—although from my description of it you can see that it wasn't capable of shedding much light on anything.

But wait! Diogenes told them that it was a magic lantern, something like Aladdin's lamp, and that if they discussed any subject while it was lighted in the room, they would be able to do so with great eloquence and logic.

Personally, I think the old boy was kidding them, in addition to unloading on them his smelly old lantern. It would appear that they were naive as well as honest.

I suppose we never will learn the truth of the matter. Diogenes hasn't been seen in these parts for a long time, and if he should come back he probably couldn't remember what he did tell them.

What I can't understand is why he pretended to bestow on them the gift of eloquence. If he really wanted to do something for them, why didn't he tell them how to distinguish an honest man from a crook?

But I suppose the old fellow was pretty well worn out with toting that old lantern around. Perhaps he couldn't see things in the right perspective. When you carry an old lantern around smoke gets in your eyes.

Maybe he had hallucinations. Perhaps he thought he was Demosthenes. Or he might have been so confused that he thought he was Isosceles, that slick old Greek mathematician who was so far from being square that they named a triangle for him.

But those three Falls Church men believed Diogenes when he told them that he could make them eloquent. It's easy for men to believe what they want to believe.

So they sat around their smoky old lantern and talked in weighty words of things worthy of great cogitation, and, like the Pharisees, they rejoiced that they were not like other men.

But finally their old lantern gave off so much smoke and such a fearful odor that they were obliged to keep it on the front porch while they talked.

The lighted lantern on the porch aroused considerable curiosity in the neighborhood. You know how neighbors are. They wanted to know what was going on. And they had various ways of finding out. The fellow across the street came over to borrow the evening paper. Another wanted a match. Another wanted a cigarette. One even wanted to know at what time the nine o'clock bus left for town in the morning.

Having come, they stayed to listen. And the three honest and eloquent men were glad to have an audience. As time went on, they permitted their not-so-honest and not-so-eloquent neighbors to chip in a word now and then, and finally the new-comers were accepted on a nearly-equal basis.

And so the club grew. It may not be the most popular club in Falls Church today but it is probably the most nearly unique. Incidentally, among those present tonight are two of the original three, and several others who might be called charter members—if we had a charter. Probably more than half of the members present have been members for more than 20 years.

And that's the legend of the lantern. As I have indicated, legends are not necessarily history. For some of them I hold no brief at all. But I feel that I can speak with authority concerning this particular legend. It happens that I wrote the thing.\*\*\*

\* \* \* \* \* \* \* \* \* \* \*

We come now to the presentation. The lantern we give to the departing member is always the *old* lantern. The reason for this might seem perfectly obvious to any one who has even seen one of them, but there is tradition involved.

Having arranged to give away our old lantern, it was necessary to buy a new one, in order that it might grace the front of the house in case any member should break down and decide to hold a meeting. Larry Laing made the purchase for us, at a cost of $3.25. It is one of the unwritten rules of this organization that we shall never have money in the treasury. In fact, we have no treasury. Any expense incurred must be borne by the host or a collection must be taken up. In this case your host chooses to have a collection made. After all, $3.25 is $3.25. Each member present will do what his individual conscience suggests.

And so Harry, the old lantern is yours. You can pick it up on your way out. As Kipling once wrote: "We gives you your certificate and if you wants it signed, we'll come and have a romp with you whenever you're inclined." And maybe you can inculcate some eastern culture into those barbarians on the west coast.

*Supplement G*

Several times during its quarter-century career the Lantern Club entered into a period of inactivity. In the interest of truth and history it must be admitted that we have had some members who were apparently willing to attend a meeting in any house but their own and who seldom or never acted as host. This attitude was a bit annoying to some of the other members who had frequently been host, and apparently those faithful members waited for some of the delinquents to make a move. Months would pass by without anybody making such a move and then somebody (usually one of the old-timers) would make an effort to get things going again.

The year 1951 was apparently one of those periods. Here is a copy of a letter which J.O. Martin wrote to Ralph Staebner on October 6 of that year:

"From time to time people ask me about the Lantern Club. One has offered to have a meeting in his house in order to get it going again. Will you please read the attached and let me know what you think. Call me up at any time and save yourself letter-writing."

Attached to the letter were the following proposed comments for use in opening the discussion if and when a meeting were held:

"As you know, we have not had a meeting for more than a year. In the mean time, several of the members have asked what has become of the Lantern Club.

The meeting tonight has been called to determine if there is sufficient interest to justify resumption of the meetings.

If we do resume the meetings I think it should be under a different arrangement from that which prevailed in the past.

Therefore, I am submitting for discussion tonight the following four points:

1. Each member should consider that he has an obligation to entertain the group once a year, in his home or elsewhere.

2. The number of members should be limited to the number which can be comfortably entertained in the average home and which will be small enough to permit general discussion.

3. If a member continues to absent himself from meetings without a satisfactory excuse his membership may be declared vacant.

4. New members should be chosen from a waiting list."

Also attached was the following:

Proposed notice to be sent to those on the membership list who are not known to have left the community:

Lantern Club<br>
October, 1951<br>
Subject for discussion:<br>
What Shall We Do About the Lantern Club?

Apparently Ralph did call J.O., as invited, for at the bottom of the letter which J.O. had written to Ralph, and which has been preserved, is the following, apparently addressed to Charles Gage:

Herewith a communication from J.O. Martin re the Lantern Club. I suggested to him that it might be well to sound out the sentiments of the "old hands" on the matter. Accordingly, he asked me to send this to you and you to Mac Smith and the latter to another and make a round robin of it. Will you call J.O.? I am not sure whether or not now is the time but would be glad to go ahead if there is enough interest in it to indicate a reasonable success.

On the other side of the sheet is a communication, quoted here in part, from Mr. Gage to Malcolm Smith:

Something along this line I think would be O.K. Perhaps a little judicious pruning of the membership list would be in order as a starter— \*\*\*. Just talked with J.O. and he suggested that this be circulated further. Your suggestion of Diehl is swell and J.O. thinks John Graham is much interested, too.

Beneath Mr. Gage's note to Mr. Smith is Mr. Smith's note quoted here in part, to Mr. Diehl:

\*\*\* I would suggest that we get together and form a closed corporation. Perhaps we should get up a tentative schedule of meetings spaced at intervals of one month. Perhaps a total list of 15 or 20 names—*good* names, would be enough. This sounds snobbish but it could mean the difference between success and failure.\*\*\* Harry Doyle of Park Avenue now has the lantern and is awaiting reactions before calling a meeting.

Bill Diehl wrote his comments, quoted here in part, under Mac's and sent the letter back to J.O. Martin:

\*\*\* A proselyte ought not be accepted to membership until he has been approved by a Committee of Membership. And to function competently in choosing persons most likely to carry on the club's best traditions this committee would have to be a small group preferably of *elder statesmen*. Perhaps we should at an annual Special Meeting elect a presiding officer for each year who could appoint this committee; he could act as archivist in addition. \*\*\*

Apparently there was a meeting, perhaps at Harry Doyle's house, but apparently the original objections (or indifference) of the members to rules continued to prevail, for the club is still without rules, and without officers and committees—and there are still long periods without a meeting.

The reader of these notes will find in them occasional references to a "membership list." As a matter of fact, there never has been what might properly be called an "official" list of members. In the beginning a history-minded member [J.O. Martin] jotted down the names of those present at meetings. Later, probably when we began to send out notices, a list was entered in a little memorandum book, with addresses, but our qualifications for membership were so vague (and, of course, unwritten) that it was difficult to keep the list accurate and up-to-date. Members would quit without notice, or fail to attend meetings for long periods, or leave the community without notice. At the beginning of each season of meetings, or at other times, we would try to clean up the list by crossing off the names of those who had left town.

## Supplement H

At a meeting held at the home of J.O. Martin in December, 1957, J.O. made the following suggestion:

"I would like to make a suggestion concerning future meetings. When we started out (I think it was in 1933) we had a meeting about every two weeks. Later we found ourselves meeting about once a month, and still later once in two or three months, or even at longer intervals. I don't know that any year went by without a meeting, although it may have happened. It is my impression, however, that in 1956 we had *only one* meeting, and I believe that our meeting here tonight is only the *third* in 1957, and the year is about gone.

I feel that we can do better in 1958, our 25th anniversary year, especially if we have some little reminder before us. With that thought in mind I have provided this little book. The January meeting has been sponsored by Oscar Kiessling. I would like signatures to the other 11 pledges. It isn't necessary to sign up tonight, but if you wish to do so please see me after the meeting. There will be other opportunities, however, for I intend to bring up the matter at subsequent meetings, until all of the months of 1958 have been provided for." (John Keller became a member at this meeting.)

Those who attended at least one meeting between January 1, 1958, and July 1, 1958:

Wm. Diehl; Howard Coyle; Malcolm Smith; Sargent White; Fred Bailey; Ralph Staebner; Larry Laing; Tom Probey; Melvin Lee Steadman Jr. (new); Donald DuBois; Chas. Gage; John Keller (new); Oscar Kiessling; Erle Prior; J.O. Martin.

## THE MASONIC ORDER

There are two Masonic Lodges in Falls Church, Kemper Lodge # 64, and Macon Ware Lodge # 192. The former, instituted June 12, 1896, is the "Mother Lodge." Macon Ware Lodge was founded April 11, 1950. The manuscript of a proposed book, *Chronicles of Kemper Lodge* by Frank M. Steadman, P.M., P.D.D.G.M., has been made available to the author. In this work Mr. Steadman has included biographical sketches of past masters and other material. When published it will be a valuable additional to local history.

Kemper Lodge was instituted in the Odd Fellows Hall, and was named in honor of Right Worshipful Kosciusko Kemper, District Deputy Grand Master of District Number One of the Grand Lodge of Virginia. Kemper became Grand Master of Masons in Virginia in 1906. The dispensation to form Kemper Lodge was issued by Most Worshipful John P. Fitzgerald, Grand Master of Masons in Virginia, on May 25, 1896 (Masonic calendar, A.L. 5896). The officers of the Lodge under dispensation were: John Henry Fisher, Worshipful Master; Benjamin W. Summy, Senior Warden; Merton E. Church, Junior Warden; George W. Mankin, Treasurer; George Stambaugh, Secretary; Rev. D.L. Rathbun, The Reverend A.M. Cackley, and The Reverend John McGill, Chaplains; and George A. Hinsch, Tiler.

The Charter was issued December 3, 1896, by Alfred R. Courtney, Grand Master. Kemper Lodge, was constituted on February 12, 1897, by Right Worshipful James E. Alexander, District Deputy Grand Master of Jurisdiction Number One. The Lodge had the following charter officers: John Henry Fisher, Worshipful Master; Merton Elbridge Church, Senior Warden; Willis Leonard Gordon, Junior Warden; George William Mankin, Treasurer; George Stambaugh, Secretary; George Tyree Mankin, Senior Deacon; George A. Hinsch, Junior Deacon; The Reverend A.M. Cackley, The Reverend John McGill, and The Reverend D.L. Rathbun, Chaplains; George B. Fadeley and Harry L. Turner, Stewards. The office of Tiler was held by Edward N. Meekins and Robert W. Summers.

The Charter Members of Kemper Lodge were: W.H. Barksdale, Charles L. Blanton, The Reverend A.M. Cackley, William J. Capner, Merton E. Church, George B. Fadeley, John H. Fisher, Willis L. Gordon, Julius Graham, George A. Hinsch, George E. King, Charles H. Lashorn, Samuel S. Luttrell, George T. Mankin, George W. Mankin, The Reverend John McGill, Edward N. Meekins, William P. Poole, The Reverend D.L. Rathbun, T.J. Hoyles-Row, John T. Schaaff, George Stambaugh, Robert W. Summers, Benjamin W. Summy, and Harry L. Turner.

The Lodge met at the Odd Fellows Hall from June 12, 1896, until December 25, 1931. On the latter date the Lodge moved to the Presbyterian Sunday School Building and occupied this building from January 8, 1932 until July 13, 1934. The Lodge moved to its first Temple at 6815 Lee Highway in East Falls Church, Arlington County in 1934/5. The Grand Lodge, by James M. Clift, Grand Secretary, authorized this move on February 13, 1935.

The new Temple was erected in 1934 at a cost of $26,989. The architect was Frank Upman of the firm of Upman & Adams. The Temple was built under the charter of the *Falls Church Temple Corporation*, which charter was granted November 24, 1933. J. Randall Caton Jr., of Alexandria, prepared the articles of incorporation for the building committee. The following were the first officers of the Corporation: Charles E. Gage, President; Olin G. Snyder, Vice President; Frank F. Shipley, Treasurer; and Ernest H. Hinkins, Secretary. Directors were: Frank Romine Taylor, Chairman; Charles E. Gage, Olin G. Snyder, Frank F. Shipley, and Ernest H. Hinkins. The building was erected by F.R. Taylor at cost.

The following article is from the *Falls Church News* of January 21, 1898, page 3:

## MASONIC RECEPTION

The members of Kemper Lodge No. 64, A.F. & A.M. gave a reception last night (Friday) to their wives and sweethearts at Odd Fellows' Hall. The affair was eagerly looked forward to by the Masons and their guests as the event of the season and they were not disappointed. The Committee in charge were composed of Messrs. Flagg, Quick, and Meekins, to whom credit should be given for making all the arrangements.

Early in the evening the guests gathered in the Society Hall on the upper floor, where the following excellent program was rendered, Mr. A.I. Flagg presiding.

Prayer by Rev. John McGill, D.D., followed by the address of welcome, delivered by Worshipful Master, M.E. Church in a cordial felicitous manner, Mr. G.W. Hawxhurst responded. Recitation, Miss Nellie Hawxhurst; vocal solos, Miss Annie Rodeffer; recitation, Miss May King of Glen-carlyn; recitation, Dr. T.C. Quick; Piano and Mandolin duet, Miss Aida Boernstein and Mr. Sig Boernstein; remarks by E.N. Meekins; recitation, Mrs. J.S. Garrison; Piano Solo, Miss Bertha Capner; address, Mrs. Lorraine J. Pitkins of Chicago, Most Worshipful Grand Matron of the General Chapter of the Western Star and Right Worthy Grand Secretary of the Eastern Star.

The Banquet tables were prettily decorated and laden with good things. Mr. Flagg acted as Toast-Master and toasts were given by Right Worshipful K. Kemper of Alexandria, Past Grand Master of the District of Columbia; Caleb Williamson, Edw. Meekins, Dr.

T.C. Quick, Dr. G.B. Fadeley, Geo. S. Hinsch, Rev. Jno. Kincheloe, Rev. A.M. Cackley, A.I. Flagg, and others.

An unique number of the program was the appearance of the goat—saddled and bridled—which all good Masons are supposed to ride when initiated.

At two o'clock the guests departed for their homes unanimously voting the Masons as jolly good fellows and hosts par excellence.

*Past Masters of Kemper Lodge*

John H. Fisher, Merton E. Church, Willis L. Gordon, George T. Mankin, George B. Fadeley, Tunis C. Quick, George M. Newell, William A. Ball, Alexander H. Barbor, Harry L. Turner, Frank M. Thompson, Pharis W. Lee, Horace E. Brown, George C. Thompson, George L. Brist, Walter T. Westcott, James W. Brown, Joseph H. Newell, Ernest H. Hinkins, Charles E. Gage, William Middleton, Macon Ware, John R. Browning, Everett E. Tillett, John J. Hughes, Mason C. Grasty, Olin G. Snyder, C.M. Sale, Everett A. Demarest, James L. Shotwell, Carl L. Campbell, Thomas M. Hodgson, Arthur P. Connelly, R.B. Turner, Benjamin F. May, Andrew T. Millard, Frank M. Steadman, Charles T. Rowell, J.A. Shockley, Homer F. Gilliam, Charles C. Smith, Creed W. Minear, Jr., Herbert Moran, Charles Martin, Chester L. Williams, and Carroll W. Pope.

*Honorary Members of Kemper Lodge*

John H. Fisher, Charles H. Callahan, Percy E. Clift, James E. Alexander, Ernest Cunningham, Harry K. Green, Frank M. Thompson, George B. Fadeley, George F. McInturff, A.H. Barbor, P.W. Lee, Ernest Hinkins, Macon Ware, and Isaac A. Rullman.

## MACON WARE LODGE # 192

Macon Ware Lodge was named in honor of Right Worshipful Macon Ware, a Past Master of Kemper Lodge, and a Past District Deputy Grand Master of Masonic Jurisdiction Number One. It was long recognized by members of Kemper Lodge that a new Lodge should be constituted for the benefit of the growing Falls Church area. In view of the need, Right Worshipful Frank McNulty Steadman, Sr., P.M.D.D.G.M., on December 23, 1949, presented a petition to Kemper Lodge signed by forty Master Masons, requesting approval of that lodge for the formation of a new lodge in the same jurisdiction. This matter was laid over for the statutory period.

A meeting of the persons who had signed the petition was called on January 4, 1950, for the purpose of selecting a name for the proposed lodge and nominating officers. Worshipful Frank M. Steadman presided. Many names were submitted for the proposed lodge, but it was agreed to apply for the dispensation under the name Falls Church Lodge, and thereafter, when the matter had crystallized, to apply for the charter in a name to be selected.

With regard to the officers of the lodge, Mr. Steadman stated that he had approached three Past Masters of Kemper Lodge and had secured their permission to place their names in nomination for the stationed offices. They were: Joshua A. Shockley, Macon Ware, and Reginald B. Turner. No other nominations were made. The ballot being taken, and Dr. Ware was elected first Master. J.A. Shockley was elected as Junior Warden. Officers selected by the Lodge included: Frank M. Steadman, Treasurer; Thomas Alexander Hughes, Secretary; James W. Brown, Jr., Senior Deacon; and Stanley W. Hudkins, Junior Deacon. The Master-designate appointed Harry T. Fleet and Clarence Montford Watkins, Stewards; John R. Archer, Chaplain; Ernest H. Hinkins, Marshal; and Howard M. Lowry, Tiler.

Kemper Lodge unanimously approved the formation of the new Lodge within their jurisdiction on January 27, 1950, and recommended that the petition for the new lodge be approved by the Grand Master. The nine surrounding lodges, Alexandria-Washington # 22, Andrew Jackson # 120, Arlington-Centennial # 81, Cherrydale # 42, Columbia # 285, Concord # 307, Henry # 57, Henry Knox Field # 349, and Sharon # 327, concurred in the recommendation for the formation of the new lodge.

A second organizational meeting was held February 8, 1950, at which Frank M. Steadman presided since Macon Ware was ill, and could not attend the meeting. The purpose of this meeting was to select a name for the lodge. The signers of the petition were requested to indicate their first, second and third choices from a list of proposed names for the lodge. A ballot was taken of those present, and the three names receiving the highest number of votes were Charles H. Callahan, Macon Ware and John Blair. All other names were dropped from consideration. A second ballot was taken, which disclosed that the name "Macon Ware Lodge" had received all but three votes. Upon a motion duly made, seconded and carried, the name "Macon Ware Lodge," was unanimously approved by those present. A committee consisting of Clarence M. Sale and J.W. Brown, Jr., was appointed to call on Dr. Ware to ascertain his wishes in the matter. The committee returned and reported that he was delighted to have the lodge named for him. The petition for dispensation of Macon Ware Lodge was transmitted to the Grand Master, through Right Worshipful William E. Sprouse, D.D.G.M. Most Worshipful Enoch Dorron Flowers, Grand Master of Masons in Virginia, issued the dispensation to open a regular lodge, designed as Macon Ware Lodge U[nder] D[ispensation].

Macon Ware Lodge U.D., was instituted on Tuesday, April 11, 1950 (Masonic Calendar A.L. 5950), by Most Worshipful John Malcolm Stewart. Mr. Stewart and The Honorable Hugh M. Reid, (Grand Senior Deacon of the Grand Lodge of Virginia) were elected to honorary membership in the lodge on April 25, '1950.

The dispensation, together with the proceedings of the lodge, was returned to the Grand Lodge. The Charter of Macon Ware Lodge # 192 was authorized by vote of the Grand Lodge, on February 14, 1951. The following day the charter was issued by James M. Hillman, Grand Secretary.

Macon Ware Lodge was constituted by Rudolph Reynolds Cooke, Grand Master of Masons in Virginia, April 10, 1951. He was accompanied by several members of the Grand Lodge, including William Moseley Brown, James N. Hillman, Clarence D. Freeman, and John M. Stewart. The Honorable Hugh M. Reid and George R. Marshall were chosen Grand Lecturer and Marshal for the occasion.

The lodge adopted a "Resolution of Gratitude" honoring Frank M. Steadman, P.M., P.D.D.G.M., "as the founder of this lodge, for his untiring efforts, his capable management, and his devotion to Masonry in general and Macon Ware Lodge in particular." This was signed by Joshua A. Shockley, S.W.; Thomas A. Hughes, Secretary; and Macon Ware, Worshipful Master.

Dr. Macon Ware for whom the lodge was named, died July 19, 1952, after a useful life devoted to his family and community. Dr. Ware owned and operated Ware's Pharmacy in East Falls Church and the Falls Church Pharmacy when he retired due to ill health in 1945. Born at Ware's Wharf, Essex County, Va., Dr. Ware was a graduate of Tappahannock High School, and Johnson's College. In 1913 he was graduated from the University of Richmond with a degree in pharmacy. Dr. Ware was president of Zeta Delta Chi fraternity during his senior year at the University of Richmond.

Dr. Ware's pharmaceutical career began in Hot Springs, Va. He settled in Falls Church in 1915 and purchased the old Mankin Pharmacy which he renamed "Ware's Pharmacy."

Dr. Ware was made a Master Mason in Hot Springs Masonic Lodge # 275 in 1915. He affiliated with Kemper Lodge in Falls Church in 1921, serving as Master in 1927. In 1930-31 he served as District Deputy Grand Master of District Number One, and in 1950-51 had the unique experience of presiding over a lodge named in his honor. For many years Dr. Ware served on the jurisprudence committee of the Grand Lodge of Virginia, and was Past Patron of Acacia Chapter # 51, O.E.S. He was past commander of the Falls Church American Legion Post, and was a loyal member of Columbia Baptist Church. An ardent student of Virginia history and genealogy, Dr. Ware collected books in this field. He also owned a large collection of guns which he displayed in the community interest. He was buried on his ancestral farm, "Bellevue," in Dunnsville, Virginia.

*Honorary Members of Macon Ware Lodge*

John M. Stewart, Judge Hugh Reid, Ernest Hinkins, Frank M. Steadman, and J.A. Shockley.

## ORDER OF DeMOLAY

The James S. Sipes Chapter, Order of DeMolay, was organized in the Masonic Temple at East Falls Church on September 9, 1948, and was founded by Frank M. Steadman. The Chapter was named in honor of James S. Sipes, only member of Kemper Lodge to be killed while serving in World

War II. Frank M. Steadman, Jr., was first Master Councilor, and Melvin Lee Steadman, Jr., was first Senior Councilor.

## ORDER OF THE EASTERN STAR

Acacia Chapter No. 51, Order of the Eastern Star, meets in the Masonic Temple. The Chapter was organized April 11, 1913, and instituted by R.S. Taylor, Grand Patron of the O.E.S. of Virginia. The Chapter was honored in 1917 when M.E. Church was elected Grand Patron of the Grand Chapter of Virginia. The following were charter members: Mrs. Marcia C. Parker, Miss Carrie A. Ball, Kate S. Barbor, Maggie Brist, Ida G. Westcott, Carrie B. Church, Katie Carrell, Anna A. Northrup, Emily T. Church, Goldie M. Thompson, Ida Q. Hawxhurst, Annie T. Garrison, Alice M. Fellows, Mary L. Haskell, Kate C. Rullman, George B. Lester, Melissa K. Beach, Ella Thompson, Grace V. Thompson, Maud Torreyson, Grace V. Sparrow, Maggie May Potter, Anna Margaret Lester, Alexander H. Barbor, G.L. Brist, H.E. Brown, George T. Mankin, F.E. Parker, M.E. Church, George C. Thompson, H.L. Kays, George N. Lester, Albert M. Lester, Henry A. Beach, Frank M. Thompson, Isaac C. Rullman, and Guy N. Church. First Matron was Mrs. A.H. Barbor.

## PATRIOTIC ORDER OF THE SONS OF AMERICA

Washington Camp Number One, Patriotic Order of the Sons of America, was organized in 1902. Officers consisted of a President, Vice President, Conductor, Inspector, Guard, Chaplain, and Trustees.

## POTOMAC FRUIT GROWERS' ASSOCIATION

This organization drew much of its membership from Falls Church. An association of citizens of Alexandria (Arlington) and Fairfax Counties, the group was formed in 1867. The following is from an unidentified clipping dated May 27, 1869:

> The Alexandria Gazette of last evening says the apple of discord was introduced at a late meeting, when it was determined to admit colored members, and the result has been that a portion of the society have withdrawn from the association, formed a new society, and will hold a meeting at Falls Church tomorrow, for the purpose of perfecting their organization. The new society will include in its membership the names of Dr. Lester Lloyd, Rev. F.M. Mills, Dr. P. Hogan, J.L. Roon, esq., Dr. L.E. Gott, and numerous others.

## UNITED DAUGHTERS OF THE CONFEDERACY

The Robert Edward Lee Chapter Number 233, United Daughters of the Confederacy, was organized in June 1898, and the object of the chapter was to assist needy widows and orphans of former Confederate soldiers. By 1904 membership included forty-three members. The Charter of this chapter was issued June 20, 1898, by Katie Cabell Currie, President, and

Mrs. John P. Hickman, Secretary, of the United Daughters of the Confederacy, with headquarters in Nashville, Tennessee. Charter members were: Mrs. George J. Head, Mrs. Armistead M. Donaldson, Mrs. Charles E. Mankin, Mrs. R.P. Buckner, Mrs. Robert B. Smith, Mrs. L.E. Gott, Miss Mary H. Smith, and Miss Lillian H. Watkins.

The chapter is still in existence.

## THE VILLAGE IMPROVEMENT SOCIETY

The Village Improvement Society was organized in the fall of 1885, and was modeled after the well-known Laurel Hill Society of Stockbridge, Massachusetts, and its object was to aid in improving the condition of the town. Under its auspices the first observance of Arbor Day in the State of Virginia was held in 1892, when the society sponsored and instituted the observance in the yard of Jefferson School. Children of the town planted memorial trees and plants in the yard.

The *Constitution and By-Laws of the Village Improvement Society of Falls Church, Va.* was published in 1907 by the Newell Printing Company of Falls Church. The following is taken from an article entitled "History" on page 1:

> Special objects are sometimes provided for by general subscriptions, but the greater part of the money raised by the Society is from voluntary dues or the proceeds of lectures and other entertainments.
>
> The Society makes a specialty of aiding in the construction of sidewalks, and has materially assisted in building many of the walks in different sections of the town. It appropriated over two hundred dollars to aid in building the board sidewalk to East Falls Church and during the past two years has paid $421.70 to aid in constructing brick walks.
>
> ... $112.00 was paid over to the Town Council to assist in the instalment of street lamps and $100.00 was paid the Council towards the cost of the survey and plat of the town. It purchased and donated a piano to the public graded school and furnished the pupils with music books. It helped to equip the public library which has over six hundred volumes upon its shelves. It makes an annual appropriation for setting out shade trees, and paid half the cost of sign boards for the streets. The total cost of the public well at East Falls Church depot, over one hundred dollars, was paid by the Society and it also keeps the well in repair.
>
> The Society also arranges each year for the proper celebration of Independence Day when an oration is delivered by some person of national reputation. A separate fund is raised for this purpose by popular subscription.
>
> Meetings are held the first Monday evening of each month, excepting July and August, at the residence of one of the members.

One dollar is paid at the time of joining and one dollar annually thereafter.

Some of the officers (as given in the booklet and found elsewhere) follow:
1885-86, W.H. Doolittle, President; D.H. Riddle, Vice President; S.V. Proudfit, Secretary; A.P. Eastman, Treasurer.
1886-87, D.H. Riddle, President; J.S. Garrison, Vice President; G.A.L. Merrifield, Secretary, A.P. Eastman, Treasurer. (Mr. Eastman served as Treasurer until 1896).
1887-88, D.H. Riddle, President; S. Duryee, Vice President; Miss Sue Riddle, Secretary.
1888-89, D.H. Riddle, President; B.W. Pond, Vice President; F.W. Tuckerman, Secretary.
1889-90, B.W. Pond, President; G.A.L. Merrifield, Vice President; F.W. Tuckerman, Secretary.
1890-91, S.V. Proudfit, President; G.A.L. Merrifield, Vice President; H.R. Center, Secretary.
1891-92, A.E. Rowell, President; G.A.L. Merrifield, Vice President; E.C. Hough, Secretary.
1892-93, A.E. Rowell, President; S.V. Proudfit, Vice President; E.C. Hough, Secretary.
1893-94, E.C. Hough, President; L.B. Parker, Vice President; S.V. Proudfit, Secretary.
1894-95, E.C. Hough, President; L.B. Parker, Vice President; S.V. Proudfit, Secretary.
1895-96, G.A.L. Merrifield, President; Dr. J.B. Gould, Vice President; E.C. Hough, Secretary.
1896-97, A.P. Eastman, President; Lieut. Barry, Vice President; Wm. Stranahan, Secretary; Mrs. A.P. Eastman, Asst. Secretary; M.E. Church, Treasurer (a position he held until 1904).
1897-98, L.B. Parker, President; G.A.L. Merrifield, Vice President; Wm. Stranahan, Secretary; Mrs. A.P. Eastman, Assistant Secretary.
1898-99, G.A.L. Merrifield, President; Dr. T.C. Quick, Vice President; J.W. Webb, Secretary; Mrs. G.W. Hawxhurst, Assistant Secretary.
1899-1900, Dr. T.C. Quick, President; P. Dodge, Vice President; Mrs. G.W. Hawxhurst, Secretary; E.C. Hough, Assistant Secretary.
1900-01, Geo. W. Hawxhurst, President; C.P. Montgomery, Vice President; G.G. Hill, Secretary; Mrs. G.W. Hawxhurst, Assistant Secretary.
1901-02, E.C. Hough, President; S.R. Copper, Vice President; G.W. Hawxhurst, Secretary; Miss Mattie Gundry, Assistant Secretary.
1902-03, G.A.L. Merrifield, President; Rev. R.A. Davison, Vice President; G.W. Hawxhurst, Secretary; G.F. McInturff, Assistant Secretary.
1903-04, Geo. B. Fadeley, President; Rev. A.W. Graves, Vice President; G.W. Hawxhurst, Secretary; Mrs. G.A.L. Merrifield, Assistant Secretary.
1904-05, M.E. Church, President; Rev. F. Noble, Vice President; Miss

B.C. Merrifield, Secretary; G.B. Fadeley, Assistant Secretary; G.W. Hawxhurst, Treasurer.

1905-06, Rev. F. Noble, President; Miss Belle C. Merrifield, Vice President; G.W. Hawxhurst, Secretary; Mrs. G.A.L. Merrifield, Assistant Secretary; Miss Mattie Gundry, Treasurer.

1906-07, A.E. Rowell, President; H.A. Fellows, Vice President; Miss B.C. Merrifield, Secretary; F.A. Whiteley, Assistant Secretary; Miss Mattie Gundry, Treasurer.

1907-08, H.A. Fellows, President.
1908-09, William M. Ellison, President.
1909-10, Dr. George Tyree Mankin, President.
1910-11, Charles A. Stewart, President.
1911-12, J.F. Hutton, President.
1912-13, E.T. Fenwick, President.
1913-14, John F. Bethune, President.

(This list is not complete. The Village Improvement Society was in existence until about 1923).

## THE VIRGINIA STATE AUDUBON SOCIETY

The Virginia State Audubon Society was organized at Falls Church on September 29, 1903. The object of the society was to protect the native birds, and to discourage the buying and wearing of ornamental feathers from birds other than the ostrich and the domesticated fowls. The society promoted a lasting interest in bird study in Falls Church. The members paid yearly dues of one dollar, and the children under sixteen paid none, but pledged not to harm birds. This organization met with great success, and continued in existence for several years. The last years of its existence were about 1914-16. Frank M. Steadman was a member at that time.

## OTHER ORGANIZATIONS

Some recent organizations include: Lions, Kiwanis, B.P.O.E., Post 130, American Legion; Sharon Chapter No. 63, OES; V.F.W., Martin-Leppert-Sipes Post No. 9274; American War Mothers, Campfire Girls, Boy Scouts, Girl Scouts, Community Theatre, Newcomers Club, P.T.A., Falls Church Music Study Club, A.A.U.W., Dramatic Club, Junior Civic League, The Leftover Club, Community Chest, Teen Canteen, Job's Daughters, Chess Club, Red Cross, Chamber of Commerce, Rebekahs, Rotary and others.

## FOOTNOTES

[1] *United States Magazine and Democratic Review.* September, 1839.
[2] With more recent additions.
[3] Hyson was a free Negro.
[4] At present (June, 1958) the picture is much different, since the trustees of the cemetery have attempted to sell this land. Lot owners and others interested have taken the matter to court. While the outcome is uncertain, it is apparent that new residents are interested in the Cemetery, and it is hoped that if the land is not sold, and is developed: they will purchase lots or continue their interest.
[5] The first building was torn down during the summer of 1958.
[6] *Northern Virginia Sun.* Thursday, March 13, 1958.
[7] Information supplied by Frank M. Steadman, Sr., 5909 N. 22nd Street, Arlington, Va.
[8] *Fairfax County Sun Echo.* December 5, 1957; *Northern Virginia Sun.* November 28, 1957 and January 22, 1958.
[9] Program in the author's file gives this date.
[10] *Northern Virginia Sun.* April 28, 1959.
[11] The Grand Lodge of Virginia was formed April 29, 1869. There were no saloons in Falls Church from 1870 until the time of World War I due to the activity of this order.
[12] From "A Few Notes Concerning The Lantern Club of Falls Church, Va.," prepared during the summer of 1958 by the late J.O. Martin, written at the author's request.

CHAPTER 14

# Rails and Ties By Fence and Field

As early as 1832[1] a railroad was advertised to begin at Leesburg in Loudoun County and extend to the Potomac River. This was proposed by the residents of Leesburg, and remained a paper project. In 1849, after much debate, the *Alexandria, Loudoun and Hampshire Railroad* was incorporated, and track laid down. This railroad has operated continuously since that time.[2]

According to the *Acts of the General Assembly of Virginia* of 1849,[3] (a session commencing December 4, 1848, and ending March 19, 1849) legislation was proposed for eleven different railroads. Among these were the Alexandria and Harper's Ferry Railroad, the Alexandria Marine Railway, and the Orange and Alexandria Railroad.

The Orange and Alexandria Railroad was incorporated by charter dated March 27, 1848 (amended March 6, 1849). The Act of Incorporation[4] states that the purpose of the company was the construction of a railroad from "Gordonsville in the county of Orange, by the way of the courthouse of that county to the courthouse of the county of Culpeper, and thence to the City of Alexandria. . ." "it shall be lawful to open books of subscription at Orange courthouse, under the direction of Philip S. Fry, David Hume, Richard Rawlings, Lewis B. Williams, Thomas Scott and Thomas A. Robinson; at Culpeper courthouse, under the direction of Thomas Hill senior, George Thomas, F.J. Thompson, George Ficklin, John Slaughter, J.C. Hansborough and W.B. Ross, and at the City of Alexandria, under the direction of Robert H. Miller, L.A. Cazenove, F.L. Smith, Robert Crupper, G.W.D. Ramsay, W.L. Powell and Robert Brockett, or any two or more of them. . ." This railroad had a definite influence on subsequent development of railroads in northern Virginia.

The Alexandria, Loudoun and Hampshire Railroad exists in part today as the Old Dominion Railroad, which operates over a stretch of track about fifty miles in length.

*The Falls Church and Potomac Railway Company* was incorporated January 24, 1888.[5] The Incorporators were W.P. Graham, George B. Ives, N.F. Graham, Schuyler Duryea, Isaac Crossman, James M. Love, D.M. Chichester, O.E. Hine, and Franklin Sherman of Fairfax County; William N. Febrey of Alexandria County, Va.; Austin Herr, George T. Dunlop and Arthur Cropley, of Georgetown, D.C. .."and such other persons as may hereafter be associated with them and their successors, are hereby constituted a body, corporate and politic, to be known as the Falls Church and Potomac railway company." The capital stock was to be twenty thousand dollars, but could be increased not to exceed one million dollars. The board of directors was to meet "in the town of Falls Church, in Fairfax County, and organize this company by electing from among the stockholders not less than five nor more than nine persons.." The *"Line of Railroad"* was "from a point at or near the Potomac river, in Alexandria county, opposite District of Columbia; thence through said county of Alexandria to or through the county of Fairfax and through the town of Falls Church, Vienna, Fairfax Courthouse, Great Falls of the Potomac, or to either or all of said points, or to any other point or points in the counties of Fairfax, Prince William, or Loudoun..."[6]

A scrapbook on local railroads, including original correspondence, newspaper clippings, and broadsides with maps, beginning August 28, 1868, and ending in 1876, is in the author's files. In it are many details concerning railroad construction in Loudoun, Fairfax, Washington, D.C., and other areas. One clipping (September 25, 1868) concerns the need for a branch of the Loudoun and Hampshire Railroad to Georgetown.

THE BRANCH RAILROAD TO GEORGETOWN. — Mr. H.W. Brewer, the officer appointed by the Corporation of Georgetown to survey a route to the Georgetown branch of the Loudoun and Hampshire Railroad, will commence next Monday to make a preliminary survey of the different routes proposed. The first route examined will be Aqueduct route, and extends past Forts Whipple and Corcoran, and strikes the main stem of the Loudoun and Hampshire road *near Falls Church*. This, we understand, seems to be the favorite route of the majority of the members of the Councils of Georgetown.

In another clipping (November 28, 1868) is this statement: "From the letters of Messrs. Blythe and Brewer it appears that the President of the Alexandria, Loudoun, and Hampshire railroad refuses to participate in even the survey of the middle or Falls Church route favored by the Committee."

It was reported November 20th, a week earlier, that Mr. Bligh, engineer of the railroad, wrote Mr. Brewer that "the route over the Alexandria Aqueduct, and from thence to Falls Church, is impracticable on account of the heavy grades (80 feet to the mile) and the deep cuttings reported as necessary on that line..."

The following article of January, 1869, is of interest, since mention is made of the proposed Lee Highway (put through in the next year) and the new town of "Rosslynn" (now called Rosslyn):

> The new Town 'Rosslynn.' — The 'Alexandria Canal Railroad and Bridge Company' who recently purchased the estate opposite Georgetown, at the southern terminus of the aqueduct bridge, known as 'Rosslynn,' have just laid out a town there, 'for the purpose,' they say, 'of making it a thriving place, in view of the important railroad and other interests to be centered there.' The new travel bridge over the aqueduct has just been finished, and is contemplated to make that structure the main railroad connection between the north and the south; while a turnpike road to Fall's Church, railroad to Alexandria, and a branch to the Loudo[u]n & Hampshire Railroad, to connect with railroads to be brought through Georgetown, are among the enterprizes soon to be inaugurated. It is also their intention to have the street cars from Washington run across the aqueduct to Rosslynn, From Messrs. Kilbourne & Latta, Real Estate Brokers, 7th and F streets, we have received a map of the new town. The plats include good business property, fine residence lots, and a number of excellent sites for suburban villas, all of which are offered by the gentlemen named above on "liberal terms."

The *EVENING STAR* of November 30, 1868 reported that a deadlock had developed in routing this new railroad, since the "middle" "or Falls Church" route favored by the committee was not favored by the company.

A clipping (not dated) in the old scrapbook gives an account of the "Fairfax and Georgetown Turnpike"[7] which was sponsored in 1869: "A meeting of the stockholders of this turnpike company was held at Fall's Church, Va., Saturday, Feb. 29, 1869, W.D. Shepherd, Esq., in the chair. The by-laws as prepared by the committee (appointed for that purpose), were read and adopted by sections. The stockholders then ratified all the acts of the Board of Directors to the present time. It was decided to petition for an extension of the capital of the company from $25,000 to $100,000, with the privilege of running a branch road to Germantown."

The *FAIRFAX CITIZEN* of February 12, 1869, reported that a meeting would be held on February 27th at Falls Church "for the purpose of considering the several interests of the road, (referring to the Fairfax and Georgetown Turnpike) and it is to be hoped, their deliberations will be perfectly harmonious.

An article of June, 1869, continues the story of Lee Highway:

FAIRFAX AND GEORGETOWN TURNPIKE COMPANY.

> The work upon this road was commenced on Tuesday, June 20, 1869, at Pin No. 3, near the Acqueduct bridge, at Georgetown, by the contractors, Messrs. Casey & Cassidy, under the direction of Messrs. Brewer & Wilson, engineers.

A glance at the map of that portion of Virginia through which this road passes will show the great importance of the undertaking to the cities of Georgetown and Washington, there being no communication, available at all times of the year, between that section of Virginia and the cities mentioned.

The road starts from the Aqueduct bridge, passes directly through the counties of Alexandria and Fairfax, crossing the 'Middle or Leesburg Turnpike,' at Falls' Church, thence directly across the country by way of 'Mills' Cross Roads,'[8] to Fairfax Court House, tapping the 'Little River Turnpike' at that place. A branch is to be run from 'Mills' Cross Roads,' by way of 'Flint Hill,' [Oakton] to Germantown [Jermantown]. The land along the route of this road is of the most fertile character, and its advantages to the business men of Washington and Georgetown, in the way of country residences, &c., are equal if not superior to that of any other section of the country in this vicinity.

A clipping dated April 23, 1873, concerning the turnpike states that: . . "The Annual Meeting of the stockholders of the Fairfax and Georgetown Turnpike Company was held on Wednesday afternoon at Falls Church, Va. A quorum of 205 votes was represented. The president reported that the road from the Aqueduct bridge to Falls Church needed considerable work on the bridges, grading, &c. The following officers were elected for the ensuing year: President, R.A. Phillips; directors, T.W. Widdecombe, Geo. Ott Wunder, Allan Pearce, Isaac Crossman, M.D. Ball, T.M. Brush and J.C. DePulton [DePutron]."

A clipping dated October, 1869, tells of a delegation of Fairfax County citizens, headed by Judge Henry W. Thomas, visiting officials concerning the proposed route of the new railroad:

RAILROAD CONNECTION WITH VIRGINIA—A delegation of citizens of Fairfax Co., Va., headed by Judge Thomas, arrived in this city yesterday and had an interview with W.W. Dungan, Esq., Secretary of the Alexandria Canal, Aqueduct, Railroad and Bridge Company, in regard to the building of a railroad from Georgetown, via Falls Church and Fairfax Court-House, to connect with the Orange and Alexandria railroad near Manassas Junction. A full interchange of views was had, after which the delegation retired, satisfied that nothing could be done at present, as the object in view could only be accomplished by the completion of the projected New Orleans and Boston through line, and as that project would fulfill their desires, they decided to abandon the idea of a distinct railroad connection.

A rough draft of a letter to Alderman T.C. Connolly (Secretary of the Citizens Railroad Association of Washington, D.C.) written by a local Falls Church gentleman, and dated January 15, 1870 gives us valuable information:

In our brief interview a few days since, you desired me to give you my views respecting the proposed connection of Washington

& Georgetown with the Alexandria, Hampshire & Loudoun Railroad.

A tax payer in this city for many years, and more recently a tax payer and resident of Virginia near the line of that Road, I have not been indifferent to the proposed action of the city in aiding its extension. That such connection with the Road and its extension would be productive of vast advantage to the District is, probably, doubted by very few. The only questions seem to be how far it shall be extended, and at what point the connection shall be made. There is very little doubt that its extension to Winchester Piedmont and the Coal fields of Hampshire County at an outlay of $3,000,000 will 'pay'; but considerably more as to its extension to Point Pleasant on the Ohio a distance of 330 miles from this city, in face of the competition of the adjacent lines on either side of the Baltimore and Ohio and Chesapeake and Ohio Roads, at an outlay of $15,000,000. The consideration of this question, however, may be postponed: but an immediate decision on the second question—At what point shall the Loudoun Road be tapped by the District cities seems imperative and must be preliminary to everything else. Shall it be at a point within four miles of Alexandria and by an elbow or switch at a cost of $200,000 and indeed already constructed or nearly so by other parties; or shall it be by a direct trunk as it were due west a dozen miles above at a possible expenditure of a million of dollars? Vast as is the disparity in expenditure there is no mistaking the tone of the press and people of the District on this subject—a million for the latter plan—not a dollar for the former. And yet, there can be no doubt that 'the elbow connection' would be far better than none and there is not a little force in the argument that whilst Alexandria will inevitably claim the coal, the markets of the District will just as inevitably claim the bulk of the wheat and other produce from the rich counties of Clarke, Loudoun, Fauquier &c, and that too even were the 'elbow' to exist at Alexandria itself instead of — miles above. But there is no reading down a matter of pride or prejudice and it seems to be a settled thing that the District cities would give a million—two millions if requisite, for a 'trunk connection' into the Loudoun Road and gladly aid in its extension to Piedmont, to say the least, when they would not given anything for the 'elbow connection' or any extension which they view as simply for the benefit of a rival city. The question for consideration therefore seems rammed down to this—the most feasible or practical connection by a direct line west from Georgetown to the Loudoun Road. And first what are the obstacles to be overcome and what the distance?

The directors of the Washington and Alexandria Canal, Aqueduct, Bridge and Railroad Company in September, 1869, passed an order "for the immediate construction of a railroad to,connect Georgetown with the Loudoun and Hampshire railroad, commencing at the Virginia terminus of the aqueduct, and running thence along the berm bank of the canal, and connecting with the . . . railroad near the Four-Mile run."

A proposed railroad, called the "Narrow-Gauge Railroad," was to carry passengers through Falls Church. Judge Joseph S. Riley gave land from his farm for this road. Work was begun on the route but not completed. On February 13, 1877, Mr. J.C. DePutron was requested by the Falls Church Town Council to address them on the proposed railroad, since he represented the company president, Mr. Barst. The most likely reason for abandonment of the route was the good service given by the "Electric Line"—which carried passengers to Rosslyn at the cost of 5¢ per ride. This connected with the old horse cars and cable cars of Washington. The horses used were replaced often as their hoofs suffered from the old cobble stone streets. They were sold cheaply to the various local farmers. The cars on the "Electric Line" to Falls Church were called "Yankee Jumpers."

A communication from "Falls Church and Neighborhood" dated March 16, 1872, by "Q," Special correspondent of the Republican gives some information concerning the railroad in Falls Church:

> The obstacles which have, for three or four years past, hindered the growth of our village are gradually being removed; and now that we shall very soon have easy and rapid communication with the capital both by rail and turnpike, we are congratulating ourselves on the prospect of being able, in less than a decade, to count our citizens by the thousand rather than by the hundred. Your readers are aware that the difficulty which has, for some time, existed in the Fairfax and Georgetown Turnpike Company has been amicably settled, and it is encouraging to know that at a meeting of the directors, held in Georgetown on Wednesday, instructions were given to Messrs. Phillips, Wonder and Febrig [Febrey] to proceed and open up the route to Falls Church as soon as the weather would permit. It is hoped that those who are in arrears will pay up promptly, so that the work may be prosecuted as speedily as possible, and the road opened to travel by May 1.
>
> In speaking of the obstacles which hinder the growth of our village, and indeed this section of Virginia, one is the want of a spirit of enterprise and accomodation on the part of the W. & O.R.R. Co., and these facts have opened the project of the Piedmont as a competing road. As to the enterprise of this road, we would state that the fare is four cents per mile, while on the A.W. & G. road it is a trifle over one cent. The accomodation train on the former has one car usually half filled; on the latter four cars full. Now the expense of running these two trains is about the same, yet the receipts of the latter is five or six times as great as the former. As to the spirit of accomodation, the Alexandria Washington and Georgetown will stop their train at any point along the line where one passenger may wish to get on or off, while it is with reluctance that the Washington and Ohio Company

stops more than once in going a distance of ten miles. The former would willingly fill its baggage car with freight, while the latter would refuse to take on board a window sash or a ten by twelve box. While these facts illustrate our point we cannot forego mentioning another still more pointed. Some time since seven gentlemen, who visit your city daily, sent in a petition requesting to have the accomodation train stop at a point nearer the village than the depot, and thus save them much time and exercise. Imagine their surprise when, after some days, they received a reply from the honorable president that 'he must decline.' Why, they were not surprised in the least. Now, we expect to see what we did see last summer, a stage running in successful competition with a great railroad company. And all this in old Virginia and in this nineteenth century.—Q.

With the completion of Lee Highway, and better service by rail, Falls Church became a center of commercial activity. By 1888, through the efforts of the late Mr. Merton E. Church, the Falls Church Telephone Company was incorporated. The Act was approved February 29, 1888.[9] Portions follow:

1. Be it enacted by the general assembly of Virginia, that Robert Morrison, W.H. Doolittle, Schuyler Duryee, E.J. Northrop, Doctor T.M. Talbott, D.O. Munson, M.E. Church, together with such persons as may become stockholders, their associates and successors, be and they are hereby created and constituted a body corporate by the name of the Falls Church telephone company, by which name it shall have perpetual succession, a common seal, may sue and be sued, contract and be contracted with.. . . The rights of the company to construct lines and poles, the liability and responsibilities of stockholders are given. The corporate stock of the company was not to be less than three hundred dollars or more than ten thousand dollars divided into shares of ten dollars each, and each share was to entitle the holder to one vote at a stockholders' meeting.

The regular annual meeting was to be held" in the town of Falls Church, at some convenient place, on the second Monday in January. . . . "

A picture owned by Mrs. Prentiss A. Shreve, taken June 18, 1904, shows the laying of the car tracks on the "Electric Line" when the service was extended to Robey Station (Idylwood).

Before going out of business (about 1940) "Auto-Railers" were put on the line and these could be converted to a bus or street car. Among the stations on the line in and near Falls Church, were West End, East Falls Church, Hyson's Station, Robey Station, Pleasant Valley, and Antrim. The right-of-way to Robey Station was cleared in 1903-04 and the late Mr. A.H. Holliday of Falls Church was foreman of the job. He had the privilege of driving the first car over the line, when extended to Fairfax, with the aid of the late

Chris Arnold of Idylwood. Mr. Holliday's son, Edward M.T. Holliday, owns the original handle from the first car.

This line was renamed (before 1904) the *"Washington, Arlington and Falls Church Railway."* In 1904 an advertisement of this route ("U.S. Mail Route") stated that it was the only "Line to Fort Myer, Va., and Short Route to Ballston, Falls Church, Dunnloring [sic], Vienna, Oakton and Fairfax Court House, Va., and Arlington National Cemetery... Take Pennsylvania Avenue or F Street cars to Aqueduct Bridge... F.B. Hubbell, Vice-President and Manager. . T. Garrett, Passenger Agent."

The *Washington, Ohio and Western Railroad,* now called the *Washington and Old Dominion Railroad,* was put through in 1857 with the intent of going on to Ohio. The point reached, however, was Bluemont, Va. The W.O. & W.R. (or as passengers tired of waiting put it: "the *W*ait *O*ver & *W*alk *R*ailroad") was later the *"Richmond and Danville Railroad"* and the *"Southern Railroad."* The name was changed to the W. & O.D. R. in 1912 when the route was leased from the Southern Railroad. At this time it was electrified. The railroad carried passengers as well as mail and freight. Passenger service was discontinued in 1952. The author had the pleasure of taking the "last ride" as far as Leesburg.

## FOOTNOTES

[1] The basic source of information for this chapter is a Scrapbook in the author's files which contains original letters, maps, and clippings concerning local railroad and road development, 1868-1876. The clippings are from the local County papers and those of Washington, Alexandria, and Baltimore.

[2] Williams, Harrison, *Legends of Loudoun,* Garrett & Massie, Inc., Richmond, 1938, page 195.

[3] *Acts of the General Assembly of Virginia,* 1848-49, Richmond, Wm. F. Ritchie, Printer, page 107.

[4] *Acts of the General Assembly of Virginia,* 1847-48, Richmond, Samuel Shepherd, Printer, page 191.

[5] *Acts and Joint Resolutions Passed By the General Assembly of the State of Virginia 1887-88,* Richmond, J. H. O'Bannon, Printer, page 43.

[6] This route was the old "Electric Car" line used extensively by residents of Falls Church. It was abandoned about 1940 and the tracks taken up. The route, near Fairfax Drive, is still visible in places.

[7] A clipping of January 3, 1869, states that a meeting was held on the past Saturday at the home of Mr. Allen Pierce in Alexandria County and reported that the engineer was directed to "proceed immediately to prepare the road to be put under contract," it states that the "road crosses the Alexandria and Leesburg Pike at the store of Mr. W.D. Shepherd. . . ." This was at Falls Church.

[8] Now Merrifield.

[9] *Acts and Joint Resolutions passed by the General Assembly of the State of Virginia 1887-88,* Richmond, J. H. O'Bannon, Printer, page 322.

CHAPTER 15

# Location and Natural Resources

The City of Falls Church is located about six miles from the Potomac River, and is situated in the extreme northeastern part of the state and in the southern part of Fairfax County. Fairfax County has an area less than 417 square miles and lies at an altitude of 300 feet above Washington, D.C. The topography of the County is gently rolling, and Falls Church shares in these rolling areas. The general land slope is toward the southeast. No section of the state is more abundantly supplied with pure, soft water.

The climate is mild, and the temperature in the coldest winter has not fallen lower than 5° below zero. The area in which Falls Church is located is not subjected to severe and prolonged droughts, but periods of excessive rain fall are rather frequent. The driest year in the history of Fairfax County (of which we have a written record) was in 1826 when the total amount of rain fall was approximately 19 inches. Recent climatic changes may have caused a deviation from this record. The wet year was 1889, the total amount of rain fall being 61 inches. The average snowfall is about 23.4 inches. The average date of the last killing frost is April 7th in the spring, and the first frost about October 21st. This gives an average growing season for homemakers of 197 days.

The land area is part of the Potomac River Basin, and is underlaid by ancient geologic formations. Near the soil surface is sedimentary rock strata—hard sandstones, and softer shales and limestones. These have been subject to massive erosion. Another type of soil is the sedentary—a very poor type formed from weathered rocks and red shale. This is the "Virginia red clay." The sedimentary soil is rich, fertilized by rotting leaves and rich top soil carried by rain water. The sub-soil of Falls Church is mixed with mica.

Granite is one of the most frequently found mineral rock deposits in the area. In former years it was quarried in considerable quantities in the localities south of the city and west of Alexandria. In these two localities the rock is similar and is of even texture and of good color. However, this stone cannot be obtained in large masses because of its tendency to split and break. It is strong and durable, and easily quarried.

The Falls Church Quarry, formerly known as Tripp's Quarry, was opened late in 1880 under the auspices of the late Mr. Silas Tripp, who owned the land. Later, "Uncle Charles" Tinner, a highly respected colored citizen, extracted stone there and some called it "Tinner's Quarry." The stone in the Falls Church Bank, Falls Church Presbyterian Church, and the 1909 building of the Columbia Baptist Church came from the quarry. Mr. Tripp, a Vestryman of the Falls Church, gave all of the stone in the Columbia Baptist Church in honor of his wife, who was an ardent Baptist.

The following is quoted from an article by Robert Willet and Donald Trask in *The Study of Falls Church* (1945):

> Quartz, granite, mica, and 'fools' gold' are also produced. Some stone is still being taken from the quarry but it is not worked as much as it was a few years ago. In the middle of the quarry there is a hole 35 feet deep. It is full of water which comes from a spring. The quarry has harmless blacksnakes, and also water moccasins.

In 1836 William Barton Rogers was appointed the first State Geologist of Virginia, and it was through his personal work in this field that the first geologic mineral sources survey of the state was made. This scientific application of the then newly discovered principles of geology, and the searches which have subsequently been made for mineral deposits, have added greatly to our knowledge of the geologic architecture of our state.

Sand and gravel are found in numerous small deposits, and are of commercial value. However, the section is too urban for an extensive operation in this field. For a number of years such a deposit was exploited just off Shreve Road at "Evans Hill" near present day Falls Hill. Soapstone deposits can also be found in this area. Two deposits, one near East Falls Church the other at West Falls Church, were used by the native Indians.

Our two main bodies of water are just small streams, the largest being historic Four Mile Run, and the other Tripp's Run. The highest altitude is at the city reservoir, 420 feet above sea level.

Falls Church has been endowed by Mother Nature with many beautiful meadows and hills. Trees have always been a main attraction along the streets.

Among the historic trees of Falls Church the most famous is the "Hangman's Tree," in the 200 block of West Broad Street, opposite Tyler Gardens. This old pin oak was used by a group of Mosby's men to execute a spy during the War Between the States. Witnesses to this hanging were alive as late as the 1930's. It is said that this hanging took place after the local "Battle of the Peach Orchard" (on the Riley place), and the victim was a Negro. Stories concerning this hanging were told to the author by his grandmother (who had obtained it from her grandmother, an eye witness); by Miss Mattie Gundry, Willis L. Gordon, E.H. Flagg, and C.A. Stewart.

During the severe storm of rain, hail, and high wind on Sunday night,

May 22, 1949, about 9:30 p.m., a combination of the elements wrenched many of the old branches off the tree—including a giant limb which overhung the street. A picture of the tree appeared in *The Washington Post* of May 24, 1949, with this caption:

> HISTORIC PAST—Hangman's Tree, grim relic of Falls Church's past where Confederate raider Mosby is said to have hanged Union spies, was casualty of Sunday night's storm. Two big limbs nearly 2 feet across were snapped off. One forked limb straddled a telephone cable which is shown being cleared away yesterday. The big oak stands beside W. Broad St., across from Tyler Gardens. Not more than one fourth of the tree was damaged.

On February 25, 1956 the tree was marked with a plaque by the Falls Church Woman's club. The guest speaker upon the occasion was Virgil Carrington Jones, author of *Ranger Mosby*.

Another famous tree is the Washington Poplar in the yard of the Falls Church. This tulip poplar is well over two hundred years old. It was here, according to reliable and consistent tradition, that Washington tied his horse when he attended services in the Church. In 1928-29 a disease appeared to be killing the old tree. Under the leadership of Mrs. John F. Bethune, then Regent of the Falls Church Chapter, D.A.R., the tree was repaired by the Davey Company. In March, 1951, some bark was peeled off the tree when a bolt of lightning struck it.

The beautiful silver maples which for many years lined Broad Street were planted in 1889 by a local nurseryman Colonel D.O. Munson, and Dr. Nodine. They were sacrificed in 1948-49 when West Broad Street was widened and repaired. Those on East Broad Street were cut in January, 1958.

CHAPTER 16

# Neighbors over the Fence

Many stories linger about neighbors of yesterday. One elderly neighbor was a noted talker. Having retired from government service, he had plenty of time to work his favorite hobby—"talking the horns off a brass monkey" (as one old-timer put it). According to the story, this gentleman, "Mr. B.," stopped a young man in front of Brown's Store one morning. Being a bitter cold day, the young man had his heavy overcoat buttoned to the chin. "Mr. B." became so interested in his subject that he talked on and on—and—on! The young man wanted to get to work, but in his enthusiasm, "Mr. B." took hold of the top button of the coat, holding the young man captive. Taking out his pen knife, the young man cut off the button. The next morning, when again on his way to work, he saw "Mr. B." still in front of Brown's Store—talking to the button!

In the early days of woman suffrage, Falls Church ladies gave battle. When two women were elected to the town council, it was their "big day." The term of one of the women was short, however, as she could not endure the smoking and tobacco chewing male members.

The other councilwoman stuck to her post, however, and served out her term. In those early days, the streets and roads of the town were poorly lighted, and many of the citizens carried lighted lanterns when they went abroad after dark. The indomitable councilwoman who remained at her post was accustomed to carry her lantern about the village at night. Not to be outdone by the smoking councilmen, one evening on her arrival at the regular meeting, she placed her lantern in the corner of the council chamber. It was not long before the room became stifling with smoke from the lantern. One of the councilmen called her attention to the smoking lantern, but she coolly replied that inasmuch as the men on the council smoked as much as they liked, and she was not a smoker herself, she had purposely provided her share of smoke for the evening. The gentlemen saw her point, had a good laugh at the joke which had been played on them, and after that time there was not as much smoking of pipes, cigars, and cigarettes during the meetings.

This lady, known as a "big tease" to her friends, was Miss Mattie Gundry.

197

Another neighbor, a local storekeeper, lived for a short length of time in a house on that part of Park Avenue which is between Little Falls Street and North Washington Street. In front of his house he put up a sign advertising "fresh country butter." This "fresh country butter" was well liked, and he made quite a profit selling it from his home. This was in 1885,[1] about the time that oleo margarine was put on the market and inspectors were sent out to check on stores selling the product. The local Inspector stopped at "Mr. Z's" one day and purchased a pound of the "fresh country butter." Upon testing it he found that it was oleo! Girls from Jefferson School thought it amusing when poor "Mr. Z." was caught. They nicknamed Park Avenue (or that portion between Little Falls Street and North Washington Street) "Butterine Alley"—a name which was used by them for a number of years.

Many stories linger about country stores of the gay 90's. Quentin and Archie Roosevelt, children of President Theodore Roosevelt, often visited the home of Dr. Rixey in Fairfax. On their way they would stop at Mr. Brown's store and buy cheese and crackers—which they ate on the front steps of the store. It is remembered how the late Mrs. Evelyn Walsh McLean (who owned the famous Hope Diamond) shocked the local ladies by stopping at Mankin's Notions & Dry Goods Store for cigarettes.

Among early merchants in Falls Church who maintained old-fashioned establishments were Jesse Owings, Charles E. Mankin, George W. Mankin, Mrs. Rawlings, and Edward Birch. Jesse Owings was the first merchant in Falls Church. He was proprietor of a general store which was where the Stratford Motel now stands on the corner of Little Falls Street and West Broad Street. This store was in operation before the War Between the States, and the building rented from Mr. Shepherd. The dwelling house was attached to the store. This building burned in the 1870's, and a Negro named John Jackson rented a tenant house near the site. The author has been told that in Colonial days this corner was a mail stop.

Joseph Westbury operated a bakery in the Mankin Notions & Dry Goods Building. Mrs. Herbert Nelson Hirst stated that the McDaniels family operated a store in 1895 on the first floor of the Tyson House, which faces North Washington Street behind Brown's Store. The Brush Saloon was purchased after the War Between the States by George W. Mankin, who sold it to his brother, Charles E. Mankin. The latter operated a candy and baked goods store there and later expanded into a notions and dry goods store. He sold the first yeast in Falls Church, which was made by his cook.

Brown's Store was opened by J.W. Brown, in 1883. The building was erected by Mr. Edward Birch, who maintained the Post Office there at one time. An interesting old hitching post once stood outside of the store. About 1887 some yeggs put six sticks of dynamite under the safe in the store and blew the corner off the building. While the damage was being repaired, the Browns stayed with their Mankin neighbors. Dr. Macon Ware had a coin that was in the safe at that time.

The old store until recently owned by Mrs. Dobkins and known as the D.G.S., was formerly the store owned by the firm of Abbott & Rawlings.

The following are some of the advertisements in *The Virginia Register* of December 5, 1885:

FOR SALE! Stock and fixtures of a FIRST-CLASS COUNTRY STORE! In the Town of Falls Church, Va., consisting of Groceries, Dry Goods, Notions, Boots, Shoes, Hats and general Merchandise, also Show Cases, Scales, Measures, and other fixtures necessary to carry on a first-class store. STORE & DWELLING FOR SALE OR RENT. The store room is 20 x 40 feet, with back room 12 x 20 feet. Dwelling has 10 rooms, some very large. Located in the centre of town. Reason for selling: Continued ill-health of proprietor. A good chance for a man of energy and means to carry on a first-class store. Apply to
GEORGE W. MANKIN,
Falls Church, Fairfax Co., Va.

J.W. BROWN, FALLS CHURCH, VIRGINIA. Dealer in Groceries, Provisions, Queensware, Hardware, Paints, Oils, and Varnishes. Keeps constantly on hand a full stock of the above, which he is selling low for cash. AGENT FOR THE REMINGTON CARBON PLOWS AND KINGSLEY BROTHERS' HAMILTON CREAMERY BUTTER. A share of public patronage solicited. Satisfaction guaranteed.

In this same paper one Oscar Johnson advertised that he was a dealer in ice cream, soda water, confectionery, tonic beer, tobacco, and cigars. "We aim to please—give us a trial!" He lists his establishment as "West Virginia Avenue, opp, Duryee Residence, Falls Church, Va." Mr. Greenbury Gaither advertised that he had "on hand a GENERAL ASSORTMENT OF GROCERIES, finest flour in the city, feed of all kinds, cigars and tobacco, writing paper, a fine line of notions, a stock of saddlery hardware on hand." He is listed on Virginia Avenue.[2] Mr. J.E. McCarty advertised—"Don't Forget:—call on J.E. McCARTY, who sells fine family groceries at lowest city prices. Fine family flours a specialty." Foote & Center "would say to the people of Falls Church and vicinity that they have on hand a stock of FLOUR, FEED AND STAPLE GROCERIES." Charles E. Mankin advertised that he was "Baker & Confectioner and Dealer in Toys & Notions."

Falls Church was a quiet community until about 1939, when the influx of new people brought about many changes. The author has in his possession a broadside of 1875 which gives a description of the village at that time. The broadside concerns the sale of "Hollywood Farm" in West Falls Church, later the Bramhall and Berry farm. This house was until recently the home of Mr. and Mrs. Stanley Rowland.

The circular reads:

FOR SALE! HOLLYWOOD FARM! One hundred acres, at Falls Church, Fairfax County, Virginia, situated on the Alexandria and Leesburg Turnpike, and on the Alexandria, Loudon

199

(sic) and Hampshire Railroad; about nine miles from Washington, D.C., and about ten miles from Alexandria, Va., and only about ten minutes walk from the R.R. Depot. 25 acres in timber—Oak, Hickory, Chestnut, Cedar, Pine, Locust, &c., and the residue in a good state of cultivation. A LARGE PEACH & APPLE ORCHARD, & OTHER FRUITS OF ALL KINDS. The farm is well watered, beautifully situated, and admirably adapted to the cultivation of Fruit, especially the Peach, the Grape, and smaller Fruit generally. The buildings and fences are, for the most part, in good condition. Society good, composed chiefly of northern people.

In the Village are Four Churches, a Lyceum, three stores, Wheelwright, Blacksmith, &c.;—in short, a place where Intoxicating Liquors are not permitted to be sold, and where lawyers and doctors do not flourish. Farm Stock and Implements also for sale. Prices low and terms reasonable. Apply to the owner, C.H. Bramhall, on the premises, or to Col. Wm. L. Bramhall, No. 517 Seventh Street, Washington, D.C.

This was a quiet Falls Church in 1875. Many of the well-remembered spots of the Village have long since faded from sight. The following are some of these well loved spots:

THE DRUG STORE — The first drug store in Falls Church (before 1878) was owned by Dr. J.B. Gardner, a lame man, in a building which once stood on the corner at the traffic light (the site of which was later Falls Church Garage and Kent's Cleaners).

Mr. M.E. Church started in business with a horse and wagon, and during the Spanish-American War sold drugs at Camp Alger. His shop was in the old building next to the Star Tavern. Mr. Church was later President of the State Pharmaceutical Association and was followed in that office by Dr. George T. Mankin, whom he trained.

The first building erected for a drug store was the brick building next to Mitchell's Barber Shop, in recent years having acquired a stone front and now used as a market. This building was erected in 1897-98 by Charles E. Mankin for his nephew and brother. The firm name was George W. Mankin & Son. The following is the announcement of the opening of the store, taken from *The Falls Church News* of January 21, 1898:

> Now open to the Public—Mankin Pharmacy—Washington Street, Falls Church, Va. G.T. Mankin & Co., Proprietors. New Store—New Stock. Prescriptions carefully compounded. 8—10:30 a.m. 12—1:00 p.m. Sunday, 8—7:30 weekdays.

Also from the same paper in this article:

> ONE WEEK SPECIAL ATTRACTION AT MANKIN PHARMACY For one week the largest display of National Capitol Cough Drops and Chewing Gum ever displayed in our Town direct from the manufacturer. To the first hundred

Fig. 51—The East End during the Spanish-American War, showing visitors coming to see soldiers at Camp Alger.

Fig. 52—Tents at East End, serving as receiving area for Camp Alger recruits.

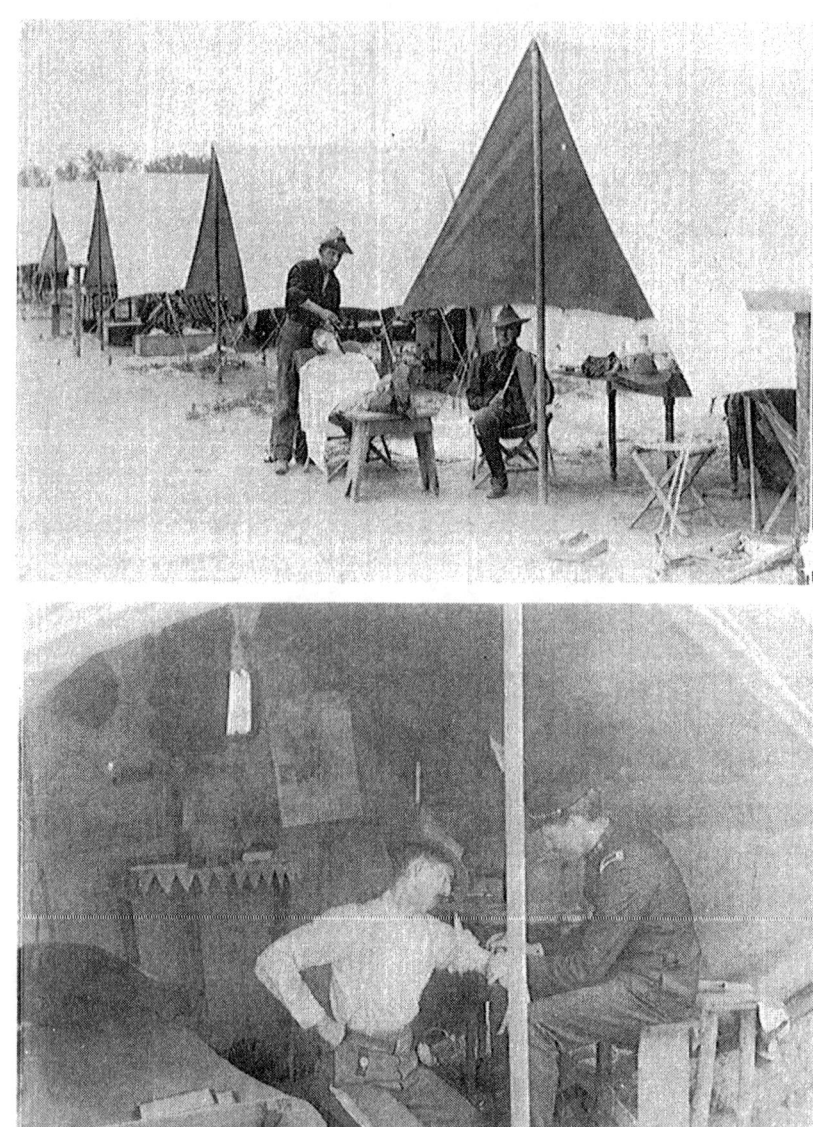

Fig. 53, a & b—Scenes at Camp Alger.

Fig. 54—Digging cut for trolley line.

Fig. 55—R.R. depots, East Falls Church, about 1921 (Penny postcard, on which the sender has written "Looks natural, eh?")

Fig. 56—4th of July celebration, Eagle House Hotel (site of State Theater); speaker thought to be Senator Daniel of Lynchburg.

Fig. 57—"Uncle Pete" Gillam, first garbage collector in Falls Church 1890.

Fig. 58—Western corner boundary stone of the original District of Columbia, erected 1791; Meridian Street, Falls Church.

Fig. 59—Brick walk on East Broad Street, 1917.

Fig. 60—Judge Joseph S. Riley, civic leader and pioneer in Falls Church incorporation in 1875.

Fig. 61—William Henry Greenbury Lynch. (Shown in his Good Templar regalia; he was a founder of Pioneer Lodge #1, the first Temperance Lodge in the state, whose first meetings were held in the Star Tavern.)

Fig. 62—Albert Wren of Longview in his Confederate uniform.

Fig. 63—Louis E. Gott, M.D., Confederate Army surgeon and physician in Falls Church for many years.

Fig. 64—Elery C. Walker in Union uniform.

Fig. 65—Minor F. Chamblin, Mayor of Falls Church, 1890.

Fig. 66—Frederick Forrest Foote, merchant, and member of Falls Church Town Council 1881-1889, serving part of the time as Secretary.

Fig. 67—Edmund Flagg, of Highland View: author, diplomat, newspaperman.

Fig. 68—America Virginia (Scott) Darne, one of the two Misses Scott taken prisoner in 1861 after they had captured a Union Captain. Buried in Episcopal churchyard.

Fig. 69—Miss Mattie Gundry, founder of the Virginia Training School, shown in her eighties.

Fig. 70—The Eastman family (l to r): **William R., Capt. Albert P., Sarah N., and Frank.**

Fig. 71—M.E. Church, founder of first Telephone Company.

Fig. 72—Harry A. Fellows, long-time Mayor of Falls Church.

Fig. 73—Ellen Lightfoot Lynch, of Big Chimneys.

Fig. 74—Ella Febrey Talbott, daughter of John E. Febrey and wife of Dr. T.M. Talbott.

Fig. 75—Joseph E. Birch, member of first town council, instrumental in founding Jefferson Institute, shown with his first wife, Delphina (Orton) Birch during the 1850s.

Fig. 76—Barbara Elizabeth (Ball) Prigg, ardent Confederate; after death of her husband operated ribbon store in Falls Church in the 1880s.

Fig. 77—Isaac Crossman, civic leader, farmer, large landowner.

Fig. 78—The Mankin brothers: (seated l to r) Alexander A., Charles E.: (standing) Benjamin A., Samuel A.

Fig. 79—William Gwynn Coe, D.D., last minister of Fairfax Chapel (1858-61), shown with his wife Anna Maria (Armstrong) Coe on their wedding day, May 4, 1853.

Fig. 80—James I. Brown, teacher at Jefferson School in the 1890s.

Fig. 81—Mrs. Louisa (Marrs) Henderson, leader in the local Negro community, shown about 1886 with her children Edwin B. (standing) and William A. Henderson.

Fig. 82—Ellison family group, 1890s: William, holding daughter Minnie; Mrs. Lillian Ball Ellison, and daughter Fannie, later Mrs. Carroll V. Shreve.

Fig. 83—Thorne family group, 1907: J. Spencer Thorne, Mildred, and Mrs. Beulah (Donaldson) Thorne.

Fig. 84—Presbyterian Picnic, July 1908, with Old Groot Hall Academy in the background.

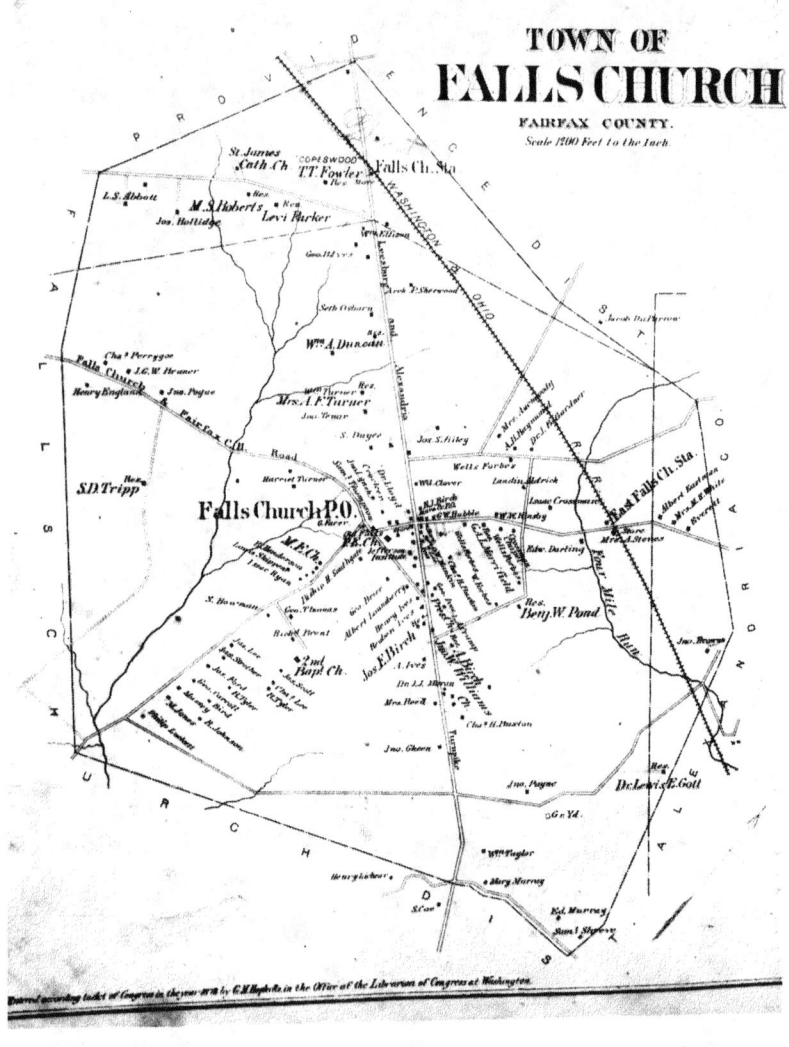

Fig. 85—1879 Map (This map and Fig. 86 are from G.M. Hopkins' Atlas of Fifteen Miles Around Washington.)

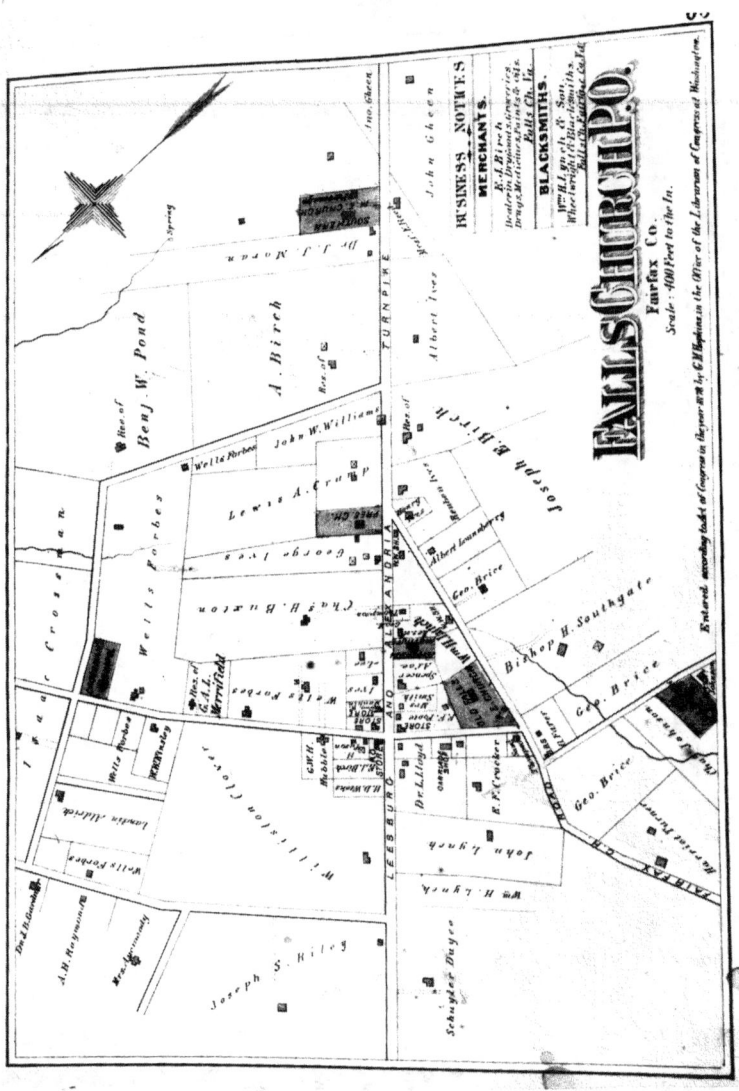

Fig. 86.—Central District of Falls Church, 1879 map.

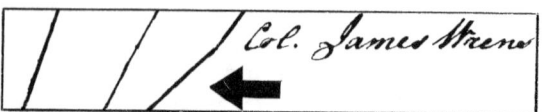

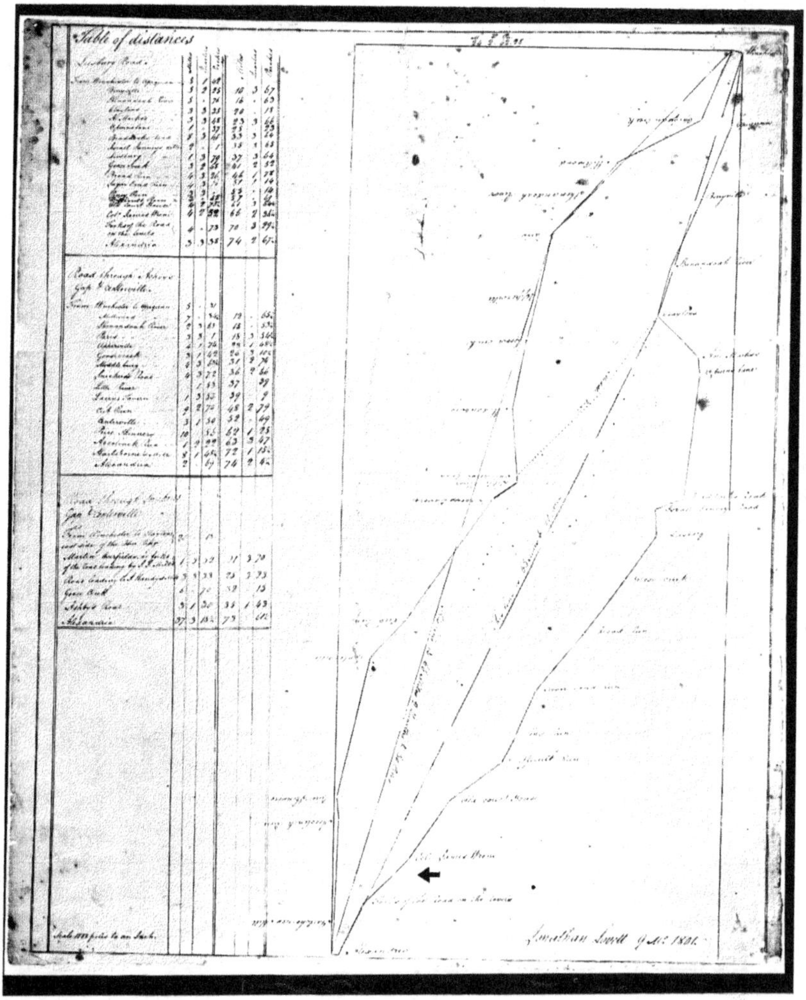

Fig. 87—Map of 1801 in which Falls Church is identified as "Wrens".

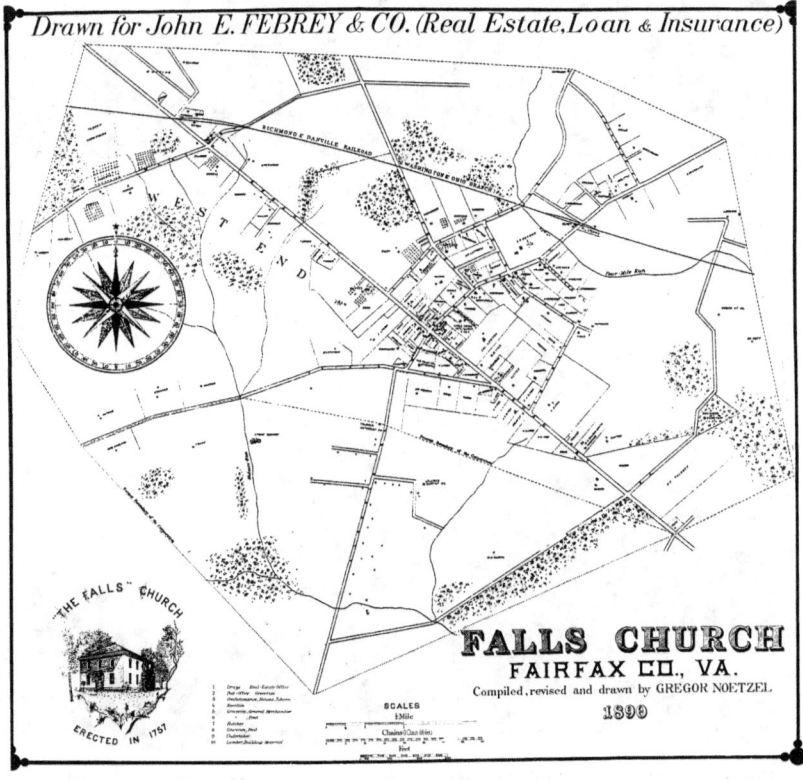

Fig. 88—Falls Church, 1890 map.

Fig. 89—Sherwood family home in 1880s, now the site of St. James Church.

Fig. 90—Charles E. Mankin Home House, about 1909. Delivery wagon of "The Sanitary Grocery Store" at right.

Fig. 91—Isaac Crossman home, nr. Columbia and N. Washington Streets, still standing. (As it appeared in the 1880's.)

Fig. 92—Eastman house, East Falls Church, Lee Highway and Washington Blvd. (As it appeared in the 1880's.)

Fig. 93—Longview (Wren-Darne house) completed 1770, home of Col. James Wren and his descendants until after 1900.

Fig. 94—1862 Brady picture of the original Columbia Baptist Church, showing (at right) rear of The Falls Church. (See also Fig. 24).

Fig. 95—1862 Brady picture of The Falls Church showing original Aquia Creek stone door framing.

Fig. 96—A third Brady view. These are the only pictures extant showing the fence which was used for firewood soon afterward. The man in Figs. 94, 95 & 96 is believed to be Matthew Brady.

Fig. 97—"Church Hill," built in 1750 by Col. Wm. Adams, as it looked during 1890s. Members of the Payne family and a former slave are standing in the yard.

Fig. 98—"Church Hill," in recent years.

Fig. 99—Bishop Horatio Southgate house, erected prior to 1860, opposite Episcopal Church on Fairfax Street.

Fig. 100—Pond House on Cherry Street in 1890, home of Rev. B.W. Pond, later home of the McGroarty family.

Fig. 101. Mankin's store as it appeared in 1904.

Fig. 102. "Cloverdale," built 1797, home of Willston Clover and of George W. Mankin; formerly faced Broad Street next to Odd Fellows Hall, moved to present Park Avenue location in 1949.

Fig. 103. Broad Street in 1860, from an original crayon picture by Miss Constance Foote. Note Columbia Baptist Church in background.

Fig. 104—First house in eastern U.S. designed by Frank Lloyd Wright.

Fig. 105—"Montpelier" (George Mason School site) picture taken in 1949.

Fig. 106—Maple trees being cut on North Washington St., 1949.

Fig. 107—"Mount Hope" during the 1880s, still standing on Oak St.

Fig. 108—"Fair Mount," still standing near 7 Corners. Built during the 1850s by John E. Febrey, later the home of Mr. A.M. Lothrop of Woodward & Lothrop.

# ANNUAL REPORT
## OF THE
## FINANCES OF THE TOWN OF FALLS CHURCH,
*Made by order of Council, June 30, 1888.*

ANSON B. NODINE, Town Sergeant, 1887-1888.

*Dr.*

| 1887. | | | | |
|---|---|---|---|---|
| July | 1. | To cash on hand, | | $152 49 |
| " | 1. | " Uncollected taxes, 1886, | | 103 14 |
| Nov. | 1. | " Taxes, 1887, turned over for collection: | | |
| | | Property Tax, | $495 14 | |
| | | Dog Tax, | 17 75 | |
| | | | | 512 89 |
| | | " Road Tax, collected in cash, | | 45 00 |
| | | | | $813 52 |

*Cr.*

| 1887. | | | |
|---|---|---|---|
| Aug. | 22. | By C. F. Wilkins, printing eight tax books, | $6 00 |
| Sept. | 19. | " Wm. M. Ellison, 3 months' salary, and printing, &c., | 13 91 |
| " | 22. | " A. B. Nodine, 14 days' work on roads, $1.75, | 24 50 |
| " | 26. | " Abatement in tax on Mrs. H. J. England's property, | 1 92 |
| Nov. | 7. | " G. Gaither, nails and shovel, | 89 |
| " | 7. | " A. B. Nodine, 14 1-2 days' work on roads, $1.75, | 25 37 |
| Dec. | 13. | " A. B. Nodine, 6 1-2 days' work on roads, $1.75, | 11 36 |
| " | 13. | " Wm. M. Ellison, 3 months' salary, | 8 84 |
| 1888. | | | |
| Jan. | 30. | " G. Gaither, 6 months' room rent and nails, | 13 41 |
| Feb. | 6. | " County Clerk fees, suit of Lloyd vs. Town of Falls Church, | 17 08 |
| " | 6. | " H. S. Rohrer, plat of town of Falls Church, | 3 00 |
| " | 6. | " A. B. Nodine, 6 days' work on roads, $1.75, | 10 50 |
| " | 6. | " Foote & Center, nails, &c., | 80 |
| April | 2. | " J. W. Brown, nails, &c., | 1 15 |
| " | 2. | " G. Gaither, 3 months' room rent, | 6 25 |
| " | 2. | " A. B. Nodine, stone and labor in improving Washington Street, | 122 90 |
| May | 7. | " Thos. Somerville & Sons, terra cotta pipe, | 6 30 |
| " | 7. | " E. G. Wheeler, 6 napping hammers, | 2 88 |
| " | 7. | " A. B. Nodine, 10 days' work on roads, $1.75, | 17 50 |
| " | 7. | " G. A. Gordon, 5 per cent. collection fee on $17.08, bill of County Clerk, | 85 |
| " | 7. | " Clerk of Circuit Court, copy of declaration, suit Lloyd vs. Town of Falls Church, | 1 75 |
| June | 5. | " Judge H. W. Thomas, for opinion as to act of the Legislature modifying boundary lines of the town, | 10 00 |
| " | 5. | " A. B. Nodine, 10 days' work on roads, $1.75, | 17 50 |
| " | 5. | " Jos. F. Anderson, sharpening tools, | 4 60 |
| " | 21. | " Robt. Morrison, docket book and blanks, | 6 75 |
| " | 21. | " Wm. M. Ellison, 7 months' salary, stationery, &c., | 21 92 |
| " | 21. | " J. W. Brown, nails, &c., | 2 08 |
| " | 21. | " H. F. D. Crocker, surveying new boundary line, | 4 25 |
| " | 21. | " Thos. Somerville & Sons, terra cotta pipe, | 7 80 |
| " | 21. | " Abatement in taxes on property of F. F. Foote, | 1 01 |
| " | 28. | " G. Gaither, 3 months' room rent, nails and shovel, | 7 01 |
| " | 28. | " Frank Burke, 67 loads of stone, at 25 cents, | 16 75 |
| " | 28. | " I. F. Norman, stone, | 18 32 |
| " | 28. | " Chas. Perrygo, 21 loads of stone, at 50 cents, | 10 50 |
| " | 28. | " A. B. Nodine, 15 days' work on roads, $1.75, | 26 25 |
| " | 28. | " F. F. Foote, Judge of Election and room rent, | 2 00 |
| " | 28. | " G. B. Ives, Judge of Election, | 1 00 |
| " | 28. | " Foote & Center, nails, &c., | 57 |
| " | 28. | " A. B. Nodine, additional compensation of 25 cents per day for 86 days' labor on roads, | 21 50 |
| " | 28. | " R. Beresford, printing Report of Committee, | 14 30 |
| " | 28. | " R. Beresford, printing Financial Statements, | 3 50 |
| " | 28. | " Cash road tax expended by order of Council for stone and labor, | 42 75 |
| " | 28. | " Taxes of 1887 uncollected, | 101 93 |
| " | 28. | " Delinquent tax, 1886, *a*, | 2 00 |
| " | 28. | " Delinquent tax, 1887, *b*, | 4 04 |
| " | 28. | " Erroneous assessment of property outside of new boundary line, *c*, | 40 46 |
| " | 28. | " A. B. Nodine, 2 1-2 per cent. commission for collection $464.67 taxes, | 11 62 |
| | | By cash on hand, | 115 95 |
| | | | $813 52 |

WM. M. ELLISON,
*Town Clerk.*

Fig. 109. Town Financial report, 1887-1888.

children under the age of fifteen calling at our store will be presented with one package of National Capitol Gum FREE. To the first ten ladies one package of National Capitol Cough Drops FREE. We need not speak of the merits of these goods, the results obtained are the most pleasing to all users.

An advertisement in the *Catalogue Of Books* of the Falls Church Library, 1903, states that G.T. Mankin & Co., Druggists, were dealers "in Drugs, Medicine, Chemicals, Toilet Articles, Soaps, Brushes, School Supplies, Etc. FINE STATIONERY."

*BARBER SHOP* The Mitchell Barber Shop was founded about the time of the first World War. In the 1880's James Johnson was proprietor of a barber shop near Lynch's Blacksmith Shop. At that time a haircut was 10¢ and a shave was 5¢. A large pole outside—partly buried in the ground—advertised the shop.

*TOWN WELL* The old Town Well stood next to Mankin's Notions & Dry Goods Store on the former drug store corner at the traffic light. The sidewalk along North Washington Street covers the old well. The well was of flint stone and had a hand pump on top. It was owned by Charles E. Mankin, but many of the local people used it.

*THE VILLAGE BLACKSMITH* The old Blacksmith shop, owned by William H. Lynch & Son, was on the site of Meese's Flower Shop; and was later owned by Robert Lee Harmon. Mr. Harmon purchased the shop in 1907 from W.N. Lynch. According to tradition, a smithy had been on the site since 1772. In 1854 the old building was purchased by W.H.G. Lynch. At that time the shop had two stories and was well fitted. Mr. Lynch hired several men to run the shop for him, and later turned it over to his son. Maurice Trammell was one of the blacksmiths. A wheelwright hired by Mr. Lynch was Albert Ives, father of Claude J. Ives. Mr. Ives sold shavings to start fires. Samuel Thompson, father of Miss Edith Thompson, was a wheelwright in the Village. Mr. Harmon was the last person to be allowed a permit to operate a smithy on the premises. After his retirement the shop was closed, much to the regret of those who love to remember "the good old days."

*FIRST TOWN HALL* Until 1953 the Falls Church Police occupied a frame building which may be recalled by some of the local residents as the Police Station. This building, on South Washington Street, was built for the first town hall. It was built about 1880 and was larger than when used by the Police Department. It originally had a gingerbread Victorian belfry tower on top. The bell was used to summon the Town Council, and as a fire bell.

*STAR TAVERN* This well-remembered building was located on the corner where the Falls Church Bank is now, and was built in the 1850's and torn down about 1926. The building was erected by Nathan Thompson and purchased by W.H. Erwin, who was proprietor until the War Between the States. It was used extensively by stage coach travelers from Leesburg and other points, en route to Alexandria. Gentlemen would ride up in the

Tally-ho, to spend the evening at games and wine. Star Tavern was similar in most respects to other Southern Ordinaries, having a broad surrounding veranda and a length of gabled house. The "public room" was just inside the front entry, and the building contained a large dining room and kitchen, with sleeping quarters upstairs. The building had a black shingle roof and a large red-brick chimney. The clapboards were painted a light cream. The namesake, the Star, was very unusual, being made of green bottle glass lighted by a candle. It stood on a length of pole to the right of the tavern. One of the last owners of the building, finding the star in an upstairs room, and not knowing what it was, threw it in the waste.

The War Between the States called a halt to business. The front porch of the tavern was the scene of the arrival of Lt. Charles Tompkins and his Company B, Union Cavalry, on June 19, 1861, and from the steps he proclaimed the village under martial law. General McClellan had his headquarters in the tavern at one time during the war.

Many stories linger from this period. One of them concerns a "yankee" who received permission to spend the night at the tavern before going on to his destination, Washington City. Mosby, the dauntless Confederate, hearing that the yankee had permission to stay there from the Union Colonel, was angered. Southern folk had not been permitted to stop there. He raided the tavern and relieved the gentleman of his money, (which happened to be one dollar)—and his pants!

The building was used for many purposes following the war. The building was remodeled and the porch torn off. A tin front was added, and Herbert N. Hirst opened a grocery store there in 1910.

*FUNERAL PARLORS* About 1890 John Wells maintained a funeral parlor at East End. E.J. Northrup owned one next to where the D.G.S. was in later years. It was moved to what is now called the Mitchell Building. In the window of Mr. Northrup's parlor was a wooden coffin which remained there about ten years. The white satin lining faded and turned yellow. This was one of the curiosities of the Village. The coffin was for a baby.

Mr. Northrup advertised in *The Virginia Register* of December 5, 1885:

> UNDERTAKING. Having purchased a FINE HEARSE, and a complete stock of coffins & caskets of all sizes, grades and prices, we are prepared to meet the wants of all who may need our services. Our stock of trimmings, linings, &c., embraces everything needed and is very fine and complete. Our previous experience enables us to GUARANTEE SATISFACTION TO ALL, very truly,
>
> E.J. Northrup & Son.

*THE EAGLE HOUSE HOTEL* was a landmark for many years in the Village. The house was on the site of the State Theater and faced the present traffic light. It was of clapboard painted yellow with a black shingle roof and green shutters. It had a cupola on the roof where the Negro help lived. The house burned about World War I. The fire was one of the largest in Falls Church and Mr. Will Edmonds stated that the paint on the back trim of his home was blistered. (Mr. Edmonds lives in the large brick house which faces East Broad Street next to Robertson's Five & Ten Cent Store.)

Mr. E.J. Northrup, the undertaker, was the proprietor of the hotel. He also operated a Livery Stable, which was later under the proprietorship of H.N. Hirst.[3]

An advertisement in *The Virginia Register* of December 5, 1885, follows:

### THE EAGLE HOUSE.

This House is newly furnished throughout and no pains are spared to provide an excellent table.

It is located high, and cool, with pleasant surroundings for summer boarders. And in winter it is heated by steam; making it a pleasant and healthful place for people of the north who desire to spend their winters in a warmer climate, near the nation's capital.

Rates reasonable.

A good, well-stocked LIVERY in connection.

Carriages will meet passengers at East Falls Church Station, on W.O. & W.R.R., on notice.

E.J. NORTHRUP & SON.

*PERRYGO'S ICE CREAM PARLOR* — This old-time popular spot was a local gathering place of the 1890's. It was opened by Mr. and Mrs. E.W. Perrygo in a building which was torn down in 1950, at which time it was known as Gerber's Falls Church Department Store. Two flavors of ice cream were served—chocolate and vanilla. It was served on tables covered with red-and-white checkered cloths, "all you could eat" for 5¢. Mr. and Mrs. Perrygo celebrated their 63rd wedding anniversary in September, 1948, at their home, 1050 Owens Road, Oxon Hill, Maryland. At that time they had 9 children, 17 grandchildren, and 10 great-grandchildren.

The 1880's, 1890's, and 1900's were good days for Falls Church—days of progress. The community was looked upon as a resort town, and people from Washington flocked here in summer. In fact, one visitor wrote a book of fiction on a summer in Falls Church. Mr. Chanell was the first person in town to have a bath room; and Mr. Hally Snyder was the first person to have an automobile. Mr. Snyder was secretary to the Secretary of War, Mr. Alger. He sold the car to Harry Turner, who in turn sold it to Dr. M.E. Church.

*GEORGE THOMAS' SHOE SHOP* — This was a spot loved by all. The small shop was attached to the Star Tavern, and was in later years owned by Dr. M.E. Church. Mr. Thomas, a colored citizen, was highly respected by local residents. He made boots and shoes for several generations of Falls Church people, and died at an advanced age. Thomas was a former slave and had served as carriage runner and gate-opener for the family of James M. Mason of Walnut Hill. The little building was moved beyond the old Police Station, and opposite the Alma Shop. It served various purposes and was partly burned in December 1951, but was repaired. George Thomas always said he wanted the marble door step to his shop for a tombstone. "All of his friends had gone over it" as one old-timer put it. No one seems to know if he got his wish.

## SOME WELL-REMEMBERED EVENTS

A Tournament was always eagerly looked forward to, and was carried out in the most festive way. The following account of a local Tournament will be of interest to the old-timers:

THE TOURNAMENT. — Our Village boys certainly had fine weather, and a fine race course, and a fine assemblage last Tuesday afternoon at their Tournament in Mr. Parker's field near the West End Depot; and there was some excellent riding by about a dozen Knights as follows: — D.B. Patterson, W.E. Parker, J. Leonard, G.W. Crossman, W. Sprangle, E.H. Flagg, H.S. Birch, W. Bernizer, E.H. Hospital, and C. Morales.

Mr. L.S. Abbott was expected to deliver the address to the knights, but being unavoidably absent Mr. Edmund Flagg at the earnest request of the Committee in Charge took his place in an off-hand and humorous speech which was well received. The riding then commenced and resulted as follows:—

Howard Flagg took 9 Rings,
Warren Bernizer took 8 Rings,
George Crossman took 7 Rings,
and James Leonard—6 in a possible 9. At the party which ensued at night at Mr. Hoagland's residence Miss Mamie Haddaway first Maid of Honor, Miss May Seaver second and Miss Libbie England third, and everything passed off excellently well. Our young friends, the Knights, wish us to express great obligations to Mr. Nat. Lynch who acted as Marshal, and Mr. Nodine, Mr. Terrett, and Mr. Thompson who acted as judges, and also to Mr. Northrup who with his large Omnibus decked with flags, filled with pretty girls and drawn by four of his fine horses contributed to render their Tournament so pleasant a success; nor will they soon forget their obligations to Mr. Flagg for his spirited speech to them in their emergency on the spur of the moment.

On the 30th of May (after the War Between the States) the entire Negro population would load wagons with flowers, and ride to Arlington National Cemetery to honor the heroic Union dead. They had a "big time," a picnic, and all the trimmings.

On Wednesday night the Protestant churches held Prayer Meeting. The congregation of Dulin Chapel did not want to appropriate money to heat the church during the winter months, so they met in private homes.

Mrs. George B. Fadeley told the author a story of interest. During the time of the temperance movement, no liquor was allowed delivered or sold in Falls Church. Word came around that a barrel of whiskey was on the porch of the train station at East End. During the night, Will Parker and another ardent temperance advocate crawled under the porch and bored a hole through the porch floor and bottom of the barrel. By morning all the whiskey was gone!

### FOOTNOTES

[1] There are interesting laws concerning the sale of Margarine, some as far back as August 2, 1886.

[2] Not Virginia Avenue of today.

[3] Another livery stable was at East End and was owned by Phil Nourse—the building of which was torn down in 1954 when the new Murphy & Ames building was erected. This livery stable was purchased by Mr. Nourse from a Mr. Purcell.

CHAPTER 17

# Friends and Neighbors At the Fireside *

There was a special place at the fireside for Mammy. She was an institution: life did not function without her. In the corner by the fire, in the best spot, was Mammy's chair. Here in slave times she nursed her "white children," gave them a growing philosophy of life, and prepared them for their place in society—a place she usually determined.

The Negro Mammy of yesterday was a basic influence on the everyday life of Falls Church. She held a respected place in the family, and her word was law. Usually a woman of superior intelligence and character, Mammy was chief among the servants (they were called slaves in legal documents).

When "Big Chimneys" was dismantled during the early 1900's, the bricks from the huge end chimneys were purchased by the Tinners and used in new Negro homes. These new chimneys were smaller, but the bricks were "at home" close to people whose forebears were part of the "Big Chimneys" fireside of other days.

Mammy at the fireside, best friend of the household, following the War Between the States became a neighbor at the fireside. The role of slavemaster was changed, but the ties of affection and friendship, could not be easily severed.

---

*In this chapter, as in references to relationships between whites and Negroes elsewhere in this book, the author has tried to reflect as faithfully as possible the actual situations as felt or recorded by contemporaries, including the terminology in common use. Probably no other aspect of American life has undergone as marked a change in the last few decades as has this one, and once commonplace words, even some indicating genuine affection, have become unacceptable in modern speech and literature. The author, far from intending any disrespect or any desire to turn back the pages of history in this connection, gladly records his satisfaction at the progress which has been made to date and his hope for a still further improvement in status and in opportunity for those whom he has ventured to describe as "Friends and Neighbors at the Fireside."

The community of yesterday, as well as the city of today, would not have its full character without the presence of its Negro citizens. For these friends and neighbors have had a vital role in the on-going of Falls Church.

The Negro people of Falls Church have always been, as a whole, a responsible citizenry. Many intelligent Negroes, former slaves, aided in the difficult adjustment following the War Between the States. They were always part of the community, even in slave times, and continued to build in the new society. One reason for the outstanding contribution of our Negro citizens was the close relationship between them and their white families. This is indicated in a deposition made by John R. Minor, of Minor's Hill, age 80 years, on January 5, 1895:[1]

> Up until the late war, when the Negroes were freed, white women and children especially used to often stay at the house of Negroes over night, and sometimes for several days and nights. The Negroes were generally their old servants, or well known to the family. The children were often left with them for several days and nights at a time, especially with their old mammys, and sometimes when children would get out with their parents they would go off and stay with old colored people in the neighborhood. I have often, myself, stayed with my old black mammy, and slept in the bed with her, even after I was quite a large boy. I remember old Frederick Foote was thought a great deal of by the white people and so was his wife, and children used to very frequently go to their house and stay all night. When he belonged to my uncle, Major Phil Minor, he had the entire charge of my uncle's place for months at a time. My uncle had a very fine place in the country (at Falls Church) but spent most of his time in the City of Washington, and as Fred was a very trusty and reliable servant, he left him in charge of everything. A great many white people used to go there when Fred and his family were there by themselves. The custom prevailed up until the late war.

This old-time Falls Church resident introduces us to some of the best known early citizens of the Negro community. Frederick Forrest Foote, Jr., served as a member of the Town Council from his appointment, August 1, 1881, until his death in 1889.[2] He served for a time as Secretary of the Council. His life history is full of interest, and a present day relative, Dr. Edwin B. Henderson, has a powder horn which came down through the Foote family, once highly prized by Mr. Foote. Dr. Henderson wrote an interesting story about the horn and the family:[3]

> [This powder horn] was the property of Col. Charles F. Broadwater, whose name and the date of manufacture (1636), is inscribed thereon. The horn was probably handed down from Broadwater's father. It was snatched by an Indian from Col. Broadwater in a fight on the Fitzhugh plantation when Chief John Logan was killed. According to legend handed down in the Foote-Hicks family, Col. Broadwater was the leader of a detachment of soldiers which left Alexandria, in 1753, to clear the In-

dians off the estate of Lord Ravensworth. In the melee, most of the Indians who were not driven away, were killed.

Among those killed was Chief John, great-grandson of Mimetou, a member of the Rappahannock tribes and Powhatan's oldest uncle. Chief John, an old man, refused to leave his wigwam and was killed. Also killed was his squaw, but his son, a papoose, was thrown aside.

An English soldier named Andrew Hicks took the papoose mentioned above, gave the baby his name and left him with the Fitzhughs to keep at Ravensworth.[4] This boy, called Andrew Hicks, married Elizabeth Mimetou Foote, a cousin of Chief John Logan. The Foote family had white and Indian blood. The Footes took their name from the family from which Admiral Foote descended.

Neither the Foote nor Hicks children were slaves at first, but living on the Fitzhugh plantation, they were kept as servants. Most of them had Indian features and hair, and some had blue eyes and light complexion. Frederick Forrest Foote, Sr., prior to his sale to the Minor family, was overseer of the slaves owned by the Fitzhughs. One of his sisters, Harriet Turner, did the buying for the Fitzhugh family. On one of her usual trips to Alexandria, with a retinue of slaves with passes, Mrs. Turner, by reason of her color and bearing, was able to flee with the group to Canada, and freedom.

John R. Minor, already quoted, made several other statements about Frederick F. Foote:

> Frederick Foote, Sr., I have known all my life. . . . Frederick Foote is a very old man. [This was in 1895]. I think he must be over 90 years of age. . . . I sold Fred Foote for Major Minor, my uncle, to a man by the name of Cook, in Washington, D.C. This was when I was a very young man. Foote was then a strong, powerful man, and I had to hand-cuff him to handle him. He must have been 35 or 40 years old at that time, but he was sold for 21, as Negroes at that age would bring a better price than older, and it was customary to sell them under age, like they do horses. Any record of his age would probably not be correct, for if he was recorded as 21 at that time it would be 10 or 15 years out of the way. . .

Mrs. Rebecca Upton Throckmorton of Washington, D.C., age 57 years, made a deposition in the Bean suit in 1893. In it she states that she was the daughter of Charles Horace and Martha Ellen Upton of Upton's Hill, and that Frederick Foote, Sr., lived near Falls Church in 1850:

> I first knew Frederick Foote and Charles Coates near Falls Church. My father and mother told me, and I have often heard others say,— that they were honest and truthful darkeys; I have never had any transactions with them, but my husband has with Frederick Foote. Frederick Foote lived with my grandfather, Captain Page for many years. When I was a little girl he was my grandfather's blacksmith, he was a very intelligent

man and considered one of the best of servants—always reliable and truthful.

In a later deposition (January 22, 1894) Mrs. Throckmorton stated that she had known him well all her life, and that "he is a man of good standing in the community, and has a remarkable memory. . ."

Frederick Foote, Sr., was born on a Fitzhugh plantation, near Burke, Virginia (probably "Cool Spring") in 1800. He died in 1895 in his home at what is now 7 Corners. Mr. Foote was twice married. By his first wife Adeline Manuel, he had issue: Rachel Foote Clay, (who had children Maggie Dutty, Joseph Clay and Caesar Clay); Ellen Foote Weston, Margaret Foote Jackson, Harriet Foote Maddox, William Foote, and Frederick Forrest Foote. By his second wife Margaret Victoria Foote, he had issue: Virginia Foote Jackson (mother of Margaret Jackson Alexander); Frank C. Foote, Sr., (father of Frederick Kenneth Foote who married Mamie Boyd); Forrest D. Foote of Linglestown, Pennsylvania (who was father of Frank and Margaret Foote); and Joseph S. Foote.

Following the Emancipation Proclamation, Frederick Foote joined the Union Army, and later received a pension. By action of the 48th Congress (Bill S.1494) relief in the amount of $1095.00 was granted Mr. Foote for supplies taken from his farm for use by the Union Army. This bill was introduced February 11, 1884. He worked for the Chesapeake and Ohio Canal on the night-shift to earn money to purchase his farm. In 1864 he purchased 33.5 acres of land at what is now 7 Corners Shopping Center for 500.00. He enlarged this to forty acres, selling some late in life. By his Will, Mr. Foote directed that the land never be sold, but must remain in the Foote family. When taxes got out of proportion, his children, Margaret Jackson, Virginia Jackson, and Frank Foote, during the 1950's, obtained release from the Will by a law suit. They sold the land for $750,000, and the 7 Corners Shopping Center was erected on it.

Frederick Forrest Foote, (called Senior), was a son of the older Frederick Foote mentioned in the depositions. When he died in 1889, the Town Council passed a resolution of honor, had it engrossed for the family, and members of the Council served as pall-bearers. Mr. Foote was not only community-minded, but owned a large grocery and provisions store on the corner of Broad and South Washington Streets (later site of Kents Cleaners). Mr. Foote was also a long-time shoemaker in Falls Church.

Mr. Foote's wife, Mary F. Foote, died in 1928. Their two children, Fred, Jr., (actually the third of that name) and his sister, Constance (called Connie) never married. Miss Constance Foote, who died in 1946, was an artist and several paintings of Falls Church of other days show remarkable accuracy. Fred Foote, Jr., died in Arlington Hospital on May 21, 1958, aged 79 years. He was buried beside his parents in the yard of the Second Baptist Church.

A long obituary appeared in *The Northern Virginia Sun*, May 25, 1958. From this we glean some details of Mr. Foote's life in Falls Church:

Fred was taught his early lessons in a school where both white and colored children attended and later went to the Falls Church colored school. . . [he] was an apt student with a bent toward scientific study and inventions. Several of his inventions are patented in the U.S. Patent office and in the Canadian Patent office.

He and his sister were great lovers of animals. He has been a large contributor to the Society for the Prevention of Cruelty to Animals.

After moving to Seven Corners Fred worked for the people in that area. For many years he was the trusted servant of Mr. Bruen, a wealthy philanthropist who built many churches, one of which is the Bruen Chapel at Merrifield.

Later Fred was in charge of the General Lane home at Seven Corners, and still later took care of grave plots in the Oakwood Cemetery. . . Fred was an avid collector of curios. He had many relics of Indians including arrow, spear heads, etc.

Fred worked for many of the older families in Falls Church, among whom were the Lichaus, Birches, Thornes and was a personal friend of most of them.

He would not have modern conveniences around him. He would not have a telephone or electricity, preferring to live as simply as did his Indian ancestors. He could tell of the Indians who migrated to the far west and Mexico coming back to call on him and his family.

He was a life-long Republican and voted each year with the exception of one year.

Mr. Foote was never affiliated with any church, and it was well known in the community that he would not lie, and kept his word. He did not smoke, drink or gamble. In later years he was a strong supporter of civil rights causes and was for many years a member of the NAACP.

Another well-known Negro family were the Coates. Old John Minor recalled Charles Coates, ancestor of all by that name in Falls Church:[5]

> I knew Charles Coates very well. He died about 3 years ago; was about 100 years old when he died; he was always considered a perfectly truthful man, and a man of excellent character. He had a most remarkable memory, and good mental faculties. I have often heard him tell of incidents that occurred during the War of 1812, and even before that time. A man by the name of Lewis, who was my father's body servant during the War of 1812, was very intimate with Coates. I have also heard Lewis tell of incidents that occurred during the War of 1812.

The Walkers were highly respected Negro citizens. John Walker, ancestor of this family, was a slave in the family of Francis Fish, Sr., and later of William Ellison (who married Elizabeth Fish).[7] Two of his eldest sons, names now forgotten, were killed while serving in the Confederate Army. They were blown up in the mine explosion at Petersburg.[8] John Walker had several other children: Aquilla Walker (who lived at Hall's Hill); George Walker (who lived in the original Fish homestead in 1894); Robert Walker, Bill Walker, John Walker, and Addie Walker. There may have been others. John Walker's granddaughter, Addie Walker, was a respected citizen of the Shreve Road Negro community (which was called "Gravel Bank").[9] Her son, Vernon Byrd Walker, lives in Falls Church.

Will Rector, who once worked for the Rowells, Birges and Rileys, was an enterprising barber at West Falls Church.[10] His children included Charlie Rector, highly respected citizen (whose wife, Hattie Rector, was loved by all); and William Rector. William Rector, better known as Brooks, had a large family by his wife, Anna Mae, many of whom live in Falls Church.

Henry and Julia Rector, husband and wife, were well-known members of this family. During ante-bellum days they were slaves of prominent families; one belonged to the Randolphs, the other to the Magills.

Aunt Fanny Robinson was a practical nurse and midwife who delivered several generations of local children. She lived with her husband, Mitchell Robinson (who, for some reason, was never called uncle), at Merrifield. Mr. Robinson farmed for Judge Riley. Mrs. Charles E. Gage recalls that Aunt Fanny was tall and thin, with gray hair, parted in the middle. She had a sweet and gentle voice, and was greatly loved. Her husband was good and honest.[11] The last baby delivered by Aunt Fanny was the late Brooks Oden.

Aunt Caroline Kerfert [Kerfoot] was another trusted and beloved citizen. A former slave, Aunt Caroline worked for most of the better known citizens of Falls Church. She was a good worker and particular about the families who hired her. She was an employee of Mrs. William H.G. Lynch for many years. Aunt Caroline never married, and it is thought she had no relatives in this country. As one old resident put it, her many friends made up for the lack of them. It is difficult to piece together the story of her long life. She was said to be the daughter of an African Chief, and brought to this country before the War Between the States. During her life-time, Aunt Caroline practiced her "religion," that of voodoo, spirit worship and animism. She arose with the sun, to worship, and also had a ritual for the sunset and full moon. If a rainbow or full moon appeared, Aunt Caroline put on a fresh white apron, and would go into the middle of Broad Street for her "spirituals." Swinging a small silver pail over her head, she would sing and chant something that sounded like: "Hello Mr. Dave, hello Mr. Will." Her spirit worship did not prevent her regular attendance at the Methodist Church.

Uncle Pete Gillam was the local garbage collector during the years prior to 1900. Uncle Pete was known far and wide. A jolly, kindly man, and a dwarf, he was loved by all. Miss Sue Riddle (sister of the local Presbyterian Minister) said that the Lord made Uncle Pete "just the right weight for sawing wood easily." He was the first garbage collector in the town.

James Lee and family were long-time and honored residents of the town. Mr. Lee was a trustee of the Second Baptist Church in 1871 and later. A modern-day descendant of this well-known family is Avon Lee, who was an employee in Brown's Store for many years. The family is recalled in Falls

Church by the James Lee Elementary School. This family has long been known for their well-kept home and grounds. The Village Improvement Society many years ago offered a prize to the family which kept the best looking lawn in Falls Church. James Lee and family won this prize in competition with all of the other homes in the entire community.

The "Hill" has long been the Negro community in Falls Church. This includes Shreve Street from Hillwood Avenue to Jefferson Village. This was part of the Dulany estate, and given originally by that family to their former Negro slaves. The Negro families on the Hill were paying monthly on this property, but had no titles. Judge Riley helped obtain titles for them and put an end to this unhappy practice whereby a white citizen (not a member of the Dulany family) took advantage of them.

The "Southgate Subdivision" was an early Negro community, developed by Dr. M.E. Church. The Brices and others owned lots in this subdivision— probably the first for Negroes in America. Negro citizens also lived at the Gravel Bank in West Falls Church, and near the Falls Church.

Among the early Negro families were those represented by James Cook, George Whitfield, Charles Lee, Clara Weaver, John Jackson, Lee Gaskins, Charles Harris, Jacob Brice, Asbury Honesty, Charles Tinner, Eli Brooks, and Robert Swails. These lived in Falls Church during the 1870's and 1880's.

The Honestys, Tinners, and Lees were superior people. The Tinners are descendants of Uncle Charles Tinner and his cousin, also named Charles. Uncle Charles Tinner and his wife, Aunt Caroline, were loved by all of the old-time residents. She had a special rocker in the Charles Mankin home with a pillow. Aunt Caroline would visit for an afternoon, rock and smoke her pipe. Uncle Charles lived on the DePutron place a number of years before moving to the Hill. He had a number of children including Wesley, Charlie, Joe, Frances Coates, Winston and Melvin who married Rose Rector. Chester, Guy, and Ollie Tinner belong to the other branch of the Tinners, that of Charles, cousin to Uncle Charles Tinner. Mr. Ollie Tinner is a well educated and prominent citizen.

One early free Negro in Falls Church was Samuel Hyson. He died in 1853 at the age of 45 years and was buried in the Fairfax Chapel Methodist Cemetery. His tombstone is still to be seen in Oakwood Cemetery on the old Chapel lawn. Hyson's Station, on the old street car line, was named for this family. Uncle Bink Hyson was a son or grandson of this Samuel Hyson.

Henry Simms, a native of Dranesville, who died April 10, 1959, at age 73 years, spent forty-three years as a smith at Harmon's Blacksmith Shop, on East Fairfax Street. He was employed by Mr. Harmon in 1915, and retired in November, 1958. In the last years he was able to shoe 25 to 30 horses a week, most of them from fashionable schools.

One long-time neighbor was George Thomas. He came to Falls Church at the close of the War Between the States and spent more than fifty-seven years as the local shoemaker. His shop, adjacent to the old Star Tavern (site of the Falls Church Bank) was a gathering place for the community. He was eighty years old and still the community shoemaker when interviewed

December 2, 1928. During this interview Mr. Thomas gave some interesting recollections of Falls Church. A copy follows:[1][2]

> I was born a slave in 1848 on the plantation of Cook Fitzhugh. The plantation consisted of more than 2,000 acres and borders on the limits of the magisterial district of the present Falls Church. I have seen as many as 150 slaves assembled on the place at one time. Neighboring plantations were owned by the Dulins, and other Fitzhughs.
>
> During the war and just before, the slaves were allowed to attend services in the rear of the old Episcopal Church at Falls Church and we occasionally heard preaching by some Negro who had been permitted to preach. Before the war there was quite a belief in the power of magic and hoodooism or voodooism. I have been taken by my mother to visit the practitioners of this art to find out things my mother wanted to know. Even today there are some people about here who believe in the power of magic. One of the Negro preachers who traveled in my day before the war was a man named Hawley.
>
> Shortly after the war began, a man named Reed, who lived on the present site of the Virginia Home for feeble minded persons, taught school for the benefit of many of the Negroes who would come to his home. He also taught Bible lessons at a Sunday School. He was Captain of the Home Guards. One night Mosby's men came into town and because of Reed's relations to Negroes, took him out into the pines about the house and shot him and two other men who lived with him.
>
> In 1865 Thomas Green and "Bill" Stuart came into the town after service in the Army and began to hold prayer meetings along with George Rumbles, and Nathan Rumbles. The first two men were Baptist, and the others Methodist.
>
> At an old house on what is now the "Pickett" Place, the four would meet with ex-slaves from the plantations and elsewhere and hold prayer meeting nearly every night. These meetings were held during the years, 1865-1866. Shortly afterwards the colored people were given an old log house which was moved piece by piece from a site near the present railroad and put on the land now belonging to Mr. William Henderson. Two rooms were built for the two white women who came into town from the north to teach Negroes. This old log building located on the railroad was used as a freedmen's camp for slaves who ran away during the war. The land now owned by Mr. Henderson [the shopping center, including the Hobby Shop adjacent to the Falls Church in 1964] belonged in those days to the Rev. Hiram Reed, a white man, then living where his relatives had been killed by Mosby's men. He would meet with the colored people in one of these rooms and exhort with them. It was here that the Baptist Church was planned and organized.

Later in 1867, the Methodist people were given the old loading platform at West Falls Church station and built a school house a little back of the present Methodist Church. It was here where Mrs. Rugg and her daughter [perhaps the white teachers from the North] taught Sunday School. The Methodist believers used this as a church building until much later on.

Shortly afterwards, Mrs. Rugg moved away and the partition was knocked from between two rooms on the present Henderson land, and regular church services conducted often by Rev. Hiram Reed were held. It was then the Second Baptist Church was organized. He encouraged Rev. Johnson then a soldier, recently returned from the war, to qualify for the ministry. Johnson was finally ordained at 19th Street Baptist Church in Washington, D.C., and took charge of the Second Baptist Church in Falls Church. In 1872 an excursion was given to Richmond which was the beginning of the attempt to build the new church.

After the building was erected it was used as a public school during the week and the school was taught by Mrs. Ada Gray of Arlington, who was the first colored school teacher in town. Johnson was thrifty. He bought a tract of land, sub-divided it and sold it to many of the colored people now living in Falls Church. Afterwards he received a call to the Metropolitan Baptist Church in Washington. After Rev. Johnson moved to Washington several ministers were called until the time of Scott. It was in his pastorage a split occurred when he was removed by the church board. His attempt to resist removal caused a civil court case but he lost out, and his followers planned another church, the Third Baptist Church which although pretentiously begun, was poorly built. This church never made much headway and today is poorly attended and its worship marked by much of emotional religion of the old days.

In the early days many white people who lived in the town from the North helped in the church and the sunday schools. Rev. Johnson a white preacher was one of the many white people who came south at the close of the war. He began his service in the town by legally marrying Negroes who had been man and wife in the old slave days and who had no legal status as married couples.

Dr. E.B. Henderson recalls the many white citizens who aided in this early attempt at establishing churches.[13] He received his first Sunday School training from Miss Sue Riddle, and heard the late Mr. Fenwick preach in the colored churches.

The land for the Second Baptist Church was one-half acre conveyed to the trustees by George Pulver. On July 7, 1871, George Brice and Harriet, his wife, conveyed a strip of land ten feet wide to the trustees in consideration of $30.00. The trustees were: Eli Blackwell, Andrew Tillman and

James Lee.[14] The deed was written and witnessed by Jesse Owings, another white friend of the Negroes.

Galloway Methodist Church (first called Watkins Chapel) was built on land donated by George and Harriet Brice (parents of Mrs. Bertie Honesty and Mattie Hunter Brown).[15] The first trustees were: George Rumbles, Robert Gunnell, and Sandy Proctor. The first minister of record was the Reverend Edgar Murphy in 1867. He was followed by Noble Watkins, Robert Wheeler, Winston Galloway; Joseph Henry, Samuel Aqualla, John H. Jackson, Bernard Martin, Benjamin Newgent, John Barnett, and John W. Galloway. The last named left in 1900.

Mrs. Harriet Brice's former master gave the timber for the building from his land. The lumber was hewn by the Reverend Mr. Watkins and others. Mrs. Bertie Honesty, daughter of the Brices, later gave land for a Parish House.

In 1871 Charles Tinner became a member of Galloway Church, having been a member of the Baptist Church in Alexandria. The Tinners have been loyal workers in the Church.

Uncle Aleck Tillman, a former slave, was a well-known resident. He moved in later life to the Gravel Bank in West Falls Church. By his wife, Aunt Alice, he had a son, Andrew, and daughters Dealy and Martha.

Aunt Caroline Granderson was another long-time resident. She was highly respected. Her grandson is Fred Dulany.

Henry Taylor was an early resident. His wife owned a store at the corner of South Washington and Fairfax Streets in the long ago.

The Jones family were also prominent in the community. Mary Jones married Frederick Foote, who was a member of the Town Council. Her family included a brother, Emory, a sister, Della, wife of Bunk Lee; and a sister who was the first wife of George Thomas.

Modern Falls Church has been blessed by many outstanding Negro leaders. Dr. Harold M. Johnson, scholar and top-flight physician, has many white patients. He was recently invited to lecture before the University of Madrid, Spain, and taught at Howard University Medical School, 1938-52. Since 1953 he has taught at Georgetown University.

No man has a higher place in state and community life than Dr. Edwin Bancroft Henderson. Dr. Henderson represents an old family. His father, William Henderson (originally named Peter Ridogruiz or Ridogruis—spelling uncertain) was the son of Shadrach Ridogruiz, a native of Portugal, and Eliza (Hicks) Ridogruiz-Henderson. William Henderson was born in Natchez, Mississippi, Semptember 27, 1860, and lived in New Orleans and Vicksburg. His father, Shadrach Ridogruiz, joined the Confederate Army from Vicksburg and never returned, probably killed in action. Mrs. Eliza (Hicks) Henderson was a daughter of Andrew and Elizabeth Mimetou (Foote) Hicks, and a granddaughter of Chief John Logan. She was almost pure Indian, with some white blood. Mrs. Henderson was thus a niece to the first Frederick Foote. She had the following brothers and sisters: Haywood Hicks, Elizabeth (Betty) Hicks, who married Mr. Collins and was the mother of Dr. Albert Collins a well-known physician; Ellen Hicks, Margaret Hicks, married Richard Moss; and Marietta Hicks, married Jenkins.

Mrs. Eliza Henderson came to Falls Church about 1900. She owned the land between the corner of East Broad and South Washington Streets extending to the old Falls Church. Her granddaughter, Mrs. Annie Henderson Briggs, has developed this property with stores in recent years. Mrs. Henderson also owned the property (now owned by Dr. E.B. Henderson) on N. Fairfax and South Washington Streets. On this property was an old log house, the old tobacco storage house of the Falls Warehouse. Mrs. Henderson owned this as a rental property many years before it was destroyed by fire. Before coming to Falls Church she owned a store at 471 School Street, S.W., in Washington, and also had property on E Street next to the Fourth Street Police Station. Her daughter-in-law, prior to World War I built a store in Falls Church which she owned for many years, and located next to the old Church.

William Henderson, the son, married Louise Mars of Williamsburg. She was the daughter of a Negro mother and white father. Her father, Mars, owned a house adjacent to the Bruton Parish Church in Williamsburg. The Williamsburg Building, recently built next to the Falls Church Library by Mrs. Annie Briggs, was named in honor of Mrs. Henderson's birthplace. Mrs. Henderson was born September 22, 1862, and at the age of 14 came to Washington, D.C. Her sisters, Alice and Mollie Mars, also came to this area. The mother, Annie, who married later to Fleming Thomas, continued to reside in Williamsburg. Mrs. Henderson was an official member of the Eastern Star, and active in community affairs. She died September 20, 1961. Mr. Henderson died February 9, 1934.

William and Louisa (Mars) Henderson had the following children: Dr. Edwin Bancroft Henderson, born November 24, 1883, married Mary Ellen Meriwether; William Alonzo Henderson, born April 2, 1885, married Louise Grant; Charles Milton Henderson, born December 30, 1890, married (1) Nettie Langston, granddaughter of Congressman Langston, and (2) Beatrice Cooper; and Annie Eliza Henderson, born June 15, 1892, married Eli J. Briggs. Mrs. Briggs lived in Atlantic City for a number of years, and was later an employee of the government. She has developed a number of stores in Falls Church and has been active in community life.

Dr. E.B. Henderson served as president of the Virginia Branch of the National Association for the Advancement of Colored People and is program chairman of the Fairfax County Council of Human Relations. He serves as a member of the Board of Directors of that same organization.

A teacher in the Washington schools for many years, Dr. Henderson served as Director of Physical Education in Negro Schools. He has written several books, among them *The Negro In Sports* (Associated Publishers, Washington, 1939 and 1949). This book is an authority in its field, and contains 507 pages.

Dr. Henderson was married in Washington on December 24, 1910. His wife has been identified with many organizations and community projects.

She is active in the League of Women Voters, the Falls Church Women's Democratic Club, the NAACP, and the Girl Scouts. In 1959 Mrs. Henderson received an award from the Fairfax County Girl Scout Council for outstanding leadership in the organization. She was the first Negro to be elected vice president of the Democratic Women's Club of Falls Church (1959). Mrs. Henderson taught in Washington schools, and for thirty years served as principal of the James Lee Elementary School in Falls Church.

Both Dr. and Mrs. Henderson were educated at Howard University and Columbia University. Mrs. Henderson also attended Virginia State College.

On December 8, 1960, Dr. and Mrs. Henderson were honored for their community service by a special party held at Annandale Methodist Church, given by their many friends.

The Hendersons have two sons: Dr. Edwin Meriwether Henderson, a graduate of Howard University, served as a Major during the Korean War, and is now a dentist on the staff of Group Health Association, Inc; and Dr. James Henry Meriwether Henderson, presently head of the Department of Biology at Tuskegee Institute. The latter received a grant from the National Science Foundation to do research at the Sorbonne in France.

The author would like to pay tribute to the many kindly Negro neighbors he knew as a child — Charlie Collins, Estelle Collins, Cindy Collins, Jim Jones, Mrs. Maggie Phillips (who often brought by delicious strawberries from her well-known garden); Aunt Matt James, Jesse James, Blue (his real name not known to the author); and many others. They made their way along the same old roads, and gave their share to the common good.

As well-diggers, farmers, carpenters, shoemakers, merchants, and educators, the Negroes have left their impress on Falls Church. Their life in Falls Church, one of friendly cooperation and usefulness, will ever be a mark of honor and distinction.[16]

[1] In the Bean law suit, "Sarah A. Dove, et al, vs. H.P. Howard et al," filed in Fannin County, Texas. (See *Murray*). This deposition, and others made in the suit, contribute valuable data on some of the early Negro citizens of Falls Church.

[2] His appointment, signed by Dr. William B. Nodine, Town Clerk, states that he was elected Councilman "to fill the vacancy caused by the refusal of Councilman-elect L. E. Gott to qualify." Foote's election certificate was signed on August 20th.

[3] MS. document in the author's files. Dr. Henderson owns the powder horn, having received it from the estate of the late Fred Foote, Jr.

[4] Ravensworth was the Fitzhugh home, and no record has been found of Lord Ravensworth. The author's best understanding is that Colonel William Fitzhugh named the plantation in honor of Lord Ravensworth, a close friend, for whom he had power of attorney. The estate was owned by his descendants, including Robert E. Lee. The widow of Dr. George Bolling Lee sold the estate in 1956.

[5] Deposition in the Bean suit dated January 5, 1895.

[6] Aunt Leah Lewis, beloved neighbor, was a daughter of this Minor slave. Aunt Leah, at age 80 years, made a deposition in the Bean lawsuit on January 10, 1890 (that portion entitled "W. W. Russell appellant vs. H. P. Howard et al"). She said she was born and raised in Fairfax County, near Falls Church. About sixty or sixty-five years earlier (ca. 1830) she lived with old Billy Gordon the tavern-keeper. William Gordon owned Taylor's Tavern (at 7 Corners) before the Taylors.

[7] Interview with Miss Minnie D. Ellison, April 21, 1963.

[8] Interview with Mrs. Leonard P. Daniel, June 3, 1964.

[9] Addie Walker washed clothes for the author's paternal grandmother. She was a highly valued person in his early childhood.

[10] Will Rector also ran a store at West Falls Church.

[11] Interview with Mrs. Charles E. Gage, November 20, 1962.

[12] Copy supplied by the Reverend C. C. Wilson, July 10, 1958. The interview was recorded by Dr. E. B. Henderson.

[13] MS. document in the author's files.

[14] Fairfax County, *Deed Book L No. 4, page 241*.

[15] Data supplied by Mrs. Estelle J. Evans, July 10, 1958.

[16] The author wishes to acknowledge the help of a number of friends. Mrs. Annie H. Briggs, in an interview July 13, 1964, was especially helpful. Her brother, Dr. E. B. Henderson, very kindly checked this chapter for errors. Dr. Henderson's MS. history, *Earliest Inhabitants of Falls Church, Va.*, dated February 20, 1948 was most useful.

# Biographical and Genealogical Sketches

Falls Church firesides are attractive in this modern day, but during the less tangled days before and following the great North-South struggle, they were warm and beautiful. The wide hearth at Big Chimneys was much like many others, and was scrubbed clean and sprinkled with clear sand. The wide logs burned with a sparkle showing up the glitter in the sand. During mid-March the first tender young greens were cooked in ham broth over the fire, with a fragrance beloved by generations of Virginians.

Mrs. Mary Lynch's salt-rising bread was baked to a golden turn in the adjacent Dutch oven. One thing long remembered by the Big Chimneys family was the fragrant fireside.

From the Big Chimneys fireside has come a variety of people, known and unknown, many of whom have been good citizens. Typically American, the *dramatis personae* form a cross section of our national life. They are typical in the sense that they have touched the life of Falls Church as planter and pioneer, banker and merchant, author and teacher, doctor and lawyer, office-holder and private citizen; few very conspicuous characters, many respectable ones, and a few over whom charity's veil may be thrown.

The Big Chimneys fireside, like the old worm fence surrounding the adjacent fields, has completely disappeared. Its embers no longer glow in the shadows of a long winter evening, nor honeysuckle and hundred-leaf roses twine over the mellow worm-turned fence rails. Yet the Big Chimneys family goes on, like hundreds of their neighbors: some of these sterling old Virginians, somewhat tarnished with the years, will be given only a "lick and a promise" here, with apology to them for no further delineation.

## THE ABBOTT FAMILY

George Abbott, ancestor of this family, was born in England, and came to Andover, Massachusetts, in 1640. He died in 1681. Joseph Abbott, one of his descendants, lived with his wife, Hannah, in Lancaster, Massachusetts. Their son, Ebenezer Abbott, born October 14, 1753, enlisted as a private in Captain Haskell's Company of Colonel Asa Whitcomb's Regiment, on April 25, 1775. He was in the Battle of Bunker Hill in June, 1775, and was discharged in December, 1775.[1] In 1780 Mr. Abbott moved to Chester, and married there on December 13, 1781, Anna Wright. In 1810 he moved to Washington, Massachusetts, and in 1826 to Cuyahoga, Ohio. Elisha Abbott, son of Ebenezer and Anna (Wright) Abbott, was born September 9, 1799, and died in St. John's, Michigan, in October, 1869. He was the father of Lewis Smith Abbott who settled in Falls Church.

Lewis Smith Abbott was born in Painesville, Ohio, on January 25, 1823, and died at his Falls Church home on January 20, 1898. Mr. Abbott lived for a time in Rowley, Massachusetts and Reading, Michigan. At age 17 he was a student in the Painesville Academy taking an intensive course in Latin and Greek. He took up Journalism, and on May 13, 1855, purchased *The Painesville Telegraph* which he edited until 1863. Mr. Abbott came to Washington, D.C., in July, 1865. He was a long-time friend and correspondent of Horace Greeley, Salmon P. Chase, and James A. Garfield. Although he studied law and was admitted to the bar, Mr. Abbott never practiced. He was an employee of the Treasury Department for many years. In 1873 he moved to a small farm, formerly part of the "Walnut Hill" (Sewall) estate, and built a house which is now the home of his granddaughter, Miss Mabel Kennedy. "Abbott's Orchard" subdivision on West Street is on this property.

Mr. Abbott "always manifested an interest in local affairs,"[2] and was correspondent for a number of western papers. He also contributed articles from Falls Church to the Washington papers.

On September 4, 1847, Mr. Abbott was married to Mary Persons Briggs, as his first wife. She was born in Wales, New York, April 18, 1823, a daughter of Simon B. Briggs. Mrs. Abbott was a brilliant woman, a writer with promise. One small volume of her work, published at Painesville, Ohio, in 1851 by Scofield, is entitled *Poetical and Prose Writings of Mrs. Mary P. Abbott*. She died on May 28, 1849.

In 1854 Mr. Abbott remarried (to his first wife's cousin), Harriet Jane Briggs. She was born August 19, 1828, and died January 22, 1912, with burial in Oakwood Cemetery. A beautiful printed booklet, *In Memoriam*, was published by her children following her death. Mrs. Abbott was an accomplished lady and an ardent member of Crossman Methodist Episcopal Church.

Lewis Smith Abbott had issue (*by Mary Persons Briggs*):

(1) Mary Loretta Abbott, born August 23, 1848, married Lawrence Wilson. Mr. Wilson served as 1st Sergeant of the 7th Ohio Volunteers. His Diary of the war is now in the Library of Congress, having been placed there by his niece, Miss Mabel Kennedy. Mr. Lawrence was the author of a two volume history, *Seventh Ohio O.V.I., 1861-1864*. Issue:

(11) Lawrence Wilson, Jr., married Ellen Wilson and had two children.

(12) Mary L. Wilson, unmarried.

(*By Harriet Jane Briggs*):

(2) Howard Briggs Abbott, born October 1, 1859, built the large house (later owned by the Cowgill family) near his home place. Mr. Abbott married (1) Mary Lou Lampman; and (2) Mattie ——. By his first marriage, issue:

(21) Walter Grant Abbott, married twice, no issue.

(22) Alta Virginia Abbott, living, unmarried.

(3) Alta Virginia Abbott, born September 7, 1862, in Reading, Michigan, died at Falls Church, April 1, 1951. She married John Kennedy, a native of Ottawa, Illinois, son of Joseph and Mary (Wolf) Kennedy. His parents were natives of Ireland and spoke

Gaelic in their home. Mr. Kennedy was a partner of Howard Briggs Abbott in a ranch in Kansas and it was there that he met his future wife. Issue:

(31) Harriet Briggs Kennedy, taught in Washington schools, and died unmarried.
(32) Mabel Louise Kennedy, taught for more than forty years in Washington schools, and is unmarried. Miss Kennedy inherited the literary inclinations of her family, and has been a frequent contributor to scholarly journals.
(33) Mary Kathleen Kennedy, died at age 3-1/2 years.

(4) Lynn Smith Abbott, born January 18, 1873, married Blanche May Freeman of Chicago. Issue:
(41) Charles Abbott, died at about age two years.
(42) Roderick Abbott.
(43) Antoinette Maine Abbott, married John Evans Hutton.
(44) Virginia Eloise Abbott, unmarried.
(45) Lynn Stratton Abbott, lived in England.
(46) Gwendolyn Jessica Abbott, unmarried.
(47) Jean Abbott, unmarried.
(48) Clifton Abbott, married twice and had a son named Lynn by his first marriage and a son by the second marriage.
(49) Yvonne Abbott, married Richard Johnson and lives in Morris Plains, N.J.

---

[1] Information taken from a *Family Bible* owned by Miss Mabel Kennedy. See also U. S. Pension File, U.S.M.S.F., #2027.
[2] *The Falls Church News*, January 21, 1898.

---

## THE ADAMS FAMILY

John Adams, ancestor of the Adams family of "Church Hill," was probably the immigrant, and owned land on Hunting Creek as early as 1677. He died in 1725 at an advanced age, leaving a family. This John Adams was not connected with the Adams family from Charles County, Maryland, whose members also lived in the same Hunting Creek vicinity of the then Stafford County.

Gabriel Adams, Sr., a son of Gabriel Adams and a grandson of the above John Adams, was a large land owner, and between 1726 and 1741, acquired over 3,000 acres of land. A modern-day descendant, Mrs. Earle T. Mutersbaugh, lives on a portion of this land. On September 19, 1730, Adams patented 790 acres on Lucky Run, a branch of Four Mile Run, including the area now owned by the Episcopal Theological Seminary. In 1731, with Simon Pearson, he purchased 708 acres including what is known as Franklin Forest (Minor's Hill). Adams is mentioned in the will of Captain Augustine Washington, father of George Washington. Captain Washington purchased a 700-acre tract in Prince William County from Adams. Adams was a vestryman of Truro Parish and was serving in this capacity in 1733 when the first Falls Church was built.

Gabriel Adams, Sr., married Priscilla Pearson, daughter of Thomas Pearson, and thus allied himself with the aristocracy of colonial Fairfax, including the Broadwaters, Wests, and others. Adams' will, dated on January 19, 1749, was probated December 27, 1750. Executors were his sons, Gabriel, Jr., and William. He also mentions his other children: John, Silvester, Catherine Earl, Simon, and Susanna Summers. He also mentions as legatees, Elizabeth Nevet and Benjamin Williams (called "Grandson"). Witnesses were John Summers, David Thomas, and John Thomas.

There may have been a son, Philip Adams, not mentioned in the will since he died before 1749. This Philip Adams signed a power of attorney for Priscilla Adams (probably his mother) to Robert Bates on May 14, 1733. His name appears first, followed by that of Gabriel Adams, Jr. This Philip Adams married Eleanor Thomas, daughter of William Thomas. She made a nuncupative will on March 6, 1749 (probated March 27, 1750). In this (according to oaths of Daniel Diskin, Mary Diskin, and Ann Thomas), she stated that she was the widow of Philip Adams and left children: Joseph, Ann, Jane, Sarah, Jacob, and William. The last four were minors and were to be reared by her brother, William Thomas. Her Testament (in 1749 owned by John Withers Harper) was to go to her son Joseph. William Thomas, in his will of January 21, 1755, mentions his wife, Catherine, and his sister's children, Joseph Adams, Ann Adams, and William Adams. William Adams at the time was under age. Witnesses to the will were Thomas Osborn, Robert Duke, and Robert Moxley. This William Adams, born, it is thought, about 1738, died in Vermilion Co., Ill., December 16, 1829. He was married in December 1799 in Harrison Co., Ky., to Nancy McCarty Crook, widow of James Crook. He probably married prior to this, but no record has been found. He was about sixty years old when he made this second marriage. Nancy Adams was born in Fairfax County about 1760 and died in Vermilion County, Illinois, May 11, 1830. Her first husband, James Crook (whom she married in 1780), died in Kentucky in 1797. She was a daughter of James and Ann (Nancy) Bozeley McCarty. Rose McCarty, born 1805, wrote in her Bible that Nancy Bozeley and Elizabeth Nevitt (Nevet) were her great-great-grandmothers, the former a native of Scotland and the latter of England. This Elizabeth Nevitt was undoubtedly the one mentioned as a legatee in the will of Gabriel Adams, Sr. William Adams, who married Nancy McCarty, purchased land at Cythianna, Harrison County, Kentucky, in 1812. He was a veteran of the Revolutionary War. Samuel Adams, only son of William and Nancy (McCarty) Adams, was born in Harrison County on April 27, 1800. He moved to Illinois in 1825 and his parents followed in 1826. Samuel Adams died in Vermilion County, Illinois, May 17, 1881. He married twice, and by his second marriage had a son, Lemuel Perry Adams, born May 2, 1854, died March 19, 1927, whose daughter, Mrs. Ethel Adams Thompson of Benton Harbor, Michigan, is tracing this branch of the family.

Gabriel, Sr., and Priscilla (Pearson) Adams had the following known children:

(1) Gabriel Adams, Jr., born 1715[1] died in Loudoun County, Virginia in 1761. Gabriel Adams made his will on March 30, 1761, and it was probated in Loudoun County on June 9, 1761 (*Will Book A, page 35*). In it he mentioned that he was sick and weak, and devised his estate to his wife, Elisabeth, and mentioned his eldest son, Philip Adams. He mentioned his three sons, "all my boys," and apparently had children by two wives. He stated in the will that "all my boys" were to stay on the plantation with their mother-in-law (i.e., step-mother) for one year, then they were to be bound to his brother, William Adams, until twenty years of age. Particular reference was made to their education. Witnesses to the will included: William Stark, William Littleton, and Benoni Dement.

Inventory of the estate of Gabriel Adams was presented to the court on March 11, 1762, by Charles Tyler, Justice of the Peace, returned by Richard Coleman, William Stark, and William Littleton. (Loudoun County, *Will Book A, page 48*). An account of this estate was returned by William Adams. In it mention is made of the widow, Elisabeth Adams (who received one third of the estate), money paid Daniel McCarty for rent, also money paid David Thomas. Reference is made to George McDonald's note (this may be George McDaniel) and James McCarty's note. The account was returned August 9, 1763, and amounted to £ 5141, 131, 11, 1½.

(2) John Adams, born ca. 1715, married Susannah—and had issue:[2]
   (21) John Adams.
   (22) George Adams (ca. 1744-1805) of Cocke County, Tennessee, who married and had eight children: William, (1766-1836); Daniel, Elizabeth, Susannah, Winifred, Sallie, George, and Nancy.
   (23) Jeremiah Adams.
   (24) Daniel Adams.
   (25) Joshua Adams
   (26) Silvester Adams.
   (27-2.11) Five other sons. Note—It may be that Samuel Adams who married Jemima Darne was a son of this John Adams and belongs here. It may be that Samuel was a son of Gabriel Adams, Jr. (1715-1761).

(3) Simon Adams.
(4) (Colonel) William Adams, married Ann Lawyer.
(5) Silvester Adams.
(6) Catherine Adams, married ————— Earl.
(7) Susannah Adams, married John Summers.

Colonel William Adams, son of Gabriel, Sr., and Priscilla (Pearson) Adams, was born in Fairfax County (at that time Stafford County) on November 3, 1723. Colonel Adams was prominent in county affairs, serving as colonel of militia and sheriff. He took oath and gave bond as sheriff of Fairfax County on November 23, 1768:[3]

> William Adams Esqr. produced a Commission from his Excellency the Governor appointing him Sheriff of this County.

Henry Gunnell and James Wren signed as co-bondsmen. On the same day Pierce Bayly, John Ratcliffe, and Augustus Darrell were appointed "Sub Sheriffs" by Adams.

Colonel Adams, like his father, was a vestryman of Truro Parish. He attended the Falls Church and in 1770, according to Washington's ledger, Adams collected £ 1 from him "By Mr. William Adams for my subscription toward decorating the Falls Church." Washington and Adams had business and friendly associations over a long period of years. "Church Hill," the Adams home, adjoined land owned by Washington. On April 4, 1799, General Washington, with adjoining land owners, Captain William Henry Terrett, Colonel Charles Little, and Adams, made a survey of his land. He wrote in his *Diary*:[4]

> Recommenced to survey at the upper end where we left off in Company with Colo. Little, Captn. Terrett and Mr. William Adams and continued it agreeably to the notes until we came to 4 Mile Run again, which employed us until dark.

Adams owned a mill near where the Columbia Pike crosses Holmes Run, and the stone ruins were in existence in 1949. William Watters conveyed this property, under terms of the will of William Adams, in a record at Fairfax Court House which shows an excellent survey of the property.[5] Adams owned large tracts of land near Bailey's Cross Roads and Chesterbrook. His home, which is still standing, was owned at one time by Mr. and Mrs. Donald Macleay. It is now known as the "Dower House," but was known in early days as "Church Hill," and by neighbors of the 1870's as the "Payne House."

Although originally a loyal Anglican, Adams became a member of the Methodist Episcopal Church before his death. Bishop Francis Asbury made the Adams home his headquarters and conducted services there, as did William Watters and others. Asbury called it "Adams Church" in his journal. It was a forerunner of Fairfax Chapel.

Bishop Asbury wrote in his Journal of Saturday, May 12, 1781:[6]

Reached Mr. Adams's about eight o'clock at night: I always come to this house weary, but generally get my body and soul refreshed. I missed my watch, but found it again at the door where I had alighted; my horse had trodden it and bruised the case, and not broken the crystal, without otherwise injuring it.

To this house rode William Watters, first native-born itinerant Methodist preacher, and here he married Sarah, daughter of William Adams. Mr. Watters was the means of the conversion of Mrs. Adams, who later was agent for the conversion of her husband and ten children. There was a special bond between Watters and his mother-in-law, and as we shall see later he wrote of her in a moving way.

Colonel Adams married Ann Lawyer of Stafford County.[7] She died December 25, 1788, at the age of 56 years. Mrs. Adams is often called the "first Methodist" of this area. Her life was one of kindness and good will. In 1773 she was converted to Methodism, although she had been a loyal member of The Falls Church. Three of her sons became Methodist preachers, and their influence was felt over pioneer Methodism. The Adams home was the first preaching place in Fairfax County. William Watters, her son-in-law, wrote in 1806:[8]

My wife's mother, Mrs. Ann Adams, departed this life December the twenty-fifth, one thousand seven hundred and eighty-eight, after being in a very weak state for several years. She was in my estimation, one of the best of women....

Mr. Adams died September 4, 1809. His will (made March 7, 1806, probated October 20, 1809) gave freedom to over twenty slaves. Both Mr. and Mrs. Adams are buried on the farm.

The Adams home later passed into the hands of descendants named Lipscomb and Payne. Edward Payne was the last of the family to reside there. The property was divided and the tract with the old home was set aside as Dower, hence the name "Dower House."

Colonel William and Ann (Lawyer) Adams had the following children:
(1) (Honorable) Simon Adams, married Catherine Wren.
(2) (The Reverend) William Adams.
(3) (The Reverend) Samuel Adams, married Hannah Wren.
(4) (The Reverend) Wesley Adams, married (1) Catherine Alexander Binns; (2) Ann Summers; (3) Elizabeth Hughes; and (4) Priscilla Larkin.
(5) John Adams, married Sarah ―――.
(6) Sarah Adams, married (The Reverend) William Watters.
(7) Edward Adams, married Jemima West.
(8) Ann Adams, married Colonel George Minor.

(9) Susannah Adams, married (1) Lewis Hipkins; and (2) Richard Wren.
(10) Margaret Adams, married (The Reverend) John Childs.

(1) (Honorable) Simon Adams, son of Colonel William and Ann (Lawyer) Adams, was born in Fairfax County about 1750. During the Revolutionary War Mr. Adams served as a soldier in Captain Thomas West's Company, 10th Virginia Regiment (which was called the 6th Virginia Regiment after 1778). He enlisted May 1, 1777, for three years, and re-enlisted at Middlebrook, December 17, 1778. Mr. Adams settled near Lexington in Shelby County, Kentucky, in 1786. He was a merchant in Shelbyville from January 1797 to December 1800. His account book is owned by a descendant in Ohio. Mr. Adams was prominent in early Kentucky politics and served in the Kentucky Territorial Legislature. Under date October 8, 1808, there is a list of patrons of a school he agreed to teach for that term (1808-1809). Another Kentucky descendant has a "Diploma" dated October 25, 1799, which states that he "had been raised to the sublime degree of a Master Mason."

Mr. Adams married Catherine (Catey) Wren, daughter of Colonel James and Catherine (Brent) Wren of "Winter Hill." She was born at "Winter Hill," about 1760, and died in Shelby Co., Ky., in 1835. She remarried on December 13, 1810, to John Hite, and the ceremony was performed by the Reverend James Blair. Mr. Adams died in December, 1809. He was en route to Kentucky from a visit to Virginia, and was robbed and murdered in the Kentucky mountains near a place now called Pineville.

Judge Thomas Scott, former minister of the Fairfax Circuit of the Methodist Episcopal Church, once met Simon Adams in after years at the home of Colonel Ebenezer Zane in Wheeling. He has left the following account of this meeting:[9]

One day when seated alone in the parlor a handsome, well-dressed intellectual looking man entered without ceremony and as he approached me he held out his hand and said "my name is Simon Adams, and I presume your name is Thomas Scott, the preacher in charge of this circuit." Being answered in the affirmative, he, at my request took a seat, and entertained me very agreeably with his conversation for about one hour, when he took his departure. He was brother to the Reverend Samuel Adams and brother-in-law to the Reverend William Watters of Fairfax County, Virginia, and was then on his journey home to Kentucky from a visit he had paid to his parents, and other relatives and friends in old Fairfax. He gave me a graphic description of Kentucky, an interesting account of the spread of Methodism over that region of country. . . .

Simon and Catherine (Wren) Adams had a number of children, but the following is the only one for which there is a record at present.

(11) (The Reverend) William Adams, married Ann Standiford.

(11) (The Reverend) William Adams, son of the Honorable Simon and Catherine (Wren) Adams, was born in Fairfax County on June 29, 1785. His obituary, published in 1836, gives the following information:[10]

His family emigrated to Kentucky at an early day, and settled near Lexington. Piously educated, he joined the Church at an early age, say fifteen, made profession of the knowledge of salvation by the remission of sins soon after, and in 1813 commenced preaching. In 1814 he joined the travelling connection, and continued regular and effective as a travelling preacher up to the period of his death. Possessed of a good, strong mind naturally, that mind was handsomely stored with valuable information. To no mean pretensions of scholarship, especially as it regards English literature, he added an admirable store of theological attainments: and few men have appeared upon the same theatre whose every day performances, throughout the year, ranked higher than those of William Adams. Although seldom overpowering in the pulpit, he was always lucid, strong, and convincing. His manner was singularly suasive and impressive. His moral and religious worth was universally known and appreciated among those who enjoyed his acquaintance. Grave and serious in manner, he was at the same time cheerful and amiable. Studious and laborious in his habits, he was always social and accessible. He lived beloved and died regretted by all who knew him well, and especially by those who knew his value as a member, and for many years the secretary, of the Kentucky Annual Conference. His death was not only peaceful, but signally triumphant.

Mr. Adams died in Shelby County, Kentucky, in August, 1835. He married in 1803 Ann (Nancy) Standiford. Mrs. Adams was a daughter of Revolutionary War Ensign David Standiford who took part in the exploring expedition of George Rogers Clark. Standiford was among the first trustees of Shelbyville, Kentucky. Mrs. Adams died in Shelby County in 1837. They had among other children, a daughter, Frances, who was born in Shelby County, November 24, 1808, and died in Troy, Ohio, March 6, 1892. On October 5, 1826, she married the Reverend William Gunn (born March 13, 1797, in Caswell Co., N.C.; died in Lexington, Ky., September 3, 1853). Descendants of this family continue to reside in Kentucky.

(2) (The Reverend) William Adams, Jr., son of Colonel William and Ann (Lawyer) Adams, died unmarried on December 3, 1779. William Watters, his brother-in-law, wrote of him as "a man of a thousand." Watters wrote of his funeral:[11]

January 1st one thousand seven hundred and eighty. I preached a funeral sermon over one of my wife's brothers, who was one of the preachers that rode Baltimore Circuit with me the two last quarters. A young man who lived holy and died happy. Many had expected that he was to be a very useful man in the vineyard; but he was cut off before he had quite reached twenty one.

Watters wrote an account of the life of William Adams, Jr., which was first privately printed, and later published in *The Methodist Magazine*. Watters wrote in his *Short Account:*[12]

Having struggled through the winter, and at last obtained help on which I could depend; in the beginning of April (1781), by making short wages, I once more visited Philadelphia, and agreed with a friendly man to print me three thousand copies of the life and death of my brother-in-law William Adams. From thence I visited my friends in several places of the Jerseys. . . .

(3) (The Reverend) Samuel Adams (called Samuel Adams, Jr.) according to Watters the eldest son of Colonel William and Ann (Lawyer) Adams, was born ca. 1755 and died August 7, 1805. He married Hannah Wren, daughter of Colonel James and Catherine (Brent) Wren. William Watters wrote of Samuel Adams:[13]

(Samuel) was a married man when he first embraced religion, and soon after began preaching the gospel. He possessed considerable preaching abilities— with a good utterance and a graceful delivery. In the early part of his life he travelled more or less for several years; but as his family concerns increased, he declined that entirely for many years. He departed this life August the seventh, one thousand eight hundred and five, after an illness of a few days, that appeared no ways alarming, until two or three days before his death. . . He was a little turned fifty years of age, a remarkably well and healthy looking man.

On December 20, 1806, Simon and Catherine Adams, Edward and Jemima Adams,[14] John and Sarah Adams, Wesley and Ann Adams, William and Sarah Watters, Richard and Susanna Wrenn, and Hannah, relict of Samuel Adams, deceased, late of Fairfax County, deeded land to John Childs of Alexandria, D.C. This deed recites that during his lifetime, Samuel Adams deeded to John Childs land which he had purchased on July 18, 1788, from James and Mary Robertson. However, Adams failed to have the deed filed. Hence, the "legal heirs and representatives" of Samuel Adams gave their consent and made a deed to Childs.

Samuel Adams ("Jr.") made his will November 20, 1791, probated September 16, 1805, in Fairfax County. A codicil was dated March 27, 1799, concerning his slaves. In the will he gave freedom to his slaves Sall and James. All other slaves (not named) were to have their freedom. He gave "Fifty pounds . . . to the building of Methodist meeting houses," and the rest of his estate was given to his wife for her lifetime. Following her death the estate was to be divided between his brothers and sisters. His "wearing apparrel" was to be divided among his four brothers.[15]

Hannah (Wren) Adams, widow of Samuel, made her will on August 12, 1812, probated February 19, 1823 (Fairfax County *Will Book N#1, page 81*). In the will she mentioned her nieces, Hannah Smith, Kitty Hughes, and Hannah Adams Hughes (the last named were sisters). Witnesses were: Wesley Adams, Betsy Adams, and William Payne.

Samuel and Hannah (Wren) Adams had no issue.

(4) (The Reverend) Wesley Adams, son of Colonel William and Ann (Lawyer) Adams, was a prominent clergyman in the Methodist Church. A notice of his family can be found in the *William & Mary Quarterly* (New Series), Vol. 6, p. 354. He married (1) on January 15, 1795 Catherine Alexander Binns of Loudoun County, daughter of Colonel Charles and Ann (Alexander) Binns. She died January 6, 1796. Mr. Adams married (2) on February 14, 1796, Ann Sommers, daughter of Simon and Elizabeth Sommers (both of whom are buried in the Falls Church yard). She was born in 1781 and died January 22, 1807. On November 24, 1808, Mr. Adams married (3) his cousin, Elizabeth Hughes, daughter of William and Elizabeth (Wren) Hughes, and a granddaughter of Colonel James and Catherine (Brent) Wren. She died in Tallahassee, Florida, February 7, 1827, and was buried at the Methodist Church, but later reburied at "Greenwood," Thomasville, Georgia. Mr. Adams remarried (4) on June 24, 1835, to Mrs. Priscilla Larkin of Tallahassee. Children:

*(By Catherine Alexander Binns):*
*(41)* Elizabeth Alexander Lawyer Adams, born January 6, 1796; married on March 11, 1813, to Richard Tidings.
*(42)* Wesley Alexander Lawyer Adams (twin of Elizabeth) was born January 6, died January 8, 1796, and was buried with his mother.

*(By Ann Sommers):*
*(43)* Susannah Adams, born December 3, 1799.
*(44)* Austin Lawyer Adams, born August 21, 1801, married on December 25, 1823, to Harriet Harding.
*(45)* Herbey Adams, died November 14, 1823.

*(By Elizabeth Hughes):*
*(46)* Ann Elizabeth Adams, born October 27, 1809; married on December 24, 1822, to Richard Harding.

*(47)* William Hughes Adams, born August 10, 1811; died September 18, 1812.
*(48)* Dr. Seth Samuel Adams, married Mary Frances Bryant.
*(49)* John Wesley Adams, born April 17, 1815.
*(4.10)* Catherine Sarah Ann Drucilla Adams, born July 21, 1818; died July 9, 1820
*(4.11)* Drucilla Amelia Adams, born April 15, 1821, died at Thomasville, Ga., September, 1841.
*(4.12)* Mary Jane Adams, born November 9, 1823.
*(4.13)* Hannah C. Adams, married on February 16, 1831, to Darius Williams of Monticello, Fla.

Of the above named children, *(48)* Dr. Seth Samuel Adams, was born May 26, 1813, and died at Thomasville, Ga., March 23, 1889. He married, on June 9, 1842, Mary Frances Bryant of Boston, Mass. Children:
(*481*) Wesley Bryant Adams, born 1843.
(*482*) Ann Elizabeth Adams, born June 9, 1845; died at Rome, Ga., Nov. 20, 1913 married William Frederick Penniman.
(*483*) George Henry Adams, died July 25, 1885.
(*484*) John William Adams, died 1867.
(*485*) Richard Adams.
(*486*) (The Reverend) Charles Darius Adams, a Methodist Minister, died December 6, 1923, at Pooler, Georgia.
(*487*) Mary Frances Adams.
(*488*) Mitchell Jones Adams, died 1890
(*489*) Samuel Wesley Adams, born May 18; died June 18, 1844.

(5) John Adams, son of Colonel William and Ann (Lawyer) Adams, was born at "Church Hill," in 1771, and died at Leesburg, age 69 years. His tombstone states that he died December 1839, age 70 (Old Stone Methodist Church Cemetery). The *Christian Advocate* (New York: March 6, 1840) states that he was "awakened" thirty-five years before on the Fairfax Circuit where his family once lived. Adams was a Class Leader in the Old Stone Church at Leesburg. His obituary states that he was a brother of the Reverend Wesley Adams of Florida. The obituary was signed by J. Berkley. John Adams married Sarah ———— (no other record).

(6) Sarah Adams, daughter of Colonel William and Ann (Lawyer) Adams, married The Reverend William Watters on June 6, 1778. Mr. Watters, first native-born itinerant Methodist minister, was born in Baltimore County, Maryland, October 16, 1751, and died at his home near what is now Chesterbrook, Fairfax County, Virginia, March 29, 1827. Mrs. Watters died October 29, 1845. There were no children of this marriage. She is mentioned a number of times in her husband's "Short Account," and from this and other records it would seem that she was a constant sufferer, and something of a saint. In 1806 Watters wrote that she was always the most sickly of the four (eldest children of William and Ann Adams), . . . . (and) is the only one of them now living.[16] She made her will on March 14, 1845, probated January 5, 1846.[17] In the will she mentions her father, William Adams, (land given her by Adams containing 57 acres). Mrs. Watters mentioned her house and lot in Alexandria on the South side of Duke Street between Royal and Fairfax Streets, "Now occupied by Benjamin Lambert." She left $100.00 to her faithful friend Nancy Magruder. She also mentioned her niece, Sarah A. Jacobs, friends Isaac Robbins and Benjamin Watters of Alexandria, the latter Executors. By this will Mrs. Watters

directed that her slaves were to be free. She also provided that the money from the public auction of her estate would be divided among the four daughters of her nephew Hugh Minor by his wife Ann: Elizabeth Minor, Martha Waring, Gertrude West, and Mary F. Clagett; also between Sarah Frazier of Kentucky and a niece, Mary Y. Wren. Witnesses to the will were John L. Ager, Joseph Longson, and James Donaldson.

(7) Edward Adams, son of Colonel William and Ann (Lawyer) Adams, married Jemima West, daughter of Hugh and Elizabeth West. On July 28, 1794, Edward and Jemima Adams conveyed to Josias Clapham of Loudoun County, for 20 pounds current money, a lot containing twelve acres near Nolands Ferry in Loudoun County. This land had been left to Jemima Adams by Colonel George West. It is also noted in this deed that Mr. Hugh West, deceased, was her father. This deed was witnessed by Thomas Gunnell, James Turley, Henry Gunnell, Thomas Asbury, and John Jackson.

On November 3, 1789, William Adams "Of Fairfax County," made a deed of gift to his son Edward, for "and in consideration of the Natural love and affection which I have, and bear unto my well beloved son Edward Adams." The land conveyed, in Loudoun County, was purchased by William Adams from William Beavers, and adjoined the lands of Captain William Ellzey. The farm was "commonly known by the name of Beavers Farm," and contained 415 acres. Witnesses to the deed were: John C. Moss, John Potts, Ann Moss, William H. Harding, Wesley Adams, and William Roper.

Edward and Jemima (West) Adams had issue (known):

(*71*) Elizabeth Adams, who was mentioned in the will of Mrs. Sybil West, widow of Hugh West, made September 16, 1786.

(8) Ann Adams, eldest daughter of Colonel William and Ann (Lawyer) Adams, was born in 1752, and died in December 1786, aged 34 years. She married Colonel George Minor of "Minor's Hill." The old house on "Minor's Hill" is still standing, though much remodeled, and is the home of the Harwood family. George Minor was a convert to Methodism and contributed the land for Fairfax Chapel. Minor was a Justice of the County in 1784. (*See Minor Sketch*) William Watters wrote of Ann Minor:[18]

... Ann Minor, wife of George Minor, Esq., departed this life in December one thousand seven hundred and eighty six, in the thirty fourth year of her age. To look at the picture of health (indicating long life) but cut off in a few days, by a violent fever, that appeared to be contagious, and was brought into the family (it was thought) by a negro girl.

(9) Susannah (Sukey) Adams, daughter of Colonel William and Ann (Lawyer) Adams, was born May 18, 1766. One record states that she died in 1849, but a family Bible gives her death as May 8, 1854, age 88 years. She married (1) January 17, 1782, to Lewis Hipkins. Mr. Hipkins was born May 20, 1753, a son of Andrew and Jane Hipkins. He died July 27, 1794. Mrs. Susannah (Adams) Hipkins remarried (2) about 1799, to Richard Wren, a son of Colonel Thomas Wren (III) and Susannah (Sanford) Wren. Mr. Hipkins was the subject of almost fourteen pages of the "Short Account" by William Watters. Hipkins died as a result of the bite of a mad dog on "the 3d or 4th of last June, (1794)[19]. . . just as he stept out of the boat at Georgetown ferry." Watters wrote that Hipkins was at the time of his marriage, and some years afterwards, "a pretty constant attendant at our Chapel (Fairfax), and was at times under good impressions. As he got into business and company, his serious impressions wore off, and for several years past, I have too much reason to fear, he had his

doubts of all revealed religion, yet not so, as openly to avow it." Even though Watters felt that his friendship with Hipkins, both as "neighbours and connexions" was from the beginning (twelve years before) sincere, he still felt it necessary to write him on the subject of his religion, "without reserve." Mr. Hipkins immediately sent the following answer, "which will show that his mind was still open to conviction":
> I am glad to hear you are so far recovered from your late illness, as to be (I trust) out of danger. Your admonitions I take as a friendly pledge of the goodness of your heart towards me, as I have always done in every instance of the sort, and always am obliged to you for every thing of the kind, as I am well satisfied they flow from a pure principle. I cannot so well express to you the language of my heart, but believe me my dear Sir, to be very affectionately,
> Your assured friend, &c.<br>LEWIS HIPKINS.

February 11, 1794

Watters writes that upon hearing of the affair at the Georgetown Ferry, he felt "much alarmed," and went immediately to see Mr. Hipkins. He found him "serious, and ... full of thought. He had been with a Doctor, and had sent to a Dutch Doctor in Pennsylvania, concerning whom he had received several letters from different Gentlemen in Georgetown, assuring him of the infallibility of the medicine, which, with the encouragement his friendly physician had given him, kept him in pretty good spirits." He was in such good spirits that he failed to continue the medicine, even with the entreaty of Watters. On Wednesday, July 23, he was "taken with a stretching, and a light chillness, something like the approach of the ague and fever." By Friday Mr. Hipkins "took to his bed," but still did not realize his danger.

> ... in the fore part of the night, being prevailed upon to take a sup of tea (for he had taken nothing all day,) as he put the cup to his lips and attempted to sip, he first perceived the hydrophobia on him, and throwing his hand and cup from his mouth, fell back on the bed, and as soon as he could well speak told his wife it was all over with him. He suffered violent pain between his shoulders, and in his breast, and thought he could not possibly live till morning. Saturday morning before I was out of my bed, a messenger came for me in all possible haste.

Watters found Mr. Hipkins full of remorse, and his condition continued to decline. On Saturday Mr. Hipkins had settled "his worldly business" and made his will. This will, on file at Fairfax Court House, is dated July 26, 1794, and was probated October 21, 1794. In this he mentions his wife, Susannah, his children, Elizabeth, Ann, Sarah, Lewis and Andrew; and named his executor, Philip Richards. Witnesses to the will were Fendall R. Young and Thomas Darne, Sr. Watters continues by saying that on Sunday morning he proposed to ride home for a few minutes, but Hipkins "absolutely refused, telling me that though I had twenty appointments I should not attend one of them that day; but after understanding that I would assuredly return in an hour or two, he reluctantly consented." Watters returned about eight o'clock, and found him "past taking any more medicine." He could not bear any kind of liquid to be near him, but was in good sense and "would answer any question and converse on any subject." He frequently "told me that he hoped that all good people would pray for him."

> The Doctor had been taking off his blister plasters, and was about to tie the handkerchief that went around his body, on his breast—he started and refused

to let him, for fear (he said) he should bite him. The Doctor replied—no—you will not bite me. He added God bless you, I would not for the world; but I am afraid I shall do it involuntarily. He then caught up a handkerchief and held it between his mouth and the Doctors' hands while he tied the knot. He frequently requested that we would confine him with ropes, lest he should hurt some of us. —But I never perceived any thing like an attempt to bite, or injure any one. As his convulsions became more violent the Doctor directed me to appoint four strong men and place two on each side the bed, to prevent his rising, to keep the clothes over and to watch him in all his movements.

Watters writes that his heart and eyes "were continually so full that I hardly knew how to contain myself in his room, without once in a while withdrawing a few minutes," and whenever he did so, Mr. Hipkins called for him. A short time later Mr. Hipkins requested him to pray, the doors were closed with a "few only in the room, the rest (for by this time many had gathered) were in the passage and in the other room," and they prayed. He confessed to Watters that he had been affected by his searching letter of a few months past, and expressed his high regard for him. Hipkins began to call upon God to have mercy, and Watters was standing by his bed about three or four o'clock on Sunday afternoon when Hipkins fell "into a violent agony of soul and body" and cried aloud "'will none of you pray for me?'"

I was awfully struck and fell on my knees with many others around his bed side, and began crying to God in behalf of his salvation. The clouds burst, and the very heavens appeared to open with blessings, and the power of God's Spirit was felt by many present. . . .

When the assembly arose from their knees they stood about the bed in a flood of tears, and he said to his wife:

. . . My dear Sukey, pray to God Almighty for my soul, and for your own soul, and for the souls of * * * * and if you should ever have another husband, I pray God he may be a better one to you than ever I have been . . . .

He continued in scriptural language to exhort, and "seldom he could repeat one verse correctly. . . I would repeat to him any part of holy writ, applicable to what he was saying, he would receive it with all possible eagerness, running before me in the repetition. When I would assist him in prayer as I stood by his bed, frequently offering up short sentences for him, he would with the greatest sincerity and fervour of soul cry out with a loud voice—Amen!—and sometimes—Amen! Amen! and I say, Amen!"

He said the spirit is willing—I answered but the flesh is weak— He replied, I think it is too strong— I added too weak to do good, but too strong in doing evil. He eagerly said—Ah! That's it—that's it.

To an old acquaintance he said: O Tommy! (probably Thomas Darne) how often we have spent our time walking about the fields scheming for the world; but we were not serving God then. Lord make me thy servant, though it be the least in all thy kingdom.

The end finally came and with "the greatest exertion of his remaining strength he cried out—Christ is the Son of God— THE ONLY SON OF GOD. And after his speech was brought down to a whisper, and his senses I suppose must have been very imperfect, I heard him distinctly, though feebly utter—CHRIST, GOD—CHRIST, GOD." Thus closes the most dramatic account of death this writer has ever seen. It should be read in full, yet the book is not available except in rare book collections.

Mrs. Hipkins-Wren made her will on May 8, 1847. It was probated May 21, 1849.[20] In it she mentions her son, Thomas S. Wren (Executor); her brother, Samuel Adams; and her son, Andrew Hipkins. Witnesses were William Nelson, John W. Marriott, and Nathan Kell.

There is a deed of record dated December 3, 1803,[21] between Philip Richard Fendall, William Watters, and Robert Young, executors of Lewis Hipkins, deceased, of the first part, and Richard Wren (who married the widow Hipkins) of the second part, conveying to Wren—for $1,344.00, the land originally owned by Captain Charles Broadwater and later by William Adams. Adams deeded this land to Hipkins on September 20, 1790. The tract was said to contain 207 acres, but a "new survey" showing 160 acres corrected this figure. By deed to John Adams, Jr., and Wesley Adams, the widow of Lewis Hipkins conveyed her dower (one equal undivided third of 207 acres, of Mills, and "the Rich Point Tract" at Little Falls).[22]

Richard Wren died about 1838. An appraisement of his estate was ordered in August 1838. George Minor, George Beard, Alfred H. Darne, Edward McMuhaney, James Payne, or any three of them were to make the appraisement. This was returned on November 6, 1838, by Payne, Beard, and Darne.[23] The sale of his estate mentioned purchasers who included Thomas Wren and Robert Darne.

Susannah Adams had issue:
*(By Lewis Hipkins)*
(*91*) John Hipkins, born April 19, 1783, died 1786.
(*92*) Elizabeth Hipkins, born February 1, 1783.
(*93*) (Captain) Lewis Hipkins, Jr., married Mary Carne.
(*94*) Ann Hipkins, born February 2, 1789.
(*95*) Sarah Hipkins, married William Fraser.
(*96*) Andrew Hipkins, married (1) — and (2) on March 5, 1848, Elizabeth Kinnard.

*(By Richard Wren)*
(*97*) Thomas Sanford Wren, married Julia Ann Wren (*see Wren*).

(*93*) (Captain) Lewis Hipkins, Jr., son of Lewis and Susannah (Adams) Hipkins, was born in Fairfax County, March 17, 1786, and died in Alexandria in May 1844. Captain Hipkins was buried in the family cemetery near his uncle, William Watters. He married Mary Carne of Alexandria August 15, 1809 (Bond filed at Arlington Court House). William Carne served as bondsman. Mr. Hipkins moved to Alexandria following his marriage and served as Captain in the War of 1812, later as Colonel of the D. C. Militia. He was prominent in Christ Episcopal Church and served as a vestryman of the Parish.[24]

(Captain) Lewis and Mary (Carne) Hipkins had issue (known):
(*931*) Lewis Hipkins (III), with his wife, Jane Elizabeth, lived in Alexandria. He had at least one son, William Lewis Hipkins, who was baptized at Christ Church on July 28, 1844. His birth date on the *Parish Register* is given as February 28, 1843.
(*932*) Mary Augusta Hipkins, married on April 10, 1832, in Alexandria Co., D.C., to William Henry Parker. Lewis Hipkins was bondsman.
(*95*) Sarah Hipkins, daughter of Lewis and Susannah (Adams) Hipkins was born

in Fairfax County on February 12, 1791, and died in Adair County, Kentucky, June 28, 1854. She married William Fraser on April 3, 1817. Mr. Fraser was born in Fairfax County on March 3, 1787, and died in Adair County, Kentucky, November 2, 1856. He was a son of William and Maria (von Rensil) Fraser. William and Sarah (Hipkins) Fraser had issue:

(951) William W. Fraser, married Mary A. Gearhart.
(952) Lewis Hipkins Fraser, born January 7, 1821, Cumberland County, Kentucky; married on September 3, 1852, Mary Jane Doslin.
(953) Thomas Anthony Fraser, born September 5, 1822; married ca. 1846, Jemima ―――――.
(954) Zebulon Montgomery Fraser, born August 8, 1825.
(955) Richard Fraser, born January 28, 1828.
(956) Susanna Fraser, born October 24, 1832.

The following account of the Fraser family was supplied by a descendant, Mrs. Francis S. Cornell:

### Fraser Genealogy

1. WILLIAM FRASER b. 1749, son of Daniel Fraser and Mary Beall (of Brandon). Daniel was the nephew of Simon Fraser, Lord Lovett, who was the last person to be executed by beheading in England. Daniel came to Westmoreland Co., Va., as a stowaway when he was only 16. He was discovered and indentured for his passage to a Mr. Beall of Brandon, whose daughter he married after his five years were served. Though only 16 when he left Scotland, he had attended the University of Edinburgh and spoke three languages. They had only one child. When Daniel died, Mary married (2) a Mr. Harrison. Young William left his step-father and came north to Alexandria, Va. He married Mary Von Rensil, who was born about 1763 in Cumberland, Md., the daughter of Dr. Von Rensil, a Saxon Baron who came to America after 1740 to escape service in the Elite Guard of Frederick the Great, for which he was selected because of his fine physique (6 ft. 4 in.). He located in the Cumberland, Md., area and became the inventor of the Rensil sheet, the first cotton sheet made in America. In some areas of the country, they are still called Rensil sheets.

William and Maria Rensil were married about 1782 and had 12 children, all born in Fairfax Co., Va.

| | |
|---|---|
| Richard | b. Dec. 29, 1783 |
| John | b. Jan. 7, 1785 |
| *William | b. Mar. 3, 1787 d. Nov. 2, 1856 m. Apr. 3, 1817 Sarah Hipkins (Daughter of Lewis Hipkins and Susanna Adams) |
| Daniel | b. Dec. 5, 1789 |
| Thomas | b. Nov. 12, 1791 |
| *Anthony Rensil | b. Nov. 12, 1793/4 d. Feb. 1, 1881 m. Presha Lee, of Leesboro, Montgomery Co., Md. Oct. 23, 1823; m. Mrs. Hoskins (Eliz.) |
| Elizabeth Beall | b. July 30, 1796 |
| James | b. June 30, 1798 |
| Sarah | b. Dec. 23, 1800 |
| John | b. Jan. 28, 1803 |
| Joseph | b. Mar. 7, 1805 |
| Mary | b. Mar. 8, 1807 |

2. *William Fraser* son of William and Mary (Rensil) Fraser was born 3 Mar. 1787 in Fairfax Co., Va., married Apr. 3, 1817 in Fairfax Co. Sarah Hipkins, daughter of Lewis and Susanna (Adams) Hipkins. Sarah was born Feb. 12, 1791 in Fairfax Co., Va., and died June 28, 1854 in Adair Co., Ky., where her husband William also died Nov. 2, 1856. They had six children:

*William W. Fraser     b. May 30, 1818 in Fairfax Co., Va., died near Bangert, Dent Co., Mo., Dec. 11, 1872, married Mary A. Gearhart abt. 1848
Lewis H. Fraser     b. Jan. 7, 1821 in Cumberland Co., Ky. (?) m. Mary Jane Doslin 9-3-1852.
Thomas Anthony     b. Sept. 5, 1822 m. Jerimiah abt 1846
Zebulon Montgomery     b. Aug. 8, 1825
Richard Fraser     b. Jan. 28, 1828
Susanna Fraser     b. Oct. 24, 1832

3. *William W. Fraser* born May 30, 1818 in Fairfax Co., Va., died, Dec. 11, 1872 and is buried in the Fraser Cemetery near Bangert. Dent Co., Mo. He married Mary A. Gearhart daughter of Samuel Gerhart (b. in Va. 1808) and Margaret Henson (b. in Ky., 1811) William and Mary Gearhart were married abt. 1848 in Adair Co., Ky. She died Dec. 24, 1898 in Salem, Dent Co., Mo. They had ten children:

*Children of William W. and Mary (Gearhart) Fraser*
Sarah Fraser
Samuel Henson Fraser     b. Dec. 14, 1851 Adair Co., Ky.
*Sylvester Adam Fraser     b. Nov. 26, 1853 Adair Co., Ky., d. Sept. 25, 1923, m. Caroline Nollner 1876
Zebulon Montgomery Fraser     b. 1856 Adair Co., Ky.
William Obediah Fraser     b. 1857 Adair Co., Ky.
L. Ellen Fraser     b. 1860 Dent Co., Mo.
Abner Harrison Fraser     b. Sept. 12, 1863 Dent Co., Mo. d. June 27, 1936
Mary Ann Fraser     b. 1865 Dent Co., Mo.
Richard Abraham Fraser     b. Dent Co., Mo.
Susanna E. Fraser     b. May 1870 Dent Co., Mo.

4. *Sylvester Adam Fraser* son of William W. and Mary (Gearhart) Fraser was born Nov. 26, 1853 Adair Co., Ky. and died Sept. 25, 1923 near Steelville, Courtoise Twp., Crawford Co., Mo. He married Caroline Lucinda Nollner in 1876 in Salem, Dent Co., Mo. She was born Apr. 24, 1857 in Izard Co., Arkansas and died in Cherry Valley Mine, Mo., on Apr. 18, 1893. She was the daughter of Alfred and Mary (Stevens) Nollner. They had three children:

*Lewis Emmett Fraser     b. July 28, 1877 at Short Bend Mo.
    d. Oct. 17, 1920
    m. July 9, 1905
Florence Anna Fraser     b. Dec. 1879
    d. Dec. 10, 1959
    m. Oct. 30, 1898 Elmer Leach
Ethel Fraser     b. Jan. 7, 1887
    d. Oct. 30, 1954
    m. 1916, Cecil Glenn Johnson

5. *Lewis Emmet Fraser* son of Sylvester Adam and Caroline (Nollner) Fraser was born July 28, 1877 in Short Bend, Dent Co., Mo., and died Oct. 16, 1920 in Miami,

Gila Co., Arizona. He married July 9, 1905 in Dillard, Crawford Co., Mo., Theresa Donahoe, the daughter of Louis B. Donahoe and Pauline Trost who was born July 15, 1881 in Monticello, Johnson Co., Kansas, and died Feb. 23, 1935, in Tucson, Arizona. They had four children:

    Alfred Nollner Fraser  b. July 8, 1906 near Steelville Mo.
                                          d. Aug. 18, 1928
    *Ona Lucile Fraser      b. May 20, 1909 near Steelville Mo.
                                          m. July 27, 1943 Francis S. Cornell
    Olga Gertrude Fraser  b. Nov. 26, 1911 in Sligo, Dent Co., Mo.
                                          d. Jan. 11, 1912
    Emmett Leroy Fraser  b. June 15, 1917 near Steelville
                                          m. Feb. 5, 1946 Regina Alice Hayden.

2A. *ANTHONY FRASER* son of William and Mary (Rensil) Fraser was born on Nov. 12, 1793 in Fairfax Co., Va. He married Presha Lee of Leesboro, Montgomery Co., Md., on October 23, 1823. Leesboro was a suburb of Washington, located between Silver Spring and Bladensburg. When he was 20 years old he enlisted in the War of 1812 on Aug. 19, 1814 and was discharged October 1, 1814. In correspondence with the pension department his address was Alexandria, Va., in 1853, 1871, and 1878. Pension records S.O. 7341. He served as a Private in Capt. Thomas West Peyton's Co., District of Columbia Militia. He received bounty land warrants #88512-40-50 and 66106-120-55.

(96) Andrew Hipkins, son of Lewis and Susannah (Adams) Hipkins was born March 27, 1794, in Fairfax County, married (1) ———; and (2) on March 5, 1848, Elizabeth Kinnard.

(10) Margaret Adams, daughter of Colonel William and Ann (Lawyer) Adams, died March 17, 1805. She married the Reverend John Childs, a Methodist preacher. He was born in Calvert County, Maryland, in 1770, was licensed to preach in 1789, located (retired from the ministry) but was re-admitted in 1816; located again in 1823, but returned to the active work in 1827. He died at the home of Mr. Thomas Jacobs in Alexandria, D.C., in 1829. William Watters wrote of Mrs. Childs:[25]

> (Margaret) was converted a little before her mother's death, and for a considerable time adorned her profession, and made her exit the seventeenth day of March, one thousand eight hundred and five, leaving eight small children behind. Her end, it is said by those present, was triumphant. She shouted aloud and gave glory to God, till within a few breaths of her last! The evening before she was walking in her garden, and a corpse before the dawn of next morning.

The Reverend John and Margaret (Adams) Childs had the following children:
*(10.1)* (Captain) William Childs.
*(10.2)* Samuel Childs.
*(10.3)* Sarah A. Childs, married George Jacobs.
*(10.4)* (The Reverend) John Wesley Childs, married Martha Binns Susannah Rives.
*(10.5)* Benjamin Childs, married.
*(10.6)* Mary Y. Childs, married John R. Wren.
*(10.7)* Elizabeth Childs, married James Allison
*(10.8)*

(*10.3*) Sarah Childs, daughter of The Reverend John and Margaret (Adams) Childs, married George Jacobs and lived at Langley, Virginia. There is a marriage bond in Arlington Court House dated September 23, 1817, where one George Jacobs married Mary A. Childs. Just who this Mary A. Childs was, has not been found. It is possible that the name was a slip of the pen. The fact that Mrs. George Jacobs was named Sarah is found in Fairfax County *Deed Book Z#2*, p. 64:

February 6, 1830. George Jacobs and Sarah his wife, John R. Wren and Mary Y., his wife, and John Wesley Childs, heirs of Margaret Childs, deceased, of Fairfax County, conveyed to William Nelson for $50.00 (paid to each) a tract of land on Pimmet Run "known as the late Saml. Adams' Upper Mill," and devised by said Samuel to his brothers and sisters and upon division, the Mill was allotted to Edward Adams (a brother), and Margaret Childs (a sister). This land was bounded by William Nelson's purchase from William Adams. Witnesses: James S. Scott and Kinsey Dyer.

(*10.4*) (The Reverend) John Wesley Childs, son of The Reverend John and Margaret (Adams) Childs, was born in Calvert County, Maryland, August 1, 1800, and died at the home of his brother, Captain William Childs, in Norfolk, Virginia, May 9, 1850, and was buried in the family burying ground of the Reverend John Early in Lynchburg. Mr. Childs was the subject of a 295 page biography by the Reverend John E. Edwards—"*Life of Rev. John Wesley Childs: For Twenty-three Years An Itinerant Methodist Minister.*" This was published in Nashville by E. Stevenson & F. A. Owen, Agents, M.E. Church, South, 1857. All quotations given here are from this book. Although the book contains a number of errors concerning the family of John Wesley Childs, it is highly interesting because of extensive quotations from his letters and Journal. Of the parents Mr. Edwards wrote:

(*page 24*) (the father) ... was a man of sterling piety, and of useful gifts as a minister of our holy religion. Mrs. Child's maiden name was Adams. She was of an old and influential Methodist family of Fairfax county, Virginia. . . . Mrs. Childs was a woman of fine sense, and was remarkable for her self-sacrificing spirit and deep devotion to the cause of God. As a mother, she understood her duty and responsibility; and most constantly and untiringly did she labour to discharge the whole measure of obligation devolving upon her in this relation of life.

In 1802, while John Wesley Childs was still an infant, his parents moved from Calvert County to Fairfax County.

At an early age John Wesley Childs was instructed in "his elementary education" under the tuition of his uncle, the Reverend Wesley Adams. Mr. Edwards says: "Under the instruction of this holy and amiable man, the moral feelings of the lad were properly developed as well as his intellect. The exercises of the school were opened and closed with prayer. The Bible was the principal text-book." At about twelve years of age John Wesley was sent to the home of the Reverend William McKenney, who in 1857 was Chaplain of the United States Navy. Mr. McKenney at the time was an extensive merchant in Georgetown. Mr. McKenney wrote to Mr. Edwards for publication that John Wesley Childs had unusual advantages because of his parents and near neighbor and relation, William Watters. Mr. McKenney wrote:[26]

Often has it been my privilege to hear Father Wat(t)ers, even after age had so obscured his vision that he could not distinguish in his congregation the features of his most beloved and intimate friends, pouring forth, in strains of deep, impassioned, and scriptural eloquence, the fullness of his soul, while explaining, enforcing, and glorying in the precious doctrines of the cross—salvation by faith, holiness of heart, and integrity of life. Unlike too many ministers of modern date, who too often aim at great things and make great displays of oratorical flourish; who elevate the cross of Christ to make themselves the more conspicuous; and who, as a necessary consequence, utterly fail, and leave their hearers as barren of spiritual comfort as the withered figtree was of fruit—he never failed. He always hit the nail on the head, and drove it home. He always fed his flock with the richest gospel food. The babe in Christ, the young men and fathers, had each his suitable portion in due season. He was always ready, and always good; so that it was commonly said of him, "He is real bacon and cabbage," a dish well known, and not lightly esteemed, in the South, and one always in season and at hand.

Can it, then, be a matter of surprise or wonder that one so favoured as was our lamented brother Childs, with such parents as his were, and such a patriarchal leader and guide of the whole neighbourhood and family circle as Father Wat(t)ers, should have been a youth of more than ordinary sedateness, humility, and fidelity?

Edwards describes Mr. Childs as "an extraordinary man . . . remarkable for his deep and influential piety . . . and especially for his *consistency* and *conscientiousness*." He says that Childs was good-looking, full six feet in height, of large frame, and well proportioned, rather light complexion—with black eyes and dark hair. Childs moved to Richmond in 1814 and lived with William Allison, Esq., but returned to Fairfax in 1822. He engaged in farming and teaching, and on April 29, 1826, entered the ministry. He married on March 13, 1834, by the Reverend John Early in the Early home in Lynchburg, Va., to Martha Binns Susannah Rives. Mrs. Childs, a sister to Mrs. Bishop John Early, was a daughter of Anthony and Mary Browne (Green) Rives, and represented an old and aristocratic Virginia family. She was born April 20, 1812. Bishop John Early, the brother-in-law, was one of the most influential men in the Methodist Church in his day, and thus another Methodist connection was formed with descendants of the unusual Adams family of Fairfax County.

The Reverend John Wesley and Martha Binns Susannah (Rives) Childs had the following children:[27]

(*10.41*) Margaret Elizabeth Childs, born January 31, 1835, died at "Forkland," Hinds County, Mississippi, n.d.

(*10.42*) Mary Antoinette Childs, unmarried.

(*10.43*) Anna Virginia Childs, born 1842, married Robert H. Aylor.

(*10.44*) Sarah Maria Childs.

(*10.45*) John William Childs, born January 9, 1845, died October 9, 1890. Mr. Childs served in the Confederate Army. He married his second cousin, Lucy Howard Brown. A child of this union was the Hon. J. Rives Childs. J(ames) Rives Childs was born at Lynchburg February 6, 1893.[28] He was a student at the Virginia Military Institute, 1909-1911, received his B.A. from Randolph-Macon College, 1912; M.A., Harvard University, 1915; graduate of the Army War College, 1917. Mr. Childs was a reporter on the *Baltimore American*, a free lance writer, and entered the American

Consular Service in November, 1923. He was appointed Consul at Jerusalem and Bucharest; 2d Secretary, American Legation, Cairo, 1930, then at Teheran and again at Cairo; Near Eastern Affairs, 1937-40; charge d'affaires, American Legation, Tangier, 1941-45; American delegate to the International Conference on Tangier, Paris, 1945; appointed Minister to Saudi Arabia, April, 1946; also to Kingdom of Yeman, October, 1946; post raised to Embassy, 1949; Ambassador to Ethiopia, 1951-53, after which he resigned from the Foreign Service. Mr. Childs is a member of Phi Delta Theta, Sigma Upsilon; honorary Phi Beta Kappa. His clubs include the Cosmos Club, Washington, D.C., and Army and Navy Country Club, Arlington, Virginia. Mr. Rives is the author of a number of works, including, *Reliques of the Rives*, 1929; *American Foreign Service*, 1948; *Restif de la Bretonne: See Critiques et sa Bibliographie* (in French), 1949, and other works. Mr. Rives married on August 13, 1922, Georgina de Brylkine.

(*10.46*) Samuel Wesley Childs, born 1847, served in the Confederate Army and married Clara Thomas.

(*10.47*) Thomas Childs, born August, 1850.

(*10.5*) Benjamin Childs, married before 1828, no other data.

(*10.6*) Mary Y. Childs, married, Washington, D.C., Sept. 1, 1827, John R. Wren.

(*10.7*) Elizabeth Childs, married on December 5, 1814 (Bond filed at Arlington Court House) to James Allison. John Childs was Bondsman.

## ADAMS—WREN—WATTERS CEMETERY

This cemetery is located near St. John's Catholic Church at El Nido (Chesterbrook). The tombstone erected to the memory of the Reverend William Watters and his wife, Sarah Adams, has already been quoted. This stone, with one to Andrew Furlong, are all that remain in the cemetery. However, this lot was used extensively in years gone by, and most of the stones disappeared long ago. The following list of some of those buried here was supplied by Mrs. Mary E. Furlong, who compiled it from papers of Mrs. Julia (Wren) Furlong (1849-1926):

The Reverend William and Sarah (Adams) Watters, Greenberry Faulkner, Charles Wren, Alice Wren, John Wren, Ellen S. Wren, Betty Faulkner, two small infants, Sarah Jacobs, Betsy Wren, Thomas Sanford and Julia (Wren) Wren, Louise Wren, Irving Furlong, Richard Wren and Susannah (Adams) (Hipkins) Wren, Julia (Wren) Furlong, Esa Clyde Furlong, Harriet Wren, Andrew Furlong, the Reverend Thomas Wood,[29] two children, Sophia Wren, Mr. and Mrs. Longston, Mr. and Mrs. Mahoney and their daughter; three bodies removed from a nearby farm; the Hipkins family (about ten members including Lewis Hipkins who died in 1794); Mr. Heath (Grandfather of Edward Heath of El Nido); and others.

---

[1] Gabriel Adams, Jr., age 33 years, made a deposition on May 1, 1748, in the suit "John Ball vs. Daniel French." This is the source of his birth year. See *Land Records of Long Standing*. (1742-1770) a volume on file at Fairfax Court House, page 113.

[2] See *Virginia Magazine*, October, 1952, Volume 60, no. 4, page 609.

[3] Fairfax County, Virginia, *County Court Record, 1768-1770*, page 67.

[4] From the *Diary* of George Washington, Volume 4, page 301, as quoted in *Four Mile Run Landgrants* by Charles Stetson.

⁵Fairfax County, Virginia, *Deed Book L #2*, page 107-108.
⁶*Journal* of Bishop Francis Asbury, Volume 1, page 424.
⁷She was not Ann Wren as has been reported. This marriage took place before August 19, 1755, and after January 1739, in Stafford County. See Stafford County *Record Book P*, pages 68-71. See also *Ancestral Proofs & Probabilities*, No. 1, (1935), page 1.
⁸*A Short Account*, etc., by William Watters, S. Snowden, Alexandria, Va., 1806, p. 111.
⁹MS. *Memoirs* of Thomas Scott, owned by the Reverend Lawrence Sherwood, Oakland, Maryland.
¹⁰*Minutes of the Annual Conference of the Methodist Episcopal Church (1829-39)*, New York: T. Mason & G. Lane, 1840, vol. 2, p. 406. This minute is for 1836.
¹¹*Short Account*, etc., p. 77.
¹²*Ibid*, p. 97.
¹³*Ibid*, p. 113.
¹⁴Arlington County, Virginia, *Deed Book 1*, page 521.
¹⁵His will was witnessed by Edward Dulin, Edward Adams, and William Watters
¹⁶*A Short Account*, etc., p. 114.
¹⁷Fairfax County *Will Book U*, p. 341. This will is indexed incorrectly under Walters.
¹⁸*A Short Account*, etc., page 113.
¹⁹*Ibid*, p. 121.
²⁰Fairfax County *Will Book V*, page 321.
²¹Fairfax County *Deed Book E #2*, p. 42.
²²Fairfax County *Deed Book A #2*, p. 342.
²³Fairfax County *Will Book T #1*, pp. 90-92.
²⁴*Lodge of Washington*, page 148.
²⁵*A Short Account*, etc., p. 114.
²⁶Edwards, pp. 28-29.
²⁷See *Reliques of the Rives (Ryves)* by J. Rives Childs, 1929, J.P. Bell Co., Inc., Lynchburg, Virginia.
²⁸See *Who's Who In America*, Vol. 28, p. 474.
²⁹The Reverend Mr. Wood was a native of England, and died in Philadelphia. He lived here during World War I, and was returned here for burial.

## THE ALBERTSON FAMILY

George Albertson was of English ancestry and was born in Pennsylvania in 1833. He died at Falls Church in 1916 and was buried in Oakwood Cemetery. Mr. Albertson was a descendant of General Nathanael Greene.

Following service in the Union Army, Mr. Albertson moved to Iowa, later coming to Falls Church. His wife was Charlotte Stoey (1848-1935). Their children included a son, and a daughter, Emma Downey Albertson who died April 3, 1912, age 34 years.

## THE ARCHIBALD LAMON ANDERSON FAMILY

Archibald Lamon Anderson (1878-1945) married Virginia Powell (1885-1943). The Anderson family lived at 300 East Broad Street. Mr. Anderson was a Civil Engineer with the Engineer Division of the War Department.

Mr. Anderson served as a member of the Falls Church Town Council, as President of the Falls Church Citizen's Association, and on the Fairfax County Ration Board during World War II. He was a member of the Falls Church and is buried in Oakwood Cemetery. He was a member of Kemper Lodge No. 64, A.F. & A.M.

The following children survived him: Mrs. Sarah Hambrick of Falls Church who has two children; Miss Virginia M. Anderson of Washington, D.C.; Mrs. Robert Smith; Lieut. A. L. Anderson, Jr., and Powell Anderson of Washington State. Powell Anderson married Caroline Smith and had two children, Robin and John Anderson.

## THE JOSEPH ANDERSON FAMILY

Joseph Anderson was a resident of Falls Church during the 1890 period, and operated a blacksmith shop on the south side of Fairfax Street. His home was next to the Falls Church Presbyterian Church. Some years afterwards, Mr. Anderson secured a position with the Post Office Department in connection with the manufacture of locks and other hardware necessary for handling the mails.

Charles F. Anderson ("Charlie"), son of Joseph Anderson, was also employed in this line of work and as a member of the Byrd expedition to the South Pole, established the post office in "Little America," and upon his death in 1943, was said to be the most "travelled man" in the world.[1]

Joseph Anderson also had three daughters, two of whom were Mamie and Hattie Anderson.

---

[1] The following is from a clipping in the author's file, n.d.: *Byrd's Antarctic Postman Retires After 48 Years.* Widely known as the man who carried the mails to the South Pole, Charles F. Anderson, 63, retired from the postal service. In the fall of 1934 he delivered mail to the expedition of Admiral Richard E. Byrd at the Little America base. His voyage to the Polar regions brought joy to philatelists because while there he cleared some 81,000 covers with the coveted Little America postmark.

A native of Clifton, Va., he went to work for the Washington post office as a helper at 15. Later he visited practically every post office in the country as a traveling expert on postal machinery. Friends estimated he covered several million miles by rail, water and air, and nominated him as the most widely traveled man in the world.

---

## THE AUCHMOODY FAMILY

In the sketch of the Erwin family, space is devoted to information concerning "Mother Auchmoody," who was the former Julia Smith, widow of Walter H. Erwin, and wife of Walter S. Auchmoody. Among the Auchmoody papers now owned by the Erwin family are several of interest. One gives the family of William L. and Ann Eliza Auchmoody. William L. Auchmoody, a resident of New York State, was of Scottish ancestry. He was born January 26, 1804, and his wife, Ann Eliza, was born April 20, 1810. They had the following children:

(1) Ellen A. Auchmoody, born July 28, 1825 at Fallsburgh, New York, married Albert Lounsbury and moved to Falls Church.
(2) Walter Auchmoody, born in New York, January 5, 1828, married in Fairfax County on October 10, 1869, to Julia L. (Smith) Erwin, widow of Walter H. Erwin and daughter of Phineas and Electa Smith. They had several children, all of whom died young except Annie Auchmoody, who married the Reverend Edward E. Eells, pastor of the Falls Church Congregational Church. She died in Pennsylvania on January 17, 1927.
(3) Mary Auchmoody, born at Wawarsing, N. Y., March 21, 1830.
(4) Wright N. Auchmoody, born at Wawarsing, N. Y., April 6, 1832.
(5) Jane S. Auchmoody, born at Dryden, N. Y., September 21, 1834, married George Ives of Falls Church.
(6) Freeman B. Auchmoody, born at Dryden, N. Y., February 23, 1837.
(7) Alonena S. Auchmoody, born at Dryden, N. Y., July 11, 1839.
(8) A. J. B. Auchmoody, born at Fallsburgh, N. Y., April 8, 1846.
(9) Adela S. Auchmoody, born at Fallsburgh, N. Y., July 20, 1850, married John Hammond.

## THE BAILEY FAMILY OF BAILEY'S CROSS ROADS

"Bailey's Cross Roads" has never been part of the corporate limits of Falls Church, but the Bailey family was long connected with the community. They were prominent members of the Dulin Methodist Church, and intermarried with many Falls Church people.

In the yard of old Falls Church are several tombstones of members of this family:[1]
In memory of Lewis Bailey, Devoted husband of Maria Bailey. Died April 8, 1870 in the 75th year of his age.
Henry L. Bailey, born March 28, 1857, died Sept. 21, 1888.
George F. Bailey, born March 23, 1849, died Nov. 29, 1891.
Gone Home (finger pointing upward) Alice, Beloved wife of Ray T. Bailey, died April 22, 1869, in the 21st year of her age. Blessed are the pure in heart, for they shall see God.

Lewis Bailey (1795-1870) was a son of Hachaliah Bailey, founder of the circus, and an early landowner in this area. Hachaliah Bailey moved here from upper New York state in 1837. On December 19, 1837,[2] he purchased a tract of land on the outskirts of Falls Church including what is now the intersection of Leesburg Pike and Columbia Pike. On this tract stood the large house known as "Bailey's Mansion," or "Maury," reputed to have originally contained one hundred rooms. This land was part of a larger tract containing 526 acres and 30 poles granted to Simon Pearson in 1729.[3]

Sometime prior to the War of 1812, Hachaliah Bailey purchased an elephant for $1,000 and named it "Old Bet." He paid this sum to his sea-captain brother (who obtained it in London for $20.00). At the time of the purchase of this elephant, Mr. Bailey was a resident of Somers, New York. He wanted a tiger to display for an admission fee, but finding the elephant to have more appeal, decided to buy it. According to the best available records, "Old Bet" appears to have been the first elephant brought into the United States. Mr. Bailey started out to show "Old Bet" with a wagon of hay, a horse to draw it, and an assistant. He left his farm in charge of other members of the family. The admission fee for an entire family was either coin or a two-gallon jug of rum. In 1808 Mr. Bailey rented two-thirds of Old Bet to Benjamin Lent and Andrew Brown, who also had a right to display her. Later, Nate Hawes of Somers, N. Y., went halves with Mr. Bailey and took "Old Bet" to Maine and collected a dime admission.

From the proceeds from displaying "Old Bet," Mr. Bailey purchased the land at Bailey's Cross Roads and also built one of the finest American Hotels ("Elephant Hotel") at Somers, N. Y. This Hotel is still standing and a granite statue of Old Bet guards the entrance, and was erected by Mr. Bailey.

One night a group of prosperous landowners in the region around Somers, N.Y., gathered at Yerkes Tavern and formed a circus syndicate. Lewis B. Lent, son of one of Mr. Bailey's partners, and interested in the success of the venture, was elected manager. By 1842 the syndicate had traveled 2,482 miles.

Hachaliah Bailey retired and Old Bet passed away. George F. Bailey, nephew of Hachaliah Bailey, managed several shows, and followed in the business. He designed a tank in which a hippo could be moved from place to place, and thus has left an imprint on circus life. Another nephew, Fred Harrison Bailey, recognized circus talent in a 13-year-old bellhop of Pontiac, Michigan, named James Anthony McGuiness. He gave McGuiness a job as his assistant, and the two traveled together for many years. Mr. McGuiness, in gratitude, took the name Bailey. By the time he was

25, McGuiness, as James A. Bailey, was a driving force in show business, and managed the circus of "Cooper & Bailey." This circus united with that of Phineas T. Barnum and formed Barnum & Bailey Circus. The circus went over the world.

After 1902 the show which James A. Bailey truly made the "greatest show on earth" joined with Ringling Brothers Circus, and today it is, as described, "tremendous, gigantic, and colossal."

It is unfortunate that Hachaliah Bailey is not given a larger place in the annals of the American Circus.[4]

Lewis Bailey, Hachaliah's son, was a prosperous farmer and man of ideas. In 1860, according to the *U. S. Census,* he had real estate valued at $20,000, and personal estate valued at $2,500. He was exceedingly proud of his nine sons and one daughter and left a handsome legacy to each. With their help he set up a community. In addition to his general farm, he carried on a profitable dairy business, serving the Willard Hotel in Washington. The Baileys worked a large number of slaves but did not own them. Their Methodist upbringing did not allow it. They rented slaves, however, from another Methodist; William Y. Dulin!

All of the young Baileys engaged in their tasks on the premises, one being a blacksmith, another a dairyman, one a carpenter, and the rest contributing their own particular talents.

The opposing forces of the War Between the States almost ruined the Baileys. The soldiers tore up the fences to build a grandstand for President Lincoln (who was served refreshments in the "Maury" mansion). The Long Branch, which meandered through the farm, was enlarged to a lake and stocked with fish. Union soldiers cut through the banks of the lake to drain it (they wanted the fish, but no fishing!). Congress later compensated the Baileys for extensive damages.

Following the war Lewis Bailey conducted a profitable summer boarding house which was an extension of the Willard Hotel. To accommodate the over-flow from the Willard who flocked to "Maury" for the summer months, Mr. Bailey moved his old Tavern from the Cross-roads and made it part of the main house. Many years later one of his descendants detached this building and moved it nearer to the Leesburg Pike. Mr. Charles F. Miller, a prominent Attorney in Washington, made this his home in after years.

The subsequent history of the old house includes the usual story of subdivision and development. Maria Bailey, widow of Lewis, sold several small parcels from the main farm. She also sold sites for a church and school. The remainder of the estate was divided following her death. The mansion and several acres was sold in July, 1897, to Millard J. Moore, U. S. Assistant Commissioner of Patents who used the partly ruined house for a summer home. At that time the central block, erected in the late eighteenth century, the addition of 1845, and several wings were in use. The earliest portion of the house was torn away.

The house burned to the ground in December, 1942. *The Falls Church Echo* of December 19, 1942, reported that the fire, of undetermined origin, occurred after the house had been vacant eight years. Five chimneys were left standing. An eyewitness told the author that the fire was started by tramps who lived in the remaining portion of the house.

What a sad end for a fine old house. During the life-time of Lewis and Maria Bailey the house was filled with beautiful antiques. Two Sheraton tables which once belonged to General Washington were in the house. These were sold about 1930 to the Lee Mansion Foundation. They were originally purchased at an Alexandria auction by Lewis Bailey.

Lewis Bailey planted acres of shrubs and trees such as althea, crepe myrtle, forsythia, hardy roses, lilacs, oaks, boxwood, and holly. A circular brick formal garden was also part of the lawn.

Lewis and Maria Bailey had issue:
(1) Elizabeth G. Bailey, the only daughter, met her soldier-lover (———— Francis) on Columbia Pike one wintry night during the War Between the States, and eloped to Alexandria where she was married.
(2) Walter T. Bailey, born in New York, 1837.
(3) Theodore B. Bailey, born in New York, 1838, had several children. The following is a clipping from the Washington, D.C., *Evening Star*, of Thursday, September 1, 1955:

### Edgar H. Bailey, Fairfax Builder

Edgar H. Bailey, 66, chief of the Building Maintenance Section, Construction Engineers, Fort Belvoir, died yesterday at his home at Bailey's Cross Roads after an illness of six months.

A native of Bailey's Cross Roads, Mr. Bailey was the son of the late Theodore and Missouri Bailey. His grandparents, Lewis and Maria Bailey, lived at Morray Farm, and established the settlement of Bailey's Cross Roads. Mr. Bailey was in construction work most of his life, working at one time for the Johnston & Terrett Construction Co. of Virginia and Florida, and the Arthur C. Moses Construction Co. of Washington.

He was a vestryman at St. Paul's Episcopal Church, Baileys Cross Roads. Surviving are his widow, Mrs. Lillye M. Bailey, and two daughters, Mrs. Dodie B. Wrenn and Miss Evelyn M. Bailey, of the home address; a sister, Mrs. Dora Terrett, 1789 Lanier place, N.W., and two brothers, S. Neale Bailey of Alexandria and French L. Bailey, Dorchester, Mass.

Funeral services will be held at 2 p.m. tomorrow at St. Paul's Church. Burial will be in Ivy Hill Cemetery, Alexandria.

(4) William Bailey, born 1841, married Ida Jane ————.
(5) Ray Tompkins Bailey, born at "Maury," in 1843, married (1) on October 27, 1869, to Alice Shreve; and (2) on December 4, 1878, to Mary E. Gordon, daughter of Daniel and Amanda E. S. Gordon. She was a sister of Eliza Gordon who married Horace U., brother of Ray Bailey. Children (by the second marriage) included: George Gordon Bailey, baptized 1878; Lewis Dean Bailey, baptized June 13, 1886, at age eight months, Harry Leroy Bailey, born 1889; and Ray Tompkins Bailey, Jr., twin to Harry, born 1889. These children were baptized at Dulin Chapel.
(6) Horace Upton Bailey, married Eliza Dent Gordon.
(7) George Bailey, born at "Maury," in 1847.
(8) Henry Bailey, born at "Maury," in 1849.
(9) Harvey Bailey, married Sarah Elizabeth Jenks.
(10) Oscar Bailey. (Note: This child may have been born after 1860, since he does not appear in the *U. S. Census* for that year. In the Census, in addition to some of the above, was the name of Jeremiah Ragan, age 22, born in Ireland, who was in the household.)

(6) Horace Upton Bailey, son of Lewis and Maria Bailey, was born at "Maury," in 1845. He married, on December 3, 1884, Eliza Dent Gordon, daughter of Daniel Smith and Amanda E. S. Gordon. They had the following children (all born at "Maury"):

(*61*) Horace Courtland Bailey, born April 8, 1886, had three children. Horace Courtland, Jr., Virginia (married MacCaley); and Robert.
(*62*) Marie Blackford Bailey, born June 8, 1888 (twin), married (The Reverend) Stephen Cartwright, an Episcopal Minister. They reside in Danville, Virginia. Children:
(*621*) Virginia Gordon Cartwright, born October 29, 1918.
(*622*) Thomas Bailey Cartwright, born January 26, 1920.
(*623*) Jane Gordon Cartwright, born May 2, 1923, married Corbett Wilkinson. Children: Ann Cartwright Wilkinson, born December 9, 1953; and Joan Lee Wilkinson, born January 31, 1955.
(*624*) Gordon Burroughs Cartwright, born April 19, 1925, had a son, Bruce Gordon Cartwright, born October 18, 1948.
(*625*) Catherine Marie Cartwright, born August 16, 1931, at Fredericksburg, Virginia, married Kenneth Oscar Woods. Mr. Woods was born in Bradley County, Tennessee, October 13, 1927, a son of Floyd Lee and Nora Jane (Owen) Woods. Children:Gordon Lee Woods, born Newport News, Virginia, April 25, 1952; and David Owen Woods, born Gettysburg, Pennsylvania, May 12, 1954.
(*63*) Lewis Gordon Bailey, born June 8, 1888 (twin), died at age one month.
(*64*) Teresa Gordon Bailey, born November 29, 1890, unmarried.
(*65*) Marguerite Gordon Bailey, born December 19, 1895, unmarried.
(*Note:* Data on the family of Horace Upton Bailey was supplied by his daughter, Mrs. F. S. Cartwright, 778 Melville Avenue, Danville, Virginia, March 5, 1956.)

(9) Harvey Bailey, son of Lewis and Maria Bailey, was born June 26, 1829. He married, on November 8, 1853, Sarah Elizabeth Jenks, only daughter of William and Elizabeth L. Jenks of Alexandria County, formerly of Lynn, Massachusetts. Her father invented the breech-loading gun. Children of Harvey Bailey included: Francis Hood Bailey, William J. Bailey, and Mamie Bailey, married William N. Young. Mrs. Sarah Elizabeth (Jenks) Bailey died in September, 1909.

---

[1] These graves were moved during the week of July 4, 1950 from their original location to another to make room for the new Parish Hall. The stones are on the side of the Church near the Alma Shop. It is said that nothing much could be found in the earliest graves.
[2] Mr. Bailey later returned to New York.
[3] By deed April 18, 1843 (*Fairfax County, Liber H. No. 3*, page 192) Hachaliah and Mary R. Bailey conveyed property to Maria, wife of Lewis Bailey, 526 acres and 30 poles, intention being to convey all the rights under the Pearson Patent except the lot conveyed to Wesley Adams and the lot of six or eight acres conveyed to Lawrence Lacy. This deed shows that the Pearson patent was granted February 17, 1729 and given by Simon Pearson to his daughter Susannah Alexander; and Susannah sold to John Luke the Elder by deed of October 8, 1773. John Luke the Elder gave it to his son John, who mortgaged it to McGruder and others, that by a decree of the Court of Fairfax County the property was sold under said mortgage to William B. Randolph (April 15, 1818) and he sold to Hachaliah Bailey. Millard J. Moore purchased "Maury" on July 17, 1897. Mr. and Mrs. Lewis Bailey sold land for a church, several farms, and schoolhouse.
[4] Passing reference is given Hachaliah Bailey, and not by name, in the W.P.A. *Guide To The Old Dominion*, page 525: "Bailey's Crossroads, 5.6. m., a store girt intersection, was named for a family one of whose members was the partner of P. T. Barnum, the circus impresario."

## THE LYMAN M. BALLARD FAMILY

Lyman M. and Mary (Andrews) Ballard came to Falls Church, from Watkins Glen, N. Y., in 1886. The family first lived in the house on Little Falls St., between Broad and Great Falls Streets, built a few years before by Mr. Garrison. In March, 1888, they moved to "Inwood," built and owned by Dr. Graham, on West Street opposite "Walnut Hill" (the old Sewall home). In the fall of 1889 the family moved to their own house which they built on land acquired from the Koon family on Haycock Road, between Broad and Great Falls Streets. Miss May Ballard sold this home in 1945, and purchased a house on Grove Avenue.

Mr. Ballard had been in Falls Church while serving in the Union Army (35th New York Volunteers), liked the little town, and returned after the War Between the States to make it his permanent home. His youngest child, Marjory, was born while the family lived at "Inwood."

Mary (Andrews) Ballard died in 1929, and Lyman Ballard in 1936. Their children were:

(1) May Ballard, unmarried.
(2) George Ballard, unmarried, deceased.
(3) Edward Ballard, unmarried.
(4) John Ballard, unmarried, deceased.
(5) Hiram C. Ballard, served in the Spanish-American War in the 3rd Virginia Volunteers, under Captain Joseph Willard, and returned to marry Agnes Armstrong of Penn Yan, N. Y. Child:
    (*51*) Frederick Ballard, married Mary Elizabeth Brackett of Minneapolis, Minn., and lived in Belle Haven, Alexandria, Va. Children:
        (*511*) Sally Ballard.
        (*512*) Mollie Ballard.
        (*513*) Julia Ballard.
(6) Marjory Ballard, married Ralph Smith of Boston, Mass., who died in 1929. She returned to Falls Church to live with May and Edward Ballard in 1944. Children
    (*61*) Ralph Smith, Jr., married Todd Crane of New Vernon, N. J., and had five children: Daniel, Leverett, Davy, Margaret, and Malcolm.
    (*62*) Polly Smith, married Peter McLane, four children: Andrew, Bruce, Gregory and Douglas.
    (*63*) Sally Smith, married James Ballantyne, four children: Lee, Jimmy, Peggy and Richard (Dick).

The Ballards are Episcopalians, and have always been active in the old Falls Church and contributed much to its growth.

---

## THE BARBOR FAMILY

Alexander Holford Barbor was born near Concord in Mercer County, West Virginia, a son of Herbert and Fanny (Grigsby) Barbor. His father, Herbert Barbor, was born and raised near London, England, and came on a merchant vessel and settled in West Virginia. He was an orphan and was apprenticed to the boat captain for one year, to pay his passage. His wife, Fanny Grigsby, was a native of Missouri.

A. H. Barbor was buried near Princeton, W. Va., in the Oakwood Cemetery. He died December 6, 1950. Mr. Barbor served as Deputy Clerk of the County Court of Mercer County when he was yet a young man. He left his paternal farm and worked on the railroad and in a coal mine. His sister, Irene H. Barbor (1868-1946) married an Englishman, Charles A. Marshall (1853-1917). Both are buried in Oakwood Cemetery in Falls Church. A daughter, Frances Elizabeth, is buried beside them. She was born August 23, 1902, died November 25, 1904. Another daughter is Mrs. Albert Lester. Mrs. Marshall settled in Falls Church and inspired her brother to come here. Mr. Barbor moved to Falls Church about 1902.

Mr. Barbor served as a Director of the Falls Church Bank, and was Sheriff of Arlington County. He was proprietor of a feed store (formerly owned by W. N. Lynch) which he rented from Colonel E. V. White of Leesburg. This store was later sold to Mrs. P. W. Lee.

Mr. Barbor married Kate Ashley Sutton, daughter of the Reverend Philip Sayers Sutton (a Methodist Minister) by his wife Victoria Mahood. Mrs. Barbor was born near Lebanon, Russell Co., Va., and was a granddaughter of the Honorable Alexander Mahood (of Irish ancestry), Judge of Giles County, Va.

## THE BARRETT FAMILY

Daniel H. Barrett purchased "Montpelier," the old Sebastian-Broadwater home (now the site of George Mason School) on January 16, 1855,[1] from John W. and Louisa F. Minor of Loudoun County. The deed calls the land a Quarter tract formerly owned by Charles Broadwater, then by William Minor, and contained 149 acres, 6 poles. Also mentioned is a division of June 8, 1816, of which this was lot 3, and Sarah Sewall received adjoining lot 2. The Barretts lived in the old Colonial dwelling which had been enlarged in 1805, and called it "Wayside." The Flagg family owned the house for many years, and Sidney Webster Flagg sold the property to the Falls Church School Board for $40,000. The family of Willis L. Gordon resided there during the 1890's, and Mr. Gordon was the source of some of this information. The house was torn down between July 5-10, 1952, to clear the front lawn of George Mason School.

"Wayside" was a well built house and had a fine entrance door of beauty. The back wing was originally the "old part," and was a story-and-half, raised to two full stories by Mr. Gordon about 1892. At that same time a front porch was added to replace the small entrance porch. This larger porch later fell away from decay, long after the house was closed. The side door frame contained bullet holes from the War Between the States. Members of the Barrett family served as targets when they attempted to go out for water from the old flint stone well. They had received a number of warnings to vacate the house, but refused to do so.

Although Daniel H. Barrett called his home "Wayside," the house was called "Barrett Hall" by his children. It is also referred to in old land records as "Barrett Hill." It is shown as Wayside on Union maps. The late George W. Shreve, born and reared in the vicinity, and a Confederate Veteran of 95 years of age, wrote in 1938:

> My battery, with Stuart's cavalry, proceeded on the Leesburg Pike as far as Barrett's Hill, just above West Falls Church, when we halted an hour or so, and then turned northwest via Dranesville to Leesburg and crossed the Potomac at Edward's Ferry. On Barrett's Hill I was only a mile from my home but could neither go there nor hear from the family."

During the War the house was occupied by both sides as a hospital and headquarters. An almost unknown cemetery was on the property, not far from the rear of the dwelling, and was pointed out to the author when he was but twelve years old by the late E. H. Flagg. He also had heard of it from Willis Gordon. When the news became public that the site was purchased for a new school, he visited the cemetery with Miss Ada Walker, Mr. Frank Maben, and Robert Lundien, a photographer, December 16, 1949.

So many such sites, consecrated by tears of other years, are often forgotten and destroyed by ruthless indifference. In order to protect this cemetery, time had come to give it publicity, and an article appeared the following week in *The Falls Church Echo*. In order to read the faint inscriptions, the stone had to be dug around, cleaned with a steel brush, and chalked in order to photograph. Credit is due to Mr. Maben, who handled these stones with great care. They were "dornick"—rough stone with crude inscriptions. Because of the interest created by the author's so-called "discovery," with subsequent publication, and the fine efforts of an interested group including Miss Ada Walker, the stones and graves were moved to the Falls Church yard. In their original situation the stones (from the Leesburg Pike) read as follows:

| 1786 | M. T. | C.T.D. |
| F Y 2 | 1776 | June 23, 1786, |
| At | | aged 85 yr. |
| DED. | | |

It was suggested that this cemetery contained bodies of the Trammell and Dyal families. The old tradition that a Revolutionary Soldier was buried there was revived.

Daniel H. Barrett and family, long associated with the old place, are buried in the Lewinsville Presbyterian Cemetery, and their tombstones contain the following data:

Daniel H. Barrett, 1808-1874.
Caroline C. Barrett, 1815-1868.
Jane Barrett, 1845-1863.
Mary Barrett, 1847-1894.
These all died in the Faith.
Catherine Barrett, 1850.
Frank M. Barrett, aged 4 yrs., 8 mos., 9 days.

Two children of Daniel Barrett, Henry and Samuel Barrett, sold the property to Edmund Flagg and moved to California where they died unmarried.

---

[1] Fairfax County *Deed Book V #3*, page 297.

## THE BARTLETT FAMILY OF "HOME HILL"

John P. Bartlett settled in Falls Church during the 1850's, and built his lovely house, now known as "Lawton Manor" (formerly the "old Buxton place") which he called "Home Hill." Mr. Bartlett was descended from a good New England family which included Josiah Bartlett of Amesbury, Massachusetts, Signer of the Declaration of Independence. Mrs. Rhoda Bartlett, mother of John P., came to Falls Church from Orleans County, New York, and died here February 20, 1868 at the age of 73 years. She is buried in the old Falls Church yard. Her son and family are buried in Ivy Hill cemetery at Alexandria.

John P. Bartlett was active in community life, and with George Ives, was responsible for saving the old Falls Church from complete destruction during the War

Between the States. The old Church, in a very real sense, is a monument to his memory.

Mr. Bartlett married twice, his first wife was Elvira Morton and his second wife was Emma Perkins. Eliza Bartlett, only child by the first wife, married Truman P. Hull, and raised a family. John P. Bartlett, Jr., was the only child of the second marriage; he married Emma Swallow and did not have children.

Letters written by members of this family from Falls Church during the War Between the States are of special interest. They follow:

Mrs. John P. Bartlett to Mrs. Truman P. Hull:

March 6th/63
Home Hill - Friday Morning

Dear Children

We received your very welcome letter last evening, glad to hear from you once more, sorry that you have been so aflicted with sickness but the more thankful that God in his mercy has seen fit to spare your life. Oh! how glad I would be to near you.

As anxious as I am for you to come here I cannot advise it—is all dark at present. But as your Father is writing he will tell you how we live, one day all is quiet, the next, we hear the boom of cannon and are looking for the Rebs. A short time ago we thought we should not be troubled again in this way but we find all things uncertain.

Don't think my dear Eliza that Ann's going away has made me doubt the government by no means. I have thought from the commencement of this horrid Rebellion that to free the slave would be necessary and I am glad it is done, but I don't want them to settle in the vicinity where I live.

In regard to Ann it was jealous-minded people, they did not like to have her stick to us because we happened to own her; but I am not sorry now I did feel bad at first —she had been with us so long, but the next week there was a poor contraband, came to me and asked me to take her in, and give her victuals & clothes. She was destitute said she would be glad to go back to her master if she could. I find her a very good girl, and perhaps I am doing good, in learning another to earn her own living, *hope so at least.*

But to the government that is another thing, what confidence can we have in an army where if they are attacked, by half, yes by a quarter of their numbers, will give themselves up without fireing a single gun, but it won't do to say all we know. So I will stop.

You will understand that I would be very glad to have Mother come here and all of you but your Father does not think it advisable at present.

Miss Manchester and I don't see a woman's face sometimes for whole months, *but each others.* I feel sometimes as though I was shut out from the world, it has been only occasionally that we have been able to make anything this winter.

Johnny might if he had not been in school earned a good deal but I am not willing to give up the chance he has now for pecunary motive, his instructions cost a good deal now but he improves well and if we let this chance pass he would get so old that he would be ashamed to go with those of his age.

We will enclose $200 dollars in this if you get it safe let us know and we will send more in our next. We shall send Mr. Warner some as soon as we can.

Johnny joyns in love to all. Remember he is a child yet and write to him, and it will be all the same to me, and he will then feel more of a responsibility to answer it, you see the force of the argument.

Direct to Falls Church next time—if the mails should be broken up we know where to find it in Wash. With much love

I am,

Emma S. Bartlett.

Mrs. John P. Bartlett to her mother-in-law:

Home Hill - Nov. 1st 1864

Dear Mother Bartlett,

Are you looking for a letter, if so, here it is. I have been thinking of writing to you so much of late, that it has farely haunted me, and now it is past 9 oc., but I am determined not to sleep untill you are in a fair way to hear from us. If you have read the papers you no doubt think the Guerillas have got us, but they have not yet but I can't say they won't for they came pretty near the other night. I did not know one while but they would have the whole Village, they came strong. They took Mr. Read a near neighbor and colored man 7 miles from home and shot them, the most cold blooded affair that we have had here. As it happened the Colored man was not killed after the ruffins left he cralled off and got back to tell the horrid tale. Mr. R. Sister and daughter a girl of 14 years went alone for the body, found it and brought it home, they could not find but one man there that would help them put it into the waggon. It was a sorry sight I asure you—may my eyes never witness another. But it is hard to tell what is in store for us. They took 7 horses from a barn across the road. It was a lovely night, I could see them as plain as though they had stood under my window. Johnnie took our horses from the barn and stood ready to escape with them should they come there. But fireing the alarm and blowing a horn, started them off. We had 250 Cavl. in half a mile of us but they were so long in getting here that they were of no use. There were too many Copperheads, among them, afraid they should hurt there friends (sic) if they came in time to fire into them. They threaten to come again and burn us out, and shoot every man in Falls Church.

There are good many moveing away but all we have is here and we shall stick by the Ship, as long as there is a stick left. John has not undressed and gone to bed for 6 weeks, he takes his blanket and curles down by some bush near where he can hear what is astirn. I wonder he stands it so well as he does. But it wears on him, he looks older some say 10 years since the war. I feel as though it would be the end of us if we don't get butchered if it lasts much longer. I had calculated to send for you this fall, but think it is well I didn't for I fear you could never bear the excitement which I have become used to. I was down to Elizas Sunday they are quite well now, Freddie has been very sick. They are doing very well and are in a safer place than we are, although they were so frightened that they packed up ready to start. Sister Emily's family are afflicted, her daughters have been sick since last July, neither one is able yet to go from their rooms. I sometimes fear they never will. Johnnie went north a week ago yesterday to go to school, so I feel safe about him as to the Rebs getting him. I have just heard from him. He is on the Hudson a little way from N. York City address Hudson River Institute, Clarrack, Columbia Co., N.Y.

Love to Mr. Sandersons family and all other friends, with love to your-self

Emma S. Bartlett

PS: Father & Mother are in Barre, somewhere. Ma has not been home over a year. Pa came home and staid two or three days last spring. Last Fall & Winter they were west in Byron last summer east."

*One Colored man they killed on the spot. I dare not let such a letter stay in the house over night for *here* they might come and find it. It is now 11 oc—if they come tonight it will be between now and 3 oc—in the morning.

## THE BEACH FAMILY

Harry A. Beach was born in New Jersey and served in the Union Army. He came to Falls Church during the 1890's and was soon active in local affairs. Mr. Beach was a long-time member of Dulin Chapel.[1] Upon his death he was buried in Arlington National Cemetery. Mr. Beach married Mary Knapp of New York. A daughter, Grace Elizabeth Beach, married George Nelson Lester of Georgia. Mrs. Lester died April 21, 1954, and is buried in Oakwood Cemetery. Mr. Lester was Mayor of Falls Church. George Nelson and Grace Elizabeth (Beach) Lester had issue:
(1) Albert H. Lester, married Helen Marshall.
(2) Anna Margaret Lester, died unmarried, January 1, 1956. Miss Lester was employed by the Falls Church Library for many years and was beloved by the community.
(3) Melissa W. Lester, married Frank Arnell Carpenter. A son is Frank Arnell Carpenter, Jr., baptized at Dulin Chapel, February 23, 1922.
(4) George Nelson Lester, Jr., died January 5, 1939 in Atlanta, Georgia. He married Katherine Vaughn and had issue: George Nelson Lester, 3rd., and Katherine Port Loche Lester.

---

[1] His mother, Mrs. Melissa H. Beach, died February 26, 1919, in Falls Church (*Dulin Chapel Records.*)

---

## THE BETHUNE FAMILY

Captain John Franklin Bethune, long a prominent citizen of Falls Church, was born in Monroe, Louisiana, and died at Falls Church on April 22, 1952, age 72. He represented an old Fauquier County, Virginia, family, long settled in Georgia.[1] Captain Bethune was a graduate of Eastern High School and George Washington University (then Columbian) Law School, having moved to Washington, D.C., in his youth. He served in the Spanish-American War and afterwards became confidential stenographer to the Secretary of the Senate. In 1908 he became special assistant to the Joint Congressional Commission of Revision of Postal Laws. He also held top clerical posts for the Lincoln Memorial Commission, the Memorial to Women of the Civil War, the Arlington Amphitheater Commission and the Arlington Memorial Bridge Commission. Captain Bethune was chief Federal Accountant in the construction of War and Navy Department annexes during World War I. At the time of his death he was Managing Director and Executive Vice President of the Arlington-Fairfax Savings and Loan Association. He was a past President of the Virginia Savings, Building and Loan League and a former member of the constitution committee of the United States Savings and Loan League. He was also a member of the Board of Directors of State Loan Company.

Captain Bethune compiled the first *Code* of Falls Church, printed in 1916. This was an important contribution to the community. He served as Chairman of the Board of Trustees of the Fairfax County Public Library, served on the Town Council, and served as Mayor of Falls Church. Captain Bethune was a Mason, member of the Falls Church Presbyterian Church, member of Kappa Sigma fraternity of George Washington University and Treasurer of Company G, District Volunteer Infantry, Richard J. Hardin Camp No. 2.

Captain Bethune married on April 29, 1904, Lucina McGroarty. Mrs. Bethune was a native of Georgetown, D.C., and a daughter of Charles Neil and Evangeline (Tweed) McGroarty and niece of William Buckner McGroarty the Alexandria Historian. Active in the Falls Church Chapter, D.A.R., Mrs. Bethune was a descendant of Nicholas Taliaferro, First Lieutenant of the Third Virginia Regiment. She served as Regent of the Falls Church D.A.R. Chapter, and took a great interest in local history. In 1923 the D.A.R. Chapter published a speech "Brief History of Falls Church" given by Mrs. Bethune on July 4th of that year. She later wrote an excellent history of the Falls Church Presbyterian Church and of the Falls Church Library.

Mrs. Bethune was a member of the Pi Beta Phi Sorority Chapter of George Washington University. She was a member of the Class of 1902.

Mrs. Bethune died at her home, 300 North Cherry Street, on November 19, 1951, age 72. She was survived by her mother, Mrs. Charles N. McGroarty, and a sister, Miss Mary Evangeline McGroarty, and other members of the family. Her mother owned the old Pond House on Cherry Street having moved here from Ohio. Captain and Mrs. John F. Bethune had a child:

(1) Catherine Jean Bethune who died January 23, 1959. She married Walter L. Phillips, a local surveyor, and they restored and lived in the old Dan McCauley House on Leesburg Pike. They had one son, Lt. Walter Lee Phillips, Jr., who married on May 11, 1957, in the Falls Church, to Electa Bacon Larcombe, daughter of Mr. and Mrs. John Franklin Larcombe. Lt. Phillips is a graduate of the University of Virginia, and his wife of Marjorie Webster Junior College. Lt. and Mrs. Phillips have a daughter, Cynthia Jean.

---

[1] "Blind Tom Bethune," born about the middle of the 19th century was a slave in this family. He was born blind and of weak mental development, but showed a remarkable aptitude for music. After hearing a piece played once, Bethune could reproduce it accurately on the piano. He was exhibited in many major cities of the United States, and died in Fauquier County.

## THE BIRCH FAMILY

The Birch family originated in King and Queen County, Virginia, and owned land there prior to 1690. The family residence may have been near Tindal's Swamp. In 1733, Robert Fullinton of North Carolina sold to William Birch of St. Stephen's Parish, King & Queen County, 340 acres on Tindal's Swamp.[1] The family spread out, some living in Westmoreland, King William, Goochland and Stafford. Samuel Birch paid tax in King William County in 1734.[2] Among the ships sailing from Kicoughtan (Hampton) on July 23, 1705, was the *Elizabeth and Ann* with sixteen men bound for Liverpool. Joseph Birch was on board.[3] The Will of Samuel Birch (probably the one listed in King William in 1734) was probated in 1739 at Goochland Court House (*Will Book 3, page 249*). A later Joseph Birch, living in Albemarle County, married Mary Rodes on November 26, 1786, and she was his cousin, daughter of Clifton Rodes of Louisa County. John Rodes, son of Clifton Rodes and brother of Mary, lived in Louisa County and married Jane Birch, sister of Joseph Birch.

John Birch, Sr., born about 1680 in what is now King & Queen County, was of English ancestry. He died in Westmoreland County in 1729. A son, John Birch, Jr., moved to Stafford County where he died in 1746. An Account of his Estate was filed in Stafford County on May 9, 1747 (*Record Book M, 1676-1790, p. 515*).[4] Mr. Birch was a Cooper.

Colonel Joseph Birch, descendant of the King & Queen County family, lived at his town house in Alexandria, but owned a large plantation in Fairfax County. He was a planter, and on July 15, 1799 was appointed Tobacco Inspector for the Town of Alexandria. His Bond to James Wood, Governor of Virginia, in the sum of $4,000 is recorded in Fairfax County *Deed Book BB #2, page 236*. Robert Bowling and Jesse Taylor signed this bond, the condition being: ". . .that whereas the above bound JOSEPH BIRCH, hath been appointed Inspector of Tobacco at Alexandria. — Now if the said JOSEPH BIRCH shall well and truly execute and perform his duty in every respect, as an Inspector of Tobacco, as is required in and by the Act of Assembly," the obligation was to be void.

On November 28, 1798, John Ball (son of Moses Ball) and Joseph Birch purchased a tract of land containing about seventy-five acres from Daniel Jennings of Nelson County, Kentucky. The purchase price was seventy five pounds current money of Virginia. This land was part of the Bricken patent of 1716 which was purchased by Daniel Jennings, Sr. It was adjacent to The Glebe, now in Arlington County. Witnesses to the deed were George Darling, Walter Pomery, Jonah Isabell, and Hugh Smith. On May 17, 1798, Joseph Birch purchased from Caleb Earp and George Wilson for 233 pounds, 10 shillings current money, "that lot of ground being upon the south side of King Street, and W. side of Royal in the Town of Alexandria, described in said Town by No. 55, containing the following bounds and distances: 74 feet westwardly of the intersection of King Street and Royal Street, and beginning upon Royal Street," the same being the dividing line between that of Caleb Earp, George Wilson and Valentine Uhler. George Darling, Joseph Thornton, Thomas Brown, and Alexander Brymer witnessed this deed.

Joseph Birch married Janet Bowmaker Robertson, daughter of James and Elizabeth (Bowmaker) Robertson.[5] Her father, James Robertson, owned vast tracts of land, including part of the present City of Alexandria. Much interesting Birch-Robertson history can be found in a law suit, "Birch vs. Alexander" filed at Manassas, Prince William County (*Minutes* of the Dumfries District Court). In 1790 the Virginia Supreme Court of Appeals decreed that the Alexander family held the title. The Birch family claimed their title through the Robertson purchase. Robertson received two contiguous patents of land, one for 800 acres (on February 27, 1729) and the other for 629 acres (on March 3, 1730). These records can be found in the *Northern Neck Land Book, B-191, C-117*. The northerly line of the patents passed through what is now Lyon Park in Arlington County. A deed to another purchase by Robertson is owned by his descendant, Mrs. Bessie Birch Haycock of Falls Church.

James Robertson died in 1769. His will is dated September 4, 1760,(*Fairfax County Will Book C, page 47*). In the will he mentions his wife, Elizabeth, his son John (to whom he gave the tract "I now live on consisting of 630 acres, except in case the Alexanders should obtain that tract adjoining Todd and Evans"); and his daughter Janet Bowmaker Robertson then unmarried, was to receive 320 acres of this tract. He left a tract of 100 acres on Four Mile Run to his granddaughter Elizabeth Robertson, daughter of his son John; the residue of his estate to his son James Robertson, Jr.

Joseph Birch also owned land in Hampshire County, Virginia, now in West Virginia. On September 5, 1810, John and Elizabeth Robertson of Alexandria conveyed to Joseph Birch, Sr., the land which James Robertson, Sr., had conveyed to his son (the said John Robertson) and "to Jennett Bowmaker Robertson, sister of John." Witnesses were J. T. Ramsey, N. C. Hunter, William Fraser and William Libby. (*Arlington County Deed Book 2, page 9*). On July 2, 1811, Ann Earp of Alexandria formerly Robertson, conveyed to Joseph Birch, Sr., all her right in the land which James Robertson left by his Will to his son John. This deed recites that Thomas, Lord Fairfax, by his patent of January 12, 1724, deeded this tract to James Robertson, Sr. The evidence submitted shows that Janet Bowmaker Robertson married Joseph Birch, Sr. This important record also gives the names of the children of John Robertson, brother of Janet Birch: James Robertson, John Robertson, Ann Earp, George Robertson (died under age); Jesse Robertson, Robert Robertson, Jane Robertson Goodrich, wife of William Goodrich; and Sarah Robertson Fosel, wife of John Fosel. Witnesses to this deed were: William Birch, John W. Compton, Arch. J. Taylor and John Birch.[6]

Colonel Joseph Birch died in 1815. On April 15, 1815, Thomas Birch signed Bond as Administrator of Joseph Birch, deceased, with James Birch, Samuel Birch, Archibald J. Taylor, Thomas Cook, Alexander Perry and Elijah Chenault, securities. (*Alexandria Will Book 2, page 54*).

Colonel Joseph and Janet Bowmaker (Robertson) Birch had issue:
(1) Joseph Birch, Jr., married Sinah Posey.
(2) Jacob Birch, died unmarried prior to 1824.
(3) Abraham Birch, died unmarried prior to 1824.
(4) (Colonel) Samuel Birch, married(1)Carey Ann Richards, and(2)Ann Cleveland.
(5) Thomas Birch, married Franzoni Hodgson.
(6) James Birch, married Priscilla Green.
(7) William Birch, married Elizabeth Alton.
(8) Caleb Birch, married Mary Bowling.
(9) Elizabeth Birch, married Archibald J. Taylor.
(10) Ann Birch.
(11) John Birch.
(12) Isaac Birch, married Elizabeth Walker.
(13) Albina Birch, married Guy Atkinson on April 7, 1807, in Alexandria County (William Birch, Bondsman).
*Note:* There may have been another daughter who married Elijah Chenault.

(1) Joseph Birch, Jr., son of Colonel Joseph and Janet Bowmaker (Robertson) Birch, died about 1831. He married on January 22, 1818, in Alexandria County, D.C., to Sinah Posey (Elijah Chenault, Bondsman). She remarried in Alexandria County on May 7, 1833, (James Birch, Bondsman) to William G. Howison. On November 4, 1818, Joseph and Sinah Birch of Fairfax County deeded to Pearson Clark of Alexandria for $1,540 land which belonged to Joseph Birch, Sr. Thomas Birch, brother of Joseph, Jr., is mentioned in the deed. Witnesses were: George H. Terrett, William H. Fitzhugh, John Allison, and Richard Kirby (*Deed Book Arlington County, 2, page 415*). On April 1, 1824, Joseph Birch, "desirous to make provisions for the support" of his wife Sinah and their child, sold to Alexander Hunter for $100 a tract of 72 acres in Alexandria County which had been allotted him by the Commissioners of his father's estate; also 700 acres of land which had belonged to his father, and located in Hampshire County. He also conveyed the interest which he held in the land of his deceased brothers, Abraham and Jacob Birch. (*Arlington County Deed Book 3, page 15*) On March 2, 1849, William H. and Sophia Birch, Joseph Edward Birch, and William G. Howison (and wife Sinah, late wife of Joseph Birch, deceased), sold to William A. Bradley for $1,500, 72 acres alloted Joseph Birch, Jr., by the Commissioners of Joseph Birch, Sr., in April, 1847, being Lot #5. Also conveyed was the interest of Joseph Birch, Jr., in the estate of his deceased brothers, Abraham and Jacob Birch. Apparently the deed of 1824 was for a loan of money, but this deed conveyed the land of Joseph Birch, Jr.

Joseph and Sinah (Posey) Birch had issue:
(*11*) William H. Birch, born before 1824, married in Washington, D. C., July 25, 1845, Sophia Cook.
(*12*) Joseph Edward Birch.

(2) Jacob Birch, son of Colonel Joseph and Janet Bowmaker (Robertson) Birch, died unmarried prior to 1824. In March, 1826, the estate of Jacob and Abraham Birch was divided among their brothers and sisters: Thomas Birch, James Birch, William Birch, Joseph Birch, Caleb Birch, Elizabeth Taylor, Ann Birch, John Birch, Samuel Birch and Isaac Birch. The final deed was recorded June 14, 1828. Witnesses were: George Minor and William Minor. (Arlington County *Deed Book 3, page 255.*)

(4) Colonel Samuel Birch, son of Colonel Joseph and Janet Bowmaker (Robertson) Birch, was born January 30, 1790, and died November 30, 1873. He is buried in the family cemetery on the Birch plantation. The original Birch home (in which he lived and died) was on the site of the home later owned by Dr. George B. Fadeley on a hill overlooking Lee Highway at Powhatan Street in Arlington County. This property was bounded by what is now Lee Highway, Lexington Street, Quantico Street, and Little Falls Road. A number of deeds are on record concerning this Samuel Birch. Three will be given here because of their interest. On August 22, 1828, William B. Richards and Priscilla[7] his wife of Fairfax County, and Ann M. (Richards) English and her husband James English, also of Fairfax County, conveyed to Samuel Birch for $200, 45 acres, part of a larger tract which belonged to their grandfather, Caleb Richards, deceased, and conveyed to their father, William Richards. Ann English and William B. Richards were the only children of William Richards, deceased. (*Arlington County Deed Book 3, page 244.*) On June 10, 1826, Samuel Birch and his wife Ann (Richards) Birch of Alexandria County sold to Alexander Tolson for $60, Lot #6 in the plat of the division of the land of the late Abraham and Jacob Birch (formerly land of Joseph Birch, Sr., and part of the tract of James Robertson.) Witnesses: Adam Lynn, John A. Sommers, and Smith Minor. (*Arlington County Deed Book 3, page 164.*) On May 10, 1838, Thomas and Elizabeth Marcey of Alexandria County sold to Samuel Birch for $100.00 land which was part of the division of Caleb Richards, and allotted to Marcey by a law suit "Hannah Richards & Others vs. Harrison Cleveland (1824)." Witnesses were: John Cox, and James Getty. (*Arlington County Deed Book 4, page 272..*)

Colonel Samuel Birch served in the War of 1812, and his pension certificate is owned by the children of Frank L. Birch. It is dated September 12, 1872, and signed by W. H. Smith, Acting Secretary of the Interior. This document states that Samuel Birch served as a soldier in Captain William Minor's Company, D.C. Militia, during the War of 1812. This pension was for $8.00 per month, and is Certificate No. 18913.

Colonel Birch married (1) on March 9, 1815, in Alexandria County, D.C., to Carey Ann Richards (Archibald J. Taylor, Bondsman). Mrs. Birch was a daughter of Caleb Richards of Alexandria. Colonel Birch remarried on September 30, 1822, in Alexandria County, to Ann Cleveland. Beale Howard was Bondsman, and Ann Howard made an oath that Ann Cleveland was over twenty-one years old. Mrs. Ann (Cleveland) Birch was born February 3, 1800, and died August 27, 1885. She is buried beside her husband.

Colonel Samuel Birch had issue:

(*By Carey Ann Richards*)
(*41*) William John Richards Birch, married Julia Ann Shreve.

*(42)* Joseph Edward Birch, married (1) Delphina Orton, and (2) Mary Elizabeth Speer.
*(43)* Carrie Birch.
*(44)* Caleb L. Birch, married Mrs. Sarah (Ball) Sherman.

*(By Ann Cleveland)*
*(45)* Samuel Birch, Jr., married Thursday Morris.
*(46)* Charles D. Birch, married ————
*(47)* Mary Frances Birch, married (1) — Myers, (2) — Birch, and (3) James Edward Murray.
*(48)* Orlando Birch, married Amanda ————.
*(49)* Margaret Birch, married Asbury Roszel Payne.
*(4.10)* Anna E. Birch, married Theodore W. Payne.
*(4.11)* Sarah Jane Birch.
*(4.12)* Elibeck W. Birch, married (1) Mary Catherine Virginia Davis, and (2) Frances Emeline America Davis.
*(4.12)* Elijah Birch, married ————.

*(41)* William John Richards Birch, son of Colonel Samuel and Carey Ann (Richards) Birch, was born January 20, 1816, and died August 14, 1916, age 100 years, 6 months, and 24 days. At the time of his birth his father resided in a house which was located near where the Ballston Presbyterian Church was later built. Mr. Birch lived his life span in Alexandria (Arlington) County. At the age of twenty, he served in the Seminole Indian War. He was married, in Washington, D. C., on December 28, 1838, to Julia Ann Shreve. Mrs. Birch was a daughter of Benjamin and Barbara (Swink) Shreve. Mr. and Mrs. Birch were active members of Fairfax Chapel Methodist Episcopal Church. He was converted and became a member in 1834.
William John Richards and Julia Ann (Shreve) Birch had issue:[8]

*(411)* Margaret J. Birch, born August 11, 1841, died March 19, 1925, and is buried in Mt. Olivet Cemetery. She married George W. Veitch. Mr. Veitch was born February 22, 1836, and died May 7, 1911. Children:

*(4111)* Julia A. Veitch, married at Ballston, June 16, 1902, to Harry R. Thomas, son of Albert G. and Alice S. Thomas. Mr. Thomas was a trial justice for twenty years, and retired in March, 1955, as associate judge of Arlington County Court. Their son, Homer Randolph Thomas, was appointed two months later to fill the vacancy. Mr. Thomas was also president of Arlington Trust Company. Mrs. Julia Veitch Thomas was a Girl Scout leader for many years and organized the first troop in Arlington County. She was an active worker on behalf of the children's ward at Arlington Hospital. She died at Arlington Hospital. She died at the age of 76 years, survived by her son, Homer R. Thomas (born September 13, 1903), four grandsons and six great-grandchildren.

*(4112)* Harry Clayton Veitch, born January 27, 1872, baptized June 10, 1873 at Dulin Chapel, died September 20, 1898.

*(4113)* Morgan Veitch.

*(4114)* Jesse Herbert Veitch, born November 9, 1868, died March 22, 1890.

*(412)* William Joseph Rowan Birch, died in 1864 in a Prisoner of War Hospital at Fort Delaware. He was a Confederate soldier. Mr. Birch married on

February 21, 1860, to Mildred Gertrude Murray (she later remarried Armistead M. Donaldson). Mrs. Birch of the old Murray family of Taylor's Tavern (granddaughter of James and Elizabeth (Street) Murray) was born November 20, 1843, and died March 27, 1929. Mrs. Birch was baptized on March 2, 1861 in Alexandria County by the Reverend William Gwynn Coe, witnessed by Julia and Margaret Birch. She became a member of Fairfax Chapel. Child:

(*4121*) Agnes Maude Birch, born in Alexandria County, January 11, 1861, died at Falls Church, April 1, 1959. She married her cousin, Robert Wilbur Birch, on February 4, 1895. He was born January 27, 1856, a son of Joseph Edward and Mary Elizabeth (Speer) Birch, and died March 12, 1924. They had two children: Guy Wilbur Birch (September 8, 1896—September 14, 1897) and Mildred Birch (March 15, 1900—November 15, 1904).

(*413*) Julia F. Birch, married on January 29, 1874, James L. Donaldson.

(*414*) Mary Elizabeth Birch, born January 9, 1847, died January 28, 1906, and is buried in Mt. Olivet Methodist Cemetery. She married John C. Sherier. Mr. Sherier was born January 22, 1840, died December 13, 1917. Mrs. Sherier wrote a history of the Birch family. There were several children, including Ethel L., born August 12, 1898, died December 17, 1916, who is buried beside her mother.

(*415*) Phoebe S. Birch, born May 3, 1849, died February 5, 1901, is buried in Mt. Olivet Methodist Cemetery. She married Joseph Fields, Children:

(*4151*) Grace Adeil Fields, baptized June 10, 1874, at Dulin Chapel, married Augustus Davis, Jr.

(*4152*) Howard Birch Fields, born 1873 at Ball's Crossroads, (later Ballston and Parkington), and was baptized June 10, 1873 at Dulin Chapel. He died November 13, 1952. Mr. Fields was Sheriff of Arlington County for twenty-four years. He married and was survived by his wife, Cora A. Fields. His foster children were: Mrs. Edna Woodyard, Mrs. Charlotte Gaines and Francis Griffith.

(*4154*) Ida Lee Fields, born May 29, 1877, married ————— Day.

(*4155*) Virgie Irene Fields, born June 3, 1879, married ————— Edwards.

(*4156*) Frank Smith Fields, born August 9, 1877, died at Fairlands, Maryland, February 16, 1958. He married Margaret Jacobs and Hazel V. —————. He was survived by children: Mrs. Josephine Marcionette, Catherine F. Fields and Frank W. Fields.

(*416*) Emma Shreve Birch, married on June 10, 1873, to Andrew W. Veitch. They had a son, Edward Veitch.

(*417*) Walter C. Birch, died at about two and one-half years of age.

(*42*) Joseph Edward Birch, son of Colonel Samuel and Carey Ann (Richards) Birch, was born in Alexandria County, May 2, 1818, and died at his home (now 312 East Broad Street) Falls Church, September 20, 1892. He married (1) in 1840 to Delphina Orton, a native of Orleans Co., N. Y., who died November 19, 1853, age 22 years. He remarried (2) on May 3, 1855 in Washington, D. C., to Mary Elizabeth Speer. Mrs. Mary (Speer) Birch was born in New York City, March 9, 1836, and died at Falls Church April 8, 1901. She was a daughter of William Pierce and Martha Mary (Dickerson) Speer. Mr. Birch was greatly loved by his Falls Church neighbors. He was one of the founders of Jefferson School, and served on the first Town Council. Mr. Birch was a Trustee of Dulin Chapel. He was one of the first in the community to see the need for a public cemetery. Mr. Birch was a farmer and blacksmith. In 1850 he was assisted by James Robey (born Virginia, age 25) and Martin Donaldson, (born Virginia, age 19). At the same time a Miss L. Constable (born New York, age 21) was his housekeeper.[9]

Mr. Birch moved to Falls Church in 1841, and lived with his father-in-law,[10] Mr. Orrin Orton. On May 31, 1852, he purchased the Orton home which is still owned by his family. This house, at 312 East Broad Street, was built before 1835. It is a large clapboard building with center hall. The price paid Orrin and Margaret M. Orton by Birch was $483.75. It is noted in the deed of transfer (*Fairfax County Deed Book Q #3, page 55*) that this land was purchased by Orton from John Butcher on May 28, 1851. The land adjoined the colonial patents of Harrison, Trammell, Reagan, and Pearson. By an earlier deed, March 22, 1849 (*Fairfax County Deed Book N #3, page 386*) Joseph E. Birch purchased two acres and 17 poles of land at public auction: "Thomas E. Scott against Thomas Murgatroid, by William H. Dulany, Commissioner of the Court of Fairfax County," to the highest bidder (Joseph E. Birch) for the "sum of one hundred and five dollars." This land was "situated on the Middle Turnpike Road near Winter Hill," and adjoined the Orton tract. By deed of May 7, 1856 (*Fairfax County Deed Book X #3, page 300*) Mr. Birch purchased for $200, eight acres from Robert F. and Ruth F. Judson, "Beginning in the Falls Church Road, corner to Page's land." Mr. Birch acquired additional land including part of the William Richards tract, *(Fairfax County Deed Book H #2, page 239).*

Joseph E. Birch had issue (all by Mary E. Speer):
(*421*) Robert Wilbur Birch, married Agnes M. Birch.
(*422*) Frank List Birch, married Flora Belle Crossman.
(*423*) Carrie Delphina Birch, married George A. Brunner.
(*424*) Mary Estella Birch.
(*425*) Minnie Marian Birch married Ernest E. Black.
(*426*) Harry Smith Birch, married Lillian Divine.
(*427*) George Crenshaw Birch, married Margaret W. Wilson.
(*428*) Eva Smithson Birch, married Tasker M. Weir.

(*422*) Frank List Birch, son of Joseph Edward and Mary Elizabeth (Speer) Birch, was born at Falls Church, May 25, 1858, and was baptized at Fairfax Chapel on December 10, 1860, by the Reverend William Gwynn Coe (witnesses: the Reverend George H. Zimmerman, Cinderella Constable, and Mrs. William Gwynn Coe). Mr. Birch died at his Falls Church home on June 26, 1939. He was married, on December 14, 1882, to Flora Belle Crossman. Mrs. Birch was born August 13, 1859, a daughter of Isaac and Mary Ann (Mutersbaugh) Crossman. She died at her home, at 312 East Broad Street, September 17, 1956, after a long and useful life. Mrs. Birch was an ardent Methodist and outstanding citizen.

Frank List and Flora Belle (Crossman) Birch had issue:
(*4221*) Essie Florence Birch, unmarried, is living (1964) in her grandfather's old home at 312 East Broad Street. Miss Birch is an accomplished artist and

many lovely oils and other examples of her work can be seen in her home. She studied art under Virgie Thompson in South West Washington.

(*4222*) Mary Nedetta Birch, born October 3, 1888, died April 23, 1957. She was an active member of Dulin Methodist Church, and for many years served as Sunday School teacher, and steward. Miss Birch served as a secretary in the Near East Division of the State Department for thirty years.

(*4223*) Isaac Franklin Birch, born October 8, 1890, died April 8, 1940. Married Elsie Wright, no issue.

(*4224*) Milton Taylor Birch married Pauline Waite. Mr. Birch is well known for his interest in justice in the community, and for many years has been a useful citizen of Falls Church. Mr. and Mrs. Birch have recently moved to the City of Fairfax. No issue.

(*423*) Carrie Delphina Birch, daughter of Joseph Edward and Mary Elizabeth (Speer) Birch, was born August 16, 1861, and died December 15, 1926. She married on November 24, 1880, George A. Brunner (1851-1929). (*See Brunner.*)

(*424*) Mary Estella Birch, daughter of Joseph Edward and Mary Elizabeth (Speer) Birch, was born September 8, 1864, and died unmarried, May 11, 1945.

(*425*) Minnie Marian Birch, daughter of Joseph Edward and Mary Elizabeth (Speer) Birch, was born April 28, 1866, and died September 24, 1954. She married on April 5, 1900 in Oklahoma City to Ernest E. Blake. Mr. Blake, of a distinguished family, was a cousin of Mrs. Walter Towner Jewell (nee Aurelia McCormick) of Arlington.

Ernest E. and Minnie Marian (Birch) Blake had issue:

(*4251*) Ernest B. Blake, married Ethel Brown and had a son, Ernest B. Blake, Jr.

(*4252*) Joseph C. Blake.

(*426*) Harry Smith Birch, son of Joseph Edward and Mary Elizabeth (Speer) Birch, was born September 3, 1869, and died October 25, 1946. He married (1) Cora Hodgkin, daughter of Dr. James B. Hodgkin of Falls Church; and (2) Mary Lillian Divine. Mrs. Lillian (Divine) Birch was born at Waterford, Loudoun County, November 19, 1876, a daughter of Joseph Tuisto and Sally A. (Roberts) Divine. Issue:

(*4261*) Joseph Vinton Birch, born November 4, 1905. Married Dorothy Walker Weaver of Pennsylvania. Mrs. Birch was born September 17, 1900. No issue. Mr. Birch is the owner of the Falls Church Garage.

(*4262*) Philip Walden Birch, born March 4, 1908, married Mary Alma Biggins (born August 25, 1909). Children:

(*42621*) Barbara Alma Birch born May 4, 1933.

(*42622*) Elizabeth Ann Birch born January 7, 1936.

(*4263*) Kathleen Virginia Birch, born September 23, 1912, married Kenneth Teachum Bolen, issue:

(*42631*) Kenneth Joseph Bolen, born April 7, 1947.

(*427*) George Crenshaw Birch, born May 23, 1875, son of Joseph Edward and Mary Elizabeth (Speer) Birch, married on April 4, 1893, Margaret W. Wilson of Maryland. Mr. Birch died December 2, 1908. Mrs. Birch died at her home in Hyattsville, Maryland, October 13, 1957. Issue:

(*4271*) (Colonel) Tyler M. Birch, married Marian, and they had issue: Stewart Birch, Phoebe Ann Birch, Betty Birch (twin), and Robert Bir ι (twin).

(*4272*) George W. Birch, married Mary Richardson, no issue.
(*4273*) Marian Birch, unmarried.

(*428*) Eva Smithson Birch, daughter of Joseph Edward and Mary Elizabeth (Speer) Birch, was born December 24, 1877, and is living. She married Tasker M. Weir (pronounced Ware). Mr. Weir was born in 1881, and died in 1921. No issue.

(*44*) Caleb L. Birch, son of Colonel Samuel and Carey Ann (Richards) Birch, was born in 1819, and died October 29, 1884. His will was probated in Alexandria County on September 27, 1886 (*Will Book 10, page 75*). In his will he mentioned his daughter, Amanda Ball Birch, his daughter Jeanette Birch, and his daughter Sarah Isabell Chapman. Witnesses were: Dr. L. E. Gott, and Francis Asbury Kirby. Mr. Birch married in Washington, D. C., November 24, 1845, to Mrs. Sarah (Ball) Sherman, widow of Daniel Sherman and daughter of Robert and Ann (Thrift) Ball. Issue:
  (*441*) Sarah Isabell Birch (1847-1922) married Henry M. Chapman (1851-1929), issue: Flora Chapman, married Walter Dulin (1873-1936); Lytton Chapman, (1876-January 4, 1899); and Lelia B. Chapman (December 18, 1884-September 13, 1924).
  (*442*) Amanda Ball Birch, unmarried.
  (*443*) Jeanette Birch (1858-1916) married John N. Gibson, who served for many years as Town Sergeant. (*See Gibson*).

(*45*) Samuel Birch, Jr., son of Colonel Samuel and Ann (Cleveland) Birch, married on June 12, 1849, to Thirry (Thursday) Morris. Issue:
  (*451*) Ida Birch.
  (*452*) Lillian (Lilly) H. Birch, died February 17, 1938, married a cousin, Morris, and had issue: Hugh Ernest Morris.
  (*453*) Richard Birch.
  (*454*) Robert Birch.
  (*455*) Alice Birch.

(*46*) Charles D. Birch, son of Colonel Samuel and Ann (Cleveland) Birch, married and had issue, one of whom was Jesse Birch, baptized at Dulin Chapel on March 16, 1877.

(*47*) Mary Frances Birch (called Fanny), daughter of Colonel Samuel and Ann (Cleveland) Birch, was born in 1836 and died April 1, 1907 (buried in Oakwood Cemetery). She married (1) ——— Myers; (2) ——— Birch; and (3) James Edward Murray, son of James and Elizabeth (Street) Murray. (*See Murray*). Myers Notes—the following are likely descendants of the Birch-Myers marriage: (*From clippings)*

*Jonathan William Myers* of 4519 Carling Spring Road, is buried in Oakwood Cemetery, Falls Church. He was a native of Fairfax County and lived for thirty-three years in Arlington. At the time of his death he was a retired Dairyman. Mr. Myers was a member of the Arlington Chapter, I.O.O.F. His widow was Margaret M. Myers and he had two brothers who survived him: Robert L. and J. Frank Myers.

*Miss Minnie Myers* died March 5, 1936 in Washington, D.C., a resident of 4519 Carlin Spring Road, Arlington. She was a daughter of the late Charles W. and Sallie Ann Myers. Miss Myers was survived by three brothers: Robert L., J. Frank and J. W. Myers.

Mary Frances Birch had issue (by her first husband Birch):

*(471)* Jacob E. Birch (1858-1912) married Frances A. Hall, daughter of Basil Hall. Her father was a large land owner in Alexandria County, where he settled in 1850. Mrs. Birch was born in 1865, and died in 1914. She is buried beside her husband in Oakwood Cemetery. Issue:

*(4711)* Oscar E. Birch, died May 26, 1955. Married Marian R., and had children:
*(47111)* Nancy Birch.
*(47112)* George Birch.
*(4712)* Clifton E. Birch, born 1885, died March 15, 1956.
Married Mark K., issue:
*(47121)* Marian L. Birch married Kraige
*(47122)* Kathleen E. Birch, married Radtke.
*(47123)* Eleanor V. Birch, married Brubaker.
*(4713)* Olive F. Birch, married W. Harry Johnson.
*(4714)* Edith Birch.

*(48)* Orlando Birch, son of Colonel Samuel and Ann (Cleveland) Birch, married Amanda, and had several children including:
*(481)* Nettie Birch.
*(482)* Minnie Birch, married Mr. Ball.

*(49)* Margaret Birch, daughter of Colonel Samuel and Ann (Cleveland) Birch, married Asbury Roszel Payne. *(See Payne)*

*(4.10)* Anna E. Birch, daughter of Colonel Samuel and Ann (Cleveland) Birch, married on May 11, 1871, Theodore W. Payne. She was born January 15, 1838, died December 3, 1881. *(See Payne.)*

*(4.11)* Sarah Jane Birch, daughter of Colonel Samuel and Ann (Cleveland) Birch, born January 18, 1825, died July 19, 1891, unmarried. She made her will on July 3, 1891 and it was probated in Alexandria County on August 3, 1891 *(Will Book 10, page 190)*. In this document she mentions her late father, Samuel Birch, her nephew Samuel French Payne, nephew Claude Taylor Payne, sister Mary F. Murray, niece Florence Murray, niece Ella Birch, brother Charles Birch, nephew Frank Payne, nephew Harry Payne, "Roswell" (Roszel) Payne, Robert Wilbur Birch, executor, and her sister-in-law, Mary Speer Birch, who was left $100 to keep the family cemetery in good order. Witnesses were Orlando Birch, J. L. Donaldson, and S. H. Stalcup.

*(4.12)* Elibeck W. Birch (called Beck), son of Colonel Samuel and Ann (Cleveland) Birch, was born December 17, 1832, and died at his home in Chantilly, September 6, 1918. Mr. Birch is buried in the Christ Episcopal Cemetery at Chantilly. He married (1) on February 28, 1860, to Mary Catherine Virginia Davis. She was born at Chantilly, November 13, 1835, and died September 2, 1864 *(Family Bible.)* Her tombstone in St. Paul's Episcopal Church Cemetery at Alexandria gives her death date as September 13, 1864. Mr. Birch remarried on March 22, 1866, his first wife's sister, Frances Emeline America Davis. The second Mrs. Birch was born December 5, 1846 at Chantilly, and died September 30, 1942, aged 95 years. The father of the two wives of Elibeck W. Birch was James Davis who lived in the Theodrick Lee Stone House (home of Mrs. Olive Wrenn) in Chantilly. James Davis was born September 13, 1806, and died May 15, 1863 (and is buried in the family

cemetery at the Stone House in Chantilly). He married on January 5, 1832, Elizabeth Cross (April 27, 1810-January 6, 1890) a daughter of Benjamin Cross of Fairfax County. The family records are in a Davis-Birch Bible, copied July 14, 1957. The Bible is owned by Ray Birch, and was published in Philadelphia by M'Carty & Davis, 171·Market Street, 1830/31.[11]

Elibeck W. Birch had issue (*By Mary Catherine Virginia Davis*):[12]

(*4.12.1*) Mary Estella Birch, married Owen Whitehall Jones.
(*4.12.2*) Blanche Birch, born June 7, 1863, died July 13, 1864.
(*By Frances Emeline America Davis*):
(*4.12.3*) Katherine Birch, married Henry E. Powell.
(*4.12.4*) Ada Florence Birch, unmarried, born March 3, 1868, died Dec. 28, 1953.
(*4.12.5*) Edwin Lee Birch, married Mary Ellen Lee.
(*4.12.6*) James Davis Birch, married Pearl Lee.
(*4.12.7*) Cora Birch, married John Hurst.

(*4.12.1*) Mary Estella Birch (called Lel), daughter of Elibeck W. and Mary Catherine Virginia (Davis) Birch, was born December 2, 1860. She married on October 14, 1883, to Owen Whitehall Jones. Mr. Jones was a son of Robert and Sarah Ellen[13] (Hitaffer) Jones. Mr. and Mrs. Owen W. Jones lived at Ravensworth (adjacent to the Fitzhugh-Lee Plantation of that name) in Fairfax County. They were intimate with the family of General Robert E. Lee. They also lived for a time in the Stone House at Chantilly. Issue:

(*4.12.11*) Anne Moore Jones, born September 29, 1886, married (1) Edward L. Santmire; and (2) Julian P. Dodge.
(*4.12.12*) Mary Ellen Jones, born at Chantilly, October 11, 1889, living in Arlington, 1961. She married on November 28, 1911, to John Henry (Harry Lewis) Brown. Mr. Brown was baptized John Henry but later changed his name to Harry Lewis. He was born January 12, 1885, and died March 2, 1946. Mr. Brown was a son of William and Catherine (Morris) Brown. Issue:
(*4.12.111*) Elmer Lewis Brown, born December 2, 1912, married his cousin, Edith May Reid. She was born on May 13, 1915, a daughter of Howard Richard and Lettie (Loy) Reid, and a granddaughter of Horatio Reid, Sr., and Gertrude (Birch) Reid. Issue: Nellie Marie Brown, married Robert F. Johnson (and had Robert F. Johnson, Jr., Lewis Johnson and a daughter); and Shirley Mae Brown, unmarried.
(*4.12.112*) Richard Lee Brown, born September 16, 1914, married Dora Mitchell Mathena. Issue: Richard Bolling Brown, married Jessie Skinner and had issue: Victoria Lynn Brown.
(*4.12.13*) Margaret Owen Jones, married (1) John Columbus, and (2) Dr. Clarence Cowper.
(*4.12.14*) Bessie Neavill Jones, married John D. King.
(*4.12.15*) Robert Edward Lee Jones, died young.
(*4.12.16*) John Thomas Jones, married Lenora V. Reid, a cousin, the daughter of Horatio Reid, Sr., and Gertrude (Birch) Reid. They were married on April 6, 1916.
(*4.12.17*) Bolling Barton Jones, married Louise Creamer.
(*4.12.18*) Marie Washington Jones, married Horatio Reid, Jr., a cousin.

(*4.12.3*) Katherine Birch, daughter of Elibeck W. and Frances Emeline America (Davis) Birch, was born January 16, 1867, and died November 6, 1942, survived by twenty-seven grandchildren and two great-grandchildren. She married Henry E. Powell, who died May 4, 1922, aged 57 years. Children:
  (*4.12.31*) Lena F. Powell, born July 4, 1892, married Garner Haines of Herndon.
  (*4.12.32*) Mamie May Powell, born May 10, 1896, died March 21, 1942, married John Frank Swart, a son of John Henry and Florence (Harrison) Swart. Issue: John Frank Swart, Jr., and Asa A. Swart.
  (*4.12.33*) James H. Powell, born February 1, 1898, married Mae Byrne.

(*4.12.5*) Edwin Lee Birch, son of Elibeck W. and Frances Emeline America Birch, was born on October 12, 1870, and died December 24, 1947. He married on April 2, 1892, to Mary Ellen Lee (called Mittie), born 1870, died 1944. She was the daughter of Franklin and Sarah (Jones) Lee. Mrs. Sarah (Jones) Lee was related to the well-known Buggy manufacturers, Jones Brothers, of Hagerstown. She was a descendant of the old Lee family of Virginia, her immediate ancestor being Lancelot Lee of "Chantilly." Her grandparents were Alexander Dove Lee and Margaret (McFarland) Lee. The grandfather was a cousin of General Robert E. Lee. Issue:
  (*4.12.51*) Alvin Ashton Birch, married (1) Mary James; and (2) Mrs. Fannie (Fincen) Sherwood.
  (*4.12.52*) Edna Birch, married Otis Brown (and had issue: Edwin Lee Brown).
  (*4.12.53*) Clarence L. Birch, died in Paterson, N. J., September 8, 1955, married Mae Maxwell, no issue.
  (*4.12.54*) Edith L. Birch, married Carl Miller, issue: Jackie Neal Birch married (1) Shirley Dye of Centreville (no issue); and (2) Barbara Robinson, and had Karyn and David Miller; and Jimmie Lee Miller; married Joyce Ann Leigh, and had Michael and James Vernon Miller.

(*4.1251*) Alvin Ashton Birch, son of Edwin Lee and Mary Ellen (Lee) Birch, was born at Chantilly, February 24, 1894, and married (1) August 30, 1918, to Mary James. She was born June 27, 1901, and died January 12, 1955, a daughter of Matthew S. and Josephine (Sherwood) James of Washington County, Virginia. Mr. Birch remarried, (2) in 1960, Mrs. Fannie (Fincen) Sherwood. She married (1) Fincen, and (2) Luther Sherwood. Mr. Birch is an active member of Pender Methodist Church and served many years as Superintendent of the Sunday School. Issue:
  (*4.12511*) Melvin Russell Birch, born June 15, 1919, married Alice Ellen Simmons, issue: Ashton Karl Birch, born October 23, 1946; Rebecca Ruth Birch, born January 28, 1948; Mary Ellan Birch, born December 15, 1953; Lee Russell Birch, born March 22, 1956; and Neal Bruce Birch, born January 14, 1957.
  (*4.12512*) Mary Louise Birch, born March 8, 1921, died April 22, 1921.
  (*4.12513*) Ray McKee Birch, born March 29, 1924, married Dorothy Sherwood, daughter of Joseph and Fleetwood Sherwood. Issue: Susan Diane Birch, born May 20, 1953; Mary Jo Birch, born March 27, 1955; Sally Ray Birch, born October 8, 1957; and Glenn McKee Birch, born April 26, 1963.
  (*4.12514*) Phylis Ellin Birch, born March 4, 1930, married on December 4, 1948, Thompson Crockett Smith. Mr. Smith was born in Chilhowie, Virginia, December 3, 1928, a son of William Gordon and Rachel (Crock-

ett) Smith. Issue: Patricia Lynn Smith, born December 24, 1953; and Debra Kay Smith, born January 18, 1957.

*(4.12515)* Ralph Wilson Birch, born September 19, 1933, married Lora Stirling (whose mother was a Birch from Richmond), issue: Pamela Birch, born May 23, 1957; Christine Birch, born August 6, 1958; Gregory Stirling Birch, born June 28, 1961; and Robert Wilson Birch, born May 12, 1963.

*(4.12.6)* James Davis Birch, son of Elibeck W. and Frances Emeline America (Davis) Birch, was born October 4, 1877, and died October 3, 1902. He married in 1899, Pearl Lee, daughter of Franklin and Sarah (Jones) Lee. Mrs. Birch was a sister to Mary Ellen Lee who married Edwin Lee Birch, brother of James Davis Birch. Mrs. Birch was born July 24, 1875, died August 16, 1950. Issue:

*(4.12.61)* James Franklin Birch (called Frank), born May 7, 1902, died unmarried, February 28, 1922.

*(4.12.7)* Cora Elizabeth Birch, daughter of Elibeck W. and Frances Emeline America (Davis) Birch, was born February 10, 1876, and married John Hurst, son of Edward Smith and Ann Virginia (Costello) Hurst. Issue:

*(4.12.71)* Frances Virginia Hurst, born July 23, 1904, married Charles O'Shaughnessy.

*(4.12.72)* Mary Hurst, unmarried.

(5) Thomas Birch, son of Colonel Joseph and Janet Bowmaker (Robertson) Birch, was born in 1774, and died June 21, 1856, age 82 years. Mr. Birch is buried in Oakwood Cemetery at Falls Church. He married in Washington, D. C., on November 5, 1834, to Franzoni (Fanny) Hodgson. She was born in 1780, and was living in 1860 with her daughter, Mrs. Taylor *(Census)*. There is a deed of record in Arlington County *(Deed Book 2, page 500)* which shows that Thomas Birch deeded land to James Birch, being the same tract given to Abraham Birch, son of Joseph Birch, Sr., deceased. This record is dated May 19, 1831. Issue:

(51) Emily Birch, born 1809, died November 27, 1891, married in Washington, D.C., January 3, 1854, to William H. Taylor. Mr. Taylor was born in 1805, died March 2, 1889, and is buried in Oakwood Cemetery. The Taylors owned Taylor's Tavern at what is now 7 Corners. They had no family, but reared the children of James W. West.

(6) James Birch, son of Colonel Joseph and Janet Bowmaker (Robertson) Birch, married in the Presbyterian Meeting House in Alexandria, on January 5, 1799, to Priscilla (Prisey) Green. Mr. and Mrs. Birch lived where the Ballston Presbyterian Church was later built. On September 12, 1849, James and Priscilla Birch deeded land to their son, Jacob Wesley Birch. (Arlington County *Deed Book 6, page 4*). On November 3, 1851, James Birch, Sr., and Priscilla, his wife, deeded land to William Bowling and John T. Birch, trustees, and Nancy Bowling, wife of William Bowling, was also a party to this document. (Arlington County *Deed Book 6, page 350*). James and Priscilla (Green) Birch had issue:

(61) Jacob Wesley Birch.

(62) James Birch, Jr., married Mrs. Aletha Buchanan (James Slatford, Bondsman), on February 4, 1823. James Birch, Sr., gave his written consent to the marriage, filed in Alexandria County, D.C.

(63) Elizabeth Birch, married on January 4, 1815, in Alexandria County, D.C., to Robert Donaldson (Thomas Donaldson and James Birch, Bondsmen). They had a number of children, some of whom were: Robert Franklin Donaldson, born September 22, 1830; Samuel Hancock Donaldson, born April 11, 1831; John Rutledge Donaldson, born September 15, 1834, and Almira America Donaldson, born December 3, 1839. These children were all baptized on July 6, 1845 at the home of James Birch. Baptized at the same time was Frances Victoria Birch, born March 16, 1845, daughter of Robert and Mary Birch.

(64) Robert Birch, married in Washington, D.C., February 16, 1833, to Mary Ann Harrison. Their children included a daughter, Frances Victoria Birch, born March 16, 1845.

(65) John Thornton Birch, married Sarah Thompson.

(66) George A. Birch, married in Washington, D. C., on May 8, 1838, to Susan Hodgson.

(67) Henry Birch, married in Washington, D. C., on July 18, 1855, to Pamelia A. Jones.

(68) Ann Birch, married William Bowling.

John Thornton Birch (65) son of James and Priscilla (Green) Birch, was born February 4, 1817, and died January 3, 1900. He made his will February 19, 1897, probated in January, 1900 (Arlington County, *Will Book 10, page 416*). In it he mentioned his deceased wife, Susan (buried in Mt. Olivet Methodist Cemetery), daughter, Paulina Gertrude Collison, wife of John Collison; daughter, Althea Gibson; son, Peter T. Birch; son, Millard F. Birch; grandson, George Bell; grandson, Theophilus Birch; grandson, John Otto Birch (who died before the will was probated); Mary Birch, mother of John Otto Birch, and his daughter-in-law, was also mentioned. Witnesses were: Samuel H. Lunt, Louis C. Barley, and R. H. Havener. Witnesses to a codicil to the will were: W. G. Duckett, William H. Baden, and James L. Clements.

John Thornton Birch was married in Washington, D. C., on January 14, 1836, to Sarah (or Susannah) Thompson. Mrs. Birch was born March 18, 1812, and died November 16, 1891. She is buried beside her husband in Mt. Olivet Methodist Cemetery. Issue:[14]

(651) Rebirta Birch, born May 2, 1847, died March 29, 1884.

(652) Paulina Gertrude Birch, married John Collison.

(653) Peter Thornton Birch, married (1) Maria Armstrong (who died in childbirth one year afterwards); (2) Catherine (Katie) L. Graves; and (3) Emma ———. By his second wife, Mr. Birch had a daughter, Daisy Maria Birch, who married Frank J. Kennedy. She died July 5, 1917, age 37 years, 10 months, and 15 days, and is buried in Oakwood Cemetery, Falls Church. Children included Bernard T. Kennedy (died October 21, 1918, age 16 years, 3 mos., and 4 days); and Emma C. Kennedy, now Berger, who lives (1959) in Vienna. Mrs. Berger, in a telephone interview on June 19, 1958, kindly supplied data on the John Thornton Birch family.

(654) Millard F. Birch, born 1856, died May 10, 1913.

(655) Sarah L. Birch, born June 19, 1851, died November 30, 1890, married ——— Beall.

(656) Althea Birch, married ——— Gibson.

(7) William Birch of "Birchland," son of Colonel Joseph and Janet Bowmaker (Robertson) Birch, died October 18, 1870, and was buried in the family cemetery (now at the corner of 37th and North Abingdon Streets, Arlington). He lived at "Birchland," or "Cooney Manor," now 3612 N. Glebe Road, Arlington.

Mr. Birch married in Washington, D. C., February 11, 1812, Elizabeth Alton.

On March 8, 1822, William Birch deeded land to the following persons (Arlington County *Deed Book 2, page 548*): William Payne, Peter Sherman, John R. Bussard, Joseph Sewell, Isaac Reed, William Minor, Alexander Boutchar (Boucher), Mrs. John Butcher, John Robertson, Sr., Thomas Elliott, Caleb Birch, Thomas Birch, Joseph Birch, Isaac Birch, William Goodrich, William Harrison, William Nelson, Thomas Mattingly and Joseph Nicholdson, a "Committee of Contributors & Builders of a Schoolhouse." This was witnessed by James Payne, Andrew Hipkins, and William Still.

Mr. Birch was called "Cooney Birch," and the crest of the hill where he lived was often called "Cooney Manor." Many of the persons who lived along the Potomac were called "Coony" probably because they enjoyed coon hunting. This seemed to have been applied to persons who lived in the Walker Chapel area. However, Albert Wren of Long View (near Merrifield) was called "Coony" Albert Wren.

Augusta McNeir Weaver wrote a charming paper entitled "Memories of Birchland," in 1896. The original is now owned by Mrs. Walter T. Weaver of Arlington. In this we have a glimpse of William ("Uncle Billie") Birch:

> Near the west end of "Chain Bridge" on the crest of the hill is a place that "before the War" was known as Kooney...In Old Colonial days an old settler, whom we will call "Uncle Billie Birch," was owner of a large portion of this place. I do not know whether he received it as a direct grant from "George III" or even earlier, but a title given at a sale a few years ago showed by the records that it had been in possession of the family for over one hundred years... I do not think I would make a wrong statement when I say that they were among the "First Families of Virginia." Now Uncle Billie had five daughters, and again the old ancestral habits showed themselves, for each daughter had the name "Ann" —given in this way: Martha-Ann, Mary-Ann, Sarah-Ann, Elizabeth-Ann, and Ann, only, as the last... For some years before his death Uncle Billie made his home (at the home of his daughter Martha Ann Titus)... and what a quaint figure he made going around early in the morning. He wore what was then called a roundabout jacket with big white buttons, while on his head was a nightcap of white flannel and then his beaver hat on top of that. He always carried a cane from natural wood. One Sunday morning he came in the sitting room and was looking for his Prayer Book upon the shelves. Not being able to put his hands right on it, he flew into a temper and something like oaths, it sounded to me; but he found it at last and sat down and found the Collect and Epistles for the day as quietly as though nothing had happened.
>
> ...His old friend Doctor Wunder would come in and the decanter would be brought from the sideboard, and hot water and sugar. Then the great question of the day—the Secession of Virginia—would be discussed pro and con until the exhausted participants would drop off in a doze, no nearer to settling the great question than when they commenced. One held that the South must have her rights, Union or no Union, while the other boldly averred that the Union

must be preserved. They would argue and shake their canes at each other and sip their grog, and when brother (Samuel) Titus would come in with a big roll of newspapers—or as he called them—"Documents from Washington," and they would read speeches from Congress . . .

Mr. Birch made his will October 18, 1870, and it was probated in Alexandria County, December 5, 1870 (*Will Book 9, page 277*). He mentioned his daughter, Martha Titus (who received land at Langley); his daughter Elizabeth J. Deeble, wife of E. S. Deeble; his daughter, Mary Downing; his daughter Sarah Hitchcock; his daughter Ann Cown (who was to receive the "old homestead"); and the following grandchildren: Maria V. Deeble, Silas W. Deeble, Ellison H. Deeble, India Sellers, Elizabeth E. Deeble, and Lucy A. Deeble. Executor was Edward K. S. Deeble. Witnesses were: T. B. J. Frye, Richard Hirst, and J. W. Sewell.

William and Elizabeth (Alton) Birch had issue:

(*71*) Elizabeth Ann Birch, married in Washington, D. C., May 31, 1838, Edward Karl Scarborough Deeble. Mr. Deeble was from the Eastern Shore of Virginia, and was a cabinet maker. He served in the Confederate Army. They had ten children: Thomas Winfield Deeble, Maria V. Deeble, Silas Wright Deeble, Ellison H. Deeble, Elizabeth E. Deeble, Lucy A. Deeble, Alice Deeble, Mildred Lee Deeble (September 18, 1855-April 17, 1955) unmarried; and America Ann Deeble who married William Ball. Mr. Ball, a son of Horatio Ball, Sr., and Elizabeth (Marcey) Ball, was born June 11, 1842 and died January 12, 1920. Mrs. America Ann (Deeble) Ball was born October 19, 1849. Children of William and America Ann (Deeble) Ball included: Maude Elizabeth Ball, married Robert E. Croson; Edward Wade Ball, married Maude Lawrence; Horatio Clark Ball, married Ida Omohundro; Senator Frank Livingston Ball, married Anna Marie Shreve; and Dallas Deeble Ball.

(*72*) Martha Ann Birch, married (1) February 4, 1843, to Joseph Edward McNeir (died October 14, 1843); and (2) Samuel Titus. Joseph Edward McNeir, Jr., a son, was born January 13, 1844. (An extensive account of this family is given in Melvin Lee Steadman's *Walker Chapel: In the First Hundred Years.*)

(*73*) Mary Ann Birch, married in Washington, D. C., July 19, 1843, to James W. Langton (called Thomas Langton in some accounts). She remarried (2) ——— Downing. A son was Samuel Langton.

(*74*) Sarah Ann Birch, married in Washington, D. C., November 16, 1847, to Thomas Hitchcock.

(*75*) Ann Birch, married ——— Crown.

(8) Caleb Birch of "Birchwood," son of Colonel Joseph and Janet Bowmaker (Robertson) Birch, married on September 6, 1806 in Alexandria County, to Mary Bowling (Joseph Bowling, Bondsman). On March 15, 1821, Caleb Birch made a deed to Thomas Janney and John Douglass Brown. (Arlington County, *Deed Book 2, page 501*). For rents, etc., Birch conveyed 37½ acres of land for the purpose of mining. This land was allotted to the "said *Taylor* Birch" in a division of his father, Joseph Birch, deceased. Witnesses were: Thomas L. Martin, John T. O. Wilbar and Silas Reed. It may be that Mr. Birch was named "Caleb Taylor Birch."

"Birch Town," an area adjacent to Glebe Road including the Country Club and

St. Mary's Episcopal Church in Arlington, was named for this Caleb Birch.
Caleb and Mary (Bowling) Birch had issue:[15]
- (*81*) John Birch, married Mary Pennington in Washington, D. C., on December 29, 1835. She was from Baltimore. Issue; Jacob Birch, Amos Birch, Caleb Birch, Lewis Birch, Edward Birch, unmarried; Lucy Birch, married Patrick Smith; Mariah Birch, married William Campbell (and had a daughter who married Ernest Marcey); Mary Ann Birch, married in Washington, D. C., December 23, 1854, Samuel Marcey; and Sarah Frances Birch, married John Elliott. Lewis and Jacob Birch married and had issue.
- (*82*) Jacob Birch.
- (*83*) Samuel Birch, married Rachel Simmons.
- (*84*) Caleb Birch, married (1) ———; and (2) Carrie ———.

Of the above, Samuel Birch (*83*) married in Washington, D. C., on February 5, 1834, to Rachel Simmons. On November 4, 1864, Samuel Birch ("of Caleb") and Rachel his wife sold to Robert Walker the "Bealer tract," part of the estate of John Birch, deceased, on the road from Ball's X Roads to Chain Bridge (Arlington County *Deed Book 8, page 338*). Issue:
- (*831*) Andrew E. Birch, died unmarried, March 19, 1920, age 59 years. He is buried in a family cemetery near old N. Summit Station in Arlington.
- (*832*) Jane Birch, died unmarried.
- (*833*) Charles Birch.
- (*834*) Caleb H. W. Birch, married Annie and had issue, among others, Belle Birch who died January 8, 1950.
- (*835*) Elizabeth Jane Birch, born November 25, 1835, died February 6, 1903. She is buried at Walker Chapel. Married James Marcey, Jr., born April 17, 1831, died March 5, 1922.
- (*836*) Richard W. Birch, born June 20, 1858, died January 18, 1932, buried at Walker Chapel. Mr. Birch married Cordelia Kidwell, born April 5, 1862, died March 28, 1937. Among their children was Joseph Walter Birch, born March 2, 1894, who married on July 25, 1916, Fannie Belle Swartz. Mrs. Birch was born in Georgetown, D. C., October 1, 1902, a daughter of Clarence Luther and Florence Lula Belle (Kerns) Swartz. Mrs. Florence L. B. (Kerns) Swartz was a sister of Mrs. Ida Jane Steadman of Falls Church. Joseph Walter Birch, Jr., born May 21, 1921, married on July 20, 1940, Jeanne Ethel Cheek and had: Joseph Walter Birch, III, born November 15, 1941; Kenneth Edward Birch, born December 17, 1942; Richard Birch, born March 15, 1944; and Donna Jeanne Birch, born August 24, 1954); and James Richard Birch, married on August 1, 1959, Linda Ann Leatherland.

(*84*) Caleb Birch, son of Caleb and Mary (Bowling) Birch, married (1) ———; and (2) Carrie ———. His widow, Carrie Birch, died in 1904. Her will was made November 26, 1903, probated April 6, 1904 (Arlington County *Will Book 11, page 25*). In it she mentions her son, Orlando Birch. Witnesses were: Edmonia Payne and Albert Williams. Issue (perhaps others):
- (*841*) Orlando Birch, son of Caleb and Carrie Birch, was born in 1846, and died September 10, 1921, age 75 years. He married at Dulin Chapel, December 28, 1869, Mildred C. Fletcher. Mr. Birch made his will February 17, 1921,

probated September 14, 1921 (Arlington County *Will Book 13, page 31*). His wife was living, and he mentioned his grandson, William E. Conserver; his son, Robert E. Birch; his daughter, Gertrude Reid, wife of Horatio Reid; his daughter, Mary Kerns; and his grandson, William E. Birch. Witnesses were: Harry R. Thomas and William C. Gloth. Issue: Robert Edwin Birch, born 1871, married and had among others, William E. Birch; Gertrude Birch, baptized March 17, 1872, at Dulin Chapel, married Horatio Reid, Sr.; and Mary Birch, married William Kerns of Baltimore.

(9) Elizabeth Birch, daughter of Colonel Joseph and Janet Bowmaker (Robertson) Birch, married Archibald J. Taylor. In November, 1822, Elizabeth Taylor deeded to Samuel Birch, in consideration "of the natural love and affection she bears to her children," for $1.00, thirty-six acres of land, one yellow slave, Louisa, one black slave, Monica, (and her child, Eliza); two cows, furniture, and other items. This was to be held in trust by Samuel Birch for Elizabeth's children, William, Robert, Mary, James, Martha, and Ann Taylor. Witnesses were: Russell Stevens, William Follin, and William Simms. (Arlington County, *Deed Book 2, page 552*).

(*11*) John Birch, son of Colonel Joseph and Janet Bowmaker (Robertson) Birch, no other record. *Note:* one John Birch married in Fauquier County, March 15, 1796, Elizabeth Benam (Roger Benam, Bondsman).

(*12*) Isaac Birch, son of Colonel Joseph and Janet Bowmaker (Robertson) Birch, lived in Georgetown, D.C. He married, in the Presbyterian Meeting House, Alexandria, September 8, 1815, to Elizabeth Walker. His guardian, following his father's death, was Elijah Chenault, indicating that Isaac was a young son. (Alexandria *Will Book 2, page 70*). Issue:

(*12.1*) Joseph F. Birch, married on June 15, 1840, in Washington, D. C., Ann E. Dunham of Maryland. Mr. Birch was an undertaker in Georgetown, and his business, established in 1841, is still owned by his descendants. Children included Isaac Birch who married Minnie Magruder Graves, and they had a daughter, Bessie Birch, who married Archibald Haycock of Falls Church.

(*12.2*) Isaac Birch.

(*12.3*) Charles I. Birch (married on January 12, 1849, Margaret E. Gill).

(*12.4*) Taylor Birch.

(*12.5*) Louisa Birch, married William Walker.

---

[1] *North Carolina Historical & Genealogical Register,* Volume 3, page 131.
[2] *Virginia Magazine,* Volume 13, page 77.
[3] *Virginia Magazine,* Volume 9, page 257.
[4] The first record was filed May 13, 1746, by Alexander Doniphan, James Hansbrough and Peter Hansbrough. (*Record Book M,* page 461). In the same book (at page 515) is the account referred to above. It was begun in September, 1745. James Grant was administrator.
[5] James Bowmaker made his will November 10, 1770, probated in Fairfax County, January 21, 1771. Legatees included: Cousin, Jennett (Janet) Bowmaker Robertson, daughter of James Robertson, Sr.; Elizabeth Robertson and John Robertson, son and daughter of the same. Executor was Elizabeth Robertson. Witnesses were: John Ball, Mary Cook, and Charles Craig.
[6] Arlington County, Virginia, *Deed Book T,* page 471.
[7] William B. Richards and Priscilla Crook were married December 19, 1820. (Note on the marriage record filed at Arlington Court House states that Priscilla's mother, Ann Crook, was guardian of her own children: Priscilla, Joseph, Elizabeth, and Bernard Crook.)

[8] There is some question as to his name—it may have been William John *Randolph* Birch.
[9] *1850 U. S. Census of Fairfax County*, page 1927.
[10] Orrin Orton (1799-June 1855) son of Luther Orton, was born in Connecticut. He came to Falls Church during the 1830's, and was a farmer. He purchased part of the old "Winter Hill" farm of Colonel James Wren.
[11] The author has extensive notes on the Davis-Cross-Fitzhugh family, which can be made available to interested persons.
[12] Some of his children are listed in his household in the 1860 *U.S. Census of Fairfax County*. (See Census, page 904). Mr. Birch was a Wheelwright in 1860.
[13] Robert Jones, Esquire, was born in England and came to America when age 14 years (with his Uncle, Dr. Owen). He married Sarah Ellen Hitaffer and lived in Loudoun County. (Mrs. Jones had brothers John and Francis Hitaffer, school teachers in New Franklin, Mo., and a sister, Elizabeth Hitaffer. Robert and Sarah Ellen (Hitaffer) Jones had issue: John Jones, Herndon Jones, Owen Whitehall Jones, and Celie Jones, married Taylor. —Notes from an interview with Mrs. Harry Lewis Jones.
[14] There may have been a son, John Birch, born in Alexandria County in 1837, who married on December 6, 1871, in Loudoun County, to Mary J. Grimes. She was age 26 years when married, a native of Fauquier County. Mrs. Birch was a daughter of Greenbury and Elizabeth J. Grimes.
[15] There is proof for the children, John and Samuel, in Arlington County, *Deed Book 9*, page 450.

## THE ALMOND BIRCH FAMILY

Almond Birch was known as "Yankee Birch," to distinguish him from the other families of that name who were natives of this area. Mr. Birch was born at Clifton Park, Saratoga County, New York, and settled in Falls Church on a twenty-acre farm in 1856. His home was part of Colonel James Wren's "Winter Hill" tract on East Broad Street, and the house is still standing. The old house now has a Cherry Street address and is in a grove of lovely old spruce trees.

The Birch family lived for a time at Aldie and was there during the War Between the States. They returned to Falls Church following the War. Two officers of the Union Army were captured at the Birch home on June 18, 1863. The official report, by Colonel James C. Rice, follows:

Headquarters, Picket Reserve, June 18, 1863.

Lieut. John M. Clark, Acting Assist. A.G.:

In accordance with directions from the Commanding Officer of the brigade I report the facts in regard to the capture of Major (William R.) Sterling and Captain Fisher, as related to me by the people of the house where they were taken.

Major Sterling and Captain Fisher were on their way to communicate with General Pleasonton when they halted at the residence of Mr. (Almond) Birch for supper and to inquire how far it was to Aldie. Having finished their supper they started for their horses which were left with their orderly at the yard gate. The horses and orderly had been removed, and before Major Sterling and Captain Fisher had reached the gate 10 or 12 Cavalrymen seized them and hurriedly mounted them and bore them off. This took place last evening at 10 o'clock, about 400 yards from the picket outpost at the house of Mr. Birch on the Little River Turnpike. Mr. Birch and family are from Clifton Park, Saratoga County, New York. They are union people, known to some of the officers of our regiment. I am satisfied that these people had no complicity with this affair, and had no knowledge of the enemy's being anywhere near their house. The capture of these officers appears to have been as unexpected to the enemy as it was to the officers captured, since the enemy was unaware of our forces being so near.

I also report that I have re-established the picket line in some respects since coming upon duty this morning, so as among other points to include the house of Mr. Birch. All is quiet upon the line.

I am, most respectively, your obedient servant,

JAMES C. RICE,
Colonel, Commanding outposts.

Among other property owned by Almond Birch was the house at 170 East Broad Street which was later owned by William H. G. Lynch, and which has long been called the "Lynch House." Mr. Birch acquired other property and was well-to-do.

Almond Birch was born October 3, 1814, and died February 15, 1907.[1] His wife, whom he married at Clifton Park, New York, in 1837, was Jane Eliza Keeler. Mrs. Birch was born September 13, 1817 and died August 10, 1889.[2] Both are buried in Rock Creek Cemetery in Washington. Issue:

(1) Ruth Ann Birch, born Clifton Park, New York, 1839, married John H. Gheen at Falls Church on October 31, 1866. Mr. Gheen was a widower, born in Chester County, Pennsylvania, 1838, a son of Benedict and Susan Gheen. He was a butcher.

(2) Sylvanus Almond Birch, born Clifton Park, New York, 1843, married and settled in Falls Church.

(3) Edward James Birch, born Clifton Park, New York, in 1846, died at Falls Church in 1923. Mr. Birch settled in Falls Church in 1866 when his father returned here. He was a merchant, and built the store later owned for many years by the Brown family. Mr. Birch was for some years Post Master of Falls Church, and also served as Mayor. He married on April 26, 1871, at Dulin Chapel, to Mary Catherine Shreve, daughter of Benjamin F. and Sarah (Simpson) Shreve. Issue:

(*31*) Herbert Almond Birch, baptized at Dulin Chapel on August 31, 1872, married Jean McFarlan.

(*32*) Alice Edna Birch, baptized February 12, 1875, at Dulin Chapel, married A. C. Bryan and lived at Brooklyn, New York. No issue.

(*33*) Nellie Shreve Birch, born April 8, 1875, died May 5, 1938. She married (1) George C. Altemus, proprietor of grocery stores in Washington and later in building and real estate. She remarried (2) Frederick S. Stitt, a patent attorney. Mrs. Stitt was a member of the Fairfax Chapter, D.A.R. Issue: G. Edward Altemus, and Catharine (Altemus) Woolwine, the latter of Nashville, Tennessee.

(*34*) Walter Edward Birch, born January 6, 1877, now deceased.

(*35*) George Albert Birch, married and had issue: Francis and David Birch.

(*36*) Mary Simpson Birch, married R. C. Newbold and lived in Wayne, Pennsylvania. Issue: Richard and Mary Carolyn Newbold.

(4) Margaret Keeler Birch, born Clifton Park, New York, in 1852, married at Falls Church in 1883 (1) —— Brown; and (2) James H. ("Mack") Crossman.

---

[1] Information on this family was supplied by George Albert Birch of Washington, D. C.

[2] Mrs. Birch was a daughter of Minor Lawrence Keeler (1796-1866) and Margaret (Shephard) Keeler (1796-1891). They were married in Clifton Park in 1816. She was a granddaughter

of Nathaniel Keeler (born 1760) and Rhoda (Lawrence) Keeler, who were married at South Salem in 1786.

## THE BOWEN FAMILY

John Thomas Bowen, descendant of an old South Carolina family, was born in Easley, in that State. Mr. Bowen married in 1911, Georgia Steedly. She was a daughter of Dr. Benjamin Steedly, a prominent physician and surgeon of Athens, Georgia. Dr. Steedly purchased a hotel in Chick Springs, South Carolina, and converted it into a private hospital. Mr. and Mrs. John T. Bowen moved to Falls Church in 1919, and resided at 209 Great Falls Street. Mrs. Bowen died in 1940.

Their daughter, Martha C. Bowen, while attending a local school, wrote the following concerning Falls Church:[1]

Six miles southwest of Washington lies the town of Falls Church—and a small town it was when I moved there twenty-three years ago. There was a highway named Lee then, as there is now; but it fell far short of the modern definition of a highway. It was narrow and it was dirt, and the ruts went deep. Citizens who lived along the highway took their duties seriously in those days and filled the deeper holes with cinders and clinkers from their furnaces. Some of the town folk in Falls Church went to Washington by automobile on Saturdays. There they visited old Center Market and bought provisions for the week.

The main connection with Washington was by the trolley which left the city from the main depot opposite the old gray stone post office at 12th and Pennsylvania Avenue. The motorman and the conductor were the same person, and he knew all his customers. You could go to sleep and he would wake you at your stop. If your land adjoined the car tracks you could have a station named for you by paying $25.00 to build the small shed (which was the waiting place). Then the car would stop at your front door.

Falls Church was dormant then, and the people liked it that way. You didn't count as one of its real inhabitants until you had been there at least fifty years. Five generations and you were good and solid—provided your grandfather fought on the right side. We had moved to Virginia from Washington, but since parents had both come from South Carolina, we were accepted on probation. The house my father bought was rooted in broom sage and weeds and their density resembled the forest that Prince Charming penetrated to get to Sleeping Beauty.

One Saturday after we had moved, my father walked to the Village to buy a scythe. Mr. (Nathan) Lynch kept a feed and hardware store there. You could usually find Mr. Lynch in front of his store leaning against a tree, chewing tobacco and the rag with the natives. When Dad told him he had come to buy a scythe Mr. Lynch said, "Why, Mr. Bowen, you don't want to buy that scythe. That scythe's expensive. Haven't the Keiths got one you can borrow?" The Keiths had the house next door to us and they probably would have been glad to lend us a scythe, but my father thought we should have one of our own.

John Thomas and Georgia (Steedly) Bowen had issue:
(1) Martha Carolina Bowen, married in 1942, to Captain Robert O. Strange, issue: John Bowen Strange and Georgia Strange. (Robert Strange, a son of Captain Strange by his first wife, is a graduate of the U.S. Naval Academy).

(2) John Thomas Bowen, Jr., married Judith Rogner, issue: William Bowen, John Bowen, and Judith Bowen.

---

[1] From a paper entitled "As I Remember It," by Martha C. Bowen, MS., Falls Church Library, written ca. 1940.

---

## THE BRAMHALL FAMILY AND "HOLLYWOOD FARM"

The Bramhall family owned property in Falls Church prior to the War Between the States. Part of their property included "Hollywood Farm," which now makes up Falls Hill Subdivision at West Falls Church, the Flagg "Highland View Farm" and adjacent land. The basis for data on the Bramhall family is statements made by the late David Leonard, and information from an old broad-side in the author's file.

According to the broadside, dated 1875 (and quoted elsewhere) the farm contained 100 acres of land, 25 acres in timber (oak, chestnut, cedar, pine and locust) with a large peach and apple orchard. The owner at the time of the 1875 sale was C. H. Bramhall, father of Colonel William L. Bramhall of Washington, D.C. A corruption of the name Bramhall is "Bramblehaw." The farm was sold on Wednesday, January 19, 1876, and the sale was made by John T. Bramhall of the stock and farm implements. This included a nine year old horse, 1 Chester-Essex Yearling Sow, an extension-seat Virginia barouche (of the "best make, leather-top, with pole and shafts"); 1 farm wagon with new box; 1 spring Market Wagon (with Torsion springs with a capacity of 1,500 lbs.); and plows, cultivator, seed-sower, corn-sheller, grindstone, 500 lb. scales and large kettle. Also for sale were the harness, saddles, corn and fodder on the grounds. Mr. E. F. Crocker was the Auctioneer.

According to tradition, the small but charming "Hollywood Farm" house was erected as early as 1750. It is the opinion of the author (having studied old records and talked with old residents) that the present house, greatly remodeled, is of a date about the time of the Revolutionary War. However, there was standing until about the time of the first World War an old log structure (used as a kitchen) which was a portion of the original house, and could have been built prior to 1750.

The present building originally had two small rooms (now one large room) each containing a fireplace. The rooms were divided by two white columns. In the corner near the stairway, Mr. Berry, an owner during the early 1900's, shot himself. He had been depressed for sometime because of the fact that the A. & F. R. R. cut his farm in half. Subsequent owners have said that his ghost still invades their privacy. The house had four small windows in the front upstairs (where a dormer window now is). It is said originally a smaller porch was on the front.

"Hollywood Farm" house is now owned by Dr. and Mrs. Nelson Podolnick.

---

## THE BROADWATER FAMILY

Captain Charles Broadwater, a merchant mariner, made a number of trips to Virginia between 1710 and his settlement here in 1717. Captain Broadwater was a native of the Village of Godalmering, Surrey, England. Some facts concerning his life are to be found in a deposition given by Abraham Lay, seventy-one year old resident of Loudoun County on May 25, 1771.[1] Lay stated that he came to this country in June, 1715, "in the capacity of a Cabbin Boy in the Ship Robert and John—Charles Broadwater, Commander, and as well as he Remembers thinks that the ship was Recommended to Messrs. Rozer and Adison or otherwise consigned to them to procure a Load of Tobacco . . . " He goes on to say that Major John West died sometime the following December (1715) and between that date and "the latter end of May, 1716," Captain Broadwater married the widow of Major West.

The Widow, Elizabeth (Semmes) West, a native of Maryland, had several children by Major West, and it is thought was his second wife. Mr. Lay testified that in the following July, near the beginning of the month, Captain Broadwater left "the country with his said Ship and proceeded to London and this Deponent with him in his capacity aforesaid."

Captain Broadwater and Lay returned in the same Ship in May, 1717, but William Mudge acted as Commander, in the place of Broadwater. Lay came along "in the capacity of an apprentice to the Caulkers Business," and continued to live with Captain Broadwater for the next four years at "his dwelling place." During this time Broadwater erected a wharf on the land which had belonged to Major West; "the said Captain Broadwater built two twelve hh° Flatts[2] and one nine hh° Flatt at the present Plaintiffs (John West's) Landing."[3]

Lay remained an apprentice for three additional years, and acted in the capacity of Overseer at a Quarter which belonged to Broadwater "about five miles distant," (near Falls Church). In 1771 John West (Jr.) had a Quarter at the same place. Lay continued in the service of Broadwater " . . . Except three or four years that he worked for himself . . . in the capacity of an Overseer, a freeman or hired," and continued until the death of his master. Lay testified that Broadwater died between 1730 and 1735.

Captain Broadwater was elected a Vestryman of Truro Parish in 1732, and died in 1733. An Inventory of his estate was filed on August 21, 1734 in Prince William County.[4] On that same day, Eliza Broadwater, widow of Captain Charles Broadwater, was awarded her third of the estate.[5] Not long afterwards she gave Bond (with John Turley and Valentine Peyton as Securities) as guardian of Charles Broadwater, Jr.[6]

Captain Broadwater had at least two children, Charles Broadwater, Jr., and Guy Broadwater. Guy Broadwater was a Surveyor in Fairfax County, but no other record has been found.

Colonel Charles Broadwater, son of Captain Charles and Elizabeth (Semmes) Broadwater, was born at his father's plantation on the south side of Great Hunting Creek in 1719. He died March 26, 1806, age 87 years,[7] and was buried at his plantation "Springfield," in what is now Vienna Woods. None of the early graves were marked, and the United States Government erected two of the three standing markers. The monument to Colonel Charles Broadwater, erected by the D.A.R., has this inscription:

Col. Charles Broadwater
Colonial Service
died 1806

A portion of the Broadwater home is standing on Frederick Street in Vienna Woods, and the graves are near the road.

By 1756, Charles Broadwater was Sheriff of Fairfax County, and a Captain of the Virginia Militia on active duty in the campaign against the French and Indians.

During that year he sent a dispatch to George Washington who relayed the information to his superiors, indicating he had "received an express from Captn Broadwater at the Gap of the Short Hills (now Hillsboro) informing me that himself and the Captns. Ramsay, Minor and Hamilton with abt (about) 100 men were at this place; that he had received dispatches to hurry on the Militia and desir'd to know wht (what) number shou(l)d be sent."[8]

Broadwater owned a slave, Samuel Jenkins, (formerly owned by a local resident of that name) who drove a team with a provision wagon belonging to his master, over the Alleghenys in the memorable campaign when Braddock was killed. Jenkins was in the Battle of Big Meadows and escaped without injury. When about forty years of age, upon Broadwater's death, Jenkins was purchased by a gentleman who took him to Ohio and freedom. He settled in Lancaster, Ohio, where he lived to a great age, said to be 115 years old at death in 1849. He was probably the last survivor of "Braddock's men."[9]

By 1774 Broadwater was Major of Militia, and shortly afterwards a full Colonel. Active in local affairs, he was made a Vestryman of Truro Parish in 1744, and served until the creation of Fairfax Parish in 1765. From 1765 until the outbreak of the Revolutionary War, Broadwater served as Vestryman in Fairfax Parish, and again in 1787.

In 1768 Colonel Broadwater and Edward Dulin were elected Church Wardens of Fairfax Parish (which included the Falls Church). He attended the Falls Church, lived nearby, and later continued to attend as long as services were held. Broadwater was in charge of the repairs on the old Falls Church, as noted earlier, but did not complete the work to the satisfaction of the Vestry. It was after this that the Vestry decided to build the present building.

Colonel Broadwater served as a Justice of Fairfax County from October, 1770, until March, 1785. He also served as a Burgess from Fairfax County from August 11, 1774, until June 1, 1775. The election, by which Broadwater and George Washington were elected as Burgesses, was held on Thursday, July 14, 1774. On that date, a young Englishman, Nicholas Cresswell, on a visit to Virginia, noted in his *Journal:*[10]

> An Election for Burgesses in town (Alexandria) (their Elections are annual.) There were three Candidates, the Poll was over in about two hours and conducted with great order and regularity. The members Col. George Washington and Major Bedwater (Broadwater). The Candidates gave the populace a Hogshead of Toddy (what we call Punch in England). In the evening the returned Member gave a Ball to the Freeholders and Gentlemen of the town. This was conducted with great harmony. Coffee and Chocolate, but no Tea. This Herb is in disgrace amongst them at present.

Just prior to the election, Washington wrote to Bryan Fairfax urging him to run against Broadwater in the pending event:[11]

> I entreated several gentlemen at our church yesterday to press Colo. Mason to take a poll, as I really think Major Broadwater, though a good man, might do as well in the discharge of his domestic concerns as in the capacity of a Legislator

This may be a hint at the deficiency of the work done by Broadwater on the Falls Church.

At a meeting of the freeholders held at Fairfax Court House (then at Alexandria) on July 18, 1774, it was decided that George Washington and Charles Broadwater, Gentlemen, "lately elected our Representatives to serve in the General Assembly," be directed to attend the Convention at Williamsburg on August 1st, and present the *Fairfax Resolves* written by Colonel George Mason.

During the Revolutionary War, Colonel Broadwater opened a recruiting headquarters in the Falls Church. After 1780 he moved to his "Springfield" plantation in present-day Vienna. Here he lived out his old age in a quiet way, and was buried in the garden there beside his wife.

Colonel Broadwater married Mrs. Ann Amelia (Markham) Pearson, a daughter of Colonel John Markham and the widow of Dr. Thomas Pearson of Fairfax County.[12] She was older than Colonel Broadwater by ten years, and died June 29, 1796, age 87 years (*West Bible*).

Mrs. E. S. Brooks wrote concerning Mrs. Broadwater:[13]

> The wife of Col. Chas. Broadwater belonged to a family of English descent, with a long line of distinguished ancestors, whose record shows frequent intermarriages with titled nobility; this fact, combined with her remarkable beauty, elegance, and dignity, gained for her great admiration and she was often styled 'Queen of Women.' Arrayed in her long trained gowns of velvet and satin, with her dainty high heeled slippers, seated in her chair of state, with a maid on either side waving peacock fans, to cool the sultry air, or put to flight the daring fly, she would graciously receive her many friends and distinguished guests.

Colonel Charles and Ann Amelia (Markham) Broadwater had issue:
(1) (Lieutenant) Charles Lewis Broadwater, married Betheland Sebastian.
(2) Margaret Broadwater, married William Henderson.
(3) Sarah Broadwater, married Colonel John West.
(4) Jane Broadwater, married Colonel John Hunter.
(5) Amelia Broadwater, married (the Reverend) Benjamin Sebastian, Jr.

*Note:* The Coat of Arms used by Colonel Broadwater follows: Argent, on a pile between two silver anchors in a base; or an anchor sable—a female figure vested in argent, the right hand pointing silver to a rainbow above her head ppz. with the left supporting an anchor gules. Motto: *Spes mea in coelo* ("My hope is in Heaven").

(1) (Lieutenant) Charles Lewis Broadwater, son of Colonel Charles and Ann Amelia (Markham) Broadwater, was born in 1751, and died September 16, 1841, aged 90 years (*West Bible*). His tombstone is near his father's at "Springfield," and was erected by the United States government: "Lieut. Charles L. Broadwater/10th Virginia Regiment/Revolutionary War."

Lieutenant Broadwater served in Captain Thomas West's Company, 10th Virginia Regiment, which was commanded by Colonel Edward Stevens. He was commissioned November 18, 1776, and discharged April 21, 1778.

Lieutenant Broadwater married Betheland Sebastian,[14] daughter of Benjamin Sebastian, Sr., Attorney at Law, and Priscilla (Elkins) Sebastian (See *Sebastian*).

The Broadwaters lived in the old Sebastian home, "Montpelier," now the site of George Mason School.

(Lieutenant) Charles Lewis and Betheland (Sebastian) Broadwater had issue:
(*11*) (Captain) Charles Guy Broadwater, married Catherine Gunnell.
(*12*) William E. Broadwater, married Margaret Darne.
(*13*) Anna Markham Broadwater.
(*14*) George Broadwater.

(*11*) (Captain) Charles Guy Broadwater, Esquire, son of Lieutenant Charles Lewis and Betheland (Sebastian) Broadwater, was born January 9, 1786, and died at his home, "Springfield," August 20, 1827.[5] His grave bears a government marker and states that he served as a soldier in the 60th Regiment of Virginia Militia during the War of 1812. Broadwater was wounded in the Battle of North Point while commanding the local Company of Militia. He was a Lawyer and lived at Providence (Fairfax Court House) before retiring to "Springfield."

Captain Broadwater married on December 18, 1808, to Catherine Gunnell. She was a native of Fairfax County, born in March, 1792, and died October 23, 1826. His children moved to Callaway County, Missouri, along with the Wrens, and others.[16]

Captain Charles Guy and Catherine (Gunnell) Broadwater had issue:

(*111*) Anna C. Markham Broadwater, born February 19, 1810, died July 12, 1890 in St. Louis, Missouri. She married on May 25, 1830, to Matthew Elgin (see *Deed Book 4 Y's, page 102*, Loudoun County). He was born at "Greenfield," Loudoun County, July 3, 1803, a son of Francis and Jane Elgin, and died April 10, 1860. Mrs. E. S. Brooks, already quoted, wrote of her: "She had a most brilliant mind, and was loved and respected by all who knew her." In the autumn of 1836 she moved to Missouri, "bringing her younger brothers with her. The weather and scenery were so beautiful . . . she walked almost all the way. St. Louis was so small then they drove on to St. Charles, twenty miles farther and gradually came back to St. Louis, as it improved." Issue: Julia Jane Elgin, born July 15, 1837, in St. Louis, married John T. Watson; John Thomas Guy Elgin, born October 17, 1842, died ca. 1845; Frances Anna Elgin, born April 16, 1846, married December 23, 1874, Everett Shepherdson Brooks of Madisonville, Kentucky. The last named had issue: Elgin Shepherdson Brooks (born February 6, 1876) married on June 3, 1908, Grace Armour of St. Louis and had two children: Shepherdson Armour Brooks and Virginia Frances Brooks; and Everett Watson Brooks, born September 10, 1881, married on April 6, 1904, Beulah Ray O'Hara and had issue: Everett Watson Brooks, Jr., born October 18, 1907.

(*112*) Charles Henry Fairfax Broadwater, born May 5, 1812, moved to St. Charles, Missouri. He married in Fairfax County, October 18, 1835, to Emily Ann Smith. Children included Colonel Charles Arthur Broadwater, who moved to Helena, Montana, in 1860. Colonel C. A. Broadwater died in 1896. He was well-to-do, and President of the Montana National and the Montana Central R. R. Companies.

(*113*) Elizabeth Broadwater, born May 12, 1814, died about 1875 in Callaway County, Missouri.

(*114*) Sally Broadwater, born January 7, 1817, died May 21, 1821.

(*115*) Arthur Broadwater, born October 1, 1819, died in 1896 at his home near Fairfax. He remained in Virginia when the rest of his family moved to Missouri. Broadwater married Catherine Bradley, daughter of Peter B. and Catherine Bradley. See Fairfax County *Deed Book M#3, page 30* (suit, "Broadwater & Graham agt. Bradley's Admr.," etc.) His will is dated March 23, 1896 and is filed in Fairfax *Will Book G#2, page 612*. Issue: Guy Broadwater, Richard F. Broadwater, died unmarried; Charles F. Broadwater (with wife, Gertrude, living near Fairfax in 1933); H. Arthur Broadwater; and Isabel F. ("Belle") Broadwater, died unmarried.

(*116*) John Chapman Hunter Broadwater, born November 11, 1821, died about 1900 at New Florence, Montgomery County, Missouri. He married on February 25, 1841 to Caroline Jackson. Issue: Guy Broadwater of Webster Grove, Missouri, 1915; Mrs. Dixie Pulliam, widow, in New York, 1915; Robert Broadwater, died before 1915; and Callie Broadwater, died before 1915.

(*117*) Thomas Jefferson Broadwater, born September 11, 1824, died in February, 1910. He married in 1859 to Martha Smoot of Scotland County, Missouri, a niece of William B. Downing (who reared her). Issue: Edward Broadwater, Thomas Broadwater, John Broadwater, Arthur Broadwater, Harry Broadwater, daughter married E. T. Bogart; Guy Lewis Broadwater, who lived in Oakland, California (and had issue: Edward, Thomas, and a daughter, Mrs. Fannie Alexander).

(*118*) Guy Lewis Broadwater, born October 6, 1826, married on September 7, 1851, Marianna Davis.

(*12*) William E. Broadwater, son of Lieutenant Charles Lewis and Betheland (Sebastian) Broadwater, died before 1833. He married in Alexandria County, D.C., November 22, 1816 (Simon Darne, Bondsman) to Margaret Darne. In 1833 his widow and three children moved to Callaway County, Missouri.

(4) Jane Broadwater, daughter of Colonel Charles and Ann Amelia (Markham) Broadwater, married Colonel John Hunter, a native of Ayreshire, Scotland. He was a descendant of the Hunters of Hunterston Castle. Colonel Hunter settled at what is now Vienna (which was once known as "Ayre Hill" in honor of his plantation). The Hunter plantation adjoined "Springfield." Ann Hunter, a daughter, married Presley Gunnell. Their daughter, Janet Gunnell, married John Haycock. A grandson, William Harrison Haycock, was a Confederate soldier. Another descendant is Archer Haycock of Falls Church who lives on that portion of the Haycock-Minor-Broadwater estate on Haycock Road which came to him in direct line of descent.[17]

---

[1] This deposition is given in "John West vs. Elizabeth Yerby," filed in a volume at Fairfax Court House entitled *Land Records of Long Standing 1742-1770*, page 338. It is noted that Lay traveled 29 miles to testify.
[2] The author is uncertain as to what an hh° Flat was, but it was suggested to him that it may refer to a floating pier.
[3] This landing was on the south side of Great Hunting Creek.
[4] Prince William County, *Will Book C*, page 8.
[5] *Ibid, Will Book C*, page 33.
[6] *Ibid, Will Book C*, page 189.
[7] From the *West Family Bible*, owned by Miss Laura West of Falls Church. So far as it is known, this is the only record of the age of Colonel Broadwater. He gave his age as "48 or 49 years" on September 19, 1771 (hence born ca. 1723), see LRLS (opp. cit.), page 347. Broadwater stated that he was born on the West Plantation.
[8] *Writing of George Washington* by Jared Sparks, Volume 1, page 345. See also *Washington And His Neighbors*, by Charles W. Stetson, Garrett & Massie, Inc., Richmond, 1956, page 236.
[9] Mrs. E. S. Brooks, 1915, MS.—copy loaned by the family.
[10] *Journal of Nicholas Cresswell, 1774-1777*. The Dial Press, New York, 1924, pages 27-28.
[11] *Writings of George Washington*, by Sparks, Volume 3, page 227.
[12] By her first marriage she had four children: Mrs. Turberville, Mrs. McCray, Captain Simon Pearson, and Captain Thomas Pearson. The latter, by his marriage to a daughter of Dr. Coates of Fairfax County, had a daughter, Mrs. Chapman, who was the mother of Dr. Nathaniel Chapman, surgeon and professor in the Medical School of the University of Pennsylvania.

[13] Written 1915, MS., copy loaned by the family.
[14] This name is found as Behethelem, Bethelan and variant spellings. Betheland seems to have been preferred by Mrs. Broadwater.
[15] Sketch by Mrs. E. S. Brooks of 4739 Westminster Avenue, St. Louis, 1915. Also records of her cousin, Julia C. Sebastian, of St. Louis.
[16] *History of Callaway County, Missouri*, National Historical Company, St. Louis, 1884, page 233.
[17] See *Virginia Magazine*, volume 47, page 234, et. seq., for an article concerning Colonel Charles Broadwater, written by a descendant, Robert Lee Haycock. See also: The Washington, D.C., *Sunday Star*, October 5, 1919.

## THE BROWN FAMILY

Two brothers, James and William Brown, came to New York from Puddington, Bedfordshire, England, at an early date. James Brown came before 1682, and in that year his brother, William Brown came here. They were children of William Brown who died in Puddington in 1662. The Brown brothers moved to Maryland about 1700. William Brown (1656-1746) married four times. By his third wife, Ann Mercer (whom he married in 1684) he was the father of Richard Brown (1693-1745). Richard Brown moved from Maryland to what was later Loudoun County, Virginia, in 1737, and settled on Ketocton Creek, near what is now Taylorstown. In 1741 Lord Fairfax granted him three tracts of land, and upon his death in 1745, he owned 2,339 acres. His first wife was Hannah Runnels (whom he married in 1717) and she died in 1726. He married twice afterwards. William Brown (1722-1794) son of Richard and Hannah (Runnels) Brown, married Elizabeth Farquhar. Richard Brown (1760-1813) son of this last named couple, married Sarah Cox. Their son, William C. Brown (1788-1851), married Sarah Piggott (1798-1877). Mrs. Brown was the daughter of William and Mary (Nichols) Piggott, and represented an old Loudoun County Quaker family. She was a granddaughter of William and Sarah Nichols. Burr Brown (1820-1899), son of William C. and Sarah (Piggott) Brown, married in 1846 to Mary Eleanor Nichols (1826-1863), his cousin. They had three children: James William Brown (who settled in Falls Church), Alberta Jeanette Brown, and Edgar Mayo Brown.

James William Brown, son of Burr and Mary Eleanor (Nichols) Brown, was born in Loudoun County in 1848, and died at his home in Falls Church on September 26, 1904. Mr. Brown moved to Falls Church in October, 1883, and established the business now operated by his grandson, Hugh R. Brown. The obituary published in *The Falls Church Monitor* of October 1, 1904, speaks of Mr. Brown as "one of the most honored and respected citizens of Falls Church." Mr. Brown served for many years as a member of the Town Council, and at the time of his death was a member of the School Board. He had served as a member of the School Board for a long time. The obituary states that he filled this position with great credit and in "testimony of the great esteem in which he was held by the school children the public schools were adjourned on the day of his funeral, and a beautiful floral memorial was contributed by the scholars."

Mr. Brown was a member of the Odd Fellows Lodge, and was a devoted member of Dulin Chapel, M. E. Church, South. His funeral services were conducted by Dr. J. W. Duffey, Presiding Elder, Dr. A. M. Cackley (a former pastor), and the Reverend W. H. Woolf.

The *Monitor* reported that the Church "was crowded to overflowing, and the floral offerings were handsome and profuse, all testifying to the high esteem in which he was held by his multitude of friends." All of the merchants of the town closed their stores during the funeral services as a mark of respect. The *Monitor* contained this tribute:

"Few men indeed, especially those engaged in public pursuits, have so conducted their personal and business affairs as to never incur the ill will or criticism of those with whom they come in contact. It can be truly said of Mr. Brown that he was thoroughly honest, conscientious and upright in all his dealings with his fellowmen. While somewhat reticent in his demeanor, he was of a lovable character and of a kind and generous disposition."

James W. Brown married at Vienna, Virginia, on March 16, 1880, to Lizzie Williams. Mrs. Brown was born in Siskiyou County, California, May 3, 1856, and died at Falls Church, July 9, 1957, in her 101st year. Mrs. Brown was a daughter of James and Catherine (Shetler) Williams.[2] They had the following children:

(1) Mary Eleanor Brown, born January 14, 1883, married Henry Scott Ryer (1882-1924). Mr. Ryer was the son of Henry Ryer, Sr. Children:

*(11)* Mary Eleanor Ryer, married David Lockling, no children.

*(12)* Henry Scott Ryer, Jr., married Florence, no children.

*(13)* James Horace Ryer, unmarried.

(2) Horace Emory Brown, born at Falls Church, August 27, 1886, and married on October 14, 1920 to Sarah Augusta Rose. Mrs. Brown was born February 24, 1885 in New York, a daughter of Hugh King and Mary (Silliman) Rose. She is of distinguished ancestry, and a descendant of John and Priscilla (Mullins) Alden who came over on the Mayflower.[3] Mr. Brown was held in high esteem by residents old and new. He served as Vice President of the Falls Church Bank, and was long active in local affairs. He was a member of the Falls Church Presbyterian Church. Mr. Brown died August 12, 1959. Mr. and Mrs. Brown had the following children:

*(21)* Horace Emory Brown, Jr., born at Falls Church, September 26, 1922, unmarried.

*(22)* Hugh Rose Brown, born at Falls Church, March 23, 1926, unmarried.

(3) (Dr.) James William Brown, Jr., born at Falls Church, May 2, 1893, died August 26, 1961. Mr. Brown married Grace Thompson, a daughter of Frank Marion, Sr., and Ella (Foley) Thompson. Children:

*(31)* (Dr.) James William Brown (III), born July 22, 1918, married Sarah Stuart, children:

*(311)* James William Brown (IV).

*(312)* Stuart Redfield Brown.

*(313)* Laurel Brown.

*(32)* Frank Redfield Brown, married Helen Simmons on February 14, 1942. No children.

*(33)* Edmund Thompson Brown, married Elizabeth Grille, children:

*(331)* Elizabeth Grace Brown (Betty).

*(332)* Robert Brown.

*(333)* Stephen Brown.

---

[1] The original store building was torn down in November-December, 1959.

[2] James Williams was wounded at the Battle of Jonesborough, Georgia, September 18, and died September 27, 1864. His wife, Catherine Shetler, was born December 16, 1831, a daught-

er of Jacob Shetler (born October 26, 1798) and Sarah (Martin) Shetler (born October 13, 1802) who were married on July 14, 1822. James Williams and Catherine Shetler were married April 16, 1854.

[3] The following is Mrs. Brown's descent from John Alden: (1) John Alden married Priscilla Mullins; (2) Elizabeth Alden, born 1624, married William Peabody (Paybodie); (3) Lydia Peabody married Daniel Grinnell; (4) Priscilla Grinnell, born 1689, married Theophilus Redfield, son of James and Elizabeth (Howe) Redfield; (5) James Redfield (1735-1788) married Sarah Grinnell; (6) James Redfield (1767-1859) married (1st) Sarah Haines, (2nd) Abigail Barlow; (7) Sarah Redfield, daughter of the second marriage, married James Smith (both are buried in the Falls Church yard); (8) Abigail Smith married Isaac Silliman; (9) Mary Silliman married Hugh King Rose; and (10) Sarah Augusta Rose married Horace E. Brown.

## THE BRUNNER FAMILY

James G. W. Brunner came to Falls Church following the War Between the States, and purchased "Hill House," formerly the residence of William H. G. Lynch. "Hill House" was on the Big Chimneys farm and was later sold to the Berryman family. The Berrymans built a large frame house on the site after "Hill House" burned. The place, known in more recent times as "Berryman's Hill" or the Lee Tract, is the site of Gibson's Apartments on Fairfax Street.

James G. W. Brunner was a contractor and built many of the turn-of-the-century homes of Falls Church. He built the old parsonage of Dulin Chapel and the Rice House ("Tall Wood") later the Eisenhower home on East Broad Street.

Mr. Brunner married Catherine J. ——— and had a number of children. One son, John B. Brunner, was president of the Peroxide Chemical Company in St. Louis during the 1930's. He was the first baby baptized in the present Dulin Methodist Church following its erection in 1869. A daughter, Matilda L. Brunner, born in Washington in 1860, married at Dulin Chapel on December 14, 1880, to Beverly A. Traylor. Mr. Traylor was born in 1857 in Petersburg, a son of Anderson and Virginia Traylor.

George A. Brunner (1851-1929), a son of James G. W. and Catherine J. Brunner, was born in Maryland. He lived in Falls Church and was a well-known builder. Henry Crocker, born in 1866, recalled the construction of Dulin Chapel Parsonage in 1873, and said he saw Mr. Brunner, then a young man, sawing lumber on the site. Brunner had on his hand a unique ring which Mr. Crocker inquired about. Mr. Brunner told him that it was given to him by Nellie Grant, daughter of President Grant. Miss Grant was married that same year, while her father was still in the White House.

Mr. Brunner married on November 24, 1880, at Dulin Chapel, to Carrie D. Birch. Mrs. Brunner was born in 1861, a daughter of Joseph Edward and Mary E. (Speer) Birch. She died December 15, 1926. Issue:

(1) Lester C. Brunner (1884-September 5, 1920) who married Mabel Viola Cox (who died September 23, 1937). Issue: Ethel (Brunner) Thom, Audrey (Brunner) Williams and George R. Brunner.
(2) Mabel V. Brunner (1885-May 2, 1937) married Ralph Garland, no issue.
(3) Leroy Brunner (1888-1900).
(4) Ruth Brunner (1891-1893).
(5) Mary Elizabeth Brunner, married on September 6, 1922, (1) Francis Olin Perkins; and (2) Nelson Webb Bishop. No issue.
(6) Joseph Earl Brunner, baptized December 12, 1894 at Dulin Chapel, died March 17, 1959. He married on October 19, 1916, to Louise B. Higgins. Issue:

Betty Louise Brunner, married Albert W. Kjar; Joseph Earl Brunner, Jr.; and James Richard (Dick) Brunner, married Norma E. Bennett, daughter of Mrs. Thaddeus Michael Dombrowski.

*Notes:* Catherine Brunner died November 30, 1918 at Falls Church. Tombstone at Cranford Memorial Methodist Church near Mount Vernon: Margaret Anna, wife of James Howard Brunner, born January 15, 1873, died August 20, 1899.

## *THE BURKE FAMILY OF ROYAL LODGE*

The quaint little brick house which is in the field opposite Miss Ada Walker's residence (917 W. Great Falls Street) is said to have been a hunting lodge of a Royal Governor of Virginia. Although this is the story told by old residents, who still call it Royal Lodge, no record has been found to prove this claim. Certainly the charm of this much remodeled dwelling cannot be denied. At any rate, it was a home of the Dye family for many years, and later owned by the Burke family. Captain Reuben Dye remodeled the old Lodge in 1808. The house originally had a small front porch, but this was torn away years ago. Captain Reuben Dye is thought to have received the property from his father, who patented the land in the 1700's. Captain Dye is buried in the Falls Church yard, and his stone has this inscription:

"In memory of Reuben Dye, who departed this life the 6th of Novr. in the year of our Lord 1815 in the 35th year of his age leaving a wife and five small children to deplore their loss."

Alexander Dye, son of Reuben Dye, is buried beside him, and he died September 8, 1816 at 4 years of age. Reuben Dye married on July 17, 1804 to Elizabeth Turner, daughter of Walker Turner of Alexandria County.[1]

John Louis Burke purchased the Lodge in 1832 from the heirs of Reuben Dye, and at that time it was a farm of several hundred acres. Mr. Burke died before 1860, and was buried in the yard. His wife was Mary Ann Rosson[2] of Baltimore, and they were married when she was 16 years old. Mrs. Burke was born in 1808, died in 1903. Mr. and Mrs. Burke and other members of the family were buried in the family cemetery, but in recent years were moved to St. James Catholic Cemetery. John Louis and Mary Ann (Rosson) Burke had the following children:

(1) Richard L. Burke, born 1828, died unmarried about 1900. He was a native of Washington.

(2) John B. Burke, born 1834, died 1904, and is buried in St. James Cemetery. Mr. Burke was unmarried.

(3) Thomas H. Burke, born 1838, died July 2, 1911, age 73 years, 6 months, and is buried in St. James Cemetery. He built the large brick house on Great Falls Street, just opposite Haycock Road. Mr. Burke married Anne Kerns of Lewinsville. No children.

(4) Francis X. Burke (Frank), born in 1842, died in 1905. He was a reporter for the Washington, D. C. *Evening Star.* Mr. Burke married a Miss Williams of Baltimore, and they had a daughter, Mrs. MacGreal.

(5) Margaret J. Burke, born 1848, died May 31, 1866 age 19 years, 6 months. She was unmarried.

(6) Ellen M. Burke (Ella), died April 9, 1943, age 97. She married in Washington,

D.C., September 26, 1856, Henry McConvey. Mr. McConvey was a native of Ireland, and served in the Union Army during the War Between the States. He was a member of George Meade Post, G.A.R., and when he died on November 10, 1904, was given a Military funeral and buried in Arlington Cemetery. Mrs. McConvey is also buried there. The death notice of Mrs. McConvey from a local paper states that she was a "niece of the late Surg. Gen. George H. Torney, USA, and a cousin of the late Commodore John Decatur Barry, USN." Children:
- (*61*) Henry McConvey, Jr., did not marry.
- (*62*) Mary E. (Molly) McConvey, did not marry.
- (*63*) Eugene McConvey.
- (*64*) George McConvey, died unmarried, age 21.
- (*65*) Charles McConvey, married Sofronia Beans, and had two daughters, one of whom is Mrs. Molly Herndon.
- (*66*) Agnes McConvey, married Alois Holderith, issue:
  - (*661*) Frances Holderith.
  - (*662*) Agnes Holderith.
  - (*663*) Burke Holderith.

---

[1] This marriage bond is filed at Arlington Court House.
[2] This name also found as Crosson.

---

## THE CHAPPEL FAMILY

The following article was clipped from a local paper dated Friday, July 1, 1938:

"*G.A.R. Veteran, Once Falls Church Resident, Back After 69 Years*

"Reminiscing of the days when Falls Church was a village of perhaps 100 persons—a cross roads center of the business life of the surrounding farm country—Charles Chappel, 91 year old veteran of the Grand Army of the Republic and former resident of the town, last Saturday paid his first visit to this section since 1869, en route to Gettysburg, where he is spending this week as one of the surviving participants of the War Between the States.

Driven by his great-grandson, William Chappel, of Long Beach, Calif., whose grandfather was born in Buckland in 1869, the spry though elderly Mr. Chappel, who showed remarkably few signs of his advanced years, hunted up Falls Church's oldest resident, Will Lynch, whom he knew as a boy; called at the bank which stands where he remembered the old tavern of his youth, and examined again the old Falls Church, which alone remains of the buildings he knew as a child.

Born in Hartwich County, N.Y. July 7, 1847, he was brought in September, '48, to Parkersburg, then in Virginia. Two years later the family crossed the mountains and settled just above Falls Church, near Lewinsville, at what was then Peach Grove Post Office, on the Merry farm. On July 11, 1854, his father was killed accidently while driving a blind mare to Washington along the old Chain Road. The family lost their farm and the mother, three sons and two daughters, moved into the village, where they had a half acre adjoining the Falls Church.

Mrs. Chappell supported her young family with difficulty, weaving carpets and making linsey cloth, the older boys helping with odd jobs. At that time the village, in addition to the tavern, boasted a wheelright shop, a blacksmith's shop and two general stores. For the spiritual life of the country-side there were the old Episcopal Church, which architecturally dominated the countryside; the Baptist Church, built in 1856 on the site of the present Episcopal Parish Hall and made of hand-hewn poplar with 8-by-8 inch sills; a two-story Presbyterian Hall, used as a church, and, further down the road, in the "tall timbers," a Southern Methodist Church. The school where the 3 R's were taught for three months in the winter was in the Baptist Church.

Every man who owned half an acre of land, according to Mr. Chappel, was expected to pay from $1 to $1.25 per month for each of his children in this school—the nearest approach to a free school that then existed. This also was a center for the social life of the town, with Friday evening spelling bees during the winter months.

According to Mr. Chappel, most of the residents of the town proper were from the north, and, when the war broke out, there was a lot of feeling. His oldest brother was 17 and faced conscription for the Southern army. His two uncles, who lived near Bailey's Cross Roads, were also northern sympathizers and left home on twenty-four hours' notice.

On April 1, 1861, his mother took her family to Washington, later going to his uncle's farm on the Chenango River, near Binghamton, N.Y. There Charles at 17 enlisted, September 7, 1864, in Company D, of the 10th New York Infantry. He was sent to Petersburg, where he did picket duty south of Petersburg until almost the end of the war when they broke camp on March 27, 1865, and his company went to the front line. He was at Appomattox when Grant received Lee's surrender. After the close of the war he was marched to Fairfax County, where he was mustered out near Bailey's Cross Roads, at what is still known as Munson's Hill, on June 30, 1865. He was sent to New York for his formal discharge and the following September returned to Virginia, drifting from Falls Church to Buckland, where, on November 21, 1868, he married the first of his three wives, Miss Amanda J. Terman.

After the birth of the first of his four sons, he took his little family to Kansas, where he took up a claim of 160 acres. In 1891 he sold out the 80 acres he still owned and moved to Oklahoma, where, in 1893, he took up another claim. At one time he owned over 400 acres, but much of the proceeds he later lost after he had moved to California in 1919. Mr. Chappel's first wife died in 1916 and the following year, at the age of 70, he married again, this time a maiden lady of 62 from Jackson, Miss., who died nine years later. After the lapse of five years, at 84, he ventured again into matrimony, this time taking as his bride a widow from Iowa. She died five years ago.

One of Mr. Chappel's father's brothers who had left Bailey's Cross Roads at the outbreak of the war for Washington, later returned to Falls Church to the Hiram Reed farm, above the village. There he was captured by Mosby's men on a raid and shot. Mr. Chappel said they gave as their reason that the uncle taught a Sunday School for Negro children.

When leaving Falls Church Saturday morning, Mr. Chappel said he intended to drive into Washington by way of Lewinsville and the new Chain Bridge. He missed the old toll house, formerly run by "Bill Williams," just below the cross roads, though he admitted that the present roads were considerably improved over the so-called macadam of the olden days, when 15 to 18 inches of rock formed the basis of the old toll and stage coach thoroughfares.

## THE CHURCH FAMILY

Dr. Merton Elbridge Church, better known as M. E. Church, was born at Derby Line, Orleans County, Vermont, February 14, 1858, a son of Joshua and Mary Elizabeth (Cobb) Church. His father, Joshua Church, was a native of Quebec, Canada, and died in the Union Army in 1862. Church left Quebec as a young man and settled in Orleans County where he was a carpenter. His death was caused by chronic dysentery. Mrs. Church was born in 1836, and died at Appopka, Florida, August 8, 1884. She was a daughter of James Paddock and Martha (Drew) Cobb.[1] She had three children by her first marriage: Merton E.; Abiah Church, born June 24, 1861; and Charles Church, who settled in Falls Church where he married Julia H. Handon. Mrs. Church remarried (2) to George S. Spofford of Vermont (who died in Fort Myer, Florida). Following this marriage she moved to Quebec (in 1870) and in 1876 moved to Herndon, Virginia. Her second family included: Addie Spofford, born 1872, and Merrill Spofford, who died October 23, 1885, in childhood.

Dr. M. E. Church, the subject of this sketch, attended schools in Orange County, Vermont, and in Fitchburg, Massachusetts. He later attended school in Quebec and worked on a farm. At the age of sixteen he was apprenticed to the jeweler's trade, and attended a private school in Quebec. In 1876, at age nineteen, he came to Herndon, Fairfax County, and remained until the following Spring, when he returned to Fitchburg and served a four year term as a Pharmacist. He returned to Herndon, opened a drug store, and did well. His trip to Herndon was made with his medicine wagon, selling enroute to pay expenses. His drug store was destroyed by fire in 1886.

He lost everything in the fire, and with his horse and medicine wagon came to Falls Church. He opened a drug store in Falls Church ("Spofford & Church") and rebuilt the one in Herndon. Dr. Church served as President of the Virginia State Pharmaceutical Association. In 1900 he sold his drug business and went into real estate.

Dr. Church was instrumental in steering the course of business in Falls Church for some fifty years or more. Endowed with an unusual business ability, Church had the vision to foresee early the importance of telephonic communication. Long before the first Bell Telephone Company was organized, Dr. Church, together with Dr. T. M. Talbott who was a personal friend of Dr. Alexander Graham Bell, established the first telephone line in Virginia, connecting Dr. Church's drug store in Falls Church with Washington, and using the Echers telephone, later purchased by the Bell company. This was in 1888. Dr. Talbott withdrew from the enterprise after the line to Washington had been established, but Dr. Church from this humble beginning developed a network of telephone companies and exchanges in Falls Church, Vienna, Herndon, Fairfax, Leesburg, Loudoun, Fauquier and Prince William Counties, as far as the Blue Ridge Mountains, serving as chief stockholder, president, and general manager. The company was absorbed by the Chesapeake & Potomac Telephone Company on December 1, 1916 when Dr. Church sold his interests.[2]

Dr. Church went into the real estate and insurance business in connection with his telephone company and much of the early development of Northern Virginia was due to his business foresight and skill. He was one of the charter members of the Alexandria, Arlington & Fairfax Realtors' Association.

Dr. Church organized the Falls Church Improvement Company, of which he was a large stockholder and general manager. Offices were in Washington. Associated with him were the Honorable Schuyler Duryee, then Chief Clerk of the U. S. Patent Office, Judge A. A. Freeman, and others. This company successfully developed the Sherwood Subdivision on West Broad Street, the first subdivision to be placed on the market in Fairfax County.

A founder of the Falls Church Bank, Dr. Church served as trust officer, vice president and director. He assisted in organizing five or six Virginia banks, and was vice president and director of the Arlington Trust Company, director and vice president of the National Bank of Fairfax, and a director of the Peoples Bank of Leesburg.

When railway service from Northern Virginia to Washington was threatened with extinction, Dr. Church took the lead in saving the service by organizing the Arlington, Fairfax Railway Company, financed by local stockholders. He served until his death as president of the company. He was also one of the most enthusiastic road builders of Virginia and a member of the original Lee Highway Association.

Dr. Church built the first electric light system in Arlington and Fairfax Counties, selling these interests in 1914 to the Alexandria Lighting Company.

Among other interests, Dr. Church served as the first president of the Fairfax County Chamber of Commerce, which he helped organize. He was a member of the Falls Church Citizens' Association, Arlington County Citizens' Association, Arlington and Alexandria Chambers of Commerce, charter member of the Arlington County Rotary Club, past mayor and member of the Town Council of Herndon, past mayor and member of the Falls Church Town Council, and member of the Falls Church Town School Board, and a trustee of the Oakwood Cemetery Association.

Always a staunch churchman, Dr. Church throughout his life was closely identified with the work of religious organizations of both local and national importance. A member of Crossman Methodist Episcopal Church, he served until his death as chairman of the board of trustees and recording steward and as superintendent emeritus of the Sunday School.

In national church affairs, Dr. Church was a member of the Board of Temperance, Prohibition and Public Morals of the Methodist Episcopal Church, serving as treasurer and member of the Executive and Finance Committees. He was trustee of the American University from its organization, serving as vice president, chairman of the Real Estate Committee and member of the Financial, Executive and Building Committees.[3] He was for many years a member of the Executive Committee of the Virginia State Sunday School Association and one of the leaders who established the week-day religious education movement in the public schools in Arlington and Fairfax Counties. He was an alternate member of the Virginia and International Conferences of Religious Education. Dr. Church was a life member of both the Virginia State Y.M.C.A. and St. Petersburg, Florida, Y.M.C.A.

Dr. Church was appointed by former Governor Harry F. Byrd as a member of the Virginia State Committee on Parks and Plans, designated as the Regional Committee. At one time he served as an active director of twenty-two different corporations.

In spite of his many responsibilities, Dr. Church found time for fraternal affiliations in both Virginia and Florida where he made his winter home for some years. He was a member and first resident Master of Kemper Lodge, and served as District Deputy Grand Master of Masonic District Number One. He was a member of Mount Vernon Royal Arch Chapter, No. 41, Alexandria; member of Old Dominion Commandery, No. 11, Knights Templar, Alexandria; he was a 32nd degree Mason, and was a member of Acacia Chapter, No. 51, O.E.W. which he helped organize. He was past Patron and past Grand Patron of the Eastern Star of Virginia, honorary member of the Grand Chapter of the Eastern Star of Florida. He was also a member of Falls Church Lodge, No. 11, I.O.O.F. In Florida he served as president of the Southland Tourists' Association at St. Petersburg, and a member of the Presidents' Union of St. Petersburg.

In Washington, D.C., he maintained membership in the Vermont State Association. Dr. Church was one of the leading Republicans of Virginia. Upon his death on September 16, 1931, it was said that he had done more for Northern Virginia than any other person. He was buried in Oakwood Cemetery and active pallbearers included Dr. Lucius Clarke, Chancellor of American University, Horace E. Brown, Ashton C. Jones, George Crossman, Dr. J. B. Gould, and Dr. George B. Fadeley. Honorary pallbearers included Honorable R. Walton Moore, Franklin Williams, Wilson M. Farr, Dr. W. Sinclair Dowen, Dr. E. L. Robey, Frederick D. Richardson, and George W. Hawxhurst.

Dr. Church left an estate of more than $200,000. He owned real estate valued at more than $175,000. American University was given $7,000 by his Will, and Crossman Church received $1,000. Other gifts were made for religious education and to friends. The bulk of his estate was left to his family.

Dr. Church married on February 14, 1884, to Carrie Belle Northrup, daughter of Eli J. and Candace A. (Barnes) Northrup. Her father, of New England ancestry, lived at Leesburg before coming to Falls Church. He was an undertaker and proprietor of the Eagle House Hotel and Livery Stable.

Dr. and Mrs. Church had issue:

(1) (Colonel) Guy Northrup Church, born at Falls Church July 26, 1889, died 1963. Colonel Church continued in the family real estate business. He served as First Lieutenant in the U.S. Signal Corps during World War I. Colonel Church was a graduate of V.P.I. Active in community affairs, he served as Chairman of the Falls Church Historical Development Commission.

Colonel Church married Mary Emilie Torreyson. (*See Torreyson*). She was born September 26, 1889, and survived her husband. Issue:

(*11*) Merton Elbridge Church, born January 5, 1915, married ——.

(*12*) Guy Northrup Church, Jr., born April 3, 1914, married Mary Ann Redington, issue:

(*121*) Michael Elbridge Church, born February 14, 1941, married Jane Connolly, issue: Kimberly Marie Church, born April 26, 1964.

(*122*) Geoffrey Northrup Church, born September 29, 1944.

(2) Lewis Eli Church, died July 19, 1894, age 5 months, and 8 days.

(3) Maybelle Amelia Church, born January 26, 1900, graduated from Goucher College. She married Kenneth Newman Mills. Issue:

(*31*) Mary Martha Mills.

(*32*) Elaine Church Mills.

---

[1] Stephen Cobb, Sr., ancestor of Mrs. Church, was a resident of Medway, Massachusetts, until about 1745 when he moved to Holliston, in the same State, where he died in 1754. His wife, Abigail, moved to Temple, New Hampshire, where she died December 31, 1783. One of their eight children was Seth Cobb, born at Medway, March 6, 1743, died January 8, 1799. By his first wife, Katherine, (probably Perry) he had a number of children. She died December 11, 1789. Seth Cobb was a Revolutionary Soldier. David Perry Cobb, a son, was born at Tem-

ple, Cheshire County, New Hampshire, and was married to Content Babcock of Stoddard, Connecticut. Their son, James Paddock Cobb, born 1807, in Branston, Quebec, died in 1858. His first wife was Martha Drew of Albany, Vermont.
[2] During the Spanish-American War, Dr. Church furnished all the telephone and telegraph facilities for Camp Alger. He was also post master there and druggist.
[3] Dr. Church gave one-tenth of his income to church and charitable purposes.

## THE CLOVER FAMILY

The Clover farm, called "Cloverdale," was located on Leesburg Pike (Broad Street) from Little Falls Street to a point near the Presbyterian Church. What is now North Washington Street at the intersection was not laid out until 1870, and the land including the State Theater, the Drug Store, and Horace Brown's, was a corn field. Willston Clover, who settled here before 1855, lived in a house which stood next to the Odd Fellows Hall. In 1949, when the Shopping Center was built, this house was moved around to the back of the lot to face Park Avenue. This building, erected about 1797, was in later years owned by George W. Mankin.

Willston Clover was a native of New York, born May 1, 1812, and died at Falls Church, August 7, 1879, and was buried beside his wife in the Falls Church yard. Armenia, his wife, was born in New York on August 29, 1811, died at Falls Church July 19, 1865. Children (known to this writer):[1]

(1) Mary Ann Clover, born in New York, 1838, married on May 19, 1866 to Samuel Forsyth. Mr. Forsyth was born in Pennsylvania in 1842, son of James and Emily Forsyth.

(2) Andrew Clover, born in New York, 1842.

(3) John Clover, born in New York in 1844.

(4) Amanda A. Clover, born January 21, 1848, died in June, 1854, and is buried in the Falls Church yard.

---

[1] Record from the 1860 U. S. Census. Samuel Shreve (1785-1862), son of Col. Samuel and Myra (Trout) Shreve, married Mary Ann Clover of Falls Church, no doubt a sister of Willston Clover.

---

## THE COE FAMILY OF "MT. HOPE"

Amzi Coe was a gentleman from the North and a Southern sympathizer during the War Between the States. He was born in Haverstraw, New York, March 7, 1795, a son of Deacon John Coe (born August, 1749, died May 2, 1839) and Mary (Halstead) Coe. The father, Deacon Coe, was an Ensign in Captain Garrett Eckerson's Haverstraw Militia during the Revolution. He married in 1786 to Mary Halstead, daughter of Caleb and Catherine Halstead. Deacon John Coe was the son of the Honorable John Coe (born Newtown, L.I., December 7, 1719, died May 11, 1782) by his wife Hannah Halstead, daughter of Jonah and Martha Halstead. The Honorable John Coe was an Elder of the Presbyterian Church and Judge of the Court of Common Pleas in Orange County, N.Y., and Delegate to the Provincial Congress of New York, May 23, 1775. He was a member of the New York Assembly and was appointed by Congress as Quarter Master General under Major General Nathaniel Green and served in the Yorktown Campaign. Honorable John Coe was a son of Lieutenant Samuel Coe (1672-1742) and Margaret (Van Zandt) Coe, daughter of John Van Zandt. Lieutenant Samuel Coe was a son of Captain John Coe (1625-1693) of Watertown, Massachusetts. He was Captain in the British action against the Dutch; was Deputy to reorganize the Long Island Government in 1664, and also served as Sheriff. Captain Coe was a son of Robert Coe, Sr., (1596-1689) the immigrant to Boston, 1634.[1]

Amzi Coe moved to Virginia about 1842. On April 13, 1842,[2] he purchased from Ruth Mills for $3,240, a tract of land near Falls Church, "Beginning in the center of Ellzeys Church road & in a line of Regans Patent." Mention is made of the adjoining lands of Pearson's Patent, J. C. Genesco, Francis Fish and the Old Leesburg Road. This tract, containing 216 acres, was sold by D. F. Dulany to J. Johnson, and by Johnson reconveyed to Dulany who sold it to Samuel Moxley "or Peter Ritter," and by Ritter it was conveyed to Ruth Mills. Mr. Coe later purchased a farm from the Sewall family and called it "Mt. Hope." The house at "Mt. Hope" is still standing on North Oak Street.

Mr. Coe was an Elder in the Lewinsville Presbyterian Church, and helped organize the Falls Church Presbyterian Church. The first services of the Falls Church congregation met in the parlor at "Mt. Hope." Mr. Coe served in the 83rd Regiment, New York Militia in 1818, and later in the Fairfax County Militia. During the War Between the States he was arrested several times and put into prison in Washington. Amzi Coe died at "Mt. Hope," June 11, 1866.

By his wife, Anna Sherwood, Mr. Coe had the following children:

(1) Spencer A. Coe, born in New York, 1837, who lived at "Mt. Hope." Mr. Coe was Administrator of the estate of his Aunt Catherine (1807-1868) in New York. He was an Elder in the Falls Church Presbyterian Church. Mr. Coe. married (1) Mariette; and (2) on May 13, 1869 at Falls Church to Margaret B. (Maggie) Thorne. Mrs. Margaret (Thorne) Coe was born in Fairfax County in 1847, daughter of Talmadge and Sarah Thorne.

(2) Henry M. Coe, died in Falls Church. Married Jane Scotten, children:
*(21)* Alfred Henry Coe, born about 1860. *(22)* Samuel Spencer Coe.

(3) Rachela Coe, died April 27, 1853 at 12 years.

(4) Catherine Coe, died April 15, 1843, age 9 mos., 5 days.

---

[1] "... descendants of Robert I are closely related, thru Lieut. Samuel Coe (1672-1742) who married Margaret Van Zandt ... The ten children of Margaret Van Zandt & Lieut. Sam Coe were her second family for she already had five children born to Mr. Smith. Their son John and his five boys fought in the same battle 'Defence of the Hudson' in the Revolution, the youngest, Matthew, being only fifteen at the time." —Letter from John E. Coe, Chicago, Ill., August 3, 1953.

[2] Fairfax County *Deed Book G #3*, p. 297.

---

## THE CROSSMAN FAMILY

Crossman (Crosman, Crossmun), is an old English name. It is said to have been taken by a soldier "of the Cross" during one of the Crusades. A great many of the defenders of the Christian faith embodied in their personal name, surname, or bore on their coat of armor some allusion or symbol proclaiming their allegiance to the Cross.

The Crossmans were early immigrants to New England. In 1637 Robert Crossman said to be ancestor of all of the name in America, settled in Dedham, Massachusetts

He married Sarah Kingsbury of Dedham, and raised a large family. The following is their Coat of Arms:

"Argent, a cross ermines between four escallops sable."

"Crest: A demi-lion ermine holding an escallop sable."

Asa Crossman, ancestor of Isaac Crossman who settled in Falls Church, was born in 1770 in Boston, and died May 29, 1828. He moved to southwest New York and later to Indiana Co., Pennsylvania, (near Cherry Tree) where he purchased 1,200 acres of land. His first purchase was the "John Drummond tract." This he later sold and bought the Isaac Carmalt farm near Punxsutawney in Jefferson County. The Cherry Tree purchase followed this. Mr. Crossman married Patience Oliver (1775-June 25, 1828) and had seven children:

(1) Cloe Crossman, married Benjamin Dwight.
(2) Asa Crossman, Jr., married Mary McHenry..
(3) Joseph Crossman, married Catherine McHenry.
(4) Rebecca Crossman, married John Piper.
(5) Oliver Crossman, married (1) Miss Foster; (2) Rachel O'Hara (and had Harry and Earl Crossman).
(6) Nathan Crossman.
(7) William Crossman.

(2) Asa Crossman, Jr., son of Asa and Patience (Oliver) Crossman, was born in Boston, October 15, 1794. He died in 1864. His tombstone has this inscription: "Yet again we hope to meet thee when the day of life is fled. Then in heaven with Joy to greet thee, where no farewell tears are shed." Mr. Crossman married Mary McHenry, a daughter of James and Elizabeth (Stuchel) McHenry, well-to-do farming people of Indiana County, Pennsylvania. Mrs. Crossman was born February 12. 1799 and died in 1869. The McHenrys lived near Perrysville, Indiana County. James McHenry was a son of Isaac McHenry who was a Major in the Pennsylvania State Militia during the Revolutionary War. Isaac McHenry was born in Scotland in 1734. He married Jane Smith. James McHenry, their son, was born February 15. 1779, and died in 1812. He married Elizabeth Stutchel (February 15, 1779-1851). in 1795. Mrs. McHenry was a daughter of John and Mary (Lydick) Stutchel. After their marriage, Asa and Mary Crossman purchased land one mile south of Perrysville, Pennsylvania, which was still in its primitive condition, but Mr. Crossman at once began to clear and improve the place. Their first home was a hewed-log house. This was afterward replaced by a comfortable farm dwelling and the land transformed into one of the finest farms of northern Mahoning township. Asa Crossman, Jr., and Mary (McHenry) Crossman had issue:

(21) Mary Crossman, born 1822 in North Mahoning Township, Pennsylvania, married (1) W. Crissman and had Eliza, who married Michael Lance of Indiana; (2) —— Barricks; (3) —— Robertson.
(22) Isaac Crossman (of Falls Church) married (1) Mary Ann Mutersbaugh; (2) Elizabeth Peffer.
(23) Nathan Crossman, born 1826 in Indiana Co., Pennsylvania, married 1852 to Rachel M.D. Bloose of Jefferson County.
(24) Asa Crossman, 3d, born 1828. He married Mary Robinson of Jefferson County. Mr. Crossman served in the Union Army during the War Between the States.

(25) Miles Crossman, born 1831, married Margaret Beck of Armstrong County and had six children.
(26) James Crossman, born 1834, married Julia Sutter of Indiana County, lived near Whiteville, Jefferson County, and had three children.
(27) Elizabeth J. Crossman, married James Chambers and had eight children.

(22) Isaac Crossman (who used the 'Crossmun' spelling of his name in early life), son of Asa and Mary (McHenry) Crossman, was born March 8, 1824, and died in Falls Church July 8, 1900. He moved to Falls Church in March, 1864. Mr. Crossman purchased the Osborn-Hunter farm and later built a new home to replace the large log house with dormers formerly on the site. (This earlier house was built about 1760). Later he purchased the Bolen tract and from time to time added to his acreage. Mr. Crossman married (1st) Mary Ann Mutersbaugh (September 13, 1828-February 25, 1864); and (2nd) Elizabeth Peffer (March 5, 1834-August 13, 1890). Soon after their marriage, Isaac and Mary Ann Crossman located on a farm near his father's in Indiana County, Pennsylvania, where he followed lumbering and farming for a number of years. They decided to move to Falls Church, but due to the strain of packing, Mrs. Crossman died. However, Mr. Crossman came as they had planned.

The following is the Obituary of Isaac Crossman from a Washington, D.C., newspaper clipping:

"Death visited three of our most prominent and esteemed families last Sunday. Although not unexpected in either case the grim messenger is never fully prepared for.

Isaac Crossman, one of the oldest and most respected citizens of Falls Church died on Sunday afternoon of cancer of the stomach, after a lingering illness of many weeks. He was seventy-six years old when he died and had been a resident of Falls Church for over thirty-five years, coming here from Indiana Co., Penna., in 1864.

He was one of the fathers of the town, a man of sterling integrity, great energy and physical ability.

A large portion of the town of Falls Church is built upon land which he originally owned. Through his thrift and industry, he accumulated quite a respectable fortune, which has been to a considerable extent divided among his large family of children.

He was public spirited and liberal in all matters of public welfare, and took an active interest in everything pertaining to the advancement of the town in which he took so much pride.

He was the founder of the Methodist Episcopal Church at this place, which bears his name and for many years the church was maintained through his liberality.

His funeral was held on Wednesday morning and was largely attended by his relatives and friends. His remains were interred in Oakwood Cemetery.

He leaves a large family to mourn his loss. His place in the community, in his church and in his family cannot easily be filled."

Mr. Crossman was identified with the post war progress of Falls Church. He gave the ground for the Crossman Methodist Church. His name is mentioned throughout this book in connection with the growth of the schools and the town. His farm was a noted show-place. The *Virginia Register* of December 5, 1885 reported:

"Next week we will give some description of another Falls Church farm, one of the best, belonging to Isaac Crossman. A new crib has just been built by friend Crossman to hold a portion of his big corn crop—estimated at 400 barrels. Yield of wheat of the farm this season is about 1,100 bushels!"

Isaac Crossman had issue:

(*By Mary Ann Mutersbaugh*):

(221) Eveline Crossman, born September 8, 1847, died August 11, 1874. She married on December 16, 1868 at Dulin Chapel William E. Vandermark. Issue:

(2211) John I. Vandermark (July 28, 1871-August 2, 1943).

(2212) George Vandermark.

(222) John Milton Crossman, born September 2, 1849, died 1933. He married Anna Forbes (1847-1930). Issue:

(2221) Nellie M. Crossman (1879-1927).

(2222) Elizabeth Crossman (Bessie) Palm.

(2223) Frances Forbes Crossman, died May 30, 1954.

(2224) Effie May Crossman, born August 22, 1880, died at age 3 months.

(223) James McHenry Crossman, born February 10, 1852, married Margaret Brown. No Issue.

(224) Marilla Jane Crossman, born July 17, 1854, died May 22, 1899, unmarried.

(225) David Clark Crossman, born December 1, 1856, died October 19, 1885.

(226) Flora Belle Crossman, born August 13, 1859 married Frank List Birch (*See Birch*).

(227) George Grant Crossman, born February 9, 1862, died January 24, 1942. Married Nellie E. Dodge, issue:

(2271) Florence Celeste Crossman, married Frank Romine Taylor.

(2272) William Clark Crossman.

(2273) George I. Crossman of Oak Park, Illinois.

(2274) Louise Crossman married Otis E. Shaw.

(228) Isaac Mutersbaugh Crossman, born February 18, 1864, died March 15, 1864.

Isaac Crossman had issue (by *Elizabeth Peffer*):

(229) Mary Elizabeth Crossman died Jan. 14, 1958, married John W. Mutersbaugh.

(22.10) Susie Ann Crossman, unmarried.

(22.11) Charles Isaac Crossman, married Pansy Payne.

(Parents of Clark Crossman).

---

## THE CRUMP FAMILY

Lewis A. Crump, an early resident of Falls Church, was born in 1823, died in 1885. He married Abigail Jenkins, a sister of Mrs. Albert H. Ives. She was born 1832, died 1883. Both are buried in Oakwood Cemetery. After the incorporation of Falls Church (1875) meetings of the Council were sometimes held in "Lewis Crump's shop." The Crump home was on the corner of East Broad and Fairfax Streets, beside the Falls Church Presbyterian Church, and on the site of a modern brick dwelling. The old pump is the only relic remaining from the old home. The house was built about 1820, torn down about 1940.

Elmer Ives Crump, son of Lewis A. and Abigail (Jenkins) Crump, was born in 1868, died 1939. He married Henrietta M. Wilson of Maryland (a sister of Mrs. George Birch of Falls Church.) Elmer Ives and Henrietta M. (Wilson) Crump had one son, Lewis Crump (1892-1900).

## THE DARNE FAMILY

It appears that the first Darne in Fairfax County was John Darne, Sr., a native of Maryland. There was a large Darne family at Darnestown, in Montgomery County, Maryland, which intermarried with the Trammell and Wren families of Fairfax County. John Darne, Sr., married Mary Gunnell, daughter of William Gunnell, who settled here in 1729. They had at least two children:
  (1) William Darne, married Sarah.
  (2) John Darne, Jr., married Hannah Follin.
Of the above, (1) William Darne died in 1808. His will was made November 7, 1807, and probated in Fairfax Court December 19, 1808 (*Will Book J, p. 163*). In the will he mentioned his wife, Sarah, and their children, Thomas Darne, William Darne, and Susanna Darne. Witnesses to the Will were Thomas Darne, John Darne, Jr., and William Minor. William Darne and Henry Darne were bonded as Tobacco Inspectors for the Falls Warehouse on September 17, 1798. George Minor countersigned for the former, and Richard Ratcliffe for the latter (Fairfax *Deed Book A #2, pp. 406-407*).

(2) John Darne, Jr., died in 1821 at an old age, surviving his son Henry. He made his will on September 24, 1818, being "old and infirm." In the will he mentions his wife, Hannah, and his children: Thomas, Henry, Elizabeth, Susan, Fanny, Corbin, and Gunnell. Executors were his sons, Thomas, Corbin, and Gunnell Darne. Witnesses to the Will were Henry Gunnell, Jr., Robert Gunnell, and "William Gunnell of William." (*Will Book M, p. 181,* probated February 19, 1821). John Darne, Jrs., married Hannah Follin, daughter of William and Bathsheba (Hurst) Follin. Children:
  (21) Thomas Darne, married Belinda ———.
  (22) Henry Darne, married Penelope Minor.
  (23) Elizabeth Darne.
  (24) Susan Darne.
  (25) Fanny Darne.
  (26) Corbin Darne.
  (27) Gunnell Darne.

(21) Thomas Darne, son of John Darne, Jr., and Hannah (Follin) Darne, died before 1819 in Alexandria County, D.C. His estate was not administered until the death of his wife, Belinda, in 1825. On March 8, 1825, Simon Darne and Allen Scott signed bond (for Simon Darne as Administrator of Thomas Darne, deceased, of Alexandria County). (Arlington County *Will Book 3, page 160*). A month earlier, on February 8, 1825, Simon Darne, Allen Scott and Alexander Hunter signed bond (for Simon) as Administrator of Belinda Darne, deceased. (Arlington County *Will Book 3, page 152*). Mrs. Darne was probably Belinda Summers, but no proof of this has been found.

Thomas and Belinda Darne had issue:

(211) Thomas P. Darne, moved to Kentucky. On April 3, 1815, Thomas P. Darne of Shelby County, Kentucky, conveyed to Allen Scott of Alexandria County, D.C., twenty acres of land on Four Mile Run, to be held with life interest by his mother, Belinda Darne. This conveyance was to secure a bond of $600.00. Witnesses were: William Minor, Simon Darne, and George Darne. (Arlington County *Deed Book #2, page 199*).

(212) George Darne, who apparently stayed in the area. On April 13, 1819, George Darne of Alexandria County, D.C., conveyed to Simon Darne for $250.00, a portion of land which George's father, Thomas Darne, lived on at the time of his death. This contained twenty acres. Witnesses were: William Minor, Samuel Shreve, and Benjamin Shreve (Arlington County *Deed Book #2, page 452*).

(213) Simon Darne, married in Washington, D.C., October 3, 1837, to Elizabeth Ann Smith.

(214) Mary Darne, married in Alexandria County, D.C., December 13, 1809 (Thomas Darne, Bondsman) to Allen Scott.

(215) Margaret Darne, married on November 22, 1816, in Alexandria County, D.C., to William C. Broadwater (Simon Darne, Bondsman). Broadwater was a son of Charles Lewis and Betheland (Sebastian) Broadwater, and died before 1833. In 1833 his widow and three children moved to Callaway County, Missouri.

(216) Nancy Darne, married in Alexandria County, D.C., December 26, 1815 (Simon Darne, Bondsman), to John Allison.

*Note:* Another Thomas Darne, who may be closely related to this family, died July 7, 1893. He married Jane Ball of Alexandria County, who was born August 6, 1816, and died August 18, 1898. Jane (Ball) Darne was the daughter of Horatio Ball, Sr., and Catherine (Marcey) Ball. Both are buried in the Ball Cemetery opposite Kann's in Arlington.

(22) Captain Henry Darne, son of John, Jr., and Hannah (Follin) Darne, died in 1806, several years before the death of his father. His coffin was made by Robert Lindsay, a neighbor, on May 23, 1806 (*Will Book J, p. 330*). He made his will December 5, 1805, and it was probated July 21, 1806 (*Will Book I, p. 510*). In it he mentions his wife, Penelope, and his children. He also refers to the fact that he was entitled to part of the estate of John Minor, deceased, and Nicholas Minor, deceased. Witnesses were John Trammell, George Beard, and Daniel Minor. The will of Penelope Darne was made November 20, 1809, and probated October 17, 1814 (*Will Book K, p. 236*). Witnesses were Thomas Moss, William Minor, and George Minor. A division of the slaves of Henry Darne is recorded in *Will Book J at page 253* (by an order of Court dated December, 1809). (Captain) Henry and Penelope (Minor) Darne had the following children:

(221) George Darne married Susanna Lane.
(222) (Captain) Robert Darne, married Verlinda Wren.
(223) (Captain) Nicholas Darne, married Amelia B. Trammell.
(224) Jemima Darne, married Samuel Adams.
(225) Elizabeth Darne, married John Saunders.
(227) Nancy Darne.
(228) Mary (Polly) Darne.
(229) Sarah (Sally) Darne.

(*221*) George Darne, son of Captain Henry and Penelope (Minor) Darne, married in Loudoun County on July 3, 1798, to Susanna (Susan) Lane. Her mother, Sarah Lane, consented to the marriage and Thomas Harper served as Bondsman. The Darnes moved to Portland, Missouri.[1]

George and Susanna (Lane) Darne had a large family, one of whom is known:

(*2211*) Catherine Darne, married her cousin, John Darne Scott, formerly of Georgetown, D.C. Scott moved to Missouri at an early age. Catherine Darne moved into the same section (Callaway County) at the age of six years. Children:
    (*22111*) Catherine Scott, married J. Notley Dutton (issue: Abbie, Chasie, and Scott, none of whom married.)
    (*22112*) Dora Scott, married Theodore ("Thee") Allen (issue: Edna Allen, married Pearl Garrett and had issue Grace and Theodore Garrett; Luna Allen, married Clifford Garrett and had issue Kathryn and John Garrett; and Theodore Allen, Jr., who married Miss Dewes of Calwood.)
    (*22113*) Anna Scott, married Theodore ("Thee") Nunnelly.

(*222*) (Captain) Robert Darne, son of Captain Henry and Penelope (Minor) Darne, born February 1778, died August 22, 1873 at his home, "Cedar Grove," formerly part of the "Long View" estate of Colonel James Wren at West Falls Church. He served in the War of 1812 under his father-in-law, Colonel John Wren. Captain Darne married Verline ("Linnie") Wren, a daughter of Colonel John and Sarah (Hite) Wren.

Captain Darne's will was made September 25, 1871, probated at Fairfax Court House in December 1873.

Captain Robert and Verlina (Wren) Darne had issue:
(*2221*) John Robert Darne, married America Virginia Scott.
(*2222*) Alfred H. Darne, died June 1, 1872.
(*2223*) Maria Louisa Darne (1815-1895), married Samuel Adams Wrenn (*See Wren Sketch*).
(*2224*) Martha Darne (1837-1903) married Augustine Augustus Wrenn (*See Wren Sketch*).
(*2225*) Eugenia Darne.
(*2226*) Sarah Frances Darne, married in Washington, D.C., January 14, 1856, to Lester Lloyd.
(*2227*) Mary Elizabeth Darne.

(*2221*) John Robert Darne (Jack), son of Captain Robert and Verlinda (Wren) Darne, was born March 9, 1829,[2] and died at "Long View," Falls Church, June 23, 1903, with burial in the family cemetery on that estate. Mr. Darne was a Confederate Soldier when he married on February 26, 1863, his cousin, America Virginia Scott. Mrs. Darne was born April 6, 1840, and died June 11, 1926 (with burial in the Falls Church yard). She was a daughter of Robert F. and Artemissa (Darne) Scott and a granddaughter of Captain Nicholas and Amelia B. (Trammell) Darne. Issue:
(*22211*) Ada Virginia Darne, born December 31, 1863, died July 8, 1865.
(*22212*) Letha Lee Darne, born January 15, 1866, married on January 2, 1895, James R. Yates (moved to California).
(*22213*) Eugene T. Darne, married Sarah Katherine King.
(*22214*) Eppa Hunton Darne, born May 11, 1875, died January 10, 1904 (buried in

Congressional Cemetery, Washington, D.C.). He married on January 28, 1902, Annie Marian (Nannie) Webster. Mrs. Darne was born March 22, 1874, died March 18, 1962. Issue: (*222141*) Eppa W. Darne, born November 11, 1902, married (1) September 3, 1927 Louise C. Hollidge (born November 19, 1909, died March 6, 1945); and (2) Frances Violet Rice. No issue by either marriage.

(*22215*) Iva Virginia Darne, born June 26, 1878, died April 8, 1944. She was called Ivy. Miss Darne married on February 12, 1913, to Charles E. Mansfield. Mr. Mansfield was born December 31, 1885, died August 29, 1938. No issue.

(*22216*) Nellie Darne, married John William (Flint) McCulloch.

(*22213*) Eugene T. Darne, son of John Robert and America Virginia (Scott) Darne, was born at Dulin's, near present-day Dunn Loring, February 8, 1869, and died in Washington, D.C., June 29, 1952. He was buried there in Cedar Hill Cemetery. Mr. Darne married on April 22, 1903, Sarah Katherine King, daughter of Richard and Julia A. (Croson) King, formerly of Gainesville, Virginia.[3] Mrs. Darne was born at Gainesville, October 6, 1874, and died at her home, 6016 North Dakota Avenue, N.W., Washington, D.C., October 24, 1938. Issue:

(*222131*) Eugene Nelson (Billy) Darne, born at the old Ford place near Dunn Loring October 26, 1904, died in Washington, D.C., March 17, 1957. He married on December 15, 1928, Dorothy O. Barton (born Oct. 13, 1907). Issue:

(*2221311*) Dorothy Jean Darne, born March 26, 1936, married (1) John Cotter and had a son. She has since remarried.

(*222132*) Ruth Evelyn Darne, born at Ballston, Virginia, June 2, 1907, married (1) May 11, 1929, Francis Ellyson Gardner (born February 7, 1905, died November 24, 1953); and (2) on November 19, 1960, Odell B. Rosser. No issue.

(*222133*) Frederick Alton Darne, born at Ballston, Virginia,[4] January 20, 1909, resides at 511 East Columbia Street, Falls Church. Mr. Darne married on May 18, 1932, to Elizabeth Sarah Crown. Mrs. Darne, a native of Washington, D.C., was born April 15, 1910, a daughter of Edgar Samuel and Rose Mary (Deakins) Crown. Issue:

(*2221331*) Richard Alan Darne, born October 9, 1942, in Washington, D.C. Mr. Darne is unmarried. He is a talented organist.

(*22216*) Nellie Darne, daughter of John Robert and America Virginia (Scott) Darne, was born June 5, 1871, and died June 5, 1955. She married on May 30, 1896, John William (Flint) McCulloch. Mr. McCulloch was born January 13, 1869, and died March 24, 1929. Issue:

(*222161*) Robert Elton McCulloch, born April 20, 1897, is living (1964) in Hermitage, Tennessee. He married (1) on July 11, 1922, Gladys Susan Smith (born February 21, 1899, died August 8, 1948); and (2) on June 4, 1953, Thelma Louise Seay Ellis (born December 17, 1904). Issue (by first wife):

(*2221611*) Dorothy Ann McCulloch, born November 27, 1934, married on December 7, 1955, Melvin Lawrence Dunteman (born December 19, 1927). Issue: Cynthia Kay Dunteman, born October 23, 1956; Phyllis Jean Dunteman, born November 7, 1958; Gary Lee Dunteman, born April 3, 1961; Brian Robert Dunteman (twin), born November 6, 1963; and Nancy Ann Dunteman (twin), born November 6, 1963.

(*222162*) Hazel Virginia McCulloch, born September 20, 1898, married on November 12, 1917, William Logan (born July 31, 1892). Issue:

    (*2221621*) John William Logan, born August 23, 1918, married on July 15, 1941, Dorothy Elizabeth Pritchard.

    (*2221622*) Florence Elizabeth Logan, born March 11, 1920, married on March 23, 1938, John Winner.

    (*2221623*) James Robert Logan, born June 10, 1923, died World War II, May 16, 1943.

    (*2221624*) Thomas Flint Logan, born July 26, 1924, married on May 9, 1959, Martha Daub Cripps.

    (*2221625*) George Elton Logan, born November 29, 1925, married on September 23, 1950, Jeanne S. James.

    (*2221626*) Louis Alexander Logan, born February 7, 1929, married on October 24, 1957, Louella Mae Wood.

    (*2221627*) Ralph David Logan, born May 14, 1930, died September 24, 1930.

(*223*) Captain Nicholas Darne, son of Captain Henry and Penelope (Minor) Darne, was born May 4, 1776,[5] and died at his home near Falls Church on April 4, 1840. He is buried in the Falls Church yard.[6] Nicholas Darne, named for his ancestor Nicholas Minor, was prominent in the early political and social life of the Falls Church vicinity. He served in the War of 1812 as Captain in the Fairfax Militia, and his extensive correspondence, including letters written from the scene of action in 1812, are owned by his descendants. One, written to his wife, and dated September 10, 1814, from Baltimore, stated that he expected to be discharged in a few days. He also wrote: "Orders was Recd' last evening to make of our Muster Roles & pay Roles and from that I think we shall not be detained.—you may inform Brother Robert that he is detailed for duty and I think he had better come on as quick as possible and make some arrangement to get a substitute at this place. Substitutes is Very high, Eighty dollars for three months..."

Captain Darne made his will July 19, 1839, and it was probated April 20, 1840 (Fairfax *Will Book T, p. 172*). Witnesses were: George Chichester, Robert Darne, and George W. Haycock.

Captain Darne married Amelia B. Trammell, a daughter of Sampson and Kerhappuch (Garrett) Trammell, of Loudoun County.

Captain Darne was Constable of the District, and signed his bond for that office on June 18, 1811. Daniel Lewis and John S. Love signed the bond as securities. (Fairfax County *Deed Book L, #2, page 137*).

In Fairfax Court records (*Deed Book M #2, page 398*, et. seq.) there is a law suit entitled "Nicholas Darne and wife vs. Childs Representatives," concerning the estate of Sampson Trammell. By an order of the Court, dated November, 1812, John Jackson, Jr., Spencer Jackson, John C. Hunter, John Dulin, and Henry Gunnell, Jr., or any three of them, were to divide the lands owned by Sampson Trammell, deceased. A survey was made March 31, 1813, and Dulin, John Jackson, Jr., and Hunter divided the land as follows: lot 1, to Walter Magruder and wife; lot 2, to Hezekiah Harris and wife; lot 3, to William Trammell; lot 4, to Nicholas Darne and wife; and lot 5, to representatives of Gabriel Childs.

Captain Nicholas and Amelia B. (Trammell) Darne had issue:

    (*2231*) Artemesia Darne, married Robert F. Scott.

    (*2232*) Leah Harle Darne, married William Henry Wrenn.

(*2233*) Robert B. Darne.
(*2234*) Emerella Darne, married Craven Ashford.
(*2231*) Artemesia Darne, daughter of Captain Nicholas and Amelia B. (Trammell) Darne, was born March 1, 1805 and died July 5, 1852. She married on August 10, 1825, to Robert F. Scott. Mr. Scott, a son of Sabert and Constant Scott, was born May 4, 1797, and died February 2, 1846. The Scotts lived in a house that was on the site of a present-day dwelling to the left of Timber Lane School on South West St. Two daughters of this couple, the Misses America and Artemesia Scott, were imprisoned by Union troops during the War Between the States. A picture of them being carried to prison in a wagon along East Broad Street was published in Harper's Weekly, Saturday, August 3, 1861. The sketch, by Harper's special artist, is entitled "Bringing in the Misses Scott as Prisoners to Fall's Church, Va." The article, "The Misses Scott" follows:

"Sometime since two young ladies of the name of Scott, residents of Fairfax County, Virginia, were the means of capturing the Captain of a volunteer regiment from Connecticut. They have now been taken themselves, and we illustrate, on this page, their appearance as they drove into our lines at Fall's Church. The account of their capture is thus given by a Connecticut boy, one of the scouting party which took them:

'After getting out of the woods we came to a corn-field, through which we crawled on our hands and knees, and we got completely *turned*, but managed to get through the greatest danger and came to a house, where we went to see what we could make out. We found there an old man, (and) we asked if any of our troops were there. He wanted to know if we were on the Southern side. Lieut. Upton told him "Yes"; (then) he told us we were about a mile from their tents, but to look out or we would be captured. We of course appeared frightened, and posted a man outside to look out. Lieutenant Upton told him he was an officer of a South Carolina regiment. The old man told him all about the United States camp, the names of all the secession neighbors, and finally said he had in his house the two Miss Scotts who took the Yankee Captain, so the old man took us into the room and introduced us to the Miss Scotts. That moment was a proud one for us, for right in our hands were those whom the whole brigade had been hunting for. But we continued to play our part, complimenting the ladies highly for further information. When, after learning the most direct road to our camp, Lieutenant Upton told them we must go, but he would like to see the whole family together to bid them good-by. Accordingly they all came out in the front porch, the old man, his wife, three sons, and daughter, and the two Miss Scotts. We just formed a circle about them, with Lieutenant Upton, drawing his sword, demanding their surrender to the United States. You ought to have seen their faces! The two Miss Scotts and the young men were all we took with us. The excitement was very great when we went into camp, and we found they had given us up for lost, and sent a company after us. With the two Miss Scotts we marched to the General's headquarters, and left the ladies there, and the men we took to the guard-house. The General sent for us in the evening, and complimented us highly for our conduct on this occasion.'

The ladies of Virginia and Maryland have been, as a rule, fiercer in their secessionism than the men. At Baltimore our troops are insulted daily by ladies.'"

Robert F. and Artemesia (Darne) Scott had issue:
(*22311*) Charles Emanuel Scott, born April 12, 1828.

(*22312*) Leah Scott, born September 15, 1834, died in California.
(*22313*) Robert Nicholas Darne Scott, born August 29, 1837, died unmarried, April 26, 1907. Mr. Scott served in the Confederate Army.
(*22314*) America V. Scott, born April 6, 1840, married a cousin, John Robert Darne.
(*22315*) Artemesia Darne Scott, born January 7, 1843, died unmarried, January 7, 1908.
(*2232*) Leah Harle Darne, daughter of Captain Nicholas and Amelia B. (Trammell) Darne, born April 27, 1806, married William Henry Wrenn, a cousin (son of James and Ann (Adams) Wrenn and a grandson of Samuel and Jemima (Darne) Adams. (*See Wren Sketch.*)
(*2233*) Robert B. Darne, son of Captain Nicholas and Amelia B. (Trammell) Darne, was born September 11, 1808, and died April 17, 1845, and is buried beside his father in the Falls Church yard. Mr. Darne was a Constable in his District. His Bond for this office is recorded in Fairfax County (*Deed Book C #3, page 9*), and is dated June 15, 1835. It was countersigned by his father, Captain Nicholas Darne. Mr. Darne may have married Mary ——, since Mary Darne administered the estate of Robert B. Darne. Mr. Darne owned land in Loudoun County. In a file entitled "Lowe's Admr. vs. Veale," (see Jewell, Records, Volume I, p. 119) there is recorded an agreement, between James R. M. Lowe and Robert B. Darne of Loudoun County. Lowe sold Darne the timber on McCarty Island in the Potomac on June 11, 1842 (agreement witnessed by W. Sidney Tebbs). No other record.

(*2234*) Emerella Darne, daughter of Captain Nicholas and Amelia B. (Trammell) Darne, was born April 16, 1811, and married in Alexandria, in 1839, to Craven Ashford. Mr. Ashford was from an old county family, and died in 1876, aged 70 years. He was a son of Francis Peyton Ashford and a grandson of Michael Ashford, an Englishman, who settled in Fairfax (Prince William) at an early date. Michael Ashford's plantation was near Mount Vernon. Francis Peyton Ashford was the only one of four brothers to survive service in the Revolutionary War. He died in 1849, aged 87 years. Craven Ashford moved in early manhood to Centreville where he engaged in business. He married (first) to Ann Elizabeth Evans, who died in 1837. In 1835 he moved to Alexandria, and in 1846 he moved to Washington City, having been appointed to a Government Clerkship. Mr. Ashford spent the remaining days of his life there, but often visited his farm in Fairfax County. A son of his first marriage, Mahlon Ashford, born at Centreville February 15, 1833, was President of the Real Estate Title Insurance Company of Washington in 1893. He is written up in *Eminent and Representative Men of Virginia and the District of Columbia Of The Nineteenth Century* (Madison, Wis., Brant & Fuller, 1893, p. 39).

Craven Ashford and his second wife, Emerella Darne, had the following children (known):
(*22341*) Nicholas Darne Ashford, born at "Wakefield," Prince William County,
(*22342*) (Dr.) Francis A. Ashford, of Washington, D.C., died before 1893. Married Belle Kelly.

(*224*) Jemima Darne, daughter of Captain Henry and Penelope (Minor) Darne, married Samuel Adams of Fairfax County, a descendant of Gabriel Adams, Sr.

Mr. Adams made his will on February 15, 1838, and in it he mentioned his wife, Jemima, and unmarried children: Gabriel Adams and Margaret Adams. He also mentioned his married daughters, Nancy Wren, wife of James Wren, Penelope Saunders, and Sally Cooksey.⁸Witnesses to the will were: Vincent Thompson, Alexander Dailey, Horatio P. Lanham, and George W. Hunter.

A list showing the division of the slaves of Samuel Adams places a valuation on them of $9,337.00. The slaves ranged in age from 8 to 70 years. Sarah, aged 70 years, was considered to have no value.

Samuel and Jemima (Darne) Adams had issue:

*(2241)* Gabriel Adams, died unmarried, November 27, 1844. (Date taken from the Wrenn Family Bible owned by Mrs. R. N. Wrenn of Herndon.) He made his will on November 2, 1844, probated December 16, 1844. In it he mentioned his sister, Margaret Brooke, who had no children in 1844, and his nieces Frances Ann and Isabella Cooksey. James Hunter was named Executor of the will, and witnesses were: Samuel Adams and Nicholas Saunders.

*(2242)* Margaret Adams (called Peggy), born 1803, died March 7, 1890, aged 87 years. She is buried in Andrew Chapel Cemetery at Kenmore. Her Wrenn relatives recall her as "Aunt Peggy Brooke." Mrs. Olive Wrenn of Flat Lick, told of a slave owned by Mrs. Brooke, named Henry. Henry was a preacher of note and was given his freedom, and that of his family. He lived for a time with the Brooke family, later moving to a piece of land near the new Pender Methodist Church (between Chantilly and Fairfax). Henry sold his children into slavery and with the proceeds of the sale, built a church (located very near the site of the new Pender Church and on the same side of the road). After the War Between the States the children returned home! Margaret Adams married Samuel Brooke. Children (perhaps others):

*(22421)* Samuel Adams Brooke, born 1846, died September 4, 1909, aged 63 years, buried at Andrew Chapel. His wife, Mary E. Brooke, is buried beside him. She was born July 25, 1852, died January 12, 1927. Issue: Grace Brooke, died January 24, 1885, aged 2 years; J. Owens Brooke, born October 25, 1891, died September 5, 1929; Samuel R. Brooke, died October 3, 1893, aged 9 months; and Upton S. Brooke, born July 27, 1894, died October 6, 1918).

*(2243)* Anne (Nancy) Adams, daughter of Samuel and Jemima (Darne) Adams, married James Wrenn (III) of Mount Rocky, a distant cousin. *(See Wren Sketch.)*

*(2244)* Penelope Adams, daughter of Samuel and Jemima (Darne) Adams, married (Nicholas?) Saunders, a cousin.

*(2245)* Sallie Adams, daughter of Samuel and Jemima (Darne) Adams, was born March 14, 1793, died December 6, 1858, and is buried in Andrew Chapel Cemetery. She married Thomas S. Cooksey (born April 11, 1798, died October 5, 1857). They had two children, Frances Ann Cooksey, who married the Reverend Alexander G. Brown; and Isabella Cooksey, married Eugene G. Ford. A sketch of these two follows:

*(22451)* Frances Ann Cooksey (Fanny), born in 1834, married at her home in Fairfax County on January 6, 1859, to the Reverend

Alexander Gustavus Brown, then a resident of Lynchburg. Dr. Brown was born at Stephensburg, Frederick County, Virginia, February 22, 1833, a son of Dr. Gustavus Alexander Scott and Ann (Murphy) Brown. He died at his home in Ashland, Hanover County, Virginia, March 16, 1900. Dr. Brown was a distinguished Methodist Clergyman and Presiding Elder, and served as Financial Secretary of Randolph-Macon College for many years. His portrait hangs in the office of the Dean at Randolph-Macon, and each year the school participates in the "Alexander G. Brown Lectures" a memorial from his family. In 1889 Dr. Brown was given an honorary Doctor of Divinity Degree by Emory and Henry College. He is written up in "*Rev. Alexander Gustavus Brown, D.C.—A Memorial*," published in Richmond in 1901. In this book he is described as a man of ". . . self reliance, strong common sense, caution, clear judgment, . . . with keen perception of human character."

Dr. Brown was of distinguished ancestry, a grandson of William and Ann (Scott) Brown who were double first cousins. Ann (Scott) Brown was a daughter of Captain James and Elizabeth (Harrison) Scott. William Brown was a son of Dr. William and Katherine (Scott) Brown who were first cousins. Dr. William Brown, distinguished Revolutionary hero and author, was a descendant of David Brown of Scotland who served in the Court of Gustavus Adolphus of Sweden, and later married Princess Christina, niece of Gustavus Adolphus. The first American ancestor of Dr. Brown was Dr. Gustavus Brown of Port Tobacco, Maryland.

Mrs. Fanny (Cooksey) Brown was an ideal wife to her husband, ". . . a blessing to him all his days, gladdening and brightening his home, and ministering with rare faithfulness to his wants in his languishing and decline." Dr. and Mrs. Brown raised a large family.

(*22452*) Isabella Cooksey, daughter of Thomas S. and Sallie (Adams) Cooksey, was born in 1836, and married on November 22, 1854, to Eugene G. Ford. Mr. Ford was also a native of Fairfax County, born in 1818, a son of Edward and Jane Ford. His father was a merchant at Fairfax Court House. Antonia Ford, the Confederate Spy, was a sister of Eugene G. Ford.

---

[1] See D.A.R. Library, Washington, D.C., MS., F.C.,"McCulloch Family-Missouri."
[2] Dates and other information supplied by Mr. Robert E. McCulloch, Hermitage, Tennessee, July 10, 1964.
[3] Richard King married (2nd) Susie Ellis of Gainesville. His first wife, Julia A. King, died May 28, 1900.
[4] Information from an interview (6/14/64), and from family papers owned by F. Alton Darne and his son, Richard A. Darne.
[5] The record of his family can be found in his Bible, published in 1825, and owned by the Rev. Raymond Fitzhugh Wrenn.
[6] His tombstone has this inscription: "In the various duties of husband, / Father and friend he was preeminent, / Beloved in life in death lamented."
[7] A great-grandson of America, Robert A. Darne of 511 E. Columbia Street, owns the autograph album which was owned originally by Miss Artemesia Scott. It is full of interest and con-

tains a partial family record. The fly-leaf is inscribed: "Miss Artie Scott from a friend, April 19, 1860." Other important notations follow: "Artemecia Scott—Virginia America Scott, Contributing Members of the First Virginia Regiment, 1st Ball of Manassas, July 18, 1861. Joseph W. Bates, Co. D, 1st Regt. Va. Vol., Richmond, Va. 2nd Battle of Manassas July 21st, 1861. Mr. R. H. Scott, a Vol. C.S.A., Fairfax Co., Va. Edward H. Collier, Co. D, 1st Regt. Va. Vol., Richmond, Va. Miss A. Scott, A Friend To the Southern Soldier."

[8] Copy of this will and papers of his son, Gabriel, are owned by Mrs. R.N. Wrenn of Herndon.

## THE DONALDSON FAMILY

The founder of this family was Andrew Donaldson of Scotland, who settled in present-day Arlington County, then part of Fairfax. Of his descendants, Benjamin Donaldson, and wife Nancy, lived near Bailey's Cross Roads. Benjamin Donaldson, although in middle age, served in the Confederate Army. He had a number of children, including a daughter, Mary H. Donaldson (born July 2, 1818, died unmarried, May 4, 1901). Another daughter was Carrie Donaldson who married Charles W. Rice and lived in Loudoun County.

Of special interest to the Falls Church community is Armistead McClellan Donaldson, a member of this family, who was a long-time resident. Records at Fairfax Court House reveal that Armistead M. Donaldson, age 29 years, son of Benjamin and Nancy Donaldson, and Mrs. Mildred J. Birch, 26 years, widow, were married on January 20, 1870, by the Reverend Benjamin Ball.

Armistead M. Donaldson was affectionately known in the community as "Arm." He was born December 14, 1839, near Bailey's Cross Roads, and died at his Falls Church home, January 7, 1906. His wife, Mildred Gertrude (Murray) Donaldson, was first married to W. J. R. Birch. During the War Between the States she fled, a refugee, with her little daughter, Agnes Birch, to the Stone House, still a well-known land-mark and scene of activity during the war. Her first husband was killed in the war. Mrs. Donaldson was born November 20, 1843, and died March 27, 1929. (*See Murray*).

Armistead M. Donaldson served as a private in Company F, 6th Virginia Cavalry. He was taken prisoner to Elmira, New York, and mustered out there on June 19, 1865. At that time he was described on the discharge (now owned by his granddaughter, Mildred T. Weaver) as 5' 8" in height, with light hair, blue eyes, and fair complexion. He was listed as a farmer and carpenter before the war.

Mr. Donaldson and family were ardent members of Dulin Methodist Church. His daughter, Beulah G. (Donaldson) Thorne was a member of Dulin Church from February 17, 1889, until her death, May 3, 1959. Mrs. Donaldson was a charter member of the Robert E. Lee Chapter, U.D.C.

Armistead McClellan and Mildred Gertrude (Murray) Donaldson had issue:
(1) Frank Clifton Donaldson, born October 30, 1870, died January 26, 1873.
(2) Victor Crenshaw Donaldson, born February 27, 1873, died December 8, 1941. He married on April 28, 1897, to Katherine May Howard, daughter of John Lewis and Hardenia (Faudree) Howard. Mr. Donaldson was a Merchant in Washington, D.C. Issue: (21) Agnes Faudree Donaldson, unmarried.
(3) Beulah Gordon Donaldson, born June 11, 1875, married on December 18, 1900, Jacob Spencer Thorne (*See Thorne).*
(4) Bernard Daniel Donaldson, born July 11, 1878, died in May, 1956. He was survived by his wife, Daisy S. Donaldson. Issue:

(41) Mildred Elizabeth Donaldson, married in 1943, C. Arthur Rolander, Jr., of McPherson, Kansas, an attorney in the Department of Justice.
(42) Audrey May Donaldson, married Lieutenant Robert Nelson Davis, U.S. M.C., son of Mr. and Mrs. George Easton Davis of Silver Spring, Maryland. Mrs. Audrey Davis attended Mary Washington College, as did her sister, Mildred.
(5) Wilbur Franklin Donaldson, born February 17, 1881, died February 14, 1926. Married on April 19, 1905, Alma Boucher.
(6) Edna Haddaway Donaldson, born September 12, 1884, died December 27, 1891.

## THE DUNCAN FAMILY

Captain William A. Duncan was a native of Ireland and a Roman Catholic by faith.[1] Prior to his removal to Falls Church (1869) he lived in Alexandria. During the War Between the States Captain Duncan joined the Confederate Army and later (while in Alexandria) deserted, according to tradition. He then joined the Federal Army and was in charge of the pay roll of a regiment. In the course of taking the pay roll from place to place, he was forced to cross through the lines. In order to avoid having the money fall into Confederate hands (as they came upon him), he buried it on a spot near the "Hollywood Farm." According to the late Willis L. Gordon, this gold was never recovered. Mr. Gordon said that Captain Duncan told him he had tried to find it after the war, but did not succeed.

Captain Duncan purchased the 95 acre "Mt. Hope" farm of Amzi Coe who was a Northern gentleman and Southern sympathizer. Mr. Coe had purchased the farm from the Sewall family.

Captain Duncan was a man of strong sentiment, and some interesting stories are told of him. He was angry at one time with his neighbor, Seth Osborn. Mr. Osborn owned "Center Hill" a fine brick home near the Duncan farm. The home of Captain Duncan (still standing on North Oak Street) originally contained only the clapboard back wing. This wing was built in 1825. Captain Duncan erected the three story brick structure in 1870. The drive way of Captain Duncan's home (now North Oak Street) bordered close to the fine home of Seth Osborn. Upon occasion it was necessary to ask aid of Mr. Osborn in winter when Captain Duncan's buggy was stuck in the mud. At one time, however, Mr. Osborn was too busy and could not aid Captain Duncan in getting his buggy on the road. This made the Captain quite angry. To "spite" Mr. Osborn (as he himself put it) he had his tenant house moved close to the line of the Osborn property. It is said that he had this building rolled on logs during the night, so that when Mr. Osborn looked out the next morning, he saw this (then unpainted) building jammed close to his fine home. Thus this building became "Spite House." "Spite House" was erected in 1808 by the Sewall family. It was torn down in 1963.

---

[1] He was possibly related to James Duncan (a farmer in Falls Church District in 1879) who came from Ireland in 1846.

## THE EASTMAN FAMILY

Albert Prescott Eastman moved to Falls Church in 1876. He boarded with the Lounsbury and Duryee families for about a year, and then built the residence in East Falls Church which was later the home of his son, Frank H. Eastman. Mr. Eastman was Lieutenant in the 1st Maine Heavy Artillery, U.S.A., Army of the Potomac. He told Mrs. Charles E. Gage that he came to Falls Church during the war, and wanted to settle here, which he did. He also said he tried to stop the damage wrought on the old Falls Church. Mr. Eastman was stationed on Analostan Island for a time, was in the Battle of the Wilderness, and wounded at Petersburg.

Mr. Eastman was active in Falls Church civic affairs, was a charter member of the old Village Improvement Society, and served as Treasurer from 1885 until 1896. He was active in the Congregational and Presbyterian Churches.

Albert Prescott Eastman was born September 6, 1841, at Derry, New Hampshire. He died at Falls Church July 13, 1915, and is buried in Oak Hill Cemetery, Washington, D.C. He married on December 24, 1869, to Sarah Norton Russell, daughter of the Reverend William and Sarah Elizabeth (Brown) Russell. She was born at East Hampton, Connecticut, July 6, 1847.

Timothy Goodhue Eastman, father of A. P. Eastman of Falls Church, was born at Deerfield, N.H., February 21, 1804. He married on March 22, 1830 to Abigail Hall, and died at Exeter, N. H., July 15, 1850. Mrs. Eastman was born November 25, 1809, and died Malden, Mass., September 13, 1852. She was a daughter of Aaron and Abigail (Pratt) Hall. Joseph Eastman, father of Timothy, was born at Kingston, N. H., in 1772. He married Sally Prescott (born March 4, 1774) and lived at Deerfield. Ephraim Eastman, father of Joseph, was born at Byfield, Massachusetts, August 4, 1747, died January 26, 1836. He married on February 28, 1771 to Elizabeth Colby, and died September 20, 1820. Jeremiah Eastman, father of Ephraim, was born at Ipswich, Massachusetts, March 30, 1704. He married on February 10, 1725 to Lydia Brown, daughter of Thomas and Elizabeth Brown. Zachariah Eastman, father of Jeremiah, was born at Salisbury, Massachusetts, August 24, 1679. He married (1st) on May 1, 1703 to Martha Thorn (who died June 6, 1718). John Eastman, father of Zachariah, was born at Salisbury January 9, 1640, died March 25, 1720. Zachariah was the child by his second wife Mary Boynton whom he married November 5, 1670. John was the son of Roger Eastman of Wales, who immigrated to Salisbury, Massachusetts (born 1611, died December 16, 1694). His wife was Sarah (Smith?) born 1621, died March 11, 1697.

Albert Prescott and Sarah Norton (Russell) Eastman had issue:

(1) Dr. William Russell Eastman, M.D., of New York. Dr. Eastman served in the Spanish-American War and World War I. He married Lottie Patten of Falls Church, daughter of Colonel Patten. In late life Dr. Eastman moved to California. Issue:

(11) William Russell Eastman, Jr.

(2) Frank Hall Eastman, born April 23, 1877, at Falls Church, died (in the room where he was born), September 10, 1960. Mr. Eastman was President of the Arlington Rotary Club, member of the Washington Round Table and of the Board of Directors of the Arlington-Fairfax Savings and Loan Association. For more than thirty years he was associated with the National Electric Supply Company of Washington, D.C. He was a member, Washington Society of Engineers, and an ardent churchman. Mr. Eastman was Superintendent of the Sunday School of the Falls Church Presby-

terian Church, and served as Elder and trustee. He married on December 7, 1903, Elizabeth McKay of Brooklyn, New York, daughter of John McKay. Mrs. Eastman was born April 26, 1880, and died December 27, 1933. Issue:
  (*21*) Eleanor Russell Eastman, born August 4, 1906 at Falls Church. She married Senator Charles R. Fenwick, son of Edward T. Fenwick. Senator and Mrs. Fenwick reside in the old Eastman home at East Falls Church. No issue.
  (*22*) Carol Elizabeth Eastman, born January 24, 1913, married William John Tate. The Tates reside on part of the Eastman home-place. Issue:
    (*221*) William John Tate, Jr., born August 12, 1940.
    (*222*) Frank Eastman Tate, born July 18, 1943.
    (*223*) Carol McKay Tate, born April 27, 1946

## THE EDMONDS FAMILY

William Fitzhugh Edmonds (born 1879), a son of Philip Mead Edmonds and Selina M. (Slade) Edmonds, is a highly respected resident of Falls Church. He married in 1907 to Maud Moss Nolan of an old Virginia family. They had issue:

(1) William Donald Edmonds, born 1908, married Kathleen Moffett and had Beverly Kathleen Edmonds, born 1938.

(2) Maud Evelyn Edmonds, born 1910, married Wells Jones, and had Donald Wells Jones.

(3) Audrey Fitzhugh Edmonds, born 1917, unmarried.

(4) Carter Moss Edmonds, born 1919, married Ruby Lee Parrott, and had Marcie Lee Edmonds.

Philip Mead Edmonds (father of William F. Edmonds) was born in 1841 and died in 1912. His wife, Selina M. Slade, was born in 1848 and died in 1912. Mrs. Edmonds was a descendant from the Fitzhugh family. Philip M. Edmonds was the son of William Foote Edmonds (1801-1868) who married his first cousin Mary Evelina Carter (daughter of Moore Fauntleroy and Judith Lee (Edmonds) Carter and descended from the family of Robert "King" Carter). William Foote Edmonds was the son of William and Hester (Foote) Edmonds of "Chestnut Grove," Fauquier County. This William Edmonds (1765-1822) was the son of Colonel William Edmonds (1734-1816) who married March 16, 1764 in Fauquier County to Elizabeth Blackwell (daughter of William and Elizabeth (Crump) Blackwell). Colonel Edmonds served as Captain in Braddock's Army in the French and Indian War and also served as Colonel of the First Battalion of Virginia Militia, 1778. He was with Washington's Army at the crossing of the Delaware, at Valley Forge, Stony Point, Brandywine, Germantown, and was with Light Horse Harry Lee at Paulus Hook. His home was "Oak Spring" near Warrenton. He was the founder of "Warren Academy" (1788) which gave the town of Warrenton its name when incorporated in 1810. Colonel Edmonds was a member of the first Vestry of Leeds Church in upper Fauquier.

Colonel William Edmonds was a son of William Edmonds (1704-1741) by his wife Catherine Miller. William Edmonds was a son of Elias Edmonds (1673-1745) who was a son of William Edmonds. This last named William was a son of Elias Edmonds who died in 1654 and left Edwin Conway as guardian of his two children. His wife was named Frances. He was among the first of the name to settle in Virginia. Sir Thomas Edmonds, an ancestor, was Ambassador to France and Comptroller to the

House of King James of England. Robert Edmonds came to Virginia in 1619 on the Ship Mary-Gold and was living on the Eastern Shore in 1623.

The home of Mr. and Mrs. William Edmonds at 133 East Broad Street was built about 1869 by George Ives. The house was later the home of Dr. Samuel Luttrell. A four room clapboard wing (perhaps older than the large brick portion) was torn down in recent years. This was attached to the back of the house.

## THE ELLIOTT FAMILY

Four brothers named Elliott came to Virginia from England. Three of them were: Perry Elliott, John Elliott, and Matthew Elliott. Matthew Elliott and the fourth brother moved West.[1]

(1) Perry Elliott and wife Rachel, lived on Georgetown Pike. Issue:
- (11) William Perry Elliott, born November 7, 1837, died April 3, 1900, and is buried at Walker Chapel. He married Margaret A. Frizzell, who was born March 1, 1834, and died August 1, 1901. Issue: Charles Elliott, Emma Elliott, Cora Elliott, and Amos Perry Elliott who married on September 25, 1894, Eva Marcey (issue: Walker Lewis Elliott, born October 19, 1900.)
- (12) Henry Elliott, married Elizabeth Bladen.
- (13) John George Elliott, (1840-1902) is buried at Walker Chapel. He married Sarah Frances Birch (1838-1892) a daughter of John and Mary (Pennington) Birch. Issue:
  - (131) William Henry Elliott, married Etta Luvnia Elliott.
  - (132) John Edward Elliott, born in October, 1864, married (1) Eliza Jane Shipman (July 17, 1862-January 15, 1886) a daughter of Charles William and Mary Ann (Fitzgerald) Shipman; and (2) Belle McVeigh Payne (1871-October 3, 1922), daughter of Amos Parker and Mary E. (Brunner) Payne. *(See Payne).* Issue *(By Eliza Jane Shipman):*
    - (1321) Carrie May Virginia Elliott, born October 18, 1885, married on October 11, 1905, Arthur Edward Dyer. Issue: John Edward Dyer, married Pearl Skillman; Hazel Odessa Dyer, born June 29, 1908, married James Samuel Magers; Frances Joseph Dyer, born December 2, 1911, married Reuben Coleman; and Carl William Dyer, born September 19, 1919, married Nina Gofernier.

    *(By Belle McVeigh Payne):*
    - (1322) Edna Marie Elliott, born April 30, 1896, died October 2, 1896.
    - (1323) Jessie Norris Elliott, born January 18, 1895, died age 3 years, 11 months, 23 days.
    - (1324) Viola Elliott, born in September, 1891, married Bruce Cornwall.
    - (1325) Grace J. Elliott, married on August 15, 1921, Owen E. Jackson.
  - (133) James Theodore Elliott, born in October, 1868, married Sarah Virginia (Donaldson) Chisman, widow. She was called Sally, and was a daughter of Dorsey Donaldson, founder of Cherrydale, and Cornelia (Dye) Donaldson. She died February 19, 1923, age 68 years. Issue:

George Mason Elliott, born December 24, 1891, died unmarried, August 18, 1936; and Lucy Elliott, married John Todd.

(134) Julian Elliott, married on February 5, 1900, Florence Garrett, issue: Florence Elizabeth Elliott, born September 25, 1904, married (1) Dewey Carter and (2) Peter Motovich; Mildred Virginia Elliott, born January 17, 1910, married (1) —— Chambers and (2) —— Harper; Lawrence Richard Elliott, born July 7, 1924, married Jean ——; and one child who died.

(14) Frank Elliott, married (1) Julia Barnes; and (2) his sister-in-law, Sarah (Barnes) Payne, widow of William Payne.

(15) Charles Elliott, died unmarried.

(16) Joseph C. Elliott, died April 17, 1924 (*Dulin Chapel Records*). He married Martha E. Harrison, daughter of William and Rebecca (Frizzell) Harrison. She died July 11, 1922. Issue:

(161) Benjamin Franklin Elliott, born March 12, 1883, died June 1, 1940, married Lillie A. Crack. Issue:

(1611) Joseph Benjamin Elliott, born June 16, 1907, died January 14, 1958; married Virginia Morris, and had a son, Joseph Morris Elliott (who had: Bradley Stephen Elliott and Elizabeth Vashti Elliott).

(1622) Albert Franklin Elliott, baptized June 12, 1921 (Dulin Chapel), living Warwick, Virginia, 1958.

(1623) J. Stephen Elliott, living Vienna, 1958.

(1624) Mary Alice Elliott, married —— Landry and lived in Birmingham, Alabama.

(162) Goldie May Elliott, born 1885, baptized at Langley Methodist Church, May 25, 1891.

(163) Luther C. Elliott, married Fannie Plaster Galleher (who died September 20, 1937 at East Falls Church). Mr. Elliott, like his brother, was a business man in Falls Church. His wife was a sister of Mrs. Marion Erwin, Miss Jennie Galleher, and Mrs. Berkeley Inge. Issue:

(1631) Luther Kenneth Elliott, baptized June 9, 1918, (Dulin Chapel).

(1632) Marion Franklin Elliott, baptized June 12, 1921, (Dulin Chapel).

(164) Florin Armstrong Elliott, born 1889.

(165) Matilda Frances Elliott, born 1890.

(166) Bertie Elliott, married (1) —— and (2) John Heath.

(167) Joseph Henry Elliott, born October 22, 1881, unmarried, living in Pennsylvania.

(168) Ida R. Elliott, married on October 31, 1900, George L. Erwin of Falls Church.

(2) John Elliott (brother to Perry Eliott) married Sophia Kirby who died in the Spring of 1890 (*Dulin Chapel Records*). She was a daughter of Richard and Jane (Bland) Kirby (*See Kirby*).
Issue:

(21) Matthew Edward Elliott, married Jane A. Shreve (April 5, 1840-April 25, 1927), daughter of Jehu and Susan (Monroe) Shreve and a granddaughter of Jehu and Anna (Ball) Shreve. Issue:

(211) Hallie May Elliott, born December 7, 1879, died September 18,

1949, married Theodore Marcey, born December 17, 1883, died February 9, 1942.
(212) James William Elliott, died at age 12 years.
(213) Ernest Edward Elliott, born January 10, 1868, died unmarried, April 15, 1926.
(214) Horace Leonard Elliott, married on February 20, 1895, Nancy Walker, daughter of Robert and Margaret Mercer (Havener) Walker of Walker's Chapel.
(215) Etta Luvnia Elliott, born April 11, 1871, living 1960, married her cousin, William Henry Elliott, born October 18, 1862, died July 22, 1957, son of John and Sarah Frances (Birch) Elliott. Had issue.
(216) John Jehu Elliott, born 1873, died 1937, married on June 3, 1895, Mary Frances Garrett (1877-March 13, 1933). Had issue.
(22) James Elliott, married Catherine Bladen (and had a daughter, Mary Elliott, who married William Caton).

[1] Interview with Mrs. William H. Elliott, February 13, 1961.

## THE ELLISON FAMILY

An early ancestor of this family, Peter Ellison, was of Irish ancestry, and lived in Westchester County, New York. He had the following children:
(1) Smith Ellison who married and had the following children: Sallie Ellison Fry; Margaret Ellison Lucke; Elijah Ellison, Thomas Ellison, George Ellison, John Ellison, Tiny Ellison Hollit; and Eliza Ellison Mason.
(2) Amanda Ellison married —— Waterbury.
(3) Fannie Ellison, married —— Barber (who had a daughter, Amanda (Barber) Allen who in turn had a son, William Allen).
(4) Sallie Ellison, married —— Brundege (who had the following children: Maria (Brundege) Goil; Deborah (Brundege) Washburn; Joseph Brundege, George Brundege, Fannie (Brundege) Brundege; and Adelia (Brundege) Fisher).
(5) Andrew Ellison, married Elizabeth Montross.

Andrew Ellison, son of Peter Ellison, was born in Westchester County, New York, October 3, 1794, and died at his home in West Falls Church, March 10, 1876, and is buried with other members of his family in the Falls Church yard. He married, on January 23, 1820, to Elizabeth (Betsy) Montross. Mrs. Ellison was born May 29, 1802, a daughter of Abraham and Patty Montross, and died July 1, 1854. William H. Ellison, son of Andrew and Elizabeth (Montross) Ellison, settled in Falls Church in 1851. The father, Andrew Ellison, followed his son to Falls Church, coming in 1855, a year after his wife died. Andrew Ellison was a cooper by trade. The record of his family, owned by the late Mrs. Carroll V. Shreve, gives his place of birth as Westchester Co., N.Y., while other records state that he was born in Marion, Ohio, and Marietta, Ohio. An Andrew Ellison, son of an immigrant, John Ellison, settled in Adams County, Ohio. Andrew and Elizabeth (Montross) Ellison had issue:

(1) Harriet H. Ellison, born October 20, 1820 died August 16, 1828.
(2) William Henry Ellison, born October 29, 1822, married Elizabeth Fish.
(3) Samuel Ellison, born October 7, 1824, died September 12, 1825

(4) Peter Ellison, born May 5, 1826.
(5) John Ellison, born July 1, 1828, died July 2, 1828.
(6) Amanda Ellison, born October 6, 1831, died June 24, 1854. (Said to be buried in the Falls Church yard.)
(7) Martha Ellison born September 4, 1835, died September 4, 1835.[2]

(2) William Henry Ellison, a son of Andrew and Elizabeth (Montross) Ellison, was born in Westchester County, New York, October 29, 1822,[3] and died at West Falls Church, Va., April 22, 1912. Mr. Ellison remained in Westchester County until he was twenty years old, having the school privileges of the time and in the meantime learning the carpenter trade, then spent one year working at his trade in Maryland. From there he moved to Alexandria where he worked as a carpenter and builder until 1851, and in that year he moved to Falls Church. In 1852 Mr. Ellison built his substantial residence here,[4] on the corner of West Broad and West Streets. Mr. Ellison did some building in Falls Church until 1866, when he purchased a farm and operated it until he retired from active business life, a few years before his death. One person said of Mr. Ellison: "He was a man of sterling character, universally respected, was a faithful member of the Methodist Episcopal Church, and all his life was loyal to the Democratic party."

As a young man, Mr. Ellison helped to build the Croton Aqueduct that supplied New York City with water. At that time he was living in Tarrytown, N.Y. Among the houses he built and owned in Falls Church was the Rowell House (the large brick house at West Falls Church, later the "Sun-Echo" office) which he later sold to George B. Ives, who started a mill nearby. Mr. Ives sold the house to Ambrose Rowell. As indicated, in 1852 he built his home on the corner of West and West Broad Streets. He built the Amanda Ellison house which stood opposite his home (now the site of McDaniel's Esso Garage). This house was the home of his father, Andrew Ellison, and his maiden sister Amanda, the latter affectionately known by her neighbors as "Miss Mandy." Mr. Ellison also built and owned the large frame house on Grove Avenue (Swimley House) now the residence of Mrs. Dr. Merry, the former Ruth Swimley.

William H. Ellison married twice. His first wife was Elizabeth Fish, whom he married in Washington, D.C., by the Rev. Mr. Morgan, on January 25, 1849. Mrs. Ellison was born in Hagerstown, Maryland in 1825, and died at Falls Church September 19, 1861, and was buried in the Falls Church yard. At the time of her death, Mr. Ellison was away from home trying to avoid the tense issue of the War Between the States, since he wished to remain neutral. Mrs. Elizabeth (Fish) Ellison was the daughter of Francis and Elizabeth (Becraft) Fish.[5] Mr. Ellison remarried, second, in February, 1863, to Emily J. Sherwood. Mrs. Emily J. (Sherwood) Ellison died April 19, 1891.

Among the old papers owned by Mrs. C. V. Shreve is a deed, dated April 1, 1852, which shows that Amzi and Anna (Sherwood) Coe deeded some property to Andrew Ellison for $250.50. There is also a deed dated September 2, 1853, from Ann B. Fish, Archibald and Lucinda (Fish) Sherwood to William H. and Elizabeth (Fish) Ellison.

William Henry and Elizabeth (Fish) Ellison had issue:
(21) Edwin H. Ellison, born at Falls Church, Va., July 19, 1852, son of William H. and Elizabeth (Fish) Ellison, died August 22, 1892. Mr. Ellison was a farmer. He married Emily Money and had issue:

(*211*) Effie Ellison, married William Ball of Chesterbrook. Issue:
    (*2111*) Elizabeth Ball, married Mr. Thompson of McLean, Va., no issue.
    (*2112*) Dorothy Ball, married Mr. Cloud, and had LeRoy Cloud and others.
    (*2113*) Raymond Ball, married twice and by his first marriage had three boys and by the second marriage had twin girls.
    (*2114*) Mabel Ball married George Boland and had a daughter.
(*212*) William H. Ellison, lives in California. He married Elizabeth Cooksey of Occoquan, Va., as his first marriage. Issue:
    (*2121*) Edwin Ellison (has children).
    (*2122*) Margaret Ellison, Mrs. Beckman, lives in Washington, D.C.
(*213*) Elizabeth Ellison, married Mr. Myers of Herndon, Va. Issue twin daughters.

(*22*) (Judge) John Francis Ellison, son of William Henry and Elizabeth (Fish) Ellison, was born at Falls Church November 29, 1853, and died in 1926. In the Falls Church Library is a book "Judge John F. Ellison" written by his wife, and published in Red Bluff, Tehama County, California, by the Record Press, 1929. On the flyleaf of the book Mrs. Ellison wrote:

"Presented to the Falls Church Library, Falls Church, Virginia — by Mrs. J. F. Ellison in recognition of Judge Ellison's Birthplace, and with the hope that the Memorial may be read by many of his old friends and neighbors and find a welcome in the two Library. March 22, 1930, Red Bluff, California."

The details of his life are taken from this book. Judge Ellison married, at Lakeview, Oregon, on August 31, 1880, to Minnie B. Cason.

Judge Ellison was educated at Richmond College and the University of Virginia, graduating from the latter in 1877. He was admitted to the California Bar in the same year, and located at Red Bluff, Tehama County, and practiced law there from 1877 until 1890. In 1890 he was elected Superior Judge of Tehama County, a position he held until his death in 1926. He was Delegate to the Republican National Convention which met in Chicago in 1888 and nominated Benjamin Harrison for President.

In his Diary Judge Ellison wrote that Falls Church was "a community noted for the sobriety, industry, and piety of its inhabitants." The following is from the *San Francisco Chronicle:*'

"A Memorial to the late Superior Judge John F. Ellison of Red Bluff, Tehama County, recently published by Mrs. Ellison for private distribution, makes a valuable contribution to California records.

For half a century the story of Judge Ellison's career was inevitably the story, in a measure, of the interesting and important district of California, where he made his home. For thirty-six years he served his community as Superior Judge, and when his distinction as a jurist became recognized beyond the confines of his own jurisdiction, so that his friends urged him to seek higher place, he declined because he preferred to continue to deal justice among the neighbors who honored and trusted him.

Intended primarily as a tribute to Judge Ellison from those who knew him most intimately, the volume goes further and gives us a glimpse, not merely of an individual, but of the straightforward and staunch character of the kind of men who furnished a firm foundation for the substantial progress of California."

(23) Amanda E. Ellison, daughter of William Henry and Elizabeth (Fish) Ellison, was born at Falls Church, October 13, 1856, and died here unmarried on January 22, 1895. Miss Ellison is buried in Oakwood Cemetery. Her home was the brick house which stood on the corner of West and Broad Streets (site of McDaniel's Garage). The back lot of the property was used at one time by Mr. George Ives for a saw mill site. This same lot was left to the Crossman Methodist Church on condition that a building be erected there in a given length of time. None was built, however, and the property reverted to the estate. After the death of "Miss Mandy," the Northrup family lived there. It was rented by various people after that. The house was of mellow red brick and the beams were hand-hewn oak. All of the doors were handmade. The iron work in the house was hand made by a Negro blacksmith. A porch was on the front of the house with four white square columns. "Miss Mandy's" house had many paned windows and shutters. The house was purchased by Mr. Noble McDaniel who had it dismantled between October 1st and 4th, 1949.

(24) William McElfresh Ellison, son of William Henry and Elizabeth (Fish) Ellison, was born at Falls Church October 3, 1859, and died here September 24, 1924. He married on November 21, 1883, to Lillian Ball, a daughter of John and Margaret Ann (Shreve) Ball. Mrs. Ellison was born March 16, 1861, died September 10, 1921. Mr. Ellison attended the public schools of Falls Church, and entered Columbian University in Washington, D.C., now George Washington University, from which he was graduated in the class of 1899 with his degree of Bachelor of Laws. He entered into practice at Falls Church and Washington, D.C., maintaining offices in West Falls Church and on the corner of Sixth and D streets in the District. Mr. Ellison had a large practice of civil and criminal law, and was a leader of the Fairfax Bar. A writeup of his life can be found on page 110 of Volume 6, *History of Virginia*, published by the American Historical Society in 1924. This says in part: "Mr. Ellison is well known in his profession as a reputable, honorable, able lawyer, and a member of the Bar Association of the Sixteenth Judicial Circuit of Virginia." Mr. Ellison was a Director of the Falls Church Bank from the time it was organized and owned large property interests in the community and developed "Ellison Heights" owning two hundred lots. He was a Steward of the Dulin Methodist Church for thirty-eight years, and was Superintendent of the Sunday School for twenty-nine years. A Democrat, Mr. Ellison served as a member of the Falls Church Town Council for twenty-five years, and on the School Board for three years and served four terms as Mayor of the Town. He was a Noble Grand of Falls Church Odd Fellows Lodge.

William M. and Lillian (Ball) Ellison had issue:

(241) Ella Elizabeth Ellison, born at Falls Church December 7, 1884, died here December 11, 1884.

(242) Fannie May Ellison, born at Falls Church June 4, 1886, married Carroll V. Shreve (*See Shreve sketch*).

(243) Minnie Duffey Ellison, born at Falls Church September 29, 1888, unmarried.

(244) John William Ellison, born at Falls Church, July 25, 1890, died here March 8, 1894.

(245) daughter Ellison, not named, born and died May 28, 1895.

(246) son Ellison, not named, born and died June 20, 1896.

(247) son Ellison, not named, born and died June 30, 1900.

[1] According to the family record, Abraham Montross died July 21, 1845; his wife, Patty Montross, died February 19, 1843. They had the following children: Daniel Montross, Lockwood Montross, David Montross (who had a son Martin Montross); Elizabeth (Montross) Ellison; Abraham Montross, Jr.; Marlin Montross (who had a son James Montross); Henry Montross, Alfred Montross, Benjamin Montross, and Jesse Montross. Jesse Montross was the father of James Elijah, and Deborah Montross. Deborah Montross, daughter of Jesse, married Mr. Gates.
[2] A date in the family record is this: "Harriet Ellison born August 16, 1828"—this cannot be placed.
[3] Mrs. C. V. Shreve, Mr. Ellison's granddaughter, stated that he told her that he was born in Marietta, Ohio.
[4] This dwelling was torn down during the week of May 20, 1955.
[5] Elizabeth (Fish) Ellison was a great-granddaughter of Jonathan Nixon, a native of England, who settled in Maryland in 1750. By his wife Mary Bentley he had seven children: Richard Nixon (no issue); Amy (Nixon) Howard (no issue); Elizabeth Nixon, James Nixon, lived in Shepherdstown, W. Va.; Hugh Nixon, lived in Iola, Ill.; Jonathan Nixon, Jr; and Mary (Nixon) Becraft. Mary (Nixon) Becraft had issue: Acquila Becraft (who lived in Jackson, Miss.); Henrietta M. (Becraft) Yander; Ann (Becraft) McElfresh; Mary (Becraft) Hitt; Jonathan Becraft; and Elizabeth (Becraft) Fish. Francis Fish was a son of William Fish.

## THE ERWIN FAMILY

Walter H. Erwin was born in Churchville, New York, in 1820. He went to California during the gold rush of 1849, and returned to the East by way of the Panama Canal. He left his wife in New York since her father refused to let her go because of the Indian menace. Maynard Erwin of Falls Church, has in his possession a very interesting old deed to Walter H. Erwin from Benjamin F. and Emily C. Erwin dated December 22, 1847. At that time Mr. Erwin was of Monroe, Ogden Co., New York. Mr. Erwin married Julia L. Smith, born in New York in 1829, daughter of Phineas and Electa Smith.

On November 23, 1852, Mr. Erwin purchased from Nathan Thompson for $100.00, two acres and buildings on the south side of the Leesburg turnpike where it intersected the "Line of the County road which runs by the School House near the Falls Church."[1] This was the famous "Star Tavern" property, now the site of the Falls Church Bank. Mr. Erwin was proprietor of this Tavern until the outbreak of the War Between the States. The old tavern included part of an earlier building where both Charles Dickens and Lafayette stayed. During the 1850's men would ride up in the "Tally-Ho," dismount, and stay for liquors, beer, and ale. The Tavern was much enlarged by Erwin in 1855.

During the War Between the States the Tavern was used by the Home Guards as their headquarters. On a number of occasions it was raided by Mosby. At the time of the First Battle of Bull Run, Mr. Erwin and his family were forced to flee to Washington for safety, as Mosby was taking all Union men as prisoners. Among those made prisoner were D. C. Munson, John B. Reed, and John Jackson, a Negro. Munson escaped enroute to Dranesville, but Reed was killed, Jackson was wounded. The Pioneer Lodge of Good Templars held their organization meeting in the building, and later met there regularly. After 1868 the Tavern was used as a Supper and Dance Hall, and one room was used as a School (taught by Miss Dinnigon).

In 1860 John Rhodes (born Virginia, age 40) and Thomas Wyatt (age 45, born New York) lived there as permanent residents. (*Census*).

The following biography of Mrs. Erwin (who later was Mrs. Auchmoody) was written in 1954 by Mrs. Charles E. Gage:

"Some of the most cherished memories of my childhood and young womanhood center around Mrs. Auchmoody—short, plump, rosy cheeked, with twinkling brown eyes, always smiling—her white hair parted in the middle with the knot at the back and two finger curls over each ear. She came to Falls Church with the wave of settlers from New York with her husband, Mr. Erwin (who was a direct descendant from the General of that name on Washington's staff) before the War Between the States, and ran the Star Tavern. It was she who hid the font of the old Falls Church during the war, when it was turned over to her by a Yankee soldier to keep for him till he went home.

Upon the death of Mr. Erwin, his widow later married Mr. Auchmoody, a brother of Mrs. Lounsbury and Mrs. George Ives, who also came to Falls Church with the wave of settlers from New York State. There were several children by Mr. Auchmoody, all of whom died young except one girl, Annie, who married the Presbyterian Minister Edward E. Eells. Annie had three girls and two boys; both of the boys became ministers. Mr. Auchmoody built the house, now 400 Great Falls St., where the family was raised. Their property extended to Little Falls St. and beyond the big brick house across the railroad built by Mr. DePutron. He also owned property on the hill where the Mt. Daniel School now stands.

Mrs. Auchmoody was always ready to help anyone in trouble or sickness, and helped to bring many babies into the world during the post war period when trained nurses were unknown—and money, too, for many people. This was then a friendly town where people were good neighbors and helped each other. Mrs. Auchmoody was loved and respected by everyone and did much to spread the friendly spirit throughout the community. God bless her!"

Mrs. Erwin-Auchmoody is buried in Oakwood Cemetery and the words "Mother Auchmoody" on a stone mark her grave.

Mr. and Mrs. Erwin had issue:
(1) Munson H. Erwin, born 1855, married Florence M. Telly, niece of Schuyler Duryee, no children. She died in Washington, D.C., August 5, 1942.
(2) Julia L. Erwin, born 1857, died young.
(3) Walter H. Erwin, married Mamie Gallaher.
(4) George Louis Erwin, married Ida Rebecca Elliott.

(3) Walter H. Erwin (1859-1927) who married Marion W. Galleher ("Mamie") daughter of Turner and Jane Galleher of Loudoun County. Mrs. Erwin died February 14, 1956, age 91. Issue:
   (*31*) Harold Erwin, founded "Erwin Ford Company" at Fairfax. Mr. Erwin is married and has three children.

(4) George Louis Erwin, married Ida Rebecca Elliott, daughter of Joseph C. and Martha (Frizzell) Elliott. Mrs. Erwin died July 14, 1958. Children:
   (*41*) Warner Elliott Erwin, born July 29, 1901, married (1) Marguerite Case and (2) her sister, Blanche Case, both daughters of Walter Case of Purcellville, Va. Children:
      (*411*) Marjorie Lee Erwin, married Wilbur Geddes.
      (*412*) Harry Case Erwin, married Peggy, and had issue:
         Michael Erwin, Deborah Erwin, and Pamela Erwin.
      (*413*) Warner Elliott Erwin, married Jean.
      (*414*) Tracey Erwin, unmarried.

(*42*) Maynard Munson Erwin, born December 15, 1904, married on September 15, 1926, Mildred Louise Ball (born at Ashburn, Virginia, April 18, 1908, of an old Loudoun County family).² No children. Mr. and Mrs. Erwin have a noted collection of Antiques.

(*43*) Virginia Elizabeth Erwin, born July 26, 1908, married Glenn Howard Wrenn. No children.

---

¹ Fairfax County *Deed Book R #3*, page 320.
² Daughter of Charles Wilmer and Edna Earle (Cross) Ball, granddaughter of Charles and Jane Ball.

---

## THE FADELEY FAMILY

The earliest known ancestor of the Fadeley family was Jacob Fadeley who was born in 1771, died 1842. Mr. Fadeley lived in Loudoun County. He married, at Leesburg, January 5, 1799, to Mary (Polly) McNeledge, daughter of James and Ann McNeledge. A January, 1799, issue of the local Leesburg paper which announced this marriage, has been passed down through the Fadeley family, and is now in the Maryland home of Dr. James McNeledge Fadeley, son of Dr. George B. Fadeley of Falls Church. James Henry Fadeley of Alexandria, son of Jacob and Mary (McNeledge) Fadeley, was born January 17, 1810 at Leesburg. His wife was a Miss Robinson of Flint Stone, Maryland. His second wife was Virginia Gray of Alexandria and they were married October 23, 1855. Mr. Fadeley was Bailiff in Alexandria. He had two children. James Fadeley, a son of James Henry Fadeley, moved to Baltimore, where he married Rebecca Hopkins a native of Manchester, England. She came to America with her mother, Jane (Mitchell) Hopkins and a large number of brothers and sisters. They had two sons, Charles Henry and George B. Fadeley.

Dr. George Beauregard Fadeley was born in Baltimore, October 8, 1861, son of James and Rebecca (Hopkins) Fadeley. He died in Washington, D.C., August 18, 1948. For many years Dr. Fadeley was a beloved physician in Falls Church. A write-up of his life can be found on page 226 of Volume XXXVII of *The National Cyclopaedia of American Biography*. Orphaned when six years old, young Fadeley apprenticed himself to a farmer in the Baltimore area, and later worked in a bakery. He attended Marston School in Baltimore, studied at the University of Maryland Medical School, and did his graduate work at Johns Hopkins University. Dr. Fadeley opened his practice in Falls Church in 1889. He lived in Falls Church for twenty-five years, and in 1920 moved to the old Martin Donaldson property. Here he lived twenty-five years. Dr. Fadeley's first office was in the Star Tavern.

On June 6, 1893, he married Marian Rice, the daughter of Yale and Helen Maria (Curtis) Rice of Falls Church. Mrs. Fadeley was born November 2, 1872 in Lewis Co., N.Y., and died March 28, 1960.

Dr. Fadeley was a founder of the Falls Church Bank, and served as its President from 1906 until 1941. He was a Director of the bank until 1947. Dr. Fadeley retired about 1935.

Dr. Fadeley was active in civic affairs in Falls Church, and was a Master of Kemper Lodge. He served as District Deputy Grand Master of Masonic Jurisdiction No. 1. The Fadeleys attended the Falls Church Presbyterian Church.

Dr. George B. and Marian (Rice) Fadeley had issue:

(1) Dr. James McNeledge Fadeley, a Surgeon in Washington, D.C. He married

(1) Marian (Polly) Parker, who was born May 2, 1896, died October 22, 1942; and (2) Shirley Sweeney of Chicago, Ill. Issue (by the second wife):
(*11*) James McNeledge Fadeley, Jr.
(*12*) Fabienne Fadeley.
(2) Charles Rice Fadeley, assistant vice president of Riggs National Bank, married Agnes McNeal, daughter of Leroy C. and Elizabeth M. (Allen) McNeal, and granddaughter of W. J. Allen, an old area resident. Issue:
(*21*) Marian Elizabeth Fadeley.
(*22*) Jane McNeal Fadeley.
(*23*) Ann Rice Fadeley.

(3) Grace Fadeley, married Robert Odil McElroy. Issue:
(*31*) Marjorie McElroy, married Eduardo De Acevedo, of Cuba. Mr. and Mrs. De Acevedo are artists, and reside in New York.

## THE FEBREY FAMILY

Nicholas Febrey, ancestor of all of that name in Virginia, was born in Alexandria County (now Arlington County) October 3, 1800 and died January 6, 1868 at Falls Church. He married twice (1) to Belinda Ball; and (2) to Amanda Ball of Ball's Cross Roads on May 15, 1860. Amanda (Ball) Febrey was born 1819, died August 12, 1882. In 1879 she was a widow living on a 120 acre farm at Falls Church. The following is a copy of an obituary of Mrs. Belinda (Ball) Febrey:

"Departed this life on the 25th instant at her residence in Alexandria County, Mrs. Belinda Febrey in the sixty third year of her age; after a long and painful illness which she bore with Christian fortitude and resignation, for five long and dreary months she was confined to the house and such was the nature of her disease that she could not lie down but a very few moments at a time, and then under very painful and distressing circumstances. Yet she was never heard to murmur at her lot but was always ready to say the will of the Lord be done and was frequently heard to say when under the most excruciating pain, Oh! Lord if it is for thy glory let it be so and thus was she submissive to the will of the Lord to the last moment and then died in the full triumph of the Christian faith and went home to . . . (torn)."

Belinda (Ball) Febrey was born in 1795, died September 25, 1858 and is buried in Oakwood Cemetery.

Mrs. Amanda Febrey died at an advanced age. She had one son who died at birth;[1] all of the children that lived were by Belinda Ball. Nicholas Febrey served in the War of 1812.

Nicholas and Belinda (Ball) Febrey had issue:

(1) (Captain) Henry Wand Febrey, son of Nicholas and Belinda (Ball) Febrey, was born November 24, 1828, died March 5, 1881, and is buried with other members of his family in Oakwood Cemetery, at Falls Church. He married on January 14, 1851, to Margaret Amelia Payne, daughter of James and Hannah Payne. She was born November 1, 1830, died April 9, 1915. The record of this family is taken from their Bible which was published by William W. Harding of Jesper Harding & Son, Philadelphia, 1860. Henry W. Febrey was commissioned Captain of the 175th Regiment of Infantry of the 5th Brigade and 2nd Division of Virginia Militia on May 21, 1849; and the original Commission, still in the family, is dated May 29, 1849, and

signed by Governor John B. Floyd. Captain Henry Wand and Margaret Amelia (Payne) Febrey had issue:
- (*11*) William N. Febrey, born November 7, 1851, died 1940. He married at Dulin Chapel on March 21, 1882, to Eliza Frances Hughes, (1859-1927). Issue:
  - (*111*) Louis Bentley Febrey born Dec. 24, 1882.
  - (*112*) Henry Febrey, lives in Washington, D. C.
  - (*113*) Louise Febrey, married Ira H. Arnold ("Dick"), of Idylwood, Va.
- (*12*) James Edward Febrey, born March 18, 1853. Mr. Febrey is written up in *History of Union Co., N.J.* by A. Van Doren Honeyman, Vol. 3, pp. 277-278. Mr. Febrey was a grocer at Elizabeth, N.J. His biography states that he attended school in his native Falls Church, and moved to Elizabeth, N.J., when he was 28 years of age. He married in Falls Church, October 25, 1882, to Emma B. Adams, a native of Ulster Co., N.Y. She died in Elizabeth, N.J., February 14, 1916. Issue:
  - (*121*) Ethel Febrey, married Morris Lynsky, and had a son, James Lynsky.
  - (*122*) Harold H. Febrey, married and had two children and lived in Newark, N. J.
- (*13*) Ida Jane Febrey, born June 18, 1855, died August 22, 1936. She married at Dulin Chapel, January 8, 1878, to William Green Bailey (1841-1909). Issue:
  - (*131*) Edna Bailey (1878-1946) married Mr. Garfield and had a son, William Bailey Garfield.
  - (*132*) Henry Febrey Bailey, born September 10, 1881, died 1934.
- (*14*) Kate Bell Febrey, born November 18, 1857, died September 29, 1915. She married at Dulin Chapel on November 13, 1877, to Joseph N. Wright. Mr. Wright was born January 11, 1854, died October 27, 1881. Issue:
  - (*141*) Ross Wright, lives in North Dakota, and has a large family.
  - (*142*) Leonora Wright, unmarried, lives in Richmond, Va.
- (*15*) Lilly Febrey, born March 11, 1859, died September 8, 1937. Married William H. Shreve. (*See Shreve*)
- (*16*) Nettie Belinda Febrey, born December 1, 1860, married on April 26, 1887 at Dulin Chapel to John L. Hughes. Issue:
  - (*161*) Eleanor Hughes.
  - (*162*) J. Leonard Hughes.
- (*17*) Amos Payne Febrey, born October 15, 1863, was a partner in Febrey Bros. Store in Elizabeth, N. J., and died April 9, 1919. By his wife Kate he had issue:
  - (*171*) Marguerite Febrey, married Robert Brinton; issue: Robert Brinton, Jr., Mr. and Mrs. Brinton reside in Texas.
- (*18*) (The Reverend) Harry Coe Febrey, born February 9, 1865, died November 5, 1948. He was a Methodist Clergyman, member of the Baltimore Conference, Methodist Episcopal Church, South. Mr. Febrey was educated at Randolph-Macon College. He was admitted to the Baltimore Conference in 1899, and during his ministry served Jarrettsville, Md.; Blue Sulphur and Piedmont, W. Va.; Buchanan, Basic and Marshall, Va. Dr. George G. Oliver wrote of Mr. Febrey: "Everywhere he went he attracted attention by his own candid countenance, his spirit of sincerity, his princely manner, and his earnest speech." Mr. Febrey married on October 9, 1895 to Nettie Schaaff. Mrs. Febrey died November 22, 1949. No children.

(*19*) Hattie Lee Febrey, born December 15, 1866, baptized by the Rev. A. B. Dolly at Dulin Chapel March 21, 1869. Married on June 23, 1887 at Dulin Chapel to Ulysses S. Walters, and moved to Langley, Va. Issue:
(*191*) Neil Walters.
(*192*) Douglas Walters.
(*193*) Pearl Febrey Walters, baptized April 15, 1895, at Dulin Chapel.
(*194*) Milton Walters.

(*1.10*) Ernest Jackson Febrey, born July 26, 1868, married at Dulin Chapel on September 10, 1889 to Grace W. Payne. Mrs. Febrey died July 27, 1933. Issue:
(*1.10.1*) Ernest Franklin Febrey, died August 18, 1893.
(*1.10.2*) Margaret Amelia Febrey, died January 15, 1913.

(*1.11*) Elsie Amelia Febrey, born February 6, 1874, married on June 25, 1901 to Sidney J. Simmonds. Mr. Simmonds died May 22, 1945. Issue:
(*1.11.1*) Albert Gordon Simmonds, born April 27, 1902. Married, no issue.
(*1.11.2*) James Henry Simmonds, born April 19, 1905. Mr. Simmonds is a lawyer in Arlington.

(2) John Edward Febrey, son of Nicholas and Belinda (Ball) Febrey, was born in 1831, died May 27, 1893, and is buried in Oakwood Cemetery. He married in Washington, D. C., January 4, 1855, to a cousin, Mary Frances Ball. Mrs. Febrey was born in Washington, D. C., September 6, 1835, daughter of John and Margaret Ann (Shreve) Ball. She died at Falls Church August 1, 1914. Mr. and Mrs. Febrey built what is now known as the "Lothrop" place near Willston. Mr. Febrey was a well-to-do farmer and real estate man, and was active in Falls Church affairs. Issue:

(*21*) Ella Ball Febrey, born October 29, 1856, died September 20, 1889. She married at Dulin Chapel, September 28, 1876 by the Reverend Benjamin F. Ball to Dr. Thomas Melville Talbott. Dr. Talbott, beloved Falls Church physician, was born October 17, 1848, died May 3, 1940. Both are buried in Oakwood Cemetery. Dr. Talbott remarried Kathleen Nourse (*See Talbott sketch.*) Issue:
(*211*) Edward Melville Talbott, born December 9, 1877.
(*212*) Ella Talbott, born March 20, 1879, died July 5, 1879.
(*213*) Infant son (not named) born February 16, 1880, died at birth.

(*22*) Annie E. Febrey, married John Franklin Shreve. They were married by their cousin, the Reverend Benjamin F. Ball at Dulin Chapel on February 10, 1881. A note on the church register states: "Church was crowded with people." Mr. Shreve was a son of Benjamin and Sarah (Simpson) Shreve and was born at Falls Church in 1857. Issue:
(*221*) Ralph Febrey Shreve, born August 14, 1882, lives at Detroit, Michigan. He has one son, Thomas Shreve, who has married twice.
(*222*) Fannie Shreve, born August 13, 1886, died at Washington, D.C. July 4, 1954. She married Francis P. Heartsill. No issue.

(3) Moses A. Febrey, son of Nicholas and Belinda (Ball) Febrey, married Caroline W. ——². He may have raised a large family, but with the exception of brief mention in the Register of Dulin Chapel, they are lost to sight. Issue:

(*31*) Alice Elizabeth Febrey, born April 22, 1857, Alexandria Co., Va., baptized December 14, 1860 by the Reverend William Gwynn Coe, witnessed by the Reverend Geo. H. Zimmerman.

(*32*) Wallis (or Wallace) Alexander Febrey, born March 8, 1859, Alexandria Co., Va., baptized December 14, 1860 by the Reverend William Gwynn Coe, witnessed by the Reverend Geo. H. Zimmerman.

---

[1] The son was Robert Ball Febrey, born February 15, 1862, died August 25, 1878, buried Oakwood Cemetery.
[2] Probably Simpson, see Fairfax County Miscellaneous papers, "Chapman & Wife vs Febrey" concerning the estate of Eliza Simpson.

---

## THE FELLOWS FAMILY

Harry Andrew Fellows, former mayor of Falls Church, was born in Livingston, Alabama, November 7, 1866, a son of Hobert and Adele Fellows. He died in the Cresdale Home November 29, 1943.[1]

Mr. Fellows attended George Washington University Law School and for twenty-two years was an employee of the Income Tax Bureau of the Treasury Department. He served as president of the Falls Church Citizens Association and the Arlington County Civic Federation. During his forty-three years' residence in East Falls Church, Mr. Fellows was identified with all that was of the public interest. He was a member of the Falls Church, a member of the District National Guard, and was an Odd Fellow. Mr. Fellows was interested in Masonry and was a Past Master of B. B. French Lodge in Washington. His term as Mayor of Falls Church lasted eight years. He was also Chairman of the Arlington County Board.

Mr. Fellows had a sister, Mrs. Zula Pence, who lived in the Falls Church area.

On June 22, 1899, at The Plains, Mr. Fellows married Alice Newton Murray of an old Fauquier family. Mrs. Fellows was born August 27, 1869, and is living in the old home place at East Falls Church (1964). She is a charming person, active in the U.D.C. and the D.A.R.

Mrs. Fellows was born at "Rock Valley," the family home at The Plains, the daughter of Enoch Milton Murray (November 19, 1834-March 1, 1926) and Virginia Sanford (Welch) Murray (January 8, 1837-January 13, 1927). Mrs. Fellows is a descendant of Sylvester Welch, Sr., a member of the First Virginia Artillery during the Revolutionary War. He served for three years, enlisting under Samuel Denny from Northumberland County in 1777. Sylvester Welch, Sr., was born May 15, 1762 and died April 19, 1834. His second wife, Ann Glascock (August 22, 1771-September 17, 1845) daughter of Thomas and Agatha Glascock, was Mrs. Fellows ancestor. They were married March 14, 1798. Their son, Sylvester Welch, Jr., (November 14, 1800-July 12, 1880) married Mrs. Rachel (Saterwhite) Rector, widow of Ludwell Rector. They were parents of Virginia Sanford Welch who married Enoch Milton Murray.

Mrs. Fellows was a descendant of Reuben Murray (born 1762, died June 3, 1845) who married Catherine Chinn (September 26, 1767-December 10, 1831). Reuben Murray also served in the Revolutionary War. Their son, Enoch Milton Murray (November 10, 1801-November 10, 1870) married Eliza Morehead and they were the parents of Enoch Milton Murray.

Harry Andrew and Alice Newton (Murray) Fellows had issue:
(1) Virginia Murray Fellows, born June 29, 1900, married on October 9, 1924, to Edward Gulager Fenwick (born November 21, 1897). Issue:

(11) Edward Gulager Fenwick, born February 22, 1927.
(12) Virginia Anne Fenwick, born July 3, 1928.
(2) Harry Andrew Fellows, Jr., born October 9, 1902, married on June 27, 1940, Jeanette Ballard Luther of Danville. She was a daughter of John T. Luther and died February 4, 1958, age 48 years. Mrs. Fellows was a supervisor in the Fairfax County Elementary Schools. No issue.

---

[1] Details of his life are taken from an obituary published in the *Falls Church Echo* of December 4, 1943.

## THE FLAGG FAMILY

Edmund Flagg was one of our most prominent citizens. Born November 24, 1815, in the little seaport town of Wiscasset, Maine, a son of Edmund and Harriet (Payson) Flagg, Mr. Flagg died at his home, "Highland View" at West Falls Church, November 1, 1890. His tombstone in the Oakwood Cemetery tells us that he was a "just man." "Highland View" is still the family home, currently the residence of his daughter-in-law, Mrs. E. H. Flagg and her daughter and son-in-law, Mr. and Mrs. Charles L. T. Edwards. The house has a side tower, long verandas, and mansard roof. It was built about 1870, by a Washington Banker, Samuel Norment, as a country home.

The Flaggs are descended from Henry de Flegg who was Prior of Norwich in 1168. The immigrant ancestor was Thomas Flagg who was baptized at Whirberg in 1615.[1] He came to Watertown, Massachusetts with Richard Carver in 1637.

Gershom Flagg, son of Thomas Flagg of Watertown, was born April 16, 1641. He was admitted a Freeman in Watertown May 27, 1676. He married on April 15, 1668 to Hannah Leppingwell, a daughter of Michael Leppingwell of Norburn, where Flagg afterwards lived. Gershom Flagg was a brave Indian fighter and was Lieutenant of the Militia. He was killed by the savages at Lamprey River, July 6, 1690. His widow afterwards remarried Ensign Isaac Walker. Gershom Flagg had nine children: Gershom, Eleazer, John, Hannah, Ebenezer, Abigail, May, Thomas, and Benoni. Of these, Eleazer was a Colonel and a Magistrate of Noburn, and John a noted citizen of Boston.

Ebenezer Flagg, fourth son and fifth child of Gershom and Hannah (Leppingwell) Flagg, was born December 12, 1678 at Noburn, and was married to Elizabeth Carter on December 25, 1700. His family were eleven in number: Elizabeth, Mary, Ebenezer, John, Gershom, Thomas, Josiah, Ruth, Hannah, Abigail.

The Reverend Ebenezer Flagg, son of Ebenezer and Elizabeth (Carter) Flagg, was born at Noburn October 18, 1704. He entered Harvard College in 1721 at the age of 17; in 1725 took his degree; studied theology and was ordained September 27, 1736 and settled over the First Congregational Church at Chester, New Hampshire, with a salary of £120. He was married on November 15, 1739, by the Rev. Mr. Hooper of Boston, to Lucretia Keyes. She was born in 1720, and died March 24, 1764. His second wife, Mary Gardner, died without issue November 10, 1783. The Reverend Mr. Flagg died November 14, 1796 after a faithful ministry of over sixty years in one church, having survived every parishioner who was active at his settlement. He had a large family.

Josiah Flagg, fourth child and third son of the Reverend Ebenezer and Lucretia (Keyes) Flagg, was born April 8, 1748. He lived on the homestead at Chester, and on March 18, 1777, married Anna Webster, daughter of Colonel John and Hannah (Fowle) Webster. Her father, Colonel John Webster, was a distinguished citizen of Chester and a brother of Ebenezer Webster, Daniel Webster's father. Mrs. Flagg was born on Sunday, February 4, 1750, and died April 1, 1799. A few months after marriage the bridegroom enlisted in Captain Moses Baker's Company which marched for Canada, near Chester, and joined the Army at Saratoga September 27, 1777. He rose to be Adjutant, and served under Washington a year. On his return Flagg lived a quiet life as a farmer and Magistrate. He died April 25, 1799. Colonel John Webster, his father-in-law, was active during the Revolution, being Muster-Master, and sometimes advanced money for bounties to the soldiers.

Josiah and Anna (Webster) Flagg had issue:

(1) Betsey Van Meter Flagg, born February 12, 1778, married Daniel French on June 30, 1805, and died April 23, 1812.

(2) Catherine Gardiner Flagg, born January 8, 1780, died September 25, 1807, married William J. Folsom.

(3) Sarah Wingate Flagg, born May 31, 1782, married on November 8, 1808 to Jonathan Bell (he died April 21, 1809). She married (2nd) on November 6, 1812, to Daniel French. (She was the grandmother of Daniel Chester French the Sculptor of Lincoln in the Memorial at Washington).

(4) Henry Flagg, born April 9, 1785, married in August, 1813 to Sarah O. Head.

(5) Edmund Flagg, born Tuesday, July 3, 1787, attended Atkinson Academy and entered Dartmouth in 1802. He graduated in 1806 second in his class and a member of Phi Beta Kappa. Mr. Flagg died December 15, 1815, on the Island of St. Croix. Flagg taught for a year at Morris Charity School at Hanover, 1806-07. He read law at Chester with Mr. French the Solicitor and subsequently the Attorney General of New Hampshire (his sister's second husband). In August, 1810, he moved to Wiscasset, Maine, to practice law. He was appointed Register of Probate in Lincoln County, Maine, in 1812. On August 1, 1813, he married Harriet Payson, daughter of Colonel David and Anna (Ingersoll) Payson.

Edmund and Harriet (Payson) Flagg had issue:

*(51)* Harriet Payson Flagg, born May 14, 1814, unmarried.

*(52)* Edmund Flagg, born, November 24, 1815.

Edmund Flagg settled at "Eastwood Farm" near Peach Grove (Tyson's Cross Roads), in 1870. His career began in 1835 when he graduated from Bowdoin College with honors. In the hope of renovating the energies of a shattered constitution, Flagg set out with his widowed mother and sister Harriet for Louisville, Kentucky. Here he began an association with the *Daily Journal* which lasted until 1861. Two months after his graduation he was teaching a Classical School in Louisville, and associated with the celebrated George D. Prentice. During the summer of 1836 he traveled on horseback through Illinois and Missouri, and contributed a series of sketches to the Journal. In 1836-7, at St. Louis, Flagg read law, taught school, and wrote for the press. In 1838 he superintended the publication of his first work (by Harper's) *The Far West* in two volumes, and with George D. Prentice commenced the *Louisville Literary News-Letter*. In 1837 he entered the bar, and edited the *St. Louis Bulletin*.

Flagg practiced law at Vicksburg, Mississippi, with the Honorable S. S. Prentiss in 1840. On March 4, 1841, while editor of the *Vicksburg Whig*, he was severely wounded in a duel with the editor of the *Gazette* at Marietta, Ohio, and later in that year wrote a series of romances for the *New York New World*, conducted by Park Benjamin. Flagg conducted the *Gazette* published at Marietta, Ohio, 1842, headed the *St. Louis Gazette* 1844-45, and was subsequently reporter at the Courts of St. Louis County, and Secretary to the Honorable Edward A. Hannegan, the American Minister to Berlin in 1848. In 1846-47 he was Secretary of a mutual insurance company, and the author of a treatise on that system. He also reported the debates in the Constitutional Convention of Missouri and wrote or adapted for the stage several plays among them being "Mary Tudor," "Catherine Howard," "Ruy Blas," "Count Julian," "Carlton," and "Castilian Honor." The first three were successfully produced at St. Louis and in southern and western cities and at New York.

In 1849 while attached as Secretary to the American Legation at Berlin, Mr. Flagg was correspondent for the New York and western presses. At that time "Edmond Dantes," a sequel to Dumas' "Count of Monte Cristo," was written by him and published by the Petersons. It was republished in 1884. In 1851 Flagg was United States Counsul at Venice and later conducted the *Democratic Times* in St. Louis. Among his works at this time were "Carrero, or the Prime Minister," "Francis of Valois," "The Howard Queen" (for which he won a prize); and "Mary Tudor." In 1850 his tale "Blanche of Artois" received a prize of one hundred dollars from the *Louisville Courier* and within the two ensuing weeks two other prizes were awarded him for poems. Among his better known poems were "Motherhood," "The Wind Harp," "Visions of Life," and "Earth's Changes."

In 1852 Flagg conducted the *St. Louis Times* during the heated Pierce and Scott presidential campaign. In 1853 he superintended the publication by Charles Scribner, at New York, of two illustrated volumes written by himself entitled "Venice, the City of the Sea," and wrote for Meyer's "United States Illustrated West" edited by Charles A. Dana.

Flagg was appointed under Secretary Marcy, to the Department of State, and in 1854 was placed as Superintendent of Statistics in charge of a report of the Commercial Relations of the United States with all Foreign Nations, ordered by Congress. These were published in four quarto volumes in 1856-57. He afterwards prepared an annual report on commercial relations, and several pamphlets on cotton and tobacco trade, and on immigration.

In 1858 Mr. Flagg was Washington correspondent for several western papers, and in 1861, was placed in charge of a library in the Interior Department. Here he remained until 1869, when he resigned and took up his residence at "East Wood Farm,"and in 1871, moved to "Highland View." In February, 1862, Mr. Flagg married Kate Adeline Gallaher, daughter of Sidney S. Gallaher of Jefferson County, Virginia. In 1888, a book, "De Molai" was published by the Petersons. Until his death in 1890, he wrote some, and superintended his somewhat extended interests in Washington and Virginia real estate. Edmund Flagg was a truly great man, and Falls Church was honored to call him a resident. He was a communicant of the Falls Church Presbyterian Church.

Edmund and Kate Adeline (Gallaher) Flagg had issue:

(521) Edmund Howard Flagg born Dec. 22, 1866, married Blanche W. Lamkin.
(522) Rose Harriet Payson Flagg born June 22, 1871, died Jan. 9, 1872.
(523) Sidney Webster Flagg born July 30, 1873? died October 20, 1950.
(524) Arthur Ingersoll Flagg born Dec. 11, 1875, died Sept. 13, 1898.

(521) Edmund Howard Flagg, born in Washington, D.C., December 22, 1866, died at "Highland View" May 21, 1949. Mr. Flagg married on March 26, 1890 to Blanche Wilmer Lamkin. Mrs. Flagg was born December 16, 1875 at historic "Maddox," Westmoreland County, of distinguished Virginia ancestry. She was the daughter of William Peyton and Cornelia Carlton (Northen) Lamkin. Her grandfather Lamkin was a native of Georgia, and her grandmother Lamkin (who was Harriet Payne of Westmoreland) was a native Virginian. Cornelia (Northen) Lamkin was the daughter of Henry H. and Margaret (Muse) Northen. A sister of Mrs. Lamkin, Clara Northen, married Ambrose Rowell and lived in Falls Church. Issue:

  (5211) Edmund Alger Flagg, born at "Eastwood Farm," near Peach Grove (now Tyson's Corners) June 16, 1891, and died in Florida, March 23, 1956. He married on September 3, 1910, to Margaret Elizabeth Copper. Mrs. Flagg is a native of Falls Church. Issue:

    (52111) Margaret Catherine Flagg, born June 21, 1911 at Falls Church, married on December 8, 1934 to John C. Elliott. Issue: (521111) Jane Lee Flagg Elliott.

  (5212) Aveline Ingersoll Flagg, born at "Highland View," August 30, 1892, married on March 20, 1918, to Charles Lewis Taylor Edwards of Bethlehem, Pennsylvania. Mr. Edwards was born at Duquesne, Pennsylvania, March 12, 1889, a son of Thomas Henry and Ella Ann (Hess) Edwards, and related to the Gallaher family of Jefferson County, West Virginia. Issue:

    (52121) Charles Taylor Edwards, born January 18, 1919, at Bethlehem, Pa., married March 15, 1943 to Marjory Ann Jolly. Children:

      (521211) Susan Flagg Edwards born August 8, 1945.

      (521212) Martha Flagg Edwards born July 31, 1947.

      (521213) Wendy Flagg Edwards born September 22, 1950.

      (521214) Charles Taylor Edwards born August 9, 1952.

    (52122) Virginia Morris Edwards born at Ensley, Birmingham, Alabama, November 1, 1920. She married on October 10, 1944 to Walter Stokes Russell of Moorestown, N.J. Children:

      (521221) Lynn Flagg Russell born October 4, 1946.

      (521222) John Masters Russell born Sept. 4, 1951.

---

[1] Son of Bartholemew & Alicia Flegg of Whinbergh & Shipdham, Norfolk Co., England; grandson of John Flegg (died 1613) married Aveline; great-grandson of Richard Flegg (died 1587) by wife Margaret; and great-great-grandson of William Flegg of Swafield, Norfolk County 1521. His son, William Flegg, was Vicar of Felthorpe, 1578.

[2] The following is from the Washington, D.C., *Evening Star* of October 20, 1950: *S. W. Flagg Dies: Was D.C. Financier.* Sidney Webster Flagg, 77, a financier and real estate man in Washington and Fairfax County for half a century, died Friday at George Washington University Hospital after a long illness. He lived at 4827 Sixteenth street, N.W.

A collateral descendant of Daniel Webster, Mr. Flagg was born on his father's farm at Tyson's Corner, Fairfax County. Edmund Flagg, his father, a poet and former newspaperman, was Consul General in Venice before his death in 1890. Mr. Flagg was reared on his father's estate, Highland View near West Falls Church, and attended Fairfax County schools. He had extensive real estate holdings in Washington and Fairfax County. For the last 20 years he had resided in this city.

A bachelor, Mr. Flagg is survived by a sister-in-law, Mrs. Edmund H. Flagg, and a nephew, Edmund A. Flagg, both of Falls Church. A niece, a great nephew, two great nieces and five great great nieces also survive. His brother, Edmund, died in May, 1949.

Funeral services will be held at 2 o'clock this afternoon in the Pearson funeral home, 472 North Washington street, Falls Church. Burial will be in the family lot in Oakwood Cemetery, Falls Church.

## THE FORD FAMILY

Clark and Lydia Ford resided during the 1880's in the house which is still standing on the corner of Idylwood Road and Leesburg Pike. Mr. Ford was interested in community welfare, and gave the ground for the "Ford School." Among their children were (1) Ella, who married Bruckner, and lived at Hastings-on-Hudson, New York. She died while visiting a sister, Mrs. Haydn, in Washington, D.C., in November, 1940. She studied at old Columbian College (now George Washington University) where she received her B.A. and M.A. Degrees. She later attended Cornell University, and was 64 years old when she died. Mrs. Bruckner was survived by the following children: Mrs. Helen S. Fagans, Basking Ridge, N.J.; Mrs. Virginia Isecke, and Mrs. Mabel Chomsland, both of Vineland, N.J., and Robert Bruckner, also of Vineland. (2) George Ford, (3) Mrs. Charles Haydn.

---

## THE DANIEL S. GORDON FAMILY

Daniel Smith Gordon was born August 26, 1811 in Greencastle, Pennsylvania, and died at his home near Bailey's Cross Roads, November 26, 1885. Mr. Gordon moved to Georgetown, D.C., before the War Between the States, and with his wife was admitted into membership of Fairfax Chapel Methodist Church on June 15, 1860. The record of that date states that he came from Georgetown. Mr. Gordon was active in Dulin Chapel Methodist Church after the War, and the Fourth Quarterly Conference of the Falls Church Circuit adopted a Resolution on February 16, 1886 as follows:[1]

"Another pillar gone to his reward above. Brother Daniel S. Gordon was born Aug. 26th 1811 in Greencastle (Franklin) Adams Co., Pa., and died at his residence in Fairfax County, Va., November 26th, 1885. The following preamble and resolutions were unanimously adopted by the Fourth Quarterly Conference of Falls Church Circuit, Washington District, Baltimore Conference, February 16th, 1886:

Whereas Almighty God the great Head of the Church, has seen fit in His wisdom to call from labor and suffering to rest & reward our brother Daniel S. Gordon, whose death occurred at his residence November 26th, 1885, and whereas Brother Gordon has been identified as Trustee for a number of years we deem it proper that this body should officially notice his death, and give an expression of sorrow at our loss therefore,

*Resolved 1st*, That in the death of Brother Gordon, we have lost from our circle a good and true man, a useful Trustee and a kind and valued citizen.

*Resolved 2nd*, That we bow submissively to the divine behest and do most sincerely regret this dispensation of providence we feel that what God wills is best and that our loss is His gain—that the peaceful close of his consistent and examplary life should afford abundant consolation to his sorrowing friends and relatives. He is now safely housed in the mansions of the redeemed and free from all earth's sorrows.

*Resolved 3rd*, That we deeply sympathize with the bereaved family in their irreparable loss, and pray that their great affliction may be sanctified to their eternal good welfare, that God's grace may comfort and sustain them while they linger on this side of the river, and that finally they may join their loved one in that land where there shall be no more death, neither sorrow nor sighing.

*Resolved 4th*, That a copy of these resolutions be spread on our conference journal and a copy sent to the Episcopal Methodist for publication and a copy sent to the bereaved family.

John E. Febrey
Joseph E. Birch (Committee)."

Mr. Gordon owned a two hundred acre farm which was well cared for and highly productive. Here he reared his large family. Daniel Smith and Amanda E. S. Gordon had the following children:

(1) Amanda Burroughs Gordon, born January 16, 1861, baptized at Fairfax Chapel March 2, 1861 by William Gwynn Coe, witnessed by Mary Eliza Burroughs and Martha Shreve.

(2) Eliza Gordon, married Horace Bailey.

(3) Mary E. Gordon, married Ray L. Bailey.

(4) Fulton Ray Gordon, born March 9, 1869, married three times, died on July 13, 1952. Mr. Gordon was a pioneer real estate developer of Chevy Chase, D.C. Taking his father's advice to "buy real estate" he made more than three million dollars in this venture. He was survived by his third wife, Mrs. Ellen M. (Gray) Gordon, and the following children: James Howell Gordon, Fulton R. Gordon, Jr., Mrs. Frances V. Elgin, and Mrs. June G. Hoke.

(5) Thomas Wood Gordon, born June 18, 1868.

(6) Robert Buhrman Gordon, baptized February 18, 1875.

The following is the death notice of Fulton R. Gordon, son of Daniel S. Gordon: (From the *Evening Star*, 7/14/1952):

"*Fulton Gordon Dies; Millionaire Came Up From Delivery Boy*

Fulton R. Gordon, 85, who started as a delivery boy and ended as a millionaire real estate man, died last night at Suburban Hospital, Bethesda. He had suffered a stroke about two weeks ago. Mr. Gordon was a pioneer real estate developer of Chevy Chase, D. C.

The tall, silver-haired man, who always wore a stiff-front shirt with wing collar, had specialized in northwest and suburban properties. During his 62 years in the real estate business, he had developed land near Laurel, Md., North Columbia Heights, Mount Pleasant Heights and an area along Sixteenth street near Walter Reed Hospital.

In 1950, he sold 500 acres of land in Oxon Hill, Md., for $1.5 million. It was one of the largest cash real estate deals in greater Washington. He had bought the land 20 years ago for $500 an acre.

Mr. Gordon, who once said Washington was the greatest real estate town in the world, was constantly proving it. To develop Chevy Chase, D.C., he bought 400 acres for $800,000. He sold it for 38 cents a square foot.

Mr. Gordon was born at Bailey's Cross Roads, Va. He was delivering milk to the White House when Benjamin Harrison was President. Once, Mrs. Harrison invited him into the East Room.

Mr. Gordon went to Episcopal High School, Alexandria. Later he took his father's advice to "buy real estate." He did and made more than $3 million.

Mr. Gordon lived at 5100 Manning place, N.W., until about two years ago when he built a home opposite Congressional Country Clubs on River road, Bradley Hills, Md. Mr. Gordon's offices were in the Colorado Building.

In 1932, Mr. Gordon disclosed that he had hit upon what he believed to be the cause and cure of crime, the root of unhappy marriage, poverty, war, insanity and other evils. He planned to write a book called "The Dawn of a New Civilization" but a stroke about four years ago kept him from finishing the project. A motion picture and stage production were to have been made from the book.

Mr. Gordon had claimed "The Dawn of Civilization" project would advance civilization in the next 50 years more than it had in the past 500.

Mr. Gordon is survived by his widow, Mrs. Ellen Marjorie Gray Gordon, his third wife whom he married in 1926; two sons, James Howell Gordon, 5803 Thirty-second street, N.W., a real estate man, and Fulton, jr., 3908 Parsons road, Chevy Chase, Md., who was in the real estate business with his father; two daughters, Mrs. Frances G. Elgin, Potomac, Md., and Mrs. June G. Hoke, 3904 Parsons road, Chevy Chase, Md., and nine grandchildren.

Funeral services will be held at 2 p.m. Wednesday at Hines funeral home, 2901 Fourteenth street, N.W. Burial will be in Glenwood Cemetery."

---

[1] From the MS records of Dulin Methodist Church, February 16, 1886.

---

## THE FAMILY OF WILLIS LEONARD GORDON

Sometime in the latter part of the seventeenth century, three brothers with the surname Gordon came to this country from Scotland on different sailing vessels. One landed in Virginia (and from this branch came Bazil Gordon, first American millionaire); and the other two, including the ancestor of Willis Leonard Gordon of Falls Church, settled in New England. This first ancestor of W. L. Gordon, lived in Southampton, New Hampshire, north of what is now Newburyport, Massachusetts. He lived with the Narragansett Indian tribe, and fell in love with an Indian maiden. They were determined to become husband and wife, but by tribal custom, this meant certain death. While on a fishing expedition, Gordon went ahead to locate a likely spot to fish. His beloved stayed behind with the tribe. As soon as was possible, she escaped and met Gordon as they had prearranged. This was during the spring at Merrimack Falls near what is now Manchester, N. H. They were married in the Episcopal Church at Newburyport, Massachusetts and moved to Maine to escape family wrath.

The son of this union, Judson Gordon, fought in the French and Indian War, and was wounded. For this wound he was granted a tract of land in New Hampshire. His son, Zebulon Gordon fought in the Revolutionary War. Mr. Willis L. Gordon tells this interesting story about his ancestor Judson Gordon:

The Captain of his Regiment was Ben Moulton. At that time, the Captain served picket duty the same as did the men, and Moulton's turn came to guard the picket. Every night of the previous week, the guard had been murdered, and Moulton did not wish to serve his turn. Judson Gordon volunteered in his place, and determined that if he should die, he would know whether it was an Indian or Frenchman that did the killing. It was thought to be the work of one man.

Gordon stationed himself in a hollow below the picket line, and hid himself. Before doing this, he put his heavy coat and hat on a pole, to resemble a man on guard. "Bang!" the coat was knocked off by a bullet. Gordon fired in the general direction of the flash, and heard a scream. When he went to look, he found a lone Indian

Chief. Gordon took the musket and wampaum belt from the Indian's body. These articles were given to the Boston Historical Society by the Gordon family.

Moulton was granted a large tract of land called "Moulton's Gore"[2] in Auburn, New Hampshire. He gave Mr. Gordon one hundred acres of this "for saving his life." He likewise gave one hundred acres to John Smith, another soldier. A daughter of this John Smith, Anne Smith, married James Gordon, son of Judson Gordon. Judson Gordon also had a brother, John Gordon, who served in the war. The following are the children of James and Anne (Smith) Gordon:

(1) George Gordon, the eldest, who had a son.
(2) Smith Gordon, married and had two children, a son and daughter. The daughter, Mrs Philbrook, had a son Roy Philbrook.
(3) Ann Gordon, did not marry.
(4) Sarah Gordon, did not marry.
(5) Leonard Shaw Gordon, born in February, 1832, died in 1906, is buried in Petaluma Cemetery, Petaluma, California. He married in Auburn, N. H., to Ellen Brown. Mrs. Gordon was born February 25, 1838, died November 27, 1894, daughter of (Episcopal) Bishop William Brown by his wife Adeline Spaulding. Leonard Shaw and Ellen (Brown) Gordon had issue:

(51) Albert Gordon, died when 5 years old.
(52) Idaho Ellen Gordon, died 1936. Named Idaho because she was born on the anniversary of the day Idaho was made a state.
(53) Willis Leonard Gordon, born at Rumney, Grafton Co., N.H., January 31, 1866, died in California, January 7, 1951. Buried at Falls Church.

Willis Leonard Gordon married Lillian Rawlings of an old and prominent Maryland family. She was born January 19, 1869. They were married on June 3, 1890 in the old Columbia Baptist Church on East Broad Street. Mrs. Gordon was a daughter of James Holliday and Matilda Riggs (Gaither) Rawlings of Maryland. This Gaither family was the one for whom Gaithersburg, Maryland, was named. The Gaither family[3] was granted a patent of land known as "Bite the Biter" near Sandy Spring, in 1692. The grant, on sheep skin, with other relics of the family, is owned by Miss Ruth L. Gordon. The Patent of 1692 is signed by Lord Baltimore. The Rawlings family came to Falls Church in 1875, the year the Town was incorporated. They opened a store where Kent's Cleaners was later located at the Traffic Light. Mrs. Rawlings, as a widow, conducted a store where the D.G.S. now is, and in the same building.

Willis Leonard and Lillian (Rawlings) Gordon had issue:
(531) Ethel Rawlings Gordon, born August 4, 1891, unmarried, died Dec. 1, 1955.
(532) Ruth Lillian Gordon, born April 3, 1894, unmarried.
(533) Arthur Ridgley Gordon, born June 17, 1899, unmarried.

Leonard Shaw Gordon (father of Willis L. Gordon) and family came to Falls Church in the fall of 1885 from Minnesota, whence they had moved from New Hampshire. During the Spanish-American War, Mr. Willis L. Gordon conducted a general grocery and meat store in a building owned by William Nathan Lynch. It was while in this business that he was given a pass (signed by President McKinley and General Graham) giving him permission to pass through any lines while delivering meat to Camp Alger.

Mr. Gordon maintained homes in Florida and California, but in his last years built a home on Hickory Street, in "Gordon's Subdivision" which he developed in West Falls Church. Mr. Gordon was identified with the development of Falls Church, and was active in building a better community.

At the time of his death, Mr. Gordon was the oldest living member and Past Master of Kemper Lodge. He circulated the petition to found the Lodge. A prominent place is given him in *Chronicles of Kemper Lodge* written by Frank M. Steadman. Mr. Gordon was made Master of the Lodge on June 24, 1898, and he served until June 23, 1899. His Masonic career began earlier, however, when he was passed into the Lodge on April 18, 1888. He was raised on May 17, 1888, and made a Master Mason July 20, 1888. Mr. Gordon was made an honorary member of Andrew Jackson Lodge #120, A.F. & A.M., of Alexandria, Va., November 3, 1938.

Mr. Gordon was a member of the American Numismatic Association, and had an extensive collection of coins. He had extended interests in history. Both Mr. and Mrs. Gordon were members of the Columbia Baptist Church and were baptized in the Tripp's Run.

[1] Interview with Willis L. Gordon, May 16, 1949.
[2] So called because it was shaped like a gore.
[3] The following tombstones of the family are in the Falls Church yard: "In memory of Sarah B. Gaither, departed this life April 13, 1887." "Maggie H. Rawlings, Died May 2, 1881, aged 17 years." "In memory of Margaret Brumley, wife of Greenbury Gaither, born Sept. 2, 1796, died Dec. 24, 1885."

## THE GOTT FAMILY

Major Richard Gott, a son of Edmund Gott of Maryland, purchased a hunting lodge near present day "White Haven" subdivision in Falls Church. This house, still standing, was called "Buena Vista," and became his home. Major Gott received an appointment to West Point through the efforts of his mother's brother, Major Hook, in 1835. Later Major Gott was an engineer of the Chesapeake and Ohio Canal project and moved from his home in Towson, Maryland, to Washington, D.C., where he was living in 1838. At the outbreak of the War Between the States Major Gott joined the Confederate Army and was given the rank of Major. He was in charge of the Commissary.

A sister of Major Gott also lived in Falls Church. She was Maria Gott, wife of the Reverend Philip D. Lipscomb, a prominent Methodist Minister. The Reverend and Mrs. Lipscomb were the parents of Susan Bond Wilson, wife of Bishop Alpheus W. Wilson of the Methodist Episcopal Church, South.

Major Gott married Ann Gordon of Fredericksburg,[1] of an old family.

Dr. Louis Edward Gott, beloved Falls Church physician, was a son of Major Richard and Ann (Gordon) Gott. He was born in Washington, D.C., August 29, 1838, and died at Falls Church on October 29, 1916.

Dr. Gott was a graduate of the University of Maryland, class of 1861.[2] His earlier education was received at William Abbott's Select School in Georgetown and Episcopal High School, Alexandria. He also attended Bloomfield Academy in Loudoun County.

Dr. Gott volunteered in the Confederate Army and served as Surgeon. He was stationed at Yorktown and Williamsburg, and in the last named place was in charge of the Confederate Hospital. When he left Williamsburg his work was taken up by Dr. Todd, brother to Mrs. Abraham Lincoln. Gott was captured at Bybee's Farm on Fairfield Road, Gettysburg, voluntarily becoming a prisoner to help the Confederate wounded. He was put into military prison at Fort McHenry in July 1863, and stayed three months. He was later exchanged, went back into the service and continued until Appomattox.

Dr. Gott was in great demand in handling typhoid cases in Falls Church when that disease was prevalent. His tombstone, in the old Falls Church yard, was erected as a "Tribute of love from his friends." The inscription says in part:

"For four years he was a surgeon in the army of the Confederate States, and for fifty-one years he practiced medicine in this vicinity, skillful, loyal, charitable, brave, he was a noble example of the COUNTRY DOCTOR."

Dr. Gott served twice as president of the Fairfax County Medical Society and served in a number of organizations in Falls Church. He was a member of the Town Council.

On October 12, 1868, at Dulin Chapel, by the Reverend W. B. Dolly, Dr. Gott married Amanda Gale Dyer. Mrs. Gott was born March 21, 1848, in Alexandria County, and died November 18, 1917. She was a daughter of William B. and Ellen Nora (Ball) Dyer, and a granddaughter of Robert Ball. Issue:

(1) Gordon Sands Gott, born December 14, 1870, died July 11, 1929, with burial in the Falls Church yard. Mr. Gott married Jessie Row (*See Row*). A son, Kenneth Gott, married Minnie Smith Glascock of an old Fauquier County family, currently living in Marshall, Virginia. Their son, John Kenneth Gott, is known for his historical interests and is an author and book collector. He is a supervisor for the public school system of Fairfax County and owns the Fauquier Book Shop. Mr. Gott is a former Librarian of J.E.B. Stuart School. Kenneth Gott remarried and had other issue.

(2) Blanche Gott, baptized at Dulin Chapel in October, 1873, was born August 5, 1873. She married —— Davis and died October 14, 1900, with burial in the Falls Church yard.

(3) Ellen Louise Gott, baptized March 6, 1877, at Dulin Chapel, died December 3, 1950.

(4) Louis Harvey Gott, baptized May 31, 1878, at Dulin Chapel, moved to Los Angeles, California.

(5) Florence Gott, born August 2, 1880, died in 1883. One record gives her birth date as August 15, 1881.

(6) Virginia Gordon Gott, unmarried, known as Virgie. For many years Miss Gott was secretary to Dr. M. E. Church.

(7) Clara Gott, born December 19, 1887, died January 4, 1892.

(8) Arthur Merryman Gott, born September 8, 1890, died 1891.

(9) Alys Elizabeth Gott (baptized Alice Elizabeth at Dulin Chapel, August 19, 1893) married John Oscar Williams. Mr. Williams was born in Venedocia, Ohio, March 10, 1885, a son of David Williams, a native of Wales, and Elizabeth Jane (Morgan) Williams. Mr. Williams was a scientist, and died in 1950. He received his B.S. degree from Ohio State University in 1908, and served for thirty-eight years with the Department of Agriculture. Mr. Williams was Chief of the Horse Husbandry Bureau. Following World War II he represented this country in the purchase of horses for UNRRA in Ireland, Great

Britain and Denmark. Mr. Williams was the author of numerous government publications and bulletins on the care and breeding of horses. His career is noted in such publications as "Who's Who in the East, 1930," and "American Men of Science, 1938." Some of his works have been translated for world use. Mr. Williams was active in Masonry. A brother is David A. Williams, vice president of Texas A. & M. College. Issue:
(91) John Oscar Williams, Jr.
(92) Anne Morgan Williams. Miss Williams is a noted actress on stage and television.

---

[1] Ann (Gordon) Gott was a daughter of William and Rebecca (Cooke) Gordon who were married in Fredericksburg in February, 1808. Cooke County, Texas, was named for Mrs. Gordon's family. One of her close kinsmen married President Diaz of Mexico.
[2] See *History of the University of Maryland*, Lewis Historical Publishing Company, Volume II, page 330.

---

## THE GUNNELL FAMILY

William Gunnell was from Westmoreland and Northumberland, and was most likely a native Virginian. He died at his plantation home near the Falls Church in 1760. Gunnell settled on his Falls Church plantation in 1729, having acquired some 1,616 acres of land on Four Mile Run. The first services for the Church of England in this area were held in his home and this was called "William Gunnell's Church." This became the congregation of Falls Church.

Gunnell made his will on March 8, 1750, probated September 19, 1760. In it he mentioned his children: William, Jr., Henry, Sarah Saunders, Elizabeth Saunders, and Mary Darne. Witnesses were: Joseph Moxley, Philip Saunders, and Daniel Jennings. Issue:

(1) William Gunnell, Jr., married Jemima Neal.
(2) Henry Gunnell, married Catherine Daniel.
(3) Sarah Gunnell, died about 1812, married James Saunders, a native of Scotland, who died in Loudoun County in 1778. Their children included: Gunnell Saunders, born 1748, who moved to Fleming County, Kentucky before 1810; James Saunders (born before 1765, and died after 1830 in Loudoun County); John Saunders (who made his will on April 7, 1797, probated June 12, 1797, wife Mary died ca. 1797); Presley Saunders; Henry Saunders; Moses Saunders (born 1810 in Fleming County, Kentucky); Aaron Saunders; Cyrus Saunders; and Barbara Saunders.
(4) Elizabeth Gunnell, married (William or Philip) Saunders.
(5) Mary Gunnell, married John Darne (*See Darne*).

(There may have been a sixth child, Ann Gunnell, who married Thomas Moxley, and had issue. Thomas Moxley died in 1750 in Fairfax County.)

(1) William Gunnell, Jr., son of William Gunnell, Sr., died in 1794 in Fairfax County. He married Jemima Neal (or Neale). Shapleigh Neal of Fairfax County, in his will dated June 8, 1777, probated August 18, 1777, mentioned his sister, Jemima Gunnell.

William Gunnell, Jr., made his will January 12, 1784, probated May 19, 1794 (Fairfax County, *Will Book F,* page 339). In it he mentioned his children: Allen Gunnell, William Gunnell, Elizabeth Wren, and a grandson, Presley Gunnell (son of

William). Executors named were: William Darne and Thomas Gunnell. Witnesses were: James Wren, John Bond, George Minor, and Thomas Darne, Sr. Issue:

(11) Allen Gunnell, married (1) Elizabeth ———; and (2) Sarah ———. He died about 1826 in Fairfax County.

(12) William Gunnell, 3rd, was commissioned Captain in the Company "lately commanded by Sampson Trammell" in Loudoun County, June 13, 1786. He had children including Presley Gunnell (died 1806) who married Ann Hunter, daughter of John and Jane (Broadwater) Hunter. Presley Gunnell had issue: Ira, father of Dr. William Presley Gunnell who married Martha A. Lindsay; Janet, married John Haycock; Sarah Broadwater (called Sally) married James McEndree of Green County, Kentucky; and William Hunter Gunnell of Washington, D.C. Dr. William Presley Gunnell, son of Ira and Margaret Gunnell, moved to Alexandria where he had an extensive medical practice. His wife, Martha A. Lindsay, daughter of Samuel Lindsay, was a granddaughter of Thomas and Martha (Scott) Lindsay of "Mount Pleasant." (*See Lindsay*). In late life Dr. Gunnell moved to Austin and still later to Waco, Texas. His children included: Jenny Lindsay Gunnell; Ada Byron Gunnell; Marian Campbell Gunnell; Dr. Mouter Gunnell; and Laura Richards Gunnell.

(13) Elizabeth Gunnell, married James Wren (*See Wren*).

(14) Henry Gunnell, died unmarried, in 1787. He made his will September 15, 1786, probated February 20, 1787. In it he mentioned his mother and father, and left land in Kentucky to his nephew, Presley Gunnell. Executors were: William Darne and Thomas Gunnell.

(2) Henry Gunnell, son of William Gunnell, Sr., was born perhaps as early as 1705 and died in 1792 at his home near the Falls Church. He married Catherine Daniel. Gunnell was a member of the Fairfax County Committee of Safety in 1774. He lived later at "Gracelands," a log and clapboard mansion at Dranesville (built 1721) owned in recent years by Rixey Smith and Dr. Summerfield. This was where he died and was buried. Henry Gunnell made his will January 21, 1792, probated February 20, 1792 (Fairfax County, *Will Book F*, page 61). Issue:

(21) John Gunnell, died in July, 1800. He was a Vestryman of Truro Parish in 1774. Mr. Gunnell was commissioned Captain of Militia in place of Thomas Lewis in Loudoun County on June 13, 1786. One John Gunnell took oath as Commissioner of Tax for Loudoun on March 18, 1789, before William Gunnell, 3rd, Justice of the Peace. (Jewell, *III*, page 163.) On October 22, 1792, Henry and Sarah West Gunnell of Fairfax County conveyed to John Gunnell of Loudoun County, in consideration of one hundred pounds, land on Goose Creek, being part of a larger tract which belonged to Hugh West, deceased, father of Sarah Gunnell. This tract of land contained 128 acres. Sarah Gunnell signed this record as Sally. Witnesses were: William Gunnell, 3rd, Robert Gunnell, Thomas Gunnell, Jr., and Thomas Gunnell, Sr.[1] On April 10, 1798, John Gunnell sold this land to Andrew Beatty of Loudoun County for three hundred seven pounds, four shillings, current money of Virginia.[2]

(22) Robert Gunnell, married Elizabeth ———.

(23) Thomas Gunnell, married Elizabeth Minor,[3] daughter of Captain Nicholas and Frances (Spence) Minor. On January 20, 1795, Bryan Fairfax of Fairfax

County leased to Thomas Gunnell, Sr., a tract of land containing 151 acres in Loudoun County, for the life of the said Thomas Gunnell and the lives of John Gunnell, Thomas Gunnell, and James Gunnell, children of the said Thomas. The yearly rent was eight hundred pounds crop tobacco. This land adjoined that of the Honorable Robert Carter. Witnesses: John Stanhope, Henry Gunnell, Jr., and Henry Gunnell, Sr.[4] Issue:

(231) Ann (Nancy) Gunnell, married John Stanhope.
(232) Henry Gunnell ("Jr."), married Mary ——, and had at least two sons, Thomas and Nicholas Minor Gunnell.
(233) James Gunnell, ("Jr."), died at sea, 1810.
(234) William Gunnell.
(235) Thomas Gunnell, Jr.
(236) Robert Gunnell, married Elizabeth ——.

(25) (Honorable) William Gunnell, son of Henry and Catherine (Daniel) Gunnell, was a member of the Virginia House of Delegates from Loudoun County in 1789/98.

(26) (Major) Henry Gunnell, Jr., son of Henry and Catherine (Daniel) Gunnell, was born July 30, 1758, died January 14, 1822. He died at the home of Colonel George W. Minor (*National Intelligencer*, Washington, D. C., January, 1822). Major Gunnell married on August 10, 1786, to Sarah (Sally) West. Mrs. Gunnell was a daughter of the Honorable Hugh West, Jr., and Elizabeth (Minor) West. She died January 17, 1837, age 72 years, in Clarke County. Burial was in the Hooe Family Cemetery in Clarke.

Sarah (West) Gunnell made her will May 25, 1830, probated April 24, 1837 (Clarke County, *Will Book A*, page 7). She mentioned: her husband, Major Henry Gunnell; children: Mary Anne Hooe; Sally Hurst; Hugh Gunnell; George Gunnell; Henry Gunnell; and Bushrod Gunnell. Mrs. Gunnell also mentioned a son-in-law, Joshua Coffer; a friend, George W. Hunter (Executor); and her late father, Hugh West, Esquire. Witnesses were: Robert P. Brooke, Presley M. Helm, and John Morgan, Jr.
Issue:
(261) Hugh West Gunnell, born 1787, married Elizabeth Moore. Their son, George West Gunnell, married a cousin, Matilda Gunnell, daughter of James and Julia Gunnell.
(262) (Colonel) George West Gunnell, born 1789, died January 8, 1878, aged 89 years. His residence was called "Chestnut Thickett." Colonel Gunnell lived in the early 1890's on the west side of Leesburg Pike above Tyson's Corner (near Ash Grove), now the site of Capper's Nursery. The old family cemetery of the Gunnell-West family was on the David Leonard Farm at West Falls Church. At one time the family owned most of the land between Falls Church and Tyson's. Colonel Gunnell married (1) Locian (Lucy or Louisiana) Ratcliffe (born 1800, died January 26, 1835, age 35 years). Mrs. Gunnell was a daughter of Richard Ratcliffe who gave the land for Fairfax Court House. Colonel Gunnell married (2) Emmaline Adams (born 1813, died November 19, 1887, age 74 years). Issue: (2621) John Gunnell; (2622) Richard H. Gunnell of Chestnut Thickett, died after 1883, issue included Fanny A., wife of (1) Jones and (2) Campbell; and Gertrude W., wife

of Coleman. (See Fairfax County *Deed Book C #5*, page 420). (2623) Charles Gunnell; (2624) Albert Gunnell; (2625) Lander Gunnell; (2626) Arthur Gunnell; (2627) Dallas Polk Gunnell, born 1844 at Chestnut Thickett, died July 15, 1915, age 71 years. He married in Loudoun County on November 26, 1878 (1) Ida Blanche Gibson (born 1854 at Berryville, died June 24, 1890 age 36 years). He remarried (2) Catherine (Kate) Young, who is buried at Andrew Chapel. The next (3rd) wife was a cousin, Miss Beck. By his wife Ida Blanche Gibson he had: J. Dallas Gunnell, died age 9 months; J. Effie Gunnell, died at 1 year, 3 months; and G. Elsie Gunnell, died at 10 years, 3 months. (2628) Martha Ann Gunnell, married Alfred Moss, Clerk of Fairfax County. She saved Washington's will by taking it in her stocking to Buckland where it was kept during the War. (For additional data see *The Sunday Star*, Washington, D. C., June 9, 1918, Part 4, page 7.)

(263) Catherine Gunnell, born 1792, married Charles Broadwater. (*See Broadwater*).

(264) West Gunnell, born 1794, died young.

(265) Sarah (Sally) Gunnell, born 1797, married James Hurst.

(266) William Henry Gunnell, born 1799 (had at least one child, Margaretta, born 1839, who married on November 17, 1868, at Falls Church, to James T. Jackson (born in Fairfax County in 1831, son of Robert R. and Matilda A. Jackson).

(267) Bushrod Gunnell, died unmarried.

(268) Mary Anne Gunnell, born 1804, married Henry D. Hooe.

(269) Amelia Gunnell, born 1809, died young.

(26.10) Eliza Gunnell, born 1811, married Joshua Coffer.

(27) Anne Gunnell, daughter of Henry and Catherine (Daniel) Gunnell, born February 16, 1744, married —— Brent.

(29) Catherine Gunnell, married —— Coffer.

During the early years of the nineteenth century, an old man named Gunnell, who was blind, lived near the Falls Church. Joseph Thomas, "the Pilgrim," an evangelist, formerly a Methodist, wrote of visiting him in September, 1811:[5]

"I came into Alexandria. My money was now expended, but finding the house of my friend W. L. though he was not at home at the time, yet I was kindly entertained by his family and recommended to some friends in Fairfax County, about Falls Church. I then went there and came to old bro. Gunnel's (sic), a blind man, but who, I found saw clearly the right way of the Lord and who was friendly and kind to me. After staying with him two days I went on my way again for the great meeting; having two dollars given me by a friend. . . ."

Thomas continued to Fredericksburg, but in October was back in Alexandria and Falls Church. He wrote:[6]

"We then went (from Alexandria) to Falls' church, and preached to a large congregation; on the same day at candlelight at brother G's, where the people were attentive, serious and solemn, and I think good impressions were made on the minds of some. Here I met with several kind and friendly brethren who appeared to be devoutly exercised by their holy calling to obtain eternal life."

After this successful mission, Thomas went on to Georgetown. Late at night on Saturday, December 13, 1811,[7] he returned to the Gunnell home, having travelled through a cold rain. On the following day he preached "in Falls' church to a large attentive assembly, but could see little effect among the people." Evangelist Thomas gives a picture of these Falls Church residents:

"The people about here are remarkable for pride, fashion and ostentation. The professors (of religion) also seem to be too much conformed to the fashion of this present world. And when I see but little difference in the dress, in formal and polite ceremony, in conversation, &c., between the professor and the non-professor, I am led to think there is but little religion in the heart."

Thomas went to Alexandria on December 23,[8] and returned to the Gunnell home on Christmas day where he held a meeting at 12 o'clock. At candlelight he held services at "brother Darns' (Darnes), a hospitable and kind friend to me." This was probably the home of Captain Nicholas Darne. Thomas continued:

" The first meeting (at Darnes) was mostly composed of young people, who by their behaviour, came together more for the purpose of seeing each other than to be affected by the word of God; and the word did not profit them because it was not mixed with faith in them that heard it. At night our meeting was attended by a number of praying people, influenced and operated upon by the Spirit of God."

This old-time evangelist stayed at the Darne home eight days and preached several times in the neighborhood.

On the first Sunday in May, 1812, Thomas was back in town, and preached at the Falls Church. He also preached several times in the community, but "saw little prospect of good being done." He went on to Alexandria, Dumfries, Stafford Court House and other points. He does not seem to have returned to Falls Church, unless it is not mentioned in his book. Later day Gunnells were members of the Methodist Protestant Church, and it may be that Joseph Thomas, Pilgrim, prepared the way, with the aid of the O'Kellyites and others.

---

[1] Loudoun County *Deed Book Y*, page 188.
[2] *Ibid, Deed Book Y*, page 237.
[3] Jewell, *I*, page 259 ("Drish vs. Taylor et. al.").
[4] Loudoun County, *Deed Book 2 A's*, page 163.
[5] *The Life of The Pilgrim, Joseph Thomas, Containing an Accurate Account of his Trials, Travels, and Gospel Labours, Up to the Present Date*, Winchester, J. Foster, Printer, 1817, page 216.
[6] *Ibid*, page 220.
[7] *Ibid*, page 227.
[8] *Ibid*, pages 228-229.

---

## THE HAWXHURST FAMILY

George White Hawxhurst was one of our best known and public spirited citizens. Mr. Hawxhurst was born June 2, 1848, and died October 2, 1932, and is buried in Oakwood Cemetery. Mr. Hawxhurst was closely identified with the temperance movement in Falls Church. He was among the group responsible for the establishment of Pioneer Lodge Number One, the first lodge in the State of Virginia. A "staunch leader of the cause," Mr. Hawxhurst was honored by the community, "en masse," for his efforts.[1]

He married (1) Sarah L. —— (born June 9, 1851, died December 17, 1895).[2] He married (2) on September 22, 1897, to Ida Jeanette Quick (*See Quick*). Mrs. Hawxhurst was born January 20, 1867, in Flemington, New Jersey, and died at the home of a nephew, Millard Quick, April 16, 1952. Mrs. Hawxhurst was organist and Sunday School Teacher in Columbia Baptist Church. She was an officer in the Baptist Woman's Mission Society, the Potomac Association, and the Fairfax County Chapter, D.A.R. She was also a member of the Falls Church Woman's Club and the Eastern Star. Among other interests, Mrs. Hawxhurst was a member of the Women's Christian Temperance Union, the Good Templars and the Rebekahs.

Mr. Hawxhurst was first cashier of the Falls Church Bank and an associate of Dr. M. E. Church. He was also mayor of Falls Church. Issue: (*By Sarah L.* ——):
(1) Nellie Esther Hawxhurst, born December 29, 1876, died October 14, 1903. According to Mrs. Charles E. Gage she married a Mr. Gerdine (or Jerdine) and had a son. Her tombstone is in Oakwood Cemetery.
(2) Flora Munson Hawxhurst, died July 4, 1874, age 5 months, 21 days. Buried in Fairfax Cemetery.

(*By Ida Jeanette Quick*):
(3) George Quick Hawxhurst, born April 6, 1908, died July 20, 1909.

---

[1] *Falls Church News,* January 21, 1898, page 13.

## THE HENDERSON FAMILY

Alexander Henderson was a vestryman of Truro Parish from 1765 to 1785. He was Church Warden 1769-1770, and 1779-1780. On February 24, 1774 he witnessed the drawing up of the deed to Washington's pew and signed that document.

Henderson has been an illustrious name in Fairfax County throughout the years. Alexander Henderson was the son of the Reverend Robert Henderson, who was a minister in Blantyre, Scotland. He settled in Virginia in 1756, and established himself as a merchant at Colchester in Fairfax County.

He married Sallie Moore of Maryland, and their son was General Henderson. During the Revolution the Hendersons retired to their farm in Fairfax County, from the fear of falling into the hands of the British, since Alexander Henderson had taken decided views against the mother country.

Henderson, with Washington and Mason, was a commissioner on the part of Virginia and met the Maryland Commissioners (Chase, Jenifer, and Stone) at Mount Vernon on March 28, 1785. This meeting was held to determine the navigation and exercise of jurisdiction in the waters of Pocomoke and Chesapeake Bay.

---

## THE HIRST FAMILY

Thomson Mason Hirst, II, who settled in Falls Church, was a descendant of settlers who came to Jamestown in 1607/8. His paternal line, that of Hirst, was ancient Anglo-Saxon. The family lived at "Greenhead Hall" Manor in Huddersfield, which was confiscated by Cromwell in 1650 and never regained by the family. The immigrant, the Reverend John Hirst, a Presbyterian Minister, was from the West Riding of Yorkshire. He held the following Arms: "Argent, a sun in splendor gules." The Crest was "A hurst of trees proper," and the Motto was "Efflorescent!" (i.e., "Blooming Forth!").

John Hirst and his wife, nee Ann Jarrett, came to Philadelphia in August, 1737. He died in 1753 at his home in Buckingham Township, Bucks County. His children included John Hirst, born August 20, 1737. This John Hirst became a Quaker to marry one. He married Mary Heston, a descendant of Thomas Hutchinson of "Hutchinson Manor," an original Proprietor of New Jersey. Through the ancestry of her mother, Elizabeth Buckman, descendants are entitled to membership in the "Welcome Society" (original settlers who came to Pennsylvania with William Penn in 1680 in the "Welcome"). Her father, Zebulon Heston, was a noted Quaker Missionary. His father was a convert from the Church of England (to marry a Quaker, the heiress Dorothy Hutchinson, daughter of Thomas and Dorothy (Starr) Hutchinson). John and Mary (Heston) Hirst were Quaker Missionaries and came to Loudoun County in 1775. They had lived at Wrightstown following their marriage on April 30, 1760. The old marriage certificate is still in the family, and is their Bible dating to 1702. The Hirsts were ancestors of many of the Janneys, Browns, Talbotts, Pierpoints, and others of Loudoun County.

Captain Thomas Hirst, son of John and Mary (Heston) Hirst, was born February 4, 1774. He was dismissed from the Friends Church for "joining in light company, in frolicking and dancing." Captain Hirst attended a dance at "Raspberry Plain" the home of his future bride. He was later a vestryman of the Episcopal Church. Captain Hirst died in Missouri August 6, 1842. He owned lots in Waterford, Salem (now Marshall), and several estates including "Springdale" in Fauquier County. His brother-in-law, Senator Stevens Thomson Mason, left him one thousand acres in Ohio. Captain Hirst married (1) on April 22, 1798, Dorothea Anna Thomson Mason, a niece of George Mason of "Gunston Hall," and a descendant of the Fowkes, Thomsons, Tabbs, Westwoods, and other old Virginia families. She was the daughter of Congressman Thomson Mason of "Raspberry Plain," and Elizabeth (Westwood) Mason. Her father, like his great-grandfather Sir William Thomson, was a student at the famous "Middle Temple" in London. He was a member of the House of Burgesses, and although not as well known as his brother, author of the Bill of Rights, he was active in the revolutionary cause. Mason was the author of the famous "Nine Letters of a British American." Mrs. Hirst was a descendant of William the Conqueror, of six Lord Mayors of London. Her ancestor, Captain Adam Thoroughgood, was a founder of Princess Ann County.

Captain Thomas Hirst remarried (2) on November 26, 1822, to Elizabeth (Priest) Hitch, of "The Hitch," Fauquier County. She was the widow of Truman Hitch. No issue by the second marriage.

Captain Thomas Hirst by his wife, Dorothea Anna Thomson Mason, had issue: Captain Thomson Mason Hirst I, married (1) Catherine Withers Payne and (2) Lavinia E. Mc. Payne; John Thomson Hirst, married Nancy Eleanor Hitch; Albert Stevens Hirst, married (1) Elizabeth Payne and (2) N. Mildred Kelly; Mary Elizabeth Hirst, married Captain James O'Bannon Nelson (and was grandmother of Congressman William Lester Nelson); Thomas Alpheus Hirst, married Lucy Mildred Payne; Augustine Smith Hirst; and Rebecca Ann Hirst, married (1) Leven Smoot and (2) Benjamin Craig.

Thomas Alpheus Hirst, born May 27, 1812, at Waterford, Loudoun County, died at his home, "Springdale," Fauquier County, September 13, 1884. He married on April 21, 1842, Lucy Mildred Payne of "Locust Shade." Two of her grandfathers were Revolutionary soldiers: Ensign Francis Payne and Lieutenant James Withers, M.D., of "Green Meadows." She was the daughter of Francis Payne, Jr., and Patsey (Withers) Payne. Her ancestors included the Norgraves, Withers, Marshalls, Scotts, and others.

Mrs. Hirst was born May 31, 1822, and died July 7, 1902. Her nephew was Honorable John Barton Payne, Secretary of the Interior under President Wilson and President of the American Red Cross.

Children of this couple included: Amelia Catherine Hirst, wife of Captain Robert Bruce Templeman of "Edgeworth" (Founder of "Edgeworth Tobacco"); Thomson Mason Hirst, II, who settled in Falls Church; Mary Nelson Hirst, who married a Payne cousin, Lewellyn L. Anderson; and Dr. Hugh Payne Hirst, married Lelia Watson.

Thomson Mason Hirst, II, son of Thomas Alpheus and Lucy Mildred (Payne) Hirst, was born at "Springdale," Fauquier County, November 27, 1851, and died at Falls Church, July 4, 1928. He was educated by private tutors and at an Academy in Fauquier. Mr. Hirst served in the famous "Black Horse Guard" of the Warrenton Rifles during the last months of the War Between the States.

He married (1) on November 18, 1874, at the Allen estate, "Ingleside," Fauquier County, to Emily Hirst Allen, a daughter of Edmund and Margaret Beavers (Jenkins) Allen. She was born October 17, 1854, and died September 16, 1904. Mr. Hirst remarried (2) to Ethel Pearl Howard (August 28, 1877-August 28, 1951) a daughter of Philip and Catherine Bradley (Graham) Howard. His first wife was a descendant of Sir Arthur Roberson, bart., of England, and of the Allen family who settled at Jamestown. Her ancestry also included the Van Buskirks, who were founders of New York.

Mr. Hirst moved to the estate of his cousin, Honorable Fitzhugh Lee, and was business manager for General Lee while he served as Governor of Virginia. Mr. Hirst later lived at "Chestnut Hill," near Annandale, and by 1901 was living in Falls Church. He became business manager for Miss Mattie Gundry at Gundry School. During his residence in Falls Church he lived for a time in the Osborn House. His children were: Edmund Alpheus Hirst (March 14, 1876-November 28, 1904); Edith Gertrude Hirst (December 13, 1877-July 9, 1878); Mary Mason Hirst (July 15, 1880-March 22, 1907) married Walter W. Caton; Herbert Nelson Hirst, married Ellen Elizabeth Mankin; Clarence Marshall Hirst, married Linda May Mankin; Norman Neil Hirst (May 1, 1886-May 5, 1907); Thomson Mason Hirst, married Edna Bennett; Mary Margaret Hirst, married (the Reverend) George G. Oliver; Lucy Mildred Hirst, married Charles William Mummaw; and Roland Gundry Hirst (child of the second marriage), born August 31, 1912, married Alice Hendricks.

Of the above children, Herbert Nelson Hirst born May 21, 1882 married Ellen Elizabeth Mankin (born at Falls Church April 7, 1883) daughter of Charles Edward and Ann Valinda (Lynch) Mankin on October 13, 1903. They had Charles Nelson Hirst who married (1) Irene Carroll Jarboe, (2) Thelma Dewey; Randle Mason Hirst, married Pauline Heyl Swann; Ruth Elizabeth Hirst, married Melvin Lee Steadman; (had Melvin Lee, Jr., Mildred Marguerite, and Ruth Ellen); Esther Mae Hirst, married Reuben Lee Clatterbuck (and had Ronald Lee and William Nelson Clatterbuck); Marian Louise Hirst; Marie Boaze Hirst, married Lieutenant Eldred Martin Yochim; Herbert Marvin Hirst, married Eleanor Greenwood Simpson (and had Ruby Lee Hirst, Elizabeth Ann Hirst, and Julian Nelson Hirst); and Clarence Marshall Hirst (II) who married Mrs. Louise (Imboden) Martin.

Another child, Clarence Marshall Hirst (I) born March 13, 1884, married Linda May Mankin (born at Falls Church May 30, 1889) daughter of Charles E. and Ann Valinda (Lynch) Mankin. They had Mildred Marshall Hirst, married Hubert Russell Bauckman, and had Brenda Mae Bauckman; and Warren Lee Hirst, married Mrs. Marjorie Elaine (Cheseldine) Nail.

Thomson Mason Hirst (born April 8, 1887) married Edna Bennett. Mr. Hirst is a real estate dealer at Annandale, Va., and his firm name is "Mason Hirst—Real Estate." Issue: Maynard Mason Hirst; and Omer Lee Hirst. The Honorable Omer Lee Hirst is a Member of the Virginia State Senate from Falls Church and Fairfax County. He married Ann Palmer and had Robin Hirst, Deborah Hirst, and Thomson Mason Hirst.

Mary Margaret Hirst (born March 28, 1889) married the Reverend George G. Oliver (former pastor at Dulin Methodist Church at Falls Church), issue: Dorsey Offutt Oliver, Evelyn Mildred Oliver, married Vance Cline; Margaret Elizabeth Oliver, married Emil Joseph Charles; Pauline Gertrude Oliver, married Lawrence Witte; and Kathleen Louise Oliver, married John McWeeny.

## THE HIETT FAMILY

The most interesting member of the Hiett family of Falls Church was "Granny" Hiett, who died July 18, 1949 aged 104 years.

Born at Winchester, Frederick County, Virginia, August 17, 1844, Flora Baker Hiett was the daughter of Henry M. Baker, artist and plantation owner. Her husband was Captain Joseph P. Hiett (who died in 1907). Both are buried at Winchester. She lived at 6732 N. 25th Street, Falls Church, until three weeks before her death, when she was removed to the Mount Shockey Nursing Home in Fairfax where she died.

On her 104th birthday in 1948, Mrs. Hiett said, "I'd trade my rocking chair any day for a ride on a spirited galloping horse." She was an ardent Confederate, and during the War Between the States was a spy for the Confederacy. She married Captain Hiett, a Confederate hero, who was "unreconstructed" to the end of his life. She liked to ride horse-back, and it is said that her father remarked upon occasion: "She would even ride the devil if she could get a bit between his teeth."

Mrs. Hiett lived through five wars, but her favorite was the War Between the States. Mr. E. H. Flagg recalled how she out-rode a regiment of Yankee soldiers who were in pursuit. Mrs. Hiett rode an excellent horse. All good horses were "appropriated" by the Union army. Mrs. Hiett's horse, however, would limp every time she was near a Yankee, and even though a beautiful animal, they had no use for a horse that limped. Mrs. Hiett told her secret after the war: she knew how to place a pin in the tender part of the hoof, so that it would cause the horse to limp, yet not hurt him!

Toward the end of her life, Mrs. Hiett was blind and deaf, but undaunted in spirit. She dressed herself, even though blind, and continued to be active.

Captain Joseph P. Hiett and Flora (Baker) Hiett had issue:

(1) Henry Lee Hiett, born December 12, 1878, died September 9, 1945. He married Margaret Watson (1882-1932). Issue:

(11) Carolyn Hiett, married Major J. N. Forrest.
(12) Barbara Hiett, married Lemuel Cooke. She was born December 21, 1915, died May 19, 1944.

(2) Catherine Lee Hiett, married Jonah Unverzagt. Mrs. Unverzagt died in 1944. Issue:

(21) William Unverzagt, lives at Arlington, Va.
(22) Henry T. Unverzagt, Vice-consul in Mexico.

## THE HULL FAMILY

Truman Parker Hull settled in Falls Church before 1857, and married Eliza, daughter of John P. Bartlett of "Home Hill." The Hull family history states that Truman P. Hull was the descendant of an English family which settled in the New England area prior to the Revolutionary War, but since they were Loyalists moved to Canada after the War. The Family Bible, published at Hartford, Conn., by Case-Tiffany & Co., 1857, does not go into detail concerning the family history. There is a note that Rebecca Hull, wife of Truman Hull, died November 4, 1809. This was probably the paternal grandmother of Truman P. Hull of Falls Church.

Truman P. Hull was a son of Truman and Philena (Parker) Hull of London, Ontario, West Canada. Truman Hull (who married Philena Parker) had a brother in Lowell, Mass., and other relatives in the United States. He died at an early age and his widow remarried to Mr. Godfrey, and died in Alexandria County, Va., April 29, 1874 aged 74 years. Truman and Philena (Parker) Hull had four children: Truman Parker Hull; Horace Hull (unmarried); Chapman Hall (married); and Sophronia Hull who married Jacob Leclear (and had at least two children: Truman Leclear and Lewis Leclear).

Truman Parker Hull was born at London, Ontario, West Canada, October 7, 1829. The family farm, "Hyde Park," was situated about five miles from London, but the family spent a good deal of time in the London community. Mr. Hull died at Aldie, Virginia, February 9, 1909. Mr. Hull married at Falls Church, September 30, 1857 to Eliza Elvira, eldest child of John P. Bartlett. The wedding certificate, in faded and beautiful writing, is owned by Mrs. A. Stuart Gibson of 206 W. Cameron Road, Falls Church. It reads as follows:

"To whom this may concern. I hereby certify that Mr. Truman P. Hull and Miss Eliza E. Bartlett were duly joined in Marriage at Falls Church, Fairfax Co., Va., this thirtieth day of Sept. 1857, by me, H. W. Read, Pastor of the Columbia Baptist Church. Witness: John Bartlett, Dexter Kingman, Samuel C. Perkins."

This is the first recorded marriage of the Columbia Baptist Church. The portraits of Truman P. and Eliza Hull, painted by a Miss Steele of Falls Church, are owned by Mrs. Gibson. Mrs. Hull was born August 14, 1837 at Elmira, Orleans County, New York, and died in Alexandria Co., Va., April 21, 1900. Mr. and Mrs. Hull had the following children:

(1) Franklin Hull, born November 6, 1858 at London, C.W., died June 23, 1860.
(2) Frederick Hull, born June 17, 1860 at London, C.W., no other record.
(3) Ella Chestlewood Hull, born May 10, 1862 at Lowell, Mass., married (1) Frank Cook, (2) Edward Denton. She died May 19, 1944. Issue:
  (31) Frederick Hull Cook, born July 9, 1885, married Ethel Patrick, issue:
    (311) Morton Cameron Cook, born October 19, 1915, married Nell Miller Shanks April 2, 1944, and had issue Ann Miller Cook and Frederick Cook.
(4) John Amos Bartlett Hull, born October 31, 1867 in Arlington (Alexandria County), Va., died at Cleveland, Ohio, April 6, 1947. He married at Macomb, Ill., June 21, 1893, Adeline V. Sommers, children:

(41) Margaret Eddy Hull, born Alexandria Co., Va., January 19, 1896.
(42) John Sommers Hull, born Alexandria Co., Va., June 21, 1899.
(43) Elizabeth Virginia Hull, born Alexandria Co., Va., January 14, 1901.

(5) Morton Truman Hull, born Alexandria Co., Va., October 3, 1870, drowned in the Gulf Stream (while serving on the ship, "Lizzy Curry") Feb. 9, 1889.
(6) George Hull, born March 10, 1873, died March 10, 1873.
(7) Emma Elvira Hull, born Feb. 13, died Feb. 26, 1875.
(8) Baby Boy Hull born and died at birth, Dec. 25, 1880.
(9) Esther Marie Hull, born December 16, 1878, living at Falls Church, Va., 1956. She married on May 25, 1908 (Alexandria Co., Va.) to the Reverend Alexander Stuart Gibson. Mr. Gibson was born at Staunton, Va., February 14, 1874, of distinguished ancestry, a son of Protestant Episcopal Bishop Robert Atkinson Gibson of Virginia, and died at Manassas, Va., March 7, 1942. Children:
- (91) Susan Stuart Gibson, born at Aldie, Va., August 27, 1909, married (1) May 25, 1936 to Robert Fox; (2) in the Falls Church, May 25, 1951 to Walter Gray; no issue.
- (92) Eleanor Bartlett Gibson, born at Aldie, Va., October 31, 1913, married at the Falls Church, September 23, 1944 to the Reverend Bancroft Pitkin Smith. No issue.
- (93) Lucy Atkinson Gibson, born at Windsor, N. C., January 4, 1918, married in the Falls Church, January 16, 1945 to Raymond Wilbur Warren. Issue:
  - (931) Lucy Atkinson Gibson Warren, born June 13, 1947.
  - (932) Eleanor Hull Warren, born September 4, 1951.

The following letter was written by Mrs. Truman P. Hull to her mother-in-law from the John Bartlett residence, later known as the "Buxton" or "Lawton House," Falls Church, Virginia.

"Home Hill Falls Church, Dec. 8th 1868

Dear Mother

Some time has already elapsed since we received your most welcome letter, and do not think our neglect has arisen from forgetfulness, for such is not the case but there has been many reasons some of which I will state—in the first place as you will see by the heading of this we have once more changed our locality—and your letter was forwarded from Lowell here. We were just getting ready to go to housekeeping there when we received a letter from Mother stating that they considered it safe here and would be glad to have us make them a visit before we settled again, and in less than a week we were on the way leaving our things packed and stored in Uncles barn.

Truman found work plenty here and wages better than there concluded to try this climate a while for his health he has been working for Mr. Munson of Munsons Hill for 1.75 per day and board—the second week he was there they were visited by Mosby and four of his men they were after old Mr. Munson who is an abolitionest—made a mistake and took his son Daniel who favors Secesh—in the meantime Truman in attempting to leave the house to give the alarm was taken and ordered to hold the horses we think it quite a joke on him to come here to hold horses for Gurrilles, but that is not the worst that has befallen him since he went there—he had the misfortune to fall from the scaffold of the house (about twenty feet) head first a week ago last Monday—was badly shocked but not seriously hurt no bones being broken as he struck the soft dirt which had been thrown from the cellars is up and about again and I suppose started for Lowell this morning. Father took him into Washington yesterday, he has gone for his money and furniture as he thinks of trying Virginia for a while has bargained for a place near Grand-fathers about four miles from Washington a place which we think if we are able to pay for we shall like for a home, contains 28 acres a house and I believe an orchard.

Truman thinks he has felt better since he came here. The children have grown fleshy fast Ellie is running around I wish I had her likeness to send but we have not been able to have it taken yet. My own I will enclose. We were very much pleased with and very thankful for yours.

I find Va. somewhat changed since I left although the little Village of Falls Church has not suffered so much as many other parts and Fathers place looks natural the trees have grown very much around the house since I left. Father and Mother are not much changed. Old Time has delt very kindly with them but—my brother—I did not know he met us at the Depot and I could hardly believe the *young man* was the same as the little boy, he has gone North to attend School this winter.

And now Mother how are all the kind neighbors: how much I would like to see them and how often I think of their many kindnesses toward me and I sincerely hope and trust the kind Heavenly Father will raise up to them friends in there time of need. I shall always cherish a respect and love for the Scotch people as a whole for I can but say they were the kindest hearted and most friendly people I have ever lived by. My best love to one and all. And for yourself Mother we are truly sorry that you should be left so desolate in your old age and I join Truman in the offer of our home if you feel that you could be content with us. But you see my sheet is full and my hand trembles so I don't write legible and must close.

Remember me in love to Jacob & Sophrona and tell little Trumie I should be delighted to get a letter from him and if our money would pass there he should not lack the means to write his—Sophronie's Children for me how is their little girls I suppose the oldest is quite a scholar, as well as Lewis. Please write soon and accept the love and best wishes of your daughter.

Eliza."

## THE IVES FAMILY

Two brothers, Reuben S. and Albert Henry Ives, came to Falls Church during the 1840's from Pennsylvania. They were the children of Sibyl and Anner Ives of Litchfield, Connecticut.[1]

Reuben S. Ives was born in Litchfield in 1799. He married at least twice, probably three times. According to the marriage record of his daughter, Elmira, she was listed as a daughter of Reuben and Ann Ives. His wife, Hannah, was born in New York in 1799, and was living in 1860 at Falls Church.[2] Mr. Ives remarried, at "Cedar Grove," the home of Levi H. York at Falls Church, on September 1, 1869, to Mrs. Mary (Liddle) Hotchkiss, a widow, age 61 years. This Mrs. Ives was born in Washington County, New York, a daughter of George and Catherine Liddle. At the time of her marriage to Mr. Ives she was a resident of Prince William. Reuben S. Ives had issue (possibly others):

(1) Daughter Ives (listed as D. Ives in the 1860 Census), born in Pennsylvania in 1830. She was a seamstress in the village.

(2) Albert Henry Ives (II), son of Reuben S. and Hannah Ives, was born in Sus-

quehanna County, Pennsylvania, in 1834. He died at his Falls Church home in 1920. Mr. Ives married in Fairfax County on November 19, 1867, at the home of James Jenkins, to Theodora Jane Jenkins. Mrs. Ives, a native of Fairfax County, was born in 1843, a daughter of James and Mary Jenkins. Her home was in that section of the County known as Spring Vale. Mr. Ives was a wheel wright for many years and was an employee of Lynch & Son. Issue:
- (21) Albert Ives.
- (22) Claude Jenkins Ives, born in Falls Church in 1875, died in Arlington on May 4, 1950. Mr. Ives was educated in Falls Church and at the Massachusetts School of Embalming, Boston. He was founder and owner of Ives Funeral Home, Arlington. Mr. Ives was a 32 degree Mason, a member of Columbia Lodge #185. He was also a member of the Arlington Rotary Club, the Eastern Star, and the Odd Fellows. He married Annie E. Pearson, and at the time of his death was survived by his widow and the following children: Claude P. Ives, Mrs. Willis H. Jordan, and Mrs. Harlan Taylor Hall. He was the grandfather of Roscoe A. Hall, Douglas L. Hall, Patricia A. Ives and Kathryn E. Ives.

(3) Elmira B. Ives, daughter of Reuben S. and *Ann* Ives, was born in 1839. She married in Fairfax County on May 16, 1856, to George K. Moony. Mr. Moony was born in New York in 1829, a son of Sylvester and Nancy Moony.

(4) Seldon S. Ives, son of Reuben S. and *Hannah* Ives, was born in Pennsylvania in 1840. He was a wagonner. Mr. Ives married in Falls Church on December 24, 1872, to Jannie L. Neal. She was born in New York in 1853, a daughter of Harrman and Mary Neal.

Albert Henry Ives (I), born June 21, 1807, died in Falls Church, April 22, 1879, was a brother of Reuben S. Ives. Mr. Ives is buried in the Falls Church yard. His wife, Kezia Ives (1791-1876) is buried beside him.

George B. Ives, son of Albert Henry and Kezia Ives, was a well known resident. He was born in Pennsylvania in 1826 and died in 1914. Mr. Ives was a Justice of the Peace in 1865. He was long identified with the building trade and built most of the brick houses in the community that were erected before 1860. These included the Rowell House, the Amanda Ellison House, the Osborn House, the Dr. Luttrell House and others. Mr. Ives was also a shoemaker. One Levi Williams, a native of England, age 18, was his apprentice in 1860. Mr. Ives married Jane Auchmoody (1834-1914). The following inscription is on a tombstone in the Falls Church yard:

Children of George & Jane Ives,
"Suffer the little children to come unto me"
Ida May, died May 4, 1863, age 2 years & 2 months.
Anna Louisa, died June 21, 1870, age 5 months & 21 days
Harry Winter, died December 13, 1872, age 5 years, & 4 months.

According to the 1860 U. S. Census, the Ives had a son, Edward W. Ives, born in Virginia in 1859.

---

[1] Parents names listed on the 1869 marriage record of Reuben Ives.
[2] *U. S. Census,* 1860, page 934.

## THE KIRBY FAMILY

There were a number of Kirby families in Fairfax County at an early day. Most of them seem to have been of Irish ancestry. James A. Kirby, M.D., came to Fairfax County from Litchfield, Connecticut, following services as a Surgeon in the Revolutionary War.[1] He married Susannah Elizabeth Boggess of an old area family. They had several children including: Robert Boggess Kirby, Ann Boggess Kirby, James A. Kirby, Jr., and a daughter who married John N. Lovejoy and had a son, John Emery Lovejoy[2]. What connection, if any, existed between Dr. James A. Kirby and Charles Kirby, the Falls Church pioneer, is not known.

Another early member of this family was Richard Kirby. He was twice married, according to tradition. Record has been found of his marriage in Alexandria County, D.C., April 30, 1819, to Jane Bland (Simon Darne, Bondsman). On September 28, 1818, Colin Auld deeded to Richard Kirby the land originally granted to Moses Ball at what is now Glen Carlyn[3]. This land, ninety-one acres, was partly in Fairfax and partly in Alexandria County. It was described as adjoining the patents of Simon Pearson and John Ball on Four Mile Run. In 1821 Kirby leased to Nehemiah Carson and Richard Veitch, 2/3rds of all minerals, ores, or precious metals, and gave them the right to work mines and sink shafts on this land[4]. It seems that Kirby did not actually reside there. Kirby died in 1831, and left a will dated December 15, 1830, probated March 10, 1831. In it he mentioned his wife, Jane, and children: Sophia, Richard, Mary, John, David, Margaret, Charlotte, and James. His friend, Wesley Carlin, was named Executor. Witnesses were: James M. Carlin, Augustus F. Bladen, and Mary Jane Bland. In 1851, two of his children, Sophie Elliott, wife of John Elliott, and Mary Kirby, conveyed their interest in the Ball tract to James Finnecy[5]. A son, Richard R. Kirby, deeded his share as late as 1871.

It is thought that Richard Kirby was an older brother of Charles Kirby. In 1860 Sallie Elliott, Nancy Elliott, and Betsey Elliott lived in the home of Joshua, son of Charles Kirby. They were probably some connection of John and Sophia (Kirby) Elliott.

A tradition of the Charles Kirby family of Kirbyville, near Falls Church, is that an ancestor farmed Mason's Island at Rosslyn.

Charles Kirby was born near Falls Church on August 9, 1797[6]. He died at his home, a six-hundred acre farm, Kirbyville, near Falls Church, July 13, 1881. Mr. Kirby was a well-to-do farmer. In early life he moved to Kentucky and stayed for a few years. He returned to Virginia, but his brother's family stayed there. By 1860 Mr. Kirby had acquired real estate valued at $10,000, and a personal estate valued at $1,000. (*Census*).

Mr. Kirby voted against secession, and was generally regarded as a "Union man," although he remained neutral during the War. A long series of depositions were made before a Congressional Committee to determine his loyalty. After three years the Committee decided: [7]

"It is plain that there is much conflict in the evidence; that there are material facts both for and against his loyalty. We have held the case for nearly three years for investigation hoping it might be made clearer, and being very reluctant to report against him if he was truly loyal. But now, upon a review of the whole evidence, we feel obliged to decide the case; and without saying that we find him actually disloyal, we deem it sufficient and feel constrained to say that his loyalty is not proved to our satisfaction, and that we must reject the case."

The depositions are especially interesting, and some of the persons who deposed were: Charles Kirby, age 73; John B. Burke, E. H. Barrett, Samuel D. Phillips, David M. Mutersbaugh, Thomas T. Johnson, Thomas J. Paine, Joshua Kirby, John C. Haycock, B. F. Johnson, Richard F. Jackson, John R. Minor, George B. Ives, Judge Richard H. Cockerille, John J. Bogen, H. W. Throckmorton, Charles D. Birch, George W. Faulkner, Mrs. Rowena Phillips, and Mrs. Ann V. Hall. The last named was a niece of Charles Kirby, aged 59 years (October 20, 1908) and living in Montross, Westmoreland County.

Some of the remarks made by Charles Kirby are of interest:

"(May 9, 1871) I voted against the ordinance of secession, and used all my influence in the neighborhood against it. Never did anything in support of the Confederate government, nor to aid any adherent of the Confederate cause. I gave support to the Union cause by feeding its men. The United States troops were first encamped on my place in September, 1861. I entertained Union officers then and subsequently, until the surrender. I have had as many as 15 or 20 Union officers in my house at one time. I never had a Confederate officer in my house. Some of the Union officers paid me for my entertainment, and some did not. I had two sons in the Confederate Army, and two in the Union Army (other evidence shows three in the Confederate Army). One lived thirty miles from home when he went into the Confederate Army, and the other one I drove from my house because he went in; he was 24 years old; they were drafted, did not volunteer.

My house at the commencement of the war was within the Confederate lines; was so for about 3 months . . . until September 1861 . . . when McClellan advanced, I staid home. I was arrested by General Stuart and taken back for a little while, and then I came back through the lines again and got home . . . I was up in the neighborhood of Sudwell (Sudley). I don't know why they arrested me. They carried me and tried me before General Longstreet, and he acquitted me.

They had a little skirmish up at Lewinsville, and I and the hands were in the field cutting off corn, about a mile and a half off, and I saw a cavalryman coming, and he came up and arrested me because I was looking on; they thought may be I was a spy; that is all they had against me . . ."

Thomas T. Johnson, aged 40 years, made a deposition on November 14, 1873. In it he gave his residence as Washington, D.C., and his occupation as United States jailor: "During the war, (I) was judge and scout in the United States army . . . while serving . . . knew Charles Kirby . . . I do not believe any one in the neighborhood will swear that Mr. Kirby was a loyal man . . . he was with all the balance of the 'Virginia Coons,' who believe in joining with the State, and determined if she went to the devil they would go too . . . While I recognize this as a pretty sweeping statement, I regard it as true."

Judge Richard H. Cockerille, until his death a well-known Rebel, stated on January 28, 1874, that Kirby stayed in his home during late 1861 and early 1862 (at Chantilly).

"He was always regarded as a Union man . . . in talking of the war, he always regretted it and the misfortunes to the country that must follow."

H. W. Throckmorton stated that Kirby "voted against the ordinance of secession, and for Mr. Upton, Union candidate for Congress, when it was almost worth a man's life to do it." The record of Kirby's vote against secession is on file at Fairfax Court

House. Throckmorton continued: "John M. Mason issued a card saying that any man who voted for any Member of Congress to the United States Government was an enemy to his country and ought to be arrested. Kirby did it. He was at that time outspoken."

Charles D. Birch, age 66 years (September 17, 1908) said his father's farm adjoined that of Charles Kirby: "I heard my father say that he believed he and old Charlie Kirby were the only two Union men in the county."

Whatever Mr. Kirby's political sentiment, he was a good citizen and an outstanding member of the Methodist Episcopal Church, South. He was a member at Fairfax Chapel and later at Langley.

On January 13, 1824, Mr. Kirby was married to Mary Sherman. Mrs. Kirby was born September 23, 1804, and died July 28, 1884. Issue:[8]

(1) John Edward Kirby, born October 21, 1824, died November 20, 1896, aged 72 years. He lived in Huntington, West Virginia. Mr. Kirby moved to Mason County as a young man and his descendants are still in West Virginia. He served in the Union Army during the War. He was twice married, the second time in 1894. *The Mirror*, of Leesburg, Virginia, on January 28, 1875, announced the marriage of Ann Virginia Kirby, daughter of John Kirby, Esquire, of Fairfax County, (at Joshua Kirby's by L. H. Crenshaw) on January 19, 1875, to Andrew J. Hall.

(2) William Henry Kirby, born October 18, 1826, was killed in the Confederate service. He was killed in the same battle at Winchester during which his brother, Walter, was killed. He was unmarried.

(3) James E. Kirby, born February 16, 1829, died (drowned) September 8, 1900. He married on February 24, 1857, to Sarah Alice Sewell (born 1838) a daughter of Joseph William and Catherine A. (Nelson) Sewell. Their children included Edwin Forest Kirby, baptized at Dulin Chapel, January 13, 1875.

(4) Joshua Kirby, married Henrietta Nelson.

(5) George F. Kirby, born March 20, 1834, died December 16, 1895. He served in the Confederate Army. Mr. Kirby married September 17, 1868, to Catherine A. Nelson (1843-1926), a daughter of Thomas Henry and Amanda (Sewell) Nelson. Mr. Kirby was proprietor of a drug store at East Falls Church (later owned by Luther Elliott). His children included a daughter, Bettie Lee Kirby, born August 11, 1869.

(6) (Lieutenant) Charles Walter Kirby, born in March, 1835, served in the Union Army and obtained the rank of Lieutenant. He was killed at Winchester. He was unmarried.

(7) Martin Kirby, born April 30, 1837, died June 9, 1837.

(8) Matthew F. Kirby, born 1838, and married Rhoda ———. No other record.

(9) Mary Elizabeth Kirby, born June 7, 1839, died December 4, 1897. She married in August, 1862, to Benjamin Franklin Johnson (1841-1921). Mr. Johnson remarried on March 8, 1899, at Mt. Zion Baptist Church near Rockville, Maryland, to Lucretia Jane Dean (1859-1900). All members of this family were buried in Oakwood Cemetery, including a Mrs. Nora Ethel (Werkin) Johnson (1872-1917). A son, Arthur Benjamin Johnson was born in 1871, died August, 1894.

(10) Nancy C. Kirby, born about 1840.

(11) Francis Asbury Kirby, married Henrietta Clay Sewell.

(12) Martha Sherman Kirby, born June 1, 1846, married on December 20, 1870, Julian May Walters (son of Thomas J. and Henrietta V. (Hirst) Walters).

(13) Rowena E. Kirby, married Charles Wesley Phillips.

(4) Joshua Kirby, son of Charles and Mary (Sherman) Kirby, was born in February, 1831, and died June 7, 1914. He was buried in the family plot in Oakwood Cemetery. Mr. Kirby was a farmer and lived in the old house formerly the home of his father. Mr. Kirby had real estate valued at $1,500 and a personal estate valued at $50.00 in 1860? Living in his household at that time were:

Sallie Elliott, (born 1795); Nancy Elliott (born 1803); and Betsy Elliott (born 1807). All of them were native Virginians. Mr. Kirby was active at Dulin Chapel, later at Langley.

He married on February 2, 1860, to Henrietta (Rhett) Nelson, (1839-1918) a daughter of Thomas and Amanda (Sewell) Nelson.[10] Issue:

(41) William W. Kirby (1861-1946) married Mary Frances Tobin (January 19, 1866-January 27, 1957).

(42) Walter Elmer Kirby, born March 20, 1865, died July 28, 1949. Married his first cousin, Minnie M. Kirby.

(43) Luther Nelson Kirby, born August 6, 1868, died May 31, 1901.

(44) Hattie Virginia Kirby, died unmarried, August 15, 1955. She was baptized as "Kate Virginia Kirby." Her birth record on file at Dulin Chapel is dated August 9, 1870. She died unmarried.

(45) Ernest Crenshaw Kirby, born January 4, 1874, died September 24, 1956 at Chesterbrook. He attended William & Mary College. Mr. Kirby married on March 29, 1930, to Lavinia B. LeHew, a native of the Shenandoah Valley (born December 17, 1906). Issue: Edna Lavinia Kirby, born January 28, 1932; and Shirley Ernestine Kirby, born August 30, 1935.

(46) Henry Clay (or Henry Charles) Kirby, born January 22, 1875, died January 18, 1895.

(47) Eppa Preston Kirby, born June 2, 1879, died July 4, 1948. Mr. Kirby was Sheriff of Fairfax County. He married Beulah Wells (1883-1955). Issue: Floyd Elmer Kirby, married Sallie B. Bradley (and had Wayne Nelson Kirby, born March 5, 1937, who married on July 13, 1957. Frances J. Cofer, born August 30, 1935); and Eula Virginia Kirby, married Dewey Lee Curtis (and had Dewey Lee Curtis, Jr., Genevieve Beulah Curtis; June Kincheloe Curtis, married Leo S. Lagana, and had Larry Leo Lagana, born May 25, 1947.

(11) Francis Asbury Kirby, son of Charles and Mary (Sherman) Kirby, was born in November, 1841, and died in 1907. He married, at the home of William Sewell at Langley, December 5, 1867, to Henrietta Clay Sewell (1844-1912). Mrs. Kirby was born near Langley, and was a daughter of Joseph William and Catherine A. (Nelson) Sewell. Issue:

(11.1) Ward Travis Kirby, born near Falls Church, September 5, 1870, and died June 21, 1933. He was an extensive farmer and owned a large farm at Langley. He married Ada Virginia Hirst, a daughter of John E. and Asburina (Payne) Hirst. Their son, Marvin Hirst Kirby, married Agnes Orrison. Mr. and Mrs. Kirby are well known for their devoted leadership in the Methodist Church and many organizations for community good. They live in McLean.

(11.2) Minnie May Kirby, born September 15, 1868, died in 1926, married her first cousin, Walter E. Kirby on April 30, 1896.

(11.3) Raymond Bernard Kirby, born 1872, died 1920.

(11.4) Harvey Casper Kirby, born June 28, 1875, died 1943.

(11.5) Ethel Ora Kirby, baptized February 23, 1890.
(11.6) Olive Pauline Kirby, unmarried.
(11.7) Foster Burton Kirby, born September 10, 1881, died January 9, 1950. He married Dorothy Row of Falls Church, a daughter of Thomas John Hoyle and Margaret Carson (Bully) Row. Issue: Ralph Kirby and Burton Kirby.
(11.8) Bertha Gray Kirby, born April 4, 1877, died unmarried, 1916.
(11.9) Norman Lee Kirby, born April 28, 1879, died November 8, 1898.

(13) Rowena E. Kirby, daughter of Charles and Mary (Sherman) Kirby, was born in 1848, and married on January 8, 1870, to Charles Wesley (Wes) Phillips. Mr. Phillips was a son of James B. and Mary Phillips of Washington, D. C. A descendant, Mrs. John H. Vetter, has a letter written by Jonathan Phillips, brother of James B., from Columbus, Ohio, August 13, 1847. This letter is full of interest and contains political and economic news from the Columbus area. Issue:

(13.1) Eugene Kirby Phillips, born October 30, 1871, died October 28, 1946, and is buried in Oakwood Cemetery. He married on November 9, 1898, Ann Salina Wren. Mrs. Phillips was born July 14, 1874, died March 13, 1950, and was a daughter of John Wesley and Lucy Salina (Payne) Wren. (*See Wren*).
(13.2) Mary Annette Phillips (May), born July 30, 1875, married Rufus Wesley Wren, son of John Wesley and Lucy Salina (Payne) Wren. (*See Wren*).
(13.3) Martha Emiline Phillips, born October 25, 1876, married John Dameron.
(13.4) Naomi Phillips, married Clarence Burroughs.
(13.5) Ina Rose Phillips, born April 1, 1881, married Michael Inscoe.

---

[1] A descendant, Mrs. Lawrence Paxton of Osceola Plantation, Leland, Mississippi, is writing a history of this family (1950).
[2] A partial record of this Kirby family can be found in *Will Book N #1*, page 379, *et. seq.*, filed at Fairfax Court House. This refers to a law suit, Kirby vs. Lovejoy, March 23, 1825. This shows that Ann Boggess Kirby of Fairfax made a will on October 7, 1823, and died thereafter. In it she mentioned: Robert Boggess Kirby, a brother (named Executor); her mother, Elizabeth Kirby; her brother, James A. Kirby; her aunt, Sarah Ann Boggess; and a nephew, John Emery Lovejoy. Reference was made to slaves and her estate on Pohick Run. Witnesses were: N. Bealle, Peter Vannesse, (or Van Ness) and J. N. Lovejoy. See also Fairfax *Will Book R #1*, page 52, George Minor, Administrator of Ann C. B. (Nancy) Kirby, decd., which refers to Robert Kirby. This was filed December 17, 1832.
[3] Arlington County, *Deed Book M #2*, page 427.
[4] Arlington County, *Deed Book L #2*, page 138.
[5] *Ibid, Deed Book S #3*, page 391.
[6] From the *Family Bible* owned by R. Vernon Palmer of McLean.
[7] "Abstract of Evidence on Loyalty," Court of Claims No. 12,332, from a typed copy made by Miss Edna L. Kirby, October, 1955, and loaned by Marvin H. Kirby. The original document is owned by Floyd E. Kirby.
[8] From the *Family Bible* and the 1860 *U. S. Census* of Fairfax County, page 992.
[9] 1860 *U. S. Census*, Fairfax County, page 993.
[10] The *Marriage Records* of Fairfax County state that her parents were Thomas and Amanda Sewell at the time of marriage. However, her maiden name is given as Nelson.

---

## THE KLOCK FAMILY

The Klock family was of German origin, and settled in Falls Church prior to the War Between the States. They purchased "The Mount," from the heirs of Robert Lindsay, and farmed the land for many years. During the War Between the States, (in 1862), Augustus Klock, described as an "estimable Falls Church citizen of known Union leanings," was arrested by Mosby. He was released with instructions to inform Federal authorities of retaliatory steps Mosby planned unless two of his men at that time held in confinement, were paroled.

Benjamin Klock, son of Augustus Klock, was born in Montgomery County, New York, August 21, 1809, and died at "The Mount," August 19, 1875. He is buried in the Falls Church yard. His wife, Sally Klock, is buried in Oakwood Cemetery. She was also a native of Montgomery County, New York, born August 20, 1810, died January 13, 1904.

Webster Klock, son of Benjamin and Sally Klock, was born May 17, 1846, died March 13, 1891. He was a farmer, and lived at "The Mount." Mrs. Webster Klock, his wife, donated the land on which Irwin Memorial Presbyterian Church was built at Idylwood.

Benjamin Irving Klock, a son of Webster Klock, was born in 1874, and died in March, 1949. He was survived by his widow, May Richards Klock, and a daughter, Mrs. Elmer (Laura M.) Cox of Idylwood.

---

[1] Record has been found of a son of Benjamin and Sally Klock, Jonathan Klock, who married in Fairfax County on August 24, 1871 to Sarah Jane Walters. He is listed as a native of New York, age 30, and she was age 31, native of Fairfax County, and a daughter of William and Rebecca Walters.

---

## THE LEE FAMILY

The Lee family of Falls Church were connected with the family of General Henry ("Light Horse Harry") Lee. A descendant, George Edward Lee, was from the Clarke County branch of the family. He was born in Tennessee after the family had moved from their home, near Berryville, to Knoxville. George Edward Lee married Harriet Satterfield. He owned a large farm at Tellicoe Plains, Tennessee, and a residence in Knoxville.

Pharis Winfield Lee, born in Knoxville, August 7, 1869, died at his Falls Church home on October 19, 1961, age 92 years. In his early manhood he attended Carson Newman College. In 1895 Mr. Lee came to Falls Church and purchased a home on South Oak Street, which burned shortly afterwards. He moved to Washington, D.C., but returned in 1901 and purchased three houses on West Broad Street (501-505- and 509). This included the large old brick house owned by the Turner family. The house at 505 West Broad Street dated back to the 1860's and the brick house was much older. The two frame houses have been torn down and the Chanel Apartments are currently (1964) being erected on the site. Mr. Lee owned fifteen acres and the three houses which he purchased for $5,500.

Mr. Lee had a varied career. He was an employee of the Southern Rail Road in Tennessee and later worked for the C. & P. Telephone Company.

Pharis Winfield Lee was married in Knoxville, November 13, 1894, to Henrietta Morris Failing. Mrs. Lee was born at Ball's Camp, Tennessee, October 25, 1870, and died at her Falls Church home on December 26, 1947. She attended Carson Newman College, and like her husband, was an ardent Baptist.

Mrs. Lee represented an old family of German origin. Her ancestor, Henrich Failing (Phailing, Fahling) was from the Rhine Valley and settled in New York in 1710. Mrs. Lee's Grandfather Failing (a native of Fort Failing in Mohawk Valley,

New York) owned a sloop. He took it full of trading goods around the Horn to Portland, Oregon, where he settled. His son, John Ellison Failing, came East from Oregon to attend Yale and Columbia. He was a physician and led an active life. He scouted with Kit Carson, crossed the Plains seven times, and once was ambushed by Indians. He was pinned to the saddle of his horse with arrows through both thighs. Later Dr. Failing served as an officer in the Union Army and moved to Tennessee. Dr. Failing married Abigail Morris, and they were the parents of Mrs. Pharis Winfield Lee.

Mr. and Mrs. Lee were greatly beloved by their Falls Church neighbors. Mr. Lee was a leader in Masonic circles. They had issue:

(1) George Ellison Lee, born April 9, 1898, in Washington D.C., died December 5, 1957. He married twice. By his first wife, Olive Hoskins, he had a son, George Ellison Lee, Jr., born in 1923. The latter has five children.

(2) Winifred Failing Lee, born August 15, 1899, married on March 22, 1923, to Philip Dana Dudley. Issue:
  (21) Dana Lee Dudley, born June 4, 1924, married Jacqueline Hastings and had issue: Justin Dana Dudley, Lisa Dudley and Nina Dudley.

(3) John Donald Lee, born October 6, 1902, married four times. His first two wives were Nancy Tazewell Ellett and Jeannette Evans. By his first wife he had issue:
  (31) Nancy Lee, married and had four children.

(4) Henrietta Merrill Lee, born February 19, 1904, married Allen Payne Chanel, son of Orson Joseph and Bertha L. Chanel of Falls Church. Issue:
  (41) Weymer Lee Chanel, born September 2, 1925, married Patricia Joynt, issue: Linda Lee Chanel, born June 29, 1952; Stephanie Chanel, born December 5, 1955; and John Merrill Chanel, born May 21, 1960.

(5) Henry Weymer Lee, born October 7, 1905, lives in Woodside Estates, Fairfax County. Mr. Lee has served as Deputy Sheriff of Fairfax County and is a Justice of the Peace. He married on January 31, 1931, Elinor Offutt Lyne. Mrs. Lee, of distinguished ancestry, was born in Oakland, Maryland, March 30, 1905, a daughter of John Julian Locke and Sue Hughes (Legge) Lyne. Mrs. Lee is Food Editor for the *Washington Post* and served for twenty years as Director of Woman's Activities for Radio Station WTOP in Washington. Issue:
  (51) Catherine Sue Lee (Kitty), born February 21, 1934, in Charlestown, West Virginia, married on December 27, 1953, Fred Stone Landess. Issue: Susan Elinor Landess, born August 27, 1957; Charles Barton Landess, born January 21, 1959; and Catherine Elizabeth Landess, born November 11, 1961.

## THE LEONARD FAMILY

David Leonard and wife, the former Agnes McKenzie, came to the Falls Church area from Boston, Massachusetts, prior to 1880. They purchased forty-eight acres at West Falls Church near Lemon Road, on which stood an old log house, very close to Leesburg Pike. In this two hundred year old "Quarter House," the family lived for a number of years, later erecting a large frame house in the oak grove behind it. The oaks are more than three hundred years old.

Mr. Leonard was a sterotypist for the Government Printing Office. The family was well liked by the community and were active in local affairs. The children attended Ford School, opposite their home, later attending Jefferson School and schools in Washington, D.C. The family were members of St. James Church.

David Leonard died in 1912 at age 76 years. His wife died in 1910, at age 69 years. Five of their children were born in Boston. The children were,[1] in order: Alexander Leonard, Margaret Leonard, Daisy Leonard (born 1867, died November 19, 1953, unmarried); James H. Leonard, for many years a lawyer in Philadelphia, married, no issue; Rose Leonard, Grace Leonard (born 1874, died March 18, 1954, unmarried); Nellie S. Leonard, married Charles Arnold of Merrifield (and had Mrs. Robert Boswell, Mrs. Earl Boswell and Leonard Arnold); David Leonard, Jr., (later); and Agnes Leonard.

David Leonard, Jr., born May 1, 1879, died August 12, 1953, was a truck farmer and lived at "Five Oaks." He is buried in the family plot in St. James Cemetery. Mr. Leonard married Mary McCauley (*See McCauley*). Issue: David Leonard, 3rd, Agnes Leonard, Daniel Leonard, Lucian Leonard, and Margaret Leonard.

---

[1] Information supplied by Miss Ada Walker, September 24, 1950.

---

## THE LINDSAY FAMILY

At the bend in Shreve Road on to Idylwood Road, about 1/3rd of a mile to the north, stood "Mount Pleasant" built in 1770 by Colonel Robert Lindsay for his son Thomas. "The Mount," in more recent times known as the "Klock Place," is nearby on Idylwood Road, and was built in 1745 by Colonel Robert Lindsay.

"The Mount" is now the home of the Stuart family, and was once the home of the maiden sisters, Miss Sarah, Miss Mary, and Miss Emeline Klock. Robert Lindsay, builder of both the "Mount" and "Mount Pleasant," was a native of Northumberland County, Virginia, and a son of Opie Lindsay.

The surname LINDSAY and LINDSEY is to be found in the oldest records of the Colony. The immigrant ancestor of Robert Lindsay was the Reverend David Lindsay of Northumberland, who settled about 1650. He was baptized in Scotland on January 3, 1603, and was a son of Sir Hierome Lindsay of "Annatland" and "The Mount" who married (1) Margaret Colville. In his Marmion, canto 4, verse 7, Sir Walter Scott gives a sketch of Sir David Lindsay of "The Mount" who was Lord Lion King at Arms.

The line of the Lindsays of Virginia is unbroken from the year A.D. 1086: Baldric de Limesay, of England, living 1086, had a son William de Lindsay of Ercildoun, 1133-47. William had a son Walter Lindsay who lived at Ercildoun, and died 1150. His son was William Lindsay who added "Crawford" to the Ercildoun estate. He married Marjory, daughter of Henry, Prince of Scotland, and sister of William the Lion, descendants of Malcolm Canmore and the Saxon Princess Margaret of England, sister of Edgar the last heir to the Saxon line. A son of this couple was William Lindsay of Luffness (1236), who had Sir David Lindsay of Luffness, who in turn had a son, Sir David Lindsay of Luffness, 1255. Sir David (2nd) had a son, Sir Alexander Lindsay of Crawford who died in 1307. His son was Sir David Lindsay (3rd) 1314-1355, who married Mary, co-heiress of the Abernethies. Their son was Sir Alexander Lindsay (2nd) of Glenesk (1382) who married (1st) Catherine, daughter of Sir John de Stivling, heiress of Glenesk and Edzell. They had a son David Lord

Lindsay First Earl of Crawford (1398) who married Princess Catherine Stuart, fifth daughter of King Robert II. Their son, Alexander Lindsay Second Earl of Crawford died January 13, 1446. He married Marietta, daughter and heiress of Sir David Dunbar of Cockburn. Their son was David Lindsay, Third Earl of Crawford, 1445. He married Marjory, daughter of Alexander Ogilvie, Chief of Clan Ogilvie.

Walter Lindsay of "Beaufort" was a son of David Third Earl of Crawford and Marjory, Lady Ogilvie. He married Isabella, daughter of William, Lord Livingstone. They had Sir David Lindsay of Edzell Castle, who married Catherine Fotheringham of Powie. They had Walter Lindsay ("the younger") of Edzell (who died on Flodden Field on September 9, 1513) and who married a daughter of Erskine of Dun. Their son Alexander Lindsay married a daughter of Barclay of Mathers, and they had David Lindsay, Bishop of Ross, who died in 1613. Sir Hierome Lindsay of Annatland and "The Mount" was a son of David Lindsay, Bishop of Ross, and married Margaret Colville as his first wife. The Reverend David Lindsay (1603-1667) of Northumberland County, Virginia, was a son of Sir Hierome Lindsay and his first wife Margaret Colville.

The first reference to The Reverend David Lindsay is in a Court Order Book of Northumberland, March 20, 1655: "Judgment is granted Mr. David Lyndsay Minister, whereby he recovers 50 pounds Tobacco from Edward Coles."

The Reverend David Lindsay was a graduate of St. Salvatore College of St. Andrew's University of Scotland, M.A., July, 1621. His Uncle-in-law, Archbishop Spotswood, was head of the University at that time. The tombstone of David Lindsay in Northumberland County reads:

> Here lyeth the body of Mr.
> David Lindsy Doctor of
> Divinity who departed this life
> the 3d of April 1667.

Colonel Lindsay, son of the Reverend David Lindsay, married and had a son Opie Lindsay. Opie was named for his Uncle, Captain Thomas Opie, husband of Helen Lindsay, eldest child of the Reverend David and Susanna Lindsay (and Executor of his will in 1667). Opie Lindsay died in 1727, and an Inventory of his estate was recorded September 20, 1727 in Northumberland. In 1743 Colonel Robert Lindsay sold "Cherry Point" his estate in Northumberland to William Taylor. He became a resident of Fairfax about 1742 (date of formation of the county). The house called "The Mount" near Falls Church was erected about 1743, replaced by the present house in 1745.

Colonel Lindsay's will dated September 11, 1784, is at the Court House at Fairfax.

"Laurel Hill" near Lorton, was the plantation of Major William Lindsay, eldest son of Robert and Susanna Lindsay of "The Mount." William Lindsay has been described as "tall and muscular, and inclined to portliness, his face was decidedly of an aristocratic type, his complexion clear, his cheeks bronzed, hair dark-brown, and he has extremely penetrating gray-blue eyes. . . ."

William Lindsay served as a Major in the Virginia Militia during the Revolution, and received a severe wound at the battle of Guilford Court-House under General Green (May, 1781).

Major Lindsay first settled at Colchester in Prince William.

On November 3, 1951 the Fairfax County Chapter, NSDAR dedicated a plaque on the "Laurel Hill" estate to Ann (Calvert) Lindsay, wife of William Lindsay, upon the site of their graves. They lie buried within the present District Reformatory grounds. Among the descendants of the Lindsays present upon this occasion were Mrs. Thomas F. Dodd and Mrs. Andrew W. Clarke of Alexandria, and Mrs. Hush Dawson of Lorton.

Major William Lindsay married about 1766 to Ann Calvert of Culpeper County, a great-granddaughter of Cecil Calvert, Lord Baltimore. She was born in 1751, and died at the home of her son-in-law, Rinaldo Grimes at Patapsco, Prince William County, in 1822, and was buried at "Laurel Hill." She was Catholic by faith and her priest would come to Alexandria about three times a month to say Mass for her.

Major Lindsay died of gout in 1792, and was buried at "Laurel Hill." Major William and Ann (Calvert) Lindsay had issue:
(1) Infant Lindsay, died at birth, 1767.
(2) Susanna Lindsay, born 1769.
(3) George Walter Lindsay, born 1771.
(4) William Henry Lindsay, born 1773.
(5) Ann Lindsay (Nancy) born 1775.
(6) Hiram Lindsay born 1778.
(7) John Lindsay, born 1780.
(8) Infant Lindsay, died young, born 1783.
(9) Sarah Lindsay, born 1785.
(10) Maria Lindsay, born 1787.
(11) Thomas Lindsay, born 1789.
(12) Catherine Lindsay (Kitty) born 1791.

Upon the death of Colonel Robert and Susanna Lindsay, "The Mount" became the home of Opie Lindsay, their second son. Opie Lindsay is described as a person of "strong characteristics, unusually handsome physique, tall, broad, and muscular..." During the Revolution he was bearer of dispatches from one position to another for the army.

Opie Lindsay married three times, (1) Margaret Lamkin (related to Lamkin and Chatam familes of Virginia); (2) Miss Jett; and (3) Miss Howerton of Montgomery County, Maryland. Opie Lindsay had issue: (*By Margaret Lamkin*):
(1) Robert Lindsay.
(2) Opie Lindsay.
(3) Thomas Lindsay.
(4) William Lindsay.

(*By Miss Jett*):
(5) child Lindsay, died in infancy and buried at "The Mount."

(*By Miss Howerton*):
(6) Fanny Lindsay.
(7) John Opie Lindsay.
(8) Hierome Lindsay.

Robert Lindsay, son of Opie and Margaret (Lamkin) Lindsay, was the founder of the Lindsays of North Carolina. He settled on the Dan River in Rockingham County, N.C., in 1790 and named his plantation "The Mount," after his home in Fairfax County.

Robert Lindsay married Elizabeth Wren, daughter of John Wren, and granddaughter of Colonel James Wren. They had five children, three of whom were William, Robert, and John Lindsay. William Lindsay, eldest son of Robert Lindsay and Elizabeth Wren, married and had two sons, George Robert Lindsay and William Carter Lindsay, both of whom had descendants. Robert Lindsay (Jr.) son of Robert Lindsay and Elizabeth Wren, was a physician, and died unmarried. John Lindsay, third son of Robert Lindsay and Elizabeth Wren, was living in 1889. He served as a Representative in the North Carolina Legislature as did a son, William R. Lindsey.

Opie Lindsay, son of Opie and Margaret (Lamkin) Lindsay of "The Mount," settled in Kentucky in 1790 with his brother Thomas Lindsay. Opie Lindsay married (1) Miss Bates of Virginia; and (2) Nancy Roder. Issue:

(*By Miss Bates*):
(21) Julia Lindsay.
(22) Samuel Lindsay.
(23) Sarah Lindsay, died unmarried.
(24) Alfred Lindsay.

(*By Nancy Roder*):
(25) Elizabeth Scott Lindsay, married Dr. De Lancy Egbert, no issue.
(26) Opie Lindsay, married Polly Delancy, and had eight children.
(27) Martha Lee Lindsay, married Morris J. Harris of Zelon, Poland.
(28) Nancy L. Lindsay, unmarried.
(29) Eveline Lindsay, married A. Smith.
(2.10) Ruben Carben Lindsay, married Belle Sparks and had child which died in infancy, and left no other heirs.

"Mount Pleasant" was named for its pleasant site, being situated on a lovely hill with a captivating view. The plantation house was erected in 1770 on a portion of "The Mount" estate by Colonel Robert Lindsay for his son Thomas.

Thomas Lindsay, son of Colonel Robert and Susanna Lindsay of "The Mount," was born at "The Mount" November 13, 1750, and was the youngest son of a large family. He is described as "a gentlemen of the old school, courteous and dignified in manner, of fine and pleasing features, tall of stature, not stout, of quick yet stately step, (and) punctilious in religious affairs." He was a vestryman of his Church and one of the respected citizens of Fairfax County. Thomas Lindsay was married to Mrs. Martha (Scott) Fox, a widow of Pennsylvania. She was born November 6, 1757, and died September 21, 1831. Thomas Lindsay died September 14, 1830 of paralysis, and was buried at "The Mount."

Thomas and Martha (Scott) Lindsay had issue the following children:
(1) Robert Lindsay, born at "Mount Pleasant" May 26, 1779; killed by lightning along with other companions while boating on the Potomac, July 17, 1805.
(2) Samuel Lindsay, born at "Mount Pleasant" November 20, 1781. He married a Miss McDougal of Virginia.
(3) David Lindsay, born at "Mount Pleasant" May 25, 1784, married Lucy Parker of Clarke County, Virginia.
(4) Nancy Lindsay, born at "Mount Pleasant" August 5, 1776, married Congressman Braddock Richmond of Rhode Island.
(5) Susanna Lindsay, born at "Mount Pleasant" February 23, 1789, married Ami Moore.

(6) Elizabeth Lindsay, born at "Mount Pleasant," March 15, 1792, married Henry Fairfax.

(7) Josiah Lindsay, born at "Mount Pleasant," November 17, 1794. Died unmarried February 22, 1813, aged 19 years.

(8) Margaret Lindsay, born at "Mount Pleasant" November 26, 1797, married William Swink.

(9) Thomas Walter Lindsay, born at "Mount Pleasant," July 22, 1800, died there August 18, 1802, and is buried at the "Mount."

Samuel Lindsay, son of Thomas and Martha (Scott) Lindsay was born at "Mount Pleasant," November 20, 1781. He was a merchant at Alexandria. By his marriage to Miss McDougal of Virginia, he had the following children:
- (21) Martha A. Lindsay, married William Presby Gunnell, a physician of Alexandria. (*See Gunnell*).

David Lindsay, son of Thomas and Martha (Scott) Lindsay, was born at "Mount Pleasant" May 25, 1784. He married Lucy Parker of Clarke County, a relation of Judge Parker of Winchester. David Lindsay and family moved to Mason County, Kentucky, where he was a well-to-do farmer.

Nancy Lindsay, daughter of Thomas and Martha (Scott) Lindsay, was born at "Mount Pleasant" August 5, 1776. She married (The Honorable) Braddock Richmond, a member of Congress from Rhode Island. Mrs. Richmond died in Washington, D.C., December 10, 1810.

Susanna Lindsay, daughter of Thomas and Martha (Scott) Lindsay was born at "Mount Pleasant" February 23, 1789. She married Ami Moore, son of the Reverend Jeremiah Moore. Ami and Susanna (Lindsay) Moore had issue:
- (51) Robert Moore (eldest child).
- (52) Thomas Moore, who was a distinguished lawyer in the county. He practiced law at Fairfax Court House under firm name of "Thomas Moore and Son." Mr. Moore married Hannah Morris of New York, a great-granddaughter of a signer of the Declaration of Independence, and a cousin of Mrs. Hamilton Fish. Thomas Moore served in the Mexican War and in the Confederate Army during the War Between the States. Thomas and Hannah (Morris) Moore had children including:
    - (521) (Honorable) Robert Walton Moore, born at Fairfax Court House February 29, 1859, and died in 1941. Mr. Moore was educated at the Episcopal High School at Alexandria, and at the University of Virginia. He was a member of the Virginia Senate from 1887 until 1890, and declined re-election. Mr. Moore was Attorney for the Town of Falls Church in 1880, having been appointed through the efforts of a Councilman, William Nathan Lynch. He received $25.00 a year as salary. Mr. Moore was admitted to the Virginia bar in 1880, and in 1911 was President of the Virginia Bar Association.

        In 1933 Mr. Moore was appointed Counselor at the State Department. Mr. Moore did not marry.
    - (522) Susanna Lindsay Moore, married Stephen Roszel Donohue of Fairfax, founder and Editor of the *Fairfax Herald* (1882).
    - (523) Jane Morris Moore, died in 1940 unmarried.
    - (524) Bessie Rutherford Moore, died unmarried.
    - (525) Helen Stuyvesant Moore, did not marry.

(526) Edith May Moore, married Thomas Randolph Keith.
(527) Lucy Kean Moore, died unmarried.
(528) Margaret Lindsay Moore, died unmarried.

(53) Francis Moore, died unmarried in 1852.
(54) daughter Moore.

Elizabeth Lindsay, daughter of Thomas and Martha (Scott) Lindsay, was born at "Mount Pleasant," March 15, 1792. She married "on the morning of the 5th of August, 1824" in the thirty-third year of her age to Henry Fairfax, Esq., of "Prospect Hill," near Dumfries, Prince William Co., Va.; and of "Freestone" in the same County. Captain Henry Fairfax was a gentleman of wealth and position, being of the family of Lord Fairfax.

On the "Mount" estate is the burial ground of the Lindsay family, which includes the resting place of Colonel Robert Lindsay, founder of the family in Fairfax County. The following stones were copied on January 14, 1950:

    (Broken stone) Sarah Gorham
    Florence Eva Downs, 1874-1911.
    Cathern Wrenn
    George Gorham.
    John Gorham.
    Francis J. Gorham, June 4, 1864-July 18, 1907
    William H. Wrenn, 1842-1929.
    His Wife, Annie E. Wrenn, 1853-1927.
    Ernest Ernie McCauley, Jan. 6, 1885-Jan.1, 1941.
Emma S. Rawlings, Died Dec. 22, 1943, beloved wife of Harry B. Gorham.
There are numerous field stones and stakes to indicate Lindsay graves.

## THE LLOYD FAMILY

Dr. Lester Lloyd, a native of New England, was born August 30, 1804, and died February 7, 1888, and is buried in Oakwood Cemetery. On May 27, 1875, the first election held in Falls Church was held in his home. At that time, the first Mayor, Dr. J. J. Moran, was elected. The home of Dr. Lloyd was formerly an Inn, later Wiltshire's Undertaking Parlor. Dr. Lloyd married on January 14, 1856, Sarah F. Darne, and had the following children (known to this writer):[1]

(1) Frances V. Lloyd, born November 30, 1856, died October 19, 1938. She married on March 5, 1878, Joseph V. Byrnes (1851-1940). Mr. and Mrs. Byrnes lived at Kirbyville.

(2) Irene M. Lloyd, born February 17, 1857, died November 19, 1887. She married on January 10, 1882 to John E. McCarty. Buried beside her is "L. M. McCarty" no dates, perhaps an infant child. They lived at McLean.

(3) Watson Lloyd.

---

[1] From the records of Dulin Chapel.

## THE LYNCH FAMILY

The Lynch family is one of the most ancient in Irish history. Eighty members of this family served as Mayors of Galway while living in the same house. The original ancestor was Olioll Olum, and the line of descent is through Mogha Corb, born in 167 A.D., King of Munster. The family bears the following Arms:
Azure, a chevron between
three trefoils slipt or.

The Crest is a lynx and the Motto is "Semper fidelis" ("Always Faithful").

The original immigrant to Maryland was Hugh Lynch who came in 1677. Hugh, as a Christian name, is used to the present generation. The family settled in Upper Prince Georges (now Montgomery County). William Hugh Lynch was the father of the two Falls Church settlers. He lost his father about 1790. An account of this incident follows:[1]

"Hugh's father was drowned when Hugh was six. His father was riding on horseback, apparently from Georgetown, with Hugh behind him on the horse. Near the Little Falls in the Potomac River, the trail was close to the river and the horse stumbled or slipped and fell into the river. Hugh fell on land and waited all night for his father to 'ride back out of the river.'

William Hugh Lynch served as Sergeant of the First Maryland Militia during the War of 1812, and participated in the "Bladensburg Races." He owned a residence in Rockville and farmed what is now the Albert Hahn farm on River Road near Potomac, Maryland. Mr. Lynch was a Democrat, member of the Town Council, and a communicant of St. Mary's Roman Catholic Church in Rockville.

William Hugh Lynch and Valinda (Linnie) Spates were married in Montgomery County on March 24, 1825. Mrs. Lynch was from a prominent family which is still represented in Montgomery County. Issue:

(1) John William Lynch, married Mary Ann Lightfoot.

(2) William Henry Greenbury Lynch, married Elizabeth Ellen Lightfoot.

(3) Ruth Ann Lynch, born January 1, 1829, married James Gingell.

(4) Henry (Harry) Lynch, born about 1834, died at age 13 years.

(5) William Thomas Lnch, born March 22, 1836, died October 16, 1919. Married (1) Mary Agnes Termon; and (2) Mrs. Sarah E. (Collins) Ingalls.

(6) Margaret Ann Lynch, married (1) Franklin Sebastian; and (2) David Lawrence.

(7) Martin Van Buren Lynch, married Susan Davis.

(1) John William Lynch, son of William Hugh and Valinda (Spates) Lynch, was born in Montgomery County, Maryland, January 29, 1826, and died at Falls Church July 13, 1910. He is buried beside his wife in Oakwood Cemetery. He married, in Washington, D. C., January 2, 1856, Mary Ann Lightfoot of Big Chimneys, a niece and heir of Nathan Thompson, Esq. She was born February 18, 1831, and died at Big Chimneys December 3, 1893. Her will is recorded in Fairfax County *Book G #2*, page 115, which she made in the name "of the Beloved Father of all." Mr. Lynch was reared in the Roman Catholic faith, but joined Fairfax Chapel Methodist Episcopal Church in Falls Church upon his marriage. His name is carried in the records of Fairfax Chapel and Dulin Chapel. He contributed largely to Church work, and on January 24, 1892 gave $75.00 to the Dulin Chapel building fund. In that day this was a very large sum of money. Mr. Lynch was a good farmer, and served as Constable of Falls Church District many years. The following description of Mr. Lynch

was sent the author by Mrs. Amelia (Payne) Thomas of Washington, D. C., in a letter dated January 18, 1950:

"I remember Uncle John Lynch very well. He was quite distinguished looking, with a long white beard and oh, how I loved him! He used to bring me hickory nuts when I was very little. He died when I was a child. . . ."

John William and Mary Ann (Lightfoot) Lynch had issue:

(11) Ida Jane Lynch, born at Big Chimneys, June 6, 1857, baptized by the Reverend William Gwynn Coe at Fairfax Chapel, February 26, 1861 (witnessed by Joseph E. Birch, James Elliott and her maternal aunt, Jane Lightfoot). She married on March 8, 1876 at Dulin Chapel to Valenchia O'Meara. He was born in Loudoun County in 1849. Their large family included Effie, Beatrice and John Raymond O'Meara. The last named, John Raymond O'Meara, was born at Big Chimneys in 1878 and baptized by the Reverend J. H. Waugh at Dulin Chapel, September 29, 1879 in the presence of John Lynch and family.

(12) Mary Valinda Lynch, born at Big Chimneys June 15, 1859, was baptized by the Reverend William Gwynn Coe at Fairfax Chapel on February 26, 1861 in the presence of Joseph E. Birch, James Elliott, and her maternal aunt, Jane Lightfoot. She married James Childress and lived in Washington, D. C. No issue.

(13) Hester Valinda Lynch, born at Big Chimneys in 1860. She died at her home in Edgewater, Maryland, May 14, 1950. She married Albert T. Marlow of Maryland. Issue: Walter William Marlow, born June 6, 1892, died at Edgewater, Maryland, November 20, 1953. He married in 1916 to May E. Finagin of Maryland. They had a daughter, Dorothy E. Marlow (born February 23, 1917) now Mrs. Tendick, who has daughters Linda and Ellen Tendick. Mr. Marlow was a Banker by profession "known widely and sincerely esteemed in the banking circles of Washington" according to historian John C. Proctor. He was a member of the Washington Board of Trade, the City Club of Washington, and Columbia Lodge #3, A. F. & A. M. He was a member of Waugh Memorial Methodist Church, a member of that Board of Trustees and Financial Secretary as well as teacher in the Sunday School.

(2) William Henry Greenbury Lynch, son of William Hugh and Valinda (Spates) Lynch, was born in Montgomery County, Maryland, in 1832, and died at his home, "Hill House," in Falls Church, March 31, 1879. Mr. Lynch was buried in the family plot in the old Falls Churchyard, but later removed to Oakwood Cemetery. Mr. Lynch was a Contractor and owned the local blacksmith shop. In 1854 he married Elizabeth Ellen Lightfoot, of Big Chimneys, a niece and heir of Nathan Thompson, Esq., and sister to Mary Ann Lightfoot who married John William Lynch. Mr. and Mrs. Lynch were members of Fairfax Chapel Methodist Episcopal Church.

During the War Between the States Mr. Lynch was a Confederate spy.[2] He was arrested several times and put into prison at Alexandria. In 1861 Mrs. Lynch was alone at "Hill House" while her husband was away on a trip. Rumors came that the Yankees were near by. In haste Mrs. Lynch pulled up some boards under the horse stall of her barn, and dug a hole in which she put a tin covered container of gold money, about $500.00. She tacked the boards back and led old "Ned" into his stall. After the war the gold was not recovered. In the July 10, 1949 issue of the *Times-Herald*, an account stated of Mrs. Lynch: "Sometime during the War Between the States a Falls Church lady with the history-book name of Ellen Lightfoot Lynch buried a pot of gold coins from marauding Union soldiers. And so far as anybody knows, it's still there." The barn was hit by a shell when Wadsworth's headquarters was under fire. Mrs. Lynch packed a wagon with family effects, took her family and some ancient family portraits with her. She joined a group of other Falls Church residents and fled to safety on the Tripp farm (then the Dulany family home). The Tripp Farm is now "Greenway Downs."

While "Hill House" was not occupied during the period the family was at the Dulany farm, Union soldiers broke in and stole numerous items, including a beautiful antique mantle clock and a new copper-studded saddle. Later, after Mrs. Lynch returned to her home, she fed a hungry Yankee Colonel. She told him that she was willing to feed any hungry person, even a Yankee, but if she continued to do so, they would have to cease running over her kitchen garden. The officer posted four men on picket about her garden while he continued to eat her food.

William H. G. Lynch died on March 31, 1879. The following obituary was written by a Dr. J. W. Gardner:

"Died, at his home, in Falls Church, on Monday, March 31, 1879 at 5 o'clock p.m., after a protracted illness, William H. Lynch, aged 46 years.

With a sad heart I announce the death of one of our most esteemed citizens, Wm. H. Lynch, who died at his residence, in this place, on Monday afternoon, 31st of March, between the hours of 5 and 6 o'clock. He had been confined to his bed for several weeks and his recovery was considered doubtful by his physicians from the first and resulted as was feared. His devoted family was unremitting and untiring in their attention to his every want, night and day. No sick man was ever nursed more faithfully, and none has ever received greater attention, from a host of friends and relatives, who constantly waited upon him. Of those one in particular deserves especial notice—one who was with him and near him, with the devotedness of a son, from the first of his indisposition to the close of his life.

Mr. Lynch was a member of the M. E. Church, South, for many years, was one among the first to organize a lodge of Good Templars in this place, and succeeded in organizing and establishing the old Pioneer Lodge No. 1, which was the first lodge of Good Templars organized in the State of Virginia, where he remained in active service until stricken down by his death illness. His pastor, Rev. J. H. Waugh, was with him at the closing hours of his life. His end was calm, peaceful, and serene. He had received the kind attention of his own pastor and Rev. Mr. Riddle, who is the Worthy Chief Templar of his lodge, frequently during his sickness.

Mr. Lynch was highly esteemed and much respected by all who knew him. Charitable and kind, ready to lend or give of his means to the various enterprises of the day—and his hands were ever open to the destitute poor—his loss will be felt by an appreciating community; but by none so much as by his heart-broken wife and sorrowing children. They have our sincere sympathy and our prayers for the guidance and blessing of Him who is too wise to err and too good to be unkind. To Him may they look and trust for succor and relief.

A FRIEND

WILLIAM H. LYNCH has gone. We shall see him lively and full of fun on our streets no more. He was a kind father, good neighbor, and a true friend, one of those you seldom meet with in this selfish generation. I cannot say half enough in his praise; words will not express my opinion of this dear friend. He was truly, in the words of a letter of recommendation I once read, 'one of nature's noblemen.'

J. W. G."

Mr. Lynch was loved by a wide circle of friends, and was a "best friend" of Mr. William Dulin who gave the ground for the Dulin Methodist Church. Mr. Lynch served as a pall-bearer at Mr. Dulin's funeral.

Of Mrs. Lynch, the late Willis L. Gordon, aged 82, wrote: "Having been a personal friend of Mrs. Elizabeth Ellen Lightfoot Lynch, I knew her as a very very good and kind person. She was everybody's friend, and anyone sick, no matter who it was, she was always on the spot, ready and willing to help. She was a very religious and good woman. I have often thought of her as an old New England saying. . . 'A regular Mother in Israel' meaning a person always somewhere doing some good work for someone. She was known to everyone as Mother Lynch, and if you mentioned her, every one knew her, as she was really outstanding. . . ."

In her will (dated July 23, 1904—*Will Book 3*, Page 187), Mrs. Lynch gave her son, William Nathan Lynch "the remainder of the Potter lot, now owned by me, and situate, lying, and being in Falls Church, Virginia, and bounded on the north by the land of Dr. W. S. Bell and the Baptist Church lot. . ." and also gave him "my large rocking chair and my mahogany bureau." To her daughter, Ann Valinda Mankin, she devised the "remainder of the land now owned by me in the rear of the land now owned by the said Ann Valinda Mankin" and her "set of silver knives and forks." To her daughter, Elizabeth Ellen Payne, she devised "all the remainder of my house lot and premises, situate, lying and being in Falls Church, Virginia, bounded on the north by Broad Street, or the Alexandria-Leesburg Pike, on the east by the late A. A. Soule; (and) on the south by the land of William N. Lynch." She also left Mrs. Payne the "residue and remainder of my personal property." To her grandson, William Newton Payne, she devised her trunk, to her grandson John Nathan Payne her "bed and bedding, except my basket quilt;" and to her granddaughter Ellen Elizabeth Payne her "low shuck bottom chair." She also devised "my basket quilt" to her granddaughter Mary Amelia Payne. George T. Mankin was executor of the estate.

Her home, to which she moved after becoming a widow, is now the office of Dr. Emanuel Newman and is next to the old Falls Church Parish Hall. The house was built in 1797. It was purchased by Mrs. Lynch from Almond Birch. On May 17, 1951, the back kitchen burned. William Henry Greenbury and Elizabeth Ellen (Lightfoot) Lynch had issue:

(21) William Nathan Lynch, born at "Hill House," Falls Church, October 31, 1855, died in Arlington Hospital, December 27, 1945. He married on April 13, 1882 to Sarah Ellen Walker at the home of her parents, Mr. and Mrs. Thomas Hartwell Walker. Her father, Thomas Hartwell Walker (1830-1913) was a soldier in the Confederate Army under Colonel John S. Mosby. Her mother was Margaret Robey (1829-1875). Mrs. Lynch was born at Vienna, December 24, 1854, died at Mt. Alto Hospital, Washington, D.C., November 10, 1937. Mr. and Mrs. Lynch are buried in Oakwood Cemetery. Mr. Lynch owned a feed store and the blacksmith shop. The Town gave a testimonial dinner for him on January 10, 1939. The following is written in the memorial book presented him at that time: "The messages and signatures in this book were written there on the evening of January 10, 1939 in the parlors of the Dulin Chapel, Falls Church, Virginia, at a testimonial dinner tendered to William Nathan Lynch by the citizens of Falls Church and vicinity in recognition of his long and faithful service to the community." A clipping from the *Washington Post* states that "flowers for the living, both verbal and floral, were heaped upon the sprightly figure of Falls Church's oldest resident when friends and neighbors of many

year's standing gathered in the Southern Methodist Church Tuesday night to pay their tributes of honor and affection to William Nathan Lynch, who, at 84, is retiring from has active business life to seek a well-merited leisure. . . . Chief orator of the occasion was Mr. Lynch's contemporary, R. Walton Moore, of Fairfax. . . . Mr. Moore traced the development of the county and town and the world at large from the days when Mr. Lynch, as a member of the Falls Church Town Council in 1880, had hired the young Fairfax lawyer to act as the town's attorney." Mr. J. O. Martin was toastmaster and was introduced by Mayor L. P. Daniel. Captain John F. Bethune introduced Mr. Moore and he was followed by Senator John Rust of Fairfax. Charles E. Gage was Chairman of the committee which arranged the celebration. William Nathan and Sarah Ellen (Walker) Lynch had issue:

(211) Lillian Margaret Lynch, born at Falls Church, February 6, 1883, died there (in the arms of her Uncle, Charles E. Mankin) February 27, 1884. Her tombstone is in the old Falls Church yard.
(212) William Henry Lynch, born at Falls Church, February 26, 1885, married on January 2, 1943, to Mrs. Lillian (Clark) Parrott. By her first marriage to William Parrott, Mrs. Lynch was the mother of Aubrey Parrott, William Parrott, and Ruby Lee Parrott (Mrs. Carter Moss Edmonds). No issue.
(213) Cora Elizabeth Lynch, born at Falls Church, February 26, 1885 (twin to her brother William) died there May 13, 1915. She married Albert Brown Piggott. Mr. Piggott was born at Silcott Springs, Loudoun County, June 9, 1885, and died at his home in Falls Church August 4, 1947. He was a teacher at McKinley High School in Washington, D. C., for 41 years. Issue:
(2131) Willard R. Piggott.
(2132) Harold Lynch Piggott, married Evelyn Elizabeth Hess.
(2133) Evelyn Piggot, married B. Franklin Good.
(214) Talbott Lynch, born at Falls Church January 15, 1887, married and died young. Talbott and Gertrude (Farrell) Lynch had issue:
(2141) Eleanor R. Lynch.
(2142) Mary Margaret Lynch.
(2143) William W. Lynch.

(22) Ann Valinda Lynch, daughter of William Henry Greenbury and Elizabeth Ellen (Lightfoot) Lynch, was born at "Hill House" Falls Church, December 14, 1860, and died at her "Home House," Falls Church, February 7, 1925. She married on December 20, 1881 at Dulin Chapel by the Reverend Presley B. Smith to Charles Edward Mankin. (*See Mankin*).

(23) Ellen Elizabeth Lynch, daughter of William Henry Greenbury and Elizabeth Ellen (Lightfoot) Lynch, was born at "Hill House," Falls Church, December 14, 1863, and died in Washington, D. C., February 7, 1936. She married in Dulin Chapel, October 25, 1893 to William Newton Payne. Mr. Payne was a native of Fairfax County, born February 12, 1853, son of William and Lavinia M. Payne. Mr. Payne died January 29, 1921 in Washington, D. C. Both are buried in Oakwood Cemetery. Issue:

(231) William Newton Payne, Jr., born April 18, 1894. Married, November 6, 1920 to Blanche Darby. Mrs. Payne was born March 13, 1894. Mr. Payne was director of the East Washington Savings Bank, of the Washington

Mechanic's Mortgage Company, and maintained other extended commercial and financial interests. Mr. Payne was affiliated with many organizations, including the Masonic Lodge, and a communicant of the Episcopal Church. William Newton and Blanche (Darby) Payne had issue:
    (2311) William Newton Payne, 3d, born in August, 1922, lived 3 days.
    (2312) Blanche Payne, born December 13, 1924, married on May 29, 1948 to Captain Robert Bruce Codling of Detroit.
    (2313) William Darby Payne, born July 18, 1927, married on June 3, 1950 in Metropolitan Memorial Church, Washington, D.C., to Mary Jane Costenbader, daughter of Mr. and Mrs. Benjamin W. Costenbader.
(232) Ellen Elizabeth Payne was born March 8, 1896. She married William Hancock Gaskins, born January 12, 1895. Issue:
    (2321) Elizabeth Ann Gaskins born March 10, 1923, married on June 19, 1948 to Dr. William Lordi of New York.
    (2322) Richard Hancock Gaskins born January 2, 1925.
    (2323) William Payne Gaskins born September 13, 1926, married in 1947 to Sally Fielder.
(233) John Nathan Payne, born December 23, 1897. Married in May, 1927 to Elsie Arnold. She was born September 5, 1898. Both Mr. and Mrs. Payne are active in Trinity Methodist Church, McLean, where Mr. Payne served as treasurer from 1933 until 1953. Issue:
    (2331) Jean Arnold Payne, born June 24, 1931.
    (2332) Betty Lou Payne, born May 21, 1936.
(234) Minnie Amelia Payne, born November 25, 1903. She married on February 16, 1929 to Don B. Thomas. Mr. Thomas was born April 22, 1902, son of Joseph Burns and Mary Charlotte (Cooper) Thomas. Issue:
    (2341) Shirley Jane Thomas, born January 3, 1933, married on October 20, 1951 to William Robert Taylor.
    (2342) Donna Lynch Thomas, born September 17, 1938.

---

[1] Letter from Norman C. Lynch, June 20, 1956.
[2] Nathan Lynch, then a child, would sit on the fence at Clover's field (the site of Brown's Store) and count the Union soldiers as they went by, and tell his father. This information was passed on to Confederate authorities.

---

## THE MABEN FAMILY

The Mabens came to Falls Church in 1885. Three brothers came here from Milford, Michigan: William, Alex, and Peter Maben. They represented an old Scottish family and the original spelling of their surname was Mayben. Pete Maben was the local barber for many years.

William Maben served in the Union Army, Second Michigan Cavalry, during the War Between the States. He married Eliza A. Bournes (Burns), who was born in Milford in 1851 and died in 1894. They were married on December 8, 1875.[1] The Mabens were good citizens and members of Columbia Baptist Church. Issue:

    (1) Walter Maben, served in the first District of Columbia Volunteers during the Spanish-American War and participated in the Battle of the Philippines. Mr. Maben was twice married and in 1954 was living in Sixes, Oregon.

    (2) George W. Maben, died 1924. Mr. Maben served in the Spanish-American War

and World War I. He married Cora E. Barr, daughter of John and Isabella Barr, who was born in Washington, D.C., in 1883, and died September 25, 1957. At her death she was survived by eight children, fifteen grandchildren and eleven great-grandchildren. Issue: Blanche (Maben) Eldridge; Dorothy (Maben) Bowler; Isabella (Maben) Herl; Helen (Maben) Thompson; Catherine (Maben) Nixon; George W. Maben; John Maben; and Edward Maben.

(3) Frank Burns Maben, born May 9, 1882, died at Falls Church on May 27, 1954. He was survived by his wife, Elizabeth. No issue.

(4) William Maben, Jr.

(5) Nellie Maben, married —— Albertson.

(6) Janette Maben, married Earl Richie.

(7) Margaret Maben, married a cousin named Maben and was living in Seattle, Washington, in 1954.

(8) May Maben, died young.

---

[1] *Fairfax Herald,* February 23, 1894.

## THE MANKIN FAMILY

Two brothers, Charles Edward and George William Mankin, settled in Falls Church after the War Between the States. They were pioneer business men of the town and settled here about 1870.[1]

The first American ancestor of this family was Colonel Stephen Mankin, who came from Scotland and settled at Port Tobacco, Charles County, Maryland before 1682. He married Mary Barker, daughter of Captain John Barker of "Barker's Rest," Charles County. On March 24, 1687, a survey is recorded for a tract of land purchased by Mr. Mankin called "Mankin's Adventure." Stephen Mankin died in 1698, and an Inventory of his estate was filed July 22, 1698. In a deposition made in 1701, Mary wife of James Stigalier gives her age as 40 years, thus giving her a birth date of 1661. Mary (Barker) Mankin married (3rd) to James Stigalier. She died in 1714. Her second husband was Thomas Howard who died after a few months. Stephen and Mary (Barker) Mankin had issue nine children: Elizabeth Mankin, born June 22, 1682; Stephen Mankin, Jr., born July 4, 1685, died 1747, married Margaret Clayton; John Mankin, born January 6, 1686; Margaret Mankin, born March 20, 1688, married John Chapman; Josias Mankin born January 18, 1690, died March 6, 1729; Mary Mankin born January 9, 1692; Hope Mankin, born January 9, 1694, married John Capshaw; James Mankin (twin of Hope) born January 9, 1694, married Jane Wood; and Tubman Mankin, born April 9, 1696, died 1747, married Jane Yopp.

James Mankin, son of Colonel Stephen and Mary (Barker) Mankin, was born at "Mankin's Adventure," January 9, 1694, and died at his plantation, "Barker's Rest," about 1752. He married Jane Wood, daughter of Colonel John Wood and Margaret (Philpot). Her father, Colonel John Wood, lived in Maryland, but purchased 2,960 acres of land in Prince William County, Virginia, in 1678, which he repatented in 1696, fearing a defective title. Captain Mark Matthews Mankin, his grandson, inherited 260 acres of this land. The will of Jane (Wood) Mankin is dated August 30, 1759, probated November 10, 1763, in Charles County. In it she mentions her daughter Elizabeth Walless (Wallace), her grandson James Mankin; her granddaughters Lydia Musgrove Mankin and Sarah Mankin (daughters of Mark Matthews

Mankin); her granddaughter Lucy Chandler; and her son Mark M. Mankin. Mark Matthews Mankin was Executor, and witnesses were Thomas Posey, Richard Cox, and Joseph Crimand.

Captain Mark Matthews Mankin, a son of James and Jane (Wood) Mankin, died at his home "Deep Hole," near Dumfries, Prince William County, in 1797. Captain Mankin settled in Virginia on part of the Wood estate. He also acquired "Deep Hole," and large tracts of land in the Woodbridge-Dumfries area of Prince William County. Captain Mankin also owned land in Loudoun County. He married Elizabeth Ann Wood, daughter of Sir John Wood of Gloucester, England, heir to an estate of several million dollars. This estate was not fully settled until after 1860. Their children were: James Wood Mankin, died unmarried; Sarah Mankin, died unmarried; Lydia Musgrove Mankin, married (1) S. Allen Puckett and (2) John Isemonger; Elizabeth Ann Mankin, married James Weedon; and Colonel Benjamin Musgrove Mankin, married Catherine Lewis French.

Colonel Benjamin Musgrove Mankin lived at "Deep Hole" on the Potomac and had a town house in Dumfries and Occoquan. The following was published in a Baltimore paper many years ago:

"Most of that part of Virginia (Dumfries) was the scene of gayety and festivity, the abode of wealthy merchants from Scotland who made it a city like that one in the mother country. Now in ruins, almost as completely as the old (Episcopal) church (nearby). Quantico Creek through which the trade from Europe came is now filled up with pines which also cover the spot where the church once stood... Dumfries was the home of Colonel Benjamin Mankin, his father living with him in his old age, who formerly lived at 'Deep Hole.' ... given him by his Grandfather John Wood of Maryland."

Colonel Mankin's wife, nee Catherine Lewis French, was a descendant of Colonel Daniel French, immigrant to Old Point Comfort in 1660, and of the Lewis and the King Carter families. Issue:

Margaret Fields Mankin, married a cousin, Samuel Lewis; Lewis French Mankin of "Creighton," Loudoun County, married Fannie Cockerille, daughter of Judge Cockerille of Loudoun County; Mark Matthews Mankin of Alexandria, married Elizabeth Ann May; Benjamin Musgrove Mankin, Jr., unmarried; James Wood Mankin, of "Rock Hill," Loudoun County, married Christiana M. Moore; William Barbour Mankin, married (1) Susan Ann Thurman and (2) Hulda H. Warring; Elizabeth Ann Musgrove Mankin, unmarried; Anna (Nancy) Mankin, married Isaac Florance of Prince William; Catherine French Mankin, unmarried; Jane Philpot Mankin, married (Honorable) Richard Nixon; and John Wood Mankin, married (1) Virginia Adeline Delaway, daughter of Admiral Delaway, and (2) Mrs. Mary Ann (Bentley) Miller.

Mark Matthews Mankin, son of Colonel Benjamin Musgrove and Catherine Lewis (French) Mankin, was born at "Deep Hole," Prince William County, March 3, 1805. Mr. Mankin died at "Creighton," in Loudoun County, November 30, 1865, and was buried in the old Presbyterian Cemetery at Alexandria. He married, by the Reverend W. C. Walton, in Prince William January 31, 1830, to Elizabeth Ann May. In the Family Bible he wrote of this day: "a day memorable for the organization of the Presbyterian Church at Occoquan." Mrs. Mankin was born in Chesterfield County, Virginia, November 23, 1811, a daughter of the Honorable Edward Arthur and Mary Edwards (Hodges) May, and died at her home, 325 South Lee Street, Alexandria,

September 20, 1900. Her father, the Honorable Edward A. May, was a wealthy land holder and owned many slaves. He was born in Plymouth, England, May 9, 1786, at "fifteen minutes after six o'clock in the evening," and died at his home in Alexandria, Wednesday morning, September 6, 1837. He married three times, his first wife whom he married in Chesterfield County April 7, 1808, was known as "Polly." Mary Edwards (Hodges) May was born in Chesterfield County September 21, 1792, daughter of Colonel James and Martha (Ashbrook) Hodges. She died December 28, 1812. Her ancestors were in Virginia by 1608. Mrs. Elizabeth (May) Mankin was a great-granddaughter of Sir Arthur and Ann May of England.

Mark Matthews Mankin was a Contractor in Alexandria. His partner in business was James Fadeley, father of Dr. George B. Fadeley who settled in Falls Church. He was associated with public affairs in Alexandria (where he settled in 1831) and was highly esteemed. Mr. Mankin attended the old Presbyterian Church in that City. Mark Matthews and Elizabeth Ann (May) Mankin had issue: James Hodges Mankin, born December 7, 1830, died May 9, 1833; Mary Elizabeth Mankin born September 27, 1832, died May 5, 1833; Alec Alexander Mankin, born June 20, 1834, died August 22, 1910, married Mariah E. Tucker; Barbara Ellen Mankin, born September 16, 1836, died April 8, 1862; Charles Edward Mankin, born July 24, 1839, died September 13, 1903, married Ann Valinda Lynch; Samuel Ashbrook Mankin, born December 20, 1841 married Phoebe Littlefield; George William Mankin, born June 9, 1844, died June 10, 1914, married Lucy A. Houchins; Ann Elizabeth Mankin, born September 7, 1846, died September 28,1853; Benjamin Acquilla Mankin, born May 13, 1849, died 1926, married Fanny Moore; Catherine Clay Mankin, born July 20, 1852, died June 3, 1862; and James Lewis Mankin, born April 11, 1855, died August 11, 1858.

Charles Edward Mankin, mentioned above, settled in Falls Church. He was married by the Reverend Presley B. Smith at Dulin Chapel, December 20, 1881, to Ann Valinda Lynch, the daughter of William Henry Greenbury and Elizabeth Ellen (Lightfoot) Lynch. She was born at "Hill House," in Falls Church, December 14, 1860 and died at her "Home House" on West Broad Street February 7, 1925. The following clipping is pasted in the May-Mankin Bible:

"Mr. Charles E. Mankin, formerly of Alexandria, but at present conducting a bakery, toy and confectionery store at Falls Church, having lived in single blessedness so long that his friends looked upon him as a confirmed celibate, has finally realized that it is not good for man to live alone and has taken to wife Miss Valinda Lynch of Falls Church, daughter of William H. Lynch, deceased. They were married on the 20th instant at Dulin Chapel at Falls Church."

Mr. Mankin was tutored in the private school of Bishop Whittle (of the Episcopal Church) at Alexandria. At the outbreak of the War Between the States he enlisted in the Mount Vernon Guards of the 17th Virginia Regiment, C.S.A. He served with distinction during the war, and was wounded. He participated in several battles, including those of Bull Run and Manassas (Second Manassas), Chancellorsville, Bloody Angle, Seven Days Fight around Richmond, Battle of Seven Pines and the Battle of Fredericksburg. He saw Stonewall Jackson shot by his own men. He was captured at Dinwiddie Court House, March 31, 1865, and put in Point Lookout (Maryland) prison. Mr. Mankin was released from military prison on May 22, 1865.

Mr. Mankin was a kind and generous man, greatly beloved by all who knew him. He was an ardent Odd Fellow and was one of the founders of the Lodge at Falls Church.

He held every office in that organization. Mr. Mankin contributed generously to the needy, and contributed to the various church functions in the community. A familiar record is this one of January 24, 1892: (Dulin Chapel) "C. E. Mankin $25.00 building fund." He was appointed Post Master at Falls Church August 27, 1885, and served until 1889. The first Post Office building in the community was built with his own funds. He wrote the following letter to Edmund Flagg (who wanted Mr. Mankin to endorse Minor Chamblin as Post Master at the new branch office at West End):

"Falls Church, Va.
August 24th/87

Mr. Flagg,
Dear Sir:
I have carefully read your letter and I cannot understand it. I have never informed the P.O. Department by writing or any other way anything in regard to you having a Post Office at West End, nor have I said anything against it to anyone nor have I talked about it. I will say to you now as I have said before that I am satisfied for the people at West End to have a Post Office, and at the same time I don't think I have any right to have anything to say about it, as I am Post Master at this place. What the Citizens here say and do I am not responsible for. While I am Post Master at Falls Church I do not intend to come in contact with the wishes of the people, I am their servant and must please them all alike to the best of my ability. I will say further that I could not endorse Mr. Chamblin.

With all due respect to you, I remain,

Yours Respectfully,
Charles E. Mankin."

The following is his obituary from the Washington, D.C., *Evening Star* of September 17, 1903:

### "Charles E. Mankin Is Dead

Mr. Charles E. Mankin, the well known, beloved and respected dry-goods merchant of Falls Church died on September 14, of a heart disease. Mr. Mankin has been sick for several months and for several weeks had been rapidly failing so that his death was not unexpected. He expired in the arms of his faithful wife, who has been so devoted to him during his long sickness, unselfishly ministering to his every comfort.

Although a severe sufferer, he was uncomplaining, insisting even to the last that he was not seriously ill. His funeral was held at the M. E. Church, South, on Tuesday, Reverend W. H. Woolf, the pastor officiating. The funeral was in charge of the Falls Church Lodge of Odd Fellows and the bearers were all members of that order. A large number of the members of that order were present to pay their last tribute of respect to their highly esteemed brother, and participated in the beautiful and impressive funeral services of that order. Probably no man in the lodge was so universally beloved and no member of the order has worked so hard and faithfully for the organization, and one of the best monuments to his memory is the hall erected almost entirely by his indefatigable efforts, and owned by the Odd Fellows lodge of this place. He has been honored with every position in the lodge and his wise and conservative counsel was sought in lodge matters on all occasions.

The floral offerings of the lodge, and friends were profuse, and beautiful. Mr. Mankin was 64 years of age and is survived by a wife and five children, who have the sympathy of the entire community in their bereavement. Mr. Mankin was a kind and

generous man, ever ready to minister to the wants of the poor and the distressed.
He will be greatly missed by the community. The interment was in Oakwood Cemetery."

The following is the obituary of Mrs. Mankin from the *Evening Star* of February 9, 1925:

"*Mrs. Charles Mankin Is Dead*
*Falls Church Woman Was Widow of Merchant—Funeral Tomorrow*

*Special Dispatch of the Star*—Falls Church, Virginia—February 9.
Funeral services for Mrs. A. V. Mankin who died Saturday night after a long illness will be held at the family residence tomorrow afternoon at 2 o'clock. Burial will be in Oakwood Cemetery.

Mrs. Mankin was the widow of Charles E. Mankin, a merchant here, and after his death continued the business as long as her health would permit.

Four children survive: Mrs. Herbert Hirst, Mrs. Clarence Hirst, Mrs. E. A. Hildebrand, and Charles Mankin.

The business which Mrs. Mankin conducted was sold to her son-in-law Clarence M. Hirst and later to E. A. Hildebrand. Mrs. Mankin was organist of the M. E. Church, South for a number of years and took an active part in all church work, aiding the sick and suffering in many ways.

She also was a member of the Robert E. Lee Chapter, United Daughters of the Confederacy."

The Mankin "Home House" in Falls Church was across from the Odd Fellows Hall. It was built in 1897 by Mr. Mankin as a gift for his wife. The ground on which it was built was part of the Big Chimney estate of the Thompson family, and was given to Mrs. Mankin by her mother, Mrs. W. H. G. Lynch. Mrs. Lynch received it by the will of her maternal Uncle, Nathan Thompson, Esq. George Simms was the Architect of the house. He also designed another house on the same plan, the Evans House across from the Rowan home on North Washington Street. The house had a steep roof and wide porch. It was originally painted a "Virginia Mode" (light gray) with dark grey trim. The shutters and roof were green. The house was opened for several weeks in the summer of 1897 to be inspected by those interested, as it was considered "modern" for its day. In 1899 George Brunner built the summer kitchen wing and the back-side porch.

The old "Mankin's Notions & Dry Goods" store on the corner was sold to Clarence M. Hirst, who sold it to his brother-in-law, E. A. Hildebrand. Mr. Hildebrand sold it in 1928 to Dr. Macon Ware and Carroll V. Shreve for an estimated $12,000. It was torn down in 1937.

Charles Edward and Ann Valinda (Lynch) Mankin had issue:

(1) Ellen Elizabeth Mankin, born April 7, 1883. Married Herbert Nelson Hirst. The author's grandparents. (*See Hirst*).

(2) Clinton Edward Mankin, born at Falls Church January 14, 1884, died there May 9, 1918, unmarried. Mr. Mankin was a member of the Falls Church Odd Fellows Lodge. He was a musician, and played the piano in the first motion picture theatre in Washington, D. C.

(3) Mary Marguerite Mankin, born at Falls Church, March 10, 1888, died March 12, 1891.

(4) Linda May Mankin, born at Falls Church, May 30, 1889, married Clarence Marshall Hirst (*See Hirst*).

(5) Ruth Cackley Mankin, born at Falls Church, April 14, 1898, married on May 26, 1924, at Mt. Vernon Place Methodist Church, Washington, D. C., to Edgar Allen Hildebrand. Mr. Hildebrand was born June 6, 1894, son of the Reverend Simpson Vietch and Lelia (Guy) Hildebrand. Mr. Hildebrand died at his home, 110 Little Falls Street, September 27, 1947. No issue.

(6) Charles Guy Mankin, born at Falls Church, June 28, 1901. Married on March 12, 1934 to Blanche Woodrow Miller of Staunton. Issue:
   (61) Blanche Ann Mankin, born August 31, 1944.
   (62) Charles Granville Mankin, born March 13, 1949.

George William Mankin, son of Mark Matthews and Elizabeth Ann (May) Mankin of Alexandria, Va., was a Contractor and Merchant in Falls Church. He was a prominent Mason, a member of Andrew Jackson Lodge in Alexandria, later a member of Kemper Lodge in Falls Church, of which he was one of the founders. He founded "Mankin's Pharmacy" at Falls Church, which was conducted by a son, Dr. George T. Mankin. He built ten or twelve houses in Falls Church, including the Keith House. George William and Lucy A. (Houchins) Mankin had issue:

(1) William Arthur Mankin, disappeared in the west. He married Elizabeth Guy and had issue:
   (11) Lucy Mankin, died unmarried.
   (12) Guy Mark Mankin, resides in Atlanta, Ga. Mr. Mankin married Helen Douglas. Mrs. Helen Douglas Mankin was a lawyer, and a member of the Georgia General Assembly, 1937-46. She was a member of the U. S. Congress, 1945-47. Issue:
      (121) Guy Mark Mankin, Jr.

(2) (Dr.) George Tyree Mankin, born at Falls Church in 1871. He attended Business College in Washington, D.C. and studied Pharmacy. Dr. Mankin served as President of the Virginia State Pharmaceutical Association. He was Clerk of the Falls Church Town Council. Mr. Mankin also served on the Board of Directors of the Falls Church Bank during its early years, and was one of the Board of Control of Thirteen of the Falls Church Library. He was a member and official member of the Falls Church Presbyterian Church. Dr. Mankin was a Fire Warden of the First Ward in 1904. He served for many years as the only Notary Public in the town. He served in that connection in the noted Murray-Bean case in Texas with Dr. M.E. Church. Dr. Mankin married Susan Davidson, daughter of Dr. Robert Allen Davidson, who served for many years as pastor of the Falls Church Presbyterian Church. He died March 9, 1918. Dr. Mankin was a prominent Mason, and affiliated with Kemper Lodge at Falls Church on May 25, 1896. He served as Fourth Master of the Lodge, succeeding W. L. Gordon in 1899. He served as District Deputy Grand Master of Masons in Virginia. Issue:
   (21) Robert Mankin.

[1] The author has found among his family papers a "Chain of Title" note of the Charles and George Mankin property which begins in January, 1833, with deed Reintzell to Mills; January, '43, Mills to Newton; May, '45, Newton to Poor; April, '46, Poor to Townshend; Oct., '47, Townshend to Steele; April, '51 Steele to Cranson; Dec., '51, Cranson to Clover; March, '75 Clover to Mankin; June, 1889, Mankin to Prigg. Thus the Mankins purchased their property in March, 1875.

## THE MARR FAMILY

James F. Marr (1827-1910) of Maryland, a real estate dealer and land owner, married twice, and resided in Falls Church. His second wife was Mary Jane Orr (1839-1914) of Pennsylvania. Both are buried in Oakwood Cemetery. Mr. Marr was of Scottish ancestry, and related to families of this name in Fauquier County, Virginia.[1] Children:

(*By first wife*):

(1) James S. Marr, married Mae Atherton, daughter of Dr. Atherton, and had two daughters and a son. Atherton Marr, the son, is a lawyer in California.

(*By second wife*):

(2) Walter Marr, eldest of this marriage.

(3) Lydia F. Marr (Lettie) (1865-1934) died unmarried.

(4) Townson O. Marr (1871-1951) married Carrie Hogan (1863-1947) daughter of Dr. Peter Hogan of Falls Church. Issue:
(41) Donald Townson Marr (who married and had issue: Barbara Marr and Kathleen Marr).

(5) Joseph H. Marr (1880-1924) married Ethel M. Payne, daughter of John D. Payne. She operated the first telephone switch-board in Falls Church. Mrs. Marr died September 17, 1958, age 75 years. Issue:
(51) James Marr.
(52) Joseph Hendricks Marr.

(6) Ralph H. Marr (1873-Nov. 10, 1948) married Mary Thorne (who married (1) James Poole).

(7) Stanley Marr, married Ethelyn Virginia Williams of "Cedar Hill," Charlottesville. Mrs. Marr is the daughter of Captain Quintius L. Williams, C.S.A., and his wife Virginia (Fitz) Williams, and a granddaughter of George Lindsay and Mary L. (Lindsay) Williams. No issue.

(8) Sarah Ellen Marr, married on January 6, 1898 at Dulin Chapel to William T. Sprankle.

(9) Carrie Marr, married —— Morris.

(10) Jane Marr.

---

[1] The following is a copy of the inscription on the Marr monument at Fairfax Court House: "This stone marks the scene of the opening conflict of the War of 1861-1865, when John Q. Marr, Captain of the Warrenton Rifles, who was the first soldier killed in action, fell 800 ft. S. 46° W., (mag.) of this spot, June 1st, 1861. Erected by Marr Camp, C.V. June 1, 1904." John Quincy Marr was a native of Fauquier County.

## THE McCAULEY FAMILY

William McCauley came to this country from County Kerry, Ireland, in 1844 with the Carlins, Monihans, and others. He landed in Boston, and moved to Connecticut.[1] After a short time the McCauleys moved to Washington, D.C., and later purchased a farm in the Pimmitt gorge (now Pimmitt Hill) at West Falls Church. The original home site is now the home of a descendant, Mrs. David Leonard, adjacent to St. Luke's Methodist Church. The present house was built of scrap lumber from Union camps and was erected following the War. William McCauley was a farmer and died at age 93 years. He is buried in St. James Cemetery.

William McCauley had issue:[2]
(1) Daniel McCauley, married Margery Carlin.
(2) John McCauley.
(3) William McCauley (Jr.), married Mrs. Mary (Monihan) Galleher, widow.
(4) Barbara McCauley, married David Patterson.
(5) Nancy McCauley, married Robert Nelson.

(1) Daniel McCauley, son of William McCauley, was born in County Kerry, Ireland, and married there to Margery Carlin[3]. They came in 1844 with the rest of the family, and their daughter, Ann Elizabeth, was born on the ship bound for Boston. Mr. McCauley is buried in Georgetown, D. C. Children:
  (11) Ann Elizabeth McCauley married Lemuel Franklin Mills. (*See Mills.*)
  (12) Mary McCauley (I), died at about 3 years of age in Connecticut, killed in some accident, details unknown:
  (13) Daniel L. McCauley, married Rachel Dugan.
  (14) William McCauley, born in Connecticut, died at Falls Church, unmarried[4].
  (15) Mary McCauley (II), married Preston Sewell.
  (16) John McCauley, died in infancy during the War Between the States (born and died at Falls Church)[5].
  (17) (1.10)—four others, died in infancy.

(12) Mary McCauley, daughter of Daniel and Margery (Carlin) McCauley (second child named Mary, the first having died young), was born in the Falls Church home-place. She married Preston Sewell. Children:
(121) Marie Alice Sewell, married Joseph Bernard Parker.
(122) Wilbur Joseph Sewell, married Cora Leigh.

(13) Daniel L. McCauley, son of Daniel and Margery (Carlin) McCauley, was born in the Falls Church home-place. He married Rachel Dugan (1856-1902) who is buried in St. James Cemetery. Children:
(131) Mary E. McCauley, married David Leonard. (*See Leonard.*)
(132) Ethel McCauley, became a Nun, Sister Mary Elizabeth.
(133) L. Willard McCauley, married Agnes Adams.

(3) William McCauley, Jr., son of William McCauley, was born in County Kerry, Ireland, and died at his Falls Church home at age 80 years. He is buried in St. James Cemetery. Mr. McCauley married Mrs. Mary (Monihan) Galleher, widow. She was born in 1807 in County Donegal, Ireland, and died at Falls Church, January 31, 1885, age 78 years. Burial was in St. James Cemetery. By her first marriage Mrs. McCauley was the mother of two Galleher daughters. One married a Carlin, the other (Eleanor?) married Ormsbee. The Galleher-Ormsbee marriage produced Mary Ellen Ormsbee (died March 8, 1934), who married John Alexander Binns (October 1, 1858-December 14, 1934) of "Green Ridge Farm," Fairfax County, a son of Charles Alexander and Mary Eleanor (Gantt) Binns, scion of the old Leesburg family of that name. John Alexander Binns and Mary Ellen Ormsbee were married in Georgetown, D.C., February 20, 1881. There is a tombstone in Arnon Cemetery, Forestville, to Mary F. Ormsbee. A reading of it, in the D.A.R. Library, apparently incorrect, gives this data: born May 15, 1831, died April 21, 1904, age 45 years.

William McCauley, Jr., and Mary (Monihan) McCauley had issue:
(31) Annie M. McCauley, unmarried (1854-1939), buried in St. James Cemetery. (There were probably others, but no record is available.)[6]

---

[1] Daniel McCauley Mills, age 91, stated (5/16/64) that his mother, daughter of Daniel and Margery (Carlin) McCauley, often stated that the family would have remained in Ireland had they been able to obtain enough "bread and clabber" to eat. The government confiscated their crops for two seasons, leaving them in a starving condition. This was during the terrible potato famine.
[2] Several of these children were adults when the family left Ireland.
[3] The Carlins settled at El Nido (Chesterbrook), some of them later buying land on the east side of Pimmitt Run (in more recent years the Redd home on the corner of Lemon Road and Leesburg Pike. According to Mrs. Arthur H. Scheid (5/16/64), the following were brothers and sisters in the Carlin family: Margery, married Daniel McCauley; Catherine, married John Peyton; William, married Mary Gleason; John, married Bridget Peyton; and James, married Mary —— (Galleher?). All born in Ireland.
[4] One source stated that he married a Miss Mary Daw.
[5] This child was ill during a skirmish of several days duration. During the night the mother was not permitted a light (since this was a possible signal to the enemy). Mrs. McCauley was forced to care for little John by the fire-place, and attributed his death to the fact that she could not see properly to measure his medicine.
[6] Buried in the McCauley lot in St. James Cemetery are: John A. McCauley (August 2, 1848-July 4, 1936); Ann E. McCauley (April 30, 1865-January 1, 1949); and William McCauley, died October 21, 1896, aged 44 years.

---

## THE MERRY FAMILY

Dr. E. R. Merry was a well known citizen of Falls Church. The following is an account taken from a clipping dated November 2, 1940:

"*Death of Dr. Merry Who Recalled Siege of Washington*

Dr. Eliphalet Remington Merry, died October 23, 1940, at his residence in West Falls Church, after a short illness. He is survived by his wife, Mrs. Bruce Swinley Merry; two sons, Eliphalet Remington Merry, Jr., of Westfield, N.J., and Harry C. Merry, of Gaithersburg, Md., and two daughters, Mrs. Katherine M. Cunningham and Miss Edith Merry, of Washington.

Identified with horses since the day he took his first horseback ride alone at the age of 2, Merry since his maturity was a trainer and trader of fine pacers and trotters. He was known as the best horse-breaker from the Potomac to the Blue Ridge and in his later years was a veterinarian.

Among his clients he numbered Dr. Alexander Graham Bell, Gardner Hubbard, Senator John Henderson, Representatives, Senators, diplomats and the social leaders of the day.

In the days when the horse was king, when transportation was still largely by stage coach, when Washington was little more than a village, Dupont Circle a corn field and Alexandria the thriving business port, Merry ran a livery and sale stable in Washington. Even as a child of 6 or 7 before the war he knew many of the old bus drivers who drove the stage from Washington to Alexandria or Alexandria to the Valley of Virginia.

One of his stories is of the Winter of 1857, when the Potomac was frozen so hard that busses ran on the ice for weeks. In those days there were no street cars and Vanderwerken ran the bus line on Pennsylvania Avenue from the old B. & O. Station to the hotels and Georgetown.

Merry was born July 26, 1851, at Peach Grove, in Fairfax County, on the Alexandria-Leesburg pike, near what is now Tyson's Cross Roads. His father, a New York man, and one of the California "forty-niners," bought a 230-acre farm. On his third trip to California in 1857 he perished in the wreck of the ill-fated Central America, the steamer commanded by Capt. Herndon of Fairfax County, for whom the town of Herndon was named and whose daughter later married President Chester A. Arthur.

His mother, Mrs. Merry, was left a widow with four children to support, became postmistress and school teacher at Peach Grove, in addition to running the farm. When the Civil War broke out, the Merry farm was located in the section over which the armies of the North and South ebbed and flowed as the tide of battle changed. The Merrys were Union sympathizers, but young "Lida" Merry was employed and imprisoned by both sides without much discrimination. Many are the battles and the guerilla warfare which harried Fairfax County. His older brother, a large lad for his age, was sent North during the war. Merry, who never weighed more than 100 pounds until he was 22, was his mother's right-hand man during the four trying years when many a day they did not know where the next meal would come from.

After Lincoln's call for volunteers, 13,000 men were stationed near Falls Church, commanded by Gen. Taylor. Soon came the army marching up the Leesburg Pike, separating on the Merry farm and on to Chantilly, where the first fight of importance occurred, to Centreville, Bull Run, Manassas and Groveton. After the retreat the Merrys were between both lines for months. When McClellan's army laid in the south defense of Washington, scouting parties from both lines came every day. Merry was messenger boy, errand boy, much of the time in the saddle, shot at by both sides, often a prisoner by the Union soldiers because he was a rebel, the next night held by Mosby's men because he was a Yankee. He had passes from both armies to get to Washington.

Fairfax County, especially the section around Ayr Hill, now Vienna, prior to the war, had been settled by many Northerners, who retained their Northern affiliations. Many of them were prisoners during the war in the old Confederate prisons, Libby, Andersonville and Thunder Castle. They used to communicate with their families by sending their mail to Washington in care of Mrs. Merry, the postmistress at Peach Grove. It was young Merry's job to ride to Washington to bring out this mail in his saddle bags and later to distribute it around the neighborhood. In 1863 he was marooned in Washington and unable to get back to Virginia. At this time he acted as a Washington Star newsboy, when the old newspaper office was on Pennsylvania Avenue and Third Street. The newsboys used to carry the Philadelphia papers and the Star to the outlying camps and sell them to the soldiers. He was one of the crowd which watched the fire that later destroyed the old Star building.

After the war Mrs. Merry and her family set to work to rebuild the farm and its fences and buildings, restock it with horses and cattle. In 1871 the country was going through the second year of a drought as bad or worse than that which this section suffered last year, and young Merry turned to Washington for employment as a contractor. He states that he hauled the first load of stone that went into the War, State and Navy Building.

During the ensuing years Merry tried his hand at many occupations. With his older brother he opened a brick factory. Many of the old houses in Northern Virginia are built of brick on which is stamped the Merry name. Always interested in horses, he opened a livery and sale stable in Washington which was patronized by the town's elite, later opening a livery and blacksmith shop in Falls Church, during the Spanish-American War. He was much in demand as a breaker of horses and handled all the mean or vicious horses in the countryside. At Waterford, Va., on one occasion he broke a class of 33 horses, four of them murderers. Sometimes he had an audience of four or five hundred to watch him work. It was during this period that Merry was waylaid one night by highwaymen on Chain Bridge Road, robbed, and left for dead. He still bears the scars of that fight on his head.

He became a pupil in veterinary science, studying at night under Charles B. Michner in Washington, former head of the Bureau of Animal Industry of the U. S. Department of Agriculture. He developed a practice that called him from the Blue Ridge Mountains to Occoquan Bay, specializing in horses and cattle. He is still active in answering calls.

To his varied trades he added that of auctioneer and many of the sales of recent years have been cried by him. Until seven or eight years ago he continued to make his headquarters on the home farm and to operate it. During his short residence in the town of Falls Church he acted as postmaster at East Falls Church and served on the Town Council. Merry says that he moved to town one Thursday and the following Tuesday was informed that he had been elected.

Merry married Miss Lizzie Center, who lived on an adjoining farm and who died last year. Four children were born, Eliphalet Remington Merry, jr., whose son E. R. Merry, 3d, is now the fourth of the family to bear his great-grandfather's name: Harry C. Merry of Rockville, Mrs. Katherine Cunningham and Miss Edith Merry, both of McLean.

It was Merry's grandmother's brother, Eliphalet Remington who invented the Remington rifle and sewing machine. Merry's older brother, Phiny Case Merry, is still active at 81, living in Maryland.

Merry has been active in Republican politics in Fairfax County ever since he cast his first vote for U. S. Grant as President. He serves each election day as one of the Republican clerks at the polls, and in spite of the fact that Fairfax County has rarely gone Republican and many of his stanchest friends are members of the opposite part, Merry has held steadfast to the principles inculcated in him by Republican forebears."

## THE MILLS FAMILY

The ancestor of the Mills family of West Falls Church was Lemuel Franklin Mills,[1] who died at his home near the Great Falls about December, 1845. His widow, Mary, purchased the old Lindsay Tavern from Albert Orcutt on March 21, 1865.[2] The tavern, almost opposite present-day St. Luke's Methodist Church on Leesburg Pike, became the family residence. Mrs. Mary Mills continued to live there until her death in 1887, and her son, Frank, continued there until he sold it for $1,000 in 1890.[3]

Mrs. Mills, called the Widow Mills by her neighbors, was born Mary E. Sherwood on May 17, 1822. She was a full sister of Mrs. William Henry Ellison (nee Emily J. Sherwood).[4] The Sherwoods came from England. Mrs. Mills died at Old Tavern on June 30, 1887, and was buried in the Falls Church yard.

Of the earlier generations of the Mills family, it is thought that they were related to the family which lived at Mills Cross Roads, now Merrifield. Lemuel Franklin

Mills (who died in 1845) had a brother, John Mills, who lived in the Dranesville area, in Loudoun County. This John Mills had at least two children, a son, Whiting,[5] and a daughter, Emma.

Lemuel Franklin and Mary E. (Sherwood) Mills had issue:

(1) Henry Mills, died unmarried.

(2) John Mills, died unmarried, and is buried in the Falls Church yard. He was a cripple and made his living operating a still behind the Old Tavern (formerly Trammell's and Lindsay's).

(3) Lemuel Franklin Mills (known as L. Frank Mills), married Ann Elizabeth McCauley.

Of the above, (3) Lemuel Franklin Mills, was born a few months following his father's death, on February 2, 1846. His birth-place was the family farm near Great Falls. Mr. Mills, after a long and useful life, died at Falls Church, August 7, 1920, and is buried in St. James Cemetery. Reared an Episcopalian, he became a member of St. James Church following his marriage to Ann Elizabeth McCauley. Mrs. Mills was born on board ship bound for Boston from Ireland, October 21, 1844. She was a daughter of Daniel and Margery (Carlin) McCauley formerly of County Kerry, Ireland. Mrs. Mills died at her Falls Church home on September 26, 1928.

Lemuel Franklin and Ann Elizabeth (McCauley) Mills had issue:

(31) Daniel McCauley Mills, married Annie Shea.

(32) William E. Mills, born December 30, 1875, died January 31, 1894.[6]

(33) John Edward Mills (Eddie), born January 31, 1877, died unmarried, April 12, 1903.

(34) Eugene Francis Mills, married (1) Lena Arnold; and (2) Anna Scherb.

(35) Mary Blanche Mills, married Arthur Henry Scheid.

(36) Joseph Julian Mills, born March 21 (or 22), 1885, died February 12, 1933. Married Blanche Money of Lewinsville.

(37) Matthew Mills, born March 21, 1887, living 1964, married Ruth Searle.

(38) Carlin Mills, born November 21, 1889, died September 20, 1891.

(39) Ray Peter Mills, born December 22, 1893, living, 1964, married Mae Howard.

(31) Daniel McCauley Mills, son of Lemuel Franklin and Ann Elizabeth (McCauley) Mills, was born in the Old Tavern on April 1, 1874. He is living, in good health, at the age of 91 years, within a short distance of his birth-place.[7] Mr. Mills served for fifty-nine years as Clerk and Judge of Elections at Lick Precinct.[8] During some of this time he was assistant to his father, who held the same office for many years. The father continued to work at the polls until his death. Mr. Mills, affectionately known as "Mac," has lived his entire life span within a mile or two of his birth-place. In 1903 he purchased, at fifteen dollars an acre, a farm of 320 acres from R.L.B. Clark.[9] He farmed this land, selling/some of it as the years passed. The George Marshall School is now on the remaining fifty acres, and Mr. Mills still retains about four acres.

Mr. Mills married Annie M. Shea (who died March 22, 1958). They had the following children: Annie, married William Monch; Margery, married William Feaster; Raymond E., married Juanita Weathers; Francis A., married Jessie Clark; Nellie, married (1) Ralph Anderson, and (2) Charles Bowman; and James J. Mills.

(34) Eugene Francis Mills, son of Lemuel Franklin and Ann Elizabeth (McCauley) Mills, was born at Old Tavern, November 16, 1879, and died August 15, 1951. He

married (1) Lena Arnold of Merrifield (sister of Chris Arnold); and (3) Anna Scherb. By his first wife Mr. Mills had issue a son, Cornelius Paul Mills who married Gertrude Nichols. By his second marriage, issue: Margaret, married Eugene Wood; and Frances Anne, married Abrasom Legg.

(35) Mary Blanche Mills, daughter of Lemuel Franklin and Ann Elizabeth (McCauley) Mills, was born at Old Tavern (the last of her family born there) November 11, 1881, and is living at the family home on Leesburg Pike at West Falls Church. As a young woman, and prior to her marriage, Mary Blanche Mills taught in the Ford School. She married Arthur Henry Scheid who was born in St. Louis, July 1, 1881, son of Philip and Augusta (Krentzer) Scheid. Mr. Scheid is living. Issue: (351) (Colonel) *Arthur Mills Scheid*, born in Cherrydale, Virginia, April 16, 1911, and married Elsie (Polly) *Nolte*. Children: Mary Christine and Richard Arthur Scheid. (352) William Edwin Scheid, Post Master of Falls Church, born December 23, 1914, married Carolyn *Adair*. Children: Suzann Carolyn ( a Registered Nurse); Nancy Jean, Teresa Ann, William Edwin and Joan-Ellen Scheid.

---

[1] There is a record in Fairfax Court of J. C. Gunnell, "Curator of the estates of Whiting Mills, deceased and Ruth Mills Scott, deceased." This shows that William, Robert, John, Henry, Peter, Alexander, Edward, and Lemuel Mills were children of Lemuel Mills, deceased. It may be, but the records are not clear, that Sarah Ann Rigg, Whiting Mills and Ruth Scott were also children. This record is dated February 13, 1854. The *Death Records* on file at Fairfax reveals that Peter Mills died May 26, 1855 in Fairfax County, aged 54 years. He was a son of Daniel & Sarah Mills and his wife, Cynthia S. Mills reported his death. He was a farmer. It is apparent that he was connected in some way with this family.

[2] Fairfax County, *Deed Book E #4*, page 329.

[3] Details from an interview with D. M. Mills, 5/16/64.

[4] Mr. Ellison's first wife was Elizabeth Fish. She had a sister who married a Sherwood.

[5] The following stones in Chestnut Grove Cemetery, Herndon, are inscribed to members of this family: Whiting A. Mills (April 11, 1854-January 10, 1923); and Ella A. Mills (August 13, 1856-February 23, 1927).

[6] William E. Mills, "gentleWillie," was killed when his horse shied at the Old Dominion train passing the crossing at West Falls Church. Miss Ada Walker, an eye-witness, gave the author some details of this tragic event in an interview with her on March 9, 1961. Miss Ada was on her way to Washington, D.C., to Woods School, and with her was Arthur Flagg, enroute to High School. Miss Ada and Arthur saw the horse jump and the buggy turned over, striking Willie on the skull. The two ran, hand-in-hand to aid Willie. It was too late—for their friend, dear and gentle Willie, had a crushed skull. It was a terrible shock to them. Miss Ada would ride on the sleigh with Arthur and Willie since they did not throw her off like the other boys. Both boys were close friends. Arthur ran to Ellison's Store, where there was a telephone, and telephoned Dr. Gott. One of the men in the store went for Mr. Mills. Even after all these years this tragedy still lingers in the minds of many who knew and loved Willie Mills.

[7] In an interview, May 16, 1964, Mr. Mills gave the author many interesting details of the Pimmitt neighborhood.

[8] Lick Precinct originally a voting place for the entire area west of Falls Church, was the scene of a number of heated political debates. Votes were cast in the Old Tavern from the time it was owned by the Lindsay family until the 1920's when it moved to Idylwood.

[9] Clark, wealthy resident on Capitol Hill in Washington, purchased a farm of 620 acres in 1866. He continued to live in his large brick mansion in the city, visiting his farm some during the summer months. In 1884 he sold 300 acres which became Dunn Loring. Mac Mills purchased the remaining 320 acres.

---

## THE MINOR FAMILY

The first American ancestor of this old family is said to have been Meindort Doodes, a sea captain, born in Holland. Doodes was naturalized in Virginia in 1673 as Minor Doodes. His eldest son, naturalized at the same time by the House of Burgesses, took the name Doodes Minor. This reversal of name was a Dutch practice.

John Minor, perhaps of this family, died in Westmoreland County in 1698. He made his will on March 30, 1697, probated February 22, 1698. His wife, Eleanor, survived him. John and Eleanor Minor had issue: Nicholas Minor, married Jemima Waddy; William Minor, John Minor, Jr., Frances Minor and Elizabeth Minor.

Nicholas Minor, son of John and Eleanor Minor, was the eldest son. He died in Westmoreland County in 1743, having acquired a large estate. Minor served as Justice in the years 1680/95. His wife was Mrs. Jemima (Waddy) (Spence) Pope, who married (1st) John Spence, and (2nd) Lawrence Pope. Issue:

(1) William Stewart Minor, deceased by 1759.
(2) (Captain) Nicholas Minor, married Frances Spence.
(3) John Minor, married Jemima Moxley.
(4) Stewart Minor.
(5) Elizabeth Minor, married —— Wherret.

Of the above children, Captain Nicholas Minor was a Justice of Westmoreland County in 1745, and was Captain of the Fairfax County Militia in 1758. He moved on to Loudoun County where he died. In September, 1757, Minor laid out a town, named Georgetown, on a tract of land surrounding his tavern at what was known as "Minor's." This became the Town of Leesburg, laid off in 67 lots. Captain Minor sold most of his lots between February and March, 1758.

Captain Minor served as a Justice of Loudoun County in 1770, an office later held by his son, John Minor.

Captain Nicholas and Frances (Spence) Minor had issue:

(21) John Minor, "the Elder," married and had at least one son, John, Jr., who died before 1807. This John Minor, Jr., had at least two sons, John and William. One John Minor married in Frederick County, Maryland, on November 29, 1796, to Mary Kale. Another married Frances Moss, daughter of John Moss. This John Minor made a nuncupative will in Loudoun County, sworn before Thomas Minor in 1782 (Loudoun County *Will Book B*, page 426). A son, probably of this one, was Thomas E. Minor, born 1755, who married in Loudoun County on March 15, 1781, Ann Jennings. This Thomas Minor was made an Ensign of the Loudoun County Militia on February 12, 1781.

(22) (Captain) Spence Minor, died intestate in Loudoun County in 1794. (See Chancery Suit entitled "Minor agt. Minor's Representatives" filed in Loudoun County Court December 12, 1798, with a report filed September 16, 1801, to which Thomas E. Minor was a witness). In 1768 Minor was living in Fairfax County (Loudoun County *Deed Book F*, page 225). He married Mary Starke, a daughter of William Starke, Sr., and Susannah (Trammell) Starke. (*See Trammell*). Early in life (1768) Minor followed the trade of a cooper. He acquired a large estate which was divided on February 8, 1799 by Thomas Gunnell, Benjamin Edwards, and Scarlett Berkeley. This was recorded on April 8, 1799. (Loudoun County, *Will Book F*, page 102). Issue: William Minor; Mary Minor, married James Stone; Nicholas Minor, under age in 1798; John Minor, under age in 1798; and Spence Minor, under age in 1798.

(23) Nicholas Minor, Jr., married Elizabeth Brewer, daughter of Henry Brewer (Loudoun County, *Will Book D*, page 325).

(24) Margaret Minor, married Charles Hansford.

(25) Elizabeth Minor, married (1) —— Edwards; and (2) Silas Wherry. Her children included: Charles Edwards; Ann Edwards; Eliza Edwards; Jane Edwards; and John Edwards.
(26) Nancy Minor, married William Hurst.
(27) Elizabeth Minor, married Thomas Gunnell (*See Gunnell*).
(28) Thomas Minor.
(29) Rebecca Minor.

(3) John Minor, son of Nicholas and Jemima (Waddy) Minor, died in Fairfax County in 1753. He made his will on March 7, 1752, probated in Fairfax Court on July 18, 1753. Witnesses were: William Ramsey, and John Dalton. Hugh West was named Executor. In his will Minor named his wife and children. John Minor married Jemima Moxley, daughter of Thomas Moxley of Fairfax County. (See the will of Thomas Moxley made February 6, 1749, probated March 27, 1750). Issue:
(31) Nicholas Minor.
(32) John Minor, died in 1780. He made his will March 14, 1799, probated February 25, 1780 in Fairfax County. He named his wife, Ann, Executrix, and George Minor and John Moss served as Executors. Thomas Darne, John Davis, and Ann Davis were witnesses. Issue: Jean Sanford Minor, John Minor and Marcia Minor.
(33) Daniel Minor.
(34) (Colonel) George Minor, married (1) Ann Adams; and (2) Mildred Heale.
(35) Penelope Minor, married Henry Darne (*See Darne*).
(36) Elizabeth Minor.
(37) Ann Minor.

(34) (Colonel) George Minor of Minor's Hill, son of John and Jemima (Moxley) Minor, was born in Fairfax County, near the Falls Church, in 1753. He married (1) Ann Adams, daughter of Colonel William Adams of "Church Hill," and Ann (Lawyer) Adams. Mrs. Minor was born in 1752 and died at her home, Minor's Hill in December, 1786. Colonel Minor remarried (2) on January 22, 1788, in Fauquier County, to Mildred Heale, daughter of Colonel George Heale.

Colonel Minor served in the Fairfax County Militia and was a Justice of Fairfax County in 1784. He gave the land for Fairfax Chapel, the first Methodist Episcopal Church in the area. His home on Minor's Hill is incorporated into a much remodeled and enlarged home, now the property of the Harwood-Hardy family.

Issue (*By Ann Adams*):
(341) (Captain) George Minor, born in 1777, died in 1861, age 84 years. He commanded a Regiment of Militia during the War of 1812 in the defense of Washington and Baltimore. He was imprisoned for disloyalty. One daughter Eliza Minor, married in 1822, George Dale. *The Genius of Liberty*, published in Leesburg, Monday, December 2, 1822, announced the marriage on the previous Tuesday of Eliza, daughter of Captain George Minor of Fairfax County to George Dale, merchant, of Leesburg, by the Reverend Mr. Allen. *The National Intelligencer* of Washington, D.C., announced the death on January 14, 1822 of Maria Minor, age 18 years (who would have celebrated her birthday on January 15th) at the residence of her father, *Colonel* George Minor. This may refer to a daughter of this George Minor who may have held the title of Colonel. He is usually found in records as Captain Minor.

(342) Daniel Minor, married and settled in the Town of Alexandria. On May 15, 1812, Daniel Minor of Alexandria County, sold to William Watters of Fairfax County, for $262.50, land on the west side of Pimmitt Run containing 26¼ acres (Alexandria *Deed Book MM #2*, page 61). On March 30, 1809, in Loudoun County, *one* Daniel J. Minor married Pleasant Nixon (George Nixon, Bondsman).
(343) (Colonel) William Minor, married Catharine West.
(344) John Minor.
(345) Hugh West Minor.
(346) Ann Minor.
(347) (Major) Philip H. Minor, married on May 9, 1816, in Alexandria County, D.C., to Sarah A. Washington. Major Minor owned a large farm near Falls Church.

(*By Mildred Heale*):
(348) Smith Minor, married in Alexandria County, D.C., November 13, 1817, to Mary (Polly) Sommers. Mrs. Minor was born about 1795 at "Sommerville," a daughter of Major Simon and Susannah (Adams?) Sommers. Smith Minor's plantation adjoined "Springfield," home of his half-brother, Major Phil Minor. Issue: Marietta Minor; Elizabeth M. Minor, unmarried; Cornelia Minor, died February 6, 1889 in Alexandria County (*See The Methodist Protestant* of July 10, 1889, page 14), she was unmarried; two sons died in infancy; Mary Jane (Mollie) Minor; and Edwin Minor.
(349) Thomas Jefferson Minor (married and went West).

For information of Colonel George Minor's descendants, see Fairfax County *Deed Book Z #2*, page 397, et. seq. There may have been a son, Joseph Minor.

Of the above named children, Colonel William Minor (343) is of special interest as he was so closely identified with the Falls Church and the community. Colonel Minor was born at "Minor's Hill," served as an officer in the War of 1812, and lived in later life at his plantation home, "Springfield," which was in Fairfax and Alexandria. Colonel Minor married in 1803, Catharine West, the daughter of Colonel John and Sarah (Broadwater) West. She was born in 1786.

A descendant wrote of her:[1]

". . . her first child, John West, was born when she was eighteen years old, she donned white net caps, tied in a little bow under her chin, and always dressed in somber colors as becoming a wife and mother . . . I remember my grandmother as being very grave and dignified. I never heard her tell a joke. Life seemed to be a very serious thing to her . . . Some people appear to have had the impression that a Southern housekeeper who owned slaves led a very idle, useless life. I never saw my grandmother idle. There was always superintending of work, clothing being cut and basted for the women to sew, knitting to be done, and many other things requiring her supervision."

This same granchild wrote of Colonel Minor:[2]

"Grandfather was just her opposite. He loved fun and was the life of every crowd that he was in. I remember him as always looking immaculate in white linen and black broadcloth . . . (Upon his death) his funeral took place on a Sunday morning, and I was told that a string of carriages extended from the Episcopal Church at

Falls Church to his home, a distance of several miles. It was the largest funeral that anyone in the community had ever known."

Issue:

(3431) (Colonel) John West Minor was born in 1804 at Minor's Hill, and died in December, 1876, at "Greenway," his home near Leesburg, with burial at Minor's Hill. *The Mirror,* of Leesburg, December 28, 1876, carried his obituary and stated that the body was buried at Falls Church in the family burying ground. Colonel Minor served in the Virginia State Legislature from Loudoun County. He was a man of great ability, and is remembered by a niece Mary Williamson Mellor, for his ruffled shirts and knee breeches fastened with silver buckles set with rhine stones. Colonel Minor married (1) Ellen Diggs of Charles County, Maryland, who died about a year following the marriage. He remarried (2) in Loudoun County on June 20, 1839, to Louisa Fairfax Catlett, a daughter of Charles J. and Ann (Fairfax) Catlett, and a granddaughter of Bryan, Eighth Lord Fairfax. Charles J. Catlett, father, was Bondsman at the wedding, with Wilson C. Selden. Witnesses were: Thomas Herttell and John Selden. There is a law suit filed in Loudoun County entitled "Mercer vs. Catlett," (March 14, 1846) showing that Charles J. Catlett died in Loudoun County in 1845. He left a widow, Ann F. Catlett, and two children: Louisa F., wife of John W. Minor, and Erskine Catlett. Reference is made to a daughter-in-law, Esther Ann Catlett. Issue (by Louisa Fairfax Catlett) included three children who died in infancy, and the following:

(34311) Fairfax Minor.

(34312) Esther (Essie) Minor, married in Loudoun County on February 26, 1867, to James Monroe Heiskell, a great-grandson of President James Monroe. They had several children who died in infancy. A son, Minor Fairfax Heiskell had his surname changed (adopted his mother's surname). As Minor Fairfax Gouverneur he was living, in 1929, in Roland Park, Baltimore.

(3432) Sarah Ann (Sallie) Minor, died at age 94 years. She married in Alexandria County, D. C., August 12, 1833, (William Minor, Bondsman) to Charles A. Newton, U.S.N. He was killed in the Confederate service. The Newtons lived at "Granite Hill," Falls Church. There were six daughters and one son of this marriage. Some of these were: Nett Newton, Margaret Newton, Ella Newton, and Catherine (Kate) Newton, who married Miles Cleveland Munson. A charming description of the Newton-Munson wedding was given by Mary Mellor:[3]

"Weddings, wedding clothes, wedding suppers were the all important subjects, for wasn't our Cousin Kate Newton, Aunt Sarah's oldest child, to soon become the bride of Mr. Miles Cleaveland Munson, and the wedding was to take place at "Springfield." We could hardly wait, we said, for the time to arrive, for we had never attended a wedding, and we had very hazy ideas what it would be like.

Finally, the night arrived. It was very cold, even the moon and stars looked frozen. The snow was so deep that we could barely see the top rail of the fences; others had broken the track so we found no difficulty in traveling. We were snug and warm as we nestled down, well wrapped in shawls and blankets, in the bottom of the large wagon body which had been transferred to a sled.

That was a joyful five miles ride, and our laughter mingled with the merry jingle of the sleigh-bells.

Upon our arrival we found the whole house lighted and sounds of merriment could be heard from within as the front door opened to welcome us.

As soon as greetings were exchanged and our wraps were removed, I looked around for the bride-to-be, thinking, of course, that she would be with the family and guests assembled, but I was told that she was dressing. The house was crowded and everyone, as "Martha" said, "was dressed in their best bib and tucker."

Everybody seemed to be in high spirits and were on "tiptoe" of expectations.

Directly, at a signal, everyone became quiet, and the bride, clad in white, with a trailing veil, and the groom entered the parlor, slowly keeping step to the soft tones of the violin.

The minister stepped forward as they took their places, and in an incredibly short time was heard to say "I pronounce you man and wife." Then the fiddler (who belonged to Grandfather) struck up the liveliest music, as the bride and groom stood for congratulations. I was so little that some kind man lifted me in his arms to witness my first wedding, and as I look back over the long years, kind people ever since, metaphorically speaking, have been lifting me up. To this day I have a very warm feeling for the memory of the man who lifted me up to witness the wedding, and for all the other "lifters."

I was the youngest girl at the wedding, and the young men of the party plied me with all kinds of good things, such as oranges, raisins, nuts and candies, until I had a large package, which some one tied up for me. With fond anticipations of the fine party I'd have the next day, I sought the lounge in the dining room, where the wedding supper was being served.

That wedding was the beginning of festivities throughout the neighborhood. I've heard mother say that they danced out the parlor carpet for the wedding at Grandfather's that winter. The musicians were to be found on the place, and it was no trouble to get a crowd together to have a dance.

A funny thing occurred soon after Cousin Kate's marriage, while she was yet a bride. She persuaded Mr. Munson to let her cut his hair. I do not know what possessed her, as she had never been known to cut anyone's hair. Believing that she could do anything he became a willing victim.

He held a Government position in Washington, and the next day when he went to his office one of his friends came up to him, and said, "Excuse me, Munson, but would you mind telling me who cut your hair?"

Mr. Munson's face beamed with joy, as he answered, "My wife."

"Pardon me," said his friend, "if you had named some barber I was going to suggest you murder him," as he turned to his desk. That was the end of Cousin Kate's haircutting."

(3433) William Joseph Minor.
(3434) Catharine Ann Minor, married on October 7, 1846, at "Springfield," to the Reverend Nicholas Lemen of Jefferson County. His family was long settled in Berkeley and Jefferson. Mr. Lemen was an early Methodist Protestant Minister in the Falls Church area. Issue:

(34341) Catharine Minor Lemen (Kate) born October 9, 1847.
(34342) Mary Colville Lemen, born 1849, died in infancy.
(34343) Mary Williamson Lemen, born April 13, 1851, married Mellor and wrote a delightful autobiography which is in manuscript. Had issue, some of whom live in the area.
(34344) John West Lemen, died at age 7 months when his nurse fell asleep and dropped him on the hearth.
(34345) (The Reverend) William Minor Lemen of the Iowa Conference of The Methodist Protestant Church.
(34346) Jacob Williamson Lemen.
(3435) Colville James Minor, died in November, 1845, at Monterey, California, of typhus. He was a graduate of West Point.

---

[1] *Once Upon A Time,* MS. autobiography of Mary Williamson Mellor, (1851-1942) of Sykesville, Maryland, written in 1929. Mrs. Mellor was a daughter of the Reverend Nicholas and Catherine Ann (Minor) Lemen, and granddaughter of Colonel William and Catharine (West) Minor. See pages 2 and 23.
[2] *Ibid,* pages 23 and 59.
[3] *Ibid,* pages 26, *et. seq.*

---

## THE MORAN FAMILY

Dr. John J. Moran was the first Mayor of Falls Church, and lived in a house on the corner of Noland and East Broad Street (now the parking lot for Dulin Methodist Church). Dr. Moran was educated in medicine, probably in Maryland. His claim to fame as Mayor of Falls Church is excelled by the fact that he attended Edgar Allan Poe at his death. Mrs. Mary Moran, his wife, read to Poe from the fourteenth chapter of St. John as the poet lay dying.[1] Hervey Allen, an authority on Poe, quotes a letter and other data about Moran's experience. Dr. Moran lectured over the country, and it seems the story was enhanced with each telling. The following are quotations from Hervey Allen:[2]

"*Dr. J. J. Moran Items*

The following letter from Dr. J. J. Moran who attended Poe on his death-bed in Baltimore, on October 7, 1849, is of interest as recording an interview with Mrs. A. B. Shelton (Elmira Royster), thirty-three years after Poe's death. *If* the doctor can be believed, Mrs. Shelton was still able to weep for Poe. This is quite possible, of course.

The point is here, however, that Dr. Moran was on one of his lecture trips in which he went about the country telling about the death of Poe. At every recital the "demise of our great poet" became more edifying. At this particular stage, a really beautiful and touching climax had been achieved. A comparison of this letter with the one which Dr. Moran wrote to Mrs. Clemm on November 15, 1849, provides an insight into the growth of a certain kind of Poe legend.

Falls Church, Va., February 27, 1882

Mr. Edward Abbott
Dear Sir
  Yours recd. did not reach me until I had returned from a lecture tour to Richmond, the home of his Annabel Lee, who yet lives, is near her three score and ten. Yet

she was at the lecture, 32 years have intervened since his death, and she and I, met for the first time after that period, it was a meeting I shall never forget—so deeply were we impressed, that our tears could not be restrained—but to the question asked in reference to the slip of paper sent, I answer, it is correct in the main or chief part. The word rode, should be arched—his decrees legibly &c. he was in my hands 16 hours, and 15 out the 16, was rational and perfectly conscious—I have some hope of getting Boston soon to deliver my lecture have been written to for that purpose—have also a letter from G. W. Childs of Pha. In haste as I have a great number of letters to answer

I remain yours<br>Respectfully—<br>J. J. Moran— "

(Courtesy of James F. Drake, Esq.)

*(Report of one of Dr. Moran's Garbled Lectures about Poe's death)*
"Dr. J. J. Moran, of Falls Church, Va., who was with Edgar Allan Poe in his dying hours, in a recent lecture said that the slander had been reiterated that Poe died while under the influence of liquor, and nothing could be further from the fact. Upon his arrival at the hospital the doctor questioned the hackman who brought him there, and he declared that Poe was not drunk, nor was there the smell of liquor about him when he lifted him into his vehicle. As Poe's last hour approached, Dr. Moran said that he bent over him and asked if he had any word he wished communicated to his friends. Poe raised his fading eyes and answered "Nevermore." In a few moments he turned uneasily and moaned, "Oh God, is there no ransom for the deathless spirit?" Continuing he said: "He who rode the heavens and upholds the universe has His decrees written on the frontlet of every human being," Then followed murmuring, growing fainter and fainter, then a tremor of the limbs, a faint sigh, "and the spirit of Edgar Allan Poe had passed the boundary line that divides time from eternity."
(Courtesy of James F. Drake, Esq.)

Dr. Moran was a man of good education and of wide interests. He was Special Agent for Virginia to adjust and determine debts or claims from the time following the War of 1812. The following letter from the author's files is of interest:

"Washington, D. C., February 20, 1886.

Hon. Fitzhugh Lee,
Governor of Virginia.
Dear Sir—I have the honor to address you as the special agent of the State, empowered by an Act of the Legislature and commissioned by the Governor, to settle, adjust and determine all debts or claims due the State of Virginia by the United States, except claims prior to 1812. I have labored faithfully and laboriously since my appointment, and have at length found to be due the State of Virginia by the U.S., on two special accounts, the sum of $2,274,466.37. The first account is under the Act of Congress of 1836, known as the "Deposit Act," and distribution of the surplus revenue whereby Virginia became entitled to $2,931,237.48, which was by contract to be paid in four equal quarterly installments of $737,809.37 each. The three-fourths was paid as they became due, and when the fourth became due and was called for, there was no money in the Treasury to pay it, and by a resolution of Congress, payment was postponed until there should be sufficient surplus in the Treasury above the expenses of the Government to pay said instalment. It was not called for until I made

the demand. The second is on account of the distribution of the sale of public lands under Act of Congress September 4, 1841. In 1842 Virginia's distributive share amounted to $41,657.37. This sum has since been drawn from the Treasury of the United States by an auauthorized party, without authority from the State, and not one dollar of the same has ever reached the State Treasury. I have an exhibit of the facts, and a copy of the warrant and draft, which will be brought to your notice in due time.

The sum from the sale of said land had amounted up to 1857, to the sum of $1,500,000, and if carried forward to the present would aggregate $4,000,000. The former sum and the $732,809.37 and $41,657, would make the gross sum of $2,931-237.48, now available and with proper effort I believe can be secured to the State this session of Congress. If our State legislature will by a resolution or otherwise, urge its representatives in Congress to take some interest in this matter and aid the State Agent in his efforts to secure this money, the State Treasury will soon be relieved of its stringency and be sufficiently able to relieve herself from present embarrassment.

My dear sir, permit me to solicit your influence in this behalf. I am, sir, most respectfully, Your obedient servant,

J. J. Moran,
Special Agent State of Virginia."

This letter clearly demonstrates that Dr. Moran was a man of great ability. At one time he was Editor of the *Loudoun Enterprise* published at Leesburg.[3]

Dr. Moran was Class Leader of Dulin Chapel Methodist Episcopal Church, South, in 1873, and died at his Falls Church home on December 12, 1888. His widow, the gentle Mary J. Moran, died March 31, 1889. A son, Charles Moran, lived in Merrifield. A daughter, Mrs. Vincent, also resided in Merrifield.

---

[1] *Israfel (The Life and Times of Edgar Allan Poe)* by Hervey Allen, Farrar & Rinehart, Inc., New York, 1934, pages 673, 674.
[2] *Ibid*, page 718.
[3] This is mentioned in *The Fairfax Herald* of October 24, 1890.

---

## THE MUNSON FAMILY

Thomas Munson, first American ancestor of the family which settled in Falls Church, was born about 1612 and died on May 7, 1685, at the age of 73 years. He was a carpenter, and served in the local Militia at his home, New Haven, Connecticut. Mr. Munson was a member of the Congregational Church. He married Joanna (born 1610, died December 13, 1678), whose sur-name is not known.

Samuel Munson, son of Thomas and Joanna Munson, was baptized August 7, 1643. He married on October 26, 1665, to Martha Bradley, daughter of William and Alice (Pritchard) Bradley. He died in 1693, and his will was dated January 10, 1693, and probated March 2, 1693. Munson was a shoemaker, and tanner, in New Haven.

John Munson, son of Samuel and Martha (Bradley) Munson, was born January 28, 1672, and died in 1752. His will is dated February 6, 1749, was probated August 6, 1752. He married, on November 10, 1692, to Sarah Cooper, daughter of (Sergeant) John and Mary (Thompson) Cooper. She was born about 1674, and died December 3, 1714. Mr. Munson was a miller in New Haven.

John Munson, son of John and Sarah (Cooper) Munson, was born July 7, 1693. He married on January 28, 1711 to Esther Clark, daughter of Samuel and Hannah (Tuttle) Clark of East Haven. She was born January 2, 1692 and died in 1747. He died in 1745/6. He was a cooper in New Haven, and Sergeant of Militia.

Timothy Munson, son of John and Esther (Clark) Munson, was born July 1, 1734. He married before March 1, 1755 to Sarah Bishop. She died February 5, 1806, aged 60 years. He married (2) Sarah ———, and she died March 2, 1819, aged 72 years. Mr. Munson died October 29, 1826 aged 92 years. He was a tailor, tavern-keeper, and farmer. He lived in New Haven, later in New Milford (now Brookfield) Connecticut and Pownal, Vermont. During the Revolutionary War he served in the 8th Regiment under Captain Josiah Smith, 5th Continental Line. Colonel Waterbury was officer in charge. Munson was made a Sergeant October 13, 1775, discharged, and later reenlisted. He was discharged again after eleven months, December 31, 1778.

John Clarke Munson, son of Timothy and Sarah (Bishop) Munson, was born in New Milford, Connecticut, in July 1774. He married in Pownal, Vermont, November 12, 1801, to Elizabeth Folsom. He died in Erie County, Pennsylvania, in 1858, aged 84 years. She died about 1866 aged 85 years. Mr. Munson was a farmer, lived in Canada, Leicester, Livingstone County, New York, and Erie, Pennsylvania.

Timothy Bishop Munson, son of John Clarke and Elizabeth (Folsom) Munson, was born in Lower Canada, June 22, 1805, and died at Falls Church, Virginia, September 18, 1867. He is buried beside his wife in the old Falls Church yard. Mr. Munson married in 1826 to Nancy Meacham. She was born December 31, 1799, died August 24, 1852, daughter of James Meacham of Hinsdale, Massachusetts. Mr. Munson was a farmer, Whig, and lived first in Leicester, New York, later at "Munson Hill," near Falls Church.

There are numerous descendants of Timothy Bishop Munson and family in Falls Church. There is a good record of the Munsons in *The Munson Record* (1637-1887) by Myron A. Munson, two volumes, published in New Haven, Connecticut, 1887, pages 568, 578, and 602.

Colonel Daniel O. Munson of New York, settled on his 180 acre farm, "Munson Hill," now site of the Munson Hill Apartments, in 1851. In 1852 he established an extensive nursery which supplied plants and trees to this and a wide area until the mid 1900's. A Catalog of 1879, published by Thomas McGill & Company of Washington, D.C., shows a wide variety of plants and shrubs available at "Munson Hill Nurseries." The old Munson Hill mansion, completed during 1862, was torn down one hundred years later, 1962, for the Munson Hill Apartments.

Colonel Daniel O. Munson married a sister of the Reverend B. F. Bittinger, local Presbyterian Minister, and of the Reverend Edmund Bittinger, Chaplain, U.S. Navy. The Reverend Edmund Bittinger left his seventy acre farm at 7 Corners, called "Shadeland," to his sisters, Mrs. Margaret Jacobs and Mrs. Daniel O. Munson. This was sold in 1893, by Colonel Munson, to James F. Marr. Colonel Munson's children included Miss Mary Jasper Munson, to whom President Lincoln wrote a letter on December 13, 1861 (the letter is now owned by a descendant of the Munsons, Munson H. Lane, Sr.). Another daughter was Lucy Eleanor, who became the second wife of Dr. Archibald Alexander Edward Taylor (1834-1903) on May 21, 1868. Dr. Taylor was a Presbyterian Minister and President of the University of Wooster, Ohio, in 1873. They had one daughter.

Miles O. Munson married Katherine Hanford. Their son, Dr. Charles Bishop Munson, a dentist in Washington, married in October, 1894, to Florence Amelia Reed. Mrs. Florence (Reed) Munson died December 1, 1949, age 80 years. She was a native of Arlington. Issue: Lillian Munson, died July 17, 1909, at 11 months, 16 days; Mrs. Thomas H. (Evangeline M.) Johnston; William Reed Munson (whose daughter, Mrs. William D. (Irene) Rouse lives in Falls Church); Boardman Munson, Charles Bishop Munson; Mrs. Mariah M. Donovan, and Mrs. Lucy M. Rose.

Miles Cleveland Munson (1831-1914) married Kate V. Newton (1834-1921) of the distinguished Minor family. (*See Minor*). A son, Dr. Reginald Munson (1858-1946) married Mary Arnold, who died in Bethesda, Maryland, May 13, 1960. Their children included Archie T. Munson, well-known resident of Falls Church; Mrs. Rosser L. Hunter, Miles A. Munson, and Colonel Reginald B. Munson, U.S.A.F.

## THE MURRAY FAMILY

Charles Murray, a well-to-do resident of Taylor's Tavern (7 Corners) area in the early days, was a native of Galloway, Scotland, born about six miles from the Town of Dumfries,[1] January 3, 1742. He came to this country during the early 1760's, and was followed by his brothers, James and Edward Murray, who came in 1764. Prior to the Revolutionary War this scion of the Murrays, grandson of Murray, Lord Broughton, lived in Baltimore. Murray died at his home near Falls Church on November 24, 1821 (or 1827). He married Elizabeth Layton.[2] Mrs. Murray was born March 4, 1749 at Urbanna, Middlesex County, Virginia, and died at her Falls Church home on March 22, 1826.

Charles and Elizabeth (Layton) Murray had issue:

(1) John Murray, born December 1, 1777, died May 18, 1813, age 36 years. He married Mildred (Millie) Pearson, issue:[3]

(11) James Murray, married Margaret Hough. Sarah A. Murray married E.G. Wheeler. Their issue with ages in 1897 were: Sarah V. Wheeler, 21; Edmond L. Wheeler, 19; Margaret Wheeler Trallis, 18; and Harriet T. Wheeler, 17. Susan C. Murray, daughter of James and Margaret (Hough) Murray married twice, and in 1897 as Susie Heywood, lived in Flemington, New Jersey. Other issue of James and Margaret (Hough) Murray included: George Murray, Allen Murray, Virginia Murray, married Moran and had a son, Clayton Moran; perhaps others.

(12) Ann Murray, married —— Ballinger.

(2) Jean (Jennie) Murray, born December 4, 1779, married William Bladen.

(3) James Murray, married Elizabeth Street.

(4) Nancy Murray, born February 12, 1784, married George Hackney and died August 9, 1820, age 37 years. Issue: Fielden P. Hackney; Martha A. married Brendman (or Brennerman); Annie M. Hackney; Sallie Hackney, married McIntosh; and Hattie (or Hettie) who married P. H. Christman.

(5) Charles Murray, Jr., born April 30, 1789, died unmarried, August 10, 1793.

(6) Winifred Murray married Colmore Bean.

*Note:* Most of this information was taken from depositions filed in the District Court of Fannin County, Texas, August 1892, No. 3702, a suit entitled "Sarah A. Dove, et. al., vs. H. P. Howard, et. al." This was the famous "Bean Law Suit." Depositions prove that there was another son of Charles Murray, not listed in the Bible record, one Thomas Murray. This Thomas Murray married twice, and his second wife was Sarah Foyles who died about 1865 in Paducah, Kentucky. He was born about 1773/4, according to deposition, in Baltimore, and died in Portsmouth, Virginia, 1849. Murray was Inspector of Provisions and Master Cooper in the Navy Yard, Washington, D.C., and later in Portsmouth. He was Captain of Artillery during the War of 1812, and participated in the Battle of Bladensburg. The author has extensive notes on his descendants.

(3) James Murray, son of Charles and Elizabeth (Layton) Murray, was born July 19, 1781, and died at his Falls Church home, July 27, 1843. He married in Fairfax County, January 31, 1813, Elizabeth (Eliza) Street. Mrs. Murray was born January 7, 1791, and died August 3, 1854. She was a daughter of Daniel and Elizabeth (Amos) Street of Harford County, Maryland. Mr. Murray, a fine looking man with dark hair and eyes, was a contractor and builder in the Falls Church area. Issue:

(31) John Murray, born November 15, 1813, died February 1, 1814.
(32) Mary E. Murray, born March 17, 1816, died February 13, 1898, at Falls Church with burial in Oakwood Cemetery. She married in Washington, D.C., August 8, 1862, to a soldier, Edward Martin. He died about six months later and she resumed her maiden name. John R. Minor of Minor's Hill, made a deposition in 1895 when he was 80 years old. In it he recalled courting her some sixty years earlier, and that she "was a very handsome girl, and very proud of her good looks." A seamstress, Miss Murray was early a member of Fairfax Chapel but later attended St. James Church.
(33) Charles Henry Murray, born April 28, 1818, died July, 1861. Murray never married and in 1850 was living with his sisters, Mary and Jane (*Census*).
(34) Jane Murray, born October 11, 1820, died unmarried, November 16, 1902. She was a seamstress.
(35) Elizabeth Ann Murray, born December 15, 1822, married a cousin, William Bladen. Issue: Ida S. Bladen, married Thomas Hoover; and Theodore Bladen.
(36) James Edward Murray, born March 4, 1824, died March 31, 1884. He married Mrs. Mary Frances (Birch) Myers, a widow, called Fanny. She was born in 1836, a daughter of Colonel Samuel and Ann (Cleveland) Birch. Mrs. Murray died April 1, 1907, with burial in Oakwood Cemetery. Issue: Florence Ardell Murray (1875-1941) married Jonathan (John) Roberts Thorne (*see Thorne*); and Irving Murray who married Della Veitch (she remarried, 2nd, Rutherford. Florence Ardell (Murray) Thorne was born April 3, 1875; Irving Murray was born January —— 1878.
(37) Franklin Murray, born December 13, 1827, died September 6, 1829.
(38) Sarah Ellen Murray (twin), born April 20, 1831, died August 21, 1832.
(39) Daniel Murray (twin), born April 20, 1831, died in Maryland, unmarried.

(6) Winifred Murray (called Winnie), daughter of Charles and Elizabeth (Layton) Murray, was born December 22, 1796. At age 16 years she ran away and married (in Washington, D.C., at Christ Episcopal Church, on November 29, 1812) to Colmore Bean. Bean, who was much older and had been previously married, was a carpenter employed by Charles Murray. They lived for a short time at Falls Church, later in Washington. In March, 1824 they were living in Heathsville, Northumberland County, Virginia, when Winifred addressed a pathetic letter to her brother,

James, asking him to intercede for her with their father. Charles Murray never accepted her after the marriage. Mrs. Bean was a very beautiful woman, tall and slim with black hair and eyes. Her niece, Mary E. Murray, daughter of James Murray, was much like her. Leah Lewis, an aged Negro neighbor testified in the Bean law suit concerning Mrs. Bean's marriage:[4]

"The reason Winnefred's (sic)·father was so much opposed to her marrying Colmore Bean was, that she being the youngest girl, she was a great favorite and pet of her father, and he did not want her to marry anyone while she was so young. Colmore Bean drank some and he opposed him on that account, and he also opposed him on account of his being older. . . and the reason he forever disowned her was because she ran away instead of marrying at home, and when old Charles Murray once made up his mind on anything he was as set as a rock and never gave in."

Winifred Murray Bean died about 1834 in Heathsville. Her husband moved West taking the three children (Oscar, Thomas C., and John) with him. John died on his way to California some years later. Thomas C. Bean died in Bonham, Texas, having accumulated a large estate there. This became the subject of a long court action. Part of the money eventually went to Misses Mary E. and Jane Murray of Falls Church, and to Mildred Gertrude (Murray) (Birch) Donaldson, wife of Armistead Donaldson, a granddaughter of James and Elizabeth (Street) Murray. (*See Donaldson*).

*The Washington Post* of Sunday, March 15, 1896, contained a story of the Bean fortune. With it was a romance, and the names Marie Conway and Agnes Ferguson were substituted for Mary and Jane Murray. During their youth both were in love with a dashing officer of the Mexican War, here called Frederick Hazelhurst. The story follows:

"*Saved By A Faded Letter—Romance of Falls Church and a Sequel*

Ten years ago there appeared in The Post a story which excited much interest and comment, entitled, "The Portrait in the Hovel; or, The Two Witches of Falls Church," Taking the plot as commonly given by the residents of the village, I am going, in my own words, to tell that story again, which is pure romance, and add to it a sequel which shall be pure reality. Then I shall leave the reader to determine whether or not it is a fact, as often asserted, that truth is stanger than fiction.

Chapter 1

Of course, if you are a worshiper at the shrine of society or pleasure, or one of the many that struggle with fierce delight for place and power in the field of political and financial activity—you would not care to live in Falls Church. But if you did not care for excitement, preferring the dreamy delight of a dozing little town, then Falls Church would appeal to your heart, and you would probably feel, could you experience its delightful serenity for one day, that a continued existence there would be all that a man with proper ideas of life could desire. Sin has not seemed to touch it with its smutty fingers; no shadow of immorality darkens the cerulean sky of its reputation, and its character is above reproach. That is why people with quiet tastes and sober habits like to live in Falls Church. They think it charming. And not one who has ever fallen beneath the spell of the influence that permeates its atmosphere has ever dared to deny it.

Within the last four years the village has caught the inspiration of our *fin de siecle* activity, and is making gentle strides to something larger and better, but ten years ago it had not opened an eye from the slumber of years. At that time there stood upon the fringe of the cluster of buildings that form the village a structure that might easily have passed for the first ever erected in the venerable State of Virginia. The shingles and the weatherboards had long since parted with their last touch of paint, and, without a thing to cover their age and nakedness, had shriveled in the sun and warped in the wind, until they were so far asunder that the sunshine and the rain, the heat, and the cold, alike, could enter and exit at will. The steps to the doorway were a wreck, the window blinds hung in helpless dilapidation, the chimney tottered to an early grave, the garden was overgrown with weeds, a swamp stretched as far as the eye could reach, and its dampness was seen engraved upon the roof of the hut in picturesque masses of dark green moss.

This was where the children of the village would tell you "the two old witches" lived. They were seldom seen in the village, but every day when the weather was good they walked out through the woods, followed by a faithful dog, the most aristocratic one of the trio. Change of circumstances, poverty, and want were nothing to him. He got his daily bone, and he was content. But the two witches walked as though the weight of some great sorrow held them down. In stature one was tall, and the other was of medium height. The tall one carried herself erect and looked about her with brilliant black eyes of piercing luster. She suggested in her carriage the movement of a belle of fashion, and one wondered if she could have been, once upon a time, the queen of some ballroom. The other was timorous. Her blue eyes were still pretty, but had lost much of the luster of youth, and melancholy seemed to have claimed her for its own.

No one in the village had ever crossed their threshold, but one day a stranger appeared at their door, and being a stranger, they took him in, lest they should turn away an angel unawares. That stranger saw many things to interest him within the mysterious recesses of that dilapidated cottage, but nothing that interested him so much as a portrait on the wall, an oil painting, framed in gilt, hanging where the light of the morning sun could tint it with the color of youth, a portrait of a young man whose proud and handsome features might well have graced the ancestral halls of some old English mansion. The forehead was broad and white, traced with the veins of gentility, from which the hair was brushed in a careless, but strikingly effective manner. The eyes were dark and somewhat cruel, the nose indicated a character strong even to recklessness, and the lips, about which a faint, sarcastic smile could be plainly traced, were the lips of a passionate man.

## Chapter II

Even with the accession of the many modern dwellings that have of late years reared themselves along the residential streets of Alexandria, some of which are really metropolitan in cost and style, there are none more desirable than the fine old mansion occupied before the War by Col. Henry Ferguson. But a short distance from this old mansion is another of almost equal pretensions to charm and grandeur, which at that time was occupied by Judge Emory Conway. I am speaking now of the time when, fifty or sixty years ago, Alexandria, as the central city of a rich farming country, the market for its cattle and produce, the port for a big shipping trade, and, as necessarily followed, a Mecca for the wealth and fashion of the time, was one of the most important cities of the South.

Between the families of Judge Conway and Col. Ferguson a bond of friendship existed that became all the stronger when Marie Conway and Agnes Ferguson, born in the same year, and, by coincidence, in the same month, within a few days of each other, grew up together and loved each other as sisters. They were inseparable It was the attraction of opposites most strikingly contrasted in the brunette and the blonde, the clinging and the independent, the tender and the strong, the merry and the sad, the laughter and the tears.

No man could ever decide within his heart which of the two was the most charming and the most lovable. If the delicate beauty, the modest manner, and the tenderness of Agnes were bewitching, the handsome figure, the dashing style, and the independence of Marie were captivating in the extreme; and one's heart was torn asunder in the effort to love both as much as each deserved without loving either less than she would have been loved if apart from the other.

Among the young men who found themselves most deeply perplexed in this sort of dual affection was Frederick Hazelhurst. He had come from Kentucky a few years before, had been admitted to the bar, and was already a lawyer of promise, although but thirty years of age. His mother had been a Creole and his father a Virginian, both of excellent birth and breeding. This combination had its effect upon the mental and physical qualities of the young man. He was handsome, reckless, poetic, artistic, tender, careless, brave and generous, passionate and impetuous. Whatever he did, he did with all his heart and soul. The result of a game at cards was as much a matter of life and death for the moment as the fate of the nation might have been had it hung in the balance of war. He could not take up a pleasure without he plunged into excess; he could not begin a task that did not end in prostration.

It is such strong yet sensitive natures that the destinies of nations are formed. The passion and tenderness make up the story of love and war. And it is men like Frederick Hazelhurst that women adore.

At any rate, Marie Conway and Agnes Ferguson loved him. I do not say that they knew it from the time it began to fill their hearts with a happiness strangely sweet and new. Very few of us recognize the insidious sweetness of Cupid's poisoned dart until the blood has become so flaming hot that nothing can cool it.

So, when Hazelhurst began paying attention to the two girls, and became assiduously devoted to each, with diplomatic avoidance of partiality to either, both closed their eyes, so to speak, like a woman when she finds uncommon rapture in a kiss, and floated, hand in hand still the same good friends, down the limpid streams of love together.

With this condition of affairs existing, Hazelhurst continued his attentions, captivated one day by Marie Conway and fascinated the next by Agnes Ferguson; honestly not knowing which he preferred, but conveying to the mind of each the impression which he really felt when in the presence of the one or the other, that she, and she alone, was the only woman on the face of the earth that he adored.

Rising rapidly in his profession, he was elected to the Legislature of Virginia. On the morning of his departure he met Miss Conway on King Street. They walked together to her home. They gained the drawing-room of the mansion, and she sank in agitation upon the sofa, trembling at the ardor of his manner. He clasped her hands and kissed away her involuntary tears. She was irresistible, and the result was inevitable. Within the hour he was betrothed to Marie Conway.

As he walked away he trod on air. He had never been so happy in his life. He flew to his room with the vigorous activity and energy of a man that love has fired, and began to pitch his things into the trunk, regardless of order in the recklessness of joy. A photograph of Agnes Ferguson stood on the mantel. As he picked it up to put it in his trunk, he remembered, with surprise at his forgetfulness, that he had not called to say good-bye to Agnes Ferguson. The impetuosity and impulsiveness of his nature, was strikingly exhibited by the immediate discontinuance of his preparations for departure and his subsequent haste in rushing to Miss Ferguson's home.

She had been watching for him all day, divided between the fear that he would not come and the hope of what he might say if he did. Meeting him in such a mood, it was impossible for him not to detect the fact that his departure would give her pain. And Hazelhurst could not bear to pain a woman. He was too susceptible, or too kind, I don't know which. And yet I have my opinion, but as I do not wish to prejudice the reader, every one can form his own opinion of this man's character by the simple statement of the fact that here within the space of a day he had met two women with tears in their eyes because he was going away, and, either unable to resist the enchantment of their soul, or in the too gallant desire to make them happy, engaged himself to each and pressed upon the lips of both the kind of kisses that only be given with the purest love.

And so he went away, with two of the fairest girls in all that section deceived, believing herself to be the queen of his heart as his promised bride.

## Chapter III

Fortune is sometimes a foe to love. The man a victor, the woman is vanquished. This is not true of all men, but it is true of such men as Hazelhurst. Political conditions during his career in the Legislature made him for the time being, at least, somewhat famous. He was looked upon as a successful man. In the days of his early career, when the struggles made a woman's love the sweeter, and really necessary to his happiness, he had clung to his dream of marriage, and, perhaps, had loved. When success came, he forgot. Gradually his correspondence with Agnes Ferguson and Marie Conway became less constant, and the letters less ardent.

The years passed, and finally his letters ceased altogether. Flushed with success, Hazelhurst had gone abroad. Ten years later he died in New York, a physical wreck from dissipation. The sputtering candle of his life went out, and the darkness came without a friend beside him, without a loving word to recall the happy days, and without a tear to show that some heart grieved.

From the day he had kissed in rapid succession the lips of Agnes Ferguson and Marie Conway, the girls had not looked upon his face. Perhaps with a sense of dishonor, he had found it impossible to face them. They waited, and watched, and the years passed, and other sweethearts came, but with that esoteric devotion of woman, so much to be pitied and yet esteemed, they enshrined the faithless in their hearts and would think of no other.

Throughout all their life these two girls had told each other their most sacred secrets, with the exception of this. And it seems to me that I could make no more complimentary comment upon their characters than that the love of their life was sacred unto themselves. But when the news of Hazelhurst's death came to them after many years, in an outburst of longing for sympathy over a grief that was still fresh, despite the lapse of time they confided in each other, and at last discovered the perfidy of the man they had loved so long.

But this sorrow only served to unite their hearts the closer. It was a common bond of sympathy, a common secret, that knitted their lives in bonds that not even the ties of home and kindred could break, and swept them finally into a secluded existence, housed in a cottage on the edge of the village. It suggested in its early days the happiness of a honeymoon, the joy of wedded love in a cottage, but the snows of many winters and the suns of many summers robbed it of its pristine prettiness, to leave it like a sad, black blot upon the loveliness of the landscape, while its owners also lost the freshness of youth, and the lustre of life in a monotonous, secluded, and saddened existence, caring only for the portrait on the wall, with its dark, cruel eyes, and its passionate lips.

### The Sequel

This act opens in the year 1812, if you please, and we will come down to the present time as rapidly as the events directly pertaining to this story will permit without the elimination of important details.

In the spring of that year Colmore Bean, a journeyman carpenter under the employ of Charles Murray, a well-to-do resident of Falls Church, had that delightful experience which the poet declares is inevitable in the spring—his thought lightly turned to love.

No, they did not lightly turn, for it was an exceedingly serious matter with Colmore. He was a vigorous, whole-souled, and manly fellow, and had a heart almost as big as himself. When he loved, he loved with the strength of a strong, honest man. In this case his love was aggravated because it was combated and attacked, as is the case when one in a lowly position seeks to aspire to the hand of a woman whose social standing is somewhat superior. The girl that won the heart of Colmore Bean was Winifred Murray, the daughter of Charles Murray, his employer.

Winifred was born in 1796. She was, therefore, just the age of sweet sixteen when she met Colmore Bean. Perhaps she was romantic, perhaps the spring had something to do with it, so far as she was concerned, too, and then, again, perhaps she really loved the young fellow. The latter supposition is probably the correct one, for Winifred Murray suffered much for Colmore Bean. She left a luxurious home for the modest environments of a cottage in the country with him. It was a runaway marriage. The wedding took place in old Christ's Episcopal Church, in Washington, and they went back to the neighborhood of Falls Church to live, where in the next eight years three sons, Thomas, John, and Oscar, were born to them. The coming of grandchildren into his life did not soften the angered heart of old Charles Murray, and when Winifred Murray and her husband moved to Heathsville, Va., in 1820, she was compelled to leave the scenes of her childhood with the curses of her father still upon her head.

No doubt his cruelty burned the poor girl's conscience and sorely wounded her affectionate heart, for she wrote a letter shortly after going to Heathsville, begging, in heart-broken words, for her father's forgiveness; but she died ten years later, without the pardon that she craved.

After her death Colmore Bean and his three sons moved to New Orleans, and subsequently lived together at Palmyra, Mo., and at Fayetteville, Ark. In 1840 they separated, Tom and his father going to Bonham, Tex., and John and Oscar to California. Oscar died a year or so afterward, and John accidentally shot himself a few months after his brother's death, and died in a strange land and was buried there.

This left Colmore Bean with only one son. In the course of a few years Colmore Bean died himself, and Tom Bean was left alone in the world.

He continued to remain alone. In and about Bonham he soon became known as a confirmed old bachelor. Not the wildest, the most dashing, the prettiest, or the most fascinating girls in all the broad prairie lands of Texas could tempt Tom Bean from bliss of single-blessedness. He seemed to have but one desire—to accumulate land. He was a surveyor by profession, and this enabled him to secure a great deal of land in the early history of Texas for almost nothing, to which he added by purchase with the money that he diligently saved from his really munificent income.

Deeds to property and acres of far-stretching prairie accumulated during the following forty years until Tom Bean was called "the millionaire land owner."

Then he died. That was in 1887. Only a few months before his death a lawyer had said to him, "Bean, you ought to make your will. What's to become of all that land when you kick the bucket?"

"To the devil with a will!" said Bachelor Tom Bean. "I have no relative in the world that I know of, and, if I have, it is no business of mine to look after their property. Let 'em fight for it."

And they did.

For Tom Bean had hardly been cold in his grave before claimants to the land by virtue of relation with the dead man sprung up all over the country. As one of the witty lawyers put it, "More Beans jumped up in a night than were ever baked in Boston in a century." Which must have been a great many Beans, indeed.

But none of the Beans seemed to have been planted in the right soil. Then J. L. Hume, an enterprising attorney of Austin, Tex., thought he would institute a quiet search for the descendants of Tom Bean's ancestors, for reasons which will be obvious to every lawyer, if not to the general public.

But whatever Mr. Hume's reasons may have been for taking up such a devious task, his shrewd work deserves the success that finally crowned his efforts. He found the two women out of all the other million women of various names in this country, and the two relatives out of all the true so-called relatives of Tom Bean, who, more than any other two persons in the world, were the most entitled to a share, if not all, of Tom Bean's estate. Probably if Mr. Hume's experiences in this search could be told they would make an interesting story in themselves; but we must hasten to say that the two women whom he selected out of the millions, as the rightful claimants to the great estate of Tom Bean, aforesaid and deceased, lived then, and live now, at Falls Church.

And the name of one is Miss Jane Murray and the name of the other is Miss Mary Murray, but in the village they are known simply as "The Misses Murray."

When Lawyer Hume discovered these two ladies they were living in a modest and rather dilapidated cottage in the suburbs of the town, all unconscious of the fortune that awaited them, simply for the asking, way down in Texas. Having found them, Mr. Hume went back home. The rest of the work in the way of securing evidence to establish the claim of the Misses Murray to the vast estate, was done by Mr. M. E. Church, a notary public of that town, and the manager of the Falls' Church Improvement Company, with an office on F street, in this city.

Mr. Church's task was almost as difficult as Mr. Hume's had been. The Misses Murray were jealous of their family treasures, and suspicious of any one who wished to examine them. But finally Mr. Church induced the two ladies to let him make a copy of the record in the old family Bible, which showed that they were the daughters of James Murray, a son of Charles Murray, and consequently brother to Winifred

Murray, who ran away and married Colmore Bean, the father of Tom Bean, bachelor and millionaire land owner.

And among their precious mementoes of the dead years the Misses Murray had that tearful, pathetic, and begging letter which Winifred Murray had written away back in 1812, begging her father's forgiveness. The letter was written to her brother, James Murray, who interceded for his sister Winifred, but without effect upon the old man's hardened heart, and then, because he had loved his sister so much, James Murray gave to his daughters, Mary and Jane, that letter on his death bed, to keep and to hold in remembrance of the golden-haired, happy girl who had played with him in his childhood and taught him a tenderness he never knew from his mother, because she died when he was a baby.

So Mary and Jane, his daughters, with first a sense of duty and then a sense of pleasure, took the letter written by Winifred Murray and placed it there in the family Bible, where Mr. Church found it half a century afterward, and we have in the resulting circumstances another instance of the fact that virtue has its reward, for it was upon the evidence of that faded, yellow letter alone that the rights of the Misses Murray were established to the fortune in Texas land which Tom Bean accumulated during his life to leave at his death as a bone for the Beans and the Beenes to quarrel over.

The fight began in the courts a few months after his death. There were claimants from exactly thirteen States, who were represented by exactly thirty lawyers. But, confident that the Misses Murray held the strongest hand, Mr. Hume, managing the matter in Texas, and Mr. Church, taking care of the case at this end of the line, struggled and fought for nine years to establish the claims of their clients, and succeeded at last. The result was the more a victory in view of the fact that shortly after Mr. Church made copies of the record in the family Bible and of the yellow letter that Winifred Murray wrote, the house occupied by the Misses Murray was destroyed by fire with all its contents, and the family Bible as well as the faded letter it had held within its pages for so many years, mingled its ashes in the ashes of all the other precious mementoes that the Misses Murray loved. This left their claim with no foundation except the copies in the possession of Mr. Church, whose sworn statement as to their correctness and authenticity is conceded to have won the case.

The decision was rendered about a month ago, and after nine years of litigation this cause celebre of Texas came to an end. By virtue of the decision the Misses Murray come into title of land variously estimated in value from $100,000 to $200,000. This was the fragment of the greater fortune that Tom Bean accumulated, after it had been torn to pieces in the extended litigation. But with the passing of time and the advancement of property values in Texas, the value of the residue will amount to the original value of the whole. Out of the amount given by the courts to Mary and Jane Murray it became necessary to take several large sums to compromise the claims of various Beans in Tennessee and a few claimants in other States. But, after all is settled, the Misses Murray will find themselves in possession of a comfortable fortune by what I am sure the reader will consider a remarkable chain of circumstances.

After the burning of their old home on the outskirts of the village they removed to a more modern dwelling within the corporate limits of Falls Church, situated upon a quiet, shady street; and there you can see them passing in and out every day, with feelings, perhaps, not unlike those of the traveler, who having long journeyed through

the darkness of dreary forest and over dangerous mountains comes at last into some pleasant valley, smiling in tranquility and peace.
—G. EDMUND HATCHER"

---

[1] The family record was written in a book, "Fourfold State," by Thomas Boston, Edinburgh, March, 1729. This record was owned by Mary E. Murray of Falls Church, and was destroyed in the fire which consumed her home in 1890. The family record gave the descent from Lord Murray. The late M. E. Church made a copy of the record prior to the fire. This was in turn copied into the Bean law suit, and a copy was loaned by a descendant, Mrs. Russell D. Weaver.
[2] One Charles Murray married an Elizabeth Robinson, daughter of Matthew Robinson and lived near this Charles Murray.
[3] Mildred (Pearson) Murray remarried to Aaron Jones and moved to Zanesville, Ohio.
[4] Deposition dated January 10, 1890.

## *THE MUTERSBAUGH FAMILY*

The earliest known ancestor of this family was John Mutersbaugh (earlier Mothersbaugh and Mutterspaugh) of York County, Pennsylvania. Mr. Mutersbaugh was born in 1800, a son of Abraham and Mary Mutersbaugh, and died October 21, 1831. He married Barbara Sprankle. Mrs. Mutersbaugh was born November 17, 1804 in York, Pa., a daughter of John and Anna (Gelhauser) Sprankle.[1] She died at Falls Church, Va., February 22, 1894, the widow Watkins, having remarried to James Watkins (*see Watkins*). Children:

(1) John B. Mutersbaugh, married Sarah Dixon.
(2) (The Reverend) David Mutersbaugh, married Ellen Louise Appleby.
(3) Abraham Mutersbaugh, married Rachel Fleck.
(4) Mary Ann Mutersbaugh, married Isaac Crossman.

(1) John B. Mutersbaugh, son of John and Barbara (Sprankle) Mutersbaugh, married Sarah Dixon of Tyrone, Pa. They came to Fairfax County in 1861 and settled on a large farm, "Thriftland," near Chesterbrook, adjoining Minor's Hill. This farm had been owned by an Army officer named Thrift who was employed in the War Department. He died at Chesterbrook March 17, 1899, and was buried in the Lewinsville Presbyterian Church yard, beside his mother. Mr. Mutersbaugh was 71 years old at the time of death. His wife died about 1903 and was buried in her native Tyrone, Pa. They did not have children but raised three orphans: Fanny M. (died Nov. 9, 1881, age 20); Daniel Divine and Mary Smith.[2]

(2) (The Reverend) David Mutersbaugh, son of John and Barbara (Sprankle) Mutersbaugh, married Ellen Louise Appleby of Georgetown, D.C. He died February 22, 1915. Mrs. Mutersbaugh was born in Georgetown, D.C., October 17, 1839, died November 4, 1914. They are buried in Lake View Cemetery, Los Angeles, California. Mr. Mutersbaugh moved from Trade City, Pa., to Fairfax County in 1858/9, and purchased a large farm near Lewinsville. He was a Local Preacher in the Methodist Church and preached without remuneration. Mr. Mutersbaugh rode from his farm at Lewinsville to Pohick Church every Sunday on horseback. He later moved to Los Angeles, California, where he was a merchant. Children:

(21) John W. Mutersbaugh, married Mary Elizabeth Crossman.
(22) Mallie Mutersbaugh.
(23) Amanda Mutersbaugh.
(24) Elizabeth Mutersbaugh.

(25) David Mutersbaugh.
(26) Emma Mutersbaugh

(3) Abraham Mutersbaugh, son of John and Barbara (Sprankle) Mutersbaugh, was born September 6, 1831, and was but one month old when his father died. He died October 29, 1903, and is buried beside his wife in the Oakwood Cemetery.[3] He married on January 13, 1853 to Rachel Fleck of Birmingham, Pa. She was born September 26, 1833, and died September 10, 1896. Children:
- (31) John Brisband Mutersbaugh, born at Tyrone, Pa., February 2, 1854, died April 14, 1855.
- (32) Georgia Etta Mutersbaugh, born August 22, 1856, Tyrone, Pa., died June 23, 1934. She married on November 25, 1879, Jonas M. Brubaker, children:
    (321) Walter Brubaker.
    (322)
- (33) Ida May Mutersbaugh, born May 22, 1858, married on December 18, 1888, Frank Lipscomb. She died March 27, 1938. No children.
- (34) Clara Virginia Mutersbaugh, born October 30, 1860, was known as Jennie. She died May 14, 1925, and is buried in Oakwood Cemetery. She married in 1905 to Brooke, and did not have children.
- (35) Ira Lincoln Mutersbaugh, born December 1, 1862, died August 11, 1863.
- (36) Ulysses Grant Mutersbaugh, born August 24, 1864, married on December 8, 1887, Cora Marsh (who died in 1943). Children (all lived in Lake Charles, La.): Alice Mutersbaugh, Alonzo Mutersbaugh, Walter Mutersbaugh, and three others.
- (37) Alonzo Sherman Mutersbaugh, born September 19, 1866, died February 8, 1950. Mr. Mutersbaugh married on December 14, 1893, to Elmira Lahrue Mason of Newport News, Va. She was born December 16, 1873, daughter of Thomas and Julia Mason and died January 28, 1958. Children:
    - (371) Earle Tanner Mutersbaugh, born August 9, 1895, married Jean Amanda Hall (no children).
    - (372) Alma Lorraine Mutersbaugh, born January 2, 1899, married on June 6, 1921, Anton Elias Groff (born June 6, 1894). Living, Dunn Loring. Children:
        - (3721) Robert Ellsworth Groff, born November 3, 1922, married (1) in 1942, Justin Stroud (two daughters live in Greenville, Tennessee); and (2) name not known to this author.
        - (3722) Freda Mason Groff, born February 21, 1928, married on March 18, 1950, Norman Andrew Smith (born August 28, 1932), children:
            - (37221) Duane Michael Smith, born July 14, 1952.
            - (37222) Carol Ann Smith, born October 22, 1953.
            - (37223) Wayne Patrick Smith, born July 26, 1955.
            - (37224) Lorraine Milly Smith, born January 3, 1957.
        - (3723) Anton Elias Groff, Jr., born May 18, 1929, married on May 27, 1950, Jean Patricia Herrell (born May 31, 1932), children:
            - (37231) Robindale Herrell Groff.
            - (37232) Laura Jean Groff.
    - (373) Emma Rachel Mutersbaugh, born September 2, 1905, married on

September 20, 1930, Horace Thaddeus Groff, brother of Anton Elias Groff. Horace T. Groff was born November 25, 1900, died December 20, 1957. Children:
(3731) Barbara Jean Groff, born September 25, 1931, married on June 14, 1952, the Rev. Earl Sanford McCary, Jr., (born June 4, 1924) of Baltimore. Mrs. McCary was graduated from Strayer's Business College, Washington, D.C., and Mr. McCary from American University and Westminster Theological Seminary. Children:
(37311) John Sanford McCary, born Deptember 14, 1954.
(37312) Lynn A. McCary, born —— 1957.
(374) Alonzo Sherman Mutersbaugh (Lonnie), born August 13, 1909, married on September 19, 1932, to Grace Odessa Evans (born January 26, 1913), children:
(3741) John Evans Mutersbaugh, born November 21, 1934, unmarried.
(3742) Lorraine Odessa Mutersbaugh, born January 7, 1937, married on September 3, 1954, Bernard Vincent Myles (born April 1, 1928). Children:
(37421) William Patrick Myles, born Feb. 16, 1956.
(375) Cline Monroe Mutersbaugh, born August 7, 1913, married on August 2, 1935, Ann Cora Moore (born September 8, 1912), children:
(3751) Cline Monroe Mutersbaugh, Jr., born Oct. 19, 1941.
(3752) Donald Gregory Mutersbaugh, born Dec. 30, 1944.

(38) Flora Belle Mutersbaugh, born January 24, 1869, died November 27, 1937, married on February 2, 1898, Lucullus Gibson, son of Owen Gibson. No children:

(39) Grace Leona Mutersbaugh, born June 13, 1872, died March 31, 1949, married on April 28, 1897, John Murray Herndon, children included Louise Herndon Watkins, and three others.

(3.10) Frank Blair Mutersbaugh, born July 3, 1875, died Sept. 3, 1876.

(4) Mary Ann Mutersbaugh, daughter of John and Barbara (Sprankle) Mutersbaugh, born September 13, 1828, died February 25, 1864, buried in Hamilton, Pa. She married Isaac Crossman of Hay City, Pa. (*See Crossman.*)

---

[1] This data is written on a lovely old Pennsylvania-Dutch birth certificate owned by Miss Ada Walker. It is decorated with hand-painted designs in vivid colors. Witnesses to this document were Michael and Mary Sprankle.
[2] Daniel Divine of Georgetown, D. C., later married Mary Smith, native of Pennsylvania.
[3] Mr. Mutersbaugh came to Fairfax County in 1858.

## *THE NELSON FAMILY*

The farm owned by William Nelson is located less than a mile North of Chesterbrook and was recently developed as a subdivision. William Nelson, Sr., purchased 1,000 acres of land from a Clergyman named Proctor who is buried in the family cemetery. Nelson erected a large Mill (known locally as Nelson's Mill). This Mill was destroyed by Union troops during the War Between the States. It must have been erected prior to the War of 1812, since old residents have stated that some of the records of the State Department were stored there on August 25, 1814.[1]

Nelson also purchased land from Colonel William Adams of "Church Hill" and on February 6, 1830, purchased the old Mill which belonged to Edward Adams, et. al., from George Jacobs and Sarah his wife, John R. Wren and Mary Y. Wren, his wife; and John Wesley Childs (Fairfax County, *Deed Book L #2*, page 64).

William Nelson, Sr., was born in 1778 and died in 1854 at the age of 76. Members of his family have a tradition that he was a relative of Secretary Thomas Nelson of Yorktown. William Nelson, Sr., married twice, first to Henrietta —— (1778-1830); and second to Valinda —— (1786-1852). They are all buried in the Nelson Cemetery.[2]

Mr. Nelson was a founder of Nelson's Chapel, Methodist Episcopal Church near Langley.

William Nelson, Sr., had the following children (known to this writer) probably all by his wife Henrietta:

(1) William Nelson, Jr., married Mary Slicer.
(2) James A. Nelson, married Sarah Ann Sewell.
(3) Thomas Henry Nelson, married Amanda Sewell.
(4) John E. Nelson, died in 1831 at the age of 10 years.

(1) William Nelson, Jr., son of William Nelson, Sr., married Mary Slicer, daughter of Henry Slicer of Washington, D.C., and moved to Washington to live. Children: (known):
   (11) Jennie Nelson, married Benjamin Ogle and resided in Washington.

(2) James A. Nelson, son of William Nelson, Sr., married Sarah Ann Sewell, daughter of Joseph A. Sewell. He is buried in the Lewinsville Presbyterian Cemetery. Children:
   (21) Catherine Nelson, married Henry Jenkins, and moved to Charlottesville during the War Between the States and died there.
   (22) James W. Nelson, served in Colonel M. M. Ball's Regiment, C.S.A., and was killed near Charlottesville.
   (23) Joseph H. Nelson, served in Ball's Regiment and died while in the service.
   (24) Henry H. Nelson, lived near Langley and died about 1902. He is buried at Lewinsville.
   (25) John E. Nelson, born April 1, 1846, died May 1, 1928, lived in the old home place. He married on January 4, 1911, to Helen Roberta Walters. Mrs. Nelson was born April 21, 1855, daughter of Thomas Jefferson and Henrietta Virginia (Hirst) Walters, and died January 30, 1933.
   (26) Annie L. Nelson, born 1852, married on January 19, 1870, to George Albert Rouzee (Rowzee). He was born in Fairfax County in 1840, son of John and Julia Rouzee.

(3) Thomas Henry Nelson, son of William Nelson, Sr., married Amanda Sewell and moved to Kentucky. Children (among others);
   (31) Henrietta Nelson, married Joshua Kirby.
   (32) Catherine A. Nelson, married George F. Kirby.

---

[1] This information can be found in an article, "The Rambler" published in the Washington, D.C., *Sunday Star* of February 4, 1917. This article contains a number of errors.

[2] Others buried here include Joseph W. Sewell (March 23, 1817-Sept. 15, 1882) and his wife,

Catherine A., (said to have been a Nelson) (April 10, 1818-May 8, 1901); William Nelson Sewell, their son (Oct. 24, 1847-Nov. 16, 1901); Laura V. Walters (Feb. 23, 1852-June 2, 1865); Mary G. daughter of T. J. and H. V. Walters, died Jan. 15, 1909, age 50; Lieut. Walter H. Reid, C.S.A. (Oct. 25, 1837-Oct. 19, 1874); Maude E. Hirst (1878-1946), and many others who have unmarked graves.

## THE NOURSE FAMILY

The Reverend Robert M. Nourse, a Congregational Minister, came to Falls Church from Illinois about 1884. He purchased "Cloverdale Farm" (now owned by the Flagg family) on Haycock Road. He was born in 1841, and died in 1902. Mr. Nourse was noted in the Village for his lecture on Dr. Jekell and Mr. Hyde. He gave it each year and the proceeds went for Village improvement. His wife was Eunice South (1835-1901). The family came to Falls Church from Illinois, but was of English origin. Issue:

(1) Rose Gertrude Nourse (1868-1909), unmarried.

(2) Kathleen Nourse, born May 14, 1872, died February 21, 1946. Married Dr. Thomas Melville Talbott who was born October 17, 1848, died May 3, 1940. Dr. Talbott was first married to Ella Ball Febrey, daughter of John E. and Mary F. (Ball) Febrey. (*See Talbott*). Issue:

(21) Gladys Talbott, born February 22, 1893, died September 3, 1893.
(22) Harold Wailes Talbott, born January 20, 1898, died June 29, 1911.
(23) Philip Talbott, Senior Vice President of Woodward and Lothrop Department Store, Washington, D.C.

(3) Margaret Roberta Nourse, 1874-1922, unmarried.

(4) Philip Beecher Nourse, born 1876, was at one time Post Master at East End and was proprietor of a Livery Stable. He was also in the Real Estate business. Mr. Hourse married Harriet F. Graham, daughter of Dr. Graham. He died Sunday, December 24, 1944, aged 68 years. Mr. Nourse was buried in National Memorial Park. His widow, Mrs. Harriet Nourse, died July 27, 1954. Issue:

(41) Harriet Nourse, married Donald E. ("Pete") Ball. Issue:
(411) Harriet Ball.
(412) Ann Ball.
(42) Eunice Nourse, married Leonard Welles.
(43) Clara Nourse, married John Busick.

## THE OSBORN FAMILY

"Center Hill" was a lovely brick home located almost opposite the St. James School, now 809 West Broad Street. To more recent residents the house is better known as the "Osborn House," or "Munson House."

Two brothers named Osborn settled in Falls Church. They were natives of Fairfield County, Connecticut, and the children of Seth and Sarah Osborn. Their mother, Sarah Osborn, is buried in Oakwood Cemetery in Falls Church. Her stone has this inscription: "Sarah, relict of Seth Osborn, a native of Fairfield Co., Ct., d. July 29, 1847 at 64 yrs." Cyrus Osborn, son of Seth and Sarah Osborn, was born in Fairfield County, June 27, 1807, and died at Falls Church, September 9, 1886. Seth Osborn, son of Seth and Sarah Osborn, was born in Fairfield County, February 24, 1819, and died at Falls Church, May 18, 1897. He moved to Falls Church prior to 1847.

Seth Osborn married Mary E. Marcy who was born in Fairfax County December 19, 1830, and died at Falls Church December 29, 1918. She was a daughter of William Marcy (died November 27, 1853 at 56 years) and Eleanor Marcy his wife (died December 15, 1879). Seth and Mary E. (Marcy) Osborn had one child, Miss Julia Osborn, who survived her parents.

George B. Ives built the "Center Hill" house for Mr. Osborn sometime prior to 1850. Apparently an older frame house had been on the site. The house was of brick with gabled ends. In the center was a small entrance porch with four square pillars. The entrance was set back in panels. About three acres of the original Osborn tract remained with the house.

When the Town of Falls Church was incorporated in 1875, Seth Osborn served on the Council. He was identified with every movement for the public good, and made a lasting contribution to the community. "Center Hill" was later the home of the Munson family and of the Thomson Mason Hirst family for a short time. "Center Hill" was torn down during the week of March 12-17, 1962. The Broadfalls Apartments now occupy the site.

## THE PAYNE FAMILY

It is an extremely difficult task to unravel the various Payne families of Colonial Fairfax. There was one Ananias Payne, ancestor of many of the Paynes of Falls Church and vicinity, who may have been connected with the family of Colonel William Payne. William Payne, Sr., and William, Jr., his son, were Vestrymen of Truro Parish on March 28, 1763, when it was decided to build the present Falls Church. In 1769, Edward Payne, of this family, was also a Vestryman. He was the one for whom Payne's Church near Fairfax Court House was named. On March 22, 1785, William Payne was a Gentleman Justice of Fairfax County. He signed the famous "Fairfax Resolves" on July 18, 1774, and was a member of the committee which was to "have power to call a general meeting, and to concert such measures as may be thought most expedient and necessary." George Washington was chairman of the committee.

The late Colonel Brooke Payne, author of *The Paynes of Virginia*, could not find the connection of the Ananias Payne family with William Payne.[1] They were certainly related. William Payne, son of Ananias, was a contemporary to several others with the same name in Fairfax County.

On May 4, 1811,[2] John Adams of Fairfax County deeded a tract of land containing 212 acres to William Payne ("of Ananias"), also of the same county. This land was granted to Charles Broadwater January 15, 1724, and to John Adams by the will of Colonel William Adams. Witnesses were: George Minor, William Minor and Smith Minor.

William Payne, son of Ananias, had a wife named Elizabeth, probably an Adams.[3] She joined him on May 4, 1811, in conveying to Colonel George Minor the above mentioned 212 acres of land.[4]

William Payne made his will on March 19, 1813, probated March 20, 1815.[5] In it he mentioned his wife, Elizabeth, and the following children: Polly, William, Elizabeth, James, Thomas, Lewis, Charity, Nancy, and John. Witnesses were: George Minor, Joseph Sewell and Richard Wrenn.

William and Elizabeth Payne had issue:[6]
(1) Mary (Polly) Payne, born February 16, 1792.
(2) William Payne, born February 7, 1794, died about 1825. He married on February 25, 1819, Catherine (Kitty) Hughes, daughter of William and Elizabeth (Wren) Hughes. An incomplete record of their family is in the *Payne Bible*. Issue:
(21) Elizabeth Payne, born January 20, 1820.
(22) Lavina Payne, born January 7, 1821.
(23) Asenath Franklin Payne, born February 25, 1822.

*Note:* William Payne's widow remarried to Joseph Sewell. (Fairfax County, *Will Book R #1*, page 373). Catherine (Hughes) (Payne) Sewell had two sons by Joseph Sewell: Franklin Sewell and John Fletcher Sewell. The Payne children were to share with the Sewell children according to the will of Joseph Sewell in 1836. Since Lavina Payne is not listed as a child, she was apparently dead by 1836.

(3) Elisabeth Payne, born November 7, 1795.
(4) James Payne, married Hannah Adams.
(5) Thomas Payne, born November 20, 1801.
(6) Lewis Payne, born November 7, 1803, died January 24, 1873.
(7) Charity Payne, born August 9, 1806.
(8) Nancy Payne, born February 26, 1808.
(9) John Payne, born March 11, 1810, married (1) Jane ——; and (2) Virginia F. Torreyson.

Of the above children, (4) James Payne, was born March 8, 1798, and died April 27, 1884. He was buried in the family cemetery, near Chesterbrook, but his remains were later removed to Walker Chapel. He married Hannah Adams. Mrs. Payne was born May 26, 1800, and according to an old family tradition, was connected with an Adams family of White Post, Virginia. She died October 6, 1882.

On January 1, 1840, George W. Hunter, Jr., Commissioner, under a law suit, "Joseph Sewell's heirs vs. Sewell's Exrs.," sold to James Payne land formerly owned by William Payne. The deed recites that William Payne devised this land to his daughters Elizabeth and Asenath, and that they agreed to take a portion under the will of Joseph Sewell. Thus they surrendered the land to be sold as part of the Sewell estate?

James Payne was an ardent Methodist and was Class Leader at Nelson's Chapel (now Trinity Church, McLean). He served in this capacity from before August 5, 1858 until after 1875. He is listed in the 1850 U. S. Census of Fairfax County as a farmer with real estate valued at $2,000. Living in his household at the time were William Deeble, a native of Washington, D.C., born 1832, a farm hand, and Alice Trammell, Negro, born in Virginia, 1810, servant.

James and Hannah (Adams) Payne had issue:[8]
(41) Mary Catherine Payne, born December 23, 1824, died unmarried.
(42) Jane America Payne, born August 23, 1828, died unmarried, June 18, 1864 (date in the *Family Bible* owned by E. P. Wren).
(43) Margaret Amelia Payne, born November 1, 1830, married Captain Henry W. Febrey *(See Febrey)*.
(44) Druannah Verlinda Payne (called Dru) born November 10, 1832, died August 4, 1900. She married John Tucker. They did not have issue, but reared Bessie Payne, daughter of Amos Parker Payne, who took the name Tucker.

(45) Amos Parker Payne, born August 14, 1838, died January 5, 1929, with burial in Arlington National Cemetery. Mr. Payne served in the Confederate Army during the War Between the States. He married (1) at Dulin Chapel, December 7, 1869, to Mrs. Mary E. (Brunner) Brunner, widow. She was born in Baltimore in 1843, daughter of Crockard Brunner. Mrs. Payne died in January 1884. Her daughter, Catherine Brunner, by the first marriage, married Francis Magarity of Lewinsville. Mr. Payne remarried (2) on December 2, 1892, to Elizabeth Katherine Gibson. She was born November 15, 1860, and died February 6, 1946. Mrs. Payne was a daughter of Owen H. and Mary E. (Hospital) Gibson who were married in Loudoun County on April 3, 1854. Her brother, John N. Gibson, was Town Sergeant of Falls Church. Mr. and Mrs. Payne were members of The Methodist Episcopal Church and attended Fairfax Chapel and Dulin Chapel. On November 13, 1887, Mr. Payne transferred to Trinity, Langley. Issue (*By Mary E. Brunner*):

(451) Cora Adams Payne, born September 18, 1870, baptized Dulin Chapel, October 10, 1870.
(452) Belle McVeigh Payne, baptized March 17, 1872.
(453) Mary Eleanor Payne (Ella) baptized January 26, 1874, married —— Gamble.
(454) Edna Payne, died in infancy.
(455) Bessie Leigh Payne, born January 5, 1884, living, 1956, surname now Tucker. She is unmarried.

(*By Elizabeth Katherine Gibson*):
(456) Zola Payne, born January 11, 1900, married on August 25, 1930, to Norman Robertson, issue: William Parker Robertson, born October 20, 1932.

(46) Lucy Salina Payne, born November 17, 1839, married John Wesley Wren (*See Wren*).

(47) Asburina Virginia Payne, born September 23, 1845, died June 6, 1901. She was named for Bishop Francis Asbury of The Methodist Episcopal Church. She married on March 19, 1868, to John E. Hirst. Mr. Hirst was born in Fairfax County, near present-day McLean, in 1833, a son of Richard and Eliza Hirst. He died in September, 1884. Mr. Hirst was a member of Trinity Methodist Church in 1869, but was later a trustee of Andrew Chapel at Kenmore. He married (1) Virginia A. (Lizzie) Reid. She was born in 1838 and died before 1872. Her only child, John E. Hirst, Jr., died shortly after birth. By his second marriage to Asburina Virginia Payne, John E. Hirst had issue:

(471) Ada Virginia Hirst, born December 24, 1872, died October 26, 1953, married Ward Travis Kirby (*See Kirby*).
(472) Arthur Nelson Hirst, born 1875, died of typhoid fever in July, 1901, unmarried.
(473) Maude Estelle Hirst, born 1878, died in March, 1946, unmarried.
(474) Henry Douglas Hirst, born January 31, 1881, is living, 1964, at Langley. He married at Portsmouth, August 15, 1923, Mafies Matilda Carper (born March 9, 1889) daughter of John Marshall and Ida Strother (Fogg) Carper. No issue.

(9) John Payne, son of William and Elizabeth Payne, was born March 11, 1810,

and died at age 62 years. He was buried on December 19, 1873 in Oak Hill Cemetery, Georgetown? Mr. Payne was a Carriage Maker for many years in Georgetown. He married (1) Jane ——, who died at age 38 years. He remarried (2) Virginia F. Torreyson, a sister of William H. Torreyson. On April 1, 1864, John and Virginia F. Payne of Georgetown, D.C., purchased "Church Hill," from William C. Lipscomb. Issue: (*By Jane* ——)

(91) William Thomas Payne, born 1835.
(92) Asbury Roszel Payne (called Ross), married Margaret Birch, daughter of Colonel Samuel and Ann (Cleveland) Birch (*See Birch*). Their son, Howard Payne, was born February 29, 1876, and died August 9, 1877, with burial in the Birch Family Cemetery.
(93) Charles R. Payne.
(94) Theodore W. Payne, died at his residence on Chain Bridge Road, April 4, 1900. He married (1) May 11, 1871, Anna E. Birch. She was born January 15, 1838, daughter of Colonel Samuel and Ann (Cleveland) Birch, and died December 3, 1881. Mrs. Payne is buried in the Birch Family Cemetery. Her sister, Margaret, married Asbury Roszel Payne, brother of Theodore W. Payne. Mr. Payne remarried (2) on January 25, 1893, to Edmonia S. Newlon, who died May 30, 1940.
(95) Julia A. T. Payne, married J. Franklin Smith. They had at least one son, James Payne Smith, born November 25, 1868, in Baltimore, baptized at Dulin Chapel.

(*By Virginia Frances Torreyson*):
(96) Samuel Winfield Payne, born October 27, 1852, settled in Falls Church on a twenty acre estate in 1865. By his wife, Mary P. Payne, he had several children including Samuel Talbott Payne, baptized at Dulin Chapel on March 11, 1888, and Walter Payne, currently a resident of Rochester, New York.
(97) Edward LeGrande Payne, born August 31, 1854, in Georgetown, died February 21, 1924. He married on June 28, 1894, Annie Cookman Jacobs, a descendant of the old Donaldson and Jacobs families. Mrs. Payne was born in Washington, D.C., January 2, 1870, and died in Arlington, July 22, 1938. Issue:
  (971) Laura Virginia Payne, born at "Church Hill," February 26, 1900, is living currently in Arlington. She married on June 28, 1921, to Hedrick Wickline Wolford, a native of Lovettsville, Virginia, born March 13, 1894. Issue:
    (9711) Hedrick Laurence Wolford, born January 12, 1923, married on June 23, 1944, Josephine Crouch of Georgia. Issue: Steven Laurence Wolford, born June 13, 1950; and Sheryl Josephine Wolford, born October 12, 1953.
    (9712) Leslie Howard Wolford, born January 15, 1926, married on June 24, 1947, Eunice Cobb of Texas. Issue: Joann Leslie Wolford, born March 5, 1951; and Patricia Lynn Wolford, born November 7, 1951.
  (972) John Howard Payne, born in Falls Church, September 4, 1904, is living in Arlington. He married Jobyna Kelley of Tennessee. Issue:

(9721) James Howard Payne, born December 15, 1929.
(9722) Virginia Ann Payne, born August 8, 1931.
(9723) Joyce Lee Payne, born January 19, 1941.
(98) Henry Clay Payne.
(99) Lydia Blanche Payne.
(9.10) Nora Larkum Payne, baptized at Dulin Chapel, June 20, 1871, died in childhood.

*Note:* For additional record of this family, including the division of "Church Hill," in June, 1876, see Fairfax *Deed Book V #4*, page 131.

### The Jacob Payne Family

Another Payne family connected with Falls Church, who gave its name "Paynes Corners," to what is now 7 Corners, was represented by Jacob Payne. These Paynes, while most likely related to the Ananias Payne family, did not claim kinship. Jacob Payne was born February 15, 1781,[10] and died May 21, 1849. He may have been a son of Josiah Payne. His wife, Ann, was born December 10, 1784, and died November 2, 1857. They had seventeen children:

(1) Chloe Payne, born November 5, 1802.
(2) Mary Payne, born April 15, 1805, died March 16, 1868.
(3) Ann Payne, born March 22, 1807, died June 11, 1877.
(4) Hannah Payne, born April 11, 1809, died November 7, 1821.
(5) James A. Payne, born January 16, 1811, died February 25, 1853.
(6) Julia A. Payne, born December 27, 1812, died October 7, 1830.
(7) Jacob Payne, Jr., born December 23, 1814, died April 17, 1842.
(8) John H. Payne, born September 25, 1816, died December 15, 1853.
(9) Harriet Payne, born January 19, 1819, died January 5, 1847.
(10) Ruth Payne, born July 29, 1820, died the same day.
(11) Charles Worthington Payne, married Elizabeth Donaldson.
(12) William H. Payne (twin), born June 27, 1821, died May 21, 1827.
(13) Louisa Payne, born August 29, 1823, died September 1, 1883.
(14) Henry Payne, born April 15, 1825, died December 13, 1898.
(15) Lewis Payne, born January 8, 1828, died March 4, 1864.
(16) William Payne, born April 26, 1829, died the same day.
(17) Elizabeth Payne, born November 18, 1830/31, died August 18, 1870.

Of the above, (11) Charles Worthington Payne, was born June 27, 1821, a twin of his brother, William. He died October 24, 1886, and was buried in Mt. Olivet Methodist Cemetery. Mr. Payne married on July 28, 1844, Elizabeth Donaldson. She was born December 24, 1823, and died April 21, 1875. Issue:

(11.1) William Harrison Payne, born May 22, 1847.
(11.2) Sarah Catherine (Kate) Payne, born August, 1849.
(11.3) Anna R. Payne, born September 23, 1851, married (1) George Lewis Walker in Georgetown, D.C., by L.W. Bates, on September 9, 1868. He was born February 14, 1844, of the Walker Chapel Walkers, and died September 26, 1872. He was a son of David and Nancy (Reid) Walker. She remarried (2) Thomas R. Sypherd. Issue:

(11.31) George Lewis Walker.
(11.32) Carrie Louise Walker, born February 10, 1871, died January 22, 1961. She married William Dulany Monroe. Mr. Monroe was born in Loudoun County, April 3, 1868, a son of James Henry and Julia (Miley) Monroe. He died June 13, 1951. Issue:
    (11.321) Anna Sypherd Monroe, born October 29, 1902, is living, unmarried, 1961, at 31st & N Streets, Georgetown.
    (11.322) Helen Walker Monroe, born July 4, 1896, married the Reverend Calvert Egerton Buck, born 1895, son of Charles Emmett and Emilie (Chesley) Buck, of Maryland. Issue: William Charles Buck, married Elizabeth Wyatt Powell of Danville and had two children, Elizabeth Ann and Susan Terry; and Helen Ann Buck, married Douglas Frank Cowley and had two children, Lawrence William Cowley, and Richard Buck Cowley.
    (11.323) William Dulany Monroe, born May 21, 1899, married (1) Emma Jane Lewis; and (2) Mabel Waddell of Middleburg. Issue (by first wife): William Dulany Monroe, III, U.S.N., married Jean Edmonds. Issue two children: William Dulany Monroe IV, and Thomas Edward Monroe.

(11.4) John Donaldson Payne, born July 8, 1853, died at Falls Church in 1938. John D. Payne was an auctioneer and gave his name to Payne's Corners. He was a mayor of Falls Church. Mr. Payne married Frances Hall, daughter of Bazil and Columbia (Birch) Hall. Children:
    (11.41) Bertha Payne.
    (11.42) Annie I. Payne, married Frank A. Twitchell. She was born in 1885 and died September 18, 1959. Mrs. Twitchell's children include Mrs. Robert Prosise and Mrs. Ralph Dubrowin.
    (11.43) Pansy E. Payne, married William C. Crossman.
    (11.44) Ethel M. Payne, married Joseph H. Marr.
    (11.45) Ruth Payne, married Paul Jones.
(11.5) Charles Wesley Payne.
(11.6) Ofealer Payne, born June 3, 1856, died February 25, 1857.
(11.7) Oliver Cox Payne, born April 24, 1858.
(11.8) George Wunder Paine, born March 14, 1860.
(11.9) William Payne, born August 15, 1862
(11.10) Lillie Payne, born October 26, 1864.
(11.11) Freddie Payne, born 1867, died June 8, 1954. She married James Cornelius Beach, who died in Tenleytown, D.C., in 1904. She was an employee of the U.S. Department of Agriculture. Children: Mrs. Harry L. Freer, Howard Payne Beach, Paul Donaldson Beach, James Elmer Beach, and John Wesley Beach.

---

[1] See page 247, et. seq.
[2] Fairfax County, *Deed Book L #2*, page 254.
[3] *The Payne Bible* of 1785 has written on the fly-leaf: "Samuel Adams 1791." This was crossed out and written underneath: "William Payne His Book price 21/." It was first an Adams Bible.
[4] Fairfax County, *Deed Book L #2*, page 282.

[5] Fairfax County, *Will Book K #1*, page 288.
[6] *The Payne Bible* is the source of the birth dates. It was published in Edinburgh, Scotland, in 1785, by Alexander Kincaid. It is owned by William Bailey Garfield of Washington, D. C.
[7] Fairfax County *Deed Book F #3*, page 366.
[8] The author has some reason to think that Mrs. James Payne was Hannah Adams Hughes, not Adams.
[9] Dulin Chapel records show that John Payne died "in peace," in December, 1873.
[10] Data from the *Family Bible* was supplied by Miss Anna Monroe, March, 1961. She stated that some years ago Ardell Payne was compiling a history of this family.

## THE PORTER FAMILY

The "Porter House" is two doors from the corner of Great Falls Street and North Washington, on the right hand side going south. This house was built about 1885 by W. W. Kingsley and purchased by David Essex Porter and Admiral David D. Porter. As a house, the edifice is not of any architectural significance. However, the Porter family is worthy of extended notice. David Essex Porter came from a long line of Yankee sea men. His father was Admiral David D. Porter of the Union Navy during the War Between the States.

Admiral David Dixon Porter was born in Chester, Pennsylvania, in 1813. He entered the navy as midshipman in 1829. From 1836 to 1841, he was employed in the coast survey of the United States and held various other appointments until the out-break of the war in 1861. Porter was then made Commander of the sloop of war "Powhatan," distinguished himself in the capture of New Orleans, and commanded the gunboat and mortar flotilla which cooperated with the squadron of Admiral Farragut in the first attack on Vicksburg. In the fall of 1862, as acting Rear Admiral, he was placed in command of all the naval forces on the river above New Orleans. At the termination of the war, he was appointed Superintendent of the U. S. Naval Academy at Annapolis. He was made Vice Admiral in 1866, Admiral in 1870, and died in 1891.

The following jingle which makes mention of Admiral Porter was of Civil War origin, and appeared in the contemporary *National Tribune* published in Washington, D.C.:

> There's Porter ever in front
> true son of a sea King sire,
> Christian Foote and Du Pont who led his ships,
> rounding the first eclipse of thunder and fire.[1]

The grandfather of David Essex Porter was Admiral Porter of Revolutionary fame. D. E. Porter married, and had at least two sons. Admiral D. D. Porter lived for a time with his son in his Falls Church home, and thus becomes a part of the Falls Church tradition.

---

[1] Part of an extensive poem on the battle of New Orleans, which Miss Ada Walker read as a young girl. She quoted this to the author on January 31, 1951.

## THE QUICK FAMILY

Jacques Voorhees Quick, Jr., of distinguished old American ancestry,[1] was born in Hunterdon County, New Jersey, October 28, 1828, and died at his home in Falls Church on September 17, 1908. He married at Readington, New Jersey, November 8, 1848, Sarah Ott Biggs, a daughter of John Ott and Ann (Laberteaux) Biggs. Mrs. Quick was born in Hunterdon County, March 8, 1832, and died at Falls Church, May 23, 1903. In 1870 the Quick family moved from their New Jersey home to Loudoun County. In 1889 they settled in Falls Church. Issue:

(1) Jacques Voorhees Quick, 3rd, born July 29, 1849, died June 13, 1918. He married on October 12, 1869, Mariah Shurts Bird (died July 23, 1920).

(2) Sarah Emma Quick, born April 25, 1851, died November 5, 1936. She married on August 10, 1888, Charles Wilson Bubb (died November 3, 1933). No issue.

(3) John Biggs Quick, born December 4, 1852, died July 9, 1899. He married on June 1, 1875, Clara E. Bubb (died 1924).

(4) Willard Augustus Quick, born May 14, 1855, died December 22, 1936. He married on May 18, 1875, Margaret Myers (died January 30, 1933). No issue.

(5) Vanderbelt Quick, born February 21, 1857, died January 20, 1930. He married on February 29, 1880, Susan Keim (born April 30, 1857, died July 29, 1938). Mr. Quick was a merchant. They had five children.

(6) Charles Bartels Quick, born August 10, 1859, died May 6, 1927. He married on October 13, 1881, Alice G. Thomas (died January 13, 1933). A daughter, Hazel Northrup Quick, "always considered one of the prettiest young ladies of the community," married William Williams Rucker of Clarendon, and their wedding was an outstanding event in the community.

(7) (The Reverend) George Washington Quick, D.D., born October 25, 1861, died November 6, 1936. He married on September 9, 1896, Kathrina Cobleigh. Mr. Quick was a distinguished Baptist Minister. Issue: Virginia M. Quick. Dr. Quick is buried in Oakwood Cemetery.

(8) Ellen Maria Quick, born June 2, 1864, married Lambert B. Nixon.

(9) Ida Jeanette Quick, born January 20, 1867, married George White Hawxhurst (*See Hawxhurst*).

(10) Dr. Tunis Cline Quick, M.D., born January 27, 1871, died February 21, 1923, a long-time resident of Falls Church. Dr. Quick was a well-known and beloved citizen. He was a school mate of President Taft, and a reception for President Taft was held in the community during his administration. The President spoke from the steps of the building now occupied by Pearson's Funeral Home.

---

[1] See *A Genealogy of the Quick Family in America, 1625-1942*, by Arthur Craig Quick.

## THE READ FAMILY

Two brothers, John B. and Hiram W. Read, settled in Falls Church before the War Between the States. The Reverend Hiram W. Read, one of the brothers, was minister of the Columbia Baptist Church.

The Reverend Hiram Walter Read was born in Jewett City, Connecticut, July 17, 1819, and was baptized at Oswego, New York, March 11, 1838. He was educated at Oswego Academy and Madison University. Mr. Read began his ministry in 1844, at

Whitewater, Wisconsin. He was pastor and chaplain to the Wisconsin Senate, and conducted extensive revivals. In 1849 he went to New Mexico and in 1852 preached to U. S. troops and to the Indians and Mexicans. He organized churches, located missionaries, established schools, explored adjacent Territories, and laid foundations for mission work.

Mr. Read returned East and labored for the Home Mission and American and Foreign Bible Societies. He settled afterwards at Falls Church and in 1857 built the Columbia Baptist Church. During the War Between the States he served the U. S. government at Washington, in the field and in hospitals; was taken prisoner, and exchanged for Dr. Broaddus, of Fredericksburg.

Mr. Read assisted in the establishment of the Territorial government of Arizona, and held positions of trust under the direction of the U. S. Treasury. He visited California in 1864 and in 1865 settled in Hannibal, Missouri. He baptized more than 1,000 persons in his revivals and was popular in Missouri as an evangelist. In 1881 he was in Virginia City, Nevada.

John B. Read, brother of Hiram W. Read, was a farmer and sometime preacher. He lived in a house on the site of the large mansion later erected by Schuyler Duryee (now Tyler Gardens). He was born in Connecticut in 1812 and was killed by some of Mosby's men in 1864, and is buried in the Falls Church yard. Details of his death are given elsewhere. Following his death, his widow, Charlotte E. Read (1821-1886) and her daughters Charlotte L. (Lottie) Read (1850-1891) and Emma Read lived in a house which was across East Broad Street from Dulin Methodist Church, the site of the modern Moffatt house. This residence, built about 1800, was much like the Clover House and the Lynch House, and was of frame. It burned after World War I.

Miss Emma Read was blind. Her eyes were damaged when a gun, held by a brother, discharged accidentally. There may have been others in this family, but no record is available.

## THE RICE FAMILY

In 1890 Yale Rice of New York purchased the ninety-five acre Gheen Farm on East Broad Street. This house, now 708 East Broad Street, is called "Tall Wood." The house is of white-painted brick. The architectural style is called Federalist. The house was built about 1870 for the Gheen family (who were related to Almond Birch) and was constructed by James G. W. Brunner. The house has great historical significance to modern Falls Church history, since it was the home of General Dwight D. Eisenhower for about six weeks when he was a Major connected with the staff of General McArthur. This was during the late 1930's and early 1940's, when "Tall Wood" was the home of his brother, Dr. Milton Eisenhower. Milton Eisenhower married a local girl, Helen Eakin (whose brother is still a resident of Falls Church). Dr. and Mrs. Eisenhower attended the Falls Church.

The immigrant ancestor of Yale Rice was Robert Royce (as the name was originally) who was born in 1590 and died in 1676. With his wife Elizabeth, he came to America in 1631. Samuel Rice, son of Robert and Elizabeth Royce-Rice, married Hannah Churchill. Their son, Samuel Rice, Jr., married Thankful Beach. Amos Rice, son of this couple, married Sarah Baldwin. Jacob Rice, son of Samuel and Sarah (Baldwin) Rice, married Sarah Morse. Their son, Benajah Rice, married on

January 31, 1793 to Sarah, daughter of Joseph and Catherine (Yale) Hough. Amos Rice, son of Benajah and Sarah (Hough) Rice, was born August 22, 1800, died May 29, 1885. He married on June 6, 1824 to Loretta Susan Andrews (born February 23, 1804, died June 9, 1867.) They were the parents of Yale Rice of Falls Church. It is of interest to their descendants to give an outline of the Yale ancestry. Sarah (Hough) Rice was a daughter of Joseph and Catherine (Yale) Hough. Catherine (Yale) Hough was born in 1721, died 1767. She was a daughter of Captain Theophilus and Sarah (Street) Yale, granddaughter of Thomas and Rebecca (Gibbons) Yale. Thomas Yale (born 1647) was a brother of Elihu Yale, for whom Yale University was named.

Yale Rice of Falls Church was born in New York December 23, 1831, son of Amos and Loretta Susan (Andrews) Rice. He died in Falls Church March 8, 1917, and is buried in Oakwood Cemetery. He married on April 18, 1860, to Helen Maria Curtis. Mrs. Rice was born September 21, 1836, died in March, 1921, and was a daughter of Judge James C. Curtis and Pamelia Calkins (Taylor) Curtis of Sullivan Co., N.Y. Judge Curtis was born October 28, 1797, died in February, 1881. Mrs. Curtis was born October 29, 1798, died January 17, 1881. They were married June 22, 1822. Mrs. Curtis was descended from Oliver Calkins, a Revolutionary Soldier. Her granddaughter, Mrs. G. B. Fadeley, has a chair which belonged to Oliver Calkins.

Mr. and Mrs. Yale Rice and family settled in Falls Church on January 1, 1891. They stayed at the "Eagle House" until their new home was prepared to receive them. Soon thereafter they settled on their farm. Yale and Helen Maria (Curtis) Rice had issue:

(1) Edward Rice, died as a child.

(2) Albert Rice, died at the same time as his brother Edward. They both died of measles.

(3) Susan Andrews Rice (1865-October 5, 1938) died unmarried. Miss Rice was a writer.

(4) Pamelia Curtis Rice (1868-1915), married Elida Crofoot Hough (1863-1926). Issue:

(41) Philip Hough, former Superintendent of "Wakefield," birthplace of George Washington. Mr. Hough married Blanche Cain, and died in 1953. Issue:
(411) Barbara Hough.
(412) Robert Laurence Hough.
(42) Laurence Cooper Hough (1891-1937), married Jennie Ponti, died in Savannah, Ga.
(43) Helen Yale Hough, unmarried. Miss Hough is a Librarian.

(5) Marian Rice, born November 2, 1872, married Dr. George B. Fadeley. Mrs. Fadeley has kindly supplied most of this information on the Rice family. She was the first child of her family born in the North Woods. Her father, Yale Rice, made his money in the tannery business. The "North Woods" were in Lewis Co., N.Y. *(See Fadeley)*

(6) John Rice (1878-1893) died unmarried.

(7) Elizabeth Rice ("Bess") lived in Washington, D.C. Unmarried.

## THE RILEY FAMILY

James Riley (Ryly), a member of the Queen's Palace Guard, and dispatch bearer for the Queen, was a native of Ireland. He married Rebecca Harvey of the family of Dr. William Harvey (1578-1657) the noted anatomist who discovered the process of blood circulation. Riley settled in Bedford County, Pennsylvania, at an early date. Issue: Sarah, Mary Ann, Samuel, Andrew, James, Isaac, Henry, and George Riley.

Andrew Riley, son of James and Rebecca (Harvey) Riley, moved from Bedford County to Western Ohio in 1825. A few years later he moved to a farm on Stony Creek, Randolph County, Indiana, and is buried there in Windsor Township. He married Margaret Schlick (1793-1881) of German ancestry, a daughter of John and Elizabeth (Wilson) Schlick. Her father represented a family whose surname was originally spelled Schleick. He was editor and publisher of a Methodist Magazine published in New York. Issue:

(1) (Captain) Reuben Alexander Riley, born in Bedford County, Pennsylvania, in 1819, was a prominent civic leader and lawyer. He married on February 20, 1844, Elizabeth Marine of North Carolina, daughter of John and Fanny (Jones) Marine. Mrs. Riley was born in 1823. Issue: John Andrew Riley, born December 11, 1844; Martha Celestia Riley, born February 21, 1847, died in childhood; James Whitcomb Riley (the poet), born October 7, 1849, died unmarried, 1916; Elva May Riley, born January 14, 1856, married Henry Eitel, a banker, and had a son, Edmund Eitel; Humboldt Alexander Riley, born October 15, 1858; and Mary Elizabeth Riley, born October 27, 1864, married —— Payne. James Whitcomb Riley, poet nephew of Judge Joseph S. Riley of Falls Church, sent inscribed copies of his works which are still owned by descendants of the Judge.[1]

(2) (Dr.) John Riley, a surgeon in the Confederate Army during the War Between the States. Dr. Riley lived to be 104 years old. He practiced medicine in Texas. His wife was Martha Colcolt of Natchez, Mississippi, and they reared a large family.

(3) Andrew Riley, Jr., was a dentist and served as Sheriff in California. He had one son who died young.

(4) George Riley, an editor and publisher of a Pennsylvania newspaper, served in the Union Army. His one son died young. Mr. Riley died in Falls Church, having moved here in his old age.

(5) James Riley went to California and reared a family.

(6) Martin Riley, married and had a family.

(7) Sarah Riley, married James Shepherd of Virginia and lived for a time in Falls Church. Their one son, James Shepherd, died unmarried.

(8) Frank Riley, married and had one daughter, Mrs. Paul.

(9) (Judge) Joseph Schlick Riley, born in Indianapolis, Indiana, March 28, 1834, and died at his "Cherry Hill," farm home (now part of the City Hall tract) on February 28, 1919. Judge Riley attended an Academy in Indianapolis, came to Washington where he owned a book store on Seventh Street. He also owned a tobacco sale and export business in Richmond.

"Cherry Hill," as originally owned by the Riley family included all the land between the Middle Pike, now Broad Street, and Great Falls Road on the East and West, extending from Little Falls Road to and slightly beyond Oak Street. The Northwest boundary adjoined the Fish tract (later the Sherwood and then DePutron tract) and was cut by the Southern Railway, now the Old Dominion. The name "Cherry Hill" derives from the large number of cherry trees around the house and bordering the lane that led to the Pike.

The farm was part of a tract originally granted John Trammell by patent from the Proprietor of the Northern Neck on January 16, 1729, and was successively owned by John Mills, Augustine Newton, (January 29, 1843); William D. Harvey, (July 16, 1845);[2] George B. Steele, (December 20, 1848, who added six acres obtained from Nathan Thompson of "Big Chimneys"); William A. Blaisdell, (July 17, 1856); William D. Shepherd, (December 18, 1865); and eighty acres of it by Judge Riley, in 1870. Judge Riley did not move to "Cherry Hill" until 1873. The Washington, D.C., *Republican* of March 16, 1872 noted in a dispatch from Falls Church signed by "Q":

"Mr. Riley (of the firm of Crandell & Riley), is soon to take possession of his farm here and contemplates cutting it up into village lots and placing them in market."

"Cherry Hill" and the old Dulany farm, "Oak Mount" (now Greenway Downs) came into the possession of Judge Riley as a result of court action brought by him to recover on large sums of money lost through the defalcations of a business partner, which ultimately necessitated sacrifice of his book store in Washington, the branch book store in Richmond, and his lucrative business of buying and selling leaf tobacco.

While living at his Washington home, Judge Riley was active in the old Metropolitan Memorial Methodist Church (then at John Marshall Place and C Street). He was always interested in the Church and was a member of Dulin Chapel at Falls Church after coming to this area. Some years later the family became members of the Falls Church.

Judge Riley was one of the most beloved citizens of Falls Church. Quiet, efficient, modest, and scholarly, he quickly won the confidence of the community. He was Magistrate and Justice of the Peace. Court sessions were held at "Cherry Hill." He was founder of the movement for a public school and first Chairman of the School Board. Judge Riley personally circulated a paper signed by the citizens by which sums of money were pledged to build Jefferson School. The following is Judge Riley's statement attached to the subscription list, one of the great recommendations for public education and a classic example of the Judge's thought and intelligence:

"*Subscription in Aid of Jefferson Institute for School Year of 1875-6.*

Recognizing the truth that the education of the masses is the only basis on which our government can expect to perpetuate the great principles on which it was founded; that general intelligence is the only safeguard of Civil and Religious liberty: that morality and all the best impulses of our nature are strengthened and controlled for greater good thereby: Knowing that to properly fit themselves for positions in life, our children must be educated: and believing that all our real prosperity, and progress as a community depends on the proper training of the youth,

We the Citizens and residents of Falls Church, and vicinity, hereby agree, and bind ourselves, to pay the sum set opposite our names, for the purpose of aiding in sustaining a public graded school in the Village of Falls Church."

Judge Riley was almost solely responsible for the incorporation of the town in 1875, and at his own expense went to Richmond to lobby the charter through the Legislature. He was made an Alderman when the town was incorporated.

On February 26, 1868, Joseph S. Riley married Mary Edwards (Molly) Pultz. Mrs. Riley was born on a plantation near "Clip" (Middleway), Jefferson County, Virginia, December 27, 1843. She was the daughter of Nicholas and Elizabeth Edwards (Bell) Pultz.[3] Mrs. Riley died at "Cherry Hill," March 6, 1927. Judge Riley met his future wife in 1863 while she was a prisoner in the Old Capitol Prison in Washington. She had written a letter to a cousin in the Confederate Army which was intercepted by the Union forces and considered by them to be information of benefit to the enemy. She was never a spy, although accused of being one. Ward Lamon, Marshal of the District and former law partner of President Lincoln, obtained her parole in his custody. Mr. Lamon was an old schoolmate of her father. The parole is dated October 13, 1863, and she was released October 31, 1863.

Mrs. Riley was a descendant of Joseph Edwards, who volunteered as a soldier in the 10th Virginia Regiment during the Revolutionary War. This Regiment became the 6th Virginia about September, 1778. It was commanded successively by Colonels William Russell and John Green. Mr. Edwards enlisted on March 17, 1777, to serve three years. He reenlisted December 18, 1778, to serve for the duration of the war. He was in the Battle of Morristown. Joseph Edwards was born in Berkeley County, Virginia (later Jefferson County, now West Virginia) in 1736, and died there on October 1, 1828. He married four times: (1) Rachel Reese, (2) in 1785, Elizabeth Vance, (3) Lydia Roberts, and (4) Ann Silver. All of these children were by Elizabeth Vance. The children were: Sarah Edwards, married Henry Bushman; Elizabeth Edwards, married Martin Payne; and Rachel Reese Edwards (1791-1872) vho married Abraham Bell. It was their daughter Elizabeth Edwards Bell (1817-1882) who married in 1843 to Nicholas Pultz (Pults) (1819-1855). Mr. Pultz was of Dutch ancestry from Philadelphia.

Mrs. Riley, daughter of the last named couple, was known far and wide as "Mother Riley." She was a woman of social graces and intellectual attainment.

Joseph Schlick and Mary Edwards (Pultz) Riley had issue:

(91) Mary Edwards Riley, born in Washington, D.C., January 3, 1869, died at Falls Church, May 10, 1946. She was baptized at Dulin Chapel July 18, 1874. She married in the Falls Church on June 8, 1892, to Samuel Holmes Styles of New York City. Mr. Styles was a native of Brooklyn, attended school in Philadelphia, and came to Falls Church in 1908. He was in the real estate business until the 1920's. Mr. Styles was afterwards an employee of the Association of American Railroads and retired as an analytical statistician in 1948. Active in local civic affairs, he was Secretary of the Fairfax County Democratic Committee and a member of the Falls Church Town Council. He was a member of the Falls Church School Board for fifteen years. He was treasurer of the Falls Church for thirty-two years, and was a long-time member and treasurer of the Odd Fellows Lodge. Mr. Styles died January 25, 1952, age 86 years. Mrs. Styles was a charter member of the Falls Church Chapter, D.A.R., and served as Regent from June 23, 1922 until June 26, 1924. She was active in maintaining a library in Falls Church and gave unstintingly of her time and money. Her children gave the site for the present city library. A plaque to her memory, in the Library, was unveiled on July 20, 1958, by her great-grandson, Nicholas Rajacich. At that time there was

an out-pouring of tributes to her memory by Mrs. Carroll V. Shreve and others. Issue:
(911) Elizabeth Morgan Styles (Betty), born 1893, unmarried. Miss Styles is well-known for her interest in charitable and civic affairs.
(912) (Honorable) Francis Holmes Styles, born 1895, served as U.S. Counsel at Antwerp, Belgium and later as American Counsel-General in Gotenborg, Sweden. He married Eleanor Lane, daughter of General and Mrs. Rufus Lane of Falls Church. Issue:
  (9121) Michael H. Styles, graduate of the University of Virginia, is an employee of the State Department. He married Nancy Howard and had issue: Thomas Lane Styles.
  (9122) David T. Styles, attended Princeton, and is currently in the U.S.A.F. He is unmarried.
  (9123) Ellen Warfield Styles, a nurse, and graduate of Johns Hopkins University. She married on January 15, 1955, Nicholas Rajacich, and had a son, Nicholas, Jr.
(92) Jeanne Elizabeth Riley (baptized Jennie), was born in Washington, D.C. November 28, 1870, and was baptized at Dulin Chapel, July 18, 1874. She married Henry Cyrus Birge (1864-1943) and resided in the large house which became the Falls Church American Legion Post. This twenty-five acre estate was known as "Woodland." Mr. Birge, known affectionately as "Harry," was an attorney and engaged in the real estate business. He died in 1943. Mrs. Birge died August 13, 1950. Issue:
(921) Warren Riley Birge, born 1898, married Margaret Hume Cooke. Issue:
  (9211) Margaret Hume Birge, married Benjamin R. Britt, issue: Benjamin R. Britt, Jr., Margaret Riley Britt and James Duncan Britt.
  (9212) Warren Riley Birge, Jr., married Frances Louise Weeks, issue: Warren Riley Birge, 3d., and John Doyle Birge.
  (9213) Thomas Worthington Cooke Birge, is a Lieutenant in the Air Force and is unmarried.
(922) Margaret Chilton Birge, born 1899, died unmarried, 1934.
(923) Morgan C. Birge, ("Happy"), born 1901, married Nellie Roberts. Issue:
  (9231) Morgan C. Birge, Jr.
  (9232) Molly Birge.
(924) Henry Edwards Birge, born 1907, died 1915.
(925) Judith Vance Birge, born 1912, married Donald H. Sides. Issue:
  (9251) Elizabeth Lynn Sides.
  (9252) Jane Edwards Sides, born March 14, 1945, died March 22, 1945.
  (9253) Kathleen Riley Sides.
(93) Joseph Harvey Riley, born at "Cherry Hill," September 19, 1873, died there December 17, 1941. Mr. Riley was unmarried. The records of Dulin Chapel show that he was baptized on July 18, 1874. Mr. Riley was a noted ornithologist and author. He was credited with 116 articles, pamphlets and books at the time of his death. He was a fellow of the American Ornithologists Union

(Lancaster, Pennsylvania) from 1919 until his death. *The Auk* official publication of A.O.U., devoted fifteen pages to his biography (Volume 60, #1, pp. 1-15, January, 1943). Mr. Riley was a member of the staff of the Smithsonian Institution for 45 years, being in charge of the Division of Birds. He graduated from Emerson Institute and was awarded a medal for outstanding achievements (1895). As one writer put it, with his characteristic modesty and diffidence in such matters, he did not attend the exercises, and Dr. Young, head of the school, came to "Cherry Hill" with the medal. Mr. Riley was leader of many expeditions for rare birds. Seven subspecies of birds were named in his honor by other Ornithologists. Mr. Riley was member of numerous clubs and civic organizations. He was a member of Kemper Lodge #64, A. F. & A. M. His library on Ornithology was one of the best in the country, and is at the University of Virginia. He was also an extensive collector of Southern history. Upon his death he provided for a Chair in Vertebrate Zoology at the University of Virginia. He left the University "Cherry Hill" estate for this purpose. He inherited "Cherry Hill" in 1927.

(94) Margaret Riley, born at "Cherry Hill," May 9, 1876, died there April 7, 1960. She married Leo Graham Parker. Mr. Parker was born November 7, 1872, and died July 25, 1940. Mrs. Parker was loved by a wide circle of friends. Part of her large collection of cook books is in the Virginia Room of Falls Church Library. No issue.

(95) Kathleen Maude Riley, born at "Cherry Hill," October 1, 1878, and is living on part of the estate, in a home called "Poverty Pines," at 401 W. Great Falls Street. She taught school at Falls Church and was an employee of the Department of Agriculture. She married on December 21, 1908, to Charles Ellsworth Gage. Mr. Gage, a descendant of the old Sanford and Gage families of New England, was born at Dorchester, Nebraska, October 12, 1882, a son of Arunah and Sarah Fidelia (Sanford) Gage. Mr. Gage was Chief Clerk, Bureau of Crop Estimates for the U. S. Department of Agriculture, 1917-19; officer in charge of field records, 1920; crop and livestock reports, 1921-26; member of the crop reporting board, 1922-29; was in charge of the newly created tobacco section, Bureau of Agriculture Economy, 1929; and served as Director of the Tobacco Board Production and Marketing Administration (formerly the Agricultural Marketing Administration), 1942-48. He has served as Agriculture Consultant for the American Tobacco Company since 1948. He was Chairman and U. S. member of the Combined Food Board during World War II, and in September, 1951, was U. S. delegate to the World Tobacco Congress at Amsterdam, Holland. He is a member of the Tobacco Advisory Committee to the Secretary of Agriculture. Mr. Gage initiated the monthly crops report series on tobacco by types. He is the author of numerous pamphlets and articles, including *American Tobacco Types, Uses and Markets* (U. S. Department of Agriculture 1933, revised 1942); *The Tobacco Industry in Puerto Rico,* 1939; and *Tobacco. Tobacco Hogsheads and Rolling Roads in Northern Virginia,* published by the Falls Church Historical Commission, 1959. Mr. Gage served on the Falls Church Town Council, 1929-38; was a member of the Planning Commission, 1938-42;

and Vice Chairman of the Historical Commission. He is a 32 degree Mason, and a member of the noted Cosmos Club of Washington, D. C. He served as President of the Falls Church Temple Corporation, 1934-44, and is a member of the American Farm Economy Association, the Agriculture Historical Society, and the Missouri State Historical Society. Mr. and Mrs. Gage have a notable library and are deeply interested in history. No issue.

---

[1] A typical inscription is in a book as follows: "For Uncle Joe/J.S. Riley, Esq./Falls Church, Va./Christmas '93."
[2] The Harvey deed from Newton mentions buildings of which there were a number, but from the moneys borrowed by Harvey secured by "Cherry Hill," it is thought that he built the greenhouse, superintendent's house (later the Riley hen house), and landscaped the grounds. It is not known when "Cherry Hill" house was erected, but it is of pre-Revolutionary architecture. Owned by the city, and the oldest house in Falls Church, almost unchanged, it should be retained for educational purposes. It could be a guest house and museum for the city. It was probably built by John Trammell.
[3] The tombstone of Mrs. Pultz is in the Falls Church yard and has this inscription: "Elizabeth Edwards Bell. To the memory of Elizabeth Edwards, daughter of Abraham and Rachel Edwards Pultz, born Jefferson Co., Va., Nov. 7, 1817, died Aug 8, 1882. Death comes not to the living soul, nor age to the loving heart."

---

## THE ROW FAMILY

Samuel Row, first known ancestor of this family, was a resident of Devonshire, England, and died May 15, 1846. He married, on January 8, 1804, to Grace Mudge. Mrs. Row was born on November 22. 1777, died October 25, 1861[1] Child (perhaps others):

(1) Thomas J. Row, married —— Hoyle. Mr. Row was connected with Lloyd's of London, lived at "Highberry Hill," and became wealthy. He died in England, October 14, 1892. Children:
(11) Wilson Row, remained in England.
(12) Daughter Row, remained in England.
(13) Thomas John Hoyle Row, married Margaret Carson Bully.
Of the children mentioned above, Thomas John Hoyle Row died March 12, 1918, at his home, "Terra Nova," near Munson Hill, Fairfax County. He was living at St. John's, Newfoundland in 1875 when his son, Thomas, was born. He came to Virginia during the 1880's. Mr. Row acquired "Terra Nova," and was a horticulturist, but lived on a pension from his family estate in England. Mr. Row married Margaret Carson Bully[2] Children:
(131) Anne Row, married George Harris, and is buried in Charlottesville, Va.
(132) Thomas J. H. Row, married Eva Terrett.
(133) Jessie Row, married Gordon Sands Gott.
(134) Susie Row, married James Cameron.
(135) Lilly Row, married John Gerns.
(136) Wilson Row, married Alice Gorham. She died March 4, 1959 at Englewood, Florida. Children:
(1361) Mary E. Row, Vienna, Va.
(1362) Daughter Row married William E. Hyde.
(1363) Thomas J. Row.
(137) Dorothy Row, married Foster Kirby

(138) Edith Row, married G. T. Rogers.
All of the above named children lived in this country.
(132) Thomas J. H. Row was born at St. John's Newfoundland, March 11, 1875, and died at his home "Terra Nova," at West Falls Church. He married Eva Terrett. Mrs. Row is a descendant of William Henry Terrett, of a family long prominent in this county.² Mrs. Row is living at "Terra Nova," in West Falls Church. Children:
- (1321) Thomas Henston Row, born December 21, 1903, married Edna O'Shaughnessy and lives on Cedar Lane, Fairfax, Va. No children.
- (1322) Wilson Terrett Row, born April 17, 1905, married Evelyn Goldsmith of England. Children:
  - (13221) Elizabeth Ann Row, married Clark Fitzhugh.
  - (13222) Audrey Lee Row, unmarried.
- (1323) Steuart Blake Row, born November 17, 1908, married Ruth Turner, issue:
  - (13231) Thomas Henry Row.

---

[1] These dates are taken from the back of an old picture of Grace (Mudge) Row owned by Mrs. Thomas J. H. Row of Falls Church.
[2] Mrs. Row had a sister living in Canada.
[3] William Henry Terrett had a son, Major George Terrett, and the latter was the father of William Henry Terrett who married Susan Bushby. They had a son, Thomas Terrett, who married Mary Catherine Bontz of Alexandria (daughter of Henry and Harriet (Scarce) Bontz). (Note: Henry Bontz married twice, and his second wife was Martha Ratrie of Loudoun County.)

---

## THE SEBASTIAN FAMILY

Colonel Benjamin Sebastian, Sr., Esquire, Attorney at Law, was born in 1706[1] in St. Paul's Parish, King George County, and died at his home, "Montpelier," (now the site of George Mason School) at West Falls Church in 1770. Colonel Sebastian represented an old family of Spanish ancestry. He married in St. Paul's Parish, King George, on February 16, 1729/30, to Priscilla Elkins. Mrs. Sebastian died at "Montpelier," in 1773.

In the early 1750's Colonel Sebastian was living in Alexandria where he owned an Ordinary.[2] He was agent for the Alexanders and a lawyer of substance. His depositions filed in several law suits show him to have been a plain spoken person, and a man of unusual conviction.[3]

Colonel Sebastian made his will September 13, 1770, probated November 19, 1770. He gave his wife, Priscilla, his home plantation, "Montpelier," and slaves. Upon her death the estate was to pass to two daughters, Elizabeth and Betheland. His land in Loudoun County, consisting of 350 acres, was to be sold by his friends, Thomas Lewis and John Moss of Loudoun. The additional 150 acres in Fairfax which he purchased of Blanch Duncan and Lettice his wife, was to be sold by his friends Thomas Wren and William Wren to pay his debts, and they were to serve as Executors of the will. Both of them refused to qualify. Witnesses to the will were: Platt Townsend, Robert H. Harrison and Mordock McPherson.

An inventory of Colonel Sebastian's estate was filed May 18, 1772, by William Payne, Jr., Benjamin Moody, and Edward Dulin.[5] An inventory of the estate of his wife, Priscilla, was filed the following year, indicating that she did not long survive him.

"Montpelier," the Sebastian home, was later owned by his Broadwater descendants. The house stood near Leesburg Pike at West Falls Church, and was torn down to make way for the erection of George Mason School. In more recent years it was known as the "Barrett" or "Flagg" House. It has been called "Wayside" and "Barrett Hall."

Part of the land was sold on October 20, 1773, by Benjamin Sebastian, of the Parish of St. Stephen and County of Northumberland, Virginia, to George McCormack. The deed noted that Benjamin Sebastian, Sr., deceased, father of Betheland Sebastian, owned in his lifetime 200 acres in Fairfax County originally taken up by John Harle, called "Montpelier." After his wife's death this was to descend to Elizabeth and Betheland Sebastian, two daughters, to be divided. Betheland, by her Power of Attorney dated April 16, 1773, authorized the said Benjamin Sebastian, "by the name Benjamin Sebastian Clerk and Rector of said (St. Stephen's) Parish." Thus for 200 pounds current money, the land was sold to McCormack.

The additional legacy of land was retained until a later time. On September 22, 1851, Thomas Moore, Special Court Commissioner, sold the "Montpelier" mansion to William Minor of Alexandria County. The deed recites that "Montpelier" was located "on the waters of Pimmits run binding on the Falls Church road the Land of the late Nicholas Darne, George W. West and others," and then in actual possession of Minor (by his tenant, N. Lemen). The deed also stated that by court action of August, 1836, wherein Matthew Elgin and wife were complaintants against certain other heirs of Charles G. Broadwater, deceased, John H. Halley was appointed commissioner to sell the land. This sale was to be made to the highest bidder on October 15, 1836. The 148 acre tract is then described as having descended to "Bethethelan" Sebastian, who "afterwards married with Charles L. Broadwater," from her father, Benjamin Sebastian, Sr. It then passed to her sons, Charles G. and William E. Broadwater, subject to life ownership of their father. Minor was the highest bidder, but Halley died before the sale was complete, and Thomas Moore was then appointed Commissioner, to make a deed. This deed was not filed, apparently, until fifteen years later. Colonel Benjamin and Priscilla (Elkins) Sebastian had issue:

(1) Ann Sebastian (Nancy), born in 1730, probably married George McCormack.

(2) (The Reverend and Judge) Benjamin Sebastian, Jr., was not mentioned in his father's will, but is identified as a son in the law suit entitled "Sebastian vs. Ellzey," filed 1759. He was a Minister of the Church of England in St. Stephen's Parish, Northumberland County, Virginia, in 1773, and by 1784 was in Washington County, Maryland. (See Loudoun County, *Deed Book O*, page 122). He owned land in Loudoun and Fairfax. He married Amelia Broadwater, sister to Lieutenant Charles Guy Broadwater. Judge Sebastian was trained in law by Patrick Henry; implicated in the Burr and Blennerhassett conspiracy and fled to the West Indies. He returned and was a Judge in Kentucky. Judge Sebastian lived to be 92 years old. His son, Dr. Charles Sebastian, was ancestor of a distinguished family, including a present-day descendant, Laura Jones Bowers.

(3) Betheland Sebastian, married (Lieutenant) Charles Guy Broadwater *(See Broadwater)*.

(4) Elizabeth Sebastian, died in 1774, unmarried. She made a will on February 23, 1773, probated May 16, 1774. In it she mentioned as legatees: George McCormack (land devised by her father, Benjamin Sebastian, in Fairfax Parish); Sarah

413

McCormack, daughter of George McCormack; John McCormack, son of George McCormack; and Amelia Watson. George McCormack was called a "friend," but was most likely a brother-in-law. Miss Sebastian left items including furniture, a silver watch, a tea chest with six silver tea spoons and one pair of silver tea tongs, and other effects. Witnesses were: John Minor, Ann Minor and Elizabeth Read.[8]

*Note:* Colonel Benjamin Sebastian probably had other children. One Nicholas Sebastian, closely associated with this family, was likely a son. This Nicholas Sebastian married Nancy Tasker. William Tasker made his will March 23, 1800, probated at Fairfax May 19, 1800, in which he mentioned as legatees Nicholas and Nancy Sebastian and their six children. Nicholas and Nancy Sebastian were named as executors and witnesses were: Thomas Sinclair and John Walker. Family tradition states that Colonel Benjamin Sebastian, Sr., was a son of Nicholas Sebastian of King George. It is noted that one Nicholas Sebastian married Anne Elliott in King George on October 29, 1726. Nicholas Sebastian died December 24, 1735. Nicholas and Anne (Elliott) Sebastian had several children recorded in St. Paul's Parish Register, King George: Thomas Elliott Sebastian, born March 20, 1730/1, and Anna Sebastian, born March 2, 1733/4. One Nicholas Sebastian, son of Richard and Elizabeth Sebastian, was born February 15, 1749/50.

---

[1] Fairfax County, *Records Of Long Standing*, page 314.
[2] Noted in papers from a law suit, "Sebastian vs. Ellzey," filed August 16, 1759.
[3] Colonel Sebastian left a number of papers which have survived to this day, some of them in the author's files. He was apparently well educated for his day and wrote with grace and apparent ease.
[4] Fairfax County, *Will Book C #1*, page 95.
[5] Fairfax County, *Will Book C #1*, page 730.
[6] Fairfax County, *Deed Book R #3*, page 40.
[7] Nicholas Lemen was a Methodist Protestant Minister and a son-in-law of Colonel William Minor. Lemen (now Lemon) Road was named for him, as it was put through the "Montpelier" estate while the Reverend Mr. Lemen lived there.
[8] One Ann Sebastian married John Read on July 21, 1748, in Overwharton Parish, Stafford County. The witness, Elizabeth Read, was likely their daughter. It is possible this Ann was a sister of Elizabeth, and thus she did not marry McCormack or he was a second husband.

---

## THE SEWELL — SEWALL FAMILY

Two families, one using the Sewell spelling and the other the Sewall spelling of the surname, lived in Falls Church and vicinity. Both were from Maryland and claimed descent from Lord Baltimore's Secretary by that name. Lewis Nicholas Sewall represented one branch of this family. He married Sarah M. (Sally) West, who died in 1890 at her home, "Walnut Hill," on South West Street at West Falls Church. She was a daughter of John West, 3d, and Sarah (Broadwater) West. Following her marriage she became a Roman Catholic. The first Mass held in Falls Church was at "Walnut Hill," and the old house was left by Miss Sybilla Sewall to St. James Church. The Sewalls also gave the site for the first St. James Church (now the cemetery site).

Lewis Nicholas and Sarah M. (West) Sewall had issue:

(1) William Henry Sewall (Harry), born April 25, 1824, died November 3, 1911, and is buried in St. James Cemetery. He was a Confederate Soldier and the gun carried by him during the war is owned by Frank M. Steadman, Sr. Mr. Sewall mar-

ried in Alexandria, November 28, 1866, Jannett D. Hunter. Mrs. Sewall was born in 1829 in Fairfax County, a daughter of John D. and S. Hunter.
  (2) John Sewall.
  (3) Joseph C. Sewall married Roberta ——.
  (4) M. Louisa Sewall, died unmarried before 1890.
  (5) Jane Sybilla Sewall, born in 1834, died January 18, 1927, unmarried, in Washington, D. C. She is buried in St. James Cemetery.
  (For a division of the Sewall estate see Fairfax County, *Deed Book J #5*, page 316)

  Joseph William Sewell represented another branch of this family. He was born March 23, 1817, and died September 19, 1882, and is buried in the Nelson-Walters Cemetery. He married Catherine A. Nelson, who was born April 10, 1818, and died May 8, 1901. Issue:
  (1) Sarah Alice Sewell, born 1838, married James E. Kirby (*See Kirby*).
  (2) Henrietta Clay Sewell (1844-1912) married Francis Asbury Kirby.
  (3) William Nelson Sewell, born October 24, 1847, died July 11, 1901.
  (4) Joseph Preston Sewell, born May 10, 1851, died September 22, 1914. He became a Roman Catholic upon his marriage to Mary E. McCauley. Mrs. Sewell was born February 15, 1854, and died February 26, 1926 (*See McCauley*).
  (5) Amanda Sewell, married Thomas Henry Nelson.

  There was also a Joseph Sewell who made his will January 21, 1836, probated February 15, 1836 (Fairfax County *Will Book R #2*, page 373). In it he reserved $800.00 from his estate to rear and educate his two youngest sons, Franklin and John Fletcher Sewell. He divided his estate between his children and "my last wifes two daughters namely Elizabeth Payne and Asneath Payne." The will also refers to their father, William Payne. Mr. Sewell mentioned his children: Elizabeth Cockrell, wife of Jesse Cockrell; Eliza Reed, wife of David Reed, a son-in-law, James Ball; and a son, Walter Sewell. Witnesses were: George Minor, Richard Reid, and John Robert Minor. A sale of his estate shows that Joseph W. Sewell, William J. Sewell, Robert B. Darne, William Nelson, Sr., William Swink, Sr., and Walter Sewell purchased from the estate (*Will Book R#1*, page 397). This would seem to connect him with Joseph William Sewell who married Catherine Nelson.
  This Joseph Sewell married (1) —— and (2) Mrs. Catherine (Hughes) Payne, who was known as Kitty. She was a daughter of William and Elizabeth (Wren) Hughes, and widow of William Payne. Apparently her only issue by Joseph Sewell were two sons, Franklin and John Fletcher Sewell. All of this family were pillars of the Methodist Episcopal Church.

---

## THE SHERWOOD FAMILY

  There were two families named Sherwood in Falls Church. The family considered in this section is that of Archibald Sherwood. The immigrant ancestor was Thomas Sherwood, who came on the Ship "Francis" in 1636. The family settled in Rye, New York. The line of descent is through Lieutenant-Colonel Isaac Sherwood, who was the father of sixteen children.[1]
  Archibald Sherwood, the Falls Church settler, was born November 21, 1812, and died March 13, 1892. He owned a 217 acre farm which was originally the home

of his wife's family.² This farm was at West Falls Church and the home was on the site of St. James Church. This became "Sherwood Subdivision, one of the first subdivisions in Virginia. Mr. Sherwood married Lucinda Fish, a daughter of Francis Fish, Sr., and Elizabeth (Becraft) Fish. She was born May 19, 1813, and died May 2, 1881.

An only child of Archibald and Lucinda (Fish) Sherwood was Mary Elizabeth Sherwood, born April 25, 1848. She died January 19, 1923. Mary Elizabeth Sherwood received a good education, and attended a young ladies' finishing school and Shepherd's School. On April 26, 1867, Mary Elizabeth Sherwood was married to Jacob Coleman DePutron. Mr. DePutron, as a member of the 79th Pennsylvania Regiment, came to Falls Church during the War Between the States, and decided to settle here.

The DePutrons were of French Huguenot ancestry, and came to this country from the Isle of Guernsey off the coast of England. Jacob Coleman DePutron was born in Philadelphia (where his family settled in 1813) on January 4, 1844, and died at Falls Church in 1926, with burial in Arlington Cemetery. He was a son of John and Sophia (Boulagier) DePutron. His mother's family came from the Isle of Sark. His second wife was Mrs. Hattie Capper, whom he married in 1914 when she was 49 and he was 70 years old.

The DePutrons owned a home at 213 Fairfax Street, Alexandria, and lived for a time in the old Fish home at Falls Church. They remodeled the old house later owned by the Schmidts and lived there while building the large brick house which still stands near the corner of Lincoln Avenue and Great Falls Street. The brick house was begun in 1893 and the family moved there in April, 1894. Mrs. DePutron would not have a fireplace installed in the mansion since she recalled the unpleasant task of polishing brass in her childhood! There were to be no brass fenders in the new home. When the slaves left after the war, twelve-year-old Mary polished the brass, a task formerly done by the servants.

Jacob and Mary Elizabeth (Sherwood) DePutron had issue:

(1) Eustis Coleman DePutron.

(2) John Jacob DePutron, born March 31, 1869, died May 18, 1870.

(3) Louis Sherwood DePutron, married Edith Miller and died while serving in the Boer War. He became a citizen of Great Britain. His children included: Cecelia, Maurice, Frederick, Louis, and three who died in infancy.

(4) Edith Sophia DePutron, married Wilbur A. Speakman.

(5) Maurice Bentley DePutron.

(6) Marian Beatrice DePutron.

(7) Lillian Corinne DePutron, born May 19, 1877, is living, 1964. She married Leonard Percy Daniel, who was a Mayor of Falls Church. Mr. Daniel was born August 23, 1874, and died April 3, 1944. He was born in Redding, Pennsylvania, while his father, a resident of Washington, D.C., was there on business. His father was William Humphrey Daniel, a native of Swampoodle, Washington, D.C., and Mary Ann (Brown) Daniel. William Humphrey Daniel was an Engineer. His wife, Mary Ann, was a cousin to William Y. Dulin of Falls Church, from whom Dulin Methodist Church was named. Mayor Daniel's grandfather was Joseph Humphrey Daniel, who was professor of music in the Washington public school system. Leonard Percy Daniel served as a Major in the 29th Division during World War II. He set up the school of sound ranging and map reproduction at Camp Humphrey (now Fort

Belvoir). Mr. Daniel was an expert engraver. Leonard Percy and Lillian Corinne (DePutron) Daniel had issue:
  (71) Audrey Virginia Daniel, born at Falls Church, April 27, 1903, married on October 17, 1923, to Theodore Clay Uhler. Issue: Theodore Clay Uhler, Jr., born January 12, 1929, married Joanne Haines and had issue: Janet Mary Uhler, Jennifer Lynne Uhler, and Theodore Clay Uhler, III.
  (72) Corinne Louise Daniel, born February 8, 1907, married in the Falls Church, April 26, 1930, to Walter Ray Granger. Mr. Granger was born in South Brooklyn, New York, December 22, 1900. Issue:
    (721) Audrey Daniel Granger, born March 19, 1934, married on March 24, 1956, Robert Graham Brents, issue: Meredith Sherwood Brents, born April 2, 1961; Allison Rae Brents, born December 28, 1962; and Robert Graham Brents, Jr., born July 30, 1963.
    (722) Lynne Granger, married on October 1, 1960, Henry Hackett Fisher. No issue.
  (8) Mary Louisa Virginia DePutron, born December 23, 1881, died December 25, 1881.

---

[1] A portrait of Mariah Esther Sherwood, wife of Lieutenant-Colonel Isaac Sherwood, is owned by a descendant, Mrs. Walter Granger.

[2] Francis Fish, Sr., settled in Falls Church long before the War Between the States. His home place, on Locust Street near the large brick house built by Jacob DePutron, had a mantle dated 1696, according to Mrs. Charles E. Gage. This house was purchased in recent years by a Mr. Schmidt and remodeled. The ancestor of the Fish family was William Fish, who was the father of nine children (descendants of whom are shown on an old family tree owned by Miss Minnie D. Ellison). Francis Fish, Sr., son of William Fish, married Elizabeth Becraft. She was a granddaughter of Jonathan Nixon who settled near Hagerstown, Maryland, in 1750. She was the daughter of Aquilla and Mary (Nixon) Becraft, and granddaughter of Peter Becraft who moved from Philadelphia to Maryland. Mrs. Elizabeth (Becraft) Fish died at Falls Church on October 2, 1868, age 67 years. She was buried with others of her family on the home place. Her remains were moved to Oakwood Cemetery after 1900. Francis Fish, Sr., and Elizabeth (Becraft) Fish had the following issue: Henrietta (Fish) Earnshaw; Ruth Fish (married (1) —— Scott and (2) —— Mills; Francis Fish, Jr.; Mary (Fish) Haines; Joel Fish; John Fish (died March 17, 1860, age 31 years); Ann B. (Nancy) Fish, died unmarried February 28, 1887; Lucinda (Fish) Sherwood; Elizabeth (Fish) Ellison; Lucie Fish (died August 17, 1865, age 32 years); and William Fish, died at age 6 years.

## THE SHOTWELL FAMILY

The earliest known ancestor of this family was William Shotwell of Madison County, Virginia. Mr. Shotwell settled about 1750 in the area near what is now Criglersville, and it is thought that he belonged to a New Jersey Quaker family. He married Betsey Jurdine. James Shotwell, son of William and Betsey (Jurdine) Shotwell, served seven years under Washington during the American Revolution. He was born about 1759, and died in December, 1841. James Shotwell married Mary Crane (who died in September, 1828).

Jeckonias Yancey Shotwell, son of James and Mary (Crane) Shotwell, married twice. His first wife was Mary E. Utz (Outz) and his second wife, whom he married on March 10, 1870, was Eliza Floyd. Mary (Utz) Shotwell died in January, 1861. Eliza (Floyd) Shotwell died April 17, 1896.

Jeckonias Lewis Shotwell, son of Jeckonias Yancey and Mary E. (Utz) Shotwell, was born near Criglersville in Madison County, 1858, and died at his home in Falls

Church, September 1, 1941. Mr. Shotwell, a contractor and a member of Columbia Baptist Church, married Anna Lee Updike, daughter of James Daniel and Mary Elizabeth (Carpenter) Updike.[1] She was born August 25, 1871 and is living (1956).

J. Lewis and Anna Lee (Updike) Shotwell were married on November 4, 1891 at Washington, Virginia. They moved to Falls Church in April, 1905.

A write-up on this family can be found on pp. 174-175 of *Annals of our Colonial Ancestors* by Ambrose M. Shotwell, 1895, (Smith & Co., Lansing, Mich.). Children:
- (1) Virgie Marie Shotwell, unmarried.
- (2) Mabel Lewis Shotwell, married George Torreyson Reeves. Issue:
    - (21) George Torreyson Reeves, Jr., married Margaret Ann Strum. Issue:
        - (211) Heather Ann Reeves, born in Bloomington, Indiana, 1954.
        - (212) Susan Reeves.
    - (22) Richard Lewis Reeves, married Mary Louise Warrick in June, 1954. Issue:
        - (221) Robin Reeves.
        - (222) Shelley Reeves.
        - (223) Deanna Reeves.
        - (224) Lauren Reeves.
    - .(23) Doris Lee Reeves, married Earl Childress. Issue:
        - (231) Earl Childress, III.
- (3) Clarence Lee Shotwell, married Mary Stuart. Issue:
    - (31) Stuart Lee Shotwell, married Lilla Holden, Issue:
        - (311) Anna Lee Shotwell.
        - (312) Margaret Blair Shotwell.
        - (313) Warren David Shotwell.
    - (32) William Lewis Shotwell, married Elizabeth McFall, April 1954. Issue:
        - (321) Robert Shotwell.
        - (322) Elizabeth Shotwell.
- (4) Ouida Shotwell, unmarried.
- (5) Etlan Shotwell, born at Falls Church, October 12, 1905, married on September 6, 1929 in the Columbia Baptist Church by the Reverend U.S. Knox, to Frank McNulty Steadman. Mr. Steadman, a native of Leesburg, was born April 12, 1903, son of Eli Stansbury and Ida Jane (Kerns) Steadman (*See Steadman.*)
- (6) James Lewis Shotwell, married Gladys Darling. Issue:
    - (62) Katherine Lee (Kassie) Shotwell.
    - (62) Robert Lewis Shotwell.

---

[1] James Daniel Updike was born November 28, 1824, died May 7, 1898. Mary Elizabeth (Carpenter) Updike was born near Woodville, Rappahannock Co., Va., August 18, 1824. She was the daughter of Jonathan and Anne (Waters) Carpenter. The parents of James Daniel Updike were John Updike (who died at Washington, Va., February 9, 1848) and Urah Waters (who died in Rappahannock Co., May 2, 1879, age 80).

---

## THE SHREVE FAMILY

This family is one of the large and well known families of this area, and has been here for several generations. They claim descent from Sir William Shreve (born 1564) and wife Lady Elizabeth Fairfax. Lady Elizabeth (Fairfax) Shreve (of Bolton Castle, Percy, England) was related to Lord Fairfax of Virginia. William Shreve, son of Sir William and Lady Elizabeth (Fairfax) Shreve, was born in the Isle of Wight, England, in 1590, and married Oara Oara, daughter of a ruling Lord of an Eastern family. Their only son, Thomas Shreve, settled in Portsmouth, Rhode Island, in 1646. He was born in 1626, married 1648. Thomas and Martha Shreve had issue: Thomas Shreve (born September 2, 1649); John Shreve (born in August, 1686) married Jane Havens and died October 14, 1739; Caleb Shreve, married Sarah Areson; Mary Shreve married on February 12, 1685 to Joseph Sheffield (and died after 1706); Susannah Shreve, died after 1714; Daniel Shreve, died 1737; Elizabeth Shreve married Edward Carter and died June 5, 1719; and Sarah Shreve, married John Moon and died June 24, 1732.

Caleb Shreve, son of Thomas and Martha Shreve, was born in Portsmouth, Rhode Island, in 1650, and died in Burlington County, New Jersey in 1741. He married in 1680 to Sarah Areson of Long Island. Mrs. Shreve, born in 1660, was a daughter of Derick and Sarah (Orrest) Areson; and granddaughter of Leendert Arenson of Holland. During the 1750's the Shreves made claim to a famous fortune in Holland which they claimed thru the Areson family. These documents are still in the Shreve family, and add interesting details to their romantic history. Caleb and Sarah (Areson) Shreve settled in Shrewsbury, N. J., and later (1699) in Mount Holly, Burlington County.

Benjamin Shreve, son of Caleb and Sarah (Areson) Shreve, was born June 9, 1706 at Mount Holly, and died in 1751. He married on February 23, 1729, to Rebecca French. Rebecca (French) Shreve was a daughter of Richard French (born 1665) of Burlington, N. J., who was made a Quaker Minister in 1723. He married Mary King, daughter of Harmanus and Mary King of Burlington County. She was the granddaughter of Thomas French (1639-1699) who came to America in 1680 on the ship "Kent," Gregory Marlowe, Master. They sailed from London August 1, 1680, and Mr. French was granted 1,200 acres of land in New Jersey. Mrs. Shreve was a great-granddaughter of Thomas and Sara French of Nether Heyford, England (the former died 1673, the latter 1653).

Colonel Samuel Shreve (brother of Israel Shreve, thus Uncle of Henry Miller Shreve for whom Shreveport, Louisiana, was named) was born at Mount Holly, January 25, 1750, son of Benjamin and Rebecca (French) Shreve. He died in 1815. Colonel Shreve was commissioned in June, 1775 as Adjutant in the 1st Battalion of Gloucester County Militia; Captain in February, 1777, and Lieutenant-Colonel later, and resigned his commission in October, 1778. He fought under Washington, and they were good friends. In 1784 when Colonel Shreve moved from New Jersey and settled at what is now Ballston, Arlington County, on a 600 acre tract acquired from the Earl of Tech, he still maintained his friendship and associations with "The Father of His Country."

"Waycroft," the plantation of Colonel Shreve (also called in records "Springfield Farm") was at Mohaw. On June 17, 1909, the Fairfax County Chapter, D.A.R., marked the grave of Colonel Shreve in the family cemetery at "Waycroft." Appropriate ceremonies were held with most of the D.A.R. chapter present, including some of his descendants. The Reverend James M. Nourse officiated during the religious services.

Colonel Shreve married on June 26, 1771 to Myra Trout of Burlington County, N. J. They were parents of five children, Benjamin Shreve; Samuel Shreve (married (1) Priscilla Payne, (2) Mary Ann Clover); John Shreve, married Ann Ball; and Mary Shreve, died unmarried.

Benjamin Shreve, son of Colonel Samuel and Myra (Trout) Shreve, died about

1825. He was a trustee of Fairfax Chapel Methodist Church in Falls Church, and was active in Church work. He owned a home in Alexandria. Mr. Shreve married (1) Miss Muse; and (2) Barbara Ann Swink. His second wife, Barbara Ann (Swink) Shreve, died March 17, 1862. She was a daughter of John William and Mary (Klein) Swink of "Madeley," Fairfax County. Her father was born in 1742 in Upper Salford Township, Philadelphia Co., Pennsylvania. He moved first to Maryland, later to Fairfax County, and served in the Revolutionary War. His family Bible is owned by a descendant, Mr. Robert J. McCandlish, Sr. His Will was probated 1822. Mrs. Shreve was a granddaughter of Hans Michael Swinck, born in the Rhine Valley in 1689, died 1773. He and wife Mary Elizabeth Swinck with other members of the family embarked from Rotterdam, Holland, on the ship "Jamaica Galley," bound for Philadelphia, on February 9, 1739.

Benjamin and Barbara Ann (Swink) Shreve were the parents of six children (by his wife Miss Muse he had a daughter Susannah, who married John Muse). Their children were: Julia Anne Shreve, married William John Richards Birch; William Henry Shreve (of "Mount Pleasant") married Mary Southern; Eliza Ann Shreve; Margaret Ann Shreve, married John Ball; and Benjamin Shreve, married Sarah Simpson. The ramifications of the Shreve family would fill several volumes, thus we must confine our attention to those who settled in Falls Church and have descendants here. They were: William Henry Shreve of "Mount Pleasant," Benjamin Shreve, and Margaret Ann (Shreve) Ball.

William Henry Shreve of "Mount Pleasant," son of Benjamin and Barbara Ann (Swink) Shreve, was born March 24, 1812, died June 29, 1890. He acquired "Mount Pleasant,"[1] the estate of Colonel Thomas Lindsay, from his daughter Margaret (Lindsay) Swink with 160 acres of land in 1838. On December 13, 1838, he married Mary Southern (1818-1904) of Alexandria County. Mrs. Shreve, daughter of Richard and Mary (Rutherford) Southern (Sothern). Her father, a native of County Durham, England, settled on Analostan Island which he leased from his friend, General John Thomson Mason, and where he raised the first tomatoes for commercial use in America. He was distinguished as a horticulturist.[2] Mr. and Mrs. Shreve lived at "Mount Pleasant" for seventy years. He was a successful farmer and fruit grower. Of the trials of the Shreve family during the War Between the States, Mrs. Prentiss A. Shreve wrote:

"Even the passing of the years has not destroyed but rather added Nature's beauty around this old home (Mount Pleasant), there is nothing to indicate that here in the early days of the Civil War, a great force of Federal troops were encamped round about. The Washington & Old Dominion Tracks, just to the south of the house, were heavily picketed and guarded by the District of Columbia Regiment, No. 2, under command of Capt. O'Hagan. This is a singular fact that the 12th Pennsylvania Regulars were encamped on this same ground during the Spanish American War. Mt. Pleasant was also the rendezvous of Colonel John Singleton Mosby and his rangers all during the War, and they usually entered from the rear or north approach. William Henry Shreve, being a true Southerner, and having two sons in the Confederate Army, and placed in a very difficult and precarious position, but he tried to remain neutral; however, he was repeatedly branded as a secessionist, and several times was arrested by the Union Forces. Once he was taken to Alexandria and kept in jail for four or five days. Another time he was taken to the Old Capitol in Washington and kept a week, but was finally released after taking the oath of allegiance to the government. It was no doubt for the sake of protection that Mr. Shreve and family would be literally eaten out of house and home for the soldiers on both sides of the conflict sought out his home for food and recreation. During the retreat of the Federal soldiers, after the battle of Bull Run, they stopped at his home, and had practically cleared the larder and had just gone, when in came Mosby with his hungry men."

William Henry and Mary Southern Shreve had issue: (The Reverend) Richard Southern Shreve, married Frances E. Epps; Barbara Anne Shreve, married Andrew Melville; George W. Shreve, married Matilda Shreve; Benjamin Rutherford Shreve, married Anna K. Ball; John Wesley Shreve, married Julia A. Berry; Virginia Coe Shreve, married James Hartwell Walker; William Joseph Shreve, married Minnie Berry; Ella May Shreve, married James L. Schaaff; and Robert Eugene T. Shreve, married Sarah Patterson.

(1) William Henry Shreve, Jr., died July 29, 1843, age 7 months.

(2) (The Reverend) Richard Southern Shreve, married on October 5, 1865 to Frances Elizabeth Epps of Nottaway County. Both were killed by a bolt of lightning on June 25, 1874. An article in the *Evening Star* of June 29, 1874, entitled "A Solemn Day at Falls Church" (written by L. S. Abbott) describes the funeral and circumstances of death of the Reverend and Mrs. Shreve. The funeral was held on Sunday morning, and all of the other churches in Falls Church closed, and each pastor took part in the service. The Reverend Richard S. and Frances (Epps) Shreve were the parents of three children: Elizabeth Shreve, married William Fletcher Doyle; Georgia Shreve, married Mr. Moore; and Richard S. Shreve.

(3) Barbara Ann Shreve was born at "Mount Pleasant." She married on September 13, 1875 to Andrew Melville (1815-1893). During the War Between the States Miss Shreve acted as a Confederate spy. This was suspected by authorities in Washington, but they could not find evidence of her activities. After the death of Lincoln, troops searched "Mount Pleasant" for John Wilkes Booth. One story is told about Miss Shreve, which is of interest. On one occasion she was able to gather together some valuable papers for Colonel Mosby, but the Yankee troops were after her. She hurried to "Mount Pleasant," and by the time the soldiers arrived, she was calm and cool, seated on a chair in the parlor. They searched every nook and cranny for the papers, but could not find them. The Captain asked Miss Shreve to stand up to be searched. She replied that a Southern Lady was never asked to stand for a gentleman, but being a Yankee, he must not be a gentleman. The Captain, wishing to prove that he was a "gentleman," asked to be excused from his request, and left. Under Miss Shreve were the valuable papers, and they were dispatched to Colonel Mosby.[3] Mr. and Mrs. Melville were the parents of Charles Melville.

(4) George W. Shreve was born at "Mount Pleasant." He married in 1875 to his cousin, Matilda Shreve. He was living in 1938 in Santa Cruz, California, at the age of 95 years. He was a Confederate soldier.

(5) Benjamin Rutherford Shreve was born at "Mount Pleasant" December 1, 1848, and died at the age of 100 years (November 19, 1949). Mr. Shreve married on April 28, 1876 to Anna K. Ball. Too young to serve in the War Between the States, Mr. Shreve, then 15 years old, became a Scout and Blockade Runner for Colonel John S. Mosby. Federal troops were never able to catch him, however. Mr. Shreve often made trips to Alexandria for such luxuries as tobacco and coffee. Benjamin Rutherford and Anna K. (Ball) Shreve had issue:

(51) Prentiss Albert Shreve, born January 11, 1878, married on June 12, 1906 to

Lellah Hancock of Mississippi. Mr. Shreve was interested in local history, and the author of numerous articles for the local papers. Prentiss A. and Lellah (Hancock) Shreve had issue: Viola Shreve, married Charles Gotthardt (and had Anne, William, Norman, Nancy, Frederick, and Linda Gotthardt); and Paul Shreve, married Lorraine Gile (and had Robert, David, and Ronald Shreve).

(52) Edgar A. Shreve, married Hattie McGinnis (and had Mary Shreve and Eleanor (Shreve) Custard.

(53) Pearl A. Shreve, married Arthur S. Jenkins of Leesburg, Va. (and had Arthur S. Jenkins, Jr.).

(6) John Wesley Shreve, was born at "Mount Pleasant." He married on June 8, 1881 to Julia A. Berry.

(7) Virginia Coe Shreve was born at "Mount Pleasant," June 25, 1859, and baptized in Fairfax Chapel August 6, 1860 by the Reverend William Gwynn Coe. She married on November 5, 1884 to James Hartwell Walker, a son of Thomas Walker. Virginia Coe Shreve and James Hartwell Walker had: Wilber Shreve Walker, George Elton Walker, Ella May Walker, Virginia Walker (Mrs. Lester Lewis Spessard); and Edna Walker (Mrs. Stenhouse).

(8) William Joseph Shreve was born at "Mount Pleasant," and married on July 5, 1881 to Minnie Berry.

(9) Ella May Shreve was born at "Mount Pleasant," and married in Dulin Chapel, May 26, 1880 to James L. Schaaff of Prince George's County, Maryland.

(10) Robert Eugene Thornton Shreve was born at "Mount Pleasant," and married Sarah Patterson, sister of David Patterson of Pimmitt Run Farm.

Margaret Ann Shreve (daughter of Benjamin and Barbara Ann (Swink) Shreve, was born in Alexandria County August 29, 1817, and died at West Falls Church, March 1, 1896. She married in Washington, D.C., October 2, 1834 to John Ball. Mr. Ball was born in Alexandria County, July 23, 1809, died January 23, 1889, and was a son of Robert and Ann (Thrift) Ball. About 1835 they moved to Washington, D. C., where Mr. Ball was associated with the government service, and served on the City Council. They returned to Virginia in 1882. John and Margaret Ann (Shreve) Ball had issue:

(1) Mary Frances Ball, born in Washington, D. C., September 6, 1835, died at Falls Church, August 1, 1914. She married in Washington, D.C., January 4, 1855, to John E. Febrey (1831-1893). *(See Febrey)*.

(2) Barbara Ann Ball, died young.

(3) (The Reverend) Benjamin Franklin Ball, a Minister in the Methodist Church, was born January 15, 1839. He married Alice Ann Hobbs (and had Ella Virginia Ball, Mary Washington Ball (Mrs. Orville M. Johnson); Fanny Ball (Mrs. Jones); and Mrs. Anderson.

(4) Barbara Elizabeth Ball, born July 28, 1841, died April 14, 1912. Married on March 9, 1863 to John Edmund Prigg (1833-1886) son of Dr. Joseph and Sophia F. (Kingsmore) Prigg. In June, 1889, as a widow, Mrs. Prigg moved to Falls Church and opened a fancy goods store. Issue: Morgan Prigg, Ada Ball Prigg (1866-1940) married the Reverend Walker Payton Conway Coe and had Elizabeth Coe, Mrs. Albert Love Ely; Honorable Conway P. Coe (U. S. Commissioner of Patents under Roosevelt) married Anna Hopton Hart; (The Reverend) Edmund Gwynn Coe; Ada Ball Coe

(married James Emerson Powell of Kentucky and had (The Reverend) James Emerson Powell, Jr.; Elizabeth Frances Powell, married Melvin Lee Steadman, Jr.; and Barbara Ball Powell (who married Kent A. Boucher); and Allen Coe; and William Benjamin Prigg, (1870-1904) married Alice Poole.
   (5) Julia Margaret Ball.
   (6) John William Ball.
   (7) Albert Shreve Ball.
   (8) Ida May Ball (1856-1890) married Augustus Davis, Jr.
   (9) Lillian Ball (1861-1921) married William M. Ellison (See Ellison).

Benjamin F. Shreve, son of Benjamin and Barbara Ann (Swink) Shreve (1819-1880) married in September 1843 to Sarah Simpson. Mr. Shreve settled on a 155 acre farm at Falls Church (now near West Haven Subdivision) in 1851. Issue:
   (1) Martha A. Shreve, born August 1, 1844, married on March 24, 1868 to Martin F. Donaldson.
   (2) Mary Catherine Shreve, born September, 1845, married Edward J. Birch. (See Birch).
   (3) Alice Shreve, born 1847, died April 22, 1869, married on October 27, 1869, Ray T. Bailey of "Bailey's Cross Roads." (See Bailey).
   (4) Benjamin Bates Shreve, born January 11, 1850, married on April 29, 1891 to Dora L. Nourse (died 1893). Issue: Ruth Lillian Shreve; Dora May Shreve.
   (5) William H. Shreve, born 1851, married on January 31, 1883 to Lillian J. Febrey. (See Febrey). Issue:
      (51) Lillian Shreve, married Burt Freeman Salsbury of Merrifield.
      (52) Carroll Veola Shreve, born at Falls Church, March 16, 1889, attended local schools and graduated from Business High School, Washington, D. C., and married (in October 1906) to Fanny M. Ellison (See Ellison). Mr. Shreve has served for several years as President of the Falls Church Bank, was Secretary of the Plumbing Board, a member of the Electrical Board of Fairfax County, and owner of Carroll V. Shreve Heating and Plumbing Co., of Falls Church. Mr. Shreve served on the Falls Church Town Council for twelve years. He is a Charter Member of the Arlington Rotary Club and past president of that organization. He is a member of Kemper Lodge #64, A. F. & A. M. Mr. Shreve is a trustee, and Steward of Dulin Methodist Church. Carroll V. and Fanny M. (Ellison) Shreve had issue:
         (521) Minnie May Shreve, born April 2, 1912, married on September 1, 1936 to Joseph Copley, issue: James Carroll Copley born June 18, 1938, died July 17, 1938; Barbara Jean Copley, born August 5, 1941; and Carol Diane Copley, born October 10, 1945.
         (522) William Carroll Shreve, born November 27, 1915, married on June 14, 1941 to Ruth Madoline Woolard, issue: William Carroll Shreve, Jr., born June 14, 1942; John Ellison Shreve, born August 20, 1946; Richard Stanley Shreve, born March 13, 1948; and Thomas Garland Shreve, born August 25, 1949.
      (53) Lawrence Shreve.

   (6) Julia M. Shreve, born 1853, married Henry William Smith.
   (7) John Franklin Shreve, born 1857, married Annie E. Febrey (and had Ralph

Shreve and Fanny Shreve, wife of Francis P. Heartsill). John Franklin Shreve died June 3, 1929, age 70 years.

---

[1] "Mount Pleasant" was burned to make way for a new road in early 1962.
[2] Tombstones in the Shreve-Southern Cemetery: Richard Southern, b. Durham Co., Eng., March 25, 1791, d. Alex Co., Va. Apr. 24, 1877. Frances (wife of R.S.) d. Aug. 16, 1874, age 90. Also In Memory of Richard, Isabella, and Frances Southern. Richard Southern was an overseer of the poor in Alexandria County in 1849, a commissioner of Election, 1862, and a member of the county court, 1862-64.
[3] Mosby had his headquarters in Williams Woods where Barbara, assisted by her brother, Benjamin, took him supplies and messages.

---

## THE SOULE FAMILY

Abram A. Soule lived in the house now owned by the Meese family on East Broad Street. Mr. Soule served as Town Sergeant of Falls Church for many years. He was born in 1836 and died in 1915. His wife, Catherine E. Soule, was born September 24, 1829; died February 3, 1886. They had several children, including Miss Mattie Soule, who was for years the village dress maker and late in life married Mr. Jones, a retired Metropolitan policeman. Other children were Mary A. Soule (1863-1904); and Mrs. Edward Kimball (who had two daughters, one named Helen Kimball).

---

## THE SPRANKLE FAMILY

The immigrant ancestor of this family is said to have been a William Sprankle (Sprengle, Sprenkel, Sprenckles) who was born in Germany and came to York County, Pennsylvania, in 1734. Of his large family, a son, Peter Sprankle, had at least two children, John Sprankle who married Anna Gelhauser and Benjamin Sprankle. The brothers, John and Benjamin, moved from York County to Indiana County, Pennsylvania, in 1808. Benjamin/Sprankle had two children, John and Samuel. Samuel Sprankle had a son, B. H. Sprankle, who was born June 23, 1859, and was living at 422 Union Ave., Knoxville, Tennessee, in 1935, as was his sister, Mrs. R. T. Eldon.

John Sprankle (until 1840 Sprengle), son of Peter Sprankle, was born about 1780, and died about 1814. His wife was Anna Gelhauser. The following is a rough translation of the "Pennsylvania-Dutch" birth certificate of his daughter Barbara:

"Johannes Sprenckel and his wife Anna, born Gilhauser, having lived in West Manchester Township, York County, in the State of Pennsylvania is on the 17th of November in the year of our Lord 1804, at 3 o'clock in the morning, as testified by this paper, a daughter into this world born which on the 15th of April Mr. Wagner, Reformest Pastor, was christened and given the name Barbara. The witnesses are Michael Sprenckel and wife Maria."

John and Anna (Gelhauser) Sprankle had issue:

(1) Solomon Sprankle, moved to Fairfax County and settled between Falls Church and Chesterbrook in 1858. He married Sarah, and had issue:
   (11) David Sprankle (lived in Kansas). His eldest son was named Walter. Two sons died in World War I.
   (12) Margaret Sprankle, died young.
   (13) William Sprankle, married Sarah Ellen Marr of Falls Church. She died May 14, 1955. Issue:

(131) Adrian Sprankle of Falls Church and Leesburg.
(14) Nellie Sprankle, unmarried.
(2) John Sprankle, Jr., lived in Tyrone, Pa.
(3) Benjamin Sprankle.
(4) Polly Sprankle married John Fetherhoof.
(5) Barbara Sprankle, born November 17, 1804, married (1) John Mutersbaugh; (2) James Watkins.
(6) Frederick Sprankle.

## THE STEADMAN FAMILY

Eli Stansbury Steadman, who settled in Falls Church, was a descendant of the ancient *Stedman* family of England and Scotland. The name was pronounced with a Scottish flavor, "Stidmon," until the early 1900's. The family name means "steadfast." The Arms of the family contain three boars heads, the most important of the Feudal symbols, indicating hospitality. The Motto, "Spes Mea In Deo," means "My hope is in God."

The first Stedman came to America in 1635, and the family has been in Northern Virginia for more than two hundred years. One ancestor, James Stedman, Sr., served in Captain John Hardin's Company from Winchester during the French & Indian War. His son, Thomas Stedman (1758-1814) was in the Revolutionary War from Harper's Ferry, Berkeley County (now Jefferson County, West Virginia). His two sons served in the War of 1812. One of them, Colonel James Stedman (1789-1857) inserted the "a" in his surname at the end of his life. The reason was political, due to certain members of the Stedman family who favored slavery. Colonel Stedman went to Indiana in 1816, and lived for a time in Jefferson County. His brother, John, and his sister, Mary,wife of James Wyckoff, also went there. The two brothers, homesick for Virginia, returned in 1821 and settled in Leesburg, Loudoun County.

Colonel James Stedman was well-to-do and owned "Steadman's Coopering Factory" which employed a large number of persons. He was Steward, Class Leader and a trustee of the famous "Old Stone Methodist Church" in Leesburg. The Stedmans were converted to Methodism from the Church of England under Bishop Francis Asbury, and their home in King & Queen County was a favorite stopping place. The Bishop also held classes at "Church Field," the Yorktown home of Christopher Stedman, Sr., after he moved from King & Queen.

Colonel James Stedman served on the Leesburg Town Council, and was a founder and trustee of the Union Cemetery.He owned a number of lots in the "new addition" to Leesburg which was called "Steadman Town." Colonel Stedman married Alice (Alsey) Fouché, of French ancestry. The name is also spelled Foushee. Her ancestor, Hugh Fouché, settled in Virginia in 1633. Her grandfather, Jacob Fouché, Sr., of Loudoun County, was a Revolutionary Soldier. Her father, Jacob, Jr., died young. His wife was Perenah Elizabeth McDaniel of Scottish ancestry, a daughter of George McDaniel of Clan McDonald.

Marshall B. Steadman (1824-1882), son of Colonel James and Alice (Fouché) Stedman-Steadman, served in the famous "Loudoun Guards" of the 17th Virginia Regiment, during the War Between the States. He was wounded on Bull Run Bridge. Mr. Steadman served on the Leesburg Town Council, carried on his father's business, and was also Town Sergeant of Leesburg following the war. He was a Mason, member of the local Odd Fellows Lodge and was an organizing member of the Temperance Lodge. His second wife's uncle, Major James F. Divine, was a national leader in the temperance movement.

Mr. Steadman was first married to Mary Elizabeth Berry who died young. His second wife was Emeline Smallwood Towner. She was something of a poet and artist. Of old American ancestry, Mrs. Steadman was a descendant of Richard Towner who settled in Connecticut in 1650. Her father, John Littlejohn Towner (1797-1866) of Leesburg married on February 25, 1828, to Sarah Ann Smallwood. The Towner ancestry included Dr. Jacob Coutsman, first physician in Leesburg, who left an estate bonded for one hundred thousand pounds. Dr. Coutsman was familiar with twenty-eight languages, and his large mansion, where he died, is standing on Market Street. Another ancestor was Lieutenant William French of Boston, one of America's early authors, who wrote "Strength Out of Weakness." Lieutenant French (born March 15, 1603) was a member of the Ancient and Honorable Artillery Company. His wife's ancestors, the Bunnells and Wilmots, were founders of Billerica, Massachusetts. Mrs. Steadman's mother, born in Waterford, Loudoun County, in 1810, was a descendant of Major James Smallwood of Charles County, Maryland, who settled in 1664. Major Smallwood's descendants are eligible for membership in the Descendants of Lords of Maryland Manors. Major Smallwood was a member of the Colonial Maryland Assembly, 1665-1714, was Commissioner of Charles County, High Sheriff, Major of Foot (1689) and made Lieutenant Colonel of Militia by 1700. Mrs. Steadman's ancestry included the first Lord Baltimore, Colonel Francis Marbury, and Thomas Greene, an early Governer of Maryland. Colonel Francis Marbury was a descendant of King Henry VII, of England. One of Mrs. Steadman's cousins was Judge Henry Wirt Thomas of Fairfax, once Lieutenant Governor of Virginia.

Mrs. Steadman's father, a merchant in Leesburg, owned the firm of "Towner and Hammerly." His winter home was on Loudoun Street in Leesburg. Summers were spent at "Springwood," the mansion owned by a cousin Major George Washington Ball.

Eli Stansbury Steadman, tenth in descent from the first Lord Baltimore, was born in Leesburg, December 2, 1857, He died at his Falls Church home, "Rose Park," December 28, 1931. He attended the Leesburg Academy and moved to Falls Church in 1904. Mr. Steadman rented the Amanda Ellison house when he settled here, later renting the Lee House at 501 West Broad Street. Before 1908 Mr. Steadman moved with his family to historic "Walnut Hill," the old Sewall home. He purchased part of the "Rose Park" tract of the Darnes and Lloyds in 1914. Mr. Steadman was a government employee in later years. He spent his early life attempting to help rear his younger brothers and sisters, as his father was never well following his war experience.

At age forty-two Mr. Steadman married the daughter of his best friend. On October 25, 1899, in Leesburg, he married Ida Jane Kerns (1881-1940), daughter of Charles Thomas and Mary Susan (Milburn) Kerns of Winchester and Leesburg. She was eighteen years of age at the time of marriage. Mrs. Steadman's family lived at Kernstown in Frederick County and were Scotch-Irish, Dutch, German and English. The many old Valley families in her ancestry included the Chapmans, Milburns, Stricklings, Sirbaughs, and others. One ancestor, John Milburn, of Milburn, New Jersey, was a Quaker from the Scottish border, related to Sir Walter Raleigh. One eccentric but interesting relative of the Milburns was Jonathan Chapman, better known as "Johnny Appleseed." Other members of this family included Bishop Paul Bentley Kern of The Methodist

Church, Dr. John Adam Kern of Vanderbilt University (also President of Randolph-Macon College). The name was originally spelled Kern, but Mrs. Steadman's father, including her brother, John Kirby Smith Kerns, used the plural spelling.

Eli Stansbury and Ida Jane (Kerns) Steadman had issue:

(1) (Honorable) Frank McNulty Steadman, born at Leesburg, April 12, 1903. Mr. Steadman received his LL.B. degree from National University Law School on June 13, 1927, and was admitted to the Virginia Bar on December 20, 1927. He was a partner in a law firm, "Steadman & Keck," at East Falls Church before entering government service. Mr. Steadman is a member of Sigma Nu Phi (Legal). He also held a Lieutenant's commission in the United States Army, and has been an Attorney in the Department of justice for more than thirty years. Mr. Steadman is an ardent Mason, founder of Macon Ware Lodge and the James S. Sipes Chapter, Order of DeMolay at Falls Church. While Master of Kemper Lodge, Mr. Steadman laid the cornerstone of Falls Church High School (May 18, 1945). He grew up an Episcopalian, and a member of the Falls Church. He has been a member of the Columbia Baptist Church for many years and served as Superintendent of the Adult Department of the Sunday School and was a long-time Treasurer of the Church. Mr. Steadman served as District Deputy Grand Master of Masonic Jurisdiction # 1, and is a Masonic historian. He is the author of numerous pamphlets and articles. On September 6, 1928, he married Etlan Shotwell, daughter of J. Lewis and Anna Lee (Updike) Shotwell of Falls Church (*See Shotwell*). Issue:

(11) Frank McNaulty Steadman, Jr., born in Newark, New Jersey (while his father was stationed there in government service), October 26, 1931. Mr. Steadman, an Attorney for the C & P Telephone Company, attended George Washington University and the University of Virginia Law School. At the University of Virginia he made the Law Review, was a member of the Order of the Coif, the Raven Society, and received honors. Mr. Steadman was an officer in the U.S. Navy and served as Prosecuting Attorney for the Navy at the Port of San Francisco. He married on February 20, 1960, in Detroit, to Patricia Sullinger. Mrs. Steadman, of early American ancestry, was born in Coral Gables, Florida, August 2, 1935, a daughter of Ferris Wood and Edna Virginia (Paulsell) Sullinger. Issue:

(111) Sarah Lynn Steadman, born in Fairfax, Virginia, September 11, 1961.
(112) Pamela Jean Steadman born in Baltimore, Maryland, July 26, 1963.

(2) Howard Elroy Steadman (who used the name Roy instead of his baptismal name Elroy), born at 501 W. Broad Street, Falls Church, November 4, 1905, died at his home on Shreve Road, December 19, 1954, with burial in Oakwood Cemetery. Mr. Steadman married on November 17, 1917 at the Falls Church, to Velva Lee Wakefield. Mrs. Steadman was a daughter of Malcolm Mallow and Lola Marie (Caton) Wakefield of Annandale, Fairfax and Falls Church. She was a granddaughter of the Reverend E.W. Wakefield founder of "Wakefield Chapel" near Fairfax. Mrs. Steadman was born at Ilda, Fairfax County, August 16, 1905, and died in Washington, D. C., June 22, 1963. Issue:

(21) Shirley Lee Steadman, born at Falls Church, January 15, 1932, married on February 4, 1951, to Howard Aubrey Hawkins. Mr. Hawkins was born in Washington, D. C., November 29, 1925, a son of Aubrey and Martha (Hudson) Hawkins of an old Rappahannock County, Virginia family. Issue:

(211) Howard Aubrey Hawkins, Jr., born July 23, 1952.

(212) Carol Anne Hawkins, born February 11, 1955.
(213) Clifford Wayne Hawkins, born July 24, 1957.
(214) Mary Jane Hawkins, born May 3, 1959.
(22) Eleanor Ann Steadman, born at Falls Church, January 30, 1935, married on April 17, 1955, to Sherwood Walter Lessig. Mr. Lessig, of old Pennsylvania Dutch ancestry, was born in Pen Argyl, Pennsylvania, December 9, 1931, a son of Claude Reese and Emily (Houck) Lessig. Issue:
(221) Amanda Lee Lessig, born January 17, 1959.
(222) Sherwood Walter Lessig, Jr., born October 14, 1963.

(3) Melvin Lee Steadman, born at "Walnut Hill," Falls Church, October 1, 1908, is living at "Antrim," at West Falls Church. Mr. Steadman attended local schools and the Ford School in Washington, D. C., and studied mechanics. He is a long-time employee of the Arlington Motor Company. Mr. Steadman married on June 14, 1929, Ruth Elizabeth Hirst. Mrs. Steadman, a descendant of the "Big Chimneys" family, was born at the Mankin "Home House," on West Broad Street, Falls Church, July 3, 1911, a daughter of Herbert Nelson and Ellen Elizabeth (Mankin) Hirst. She is a granddaughter of Charles Edward and Ann Valinda (Lynch) Mankin and of Thomson Mason and Emily Hirst (Allen) Hirst. (*See Mankin, Lynch, Thompson, Hirst*). Issue:
(31) (The Reverend) Melvin Lee Steadman, Jr. (author of this book), born at "Sprucewood," Falls Church, May 14, 1932. Mr. Steadman attended public and parochial schools in Falls Church and attended American University. He received his B.A. from Randolph-Macon and his S.B.T. degree from Wesley Theological Seminary. Mr. Steadman, a Methodist Minister, was baptized in the Falls Church, since his father's family were Episcopalians. He became a member of Dulin Chapel in 1941, and served there as a student minister, 1949-1954. Mr. Steadman was granted a Local Preacher's License on September 15, 1949. He was employed by the D. C. Public Library for several years, and is the author of numerous articles and pamphlets. Since 1951 he has been a member of the National Genealogical Society, and holds membership in eighteen other societies devoted to historical interests. Mr. Steadman is Historiographer of the Methodist Church in Virginia. He is a Mason, and a member of Henry Lodge #57, Fairfax. Mr. Steadman married, at Dulin Methodist Church, August 29, 1953, to Elizabeth Frances (Beth) Powell. The groom's uncle, the Reverend George G. Oliver, and the bride's brother, the Reverend James Emerson Powell, Jr., officiated at the wedding. Mrs. Steadman was born in Washington, D.C., July 1, 1932, a daughter of James Emerson and Ada Ball (Coe) Powell. She is a descendant of pioneer Falls Church families including the Shreve and Ball clan. Her grandmother, Mrs. Walker Peyton Conway Coe, was a niece of Mrs. William H. Ellison. Her father, a graduate of Washington & Lee University, is a native of Kentucky, related to the Powell and Harrison families of Loudoun County. A great-grandfather, the Reverend William Gwynn Coe, D.D., was minister of Fairfax Chapel in Falls Church prior to the War Between the States. Other local connections include the families of Birch, Veitch, Febrey, and many others. Mr. and Mrs. Steadman reside at Lake View Estates, Gainesville, with their children, John Payton (born in Arlington, July 14, 1958) and Elizabeth Lee (born in Williamsburg, December 16, 1961).

(32) Mildred Marguerite Steadman, born at "Sprucewood," Falls Church, January 22, 1936. She attended the American Institute of Banking and was an employee of the Old Dominion Bank. She married on November 3, 1962, to Ernest George Pappas. Mr. Pappas was born in Wilson, North Carolina, of Albanian ancestry, a son of George Anastas and Lambrini (Lambra) (Dima) Pappas. He was born March 17, 1937. Mrs. Mildred S. Pappas is a member of the Falls Church Chapter, D.A.R.

(33) Ruth Ellen Steadman, born in Washington, D.C., November 9, 1945, was a charter member of the Falls Church Chapter, C.A.R. Miss Steadman is an employee of the Old Dominion Bank.

## THE STEWART FAMILY

Charles Alexander Stewart settled in Falls Church in September 1892. His home was at 6857 N. Washington Blvd., Arlington, which was formerly within the corporate limits of Falls Church. Mr. Stewart was active in every movement for good in the community. He served for many years as a Vestryman of the Falls Church. Mr. Stewart was formerly Chairman of the Falls Church School Board, and was active in building Madison School. Charles A. Stewart School on North Underwood Street, Arlington, was named for him. At his death, the school was closed one-half day and the flag placed at half-staff.

Mr. Stewart was the author of *A Virginia Village*, published in 1904, the first history of Falls Church. A writeup of his life can be found on pages 12-13 of *Family History of The Stewarts of Beechwood* privately printed by him in 1897. Mr. Stewart was educated at public and private schools in Norfolk, Virginia, and Eaton and Burnett's Business College, Baltimore. In 1878 he printed and published a small weekly paper at Wallaceton, was afterwards on the reportorial staff of *Portsmouth Daily Times* as local editor, and resigned this position in the fall of 1879 to take over the management of "Beechwood Farm" his ancestral home.

Mr. Stewart was a delegate to the Democratic Congressional Convention at Virginia Beach in September, 1884 and the Gubernatorial Convention at Richmond in 1885 which nominated Fitzhugh Lee. On September 1, 1886, he was appointed to a clerkship in the U. S. Treasury Department, and assigned to the office of the Comptroller of the Currency, having passed successfully an examination before the U. S. Civil Service Commission in March of that year. He received rapid promotions so that by February 20, 1893, he was promoted to class 4, the highest at that time under Civil Service Rules, the result of a competitive examination.

Mr. Stewart took a law course at the old Columbian University (now George Washington University) in Washington. He served many years as Chief Clerk in the Treasury Department, and in 1919 was appointed a national bank examiner, a position he held until his retirement in 1931.

Mr. Stewart was a native of Norfolk County, Virginia, born on November 19, 1860, and died at East Falls Church, April 17, 1950. He came from an old Virginia family. His ancestor, Charles Stewart, born about 1730, married Martha Foreman, a daughter of Alexander Foreman. He was a soldier in the Revolution and was commissioned as Ensign in Captain William Grimes' Company of the 15th Virginia Regiment of Foot, commanded by Lieutenant Colonel James Innes. His name first appears on the roll for July 1, 1777, with the remark: "Commissioned April, 1777." On the roll for

August, 1777, he is reported as "Looking after the sick in Philadelphia." By D cember, 1777, he was a 2nd Lieutenant. He was granted 2,666-2/3 acres of land ( April 10, 1819, for his three years service as Ensign, (Virginia Military Warra No. 6308). Charles Stewart died in February 1801. He had issue:
(1) William Stewart, born August 11, 1780.
(2) Charles Stewart, born August 30, 1782.
(3) Joseph Stewart, born May 20, 1784, died in infancy.
(4) Ann Stewart, born July 12, 1786, died in infancy.
(5) Alexander Stewart, born March 8, 1788.
(6) John Stewart, born December 9, 1791, died in infancy.

Alexander Stewart, son of Charles and Martha (Foreman) Stewart, was born Mar 8, 1788, and died in 1813. He married in 1807 to Lauretta Wallace (who remarri twice after his death). She was born March 3, 1786, died June 6, 1857. Alexand Stewart was a soldier in the War of 1812 and died from a cold contracted while service. Alexander and Lauretta (Wallace) Stewart had issue:
(51) Joseph Stewart, born 1808.
(52) William Charles Stewart.
(53) Caroline Frances Stewart, born October 17, 1812.

(52) William Charles Stewart, a son of Alexander and Lauretta (Wallace) Ste art, was born September 21, 1810 in Norfolk County, Virginia. He served as a Li tenant of the State Volunteers in the Mexican War but his command was not call into service. He married on September 13, 1837 to Catharine Matilda Garrett daughter of Henry and Ann (Wilkins) Garrett. She was born June 27, 1818, in N folk County. Her father, Henry Garrett, was a native of Accomac County (born 17 died August 1, 1855, aged 74 years). He was an early settler near Deep Creek Norfolk County and was for many years Superintendent of the Dismal Swamp Can He married twice. His first wife, Ann Wilkins (the widow Smith) was a daughter Captain Willis Wilkins of New Mill Creek, Norfolk County, and Blandinah the wid of The Reverend John Braidfoot and daughter of Arthur Moseley 2nd. Arthur Mo ley, 2nd, died 1757, was descended from William and Susan Mosely who settled Virginia from Rotterdam, Holland, in 1649, and settled in Lower Norfolk Coun later Princess Anne. Henry Garrett and Ann (Wilkins) Smith were married on I cember 29, 1814 and she died July 31, 1829.

William Charles Stewart (who married Catharine M. Garrett) was a farmer a died at his farm "Beechwood," at the intersection of the Dismal Swamp and Nor west Canals, in St. Brides Parish, Norfolk County, June 29, 1865. During the W Between the States Mr. Stewart was imprisoned at Old Point Comfort by Gene Butler because of his loyalty to the South. William Charles and Catharine Mati (Garrett) Stewart had issue:
(521) William Henry Stewart, born September 25, 1838. (Lieutenant Colo William H. Stewart married twice, by his wife Annie Wright Stubbs—who v a daughter of John S. and Stella L. H. (Armistead) Stubbs—he had issue R ert Armistead Stewart, born March 9, 1877, and died at the home of his Unc Charles A. Stewart at East Falls Church, in January, 1950. Mr. Stewart was authority on Virginia genealogy and author of numerous books.)
(522) Nannie Garrett Stewart, born December 1, 1840, died unmarried Janu 30, 1897.

(523) Sarah Catharine Stewart, born June 5, 1843.
(524) Charles Alexander Stewart, born November 19, 1860 (settled in Falls Church).
(525) Robert Edward Bruce Stewart, born July 20, 1863.

Charles Alexander Stewart, the son of William Charles and Catharine Matilda (Garrett) Stewart, is the subject of this sketch. He was a member of the Virginia Society, Sons of the American Revolution,[1] and served three years' service in the National Guard of the District of Columbia as a private. He married on December 6, 1887, to Mary Isabella Tabb, daughter of Dr. Robert Bruce and Elizabeth Anne (Warden) Tabb, his wife. The tombstone of Dr. Tabb (in Oakwood Cemetery, Falls Church) states that he was born in Elizabeth City County, Va., August 10, 1833 and died at Falls Church November 12, 1906. He was a "Soldier, Legislator, Physician, for 40 years an honored resident of Lower Norfolk County." His wife, Elizabeth Anne Warden, was born March 12, 1837, died April 10, 1891, was a daughter of William West and Isabella (Morris) Warden. Mrs. Stewart was born in Norfolk County, July 19, 1866, died at her home in Falls Church November 17, 1939. Charles Alexander and Mary Isabella (Tabb) Stewart had issue:

(5241) Mary Agnes Stewart, born December 11, 1888.
(5242) Elizabeth Tabb Stewart, born March 6, 1890, resides at the family home on N. Washington Blvd., unmarried.
(5243) Catharine Maud Stewart, born November 23, 1891, died 1931, unmarried.
(5244) Marie Louise Stewart, born July and died August 1893.
(5245) John Robert Bruce Stewart, born August 13, 1895.
(5246) Charles Alexander Stewart, Jr., born July 30, 1900, died at Camp Devens, Massachusetts, July 14, 1920.
(5247) Henry Edward Stewart, married Elizabeth Bland Fitzhugh Stuntz. Issue:
    (52471) Elizabeth Bland Stewart.
    (52472) Anne Catherine Randolph Stewart.
    Mr. Stewart lives in Campana, Argentina.
(5248) William Moseley Stewart, married Elsie Lucille Banks, daughter of Nathan Banks of East Falls Church. Issue:
    (52481) Sally Anne Stewart.
    (52482) William Mosely Stewart, Jr.
    (52483) David Tabb Stewart.
(5249) Robert Tabb Stewart, married Mary Elizabeth Townsend, issue:
    (52491) Catherine Townsend Stewart.
(524.10) Clara Fenwick Stewart, married Roy R. Keith.
(524.11) Robert Bruce Stewart, died in infancy.

---

[1] Became a member of the Virginia Society, S.A.R. in 1915; and later transferred to the D.C. Chapter. In 1944 he was honored as having been a member for over a quarter of a century.

## THE TALBOTT FAMILY

Dr. Thomas Melville Talbott was a well-known physician in Falls Church where he practiced for 67 years. Dr. Talbott represented an old Maryland family. He was born in Maryland on October 17, 1848, a son of Benson and Marie (Hyde) Talbott. Dr. Talbott died May 3, 1940.

Dr. Talbott built a large home on a portion of the farm owned by his father-in-law, John E. Febrey, at what is now 7 Corners. He married (1) to Ella Ball Febrey, considered to be the most beautiful woman in Falls Church. Dr. Talbott remarried (2) Kathleen Nourse. She was born May 14, 1872, and died February 21, 1946. Issue:

*(By Ella Ball Febrey)*:

(1) (Colonel) Edward M. Talbott, born in 1878, died August 17, 1958, in San Francisco, aged 80 years. Colonel Talbott was educated in medicine and was in private practice in San Francisco by 1922. Upon his graduation from Georgetown University, he practiced medicine with his father. He later attended the Army Medical School in Washington and was an eye specialist in the Army. He was survived by his wife, Grace Talbott, and no issue.

*(By Kathleen Nourse)*:

(2) Gladys Talbott, born February 22, 1893, died September 3, 1893.

(3) Harold Wailes Talbott, born January 20, 1898, died June 29, 1911.

(4) Philip M. Talbott, born February 12, 1896, has lived in Arlington County during his entire life. Mr. Talbott has been one of Washington's foremost civic leaders. He served in World War I, and on September 21, 1914, became an employee of Woodward & Lothrop Department Store. He served continuously in that firm until he retired recently. His education at Randolph-Macon Academy gave him a good background for his long career. He served in a variety of executive posts, including secretary and general manager at Woodward & Lothrop. He was elected a Director in 1934, and Senior Vice President in 1950. Mr. Talbott, during his 44 years with this fashionable store, aided in its growth from one store to a Washington area chain of six stores.

Mr. Talbott served as President and Chairman of the Board of the U. S. Chamber of Commerce, as President of the National Retail Dry Goods Association, and headed the Washington Board of Trade. He has served as Chairman of the Board of the Suburban Savings & Loan Association, chairman of the business advisory board of the American University School of Business, first vice president of the Merchants & Manufacturers Association, director of the Potomac Electric & Power Company, member of the advisory board of branches of Riggs National Bank, and a director of the Springfield Bank.

Mr. Talbott received the Gold Medal Award of the National Retail Dry Goods Association, regarded as retailing's highest honor.

Mr. Talbott's wife was Miss Thompson.

(5) Daughter Talbott, married (1) —— Bowman, and (2) Wallace Linfoot.

## THE TAYLOR FAMILY

John Taylor, born in Maryland in 1824, was living in Falls Church by 1860, and was a farmer. His wife, Catherine, was a native Virginian, born in 1821. Their children as listed in the 1860 U. S. Census were: John Taylor, Jr., born 1844, Mary A. Taylor, born 1848, Eli Taylor, born 1858, and S. A. Taylor, born 1857.

Summerfield Taylor, called Stump, was in the grocery business in Falls Church for many years. He died October 19, 1948, at his home 120 N. Washington Street. He married Alice Boucher and was the father of John E. Taylor, former Sheriff of Fairfax County, and Rudolph S. Taylor

Another member of this family, James William Taylor, lived at 115 W. Park Avenue, where he died March 10, 1946. He was the husband of Lola T. Taylor and had children including Madeline L. Taylor and Roger E. Taylor. A son, James W., Jr., died at Camp Lee, Virginia, July 9, 1942.

## THE TERRETT FAMILY

This distinguished old Virginia family is much in need of a historian. The Terretts owned land in the area between Falls Church and Bailey's Cross Roads, and in other sections of Northern Virginia. William Henry Terrett, ancestor of most of this name, was Deputy Clerk of Fairfax County at the time of its organization. In 1741 he patented 982 acres near Great Hunting Creek and in 1746 acquired an additional 127 acres. In the same year, 1746, he acquired 300 acres from Gabriel Adams. Captain Terrett married Margaret Pearson, daughter of Captain Simon Pearson, also of a well known local family. Their children included Pearson Terrett (who died unmarried before his father's death); William Henry Terrett, Jr., and Nathaniel Terrett.

Captain William Henry Terrett made his will February 7, 1755, probated 1758. He left a plantation of one thousand acres to his son, William Henry, Jr., and provided for "the child my wife now goes with." If this child was male, he was to have "the land whereon John Summers now dwells." His widow remarried to John West (*See West*). Her will, probated in 1798, mentions her children: William Henry Terrett, Nathaniel Terrett, Constant Washington, Anna Powell, Susanna Terrett and Roger West.

Grandchildren of William Henry Terrett, Jr., are yet living. In 1830 Gibson A. Terrett, a descendant, settled on a farm of 75 acres in Falls Church. His children included a son, Victor Terrett. Another William Henry Terrett who lived in the Falls Church neighborhood was a son of Hunter and Anna Elizabeth Terrett. He was born at Falls Church in 1847 and married on February 25, 1869 at Langley, to Priscilla G. Richards. Mrs. Terrett was born in 1847 a daughter of John and Mary E. Richards, of an old family.

Thomas Terrett, who was connected with the prominent Bontz family of Alexandria, was a long-time resident of the area. His grandfather was William Henry Terrett, Jr. This Thomas Terrett had a number of children, some of whom are active in community life. A son, Thomas Terrett, Jr., died in August, 1955, at 86 years of age. He was born August 10, 1868, on the farm originally owned by his Grandfather, William Henry Terrett. He later took over the stock and general farm there as well as another farm in Accokeek, Maryland. At one time Mr. Terrett owned the Barcroft grain mill in Fairfax County He was in the real estate business for several years. Mr. Terrett moved to Washington in 1920. In early life he was a Vestryman of St. Paul's Episcopal Church at Bailey's Cross Roads. His wife was Maude White, whom he married in 1900. Their children included Thomas Vernon Terrett, Robert Walton Terrett, Mrs. Sherod L. Earle, II, and Mrs. Arthur C. Parsons.

Mrs. Thomas Row, long-time member of the choir of the Falls Church, and still an active communicant of the Church, is a sister to Thomas Terrett, Jr., mentioned above. Others of this family included Mrs. Vernon Rector, Mrs. J. A. Pearson, Henry Bontz Terrett, Mrs. Leon McCoy and Mrs. Howard B. Clapp.

## THE THOMPSON FAMILY OF "BIG CHIMNEYS"

In 1662 Colonel George Thompson was granted 1,000 acres of land including part of the present City of Washington. This estate, known as "Blew Playne" (Blue Plain) was on the Eastern Branch of the Anacostia River and lay between there and Oxon Creek. In 1663 Thompson patented "Duddington Manor" of 1,000 acres. He also owned "Duddington Pasture" of 300 acres and "New Troy" of 500 acres. In 1670 Thompson leased "New Troy" to Thomas Notley for one thousand years!

Colonel Thompson's descendants moved into the Hunting Creek area and lived in that section which became Alexandria. A descendant, William Thompson, who died in 1785, married Mildred Ball, daughter of John and Elizabeth (Payne) Ball who owned land in what is now Glen Carlin in the 1740's. This John Ball was a son of John and Winifred (Williams) Ball and a grandson of Richard and Elizabeth (Linton) Ball. His brother was Moses Ball, ancestor of all by that name in present day Arlington.

William Thompson lived at "Big Chimneys," and also owned land in Glen Carlin. His descendants owned the farm which in more recent years was known as the Torreyson Farm on Arlington Boulevard. During certain periods the family did not reside at "Big Chimneys," but used it as a rental property. They had a way of returning to it, however. The house was a Tavern at one time during its long history.

Richard Thompson (ca. 1760-1835), son of William and Mildred (Ball) Thompson, also lived at "Big Chimneys." He had other properties in the vicinity of Falls Church. His brother, George Thompson, also owned large tracts in the area. Richard Thompson's family included the following children: Nancy Thompson, who died at "Big Chimneys" before 1850, unmarried; Mary Thompson born 1791, died at "Big Chimneys," in February, 1861, unmarried; Nathan Thompson, born in 1800, died at "Big Chimneys," unmarried, in 1854, and Ellen (Thompson) Lightfoot, the latter the only one to marry.

Nathan Thompson reared his nieces, Elizabeth Ellen, Mary Ann, and Jane Lightfoot, who became heirs to "Big Chimneys." He added considerably to their estate. On May 28, 1839, he purchased property of Richard Thompson from George H. Thompson;[1] and on January 13, 1845, purchased two tracts of land from James and Rebecca Gordon of Washington.[2] The land cost $1,100, and the first tract was "in the neighborhood of the Falls Church, contained 70 or 75 acres; and the second, "adjoining the farm of John Haycock," contained about 78 acres. On January 22, 1845, Thompson purchased from Alfred Moss (trustee for Ruth Scott, formerly Mills) "the Gordon tract," for $4,050, containing 78 acres, 3 rods, and 36 poles.[3]

On February 3, 1846, Thompson purchased a tract of land containing nine acres, three rods, and thirty-two poles from Henry P. Townsend of New York City and John M. and Harriet H. Poor of Fairfax County.[4] This land was opposite the south west corner of the Falls Church lot and adjoined Thompson's other land. In an effort to square his property, Thompson purchased from William H. and W. F. Dulany a tract of one acre, "situate and lying and being in the said County of Fairfax, being that portion of the 'Centre Lodge Tract' lying north of the road leading from Fairfax Court House to the Middle Turnpike."This was on February 27, 1849.[5] He purchased four and one-half acres from Verlinda Atkinson and Ann Reese on May 25, 1852.[6]

Thompson owned the "Star Tavern" property, once a corner of "Big Chimneys" farm, now the site of the Falls Church Bank. On November 23, 1852, he sold this to Walter H. Erwin for $100.00. The tract sold Erwin contained two acres of land and buildings, beginning at a "Line of the County road which runs by the School House near Falls Church," on the south side of the Turnpike where it was intersected.[7] On December 16, 1852, Thompson sold a tract of one rod and eleven poles to A. L. Brent, William F. Dulany, L. L. Somers, J. C. Chichester, and F. M. Fitzhugh, trustees of "the Episcopal church known and designated as the 'Falls Church' " for $5.00. This land was "contigerous to said church. . ."[8]

Bachelor Thompson acquired a large estate which he left by will dated July 19, 1853,[9] to his sister, Mary Thompson, and his three Lightfoot nieces, in equal proportions. He instructed that his sister, Mary, "occupy and control the House and Household affairs" at "Big Chimneys."

On February 16, 1860, Mary Thompson, Jane Lightfoot, John W. Lynch and Mary Ann, his wife, and William H. Lynch and Elizabeth Ellen his wife, sold to Hiram W. Reed a tract of land which was adjacent to Reed's other land, being that which Mary Thompson had a life interest in until her death.[10] This tract is now the site of Tyler Gardens Apartments and the Falls Church Post Office.

The "Big Chimneys" farm at one time had the following approximate boundaries: beginning at the corner, now the site of the Falls Church Bank, and continuing along West Broad Street to a point at North Oak Street, then along North Oak Street to Tripp's Run, and following the Run to a point about opposite the Quarry, then to the Bank site.

"Big Chimneys" became known as "John Lynch's Old Log House" following a long occupancy by Mr. Lynch. He acquired that portion containing the old log house following the death of Nathan Thompson and his sister, Mary. The three Lightfoot nieces were the only heirs, and one, Jane, never married.[11]

The "Big Chimneys" house was built in 1699, according to a date stone in one of the large end chimneys. It was remembered as "the first house in Falls Church." "Big Chimneys" was picturesque, built of hand-hewn logs, squared and painted white. The logs were put together with wood pins, two feet long. The pins were split in the end while green, and in the process of aging and swelling, held the building together. Hand wrought nails were in the door and other frames. The glass windows were hand made and set in lead.

The chimneys were the outstanding feature of the house. They were twenty feet long at the base and tapered to the cap. The sides were lined with slabs of stone which glittered with mica. The windows had panel (solid wood) shutters, called "Dutch Blinds." These were removed during the years following the War Between the States. The doors had brass knobs which were polished each day by some of the house servants. The roof was of wood shingles which were covered with moss. The main door step was a large flat stone. The foundation had a native rock base.

The house was built on a slight rise in the rolling pastures, and was amid a garden. Vines grew on the old salmon colored brick chimneys, as did roses in abundance. One rose covered the west window, climbing a special arbor. The house was surrounded by dependencies, including a smoke house and wash house. To the left of the house in a cedar grove, was a stone spring house covered with honey-suckle and rambler roses. A well was also in the yard, a product of progress about 1800. Under the cedar trees near the spring house the Thompsons and their descendants had "butter" tables, where the butter was made. Under the cool water, milk, butter and other foods were kept in crocks. Apples were kept there to cool and were a delight.[12]

"Big Chimneys" was almost concealed from Leesburg Pike (Broad Street) by lilac and box bushes. All of the old-fashioned flowers grew in the gardens. The drive way to the house was once part of the original Little Falls Road. A worm fence, replaced in the years following the War Between the States, originally surrounded the farm. The front gate posts were made of locust wood and were tall and circular. Bird houses were carved in the posts. On the fence were many old roses such as "hundred leaf" and "Macrophylla." Wisteria and other vines were in abundance.

Mrs. John W. Lynch inherited the furnishings left by her Thompson relatives. The description given by Mrs. Ellen Mankin Hirst is of the house during the occupancy of the Lynch family. In the parlor ("great room"), a low ceiling room like all of them, was a Virginia sofa, cherry drop-leaf table, and wing back chairs. A milk-glass type lamp was kept on the table. A scenic paper was on one wall. Blue and white ginger jugs and a family portrait were over the black walnut mantle.

The "Chamber," where the head of the house had his bed, was at one time a hall. In it was a tall bed and trundle. Ladder back chairs were in all of the rooms. A Grandfather's Clock stood in the hall next to the box (enclosed) stair.

The kitchen must have been a delightful place. The entire side wall was a fireplace and Dutch Oven. Connected with it in more recent years was a large iron wood range. Rocking chairs made the room comfortable. The kitchen had a scallop corner cupboard. An exact plan of each room is in the author's file.

Following the death of Mrs. Lynch, her husband moved to Washington. The old house was not desirable, as the family were enamored by the "gingerbread" era. The house was rented by various people and finally abandoned. Ida Jane (Lynch) O'Mearer gave the house to her cousin, Ellen Mankin Hirst, who hired Dick Digges to tear it down. The bricks from the chimneys were sold to Joe Tinner for $10.00 and the smoke house moved to the Mankin "Home House." The house was torn down about 1908/9. Later Mrs. O'Mearer sold the site to Dr. M. E. Church.

[1] Alexandria, Virginia, *Deed Book Z #2*, page 281.
[2] Fairfax County, *Deed Book J #3*, page 304.
[3] Fairfax County, *Deed Book K #3*, page 346.
[4] Fairfax County, *Deed Book L #3*, page 207.
[5] Fairfax County, *Deed Book O #3*, page 170.
[6] Fairfax County, *Deed Book R #3*, page 260.
[7] Fairfax County, *Deed Book R #3*, page 320.
[8] Fairfax County, *Deed Book S #3*, page 379.
[9] Fairfax County, *Deed Book X #1*, page 173.
[10] Fairfax County, *Deed Book C #4*, page 138.
[11] The Lightfoot children were reared by the bachelor uncle. Their father remarried and moved to Georgetown. Their father's side of the family included descent from Richard Lee (1600-1664) by his son, Hancock Lee of "Ditchley," and the latter's daughter, Anna, wife of William Armistead of Eastmost River, Matthews County. Mary Armistead, a daughter, married (1st) James Burwell and (2nd) Colonel Philip Lightfoot, son of Colonel Philip and Alice (Corbin) Lightfoot, member of the Council, etc.
[12] On August 8, 1947 the author's grandmother, who often ate a picnic lunch on the butter tables, gave the description of "Big Chimneys" used here. She helped sketch the building and grounds, and recalled that a wealthy man from Maryland had exact drawings made about 1900 to use in building a similar dwelling in Maryland. The grandmother, Ellen Mankin Hirst, was a granddaughter of Elizabeth Ellen (Lightfoot) Lynch, of "Big Chimneys."

## THE THORNE FAMILY

Talmadge Thorn (later spelled Thorne), settled at Pleasant Valley, Fairfax County, in 1849. In a letter written to his brother, James H. Thorn of Sparta (now Pittsford), Michigan, dated from Pine Plains, New York, May 5, 1849,[1] Mr. Thorn said that because his wife was a "tender plant," and in poor health, he considered moving South. He contemplated moving in the fall:

"I like the country very much, it is an old settled State and good markets and land cheap, water good . . . I expect I shall goe (there) the 29th of this month to make a payment—then by moving this fall I shall have to be very much engaged, this reason I have the refusal of a farm in Virginia—two hundred and twelve ackers, at two thousand dollars, there is seventy five ackers of timber land—first rate oak and hickory. And I think the land is as good as any I saw in Michigan and climate good—I like the face of the country."

He settled at Pleasant Valley, as indicated by two letters he wrote from there to his friend Governor William Eno of California, May 16 and June 8, 1857.[2] By the close of the War Between the States he lived on a farm at Falls Church. His letter to William Eno, dated February 8, 1866, has already been quoted. His home was at what is now 7 Corners, and was later the home of General Rufus Lane.

Talmadge Thorn was jailed by the Confederacy for scouting for Union troops. He was an ardent Republican, and served for a time as Sheriff following the War Between the States.

Talmadge Thorn's mother was a Coe, according to family tradition, a near relative of Spencer A. Coe, who settled in Falls Church.

Mr. Thorn married Sarah Storey Cornwell and had issue, among others, Jacob Moses Thorne.

Jacob Moses Thorne was born October 17, 1845, in New York, son of Talmadge and Saray Storey (Cornwell) Thorn. Mr. Thorne lived at "The Oaks," a fine farm at 7 Corners, now "Buffalo Hills" subdivision. He died there on March 19, 1907.

Jacob Moses Thorne and Mary Ella Roberts were married on July 31, 1867. Mrs. Thorne, called Mell by her friends, was born August 17, 1848, and died January 22, 1929. She was a daughter of Jonathan and Abigail (Haines) Roberts.

Waldo Thorn, who visited the family in 1896 and 1900, wrote of the family at "The Oaks":[3]

"Jacob and his wife . . . were very proud of their large family of ten children, all of whom were then living and appeared to be strong, healthy girls and boys . . . I found them all socially disposed and religiously inclined. I recollect very clearly one feature of my entertainment wherein it was noticeable how carefully the children were trained to be polite and useful. At the dining table each of the youngest daughters had her assigned duties to perform, one pouring out the coffee, the other baking the cakes and waiting upon those who were partaking of the good things provided to satisfy the appetite."

Jacob Moses and Mary Ella (Roberts) Thorne had issue:

(1) Virginia (called Jennie) Thorne, born May 17, 1868, died December 8, 1934. She married on April 21, 1897, Dr. Tunis Cline Quick. Dr. Quick was born January 27, 1871, and died February 21, 1923. He was a son of Jacques Vorhees and Sarah Ott (Biggs) Quick. After their marriage they settled in Falls Church. They later resided at Hoboken, New Jersey, Buffalo, New York, Fort Bayard, New Mexico,

and in Washington, D.C. Dr. Quick was Lieutenant Colonel in the Medical Corps of the U.S. Army, and at the time of his death was Surgeon in the United States Public Health Service. Mrs. Quick was Postmaster of Falls Church for several years. No children.

(2) Maude Gertrude Thorne, born August 13, 1869, died in Washington, D.C., January 31, 1960. She married on October 17, 1893, Warren Frazier Brenizer. Mr. Brenizer was born July 29, 1866, a son of John and Margaret Susanne (Indermauer) Brenizer. Mr. Brenizer was a general contractor and the senior member of the firm of Warren F. Brenizer Company of Washington, D.C. Issue:

>   (21) Warren Spencer Brenizer, born May 5, 1896, married on October 12, 1921, Marie Louise Burke. Mrs. Brenizer was born January 2, 1898, a daughter of Charles Durfee and Mary Elizabeth (West) Burke.

(3) Jacob Spencer Thorne, born March 12, 1871, died July 6, 1949. He married on December 18, 1900, to Beulah Gordon Donaldson. Mrs. Thorne was born June 11, 1875, and died May 3, 1959. She was a daughter of Armistead M. and Mildred Gertrude (Murray) Donaldson. Issue:

>   (31) Mildred Thorne, born August 19, 1905, married on June 15, 1940 to Russell Darwin Weaver. Mr. Weaver is a son of the late Charles Darwin and Mary Catherine (Davis) Weaver. No issue.
>
>   (32) Tunis Donaldson Thorne, born May 24, 1912, married on July 4, 1936, to Mildred Pauline Herrell. Mrs. Thorne was born January 9, 1916, a daughter of Smith Addison and Maude Myrtle (Greenlease) Herrell. Issue:
>
>   >   (321) Donald Tunis Thorne, born August 30, 1940. Married December 24, 1961 Ann Elizabeth LeGette, from Latta, South Carolina. Issue: (3211) William LeGette Thorne, born June 12, 1963.
>   >
>   >   (322) Brent Herrell Thorne, born September 18, 1947.

(4) Jonathan Roberts Thorne (John), born July 18, 1873, died September 28, 1949. He married on July 14, 1896, Florence A. Murray. Mrs. Thorne, a descendant of the well-known Murray family of Falls Church, was born April 3, 1875, and died April 19, 1941. She was a daughter of James Edward and Mary Frances (Birch) Murray. Issue:

>   (41) Talmadge Milton Thorne, born November 21, 1896, and was an Attorney in Washington, D. C. He married on May 1, 1926, Mrs. Sara (Puckett) Randall, daughter of Charles Davidson and Margaret Elizabeth (Lentz) Puckett. She was born April 3, 1897, and died April 5, 1947.
>
>   (42) Kathleen Inez Thorne, born October 18, 1899, died May 2, 1904.

(5) Margaret Boyce Thorne, born November 14, 1875, died February 20, 1926, married on September 8, 1896, to Alfred Dealy Swift. Mr. Swift was born August 7, 1872, a son of James Alfred and Sophia (Garner) Swift. He died at his residence, 301 West Fairfax Street, April 1, 1958. The James A. Swifts were living in Falls Church on September 14, 1884, when they became members of Dulin Chapel. In September, 1890, James A. and "Libbie" E. Swift were in Washington, D.C., according to records at Dulin Church. Mrs. Sophia Swift was a daughter of Mrs. Martha A. Garner of Falls Church. Among the children of James A. and Sophia Swift, other than Alfred D., were: Frank D. Swift of Vashon, Washington; Mrs. Edith Elliott, of Van-

couver, British Columbia; Mrs. Matilda Smith, of Vancouver; and Mrs. Dasie Chapman of Vancouver. Issue:
(51) James Alfred Swift, born June 19, 1897, died October 26, 1957. He married on June 29, 1920 to Irene Gessford. She was born April 1, 1896, daughter of William Chillenworth and Isabelle (Casey) Gessford. Issue:
(511) James Gessford Swift, born September 23, 1921.
(512) Charles Linwood Swift, born April 23, 1923.
(513) Ethel Jeanette Swift, born January 8, 1925, married (1) Robert Payne, and (2) Edward Fagiola.
(514) Alfred Boyce Swift, born December 12, 1926.
(515) Frank Dealy Swift, born February 13, 1930.
(52) Carroll Swift, born October 6, died October 8, 1901.
(53) Dorothy Virginia Swift, born September 30, 1902, married on January 15, 1921, Olin Grant Snyder. Mr. Snyder was born July 6, 1899, a son of Jay Grant and Luella (Weeks) Snyder. Mr. Snyder was founder of Snyder's Hardware Store at East Falls Church. Issue:
(531) Jay Alfred Snyder, born June 30, 1921, died November 1, 1927.
(54) William Harvey Swift, born October 31, 1906, married in June, 1932, to Dorothy B. Davis. Mrs. Swift was born August 6, 1907, a daughter of George S. and Bertie (Mishler) Davis.
(55) Mark Martelle Swift, born April 1, 1909, died June 28, 1909.
(56) Frank Linwood Swift, born April 29, 1910, married on June 21, 1932, to Edith D. Miller. She was a daughter of Samuel and Luvina Miller.
(57) Margaret Lydia Swift, born September 11, 1912, married on June 4, 1927, to Alvin W. Tasker. Mr. Tasker was born August 29, 1910, a son of Wilbert C. and Annie (Reed) Tasker. The father, Wilbert C. Tasker, died January 11, 1951, in Washington, D.C., and was survived by his children, Alvin Tasker, Wilbert Tasker, Mrs. Dorothy Kerr of Maryland and Catherine Snippes of Maryland. He was also survived by his brother, Charles, of North Carolina, and a sister, Mrs. Emma Lowe of Washington, D.C. Issue:
(571) Margaret Ann Tasker (Peggy), born July 31, 1928, married the Reverend Robert J. Stith, son of Dr. and Mrs. M. Chandler Stith. Mrs. Stith attended Mary Washington College. Mr. Stith is Minister of the Leesburg Baptist Church.
(572) Ruth Tasker, born January 8, 1931.
(573) Ellen Tasker, born December 15, 1931.
(574) Alvin Tasker, born January 13, 1933.
(575) Wilbert Tasker, born May 29, 1934.
(576) John Tasker, born August 15, 1936.
(577) Virginia Tasker, born November 3, 1940.
(578) Douglas Tasker, born April 8, 1942.

(6) Mary Haines Thorne, born March 18, 1878, died ——. She married (1) on October 14, 1896, to James Amos Poole. Mr. Poole was born September 24, 1873, a son of George Wallace and Janet (Hutchison) Poole. She remarried (2) Ralph Marr. Issue:
(61) Maud Jeanette Poole, born September 21, 1897, died July 13, 1960. She married (1) on May 5, 1915, to Wilson Oliver Tolford. Mr. Tolford was

born January 1, 1893, a son of Wilson Oliver and Mary Wright (Olmsted) Tolford. She remarried (2) Thornton M. Hudson. Mrs. Hudson taught ballet with Miss Minnie Hawke in the early 1900's, and later at Congressional School. She established the Tiny Tot Hospital in Arlington in 1950 (said to be the only hospital in Virginia that specialized in caring for infants from two weeks to two years of age). Issue:

(611) James Wilson Tolford, born January 8, 1916.

(7) George Kendall Thorne, born June 20, 1880, died November 16, 1910. Married Elizabeth Ricker. No issue.

(8) Sarah Ann Coe Thorne, born November 19, 1882, married (1) on August 25, 1909, John Grafton Hall (divorced September 18, 1913); and (2) on January 25, 1915, William Sylvanus Brown. Mr. Brown was born March 15, 1885, died December 4, 1941. Mr. Brown was a son of John Calvin Head and Margaret Keller (Birch) Brown. (*See Almond Birch*). No issue.

(9) (The Reverend) Milton Martelle Thorne, born August 3, 1885, married, in Salt Lake City, Utah, January 29, 1914, to Bertie Estella Thomas. Mrs. Thorne was born March 23, 1887, a daughter of James Oney and Barbara Jane (Bowers) Thomas. Mr. Thorne was ordained a Minister in the Methodist Episcopal Church and has served in Idaho, New Mexico, Oklahoma, and Kansas. Issue:

(91) Milton Martelle Thorne, Jr., born February 1, 1916.
(92) Ralph Jacob Thorne, born April 13, 1921.
(93) Warren Wayne Thorne, born August 20, 1923.
(94) William Jewell Thorne, born June 22, 1932.

(10) Ruth Anita Thorne, born September 17, 1887, died unmarried, August 24, 1906.

---

[1] A copy of this letter and other genealogical materials was sent to Mr. and Mrs. Jacob S. Thorne by Waldo Thorn of Shawnee, Oklahoma, April 26, 1937. These materials were kindly loaned the author by Mrs. Russell D. Weaver. Waldo Thorn retained the old spelling of his surname.
[2] Letters are in the author's files, having been purchased from Alvin Lohr of Hagerstown, Maryland.
[3] From a MS. history entitled "Descendants of Jacob M. and Mary Ella Thorne," written by Waldo Thorn. This was loaned by Mrs. Russell D. Weaver.

---

## THE TORREYSON FAMILY

William H. Torreyson was born in Loudoun County on June 29, 1835, and died on his farm near Falls Church, August 24, 1910. His farm, formerly the home of the Ball-Lightfoot family, was near 7 Corners. He attended Dulin Chapel. Mr. Torreyson married Mary Elizabeth Burroughs. She was born May 29, 1835, and died December 29, 1921, and is buried beside her husband in Oakwood Cemetery. Issue:

(1) Norman B. Torreyson, born December 30, 1867, baptized at Dulin Chapel May 8, 1868. He died July 10, 1869, and was buried in the Falls Church yard.

(2) Andrew Duke Torreyson, born in 1868, died January 23, 1951, at his residence in Sarasota, Florida. Mr. Torreyson moved to Florida in 1919. He was a former Arlington (Alexandria) County official and owned a dairy farm in Arlington. He was in the real estate business in Sarasota and was secretary and treasurer of the

Sarasota Building & Loan Association. Mr. Torreyson was also a County Court Judge. In his early life he served as land assessor and registrar of Alexandria County, and in 1919 was unsuccessful candidate for County Commissioner of Revenue. He was a leader in the Virginia Constitutional Convention of 1901/02. Mr. Torreyson was a founder and first president of the Maryland and Virginia Milk Producers Association. He was a founder of Arlington's first bank, now the Arlington Trust Company. He was also a director of the fore-runner of the Virginia Electric and Power Company. His farm, near Westover, was well kept and beautiful. Mr. Torreyson had other interests and was secretary and treasurer of the Rosslyn Milling Corporation. He was a founder of the Washington Golf and Country Club and a member of Columbia Lodge #285, A. F. & A. M. On November 30, 1887, he married Blanche Emilie Schutt of Alexandria County, daughter of Frances Granger and Elizabeth T. Schutt. Issue:

(21) Elizabeth Maude Torreyson, born November 16, 1894, died May 23, 1940. She married Lyman M. Moore and had issue: Emilie Moore, married Ray R. Fearson; Dorothy Moore, Eleanor Moore, and Eileen Carolyn Moore who married William Middleton Hill, son of Assistant Secretary of Agriculture and Mrs. Grover B. Hill of Falls Church and Amarillo, Texas.

(22) William Francis Torreyson, baptized at Dulin Chapel October 16, 1898.

(23) Emilie Torreyson, married Colonel Guy N. Church (*See Church*).

(3) Lucy Ellen Torreyson, born May 29, 1869, married on October 25, 1894, George R. Reeves. Mr. Reeves died June 10, 1949, age 86 years. He was born near Chaptico, St. Mary's County, Maryland, and moved to Alexandria County in 1898. His farm was at 303 North Montague Road. Issue:

(31) George Torreyson Reeves, married Mabel Shotwell (*See Shotwell*).

(32) Nelson E. Reeves, married on October 18, 1929, Claire L. Sprigg.

(33) Ruth Reeves, baptized at Dulin Chapel on March 29, 1899, married there on May 24, 1923, Munson H. Lane. (*See Munson*).

(4) William Dent Torreyson, baptized January 17, 1873 at Dulin Chapel, died July 16, 1873, age 8 months, 20 days. He is buried in the Falls Church yard.

(5) Eliza Ruth Torreyson, baptized February 18, 1875 at Dulin Chapel, married in June, 1905, the Reverend James Burnette Hupman, a Methodist Minister.

## THE TRAMMELL FAMILY

John Trammell, Sr., Gentleman, owned large tracts of land in Falls Church and vicinity, as did his brothers, Sampson, Gerrard, and William.[1] In 1733 Alexander Scott conveyed to John Trammell, Sr., and Susanna, his wife, of Truro Parish, 200 acres near Pimmitt Run.[2] Trammell had patented land in the vicinity (then Stafford County) in 1728, as witnessed by a statement in a deed dated September 1, 1766, from his son, John Trammell, Jr., to another son, William, of Loudoun County. This deed was for 464 acres of land "originally taken up by John Harl of Stafford," patented in 1728 by John Trammell, Sr., "who devised it to John Trammell, Jr., to have & to hold unto the said William Trammell. . ."[3] On July 11, 1735, Trammell leased a tract of land from Alexander Scott of Overwharton Parish, Stafford County.[4] He continued to add to his land and his home was probably the "Cherry Hill" residence of the later day Riley family (now next to the City Hall). The Trammell tract included the Reagan Patent, and since Michael Reagan failed to file a deed to the Vestry, Trammell owned the Falls Church which he deeded to the Vestry.

John Trammell, Sr., "Gentleman," died in 1753,[5] and his will was made by Thomas Wren on April 9, 1753, probated May 20, 1755.[6] His estate was appraised by Captain Charles Broadwater on December 19, 1758.[7]

John Trammell, Sr., and wife Susanna (probably nee Harle) had issue:

(1) William Trammell.

(2) Sampson Trammell, Jr., died in 1794 in Loudoun County. He married Kerhappuch (Caron or Keron) Garrett, daughter of Nicholas and Mary Garrett. Nicholas Garrett made his will December 20, 1786, probated May 18, 1795, in which he mentioned his wife, Mary, and legatees: Ann, wife of Timothy Carrington, Kerhappuch, wife of Sampson Trammell, Jr., and a grandson, Thomas Garrett. Executors included his wife and Timothy Carrington. In 1761 Trammell owned land in Loudoun County, although he did not live on it. John Harle was his Overseer (*Tithe List*, 1761, Loudoun County). He had a number of slaves on his Loudoun "Quarter Tract." References to his children can be found in Loudoun County, *Order Book U*, page 31, and in several law suits. William Gunnell was guardian of the younger children. In a note addressed to the Court, July 14, 1794 (*Jewell*, Volume IV, page 160), Caron Trammell, widow of Sampson Trammell, Jr., refused to administer the estate, and asked that William Gunnell, Jr., of Loudoun County be asked to qualify. This note was witnessed by W. Hall and Nancy Trammell. Issue:

    (21) Ann (Nancy) Trammell, died in Vincennes, Indiana, June 25, 1834. She married John S. Cartwright, and they moved to Dandridge, Jefferson County, Tennessee, in 1816. By 1832 they were living near Carlisle, Indiana. Their children included: (Dr.) John N. Cartwright (who had Oswald Cartwright, Aeolphus Cartwright who died June 25, 1834 in Natchez, Mississippi, age 9 months, two others born dead and one who died in infancy); Ann Noland Cartwright, married Dr. Thistle of Maryland; Sarah Cartwright who married Henry Slaughter Doniphan (issue included Edgar Cartwright Doniphan born ca. 1845); Dr. Noland Cartwright; Julia Cartwright, married a Major Haddon; John Cartwright, died at New Madrid, Missouri, in the Spring of 1832, "... a very promising young man & beloved by every person who knew him"; Thomas Cartwright, in New Orleans in 1832, unmarried in 1845; Samuel Cartwright, William Cartwright, and Baldwin Harle Cartwright, born in December, 1822.

    (22) Amelia B. Trammell, married Captain Nicholas Darne (*See Darne*).

    (23) William John Trammell, in 1816 was in Knoxville, Tennessee. He did not marry.

    (24) Eliza Trammell.

    (25) Sarah Trammell, married Hezekiah Harris.

    (26) Daughter Trammell, wife of Walter Magruder of Maryland

    (27) Daughter Trammell, wife of Gabriel Childs.

(See Fairfax County *Deed Book M #2*, page 398 for references; also Fairfax County law suit, "Nicholas Barne & wife vs. Childs Representatives, November 1812-March 13, 1813.)

(3) John Trammell, Jr., died in February, 1784, in Frederick County, Maryland. Trammell was a large land owner, and made his will January 1, 1784, probated February 24, 1784 (Frederick County, Maryland, *Will Book GM #2*, page 53). He men-

tioned his friend, William Drown, Sr.; housekeeper, Cumfort Walker; nurse, Jemima Tracey; sister, Milcah Pearson (given 100 acres); granddaughter, Susannah Mackall, daughter of James Mackall, deceased, all of his Fairfax County land except 100 acres given Milcah Pearson; also to said Susannah Mackall lands purchased from William Gladding on Difficult Run in Loudoun County, and a Mill, also land purchased of John Hanby and Margaret St. Clare (Sinclair) on Clerks Run in Loudoun, whereon John Tucker and Thomas Edelen lived in 1784. He left Susannah Mackall one undivided fourth part of his copper mines on land purchased from Stephen Richards, also the Broken Islands in the Potomac, Negroes, etc. In the event of Susannah's death, this portion of the estate would go to his granddaughter, Sarah Delashmutt, wife of Lindsay Delashmutt. He mentioned his land called "Trammells Conoy Islands" in the Potomac, where John Unglesby was tenant. Mr. Trammell gave Conoy Island, part of Trammell's Conoy Islands to his grandson, Trammell Delashmutt. This grandson was also given 100 acres of timber, part of a larger tract on the east side of Kittocton Mountain near the Potomac; also 100 acres "which Begin's at the Mouth of a Gutt which makes into Potowmack River called Dunkins Gutt," to include the place where William Adams was living; also a field called Conoy Field between the Potomac River and Arthur Nelson's land. This same grandson received 90 acres called "Wood Land" and "now called Rock Hall" on the Potomac, and "most Convenient to the Conoy Island." Trammell directed his Executors to lay out 400 lots for a town, each lot to be 60 feet in front and 120 feet in back, with streets and alleys, this to be on part of his Conoy Island and the woodland "Between a Tract of Land Called Sweeds Folly" and Potomac River at the Point of Rocks. The lots were to be sold by his Executors for eight silver dollars per lot, or a rent of eighteen shillings, sterling. He gave Trammell Delashmutt half of the lots, also part of the Copper Mines, and land purchased of Stephen Richards. This same favorite grandson also received eight Negroes. His daughter, Sarah, was given a large quantity of Negroes. Executors were Sarah and Lindsay Delashmutt. Witnesses: Josiah Clapham, John Steere, Isaac Steere, William Jenkins and Samuel J. Thomas. Issue:

(31) Daughter Trammell, married James Mackall (and had issue including Susannah Mackall).

(32) Sarah Trammell, born about 1760, died after 1791. She married in Frederick County, Maryland, February 22, 1779, Lindsay Delashmutt who died in 1791. He made his will October 5, 1791, probated November 10, 1791 (Frederick County, Maryland, *Will Book GM #2*, page 398). He mentioned his wife, Sarah, his son Trammell (under 21 years); son John, son Sampson, and a daughter, Jean. Witnesses were: Samuel S. Thomas, John Whitenack, and John Brunner.

(4) Susanna Trammell, called Sukey, died June 2, 1794 in Loudoun County. She married (1) William Starke and (2) William Carnan. Her family is recorded in a suit in Loudoun County, "Stark adv. Blincoe & wife," filed November, 1797, with a decree dated April 16, 1800. Her first husband, William Starke, made his will on April 1, 1772. Children: Elizabeth Starke, married Benjamin Blincoe; Ann Starke, married Burgess Mason; William Starke, Jr., died young, ca. 1773; John Starke, Susannah Starke, married Christopher Cockerille; Mary Starke, married Spence Minor; and Sinah Starke, married John Veale.

(5) Elizabeth Trammell (Betty), married (1) —— Ellzey and (2) Ezekiel Hickman.

443

(6) Lettice Trammell, married —— Offutt.
(7) Milcah Trammell (Milkey) married wealthy Simon Pearson, son of Captain Thomas Pearson, and this marriage ended in divorce.

Gerrard Trammell, a brother of John Trammell, Sr., was born about 1702,[8] and died near Falls Church in 1786. He made his will on November 16, 1775.[9] In it he mentioned his wife, Mary, and the following children: Philip Trammell, Ann Thrift, Rebecca Trammell, Mary Conn, Gerrard Trammell, Thomas Trammell, Priscilla Dyal, and Margaret Jenkins. He also mentioned a grandson, Gerrard Trammell, who was left his "Still & warm Pone mash." Other grandchildren mentioned were: Mary Fields Dyal and Nimrod Trammell Dyal. Colonel James Wren furnished a burying sheet for Mr. Trammell. An inventory of his estate was made December 16, 1786, by Charles Broadwater and Thomas Gunnell.

The children of Gerrard and Mary Trammell included Philip, Ann Thrift (ancestor of the Balls of Arlington including the author's wife); Rebecca, Mary Conn, Gerrard, Jr., Thomas, Priscilla Dyal and Margaret, wife of Samuel Jenkins.

Mary Trammell married Hugh Conn (who died in Loudoun County in 1772). Conn lived near Bladensburg, Maryland, and moved to Fairfax at an early day. He owned a "vessell" on the Potomac which he had for hire in 1760. Their children included Josias Conn, Hugh Conn, Jr., Ruth Conn, Coxon Conn, Gerrard Trammell Conn, and Jane Conn who married Michael Ashford before June 12, 1772. Jane and Michael Ashford's descendants intermarried with descendants of Sampson Trammell, Jr. One descendant was Margaret Conn, wife of Captain Rezin Wilcoxon.

Captain Sampson Trammell, Sr., a brother to John Trammell, Sr., and Gerrard Trammell, Sr., lived in 1784 two miles west of Falls Church and George Washington and Dr. Craik were entertained there with dinner enroute to Washington's western lands.

There are numerous descendants of the Trammell family in Falls Church. A recent member of the family was James Philip Trammell (March 31, 1843-September 18, 1912) who is buried beside his wife, Elizabeth, (May 19, 1850-December 16, 1929) in Oakwood Cemetery.

---

[1] William Trammell, one of the brothers, was born about 1704, (see *Land Records of Long Standing*, page 115, Fairfax Court House). He was an early resident and was alive, age 44 years, when he made a deposition April 16, 1748.
[2] Prince William County, *Deed Book B*, page 136.
[3] Fairfax County, *Deed Book G*, page 60.
[4] Stafford County, *Lease Book, 1733*, page 136.
[5] See Loudoun County, Virginia, law suit, "Pearson & ad. ver. Trammells" filed March 14, 1760, abated October, 1798.
[6] Fairfax County, *Will Book B*, page 85.
[7] *Ibid, Will Book 1*, page 85.
[8] Fairfax County, *Land Records Of Long Standing*, page 256.
[9] Fairfax County, *Will Book #E #1*, page 148.

---

## THE TRIPP FAMILY

Mr. Silas D. Tripp was a native of Dutchess County, New York. He settled in 1869 on the 109 acre farm formerly owned by the Dulany family. Mr. Tripp was a vestryman of the old Falls Church, and an ardent church worker. He had a son,

Percy Tripp, a Missionary to China, who married a Chinese Princess, "Susie," and remained there.

Percy and Susie Tripp had issue (some born in Falls Church, the rest in China): John Tripp, born 1917; Helen Tripp, born 1919; Virginia Tripp born 1922; Myrtle Tripp born 1924; Eunice Tripp born 1927; Bernice Tripp born 1930, and Kenneth Tripp born 1932.

## THE TURNER FAMILY

A. F. Turner, native of Washington, D.C., settled in Falls Church in 1863 on 160 acres of land on Broad Street. He was a farmer, real estate man, and also owned a livery stable in Washington. Mr. Turner moved back to Washington, but returned to Falls Church after his second marriage and lived in the brick house on the south side of Leesburg Pike next to the P. W. Lee house. Mr. Turner married sisters named Havenner of Alexandria, Va. They were related to Mrs. E. H. Flagg. Harry Turner, only son of Mr. A. F. Turner by his second wife, inherited considerable property in the town. He married and had one child who died in infancy. He later sold all of his Falls Church land and moved to California where he died.

By his first marriage, A. F. Turner had a son Henry Turner, who with his wife lived and died on Little Falls Street in the house now owned by Miss Agnes Smith.

The following Turners are buried in Oakwood Cemetery (but not related to the above family):

"Walter Lee Turner, Sr., 1862-1945."
"Daisy V., wife of J. V. Turner, died Jan. 10, 1915 at 37 years."

## THE WAKEFIELD FAMILY

Malcom Mallow Wakefield and wife moved to Falls Church in 1922. They came from Ilda, near Fairfax. Their first home here was the old Morgan Steves house at East End (on the corner now a vegetable market) and their second home was the large white clapboard house on Lincoln Avenue next to the home of the late Dr. John P. Smallwood. Mr. and Mrs. Wakefield later lived at East End in the house which is now the home of their grandson, Paul Allen Wakefield.

The first ancestor of this family was John Wakefield of Wakefield, who was born in Gravesend, Kent County, England, in 1614. He moved to Martha's Vineyard, Massachusetts and later to Maryland, where his brother resided. He later returned to Massachusetts with his wife, Ann. A writeup of this family can be found in *The Wakefield Memorial* by Homer Wakefield, M.D., published in Bloomington, Illinois, 1897.

John Wakefield, son of John and Ann Wakefield, was born either in Maryland or near Edgartown, Mass., about 1640. He moved with his parents to Boston before 1651 and died in 1691. His wife's name was Deliverance. John Wakefield son of John and Deliverance Wakefield, was born in Boston, January 27, 1668. He married, on November 23, 1693, to Elizabeth Walker, daughter of Thomas and Elizabeth (Collins) Walker. The ceremony was performed by the Reverend Cotton Mather.

Joseph Wakefield, son of John and Elizabeth (Walker) Wakefield, was born in Boston June 9, 1701. He was baptized in old North Church on June 15, 1701. He married on December 7, 1726 to Mrs. Copia Love, widow of Richard Love, and daughter of the Reverend Thomas and Elizabeth (Turner) Bridge. Mr. Wakefield died in April, 1732. Thomas Wakefield, son of Joseph and Copia (Bridge) Wakefield, was born in Boston August 5, 1727. He married, at Reading, Massachusetts, on March 24, 1750 to Dorcas Pratt, daughter of Timothy and Tabitha (Boutwell) Pratt. He died in September 1791.

Peter Wakefield, a Revolutionary Soldier, was the son of Thomas and Dorcas (Pratt) Wakefield. He was born in Amherst, New Hampshire, August 7, 1764, and died at Windsor, Lawrence County, Ohio, in January, 1847. He married on March 3, 1792 to Keziah Burns. Mr. Wakefield enlisted in September 1781 as a private in Captain John Mills Company, Colonel Rumnels New Hampshire Regiment. He received a pension for his services in 1832. He moved to Ohio in 1806, and was a magistrate.

Elhanen Winchester Wakefield, son of Peter and Keziah (Burns) Wakefield, was named for the Reverend Elhanen Winchester, a noted Clergyman. He was born in Clairmont, N. H., August 1, 1799, and died at Proctorsville, Ohio, September 5, 1883. He married on September 30, 1827 to Candance Gillette, daughter of Joel and Chloe (Griswold) Gillette.

The Reverend Elhanen Winchester Wakefield (Jr.), son of Elhanen Winchester and Candance (Gillette) Wakefield, was born in Ohio on July 2, 1834. He married Mary Rebecca Tennison (1842-1907).

The following Arms used by The Reverend Mr. Wakefield:

Barry of six arg. and gu. on a chief of the second
three owls of the first.
CREST: A bat displayed or.
MOTTO: "Be just and fear not."

There have been many colorful figures in Virginia Methodism, among them the late Elhanen Winchester Wakefield. E. W. Wakefield was a remarkable man: he could endure great hardships, preach a scholarly sermon, build a house, or plow a field. He was the last of the old school Methodist preachers in Fairfax County. Toward the end of his life he settled on a farm near Annandale, and rode a wide circuit between Falls Church and Fairfax Court House. That is, except on Sunday. According to a granddaughter, Mrs. Howard R. Steadman, when the Sabbath dawned, Mr. Wakefield's horse was in pasture, and rain or shine, one mile or ten, the tall figure of this remarkable man hurried down the road on foot. He always wore a long black cape, and black suit. He did not cut his hair or beard. This was to him a sin, as his hair was a "glory to God." The early background of Mr. Wakefield was as colorful as he was.

Wakefield went west in the gold rush of 1849, fought Indians in the Black Hills of North Dakota, joined the Union Army, and was seriously wounded at Tom's Brook, Virginia, was half buried in a common grave when the men filling in the earth found him still alive.

His wife, Mary Rebecca Tennison, was a "discovery" of his. Riding by a farm house in the County one day, Mr. Wakefield was attracted by a lovely voice and the sweet melody of a piano. He decided that the lady with that voice would be his wife. Stopping, he knocked on the door and told the young lady his purpose. Miss Tennison was indignant. However, after an ardent courtship, she consented to be his bride.

According to Homer Wakefield, M.D., E. W. Wakefield moved to Kansas in 1856, then back to California. In the sketch of him given by Dr. Homer Wakefield[1] it is stated that he was proprietor of a Grocery Store in Washington, D.C., and "In 1896 he was at Annandale, Fairfax Co., Va."

Mr. Wakefield enlisted in Company F, 2nd Regiment of Massachusetts Calvary, mustered into service May 10, 1862 by Captain D. E. Merritt. He joined for duty February 9, 1863, at San Francisco, California, for a three year term. He appears on the first Company Muster Roll dated from San Francisco April 22, 1863. He is next listed as Sergeant on June 30, 1863. For September, and October, 1863, he is listed as "absent, on detachment service at Camp Vienna Vir. by order of Col. C. R. Lowell, Junr." He was in Vienna until June, 1864. For July and August, 1864, he is noted as "absent on detached service as Brigade Wagon-Master for Brid. Ord. No." He was transferred to Company K in September, and October, 1864 by order of "Lt. Col. Brownshend, Comdg. Brig."

In the latter part of September, and in October, 1864, he was noted as "absent, wounded in Hospl. Balto. Md." He was wounded on October 8, 1864, and was in the hospital at Baltimore until February, 1865. It is noted that $16.04 was furnished him by Captain Burton. He was discharged for his wounds and on March 28, 1865, was put on the D. and D. R. Railroad for home. He appears in other files as Sergt/ Co. F, Muster Roll dated Fairfax Court House, Va., July 20, 1865. Noted: "Discharged Annapolis, Md. U. S. Genl. Hospl. Mch. 28/65 per Surg. Certif. of Dr's." At this time he is described as 5 feet, 9-1/4 inches in height, of light complexion, with grey eyes, and brown hair. The record shows that he was born in Lawrence, Ohio, and was by occupation a carpenter when he entered the U. S. Army.

The following is in his personal file at the National Archives in Washington:

"I certify that I have carefully examined the said Sergt. Elhannan W. Wakefield of Lieut. Saml. Tucker's Company, and find him incapable of performing the duties of a soldier because of penetrating gun shot wound of left lung, received in action at Fisher's Hill, Va., Oct. 8th, 1864, followed, up to the present time, by frequent haemonhages (sic). This man is not a fit subject for the Veteran Reserve Corps. Disability total. John Bell, Asst. Super. Comm. in Charge Rulison Genl. Hospt. Discharged this twenty eighth day of March 1865 at Annapolis, Md.

Soldier desires to be addressed town: Alexandria, State: Virginia."

Mr. Wakefield wrote a book of his experiences. He gave a lecture using the title of his book: "The West As I Saw It."

As already noted, Mr. Wakefield married Mary Rebecca Tennison. Her tombstone in the Annandale Methodist Cemetery reads: "Wakefield (Mother) Mary R. Tennison, wife of Rev. E. W. Wakefield 1842-1907." The tombstone of her mother, in the same plot, reads: "Tennison—In memory of Our Mother, Lucinda Marts Tennison,[2] born June 23, 1798, died June 11, 1890." Also these stones: "In memory of Blanche L. Wakefield, beloved wife of Harrie A. Bacon, born Jan. 2, 1869, died Jan. 3, 1902." "Dorothy Jean Bacon, born Dec. 17, 1900, died July 2, 1901." "In memory of Our Daughter, Teresa May Wakefield, born Jan. 24, 1881, died Oct. 30, 1886."

The "Wakefield Chapel" Methodist Church on Little River Turnpike near Fairfax was built by Mr. Wakefield, and he gave the materials and did most of the work.

Elhanen Winchester Wakefield married (2) to Ada Haines. All his children were by the first wife. Issue:

(1) Malcom Mallow Wakefield, born October 5, 1865, died August 17, 1944. He married Lola Marie Caton (born in Loudoun County, December 22, 1868, died October 7, 1941). Both are buried in the Flint Hill Cemetery near Oakton. Mrs. Wakefield was a daughter of John and Sarah Jane (Thompson) Caton. Issue:
  (11) Elton Holland Wakefield, married Mamie Grace Much, and resided at Annandale. Issue:
    (111) Helen Elizabeth Wakefield, married Preston Poole, issue:
      (1111) Beverly June Poole.
      (1112) Faith Ann Poole.
    (112) Leona Mae Wakefield, married Millard Wyant. Issue:
      (1121) Nancy Carol Wyant.
    (113) Edith Lucille Wakefield, married twice, first to Charles Chaney.
    (114) Florence Louise Wakefield, married Irvin Payne of Bailey's Cross Roads. Issue:
      (1141) Joyce Grace Payne.
    (115) Velva Jean Wakefield, married Robert Blackwell. Issue:
      (1151) Brenda Mae Blackwell.
    (116) Joseph Elton Wakefield, unmarried, serving in the U. S. Army.
  (12) Minnie Rita Wakefield, daughter of Malcom M. and Lola M. (Caton) Wakefield, married William Henry Lillard, issue:
    (121) Lola Virginia Lillard, died at 6 years.
    (122) Rita Pauline Lillard, married Joseph Ballard, issue:
      (1221) Virginia Pauline Ballard.
      (1222) Joseph Robert Ballard.
    (123) William Maurice Lillard, married Lucille, and had issue:
      (1231) Rita Lucille Lillard.
  (13) Ellis Allen Wakefield, son of Malcom M. and Lola M. (Caton) Wakefield, married Edna Marie Tobin, issue:
    (131) Paul Allen Wakefield, married Kathleen Reichman. Issue:
      (1311) Paul Allan Wakefield, Jr.
  (14) Vernon Ridgley Wakefield (1896-1922), married Ruth Virginia Moore (1900-1918), no issue.
  (15) Anna Wakefield, died in infancy, 1900.
  (16) Effie Wakefield, died in infancy, 1898.
  (17) Bessie Tennison Wakefield, daughter of Malcom M. and Lola M. (Caton) Wakefield, married Delbert Alonzo Kidwell-Walker (adopted son of the Walkers and son of Andrew Kidwell). Issue:
    (171) Dorothy Ellen Kidwell-Walker, married Ray Farmer, issue:
      (1711) Barbara Ellen Farmer.
      (1712) Rodney Ray Farmer.
  (18) Velva Lee Wakefield, born August 16, 1905, near Ilda, Fairfax County, daughter of Malcom M. and Lola M. (Caton) Wakefield, married on November 17, 1928, at Falls Church, to Howard Elroy Steadman, a son of Eli Stansbury and Ida Jane (Kerns) Steadman. She remarried (2) February 9, 1957, to Harold Stern. (*See Steadman.*)
  (19) Grace Winchester Wakefield, daughter of Malcom M. and Lola M. (Caton) Wakefield, married Paul Amos Bowbeer, issue:

(191) Donna Grace Bowbeer.
(192) Sandra Wakefield Bowbeer.

---

[1] Page 98, person 315.
[2] She was the widow of Samuel Tennison.

---

## THE WALKER FAMILY OF "CHESTNUT GROVE"

Gilman E. Walker was a native of "Walker Mountain," Wallingford, Rutland County, Vermont. He was married at Danby, Vt., January 15, 1837 by the Reverend Orrange Green to Amanda Staples. Mrs. Walker was born at Dorset, Vt., March 4, 1816, daughter of Elery and Almira (Skeels) Staples, and a descendant of Jonathan Staples, a foot soldier for seven years during the Revolutionary War. Gilman E. Walker moved to Troy, Pa., where he owned a Fulling and Carding Mill. Here he died in February, 1846. Mr. Walker is buried at Troy, Bradford Co., Pa. Mrs. Amanda (Staples) Walker remarried (2) to the Reverend George S. Bessey, a Methodist minister. By the second marriage she was the mother of the Reverend Francis Eugene ("Frank") Bessey, Dr. Herman Bessey, and Albert D. Bessey. The Reverend George S. Bessey was born in Nichols, N.Y., in 1810, lived at Monroeton, Pa., where he owned a farm. He also operated a saw mill to support his ministry. Amanda (Staples) (Walker) Bessey died March 22, 1866 and is buried at Lewinsville, Va., beside her sister. Gilman E. and Amanda (Staples) Walker had the following children:
 (1) Elery Chandler Walker married Harriet Watkins.
 (2) (The Reverend) George W. Walker married Mary La Porte.
 (3) Amanda Walker married Albert Peacock.

(1) Elery Chandler Walker was born October 30, 1840, on a farm near Danby Four Corners, Vt., in a house which burned in 1935. Mr. Walker served as a Private in Captain L. B. Blanton's Company, K, of the 9th Regiment of the Veteran Reserve Corps. He was enrolled in Captain A. J. Swart's Company, C, 141st Regiment of Pennsylvania Volunteers on August 7, 1861, and was discharged on June 28, 1865 at Washington, D.C. On his discharge Mr. Walker is described as being 5'5" in height of light complexion, with blue eyes and brown hair. When he enrolled his occupation was listed as a farmer. Mr. Walker was wounded May 3, 1863 at Chancellorsville when he caught up the colors when the bearer fell. He had a bullet in both legs. Following his discharge Mr. Walker moved to the farm of his Aunt, Mrs. Dorr Crocker (Sarah Staples)[1] near Falls Church.

On May 3, 1866, Mr. Walker married Harriet Watkins. Mrs. Walker was born at Trade City (then Davidsville), Indiana County, Pa., October 11, 1847. She came to Virginia when but eleven years of age and the family lived in a log house with log chimneys which was formerly a Nelson home and erected before the Revolutionary War. This house was at "Lincolnville," now Chesterbrook, and was the birthplace of Henrietta Nelson, wife of Joshua Kirby. Mrs. Walker was a daughter of James and Barbara (Sprankle) Watkins.

Mr. Walker purchased the Jay Smith farm "Chestnut Grove," which was located half way between Lewinsville and Falls Church. He purchased it in 1868, and later built the main two story portion of the house. The kitchen portion was erected before the War Between the States. It was called "Chestnut Grove" because of four-

teen large Chestnut trees in the yard. Often Indian arrow heads and other relics were found near these old trees. Miss Ada Walker, daughter of E. C. Walker, still resides in the old home. Mr. Walker was a truck farmer, and was active in community affairs. He contributed team work and $50.00 to the project of building "Ford School," and was a member of the Lewinsville Presbyterian Church. He was also liberal in contributing to other churches, including St. James Roman Catholic Church. Mr. Walker died May 3, 1903, and his widow died June 2, 1932. Children:
- (11) Edwin Chandler Walker, born February 12, 1868, died January 28, 1940. He married (1) on November 25, 1897, Laura Setzler of Ohio (who died in 1900); and (2) Lottie Clifton of Cincinnati, Ohio. No children.
- (12) John Watkins Walker, born August 6, 1870, died March 6, 1935. He married (1) on August 27, 1896 to Lucinda Belle Alcock (born at Masonville, Iowa, August 28, 1875). Children:
  - (121) Elery Clyde Walker, born Lake Charles, La., July 8, 1899, served in World War I. He married (1) Lucy E., and (2) Ella.
  - (122) Merle Evelyn Walker, died at 6 months of age, buried Lake Charles, La.
  - (123) Pearl Emma Walker, born November 10, 1903, lives at Beaumont, Texas. She married on April 23, 1923 to Lloyd D. Bowers, children:
    - (1231) Merlwyn Earles Bowers, born January 20, 1925.
    - (1232) Elery Coatney Bowers, born June 18, 1926.
    - (1233) Lois Lucinda Bowers born November 28, 1927.
    - (1234) Walter Clayton Bowers, born December 22, 1931.
  - (124) Mildred Winifred Walker, died at age 16.
  - (125) Edna Irene Walker, born November 17, 1913, married on June 7, 1932 to Harry Smith.
- (13) George Murray Walker, born December 12, 1872, died April 8, 1932. He married Elizabeth Hall of Alexandria, Va. Children:
  - (131) Lawrence Adelbert Walker, born June 4, 1899, married on September 20, 1922, Catherine Gibbs, children:
    - (1311) Betty Jean Walker born September 24, 1927.
- (14) Ada Walker, born December 12, 1875, is living on the old home place, 1964. She attended the Ford School and Jefferson School at Falls Church for her early training, and attended Woods Commercial College, Washington, D.C. She graduated from the last named institution with honors, and won the gold medal for stenography, Class of 1894. During the "clean up" movement of the 1920's, when the County government was reformed, no one had a more active interest or did more to aid the "cause" than did Miss Ada Walker. A master of satire, she took keen delight in painting *Pen Portraits of Politicians.* Miss Walker won many friends as she did not deal in personalities. Adhering strictly to the truth, she made few enemies. Miss Walker has been active in every cause for community good.
- (15) Harry Jabez Walker, born December 1, 1878, died January 11, 1939. He married Helen Faulkner who died Nov. 28, 1958. Children:
  - (151) Avis Elery Walker, married Russell Hill. Issue:
    - (1511) Harry Russell Hill.

(About 1902 President Theodore Roosevelt stopped at "Chestnut Grove" enroute to the farm of his physician friend, Dr. Rixey. After his request for a drink of water was filled, he looked over the farm, and soon came upon the arbor of "Walker's Best" grapes. Before leaving he enjoyed some of these grapes. The President often passed while enroute to the farm with Dr. Rixey, usually after having been to the Country Club.)

(2) (The Reverend) George W. Walker, son of Gilman E. and Amanda (Staples) Walker, was born at Troy, Bradford Co., Pa., February 8, 1842. He attended school at Monroeton, Pa., and Starkey University, N. Y. On August 10, 1861 he enlisted in Company K, 50th Regiment of Pennsylvania Volunteers, and was later discharged because of poor health. He taught school in Pennsylvania and Missouri for a time, then entered the Methodist ministry. Mr. Walker was recommended by the Quarterly Conference of La Porte Circuit, Macon District, Missouri Conference, February 23, 1867. He was ordained a Deacon by Bishop Clark at Macon City, Mo., March 19, 1870, and later transferred to the North Ohio Conference. He married on November 17, 1868, to Mary La Porte, and died at Danville, Ohio, September 1, 1895. Children: Ella, Esther, Estella, and Edith. All four daughters married Methodist ministers.

(3) Amanda S. Walker, daughter of Gilman E. and Amanda (Staples) Walker, was born in 1844. She married Albert Peacock who lived in the Great Falls area. They lived in Lewinsville, and had children:
(31) Thomas D. Peacock (1864-65).
(32) James E. Peacock (1866-66).
(33) Rose C. Peacock (1867-1883).
(34) Anna E. Peacock (1872-1878).
(35) Albert Peacock, Jr. (1878-1878).
(36) Harvey D. Peacock (1881-1881).
(37) Molly Peacock.

---

[1] In the Lewinsville Presbyterian Cemetery there is a stone to J. D. Crocker (1813-1880) and his wife Sarah (1812-1875).

---

## THE WATKINS FAMILY

James Watkins was born in Merthyr Tydvil, south Wales, in 1799, and died at Alexandria, Pennsylvania, February 15, 1854. He had two brothers, Wesley Watkins, killed in the Mexican War, and Nathaniel Watkins. By a former marriage Mr. Watkins had two children, James, Jr., and Nathaniel Watkins. Mr. Watkins remarried at Sinking Spring, Blair Co., Pa., to Mrs. Barbara (Sprankle) Mutersbaugh, widow of John Mutersbaugh. Children:
(1) Maria Watkins, married Alexander Thomson.
(2) Sprankle Watkins, married (1) Lydia McBriar, (2) Eliza Mitchell.
(3) Barbara Ellen Watkins, married Archibald McNeal.
(4) Ruth Ann Watkins, married William White of New York.
(5) Jabez Bunting Watkins, married Elizabeth J. Miller.
(6) Harriet Watkins, married Elery C. Walker.

(1) Maria Watkins, daughter of James and Barbara (Sprankle) Watkins, was born at Sinking Valley, Blair Co., Pa., March 10, 1836. She came to Falls Church with

other members of her family in 1858. During the War Between the States she kept a tobacco and candy store at Falls Church, and was a spy. One of Mosby's men, John Munson, admired her, and let slip a number of important pieces of information. Apparently she did not have much competition in her business, as Falls Church was described by a soldier writing home from camp on December 4, 1861:

"We reached Falls Church. This is a small Virginia village. A few goodlooking houses, one church and one store, a one-story building with the glass half broken out, and three apples, two cakes and one paper of tobacco on the window sill, seemed to be the stock in trade. A charcoal sign 'Store' over the door was all that would lead anyone to suppose it was a mercantile establishment."

Maria Watkins married in Racine, Wisconsin, on March 28, 1870, to Professor Alexander Thomson. He taught engineering at Ames, Iowa, Agricultural College and Mrs. Thomson was Matron of the College. In the early 1880's they moved to Lake Charles, La., and lived at 625 Broad Street, the first plastered house in the town. Children:

(11) Zena Thomson, born January 2, 1871, died at Lake Charles, La., August 6, 1926, and is buried there in the Orange Grove Cemetery.

(2) Sprankle Watkins, son of James and Barbara (Sprankle) Watkins, was born in Trade City, Pa., August 3, 1838. He married (1) Lydia Jane McBriar, who died June 30, 1862, age 22 years, and is buried with her family in the Brick Church yard, Oliveburg, Jefferson Co., Pa. By this marriage there was one child, Hannah Watkins, born August 20, 1861. She married Osborn, and had one child, Lula Kuntz. Mrs. Osborn is buried in the Rumberger Cemetery, DuBois, Pa. Mr. Watkins remarried (2) to Eliza Mitchell, and their only child died at birth. He died June 13, 1873 and is buried in the Neal Cemetary at Hamilton, Pa. His widow survived him by many years, and lived in Indianatown, Indiana Co., Pa.

(3) Barbara Ellen Watkins, daughter of James and Barbara (Sprankle) Watkins, was born in Trade City, Pa., in 1841. She married Archibald Haddon Neal of Hamilton, Pa., on April 11, 1861, at Frostburg, Pa., by Squire Michael. Mrs. Neal refused to come to Virginia with the rest of her family as she feared living "among the Colored people." She is buried on the Neal farm at Hamilton, Pa..Children: Della A.; Harriet A.; Ada, Ruth, Lillie V.; James H.; and Kate. Ada and Harriet died in 1876, the same year as their mother. Mr. Neal was born on a farm near Punxsutawnay, Pa., February 25, 1839, and died in 1908, a son of James C. Neal (born 1813) and his wife Catherine H. Neal (born 1813). He was a Master Logger, and took many rafts of logs to Pittsburgh.

(4) Ruth Ann Watkins, daughter of James and Barbara (Sprankle) Watkins, was born at Trade City, Pa., February 28, 1843. She married William C. White of New York.

(5) Jabez Bunting Watkins, son of James and Barbara (Sprankle) Watkins, was born in Trade City, Pa., June 25, 1845, and was named for the noted Methodist clergyman, the Reverend Jabez Bunting. He attended Dayton, Pa., Academy, 1864-66, and received his LL.B degree from the University of Michigan in 1869. Mr. Watkins practiced law at Champaign, Ill., 1870-73. He became wealthy, and invested in land mortgages and purchased 1,500,000 acres in the section near Lake Charles, La., in 1883. In 1890 he built and operated the 100 mile Rail Road from

Lake Charles to Alexandria, La. Mr. Watkins established the Watkins Bank of Lake Charles in 1884 and served as President. He was the author of "The True Money System," published for the United States in 1896. This member of the Watkins clan was a Democrat and a member of the Baptist Church. He married at the age of 64, on November 10, 1909, at Brooklyn N.Y., to Elizabeth Josephine Miller of Lawrence Kansas. Mr. Watkins died in Lawrence Kansas, February 7, 1921, and is buried there in the Oak Hill Cemetery. No children.

---

[1] Alexander Thomson was born in Canada, July 29, 1841, and died at Shreveport, La., July 29, 1917, and is buried in the Orange Grove Cemetery at Lake Charles. He was Vice President of the Watkins Bank of Lake Charles, founded by his brother-in-law, J. B. Watkins, who developed Lake Charles. He had a nephew J. Stuart Thomson and a niece Charlotte McCloud.

---

## THE WEST FAMILY

Major John West, ancestor of the family that settled in Falls Church, lived in Stafford County at an early date. He was probably a member of the family of Captain John West who served as Governor of the Colony from 1635 until 1638. While printed sources state that the origin of Major John West is unknown, and deny a possible connection with Governor West, yet this writer is convinced that Major West was probably of the fourth generation in descent. The basis for this is one reference in the Will of Major John West, who left his "500 acres at Pamunky" to his son, John West.

Governor John West was granted 3,000 acres of land, including the old town of Cinquotek, the extreme eastern tip of the Neck where the town of Delaware (now West Point, King William County) was laid off some 50 years later. This grant, dated March 6, 1653, was to land in "Pamunkey Necke," on Pamunkey River, and was named "West Point Plantation." All of the Governor's family held portions of this land by descent, and it is unlikely that a West holding this land at an early date was not a member of this old and honorable family.[1]

Governor John West (1590-1659) was a son of Sir Thomas West, Lord Delaware,[2] and a brother to Thomas West, Jr., Lord Delaware, first Governor of Virginia. Governor John West was born in Hampshire, England, received his B.A. from Oxford in 1613, and served on the King's Council of Virginia for twenty-nine years (1630-1659). He was a descendant of Sir Thomas Boleyn by his daughter, Mary, sister to Queen Anne Boleyn, of Thomas Mowbray, Duke of Norfolk, and other prominent people.

By his wife, Ann, Governor John West had at least one son, said to have been an only child, Colonel John West (II). This John West was of West Point, which he inherited, and was born at "Bellefield," Chyskiack, Virginia, in 1633, the first white child born on York River. He died in 1691. West was Senior Justice of the Colonial General Court, sat on the court-martial which tried Bacon's rebels, and was a member of the House of Burgesses. In 1660, this John West was accorded official exemption from taxation for life, because of "the many important former services to the countrey of Virginia by the noble family of West, predecessor of John West, the now only survivor." Colonel John West (II) married Ursula (Unity) Croshaw, daughter of Major Joseph Croshaw (member of the House of Burgesses, 1659-60, Justice of the Peace, Major of Militia) of "Poplar Neck, York County. Colonel John West (II) and Ursula (Croshaw) West had four children: John West (III), Nathaniel West, Thomas West, and Anne West who married Henry Fox.

John West (III) inherited the West Point Plantation after the death of Colonel John West (II). He was a member of the House of Burgesses from New Kent, and first Sheriff of King & Queen County (formed from New Kent) in 1691. He married on October 15, 1698, to Judith Armistead, daughter of Anthony and Hannah (Elliason) Armistead, and had one known son, Charles West.

Major John West of Stafford County was probably a son of Thomas West, or Nathaniel West, mentioned above[3] Major West acquired large tracts of land in Stafford County (including what is now Prince William, Fairfax, and Loudoun). Major West made his will November 16, 1715, probated February 13, 1716 in Stafford.[4] In it he mentions his Grandson, Hugh West, to whom he left 300 acres of the north side of "Aquatinck" (Accotink) Creek; his Grandson, John West; his "Daughter in Law" Ann Turley (to inherit at age 16 or upon marriage); son, John West, land on Hunting Creek and "500 acres at Pamunky"; and also left to John "all my lands above the Potomac & 100 acres below the aforesaid Falls." Legatees included Benjamin Blake or his brother John Blake; William Harrison, Jr.; Burr Harrison, son of Captain Thomas Harrison; Thomas West; James Turley; John Turley; "Seith" Harrison, wife of Capt. Thomas Harrison; Seith Anderson, daughter of Jacob Henderson; Seith Lucas; William Custes (Custis); David Innis; and Francis Ballenger. He also mentions a Godson, John Symmonds (Simmonds) son of Thomas Symmonds. Major West also speaks of his wife, Elizabeth West. There is also this interesting reference to his son John West:

"I ordain my loving . . . friends Capt. Thomas Harrison & Mr. Simon to be assistants unto my wife Elizabeth West & that my wife bring up and educate my son John West in the reform'd religion according to the doctrine of the Church of England & in case of failure that my good friend the Reverend John Frazer take special care of his sound education at the charge of the Estate."

Witnesses to the will were James Turley, Lewis Saunders, David Annise, Mary Mitchison, and Elizabeth Woodward.

Major John West married twice, first to Margaret Pearson, and second to Elizabeth Semmes,[5] of Maryland. The widow, Elizabeth (Semmes) West, remarried to Captain Charles Broadwater. Major John West had issue (*known*):

(*By Margaret Pearson*)
(1) Pearson West.
(2) (Colonel) Hugh West, married Sybil Harrison.

(*By Elizabeth Semmes*)
(3) (Colonel) John West, married (1) Ann Harris and (2) Mrs. Margaret (Pearson) Terrett. (There may have been a daughter, Ann, who married (ca. 1730) Thomas Owsley, II.)

(2) (Colonel) Hugh West, son of Major John and Margaret (Pearson) West, was born March 18, 1705, and died August 25, 1754. Colonel West was a large landowner and was prominent in local affairs. He was a Vestryman of Truro Parish in 1744. West was named a trustee of Alexandria when it was laid out in 1749. Colonel West owned lots 68 and 76 in Alexandria, being on Duke and Royal. Here he owned an Ordinary. His home plantation was on Dogue and Piney Runs. On some of his land adjacent to Alexandria he erected a Tobacco Warehouse, the largest in this area. Colonel West served as Burgess from Fairfax County in 1752, 1753, and 1754.[6]

Colonel West married on December 29, 1725, to Sybil Harrison, of the Northern Neck Harrisons. She was born February 3, 1705, a daughter of Captain William and Sarah (Hawley) Harrison. She died May 27, 1787. Her mother, Sarah (Hawley) Harrison, remarried (2) to Thomas Lewis.

Hugh West made his will on February 9, 1754, probated November 21, 1754. In it he names his sons, John, Hugh, George, and William; also a daughter, Sybil West. Nathaniel Chapman was named Executor, and witnesses were: Richard Sanford, Robert Sanford, and William Sewell. Mrs. West made her will on September 16, 1786, probated January 18, 1787. Legatees included her son, William West, granddaughters, Margaret and Sybil, who were children of William, great-granddaughters, Catherine and Ann West, children of Thomas and grandchildren of John West; granddaughter Catherine Dade, and her daughters, Catherine and Elizabeth. She also mentioned her son, Hugh's children: Sybil Deneale (and her daughter Elizabeth Deneale); Jemima Adams (and her daughter Elizabeth Adams); and son William West was named Executor. Witnesses were: Peter Wise, Robert Allison, and John McKinsey.[7]

Colonel Hugh and Sybil (Harrison) West had issue:

(21) (Captain) John West ("Junior"), married Catherine Foster-Colville.
(22) (Honorable) Hugh West, Jr., married Elizabeth Minor.
(23) George West, married (1) Anne Fowke Dade; and (2) Penelope Payne.
(24) (The Reverend) William West, married Susanna Walker.
(25) Sybil West, married Colonel John Carlyle.

(21) (Captain) John West (called Junior to distinguish him from his uncle of the same name whom George Washington called Colonel John West) lived at "West's Grove," on Little Hunting Creek. Captain West was Assistant Surveyor of Fairfax County and laid off Alexandria with the aid of young George Washington. He held a pew in Christ Church for which he paid L33. Captain West was sent to the Virginia Assembly in 1776 in place of his uncle, Colonel John West, who resigned.

Captain West married before 1755, Catherine Foster-Colville, daughter of Colonel John Colville of "Cleesh," and Mary Foster.[8]

Captain West and George Washington were named Executors of the will of Thomas Colville, an uncle of Mrs. West.

Captain West made his will April 26, 1775, probated February 18, 1777. In it he mentioned his children: Thomas (eldest), Hugh, John, Catherine, Frances, and Sarah. He also mentioned his brothers, George West and the Reverend William West. The latter two were named Executors. Witnesses were: Sarah Lewis, Sybil West, and William Triplett.

Captain John and Catherine (Foster-Colville) West had issue:

(211) (Captain) Thomas West, married Anna Payne.
(212) Hugh West, married Anne ——.
(213) John West, married Sarah Broadwater.
(214) Catherine West, married Baldwin Dade, and had daughters Elizabeth and Catherine Dade in 1786.
(215) Frances West, married Charles Turner, Sr., September 11, 1795, and lived in Alexandria.
(216) Sarah West.

(211) (Captain) Thomas West, son of Captain John and Catherine (Foster-Col-

ville) West, married in 1779, Anna Payne. Mrs. West was born July 4, 1759, and died in 1788. They had at least two children, Catherine and Ann, mentioned in the will of their great-grandmother West.

(212) Hugh West, son of Captain John and Catherine (Foster-Colville) West, married Anne ——, and died about 1807. At least one son, John H. West.

(213) John West (III), son of Captain John and Catherine (Foster-Colville) West, was born in 1760, and died June 9, 1806, age 46. He lived on a tract of land including the present day boundaries of Little Falls Street almost to Tyson's Corners (the right side enroute from Falls Church to Tyson's). His grandson, James William West, owned 500 acres of this tract before his death in the 1890's. Some of this land he acquired by his marriage to a daughter of Colonel Charles Broadwater. He married twice, first to Sarah (Sallie) Broadwater, daughter of Colonel Charles and Ann Amelia (Markham) Broadwater, who died May 6, 1796, age 36 years. His second wife was named Elizabeth. In his will, probated July 21, 1806, West names the following children: George W. West, Mary West, Catherine A. West, Marian P. West, and Matilda Anne Broadwater West. John and Sarah (Broadwater) West had the following children:

(2131) George William West, married Nancy.
(2132) Mary West.
(2133) Catherine A. West, married Colonel William Minor.
(2134) Marian P. West.
(2135) Matilda Anne Broadwater West, married. Clyne.[9]
(2136) Sarah M. West, married L. Nicholas Sewall. (*See Sewall*).

(2131) George William West, son of John and Sarah (Broadwater) West, was born near Falls Church on February 19, 1785.[10] He married by the Reverend Edward Gantt, on July 31, 1808 to Nancy ——.[11] She was born January 12, 1790, died June 2, 1847. Mr. West died September 20, 1871, and was buried in the Falls Church yard. He lived in a house, partly of log, which adjoined the Flagg tract near Idylwood Road. According to a plat of the division among the heirs of Colonel Charles Broadwater, it would appear that "Hollywood Farm" was part of this tract and thus the house built either by a Broadwater or West. George William and Nancy West had issue:

(21311) Jane Elizabeth West, married Jacob Bowers.
(21312) John Thomas West, born September 24, 1811, died July 25, 1820.
(21313) Charles Broadwater West, born July 13, 1814, died in the Mexican War service at Camp Buena Vista, Mexico, August 7, 1847.
(21314) Mary Ann Broadwater West, born March 15, 1817.
(21315) George William West, Jr., born February 27, 1820, died July 27, 1820.
(21316) Catharine Matilda West, born December 31, 1821, died November 5, 1825, age 3 yrs., 10 mos., 5 days.
(21317) Eliza Sybil West, born March 2, 1824.
(21318) James William West, married (1) Eliza Mills, and (2) Catherine Dove.
(21319) Arthur Broadwater West, born May 6, 1831, died unmarried about 1897 and is buried in the Falls Church yard.

(21311) Jane Elizabeth West, daughter of George William and Nancy West, was born June 12, 1809. She married Jacob Bowers and moved to Philadelphia, Pa.[12]
Issue:
(213111) Laura Bowers.

(21318) James William West, son of George William and Nancy West, was born November 2, 1827 at Falls Church, and died December 30, 1898. He married (1) Eliza Mills of Mills Cross Roads (Merrifield), and (2) Catherine Dove, daughter of Samuel and Mary Dove of Fairfax County. Catherine (Dove) West died about 1898, and her children were raised by William H. Taylor of Taylor's Tavern (7 Corners). Mrs. Taylor, the former Emily Birch, was a kind and affectionate foster mother, and Mr. Taylor, a long-time friend of James William West, a kindly father. Early in life Mr. West served in the Mexican War, and received bounty land which helped support his children. Issue: (*By Eliza Mills*)

(213181) James West, died unmarried.

(213182) Charles Broadwater West, married Catherine (Kate) Dance, and had issue: Guy West, Washington, D.C.; Bernard West, U.S.N.; Gertrude (West) Lawrence: Ethel (West) Hines; Nettie (West) Clutz; Mildred West, unmarried; Charles Broadwater West, Jr.; George West; Howard West; Linton West; and Harry West.

(213183) Anne West, married —— Blair.

(213184) Daughter West, married —— St. Clair.

(213185) Martha West, married ——.

(*By Catherine Dove*)

(213186) Laura West, born at Falls Church, January 27, 1872, and is living at Oakton. Miss West is unmarried.

(213187) Thomas West, died young and is buried in an unmarked grave in the Annandale Methodist Church Cemetery.

(213188) Marian West, born at Falls Church, November 23, 1875, and died April 5, 1934. She married Abner Harrison of Cherrydale, Virginia. Issue:

(2131881) Laurence W. Harrison ("Dick"), born March 13, 1898, lived in Falls Church. He married Lillian Cooksey of a Loudoun County family.

(2131882) Emily Harrison, born December 14, 1899.

(2131883) Henry Abner Harrison, born February 9, 1909.

(213189) Lena West, born July 7, 1873, died August 19, 1893, aged 19 years.

(22) (Honorable) Hugh West, Jr., Esquire, Attorney-at-Law, was a son of Colonel Hugh and Sybil (Harrison) West, and a well known figure in political circles of the County. Mr. West died June 10, 1767, after having made his will on May 19th, probated July 20th, of the same year.[13] In his will he named his wife, Elizabeth, and children: Sybil, Jemima and Sarah. Mr. West also referred to an unborn child. His brothers, John, George, and William were named executors. Witnesses were: Sarah Manley, Sybil West, William Rumsey, James Colquhoun and William Triplett. By his will he disposed of landed estate which was in Alexandria, Fairfax, and Leesburg.

West married Elizabeth Minor, daughter of John and Jemima (McCarty) Minor (*See Minor*). Issue:

(221) Sybil West (There is a Sybil West whose birth on October 21, 1762 is noted in the Bible of the Reverend William West). She married Captain William DeNeale (Deneale), an officer in the Revolutionary War. He was of a distinguished family, and a brother to Colonel George DeNeale. Children included: Theodosia DeNeale, married Blinker; Jane DeNeale, married

Huff; Catherine DeNeale, married Marshall of Kentucky; James DeNeale, married Miss Young; and Elizabeth DeNeale, wife of Captain Rezin Willcoxon of the War of 1812, son of Rezin and Margaret (Conn) Willcoxon (*See Trammell*). Some records show a daughter, Sybil West DeNeale, married Hunter. Captain William DeNeale was born August 10, 1756, and died in September, 1814.

(222) Jemima West, married Edward Adams and had a daughter, Elizabeth Adams, perhaps others.

(223) Sarah West, born 1765, died August 18, 1786, married Major Henry Gunnell (*See Gunnell*).

(224) James West.

(23) George West, son of Colonel Hugh and Sybil (Harrison) West, made his will on April 13, 1786, probated April 18, 1786. He stated that the estate of his late wife, Penelope Payne West, was to revert to her family. He also mentioned his brothers, John and Hugh; nieces Catherine and Sarah West, daughters of John West; nephew, George William West; and named as Executors: Charles Little and the Reverend William West. Witnesses were: Penelope French, Mary Little, and William Herbert.

Mr. West married (1) Mrs. Anne (Fowke) Dade; and (2) Penelope Payne. Penelope (Payne) West, daughter of William Payne, was born December 7, 1757, and died in 1782. Her sister, Anna, married Capt. Thomas West. No issue.

(24) (The Reverend) William West, D.D., son of Colonel Hugh and Sybil (Harrison) West was born in Prince William (now Fairfax) County, August 17, 1737, and died at his home in Baltimore, March 30, 1791. He was buried in Baltimore in a vault in the south end of the chancel of St. Paul's Episcopal Church[14] Dr. West married on April 28, 1768, to Susanna Walker. Mrs. West was the fourth child of Dr. James and Susanna (Gardner) Walker,[15] and was born February 26, 1738. She died in Baltimore on July 13, 1787, "A valuable and beloved wife." (*Family Bible*). Mrs. West was buried beside her husband.

The Reverend Mr. West received an excellent classical education, and was ordained a Clergyman of the Church of England in 1761. On September 12, 1762, the Governor of Maryland informed Lord Baltimore that Mr. West, "a well behaved young man," had come to him with recommendations from Colonel George Washington, and that he was serving the Reverend Theophilus Swift as a Curate in Port Tobacco and Durham in Charles County. Following Swift's death in 1762, Mr. West became incumbent of the Parish, remaining until his appointment to St. Andrew's Parish in St. Mary's County in 1767. In 1772 he was appointed to St. George's Parish in Harford County. He became Rector of old St. Paul's, Baltimore, on June 7, 1779, and remained there until his death.

Dr. West became one of the best known Clergymen in Maryland. He labored diligently to keep the Methodist Societies within the Church. He presided over the Convention which adopted the Constitution of the Diocese of Maryland on June 23, 1783, after the separation from the Church of England. Had he lived, Dr. West would likely have been elected first Bishop of Maryland.

The Reverend Mr. West made his Will on March 29, 1791, probated May 27, 1791 (Fairfax County, also probated in Baltimore, *Will Book O, page 541*). In it he mentioned his son, George William West (named Executor); and daughters Sybil

and Margaret. He also appointed his friends, John Merryman and William Gibson as Executors. Dr. West spoke of "Elizabeth Chambers who lives with me" and his share in the estate of Thomas Harrison, deceased. This share was to go to the children of John Harrison of Norton Place, Lincolnshire, England (except the eldest son of the said John); also to Mrs. Elizabeth Irvin, sister of John Harrison. His son, George William, was given his lands in Virginia, and daughters Sybil and Margaret were given land in Anne Arundel County, Maryland. Witnesses to the will were: Hercules Courtenay, Samuel Johnston, and Dr. Samuel Springer Coale.
Issue:
(241) George William West, born January 22, 1770, St. Mary's County, Maryland, died August 1, 1795 in Baltimore. He was unmarried. His nuncupative will was filed August 20, 1795, probated September 20, 1796, at Fairfax Court House. In it he named his sister as legatee, but only one by name: Betsy Chambers. She is not mentioned in the will of the Reverend Mr. West. He also mentioned his friends: James House and Samuel Stringer Coale and the heirs of his uncle, Charles Walker. Witnesses were: Margaret Walker and Mary Kelso.
(242) Margaret West, born at Westminster, St. Margaret's Parish, Anne Arundel County, Maryland, July 9, 1773, married on September 28, 1796, to John Beale Howard, Jr.
(243) Sybil West, born in Harford County, Maryland, August 4, 1774, no other record.
(244) Susanna West, twin of Sybil, born August 4, 1774, died August 20, 1774.
(245) John West, born April 24, 1780 in Baltimore, died there August 6, 1780.
(246) Elizabeth (Betsy), married Chambers. *Note:* The Reverend Mr. West does not mention her as a daughter, but refers to "Elizabeth Chambers who lives with me." However, George William West (1770-1795) refers in his will to his "sister Betsy Chambers." She is not mentioned in the Family Bible. She was probably a foster daughter.

(25) Sybil West, daughter of Colonel Hugh and Sybil (Harrison) West, in her middle age became the second wife of Colonel John Carlyle of Alexandria. Colonel Carlyle was first married to Sarah Fairfax, daughter of the Honorable William Fairfax of Belvoir. The only child of the second marriage was a son, named for George William Fairfax, a brother-in-law of Colonel Carlyle by his first marriage. Colonel John and Sybil (West) Carlyle had issue:
(251) George William Carlyle, who at the age of 17 years was killed while an officer in the Continental Army at Eutaw Springs, 1781. He was heir to vast estates including the title Lord Carlyle. The estates were inherited by the Whiting grandchildren of Colonel John Carlyle by his first marriage.

(3) (Colonel) John West, son of Major John and Elizabeth (Semmes) West, died in 1777. He made his home at the "Bush Hill" estate, still located near Franconia. The present mansion at "Bush Hill" was erected in 1762 by West. Colonel West was a vestryman of Truro Parish, and served as Burgess and later as a member of the Virginia Assembly. He retired from the Assembly because of ill health in 1776. Colonel West made his will on March 27, 1776, probated August 18, 1777.[16] In the will he mentions his daughters: Ann, wife of Daniel Talbut (Talbott); Hannah, wife of John Ashton; Mary, wife of Richard Conway; and also a son Roger West. George

Washington was appointed guardian to Roger West. Colonel West also mentioned his grandchildren, John Talbut, Monica Talbut, and Elizabeth Talbut. Executors to the will were George Washington, Daniel Talbut, Richard Conway, and John Ashton. Witnesses were: Daniel McCarty, Peter Wagener, and John Muir.

Colonel West married (1) Ann Harris and (2) Mrs. Margaret (Pearson) Terrett, widow of Captain William Henry Terrett and a daughter of Simon Pearson. She was born in 1720, her will is dated 1796, probated 1798. Issue:

(*By Ann Harris*)
(31) Ann West, married Daniel Talbott.
(32) Hannah West, married John Ashton
(33) Mary West, married Richard Conway.

(*By Margaret Pearson*)
(34) (Colonel) Roger West, married (1) Nancy McRae and (2) Mariamne Craik.
(35) Ann (Nancy) West, married —— Powell (?). One record shows this.

(31) Ann West, daughter of Colonel John and Margaret (Pearson) West, married Daniel Talbott, of an old Maryland family. Mr. Talbott was twice married, but little information is available concerning his second marriage, if, indeed, it was a second marriage. His wife, Ann West, may have been the second wife. At any rate, he was twice married, and died at his home between Falls Church and Alexandria, of smallpox, on May 22, 1777![17] He was a Class Leader in the early days of Methodism, and his home was one of the first preaching places in Fairfax. John Littlejohn, later his son-in-law, preached at Talbott's as early as 1775. Daniel and Ann (West) Talbott had issue:[18]

(311) John Talbott.
(312) Monica Talbott, married on December 7, 1778, the Rev. John Littlejohn.
(313) Elizabeth (Betsey) Talbott.
(314) Frances (Fanny) Talbott, married John Towner of Leesburg.

(312) Monica Talbott, daughter of Daniel and Ann (West) Talbott, married on December 7, 1778, to the Reverend John Littlejohn. Mr. Littlejohn was born in Penrith, County Cumberland, England, December 7, 1756, a son of John and Catherine (Carney) Littlejohn. His parents brought him to America, living at Port Tobacco, Maryland, and Prince Georges County, Maryland. He was a grandson of James Littlejohn (of Scottish ancestry), who lived in Cumberland, and was a Lieutenant in Honorable Colonel Collenbines Regiment of Foot. James Littlejohn, who held a Coat-of-Arms, was well-to-do, and married Dorothy Graves of Penrith. He died there on February 23, 1745/6, at the age of 74 years, leaving a son (one daughter died at the age of five years).[19] John Littlejohn, Sr., died in Prince Georges County, Maryland, September 1, 1769, leaving his widow, Catherine, with eight children. Of the children, Catherine married John Weatherburn, a Merchant of Baltimore; Dr. Miles Littlejohn was a distinguished Surgeon in Baltimore; the eldest son, James, was also a Surgeon, and died while on a Guinea Ship. Others included Sarah (died single in Baltimore); Thomas, who married but died in Baltimore without issue; William, who died young in Baltimore; Carney, and Mary Littlejohn.

John Littlejohn was a distinguished minister of The Methodist Episcopal Church, and died in Kentucky. He was a resident of Leesburg in Loudoun County between 1778 and 1818. He was a Justice, Sheriff, and held important offices.

John and Monica (Talbott) Littlejohn had a number of children.

(34) (Colonel) Roger West, of "West Grove," Fairfax County, was a son of Colonel John and Margaret (Pearson) West. He was a Justice, and a Delegate to the Virginia Legislature in 1788. Colonel West made a will which was probated in 1801. He married (1) Nancy McRae, daughter of Allen and —— (Washington) McRae; and (2) to Mariamne Craik, daughter of Dr. James Craik, physician to George Washington. His children included a son by the second marriage, James Craik West, who married Eliza Payne.

---

[1] An excellent article on West Point and the West family can be found beginning on page 6, *Program—250th Anniversary Of The Founding of King William County, Virginia*, April, 1952, an article by Elizabeth Stuart Gray: "West Point's History."
[2] *The Armistead Family 1635-1910* by Virginia Armistead Garber, Whittet & Shepperson, Richmond, Virginia, 1910, page 114.
[3] One descendant says that Major West was a son of John West I, who died before 1698 in Northumberland County, Virginia, by his *second wife*, Susannah Pearson, daughter of Thomas Pearson, I, and Susan (Bland) Pearson.
[4] Fairfax County, *Land Records Of Long Standing (1742-1770)*, page 208.
[5] She may have been married to —— Turley. The "Daughter in Law," Ann Turley, may have been a god child or a child by a wife's previous marriage.
[6] References to his life can be found in *Landmarks of Old Prince William*, by Fairfax Harrison, Volume 1, page 138, etc.
[7] From notes in the manuscript files of the Alexandria Library, reviewed September 19, 1958.
[9] See Fairfax County *Will Book B*, page 97.
[8] Matilda Anne Broadwater (West) Clyne died April 24, 1870, at an advanced age. Her picture is owned by Miss Laura West of Oakton, Virginia.
[10] This date and others in this sketch can be found in the George William West Bible ("The West Bible") published in 1814 and owned by Laurence W. Harrison of Falls Church.
[11] Mr. West took great pain to record the name of the Clergyman, but failed to record his wife's surname. This name has been forgotten by the family, and with the destruction of the early Fairfax marriage records, this writer has been unable to find reference to her.
[12] This information given by Miss Laura West. One account states that Jane Elizabeth West married —— Horseman, and had issue: George Henry Horseman.
[13] Fairfax County, *Will Book C #1*, page 7. Also there is a division of the land owned by West (1783 and 1791), *Deed Book Q*, page 202.
[14] Dates, including those of his parents, are from his Bible, owned by Miss Jean Rumsey (quoted in *The Reverend William West of St. Paul's Parish, Baltimore, Maryland, 1737-1791* by Mabel Van Dyke Baer, 1959, D.A.R. Library, Washington, D.C.)
[15] Dr. Walker lived on the south shore of Patapsco (south of Baltimore). He was born in Peterhead, Scotland, May 11, 1705, and died near Baltimore, January 14, 1759. He married Susanna Gardner (born in Maryland, March 12, 1713). (*West Family Bible*—Rumsey).
[16] Fairfax County, *Will Book D*, page 25.
[17] From the MS. *Journal of John Littlejohn*, Louisville Conference Historical Society, Louisville, Kentucky.
[18] Daniel and Ann Talbott are mentioned in the Will of Col. John West, as well as the three first named Grandchildren: John, Monica, and Elizabeth. One son was the Reverend William Talbott of the Methodist Church, who married Miss Boydstone, and went to Pike Co., Ohio, before 1801; another was the Reverend Benjamin Talbott; and two others were the wives of John Hite and Benjamin (?) Boydstone. These are mentioned, with Nancy (Talbott) Welsh, as sisters of Monica Littlejohn in the MS.. *Journal* of Thomas Scott (owned by Lawrence Sherwood, Glenville, West Virginia). However, John Littlejohn definitely states that Nancy Talbott (later Mrs. Welsh) was a half-sister of Monica Littlejohn.
[19] MS.. *Journal of John Littlejohn* ("Revisal & Abridgement of My Old Journals Commenced in Logan Co., Kentucky in May, 1829.")

---

## THE WHEELER FAMILY

Arthur Middleton Wheeler, Sr. (1851-1927), lived in Georgetown, D.C., and moved to Falls Church during the 1870's. After a short stay here he returned to

Georgetown, but about 1890 moved back to Falls Church. Mr. Wheeler is buried with other members of his family in Oakwood Cemetery.[1]

Arthur Middleton Wheeler, Jr., (1872-1932), married Marian Edna Johnson (1874-July 24, 1942) of Georgetown. She was related to John Quincy Adams and Meade Johnson. One of her two brothers was named Adams Johnson. Her parents died when she was but three years old. Mrs. Wheeler was a lovely Christian lady, an ardent communicant of the old Falls Church, and well known for her good works.

Mr. and Mrs. Wheeler had ten children, seven boys and three girls, all reared in Falls Church. They lived on land at West End which they purchased of Mr. Compton, until 1914. In that year they moved to a farm near Masonville where they stayed five years, and then moved to the old Lynch-Shotwell house next to the old Falls Church. A grandchild, Mrs. Lester Gorham, still lives on part of that property.

Arthur Middleton, Jr., and Marian Edna (Johnson) Wheeler had the following children:
(1) Keith Compton Wheeler (1897-1940) married and had:
    (11) Keith Compton Wheeler, Jr.
    (12) Arthur Wheeler.
    (13) Mrs. Lester Gorham (and others).
(2) Morris C. Wheeler (1899-1917).
(3) Stuart C. Wheeler, currently in the Air Force and stationed in Florida.
(4) Ruel S. Wheeler of Hyattsville, Md.
(5) Arthur Middleton Wheeler, III, of Hyattsville, Md.
(6) Marian C. Wheeler, a career Navy Nurse stationed at the Great Lakes Naval Center, Evanston, Ill.
(7) Creighton L. Wheeler, went down on the Juneau with the five Sullivan brothers during the Solomons campaign in World War II.
(8) Sue Creighton Wheeler, married J. M. Brown, and died in 1946.
(9) Valerie L. Wheeler, died 1953.
(10) The Reverend Temple G. Wheeler. Mr. Wheeler writes:

"I was born in our home at West End or West Falls Church, being between the old Henry Sewell home and that of Mr. John? Davenport close to the Roman Catholic Cemetery, April 12, 1904. I was married in the Falls Church May 1, 1928 to Helen Caljouw of Dutch birth in Holland. She was born there Jan. 3, 1910, and emigrated to America at age nine months. We have one son, Arthur Louis, born May 28, 1939. I am reportedly the first man to be ordained in the Falls Church and in 1936. Almost certainly I am the only one who was baptized, confirmed, married and ordained in the little church."

After seven years of parish work, Mr. Wheeler decided to make a specialty of youth work among underprivileged children. He organized Children's Haven near Charles Town, West Virginia, in 1943, which has been highly successful. Upon an offer of the Trustees of the Paxton Home, Leesburg, Va., he moved to that lovely place in June, 1955, as an experiment to see whether this would be a suitable place for his home. However, finding the location at Charles Town to be better suited to the needs of his charges, he moved back in June, 1956. Mr. and Mrs. Wheeler have been parent and friend to numerous young people, and their work has been highly successful.

---

[1] This information, and most of the other data in this article, is based on a letter from the Reverend Temple G. Wheeler of Leesburg, Va., dated April 13, 1956.

## THE WREN (WRENN) FAMILY

Jonathan Lovett, a Quaker Surveyor of Loudoun County, made a map, in September 1801, showing the roads from Winchester to Alexandria.[1] When he arrived at Falls Church, he gave it another name: "Col. James Wrens." At that time Wren was not only one of the most prominent citizens of the area, but Wren's Ordinary (Tavern) was a noted stopping place, recommended by Thomas Jefferson.[2]

Lovett noted that the distance from Winchester to Colonel Wren's was 66 miles, 2 quarters and 36½ perches. It was 4 miles, 2 quarters and 52 perches from "Old Court House" (Tyson's Corner) to Wren's; and 4 miles, 2 quarters, and 73 perches from Wren's to the "Forks of the Road on the levels" (now Bailey's Cross Roads).

Very little has been written about Colonel James Wren. His connection with the life of Falls Church and Northern Virginia is yet to find its place on the printed page. Any man is a product of his family environment. This is especially true of Colonel Wren, for good architecture was in his blood, as the old folks used to say. His roots include Sir Christopher Wren, distinguished English Architect.

The earliest known ancestor of Sir Christopher Wren was one Cuthbert Wren, who died in 1558. He was a haberdasher with a corner stall "next unto Cheap-Crosse." His ancestors came from Denmark and settled in County Durham, England, in the 15th Century. Cuthbert Wren settled at Monk's Kirby, Warwickshire. The name is found in old records as Wren, Wrenn, and Wrenne. Present day descendants in Virginia use Wren and Wrenn, the latter being most popular.

Francis Wren (1553-1624), a son of Cuthbert Wren,[3] was a London Mercer. By his wife, Susan, he had at least three children: Matthew Wren, Bishop of Ely; Susan Wren, married William Holder the mathematician; and the Rev. Christopher Wren, father of Sir Christopher Wren.

Of the three above named, Bishop Matthew Wren was the most noted. He was born December 23, 1585, baptized at St. Peter's Cheap, London, January 2, 1586, received a good education, and became a Clergyman in the Established Church. He was imprisoned in the Tower by Cromwell because of his loyalty to the English Crown. Bishop Wren married on August 17, 1628, Elizabeth Cutler Brownrigg, daughter of Thomas Cutler and widow of Robert Brownrigg. She was a native of Ringshall, Suffolk, and born October 17, 1604. Mrs. Wren died December 8, 1646. Wren was created Bishop of Ely, and wielded considerable power over the Crown. He died at Ely House, Holborn, April 24, 1667. Bishop Wren was father of nine children, some of whom died in infancy. Matthew Wren (Jr.), the eldest (1629-1672), received his M.A. from Oxford, on September 9, 1661. He was a Member of Parliament, an author, and at one time Secretary to James, Duke of York. Wren died June 14, 1672. Thomas Wren, another son of Bishop Matthew Wren, was born in 1633, and died in 1679. He held degrees of M.D. and LLd, and was an original member of the Royal Society. He was Archdeacon of Ely in 1663. Charles Wren, another son of Bishop Matthew Wren, died in 1681, and no record has been found concerning his life, perhaps being overshadowed by his more prominent brothers. The final child to be mentioned is Sir William Wren (1639-1689) who was knighted in 1685, served as a member of Parliament from Cambridge, and left an honorable record. He worked closely with his brother-in-law, Sir Robert Wright (who married Susan Wren), and had an outstanding career.

The Reverend Christopher Wren, son of Francis and Susan Wren, and brother

463

to Matthew, Bishop of Ely, was born in 1591, and died on May 29, 1658. He held the following Arms:

*Coat of Arms*— "Argent, on a Chevron sable between three lion's heads erased purpure, as many wrens of the field, a chief gules charged with three crosses - crosslet or."

*Crest* "A lion's head erased collared gules, pierced through the neck with a broken spear of the last, headed of the first, vulned of the second."

The Reverend Mr. Wren was educated at Merchant Taylor's School, 1601-09, and St. John's College, Oxford. He was Chaplain to Charles II, and in 1620 was Rector of Fonthill, Wiltshire. In 1623 he was installed in the living at East Knoyle. On April 4, 1635, Wren was installed Dean of Windsor in succession to his elder brother, Matthew. Mr. Wren married Mary Cox, a daughter of Robert Cox of Fonthill Abbey. They had at least two children: Sir Christopher Wren, and Elizabeth Wren, the latter born on December 26, 1634.

Sir Christopher Wren, a son of the Reverend Christopher and Mary (Cox) Wren, was born near Tisbury, East Knoyle, Wiltshire, England, October 20, 1632. He led a varied life, and contributed much to his day. The reader is referred to the excellent article on his career which is to be found in the *Dictionary of National Biography*. No attempt will be made here to fill in the details of his many services as statesman, churchman, and distinguished architect. Wren married twice, first, in December 1669, to Faith Coghill, daughter of Sir John Coghill. By her he had two children, Gilbert, born 1672, and died before the age of two years; and Christopher, born February 18, 1675. Sir Christopher Wren remarried to Jane Fitz William, daughter of Lord Fitz William, in 1676. She died in 1680. By her he had at least two children: Jane Wren, born 1677, died unmarried on December 29, 1702; and William Wren (1679-1738), ancestor of Colonel James Wren of Fairfax County, Virginia.

Christopher Wren, Jr. (1675-1747), was educated at Eton, and was a Member of Parliament. He was the author of his family history, and left a good record of scholarship. He married twice, first to Mary, daughter of Philip Musard, Jeweller to Queen Anne; and second, to Constance Middleton, daughter of Sir Thomas Middleton, and widow of Sir Roger Burgoyne. She died May 23, 1734. They had a son, Stephen Wren.

William Wren, son of Sir Christopher and Jane (Fitz William) Wren, was born in 1679, and died March 15, 1738. He is the one of greatest interest to the Fairfax County family, since they claim him as their ancestor.[4] He had several children who settled in Virginia, and came himself but, it is said, returned to England. It should be said here that members of the Wren family were in Virginia at a much earlier time. James Wren was in Accomac County on the Eastern Shore in March 1642, coming with Henry Weede. Among "Licences to go beyond the Seas 10 August 1635" there is underwritten names of those to be "transplanted to Virginia imbarqued in the 'Safety,' John Grant, Master"; and these include Thomas Wren, age 20 years (born 1615). He was probably the father of Francis Wren of Surry County, whose descendants are in legion. The Francis Wren family belongs to the Sir Christopher Wren group, and the given name Francis, being brought into the family by Francis Wren, grandfather of Sir Christopher Wren, continues to this day in the Surry County family.

There was a Nicholas Wren transported by William Bauldwin (Baldwin) of York

County, October 26, 1652. It is noted that the Fairfax Wrens used the given name Nicholas. Records of this family are apparently in Lancaster County: Nicholas Wren Sr., Will, 1701; William Wren, Will, 1710/11; and William Wren, Will, 1736. These records should be considered when a complete history of this old family is written.

William Wren (1679-1738), son of Sir Christopher and Jane (Fitz William) Wren, is credited in family records with at least two children. John Wren (I) (died 1750), married Ann Turner; and Thomas Wren (I), (died 1768), married Jean ———.

John Wren (I), was born about 1701, and died in 1750. The first record of his life in Hanover Parish, King George County, Virginia, is a record of lease and release for eighty acres from Samuel Wharton of the same place. He is called John *Wrenn* in this record. The land was bounded by Thomas Turner and Henry Long. This document was made March 5, 1734/5, and recorded March 7, 1734/5. Witnesses were: Benjamin Adie, James Strother, and Harry Turner.[5] On January 31, 1738/9, William Wharton of Hanover Parish conveyed to John *Wren* twenty six acres. Witnesses were: George Tankersley, Thomas Bartlett, and John Thornley.[6]

On April 1-2, 1742, Francis and Ann Balthop of Hanover Parish, King George, conveyed to John Wren of the same place, seventeen acres, adjacent to land owned by Wren. Witnesses were: Harry Turner, and John Moor.[7] On March 28-29, 1746, Thomas Thatcher and Catherine, his wife, of Hanover Parish conveyed to John Wren, one hundred acres. Witnesses were: William Longmire, James Butler, and George Tankersley.[8] On December 4-5, 1746, Francis Balthrop and Verlinda, his wife, of Hanover Parish, King George, conveyed to John Wren sixty acres (corner to Colonel Thomas Turner). Witnesses were: William Longmire, Robert Strother, and William Mumford.[9] On November 1, 1747, John Wren of Hanover Parish, King George, conveyed to his son, John Wren, Jr., for love and affection, the one hundred acres purchased from Thatcher on March 28-29, 1746. Witnesses: William Longmire and George Tankersley.[10]

John Wren's estate received two inventories and appraisals: the first, December 7, 1750, was by John Thornley and George Tankersley. Mention is made of "cash in Col. Turner's hands."[11] The second was dated March 5, 1752.[12]

John Wren (I) married Ann Turner of King George.[13] Issue: (*perhaps others*)

(11) John Wren (II) married Ann Lloyd.
(12) William Wren, married Mary Strother.
(13) (Colonel) James Wren, married (1) Catherine Brent; (2) ———; and (3) Sarah Jones.
(14) Kilbree Wren.

John Wren (II) (called Junior) son of John and Ann (Turner) Wren, was born about 1720, possibly in Westmoreland County, Virginia. He died in 1752 in Hanover Parish, King George County. His wife was Ann Lloyd,[14] daughter of Samuel Lloyd. She remarried (2) Alexander Hansford.

John Wren of Hanover Parish, King George, made his will which was probated on August 6, 1752.[15] In it he mentioned his wife, Ann (who was pregnant), daughters, Sarah and Ann Wren, and a son, John Wren. His son John was to have the land on which John Wren (II) resided. Captain Edward Dixon was to "have the bringing up of my Son John Wren of a Wrighter (writer) in his Store of a Joiner (carpenter or architect) which he shall think proper." Executors were his wife, Ann, Captain Edward *Dickson* (Dixon) and Thomas Turner. Witnesses were: Thomas McClanaham(n), Robert Brinson and Enoch Berry.

465

An Inventory of John Wren's estate was made by Enoch Berry, Samuel Hoyle, and Joseph Berry, August 6, 1752 (recorded November 2, 1752).[16]

On November 30, 1758, Alexander Hansford and Ann, his wife (late Ann Wren, widow of John Wren), made an indenture concerning Ann's dower. In this document it is stated that John Wren left "sundry" children, and Ann occupied the Manor House. It was noted that in 175——, she married Hansford. They conveyed, by this record, her dower to Joseph Jones, the dower being a *one-third interest*. Witnesses were: William Mackay, John Davis, and Walter Anderson. This was recorded July 5, 1759.[17]

John Wren (II) and Ann (Lloyd) Wren had issue: *(perhaps others)*
(111) John Wren (III) married Hannah ——.
(112) Sarah Wren.
(113) Ann Wren.
(114) William Wren, born 1752/3.

(111) John Wren (III) sometimes called John Wren, Jr., son of John Wren (II) and Ann (Lloyd) Wren, was born about 1747 in King George County. He was living as late as 1826 in Fauquier County. Wren married before June 17, 1776, to Hannah —— (living in 1826 in Fauquier County).

At a Court held April 7, 1763, one John Wren, probably this one, bound himself (with the approbation of the Court) to James Wren, to "Learn the Trade of a Carpenter and Joiner."[18] Due to the long and close association of this John Wren with Colonel James Wren the Architect, it is most likely that he was apprenticed to him.

On November 7, 1771, John Wren, *of Fairfax County*, son and heir of John Wren, late of King George (said John Wren of Fairfax and Hannah, his wife) sold to Alexander Rose of King George one hundred acres of land. This land was originally owned by the Micou family and was sold by Thomas Thatcher by deed of lease and release dated March 28-29, 1746, to John Wren (grandfather of John Wren party to the deed). The tract in question was listed in Hanover Parish. Witnesses were: Seymour Hooe, William Bernard, Thomas Hodge, Alexander Hansford, and Baldwin Berry. The document was recorded March 5, 1772.[19]

In June 1772, Wren purchased several tracts adjacent to Colonel James Wren's land on Pimmitt Run, but complete details are not available since the deed book is damaged.[20] A portion of a lease of June 1772, is on file, from Augustus and Sarah Darrell. Witnesses were: John Searle, William Payne, and John Minor.[21] On June 17, 1772, Augustus and Sarah Darrell signed a release for this land (in the name of John Wren, junior) in consideration of 190 pounds current money of Virginia. This tract contained 190 acres. The same witnesses signed the release.[22] Mr. and Mrs. Wren sold this land on June 17, 1776, to Richard Conway for 296 pounds of tobacco. Witnesses were: William Ellzey, John Muir, Peter Wagener, and Sampson Darrell.[23]

Before April 8, 1780, Wren moved to Loudoun County, and on this date, "John Wren of Loudoun County" purchased from John Hough of the same County for 250 pounds current money of Virginia, land on Goose Creek and Stoney Branch, then in possession of Wren. This tract contained 290 acres.[24] On October 8, 1789, Wren sold part of this land to a tenant, Peter Herbert (Harbourt) for 140 pounds current money of Virginia. Witnesses were: Samuel D. Harriman, John Albritain, and John Urton.[25] On August 6, 1792, Wren sold the remainder to Samuel Dorsey Harriman for 250 pounds current money of Virginia. Witnesses were: Turner Wren, John Harris, and Elijah Hall.[26]

John Wren's name appeared on the *Tax List* made in 1782 by Josiah Watson in Fairfax County. At that time he paid tithe on eleven whites and six slaves.[27] He appears on the Loudoun County *Tithe List* in 1783 with John Urton, Overseer, and paid for three Negroes (five tithes in all). In 1786 he paid in Loudoun County for himself and Negroes : James, Peter, and Frank.[28]

There is also a record in Loudoun County of Samuel Chun being apprenticed to John Wren:[29]

"I do hereby Certifie that Mary Chun the Mother of Samuel Chun is willing that he shall be bound to John Wren of Loudon County to learn the trade of a carpenter, he is twelve years old the nineteenth day of March Next 1785. James Wren."

On July 29, 1793, Gray Douglass conveyed a wagon and team and other items to John and Thomas Wren. Merchants, of Loudoun County (Witness: Simon Triplett).

On September 8, 1795, Wren, and wife Hannah, then of Fauquier County, sold to Francis Harriman of Loudoun County, for 200 pounds, the same tract sold Samuel Dorsey Harriman in 1792. The deed recites that the land was sold by Court decree and repurchased by Wren. The land is here further described as being on the northeast side of the main road leading from Leesburg to Alexandria. This deed made an exception of one acre which Wren sold to Colonel Thomas Ludwell Lee. Witnesses were: John Littlejohn, Benjamin Edwards, and John Fry.[30] On February 11, 1796, John and Hannah Wren sold to Colonel Thomas Ludwell Lee one acre on Goose Creek for a mill. On August 17, 1793, Samuel Dorsey Harriman had made a deed to Lee, but later died without fully paying Wren who reclaimed the property. Witnesses were: Charles Binns, Jr., Thomas Swann, and William A. Harding.[31]

On October 26, 1793, Mrs. Jane Carter, Landon Carter, Jr., and Robert Carter of Bull Run, and others, sold to John Wren, then of Fauquier County, a tract of 277 acres of land on Goose Creek. The deed recited that John Carter during his life time had obligated himself to Wren to sell the land confirmed by this deed. The lease was made for the life time of John Wren, his wife Hannah, and son James Wren.[32] Witnesses were: John McEndree, George McKenny, and William DeBell.

On May 13, 1800,[33] Landon Carter, Jr., and Robert Carter of Bull Run, made a conveyance to John Wren. This states that John Carter during his life time obligated himself to lease to John *Duland* (Dulin) a tract of land and Dulin conveyed this to Wren. The said Wren refused to "pay rent," unless the lease to Dulin was legally executed. This instrument was made to correct any defect in title. Witnesses: Elijah Newlon, Samuel Henderson, and George Newlon.

On May 23, 1806,[34] Robert Donaldson of Fauquier County conveyed to John and Turner Wren, for 525 pounds, several tracts of land on Goose Creek at Ivey Clift. Witnesses: Samuel Harris, John Bishop, and Samuel Berry.

On July 21, 1809,[35] John Wren conveyed to Robert Fletcher a tract of land leased from John Carter, deceased (to said Wren, his wife Hannah, and son James). Witnesses: John Talbert (Talbott); George Dulin, William Fletcher, Stephen Bowen and Samuel Berry.

On February 9, 1810,[36] Edward Carter of Fauquier County conveyed to John Wren for $15.00, land on Goose Creek. Witnesses: Stephen Bowen, John Talbert (Talbott) and Robert Fletcher.

On September 28, 1815.[37] John and Hannah Wren and Turner Wren sold to James Lake, Sr., for $450.00, part of a tract they had purchased from Donaldson. Witnesses: Philip Fishback, Samuel Harris, and James Wren.

By a deed of the same date,[38] John and Hannah Wren, and their son, Turner Wren, sold to James Lake, Sr., for $450.00, land on Goose Creek, part of a larger tract they had purchased from Donaldson. Witnesses: Philip Fishback, Samuel Harris, and James Wren.

By a deed dated April 19, 1817,[39] John Bishop, John Wren and Turner Wren, all of Fauquier, sold to Jesse Jones for $63.59, land on Goose Creek, containing 2 acres, 2 roods, and 7 poles. Witnesses: Charles Green, Moses Glascock, and Aquilla Bishop.

On May 1, 1817,[40] John and Hannah Wren of Fauquier County sold to their son, James Wren, of the same place, for $912.00, land which said John and Turner Wren purchased of Donaldson. Witnesses: Turner Wren, Philip Fishback, Jr., Samuel Henderson and Willis Hoff.

By a lease of October 7, 1818,[41] Aquila Glasscock conveyed to John Wren (for the life of said Wren and his wife Hannah), for $81.00 per year, a tract of land. Witnesses: Burr Powell, Benjamin Glasscock and Asa Rogers. On the same day, John and Hannah *Wrenn* conveyed to Aquila Glasscock for $1,350.00, the land Wren resided on (conveyed to him by Edward Carter) being on the road from "Winn Old Mill (now Haines)," leading to Upperville. Witnesses: Benjamin Glasscock, Burr Powell and Asa Rogers.[42]

By a deed dated January 16, 1821,[43] John Wren conveyed to his daughter, Lucinda Wren, certain slaves. Witnesses: Aquila Glasscock, Robert Fletcher and William Rust.

On March 4, 1823, Alfred and Sarah Rector sold John Wren a tract of land on Goose Creek at Henderson's Ford (adjoining James Wren, John Wren and others). This land cost $250.00. Witnesses: Ludwell Rector, George Tolle and John Kincheloe.[44]

On September 17, 1823, John Wren conveyed to Robert Fletcher his lease for fifty or sixty acres (where Wren lived). This lease was the remainder of a larger tract conveyed to Wren, his wife Hannah, and son James, on October 26, 1793. Witnesses: Samuel Smith, William Fletcher, Jr., Matilda Fletcher, and Agnes Martin.[45]

By a deed of October 13, 1826, John and Hannah Wren conveyed property, with their son, Turner, to James Lake. The deed mentions James Wiatt.[46] This is the last record found for them.

John and Hannah Wren had issue:

(1111) James Wren, married Elizabeth ——. On August 16, 1821,[47] James Wren and Elizabeth, his wife, sold land on Goose Creek, immediately below Henderson's Ford, and lately occupied by said Wren. This was conveyed to Alfred Rector for $24.00. Witnesses: Nancy Jones, Fenley Bishop and Harriet Dawson. James Wren was probably the eldest child, and was mentioned in Carter's deed to John Wren dated October 26, 1793. No other record.

(1112) Turner Wren, who was one of the older children of John Wren, first appears in the records of Fauquier County as Bondsman for his cousin, Delilah Strother, when she married Joseph Carr (September 10, 1796). (*Marriage Book #2*, page 62). On May 15, 1819,[48] John and Hannah Dawson conveyed a mortgage to Turner Wren. Witnesses: James Wren, Aquilla Bishop and Tenley Bishop. Apparently Turner Wren conveyed this mortgage to James Wren. At any rate, on October 27, 1821,[49] John Dawson and James Wren, of the first part, Turner Adams, Administrator of Thomas Adams, Jr., deceased, of the second part, conveyed to Michael Rickard for

$1.00, items including mill weights, carpenters tools, rights to a mill, etc. (by purchase of Turner Wren and others). Wren was alive in Fauquier County in 1826 and joined in deeds with his parents.

(1113) Thomas Wren, married in Fauquier County on March 29, 1798, to Nancy Turley, a daughter of William Turley. James Kincheloe was Bondsman. (*Marriage Book 2*, page 124, contains the Bond dated March 26, 1798, and the record of marriage is in *Book 1*, page 454). On August 6, 1821,[50] Thomas and Nancy Wren (late Turley) of Fauquier County, sold to Isaac Lake for $900.00, land on which William Turley, deceased (father of said Nancy), formerly resided. Witnesses: John Entsminger and Joseph Dance.

(1114) Sarah Wren, married in Fauquier County on November 7, 1796, Isaac Harris (John Wren, Bondsman). (*Marriage Book 2*, page 68).

(1115) Frances Wren, called Fanny, married in Fauquier County on February 7, 1812, to Addison P. Harrison (Samuel Harris, Bondsman; William Wren and Jonathan Lewis, witnesses). (*Marriage Book 3*, page 183). On January 16, 1821,[51] John Wren, father of Fanny Harrison, deeded certain property to his grandchildren: Harriet Turner Harrison, Eliza Peyton Harrison, Juliet Laura Harrison, and William Henry Harrison, Witnesses: Aquila Glasscock, Robert Fletcher, and William Rust.

(1116) Mary Wren, married in Fauquier County on September 14, 1816, James Wiatt (Wyatt). John Wren, father, was witness, and Samuel Harris was Bondsman. On January 16, 1821,[52] John Wren conveyed certain property to his grandchildren, children of his daughter, Mary Wiatt, by name: Eliza Hamilton Wiatt, and Turner Washington Wiatt. Witnesses: Aquila Glasscock, Robert Fletcher, and William Rust.

(1117) Daniel Wren, married Elizabeth Bishop in Fauquier County on February 11, 1796 (*Marriage Book #1, page 40* contains the Bond dated February 3, 1796; *Marriage Book #1*, page 453, contains the return of marriage). John Bishop acted as Bondsman. One Daniel Wren, unplaced in this history, had a wife named Eleanor. It is possible this is a record of this Daniel Wren. The following is from a tombstone in Christ Church yard, Alexandria: "Erected to the memory of Eleanor Wrenn, the wife of Mr. Daniel Wrenn, who departed this life on the 7th day of April in the year of Our Lord 1798, aged 32 years. Revelation, Chapter 14, verse XLII. This stone was placed over her by the order of her disconsolate husband, who was left with two children, to lament his loss—John Renweld her son being only three years old when his mother departed this life, and Dinah Eleanor the daughter aged seven days." This may be Daniel, son of William and Mary (Strother) Wren.

(1118) Lucinda Wren, died unmarried. On January 16, 1821.[53] John Wren deeded certain Negroes to his daughter, Lucinda Wren. Witnesses: Aquila Glasscock, Robert Fletcher and William Rust.

(1119) Elizabeth Wren, married in Loudoun County on January 13, 1803, to Samuel Harris.

(111.10) Samuel Wren, married Barbara Warrenburg in Loudoun County, December 1, 1805. Frances Wren and "Sister Wren, consort of Br. Samuel Wren" were received into membership into Goose Creek Baptist Church at Upperville, on November 3, 1804 and May 2, 1807. (John K. Gott, *Goose Creek Baptist Church Records, Upperville, Virginia, 1775-1842*). On September 11, 1803, Samuel Wren was baptized there by John Hickerson. He was dismissed October 5, 1811. Frances

Wren and "Barbary" Wren were dismissed the same day. It is noted that Samuel Wren pledged $5.00 to build a new Church in April, 1805. No other record.

*Note:* There may have been a John Wren, Jr. There is a tombstone in Christ Church Yard, Alexandria, to the memory of Sarah, wife of John Wrenn, who died August 13, 1792, age 28 years.

(12) William Wren, son of John Wren (I) and Ann (Turner) Wren, was born about 1725 and died in 1766 in Hanover Parish, King George County. He married before November 30, 1749, to Mary Strother (died in Fauquier County after 1814).[54] On November 30, 1749, Grace Berry of Hanover Parish, King George, conveyed to her granddaughter, Mary Wren, late Mary Strother, and wife of William Wren, a Negro named Pegg. Witnesses: Joseph Strother, Robert Strother, and James Stigler.[55] On October 4, 1758, there was recorded a deed between James Wren and William Wren of Hanover Parish, King George, to Zaccheus Wharton, for sixty acres in the said county (corner to Thomas Turner). Witnesses: Benjamin Berry, Withers Conway, and Robert Strother. This was recorded March 2, 1759.[56]

William Wren made his will on September 4, 1766, when he was of Hanover Parish, King George County. This was probated September 4, 1766.[57] In it he mentioned his wife, Mary, and children: Nicholas Wren, William Wren, and John Wren. His son Nicholas was to pay his brother, William, ten pounds when age 21 years. Wren also refers to "my children" perhaps meaning others. Executors were his son, Nicholas, his wife, Elias Gravatt and James Wren. Witnesses: Lawrence Catlett, John Casey and William Vaughan.

William and Mary (Strother) Wren had issue:

(121) Nicholas Wren.

(122) (The Reverend) William Wren, never married. Mr. Wren died about 1777. He was a Methodist Minister, admitted on trial in 1776 and served Kent Circuit with Nicholas Watters and Joseph Hartley.

(123) John Wren, born about 1752 in King George County, died after 1829 in Albemarle County. He married (1) Mary -- (traditionally from Wales); and (2) Elizabeth ——. On March 7, 1777,[58] John Wren of King George conveyed to Eliza Arnold of the same place, thirteen acres in Hanover Parish, which came to said Wren from his brother, William Wren, deceased. Witnesses: Minney Arnold, Lettis Cullom, William Boon, Thomas Smith, William Green, and William Shropshire.[59] On November 2, 1780,[60] John Wren and Mary, his wife, of King George, conveyed to John Clift of Caroline County, fifty acres "being the Tract or Dividend of Land that Mary Arnot the Elder purchased of John Wren and Mary his wife for Jemima Arnot, now Jemima Clift," wife of the said John Clift. On February 24, 1783, John Wren and Mary, his wife, of King George, conveyed 24½ acres of land to Aaron Thornley.[61] This was part of a plantation on which Wren was living, which was the property of William Wren, deceased, and descended to said John, his heir-at-law. Witnesses: Francis Conway, Thomas Berry, J. Skinker, James Edwards and E. Thornley. On March 22, 1784,[62] John Wren and Mary, his wife, conveyed to Aaron Thornley (recorded May 6, 1784). Witnesses: Epaphroditus Thornley, John Gravatt and George Strother. About 1785 John Wren moved to Spotsylvania County from King George, where on October 12, 1785, he purchased one hundred acres (listed as of King George at that date).[63] On March 2, 1786, Wren purchased two acres in Spotsylvania, and on November 20, 1787, sold land there.[64] On June 3, 1794, John Wren

of Spotsylvania County sold 106 acres to Edward Hyde.[65] On November 24, 1797, a deed for 1,231 acres was recorded of a purchase from ten men, including John Wren (recorded July 3, 1798).[66] About 1829 John Wren moved to Albermarle County, Virginia, where he died. It appears that the Wrens of Fredericksburg and Spotsylvania belong to the family of John and Mary Wren. Two brothers, John Wren (1792-18——) and Edward Wren (1795-1881) were born in Spotsylvania County and married sisters, Ester and Lucy Lloyd. (Information on these Wrens has been supplied by Edward's descendant, Mrs. Anna Diehl, 1727 Thomas Road, Medford, Oregon). Of the seven children (tradition) of likely this John, John Wren(n) was born in Spotsylvania County, as indicated, in 1792 and served in the war of 1812. He married Ester Lloyd in Orange County. The brother, Edward Wren, enlisted from Spotsylvania County in the War of 1812. He married Lucy Lloyd of Orange County and died in 1881 in Shelby County, Ohio. Edward and Lucy (Lloyd) Wren had a large family, including: Thomas, James, John, William, Isaac, Joseph, Edward, Jr., Benjamin, and Tabitha Ann.

(13) (Colonel) James Wren, the Architect of Falls Church, was born about 1728, a son of John Wren (I) and Ann (Turner) Wren. He died at his Falls Church home, "Long View," in 1815. Colonel Wren established a large plantation, "Winter Hill," on that tract which includes the present site of Dulin Methodist Church. His mansion house was on the site of the present-day Ankers House in the 300 block of East Broad Street. The Birch home at 312 East Broad Street was an early building on the "Winter Hill" tract.

The first record of Colonel Wren is on a Poll (nature not indicated), one of many names, January 10, 1751 (King George County, *Deed Book 3*, page 469). He is listed thus: "James Wren—107." On May 17, 1753, there is a record, an Indenture of Apprentice, between David Bronaugh and Thomas Bronaugh (cousin of said David) both of King George, and James Wren, also of King George. The said David Bronaugh apprenticed the said Thomas Bronaugh to Wren, to be taught the "trade Suince (Science) or Occupation of a Carpenter and Joiner." Recorded September 6, 1753.[67]

On October 2, 1755, Thomas Wren was bound to James Wren, as an apprentice, until age 21 years, to learn the trade of "Joiner and Carpenter."[68]

On July 6, 1758, *Kilby* (Kilbree) Wren, son of John Wren, late of Hanover Parish, King George County, and James Wren, of *Truro Parish, Fairfax County*, joined in an Indenture of Apprentice. Kilbree Wren was apprenticed to James Wren, "to be taught the trade science or occupation of a Joiner & Carpenter which he the said James Wren now useth . . . " for five years. The signature of Kilbree Wren gives the correct spelling of his name. Witnesses were: Nathaniel Harrison, Thomas Bronaugh, and William Brent. [69]

On October 4, 1758, there is a deed of record between James Wren and William Wren of Hanover Parish, King George, to Zaccheus Wharton, for 60 acres (corner to Thomas Turner). This has already been given in detail.

John Wren, with the approbation of the Court, bound himself to James Wren on April 7, 1763, to "Learn the Trade of a Carpenter and Joiner." This, too, is detailed elsewhere.

The first reference to Colonel James Wren in the Fairfax County land records is a deed dated June 15, 1756, in which James Scott conveyed to Wren (then of Truro Parish) the land Wren was living upon. The land is described as 200 acres adjacent to John and Gerrard Trammell. James Wren, Catherine Wren, and their son, Charles

Wren, are mentioned in the deed. Witnesses to the deed included the Honorable Thomson Mason, George Johnston and John Marky.[70] On June 18, 1759, Benjamin Sebastian and Charles Broadwater, Executors of William Harle, deceased (by his will dated June 29, 1749), sold to James Wren, "Joiner," for 48 Pounds current money 200 acres of land. This land adjoined that of John Colville, Gentleman, Simon Pearson, Owen Williams, and others, on the middle run of Holmes Run. This tract was originally granted Harle on June 18, 1741, by the Proprietors of the Northern Neck.[71]

The *Register* of Overwharton Parish, kept at old Aquia Church, shows that James Wren and Catherine Brent were married on March 27, 1753. Mrs. Wren was born in Stafford County on January 13, 1729, a daughter of Charles and Hannah (Innes) Brent.[72] Her father, Charles Brent, made his will in Overwharton Parish, Stafford County, on August 28, 1755, and this was probated April 13, 1756.[73] In the will he mentions his children: Charles Brent, Hugh Brent, William Brent, George Brent, Mary Brent, Ann Brent, Catherine Wren, and his wife, Hannah Brent. He also mentions his friend and neighbor, Peter Daniel. Brent left his daughter, Catherine Wren, three Negroes: Sarah, Moll, and Hannah; also one equal part of all his household goods and stock, "including what she hath already received to be part of the same." Witnesses to the will were: John Anderson, Clement Cheverel, Mary Cheverel, Sarah Daniel, and Mary Carter.

About 1771/74, Colonel Wren remarried (no record available). Colonel Wren married (third) in Alexandria, D.C., on March 4, 1804, to Sarah Jones.[74] George Deneale was Bondsman at the time of this marriage.

Colonel Wren was listed as a Vestryman and Church Warden for Fairfax Parish on December 20, 1769. His election to the Vestry was on November 15, 1766, to replace Edward Blackburn, a former Vestryman. This election serves as additional evidence of his loyalty and interest in the Anglican Church. As noted earlier, Wren designed Falls Church and built it. His plan was also used in Christ Church at Alexandria, and Pohick Church.

Although Wren was the Architect of Christ Church, it was built by James Parsons. Wren did, however, letter tablets on either side of the "three windows," and the chancel of Christ Church, for which he was paid 8 pounds in 1773. The bricks for the Falls Church were burned in his brick kiln on Shreve Road, near "Long View," which tradition states he owned in proprietorship with his brother, William Wren. As an Architect, Wren had been influenced by works in print in his day, and it is thought by this writer that he may have come under the influence of William Buckland who designed George Mason's "Gunston Hall." In 1759 Buckland completed work on the Truro Parish Glebe which much later (under provision of the Act of 1802), was purchased by Wren.[75]

Colonel Wren was Commissioner of Provisional Law for Fairfax County during the Revolutionary War, and the D.A.R. records also call him an Artificer and Soldier. Certificates are on file in the Virginia State Library at Richmond (under *Public Claims*) showing that Wren received rye "for the use of the army," from his son, James Wren, Jr., on October 16, 1780. He signed both certificates under this date as "Jas. Wren, Commissioner." Wren was appointed Lieutenant of the Fairfax County Militia and took Oath April 16, 1787.[76] It is known that he held the commission of Captain during the early part of the Revolutionary Conflict. Samuel Barker Davis in his deposition made February 2, 1833,[77] states that he enlisted in Fairfax County on July 10, 1775, under Captain James Wren, and took part in the defense of Alexandria.

Wren purchased several tracts of land in the Falls Church area as he extended his interests in social and political affairs. He must have been a well-educated man, with a good business sense, judging from the following extract of a letter he wrote from "Winter Hill" on November 5, 1797, to his son-in-law, Simon Adams:

"Mr. Talbot (another son-in-law) informs me that you are selling goods fast, but must remind you that selling is one part of the business and receiving is another, and you had but a small capital to begin with, so that in the end you may find it a disagreeable business if you are not very cautious who you trade with. I cant help but remind you of old John Muir's opinion 'that a man had better cry over his goods than after them.'"

Wren owned land in Loudoun County, and the *Tithe List* for 1780 (page four) gives reference to the Quarter owned by Colonel James Wren "of Fairfax" and he paid four tithes, on John Hubbard (probably his Overseer) and three Negroes: Jack, Mary, and Winny. The *Tithe List* for Loudoun County (1782, Part I), gives this information: "Colo. James Renn (Fairfax), David Allen, Overseer." Negroes named Jack, Moll, and Winny were living at this "Quarter" tract in Loudoun in 1782. He paid six tithes in 1785, and John Win (Winn) is listed as Overseer. Apparently this land was the 200 acre tract in Cameron Parish (near the Fairfax border) on Difficult Run, which he purchased on February 21, 1774.[78] The deed of that date was from Benjamin Cockrill of Loudoun to James Wren of Fairfax, in consideration of 80 Pounds, current money. Witnesses to the deed were Robert H. Harrison, Bailey Donaldson, Edward Dulin, Philip Adams, William Ellzey, William Gunnell, and William Payne.

On May 28, 1787, James and Mary Hurst conveyed to James Wren land in Fairfax County on Four Mile Run. Boundaries included: Pearson, Harrison & Reagan, Trammell, and along the Run to Gunnell's corner (on the North side of the Run). This tract contained 145 acres, 35 perches, and was originally granted to George Harrison. Witnesses were: George Minor, Henry Darne, and Thomas Grafford.[79]

On February 23, 1788, James Wren, Gentleman, took oath as a Commissioner of Tax for Fairfax County, and his Bond was countersigned by Colonel George Minor.[80] He was appointed Sheriff of Fairfax County by Governor Henry Lee, and his Commission was dated November 13, 1792. His Bond in the amount of 20,000 pounds current money was dated November 19, 1792, and addressed to the Gentleman Justices of Fairfax County: David Stuart, William Herbert, and Richard Conway. The Bond was countersigned by: Benjamin Dulaney, William Payne, George Minor, and Richard Ratcliffe.[81]

On February 7, 1791, Charles and Ann Broadwater conveyed to James Wren for 90 pounds current money, 100 acres of land, being part of a lease formerly granted by Thomas Pearson to Abraham Lay, "& now in possession of said Wren," adjoining the other land owned by Wren, and that of Thomas and Opie Lindsay. Witnesses included: John West, Thomas Graffort, George Smith, William Crum, and William Tasker.[82]

There is an interesting record on file at Fairfax[83] which recites that at the request of James Wren, Charles Lee, and Joseph W. Harrison, Gentlemen, the subscribers (surveyors Charles Little, George Minor, and Simon Sommers) met at "Winter Hill" on August 28, 1797, to settle and adjust the bounds of their land, then in dispute.

This land is described as on the North Branch of Holmes Run and was surveyed by Colonel William Payne. Mention is made of the Emms Patent and the Harle Patent ("now Harrison & Lee"), and also of Thomas Lindsay's meadow. This information was filed "at the request of Colo. James Wren, he having lost the Copy formerly given him," on January 22, 1800.

Between 1797 and 1815 (*Deed Book F 2*, page 193—book lost, only the index is extant) Wren deeded part of the tract purchased from Hurst to the trustees of the Methodist Society.[84]

Little else is known of Colonel James Wren, excepting that he served as a Justice of the Peace of Fairfax County, and was a Trustee of the stillborn Town of Turberville, laid off near the Little Falls of the Potomac in 1798.

The only house owned and lived in by James Wren, which is standing,[85] is "Long View" on Shreve Road. This house was erected in 1770, and became his home after his second marriage. His son, John Wren, later lived at "Long View" after the death of his step-mother. "Long View" has changed little over the years. The original front was from what is now the Lee Highway area, and the house was approached by an avenue of cedar trees. The family cemetery was to the left of the entrance. Stones which were standing as late as 1949 have disappeared, but twelve graves with dornick stones are still to be seen. A twisted piece of box, burned many times, but still coming back, marks the grave of Colonel Wren. Also buried in the cemetery are Mrs. Robert Reid and children, Sarah (Jones) Wren, members of the family of John Wren, and also descendants of Robert and Verlinda (Wren) Darne.[86] Mr. John Robert Darne (always known as "Jack" Darne), was the last member of the Wren family buried there. Mr. Darne was a great-grandson of Colonel James Wren. "Long View" is now the home of Mr. and Mrs. Charles Bretschneider.

One of the last records made by Colonel Wren was a deed in connection with the final settlement and sale of the old Glebe of Fairfax Parish, made a few months before his death. At that time, April 25, 1815, Wren was too feeble to sign his name, and signed with an "x." The deed[87] recites that James Wren of Fairfax County, "surviving trustee" of the Glebe of Fairfax Parish, for $100.00, released all rights to the property he held as trustee. This deed, to George Deneale and John Muncaster of Alexandria, D.C., Church Wardens of Christ Church, was the same conveyed by Daniel Jennings to Townshend Dade, Sr., and James Wren (then a Church Warden) on September 18, 1770, and located on Lubbers Branch (now Lubber Run). Deneale and Muncaster are described as legal successors to Dade and Wren, and acting under a decree of the U.S. Supreme Court from the February term, 1815. This decree was rendered in the case of George Deneale, John Muncaster, and James Wren (surviving trustee) who were defendants, and the Overseers of the Poor of Fairfax County (William Henry Terrett, George H. Terrett, George Triplett, George Summers, John Jackson, Jr., Humphrey Peake, John Wrenn, and Thomas Coffer) were Complainants. Also named in the deed are the members of the Vestry of Christ Church: George Taylor, William Herbert, Charles Simms, Thomas Swann, William S. Moore, Charles Alexander, Augustine J. Smith, John Tucker, Cuthbert Powell, and Edmund Jennings Lee. Witnesses to the deed were: William Herbert, Anthony Crease, Charles Simms, and Oliver Morris.

James Wren made his will on March 9, 1808, probated November 21, 1815, by oath of Thomas Lindsay, John Wood, John Wren, Robert Darne, and David Lindsay.[88] He loaned to his "dear and well beloved wife" Sarah Wren "the tract of Land whereon I live on for her to work her people on during her life, likewise I lend her Two horses, Jolly and the young sorrel horse and the riding chaise and Harness and her saddle and her choice of a Feather bed and furniture, Two tables, Six Chairs, the Cupboard in the little Room and the China Earthen and glass ware in this house and Kitchen furniture and as much provision as will last her and family to the end of the year, and as much provisions as will serve her and her family the ensuing year, also her choise of Two Cows, one sow and pigs and her choise of Six Sheep..." Wren also loaned her the use of Charles the blacksmith and his tools for three years "if he lives so long and at the expiration of that time to be given up and his tools to his wife Sarah Piper not as a slave but as her husband." [89] Wren also loaned to his wife all the fowls on the home plantation, and directed that she not rent "out any part of the land nor suffer any waste of the timber to be done on the land..." He directed also that the land was to belong to his son, John Wren, following the death of his wife, and that her estate which he received at the time of marriage, "be given up to her or her heirs at my death agreeable to Contract by my Executors."

Wren gave his son, James Wren, his watch and all his "wearing apparrell," his riding Saddle, and three Negroes (already in his son's possession): Nelly, Kitty, and Lilly. To his daughter, Hannah Adams, he gave three Negroes, Sall (and her two children, Ione and Hamon) already in Hannah's possession, and also $200 out of his estate. Wren gave his daughter Mary Dulin two Negroes, Milly and Anna and their increase, these Negroes already owned by Mary, and also $200. Daughter "Catey" Adams during her life was to have right and title "to a small tract of land lying and being in the state of Kentucky, Shelby County," and was loaned three Negroes "which is in her possession named Sarah, Maryann and Reubin," which after her death were to belong to William Adams, her son. Another daughter, Sarah Talbott, was given Negroes Lewes and Anny, already in her possession, and $200.

The main provision of the will was for John Wren, who apparently received more than his brother James. It may be, however, that Colonel Wren provided for James, Jr., during his lifetime. John Wren was to receive the home plantation and all items "loaned" his step-mother during her life, also "the tract of land I purchased of Mr. James Hurst Except one quarter of an acre I gave to the Methodist Society to build their Church on—likewise one tract of Land I took up adjoining Benjamin Dulany Esq. Col. Broadwater and Col. Little—likewise the land I purchased of Col. Broadwater—also one Small tract I took up adjoining Charles Lee Esqr. Mr. Thomas Lindway and myself—also the tract of Land I live on after the death of my wife..." He also left John two Negroes, John and Julet, already in John's possession, and by a codicil of December 28, 1810, gave him a tract of land purchased from Andrew Rounsaville containing eleven and three quarters acres.

Wren also provided for the heirs of his daughter Betty Hughes, giving her children "Two Negroes named Will and Tonney that I let William Hughes have in the Spring (of) 1806 and at his death they and Jeneys Increase to be equally divided amongst her (Betty's) children. He also gave the Hughes grandchildren $200 to be paid them in equal portions "at their comeing of age or day of Marriage."

To a favorite grandchild, Verlinda Wren, daughter of John Wren, Colonel Wren left six silver table spoons. He also gave a soup ladle to Virlinda McGruder, daughter of Daniel McGruder. Wren also provided that his debts be paid and "then whatever remains of my Estate that has not been mentioned be sold on Twelve months Credit taking bond and good security and the Money arising from the Sale thereof together with bonds or debts that may be owing to me after they are collected by my Executors and the amount thereof," be equally divided into six parts for his children, James, Mary Dulin, Caty Adams, Sarah Talbott, and his Hughes grandchildren. Since he mentions six parts, but does not name his son John, the only heir not so mentioned, it is assumed this was an omission.

John Wren and son-in-law William Dulin were named Executors of the will, and it was witnessed by Opie Lindsay, Thomas Lindsay, John Wood, Thomas Sinclair, and John Wren. Witnesses to the codicil were: Opie Lindsay, Thomas Lindsay, Robert Darne, David Lindsay, and Hierome Opie Lindsay.

In the probate records of Fairfax County is a record of the Appraisal and Sale of the estate of Colonel James Wren, but it was not recorded until December 18, 1837. The document recites that a sale was held December 19, 1815 (by Court order of November, 1815), and the paper was found in the desk of John Wren, deceased, Executor of James Wren, by John's Executor, Thomas Moss. The slaves mentioned were: Charles, Thomas, Edward, Henry, David, Jack, Joseph, Juday, and Hannah. These were apparently the remaining slaves mentioned as twenty-five in all, in the so called 1790 "Census."[90] Among the purchasers at the Sale were the following: Richard L. Washington, John Wren, John Wood, G. W. Hunter, George Darne, Mrs. Wren, Mrs. Hannah Adams, William Donaldson, Daniel Dulaney, Wesley Adams Kitty Hughes, Thomas Nelson, William Nelson, John Crump, John Dulin, Nicholas Darne, Richard Kirby, Dabney Ball, John A. Summers, Daniel M. Chichester, Sarah Wren, and Thomas Moss.[91] The Estate Account[92] notes that the coffin for Col. Wren cost $31.00, and was paid for on November 16, 1815. Since this large sum was expended, the coffin must have been of copper or some metal. John Littlejohn was paid taxes in 1816, and it is noted that Nicholas Darne "cried the sale" for several days. This record is signed by Richard Ratcliffe and dated December 18, 1837.

The will of "Sally" Wren, widow of James Wren, was made March 3, 1815, and probated May 20, 1816, showing that she survived him but a few months.[93] By this will she stated that all her slaves were to be free upon her death. She left all of her estate to her brothers' and sisters' children, excepting Frances Hays, daughter of her sister, Frances Lampkin.[94] Her friend, John Dulin, was named Executor. Witnesses were: Edward Dulin, Ashaddia Moore, and Thomas Lindsay. By order of the Fairfax County Court of May, 1816,[95] Thomas Lindsay, Robert Darne, John Sommers, and Edward Dulin were appointed to make an Inventory of the estate of Sarah Wren, widow of Colonel James Wren, deceased. Lindsay, Dulin and Darne qualified for this purpose on May 30, 1816. A sale of the estate was held on May 30, 1816. Purchasers included: John Dulin, Robert Darne, James Gordon, John Haycock, Edward Dulin, Richard Thompson, John Summers, Hugh W. Minor, and Daniel F. Dulaney, all of the Falls Church neighborhood. An account of the estate was filed on February 14, 1822, by John Dulin, Executor.[96] This shows that her coffin was paid for, with other funeral expenses, on April 29, 1816. On May 22, 1816, an amount was paid for advertising the sale of her estate. In the Account is mentioned George Darne, and "Samuel Shreve's Note." Witnesses included Thomas Moss, Thomas Lindsay, and John A. Sommers.

Colonel James Wren had issue (all by Catherine Brent):[97]

(131) Charles Wren (mentioned in the 1756 deed from Scott to Wren. He may have been the eldest son and died young.)

(132) James Wren, Jr., married (1) Elizabeth Gunnell and (2) Verlinda Barry.

(133) John Wren, married Elizabeth (Gunnell?).

(134) Hannah Wren, married (The Reverend) Samuel Adams. (*See Adams*).

(135) Mary Wren, married William Dulin. She died in Fairfax County in 1814. Mr. Dulin was born in Fairfax County, near Falls Church in 1765 and died in Loudoun County in 1812. He was a son of Edward and Sarah (Hurst) Dulin. He made his will on May 28, 1812, probated September 14, 1812 in Loudoun County (*Will Book K*, page 153). He mentioned his wife, Mary; daughter, Hannah; son, Edward; brother, John; and grandchildren, William Wren and Mary Wren. Witnesses were: William Minn (Winn?), George Weeagley (Wageley), and William A. Summers. Children: Edward Dulin (no record); Hannah Dulin, married William Smith, and he died in Loudoun County in 1810. Mr. Smith's will was made July 21, 1810, probated in Loudoun County, October 8, 1811 (*Will Book I*, page 271). He mentioned his estate in Fairfax County; son, George Dulin Smith (under 21 years to have a liberal education and 1,000 acres in Kentucky); wife, Hannah; daughters under age 18 years; father-in-law, William Dulin and wife were named as Executors. Smith also referred to land he resided on and a tract with Sanford Wren as tenant ("which my father-in-law has promised I may dispose of") which was to be equally divided between his daughters, Catharine Wren Smith, Mary Dulin Smith, and Sarah Ann Smith. Witnesses: William Noland, William Williams, and George Sinclair. Thus issue included: George Dulin Smith, Catharine Wren Smith, Mary Dulin Smith and Sarah Ann Smith. Sally Dulin, another child of William and Mary (Wren) Dulin, married in Loudoun County on March 14, 1799, to a cousin, Sanford Wren, son of Thomas and Susanna (Sanford) Wren. (See *Guardian Accounts A (1759-1821)* page 251, Loudoun County, which shows William and Mary Wren in account with the estate of Mary Dulin, their guardian, 1814, in William Dulin's estate.) Issue, thus, included: William Wren (married his cousin, Evalina Wren) and Mary Wren.

(136) Catherine Wren, married (1) Colonel Simon Adams, and (2) John Hite (*See Adams*).

(137) Elizabeth Wren, married William Hughes (*See Payne* and *Adams*).

(139) Sarah Wren, born March 3, 1768, at "Winter Hill," died in Kentucky in 1832. She married on January 11, 1790, Nathaniel Talbott of Fairfax County. Her obituary, giving a lengthy account of her life, is in *The Christian Advocate & Zions Herald* of February 17, 1832, page 100. This article gives a clue concerning her father's second wife of ca. 1771/74. Mrs. Talbott was a distinguished Methodist.

(132) James Wren, Jr., son of Colonel James and Catherine (Brent) Wren, was born in Stafford County, Virginia, and was baptized there on December 21, 1758, in Aquia Church, by the Rector of Overwharton Parish. Mr. Wren acquired land in the western end of Fairfax County, in the present day neighborhoods of Vale and Chantilly. He died at his Plantation near Chantilly ("Flat Lick") about 1820.

On April 5, 1790,[98] James Wren, Jr., and Verlinda, his wife, of Fairfax County, sold to James Wren, Sr., for 100 pounds, a tract of land in Loudoun and Fairfax County, on the waters of Difficult Run. The tract conveyed by this deed was originally granted in 1727 to William Moore, and he sold to Edward Barry of "Huntingdon." Barry, by his will, left the tract to John Barry, who conveyed to William Barry. The latter conveyed it to Verlinda Barry who married James Wren, Jr., on

May 17, 1778. Witnesses to the 1790 deed of Wren to Wren included Charles Lewis Broadwater, John W. Douglass, Thomas Lindsay, Charles Broadwater, and William Payne.

Apparently James Wren, Jr., retained a portion of this land, for it was conveyed by him and his wife to Thomas Smith for 150 pounds, 6 shillings. This deed, of April 17, 1797, describes the land as in Truro Parish at the "Head of the South Ford of Difficult Run," and formerly owned by patent of William Moore. Witnesses to this deed were: George Minor, Charles Little, and Carlyle F. Whiting.[99] The house on this property was erected in 1727,[100] subsequently enlarged, and is still standing. It is on the road from "Burnt School House" triangle to Vale Church, and in more recent years was known as the "Alfred Kitchen Place." The house is of log and clapboard with an immense stone chimney. It was the home of Gabriel Fox, Captain Jack Barnes, the Waples, and others. It is now being restored by C. J. Reeder.

There is little else of record concerning James Wren, Jr. His father in his will left him all his "wearing apparrell," his watch, his riding saddle, and some Negroes. In 1785 ("1790 Census")[101] James Wren, Jr., is listed with 7 whites in his household, 1 dwelling house, 2 other buildings, and no slaves noted. In 1782,[102] he is listed on John Gibson's List with 5 whites and 4 slaves.

James Wren, Jr., married (1) Elizabeth Gunnell; and (2) before 1790 (see Fairfax County *Deed Book S 1*, page 152) to Verlinda Barry. His second wife was living in Ohio in 1836 with a son, Richard Wren.

Mrs. Olive Wrenn tells a charming story of a visit by Colonel Henry Gunnell, a member of the Virginia Legislature, to his nephew, James Wren (III) who married Anne Adams. Uncle Henry was in his cups and quite disagreeable. Young Wren would have none of it, and in a fit of anger, Colonel Gunnell struck his horse with his stick, and the family remembered the scene: Uncle Henry's wrap-rascal (cape) sailing in the breeze and his high white beaver hat bouncing on his head!

James Wren, Jr., had issue *(By Elizabeth Gunnell)*:[103]
(1321) Thomas Wren, married Joanna Brent.
(1322) James Wren (III), married Anne Adams.
(1323) Robert Wren, married Sarah ——.
(1324) John Wren, married Elizabeth Carr Lane.
(1325) Allen W. Wren, went West.
(1326) Margaret Wren, married Isaac Fox.
(1327) Elizabeth (Betty) Wren, married —— Fennell (had a son in 1832, according to an old letter).

*(By Verlinda Barry)*:
(1328) William Wren.
(1329) Richard Wren, married Patty Peake.
(132.10) Nancy Wren, married —— Askins (They were in Fayette County, Kentucky, by 1818. They had three daughters, and one, Betsy, was married in 1832.)
(132.11) Mary Wren.
(132.12) Jane Wren.

(1321) Thomas Wren, son of James, Jr., and Elizabeth (Gunnell) Wren, died at Middletown, Ohio, September 9, 1824. He married Joanna Catherine (Caty) Brent, a daughter of George and Joanna (Wale) Brent.[104] Mrs. Wren was born October 4, 1775, and died September 22, 1822. Mr. Wren moved to Kentucky, and later to

Ohio. Thomas Wren and William Wren were merchants in Leesburg in 1795/6. (See *Wrenn vs. Neale.* ) Thomas and Joanna Catherine (Brent) Wren had issue:
(13211) Martha Newton Wren, married Francis S. Adams.
(13212) Martin Wren.
(13213) Allen Smith Wrenn, married.
(13214) Hugh Brent Wren, married Harriet Wren.
(Perhaps others)

(13211) Martha Newton Wren (Patsy), was born at Centreville in 1796, and died in Loudoun County on July 3, 1854, age 58 years. She married Francis S. Adams[105] on December 2, 1834 in Fauquier County.

(13212) Martin Wren (called "Yankee Wren"), born 1805, was named for an Uncle, Martin Brent. He married Julia —— (born Virginia, 1810). Children (1850 Census): Catharine, born 1838; Mary, born 1840; Betsy, born 1848; and female, born 1850. Mr. Wrenn was a carpenter.

(13213) Allen Smith Wrenn, was born at Westchester, Virginia (now West Virginia), and died in Middletown, Ohio. He married and had issue:[106]
(132131) Catherine Brent (Kate) Wrenn, living, unmarried, in 1927.
(132132) Thomas A. Wrenn, died September 17, 1918. He married and had issue:
(1321321) Thomas Newton Wrenn, living, 1934, in South Norwalk, Connecticut. Mr. Wrenn was then owner of the Family Bible of Thomas and Joanna (Brent) Wren.

(1322) James Wrenn (III) (called "Mt. Rocky James"),[107] son of James, Jr., and Elizabeth (Gunnell) Wren, was born in 1776, and died September 30, 1843, age 67 years. He is called "James Wren, Sr.," in some later records. This James Wrenn was an officer in the War of 1812, and the following is from his note book kept at that time:[108]

"Camp Leanord (Leonard) Town
    Lieutenant Wren has leave of absence for fifteen days December the 2, 1814.
Sir please to pay James Wren six shillings on my accompt when you receive money due me from the United States.

                                                            his
                                                  Samuel x Walker
Capt. Thos. Coffer.                                      mark "

It would appear that James Wrenn served as Lieutenant in Captain Thomas Coffer's Company, on duty at Leonard Town, Maryland, in December 1814.

On November 21, 1831,[109] Wrenn purchased "Mount Rocky," near Chantilly, from George M. Hunter, trustee for George Lee Turberville. On October 18, 1830, Turberville made a deed to Hunter "for the purpose of providing a fund for the payment of his debts" and for future support of the 480 acre "Mount Rocky" tract, and other considerations. "Mount Rocky" was formerly "the Cockerille Lease," and is described as near Little River Turnpike. Witnesses to this deed were: John Haycock and Joshua C. Gunnell.

In Fairfax County records[110] is a map of the "Mount Rocky" estate. Also in the same book is a record of the law suit of January 1860,[111] "Ann (Adams) Wrenn vs. James Wrenn." Those making complaint with Ann Wrenn were: Ann Elizabeth Wrenn, Mary V. Wrenn, John W. Wrenn, Gabrielanna Wrenn, William A. Wrenn, James N. Wrenn, and Robert Wrenn. Defendants were: James Wrenn, Samuel

479

Wrenn, Augustine Wrenn, William A. Hutchison (husband of Martha Ann Wrenn), Leah H. Wrenn (wife of William H. Wrenn) and James W. Wrenn. It was ordered by the Court that the "Mount Rocky" tract of which "James Wrenn the elder died seized," be partitioned to the heirs. One-sixth was awarded to James Wrenn, one-sixth to Samuel Wrenn, and the remainder to the children of Gabriel A. Wrenn, with the exception that Ann (Adams) Wrenn was to have the use of the house and garden "where she now lives" during her life time. Albert Wrenn and James R. Wrenn acted as Commissioners. Also in the same book is a deed of August 30, 1860, where Anne (Adams) Wrenn conveyed certain property.[112]

There was an *Agreement* between William Ellzey and James *Wren* whereby Ellzey sold to Wren a small tract of land adjoining the land of Reid, Ashton, and Stuart. This paper is dated January 29, 18— (torn), probably before 1835. Wren agreed to pay $10.00 per acre in five years from the first of "January last," and to be paid in annual installments. Ellzey agreed in the meantime to ascertain the "quantity of acres & convey the same with a general warranty," to Wren. The paper is signed by W: Ellzey and James *Wrenn*. The deed for this land was drawn on May 30, 1835, between William Ellzey of Loudoun County and James Wren of Fairfax County. Ellzey conveyed to Wren for $463.33, land in Fairfax County between Reid, Steuart, Ashton, and Talbot, containing 46 acres, and 54 poles. Witnesses were: Hugh Mitchell, Benjamin Cross, William H. Wrenn, and James Wrenn.[113]

Mr. Wrenn made his will on May 12, 1843, and it was probated on October 16, 1843.[114] In this he mentions his wife, Nancy, and his children: Gabriel Adams Wrenn, William Henry Wrenn, James Wrenn, Samuel Wrenn, Martha Ann Wrenn, and Augustine A. Wrenn. Witnesses to the will were: Benjamin Cross, William S. Daniel, and Robert Mitchell.

James Wrenn (III) of "Mount Rocky" married Anne (Nancy) Adams, a daughter of Samuel and Jemima (Darne) Adams (*See Darne*). Issue:

(13221) Martha Ann Wrenn, born about 1810, married William A. Hutchison, of "Burnt Wood" farm, Loudoun County. He was called "Burnt Wood Billy" Hutchison. Issue included: Margaret L. Hutchison, married John Wallace Wrenn; James E. Hutchison, married Gabrielanna Wrenn; William Henry Hutchison who married Augusta Meade Wrenn; and Philip A. Hutchison who married (1) —— Bradshaw and (2) Ora Fleming of Loudoun County. Philip A. Hutchison's children included: Alice, married (1) Irving Harrison and (2) —— Wheeler; Philip, Jr.; Hugh Hutchison of McLean; and Edna Hutchison.

(13222) Gabriel Adams Wrenn, married Julia Ann Darne.
(13223) William Henry Wrenn, married Leah Harle Darne.
(13224) Augustine Augustus Wrenn, married Martha Darne.
(13225) James Wrenn (IV) ("Junior"), married Lucinda Mitchell.
(13226) Samuel Adams Wrenn, married Maria Louisa Darne.

(13222) Gabriel Adams Wrenn was born May 9, 1810, and died July 25, 1845.[115] An *Appraisal* of his estate was ordered by Fairfax County Court in August 1845, and was returned on December 3, 1845.[116] It was submitted by James Davis, Alexander Turley, and Benjamin Cross. A sale of the estate was held in December 1845,[117] and purchasers included: William H. Wrenn, William F. Lee, Augustine A. Wrenn, James Wrenn, and Mrs. Julia Wrenn. On August 18, 1847,[118] William H. Wrenn, Administrator of Gabriel A. Wrenn, returned an *Account* of the estate. In it are

mentioned the widow, Julia Ann Wrenn, James Wrenn, guardian of Mitchell's children; Samuel Wrenn, and Ann Wrenn. Gabriel Adams Wrenn married Julia Ann Darne. Issue:
(132221) Charles Wrenn (1835-November 6, 1839).
(132222) John Wallace Wrenn, married Margaret L. Hutchison.
(132223) Gabrielanna Wrenn, married James E. (Cook) Hutchison.
(132224) Mary V. Wrenn (Molly), unmarried.
(132225) Ann Elizabeth Wrenn, unmarried.
(132226) James William Wrenn, married Ella Calvert.

(132222) John Wallace Wrenn, was born February 2, 1843, and died March 12, 1908. He is buried beside his wife in Chestnut Grove Cemetery, Herndon. Mr. Wrenn married his first cousin, Margaret L. Hutchison. She was born December 5, 1855, died April 1, 1924, and was a daughter of William A. and Martha Ann (Wrenn) Hutchison. No children.

(132223) Gabrielanna Wrenn (Teasie), born 1846, married at "Mrs. Wrenn's," on December 14, 1869, to James E. Hutchison (Cook), her first cousin. Mr. Hutchison was born in Loudoun County in 1848, died 9-27-1870, buried at "Mount Rocky," and was a son of William A. and Martha Ann (Wrenn) Hutchison. Children (others):
(1322231) Moss Hutchison, married ——Pennington.
(1322232) Julia Hutchison, married his cousin Bernard Johnson Fox.

(132226) James William Wrenn, married Ella Calvert of Maryland. Issue:
(1322261) Julia Marguerite ("Rita") Wrenn, died October 9, 1949 in Washington D.C., unmarried.

(13223) William Henry Wrenn was born August 16, 1811, and died September 8, 1855.[119] He lived at "Mount Rocky," near Chantilly, where he raised his family. He married on June 18, 1840, Leah Harle Darne. Mrs. Wrenn was born at Falls Church on April 27, 1806, and was a daughter of Captain Nicholas and Amelia B. (Trammell) Darne. She died in 1875, and is buried with other members of the family at "Mount Rocky."[120]

On March 1, 1833, George Hunter, Trustee for George Lee Turberville, leased to Mr. Wrenn the "Leeton" estate, to terminate in 1836, on January 1st, at a rent of $25.00 per year for three years. He was then permitted to lease the land for two years at $30.00 per year. An interesting reservation was made in the lease that "The House now occupied by an old Servant of the Said Turbervilles Ancestors for her use and habitation," provided for her and husband, with a garden and small corn patch, was to remain in her possession. Witnesses to the lease were: Henry D. Hooe, Margaret Hunter, and Margaret Weatherby.[121]

On May 23, 1835, Mr. Wrenn was appointed "Captain of Patrole," with James Wren, Gibson A. Whaley, John B. Stuart, Charles W. Turley, and John B. Trott, and was directed by Joshua Hutchison, who signed the order, as follows:[122]

"... you are to patrole all Negro quarters, and other places Suspected of entertaining unlawfully, assembly of slaves, servants, or other disorderly persons as afsd. (aforesaid), and also to govern your company as the law directs..."

On August 11, 1852, Alfred Moss (Court Commission in the suit of Edward Sangster and others against Harriet Padgett and others) conveyed to Mr. Wrenn Lot Number 6, in the division of the real estate of George W. Turley. This Lot was alloted to James Horseman, and contained forty acres of land. The deed was signed by

Moss, David D. Lane, and Lucinda Lane. It was sworn before Alexander D. Lee and Lewis F. Mankin, Justices.[123]

On December 20, 1852, Wrenn purchased for $125.00, Lot Number 4 of the Turley division, and allotted to Charles A. Turley, who conveyed it to Charles A. Whaley on September 23, 1847. This deed, Whaley to Wrenn, was for 52 acres.[124]

William Henry and Leah Harle (Darne) Wrenn had issue:

(132231) William Asbury Wrenn, born June 2, 1841, died unmarried, Dec. 26, 1878.

(132232) James Nicholas Wrenn, born October 2, 1843, died February 2, 1865 (Bible—Fairfax records state February 1, 1866). He was arrested as a civilian and placed in Point Lookout Prison where he died. He was unmarried.

(132233) Robert Wrenn, married (1) Sarah Elizabeth Cross; and (2) Anna Harrison Fitzhugh Cross.

(132233) Robert Wrenn, son of William Henry and Leah Harle (Darne) Wrenn, was born on the "Willard Farm," located between Arcola and Floris (Frying Pan), on September 30, 1846. He died on March 11, 1925, and is buried at "Sunnyside" Farm, located on the South East corner of Stringfellow and Poplar Tree Roads between Chantilly and Centreville. Mr. Wrenn lived at "Walnut Grove," (part of "Mount Rocky") which he inherited from his Grandfather Wrenn. He was an ardent member of Centreville M.E. Church, South, holding various official positions in that Church. He donated the land for Pender M. E. Church, South, which was erected in 1907. The deed to the Pender Methodist Episcopal Church, South, is recorded in Fairfax County *Deed Book O 6*, pages 535/6, and is between Robert Wrenn of the first part, and Everett B. Whaley, Charles Stewart, Edward S. Hurst, and Sylvester Fox, trustees, of the second part. The deed is dated December 14, 1903.

Mr. Wrenn married: (1) on October 9, 1872, Sarah Elizabeth (Lizzie) Cross (1846-1886); and (2) on June 8, 1887, Anna Harrison Fitzhugh Cross (1845-1893). They were sisters, and daughters of James Lewis Cross (1813-1894) by his wife Lucy Byrd Mayo (Fitzhugh) Cross (1821-1883) of "Sunnyside," near Chantilly. They were descendants of the Harrison and Fitzhugh families.

Robert Wrenn had issue:

*(By Sarah Elizabeth Cross)*:
(1322331)  James Wrenn (born and died, 1874)
(1322332) Mabel May Wrenn, born September 29, 1876, died February 12, 1942, married Harry Bernard Mitchell on August 1, 1907.
(1322333) Robert James Wrenn, born September 24, 1880, died February 3, 1881.
(1322334) Raymond Nicholas Wrenn, married Winnie Varina Holden.

*(By Anna Harrison Fitzhugh Cross)*
(1322335) Robert Fitzhugh Wrenn, born about 1889, living, 1958, unmarried, at Chantilly.

(1322334) Raymond Nicholas Wrenn was born at "Walnut Grove," September 9, 1884, and died at Herndon, November 26, 1956. Mr. Wrenn served as Mayor of Herndon from 1919 until 1921, and served on the Town Council. He was a Deacon in the Herndon Congregational Church, a Real Estate Broker, and active in Civic affairs.

Mr. Wrenn married, on October 11, 1915, Winnie Varina Holden. She was born in Fairfax County on July 23, 1886, a daughter of Thomas and Isabella Johnson (Summers) Holden, and is living, 1958. Children:

(13223341) (The Reverend) Raymond Fitzhugh Wrenn, married Rena DeShazo Lynch.
(13223342) Robert Holden Wrenn, married Mary Craig.
(13223343) Thomas Randall Wrenn, married Margaret A. McMurray.

(13223341) (The Reverend) Raymond Fitzhugh Wrenn was born June 25, 1918, and married on September 17, 1949, to Rena DeShazo Lynch. Mrs. Wren was born in Fairfax County on November 29, 1916, a daughter of Vernon Montgomery and Minnie Isabella (Williams) Lynch. The Reverend Mr. Wrenn is Executive Secretary of the Northern Virginia Methodist Board of Missions. Issue:
(132233411) Richard Fitzhugh Wrenn, born September 27, 1950, at Alexandria.
(132233412) Elizabeth DeShazo Wrenn, born February 23, 1952.
(132233413) Katharine Lynch Wrenn, born November 5, 1956.

(13223342) Robert Holden Wrenn, was born June 15, 1923, and married on May 23, 1944, Mary Craig, daughter of James C. and Martha May (Speer) Craig. Children:
(132233421) Pamela Jane Wrenn, born December 19, 1947.
(132233422) Nancy Jean Wrenn, born April 24, 1950.
(132233423) Roberta Lee Wrenn, born May 19, 1961.

(13223343) Thomas Randall Wrenn was born September 12, 1924, and married on August 10, 1945, Margaret Almeda McMurray of Forest City, N.C. Issue:
(132233431) Thomas Roger Wrenn, born November 29, 1946.
(132233432) Leah Carol Wrenn, born February 25, 1951.
(132233433) Douglas McDonald Wrenn, born September 12, 1952.
(132233434) Wendy Susan Wrenn, born April 16, 1956.

(13224) Augustine Augustus Wrenn, son of James and Anne (Adams) Wrenn, was born at "Mount Rocky," and died in 1866. He married a cousin, Martha E. Darne, daughter of Robert and Verlinda (Wren) Darne. She was born February 20, 1837, died on her birthday, February 20, 1903, and is buried at "Mount Rocky." Issue:
(132241) Charles Augustus Wrenn, born August 24, 1854, died May 13, 1928, buried at "Mount Rocky." He married Mary Jane (Minnie) James (July 13, 1859-January 19, 1931). No issue.
(132242) Alice V. Wrenn, born May 17, 1857, died November 12, 1923, buried Chestnut Grove Cemetery, Herndon. Unmarried.
(132243) Lucretia Wrenn.
(132244) Ellen Eugenia Wrenn, born 1849, married at "Mount Rocky," on June 3, 1869, Benedict D. Utterback, Jr. He was born in Fairfax County in 1849, a son of Benedict (or Benjamin) D. and Susan Utterback.
(132245) Helen Wrenn, died young.

(13225) James Wrenn (IV) (called "Flat Lick James"), son of James and Anne (Adams) Wrenn, was born in 1813, and died February 8, 1887, at Chantilly, and is buried there in the Christ Episcopal Church Cemetery. Mr. Wrenn married on January 16, 1838, Lucinda Mitchell. Mrs. Wrenn was born May 13, 1818 (*Bible*), and died November 17, 1908. She was the daughter of Hugh and Emily (Wooster) Mitchell of Chantilly, and granddaughter of Benjamin and Betty Neville (Jones) Mitchell.

James Wrenn brought suit against his mother-in-law concerning the settlement of the Hugh Mitchell estate. This suit, "Wren vs. Mitchell," is on file at Fairfax, and contains interesting data concerning this family.[125]

James Wrenn (IV) and Lucinda (Mitchell) Wrenn had issue:
(132251) Mary Frances Wrenn, born June 20, 1839 at "Stone House" Chantilly, died unmarried in the Dower House, Chantilly, May 28, 1932. She is buried in Christ Church yard, Chantilly.

(132252) (Lieutenant) Albert Wrenn, married (1) Lucy Fox; and (2) Hannah Harrison.

(132253) Victoria Wrenn, born at Dower House, Chantilly, October 1, 1842, died there, unmarried, September 26, 1918. She is buried in Christ Episcopal Church yard, Chantilly.

(132254) Ann Eliza Wrenn, born at Dower House, Chantilly, May 27, 1844, died there, unmarried, May 8, 1890. She is buried in Christ Episcopal Church yard, Chantilly.

(132255) Arthur Wrenn, married Annie May Yates.

(132256) Adelaide Wrenn, born at Dower House, Chantilly, March 26, 1849, died there, unmarried, April 18, 1930. She is buried in Christ Episcopal Church yard, Chantilly.

(132257) Rose Anna Wrenn, born at Dower House, Chantilly, June 8, 1851, married Massie Riley. His sister, Jane, married Hugh Mitchell, Jr., brother of his mother-in-law, Lucinda (Mitchell) Wrenn! Mrs. Riley died in child-birth and is buried, with her infant, in Christ Church yard, Chantilly.

(132258) Roberta Wrenn, born at Dower House, Chantilly, October 8, 1854, died there, unmarried, in December 1941. She is buried in Christ Episcopal Church yard, Chantilly.

(132259) Catherine Della Wrenn (Kate) born at Dower House, Chantilly, April 17, 1857, died there, unmarried, in 1942. She is buried in Christ Episcopal Church yard, Chantilly.

(13225.10) Lucy Emma Wrenn, born at Dower House, Chantilly, March 13, 1860, died there, unmarried, April 10, 1930. She is buried in Christ Episcopal Church yard, Chantilly.

(132252) (Lieutenant) Albert Wrenn, was born at "Stone House," Chantilly, September 7, 1840, and died November 6, 1910. He was a member of Mosby's Scouts, in the Confederate Army. Mr. Wrenn married (1) in 1866, his cousin, Lucy Fox (1842-1881). She was a daughter of John and Matilda (Barker) Fox and a granddaughter of Isaac and Margaret (Wrenn) Fox. Mr. Wrenn remarried (2) on May 15, 1882, to Hannah Harrison. The second Mrs. Wrenn was born in Fairfax County in 1853, a daughter of J. S. and Catherine Harrison. Issue:

(*By Lucy Fox*)
(1322521) Milton Wrenn (1862-1915), unmarried.
(1322522) Edith Wrenn, unmarried.
(1322523) Claude Wrenn, married Lenah Middleton (and had issue a son, Albert Middleton Wrenn, who was killed in an accident while a student at the University of Virginia).
(1322524) Sidney Wrenn, married his cousin, Olive Wrenn. Mr. Wrenn was born April 20, 1873, died April 18, 1955. No issue.

(*By Hannah Harrison*)
(1322525) Page Wrenn, married Carrie Hutchison, daughter of Lycurgus and Sarah

E. (Benton) Hutchison. Issue: Lyle Wrenn, Richard Wrenn, Martha (Wrenn) Pearson, and Hannah Ann (Wrenn) Monroe.

(1322526) Carroll Wrenn, married and has one son who is living in Pennsylvania.

(132255) Arthur Wrenn, born July 13, 1846, at Dower House, Chantilly, died "Stone House," Chantilly, in 1908. He married a cousin, Annie May Yates. She was born in Washington, D.C., a daughter of William and Margaret (Smith) Yates, and a descendant of the Brent family. Issue:

(1322551) Olive Blanche Wrenn, born at Chantilly, September 6, 1882, is living there in the historic "Stone House" of her ancestors, 1962. She married her first cousin, Sidney Wrenn, son of Lieutenant Albert and Hannah (Harrison) Wrenn. No issue.

(13226) Samuel Adams Wrenn, died August 20, 1864, and is buried at "Mount Rocky." He lived near Chantilly on "Cherry Grove" farm (house is now a tenant house on the north side of Route 669 about a mile east of its crossing with route 645, about a mile north of Route 50.) This is part of James B. Franklin's "Dairylou Farm." Mr. Wrenn married a cousin, Maria Louisa Darne, daughter of Robert and Verlinda (Wren) Darne. She was born October 28, 1815 and died December 26, 1895, with burial at "Mount Rocky." Issue:

(132261) James Robert Wrenn, eldest, married and went North.

(132262) Gabriel Hite Wrenn, died February 22, 1939, age 89 years. He is buried in Union Cemetery, Leesburg. He married on March 11, 1875, a cousin, Laura Fox (1853-1901). She was a daughter of John and Jane Hervey (Summers) Fox and a granddaughter of Isaac and Margaret (Wren) Fox. Issue:

(1322621) Minnie Jane Wrenn, married (1) George Taylor; and (2) Charles T. Moriarty. No issue.

(1322622) Ona Wrenn (Onie), married Frank Odor; issue: Laura Odor, married Frederick Thaler; Franklin Odor, married Frances Harlan; Hammond Odor, married Virginia Maloney (and had a son, David); and Louise Odor, unmarried.

(1322623) Oceola (Ocie) Wrenn, married Robert L. Schepmoes; issue: Douglas Schepmoes, married Ethel Merchant; Oceola Schepmoes, married Nelson Howard (had a son, Philip); Robert L. Schepmoes, Jr., married Dorothy Plaugher (had Robert L. III, James and Barbara); and Marjorie Schepmoes, married Lynn Karge.

(1322624) Rufus Wrenn, married Lucy Bryant and lives in Purcellville. One son, Stanley, died in infancy, and another grew to maturity.

(132263) John Philip Wrenn, died in February 1853, aged 4 months.

(132264) Washington Clay Wrenn, born in 1856, died in 1919. He married on December 21, 1881, Susan Lane Utterback. Mrs. Wrenn was born in Fairfax County in 1861, died 1926, and was a daughter of Benedict D. and Susan Utterback. They are buried in Chestnut Grove Cemetery, Herndon. Issue: Virginia Wrenn, married Walter W. Wyatt of North Carolina. Their son, Wrenn Wyatt, is a civilian Civil Engineer at Homestead Air Force Base, Florida. Vernon Wrenn, another child of Washington Clay Wrenn, married but had no issue.

(132265) Martha Wrenn, unmarried.

(132266) Josephine Wrenn, married Albert Powell; issue included: Sash Powell, married, two issue; Henry Powell, married Kate Birch; Maude Powell, married

Harry Alden, two issue; and Blanche Powell, married a cousin, Robert Utterback, and had two sons, William and Roland Utterback.

(132267) Samuel Allen Wrenn, Commissioner of Revenue of Fairfax County for many years. Unmarried.

(1323) Robert Wren, son of James Wren, Jr., and Elizabeth (Gunnell) Wren, died in Loudoun County in 1821. His wife, Sarah (Sally), was living in 1821. On November 12, 1821, Joseph Beard was appointed Administrator of Robert Wren, deceased (Bond in the amount of $5,000). Securities were: William Cooke, Samuel M. Edwards, and John Thomas. Sally Wren, widow, relinquished her right to administrate the estate (witness: James Adams).[126] An Inventory returned December 11, 1811 by Jacob Fadeley, Joseph T. Newton and Edward Hammat.[127] Issue: (probably others)[128]
(13231) James Oscar Wrenn, married Martha E. ——.
(13232) Philip Wrenn, married Susan C. Vermillion.

(13231) James Oscar Wrenn, son of Robert and Sarah Wren, was born in 1811 and died August 14, 1871, age 60 years, at his residence, Fairfax Court House.[129] His wife, Martha E., died after 1871. By deed dated September 19, 1871,[130] John R. Wrenn and Martha E. Wrenn of Randolph County, Missouri, deeded property to Mrs. Martha E. Wrenn, widow of James O. Wrenn. Issue:

(132311) James Oscar Wrenn, Jr., born in Fairfax County, about 1846/8, died in 1909 and was buried in Chestnut Grove Cemetery, Herndon. He married in Fairfax County on August 27, 1872 (reported in *The Mirror*, Leesburg, August 28, 1872), to a cousin, Lula Wrenn. Mrs. Wrenn was born in Prince William County in 1849 and died in 1924. She was a daughter of Philip and Susan C. (Vermillion) Wrenn. Issue: Leola Wrenn, married Clarence Daffer of Dranesville; Cecil Wrenn, married (1) Walter Stutz (four children) and (2) A. Branch Burton; Ruth Wrenn, married Henry Lieber (no children); Stanley Wrenn, married Mamie Estes; and Clyde Wrenn, married Lillian Stutz.

(132312) Sarah A. Wrenn, born 1850, married at her mother's residence in Fairfax County, October 17, 1871, to Charles William Cockerille. Mr. Cockerille was born in Fairfax County in 1841, a son of William H. and Julia Ann (Wren) Cockerille of Willard, Fairfax County.

(132313) John R. Wrenn, was living in Randolph County, Missouri, in 1871.

(132314) Martha E. Wrenn, was living in Randolph County, Missouri, in 1871.

(13232) Philip Wrenn, son of Robert and Sarah Wren, was born in Prince William County in 1824 and died in Fairfax County in 1876. He was buried in Chestnut Grove Cemetery, Herndon. Mr. Wrenn married Susan C. Vermillion, a native of Fairfax County, born in 1830, died in 1903. She was related to John Quincy Adams, according to tradition.[131] Mr. Wrenn lived on Russell Road, Alexandria, and his house was on the site of the present-day St. Mary's Girls' School. He later lived at Dranesville, Fairfax County. Issue:

(132321) Lula Wrenn, married James Oscar Wrenn, Jr.

(132322) James Hamilton Wrenn, born in Prince William County on September 4, 1857, died at Waxpool, Loudoun County, July 15, 1920, with burial in Chestnut Grove Cemetery, Herndon. Mr. Wrenn married in Fairfax County, (1) on December 16, 1884, Anna Roberta (Bert) Hurst. Mrs. Wrenn was born in Fairfax County, November 18, 1859, and died in Loudoun County, August 14, 1897. She was a daughter of John Henry and Ann Virginia (Bicksler) Hurst.[132] Mr. Wrenn remarried (his first wife's sister), Alice Virginia Hurst. Issue (by first marriage):

(1323221) Wade Hampton Wrenn, born April 27, 1897, died August 6, 1897, buried Chestnut Grove Cemetery, Herndon.

(1323222) James Clayton Wrenn, married Julia Newman, no issue.

(1323223) Della Virginia Wrenn,[133] married Odilon Joseph Rogers (this family surname was originally Roger). Issue:

(13232231) Jane Hamilton Rogers, born September 6, 1922, died January 3, 1959, married George Robert Stinemeyer, issue: Nancy Kay Stinemeyer.

(1323224) Audrey Rae Wrenn, married John Herbert Mills. Issue:

(13232241) Grayson Hurst Mills, married Edna Thompson.

(13232242) Thelma Rae Mills, married Manton Wyvell.

(13232243) Bernice Virginia Mills, married Bernard Hillyard.

(13232244) Dorothy Hamilton Mills, married Robert McClelland Fields.

(13232245) Margaret Mills, married Meredith Walker.

(132323) Mary C. Wrenn (1859-1873), unmarried, buried at Chestnut Grove, Herndon.

(132324) Rosa M. Wrenn, died unmarried, January 1, 1920, buried at Chestnut Grove, Herndon.

(132325) Augusta Meade Wrenn, married William Henry Hutchison.

(132326) Moultrie Franklin Wrenn, married (1) Rachel Lefever; and (2) Mary Walker. Issue: (*By Rachel Lefever*):

(1323261) Leroy Wrenn, married Ruth —— and had two sons, one named Edwin.

(*By Mary Walker*):

(1323262) Moultrie Franklin Wrenn, Jr., married and has issue.

(1323263) Philip Wrenn, married Mamie —— and is living at Yorktown, Virginia, 1962 with two children: Nancy and Philip.

(1323264) John Walker Wrenn (Jack), married Mary —— and had three children. He lives in Florida.

(1323265) Richard Wrenn, married, had a son, and a daughter, Nancy.

(1323266) Margaret Wrenn, married (1) —— Bard of Clarksburg, Pennsylvania, and had a daughter, Julia Lynn Bard; married (2) Samuel Zadger of Harrisonburg, Virginia and has three children by this marriage.

(1323267) Mary Susan Wrenn, married —— McDonald of England, a DuPont official. They have two children.

(132327) Beverley Wrenn, unmarried.

(132328) Lillian Wrenn, married Catesby Rowzee. Issue: Helen Rowzee, married (Major-General) Charles L. Dasher. They are living at 7812 Old Chester Road, Bethesda, Maryland. Issue: Beverley Ann Dasher, married William Priest and lives near Birmingham, Alabama; and Charlene (Dasher) Hyatt.

(132329) Samuel Wrenn, went to Seattle, Washington, became wealthy in the lumber business, married and had issue.

(13232.10) "Bud" (real name not recalled by the cousin who supplied this data) Wrenn, married and moved to Missouri, later returning to Virginia. His children were: Walton Wrenn, William Wrenn, Charles Wren, Nellie Wrenn, and another son and daughter.

(13232.11) Mary Wrenn, died young in Alexandria, and her body was moved in recent years to Chestnut Grove, Herndon.
(13232.12) Fanny Wrenn, married —— Wrenn, settled in Nebraska.
(13232.13) Walton A. Wrenn, born October 2, 1863, died December 24, 1919. He is buried in Union Cemetery, Leesburg. Mr. Wrenn married (1) Lula E. Smith (born September 24, 1867, died December 6, 1897); and (2) (his first wife's sister), Blanche E. Smith (born February 18, 1871, died July 17, 1940).

Issue (*By Lula E. Smith*):
(13232.13.1) Hammond Wrenn, married Margaret ——.
(13232.13.2) Pearl Wrenn, married Archie Myers
(13232.13.3) Maude Wrenn, married Harry Harvey.
(13232.13.4) Nellie Wrenn, married, moved West.
(13232.13.5) Mary Wrenn, married Frederick Wightman.
(13232.13.6) Edna Wrenn, married ——.
(*By Blanche E. Smith*):
(13232.13.7) Eleanor Wrenn, married a dentist in Lynchburg.

(132325) Augusta Meade Wrenn, daughter of Philip and Susan C. (Vermillion) Wrenn, married her cousin, William Henry Hutchison, son of William A. and Martha Ann (Wrenn) Hutchison. They are buried in Fairfax Cemetery. Issue:
(1323251) Oden Henry Hutchison, born June 8, 1882, near Aldie, Loudoun County, died April 16, 1963. Mr. Hutchison owned "Mount Rocky," Chantilly, the home of his Wren ancestors. He married on December 15, 1917, in Washington, D.C., Bessie Leanah (Lee) Jones. She was born in Fairfax County, January 16, 1886, a daughter of Emanuel Henry and Ellen (Brooks) Jones. Her mother's first cousin was the distinguished Dr. Brooks, a well-known physician in the Fairfax area. Mrs. Hutchison is living at "Mount Rocky" (1964). Issue:
(13232511) Helen Brooks Hutchison, born at "Mount Rocky," March 4, 1926, married in South Carolina, March 15, 1947, Edward Alexis Smith. Mr. Smith was born near Alexandria, November 29, 1918, a son of Sidney Harmon and Clara Maude (Polklaesner) Smith. Issue: Alexandra Rider Smith, born in Washington, D.C., July 7, 1948.
(13232512) Joseph Oden Hutchison, born at "Mount Rocky," April 18, 1921, married Christine Popovitch. Issue: Sandra Lee, Joseph Oden, Jr., and Timothy Preston Hutchison.

(1323252) Eva Hutchison, married Frank Gingrich and lives at Reisterstown, Maryland. Issue. John Gingrich, Bessie Gingrich, Mabel Gingrich, and Frances Gingrich (all of whom are married).
(1323253) Mattie Hutchison, married Frederick Hagmann, had two children: a son, died young; and Ralph Hagmann, married, and living in Winchester (1962).
(1323254) Cora Hutchison, married John Stedman Collins. He married (1) and had a son, Linwood Collins. Following the death of his wife, Cora Hutchison, Mr. Collins remarried (3) Mrs. Ruby (Payne) Shaver, a sister of Pearl Payne who married Eugene Archie Hutchison, a brother of Cora (Hutchison) Collins. Issue:
(13232541) Isabelle Collins, married on November 5, 1932, Martin Towner Prosise. Mr. Prosise was born in Washington, D.C., February 26, 1910, died at Arlington Hospital, July 5, 1961. He was a son of Robert Edward Lee and Maude Elizabeth (Martin) Prosise. His grandparents were Benjamin and Virginia Flor-

ence (Towner) Prosise, related to the Smallwoods, Wrights, Steadmans, and others. Issue: Nancy Gail Prosise, born February 9, 1935; and Carol Lee Prosise, born December 8, 1943.
(13232542) Vera Collins, married (1) Colin Hamilton; (2) Joseph Bailey (had issue Jay Bailey); and (3) George Purcell.
(13232543) Child Collins, died in infancy.
(1323255) Katherine Hutchison, married —— Downs, no issue.
(1323256) Fanny Hutchison, died unmarried, and was killed when her horse was frightened by a street-car and her buggy over-turned. Miss Hutchison was returning from attending a funeral. She was buried in Fairfax Cemetery.
(1323257) Bertha Hutchison, married Harry Cross (no issue).
(1323258) William Hutchison, married Virgie Rector of Centreville, issue: Catherine Hutchison, married George Shumate, Sheriff of Prince William County (two children); Hilda Hutchison, married; and a third daughter.
(132325.9) Ossie Hutchison, married Harvey Cross (brother of Harry Cross who married Bertha Hutchison). Issue: Glenn Wood Cross, and Florence Cross.
(132325.10) Eugene Archie Hutchison (Gene), married Pearl Payne, issue: Frances Hutchison, married Francis Witham; Janet Hutchison, married Robert Miller; Augusta Meade Hutchison, married Norman DeLeon; Buckey Gwynn Hutchison, married Gwendolyn; and two others that died in infancy.
(There were three other children of William Henry and Augusta Meade (Wrenn) Hutchison—two boys and a girl—that died in infancy.)

(1324) John Wren (Jack), son of James Wren, Jr., and Elizabeth (Gunnell) Wren, went West. He lived for a time near Centreville, Fairfax County. Mr. Wren married Elizabeth Carr (Lane) Lane, widow of Philo Lane, and a daughter of Captain William Lane, a Revolutionary Officer, and Susanna Linton (Jennings) Lane. She was a granddaughter of James de Moville and Patsy (Carr) Lane.[134] On February 20, 1830, Humphrey and Ann L. (Nancy) Peake, John and Elizabeth Wren, Benedict and Susanna Lane, Patsy Bailey, William H. Lane, Susanna Lane, and Catherine Lane, surviving children of Captain William Lane, conveyed property near Centreville to their mother, Susanna Lane.[135] John and Elizabeth Carr (Lane) Wren had issue (probably others):
(13241) William Wren.
(13242) Robert Wren.

(1325) Allen W. Wren, died about 1816. An Administration account of his estate was filed August 20, 1816, by Jane Wren, Administratrix.[136] An account was filed by Mrs. Jane Wren on October 20, 1818, and signed by George Millan, James Wren, Joseph Bennett, George Summers and Daniel Lewis.[137] In it William Wren is mentioned, and a notation shows that the coffin for Allen Wren was paid for on August 20, 1816. Names of the children born to Allen W. and Jane Wren, if any, are unknown.

(1326) Margaret Wren (Peggy), daughter of James Wren, Jr., and Elizabeth (Gunnell) Wren, died in 1833. She married in 1794,[138] Isaac Fox. Mr. Fox died in 1806. Issue:
(13261) John Fox, born November 24, 1795, died April 6, 1877. He married (1) in 1829, Matilda Barker (1810-1845); and (2) in 1847, Jane Hervey Summers (1821-1883). Issue: (*By Matilda Barker*)
   (132611) Elvira Fox (1831-1865) unmarried.

(132612) Adrianna Fox (1832-1880) married, in 1859, Mack Wooster and had issue one girl and two boys.
(132613) John Fox, Jr., born 1834.
(132614) Alfred Fox, born 1837, died in Pike's Peak, Colorado
(132615) Sydney Fox, born May 1839, died 1902. He married Frances (Fannie) Scott, issue:
    (1326151) Beulah Fox, married Hubert H. Halley and had one child, Lucille Halley.
    (1326152) Lucy Fox, married H. V. Baker, and had one child, Sydney Baker.
    (1326153) Alfred Maurice Fox, married his cousin, Alma Fox, daughter of William Hervey and Catherine Mildred (Johnson) Fox. He lived in Mineola, Missouri. Issue:
        (13261531) Frances Idelle Fox, married Robert Louis Clingerman, no issue.
        (13261532) Myldred Maurine Fox, married Frank Fairchild, and had issue: Virginia Dale and Maurine Fox Fairchild.
        (13261533) Sydney Eugene Fox, married Dorothy Evans, and had issue: Joan Janet, Judy Catherine, and Sydney Eugene Fox, Jr.
        (13261534) Alfred Maurice Fox, Jr., died at age 19 years.
    (1326254) Frank Fox, married Uda Oliver, issue: Clyde Fox and Alma Fox who married Lorenz Zink.
    (1326155) Scott Fox, married Ruth Miller, issue: Carolyn Fox.
    (1326156) Egland Fox, died in childhood.
    (1326157) Nettie Fox, died in childhood.
    (1326158) Eugenia Fox, died in childhood.
    (1326159) Clyde Fox, died in childhood.
(132616) Lucy Fox (1842-1881) married her cousin, Albert Wrenn, son of James Wrenn (IV) and Lucinda (Mitchell) Wrenn of "Flat Lick."

(*By Jane Hervey Summers*):
(132617) William Hervey Fox, born June 8, 1848, died 1928. He married (1) January 9, 1872, Catherine Mildred Johnson, of distinguished ancestry. She was a daughter of Moses and Susan Amanda (Childs) Johnson of Warrenton. Mrs. Fox had the following brothers and sisters: Robert F. Johnson; Nannie Johnson; William Johnson and James Mars Johnson (named for Lady Mars of Scotland, an ancestor). Mr. Fox remarried (2) on March 5, 1909, a cousin, Gertrude Taylor, daughter of Timothy and Georgiana (Fox) Taylor. Issue (*all by Catherine Mildred Johnson*):
    (1326171) Eugene Fox, died age 4 years.
    (1326172) Eolene Fox, died January 3, 1955, married R. W. (Webb) Baker of Mineola, Missouri, no issue.
    (1326173) Frank Fox, died age 1 year.
    (1326174) Alma Fox, married Alfred Maurice Fox.
    (1326175) Susan Jane Fox, living, 1955. She married, on December 18, 1901, Sydney Marvin Follin. Mr. Follin, a descendant of John Follin, Revolutionary Hero, was born May 23, 1875, and died January 5, 1931. He was a son of Albert F. and Catherine C. (Follin) Follin. Issue:
        (13261751) William Albert Follin, born October 18, 1903, died July 1910.
        (13261752) Katherine Olivia Follin, born April 22, 1905, married on August 5, 1933, John W. Greene. Issue: Susan Greene, born June 3, 1938 and Ellen Greene, born February 8, 1944.

(13261753) Eolene Rebecca Follin, born May 31, 1909, married Bernard Joseph Vincent (who died March 12, 1949). Issue: Michael Childs Vincent, born November 18, 1943.

(13261754) Dorothy Eleanor Follin, born February 27, 1911, married on January 26, 1935, Wilson P. (Scotty) Kilgore (who died in September, 1949). Issue: Susanne Kilgore, born September 28, 1940 and Camella Rae Kilgore, born February 23, 1946.

(13261755) Sydney Marvin Follin, Jr., married on January 10, 1942, Edna Vogt. Issue: Linda Jane (Follin) Thompson, born October 26, 1944; Sydney Marvin Follin, 3d, born March 10, 1945, died age 6 years; Wayne Sanford Follin, born June 3, 1948; and Melissa Eolene Follin, born October 7, 1952.

(13261756) Albert Fox Follin, married on November 16, 1936, Elsie Adrian. Issue: Joyce Gayle Follin, born September 30, 1937; Adrianne Charlotte Follin, born January 6, 1941; and Albert Fox Follin, Jr., born September 6, 1946.

(1326176) Bernard Johnson Fox, married on April 22, 1908, his cousin, Julia Hutchison, daughter of James E. and Gabrielanna (Wrenn) Hutchison. She was a granddaughter of Gabriel Adams and Julia Ann (Darne) Wrenn and of William A. and Martha Ann (Wrenn) Hutchison. Issue:

    (13261761) Mildred Rosebud Fox, married on November 23, 1935, Eugene Brown (no issue).

(1326177) Maurice William Fox, married on January 25, 1910, Wilhelmina Smith. Issue:

    (13261771) Catherine Jeanette (Kitty) Fox, married on June 28, 1937, Colonel Martin Levering Green, issue:

        (132617711) Martin Levering Green, Jr., born July 9, 1941.

        (132617712) Maurice Fox Green, born July 1, 1944.

        (132617713) Jeanette Trenholm Green, born December 31, 1947.

    (13261772) Wilma Aileen Fox, married on December 27, 1945, Walter Herman Rousch. Issue:

        (132617721) John H. Rousch, born May 18, 1949.

        (132617722) Walter Herman Rousch, Jr., born May 15, 1952.

    (1326178-9) Twins Fox, died in infancy.

(132618) Jane Elizabeth (Betty) Fox (1850-1925), married in 1877, Joseph Bennett and had issue: Summers Bennett (1879-1902).

(132619) Montgomery Fox, born 1856, died 1933, married on March 16, 1887, Frances (Fannie) Taylor. Issue:

    (1326191) Walter Fox, married on November 26, 1913, Ona Thompson, issue:

        (13261911) Margaret Fox, married on January 23, 1935, Isaac Fletcher (issue: Margaret Anne Fletcher).

        (13261912) Corliss Fox, married on June 17, 1944, Louise Shuttz (issue: Richard Fox, Donald Fox and Roland Fox).

    (1326192) Emily Fox, died in youth.

    (1326193) Corliss Fox, died in World War I.

    (1326194) Jane Hervey Fox, married J. M. (Mac) McMahon, issue: Betty Ann McMahon and Maurice Joseph McMahon.

(13261.10) Laura Fox, married her cousin, Gabriel Hite Wrenn.

(13261.11) Isaac N. Fox (1858-1900) married Annie Studds, no issue.

(13261.12) Rufus Fox (1860-1944) married in 1897, Annie Guy Horton (died 1933)

Issue: Edith Fox, died as a child; Ruth E. Fox, married on September 8, 1920, Roy Wise, no issue; and Isaac Fox.

(13261.13) Walter Fox (1851-1852).

(13262) James Fox, son of Isaac and Margaret (Wren) Fox, married Ann (Nancy) Millan, on November 6, 1828. She was a daughter of Thomas and Susanna (Summers) Millan of "Oakley," and born April 4, 1806. Mr. Fox died August 12, 1878. Issue:

(132621) Georgiana Fox, married Timothy Taylor, issue:

(1326211) Annie Taylor, married William Steibeling.

(1326212) Gertrude Taylor, married her cousin, William Hervey Fox.

(1326213) James Taylor, died unmarried.

(132622) Lyle Fox, married Susan Rigg and moved to Missouri.

(132623) Gertrude Fox, unmarried.

(132624) Hervey Fox, unmarried.

(132625) Jennie Fox, unmarried.

(1328) William Wren, son of James Wren, Jr., and Verlinda (Barry) Wren, died in Kentucky, unmarried, in 1832. Mr. Wren was a dealer in horses and was in Lexington, Kentucky, by 1818. Several of his letters are extant and follow:

(This letter is torn)

"July the 10 1832

Dear Brother

I take my pen in hand to inform you of the death of Brother William he taken sick Last summer we was to see him and staid a week he got so he could go about he wishd us to live with him again as he had ever done the prospect was gloomy we told him we would go home and do the fall sewing and then we would go and stay the winter winter (sic) with him thinking we would live with him again as to appearance his health was gone but he did not send for us for —— several Reasons in febuary he Left that place and Boarded —— ather admitted of his Comeing to Lexenton he mentioned he wishd us to live with him a little before this he hierd out his woman and girl we thought we was not to do the house work and wait on him his health was bad though he could go about we afterwards thought(t) we we (sic) would live with him and told him if he could get a house we would live with him but he could not get such as suited. We had but one Room and that upstairs wich did not suit him as it was with difficulty he could get up and down the steps we told him we would go in the country with him wich we would Rather have done he then concluded he would go 4 miles in the country and Board with a man he had been acquainted with ever since he had been in the state intending comeing back in about a month before that time he was taken very ill we was sent for Jane went he was better when she got there she sould not stay with him as she was not well I was unwell at that time the person he was with promisd to Let us know weather he got better or worse. Brother had a boy with him we heard once he was still better—the ninth day the news came he was dead the Reason they gave for not sending for us was they saw but little alteration only he got weaker the day before he died he walkd from one bed to one and talkd pearter than he had done for some days—he has not Left much property there is one old Black man and woman I expect between fifty and sixty years old there is one boy and girl that is grown or nearly so one hors and waggon he had not one cent of money that we know of from what we can see from his papers there is but very little oweing about here; what Claims may Come against the state we cant tell he has sufferd by going security for Benjamin Grafford and I expect others his papers shows he has payd hundreds of dollars about the Land suit of Lanes heirs this I would sopose might be Recoverd: you have a better chance to know than any person here in consequence if there misfortunes and the disapointments we met with in Receiving money from Virginia he had to sell a likely young woman we have heard Bro. William say several times he had expected money from you and was at a loss to know the cause of your not sending it. I think papers shows you have several hundred dollars in your hands—the memorandom states you had Collected six hundred and seventy nine dollars and 37 cents; I seen in one Letter you sent 145 Dollars I likewise saw where you had paid John Woster one hundred dol. and Mr. Pritchard seventy dollars and Robertson ten. You may have collected this memorandom money since you paid Woster this you know I hope—be hurt with me I have give you a true statement of what is here or there, may be some little articles I have omitted: I saw in one of your Letters that you was dissatisfied about some Land Bro. William sold of our fathers I have Read a letter from Ann —— to William that Dunlap had been there and denied W. power to sell the Land and that his father had bought it again from (Jun?) and and (sic) Requested W. to come down and let them know what they had to depend on this Letter was dated 1828: Brother Left no will we want to hear from you all what fix is to be made; I expect there is not one as needy as Jane and myself and there is not one that had the trouble with his horses that we had we work hard and we have no dependance now but our work we had though(t) before we found you had money in your hands that you and sister Peggy Relinguish your part to us—I would sopose B. Thomas would never think of wanting one cent I would likewise think B. John would not especialy as he had a boy of fathers I tho-- is account (amount?) against him here we have heard nothing of B. Richard since you mentioned he had gone to the Ohio if you have heard please to inform us; there is Roberts children we mention this as you may all make up your minds and Let us know. A person we heard a few days past that Mr. Askins family was well as Common Nancy dont have her health Betsy is married and has a son; Sister Jane nor myself don't enjoy good health: we want to hear from you all I hope you will write as soon as you can after you get this Letter: I now Leave this subject and turn my attention to Religion it has been our Consolation under discourageing Circumstances I bless the Lord we have a sure hope that when we are done with this world we shall be admitted in our heavenly fathers kingdom where sorrow nor pain will never be felt a(nd) may we meet one and all of you in that Blest world

(another page missing?)

The following letter, concerning the death of William Wren, was written by Allen W. Wren, son of James Wren, Jr., and Elizabeth (Gunnell) Wren (thus a half-brother to William Wren):

Address: Lexington January 10 Kentucky (stamp mark) 25
Mr. James Wrenn
Fairfax County Virga
Near the Court House in said Cty.

Dr Sr (Dear Sir) I have enclosd order on Those men who I left Notes in the hands of Thos Wren on — he informs me the Notes are lost if so or Not, do all you can to obtain the Money, as I doe not want him to collect it, as I have to pay the money that that (sic) was intended to pay, I have been in Virga twist since last Aprill, with

Horses, and shall start again about the middle of Febuary, and perhaps may be in Fairfax. The Girls are well, allso John, & Askins, & Family. Askins had the Barn burnt where he lives, loss to him $120. Nancy has been much dissatisyed, she has not had good health and Askins conduct been disagreeable, has been measurable the Cause, The Girls appeare to be satisfyed,—There is a plenty of preaching in the Neighbourhood, they have not had a letter from you, they appear to wish to hear from you, there oald mare I expect started to Virga in the summer she has run of(f) Askuns hired the oald woman for 40$ pr. year. Frank has been hired several times and returnd, he hardly Earns his Victuals & Clothes, if you Collect the Money, there will be Considerable Interest, corn (cane?) are selling heare from nine to twelve shillings pr. Busl. Askins made about 300 Balls. & about 20001. Toba (tobacco), the latter all burnt & his Hay, Fodder, Gear &c—I did not recollect pools given name, Insert it in the order, I should be glad to heare from you

Yours with Respect<br>Wm. Wren

Fayette County Jan. 10th 1818

Messrs. Wm & Guy Broadwater Gentl. Please to pay to my Brother James Wren the Amt. of your Note given to me in the Fall of the year 1815 for $85 and his Receipt shall be good for The same & in full discharge of said Note—

Jan.y 10th 1818— Yours &c<br>Wm. Wren

Mssrs. James Williams & Benja. R. Davis
Gentlm. Please to pay my brother James Wren the Amt. of your Note given to me in the Fall of The year 1815 for $52.50 and his Receipt shall be good for The same and in full discharge of said Note—    Yours &c
Jany. 10th 1818—    Wm. Wren

Mssrs            Pool and John Standhope   Gentlm.
Please to pay to my Brother James Wren The Amts. of your Three notes for Twenty dollars each given to me in The Fall of the Yeare 1815, and his Receipt shall be good for The same and in full discharge of said Note—

Yours &c

Jny. 10th 1818.    Wm. Wren
Mr. Jno Wren
Orange Ct. House 25th March 1822

Sir I Intended to come on to Fairfax, and perhaps may, But uncertain Meeting with Mr. Shortrigner (?), who will Deliver you some papers, which I wish you to act on, as I could myself—which are related To a Debt, or Debts due me from B. R. Davis whom I am Inform'd am Dead—I wish, you to apply for the money. If not Obtained, to Bring suit, &c, Get Robt. Wren will prove the contract,—that he was to Forward the papers from the Office of Fairfax to Enable me to Obtain the Money & *He* has not sent on the papers.

Respectfully &c

In Haste (all well)    Wm. Wren
Mr. Jno. Wren

July 21st 1824    Lexington (?) Kentucky

Dr. Sir. I have been long looking for a letter from you, to Inform me the situation of my affairs there, Respecting money owing me, I have wrote to you, to Inform the situation thereof; a considerable time past, and have not recd. an answr Though Angeious (anxious) to hear from you on that subject. Being in particular want of the money, most particular on our sisters acct., I have been, trading and severally from home, seing they have been with me, which is Disagreeable to them, only haveing a Negro or two with them, I have Just purchased two or three negores, and if I could get the money, under your care, I shall purchase a place this fall & settle myself for life, which, is but short, agreeable to the cours(e) of nature, but have a wish to make them comfortable, as they Depend on me only. If you have recd. the money for me, and willing to part from it, as to parting from it, you will understand me, from what was namd in my former Letter) If you have any for me the most speedy way, and the safest, at least a plan that I would greatly prefer, would be to Deposit it in United States Branch Bank in Washington Cty., to my Credit and and (sic) send me the Cashiers Certificate of Deposit. It must be in my name or I cannot make use of It, if Executed in this way I can get the money from our Merchants, amediately after the receipt thereof—I hope you will not fast writing to me (?) amediatly on the subject, as I am Truly ancious to hear from you, we are all well. Askins & Family allso, our Brother John, I have not heard from for nine Months, (he?) has sold Hundly, I do not Know who to nor where he is, I Expect he has Been Taken Down the river to Orleans, to prevent M. Foxs Geting him.

              Yours with Respecs &c.
Mr. James Wren         Wm. Wren"

(1329) Richard Wren, son of James Wren, Jr., and Verlinda (Barry) Wren, was born in 1792 in Fairfax County, and died in Ohio in 1850. Mr. Wren married Martha (Pattie) Peake (1796-1850), a daughter of George and Fannie (Sears) Peake.[139] They were in Northfield, Brandywine, Portage County, Ohio, by 1836. Issue (*probably others*):

(13291) Alfred Wren, married ——.
(13292) Amanda Wren, married ——.
(13293) Martha (Patty) Wren, married ——.
(13294) Richard Cornelius Wren (1816-1894), married on January 1, 1840, Mary Magdaline Kenninger (1820-1894). Their children included Lucinda Jane Wren (1846-1935), who married in 1867, at Waverly, Missouri, Thompson G. Martin. A daughter of this couple, Winifred Martin, married Glenn F. May.

The following is a letter which Richard Wren sent his brother James (note—he apparently used the Wrenn spelling of the surname):

    "Northfield Brandywine  Portage Co. Ohio  October the 28 1836
Brother

I take this opportunity of informing you that we yet Live and are injoying good health at this time for which we ought To Be very thankfull to our preserver of Life and health. We hope those Lines will find you and all the family Injoying the same With all the Rest of our friends. Patty, Mother and Sister Mary Lives in part of our house and Likewise Alfred and his Familly; Amandy is Married and Lives in one Mile and half; the Rest is not home. We are in 20 Miles of the Lake Erie it is very healthy But cold. We had very Cold and Wete spring owing to that the Crops of Corn is short wheat and oats are Good. Wheat is worth $1.25 cents per Bushel Corn 75 cents oats 37½. I think it a Better Country than Virginia. I should like it Better If the winter Season was not so Long we have to feed our stock From five to six Months; Cattle sell high Milk Cows from 15 to 30 Dollars and other Cattle in proportion. Pork sells at Six Dollars per hundred; I have often wishd we had some of the potomac fish. I (could?) a Bought four hundred Bushel of wheat this year or bought five hundred of oats. I think we will have about 7 hundred of corn 300-50 Bushels of potatoes. We will Be glad to hear from you and wish you to inform us Respec(t)ing of all our Relations. If you have heard from our Sister in kentucky I will be glad to here. I will Be glad if you Will try to find out of Sandiford Paines family What part of Kentucky the Peake family Live and Let me know. We all joyn In Love to you and Nancy all of the family and our friends

                                                Richd. Wrenn

Brandywine Mills O. Oct 27   25
                    Mr. James Wrenn
          Fairfax County Virginia Providence Post Office "

(133) (Colonel) John Wren, son of Colonel James and Catherine (Brent) Wren, died about 1815. He married Elizabeth (Gunnell?).

On March 23, 1786, John Wren of Fairfax County, and Elizabeth, his wife, conveyed 275 acres to James Hurst. This tract was an original patent of Gerrard Trammell and William Harle. Trammell and Harle sold it to the Reverend John Moncure of Stafford and he devised it to his daughters Ann Moncure and Jane, wife of James Wood. The latter two conveyed to Wren. Witnesses: James Wren, Charles Broadwater, Thomas Pearson, John West and Charles Lewis Broadwater.[140]

On the same day, John Wren conveyed to James Hurst an additional portion of the same tract which he had purchased from Ann and Jane Moncure (the latter married Wood) of Overwharton Parish, Stafford County, on January 23, 1775. This land, 347 acres, was the tract whereon Samuel Talbott[141] lived, and was part of a patent owned by Gerrard Trammell and William Harle. This was leased to Wren during the lives of the said John Wren, Mary his daughter, and Thomas his son, etc. Witnesses: James Wren, Charles Broadwater, Thomas Pearson, John West, and Charles Lewis Broadwater.[142]

John Wren received several tracts of land by the Will of his father. These includ- that land purchased from James Hurst (excepting one-quarter acre given the Methodists) and that adjoining Benjamin Dulany, Colonel Charles Broadwater, and Colonel Charles Little. Colonel James Wren also gave his son land adjoining Charles Lee and Thomas Lindsay and the home place following the death of his step-mother (this was "Long View"). He also gave him land purchased from Andrew Rousavill and slaves.

On February 28, 1806, John Wren conveyed to James Horseman, for $350.00, a Negro named Sam. (Witnesses: John DeBell, and Thomas Violett.[143]) A family tradition states that John Wren died from the effects of drinking bad water while in the Army during the War of 1812.

Colonel John and Elizabeth Wren had issue *(probably others)*:
(1331) John S. Wren, married Sarah Hite.
(1332) Verlinda Wren.[144]
(1333) Mary Wren (eldest child).
(1334) Thomas Wren.

   (1331) John S. Wren, son of Colonel John and Elizabeth Wren, died at "Long View," in 1822. In early life he may have lived in Rockingham County. One descendant found deeds of 1797 and 1806 for John Wren in Rockingham. By 1813 he was in Fairfax County but retained landed interests in Rockingham County.

An *Account* of John Wren's estate was filed on February 19, 1825 (by Court Order of December, 1824), by Thomas Moss, Administrator.[145] This shows that a sale was held on January 12, 1822, and the coffin was paid for on July 22, 1822. Also mentioned was the balance due John Dulin (from a legacy of Colonel James Wren to William Dulin); the same to Sarah Hughes, Administrator; also to Isaac Harrison, John Hite, Jacob Snider and wife; and the balance due to Hugh B. Wren, "in part of James Wrens legacy d(itt)o."

An Inventory of the estate of John Wren was filed by Thomas Moss, J. McLain, John Johnson, and Daniel F. Dulany.[146] The Sale Account of May 19, 1823, contains the names of numerous neighbors, among whom were: William Nelson, Sarah Wren, Robert Darne, Samuel Childs, W. Ball, Joseph Sewell, Robert Blackborn, Samuel Shreve, Joseph Birch, Armistead Donaldson, William Payne, Richard Kirby, George Crump, and James Wren.

John S. Wren married Sarah Hite, of an old Valley family,[147] in Frederick County on January 14, 1790. Sarah S. Wren died in 1843. She made her will on April 15, 1842, and it was probated on May 15, 1843.[148] In this document she mentions some of her children: Susan, Elizabeth, Charles B., Jane Davis, George W. (and his wife, Catherine A.); and Albert Wren. The last named was to serve as Executor, and witnesses were: James Thrift and John Crump. Purchasers from her estate included the following neighbors and relatives:[149] James Donaldson, Colonel Crump, Charles Wren, Col. William Minor, Joseph Birch, Susan Wren, Robert Birch, William Skidmore, Lewis Skidmore, Samuel Birch, Jr., Nathan Thompson, Presley Haycock, John Darne, George Thompson, Thomas Wren, and William Birch.

In Fairfax County[150] records there is an interesting law suit showing that Robert and Verlinda (Wren) Darne, and James Wren, instituted suit against their mother, Sarah S. Wren, and others, on October 18, 1831, to force a division of the estate of John S. Wren, of Fairfax County, and "late of Fauquier County," deceased. Other parties to the suit were: Susan Wren, Elizabeth Wren, George W. Wren, John H. Wren, Albert Wren, Horatio Nelson Wren, Evalina Wren, Mary Jane Wren, Julia Ann Wren, Charles B. Wren, and "absent," Hugh B. and Harriet Wren. By a decree of Court, 1/3rd of the land "commonly called Winter Hill," was to be owned by Sarah Wren, widow of John Wren, in right of her dower. Out of the "Mansion House tract" on Shreve Road were carved a number of lots by Commissioners James Hunter, Robert Hunter, Nicholas Darne, and Mottrom Ball. The "Mansion House tract" was "Long View," on Shreve Road, and boundaries at the time of suit included the land of Thomas Lindsay ("Now Swink"), Wren, Sewell, Moxley, Dulany, Walters, and stakes "south of the Falls Church road."

There is an interesting record of some of this land which was condemned by the Middle Turnpike Company, and it is shown (by record of March 19, 1829) that Nelson Wren, Evalina Wren, Jane Wren, Julia Wren, and Charles Wren (under the age of 21 years, and with no guardian), and Hugh B. Wren (by Harriet his wife), the latter not in Fairfax County, "all having an interest as children and heirs of John Wren, deceased, were notified of action by the Company." This document shows that "no damages" were sustained.[151] On July 19, 1830, Thomas Blackburn made oath that on the 9th he delivered to Elizabeth Wren, George W. Wren, and Charles Wren, a true copy of a notice concerning land condemned by the Turnpike Company, "damages awarded," and this was returned on July 15, 1830.[152]

John S. Wren had issue:

(13311) James Wren, married (1) Sarah McCarty Lee; and (2) Mariah Williams.
(13312) Verlinda Wren, married (Captain) Robert Darne.
(13313) John Hite Wren, married Lucinda Davis.
(13314) Harriet Wren, married a cousin, Hugh Brent Wren, and died in Missouri, without issue, before June, 1839 (see Fairfax County, *Chancery Suit 22, Darne vs. Wren,* filed in June, 1839).
(13315) Susannah Wren, married Robert Reid. Mrs. Reid and several small children died from small pox. Mr. Reid conveyed his interest in "Long View" to the Wren heirs. The Reids lived in a house later owned by Smith Harrell, which was torn down during the 1950's.
(13316) Elizabeth Wren, married Robert Lindsay (*see Lindsay*).
(13317) George Washington Wren, married Catherine Ann Lee, a daughter of Hancock and Sinah Ellen (Chichester) Lee, thus a sister of Sarah McCarty Wren who married James Wren, a brother of George.
(13318) Albert Wren, married (1) Mary Coward; (2) Sally Sisson; and (3) Elizabeth M. Lewis.
(13319) Mary Jane Wren, married Norman R. Davis.
(1331.10) Charles Brent Wren, married Catherine Lindsay.
(1331.11) Julia Ann Wren, married Thomas Sanford Wren.
(1331.12) Evalina Wren, married William Wren.
(1331.13) Horatio Nelson Wren, married Phoebe ——.

(13311) James Wren, son of John S. and Sarah (Hite) Wren, was born in 1796,[15.] and died in Callaway County, Missouri, in 1875. He settled in Callaway County in 1833, along with a large number of former Fairfax County residents. Mr. Wren married (1) Sarah McCarty Lee; and (2) Dec. 5, 1870, Mariah Williams, widow. His first wife, Sarah McCarty Lee, was a daughter of Hancock and Sinah (Chichester) Lee; and a granddaughter of Kendall and Betty (Heale) Lee. Her mother, Sinah Ellen Chichester, was a daughter of Colonel Richard and Sarah (McCarty) Chichester of Fairfax County, of prominent families. Mrs. Hancock Lee made her will on July 12, 1851, probated at Fairfax on August 18, 1851.[154] George Washington Wren, brother to this James Wren, married Catherine A. Lee, sister to Sarah McCarty (Lee) Wren. On October 5, 1833, James Wren and Sarah McCarty Wren his wife, deeded to her mother, Sinah Ellen Lee, for $400.00, a tract of 113 acres and 100 poles of land, formerly Lee property. Witnesses were William A. Wren, John H. Wren, and William Lee.[155] On March 13, 1839, James and Sarah M. Wren of Callaway County, Missouri, sold to Robert Darne for $150.00, Lot #4 of the division of the estate of "the father of said James," and known as "Cedar Grove," containing 39 acres.[156]

James Wren served in the War of 1812, and left an honorable record.

James and Sarah McCarty (Lee) Wren had issue:
(133111) Sarah E. Wren, married Honorable William J. Jackson.
(133112) James Wren.
(133113) Mary C. Wren.
(133114) John E. Wren.

(133111) Sarah E. Wren, daughter of James and Sarah McCarty (Lee) Wren, was married October 31, 1839, to the Honorable William J. Jackson.[157] Mr. Jackson, a native of Kentucky, was born July 14, 1818, son of Richard B. and Clarissa (Greenwell) Jackson. William J. and Sarah E. (Wren) Jackson had issue:

(1331111) Henrietta Jackson, married W.W. McCall.
(1331112) Eleanor A. Jackson, married J.B. Goodrich.
(1331113) Eldorado Jackson, married Robert Berry.
(1331114) Sallie Jackson, married John S. Payne.
(1331115) Kittie Lee Jackson.
(1331116) Ida W. Jackson.
(1331117) William J. Jackson, Jr.

(13313) John Hite Wren, son of John S. and Sarah (Hite) Wren, was born about 1799, and died in Fairfax County in 1836. Mr. Wren made his will on February 8, 1836, probated June 18, 1836.[158] In it he mentions his wife, Lucinda, his children (not named), his brother, George Washington Wren, and his wife's brother, Norman Davis. The last two named were appointed Executors. Witnesses were: Lee H. Monroe, George Beard, Robert Blackburn, and John Blackburn. An *Appraisement* of his estate was returned on October 12, 1836, by William Warren Ball, John Haycock, and John Horseman.[159]

Mr. Wren married, in 1833, Lucinda Davis, a daughter of Benjamin Reeder and Jane (Monroe) Davis. Mrs. Wren moved to Callaway County, Missouri, in 1837, taking her two infants with her, and lived there with her brother, Norman Reeder Davis, who married Mary Jane Wren. Mrs. Lucinda (Davis) Wren remarried (2) in 1838, William Dyson;[160] and (3) in 1863, Joseph Everhart. She died on April 11, 1899.[161]

On February 10, 1860, John W. Cook and Sarah Jane (Wren) his wife, John Reeder Wren, and Fannie C., his wife, all of Callaway County, Missouri, sold land in Fairfax County (at Falls Church) to Joseph E. Birch, containing 27 acres, 2 roods, and 32 poles.[162] This land was part of the Birch tract (now including 312 East Broad Street), and is called "Winter Hill," having been part of that estate. Mention is made in the deed of the mother, Lucinda, and the late father, John H. Wren.

John H. and Lucinda (Davis) Wren had issue:
(133131) John Reeder Wren, married Fannie Catherine ——
(133132) Sarah Jane Wren, married (1) Reverend John William Cook, and (2) Henry H. Hayden.

(133131) John Reeder Wren, son of John H. and Lucinda (Davis) Wren, was born in Fairfax County, Virginia, in 1836, and was taken to Missouri by his mother when he was one year old. He married in Callaway County, Missouri, to Fannie Catherine ——. Children:
(1331311) Sally Wren, born 1858, married J. H. Buchanan.
(1331312) Lucy Wren, born 1860, married Charles Craig.
(1331313) Alice Wren, born 1863, married George Garrett.
(1331314) John Reeder Wren, Jr., is said to have married and left descendants.

(133132) Sarah Jane Wren, daughter of John H. and Lucinda (Davis) Wren, was born in Fairfax County, Virginia, May 25, 1834, and was taken to Missouri in 1837 by her Mother. She died in Fulton, Missouri, August 10, 1910. A picture of her, owned by her grandson, John Wren Cook, shows that she was a lovely woman with thick dark hair. She married (1) in 1852, to the Reverend John William Cook of the Methodist Church. Mr. Cook was born in Greens County, Alabama, August 4, 1830, and died in the Confederate Service in June, 1862. He was the founder of churches in St. Charles, and Montgomery City, Missouri. Mrs. Cook remarried (2)

in 1870, Henry H. Hayden. He died in 1905, and they did not have children. The Reverend John William and Sarah Jane (Wren) Cook had issue:
(1331321) Willie Cook, died in infancy.
(1331322) Eddie Cook, died at age 10 years.
(1331323) Della Cook, died in infancy.
(1331324) Emma Price Cook, married George W. Lee.
(1331325) John Wilson Cook, married Mary Ann Crump.

(1331324) Emma Price Cook, daughter of the Reverend John William and Sarah Jane (Wren) Cook, was born in Callaway County, Missouri, September 1, 1860, and died in 1905. She married, in 1889, George W. Lee. George W. and Emma Price (Cook) Lee had issue:
(13313241) Earl Lee, born June 7, 1892.
(13313242) Ruth Lee, born March 8, 1895, married Bert Valentine, and she died in 1931.
(13313243) Lillian Lee, born October 10, 1897, married Grady Nun.
(13313244) Lucille Lee, twin of Lillian, born October 10, 1897, married James Strather.
(13313245) Sarah Lee, born April 17, 1900, married Edbert Betts.

(1331325) John Wilson Cook, son of the Reverend John William and Sarah Jane (Wren) Cook, was born in Callaway County, Missouri, January 12, 1863, and died August 3, 1953. He married, on February 2, 1887, Mary Ann Crump. She was born January 1, 1868, died November 6, 1931.[163] Child:
(13313251) John Wren Cook, born in Callaway County, Missouri, April 27, 1906, married on September 5, 1929, to Lorraine Adele Ford [164] daughter of James G. and Anna Leora (Armstrong) Ford. Mr. and Mrs. Cook are living currently in Alexandria, having moved here in 1957 from Missouri. Children:
   (133132511) John Ford Cook, born October 7, 1931, Mexico, Missouri. He married on January 4, 1952, Betty Wise, of Piedmont, California. Children:
      (1331325111) Sherrill Ann Cook, born August 8, 1955.
      (1331325112) John Wilson Cook, born November, 1957.
   (133132512) Jan Wilson Cook, born July 25, 1936, Fulton, Missouri, married on June 7, 1958, Lore Mulhauser.

(13318) Albert Wren ("Cooney Albert"), son of John S. and Sarah (Hite) Wren, died in 1892 and is buried in an unmarked grave in Oakwood Cemetery, Falls Church. Mr. Wren married three times: (1) in Trinity Methodist Episcopal Church, Alexandria, Mary Coward; (2) Sally Sisson; and (3) in Washington, D.C., November 2, 1857, Elizabeth M. Lewis.

His second wife, Sally (Sisson) Wren, was born in Fairfax County in 1824, a daughter of Robert T. and Minta (Boswell) Sisson,[165]and died in child-birth on August 20, 1854. Mrs. Elizabeth M. (Lewis) Wren, the third wife, died December 9, 1892.

Mr. Wren built a home on a portion of the "Long View" estate which is now included in the "King David" section of National Memorial Park Cemetery. This house burned about 1854. In 1855 Mr. Wren erected another house on the site which was later the home on S. V. Rollins. This last house, which stood on a hill surrounded by holly trees, was torn down in 1952 when land was cleared for cemetery expansion. The 1855 house was a story-and-half building.

There are numerous deeds to and from Albert Wren on record. Among those most helpful to the genealogist are those dealing with the estate of his father. On December 20, 1839, Charles B. and Catherine H. Wren conveyed Lot #11 to Albert Wren.[166] On February 24, 1838, Albert and Mary Wren deeded Lot #2 to Susan Wren.[167]

On March 29, 1842, William B. Adams of Kentucky, Johnson S. Adams of Illinois, and Thornton W. Adams (the latter a brother of William B. Adams) conveyed land on Little Pimmitt Run and a new Mill to Albert Wren. This land was allotted to John Adams, deceased, in the distribution of the estate of Samuel Adams, deceased.[168] On August 4, 1845,[169] Albert Wren conveyed to Thomas L. Orr land on the headwaters of Holmes Run (corner of Henry Fairfax and Wren in Sewell's line), and mention is made of a dispute between Albert Wren and Mrs. Sarah M. Sewell, this being the same land sold by Charles B. Wren to Albert Wren on December 20, 1839 (recorded January 20, 1849).

Albert Wren served in the Confederate Army and his picture is elsewhere in this book.

Mr. Wren made his will on March 17, 1889, probated in February, 1892.[170] In it he mentioned his wife, Elizabeth, and children: George W. Wren, John W. Wren, and Lewis E. Wren. Witnesses were: J. W. Roby, J. A. Caton and Thomas H. Walker.

Albert Wren had issue: (*By Mary Coward*)
(133181) Ann Azalia Wren, born December 17, 1831, died unmarried.
(133182) John Washington Wren, born January 20, 1836, died young.
(133183) James William Wren, born December 5, 1837, and may have died while serving in the Confederate Army. One full brother of John Wesley Wren died during the war, name not recalled.
(133184) John Wesley Wren, married Lucy Salina Payne.
(133185) Nelson H. Wren, born November 24, 1842, no other record.
(133186) Mary Jane Wren, born October 23, 1844.

(*By Sally Sisson*):
(133187) George Washington Wren, married Caroline Bezler.

(*By Elizabeth M. Lewis*):
(133188) Lewis Edward Wren, married Mary D. Milholland. (There was a child by Sally Sisson which died in infancy).

(133184) John Wesley Wren, son of Albert and Mary (Coward) Wren, was born February 21, 1840, and died June 21, 1917, at Falls Church. He is buried in Oakwood Cemetery. Mr. Wren married Lucy Salina Payne, daughter of James and Hannah (Adams) Payne. (*See Payne*). Mrs. Wren was born November 17, 1839, and died April 21, 1898. Issue:
(1331841) Elwin Parker Wren, married Georgie Alice Faulkner.
(1331842) Wyatt Adams Wren, married Elizabeth McCuen. Mr. Wren was born November 24, 1868, and died in 1943 with burial in Oakwood Cemetery. No issue.
(1331843) Delfina Wren, married William Gotleib Berg.
(1331844) Ann Salina Wren, married Eugene Kirby Philips.
(1331845) Rufus Wesley Wren, married (1) May A. Philips; and (2) Katherine S. Foster.

(1331841) Elwin Parker Wren ("John"), born June 14, 1864, died March 24, 1956. Mr. Wren married, on December 16, 1886, Georgie Alice Faulkner of Chesterbrook. Mrs. Wren was born March 17, 1864, and died February 17, 1935. She was a daughter of George and Sarah (Hager) Faulkner. Mr. Wren was reared at Dunn Loring in the old home place of Albert Wren. Issue (*some use Wrenn*):

(13318411) Howard Parker Wrenn, born November 2, 1887, died August 18, 1944. He married on November 24, 1909, Mary Katherine Zimmerman, issue:
    (133184111) Dorothy Catherine Wrenn, born October 1, 1910, married Joseph J. O'Meara (issue: Michael Patrick O'Meara).
    (133184112) Glen Howard Wrenn, born January 12, 1913, married Virginia Erwin, no issue.
    (133184113) George Elwin Wrenn, born January 15, 1922, married a cousin, Betty Hall, issue: George Wrenn.
    (133184114) Betty Lou Wrenn, born May 8, 1925, married Lloyd Henry, issue: William Henry and another son.
(13318412) Frederick Clements Wren, born February 16, 1889, married on January 18, 1909, Lucy Esther Loomis, issue:
    (133184121) Esther Wren, born November 13, 1909, died February 21, 1933. Married Ralph Bennie, issue: Ralph Thomas Bennie, born September 29, 1928.
    (133184122) Willis Frederick Wren, born December 19, 1911, died the next day.
    (133184123) Minnie Elizabeth Wren, born June 8, 1913.
    (133184124) Thelma Verona Wren, born September 4, 1919, married Orrin K. Rhodes, issue: Kenneth Edward Rhodes, Wayne Rhodes, Milton Orrin Rhodes, Peggy Ann Rhodes, Judith Lee Rhodes, Larry Kemper Rhodes, Patricia May Rhodes, and Roy Eugene Rhodes.
(13318413) Ethel Eleanor Wren, born October 14, 1891, married on June 17, 1914, David Frederick Wetzel. Mr. Wetzel was born in Georgetown, D.C., July 8, 1889, a son of Charles Frederick and Clara (Jones) Wetzel. No issue. Mrs. Ethel Wetzel owns the Bible presented to Elwin P. Wren by his Aunt, Jane A. Payne. This Bible contains the birth dates of the children of Albert Wren. It also records the death of Martha Ellen Hutchins, March 10, 1856 (relationship unknown). The Bible was published in 1854 by the American Bible Society.
(13318414) Marian Evelyn McGregor Wren, born April 21, 1894, married (1) on April 21, 1914, Francis Joseph Schwalenberg; and (2) Leon Hager. Issue: Francis Elgin Schwalenberg, born April 16, 1915; and Ralph Joseph Schwalenberg, born August 4, 1918.

    (1331843) Delfina Wren, daughter of John Wesley and Lucy Salina (Payne) Wren was born April 20, 1870 and died February 19, 1941. She married on April 16, 1890, William Gotleib Berg. Mr. Berg was born June 23, 18—. Issue:
(13318431) Wade Hampton Berg, born January 22, 1891, died at Shadyside, Maryland, April 18, 1959. He was survived by his wife, Caroline R. Berg.
(13318432) Anne Salina Berg, born January 30, 1893, died July 16, 1959. She married (1) Washington Columbus Herdle and (2) John F. Jennings. Issue: Child Herdle, died in infancy; Child Herdle, died in infancy; Louise Delfina Herdle, married Thomas Gilbert Walker; Ann F. Jennings, married —— Umphries; Joseph F. Jennings and John F. Jennings.
(13318433) Louise Henrietta Berg, born September 15, 1896, married —— Powers
(13318434) William Wesley Berg, born September 24, 1898. (This information was supplied by Mrs. Annie Jennings).

    (1331844) Ann Salina Wren, daughter of John Wesley and Lucy Salina (Payne) Wren, was born June 14, 1874, and died March 13, 1950. She married Eugene Kirby Philips (1871-1946), a son of Charles Wesley and Rhoda (Kirby) Philips *(See Kirby)*. Issue:

(13318441) James Albert Philips, born November 19, 1899, married on June 22, 1922, Lona Maybelle Furlong, a cousin. Mrs. Philips was a daughter of Charles H. and Mary E. (Reid) Furlong, and a descendant of Thomas Sanford and Julia Ann (Wren) Wren. Issue:
   (133184411) Charles Wilbur Philips, born March 2, 1925, married (1) Mary Elizabeth —— and (2) ——.
   (133184412) James Irving Philips, born November 16, 1926.
   (133184413) Roy Eugene Philips, born April 27, 1929, married in June 1950, Norine Kidwell, issue: Peggy Lee Philips, Shirley Ann Philips, and Norma Jean Philips.
   *Note:* Lona Maybelle (Furlong) Philips was born August 25, 1905 and remarried (2) George Edward Kushnereit on November 10, 1950.
(13318442) Lois Eugenia Philips, burn July 17, 1905, married on September 8, 1926, John Henry Vetter. He was born April 21, 1904, a son of Jacob and Mary Elizabeth (Swartz) Vetter of Strasburg, Virginia. Issue:
   (133184421) Elizabeth Ann Vetter, born September 8, 1927, married on July 26, 1952, Marvin Alfred Poole (born April 5, 1926). Issue: Dennis Alfred Poole, born July 22, 1956.
   (133184422) Alvin Eugene Vetter, born January 30, 1930, married on May 1, 1951, Anna Virginia Harris (born July 3, 1930).

(1331845) Rufus Wesley Wren ("Jim"), son of John Wesley and Lucy Salina (Payne) Wren, was born October 23, 1876, and died at his home, 3307 North Rochester Street, Falls Church, June 15, 1960. Mr. Wren married (1) May A. Philips (1875-1930) daughter of Charles Wesley and Rhoda (Kirby) Philips *(See Kirby).* He married (2) Mrs. Katherine S. Foster, widow. (She had issue including: Mrs. Pearl Kochlek, Mrs. Emma M. Wren, Mrs. Myrtle Crawford, and Mrs. Mildred D. Barricman.) Issue *(By May A. Philips):*
(13318451) Irene Wren, married Morrell Magarity, and had issue including: Eugene, Chester, and Robert Magarity.
(13318452) Cline E. Wren, married Emma Foster (daughter of Mrs. Rufus Wesley Wren by her first marriage). Issue: James, Betty, Norma Jean, Catherine, Virginia, Robert, William and Irene Wren.
(13318453) Virginia Wren, married George William Snyder (Buck) Frazier, no issue.
(13318454) Joseph E. Wren (1917-1924).
(13318455) Wyatt W. Wren (1910-1936).
(13318456) Annette Wren, married William Karns.
(Data supplied by Rufus Wesley Wren).

(133187) George Washington Wren, son of Albert and Sally (Sisson) Wren, was born January 13, 1852, and early in life moved to Callaway County, Missouri, where other Wrens had settled earlier. He visited with his Jackson cousins there before establishing his home. Mr. Wren died in 1929. He married Caroline Bezler (1858-1942). Issue:
(1331871) Rosa Lee Wren, born 1879
(1331872) Mary Alice Wren, born 1881, married John William Payne (born 1878). Issue:
   (13318721) Floyd Payne, born 1900, married Lorene Scott, born 1903 (issue: John Scott Payne, born 1945).

(13318722) Delbert Payne, born 1905, married Lucy Amy Craigo (born 1908). Issue: Betty Lou Payne, born 1930, married Donald Dean Duff (born 1928) and had two children: Marise Rene Payne, born 1955 and Marsha Jayne Payne, born 1957.

(1331873) John Robert Wren, born 1882, married Maud Wheeler, born 1886. Issue:
(13318731) John Robert Wren, Jr., born 1921, married Betty Hape, born 1923, issue: Martha Lynn Wren, born 1949; David Barton Wren, born 1950; and Leslie Ann Wren, born 1954.

(1331874) Albert Edward Wren, born 1884, married Madge Pasley, born 1885, issue:

(13318741) Walter Ray Wren (1907-1922).

(13318742) Paul Burten Wren, born 1910, married Georgia Lee Harwell, issue: Kathleen Joyce Wren, born 1941.

(13318743) Harold Edward Wren, born 1915.

(13318744) Kenneth Russell Wren, born 1923, married Evelyn Lorene Burre, born 1924, issue: Kevin Edward Wren, born 1953.

(1331875) William Davis Wren, born October 8, 1886, married Ola Frances Hatfield, born March 20, 1889. Issue:

(13318751) Helen Lorraine Wren, born July 20, 1911, married Mervin Elbert Cary son of James Franklin and Bessie (Anders) Cary, born October 30, 1909. Issue:

(133187511) Barbara Dale Cary, born December 1, 1936, married William Marvin Harbaugh, born November 20, 1931. He was a son of Martin Edward and Mary Elizabeth (Hicks) Harbaugh. Issue: Michael Edward Harbaugh, born May 16, 1959.

(133187512) Deanna Leigh Cary, born July 31, 1939.

(133187513) Billie Joyce Cary, born January 9, 1941, married Lonzo Neil Simmons, born August 3, 1938.

(133187514) Mervin Wren Cary, born April 11, 1943.

(1331876) Martin Lee Wren, born 1890, married Julia Elmira McCall, born 1890, issue:

(13318761) Dorothy Evelyn Wren, born 1914, married C. Frank Schulte, born 1910.

(1331877) David Omer Wren, born 1891, married (1) Mattie Eunice Coats (1893-1921) and (2) Elsie Mae Krebs, born 1898. Issue (by Mattie Eunice Coats): Lelmael Leland Wren, born 1917, married Bernice Helen Tate, born 1917, and had issue: George David Wren, born 1954.

(1331878) Russell Lloyd Wren, born 1893, married Ula Thompson, born 1896. Mr. Wren lives in Jefferson City, Missouri and owns Wren Insurance Agency in that City. Issue:

(13318781) Caroline Jane Wren, born 1925, married Bill Lee Todd, born 1926, issue: Candace Kay Todd, born November 1, 1960; and Christopher Andrew Todd, born November 1, 1960; and Christopher Andrew Todd, born May 3, 1964, died May 12, 1964, Jefferson City, Missouri.

(1331879) Julian Thomas Wren, born 1895, married (1) Winnie Bingelli (1895-1931) and (2) Blanche Taylor, born 1901. Issue: (*By Winnie Bingelli*)

(13318791) Clyde Eugene Wren, born 1920, married Mildred Joan Means, born 1923.

(13318792) Julian Clayton Wren, born 1931, married Gloria Plybon, born 1935, issue: Debra Sue Wren, born 1954.
*(By Blanche Taylor):*
(13318793) Clifford Taylor Wren, born 1936.

(133188) Lewis Edward Wren, son of Albert and Elizabeth M. (Lewis) Wren, was born August 16, 1858, and died January 17, 1912. Mr. Wren is buried in Merrifield Cemetery. He married Mary D. Milholland (1861-October 4, 1919).[171] Issue:
(1331881) Albert Lewis Wren, born January 21, 1879, died July 23, 1879, age 6 months, 3 days (*The Mirror,* Leesburg, August 7, 1879).
(1331882) Clarence E. Wren (1881-1935) married Sarah E. —— (1888-July, 1957) who remarried —— Taylor.
(1331883) Edward Wren.
(1331884) Effie Wren.
(1331885) Grace D. Wren, married (1) John B. Gill (died December 9, 1910, age 30 years, and is buried in Merrifield Cemetery). She remarried (2) Frederick Oliver. Mrs. Oliver died May 22, 1958, and was survived by the following children: Albert Gill, Clifton Gill, Clarence Gill, and Mrs. Lucy Mayo. She was also survived by six grandchildren and three great-grandchildren. Others included: Luther E. Gill, died August 4, 1902, age 4 months. The son, Albert Gill, died January 7, 1959.

(13319) Mary Jane Wren, daughter of John S. and Sarah (Hite) Wren, married Norman Reeder Davis, son of Benjamin Reeder and Jane (Monroe) Davis. He was a brother of Lucinda Davis who married John Hite Wren, brother of Mary Jane Wren.

In a very interesting letter written from Callaway County, Missouri, August 9, 1842, Mrs. Davis expressed great concern about her mother, Sarah Wren. The letter was addressed to "Miss Susannah Wren, Annandale, Fairfax County, Va.," and is post-marked Portland, Missouri, August 16, 1842. In the body of the letter Mrs. Davis gives advice concerning her mother, apparently ill with cancer, and mentions a number of relatives. She states that "last Thursday" Miss Amanda Blackburn (apparently formerly of Fairfax County) married a Mr. Bell, a school-master, originally from Virginia, and resident of Callaway County, Missouri. She also mentions that Zeder (or Teder) apparently a relative, had married Miss Ann Darby, a cousin of Mr. Dyson, in Missouri. Her mother-in-law, Mrs. Davis, sent much love to Sarah Wren and to "Betsey" (sister of Mary Jane (Wren) Davis). She mentions her sister-in-law, Lucinda (Davis) (Wren) Dyson, also living near them in Missouri, states that she had a large family, and thus had not written. She also stated that Lucinda was preparing to go to Camp Meeting "to commence next Thursday," showing that apparently they remained loyal Methodists in Missouri. The letter also mentions Albert and Mary Wren, Thomas Wren, Sarah and John, apparently children of the writer. She states that she "saw Margaret Fish" that morning, another Fairfax native. Mrs. Davis also writes of her sister, Evelina, of William and James Wren. She concludes her letter with advice for her brother, Charles Wren, and inquires of Fanny Lindsay and "John." The Susannah Wren to whom it was addressed may have been her sister, who later married Robert Reid, or it may have been Susannah (Adams) (Hipkins) Wren. This very interesting letter is owned by Mrs. Earle T. Mutersbaugh.

Mrs. Davis mentions her children in the letter, including a son "large enough" to ride behind her on a horse. No children are mentioned by name, however.

(1331.10) Charles Brent Wren, son of John S. and Sarah (Hite) Wren, married in

Washington, D.C., on November 28, 1839, Catherine Lindsay (*See Lindsay*). Issue (*probably others*):

(1331.10.1) William H. Wren (Billy), born 1842, died 1929, and is buried in the Lindsay Family Cemetery at "The Mount," He married, on April 10, 1873, Ann E. Clarke, daughter of W. T. Clarke. She was born in 1853, and died in 1927. Issue:

(1331.10.11) Florence Eva Wren (1874-1911) married on July 25, 1893, George Downs, and is buried at "The Mount."

(1331.10.12) Elmer Clarke Wren, born 1877, baptized at Dulin Chapel, September 16, 1879.

(1331.10.13) Edna Dean Wren, born 1879, baptized at Dulin Chapel, September 16, 1879, married Chris Arnold of Idylwood.

(1331.10.14) Roy Wren.

(1331.10.15) Ray Wren, married Imogene Bartlett and lived at Bel Air, Maryland.

(1331.12) Evalina (or Evelina) Wren, daughter of John S. and Sarah (Hite) Wren, married a cousin, William Wren, son of Sanford and Sally (Dulin) Wren, and a grandson of William and Mary (Wren) Dulin. In *Fairfax Deed Book C 3,* at page 496, there is a deed of April 5, 1836, when William Wren and Evelina his wife, deeded land, part of that "lately divided" which belonged to John Wren, deceased. This was the Lot (number 10) awarded Evelina Wren. This was sold to Albert Wren, brother of Evelina, for $150.00. Witnesses: Robert Blackburn, Mottrom Ball, and John Gant. They are said to have raised a large family, but records have not been brought to light concerning them.

(1331.13) Horatio Nelson Wren, son of John S. and Sarah (Hite) Wren, died before 1842. In *Fairfax Will Book U,* page 181, there is a Guardian Bond of Phoebe Wren, guardian of John Thomas and Sarah Hill Wren, dated July 15, 1844. Peyton Ashford and Noah Martin served as Trustees. Nelson Wren made his will October 16, 1841, recorded in *Will Book U,* page 42. This document was probated October 17, 1842. In it he mentions his wife, Pheby, and two children: John Thomas Wren and Sarah Hill Wren. Witnesses were William Shreve, Lewis Sewall, and James O. Tucker. On February 24, 1838, Nelson and Phoebe Wren, and Susan Wren (sister of Nelson Wren) deeded to Albert Wren for $150.00, Lot 8 (owned by Nelson Wren) which was part of the division of the estate of John Wren, deceased. This Deed is recorded in D #3, page 472. It also deeded Susan Wren's Lot #9. Issue:

(1331.13.1) John Thomas Wren.

(1331.13.2) Sarah Hill Wren, born 1841, married on September 3, 1867, at St. Mary's Church, Alexandria, to Thomas L. Fenwick. He was born in Fairfax County in 1836, son of Ret (or Robert?)[172] and Mary Fenwick.

(2) (Colonel) Thomas Wren (I) (sometimes called Junior) was born in 1703, and died at his home near Falls Church in 1768. His wife, Jean, died after 1768.[173] One of the first references to Colonel Thomas Wren in Fairfax (then Prince William) is a record dated June 22, 1741.[174] On that day Thomas Wren, Edward Emms, and William Harle appraised the estate of William Williams, deceased. The appraisal was returned to the Prince William Court on July 27, 1741.

On October 25, 1742, the Prince William Court ordered an Inventory made of the estate of Rodham Neale. This was returned to the Court on March 28, 1743, by Thomas Wren, Owin Williams, and Walter English.[175] On February 19, 1749, Thomas Wren was listed as a Vestryman of Truro Parish.

The Fairfax Court orders contain some reference to Colonel Wren during the

1750's. On February 20, 1754, Wren was awarded 2 pounds, 11 shillings, 5 pence, and 109 pounds of tobacco in a suit against Pierce Noland.[176] A suit was brought against Wren by John Pagan on February 20, 1754. Wren was to give special bail before he was allowed to appear in the suit, "Whereupon Robert Boggess came into Court & undertook for the said Thomas to pay the condemnation of the Court if he should be cast in this suit or deliver up his body in Execution." [177]

On December 10, 1759, Thomas Wren made an interesting deposition before Edward Blackburn and Lee Massey in a lawsuit, "George West Against Orsin alias William Holyfield & Valentine Holyfield."[178] This suit, recorded in Loudoun County, is the only proof for the birth year of Thomas Wren. His deposition ("Thomas Wren of Fairfax, aged 56 years"), was recorded on Thursday, March 12, 1761, but was made on December 10, 1759, at the institution of the suit. The suit is of special interest. Orsin (an assumed name of William) Holyfield (or Holifield), and Ralph Holyfield conveyed to Hugh West some land in Loudoun County which had been the property of their parents, Valentine and Elizabeth Holyfield. However, question had been raised over their right to convey the property, since, as Wren, and others testified, they were "Bastard children," born before their parents were married by license. Valentine and Elizabeth (———) Holyfield were indentured servants brought into this country by Thomas Worthington of Maryland. They lived together without ceremony, since indentured servants were not permitted to wed. Two children were born during this time, Ralph and William (Orsin). After completion of the indenture, the family moved across the Potomac to what is now Fairfax County, and were married here by the minister of Truro Parish. They were hired as servants by Edward Emms, a neighbor to Thomas Wren, and thus came into contact with settlers in what is now the Falls Church neighborhood. Gerard Trammell (age 57 years "and upwards" on December 10, 1759), and Samuel Jenkins, age 47 years, on the same date, both gave other details. Samuel Jenkins testified that Ralph Holyfield lived with him as a hired hand at one time. It was during this time that he was Godfather at the baptism of William ("now Orsin") Holyfield. After the marriage, Valentine and Elizabeth had three more children: Daniel, Valentine, and Elizabeth. Daniel, the eldest child (after the marriage) was considered by Thomas Wren to be legal heir to the father. It was further testified that Valentine Holyfield, Sr., died at the house of a sister of Jacob Lasswell at the age of 56. Since he was called a close friend of Lasswell, it may be that Elizabeth Holyfield was a Lasswell. At any rate, this suit covers several pages and gives us a glimpse of the conditions and customs of the day.

On March 28, 1763, Thomas Wren (with his fellow Vestrymen, including George Washington) voted to build the present Falls Church, according to Colonel James Wren's plan. On November 30, 1765, Wren, now a Vestryman of the new Fairfax Parish, which was formed from the older Truro Parish, was appointed Reader at the Falls Church, with an annual salary of 250 pounds of tobacco. On October 16, 1766, Thomas Wren was appointed Clerk of the Falls Church with an annual salary of 1,000 pounds of tobacco.

On September 8, 1767, Colonel Wren made his Will, probated May 16, 1768.[179] In it he mentioned his wife, Jean, and the following children: Thomas Wren, Nicholas Wren, William Wren, John Wren, Travis ("Traverse") Wren, Isaac Wren, Mary Wren, Ann Wren, and Winney Athill (or Atwell). Witnesses were: Colonel James Wren, James Donaldson and Colonel Robert Lindsay.

Colonel Thomas and Jean Wren had issue:
(21) (Colonel) Thomas Wren (II) married Susanna Sanford.
(22) Nicholas Wren married Elizabeth Jenkins.
(23) William Wren.
(24) John Wren.
(25) Travis Wren.
(26) Isaac Wren.
(27) Mary Wren.
(28) Ann Wren.
(29) Winifred Wren, married —— Athill (or Atwell).

(21) (Colonel) Thomas Wren (II), son of Thomas Wren, Jr., and Jean Wren, died in Loudoun County, in 1779. On March 8, 1761, Simon Pearson conveyed to Thomas Wren (both of Truro Parish, Fairfax County) by lease, two hundred acres of land in consideration of 630 pounds of tobacco to be paid on March first of each year, beginning in 1763. This land is described as "Beginning at a marked Poplar in the main Road that leads from Falls Church to the Ox road thence along the line of James Wren's to his Corner thence with a line of John Fitzhugh to Gerrard Bowlings line and along the said Line to the main Road and along the said Road to the Beginning." This lease was effective during the life of the said Thomas Wren, "James Wren Junr. & Hanah Wren and the Longest Liver of them." This lease was proved on March 16, 1762, and ordered recorded. Witnesses were William Wren, James Wren, and John Wren.[180]

On October 3, 1774, Thomas and Ann Johnson of Loudoun County sold to Thomas Wrenn of Fairfax County for 200 pounds current money, a tract in Loudoun County containing 288 acres. Witnesses to this deed were Isaac Sanders, Travis Wren, Samuel Helen, Patrick Carty, Thomas Matthews, and David Carty.[181] Wren and wife, Susanna, sold this land for 400 pounds current money on May 6, 1778, to Alexander McIntyre. Witnesses were Joseph Morehouse (or Morehane), Henry Eaton, and Joseph Butler, Jr.[182]

On April 13, 1779, Susanna Wren, widow of Thomas Wren, with John Wren and Daniel Sanford, her Securities, gave Bond as Executrix of the estate of Thomas Wren.[183] She must have died shortly afterwards, for an inventory of her estate was returned with one of her husband on August 10, 1779.[184] The Inventory was signed by Alexander McMakin, Joseph Wildman, and Francis Elgin. An Account of the estate of Thomas Wren was rendered on November 1, 1788, by Thomas Sandford, Administrator. John Wren is mentioned in this final Account.[185]

Colonel Thomas Wren (II) and Susanna (Sanford) Wren had issue:
(211) James Wren (called Junior).
(212) Hannah Wren.
(213) Richard Wren, married Mrs. Susannah (Adams) Hipkins.
(214) John Wren.[186]
(215) Sanford Wren, married in Loudoun County, May 14, 1799, Sally Dulin.

(213) Richard Wren, son of Colonel Thomas Wren (II) and Susanna (Sanford) Wren, married about 1799, Mrs. Susannah (Adams) Hipkins, widow of Lewis Hipkins. She was a daughter of Colonel William and Ann (Lawyer) Adams of "Church Hill," and died in 1849. (*See Adams*)

On October 20, 1796, Richard Wren of Alexandria purchased from James Irvin for forty pounds, a lot on the East side of Washington Street.[187] On December 19,

1796, James Irvin conveyed to Richard Wren additional land on Washington Street.[188] On March 29, 1799, Thomas Ramsey of Alexandria appointed Richard Wren, then of Fairfax County, his Attorney.[189]

Mrs. Susannah (Adams) Wren made her will May 8, 1847, probated May 21, 1849.[190] In it she mentioned her son, Andrew Hipkins, a brother, Samuel Adams, and named her son, Thomas S. Wren, Executor. Witnesses were: William Nelson, John W. Marriott, and Nathan Kell.

Richard Wren predeceased his wife by about ten years. He died about 1838. An appraisal of the estate of Richard Wren was filed November 6, 1838.[191] George Minor, George Beard, Alfred H. Darne, Edward McMuhaney and James Payne, or any three, had been ordered to make the appraisal at the August Court, 1838. Beard, Payne, and Darne returned to appraisal. The sale account of the estate of Richard Wren shows persons who purchased items, including Thomas Wren and Robert Darne.[192]

Richard and Susannah (Adams) Wren had issue:

(2131) Thomas Sanford Wren, married Julia Ann Wren. (There may have been a daughter who died in infancy)

(2131) Thomas Sanford Wren, son of Richard and Susannah (Adams) Wren, was born at "Salona," near present day McLean, on May 19, 1808, and died at his Langley home, "Mount Pleasant," August 5, 1887.[193] Mr. Wren married in Washington, D.C., on December 5, 1833, a cousin, Julia Ann Wren. Mrs. Wren was born at "Long View," Falls Church, December 8, 1813, a daughter of John S. and Sarah (Hite) Wren. She was a granddaughter of Colonel James Wren. Mrs. Wren died September 8, 1881.

Mr. Wren was an official of Nelson's Chapel Methodist Episcopal Church and later at Langley. His will, recorded in Fairfax,[194] shows that he gave his "Mount Pleasant" estate to a daughter, Julia Furlong. Witnesses to the will were: Thomas C. Faulkner and William S. Smoot.

Thomas Sanford and Julia Ann (Wren) Wren had issue:

(21311) Harriet S. S. Wren, born November 12, 1837, died unmarried, October 18, 1864.

(21312) Charles W. Wren, born October 16, 1831, died unmarried, June 4, 1857 (Bible Record). The *Death Records* at Fairfax Court House recorded his death as June 19, 1857, age 20 years.

(21313) Martha Ellen Wren, born February 26, 1839, died May 9, 1839.

(21314) Sarah Adams Wren, married James Nathaniel Hall.

(21315) Lucy Ann Wren, born February 27, 1842, died October 18, 1843.

(21316) Mary Frances Wren, born April 13, 1844, died November 8, 1845.

(21317) Sophia Smith Wren, born August 30, 1846, died August 9, 1860. The Reverend William Gwynn Coe, Minister on the Fairfax Circuit of the Methodist Episcopal Church, noted in his *Sermon Book* on August 11, 1860: "Dwelling of Thos. Wrenn near Nelson's Ch(apel) fun(era)l of his daughter Sophia, aged 14 yrs. Heb(rews) XII, 5." This last is the text of his funeral sermon.

(21318) Julia Thomas Wren, married Charles Irving Furlong

(21319) Alice Virginia Wren, born February 17, 1851, died June 11, 1851.

(2131.10) John Richard Wren, born June 16, 1852, died August 20, 1861. One record, probably incorrect, notes his dates as June 16, 1862-August 20, 1862.

(21314) Sarah Adams Wren, daughter of Thomas Sanford and Julia Ann (Wren)

Wren, was born January 23, 1841, and died at Langley, February 17, 1907. She married, on August 6, 1868, James Nathaniel Hall. Mr. Hall was born in Prince William County, March 13, 1843, a son of William Travis and Mary Ann (Ellis) Hall. He remarried (2) to Ann (Jeffries) Davis. By her first marriage Mrs. Hall was the mother of Effie Davis. Mr. Hall died at Langley on May 5, 1919. Issue:
(213141) William Hall, died at age 8 or 9 years.
(213142) Joseph Edward Hall, married Margaret Jane Minor.
(213143) James Lucien Hall, married Mary Estella Mayhugh.
(213144) John Washington Hall, married Florence Trussell.

(213142) Joseph Edward Hall, son of James Nathaniel and Sarah Adams (Wren) Hall, was born August 31, 1874, and died March 26, 1943. He married in 1898, Margaret Jane Minor. Mrs. Hall was born near Falls Church, January 26, 1871, died August 18, 1948, and was a descendant of Colonel George Minor of "Minor's Hill," and a cousin of her husband. Issue:
(2131421) Mildred Elizabeth Hall, born February 16, 1901, unmarried.
(2131422) James Edward Hall, born May 14, 1903, died unmarried July 26, 1955.
(2131423) John Wesley Hall, born February 28, 1905, married on December 25, 1939 to Hilda Elizabeth Prichard. Issue:
   (21314231) Anne Margaret Hall, born July 26, 1941.
   (21314232) Linda Elizabeth Hall, born July 17, 1942.
(2131424) Edna Estelle Hall, born December 12, 1907, married (1) August 1, 1922, Frank Doyle (divorced); and (2) on May 10, 1948, George Charles Sullivan (born October 11, 1905). Issue:
   (21314241) Margaret Catherine Doyle born February 21, 1923.
   (21314242) Frank Edward Doyle born July 15, 1925.
   (21314243) John Daniel Doyle born April 29, 1935.
   (21314244) George Charles Sullivan, Jr., born July 18, 1949.
(2131425) Daniel Minor Hall, born July 23, 1909, married on April 6, 1943, Olga Grace Pascoe (born May 26, 1912). No children.

(213143) James Lucien Hall, son of James Nathaniel and Sarah Adams (Wren) Hall, was born at Langley, February 23, 1875, and died at McLean, July 31, 1942. He married on September 12, 1895, Mary Estella Mayhugh of Fauquier County. She was born at Greenwich, Fauquier County, May 31, 1878, died July 25, 1949. Mrs. Hall was a first cousin to her husband, being the daughter of George and Jane Amanda (Hall) Mayhugh. Her father, George Mayhugh, died January 4, 1904. Her mother, Jean Amanda (Hall) Mayhugh was born April 5, 1853, died September 10, 1936. Issue:
(2131431) Mary James Hall, born January 14, 1897, died August 6, 1908.
(2131432) George Vernon Hall, born March 31, 1898, married July 19, 1926 to Althea Faulkner, daughter of Wilfred Faulkner. Issue:
   (21314321) Virginia Dale Hall, born March 17, 1927, married October 16, 1949 to Robert Triplett. Issue:
      (213143211) Robert Wesley Triplett, born August 20, 1950.
      (213143212) Wayne Lee Triplett, born December 4, 1951.
      (213143213) Mary Ann Triplett, born October 12, 1955.
   (21314322) Audrey Ruth Hall, born February 5, 1929, married on July 25, 1948, to Robert Harnar, Issue:
      (213143221) Margaret Susan Harnar, born October 25, 1949.

(213143222) Karen Elizabeth Harnar, born January 25, 1953.
(213143223) Robin Cheryl Harnar, born September 27, 1954.
(21324323) George Vernon Hall, Jr., born June 24, 1933, married on January 7, 1956, Margaret Ann Reedy, no children.
(2131433) Jean Amanda Hall, born October 17, 1903, married on October 17, 1924, Earle Tanner Mutersbaugh, no children.
(2131434) Joseph Lucien Hall, born January 22, 1906, unmarried.
(2131435) Douglas Adams Hall, born May 19, 1907, died July 18, 1955. Married Essie Craven (widow) on November 5, 1943. (She had children by her first marriage, Ernest Craven, Charles Craven, and Robert Craven).
(2131436) Sarah Adams Hall, born May 6, 1910, married July 17, 1937, Edward Irving Smith, children:
   (21314361) Edward Irving Smith, Jr., born February 14, 1939.
   (21314362) James Lucien Smith born May 29, 1945.
(2131437) William Travis Hall, born October 7, 1911, married on June 17, 1937, Neota Silvers. She was born in Fonda, Iowa, May 16, 1910. Issue:
   (21314371) Neota Silvers Hall, born October 26, 1942.
   (21314372) Mary Alene Hall, born March 7, 1945.
   (21314373) William Travis Hall, Jr., born August 9, 1946.
(2131438) Bernice Lee Hall, born July 25, 1913, died December 27, 1913.
(2131439) Thomas Sanford Hall, born November 7, 1914, died September 24, 1915.
(213143.10) Eunice Elizabeth Hall (Betty), born January 8, 1917, married on June 21, 1946, George Elwin Wrenn. Issue:
   (213143.10.1) George Elwin Wrenn, Jr., born February 2, 1955. (Note: George Elwin Wrenn, Jr., is a descendant of John Wren, son of Colonel James Wren, by two of his children, Albert Wren and Julia Ann Wren, and from Thomas Wren (thru Thomas Sanford Wren).

(213144) John Washington Hall, son of James Nathaniel and Sarah Adams (Wren) Hall, was born December 13, 1879, died January 23, 1953. He married on June 21, 1905, Florence Trussell (born June 1, 1887). Issue:
(213144) Mary Virginia Hall, born December 10, 1906, married on January 30, 1926, George William Clinton Florance (born February 9, 1905). No children.
(2131442) Frances Elmira Hall, born July 19, 1909, married on June 23, 1931, Dudley Heath Rector (born January 13, 1910). Issue:
   (21314421) Betty Frances Rector, born January 1, 1934, married on June 9, 1954, George Sanford Tever (born February 27, 1929). Issue:
      (213144211) Vickie Jean Tever, born February 10, 1957.
(2131443) John Trussell Hall, born March 25, 1915, married on May 11, 1940, Edna May Chapman (divorced). Child:
   (21314431) Virginia Ann Hall, born November 8, 1943.

(21318) Julia Thomas Wren, daughter of Thomas Sanford and Julia Ann (Wren) Wren, was born January 22, 1849, died October 26, 1926. She married Charles Irving Furlong of Chester Co., Pennsylvania. Mr. Furlong died February 1, 1923, age 74. Issue:
(213181) Andrew Thomas Furlong, born August 14, 1879, in Pawling, New York, died June 2, 1932. He married Florence Martin (or Norton—record not clear). His widow remarried William Harrison. Children included Geraldine and Beatrice Furlong.

(213182) Charles Herbert Furlong, born August 2, 1882, died December 28, 1942. He married, on August 11, 1901, Mary Ella Reid, daughter of George W., Jr., and Mary Elizabeth (Ball) Reid of Langley, of an old and prominent family. Mrs. Furlong supplied information on this branch of the Adams-Wren family. Issue:
  (2131821) Ralph Furlong, born March 21, 1903, married on November 2, 1929 Lillian Cozzins. He died December 24, 1940. Issue:
    (21318211) Marion Furlong, born January 22, 1930, married Shirley Bennett, children:
      (213182111) Edward Parke Furlong.
  (2131822) Charles Vernon Furlong, married on September 12, 1936, Pauline Reid of Vale, daughter of Eskins and Eva (Thompson) Reid. Issue:
    (21318221) Charles Lee Furlong, born April 11, 1937.
(2131823) Lona Maybelle Furlong, born August 25, 1905, married on June 22, 1922, James Albert Philips (son of Eugene Kirby and Ann Salina (Wren) Philips): and (2) November 10, 1950, George Edward Kushnereit. Issue:
  (21318231) Charles Wilbur Philips, born March 2, 1925.
  (21318232) James Irving Philips, born November 16, 1926.
  (21318233) Roy Eugene Philips born April 27, 1929.
(2131824) Olive Furlong married Roy Thompson, no children.
(2131825) Lois Elizabeth Furlong, married on November 24, 1943 to Gilbert Gray. Issue:
  (21318251) Ralph Daniel Gray, born October 18, 1947.
  (21318252) Linda Ann Gray, born November 3, 1948.

(22) Nicholas Wren, son of Colonel Thomas and Jean Wren, was born April 26, 1731, and died in Warren County, Kentucky, June 19, 1809. He married, on November 14,1756, Elizabeth Jenkins. Mrs. Wren (whose mother was Elizabeth (Payne) of an old Fairfax County family) was born January 15, 1738, and died in Kentucky, April 17, 1819.[195] This family moved to Albermarle County and later to Amherst County. On June 10, 1772, *one* Nicholas Wren was Overseer for Colonel Francis Lightfoot Lee in Cameron Parish, Loudoun County (*Tithe List*). Issue:
(221) John Wren, born April 15, 1763.
(222) Elizabeth Wren, born May 27, 1765, married on December 25, 1783, John Jones, son of Hezekiah and Mary Ann (Sowell) Jones. His brother, William, married Elizabeth Wren's sister, Nancy. Issue: Tilman Jones, Nancy Jones, Mary (Polly) Jones, Robert Jones, Margaret Jones, Elizabeth Jones, Hezekiah Jones, and William Jones.

(223) Nancy Wren, born March 1, 1767, died April 12, 1843. She married on November 29, 1785, William Jones. Mr. Jones was born June 19, 1764, a son of Hezekiah and Ann (Sowell) Jones. They followed George Rogers Clark to Kentucky and their son, John, born 1786, was, by family tradition, the first white boy born in what is now Louisville. They lived near Glasgow, Kentucky, and in Green County. Issue:
  (1131) John Jones, born September 9, 1786, in what is now Louisville, Kentucky, died September 29, 1843 in Grandview, Iowa. His wife died the same day and was buried in the same grave. He married Polly Young (born May 30, 1793). They went from Barren County, Kentucky, to Louisa County, Iowa, in 1842. Issue:
    (22311) Angeline Jones, born September 10, 1814, died July 26, 1890, married Philip Grinstead.

(22312) William Boon Jones, born February 14, 1816, died September 10, 1907. Married (1) —— Lewis; and (2) —— Mann.
(22313) Keziah Jones, born December 20, 1817, died May 19, 1863. Married John Jameson.
(22314) Charlotte Jones, born December 18, 1819, died January 15, 1913. She married (1) Thomas Jameson; and (2) John S. Bohannon.
(22315) Edward Jones, born July 22, 1822, died May 12, 1903. Married Martha Ann Kendall.
(22316) Elizabeth Jones (twin), born June 17, 1824, died May 21, 1910. She married —— Evans.
(22317) Nancy Jones (twin), born June 17, 1824, died November 27, 1907. She married in Grandview, Louisa County, Iowa, on March 7, 1844, Andrew Kendall. Mr. Kendall was born November 18, 1814, died September 2, 1889, and they lived in Washington, Iowa. Issue:

(223171) Sarah Elizabeth Kendall, born August 8, 1845, died unmarried, December 8, 1887.
(223172) Martha Ann Kendall, born December 11, 1846, died September 19, 1918, married Robert Anderson.
(223173) William Andrew Kendall, born April 9, 1850, died May 13, 1852.
(223174) Margaret Angeline Kendall, born October 17, 1853, died March 23, 1855.
(223175) Infant son, born and died June 7, 1857.
(223176) Elvira Ellen Kendall, born April 19, 1859, died February 12, 1897, unmarried.
(223177) Addie Emily Kendall, born May 25, 1864, in Washington, Iowa, died in Chicago, Illinois, January 16, 1946. She married in Washington, Iowa, May 4, 1886, Robert Wilson Gibson. Mr. Gibson was born in Newcastle, Pennsylvania, March 26, 1862, and died in Chicago, October 31, 1926. Issue:

(2231771) Ralph Andrew Gibson, born July 12, 1887, in Chicago, living, Casper, Wyoming.
(2231772) Marian Gibson, born October 8, 1889, in Chicago, died May 16, 1954 in Indianapolis. Indiana.
(2231773) Bayard Kendall Gibson, born April 18, 1892, is living in Chicago, 1956. He is an Architect. Mr. Gibson married on September 28, 1915, Ruth Elizabeth Gleeson. She was born in Chicago on December 16, 1892. Issue: Owen Bayard Gibson, born July 17, 1916; Charles Robert Gibson, born July 4, 1919; and Howard Kendall Gibson, born August 18, 1923, died December 13, 1944, in France, buried in Arlington National Cemetery.
(2231774) Robert Lawrence Gibson, born October 19, 1893, died June 4, 1919. Married a cousin.
(2231775) Adaline Gibson, born December 6, 1894.

(223178) Mary Gertrude Kendall, born February 7, 1868, unmarried.
(22318) John Young Jones, born September 10, 1826, died April 24, 1887. Married Ann Young.
(22319) Robert Jones, born July 3, 1828, died October 1, 1890, married —— Bohannon.

(2231.10) Samuel Emerson Jones, born September 22, 1832, died May 30, 1866, married Emily Ronald.
(2231.11) Christopher Tompkins Jones, born September 11, 1837, died September 16, 1915. Married Gertrude Reister.
(2232) Sophia Jones, born January 15, 1790, died in October, 1819.
(2233) Elizabeth Jones, born December 25, 1791, died June 28, 1835, married ——Shirl.
(2234) Charlotte Jones, born November 2, 1793, died August 7, 1863, married William Hawx.
(2235) Robert Jones, born August 18, 1794, died May 30, 1877.
(2236) Anna Jones, born June 6, 1798, died September 5, 1870.
(2237) William Sowell Jones, born September 19, 1800, died February 7, 1888. His children included a daughter, Mellisa Jones.
(2238) Mary Ann Sowell Jones, born September 22, 1802, died December 25, 1875.
(2239) Nicholas Wren Jones, born March 17, 1805, died March 12, 1884, married Mary Graysbrook.
(223.10) Thomas Jones, born March 17, 1808, died May 1, 1873.
*(Continue children of Nicholas and Elizabeth (Jenkins) Wren):*
(224) Nicholas Wren, Jr., born May 11, 1770.
(225) James Wren, born January 8, 1773.
(226) Winnifred Wren, born June 9, 1775.
(227) Isaac Wren, born October 2, 1777.
(228) Margaret Wren, born May 16, 1780.
(229) Thomas Wren.
(22.10) Mary (Polly) Wren.
(22.11) William Wren.

(23) William Wren, son of Colonel Thomas and Jean Wren, probably moved to South Carolina. On June 13, 1775, James Scott of Dittengen Parish, Prince William County, Clerk, sold to William Wren of Truro Parish, Fairfax County, a plantation "whereon he (Wren) now Dwells," containing two hundred acres and being part of a greater tract on Pimmit's Run, bounded by John Trammell and Gerrard Trammell. Wren paid 950 pounds of crop tobacco for this lease. Witnesses were: Nathaniel Popejoy, Jr., John Seignior, and Nathaniel Popejoy, Jr.[196]

An Order of the Fairfax Court dated March 18, 1770, bound James Garrison, "five years old the last of this month," and Sarah Gameron, three years old, orphans, to William Wren, "to learn them to read and write, and the said James the trade of a shoe maker."

No other record.

(25) Travis Wren, son of Colonel Thomas and Jean Wren, lived in Loudoun County during the 1780's (*Virginia Tax Payers,* page 140). There was also a Travis Wren in Lunenburg County at the same time. Travis Wren and Isaac Wren gave bond in Loudoun County, in the amount of 11 pounds, 14 shillings and 9 pence on October 6, 1791. Witnesses were: Elijah Smallwood and Daniel Wren. Wren married and had issue (*probably others*):
(251) James Wren, probably the one by this name who married Elizabeth Jacobs, in Loudoun County on August 10, 1812.
(252) William Wren, died unmarried in Loudoun County in May 1805. He made a

nuncupative Will on May 3, 1805, before Augustine Love and Amos Harriss. This was probated May 13, 1805 (Loudoun County *Will Book G*, page 355). In it he mentioned his parents, a brother, James, a sister, Jane and a sister, Margaret. On May 13, 1805, Travis Wren gave bond (with Amos Harriss and Augustine Love) for $700.00, as administrator of the will of William Wren, deceased.
(253) Margaret Wren, married in Loudoun County, August 22, 1805, Robert Neale.
(254) Jane Wren, married in Loudoun County on May 23, 1805, Amos Harriss.

(26) Isaac Wren, son of Colonel Thomas, and Jean Wren, moved to Loudoun County where he reared his family. On October 13, 1777, William Morlan (or Moreland) of Loudoun County, farmer, made a contract with Isaac Wren of Fairfax County, farmer, to farm-let to Wren a tract of land on "Siccolon" Run in consideration of a yearly rent. Witnesses to the lease were: James Megeath, Edward Cavans, and Elisha Edwards.[197] Wren must have moved to Loudoun County shortly after making this lease. On the list of *Virginia Tax Payers* ("Census of 1790")[198] taken in 1782 and 1787, Isaac Wren is listed in Loudoun County paying tax for himself and four slaves.

The only other record of Isaac Wren yet found, is in a *Judgement* suit recorded in Loudoun County in 1795, "Sudduth v. Wrenn." A note in connection with this states:
"Mr. Isaac Wren: Sir, Be pleased to take notice that I shall make a motion to the next Loudoun Court on the first day of the Court for your not producing property on the day of Sale.   William Sudduth
Mr. Isaac Wren, May the 25th, 1795."

Isaac Wren, with John Wren as co-bondsman, made a bond to William Sudduth on May 26, 1794 (witnessed by Samuel Boggess), in the sum of thirteen pounds and one shilling. According to the bond, Sudduth had recovered against Wren on one mare and a roan horse, which Wren apparently did not deliver on the day of sale.

*Note:* This is a highly condensed sketch of the Wren family. The author has an abundance of material in his files for a contemplated full-scale history. Corrections and additions for this purpose would be appreciated.

---

[1] The original map is owned by the Purcell family of Round Hill. It was taken to the Library of Congress by Charles E. Gage in 1958, and repaired. A copy was placed on permanent file there.
[2] In a letter, written in 1802, Jefferson recommended Wren's to a friend.
[3] The Wren family has received good treatment in an early work, *Parentalia; or Memoirs of the Wrens*, by Sir Christopher Wren's son, Christopher Wren, Jr. (1675-1747), and published in 1750. A copy is in the Library of Congress, and one was on exhibition in 1957 at the Jamestown Celebration.
[4] This writer has not attempted to search the ramifications of the William Wren career. This information has been supplied by members of the family in Virginia. More data would be desirable.
[5] King George County, Virginia, *Deed Book 1-A*, pages 322/23.
[6] *Ibid, Deed Book 2*, pages 241/42.
[7] *Ibid, Deed Book 2*, pages 414-15.
[8] *Ibid, Deed Book 3*, pages 132-33.
[9] *Ibid, Deed Book 3*, pages 163-65.
[10] *Ibid, Deed Book 3*, pages 254-55.
[11] *Ibid, Deed Book 6*, page 73.
[12] *Ibid, Deed Book 6*, pages 92 .
[13] This marriage is mentioned in several MS. sketches of the Wren family. This writer has found no proof of it, but the many records on file which included witnesses, etc., of the Harry Turner clan, certainly indicates a close friendship or kinship.

[14] Spotsylvania County, Virginia, *Deed Book 26*, page 26.
[15] King George County, *Will Book 1*, page 16.
[16] *Ibid, Deed Book 6*, page 101.
[17] *Ibid, Deed Book 4*, page 397.
[18] *Ibid, Order Book (1759-1765), Part 3*, page 1057.
[19] *Ibid, Deed Book 5*, page 911.
[20] Fairfax County, Virginia, *Deed Book K 1, page 100* (this page is missing).
[21] *Ibid, Deed Book K 1*, page 101.
[22] *Ibid, Deed Book K 1*, page 102.
[23] *Ibid, Deed Book M 1*, page 233.
[24] Loudoun County, Virginia, *Deed Book N 1*, pages 113-115.
[25] *Ibid, Deed Book R 1*, page 410.
[26] *Ibid, Deed Book U 1*, page 110.
[27] *U. S. Census*, Virginia, 1790, page 18.
[28] *Tithe List*, on file at Leesburg, Virginia (Loudoun County Court House).
[29] *Loose papers* on file in the Archives Room, Court House, Leesburg, Virginia, entitled "Bindings Out."
[30] Loudoun County, Virginia, *Deed Book A 2*, page 24.
[31] *Ibid*, page 26.
[32] Fauquier County, Virginia, *Deed Book 11*, page 431.
[33] *Ibid, Deed Book 15*, page 340.
[34] *Ibid, Deed Book 16*, page 412.
[35] *Ibid, Deed Book 17*, page 506.
[36] *Ibid*, page 505.
[37] *Ibid, Deed Book 20*, page 141.
[38] *Ibid, Deed Book 21*, page 180.
[39] *Ibid, Deed Book 20*, page 237.
[40] *Ibid, Deed Book 22*, page 29.
[41] *Ibid, Deed Book 23*, page 49.
[42] *Ibid, Deed Book 25*, page 50.
[43] *Ibid*, page 237.
[44] *Ibid, Deed Book 27*, page 44.
[45] Unrecorded deed.
[46] Fauquier County, Virginia, *Deed Book 29*, page 139.
[47] *Ibid, Deed Book 26*, page 423.
[48] *Ibid, Deed Book 23*, page 307.
[49] *Ibid, Deed Book 26*, page 6.
[50] *Ibid*, page 26.
[51] Unrecorded Deed.
[52] *Ibid*.
[53] *Ibid*.
[54] Mary (Strother) Wren was alive as late as July 6, 1814, when (with Fanny Lloyd) she witnessed the marriage of Joshua Windsor to Betsey, daughter of Reuben Strother (William Strother, Bondsman). Fauquier County, *Marriage Book 3*, page 230.
[55] King George County, Virginia, *Deed Book 3*, page 326.
[56] *Ibid, Deed Book 4*, page 389.
[57] *Ibid, Will Book 1*, page 234.
[58] *Ibid, Deed Book 5*, page 1213.
[59] William Shropshire, the witness may have been related. There is a will of record in King George (*Will Book 2*, page 63) of an unplaced Margaret Wren, of the said County. She was about to bear a child, and ordered that it be baptized Sally. If the child died, her estate was to be divided among James Shropshire, William Shropshire and Nicholas Shropshire, children of William Shropshire. Witnesses: William Boon, Ann Rawley and Laurance Balthrope. The will was dated December 16, 1780, probated May 2, 1782.
[60] King George County, Virginia, *Deed Book 6*, page 314.
[61] *Ibid*, page 335.
[62] *Ibid*, page 364.
[63] Spotsylvania County, *Deed Book L*, page 394.
[64] *Ibid*, page 415.
[65] *Ibid, Deed Book N*, page 468.
[66] *Ibid, Deed Book P*, page 502.
[67] King George County, Virginia, *Deed Book 4*, page 61.
[68] *Ibid, Order Book (1751-65)*, page 568.

⁶⁹ *Ibid, Deed Book 4*, page 338.
⁷⁰ Fairfax County *Deed Book D (Part I)*, page 305.
⁷¹ *Ibid (Part II)*, page 598.
⁷² Charles Brent (ca. 1695-January 13, 1756), married Hannah Innes (or Innis), about 1725. She was a daughter of James Innes of Richmond County, who died in 1710. Mrs. Brent died in 1762. Charles Brent was a son of Hugh Brent (ca. 1660-1716) of Lancaster County, who married Catherine. He was a grandson of another Hugh Brent (ca. 1620-1671) of Isle of Wight County, who married on June 20, 1642, Mary Ocherson. See *The Descendants of Hugh Brent*, by Charles Horton Brent, Tuttle Publishing Company, Rutland, Vermont, 1936, pages 56-58.
⁷³ Stafford County, *Will Book O*, page 317.
⁷⁴ The original bond is on file at Arlington Court House, and contains one of the few extant signatures of Wren.
⁷⁵ *The Falls Church (1733-1940)* by Charles A. Stewart (MS), February, 1941, page 53.
⁷⁶ Fairfax County, *Orders, Book 3*, page 3.
⁷⁷ *Revolutionary War Pension #W 1728-Va.*, filed in the National Archives, Washington, D.C.
⁷⁸ Fairfax County, Virginia, *Deed Book Q 1*, page 398.
⁷⁹ Loudoun County *Deed Book K*, page 93.
⁸⁰ Fairfax County *Deed Book U*, page 446.
⁸¹ *Ibid*, page 446.
⁸² *Ibid, Deed Book T 1*, page 152.
⁸³ *Ibid, Deed Book B 2*, page 480.
⁸⁴ On February 22, 1963, when the new Methodist Building at 5001 Echols Avenue, Alexandria, was opened, the James Wren Chapel was dedicated to his memory. He was a convert to Methodism. The D.A.R. erected a plaque in the Falls Church to his memory.
⁸⁵ Wren also owned the large frame and log house which in recent years was called the "Kitchen Place," on the Vale Road in western Fairfax County. This house, now being restored by C. J. Reeder, was purchased by Col. James Wren on April 5, 1790. from his son, James Wren,Jr.
⁸⁶ An infant of Mr. and Mrs. Morgan Nalls was buried there after 1900. The Nalls family held "Long View" under rent, and received permission to bury their son from Mrs. Molly Wren.
⁸⁷ Alexandria, Virginia *Deed Book z*, page 83.
⁸⁸ Fairfax County, *Will Book K*, pages 363-367.
⁸⁹ Charles Piper, Blacksmith, is mentioned in the will of his master, Harry Piper, made November 1, 1774, probated in Fairfax Court February 22, 1780, by which he was given his freedom. He may have been hired by Wren after 1780, or, as was sometimes the case, sold himself into slavery.
⁹⁰ As a matter of record, Wren is listed with four slaves in Loudoun County (on his Quarter) in 1782-87 (*Virginia Tax Payers*, page 140); and at the same time, on the list of Thomas Lewis, with 6 white tithes and 25 slaves in Fairfax (*Virginia 1790 Census*, page 17). The tax list for Fairfax County in 1785 (list compiled by Wren) gives him 8 white tithes, 1 dwelling house, and 13 other buildings (Ibid, page 86).
⁹¹ Fairfax County, *Will Book S 1*, page 274.
⁹² *Ibid*, page 414.
⁹³ *Ibid, Will Book L*, page 53.
⁹⁴ George C. *Lamkin*, made his will which was probated November 21, 1814 (*Will Book K 1*, page 242). In it he writes that he was about to be "called in defence of my much injured Country," (War of 1812), but the will is not dated. He mentioned his "Aunt Sarah Wren," to whom he gave $50.00, his sister, Frances Hays of Fauquier County, sister Sarah Parker of Ohio, and their children. He also mentioned sisters Betsy Pepper and Charlotte Craig of Kentucky. W. Richard Wren was named Executor. Witnesses were: Thomas Lindsay, John Wood, and Rebecca S. Hampton.
⁹⁵ Fairfax County, *Will Book M*, page 312.
⁹⁶ Fairfax County, *Will Book M*, page 317.
⁹⁷ No evidence that issue came from the second marriage. A daughter, Sarah, born March 3, 1768, had a step-mother when but a small child, and this daughter was the last known child of Colonel Wren.
⁹⁸ Fairfax County, Virginia, *Deed Book S 1*, page 152.
⁹⁹ *Ibid, Deed Book Z 1*, page 398.
¹⁰⁰ A log was found in the house with the date 1705, according to members of the Kitchen family.
¹⁰¹ *U. S. Census of Virginia*, 1790, page 86.
¹⁰² *Ibid*, page 18.
¹⁰³ The children were assigned to each mother from old letters and papers owned by the Reverend Raymond Fitzhugh Wrenn, May 1964.

[104] George Brent was born November 4, 1745 in Lancaster County, Virginia, and belonged to the same family as did Catherine Brent, wife of Col. James Wren. He was a son of Thomas and Ann (Yerby) Brent, and died in 1785 in Loudoun County. Mr. Brent married Joanna Wale (who married a second husband, James Lewis). Mrs. Joanna (Wale) (Brent) Lewis made her will April 7, 1827 (codicil April 9, 1827), probated in Loudoun County on May 14, 1827. In this she mentioned her friend, John P. Dulaney, her granddaughter, Patsy Newton Wren; her son, Hugh Brent; her "four present children;" her daughter, Sarah Powell (and her children); son Willis Brent; son-in-law, Thomas Wren; and named John M. Green, Executor. Witnesses were: Edward Hall, Henry Smith, and John P. Dulaney. (Loudoun County, *Will Book Q*, page 301). By George Brent, Mrs. Lewis had the following children: Sarah (Brent) Powell; Joanna (Brent) Wren; Thomas Brent; Willis Brent; Martin Brent; and Hugh Brent.

[105] Proof of this can be found in Loudoun County *Death Records*, record number 306. In Arlington County Court House is a marriage bond of Francis Adams to *Mary Ricketts Newton*, William Newton, Bondsman, on December 20, 1814.

[106] This information, and other on this family, can be found in *The Descendants of Hugh Brent* by Chester Horton Brent, Tuttle Publishing Company, Rutland, Vermont, 1936, pp. 95-96.

[107] Mr. Wrenn used the double "n" spelling.

[108] Wrenn Papers. This notebook has written on the fly leaf: "James Wren Pocket Book August 14, 1800" — "James Wrens Book May the 19, 1801——."

[109] Fairfax County, Virginia, *Deed Book A 3*, page 14.

[110] *Ibid, Deed Book C 4*, page 455.

[111] *Ibid*, page 206.

[112] *Ibid*, page 366.

[113] *Ibid*, Deed Book D 3, page 38.

[114] *Ibid, Will Book U*, page 137.

[115] One record states July 12, 1845.

[116] Fairfax County, Virginia, *Will Book U*, page 344.

[117] *Ibid*, page 345.

[118] *Ibid, Will Book V*, page 206.

[119] This date, and others in this section, can be found in the *Wrenn Family Bible*, published in 1831, and owned by Mrs. R. N. Wrenn of Herndon. A notation in the front shows that it was purchased on August 9, 1836.

[120] "Mount Rocky," on the road from Chantilly to Centreville, is still owned by a Wrenn descendant, Oden Hutchison.

[121] *Wrenn Papers.*

[122] *Ibid.*

[123] Fairfax County, Virginia, *Deed Book R 3*, page 264.

[124] *Ibid*, 273.

[125] This shows that the *Estate Account* of Hugh Mitchell, deceased, was filed on February 4, 1838, by Emily Mitchell, Widow. Hugh and Emily (Wooster) Mitchell had the following children, listed among the suit papers: (1) Lucinda, wife of James Wrenn; (2) Robert Mitchell; (3) Jane Elizabeth, wife of Wesley Hutchison; (4) Eliza, wife of George W. Kipps; (5) Benjamin F. Mitchell; (6) Francis A. Mitchell; (7) James W. Mitchell; (8) Mary Mitchell; and (9) Hugh Mitchell, Jr. The last five named were young when their father died on December 25, 1837. This suit was filed May 17, 1847. Ann Mitchell, daughter of Benjamin and Betty Neville (Jones) Mitchell, married William Lewis. A descendant of this couple, Francis Lewis of Prince William County, is currently writing a history of the Mitchell family.

[126] From the loose papers of Loudoun County (no index).

[127] Loudoun County, Virginia, *Will Book O*, page 3.

[128] There may have been an Elizabeth A. Wren, daughter of this Robert. Elizabeth A. (Wren) Minor of Alexandria County, made her will November 12, 1885, probated May 24, 1886 (Arlington County, *Will Book 10*, page 72). In it she mentioned her brother, James Q. (O?) Wrenn, a brother, S. H. Wrenn, a daughter, Mord M. Minor; and six children (not named). Witnesses were: John Powell, W.T.S. Duvall, and F. A. Clarvore.

[129] See *The Mirror*, Leesburg, August 30, 1871.

[130] Fairfax County, *Deed Book N 4*, page 341.

[131] Note of Mrs. O. J. Rogers, July 6, 1962.

[132] John Henry Hurst was born December 23, 1831, died January 6, 1914. His wife, Ann Virginia Bicksler, was born May 24, 1832, died November 28, 1905. They are buried at Chestnut Grove, Herndon. Among their children were: William Hurst; Eppa Hurst; Frank Hurst; Alice Virginia (Hurst) Wrenn; Anna Roberta (Hurst) Wrenn; and Benjamin Hurst who married Frances Thrift. Benjamin's children included: Hazel Hurst, married Lacy Ferguson (had Ann (Ferguson) White of Herndon); and Lester Hurst who married Lethia Alexander.

133 Interview, Mrs. O. J. Rogers, July 6, 1962.
134 *Notes.* William Lane, an early Prince William resident, married a de Moville, and had two sons (perhaps others): James de Moville Lane who married Patsy Carr and William Lane, who married Mary Carr. James de Moville and Patsy (Carr) Lane had three children: Captain William Lane, married Susanna Linton Jennings; Joseph Lane, married Miss Prince of Princeton, New Jersey (whose only child married Peter Jett of Rappahannock County); and Ellen Lane who married Colonel Simon Triplett. Of these, Captain William Lane by his wife, Susanna Linton Jennings, had eleven children: James Lane, married Mrs. Catherine (Triplett) Alexander; Anne Linton Lane, married Humphrey Peake; Ralph Lane, married Susan Triplett; Patsy Carr Lane, married John Bailey; Elizabeth Lane, married (1) a cousin, Philo Lane, and (2) John Wren; Catherine Lane, unmarried; Susan Lane, unmarried; Alfred Lane, unmarried; Harrison Lane, married Lucinda Carter; Sarah Lane, unmarried; and Benedict Middleton Lane, married (1) Anne Adams and (2) Susan Cockerille. William Carr (1771-1855) was related to this Lane family. He married (1) Margaret Wrenn and (2) Mrs. Mary (Dyer) Hughes. Issue: David Carr; Wesley Carr; Rachel Carr, married David Nixon; E·elina Carr, married —— Claggett; Jane Carr, married David Fulton; William Carr, Jr.; Mary Ellen Carr, married Joseph Helm; Josephus Carr; and John Henry Carr.
135 Fairfax County, *Deed Book Z 2*, page 151.
136 *Ibid,* Will Book L, page 79. This record is dated October 27, 1815.
137 *Ibid, Will Book O*, page 354.
138 See *Branches and Twigs on the Fox Family Tree* by Susie Fox Follin, March, 1955.
139 George Peake married Fannie Sears (born Fairfax County, 1770). They went to Ohio. Issue: Alexander Peake, William B. Peake, Martha (Pattie) Peake, married Richard Wren; Bettie Peake, married —— Harman; and Mary Peake. See *William & Mary Quarterly*, (second series), volume II (1931), page 72.
140 Fairfax County, *Deed Book Q*, page 175.
141 One family tradition asserts that John Wren's wife was a Talbott. This indicates Samuel Talbott was a neighbor, and may tend to confirm the tradition.
142 Fairfax County, *Deed Book Q*, page 179.
143 *Ibid, Deed Book G 2*, page 292.
144 There may have been a Magruder connection, hence the use of the given name Verlinda, a favorite Magruder name. In *Will Book 2*, Jefferson County, Kentucky, is the will of Ann Harding. She left property to Sarah Ann Wrenn; niece, Malinda W. Wren; Hezekiah Magruder; nephew, Josiah Harding Magruder; remainder to nephews and nieces: Hezekiah Magruder, Josiah Harding Magruder, and Verlinda W. Wren, sons and daughters of Daniel Magruder. Executors: Hezekiah and Josiah H. Magruder. This will was made October 15, 1821, probated November 12, 1821. It is to be noted that Colonel James Wren left a piece of silver to Verlinda Magruder, daughter of Daniel Magruder.
145 Fairfax County, Virginia, *Will Book O 1*, page 68.
146 Fairfax County, Virginia, *Will Book N 1*, page 106.
147 One tradition in this family states that some of the Wrens adopted the "Wrenn" spelling due to this marriage to a Dutch Hite!
148 Fairfax County, *Will Book U*, page 108.
149 *Ibid,* page 352.
150 Filed in *Will Book C*, page 451, and in miscellaneous suits.
151 Fairfax County, *Deed Book Y 2*, page 193.
152 *Ibid, Deed Book Z 2*, page 138.
153 *History of Callaway County, Missouri,* National Historical Company, 1884, St. Louis, Missouri, page 246.
154 *Lee of Virginia,* by Edmund J. Lee, 1895, *Vol. 2,* pp. 546-547.
155 Fairfax County, *Deed Book B 3*, page 201.
156 *Ibid, Deed Book F 3,* page 146.
157 *History of Callaway County, Missouri,* National Historical Company, St. Louis, 1884, page 546.
158 Fairfax County, Virginia, *Will Book R 1*, page 410.
159 Fairfax County, Virginia, *Will Book S 1*, page 51.
160 Mrs. Lucinda (Davis) (Wren) Dyson had eight children by William Dyson: (1) Joseph H. Dyson, married Molly Walthal; (2) Mary Dyson, born 1841, married 1863, W. H. Garrett (born October 11, 1837, died 1924) and died in 1917; (3) Alice Dyson, born 1844, died January, 1902, married in 1860 to D. R. Knox (born September 9, 1843) and had Mrs. J. C. Brashear, E. H. Knox, J. H. Knox, Samuel Knox, and Mrs. Harold Ellis; (4) Lucy Dyson, born 1847, married 1869, Zedekiah Randolph Kidwell (born December 6, 1845, died August 7, 1897) formerly of Fairfax County; (5) Samuel A. Dyson, born 1849, married Henrietta Singleton;

(6) William Dyson, born 1851, married Alice Bryant; (7) Lillie Dyson, born 1854, married L. D. Farmer; and (8) Dorsey Dyson, died young.

[161] Information supplied by Mr. John Wren Cook of Alexandria, Virginia, formerly of Callaway County, Mo., October 18, 1958.

[162] Fairfax County, Virginia, *Deed Book C 3*, page 451.

[163] Mrs. Mary Ann (Crump) Cook was a daughter of James Smith Crump (February 10, 1814-September 4, 1883) who married on September 15, 1842, Polly Ann Martin (March 22, 1820-May 25, 1907) daughter of John P. and Sarah (Hatcher) Martin. She was a granddaughter of Richard Crump of Fauquier County, Virginia, born March 13, 1762, died October 22, 1828, and who moved to Missouri in 1820. Richard Crump married, in 1796, Sarah Smith (born June 12, 1776, died November 12, 1839).

[164] James G. Ford, father of Lorraine A. Cook, was born in Kentucky on November 31, 1864. He moved with his parents to Missouri and settled near McCredie, and married Anna Leora Armstrong on April 26, 1905. He died February 14, 1953.

[165] Minta Sisson died April 7, 1853 in Fairfax County, age 66 years. She was a daughter of Matthew and Sally Boswell. Mrs. Sisson was born in Fairfax County. Her husband, Robert T. Sisson, reported the death. (Fairfax County, *Death Records*)

[166] Fairfax County *Deed Book F 3*, page 37.

[167] *Ibid*, *Deed Book D 3*, page 474.

[168] *Ibid*, *Deed Book H 3*, page 17.

[169] *Ibid*, *Deed Book N 3*, page 210.

[170] *Ibid*, *Will Book F 2*, page 364.

[171] The surname Milholland was given by Rufus W. Wren. *The Mirror*, Leesburg, Virginia, for March 7, 1878 announces this marriage, which took place in Metropolitan M.E. Church, Wlshington, D.C., February 22, 1878, as *Edward L.* Wren of Fairfax County to Miss Mary D. *Holland* of Leesburg.

[172] Name on the marriage bond filed at Fairfax is not clear.

[173] Various accounts state that Wren married "the widow Curtis," "Frances Curtis," etc. None of these can be proved from records examined.

[174] Prince William County, *Will Book C*, page 320.

[175] *Ibid*, page 398/99.

[176] Fairfax County, *Court Orders (1754-56) Part I*, page 45.

[177] *Ibid*, page 36.

[178] Loudoun County, Virginia, *Land Cause Book No. 1 (1757-after 1783)*, pages 24, 25, and 26.

[179] Fairfax County, *Will Book C*, page 26.

[180] Fairfax County, Virginia, *Deed Book E 1*, page 52.

[181] Loudoun County, Virginia, *Deed Book K*, page 385.

[182] Recorded in Loudoun County records.

[183] *Order Book G*, page 159 (Loudoun County). Thomas Sanford was later appointed Administrator.

[184] His Inventory was filed in *Will Book B*, page 279, and that of Mrs. Wren in *Will Book B*, page 301.

[185] Loudoun County, *Will Book D*, page 20.

[186] This may be the John Wren whose wife is buried in Christ Church yard, Alexandria (*See elsewhere*).

[187] Alexandria, *Deed Book H*, page 147.

[188] *Ibid*, page 152.

[189] *Ibid*, *Deed Book B 2*, page 157.

[190] Fairfax County, *Will Book V*, page 321.

[191] *Ibid*, *Will Book T 1*, page 90.

[192] *Ibid*, page 92.

[193] From a Bible Record owned by Mrs. Earle T. Mutersbaugh.

[194] Fairfax County, *Will Book E 2*, page 439.

[195] Information on this family was supplied by Mrs. B. K. Gibson, and Mrs. Theodore A. Dunst. *Note:* Elizabeth (Jenkins) Wren had sisters named Melissa and Nancy Jenkins.

[196] Fairfax County, *Deed Book M 1*, page 140.

[197] Loudoun County, Virginia, *Deed Book M*, page 76.

[198] *Census of 1790* (Virginia Tax Payers), page 140.

# At the End of the Fence Row[1]

The fence row by Big Chimneys ended opposite the Quarry. Other and somewhat longer fence lines were over the hill and as far as human eye could see: a point at lane's end. Other neighbors, other firesides, but none quite like Falls Church.

The old-time hundred leaf roses are gone, the much more striking roses of today grace our many gardens. The old firesides are gone, too, but the gleam and glow returns in changing patterns. Old ways blend with the new, and demand a new look.

In May, 1950, a member of the City Council, recalling the days of long ago, proclaimed that he wanted a community "like Melvin Steadman's Falls Church." This rather personal feeling is an echo of a dear friend of other days, Mrs. John F. Bethune, and will speak for the author's Falls Church:

"... we seem to hear a voice from the olden days saying, Virginians, your glory is not all in the past; your sons are carrying on the traditions of their fathers, and will, as long as old monuments endure and old institutions are cherished."

We cannot and will not return to the past . . . we will cherish the best from fence and fireside, confident in the after-glow.

---

[1] History knows no end. Life goes on, and each new generation brings to life its own story. The author regrets that a large portion of his manuscript could not be used because of space limitations. He takes no responsibility for the family data, most of which was supplied to him by subject families. To this he had added names and dates from court and church records. Additions and corrections will be welcome.

# APPENDIX

## BIBLIOGRAPHY

Hundreds of books have been examined—from public and private collections. Old tombstones, court records, letters, and collections of private papers have been sifted. Areas of research included the manuscript collections at Duke University, the University of North Carolina, the University of Virginia, the Library of Congress and the D.A.R. Library. The author has in his personal files several thousand original documents pertaining to Falls Church, and correspondence from all over the United States.

The Bibliography listed is of secondary sources, and is not complete. The author's file on Falls Church will ultimately be deposited in the Virginia Room of the Falls Church Library. Thus, "after a time," these papers will be available for additional study.

    Andrews, Marietta Minnigerode, *George Washington's Country*, E.P. Dutton & Co., Inc., New York, 1930.

    Architectural Forum Magazine, article, December 1948 issue, on Tyler Park.

    Bethune, Lucina M. (Mrs. John F.), *A Brief History of Falls Church*, printed by the Falls Church Chapter, D.A.R., 1923. Mrs. Bethune read this address at the 4th of July celebration on the steps of the Lawton House in 1923.

    Bethune, Lucina M. (Mrs. John F.) *Golden Jubilee History—Falls Church Presbyterian Church, 1884-1934.*

    Brock, Irving, *Colonial Churches in Virginia.*

    Brydon, George Maclaren, *Virginia's Mother Church and the Political Conditions Under Which It Grew,* Philadelphia, Church Historical Society, 1952.

    *Calling All Girls Magazine,* article, February, 1949, on the Teen Canteen in Falls Church.

    Chastellux, Francois Jean, Marquis de, *Travels in North America, in the years 1780-82,* New York, 1928.

    Choate, Columbus D., *Historic Fairfax County.*

    Cook, John Esten, *Virginia, A History of the People* (American Commonwealths Series), Boston, Houghton-Mifflin & Co., 1899.

    Elliot, Jonathan, *Historical Sketches of the Ten Miles Square Forming the District of Columbia,* 1830.

    Embrey, Alvin T., *Waters of The State,* Old Dominion Press, Inc., Richmond, Va., 1931.

    Eubank, H. Ragland, *Touring Historyland; The Authentic Guide Book of Historic Northern Neck of Virginia; The Land of George Washington and Robert E. Lee,* issued by The Northern Neck Association, Colonial Beach, Va. Richmond, Va., Whittet & Shepperson, 1934.

    Ford, Paul Leicester, *The True George Washington,* Philadelphia, J. B. Lippincott Co., 1900.

    Freeman, Douglas Southall, *George Washington; A Biography,* New York, Charles Scribner's Sons, 1948-55.

    Groome, H. C., *Fauquier during the Proprietorship; a Chronicle of the Colonization and Organization of a Northern Neck County,* Richmond, Old Dominion Press, 1927.

    Gutheim, Frederick, *The Potomac,* 1949.

    Harrison, Fairfax, *Landmarks of Old Prince William; a Study of Origins in Northern Virginia.* Richmond, The Old Dominion Press, 1924, two volumes.

    Hayes, Francis W., Jr., *An Historical Sketch of Falls Church, At Falls Church, Va.,* 1948.

    Hayes, Francis W., Jr., *A Year Book for 1948 and Historical Sketch of the Falls Church, Falls Church, Va.*

    Hopkins, G. M., *Atlas of 15 Miles Around Washington,* etc., Philadelphia, 320 Walnut St., 1879.

    *House Beautiful Magazine,* August, 1948 (vol. 90 #8), on the Frank Lloyd Wright house in Falls Church, page 32, *et. seq.*

    *The Iron Worker,* Fall Issue, 1950, Vol. XIV, No. 4, contains article on Falls Church.

    Johnston, F., *Memorials of Old Virginia Clerks,* J. P. Bell Co., Lynchburg, Va., 1888.

    Konwiser, Harry M., *Colonial and Revolutionary Posts,* Richmond, Va., The Dietz Press, 1931.

Lancaster, Robert A., Jr., *Historic Virginia Homes and Churches*.
Lee, Mrs. Dorothy Ellis, *A History of Arlington County, Va.*
Madison Elementary School, Mrs. Margaret V. Hartman's 7th grade class, 1945, *The Study of Falls Church*, printed in May, 1945 by the Jodizes "Arlington Letter Service Press," Clarendon, Virginia.
Martin, J. O., *Over the Concrete*, C. & P. Telephone Company.
Meade, William, *Old Churches and Families of Virginia*, Philadelphia, 1857, J. B. Lippincott & Co.
McAtee, W. L., *A Sketch of the Natural History of the District of Columbia*, May, 1918, Washington, D. C.
Moore, Gay Montague, *Seaport in Virginia; George Washington's Alexandria*, Richmond, Va., Garrett and Massie, Inc., 1949.
Nannes, Caspar, article in the *Evening Star*, Washington, D.C., of June 29, 1947—"Falls Episcopal Church at Falls Church, Va., Had the Rev. Charles Green as First Rector" with a sketch by artist Leslie Bontz.
Nickell, Lehman, & Randolph, Cary J., *An Economic and Social Survey of Fairfax County*, University of Virginia, Record Extension Series, May 23, 1924.
Olesen, Don, article in the *Washington Post*, Washington, D. C., of August 15, 1948, "18th Century Village of Falls Church Becomes a City Tonight."
Page, Thomas Nelson, *The Old Dominion, Her Making and Her Manners*, Chas. Scribner's Sons, N.Y., 1908.
Proctor, John C., and others, *Washington Past and Present*, Lewis Historical Publishing Co., Inc., New York, 1930.
W.P.A., *Prince William; the Story of its People and its Places*, Richmond, Va., Whittet & Shepperson, 1941 (The Bethlehem Good Housekeeping Club, Manassas, Va.).
Richmond & Danville Railroad Co., *Country Homes Near The Nation's Capital*, Richmond, Va.
Rollings, Robert C., article in the *Evening Star* of Washington, D.C., March 6, 1947, "150 Year Old Fairfax Grist Mill to be Restored and Operated."
Shuster, Ernest A., article in *National Geographic Magazine*, Volume XX, April, 1909, pp. 356-359, "Original Boundary Stones of the District of Columbia."
Smith, Captain John, *The General History of Virginia, New England, etc.*, 1624.
Snowden, W. H., *Some Old Historic Landmarks of Virginia and Maryland*, 3rd edition, Alexandria, Va., printed by G. H. Ramey & Son, 1902.
Stetson, Charles W., *Four Mile Run Land Grants*, Mimeoform Press, Washington, D.C., 1935.
Slaughter, Philip, *The History of Truro Parish*, edited by Edward L. Goodwin, Historiographer of the Diocese of Virginia, was published in 1907-1908 by George W. Jacobs & Co., Publishers, Philadelphia, Pa. Copies are in all good libraries. This is recommended for further study.
Townsmen of Fairfax, Va., *A Brochure on Fairfax County*.
U. S. Army Engineers, *Potomac River and its Tributaries*, House Document, No. 622, 79th Congress, 2nd Session, 1946.
*Virginia: A Guide to the Old Dominion*, W.P.A., New York, Oxford University Press, 1940.
Washington, George, *The Diaries of George Washington, 1748-1799*, John C. Fitzpatrick, Editor, published for the Mount Vernon Ladies Association of the Union, Boston, Houghton Mifflin Co., 1925.
*Washington Daily News*, article, June 1, 1947, page 26, "The Story of a Home."
Waterman, Thomas Tileston, *The Mansions of Virginia, 1706-1776*, Chapel Hill, The University of North Carolina Press, 1946.
*West Virginia; A Guide to the Mountain State*, W.P.A., Oxford University Press, 1941.
Wigmore, Francis M., *The Old Parish Churches of Virginia*, The Library of Congress, Washington, D. C., 1929.
Wilstach, Paul, *Tidewater Virginia*, Blue Ribbon Books, Inc., New York, 1929.
Wilstach, Paul, *Potomac Landings*, Tudor Publishing Co., N.Y., 1937.
*Yearbook, Fairfax County Police Association*, 1947.

# ROLL OF ELECTED MAYORS

Dr. John J. Moran, elected by acclamation, Chairman pro. tem. April 13, 1875, elected Mayor July 1, 1875. Served until July 1, 1876.
T. T. Fowler (July 1, 1876 — July 2, 1877).
Dr. John J. Moran (July 2, 1877 — July 1, 1878).
T. T. Fowler (July 1, 1878 — May 26, 1879).
Wells Forbes (May 26, 1879 — July 1, 1879).
Lewis S. Abbott (July 1, 1879 — Aug. 18, 1879).
George B. Ives (Aug. 18, 1879 — July 1, 1881).
William P. Graham (July 1, 1881 — July 5, 1881).
W. A. Duncan (July 5, 1881 — July 1, 1882).
Seth Osborn (July 1, 1882 — July 6, 1882).
Edward J. Birch (July 6, 1882 — July 1, 1884 and probably afterwards).
*(July 1, 1884 to July 1898 minutes are missing; the following names are from other sources.)*
On June 12, 1890 George W. Hawxhurst was Mayor. His term ended July 1, 1890.
On July 1, 1890 Minor F. Chamblin was Mayor. His term extended to July 1, 1891, and perhaps later.
Merton Elbridge Church served as Mayor in this period.
William M. Ellison served *four* terms as Mayor—the first probably here.
*(The following are from extant minutes):*
George W. Hawxhurst (July 1898 — July 2, 1900).
Harry L. Turner (July 2, 1900 — March 10, 1902).
Wm. M. Ellison (March 10, 1902 — July 7, 1902).
C. C. Walters (July 7, 1902 — Sept. 1, 1904).
George N. Lester (Sept. 1, 1904 — April 15, 1905).
Wm. M. Ellison (April 15, 1905 — Sept. 1, 1905).
George W. Hawxhurst (Sept. 1, 1905 — Sept. 9, 1906).
John D. Payne (Sept. 9, 1906 — Sept. 2, 1907).
George L. Erwin (Sept. 2, 1907 — Sept. 1, 1908).
Thomas A. Williams (Sept. 1, 1908 — Sept. 1, 1909).
George W. Hawxhurst (Sept. 1, 1909 — May 12, 1913).
Harry A. Fellows (July 14, 1913 — July 13, 1914).
J. B. Herndon (July 13, 1914 — June 12, 1916).
Capt. John Franklin Bethune (June 12, 1916 — June 22, 1916).
Dr. S. S. Luttrell (June 22, 1916 - Nov. 12, 1917)
J. Edward Thomas (Dec. 12, 1917 —— ).
Wm. M. Ellison (was Mayor on Jan. 14, 1918).
Carroll V. Shreve (was Mayor on July 8, 1918).
J. Edward Thomas (Sept. 1, 1918 — Sept. 1, 1920)
Harry A. Fellows (Sept. 1, 1920 — June —, 1926).
Harmon B. Green (June —, 1926 — March 14, 1927).
Richard C. L. Moncure (March 14, 1927 — June 12, 1928).
Capt. John Franklin Bethune (June 12, 1928 — June 10, 1930).
Leonard Percy Daniel (June 10, 1930 — July 11, 1940).
Burns Nixon Gibson (July 11, 1940 — Feb. 8, 1943).
J. H. McCarthy (Acting Mayor) (Feb. 8, 1943 — April 12, 1943).
Martin H. Haertal (April 12, 1943 — June 11, 1946).
Fenner Hazelgrove (June 11, 1946 — Sept. 1, 1948).
Albert H. Orme (Sept. 1, 1948 — Sept. 4, 1951).
Charles E. Kellogg (Sept. 4, 1951 — Sept. 1, 1953).
Eldon Colby (Sept. 1, 1953 — July 11, 1955).
Herman Fink (July 11, 1955 — Sept. 2, 1957).
Thomas O'Halloran (Sept. 2, 1957 — Sept. 1, 1959).
Charles M. Hailey (Sept. 1, 1959 — present, 1964).

*This roll includes only elected Mayors. The Falls Church Public Library has in its files a more complete list which includes temporary officers of the Council who served in the absence of the elected Mayor.

## LOCAL POPULATION SHIFT

| Year | Washington[1] | Fairfax Co.[2] | Arlington Co.[3] | Alexandria[4] | Falls Church[5] |
|---|---|---|---|---|---|
| 1790 | | 12,320 | | | |
| 1800 | | 13,317 | | | |
| 1810 | | 13,111 | | | |
| 1820 | 13,247 | 11,404 | | 8,218 | |
| 1830 | | 9,204 | | | |
| 1840 | | 9,370 | | | |
| 1850 | | 10,682 | | | |
| 1860 | | 11,834 | | | |
| 1870 | 109,199 | 12,952 | 16,755 | 13,570 | |
| 1880 | | 16,025 | | | |
| 1890 | | 16,665 | | | 792 |
| 1900 | 278,718 | 18,580 | | 14,528 | 1,007 |
| 1910 | | 20,536 | 10,231 | | |
| 1920 | | 21,943 | 16,040 | | 1,659 |
| 1930 | | 25,264 | 26,615 | | 2,019 |
| 1940 | 663,091 | 40,929 | 57,040 | 33,523 | 2,576 |
| 1950 | | 98,557 | | | 7,535 |

[1] Washington, D. C., coextensive with the District of Columbia since 1895.
[2] Statistics on Fairfax County can be found in the 1953 Report of the Secretary of the Commonwealth of Virginia (Note population jump between 1940 and 1950—an increase of 140.8%.)
[3] The 1870 figure for Arlington County (then Alexandria County) included the city of Alexandria with 13,570 people.
[4] The City of Alexandria was part of the District of Columbia from 1791 to 1846.
[5] In 1904 there was an estimated population of 1,100 in Falls Church. By special enumeration in 1948, the population was 5,338. The purpose of this enumeration was to determine if there was sufficient population to justify Falls Church being made a second class city.

In 1950 the median income for Falls Church was $5,098.00. Only 10.9% of the population had an income below $2,000.00.

The increase in population for Falls Church, during 1940/50, was 192.5%. The *Falls Church District* for 1930-50 had the following increase:

    1930 .................................................................... 4,173
    1940 .................................................................... 7,614
    1950 ....................................................................26,617

See the following for additional material: *Fairfax Herald*, February 22, 1901, and *Census Of Population: 1950*, Volume II, part 46 (G.P.O., 1952), page 46:11-13.

### ASSESSED VALUATION TAXABLE VALUE
### AS OFFICIALLY REPORTED FOR FALLS CHURCH

    1900 ..................................................................442,504
    1905 ..................................................................455,671
    1910 ..................................................................558,801
    1915 ..................................................................742,715
    1920 ..................................................................838,165
    1923 ................................................................1,069,531

The above figures were given in a School Board Circular dated September 23, 1924.

*The *Fairfax Herald* of August 18, 1899 reports "The total assessment of real and personal property in the town of Falls Church is $438,357."

## LIST OF TITHABLES, 1748/9 (See End Paper Map)

Appended to the Reverend Charles Green's report concerning the condition of his Parish is a listing of the tithables, persons in his care, and a number of notations concerning their religious and political affiliation. All of the persons listed were, by law, in Mr. Green's charge. Thus we have a valuable account, in a sense a "census" of Northern Virginia for 1748/9. Since many of the records of this period are missing, Mr. Green's list will have particular value to historians.[1]

### Page 1, Column 1

| Name | White | Negro | Remarks |
|---|---|---|---|
| Angel, Cha | 1 | | |
| Adams, Gab | 2 | | formerly a Vestryman |
| Adams, Abra | 1 | | |
| Adams, Jno | 2 | | |
| Adams, Abedno | 2 | | |
| Awbrey, Tho | 1 | 4 | Vestryman, Upper Parish |
| Awbrey, Hen | 2 | 3 | 1 Papist, Petr Lane, Upper Parish |
| Ashton, Hen | 1 | 2 | of Westmoreland |
| Alexander, Phil Jr | 1 | 8 | Maj. in Stafford |
| Alexander, Jno Jr | | 6 | of Stafford |
| Alexander, Gerd | | 12 | Justice |
| Aylets, Heirs | 1 | 14 | of Westmoreland |
| Ashford, Jno | 3 | 1 | 1 Papist Michl Monchera, Lower Parish |
| Ashford, Mich | 1 | | Papist comes sometimes to Church Lower Parish |
| Ashford, Wil | 1 | | Papist comes sometimes to Church Lower Parish |
| Anderson, Bapt. | 2 | 1 | |
| Anderson, Jno | 2 | | Presbyterian, Upper Parish |
| Alexon, Tho | 1 | | |
| Ansdale, Dan | 1 | | |
| Arpe, Josh | 2 | | |
| Arpe, Jo | 2 | | |
| Arpe, Tho | 2 | | |
| Booth, Jno | 1 | | Quaker Upper Parish |
| Brown, Hen | 1 | | Quaker Upper Parish |
| Brown, Wm | 1 | | Quaker Upper Parish |
| Brown, Jno | 1 | | Quaker Upper Parish |
| Bryan, Phil | 1 | | Papist Upper Parish |
| Bivin, Ja. | 2 | | Papist Upper Parish but comes to Church of Late |
| Barnet, Jno | 1 | | Quaker Upper Parish |
| Beasley, Wm | 1 | | Anabaptist Upper Parish |
| Burster, Tho | 4 | 2 | |
| Barry, Wm | 1 | | |
| Barry, Wido | 3 | 2 | 1 a Papist Jas Delany Lower Parish |
| Bolen, Jo | 2 | | |
| Bolen, Gerd | 1 | | |
| Boilstone, Wm | 2 | | |
| Baker, Tho | 1 | | |
| Brian, Tho | 1 | | |
| Butrfield, Wm | 2 | | |
| Broadwater, Guy | 1 | | Presbyterian Lower Parish |

[1] The original list is on file in the manuscript collection in the Library of Congress. The first mention of it, found by the author, is in Dr. Douglas S. Freeman's life of Washington, Vol. I, p. 139.

| | | | |
|---|---|---|---|
| Berkley, Wm | 2 | 3 | |
| Berkley, Wm. Jr | 1 | | |
| Berkley, Burges | 1 | | Vestryman Upper Parish |
| Bailey, Tho | 3 | | |
| Bailey, Jo | 1 | | |
| Bailey, Tho | 1 | 1 | |
| Bailey, Wm | 1 | 3 | |
| Bennet, Rob | 1 | | |
| Brown, Tho | 3 | 3 | |
| Brown, Rd | 3 | | |
| Brown, Wm | 1 | | |
| Brown, Ja | 2 | | |
| Buckley, Ja | 1 | | |
| Blackburn, R | | 6 | Colo of Prince William County |
| Berryman, Heirs | 1 | 11 | |
| Buckley, Abra | 1 | | |
| Brooks, Jos | 1 | | Presbyterian Upper Parish |
| Batnet, Tho | 1 | | |
| Brummit, Wm | 2 | 1 | |
| Boseley, Tho | 3 | | |
| Bogess, Robt | 8 | 9 | 3 Presbyterians, Merchant, 1 Papist, Ja McCarty Vestryman Lower Parish |
| Bogess, Hen | 2 | 1 | |
| Bronough, Jere | 2 | 5 | Vestryman, Lower Parish. Justice. Captain |
| Bronough, Wm | 4 | | |
| Barnes, Abra | 3 | 12 | Vestryman, Lower Parish |
| Behoe, Moses | 1 | | Presbyterian, Lower Parish often at Church |
| Ballenger, Wm | 1 | | |
| Butcher, Wido | 1 | | |
| Ball, Geo | 3 | | |
| Ball, Jno | 1 | | |
| Ball, Jas | 2 | | |
| Burk, Wm | 1 | | Papist Lower Parish comes to Church |
| Bum, Dan | 2 | | Papist Upper Parish comes to Church often |
| | 124 | 111 | |

*Page 1 Column 2*

| | | | |
|---|---|---|---|
| Barton, Wm | 1 | | |
| Bradley, Mat | 1 | | |
| Broadwater, Cha | 3 | 11 | Vestryman Lower Parish. Justice |
| Butler, Ed | 2 | 1 | Papist Lower Parish, often comes to Church |
| Butler, Corns | 1 | | Papist Lower Parish, often comes to Church |
| Bosman, Tho | 2 | | |
| Brent, Hen | 2 | | Papist Lower Parish |
| Baker, Wm | 1 | 1 | |
| Buckley, Wm | 1 | 1 | |
| Cockerill, Jno | 2 | 3 | |
| Cockerill, Jos | 2 | | |
| Cash, Moses | 1 | | |
| Cash, Jos | 2 | | |
| Connel, Tho | 1 | | |
| Canterberry, Sam | 1 | 3 | |
| Christmas, Cha | 3 | | |
| Connor, Sam | 3 | 2 | 1 Papist Lower Parish Wm Keip |
| Carpenter, Rd | 2 | | |
| Crook, Jno | 1 | | Quaker Upper Parish |
| Culverhouse, Th | 1 | | |
| Connor, Terence | 1 | | |
| Carroll, Wm | 1 | | Papist Lower Parish, comes to Church often |
| Cocke, Catesby | 4 | 14 | Colo. Justice if he swears pr. Com. |

| Name | | | Notes |
|---|---|---|---|
| Combs, Jno | 1 | | |
| Coffer, Tho | 1 | 2 | |
| Carter, Rob Jr | 1 | 10 | Westmoreland |
| Carter, Tho | 1 | | |
| Carter, Chas Jr | 1 | 5 | Colo. King George |
| Curry, Barn | 1 | | Papist Upper Parish, comes to Church often |
| Colclough, Robt | 1 | 3 | |
| Chamben, Tho | 1 | | |
| Carroll, Dempsey | 1 | 3 | Papist, comes to Church often |
| Cambden, Jno | 1 | | |
| Caldwel, Hugh | 1 | | Anabaptist Upper Parish |
| Chinn, Elisha | 1 | 4 | |
| Canady, Jno | 2 | | formerly a Papist now comes to Church |
| Curk, Wm | 2 | | Quaker Upper Parish |
| Crutcher, Jadn | 2 | 2 | |
| Coalman, Rd | 1 | 3 | Vestryman Upper Parish |
| Clapham, Josia | 3 | 2 | |
| Crosley, Jo | 1 | | Presbyterian Upper Parish |
| Callahan, Jno | 1 | | Papist Upper Parish |
| Cox, Herman | 1 | | Quaker Upper Parish |
| Cleaves, Tho | 1 | | Quaker Upper Parish |
| Chilton, Geo | 1 | | Quaker Upper Parish |
| Cotton, Wm | 1 | | |
| Cotton, Jno | 1 | | |
| Chapman, Nat | 2 | 5 | |
| Collum, Hen | 3 | | |
| Champy, Wm | 1 | 1 | |
| Coburn, Wm | 1 | | |
| Connoly, Ja | 2 | | Quaker Upper Parish |
| Carty, Dan | 2 | | |
| Compton, Sam | 4 | | |
| Cotter, Tho | 2 | | |
| Clifton, Wm | 3 | 6 | Papist Lower Parish |
| Carney, Jno | 5 | | Papist Lower Parish |
| Colvil, Jno | 5 | 29 | Presbyterian, Colo, Justice & formerly a Vestryman, Lower Parish |
| Carlisle, Jno | 2 | 7 | Presbyterian, Capt Justice, Lower Parish Merchant |
| Carter, Peter | 1 | 1 | |
| Clark, Gidney | 1 | 14 | Barbadoes |
| Dalton, Jno | 2 | 6 | Presbyterian, Merchant, Lower Parish |
| Dougle, Tho | 1 | | |
| Dorrel, Susan | 5 | 2 | |
| Downs, Tho | 4 | | |
| Donalson, Jas | 4 | 2 | |
| Doolin, Wm | 5 | 1 | formerly Papist now comes to Church Lower Parish |
| Doolin, Ed | 1 | | |
| Donalson, Wm | 1 | | |
| Daly, Hu | 2 | | Papist Upper Parish |
| Davis, Ja | 2 | | |
| Davis, Tho | 4 | | |
| Davis, Sam | 1 | | Quaker Upper Parish |
| | 135 | 143 | |

Page 2 Column 1

| | | | | |
|---|---|---|---|---|
| Dade, Badn, Jr | 1 | 3 | Stafford | |
| Dade, Townsd | 2 | 4 | Justice | |
| Dixon, Ja | 3 | | Quaker Upper Parish | |
| Duncan, Wm | 1 | | Quaker Upper Parish | |
| Duncan, Blansr | 2 | | | |
| Duncan, Joshr | 2 | | | |

| Name | | | Notes |
|---|---|---|---|
| Dodd, Wm | 1 | | Quaker Upper Parish |
| Dainty, Jno | 1 | | |
| Dibell, Jno | 1 | | |
| Duren, Jno | 1 | | |
| Dosier, Leond | 1 | 2 | Vestryman Upper Parish |
| DeWit, Ja | 2 | | |
| DisKin, Danl | 1 | | |
| Daniel, Jno | 1 | | |
| Evans, Wido | 2 | | Presbyterian Lower Parish comes to church |
| Evans, Tho | 1 | | |
| English, And | 1 | | |
| English, Waltr | 1 | | |
| Ellsey, Lewis | 3 | 9 | Vestryman, lately Justice, Capt. Lower Parish |
| Ethey, Ja | 1 | | |
| Elliot, Jno Jr | | 3 | Westmoreland |
| Elliot, Jno | 1 | | |
| Ellet, Wm | 1 | | |
| Ellrey, Fra | 3 | 4 | Vestryman Upper Parish |
| Estes, Jas | 2 | | Quaker, Upper Parish |
| Eskridge, Wido | 1 | 2 | Westmoreland |
| Faihunt, Jere | 1 | | Quaker Upper Parish |
| Fields, Tho | 2 | | Papist, Upper Parish, sometimes comes to church |
| Ferguson, Jno | 1 | 5 | |
| Forrester, Mat | 2 | | |
| Fitzhugh, Wm Jr | 3 | 18 | Westmoreland Collo |
| Fitzhugh, Wm Jr | 2 | 19 | Stafford |
| Fitzhugh, Hen Jr | 1 | 19 | Stafford |
| Fitzhugh, Heirs | 2 | 28 | Stafford |
| Fryer, Wm | 1 | | |
| Frisell, Isaac | 3 | | Sectaries of some sort in Upper Parish |
| Frisell, Jno | 1 | | |
| Fairfax, Lord | 10 | 15 | |
| Fairfax, Honble | 2 | 7 | |
| Floid, Jno | 3 | 1 | |
| French, Danl | 1 | 3 | Vestryman Lower parish |
| Fry, Ja | 1 | | |
| Farmer, Ja | 1 | | |
| Fearson, Sam | 1 | | |
| Garret, Ed | 2 | | Quaker Upper Parish |
| Gunnel, Wm | 3 | 2 | |
| Grafford, Tho | 2 | | |
| Gaslin, Rob | 2 | | |
| Grayson, Ben Jr | 2 | 3 | Colo Prince William |
| Gossom, Wm | 2 | | |
| Gates, Isaac | 2 | | |
| Grimsley, Ja | 2 | | Papist comes often to church |
| Godfrey, Wm | 3 | 2 | Formerly vestryman & Justice Lower Parish |
| Guest, Jno | 2 | | |
| Graham, Jno | 2 | 10 | County Clerk |
| Guest, Wido | 1 | | |
| Grant, Alexr | 2 | | |
| Gardner, Ja | 1 | 2 | |
| Green, Chas | 2 | 6 | |
| Griffith, Chas | 1 | | Formerly Papist now churchman, Lower Parish |
| Gibson, Jno | 1 | | |
| | 121 | 184 | |

*Second Column Page 2*

| Grimes, Nic | 5 | |
| Gunnel, Henry | 6 | 1 |

| Name | | | Notes |
|---|---|---|---|
| Going, Jas Alex | 2 | | |
| Grimes, Rob & Ed | 2 | | |
| Gardner, Sil | 1 | | |
| Greg, Geo | 1 | | Quaker Upper Parish |
| Gladden, Fra | 1 | 2 | |
| Gladden, Wm | 2 | | |
| Gray, Jno | 2 | | |
| Gladden, Wido | 3 | | |
| Graham, Wil | 1 | | Papist Upper Parish |
| Green, Ja | 1 | | |
| Grant, Ja | 1 | | |
| Gladden, Jno | 1 | | |
| Goreham, Jno | 1 | | |
| Gore, Josh | 1 | | Quaker Upper Parish |
| Gore, Tho | 1 | | Quaker Upper Parish |
| Hays, Wm | 1 | | |
| Haswell, Sampn | 1 | | Presbyterian Upper Parish |
| Harrison, Tho | 1 | | |
| Henry, Aaron | 1 | | |
| Hicks, Tho | 1 | | |
| Hamilton, Jas | 6 | 2 | Vestryman Lower Parish |
| Horseman, Wil | 1 | | |
| Harrison, Wido Jr | 1 | 2 | Stafford |
| Holifield, Orson | 1 | | |
| Hirst, Jno | 3 | 2 | |
| Harness, Jno | 1 | | |
| Harle, Jno | 5 | | |
| Helms, Sam | 1 | | |
| Higgerson, Jno | 1 | | |
| Hampton, Jere | 1 | | |
| Halling, Wm | 3 | | |
| Hough, Jno | 2 | | Quaker Upper Parish |
| Hague, Fra | 3 | | Quaker Upper Parish |
| Harrington, Jno | 2 | | Papist Upper Parish |
| Harding, Wm | 1 | | |
| Hatcher, Wm | 1 | | |
| Houton, Hen | 1 | | |
| Harrison, Sam | 1 | | |
| Haney, Tim | 1 | | Quakers Upper Parish |
| Handy, Wm | 1 | | |
| Hall, Jno | 1 | | |
| Hutchinson, Jno | 1 | | |
| Hutchinson, Andw | 4 | 3 | Late vestryman, Justice |
| Hutchinson, Daniel | 3 | | |
| Halley, Ben | 2 | 2 | |
| Holifield, Dan | 1 | | |
| Hall, Elisha | 1 | 10 | Quaker Upper Parish Sometimes comes to church |
| Holly, Jno | 3 | | |
| Hartshorn, Jno | 1 | 2 | |
| Hollis, Moses | 1 | | |
| Hamton, Hen | 1 | | |
| Hereford, Jno | 4 | 2 | |
| Harrison, Wido | 1 | 4 | 1 Papist Ed barret Lower Parish Comes to church |
| Hamton, Ja | 2 | 2 | |
| Holefield, Ra | 1 | | |
| Hamlet, Jno | 1 | | |
| Hughes, Ed | 1 | 1 | Vestryman Upper Parish |
| Henwood, Jno | 1 | | |
| Hall, Wm | 1 | 2 | |
| Hardage, Ja | 2 | | |
| Hart, Jno | 2 | | |
| Jenkins, Hamess | 1 | | |
| Jenkins, Jno Jr | 1 | | |

| | | |
|---|---|---|
| Jenkins, Jas | 3 | |
| Jenkins, Enoch | 4 | |
| Jenkins, Jno Sr | 1 | 5 |
| | 119 | 42 |

*Page 3 Column 1*

| | | | |
|---|---|---|---|
| Jenkins, Mary | 1 | | |
| Jenkins, Jno | 4 | | |
| James, Danl | 5 | 2 | |
| Jay, Wm | 1 | | Quaker Upper Parish |
| Jonston, Wm | 1 | | |
| Jonston, Robt | 1 | | Presbyterian Lower Parish |
| Jennings, Alex | 3 | | Presbyterian Upper Parish Comes to Church |
| Jennings, Danl | 3 | 8 | Justice |
| Janney, Wido | 2 | | Quaker Upper Parish |
| Janney, Jacob | 1 | | Quaker Upper Parish—Preacher |
| Janney, Jacob, Jr | 1 | | Quaker Upper Parish—his wife a Preacher |
| Johns, Tho | 4 | | Quaker Upper Parish |
| Jackson, Jno | 1 | 2 | |
| Jonston, Sam | 1 | | |
| Jones, Ja | 1 | | |
| Jewel, Wm | 1 | | |
| Jones, Wm | 1 | | |
| Jennings, Hen | 1 | | |
| Jennings, Kelly | 2 | | Formerly a Preacher of what sect I know not now comes to church |
| Jacob, Ja | 1 | | |
| Keith, Ja Jr | 1 | 4 | Clerk Prince William |
| Kent, Absm | 1 | | |
| Kent, Ben | 1 | | |
| Kent, Rd | 1 | 1 | |
| Kessey, Jno | 1 | | |
| Kirkland, Ed | 1 | | |
| Kirkland, Rob | 1 | 1 | |
| Kitchen, Wm | 1 | | |
| Kent, Wil | 1 | | |
| Kirk, — | 1 | | Quaker Upper Parish |
| King, Ja | 1 | | |
| Kesmington, Wil | 1 | | |
| Knighton, Tho | 1 | | |
| Keen, Jno | 3 | | |
| Keen, Jas | 2 | 1 | |
| King, Wil | 1 | | Papist Lower Parish |
| Kidwell, Wm | 1 | | |
| Kerford, Sam | 1 | | |
| Kelly, Tho | 2 | 3 | Papist Upper Parish |
| Littleton, Ch & W | 2 | | |
| Lammum, Wm | 1 | | |
| Leister, Jno | 1 | | |
| Loid, Hen | 2 | | |
| Lucas, Jno | 1 | 1 | |
| Love, Tho | 1 | | |
| Lewis, Tho | 1 | | |
| Lewis, Thos Jr | 2 | | |
| Lewis, Stephn | 2 | 9 | Presbyterian, Justice Lower Parish |
| Lewis, Tho | 3 | 3 | Presbyterian Lower Late a Vestryman |
| Lewis, Peter | 1 | 1 | |
| Lewis, Vincent | 4 | 3 | |
| Loyal, Manass | 1 | | |
| Lay, Abra | 7 | | |

531

|  | | | |
|---|---|---|---|
| Lee, Tho Jr | 4 | 61 | Honorable, Westmoreland |
| Lee, Rich Jr | 1 | 5 | Westmoreland |
| Lamb, Robt | 1 | | |
| Llewellin, Tho | 1 | | Wife Quaker Upper Parish |
| Lane, Jas | 1 | | |
| Littlejohn, Hen | 1 | | |
| Littlejohn, Moses | 1 | | |
| Laswell, Jno | 1 | | |
| Laswell, Jacob | 1 | | |
| Laswell, Abra | 1 | | Anabaptist Upper Parish |
| Lewis, Turley | 2 | | |
| Lewis, Rd | 1 | | |
| Long, Lockr | 1 | | |
| Lindsay, Robt | 2 | | |
| Linton, Moses | 5 | 7 | Vestryman Upper Parish Justice |
| Mitchel, Adm | 2 | | |
| McMillon, Wm | 2 | | |
| | 117 | 119 | |

*Second Column Page 3*

|  | | | |
|---|---|---|---|
| Morton, Jas & Jno | 2 | | |
| Middleton, Tho | 2 | | |
| Mahoney, Wm | 2 | | |
| Moon, Wm | 2 | | |
| Mercer, Jno Jr | 1 | 9 | Stafford |
| Mason, Ben | 2 | 2 | |
| Minor, Nic, Jr | 1 | 4 | Westmoreland |
| Mead, Wm | 1 | | Quaker Upper Parish |
| Mead, — | 2 | | Quaker Upper Parish |
| Middleton, Jno | 2 | | Lately Justice |
| Massey, Cha | 1 | | |
| Morris, Jno | 2 | | |
| McGarth, Ja | 1 | | Presbyterian Upper Parish |
| Masterson, Ed | 6 | 3 | |
| Mills, Rob | 3 | | |
| Maskey, Dan | 1 | | Quaker Preacher Upper Parish |
| Moxley, Wil | 1 | | |
| Maddy, Wil | 1 | | |
| Monday, Wm | 3 | | |
| Martin, Nic | 2 | 1 | |
| McDanl, Tho | 1 | | |
| Moxley, Ja | 1 | | |
| McCasty, Jere | 1 | | |
| Massey, Rd | 1 | | |
| Monroe, — | 1 | 3 | Collo Westmoreland |
| Mills, Dan | | | |
| Mason, Cha | 2 | | |
| Minor, Jno | 1 | 4 | Late Vestryman, Justice |
| McCarthy, Dan | 3 | 12 | |
| Moody, Wm | 1 | | |
| Manley, Jnol | 3 | | |
| Moore, Wm | 2 | 2 | |
| Moxley, Sam | 3 | 1 | |
| Marshall, Tho | 1 | 6 | Maryland |
| Mason, Geo | 2 | 11 | |
| Moxley, Tho | 3 | 2 | |
| Moss, Jno | 1 | 3 | |
| McLaughlin, Jno | 1 | | Presbyterian Upper Parish |
| Morris, Jno | 2 | | Presbyterian Upper Parish |
| McMillan, Sten | 1 | | Papist comes to Church sometimes Upper Parish |

| Name | Col1 | Col2 | Notes |
|---|---|---|---|
| McSherry, Dan | 1 | | Quaker Upper Parish |
| Newton, Will Jr | 4 | 11 | Westmoreland |
| Nelson, Rd | 3 | | |
| Nelson, Josa | 1 | | |
| Nelson, Reass | 1 | | |
| Neekton, Aaron | | | |
| Norton, Ed | 1 | | Quaker Upper Parish, Wife a Preacher |
| Noland, Phil | 2 | 3 | Papist Upper Parish now comes to Church |
| Noland, Peter | 1 | | Papist now comes to Church, Upper Parish |
| Noland, Jas | 1 | | Papist Lower Parish |
| Nichols, Sol | 1 | | |
| North, Jas | 2 | | |
| Neal, Chr | 2 | 8 | |
| Neal, Danl | 1 | 8 | |
| Night, Jno | 1 | | |
| Noddin, Wm | 1 | | |
| Oliver, Wm | 3 | | |
| O'Daniel, Jno | 2 | | |
| Owins, Jno | 1 | | |
| Osborn, Rd | 2 | 5 | Major, Justice, Vestryman |
| Osborn, Jno | 1 | | Presbyterian Upper Parish |
| Osborn, Jas | 1 | | Presbyterian Upper Parish |
| Pollard, Qr. | 1 | 6 | Jo Watkins Overseer, Justice and Vestryman Upper Parish |
| Pearl, Wm | 1 | | |
| Pinkston, Val | 1 | 4 | Prince William |
| Paget, Fra | 1 | 1 | |
| Power, Ja | 1 | | Quaker Upper Parish |
| | 118 | 111 | |

*Page 4 Column 1*

| Name | Col1 | Col2 | Notes |
|---|---|---|---|
| Pattison, Cha | 4 | | |
| Payne, Jno | 1 | | Quaker Upper Parish |
| Parker, Nic | 1 | | Quaker Upper Parish |
| Philips, Jno | 2 | | Quaker Upper Parish |
| Poultney, Jno | 1 | | Quaker Upper Parish |
| Potts, David | 2 | | Quaker Upper Parish |
| Potts, Jas | 1 | | Quaker Upper Parish |
| Pyborne, Rd | 2 | | Presbyterian Upper Parish |
| Poston, Jno | 1 | | |
| Preston, Jno | 1 | | |
| Paul, Jas | 1 | | |
| Peake, Jno | 1 | 3 | |
| Peake, Wm | 3 | 6 | |
| Payne, Wm, Jr | 1 | 5 | Vestryman Lower Parish, Lately a Justice |
| Preston, Rob | 1 | | |
| Popjay, Nat | 1 | | |
| Pettwith, Jno | 1 | | Quaker Upper Parish |
| Porter, Fra | 2 | | |
| Pagan, Jno | 3 | | Presbyterian Merchant Lower Parish |
| Potter, Wm | 1 | | |
| Pearson, Simon | 1 | 5 | |
| Rust, Ben, Jr | 1 | 1 | Richmond |
| Rogers, Rd | 1 | | |
| Regan, Mic | 2 | | |
| Regan, Wm | 1 | | Papist Lower Parish |
| Regan, Jno | 1 | | |
| Remy, Sanfd | 2 | 2 | |
| Rairdon, Wm | 3 | 2 | |
| Rairdon, Hen | 1 | | |

| | | | |
|---|---|---|---|
| Robertson, Jno | 1 | | |
| Reiley, Jno | 1 | | |
| Ramsey, Ja | 7 | 7 | Presbyterian, Merchant, Justice, Lower Parish |
| Ratcliff, Jno | 2 | | Quaker Upper Parish |
| Ramsay, Jas | 1 | | Papist Lower Parish Sometimes comes to Church |
| Roberts, Jno | 1 | | |
| Roberts, Wm | 1 | | |
| Reid, — | 2 | | Presbyterian Lower Parish |
| Remy, Ben | 1 | | |
| Russell, Antho | 1 | 4 | Vestryman, Justice Upper Parish |
| Roberts, Geo | 1 | | Quaker Upper Parish |
| Remey, Wm | 1 | | |
| Russell, Wm | 1 | | |
| Reader, Swinn | 1 | | |
| Remey, Jacob | 2 | 3 | |
| Reeves, Tho | 1 | | Quaker Upper Parish |
| Russell, Cha | 1 | | |
| Roberts, Jno | 1 | | |
| Roach, Rd | 1 | | Quaker Upper Parish |
| Reiley, Jno | 2 | | Papist Upper Parish |
| Rdson (Richardson), Da | 2 | | |
| Rdson, Jno | 1 | | Presbyterian Upper Parish |
| Ross, Fra | 3 | | |
| Ross, Wm | 4 | | |
| Redmand, And | 1 | | |
| Ratcliff, Jno | 1 | | Quaker Upper Parish |
| Roberts, Rd Junr | 1 | | |
| Robertson, Wm | 1 | | Quaker Upper Parish |
| Ready, Cornl | 1 | | Papist, comes to Church sometimes Upper Parish |
| Robertson, Jas | 2 | | Presbyterian Lower Parish |
| Reynolds, Rd | 2 | | |
| Rooson, Jno | 1 | | |
| Sibley, Jno | 3 | 1 | 1 Papist Martin Duleney Lower Parish |
| Sanders, Lewis | 1 | | |
| Sanders, Tho | 1 | | |
| Sanders, Wm | 2 | | |
| Scot, Jas Jr | 1 | 5 | Clerk, Prince William |
| Shortridge, Wm | 3 | | |
| Steptoe, Jas Jr | 1 | 12 | |
| Simson, Wm | 3 | | |
| Simson, Baxt | 2 | | |
| | 114 | 54 | |

*Column 2 Page 4*

| | | | |
|---|---|---|---|
| Stevens, Rd | 3 | | |
| Smith, Tho | 3 | | |
| Smith, Jno | 4 | | |
| Smith, Jno Jr | 2 | | |
| Simson, Gilbert | 1 | | |
| Sanford, Rd | 1 | 1 | |
| Scot, Wm | 4 | | |
| Sebastan, Ben | 3 | | |
| Sanford, Robt | 1 | 3 | |
| Squire, Tho | 1 | | |
| Snow, Jno | 1 | | Papist Lower Parish |
| Smith, Jno | 1 | | |
| Sherndon, Jno | 1 | | Papist Lower Parish |
| Salter, Peter | 1 | | |
| Sparrow, Wm | 1 | | |
| Shelton, Ja | 1 | | |

| Name | Col1 | Col2 | Notes |
|---|---|---|---|
| Simson, Rd Jr | 1 | | |
| Shorley, Rd | 1 | | |
| Stevens, Jno | 2 | | |
| Sanders, Danl | 3 | | |
| Smith, Ja | 1 | | |
| Sanders, — | 1 | | |
| Sewell, Phil | 1 | | |
| Stranghan, Jno | 3 | | |
| Story, Cha | 1 | | |
| Speake, Tho | 1 | 1 | |
| Smith, Nat | 1 | | |
| Sands, Edmd | 1 | | Quaker Upper Parish |
| Shelton, Jno | 3 | | |
| Sears, Ja | 2 | | |
| Stark, Wm | 3 | | |
| Sadd, Wm | 1 | | |
| Self, Tho | 1 | | |
| Snow, Tho | 1 | | |
| Sanders, Ja | 1 | | |
| St. Clair, Wido | 2 | | |
| Snow, Hen | 2 | | |
| Speer, Ja | 2 | | |
| Summers, Fra | 2 | 4 | Vestryman Upper Parish |
| Simms, Jno | 1 | | Quaker Upper Parish |
| Simms, Jno | 1 | | Quaker Upper Parish |
| Sanders, Fra | 1 | | Quaker Upper Parish |
| Sutterfield, Ja | 2 | | |
| Sutterfield, Wm | 2 | | Presbyterian Upper Parish |
| Shrive, Wm | 2 | | |
| Steers, Isaac | 1 | | Quakers Upper Parish |
| Simmonds, Tho | 3 | | |
| Shaw, Ra | 1 | | Quaker Upper Parish |
| Stevens, Rob | 2 | 2 | |
| Simson, P Rd Sr | 2 | 3 | |
| Spencer, Ja | 4 | | |
| Shaw, Ja | 1 | | |
| Sparks, Jere | 3 | | |
| Smith, Wil | 1 | 2 | |
| Simmonds, Isaac | 1 | | |
| Sweet, Jno | 2 | | |
| Smith, Jno | 2 | | |
| Scandal, Mich | 1 | | Papist Lower Parish comes to Church sometimes |
| Thomas, Wm | 2 | | |
| Timms, Jno | 3 | | |
| Thomas, Owin | 1 | | |
| Thomas, Jno | 2 | 3 | |
| Thomas, Fra | 1 | | Quaker Upper Parish |
| Thomson, Ed | 1 | | Quaker Upper Parish & wife both Preachers |
| Tramell, Jno Jr | 3 | | |
| Tramell, Jno | 4 | 6 | |
| Tilley, Elis | 1 | | |
| Tiler, Cha | 3 | 1 | |
| Tillet, Ja | 1 | 1 | |
| Turley, Peter | 1 | 1 | formerly Papist now comes to church Upper Parish |
| | 124 | 35 | |

*Page 5 Column 1*

| Name | Col1 | Col2 | Notes |
|---|---|---|---|
| Taylor, Jno Jr | 1 | 8 | 1 Papist Fred O'Neil overseer Upper Parish |
| Tillet, Sam | 1 | 1 | |
| Thomas, Rob | 3 | | |

| Name | | | Notes |
|---|---|---|---|
| Tramell, Jno | 1 | | |
| Turner, Field | 3 | 2 | |
| Tap, Ja | 3 | | |
| Turley, Ja | 3 | | formerly a Papist now comes to Church Upper Parish |
| Turley, Paul | 2 | 2 | formerly a Papist now comes to Church Upper Parish |
| Thomas, Ha | 3 | | |
| Thomas, Dan | 1 | 1 | |
| Thomas, Rob Jr | 1 | | |
| Thomas, Dan | 2 | | |
| Triplet, Tho | 1 | | |
| Triplet, Fra | 3 | 1 | |
| Triplet, Jno | 1 | | |
| Taylor, Hen | 1 | 1 | |
| Taylor, Geo | 2 | 1 | |
| Taylor, Hen Jr | 2 | 2 | |
| Terret, W.H. | 2 | 5 | Justice, 1 Papist W. Malohone, Overseer, Lower Parish |
| Thomas, Jane | 1 | | |
| Thomas, Jacob | 1 | | |
| Talbot, Wm | 2 | 2 | |
| Turley, Saml | 1 | 4 | |
| Turley, Jno | 2 | 2 | formerly Papist now Vestryman Lower Parish |
| Tren, Hen | 1 | | |
| Tramel, Wm | 2 | | |
| Taylor, Ja | 3 | | |
| Taylor, Ja Jr | 1 | | |
| Thrift, Cha | 1 | 2 | |
| Thrift, Jere | 1 | | |
| Talbot, Nat | 1 | | |
| Vermillion, Wm | 2 | | |
| Violet, Ed | 3 | 1 | |
| Vanlandigm, Mic | 2 | | Papist Sometimes comes to Church Upper Parish |
| Vincent, Ben | 2 | | |
| Vinyard, Steo | 1 | | |
| West, Wil | 2 | 3 | 1 Papist R. McVoy, Overseer Upper Parish |
| West, Hu | 4 | 10 | Vestryman Lower Parish |
| West, Jno | 3 | 5 | formerly Papist, Lately Vestryman, Justice, Captain Lower Parish |
| Wilkinson, Wil | 2 | | |
| Williams, Wil | 2 | | |
| Williams, Wil | 1 | | Secretary Preacher, formerly Anabaptist Upper Parish |
| Watts, Jno Jr | 1 | 5 | Westmoreland |
| Windsor, Wm | 1 | | |
| Wilks, Fra | 1 | | Quaker Upper Parish |
| Williams, Wat | 3 | | |
| West, Ja | 2 | | Quaker Upper Parish |
| Walker, Isaac | 1 | | Quaker Upper Parish |
| Walker, Wido | 1 | | Quaker, Upper Parish |
| Warnsfield, Ben | 1 | | Quaker Upper Parish |
| Ware, Wm | 1 | | |
| White, Rd | 1 | | Quaker, Upper Parish |
| Williams, Wil | 1 | | Quaker Upper Parish |
| Wiginton, Rogr | 4 | 5 | |
| Williams, Tho | 1 | | |
| Washington, Tho | 3 | 2 | |
| Wells, Tho | 1 | | |
| Wheeler, Rd | 3 | 1 | |
| Woodwd, Fra | 1 | | |
| Williams, Own | 1 | 3 | |
| Willis, Mary | 3 | | |

| | |
|---|---|
| Wilkins, Ja | 1 |
| Winsor, Hen | 2 |
| Wilson, Gd | 1 |
| Williams, Wm | 2 |
| Ward, Geo | 1 |
| Washington, Law | 2......27 |
| | 120    96 |

*Column 2 Page 5*

| | | |
|---|---|---|
| Woodbridge, Jno | 1......11 | Richmond |
| Ward, Jno | 1 | |
| Wadlinton, Tho | 1 | |
| Wiar, Ja | 3 | |
| Williams, Ed | 2 | |
| ——(torn) | 2 | |
| Ward (?) — (torn) | 1 | |
| Wright, Hen | 2 | |
| Wade Wid | 3......2 | Presbyterian |
| Wren, Tho | 4......2 | Vestryman Lower Parish |
| Wren, Tho Jr | 1......1 | |
| Wright, W | 1......1 | |
| | 38    18 | |

|  | White | Negro |
|---|---|---|
| Total | 1122 | 913 |

in Fairfax of wch in Truro Parish .................................................................1207
in ye upper cameron Parish ............................................................................928
Total ..............................................................................................................2035

In 1738 when Charles Green came up as Minister of Truro Parish was Tithables ........621

Increase in Eleven Years ..............................................................................1414

The Quakers all live in Cameron or the upper Parish & scarcely one man of them come to Church in my time except Elisha Hall.

Before the parish was divided there was four Churches in it 2 wherof now in the Parish of Cameron — at Goose Creek Church I never had one Communicant — tho Several times prepared to Administer the Sacrament.

At Rocky run Church built abt 3 Years Since — about ——(torn) ——

At the 2 Churches in the Lower Parish — the falls Church & Pohic Church about 120 Constant Communicants ——

Cha Green.

the Country born Negros are chiefly Baptized

*NOTE: This has been reproduced as written by Dr. Green. No changes or corrections (surnames, punctuation, etc.) were made.*

Facsimile of Vestry Book; 1733 agreement to build the first Falls Church.

Majr Wst & Capt Broadwater appointed Church Wardens for ensuing year. William Payne Junr & Henry Gunnell Chosen Vestrymen instead of Capt Turly & James Hamilton.

Richard Lewis exempt from paying Parish Levy

Ordered that the Church Wardens have Seats made for the Church at Alexandria.

      Cha Green

      John Wsh. C.W.

A True Copy taken from the Minute Book, Recorded

    by John West Renr Ch. Vestry.

At a Vestry held for Truro Parish Novr 28th 1757

 Present Revd Mr Charles Green Minister

Charles Broadwater, Danl McCarty, William Payne, Thos West, John West, Wm Payne Junr, Henry Gunnell — Vestrymen

### Truro Parish          Dr

| | |
|---|---:|
| To the Revd Mr Charles Green for his Sallary & Cask | 17,280 |
| To John Berry Clk at Pohick | 1000 |
| To Wm Jas Lunsley Clk at Falls Church & Alexandria | 2000 |
| To James Palmer Sexton at Falls Church | 560 |
| To Jane Lewis Sexton at Pohick | 560 |
| To William Gladen Sexton at Alexandria | 560 |
| To William Henry Terrett Clk of the Vestry | 500 |
| To Mr Hugh West & Accot | 1800 |
| To Mrs Jno West & Account | 1380 |
| To James Sanders & Account | 400 |
| To Majr Peter Wagener & Account | 1052 |
| To Capt Broadwater for Eliz Collins Attendance at ye Church Wardens Suit vs Cole | 175 |
| To Drummond Wheeler for Attendc at the Ch Wardens Suit vs Cole | 250 |
| To Messrs Carlyle & Dalton & Accot | 720 |
| To Joseph Good & Accot | 880 |
| To Messrs Carlyle & Dalton for Hittendon Mondays Claim | 704 |
| To Benj Sebastian & Accot | 600 |

Facsimile of Truro Parish Vestry Book: First use of name "Falls Church," 1757.

At a Vestry of Truro Parish held at the Falls Church
March 28th 1768

Present Henry Gunnell } Ch. Wardens    Thos. Wren
        Wm. Payne Junr. }               Abra. Barnes
        John West                       Danl. McCarty      } Vestry Men
        William Payne                   Robt. Boggess
        Chas. Broadwater                Geo. Washington

We being there met to examine into the State of the said Church
greatly in decay & want of repair, & likewise whether the same
should be repaired, or a new one built, and whether at the same
place, or removed to a more convenient one, and likewise to view
the Addition built by Mr. Charles Broadwater, and what he
hath been deficient in the Work.

Resolved it is the Opinion of this Vestry, that the old Church is rotten
and unfit for repair; but that a new Church be built at the same place.

Resolved that James Wren and Owen Williams do value the work
to be done by Mr. Broadwater on the new Addition, that is, the price
of Glazing the Windows & Plaistering the said House, together
with materials necessary for the same; and make report to the next
Vestry.

Ordered that the Clerk of the Vestry Advertise in the Virginia and
Maryland Gazettes for Workmen to meet at the said Church on
the 29th Day of August next, if fair, if not the next fair day, to
undertake the Building a Brick Church to contain 1600 feet
on the Floor, with a suitable Gallery being a fourth of the Church
and price made up to the same.

Ordered that the Church Wardens employ Workmen to repair
the Windows on the North side of the East End of the old Church and
repair the Shutters of the new Addition.

                                    Henry Gunnell
    Copy.                           W. Paynes

N.B. This Vestry was held when I was sick, and could not attend, the above orders
were sent as above, signed by Messrs. Gunnell & Payne, and I thought fit
to record the same — tho' in point of Time it should have been before the
last one.        John Wedgwood

**Facsimile of Vestry Book: Order to build the present brick church, 1768.**

# FOR SALE!
# HOLLYWOOD FARM!
## ONE HUNDRED ACRES,

At Falls Church, Fairfax County, Virginia,

Situated on the **ALEXANDRIA AND LEESBURG TURNPIKE**, and on the **ALEXANDRIA, LOUDON AND HAMPSHIRE RAILROAD**; about nine miles from Washington, D. C., and about ten miles from Alexandria, Va., and only about ten minutes walk from the R. R. Depot.

25 Acres in Timber—Oak, Hickory, Chestnut, Cedar, Pine, Locust, &c., and the residue in a good state of cultivation.

## A LARGE PEACH & APPLE ORCHARD, & OTHER FRUITS OF ALL KINDS

The farm is well watered, beautifully situated, and admirably adapted to the cultivation of Fruit, especially the Peach, the Grape, and smaller Fruit generally. The buildings and fences are, for the most part, in good condition. Society good, composed chiefly of northern people.

In the Village are Four Churches, a Lyceum, Three Stores, Wheelwright, Blacksmith, &c.;—in short, a place where Intoxicating Liquors are not permitted to be sold, and where lawyers and doctors do not flourish.

Farm Stock and Implements also for sale.

Prices low and terms reasonable. Apply to the owner,

**C. H. BRAMHALL,**

On the premises, or to

Col. **WM. L. BRAMHALL,**

No. 517 Seventh Street, Washington, D. C.

Broadside offering "Hollywood Farm" for sale in 1876.

# Index

This index covers the principal references to persons and organizations in the 17 chapters of the main text, and the main family references in the genealogical section. Introductory material and the Appendix are not indexed. The most important item in the Appendix is a list of residents ("tithables") in Northern Virginia in 1748/49, hitherto unpublished and largely unknown. While not indexed, this list is in alphabetical order. The publisher contemplates the preparation and separate issuance of a more comprehensive reference index.

Abbott Family, 219-221
Abbott, David 103
Abbott, Mr. & Mrs. L.S., 75, 204
Adams-Wren-Watters Cemetery, 238
Adams Family, 221 to 233
Adams, Gabriel, 6, 12, 13
Adams, Harry D., 83
Adams, John, 95
Adams, K., 105
Adams, Robert I., 83
Adams, Wesley, 95
Adams, William & Mrs., 19, 23, 35, 93, 95, 108
Albertson Family, 239
Alexander, Charles, 19
Alexander, John, 6
Alexandria, 1, 5, 8, 11, 13, 18, 19, 22, 24, 26, 27, 30, 33, 41, 45, 75, 110
Alger, (Camp) Russel A., 81, 85, 86, 87
Allen, Jacob I., 83
Allen, William J., 120, 152
Allison, Mary, 96
Altfather, Alton B., 119
Alves, J. Hodge, 25, 73
Amos, J.E., 107
Anderson, Archibald Lamon, 239
Anderson, James, 114
Anderson, Joseph—Family, 240
Anderson, S.H., 153
Andrew, J.R., 106
Archer, Maggie, 72
Archer, Mattie Frances, 72
Arlington, 2, 9
Arlington Mills, 55
Ariss, John, 6
Ariss, John, Jr., 6
Armstrong, Charles A., 83
Armstrong, James E., 98, 106, 108
Arnold, Charles P., 83
Arnold, Chis, 193
Arnold, Christian F., 83
Arnold, Miss, 138
Arrell, Richard, 24

Asbury, Francis, 92, 93, 103, 108
"Ash Grove" Home of Fairfax, 12, 13
Ashford, Michael, 12, 13
Auchmoody, Mrs., 66
  see also Erwin, Mrs. W.H.
Auchmoody Family, 240, 311
August, Peter F., 105
Austin, Byron, 147
Austin, Virginia, 147
Awbrey, Francis, 12, 14
Awbrey, John & Mary, 39

Baggott, James W., 83
Bailey, Captain, 52
Bailey, Edward, 103
Bailey Family, 241, 244
Bailey's Cross Roads, 55, 59
Baker, H.P., 106
Ball, Amanda, 96
Ball, Benjamin, 96
Ball, Mrs. C.C., 101
Ball, C.W., 107
Ball, Carrie, 100, 101, 153
Ball, D., 58
Ball, Elizabeth, 96
Ball, Frank L., 27
Ball, Horatio, 95, 109
Ball, Ida N., 138
Ball, John, 24, 98
Ball, Louisa (Lou), 96, 130
Ball, M.D., 189
Ball, Martha, 119
Ball, Mary, 72
Ball, Mr. & Mrs., 118
Ball, Samuel A., 107
Ball, Sarah, 96
Ball, William, 96, 154
Ballard, Hiram C., 83
Ballard, James W., 83
Ballard, Lyman M.—Family, 245
Baltimore, 5, 6
Banneker, Benjamin, 7
Baptist Church, 49
Barbor, A.H., 153
Barbor Family, 245
Barbor, S.J., 115

Barnes, Abraham, 15, 16, 17, 18
Barrett, Daniel H., 38
Barrett Family, 246
Barrett, Henry, 139
Barrett, Lewis Sewall, 37
Barrett, Mr. & Mrs., 118
Bartlett, John, 66
Bartlett, Mrs. John P., 112
Bartlett Family, 247-249
Bartlett, W.A., 117
Barry, Edward, 12, 13, 14
Bates, Edward, 95
Baxter, James, 14
Bayton, Thomas J., 105
Beach Family, 250
Beall, M.E., 118
Bean, Edith, 101
Beard, Callie, 114
Beattie Family, 123
Beckwith, J.H., 105
Bedle (Beedle) Andrew, 38
Bell, John, 104
Bennett, James, 112
Bennett, Mary, 15, 16
Benton's Tavern, 58
Berger, Charles A. & Mrs., 113, 114
Berkeley, William, 6
Berkley, Frank, 115
Bernizer, W. 204
Berry, Mrs. 112
Besley, James L., 83
Bethune Family, 250-251
Bethune, John F. Mrs., 65, 89, 116, 121, 129, 144, 155
Bibbins, Mrs. Arthur, 108
Billingsley, Billy, 157
Binns, John Alexander, 5, 10
Birch, Almond—Family, 99, 157, 269-271
Birch, Edward J., 147, 198
Birch, Essie, 98, 150
Birch Family, 251, 269
Birch, Frank L., 91, 152
Birch, Mrs. Frank, 41, 151
Birch, H.S., 204
Birch, J.E. & Mrs., 75, 76, 77, 78, 79, 80, 81, 96, 97, 98, 109, 133, 151

542

Birch, Julia, 96
Birch, Kathleen Virginia, 101
Birch, Lillian, 101
Birch, Mrs. Lillian Divine, 138
Birch, Margaret, 101
Birch, Mary, 96, 98
Birch, Mildred, 98
Birch, Minnie, 138
Birch, Samuel, 96
Birch, William, R., 96, 109
Bittinger, B.F. 117, 118, 119
Bittinger, Henry E. (Mr. and Mrs.) 118, 119
Black, Richard Blackburn, 14
Blackburn, 47, 16
Blackburn, Edward, 21
Blackburn, Jane Charlotte, 14
Blackburn, Julia Anne, 14
Blackburn, Richard, 13, 14
Blackburn, Thomas, 14
Blackford, L.M., 72
Blackwell, Eli, 214
Blackwell, John D., 105
Blenkers, Gen., 60
Bloodgood, John, 103
Blumfield, Joseph, 24
Boggess, Robert, 15, 17
Boernstein, Sigismond, 83
Bond, B.W., 106
Bond, John W., 104
Bond, R., 104
Bond, Richard, 104
Bonnell, John W., 156
Booker, S.L., 104
Bowen, 75
Bowen Family, 271, 272
Bowen Thomas, 103
Bowler, John, 124, 127
Boyd, J.H., 106
Braddock, Edward 33, 45
Bramhall, Charles, 37
Bramhall, Family, 272
Brawner, John, 23
Brechin, James, 28
Breeze, Samuel, 103
Brent, Arthur Lee, 48, 119
Brent, Giles, 4
Brice, George and Harriet, 214
Brinkerhoff, M.H. 121
Broadwater, Charles, 12, 15, 16, 17, 18, 19, 21, 23, 24, 35, 46, 47, 207
Broadwater Family, 272-278
Bronaugh, Jeremiah, 14
Brooke, Benjamin F., 104
Brooke, Earnest A., 83
Brooks, Frank 64
Brown, Alexander, G., 105
Brown Family, 278, 280
Brown, H.E., 120, 153, 198
Brown, Ivy, 133

Brown, J.W., 138, 146, 199
Brown, James Isaac 130, 136, 138
Brown, John (J.A. & Mrs. J.H.C.), 75
Brown, Mary Byrd, 133
Brown, Myrtle, 133
Brown, R.L., 25
Browne, Charles E., 104
Browning, Lewis, 103
Brunner, Catherine Jane, 98
Brunner, Family, 280-281
Brunner, George, 98
Brunner, James, 98
Brunner, Mrs. James, 81
Brush, John D., 81, 91
Brush, Truman M., 97, 189
Bryan, Corbin Braxton, III, 89
Bryan, W.B., 35, 43
Buckland, William, 4, 31
Buchwald, Maurice, 83
Budd, Daniel C., 89
Buggs, Fannie, 138
Bull, John W., 105
Bunn, Seely, 104
Burch, Robert, 104
Burke Family, 123, 281
Burke, John B., 38
Burke, Lt. Col., 55
Burns, Richard K., 156
Butler, Gen., 87
Buxton, Charles H., 80, 99, 117, 120
Byers, E.P., 107

Cackley, A.M., 106
Callinder, W.E., 25
Cameron, Baron of (Thomas, Lord Fairfax) 2, 15
Campbell, C.L., 82
Campbell, Ernest F., 113
Cannon, C.H., 106
Cannon, George, 103
Cappelmann, Eimer, 114
Carlin Family, 123
Carlin, William, 95
Carlyle, John, 7
Carmichael, Richard H., 83
Carnegie, Andrew, 100
Carpenter, Anna M., 119
Carpenter, B.D., 119
Carpenter, B.L., 118
Carpenter, Sarah, 119
Carrell, Kate, 101
Carrico, John A., 83
Carroll, Daniel, 8
Carroll, John L., 83
Carter, J.J., 75, 76, 78
Carter, Robert "King," 5
Cartwright, The Rev. and Mrs., 244
Castleman, Mamie, 130, 138

Castleman, R.A., 25, 142
Caton Family, 139
Caton, Sarah Jane (Thompson), 127
Chalmers, John, 103, 104
Chanel, Helen May, 101
Chanel, Louise Catherine, 101
Chantilly, 1
Chappel Family, 282, 283
Cheatham, Henry C., 106
Chickering, J.W., Jr., 120, 121
Chester, Dr. John, 117
Chichester, D.M., 187
Chichester, John C., 83
Child, Mr. & Mrs., 118
Children of the American Revolution, (CAR) 157
Children of the Confederacy, 157
Childs, 236
Childs, John—Family, 95, 236
Chinn, William Ulysses, 89
Christian Endeavor Society, 158
Christian, L.H., 116, 119
Church Family, 284-287
Church, Emilie, 101
Church, M.E., 100, 101, 113, 140, 146, 147, 151, 152, 153, 156, 192, 200, 212
Church, Maybelle, 101
Church, Merton E., Jr., 101, 154, 192, 203
Clark, R.B., 114
Cloud, Adam, 103
Clayton, J.B., 115
Cleveland, William E., 83
Chew, Thomas S., 103
Clewlow, Carl W., 156
Clover Family, 287
Clover, Williston Farm, 49
Coates, Charles, 210
Cobb, Jane, 101
Coe Family of Mount Hope, 287, 288
Coe, Amzi, 116, 117, 302
Coe, Annie, 138
Coe, Eliza, 119
Coe, Henry, Mariette, 119
Coe, Spencer A., 117, 119, 120, 152
Coe, Mr. & Mrs., 118
Coe, Walker Peyton Conway, 109
Coe, William Gwynn, 49, 96, 98, 105, 108, 115
Coggins, Major, 127
Cogswell, Teco, 101
Coke, Thomas, 93
Colby, Edith, 114
Collins, Edward L., 83
Collins, Harry, 83
Colville, John, 7

543

Compton, A., 104
Conn, Hugh, 35
Conway, Richard, 24
Cook, Ambrose, 97
Cooksey, Corrie, 100
Cooper, John, 103
Corcoran, William, 79
Cornelius, Thomas, 105
Courtney, W.S., 106
Cowling, Stephen, 100
Cox, Philip, 103
Craik, Dr., 7
Crenshaw, L.H., 106
Cresswell, Nicholas, 41, 44
Crimmins Family, 123
Crocker, Anna, 119
Crocker, Aurelia R., 118
Crocker, Charley, 119
Crocker, Dorr, 119
Crocker, E.F., 72, 75, 76, 78, 80, 147
Crocker, Ellen H., 119
Crocker, Francis, 119
Crocker, James H., 119
Crocker, Sarah D., 118, 119
Crocker, Scott, 119
Crocker, William C., 118
Crombie, James, 118
Crombie, Mary C., 119
Cropley, Arthur, 187
Crossman Family, 288-291
Crossman, G.W., 204
Crossman, Isaac, 3, 75, 76, 99, 108, 151, 152, 187, 189
Crossman, Mack, 63
Crossman Methodist Church, 96, 97, 98
Crossman, Nellie, 101
Cromwell, 4
Crowell Family, 123
Crowell, Harvey M., 83
Crump, Abby, 96
Crump Family, 291, 292
Crump, Lewis (Mr. and Mrs.) 77, 96, 99, 151
Cuervas, Valentine, 126
Culpeper, Lord, 2, 4, 34
Cunningham, Thomas J., 89
Cushing, Caleb, 30
Custis-Lee House, 9
Custis, Nellie, 33
Curtiss, Harvey E., 83

Dade, Baldwin, 24
Dade, Townshend, 19, 23, 24, 25, 26, 27, 35
Dagworthy, Capt., 45
Dalton, John, 16, 19, 23, 35
Daniels, E.L., 114
Danty, John Wilber, 15, 16
Darling, Mr. & Mrs. E.D., 99, 100, 101

Darling, Frances, 101
Darne Family, 139, 292-301
Darne, John R., 38
Darne, Nicholas, 47
Darne. Robert, 7, 37, 38, 47
Darrell, William, 24
Daughters of the American Revolution, Regents, Falls Church Chapter, 159, 160
Davenport, J.L., 153
Davis, Alice, 157
Davis, Augustus Jr., 98
Davis, C.A., 104
Davis Family, 44
Davis, George, 118
Davis, George W., 83
Davis, John, 104
Davis, John P., 83
Davis, Lawrence E., 83
Davis, O.H., 149
Davis, Olin, 83
Davis, Samuel E.,
Davis, Thomas, 24, 25, 47
Davison, Robert A., 119
Dawson, Lewis, 103
DeButts, Lawrence, 12, 24
Dechert, H.P., 117, 119, 120, 130
Dennison, Henry, 48
DePutron, Jacob C., 37, 72, 73, 75, 79, 189, 192, 312, 416
DeRussy, Brig. Gen. G.A., 112
Der, Tatevasion, Roosevelt, 150
Dickenson, John, 145
Dickinson, Hattie, 101
Dickinson, Marguerite, 101
Dickson, Samuel, 105
Diggs, Bessie, 139
Dillon, Dale C., 114
Dinwiddie (Gov.), 33, 45
District of Columbia, 3, 5, 7, 8, 30
Dodge, Pickering, 154
Dolly, Andrew B., 99, 105
Donaldson Family, 301, 302
Donaldson, James, 35, 38
Donaldson, William, 16
Donohue, John, 114
Donohue, Second Lieut. Stephen R., 83
Donovan, William, 83
Doolittle, Ruth, 132
Doolittle, W.H., 156, 192
Douglas, Henry H., 156
Douglass, A.P., 117, 120
Dranesville, 32, 34
Duffey, J.W., 106
Duke, William, 92, 103
Dulany, M.N., 118
Dulin Chapel, 81, 91, 96, 97, 98

Dulin, Edward, 23
Dulin, William, 96, 97
Dumfries, 5, 6, 38, 39
Dunbar, Col., 45
Duncan Family, 302
Dunlop, George T., 187
Dunn Loring, 23
Duryee, Schuyler, 74, 81, 117, 143, 156, 187, 192
Duryee, Sackett, 72, 64
Duvall, Daniel, 103
Dyer, Lottie, 138

Early, William, 112
Eastman Family, 303, 304
Eastman, Mark H., 120, 121
Eastman, Mr. and Mrs. Albert P., 89, 121
Eaton, Richard, 150
Edmonds Family, 304 to 305
Edmonds, Phillip, 73, 74
Edmonds, Mr. and Mrs. William Fitzhugh, 73, 130, 202
Edwards, Charles, 45
Eels, R.E., 121
Eisenhower, Dwight, D., 89
Eisenhower, Milton, 89
Ellicott, Andrew, 7, 8
Ellicott Family, 305 to 307
Ellis, Michael, 103
Ellison, Amanda, 118
Ellison, Andrew, 96
Ellison, Elizabeth, 96
Ellison Family, 307 to 311
Ellison, John Francis, 112
Ellison, Lillian B., 98
Ellison, Minnie D., 218
Ellison, William H., 37, 96, 102, 130, 131, 132
Ellison, Mr. and Mrs. William, 99
Ellison, Wm. M., 98, 101, 148, 153
Ely, Mr. and Mrs. Geo. G., 72, 73
Embrey, Alvin T., 10
Emms, Edward, 12, 13
England, H.J., 72, 75, 77, 79
England, Mrs. Henry, 75
England, Jessie, 74
England, Libbie, 204
Eno, William, 71, 72
Erwin Family, 311 to 313
Erwin, M.M., 120
Erwin, W.H., 201
Erwin, Mrs. W.H., 66 (later Mrs. Auchmoody)
Eskridge. Isabella, 96
Eskridge, Margaret, 96
Essex, Benjamin, 104
Eubank, W.C., 114
Evans, Edward G., 83

544

Evans, J.E., 107
Evans, William, 104
Everett, C. Roy Jr., 107
Everett, Joseph, 103
Everett, Lloyd T., 83
Everett, Mr. and Mrs. S.S., 112, 114
Ewalt, Floyd W., 119
Ewell, Col., 51

Fadeley Family, 313, 314
Fadeley, Dr. and Mrs. George B., 120, 152, 153, 154, 155, 204
Fairfax, Bryan, 24, 25, 26, 35, 46
Fairfax Circuit, Methodist, 92, 93
Fairfax County, 1, 2, 4, 6, 13, 16, 18, 21, 23, 26, 32, 33, 34, 42, 43, 46, 75, 110
Fairfax Courthouse, 50, 53
Fairfax, George William, 18, 33
Fairfax, Henry, 46, 47, 48, 50
Fairfax Light Inf. USA Co 1 Third Va. Vol. Inf. Spanish War 1898, 75 names, 83
Fairfax Meeting House (Chapel), 95, 96, 99
Fairfax, William, 25
Fairfax, Thomas, Sixth Lord, Baron of Cameron, 2, 15, 33
Falls Church Echo, 43; Footnote 2, p.3
Falls Church (Episcopal), 49, 94, 95, 96
Falls Church Historical Society, 160
Falls Church Lodge, 178
Falls Church Poultry Association, 161
Falls Church Town, Boundary 1894, 75
Falls Church Womans Club, 161
Farr, Richard Ratcliffe, 89, 130
Farrall, Patrick, 83
Farquhar, Charles B., 83
Febrey, Caroline, 96
Febrey, Ernest J., 98
Febrey, Ernest F., 98
Febrey Family, 314 to 317
Febrey, Grace W., 98
Febrey, Mrs. Henry W., 81, 96, 97, 98, 109
Febrey, Mr. and Mrs. John E., 81, 96, 97, 151
Febrey, Margaret, 96, 98
Febrey, Mary F., 96
Febrey, Moses, 96

Febrey, Nicholas, 96
Febrey, William N., 151, 152, 187
Fellows Family, 317, 318
Fellows, H.A., 141, 142, 144
Fendall, Philip R., 24
Fenwick, Edward G., 89, 114
Fenwick, Edward Taylor, 113, 114
Ferguson, L.M., 101, 107
Fidler, John, 103
Fink, J.C., 107
Fish, Nancy, 119
Fisher, Samuel T., 84
Fitzhugh, John, 6
Fitzhugh, Nicholas, 24
Fitzhugh, William, 5, 6
Flagg, Arthur I., 83
Flagg, E.H., 63, 139, 143, 144, 147, 148, 152, 158, 195, 204, 247
Flagg Family, 318-321
Flagg Family, 139
Flagg, S.W., 139, 246
Fleming, Thornton, 103
Fletcher, Palmer, 114
Follin, E.H., 101
Follin, Harvey, 101
Follin, Hattie, 101
Follin, J.C., 101
Follin, John, 46
Follin, Vernon, 84
Follin, Walter, 39
Foote, F.F Jr., 80
Foote, Frederick, 207, 208
Foote, Wm. G., 105
Forbes, Mrs., 140
Forbes, Wells S., 78, 80
Force, Peter, 10
Ford, Antonia, 83
Ford, Clark, 139
Ford, Charles. F., 83
Ford, Ernest. R., 84
Ford Family, 322
Ford Family, 139
Ford, John, 84
Fornerdon, Adam, 103
Forrest, Jonathan, 103
Forsythe, Wm. F., 107
Four Mile Run, 3
Franks, Cecil H., 115
Fraser, Genealogy, 233-235
Fravel, Mrs. W.A., 142
Fredericksburg, 1
Frye, Christopher, 104
Frye, Edward M., 84
Frye, Joseph, 104
Frying Pan Baptist Church, 111
Fought, William S., 89
Fowler, T.T., 72, 75, 76, 77, 78, 80
Fox, W.L., 101

Freeman, A.A., 75
Freeman, Douglas Southall, 13
French, Daniel, 19, 23, 35, 36
Furlong, Mary, Julia (Wren), 238

Gacen, Mr. And Mrs., 119
Gage, Mrs. Charles E., 41, 43, 76, 140, 144, 156, 218
Gaither, Greenbury, 112
Galpin, Charles, 85
Galpin, Mrs. E., 72
Galpin, E.J., 114
Galpin, Mrs. Josiah, 111
Gardner, J.B., 200
Gardner, J.S., 105
Gardner, William, 19, 78
Garner, John M., 140
Garrett, T., 193
Gaston, Mrs. Vernon H., 157
Gatch, Philip, 92, 103
Gates, Capt., 45
Gough, Harry Dorsey, 93
Gaylord, J.W., 37
Georgetown, 7
Gibson, Burns N., 30
Gibson, Churchill J., 27
Gibson, John, 23
Gibson, James, 123
Gibson, U.P., 114
Gilbert, B., 116
Gilbert, John, 119
Gilbert, Roy L., 89
Gilbert, Mrs. Sarah C., 118
Gill, William, 103
Gillam, Pete, 211
Godfrey, William, 12, 13, 14
Goodwin, Harry I., 84
Goose Creek, 14, 16
Gorden, Daniel S., 96, 98, 151
Gordon, Amanda S., 96
Gordon, Daniel S., Family, 322-324
Gordon, Ellen, 75
Gordon, Willis L., Family, 324
Gordon, Willis L., 56, 57, 63, 85, 127, 195, 246, 247
Gorham, Mrs., 119
Gorham Family, 139
Gorham, Mrs. I.K., 119
Gott, L.E., 75, 76, 77, 78, 80, 218
Gott Family, 326
Gould, James Burr, 72, 153, 154
Govaert, Joseph, 126
Graffort, Peletiah, 7
Graham, Alfred M., 84
Graham, Clara, 130
Graham, Hattie, 130
Graham, N.F., 72, 187
Graham, W.P., 114, 152, 187

545

Grandenson, Caroline, 215
Grandin, Joshua M., 105
Grant, Dr. and Mrs., 118
Graves, A.W., 115
Gray, L.C., 43, 44
Great Falls, 2
Green, Charles, 14, 15, 17, 18, 23, 25, 26
Green, Thomas, 213
Green's Blacksmith Shop, 78
Griffith, Alfred, 104
Griffith, David, 25, 31, 93
Grinnan, Andrew G., 25
Groah, W.J., 107
Groot, Hall Academy, 111
Groot, Simon J., 49, 116, 130, 146, 147
Groves, William, 84
Gundry, Mattie, 64, 74, 143, 144, 153, 195, 197
Gunnell Family, 328-332
Gunnell, Henry, 17, 18, 23, 35, 223
Gunnell, Moss, 84
Gunnell, William, 7, 12, 13
Gunston Hall, 4, 5, 15

Haddaway, J.S., 106
Haddaway, Mamie, 204
Harper's Livery Stables, 2
Halket, James, 46
Halket, Sir Peter, 33, 45, 46
Hall, Cleveland J., 25, 74
Hall, Daniel, 104
Hall, M.D., 138, 142
Hall, Quincy, 84
Hamilton, Andrew, 145
Hamilton, James, 15
Hamilton Parish, 11, 13
Hamilton, M.G., 105
Hammond, Wesley, 105
Hammond, Wm. G., 106
Hamon, Samuel, 21
Hampton, Anthony, 16
Hamtramck, John F., 48
Hangman's Tree, 49
Hansberger, Layton, 104
Harle, John, 15
Harley, Robert, 3
Harman, Robert L., 154, 201
Harper, John, 7
Harrell, W.A., 107
Harrison, Thomas, 16
Hart, Harris, 142
Haskell, Dorothy, 101
Haskell, Edith, 101
Haskell, Louise, 101
Hatch, Mr. and Mrs., 118
Hawley, Warren L., 89
Hawxhurst, George W., 113, 120, 147, 153, 154, 155
Hawxhurst Family, 332-336

Hawxhurst, Nellie, 155
Hayes, Edmund, 110
Hayes, Francis W., 25
Hayes, Joseph, 104
Haycock, J.C., 38
Heaton, Prof., 138
Heavener, U.S.A., 100, 107
Hedrick, D.C., 101, 107
Helmintoller, P.C., 106
Hefner, Clistie, 140
Hemphill, Andrew, 104
Hen, Robert, 4
Henderson, Alexander, 23
Henderson, Edwin B., 207, 214, 216, 217, 218
Henderson, William, 213, 216
Hendricks, J.R., 107
Henning, John A., 104
Henry, J.B., 106
Henry, Patrick, 111
Herbert, William, 24
Herndon, J.G., 114
Herr, Austin, 187
Heryford (Hereford), John, 12, 13
Hiett Family, 336, 337
Higley, Rev. H.P., 121
Hild, J.E., 114
Hildebrand, S.V., 106
Hill, Stephen Prescott, 111, 115
Hillier, Thomas, 112, 113, 114, 127
Hine, O.E., 187
Hipkins, Lewis, 230, 232 (Mrs. Hipkins-Wren)
Hirst, Ellen Mankin, 91, 121, 130, 144, 198, 202, 203
Hirst, Mason, 34
Hitt, Daniel, 104
Hoagland, Mr., 204
Hobbs, Miss, 142
Hodges, Asa, 112
Hodgkin, Dr., 75
Hodgkin, Miss Maude, 74
Hoffman, Morris W.H., 84
Hogan, Peter, 112
Hoge, W.S. Jr., 113, 114
Holliday, A.H., 192, 193
Holliday, Edward\M.T., 192, 193
Hollins, H.A., 120
Holmes, John, 24
Honesty, Bertie, 215
Hooe, Robert T., 24
Hooiser, Harry, 93
Hoover, John W., 105
Hopkins, Mrs., 26
Hopkins, Marcus S., 72
Hosier, Harry, 93
Hospital, E.H., 204
Hoskinson, Robert, 130

Hough, E.C., 120, 154
Houseweart, John, 104
Houston, H.C., 101, 108
Howard, O.O., 51
Howe, Julia Ward, 62
Howe, Morris, 104
Howe, Wesley, 104
Howsing, Robert, 6
Huber, Mrs., 73
Hubbell, Elizabeth, 99
Hubbell, F.B., 193
Hubbell, George W., 99
Hughey, Major, 53
Hubbert, Archer B., 43
Hull Family, 337-339
Humphrey, N., 38
Hunter, John, 16, 24
Hunter, N.C., 38
Hunters Hill, 69
Hunting Creek, 6, 16, 32, 35, 39
Huntington, Guy, 83
Hutchison, Andrew, 16, 20
Hutchinson, Robert Lee, 841
Hylton, E.L., 107
Hyson, Samuel, 150, 212

Independent Order of Odd Fellows, 161
Independent Order of Good Templars, 161
Israel, G.W., 104
Ireton, Peter L., 126, 127
Ives, Mr. and Mrs., 118
Ives Family, 339-340
Ives, Albert H., 117, 119, 201
Ives, Claude J., 201
Ives, George B. and Mrs., 66, 75, 76, 77, 78, 79, 80, 81, 117, 147, 187

Jackson, John, 198
Jacobs, Mr. and Mrs. George, 236
James, Sandy, 81
Jefferson County, 4
Jefferson Institute, 109
Jefferson, Hamilton, 104
Jefferson, Thomas, 5, 7, 30, 41, 46
Jenkins, J.H., 121
Jennings, Daniel, 27, 28
Jewell, Aurelia (Mrs. Walter Towner), 101, 108
Johns, John, 27
Johnson, Benjamin F., 38
Johnston, George, 19
Johnson, Harold M., 215
Johnson, James, 201
Johnson, Joseph, 14
Johnson, Oscar, 199

Johnson, Thomas, 8
Jonas, Joseph, 84
Jones Family, 215
Jones, Mrs. Frederick W., 155
Jones, M.T., 119
Jones, Mark C., 119
Jones, Mrs. Mary W., 119
Jones' Point, 8
Jones, Thomas A.C., 116, 119
Jones, Virgil Carrington, 196
Jones, Walter, 30
Jordan, Edward B., 126
Jordan, Wm. W., 121
Judkins, Wm. E., 105
Judson, Robert, 118

Kalbfus, Charles, 104
Kane, John Dennis, 122, 123, 127
Kearnes, William S., 115
Keene, W.D., 106
Keith, James, 12, 24
Keith, Thomas R., 10, 83
Kelly, J.W., 105
Keller, Paul, 127
Kemp, Fletcher, 142
Kemper Lodge, 178
Kemper Lodge, Past Masters, 178
Kendall, John F., 84
Kendrick, Robert E., 154
Kennedy, Mabel, 101
Kennedy, Samuel, 104
Kenyon, Howland, 84
Keppel, Commodore, 45
Kerfert (Kerfoot) Caroline, 211
Kerr Mill, 78
Kerr, Walter, 138, 139
Key Bridge, 40
Key, Francis Scott, 26, 40
Kibler, J.L., 106
Kidwell, Wm. W., 84
Kidwell, J. Thomas, 139
Kidwell, Rose, 139
Kimball, Edward, 154
Kinckle, W.H., 27
Kincheloe, J.W., 115
King, John, 103
King, W.D., 106
King, Wallace, 84
Kingman, Deacon and Mrs. Dexter, 111, 112
Kingman, Mr. and Mrs. William, 111
Kingsley, W.W., 80, 154
Kinsloe, James L., 84
Kinsolving, Bishop of Brazil, 27
Kirby Family, 139, 341-345
Kirby, Charles, 38, 97
Kirby, Francis A., 38
Kirby, Walter, 139

Kittlets, Rudolph F., 100
Klock, Mr. and Mrs., 118
Klock Family, 345, 346
Klock, Augustus, 65
Klock, Benjamin, 38, 39, 42
Klock, Mary Child, Lucy, 118
Klock, Webster, 139
Knotts, James H., 105
Koon, John L., 38
Koon, Jabez, 73
Koutsos, John, M., 89
Knox, Ulysses S., 113, 115, 142

Lackey, Father, 124, 126
LaFayette, Marquis de, 47
Laing, Walter, 84
Lambert, Benjamin, 228
Landstreet, John, 105
Landess, S.S., 114
Lane, Charles Harmon, 113
Laney, Wm. H., 104
Lanning, Gideon, 104
Lantern Club, 162-176
Lawton House, 50
Lawton, Henry Ware, 85
Lee, Cassius F., 73
Lee Family, 346-347
Lee, Charles, 30
Lee, Donald, 157
Lee, James, 211, 212, 215
Leeds, Florence, 138
Leesburg Pike or Road, 1, 3, 7, 11, 13, 32, 33, 34, 38, 39, 40, 41, 45, 108
Lemon Road, 40
L'Enfant, Charles Pierre, 7, 8
Leonard Family, 347, 348
Leonard, David, 40, 41, 42, 127, 139
Leonard, J., 204
Leppert, Norman E., 89
Lester, Robert T., 83
Lewis, John, 12, 14, 16
Lichau, P.H. Emma and Annie, 98
Lightfoot Family, 123
Lightfoot, Ellen (later Mrs. W.G.H. Lynch), 128, 129, 144
Lightfoot, Jane, 128
Lightfoot, Mary Ann (later Lynch), 128
Lindsay Family, 348-353
Lindsay, Robert, 7, 39, 412
Lipscomb, Mr., 53
Lipscomb, R.M., 105
Lippit, Edward, 25, 26, 48
Little, Charles, 7, 46, 82
Little Falls, 2
Livingston, Bertha (Miss), 101

Livingston, Boynton Parke 101
Livingston, O.B., 101, 147
Lloyd Family, 353
Lloyd, Dr. (Barn), 77, 78
Lloyd, H.W., 140
Lloyd, Lester and Sarah (Darne), 111, 112
Lockwood, William F., 25
Longstreet, Gen., 58
Longstreets Hdqtrs, 50
Lothrop, A.M., 153
Loudoun County, 1, 2, 4, 5, 13, 33, 40, 72
Lounsbury, A.E., 30, 81, 116, 117, 119, 120, 147
Love, James M., 76, 187
Love, Thomas B., 83
Lowe, Laura, 101
Lumley, John, 13, 16
Lumsden, W.O., 104, 105
Lusby, O.W., 106
Luttrell, S.S., 100
Lyell, Thomas, 104
Lynch Family, 354, 359
Lynch, Ann, Valinda, 38
Lynch, Elizabeth, 96
Lynch, Ellen (Ella), 140
Lynch, Mr. and Mrs. John W., 73, 96, 128
Lynch, William Nathan, 31, 41, 49, 63, 73, 96, 201, 204
Lynch, Mrs. William H.G., 81, 97, 128, 201, 211
Lynch, William H.G., 49
Lynn, Andrew M., 84

Maben Family, 359, 360
Maben, Frank, 247
Maben, George, 83
Mabin, Blanche, 101
Mabin, John Wesley, 101
M'Allister, Richard, 104
McCabe, Harry, 41
M'Cann, James, 104
McCarty, Daniel, 15, 17, 23
McCarty, Dennis, 12, 13, 14
McCarty, Family (J.E.), 123, 199
McCauley Family, 123, 139, 366, 368
McCauley, William, 38
McClellen, Clarence S., 25
McClellan, Geo. B., 50, 53, 56
McClure, Thomas, 103
McCook, Col., 53
McCormick, Hugh P., 115
McDowell, Gen. 49, 50, 52, 53, 57
McElroy, Wm. R., 119
M'Falls, Thaddeus B., 105

McGill, John, 25, 74
McGroarty, Charles N., 120, 142
McGroarty, Stephen, 89, 119
M'Gruder, W.C., 105
McKay, Herman, 107
Macklefresh, John, 104
McNary, J.V., 120
M'Nemar, Harrison, 105
Madison, Dolley, 33
Madison, James, 27, 47
Maffit, William, 116
Mankin, Benjamin Musgrove, 6
Mankin, Mr. and Mrs. Charles E., 6, 38, 47, 80, 87, 130, 146, 147, 198
Mankin Family, 360-365
Mankin, Ellen, 139, 140
Mankin, George T., 153, 154, 200, 201
Mankin, George W., 6, 47, 80, 81, 87, 198, 199, 200
Mankin, Henry, 6, 10
Mankin, Lula, 150
Mankin, Ruth C. (Mrs. E.A. Hildebrand), 146, 147
Manly, Charles G., 150
Manley, Eddie R., 84
Marcey, Samuel, 95
Markham, John, 275
Marks, August S., 84
Marr, Carrie, 139
Marr Family, 366
Marr, Mrs. J.H. (Ethel Payne —see Payne), 153
Marr, Sarah, 139
Mary Callesta, 127
Marshall, Mrs. Charles, 155
Marshall, Lindon R., 89
Marshall, John, 12
Martin, Congressman, 102
Martin, Ernest S., 84
Martin, Eugene L., 84
Martin, J.O., 33, 34, 39, 44, 122, 124, 126, 127
Martin, Paul F., 89
Martin, Raymond Jacques, 89
Maryland, 1, 3, 4
Maryland Gazette, 18
Maryland Rangers, 45
Mase, Mr. and Mrs., 119
Mason, George, 1, 4, 5, 15, 18, 28, 30, 41, 46, 143, 274
Mason, James M., 73, 203
Mason, John, 30
Massey, Lee, 25
Massie, W.C., 114
Matthews, E., 104
Matthews, Thomas, 3, 4
May, B. Frank, 147
May, Edward Arthur, 47
Mays, A.R., 107

Meade, William, 13, 20, 22, 26, 47
Melville, Charles B., 84
Melville Family, 139
Merrifield, Belle C., 154, 155
Merrifield, Mr. and Mrs. G.A.L., 72, 89, 121, 152, 153, 154
Merry Family, 368-370
Mary, George, 40
Methodist Chapel, 49
Meyers, 72
Miller, Charles F., 242
Miller, W.F., 107
Mills, Blanche, 139
Mills, D.M., 44
Mills Family of Old Tavern, 370-372
Mills, John C., 38
Mills, Lemuel, 38
Mills, Mary E., 38
Milstead, Ernest, 84
Mines, Dr., 25, 51
Minor Family, 372-378
Minor, George, 95
Minor Heirs: Daniel, William John, Hugh, Ann, Phillip H., Smith, Thomas—95, 229
Minor, Hugh, 229
Minor, John R., 207, 208
Minor, Philip, 207
Minor, Launcelot, 25, 26, 93
Mitchell, George D., 152
Mitchell, Russel Edward, 141
Mix, Charles H., 120
Moffatt, Reuben C., 89
Moffett, Carl G., 83
Moncure, Richard C.L., 83, 149
Money Family, 139
Monroe, John, 18
Moore, Alfred, 38
Moore, Beverly J., 84
Moore, Ella, 73
Moore, Elizabeth, 73
Moore, Gertrude, 73
Moore, J.B., 114
Moore, Jeremiah, 110, 111
Moore, John, 38, 47
Moore, Kate, 139
Moore, Dr. Robert, 156
Moore, Robert L., 84
Moore, R. Walton, 111, 142
Moore, William, 16, 147
Moore, William and Angelia, 110
Morales, 204
Moran Family, 378-380
Moran, John J., 75, 76, 77, 78, 80
Moran, Wm., 55
Morgan, L.F., 104

Morrison, Robert, 156, 192
Mortimore, Virginia, 96
Mount Vernon, 2, 4, 5, 6, 13, 18, 47, 94
Muir, James, 8
Muir, John, 24
Mullarkey, E.V., 127
Munroe, Lamor, 83
Munson Hill, 50, 51, 57, 58, 59
Munsey, Dr., 98
Munson, Daniel O., 117, 156, 192, 196
Munson Family, 380-382
Munson, Ira F., 117
Munson, Miles C., 117, 118, 119
Munson, Timothy—Ann, 119
Murphy, Edgar, 215
Murphy, R.R., 105
Murray Family, 382-391
Mutersbaugh, David M., 99, 107
Mutersbaugh Family, 391-393
Myers, Mrs. Harry, 156

Neale, Thomas, 145
Nelson, Cleveland K., 48
Nelson Family, 123, 393, 394
Newell, Geo. M., 89
Newlon, Samuel R., 147
Nichols, Andrew, 103
Nickell, Lehman, 10
Nicholson, J.C., 75
Nicolson, George, 74
Nixon, R.T., 105
Noble, Franklin, 121
Noble, Henry P., 120
Nodine, Mr., 204
Noding, William, 35
Noland, Timothy W.T., 115, 196
Norman, Isaac, 87
Norris, Richard, 100
Northern Neck, 2, 4, 6
Northrup, Eli J., 114, 146, 152, 156, 202, 203
Northrup, T.J., 113
Northumberland, 2
Nourse, Gertrude, 121
Nourse, Phil, 205
Nourse, Robert, 40

O'Bannon, J.H., 193
O'Connor, Thomas L., 84
Oden, Mrs. James, 75
O'Hara, Barrett, 86, 87
Old Rice House "Tallwood," 89
Old Stone Church, 108

Oliver, Charles Y., 83
Oliver, George G., 98, 106
Order of DeMolay, 180
Order of the Eastern Star, 181
Ortolani, Sally, 34
Orton, Charles A., 147
Osborn, Richard, 12, 14
Osborn, Mr. and Mrs. Seth, 37, 78, 79, 80, 117, 119
Osborne, Cyrus, 119
Osborne Family, 395-396
Osborne, John W., 104
Owens, Mr. and Mrs., 130
Owings, Jesse, 198, 215
Owings, Richard, 92, 103, 108

Packard, Joseph, 26, 27, 97
Paddock, Capt., 52
Page, Bernard, 24
Page, Frank, 25
Painter, (Paynter), G.S., 104, 107
Palmer, D.P., 119
Palmer, Mrs. Julia, 118
Palmer, William, 117
Park, A.L., 121
Parker, Mr. and Mrs., 118
Parker, Carrie, 73, 74, 119
Parker, F.E., 101
Parker, Henry, 99
Parker, Mr. and Mrs. Levi, 38, 72, 73
Parker, Mrs. Marcia, 101
Parker, Mary F. 73, 138, 139
Parker, W.E., 204, 205
Parkinson, C., 104
Parmelee, Julius H., 157
Parrott, Lt. Col., 52
Parrott, J.S., 114
Parrott, W.T., 114
Patriotic Order of the Sons of America, 181
Patterson, David B., 4, 154, 204
Patterson Family, 139
Patterson, Jos. W. Jr., 89
Pattie, Mrs. N. Currell, 157
Patton, George J., 84
Patton, W.S., 75
Pascoe, J.M., 107
Payne Family, 396-399
Payne Family, Jacob, 400, 402
Payne, William N., 358, 359
Payne, Edward, 19
Payne, Ethel M., 100, 101, 153
Payne, James, 38, 109
Payne, John B., 84
Payne, Minnie, 73
Payne, William, 15, 17, 18, 19, 21, 23, 24

Peach Orchard, Battle of, 65, 68
Peake, William, 16
Pearson, John, 7
Pearson, Thomas, 12, 221
Pearson, Simon, 6, 7
Pease, Capt., 52
Pergrande, Philip E., 89
Perkins, Mr. and Mrs., 118
Perkins, Thatcher, 112
Perrigo, Mrs. Chas., 99
Perrygo, E.W., 203
Perrin, James, 114
Persinger, Mrs. Mary, 156
Peterkin, Joshua, 25
Pettit, John M., 84
Peyton Family, 123
Phelps, Mr. and Mrs., 118
Phelps, E.P., 107
Philips, John, 104
Phillips, G.B., 118
Phillips, R.A., 189
Phillips, Mrs. Sarah C., 119
Pierce, Allen, 193
Piggott, Lt. A.B., 89
Pigman, Ignatius, 103
Pile, Simon, 103
Pimmitt, Mr., 4
Pitts, John, 104
Plaskett, Susan Annie, 20
Platt, L.B., 121
Pocahontas, 2
Polk, James K., 8
Paison, Capt., 45
Palson, Capt., 45
Pasey, John, 19
Pohick Church, 13, 15, 20, 24, 35
Porter, A.J., 100, 107
Porter Family, 402
Porter, George E., 72
Porter, Ida, 100
Porter, Robert S., 38
Potomac Fruit Growers Association, 181
Potomac River, 2, 4, 6, 7, 11, 16, 34, 35, 36, 38, 39, 43, 47
Potter, Arthur Jr., 101
Potter, A.J., 101
Pound, Benj. W., 72
Powell, E.O., 38
Powell, Elisha, 24
Powell, G.C., 38
Powell, Mary G., 31
Powell, Robert L., 121
Powell, William F., 84
Powhatan Springs, 2
Poythress, Francis, 103
Presbyterian Church, 49
Prettyman, Wm., 105
Price, Thomas, 19, 21
Prince William County, 2,
11, 33, 39
Proctor, John Clagett, 10
Proudfit, Samuel Victor, 3, 10
Proudfit, S.M., 114
Pruden, Dr. Edward H., 114
Pulver, George, 214

Quick, Charles B., 113
Quick Family, 403
Quick, Tunis Cline, 154
Quick, Van Vanderbeet, 113, 147
Quick, Virginia T., 147

Randolph, Cary J., 10
Ransom, Mr. and Mrs., 119
Rankin, Thomas, 103
Rappahannock River, 2
Rathbun, David L., 119
Rawlings, 325
Rawlings, Mrs., 112, 198
Rawlings, Sally, 112, 198
Ray, Benjamin, 28
Raymond, Mrs. Helen C., 121
Read, Charlotte, 63, 65, 81, 112, 115
Read, Emma, 149
Read Family, 403, 404
Reagan, Michael, 12, 13
Rector, Henry and Julia, 211
Rector, Will, 211
Redman, Stuart, 103
Reed, Mr. and Mrs. Caleb, 111
Reed, Emma, 63, 65, 112
Reed, H.W., 111, 112, 115
Reed, John, 81, 56
Reed, John B., 56, 64
Reed, Wm. N., 151
Reese, A.A., 104
Reeves, Mrs. George R., 41
Reeves, G. Torreyson, 30, 11
Reid, Silas L., 84
Renney, Elton, 83
Renney, John E., 30
Reynolds, Benedict, 104
Rhodda, Martin, 92
Ribble, W. Leigh, 25
Rice Family, 404, 405
Rice, John, 119
Rice, Mr. and Mrs. Yale, 119
Richards, John, 104
Riddle, David Hoge, 117, 118, 119
Riddle, Elizabeth Brown, 118, 119
Riddle, Sue, 118, 214
Rice, Bessie, 130
Richards, Charles, 139
Riddell, Henry, 35

549

Riley Family, 406-411
Riley, Joseph S., 75, 76, 78, 79, 81, 138
Riley, Maggie, 133
Riley, Mary Edwards, 74
Riley, Maude (Gage), 138
Rippon Lodge, 14
Ritchie, Joshua A., 84
Ritchie, Wm. F., 193
Rives, Anthony and Mary, 237
Rixey, Dr., of Fairfax, 198
Roach, A.P., 107
Robert, Milton S., 72, 89
Roberts, Fannie, 114
Roberts, Capt. and Mrs. M.S., 99, 119
Robertson, John H., 84
Robertson, Richard M., 106
Robinson, Mitchell and Fanny, 211
Roby, Tobias, 38
Roby, James, 96
Rouchefoucauld, Duc de la, 43
Rockwell, (Miss), 138
Rogers, Nellie, 114
Rogers, Wm. B., 195
Rogers, W.H., 101
Rohr, Wesley, 104
Rohwer, S.A., 141, 142
Rolfe, John, 2
Rollins, Geo. F., 89, 121
Rollins, Isaac, 103
Rorebeck, Mrs. A.C., 121
Rorebeck, Edward F., 149
Rosslyn, 32
Round, G.C., 101
Row Family, 411, 412
Rowen, Joseph, 104
Rowland, Kate Mason, 10
Rowland, Mr. and Mrs. Stanley, 199
Rubright, Leonard, 114
Ruff, Daniel, 103
Rullman, Isaac, 120
Rumbles, George, 213
Rumbles, Nathan, 213
Rutherford, Capt., 45
Ryan, Mrs. Thomas Fortune, 123
Ryer, H.C., 31
Ryer, H. Scott, 153
Ryland, J.E., 105

Saemmerer, H. Paul, 10
Sage, Mr. and Mrs., 119
Sale, Clarence M., 147
Sanborn, Merton C.,
Sanford, Richard, 19, 23
Sangston, Lawrence, 84
Sangster, Judge, 138
Sargent, James W., 120

Schenck, Robert C., 52, 53
Schooley, Wm. T., 107
Schmavonian, Arsene, 121
Scott, Lt. Gen., 52
Scott, R.A., 99, 107
Scheid, W. Edwin, 147
Seabury, Bishop, 26
Sealock, Walter, 147
Seaver, May, 204
Seaymaker, Mr. and Mrs., 118
Sebastian Family, 412-414
Segal, H.J., 56
Selecman, Harry T., 83
Selecman, John R., 84
Selecman, Odie L., 84
Seoane, Mr., 113
Sewall Family, 123
Sewall, Lewis, 37
Sewall, James, 104
Sewall, Sabilla, 122, 123, 127
Sewell, (Sewall) Family, 414-415
Sewell, 75
Shadford, George, 103
Shattuck, L.B., 56
Shaw, S.B., 150
Shaw, Thomas, 23
Sheers, William P., 89
Shepherd, Samuel, 193, 198
Shepherd, W.D., 188, 193
Sherman, Alvord, 48
Sherman, Caroline, 118
Sherwood Family, 139
Sherwood Family, 415-417
Sherwood, Mr. and Mrs., 119
Sherwood, Archibald, 37, 38
Sherwood, Robert, 38
Shinn, George W., 27
Shipman, Stephen P., 107
Shotwell, Clarence L., 114
Shotwell Family, 417-418
Shotwell, J.L., 113, 114
Shreve Family, 418-424
Shreve Family, 139
Shreve, Barbara, 66, 96
Shreve, B.F. and Benj. R., 66, 78, 95, 96, 97, 109, 130
Shreve, Carroll V., 153
Shreve, George W., 246
Shreve, Mary, 96
Shreve, Mrs. Prentiss A., 39, 95, 130, 192
Shreve Road, 23, 37
Shreve, Sarah, 96
Shreve, Susan, 96
Shreve, Bessie, 139
Shreve, William Henry, 37, 38, 97, 98
Simms, Charles, 46
Simms, George, 81
Simms, Henry, 212

Sinclair, J.C., 107
Sinclair, John W., 96
Sine, E.C., 138
Skinner, Major, 58
Skinner, Emmett W., 147
Slade, Selina M., 74
Sloper, Thomas E., 84
Smith, Andrew M., 120
Smith, George H., 84
Smith, James, 104
Smith, James W., 106
Smith, John, 2, 3,
Smith, Nathaniel, 16
Smith, Presley, 106
Smith, Ralph F., 89
Smith's Division, Gen. W.F., 53, 55, 56
Smithson, Rumsey, 106
Smoot's, 33
Smoot, Mrs. Steven Thomas, 112
Smyth, Mrs. Peverel H., 155
Snelling, Benjamin, 103
Snoddy, T.B., 113
Snyder, Hally, 203
Somerville, George S., 25, 30
Soule Family, 424
Southgate, Horatio, 25, 27, 30
Southgate, H.S., 106
Southron, Richard, 96
Spalding, George C., 84
Spanish War—1898, Fairfax Light Inf. USA Co. I., Third Va. Vol. Inf., 75 names, 83
Sparks, Elijah, 103
Speer, Horton, 98
Speer, George B., 84
Speer, William, 97
Spencer, Frances, 6
Spencer, John, 6
Spencer, Linwood F., 89
Spencer, Nicholas, 4, 6
Spindle, Zeno H., 84
Sprangle, Mrs. Sarah, 99
Sprangle, W., 204
Sprankle Family, 424, 425
Sprigg, Clarence B., 84
Squier, Mr. and Mrs., 119
Stafford, 2, 6, 9, 11, 33
Stalcup, Benjamin S., 89
Stambaugh, Ralph, 89
Star Tavern, 49, 50, 78
Steadman Family, 425-429
Steadman, Frank M., 114, 115, 157, 185
Steadman, Mrs. Howard R., 127
Steadman, Melvin Lee Jr., 10, 86, 108
Steadman, Velva Lee (Wakefield), 127
Steele, Mr. and Mrs., 118

Stephenson, Richard M., 115
Stetson, Charles, 7, 10, 39, 44
Stevens, Allen, 101
Stevens, Frannie, 101
Stewart Family, 429-431
Stewart Family, 123
Stewart, Charles A. (Miss Elizabeth Tabb), 20, 31, 50, 67, 87, 91, 121, 140, 143, 195
Stewart, Lula, 139
Stier, Frederick, 104
Stone, George, 84
Stone, Joseph, 104
Storer, Mrs., 119
Stoughton, Edwin, 83
Strawbridge, Robert, 92, 93
Stuart, Bill, 213
Stuart, Lawyer, 72
Stuart, J.E.B., 51, 58, 59, 97
Stuart, David, 8
Sturmon, John, 12, 13, 14
Styles, Elizabeth M., 147, 156
Styles, Francis, H., 156
Styles, Mr. and Mrs. Samuel Holmes, 74, 155
Summers, John A., 95
Swift, Dorothy, 101
Swift, Margaret L., 101
Swink, Martha S., 119

Talbott Family, 432
Talbott, T.M., 156, 192, 284
Tallwood, Old Rice House, 708 E. Broad, 89
Tavenner, Sarah (Mrs. Brown), 133
Taylor, 75
Taylor Family, 432
Taylor, Henry, 215
Taylor, J.H., 112
Taylor, William, 148
Taylor's Tavern, 53, 96
Tenant, Mr. and Mrs., 118
Terrett Family, 123, 204, 433
Terrett, Mrs. Gibson, 102, 103
Thomas, David, 104, 105, 110
Thomas, George, 203, 204, 212
Thomas, Hugh, 20
Thomas, James, 103
Thomas, Russell, 113
Thomas, William, 222
Thomas, W.S.O., 112, 113, 115
Thompson Family, 434-436
Thompson, Amos G., 103
Thompson, Edith, 201
Thompson, George M., 79, 80
Thompson, J.P., 120
Thompson, Lightfoot, 47

Thompson, Nathan, 128, 201
Thompson, Richard, 95
Thompson, Samuel, 201
Thorne Family, 437-440
Thorne, Mr. and Mrs. Jacob M., 99, 100, 101, 151
Thorne, Jennie, 100
Thorne, Mr. and Mrs. Talmadge, 71, 72, 99, 151
Throckmorton, Rebecca Upton, 208, 209
Tidewater, 6
Tidings, Richard, 104
Tierney, Edward, 124, 127
Tilghman, Henry S., 84
Tillet, Everett E., 120
Tillett, Giles, 12, 13
Tillman, Andrew—Family, 214, 215
Tinner, 206, 212, 215
Tompkins, Lt. Charles, 51, 202
Tongue, Rev. John W., 105
Torreyson Family, 440, 441
Torreyson, Mrs. A.D., 81
Torreyson, Mary E., 98
Torreyson, Wm. H., 98
Trammell, Albert W., 84
Trammell Family, 441-444
Trammell, Gerard, 16, 18, 21, 24, 42
Trammell, John, 13, 14, 15
Trammell, Sampson, 7, 35
Trammell, William, 35
Tripp Family, 444
Tripp, Percy, 130
Tripp, Silas D., 59, 73, 74, 195
Tripp, Mrs. Silas D., 112
True, Rodney H., 10
Truett, George E., 115
Truman, John, 4, 13, 14
Trumble, Edwin, 84
Truro Parish, 11, 13, 17, 18, 19, 20, 23, 34, 39, 41
Tuckerman, F.W., 121
Turley, John, 15
Turner Family, 445
Turner, Harriet, 208
Turner, Harry, 203
Turner, Henry, 100
Turner, Ralph McMillan, 38
Twitchell, Annie, 101
Tyler, Gen., 53
Tyler, George T., 106
Tyson's Corners, 41

Uber, Mrs., 73
United Daughters of the Confederacy, 181
Updike, E.M., 114
Upper Church, 13, 15, 16, 18, 34, 39

Upton, Charles Horace, 146, 147, 208

Van de Vyver, Augustus, 124
Vandivere, Edgar, 156
Van Herblis, A.O., 123
Van Ingelgem, A.J., 124, 125, 126
Van Ness, John Peter, 31
Van Voast, Nicholas, 117
Veitch, E.R., 104
Via, Lila Mae, 114
Via, Roy S., 114
Viands, Mrs. Sallie B., 101
Vienna, 52
Village Improvement Society, 182, 183, 184
Virginia Rangers, 45
Vroom, G.D. and K.R. (Kate Vroom Riddle), 118

Wade, W.A., 106
Wadsworth, Gen., 109
Waite, Thomas, 31
Wakefield Family, 445-449
Wakefield (Mrs.), 41
Wakefield, Roy, 83
Walker, Ada, 33, 85, 129, 130, 131, 132, 133, 134, 139, 247
Walker, Ellery C., 139
Walker, Ewell, 123
Walker Family, 139
Walker Family of Chestnut Grove, 449-451
Walker, Harry, 85
Walker, John, 210, 211
Walker, Thomas Hartwell, 123, 127
Walling, H.C., 41, 95, 108
Walters, M.R., 114
Walters, C.C., 31
Wandling, Miss, 101
Ward, Edwin M., 89
Ware, Macon, 178, 198
Warner, Paul, 106
Washington, Augustine, 14, 17
Washington, Bushrod, 14
Washington, George, 1, 2, 4, 5, 7, 8, 10, 13, 14, 16, 17, 18, 19, 20, 23, 31, 33, 34, 37, 41, 45, 94, 116, 274
Washington, John, 4, 6, 14
Washington, Lawrence, 17
Washington, Lund, 17
Waters, Thomas, 125
Watkins Family, 451-453
Watson, Boyd, 83
Watson, John, 104
Watson, Samuel, 103

551

Watt, John G., 104
Watters, William and Wife (Sarah Adams), 92, 93, 94, 95, 103, 108, 224, 228, 238
Watts, James, 104
Waugh, J.H., 81, 106
Weedon, Fannie, 138
Weeks, H.D., 79, 80
Welch, Homer, 98, 106
Welch, Mary, 7
Weller, Miss, 143
Wells, John, 202
Welsh, Washington W., 105
Wescott, Milton Roberts, 89
West, 7
West, Arthur B., 38
West, Benjamin, 24
West Family, 453-461
West, George, 28, 38
West, Hugh, 15, 35, 229
West, John, 17, 18, 19
West, John Jr., 24
West, Roger, 24
West, William, 25
Westbury, Joseph, 198
Westmoreland, County, 2, 6, 12, 28
Weston, Mr. and Mrs., 111
Wharton, Dr. H.M., 112
Wheeler, A.M., 114
Wheeler Family, 461-462
Wheeler, Thomas, 104
White, G.D., 106

White, John, 104
Whiting, Carlyle, Fairfax, 7
Whitmer, James V., 89
Whitworth, Abraham, 103
Wickling, Rev. and Mrs. J.S., 100, 107
Widdecombe, R.W., 189
Willard, Jos. and wife, Antonia Ford, 82
Willard, Jos. E., 82, 83
Willet, Julius, 38
Williams, Mrs. Abigail, 118
Williams, B.E., 149
Williams, Curtis, 104
Williams, Ernest, 84
Williams, Frank, 56
Williams, Franklin Jr., 114
Williams, Gladstone Ellis, 101, 107
Williams, G. Ellis, 100, 108
Williams, John and Mary, 38
Williams, J.T., 106
Williams, Owen, 17, 35
Williams, Robert, 103
Williamsburg, 45
Willis, Nicholas, 104
Wilmer, Richard, 27
Wilson Boulevard, 2, 28, 39
Wilson, Daniel B., 84
Wilson, Mrs. Norval, 119
Winn, Pauline, 114
Winslow, Lt. Col. B., 56
Wood, J.R., 106
Woodward, Lt., 52

Woodworth, Harriet, 118, 119
Woodworth, Malcolm, 119
Woodworth, Mary A., 119
Woodworth, Milton, 118
Woodworth, Oliver, 104
Woodworth, Mrs. Sharley G., 118
Woodworth, Mr. William, 119
Woolf, W.H., 102, 106
Wren, Albert, 37, 96, 152
Wren, Elizabeth, 37, 38
Wren, James, 17, 18, 19, 21, 22, 23, 27, 41, 96, 223
Wren, John, 47, 236
Wren, Thomas, 15, 17, 18, 21, 229, 232
Wren, Richard, 229, 232
Wren, William, 23
Wrenn, Nelson,
Wright, Mr. and Mrs., 112, 118
Wright, Richard, 103
Wright, Ross, 154
Wunder, Ott., 189

Yates, R.J., 138
Yearbry, Joseph, 103
Young, Charles B., 104
Younglove, Mr. and Mrs., 119

Zimmerman, G.H., 105

This is the first book to be set in type by means of the "Alphatype," an electronic photo-composing machine. The type face used is Times Roman. The text pages in the regular edition are printed on 50# Pinnacle offset paper. The illustrations in both the presentation and the regular edition are printed on 70# Lustro Offset Enamel, Gloss finish paper.

www.ingramcontent.com/pod-product-compliance
Lightning Source LLC
Chambersburg PA
CBHW071711300426
44115CB00010B/1383